Vision Science

Photons to Phenomenology

Vision Science

Photons to Phenomenology

Stephen E. Palmer

A Bradford Book
The MIT Press
Cambridge, Massachusetts
London, England

This book was set in Baskerville by Asco Typesetters, Hong Kong, and was printed and bound in the United States of America.

Library of Congress Cataloging-in-Publication Data

Palmer, Stephen E.
    Vision science—photons to phenomenology / Stephen E. Palmer.
        p.   cm.
    Includes bibliographical references and index.
    ISBN 0-262-16183-4
    1. Vision. 2. Visual perception. 3. Cognitive science.
I. Title.
QP475.P24   1999
612.8'4—dc21   99-11785
                                                    CIP

In loving memory of my mentor, colleague, and friend, Irvin Rock (1922–1995), who taught me more about visual perception than everyone else combined and who showed me by example what it means to be a scientist.

Brief Contents

Contents

II Spatial Vision 143

6 Organizing Objects and Scenes   254

7 Perceiving Object Properties and Parts   311

Contents

Preface

Writing this book has been a long and difficult undertaking. Because several good textbooks are available that present the basic facts about vision in a clear and readable fashion, the reader may wonder why I embarked on this journey. Indeed, I often wonder myself! It was not that I thought I could do a better job at what these other books do. Truthfully, I doubt I could. It was that I felt the need for a different kind of textbook, one that accurately reflects the way most modern research scientists think about vision. In fact, the scientific understanding of visual perception has changed profoundly over the past 25 years, and almost all the current textbooks are still in the "old" mold in both structure and content. New results are included, of course, but the new approach to vision is not.

So what is this new approach? The change in the nature of visual research began in the 1970s, resulting from the gradual emergence of an interdisciplinary field that I will call vision science. It arose at the intersection of several existing disciplines in which scientists were concerned with image understanding: how the structure of optical images was (or could be) processed to extract useful information about the environment. Perceptual psychologists, psychophysicists, computer scientists, neurophysiologists, and neuropsychologists who study vision started talking and listening to each other at this time because they began to recognize that they were working on the same problem from different but compatible and complementary perspectives. Vision science is a branch of a larger interdisciplinary endeavor known as cognitive science that began at about the same time. Cognitive science is the study of all mental states and processes—not just visual ones—from an even greater variety of methodologically distinct fields, including not only psychology, computer science, and neuroscience, but also linguistics, philosophy, anthropology, sociology, and others. In my own view, vision science is not just one branch of cognitive science, but the single most coherent, integrated, and successful branch of cognitive science.

Central to this new approach is the idea that vision is a kind of computation. In living organisms, it occurs in eyes and brains through complex neural information processing, but it can, at least in theory, also take place when information from video cameras is fed to properly programmed digital computers. This idea has had an important unifying effect on the study of vision, enabling psychologists, computer scientists, and physiologists to relate their findings to each other in the common language of computation. Vision researchers from disparate fields now read and cite each other's work regularly, participate in interdisciplinary conferences, and collaborate on joint research projects. Indeed, the study of vision is rapidly becoming a unified field in which the boundaries between the component disciplines have become largely transparent.

This interdisciplinary convergence has dominated the cutting edge of vision research for more than two decades, but it is curiously underrepresented or even absent in most modern textbooks about perception. One reason is that most textbooks that cover vision also include hearing, taste, touch, and smell. With the exception of hearing, the computational approach has not yet gained a firm foothold in these other sensory modalities. The attempt to provide a consistent framework for research in all modalities thus precludes using the computational approach so dominant in vision research.

Another reason the computational approach to vision has not been well represented in textbooks is that its essential core is theoretical, and introductory textbook authors tend to shy away from theory. The reasons are several, having to do partly with many authors' lack of computational background, partly with the difficulty of presenting complex quantitative theories clearly without overwhelming the reader, and partly with students' desire to learn only things that are "right." In the final analysis, all phenomena are "right," and all theories (except one) are presumably "wrong"—although some are "wronger" than others. Students are understandably wary of expending much effort on learning a theory that is surely flawed in some way or other. Such considerations have led to a generation of textbooks that are as theoretically neutral as possible, usually by being as atheoretical as possible. But the importance of theories in science lies not so much in their ultimate truth or

falsity as in the crucial role they play in understanding known phenomena and in predicting new ones. Given that we have few, if any, truly adequate theories in vision science yet, virtually every insight we have into known phenomena and every predicted new one have been generated by incorrect theories! They are, quite simply, an essential component of vision science.

In this book I have therefore taken the position that it is just as important for students of vision to understand theories as to know about phenomena. Most chapters include a healthy dose of theory, and some (e.g., Chapters 2 and 8) are almost entirely theoretical. But I have tried to do more than simply catalog bits and pieces of existing theory; I have tried to present a theoretical synthesis that is internally consistent and globally coherent. This is a tall order, to be sure, for the classical theories of visual perception seem so different as to be diametrically opposed. Structuralist theory, for example, claimed that wholes are nothing but associations of elementary parts, whereas Gestalt theory championed the primacy of wholes over parts. Helmholtz's theory of unconscious inference claimed that vision is mediated by thoughtlike deductions, whereas Gibson's ecological theory countered that perception is direct and unmediated. How can a theoretically coherent position be fashioned from such diverse and contradictory components? I do not claim to have succeeded completely in this synthesis, for I do have to deny some important tenets of certain positions. But not many. Much has been made of differences that are more apparent than real, and I believe that the computational approach presented in this book can span the vast majority of them without strain. The strong form of Gibson's claim for direct perception is an exception, but weaker forms of this view are quite compatible with the computational view taken in this book, as I explain in Chapter 2.

The unified theoretical viewpoint I present is not so much my own theory as my construction of what I think of as the current "modal theory." Experts on vision will naturally find aspects of it to which they take exception, but I believe the vast majority will find it consistent with most of their firmly held beliefs. The theoretical framework I advocate owes much to the influential proposals of the late David Marr and his colleagues at MIT, but this is true of the field in general. In many cases, I have generalized Marr's specific proposals to make clear how his own detailed theories were examples of a more general framework into which a variety of other specific theories fit quite comfortably. Even so, I do not consider the view I describe as exclusively or even primarily Marr's; it owes just as much to classical perceptual theorists such as Helmholtz, Wertheimer, Gibson, and Rock. The interweaving of such diverse theoretical ideas is not difficult to achieve, provided one avoids divisive dogma and instead concentrates on the positive contributions of each view.

Because the book is much more theoretical and interdisciplinary than most perception textbooks, it is correspondingly longer and more difficult. It is designed for an upper division undergraduate course or an entry-level graduate course on vision, most likely as part of a program of study in psychology, cognitive science, or optometry. I have tried to explain both theories and phenomena clearly enough to be understood by intelligent, motivated students with no prior background in the field of vision. I do presume that readers have some basic understanding of behavioral experiments, computer programming, and neurobiology. Those who are unfamiliar with this material may find certain portions of the text more difficult and have to work harder as a result, but the technical prerequisites are intended to be relatively few and low-level, mainly high school geometry and algebra.

Despite the strongly interdisciplinary nature of this book, it is written primarily from a psychological perspective. The reason is simply that I am a psychologist by training, and no matter how seriously I have read the literature in computer vision and visual neuroscience, the core of my viewpoint is still psychological. In keeping with this perspective, I have avoided presenting the complex mathematical details that would be central to a computer scientist's presentation of the same topics and the biological details that would figure prominently in a neuroscientist's presentation. By the same token, I have included details of experimental methods and results that they might well have omitted by nonpsychologists. Vision science may have made the boundaries between disciplines more transparent, but it has not eliminated them. Psychologists still perform experiments on sighted organisms, computer scientists still write programs that extract and transform optical information, and neuroscientists still study the structure and function of the visual nervous system. Such methodological differences will not disappear. Indeed, they should not disappear,

because they are precisely what makes an interdisciplinary approach desirable. What is needed is a group of vision scientists who are well versed in all these disciplines. It is my sincere hope that this book will help create such a community of scientists.

In addition to being used as a textbook, I hope that this book will be useful as a reference text for members of the expanding vision science community. Although the sections describing one's own field of specialization may seem elementary, the rest of the book can provide useful background material and relatively sophisticated introductions to other areas of vision research. The coverage is not intended to be at the same level as a professional handbook, in which each chapter is expected to be a definitive treatment of a specific topic written by a world-class expert for an audience of other experts, but it is also more accessible and internally consistent than any handbook I have ever seen. It is therefore particularly useful for someone who wants to get a global view of vision science—the "lay of the land," if you will—within which the focused chapters that one finds in professional handbooks will fit comfortably and make more sense.

Organization of the Book

Because the aim of this book is to integrate material across disciplines, each chapter includes findings from many different approaches. There is no "physiology chapter," no "psychophysics chapter," no "developmental chapter," no "neuropsychology chapter," and no "computational chapter" in which the separate and often conflicting mini-views within each of these disciplines can be conveniently described in isolation. I have avoided this approach because it compartmentalizes knowledge, blocking the kind of synthesis that I am trying to achieve and that I view as essential for progress in the field. Rather, the topic of each chapter is discussed from the perspectives of *all* relevant disciplines, sometimes including those that writers of textbooks on vision traditionally ignore, such as computer science, philosophy, and linguistic anthropology. Even within the more standard visual disciplines, the coverage is not uniform because the distribution of knowledge is not uniform. We know a great deal more about the physiology of early image processing, for example, than we do about the physiology of categorization and visual imagery.

This unevenness is merely a reflection of the current state of understanding.

The overall organization of the book is defined by its three parts: Foundations, Spatial Vision, and Visual Dynamics.

Foundations. The Foundations section covers a basic introduction to the interdisciplinary science of vision. Chapter 1 introduces the problem of visual perception and sets forth an interdisciplinary framework for approaching it. It covers many of the most important perceptual, optical, and physiological facts on which vision is based. Chapter 2 then discusses theoretical approaches to vision from an historical perspective. It covers the classical theories of vision as well as the information processing (or computational) approach, including several important proposals from the work of the late David Marr (1982) that play a large role in defining the superstructure of the rest of the book. The key idea is that visual perception can be analyzed into a sequence of four basic stages: one that deals with extracting image structure (Marr's "primal sketch"), one that deals with recovering surfaces in depth (Marr's "2.5-D sketch"), one that deals with describing 3-D objects (Marr's "volumetric descriptions"), and one that deals with identifying objects in terms of known categories. This sequence of processes—which I call *image-based, surface-based, object-based*, and *category-based*—is then traced for each of the major topics covered in the book: color, space, and motion perception. The final chapter of the Foundations section, Chapter 3, is a long but important one. It tells "the color story," which spans vision science from the physiology of retinal receptors to the linguistic analysis of color names in different cultures of the world. Its importance derives from the fact that the current understanding of color processing illustrates better than any other single example in all of cognitive science why an integrated, interdisciplinary approach is necessary for a complete understanding of a perceptual domain.

Spatial Vision. Chapters 4 through 9 cover spatial perception as a sequence of processes: extracting image structure (Chapter 4), recovering oriented surfaces in depth (Chapter 5), organizing perception into coherent objects (Chapter 6), perceiving object properties and parts (Chapter 7), representing shape (Chapter 8), and identifying objects as members of known categories

(Chapter 9). This material on spatial processing of images is the heart and soul of classical visual perception. Because it is much more complex than color processing, we understand it much less well. It is hard at times not to be overwhelmed by the mountains of facts and frustrated at the lack of good theory, but I believe we are beginning to get some clearer notion of how this all fits together.

Visual Dynamics. The final section concerns perceptual dynamics: how visual perception and its aftereffects change over time. Perception of motion and events is the first topic considered (Chapter 10), being essentially an extension of spatial perception to the domain of space-time. Then we discuss ways in which the visual system selects different information over time by making overt eye movements and covert attentional adjustments (Chapter 11). Next we consider memory for visual information within a multistore framework—iconic memory, short-term visual memory, and long-term visual memory—and examine how such stored information can be reconstructed and transformed in visual imagery (Chapter 12). Finally, Chapter 13 takes up what is perhaps the most fascinating of all topics: the nature of visual awareness (and its absence in certain neurological syndromes) and various attempts at explaining it. This topic is very much on the cutting edge of modern vision science and is finally getting the attention that it deserves.

Tailoring the Book to Different Needs

Because the book contains more topics and material than can comfortably fit into any single-term undergraduate course, instructors are encouraged to be selective in using it. I have included too much rather than too little because I find it easier to skip what I do not want to cover in a single unified textbook than to find external readings that cover the desired material at an appropriate level and in a framework that is compatible with the main textbook—a nearly impossible task, I have found.

There are several ways of tailoring the present book to different needs. Most obviously, certain chapters can be skipped in their entirety. For example, if color is not a high priority, Chapter 3 can be omitted with only minor ramifications for later chapters. Chapter 10 on motion perception is likewise reasonably independent of the rest of the book. For courses that are restricted to classical visual perception, Chapter 11 on eye movements and attention and Chapter 12 on memory and imagery are probably the least relevant. A course emphasizing high-level vision can reasonably omit Chapter 4 on image-based processing.

Another approach to selective coverage is omitting subsections within chapters. For traditional courses on the psychology of vision, the sections on computational theory and other technical material may be eliminated or assigned as optional. (One effective approach I have used is to teach an honors section of the course for additional credit in which the more difficult material is required and other sections for which it is not.) Eliminating this material has the advantages of making the book substantially shorter and easier to understand for students with less technical backgrounds. The developmental sections can also generally be omitted without much affecting the book's continuity and cohesion.

For students with strong scientific backgrounds who are highly motivated to learn about modern vision science, I encourage instructors to use as much of the book as possible. It is perfectly reasonable, for example, to cover the entire book in a graduate course on vision that lasts a full semester.

Acknowledgments

There are many people I wish to thank for helping me in various phases of writing this book. First and foremost, I gratefully acknowledge my debt to my late colleague and friend, Irvin Rock, to whom this book is dedicated. Irv not only taught me about perception in his own gentle, probing, inimitable way, but he also read and commented on earlier drafts of the first nine chapters before his death in 1995. Moreover, his 1975 textbook *An Introduction to Perception* served as a model for this one in certain important ways. In that book, Irv tried to present the phenomena of visual perception at an introductory level yet within a coherent and principled theoretical view of perception as a problem solving process. While it was still in print, it was my favorite perception text, and I know that some instructors continue to use it in photocopied readers to this day.

Irv's influence on this book has been substantial, as careful readers will surely discover. Had he lived, I believe his continued contributions would have improved it further and kept me from making some mistakes I doubtless have made in his absence. After Irv's death, Arien Mack, one of Irv's most distinguished students and collaborators, became my primary reviewer for the remaining chapters of the book. One or the other of them has read and commented on every chapter.

Many other experts in vision science have also read more limited portions of the book, either at my own request or at that of MIT Press, and provided valuable comments on material in their specialty areas. I wish to thank the following scholars, plus several anonymous reviewers, for the time and effort they spent in evaluating portions of the manuscript:

Chapter 1: Irvin Rock, Jack Gallant, Paul Kube
Chapter 2: Irvin Rock, James Cutting, Ulric Neisser, Paul Kube, Jitendra Malik, and an anonymous reviewer
Chapter 3: Irvin Rock, Karen DeValois, Alan Gilchrist, C. Lawrence Hardin, Paul Kay, and an anonymous reviewer
Chapter 4: Irvin Rock, Jitendra Malik, Jack Gallant, Ken Nakayama, and an anonymous reviewer
Chapter 5: Irvin Rock, Jitendra Malik, Ken Nakayama, and an anonymous reviewer
Chapter 6: Irvin Rock, Jitendra Malik, and Michael Kubovy
Chapter 7: Irvin Rock, Arien Mack, and an anonymous reviewer
Chapter 8: Irvin Rock, John Hummel, and an anonymous reviewer
Chapter 9: Irvin Rock, John Hummel, and an anonymous reviewer
Chapter 10: Arien Mack, James Cutting, Dennis Proffitt, and an anonymous reviewer
Chapter 11: Arien Mack, Michael Posner, Anne Treisman, and William Prinzmetal
Chapter 12: Arien Mack and Martha Farah
Chapter 13: Arien Mack, Alison Gopnik, John Watson, Bruce Mangan, Bernard Baars, and C. Lawrence Hardin
Appendix A: Ken Nakayama and Ervin Hafter
Appendix B: John Kruschke and Jerome Feldman
Appendix C: Alan Gilchrist

Several students, postdoctoral fellows, and visitors in my lab have also taken the time to comment on various portions of the book. Without differentiating among chapters, I wish to thank Daniel Levitin, Elisabeth Pachiere, Joel Norman, Akira Shimaya, Diane Beck, Justin Beck, Sheryl Ehrlich, Craig Fox, Jonathan Neff, Charles Schreiber, and Christopher Stecker for their helpful comments. In addition, I would like to thank Christopher Linnett, Sheryl Ehrlich, Diane Beck, Thomas Leung, William Prinzmetal, Gregory Larson for doing some of the more complex and technical illustrations, Lisa Hamilton for working on design issues, and Richard Powers for improving my work environment. For their help in copy editing and preparing the final manuscript for production, I would like to thank Barbara Willette and Peggy Gordon, respectively. Last, but not least, I must thank Edward Hubbard for his tireless help in tracking down references, obtaining permission to reprint figures, checking page proofs, and generally overseeing the final stages of preparing the manuscript for publication.

This book took a long time to write—certainly a good deal longer than I had planned or than I would like to admit—and its writing put a significant strain on all other aspects of my life. During this time, many people have contributed emotional support and understanding, for which they are due both thanks for their help and apologies for the time this project has stolen from them. They include Paul Harris, Stephen Forsling, David Shiver, and Andy Utiger, as well as Linda, Emily, and Nathan Palmer.

Part I

Foundations

An Introduction to Vision Science

Most of us take completely for granted our ability to see the world around us. How we do it seems no great mystery: We just open our eyes and look! When we do, we perceive a complex array of meaningful objects located in three-dimensional space. For example, Figure 1.1.1 shows a typical scene on the Berkeley campus of the University of California: some students walking through Sather Gate, with trees and the distinctive Campanile bell tower in the background. We perceive all this so quickly and effortlessly that it is hard to imagine there being anything very complicated about it. Yet, when viewed critically as an ability that must be explained, visual perception is so incredibly complex that it seems almost a miracle that we can do it at all.

The rich fabric of visual experience that results from viewing natural scenes like the one in Figure 1.1.1 arises when the neural tissues at the back of the eyes are stimulated by a two-dimensional pattern of light that includes only bits and pieces of the objects being perceived. Most of the Campanile, for example, is hidden behind the trees, and parts of the trees are occluded by the towers of the gate. We don't perceive the Campanile as floating in the air or the trees as having tower-shaped holes cut in them where we cannot currently see them. Even objects that seem to be fully visible, such as the gate towers and the students, can be seen only in part because their far sides are occluded by their near sides. How, then, are we able so quickly and effortlessly to perceive the meaningful, coherent, three-dimensional scene that we obviously do experience from the incomplete, two-dimensional pattern of light that enters our eyes?

This is the fundamental question of vision, and the rest of this book is an extended inquiry into its answer from a scientific point of view. It is no accident that I began the book with a question, for the first step in any scientific enterprise is asking questions about things that are normally taken for granted. Many more questions will prove to be important in the course of our discussions. A few of them are listed here:

- Why do objects appear colored?
- How can we determine whether an object is large and distant or small and close?
- How do we perceive which regions in a visual image are parts of the same object?

Figure 1.1.1 A real-world scene on the Berkeley campus. Viewers perceive students walking near Sather Gate with the Campanile bell tower behind a row of trees, even though none of these objects are visible in their entirety. Perception must somehow infer the bottom of the bell tower, the trees behind the gate towers, and the far sides of all these objects from the parts that are visible.

- How do we know what the objects that we see are for?
- How can we tell whether we are moving relative to objects in the environment or they are moving relative to us?
- Do newborn babies see the world in the same way we do?
- Can people "see" without being *aware* of what they see?

Posing such questions is just the first step of our journey, however, for we must then try to find the answers. The majority of this book will be devoted to describing how vision scientists do this and what they have discovered about seeing as a result. It turns out that different parts of the answers come from a variety of different disciplines—biology, psychology, computer science, neuropsychology, linguistics, and cognitive anthropology—all of which are part of the emerging field of **cognitive science**. The premise of cognitive science is that the problems of cognition will be solved more quickly and completely by attacking them from as many perspectives as possible.

The modern study of vision certainly fits this interdisciplinary mold. It is rapidly becoming a tightly integrated field at the intersection of many related disciplines, each of which provides different pieces of the jigsaw puzzle. This interdisciplinary field, which I will call **vision science**, is part of cognitive science. In this book, I try to convey a sense of the excitement that it is generating among the scientists who study vision and of the promise that it holds for reaching a new understanding about how we see.

In this initial chapter, I will set the stage for the rest of the book by providing an introductory framework for understanding vision in terms of three domains:

1. phenomena of visual perception,

2. the nature of optical information, and

3. the physiology of the visual nervous system.

The view presented in this book is that an understanding of all three domains and the relations among them is required to explain vision. In the first section of this chapter, we will consider the nature of visual perception itself from an evolutionary perspective, asking what it is for. We will define it, talk about some of its most salient properties, and examine its usefulness in coupling organisms to their environments for survival. Next, we will consider the nature of optical information, because all vision ultimately rests on the structure of light reflected into the eyes from surfaces in the environment. Finally, we will describe the physiology of the part of the nervous system that underlies our ability to see. The eyes are important, to be sure, but just as crucial are huge portions of the brain, much of which vision scientists are only beginning to understand. In each domain, the coverage in this introductory chapter will be rudimentary and incomplete. But it is important to realize from the very beginning that only by understanding all three domains and the relations among them can we achieve a full and satisfying scientific explanation of what it means to see. What we learn here forms the scaffold onto which we can fit the more detailed presentations in later chapters.

1.1 Visual Perception

Until now, I have been taking for granted that you know what I mean by "visual perception." I do so in large part because I assume that you are reading the words on this page using your own eyes and therefore know what

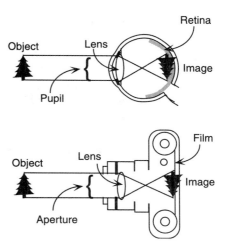

Figure 1.1.2 The eye-camera analogy. The eye is much like a camera in the nature of its optics: Both form an upside-down image by admitting light through a variable-sized opening and focusing it on a two-dimensional surface using a transparent lens.

visual experiences are like. Before we go any further, however, we ought to have an explicit definition.

1.1.1 Defining Visual Perception

In the context of this book, **visual perception** will be defined as the process of acquiring knowledge about environmental objects and events by extracting information from the light they emit or reflect. Several aspects of this definition are worth noting:

1. Visual perception concerns the *acquisition of knowledge*. This means that vision is fundamentally a cognitive activity (from the Latin *cognoscere*, meaning *to know* or *learn*), distinct from purely optical processes such as photographic ones. Certain physical similarities between cameras and eyes suggest that perception is analogous to taking a picture, as illustrated in Figure 1.1.2. There are indeed important similarities between eyes and cameras in terms of optical phenomena, as we will see in Section 1.2, but there are no similarities whatever in terms of *perceptual* phenomena. Cameras have no perceptual capabilities at all; that is, they do not *know* anything about the scenes they record. Photographic images merely contain information, whereas sighted people and animals acquire knowledge about their environments. It is this knowledge that enables perceivers to act appropriately in a given situation.

2. The knowledge achieved by visual perception concerns *objects and events in the environment*. Perception is not merely about an observer's subjective visual experiences, because we would not say that even highly detailed hallucinations or visual images would count as visual perception. We will, in fact, be very interested in the nature of people's subjective experience—particularly in Chapter 13 when we discuss visual awareness in detail—but it is part of visual perception only when it signifies something about the nature of external reality.

3. Visual knowledge about the environment is obtained by *extracting information*. This aspect of our definition implies a certain "metatheoretical" approach to understanding visual perception and cognition, one that is based on the concept of information and how it is processed. We will discuss this **information processing** approach more fully in Chapter 2, but for now suffice it to say that it is an approach that allows vision scientists to talk about how people see in the same terms as they talk about how computers might be programmed to see. Again, we will have more to say about the prospects for sighted computers in Chapter 13 when we discuss the problem of visual awareness.

4. The information that is processed in visual perception comes from the light that is *emitted or reflected by objects*. Optical information is the foundation of all vision. It results from the way in which physical surfaces interact with light in the environment. Because this restructuring of light determines what information about objects is available for vision in the first place, it is the appropriate starting point for any systematic analysis of vision (Gibson, 1950). As we will see in Section 1.2, most of the early problems in understanding vision arise from the difficulty of undoing what happens when light projects from a three-dimensional world onto the two-dimensional surfaces at the back of the eyes. The study of what information is contained in these projected images is therefore an important frontier of research in vision science, one that computational theorists are constantly exploring to find new sources of information that vision might employ.

1.1.2 The Evolutionary Utility of Vision

Now that we have considered what visual perception *is*, we should ask what it is *for*. Given its biological importance to a wide variety of animals, the answer must be that *vision evolved to aid in the survival and successful reproduction of organisms*. Desirable objects and situations—such as nourishing food, protective shelter, and desirable mates—must be sought out and approached. Dangerous objects and situations—such as precipitous drops, falling objects, and hungry or angry predators—must be avoided or fled from. Thus, to behave in an evolutionarily adaptive manner, we must somehow get information about what objects are present in the world around us, where they are located, and what opportunities they afford us. All of the senses—seeing, hearing, touching, tasting, and smelling—participate in this endeavor.

There are some creatures for which nonvisual senses play the dominant role—such as hearing in the navigation of bats—but for *homo sapiens*, as well as for many other species, vision is preeminent. The reason is that vision provides spatially accurate information from a distance. It gives a perceiver highly reliable information about the locations and properties of environmental objects while they are safely distant. Hearing and smell sometimes provide information from even greater distances, but they are seldom as accurate in identifying and locating objects, at least for humans. Touch and taste provide the most direct information about certain properties of objects because they operate only when the objects are actually in contact with our bodies, but they provide no information at all from farther distances.

Evolutionarily speaking, visual perception is useful only if it is reasonably accurate. If the information in light were insufficient to tell one object from another or to know where they are in space, vision never would have evolved to the exquisite level it has in humans. In fact, light is an enormously rich source of environmental information, and human vision exploits it to a high degree. Indeed, vision is useful precisely because it is so accurate. By and large, *what you see is what you get*. When this is true, we have what is called **veridical perception** (from the Latin *veridicus* meaning *to say truthfully*): perception that is consistent with the actual state of affairs in the environment. This is almost always the case with vision, and it is probably why we take vision so completely for granted. It seems like a perfectly clear window onto reality. But is it really?

In the remainder of this section, I will argue that perception is *not* a clear window onto reality, but an actively constructed, meaningful model of the environment that allows perceivers to predict what will happen in the future so that they can take appropriate action and thereby increase their chances of survival. In making this argument, we will touch on several of the most important phenomena of visual perception, ones to which we will return at various points later in this book.

1.1.3 Perception as a Constructive Act

The first issue that we must challenge is whether what you see is *necessarily* what you get: Is visual perception unerringly veridical? This question is important because the answer will tell us whether or not vision should be conceived as a "clear window onto reality."

Adaptation and Aftereffects. One kind of evidence that visual experience is not a clear window onto reality is provided by the fact that visual perception changes over time as it adapts to particular conditions. When you first enter a darkened movie theater on a bright afternoon, for instance, you cannot see much except the images on the screen. After just a few minutes, however, you can see the people seated near you, and after 20 minutes or so, you can see the whole theater surprisingly well. This increase in sensitivity to light is called **dark adaptation**. The theater walls and distant people were there all along; you just could not see them at first because your visual system was not sensitive enough.

Another everyday example of dark adaptation arises in gazing at stars. When you leave a brightly lit room to go outside on a cloudless night, the stars at first may seem disappointingly dim and few in number. After you have been outside for just a few minutes, however, they appear considerably brighter and far more numerous. And after 20–30 minutes, you see the heavens awash with thousands of stars that you could not see at first. The reason is not that the stars emit more light as you continue to gaze at them, but that your visual system has become more sensitive to the light that they do emit.

Adaptation is a very general phenomenon in visual perception. As we will see in many later chapters, visual experience becomes less intense[1] as a result of prolonged exposure to a wide variety of different kinds of stimulation: color, orientation, size, and motion, to name just a few. These changes in visual experience show that visual perception is not always a clear window onto reality because we have different visual experiences of the same physical environment at different stages of adaptation. What changes over time is our visual system, not the environment. Even so, one could sensibly argue that although some things may fail to be perceived because of adaptation, whatever *is* perceived is an accurate reflection of reality. This modified view can be shown to be incorrect, however, by another result of prolonged or very intense stimulation: the existence of visual aftereffects.

When someone takes a picture of you with a flash, you first experience a blinding blaze of light. This is a veridical perception, but it is followed by a prolonged experience of a dark spot where you saw the initial flash. This **afterimage** is superimposed on whatever else you look at for the next few minutes, altering your subsequent visual experiences so that you see something that is not there. Clearly, this is not veridical perception because the afterimage lasts long after the physical flash is gone.

Not all aftereffects make you see things that are not there; others cause you to misperceive properties of visible objects. Figure 1.1.3 shows an example called an **orientation aftereffect**. First, examine the two striped gratings on the right to convince yourself that they are vertical and identical to each other. Then look at the two tilted gratings on the left for about a minute by fixating on the bar between them and moving your gaze back and forth along it. Then look at the square between the two gratings on the right. The top grating now looks tilted to the left, and the bottom one looks tilted to the right. These errors in perception are further evidence that what you see results from an interaction between the external world and the present state of your visual nervous system.

Reality and Illusion. There are many other cases of systematically nonveridical perceptions, usually called **illusions**. One particularly striking example with which you may already be familiar is the **moon illusion**. You

---

[1] It may be confusing that during dark adaptation the visual system becomes *more* sensitive to light rather than less. This apparent difference from other forms of adaptation can be eliminated if you realize that during dark adaptation the visual system is, in a sense, becoming less sensitive to the *dark*.

An Introduction to Vision Science

Figure 1.1.3 An orientation aftereffect. Run your eyes along the central bar between the gratings on the left for 30–60 seconds. Then look at the square between the two identical gratings on the right. The upper grating should now appear tilted to the left of vertical and the lower grating tilted to the right.

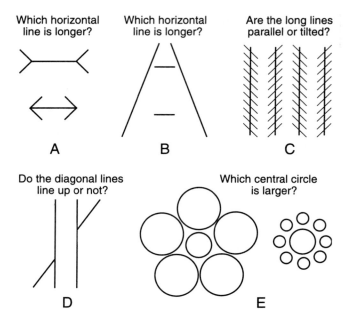

Figure 1.1.4 Visual illusions. Although they do not appear to be so, the two arrow shafts are the same length in A, the horizontal lines are identical in B, the long lines are vertical in C, the diagonal lines are collinear in D, and the middle circles are equal in size in E.

have probably noticed that the moon looks much larger when it is close to the horizon than it does when it is high in the night sky. Have you ever thought about why?

Many people think that it is due to refractive distortions introduced by the atmosphere. Others suppose that it is due to the shape of the moon's orbit. In fact, the optical size of the moon is entirely constant throughout its journey across the sky. You can demonstrate this by taking a series of photographs as the moon rises; the size of its photographic image will not change in the slightest. It is only our perception of the moon's size that changes. In this respect, it is indeed an illusion—a non-veridical perception—because its image in our eyes does not change size any more than it does in the photographs. In Chapter 7, we will discuss in detail why the moon illusion occurs (Kaufman & Rock, 1962; Rock & Kaufman, 1962). For right now, the important thing is just to realize that our perception of the apparent difference in the moon's size at different heights in the night sky is illusory.

There are many other illusions demonstrating that visual perception is less than entirely accurate. Some of

these are illustrated in Figure 1.1.4. The two arrow shafts in A are actually equal in length; the horizontal lines in B are actually the same size; the long lines in C are actually vertical and parallel; the diagonal lines in D are actually collinear; and the two central circles in E are actually equal in size. In each case, our visual system is somehow fooled into making perceptual errors about seemingly obvious properties of simple line drawings. These illusions support the conclusion that perception is indeed fallible and therefore cannot be considered a clear window onto external reality. The reality that vision provides must therefore be, at least in part, a construction by the visual system that results from the way it processes information in light. As we shall see, the nature of this construction implies certain hidden assumptions, of which we have no conscious knowledge, and when these assumptions are untrue, illusions result. This topic will appear frequently in various forms throughout this book, particularly in Chapter 7.

It is easy to get so carried away by illusions that one starts to think of visual perception as grossly inaccurate and unreliable. This is a mistake. As we said earlier, vision is evolutionarily useful to the extent that it is accurate—or, rather, as accurate as it needs to be. Even illusory perceptions are quite accurate in most respects. For instance, there really *are* two short horizontal lines and two long oblique ones in Figure 1.1.4B, none of which touch each other. The only aspect that is inaccurately perceived is the single illusory property—the relative lengths of the horizontal lines—and the discrepancy between perception and reality is actually quite modest. Moreover, illusions such as these are not terribly obvious in everyday life; they occur most frequently in books about perception.

All things considered, then, it would be erroneous to believe that the relatively minor errors introduced by vision overshadow its evolutionary usefulness. Moreover, we will later consider the possibility that the perceptual errors produced by these illusions may actually be relatively harmless side effects of the same processes that produce veridical perception under ordinary circumstances (see Chapters 5 and 7). The important point for the present discussion is that the existence of illusions proves convincingly that perception is not just a simple registration of objective reality. There is a great deal more to it than that.

Once the lesson of illusions has been learned, it is easier to see that there is really no good reason why perception *should* be a clear window onto reality. The objects that we so effortlessly perceive are not the direct cause of our perceptions. Rather, perceptions are caused by the two-dimensional patterns of light that stimulate our eyes. (To demonstrate the truth of this assertion, just close your eyes. The objects are still present, but they no longer give rise to visual experiences.) To provide us with information about the three-dimensional environment, vision must therefore be an **interpretive process** that somehow transforms complex, moving, two-dimensional patterns of light at the back of the eyes into stable perceptions of three-dimensional objects in three-dimensional space. We must therefore conclude that the objects we perceive are actually interpretations based on the structure of images rather than direct registrations of physical reality.

Ambiguous Figures. Potent demonstrations of the interpretive nature of vision come from **ambiguous figures**: single images that can give rise to two or more distinct perceptions. Several compelling examples are

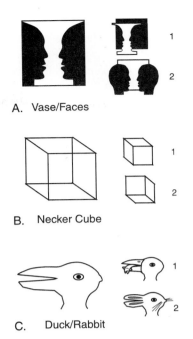

A. Vase/Faces

B. Necker Cube

C. Duck/Rabbit

Figure 1.1.5 Ambiguous figures. Figure A can be seen either as a white vase against a black background or as a pair of black faces against a white background. Figure B can be seen as a cube viewed from above or below. Figure C can be seen as a duck (facing left) or a rabbit (facing right).

shown in Figure 1.1.5. The vase/faces figure in part A can be perceived either as a white vase on a black background (A1) or as two black faces in silhouette against a white background (A2). The Necker cube in Figure 1.1.5B can be perceived as a cube in two different orientations relative to the viewer: with the observer looking down and to the right at the cube (B1) or looking up and to the left (B2). When the percept "reverses," the interpretation of the depth relations among the lines change; front edges become back ones, and back edges become front ones. A somewhat different kind of ambiguity is illustrated in Figure 1.1.5C. This drawing can be seen either as a duck facing left (C1) or as a rabbit facing right (C2). The interpretation of lines again shifts from one percept to the other, but this time the change is from one body part to another: The duck's bill becomes the rabbit's ears, and a bump on the back of the duck's head becomes the rabbit's nose.

There are two important things to notice about your perception of these ambiguous figures as you look at them. First, the interpretations are *mutually exclusive*. That

An Introduction to Vision Science

is, you perceive just one of them at a time: a duck *or* a rabbit, not both. This is consistent with the idea that perception involves the construction of an interpretive model because only one such model can be fit to the sensory data at one time. Second, once you have seen both interpretations, they are **multistable perceptions**, that is, dynamic perceptions in which the two possibilities alternate back and forth as you continue to look at them. This suggests that the two models compete with each other in some sense, with the winner eventually getting "tired out" so that the loser gains the advantage. These phenomena can be modeled in neural network theories that capture some of the biological properties of neural circuits, as we will see in Chapter 6.

1.1.4 Perception as Modeling the Environment

Ambiguous figures demonstrate the constructive nature of perception because they show that perceivers interpret visual stimulation and that more than one interpretation is sometimes possible. If perception were completely determined by the light stimulating the eye, there would be no ambiguous figures because each pattern of stimulation would map onto a unique percept. This position is obviously incorrect. Something more complex and creative is occurring in vision, going beyond the information strictly given in the light that stimulates our eyes (Bruner, 1973).

But *how* does vision go beyond the optical information, and *why*? The currently favored answer is that *the observer is constructing a model of what environmental situation might have produced the observed pattern of sensory stimulation.* The important and challenging idea here is that people's perceptions actually correspond to the models that their visual systems have constructed rather than (or in addition to) the sensory stimulation on which the models are based. That is why perceptions can be illusory and ambiguous despite the nonillusory and unambiguous status of the raw optical images on which they are based. Sometimes we construct the wrong model, and sometimes we construct two or more models that are equally plausible, given the available information.

The view that the purpose of the visual system is to construct models of the environment was initially set forth by the brilliant German scientist Hermann von Helmholtz in the latter half of the 1800s. He viewed perception as the process of inferring the most likely environmental situation given the pattern of visual stimulation (Helmholtz, 1867/1925). This view has been the dominant framework for understanding vision for more than a century, although it has been extended and elaborated by later theorists, such as Richard Gregory (1970), David Marr (1982), and Irvin Rock (1983), in ways that we will discuss throughout this book.

Care must be taken not to misunderstand the notion that visual perception is based on constructing models. Invoking the concept of models does *not* imply that perception is "pure fiction." If it were, it would not fulfill the evolutionary demand for accurate information about the environment. To satisfy this requirement, perceptual models must (a) be closely coupled to the information in the projected image of the world and (b) provide reasonably accurate interpretations of this information. Illusions show that our models are sometimes inaccurate, and ambiguous figures show that they are sometimes not unique, but both tend to occur only under unusual conditions such as in the books and laboratories of vision scientists. Everyday experience tells us that our perceptual models are usually both accurate and unique. Indeed, if the sensory information is rich and complex enough, it is nearly impossible to fool the visual system into interpreting the environment incorrectly (Gibson, 1966).

Visual Completion. Perhaps the clearest and most convincing evidence that visual perception involves the construction of environmental models comes from the fact that our perceptions include portions of surfaces that we cannot actually see. Look at the shapes depicted in Figure 1.1.6A. No doubt you perceive a collection of three simple geometrical figures: a square, a circle, and a long rectangle. Now consider carefully how this description relates to what is actually present in the image. The circle is partly occluded by the square, so its lower left portion is absent from the image, and only the ends of the rectangle are directly visible, the middle being hidden (or *occluded*) behind the square and circle. Nevertheless, you perceive the partial circle as complete and the two ends of the rectangle as parts of a single, continuous object. In case you doubt this, compare this perception with that of Figure 1.1.6B, in which exactly the same regions are present but not in a configuration that allows them to be completed.

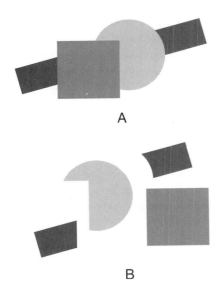

A

B

Figure 1.1.6 Visual completion behind partly occluding objects. Figure A is perceived as consisting of a square, a circle, and a rectangle even though the only visible regions are those shown separated in Figure B.

This perceptual filling in of parts of objects that are hidden from view is called **visual completion**. It happens automatically and effortlessly whenever you perceive the environment. Take a moment to look at your present surroundings and notice how much of what you "see" is actually based on completion of unseen or partly seen surfaces. Almost *nothing* is visible in its entirety, yet almost *everything* is perceived as whole and complete.

You may have noticed in considering the incompleteness of the sensory information about your present environment that visual perception also includes information about **self-occluded surfaces**: those surfaces of an object that are entirely hidden from view by its own visible surfaces. For example, only half of the cube that you perceive so clearly in Figure 1.1.7A is visible. Your perception somehow manages to include the three hidden surfaces that are occluded by the three visible ones. You would be more than a little surprised if you changed your viewpoint by walking to the other side and saw that the cube now appeared as in Figure 1.1.7B. Indeed, there are infinitely many possible physical situations that are consistent with Figure 1.1.7A, yet you automatically perceived just one: a whole cube.

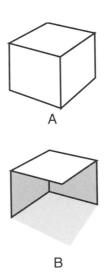

A

B

Figure 1.1.7 Visual completion due to self-occlusion. Figure A is invariably perceived as a solid cube, yet it is physically possible that its rear side looks like Figure B.

Completion presents an even more compelling case for the model-constructive view of visual perception than do illusions and ambiguous figures. It shows that what you perceive actually goes a good deal beyond what is directly available in the light reaching your eyes. You have very strong expectations about what self-occluded and partly occluded surfaces are like. These must be constructed from something more than the light entering your eyes, because the image itself contains no direct stimulation corresponding to these perceived, but unseen, parts of the world.

Impossible Objects. There is another phenomenon that offers an especially clear demonstration of the modeling aspect of visual perception. **Impossible objects** are two-dimensional line drawings that initially give the clear perception of coherent three-dimensional objects but are physically impossible. Figure 1.1.8 shows some famous examples. The "blivit" in Figure 1.1.8A looks sensible enough at first glance, but on closer inspection, it becomes clear that such an object cannot exist because the three round prongs on the left end do not match up with the two square ones on the right end. Similarly, the continuous three-dimensional triangle that we initially perceive in Figure 1.1.8B cannot exist because the surfaces of the locally interpretable sides do not match up properly (Penrose & Penrose, 1958).

An Introduction to Vision Science

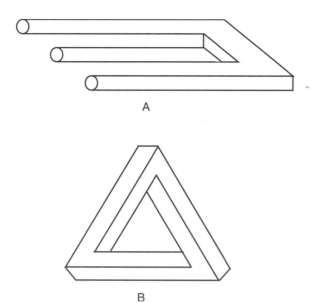

A

B

Figure 1.1.8 Impossible objects. Both the objects shown in this figure initially produce perceptions of coherent three-dimensional objects, but they are physically impossible. Such demonstrations support the idea that vision actively constructs environmental models rather than simply registering what is present.

One of the most interesting things about impossible objects is how clearly they show that our perceptions are internal constructions of a hypothesized external reality. If visual perception were merely an infallible reflection of the world, a physically impossible object simply could not be perceived. It would be as impossible perceptually as it is physically. Yet people readily perceive such objects when viewing properly constructed images. This fact suggests that perception must be performing an interpretation of visual information in terms of the three-dimensional (3-D) objects in the environment that might have given rise to the images registered by our eyes. Moreover, the kinds of errors that are evident in perceiving impossible objects seem to indicate that at least some visual processes work initially at a local level and only later fit the results into a global framework. The objects in Figure 1.1.8 actually make good sense locally; it is only in trying to put these local pieces together more globally that the inconsistencies become evident.

Predicting the Future. Supposing that the visual system does construct hypothetical models of reality rather than just sticking to information available in sensory stimulation, why might such a system have evolved? At some level, the answer must be that the models are more useful from an evolutionary standpoint than the images that gave rise to them, but the reason for this is not entirely clear. The usefulness of visual completion, for example, would seem to be that 3-D models representing hidden surfaces contain much more comprehensive information about the world than purely stimulus-based perceptions. The additional information in the constructed model is valuable because it helps the perceiving organism to predict the future. We have already considered one example in our discussion of Figure 1.1.7. Perceiving a whole three-dimensional cube provides the basis for expecting what we would see if we were to move so that new surfaces come into view. This is terribly important for creatures (like us) who are constantly on the move. A stable three-dimensional model frees us from having to reperceive everything from scratch as we move about in the world.

A perceptual model of the three-dimensional environment does not need to be modified much as we move around because the only thing that changes is our viewpoint relative to a largely stable landscape of objects and surfaces. In fact, the only time the model needs major modification is when model-based expectations are *disconfirmed* as unexpected surfaces come into view. Everyday experience tells us that this does not happen nearly as often as confirmation of our expectations. Thus, although constructing a three-dimensional model of the environment may initially seem like a poor evolutionary strategy, its short-term costs appear to be outweighed by its long-term benefits. It takes more time and effort to construct the complete model initially, but once it is done, it requires far less time and effort to maintain it. In the final analysis, the completed model is a remarkably economical solution to the problem of how to achieve stable and accurate knowledge of the environment.

The ability to predict the perceptual future is also evolutionarily crucial because we live in a world that includes moving objects and other mobile creatures. It is useful to know the current position of a moving object, but it is far more useful to know its direction and speed so that you can predict its future trajectory. This is particularly important when something is coming toward you, because you need to decide whether to approach, sidestep, flee, or ignore it. Without a perceptual model that somehow transcends momentary stimulus information, vision would not be able to guide our actions appropriately.

The view that the purpose of the brain is to compute dynamic, predictive models of the environment was set forth by British psychologist Kenneth Craik in 1943. He argued forcefully that organisms that can rapidly extrapolate the present situation into the future have an evolutionary advantage over otherwise identical organisms that cannot. An organism that can predict accurately is able to *plan* future actions, whereas one that cannot predict can only *react* once something has happened. There is an important caveat here, however: The process of extrapolation must work faster than the predicted event to be useful. Not surprisingly, then, most perceptual predictions are generated very quickly. Indeed, they are usually generated so quickly that we have no conscious experience of them unless they are violated. Even then, our conscious experience reflects the violation rather than the expectation itself.

1.1.5 Perception as Apprehension of Meaning

Our perceptual constructions of the external world go even further than completing unseen surfaces in a three-dimensional model, however. They include information about the meaning or functional significance of objects and situations. We perceive an object not just as having a particular shape and being in a particular location, but as a person, a dog, a house, or whatever. Being able to *classify* (or *recognize* or *identify*) objects as members of known categories allows us to respond to them in appropriate ways because it gives us access to vast amounts of information that we have stored from previous experiences with similar objects.

Classification. Perhaps the easiest way to appreciate the importance of classification is to imagine encountering some completely foreign object. You could perceive its physical characteristics, such as its color, texture, size, shape, and location, but you wouldn't know what it was or what you should do with it. Is it alive? Can it be eaten? Is it dangerous? Should you approach it? Should you avoid it? Such questions can seldom be answered directly from an object's physical characteristics, for they also depend on what kind of object it is. We em-

brace loved ones, flee angry dogs, walk around pillars, eat hamburgers, and sit in chairs. All this is so obvious that it scarcely seems worth mentioning, but without perceptually classifying things into known categories, it would be difficult to behave appropriately with the enormous variety of new objects that we encounter daily. We can simply walk around the pillar because past experience informs us that such objects do not generally move. But angry dogs can and do!

Classification is useful because objects within the same category share so many properties and behaviors. All chairs are not exactly alike, nor are all hamburgers, but one chair is a lot more like another than it is like any hamburger, and vice versa. Previous experience with members of a given category therefore allows us to predict with reasonable certainty what new members of that same class will do. As a consequence, we can deal with most new objects at the more abstract level of their category, even though we have never seen that particular object before.

Classifying objects as members of known categories seems simple, but it is actually quite an achievement. Consider the wide variety of dogs shown in Figure 1.1.9, for example. How can we recognize almost immediately that they are all dogs? Do dogs have some unique set of properties that enable us to perceive them as dogs? If so, what might they be? These are problems of object identification, one of the most difficult—and as yet unsolved—puzzles of visual perception. In Chapters 8 and 9, we will consider some current ideas about how this might happen.

Attention and Consciousness. It is an undeniable fact that the visible environment contains much more information than anyone can fully perceive. You must therefore be *selective* in what you attend to, and what you select will depend a great deal on your needs, goals, plans, and desires. Although there is certainly an important sense in which a hamburger is always a hamburger, how you react to one depends a great deal on whether you have just finished a two-day fast or a seven-course meal. After fasting, your attention would undoubtedly be drawn immediately to the hamburger; right after a big Thanksgiving dinner, you would probably ignore it, and if you did not, the sight of it might literally nauseate you.

This example demonstrates that perception is not an entirely **stimulus-driven process**; that is, perceptions

Figure 1.1.9 Many kinds of dogs. Visual perception goes beyond the physical description of objects to classify them into known categories. Despite the substantial physical differences in their appearance, all these animals are readily perceived as belonging to the category of dogs.

are not determined solely by the nature of the optical information present in sensory stimulation. Our perceptions are also influenced to some extent by **cognitive constraints**: higher-level goals, plans, and expectations. It would be strange indeed if this were not so, since the whole evolutionary purpose of perception, I have argued, is to make contact between the needs of the organism and the corresponding opportunities available in its environment. There are countless ways in which such higher-level cognitive constraints influence your perception, many of which involve the selective process of visual attention. As the hamburger example suggests, we look at different things in our surroundings depending on what we are trying to accomplish, and we may perceive them differently as a result. This point is perhaps so obvious that it goes without saying, but it is important nevertheless.

One of the functions of attention is to bring visual information to consciousness. Certain properties of objects do not seem to be experienced consciously unless they are attended, yet unattended objects are often processed fully enough outside of consciousness to attract your attention. Everyday examples abound. You may initially not notice a stationary object in your visual periphery, but if it suddenly starts moving toward you, you look in its direction without knowing why, only then becoming consciously aware of its presence. While driving your car, you sometimes look over at the car next to you without knowing why, only to find that the driver has been looking at you. In both cases, visual processing must have taken place outside of consciousness, directing your attention to the interesting or important aspects of the environment: the moving object or the person looking at you. Once the object is attended, you become conscious of its detailed properties and are able to identify it and discern its meaning in the present situation.

Attending to an object visually usually means moving your eyes to fixate on it, but attention and visual fixation are not the same. You are probably familiar with the fact that you can be looking directly at something without attending to it in the slightest. Your thoughts may wander to some completely different topic, and once attention returns to the visual information, you may realize that you had no awareness of what was in your visual field during the diversion. Conversely, you can attend to an object without fixating on it. To demonstrate this, hold your hand out in front of you and fixate directly on your middle finger. Now, without moving your eyes, try attending to each of the other fingers in turn. It is not terribly easy, because you want to move your eyes at the same time as you shift your attention, but it clearly can be done.

Many high-level aspects of perception seem to be fully conscious. For example, when you look around the room trying to find your keys, you are certainly aware of the key-finding goal that directs your attention to various likely places in the room. Other aspects of perception are clearly *not* conscious, even in the same situation, such as knowing what makes an object "keylike" enough to direct your eyes at it during this visual search. In general, lower levels of perception do not seem to be accessible to, or modifiable by, conscious knowledge and expectations, whereas higher levels do.

Not much is yet known about the role of consciousness in perception. Indeed, we know surprisingly little even about the evolutionary advantage of conscious perception. There is a general belief that there must be one, but nobody has yet managed to give a good account of what it is. The basic question is what advantage there might be for a consciously perceiving organism over one that can perform all the same perceptual tasks but without having conscious visual experiences. The unconscious automaton can, by definition, engage in all of the same evolutionarily useful activities—successfully finding food, shelter, and mates while avoiding cliffs, predators, and falling objects—so it is unclear on what basis consciousness could be evolutionarily selected.

One possibility is that the problem is ill-posed. Perhaps the automaton actually could *not* perform all the tasks that the consciously perceiving organism could. Perhaps consciousness plays some crucial and as-yet-unspecified role in our perceptual abilities. We will return to these conjectures in Chapter 13 when we consider what is known about the relation between consciousness and perception.

1.2 Optical Information

Our definition of visual perception implies that vision depends crucially on the interaction among three things: light, surfaces that reflect light, and the visual system of an observer that can detect light. Remove any one of these ingredients, and visual perception of the environment simply does not occur. It seems reasonable, therefore, to begin our study of vision by considering some basic facts about each of them. The present section will describe how light interacts with surfaces to produce the optical events that are the starting point of vision. The next section will describe the overall structure of the human visual system that processes information in these optical events. The remainder of the book discusses in detail how the visual system goes about extracting relevant information from light to produce useful perceptions of environmental scenes and events.

I argued in the preceding section that the evolutionary role of visual perception is to provide an organism with accurate information about its environment. For this to happen, the light that enters our eyes must somehow carry information about the environment. It need not carry *all* the information we ultimately get from looking at things, but it must carry enough that the rest can be inferred with reasonable accuracy. In this section, we will consider how light manages to carry information about the world of visible objects around us.

1.2.1 The Behavior of Light

The science concerned with the behavior of light is a branch of physics called **optics**. According to prevailing physical theory, light consists of minute packets of energy called **photons** that behave like waves in some respects and like particles in others. Throughout most of this book we will be concerned mainly with the particle behavior of photons, although the discussion of color vision in Chapter 3 will require consideration of its wavelike properties as well. Photons radiate outward from their source—a hot body such as the sun, a fire, or the filament of an incandescent light bulb—like infinitely tiny bullets that travel through air in perfectly straight lines at the enormous speed of 186,000 miles per second. When photons strike the surface of an object, we say that it is *illuminated*. The amount of visible light—that is, the number of photons—falling on a given surface per unit of time is called its **luminance**. The luminance of a light covaries to some degree with its perceived brightness, but the relation is far from simple, as we will discover in Chapter 3.

Illumination. Illumination refers to the lighting conditions in the environment. The simplest condition from an analytical standpoint is called **point-source illumination**. It refers to an idealized situation in which all the light illuminating a scene comes from a single, point-sized light source at a specific location. A single incandescent light bulb in an otherwise dark space would be a reasonable approximation, as would the sun on a cloudless day. Point-source illumination produces dark, well-defined shadows behind illuminated surfaces and strong shading effects on the illuminated surfaces themselves, as illustrated in Figure 1.2.1A. Both effects result from the fact that all of the direct (nonreflected) light is coming from a single location. In fact, one seldom encounters lighting conditions this simple in the real world. Point-

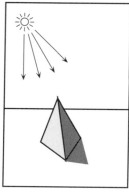
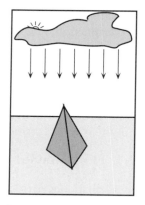

A. Point-Source Illumination B. Spatially Extended Illumination

Figure 1.2.1 Point-source illumination versus diffuse illumination. A single point source creates well-defined shadows (A), whereas spatially extended illumination does not (B).

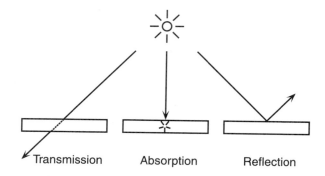

Transmission Absorption Reflection

Figure 1.2.2 Interactions between light and surfaces. A photon can be transmitted through a surface, absorbed by it, or reflected off it.

source illumination is primarily of interest to vision theorists as a way to reduce the mathematical complexity of certain problems. It is used as a simplifying assumption, for example, in determining the shape of an object from the shading on its illuminated surfaces. If there are multiple point sources, such as a room with two or more incandescent lights, there are correspondingly two or more different shadows and shading patterns for each surface. Each additional light source thus complicates the optical structure of the environment.

In many real situations, light comes from **diffuse illumination**, in which light radiates from a relatively large region of space. To take an extreme example, the light of the sun on an overcast day is diffused almost uniformly over the entire sky, so nearly equal amounts of radiant light are coming from everywhere in the whole upper half of the visual environment. Under such conditions, both the shadow cast by illuminated surfaces and the shading on the surfaces themselves are much weaker and less well defined than under point-source illumination, as illustrated in Figure 1.2.1B. If you are a skier, you have probably noticed one of the effects of diffuse illumination under cloudy skies: It reduces the optical information that allows you to perceive the undulations in the snow surface (called "moguls") that cause a large proportion of falls. In fact, skiers have so much more trouble negotiating the slopes on cloudy days that they have invented an apt name for the situation: "flat light."

Interaction with Surfaces. We said that photons travel in perfectly straight lines, but only until they strike the surface of an object. In almost every case, the surface produces a radical change in the behavior of the photons that strike it. It is these surface-induced changes in the behavior of photons that ultimately provide vision with information about the surfaces in the environment that produced them. The only surfaces that do not change the behavior of photons are completely transparent ones, and such surfaces would be literally invisible—if they existed. All real surfaces interact with light strongly enough under most conditions that they are visible to a vigilant observer.

When a photon strikes the surface of an object, one of three basic events takes place: It is either *transmitted* through the surface, *absorbed* by it, or *reflected* off it (see Figure 1.2.2). Transmitted light can either pass straight through the surface or be bent (*refracted*), as it is in Figure 1.2.3, which shows the lower part of a spoon in a glass of water as being displaced laterally. Of these photon-surface interactions, reflection is the most important for vision for two reasons. First, reflected light has been changed by its interaction with the surface, so it contains information about the surface. Second, reflected light is subsequently available to strike the receptive surface of an observer's eye, so it can transmit that information about the surface to the visual system. Nonreflected light is also important for understanding certain aspects of visual perception—absorbed light for color vision and transmitted light for perception of transparency—but in the present discussion, we will concentrate on the optical information in reflected light.

Figure 1.2.3 Refraction of light. When light is transmitted through an object, it can be bent (refracted), leading to erroneous perceptions, such as the misaligned appearance of the spoon handle in this glass of water.

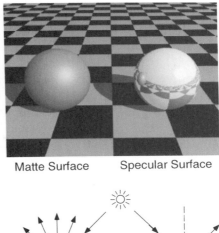

Matte Surface   Specular Surface

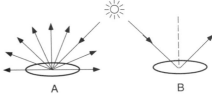

A   B

Figure 1.2.4 Matte versus specular surfaces. The two spheres in the picture differ only in how their surfaces reflect light. The matte sphere on the left reflects light equally in all directions, whereas the specular sphere on the right reflects it coherently, so that the angle of reflection equals the angle of incidence.

The change that a surface produces in a reflected photon is to alter its trajectory: The photon bounces off the surface in a direction that depends on both the direction from which it came and the microscopic structure of the surface. If the surface is highly polished, or **specular**, such as a mirror, the light is reflected in the single direction that is symmetric to the direction from which it came (see Figure 1.2.4B); the angle of incidence is equal to the angle of reflection. On the other hand, if the surface is dull or **matte**, such as a typical piece of paper, the light is scattered diffusely in many directions (see Figure 1.2.4A). Perfectly specular and perfectly matte surfaces are just the two idealized endpoints of a continuum, and all real surfaces fall somewhere in between. Figure 1.2.4 shows how different the same spherical shape looks with a highly specular surface compared to a highly matte surface. The reflectance properties of surfaces are actually even more complex than we have considered here because the degree of specularity can vary as a function of the angle of incident light, as is the case with semigloss surfaces. When viewed in a direction nearly parallel to the surface, they are much more specular than when viewed nearly perpendicular to it.

Let us now try to put together what we have said about light radiation from sources of illumination and light reflection by surfaces to come to a more complete understanding of the behavior of light in a real environment. All surfaces reflect some light except completely black ones (which absorb it all) and completely transparent ones (which transmit it all).[2] And most surfaces are more matte than specular. Together, these facts imply that some light bounces in almost every direction off almost every surface in the environment. As a result, light does not come just from the direction of radiant light sources, such as the sun and light bulbs; it also comes by reflection from virtually every surface in the environment. Surfaces thus act as **secondary light sources** by illuminating other surfaces with their reflected light. Moreover, all of these photons are bouncing from sur-

---

[2] In reality, there are neither totally black surfaces nor totally transparent ones. Even seemingly jet-black surfaces reflect a few percent of the pho-

tons that fall on them, and even seemingly crystal-clear glass or plastic reflects and absorbs a few percent of the incident photons.

An Introduction to Vision Science

face to surface at enormous speed, often being reflected off many surfaces before finally being absorbed.

Color Plate 1.1 illustrates the sometimes profound effect of different levels of light reflection in the appearance of a bathroom scene. Image A was generated by a sophisticated computer program that shows only the direct illumination entering the eye from the light source, before any light from the fixture has been reflected from surfaces into the eye. Image B shows the same scene with the addition of primary reflections from nonluminous surfaces. Image C then adds secondary reflections, and image D adds further reflections up to the fifth-order. Notice that nonluminous surfaces do not appear in the image until the primary reflections are included, that the reflection in the mirror does not appear until secondary reflections are included, and that specular highlights on the shower door are not apparent until higher-order reflections are modeled. Thus, the rich appearance of natural scenes depends importantly on the complex interactions of ambient light with the structure of the physical environment.

The net effect of all these reflections is that light is reverberating around the environment, filling it with light from virtually every direction. This fact is of paramount importance for vision, because it is this complex optical structure that enables vision to occur. More light comes from some directions than others, and that is why we are able to see surfaces of different colors in different directions. Equal amounts of light from all directions, called a **Ganzfeld**, just looks like an all-encompassing gray fog.

The Ambient Optic Array. The pioneering perceptual psychologist James J. Gibson conceptualized the optical information available in light in terms of what he called the **ambient optic array** (or **AOA**). The AOA refers to the light coming toward a given point of observation from all directions. It is called "ambient" because the observation point is literally surrounded by light converging on it from all directions. This means that if your eye were at this observation point, either light reflected from environmental surfaces or light emitted directly from the radiant source would be available from every direction. Vision is possible at that observation point because environmental surfaces structure the light in the AOA in complex, but lawful, ways. This lawfulness in the optical structure of the AOA provides the information that enables vision to occur.

When conceived in this way, vision can be likened to solving a puzzle. Surfaces in the world alter light by reflecting it in a way that forms the AOA at the current observation point with a particular complex structure. The visual system registers this structure and then tries, in effect, to reverse the process by determining the arrangement of surfaces that must exist in the environment to have structured the AOA in just that way. This all happens so quickly and effortlessly that we have no conscious knowledge about how it is done.

To appreciate more fully the nature of the AOA, let us consider a few examples. Figure 1.2.5A shows schematically the structure of the AOA from an observer's perspective in a room containing a stool and a window that looks onto a tree. Notice that light comes from *all directions* toward the point of observation and that the AOA defined at this point exists independently of an observer occupying it. Figure 1.2.5B illustrates the relationship between an observer's view of the world and the AOA: The eye samples a directional subset of the AOA. The shaded part of the AOA is not currently visible because the eye admits light only from the front. Figure 1.2.5C shows the resulting pattern of light that would be entering the observer's eye at this observation point. It depicts the momentary optical image that falls on the light-sensitive cells at the back of the eye. This is the starting point of vision, at least for that instant in time.

It is important to realize that *there is a differently structured AOA at every point in the environment*. Each one is unique, providing slightly different information about the environment. To illustrate this fact, consider what happens when this observer stands up. As he or she rises, the eye moves along a trajectory of different observation points, and visual stimulation is determined at each one by its unique AOA. Figure 1.2.5D depicts the final AOA of this event with solid lines, showing how certain parts of surfaces that were previously visible have become occluded and how other parts of surfaces that were previously occluded have now become visible. Figure 1.2.5E shows what optical image is entering the observer's eye at this moment so that you can see how it has changed.

The changes in optical information caused by the change in observation point highlight a distinction of great importance between the momentary static AOA and the temporally extended, dynamic AOA. Whereas

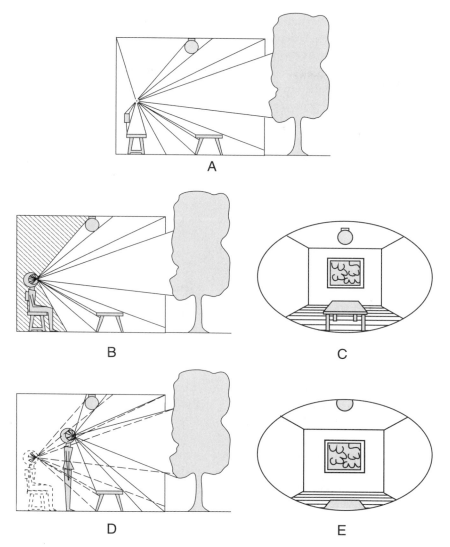

Figure 1.2.5 The ambient optic array (AOA). (A) All light converging at a given point defines the AOA at that position. (B) When an observer's eye is at that position, it samples the part of the AOA in front of the observer. (C) This sample is registered on the observer's retina as an image. (D) If the observer moves (for example, by standing), the AOA changes as illustrated. (E) This change in the AOA results in corresponding subtle changes in the observer's retinal image. (A, B, and D from Gibson, 1979.)

the static AOA can be characterized by a pattern of light converging at the observation point, the dynamic AOA can be fully characterized only by the **optic flow** of light over time. Thus, the dynamic AOA provides the observer with information from an additional dimension that unfolds over time. This turns out to be enormously important for many perceptual phenomena, such as our ability to perceive the third dimension of the environment (depth or distance from the observer), to deter-

mine the shapes of moving objects, and to perceive our own trajectory through the environment as we move. We will consider each of these topics more fully in Chapters 5 and 10 when we discuss perception of depth and motion in detail.

1.2.2 The Formation of Images

If vision is to provide accurate information about the external world, then there must be a consistent relation-

An Introduction to Vision Science

ship between the geometry of environmental surfaces and the light that enters the eye at a particular observation point. Indeed, there is. Figure 1.2.5 depicts the nature of this relationship by illustration. In this section, we will take a closer look at how optical images are formed on the back of the eye and how the laws of perspective projection describe this image formation process.

Optical Images. The situation involved in image formation is diagrammed in Figure 1.2.6. The external world has three spatial dimensions. Illumination bathes the objects in this three-dimensional space with light, and that light is reflected by surfaces into the observer's eye along straight lines (Figure 1.2.6A). Photons pass into the eye to form a two-dimensional, upside-down image on its back surface (Figure 1.2.6B and C). The object in the external world is often referred to as the **distal stimulus** (meaning distant from the observer), and its optical image at the back of the eye as the **proximal stimulus** (meaning close to the observer). As Figure 1.2.6A illustrates, the size of an object's image in the eye is usually specified by its **visual angle**: the number of degrees subtended by the image from its extremes to the focal point of the eye. It is important to understand that this angle measures the spatial dimensions of the proximal stimulus, not the distal stimulus. The same external object will subtend a smaller angle when it is farther away and a larger angle when it is closer to the observer's eye. This relationship between object size, object distance, and image size is important in understanding how we perceive the size and location of objects, as we will see in Chapter 5.

Perhaps the most important fact about the image formation process for understanding the problem of vision is that the image on the back of the eye has only *two* spatial dimensions rather than three; that is, the optical image on the back of the eye is like a slide projected onto a curved screen. This means that vital spatial information has been lost in going from the real, 3-D world to the eye's 2-D image of it. The dimension that is missing in the image is *depth*: the distance outward from the focal point of the observer's eye to the location of the environmental surface that reflected light into the eye. To perceive the world three dimensionally—which we obviously do—the dimension of depth must somehow be recovered from the information in the two spatial dimensions of the optical image.

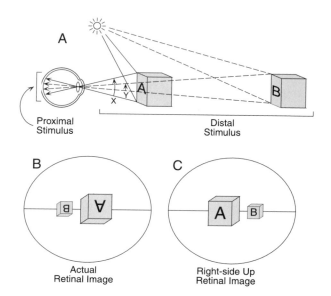

Figure 1.2.6 Image formation and the size-distance relation. Light is reflected by 3-D objects (the distal stimulus) into the eye, projecting a 2-D image (the proximal stimulus) onto the retina (part A). Because the distance to an object is not directly represented in its 2-D projection, environmental objects of the same size at different distances project images of different sizes, as illustrated in parts B and C.

Projective Geometry. The image formation process that maps the 3-D world to the 2-D image is highly lawful, and like most lawfulness, it can be analyzed mathematically. The most appropriate mathematics for the task is **projective geometry**: the study of how a higher-dimensional space is mapped onto a lower-dimensional one. In the case of static vision, the projective mapping of interest is from the 3-D space of the environment onto the 2-D space of the image plane. Projective geometry can therefore specify for a given 3-D scene of objects exactly where each point in the scene will project onto a given 2-D image plane and what properties of these images will be invariant over different projections. In dynamic vision, the projection of interest is from the 4-D structure of space-time onto the 3-D space of optic flow that unfolds over time on the 2-D surface at the back of the eye.

Projective geometry thus seems to be the ideal mathematical tool for understanding image formation. The problem is that projective geometry alone cannot model the full complexity of optical phenomena because it does not contain the appropriate structure for modeling reflection, absorption, or refraction of light. In a world filled with opaque surfaces, for example, only light reflected from the *closest* surface in a particular direction will enter the eye. Photons from all farther points will be either absorbed or reflected by the next closer surface, thus preventing them from reaching the eye. The complications that are introduced by the interaction of light with surfaces make projective geometry only partly useful for modeling the process of forming 2-D optical images from the 3-D world. Rather, one must understand in more detail how light from the 3-D world forms an image when it is projected onto a 2-D plane.

Perspective and Orthographic Projection. One way to form a 2-D image of the 3-D world is to place a pinhole at a given distance in front of an image plane or other 2-D surface inside an otherwise lightproof box. Such a device is called a **pinhole camera**. Because photons travel in straight lines, the light falling on each point of the image plane of the pinhole camera got there by being reflected (or emitted) from a particular point in environmental space. That point lies along the ray starting at its image-plane point and passing through the pinhole (see Figure 1.2.7A). This situation gives the basic geometry of **perspective projection** (or **polar projection**): the process of image formation in which the light converges toward a single focal point (or pole).

Good pinhole images are not as easy to create as the above description makes it seem. To get a crisp, clear image, the pinhole must be very small; about 0.4 mm in diameter is ideal. Because of this small aperture size, however, very little light falls on the image plane, so it must be observed under very dark conditions.[3] If the hole is made larger to let more light in, the image becomes blurred because all the light no longer goes through the single point of the pinhole but through many different points (see Figure 1.2.7B). This problem can be overcome by supplying the camera with a transparent convex **lens** at its opening to bend the incoming light inward to a point (called its **focal point**) some distance behind the lens (see Figure 1.2.7C). Thus, the lens provides a "virtual pinhole" at its focal point that makes

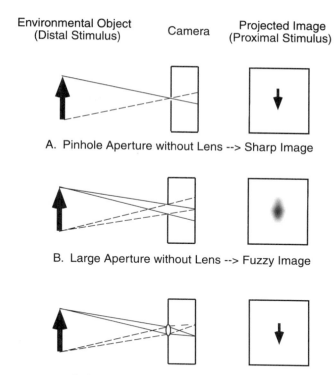

A. Pinhole Aperture without Lens --> Sharp Image

B. Large Aperture without Lens --> Fuzzy Image

C. Large Aperture with Lens --> Sharp Image

Figure 1.2.7 The optics of pinhole cameras and lenses. (A) A pinhole camera with a small aperture produces sharp images without a lens. (B) A camera with a larger aperture but no lens produces fuzzy, out-of-focus images. (C) A camera with a large aperture and a lens can produce clear, well-focused images if the focal length of the lens is appropriate for the distance to the imaging surface.

the projected image at the back sharp and clear again, like the pinhole camera's image, only brighter because more light comes through the larger opening. As we will see in Section 1.3, the human eye contains such a lens whose job is to focus the image on the back surface of the eye.

Assuming that the complicating effects of light-surface interaction can be incorporated into the model, the mathematics of perspective (or polar) projection are useful for modeling image formation by the human eye (see Figure 1.2.8A and B). Unfortunately, they are also

[3] A good way to do this is to make a light-tight box with a single pinhole on one side and a translucent flat surface behind it. When the back surface is viewed under darkened conditions—such as with a dark cloth covering one's head and the back of the box—you can observe the upside-down and backward image on the translucent surface.

An Introduction to Vision Science

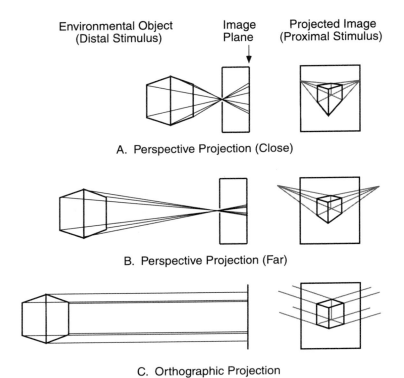

Environmental Object
(Distal Stimulus)

Image
Plane

Projected Image
(Proximal Stimulus)

A. Perspective Projection (Close)

B. Perspective Projection (Far)

C. Orthographic Projection

Figure 1.2.8 Perspective and orthographic projection. Perspective projection through a pinhole (A and B) produces convergence of parallel lines to a vanishing point, but close perspective (A) yields more convergence than far perspective (B). Orthographic projection (C) is based on parallel light rays and produces no convergence of parallel lines in the image.

rather complex, much more so than has been alluded to here. To simplify matters, visual theorists often employ **orthographic projection** (or **parallel projection**) instead of perspective projection to model the geometry of image formation (see Figure 1.2.8C). In this case, the image is conceptualized as being formed by light rays that travel parallel to each other and perpendicular to the image plane, rather than rays that converge at the pinhole.

The mathematical simplification that results from orthographic projection is that the depth dimension of the world—distances from image to objects—is simply ignored, whereas all spatial information in the plane perpendicular to the viewing direction is preserved without change. This means that when the distance from the image to the object is large relative to the depth of the object (Figure 1.2.8B), orthographic projection is a good approximation of perspective projection. Close up, however, the differences between orthographic and perspective projection become quite significant, as illustrated in Figure 1.2.8A.

One way of understanding the relationship between perspective and orthographic projection is to consider what happens when an object is moved farther and farther away from the pinhole of perspective projection (compare Figure 1.2.8A and Figure 1.2.8B). As this happens, the light rays projecting through the pinhole become more and more parallel so that, at an infinite distance, the light rays would be parallel, as they are in orthographic projection (Figure 1.2.8C). Thus, orthographic projection can be conceived as a limiting case of perspective projection, at which the distance between object and focal point is infinite. The important difference is that the perspective image of an object at an infinite distance is a single point, unlike its true orthographic projection which results in a spatially extended image.

1.2.3 Vision as an "Inverse" Problem

We have now described how light reflected from the 3-D world produces 2-D images at the back of the eye where vision begins. This process of image formation is completely determined by the laws of optics, so for any given scene with well-specified lighting conditions and a point of observation, we can determine with great accuracy what image would be produced. In fact, the field of **computer graphics** is concerned with exactly this problem: how to render images on a computer display screen that realistically depict scenes of objects by modeling the process of image formation. Many of the problems in this domain are now very well understood, as one can appreciate by examining some examples of state-of-the-art computer images that have been generated without recourse to any real optical processes whatsoever. The images in Color Plate 1.1, for example, were rendered by a ray-tracing algorithm that simulates image formation from an internal model of the surfaces in the room and the behavior of the light that illuminates them. In effect, the program simulates the optical events of photon emission, reflection, transmission, and absorption to construct an image of a "virtual" environment that does not exist in the physical world. Such programs allow the effects of different orders of light reflection to be illustrated (e.g., in Color Plate 1.1A–D) because the program can be stopped after each cycle of simulated reflection to see what the image looks like. This is not possible with real optical image formation.

The early stages of visual perception can be viewed as trying to solve what is often called the **inverse problem**: how to get from optical images of scenes back to knowledge of the objects that gave rise to them. From this perspective, the most obvious solution is for vision to try to *invert* the process of image formation by undoing the optical transformations that happen during image formation.

Unfortunately, there is no easy way to do this. The difficulty is that the mathematical relation between the environment and its projective image is not symmetrical. The projection from environment to image goes from three dimensions to two and so is a well-defined function: Each point in the environment maps into a unique point in the image. The inverse mapping from image to environment goes from two dimensions to three, and

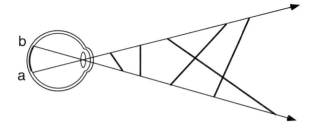

Figure 1.2.9 An illustration of inverse projection. A single line segment on the retina can be the projection of an infinite variety of lines in the environment.

this is not a well-defined function: Each point in the image could map into an infinite number of points in the environment. Therefore, logic dictates that for every 2-D image on the back of our eyes, there are infinitely many distinct 3-D environments that could have given rise to it.

Figure 1.2.9 illustrates the indeterminacy of inverse projection by showing that a single line segment in an optical image could have resulted from the projection of an infinite number of lines in the environment. The reason is that the inverse problem is *underspecified* (or *underconstrained* or *underdetermined*) by the sensory data in the image. There is no easy way around this problem, and that is why visual perception is so complex. In fact, were it not for the fact that our brains manage to come up with the correct solution most of the time, it would be tempting to conclude that 3-D visual perception is simply impossible!

We know that 3-D perception *is* possible precisely because the human visual system manages to do it with such remarkable accuracy under most circumstances. How does it solve this seemingly insoluble problem? Different theorists have taken different approaches, as we shall see in Chapter 5, but the dominant one is to assume that 3-D perception results from the visual system making a lot of highly plausible assumptions about the nature of the environment and the conditions under which it is viewed. These assumptions constrain the inverse problem enough to make it solvable most of the time. If the assumptions are true, the resulting solution will be veridical. Vision is thus a **heuristic process** in which inferences are made about the most likely environmental condition that could have produced a given image. The process is *heuristic* because it makes

An Introduction to Vision Science

use of inferential rules of thumb—based on the additional assumptions—that are not always valid and so will sometimes lead to erroneous conclusions, as in the case of perceptual illusions. Under most everyday circumstances, however, the assumptions *are* true, and so normal visual perception is highly veridical. We will encounter these additional assumptions throughout the book, particularly in Chapter 5 when we discuss depth perception in detail. Then we will be able to see in what sense they allow the visual system to go beyond the information given in the optical image so that the seemingly impossible inverse problem can be solved.

1.3 Visual Systems

We know that the inverse problem can be solved because the human visual system solves it—maybe not all the time and maybe not with perfect accuracy, but enough of the time and with sufficient accuracy to provide us with excellent information about the environment. Much of the rest of this book is concerned with what is currently known about how the visual system accomplishes this feat. To begin, we will now take a quick look at the overall structure of the part of the nervous system that is known to be involved in processing visual information. The description that we give here will be brief and superficial in many respects. This is intentional. Its purpose is merely to provide a scaffolding of background knowledge about the biological structure of the visual system so that it will be available for later discussions that complete the picture. Once we have mastered some of the basic facts about the "hardware" of this system—its **anatomy** or physical structure—we can begin to ask better informed questions about what it does—its **physiology**, or biological function.

1.3.1 The Human Eye

Although it has been known since antiquity that eyes are the sensory organs of vision, an accurate understanding of how they work is a relatively recent achievement. The Greek philosopher Plato (427–347 B.C.) believed that an "inner fire" gave rise to rays that emanated from the eye toward perceived objects. Epicurus (341–270 B.C.) rejected this emanation theory, believing instead that tiny replicas of objects were somehow transmitted rapidly into the mind through the eyes. Galen (A.D. 130–200)

later elaborated these ideas with physiological details, proposing that after the rays emanated from the eye, they interacted with the object and then returned to the eye. In the lens of the eye, he believed, these rays interacted with a "visual spirit" that flowed from the brain to the eye and back, bringing with it the replicas of perceived objects.

The modern era of physiological optics did not really begin until the brilliant Arabic philosopher Alhazen (A.D. 965–1040) hit upon the idea that the eye is like a pinhole camera, as we discussed in Section 1.2.2. The important insight that he achieved was that vision occurs when light from external sources is reflected from surfaces of objects and enters the eye. Even so, an accurate understanding of the optics of the eye required the invention and understanding of lenses. The noted astronomer Johannes Kepler (1571–1630) finally put these elements together into a reasonable approximation of the modern theory of physiological optics, discussed below.

Eye and Brain. Although Galen had many important facts about vision wrong, he was right in believing that both eyes and brain are essential (see Figure 1.3.1). We now know that optical information from the eyes is transmitted to the primary visual cortex in the occipital lobe at the back of the head, as shown in Figure 1.3.1. This information is then sent to many other visual centers located in the posterior temporal and parietal cortex, as illustrated in Figure 1.3.2. Some estimates put the percentage of the cortex involved with visual function at more than 50% in the macaque monkey (DeYoe & Van Essen, 1988; Van Essen et al., 1990), although it is probably slightly lower in humans. The complete visual system thus includes much of the brain as well as the eyes, and the whole eye-brain system must function properly for the organism to extract reliable information about the environment from the ambient optic array. The eyes must collect and register information contained in light, and the brain must then process that information in ways that make it useful for the organism.

The fact that both eye and brain are required for vision means that a person who has normal eyes but damage to visual parts of the brain might be as "blind" as a person who has a normal brain but eyes that fail to work. Indeed, both sorts of blindness exist. Damage to the eyes from accidents or disease sometimes prevents

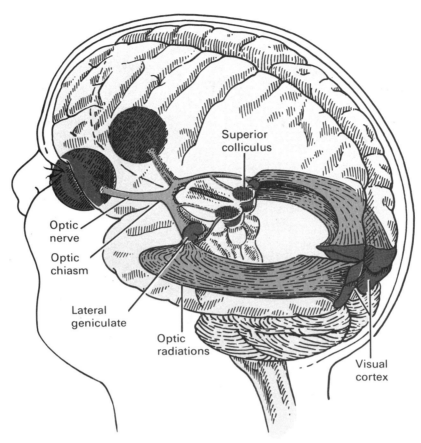

Figure 1.3.1 The human visual system. Visual processing begins in the eyes and is relayed to the brain by the optic nerve. The primary visual pathway then goes from the lateral geniculate nucleus to occipital cortex via the optic radiations. From there, visual information travels to other parts of the brain. A secondary pathway goes from the optic nerve to the superior colliculus and then to other brain centers. (From Rosenzweig & Leiman, 1982.)

them from doing their job of registering optical information and/or sending it on to the visual areas of the brain. Such conditions cause the sort of blindness most people know about: lack of sight because no information from light gets into the system. Although far less common, there are also people who cannot see—or at least do not have visual experiences—yet have eyes that work quite normally. This kind of blindness—called **blindsight**—results from damage to certain critical parts of the visual cortex due to disease, surgery, or stroke (see Section 13.2.2). Damage to other parts of visual cortex does not result in blindness but can cause debilitating selective deficits in perception. Some patients can see well enough to describe faces accurately but cannot identify even members of their own family by sight (see Section 9.2.5). Others can describe and draw simple everyday objects but cannot name them or use them properly. It has even been reported that some people see stationary scenes perfectly well but cannot perceive motion, experiencing instead a series of frozen snapshots (see Section 10.1.4). We will discuss these fascinating problems in more detail at appropriate places throughout the book, particularly at the end when we consider conscious experiences of seeing.

Anatomy of the Eye. There are some obvious anatomical facts about the eyes that almost everyone knows. Humans have two eyes, which are approximately spherical in shape except for a bulge at the front. Located at about the horizontal midline of the head, they sit in nearly hemispherical holes in the skull, called the **eye sockets**, that hold them securely in position yet allow

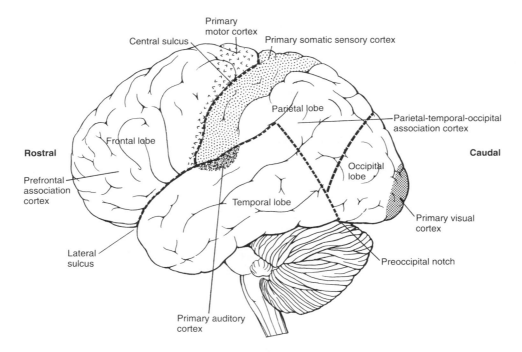

Figure 1.3.2 Visual areas of the human cortex. From primary visual cortex in the occipital lobe, visual information separates into two major pathways: a lower (ventral) one that goes to the inferior regions of the temporal lobe and an upper (dorsal) one that goes to the parietal lobe. Both pathways eventually make their way to the frontal lobe. (From Kandel, Schwartz, & Jessell, 1991.)

their direction to be changed by rotation. Each eye is moved by the coordinated use of six small, strong muscles, called the **extraocular muscles**, which are controlled by specific areas in the brain (see Section 11.1.2). Eye movements are necessary for scanning different regions of the visual field without having to turn the entire head and for focusing on objects at different distances. Eyelids and eyelashes protect the eyes, and tears keep them moist and clean.

Few of these simple facts are universally true of nonhuman eyes, however. Some species, such as pigeons and owls, cannot move their eyes in sockets but must move their whole heads. This limits the rate at which new views of the world can be registered, simply because heads are so much heavier and harder to turn than eyes. Eye position also differs in important ways across species. Although human eyes are both positioned at the front of our heads, many animals have their eyes located very much nearer the sides. Frontal placement provides two visual fields with a large area of overlap, as shown in Figure 1.3.3 but a correspondingly smaller total view of the environment. The benefit of over-

lapping visual fields is that binocular ("two-eyed") vision is important for precise depth perception, as we will discover in Section 5.3. Being able to gauge the distance to an object precisely is evolutionarily advantageous for predators, who need this information for an effective attack, and so the eyes of hunters tend to be placed frontally with overlapping fields. In contrast, panoramic visual fields are advantageous for the hunted to monitor as much of the world as possible for danger, and so prey tend to have laterally placed eyes. Other animals have frontally or laterally placed eyes for a variety of reasons, all of which reflect the same tradeoff between accuracy of depth perception and coverage of the visual world.

Physiological Optics. Because they constitute the "front end" of the visual system, the eyes have two important optical functions in common with cameras: to gather light reflected from surfaces in the world and to focus it in a clear image on the back of the eye. If insufficient light is admitted, the image will be dim and ineffective for vision. If the image is not clearly focused,

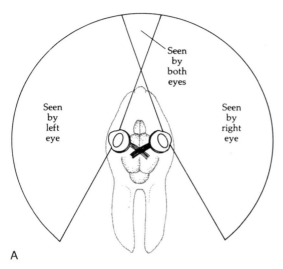

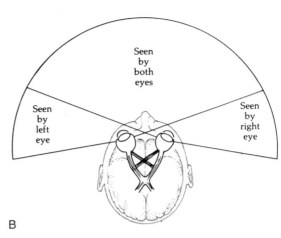

A

B

Figure 1.3.3 Overlap of monocular visual fields. In rabbits (A), lateral placement of the eyes produces a wide field of view but little binocular overlap. In people (B), frontal placement of the

eyes produces a narrower field of view but a large area of binocular vision. (From Sekuler & Blake, 1985.)

fine-grained optical information will be irrevocably lost, and spatial perception will suffer.

There are many parts of the eye that accomplish different optical functions (see Figure 1.3.4). To find out how the eye is constructed and how it registers light, let's follow a photon through its various structures. First, light enters the **cornea**, a transparent bulge on the front of the eye behind which is a cavity filled with a clear liquid, called the **aqueous humor**. Next it passes through the **pupil**, a variably sized opening in the opaque **iris**, which gives the eye its external color. Just behind the iris, light passes through the *lens*, whose shape is con-

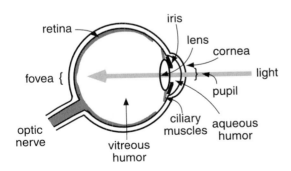

Figure 1.3.4 A cross section of the human eye. Light enters the eye through the cornea, aqueous humor, lens, and vitreous humor before striking the light-sensitive receptors of the retina, where light is converted into electrochemical signals that are carried to the brain via the optic nerve.

trolled by **ciliary muscles** attached to its edge. The photon then travels through the clear **vitreous humor** that fills the central chamber of the eye. Finally, it reaches its destination, striking the **retina**, the curved surface at the back of the eye. The retina is densely covered with over 100 million light-sensitive **photoreceptors**, which convert light into neural activity. This information about the light striking the retina is then sent to the visual centers in the brain.

Each of the eye's components performs a critical role in the eye's sensory capabilities. The amount of light striking the retina is controlled by the iris and pupil. When illumination is low, the pupil dilates so that more light strikes the retina. When illumination is high, the pupil constricts so that less light strikes it. Interestingly, pupil size also changes in response to psychological factors. For instance, positive emotional reactions dilate the pupil, as shown by the fact that most men's pupils dilate when viewing pictures of nude females and most women's pupils dilate when viewing pictures of nude males (Hess & Polt, 1960). Pupil size also reflects mental effort, dilating when concentration is intense (Hess & Polt, 1964; Kahneman & Beatty, 1967). All of this occurs without our knowledge, since we have no conscious control over the mechanisms that alter the size of our pupils.

Light entering the eye is useful only if it is focused on the retina in a reasonably sharp image. Because the

An Introduction to Vision Science

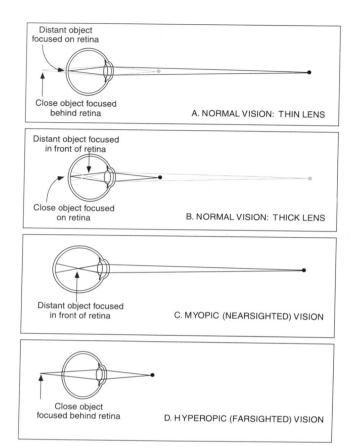

Figure 1.3.5 Focusing light by the lens. In a normal eye (A), a thin lens focuses light from distant objects, but not from close objects, on the retina. In a normal eye (B), a thick lens focuses light from close objects, but not from far objects, on the retina. In an uncorrected myopic (nearsighted) eye (C), light from distant objects is focused in front of the retina. In an uncorrected hyperopic (farsighted) eye (D), light from near objects is focused behind the retina.

pupil is much bigger than a pinhole, the light must be bent inward toward the center of the eye to focus it on the retina (see Figure 1.3.5). The curvature of the cornea does most of the job, and the lens does the rest. The lens is particularly important, however, because of its *variable focusing ability*. The lens's optical properties can be altered by changing its shape, a process called **accommodation**. To bring distant objects into focus on the retina, the lens must be thin (see Figure 1.3.5A). This is accomplished by relaxing the ciliary muscles. To focus on nearby objects, the lens must be thick (see Figure 1.3.5B). This is accomplished by contracting the ciliary muscles. People who are nearsighted (or **myopic**) have

excellent near vision but cannot focus distant objects properly because their lens is too thick for the depth of their eye (see Figure 1.3.5C). People who are farsighted (or **hyperopic**) can see well far away but cannot focus on nearby objects properly because their lens is too thin for the depth of their eye (see Figure 1.3.5D). As people get older, the lens gradually loses its elasticity, so it cannot become thick enough for near vision—a condition known as **presbyopia**. At about 40–50 years of age, many people who have never worn glasses before begin to need them for reading and other near work, and many people who already wore glasses must switch to bifocals.

Most of the light that comes though the pupil gets absorbed by photoreceptors in the retina and causes neurochemical responses in them. Some gets absorbed by the lens, vitreous humor, blood vessels, and various nonreceptor cells in the retina. This is to be expected, because none of these structures are perfectly clear, and some of them (like blood vessels and the pigment epithelium) are quite dark, absorbing a great deal of light. But the majority of light entering the eye makes it through to the retina.

1.3.2 The Retina

After the optics of the eye have done their job, the next critical function of the eye is to convert light into neural activity so that the brain can process the optical information. To understand how this occurs, we must briefly explain the basic building blocks of the brain and how they work.

Neurons. The main functional component of the brain is generally believed to be the **neuron**: a specialized type of cell that integrates the (input) activity of other neurons that are connected to it and propagates that integrated (output) activity to other neurons. This process of integration and transmission is accomplished by a complex series of biochemical events within the neuron. The parts of a neuron are illustrated in Figure 1.3.6, and their function can be described as follows:

1. The **dendrites** are thin protrusions from the cell body that collect chemical signals from other neurons and convert them into electrical activity along the thin membrane that encloses the cell. This electrical activity is a **graded potential**: an electrical difference between

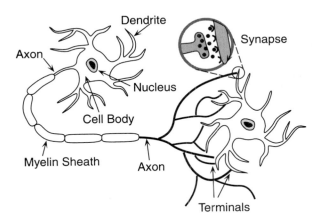

Figure 1.3.6 A typical neuron. A neuron is a cell that consists of a cell body that integrates graded electrical signals from its dendrites and transmits the result via discrete action potentials. These spikes travel along an axon, which is encased in a myelinated sheath, to terminals, where neurotransmitters are released at synapses to stimulate the dendrites of other neurons.

the inside and outside of the dendrite whose value can vary continuously within a range, depending on how strongly the dendrite has been stimulated by other neurons.

2. The **cell body** contains the nucleus and cellular machinery. The membrane around the cell body integrates the electrical signals arriving from all the dendrites, again coded in terms of a graded potential, and converts it into a series of all-or-none electrical potentials (called **action potentials**, **nerve impulses**, or simply **spikes**) that are propagated along the axon.

3. The **axon** is a long, thin projection of the neuron along which action potentials are propagated to other neurons, often over a considerable distance. Most of the axon of most neurons is covered by a **myelin sheath**, which speeds the conduction of action potentials. The strength of the integrated signal that the axon transmits is encoded primarily in its **firing rate**: the number of electrical impulses it generates in a given amount of time (e.g., spikes per second).

4. The **terminals** are the branching ends of the axon at which the electrical activity of the axon is converted back into a chemical signal by which it can stimulate another neuron. This is accomplished by releasing a **neurotransmitter** into the small gap between the terminal and the dendrite of the next neuron. Neurotransmitters are chemical substances that are capable of

exciting the dendrites of other neurons. The signal strength transmitted at the terminal is determined by the amount of neurotransmitter released.

5. The **synapse** is the small gap that exists between the terminals of one neuron and the dendrites of another. The neurotransmitter that is released into the synapse rapidly crosses the gap and affects the next neuron's dendrite by occupying specialized sites on its membrane. This is where the chemical signal from one neuron is converted to an electrical signal in the next, as described in item 1 above.

Neurons thus receive input from some neurons and send their output to other neurons. But before any of this neural activity can occur, something must convert energy in the environment into the form needed by these neurons. In the visual system, this function is carried out by *photoreceptors*: specialized retinal cells that are stimulated by light energy through a complex process that we will describe shortly. Once the optical information is coded into neural responses, some initial processing is accomplished within the retina itself by several other types of neurons, including the **horizontal**, **bipolar**, **amacrine**, and **ganglion cells**, all of which integrate responses from many nearby cells (see Figure 1.3.7). We will consider the function of these other neurons in the retina in later chapters (e.g., Chapters 3 and 4). The axons of the ganglion cells carry information out of the eye through the **optic nerve** and on to the visual centers of the brain.

Photoreceptors. There are two distinct classes of photoreceptor cells in the retina: **rods** and **cones**. Their names were chosen to describe their shapes, as shown in the scanning electron micrograph in Figure 1.3.8. Rods are typically longer and have untapered (rodlike) ends, whereas cones are shorter, thicker, and have tapered (conelike) ends. Rods are more numerous (about 120 million), extremely sensitive to light, and located everywhere in the retina except at its very center (see Figure 1.3.9). They are used exclusively for vision at very low light levels (called **scotopic conditions**): at night, at twilight, or in dimly lighted rooms. Cones are less abundant ("only" 8 million), much less sensitive to light, and heavily concentrated in the center of the retina, although some are found scattered throughout the periphery (see Figure 1.3.9). They are responsible for

An Introduction to Vision Science

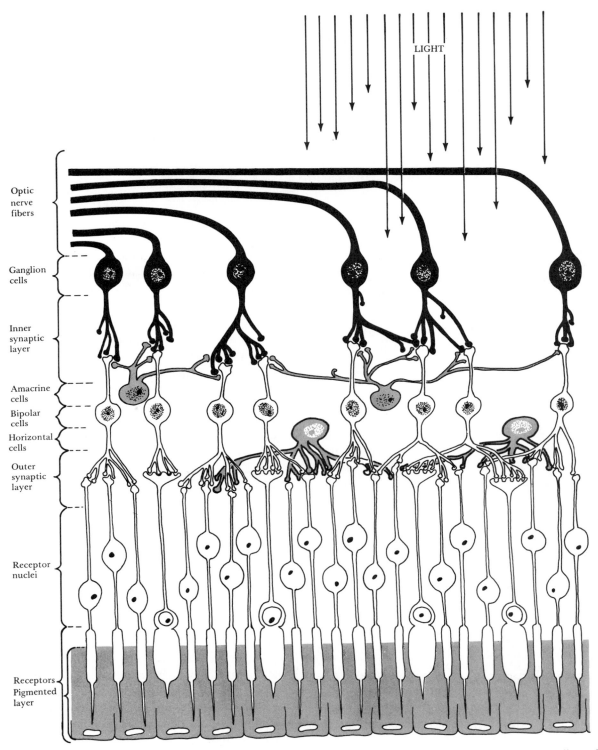

LIGHT

Optic
nerve
fibers

Ganglion
cells

Inner
synaptic
layer

Amacrine
cells

Bipolar
cells

Horizontal
cells

Outer
synaptic
layer

Receptor
nuclei

Receptors
Pigmented
layer

Figure 1.3.7 The human retina. The retina consists of five major types of neurons: receptors (the rods and three kinds of cones, shown near the bottom), bipolar cells, ganglion cells, horizontal cells, and amacrine cells. (From Lindsay & Norman, 1977.)

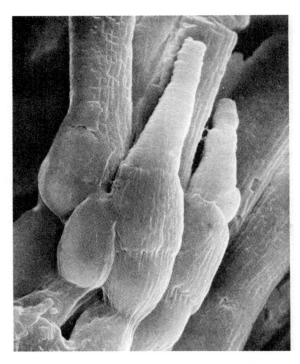

Figure 1.3.8 Scanning electron micrograph of rods and cones. The outer segments of rods have an untapered cylindrical shape, and those of cones have a tapered conical shape. (From Lewis, Zeevi, & Werblin, 1969.)

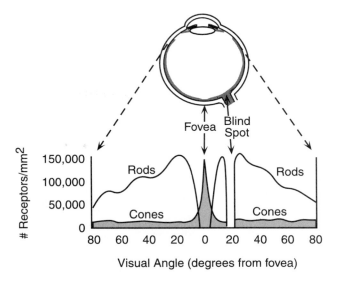

Figure 1.3.9 Distribution of rods (solid curve) and cones (shaded region) in the human retina. Notice that the fovea is populated almost exclusively by cones and that rods are much more plentiful than cones in the periphery.

our visual experiences under most normal lighting conditions (called **photopic conditions**) and for all our experiences of color. There is a small region, called the **fovea**, right at the center of the retina that contains nothing but densely packed cones (see Figure 1.3.9). The visual angle covered by the fovea is only about 2 degrees, the size of your thumbnail held at arm's length. It is more important than its small size would suggest, however, because it is here that both color and spatial vision are most acute.

The obvious question at this point is *how* photoreceptors manage to change the electromagnetic energy of photons into neural activity. It is a complex and truly ingenious process that is now reasonably well understood. Both rods and cones have two basic parts, as shown in Figure 1.3.10: the **inner segment** which contains the nucleus and other cellular machinery, and the **outer segment** which contains billions of light-sensitive pigment molecules. These pigment molecules are embedded in the membranes of hundreds of disks

stacked like pancakes perpendicular to the long axis of the outer segment.

The pigment in rods is called **rhodopsin**, and a great deal is now known about how this photosensitive molecule converts light into electrochemical energy. When a photon strikes a rhodopsin molecule and is absorbed by it, the molecule changes its shape in a way that alters the flow of electric current in and around the pigment molecule. We will not be concerned with the details of this complex biochemical reaction except to note that its result is to produce electrical changes in the outer membrane of the receptor. These changes are then propagated down the outer membrane to the synaptic region of the receptor, where chemical transmitters affect the next neuron.

The electrical changes that result from many photons being absorbed within the same receptor are integrated in the response of its outer membrane. The resulting overall change in the electrical potential between inside and outside of the cell is *graded*, in that it is continuous (rather than discrete), unlike that in most other parts of the nervous system. In quantitative terms, the graded response of a photoreceptor is a *logarithmic function* of the number of photons absorbed. This means that the same overall increase in output will require very few addi-

An Introduction to Vision Science

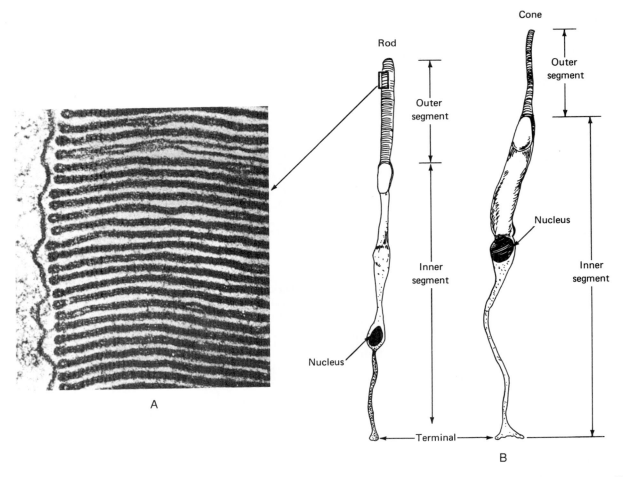

Cone

Rod

Outer segment

Outer segment

Inner segment

Inner segment

Nucleus

Nucleus

Terminal

A

B

Figure 1.3.10 The anatomy of rods and cones. The outer segment contains thin disks with pigment molecules embedded in them. Absorption of light by these molecules results in chemical changes that cause electrical changes in the inner segment. These electrical signals are transmitted to neurons via the terminal. (From Allen, 1967.)

tional photons at low light levels but lots of additional photons at high light levels (see Figure 1.3.11).

This complex chain of events in the outer segment is called **pigment bleaching** because the change in molecular shape brought about by light also causes the molecule to change color. Before a rhodopsin molecule is bleached by absorbing light, it looks deep purple; afterward, it is almost transparent. Because it becomes transparent when it absorbs a photon, it is very unlikely to absorb another photon after it is bleached. Once bleached, the pigment molecules are restored to their prior unbleached state by the action of enzymes in the **pigment epithelium** behind the retina.

These changes in pigment bleaching can actually be measured in the eyes of living humans by a process called **retinal densitometry** (Rushton & Campbell, 1954). A beam of light with known intensity is focused on the retina. Part of the light is absorbed by the receptors (and pigment epithelium), and the rest is reflected back out the eye. The intensity of the reflected beam can then be measured. By making this measurement at different times after a bright flash of light that bleaches most of the pigment molecules, the rate at which pigment regeneration takes place can be determined. Full regeneration takes about 30 minutes in rods; it takes only about 6 minutes in cones.

These differences in regeneration time in the rods and cones result in the uneven course of dark adaption alluded to in Section 1.1.3. The precise development of

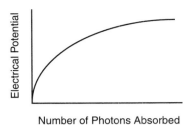

Electrical Potential

Number of Photons Absorbed

Figure 1.3.11 The logarithmic relation between absorption of photons by receptors and their output. When few photons are absorbed, small changes in input produce large changes in output. When many photons are absorbed, large changes in input produce small changes in output.

dark adaptation in visual experience is measured objectively by finding the observer's **absolute threshold**—the dimmest light that can be seen—at various times after an observer is placed in a dark room. The results from such an experiment are shown in Figure 1.3.12. The intensity of the dimmest visible light is plotted as a function of how long the observer has been in darkened conditions. This graph reflects dark adaptation in the fact that the threshold curve decreases over time: The longer the observer has been in the dark, the dimmer is the spot that the subject can just barely see. Notice, however, that this decrease in threshold is not smooth, having two distinct parts: one from 0 to about 8 or 10 minutes and the other from 10 to about 40 minutes. Many further experiments have shown that these two

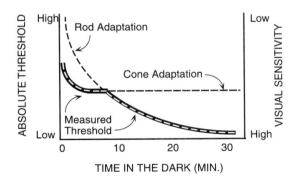

Figure 1.3.12 The dark adaptation function. Visual threshold (left scale) and sensitivity (right scale) are plotted as a function of time in the dark. The function results from two different components. Cones adapt rapidly but reach only a moderate level of sensitivity. Rods adapt more slowly but reach a high level of sensitivity (low threshold).

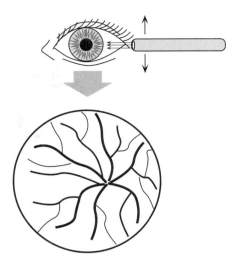

Figure 1.3.13 Seeing your retinal blood vessels. To see the blood vessels on your retina, carefully place a small penlight against the outer corner of your eye and gently shake it up and down. The weblike lines that you then see are caused by the shadows of your retinal blood vessels.

parts reflect the different time courses of dark adaptation in rods and cones, as described above.

Peculiarities of Retinal Design. Although the human eye is an excellent organ for detecting light, certain aspects of its design seem peculiar enough to warrant special mention. For example, one would logically expect the receptor cells to be the *first* layer of the retina that incoming light encounters, but they are actually the *last* (see Figure 1.3.7). Not only that, but both rods and cones appear to be pointing *backward*; the light-sensitive outer segment is the most distant part of the receptor cell from incoming light. The reason for this unusual arrangement is probably that the enzymes that are needed for pigment regeneration are in the pigment epithelium, which is opaque. Because the receptor disks must be adjacent to this vital biochemical resource, they must also be at the back of the retina. Luckily for our visual abilities, the retinal cells and axons in front of the receptors are fairly transparent, so the optical quality of the image does not suffer as much as one might imagine.

In addition to the nearly transparent retinal cells that lie in the path of incoming light, however, there are also many blood vessels that nourish the retina. Because

33 An Introduction to Vision Science

Figure 1.3.14 Spotting your blind spot. With your right eye closed, fixate the upper cross with your left eye. Starting with the book close to your face, move it slowly away. At a distance of about 9 inches, the spot on the left will disappear. Doing the same thing with the lower display will cause the gap in the line to fill in so that it appears complete and uninterrupted.

these are dark, one would expect them to be clearly visible all the time. The reason we do not normally see them is that the brain adapts completely to their presence and fills in the part of the image over which the blood vessels cast their shadows. In fact, you *can* see your retinal blood vessels under the proper circumstances. When you get an eye examination, for example, you can see them quite vividly as the ophthalmologist shines a light into your eye at unusual angles. You can also see them for yourself using the following procedure: Look at a uniform surface (a plain wall or blank piece of paper will do) and shine a pen flashlight directly into the white of your eye against the outside corner, as illustrated in Figure 1.3.13. When you gently shake the penlight up and down, you will be able to see the blood vessels clearly because their shadows are now moving over different receptors, ones to which the brain has not adapted.

Another curiosity in the anatomical design of the eye exists where the axons of the ganglion cells leave the eye at the optic nerve. This region is called the **optic disk** (also known as the **blind spot**) and it contains no receptor cells at all. However, we do not experience blindness there, except under very special circumstances. There are two reasons for this: First, the blind spots are positioned so that receptors in one eye register what is missed in the blind spot of the other eye. Second, the visual system fills in this region with appropriate sensory qualities, just as it does the shadows of the blood vessels. We do not yet know how this is accomplished, but it works quite effectively.

To spot your blind spot, hold this book near your face, close your right eye, and fixate on the upper-right cross in Figure 1.3.14 with your left eye. Now move the book slowly further away while continuing to focus on the upper-right cross. When the circle on the left is in your blind spot, it will disappear. Notice how the visual system fills in this area with the background whiteness of the page. This is a curious fact, since it is not obvious how the visual system can "see" the white page, which is *not* there, and fail to "see" the dot, which *is*.

Higher brain processes, probably in visual cortex, seem to fill in the part of the visual field corresponding to the blind spot with appropriate information, which is then experienced consciously. You can convince yourself of this using the lower-right cross and the broken line next to it. Again, close your right eye and fixate the cross with your left eye as you move the book further away. When the gap in the line is in your blind spot, the gap will disappear. It is filled in with an illusory line that completes the broken one. As we said before, what you see isn't always what you get!

Yet another peculiarity of retinal physiology concerns the encoding of information about light intensity. Since the task of the eye is to convert light into neural responses, the natural expectation is that receptors would not respond in darkness and would increase their synaptic output as the intensity of light increases. But exactly the opposite actually occurs in the receptors of vertebrates (Toyoda, Nosaki & Tomita, 1969). The response to a flash of light is a *decrease* in synaptic activity at the receptors' output. Although this result greatly surprised visual scientists, it probably should not have. The important fact is only that neural activity should preserve the information present in light intensities over the visual field, and this task can be accomplished equally well by either positive or negative correlations between neural activity and light intensity. As it turns out, receptors in invertebrate eyes work in the opposite—and more intuitively obvious—way, increasing their output for increases in light intensity. And the seeming anomaly of decreased activity in vertebrate receptors is rectified by the next synapse in which increased light produces increased release of neurotransmitter.

Pathways to the Brain. The axons of the ganglion cells leave the eye via the optic nerve which leads to the **optic chiasm**, named for its resemblance to the Greek letter χ ("chi," pronounced "kye" as in "sky"). Here the fibers from the nasal side of the fovea in each eye cross over to the opposite side of the brain while the others remain on the same side (see Figure 1.3.15). The result is that the mapping from external visual fields to the cortex is completely crossed: All of the information from the left half of the visual field goes to the right half of the brain, while all the information from the right visual field goes to the left half of the brain.

From the optic chiasm, there are two separate pathways into the brain on each side. The smaller one (only a few percent) goes to the **superior colliculus**, a nucleus in the brain stem. This visual center seems to process primarily information about where things are in the world and to be involved in the control of eye movements. The larger pathway goes first to the **lateral geniculate nucleus** (or **LGN**) of the thalamus and then to the **occipital cortex** (or **primary visual cortex**). We will have much more to say about the extensive processing that goes on in the visual cortex in Chapter 4, but for now we will merely describe the gross anatomical and physiological organization of this complex structure.

1.3.3 Visual Cortex

Two facts about the human cortex are obvious from inspecting it with the naked eye. The first is that its surface is highly convoluted or folded. This is because the cortex is actually a layered sheet of neurons, and the convolutions result from trying to fit a large sheet of cortex into an small inflexible skull. A second obvious macroscopic feature of the cortex is that it is divided into two halves, or **cerebral hemispheres**, that are approximately symmetrical. Otherwise, the cortex looks pretty much homogeneous, and it is completely unclear from looking at it how it might work. Indeed, its mechanisms are so obscure that early scientists failed to realize that the brain was the organ of mental functioning. Aristotle

believed that the seat of mental capacities was in the heart and that the brain was essentially a heat sink to cool the blood!

Localization of Function. One of the first questions to be raised about the brain, once its true importance was realized, was whether or not its functions are *localized*: Are different mental faculties located in different anatomical regions, or are all functions spread throughout the entire brain? Early pseudoscientific support for the localization hypothesis came from **phrenology**, the study of the shape of people's skulls. Phrenologists claimed that the size of the lumps, bumps, and bulges on a person's skull indicated the size and development of the brain structures underneath. Their approach was to find correspondences between skull measurements and assessments of mental attributes, such as "ambition," "calculation," and "spirituality." The result was a collection of bizarre phrenological maps, as shown in Figure 1.3.16, charting the position of such functions. These supposed correlations were generally unfounded, however, and real scientific support for the concept of localization of function did not appear until the effects of brain damage were studied systematically during the late nineteenth century.

The scientific basis of localization of function was established when physicians began to perform postmortem analyses of the brains of patients who had acquired specific mental disabilities during their lifetimes from strokes or head injuries. They found that certain types of deficits were very strongly correlated with damage to certain regions. Among the findings was that visual dysfunction characteristically occurred when there was damage to the posterior parts of the brain, mainly in the occipital lobe (see Figure 1.3.2). Particularly important was a study by a young Japanese physician of visual impairments in soldiers resulting from gunshot wounds to the head in the Russo-Japanese War of 1904–1905 (Glickstein, 1988). As a result of this and other neuropsychological studies, it is now well established that the occipital lobe is the primary cortical receiving area for visual information and that there are other cortical areas that are similarly specialized for the other sensory modalities: audition, taste, touch, and smell.

Still, there has been considerable controversy as to whether or not there is further localization of function.

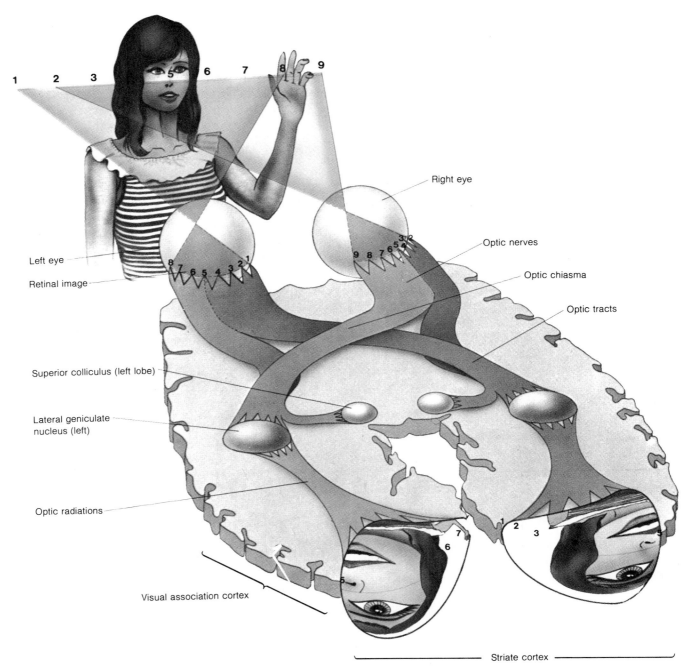

Figure 1.3.15 Neural pathways from the eye to visual cortex. Information from the inner (nasal) portion of each retina crosses over to the opposite side of the brain so that each side of the brain receives input only from the opposite half of the visual field.

Note that the representation of the central portion of the visual field receives disproportionate representation in visual cortex. (From Frisby, 1979.)

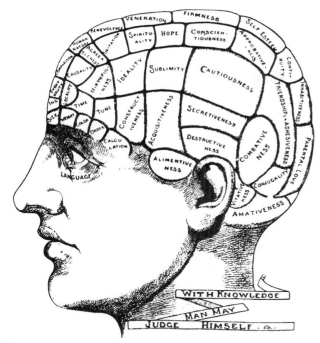

Figure 1.3.16 A phrenological map. Phrenologists believed that they could determine the location of brain functions by measuring characteristics of the skull and correlating them with psychological abilities. (From Kolb & Whishaw, 1996.)

In a well-known series of studies, the physiological psychologist Karl Lashley and his colleagues tried to localize memories—visual and otherwise—for the information that rats learned from running mazes (Lashley, 1929, 1931, 1950). They removed various amounts of cortex at various different locations and never found any specific locus that seemed to correspond to those memories. The only variable that seemed to make a difference was the total amount of cortex that was excised: The more brain tissue that was removed, the worse the animal performed, a result that Lashley christened the "law of mass action." Because of this finding, he questioned the notion that memories are localized at all, instead proposing that they are distributed more or less equally over the whole cortex.

We still do not know the extent to which function is precisely localized, but the evidence increasingly supports the view that it is. In visual cortex of monkeys, for example, over 30 different visual areas have been identified, with more being discovered each year (Van Essen & DeYoe, 1995). The best known and understood of

these visual centers lie in the **occipital**, **parietal**, and **temporal lobes** of the cortex, the locations of which are indicated in Figure 1.3.2.

Occipital Cortex. The most complete anatomical and physiological data about visual cortex come from old-world monkeys, such as the macaque. Behavioral analyses have shown that their visual abilities are strikingly similar to those of humans, making them a good animal model for the human visual system (De Valois & De Valois, 1988). Since the cellular exploration of visual cortex began more than two decades ago with the pioneering studies of Hubel and Wiesel (1959, 1962), a great deal has been learned about both the anatomy and the physiology of various mammalian visual systems. The structure and function of dozens of distinct visual areas are being explored, and their interrelationships are being determined by a variety of techniques. Although it would be a gross overstatement to say that we understand how visual cortex works, we are at least beginning to get some glimmerings of what the assorted pieces might be and how they might fit together.

The first steps in cortical processing of visual information take place in the **striate cortex**. This part of the occipital lobe receives its input from the LGN on the same side of the brain, so the visual input of striate cortex, like that of LGN, is completely crossed: The left visual field projects to the right striate cortex, and the right visual field projects to the left striate cortex (see Figure 1.3.15). Both sides are activated by the thin central vertical strip, measuring about 1 degree of visual angle in width, that separates the two sides of the visual field. The cells that are sensitive to this strip in one side of the brain are connected to the corresponding cells on the other side of the brain through the **corpus callosum**, the large fiber tract that allows communication between the two cerebral hemispheres.

The mapping from retina to striate cortex is *topographical* in that nearby regions on the retina project to nearby regions in striate cortex. This transformation preserves *qualitative* spatial relations but distorts *quantitative* ones, much as an image on a rubber sheet can be distorted when it is stretched without being torn. Figure 1.3.15 depicts the approximate distortion produced by this topological transformation: The central area of the visual field, which falls on or near the fovea, receives

An Introduction to Vision Science

proportionally much greater representation in the cortex than the periphery does. This is called the **cortical magnification factor**. It reflects the fact that we have more detailed spatial information about objects in the central region of the retina than about those in peripheral regions.[4] It does *not* imply that perception of environmental space is somehow distorted so that objects in the center of the visual field appear to be bigger than those in the periphery. You can convince yourself of this simply by holding your two hands out at arm's length and focusing on one of them. If perception of space were distorted by the cortical magnification factor, the hand that you focus on would seem much larger than the other hand, but this does not happen. Instead, you merely perceive the fine details of the focused hand more clearly, such as its lines, veins, and fingernails.

This is but a small part of what is known about the internal structure of striate cortex. We will save the rest of the story for Chapter 4, in which the physiology of this area of cortex plays a central role in our understanding of image-based processing. Its output projects to many other parts of the visual cortex, including other areas in the occipital lobe as well as parts of the parietal and temporal lobes. Different areas are involved in different sorts of visual processing. One of the important features that marks such areas as "visual" is that, like striate cortex, they are organized topographically with respect to retinal locations. Indeed, visual cortex is a veritable patchwork quilt of small maps that code different aspects of retinal stimulation, including brightness, color, motion, depth, texture, and form.

Parietal and Temporal Cortex. Part of the "big picture" about how cortical functioning is organized has come from lesion studies by physiologists Mortimer Mishkin, Leslie Ungerleider, and their colleagues. They have reported convincing evidence of a pronounced difference between the function of the visual areas in the temporal versus parietal lobes of the monkey's cortex (Figure 1.3.17A). The inferior temporal centers in the lower (ventral) system seem to be involved in *identifying objects*, whereas the parietal centers in the upper (dorsal)

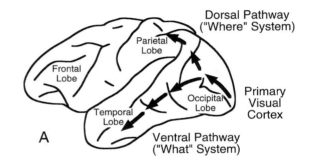

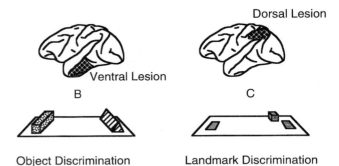

Figure 1.3.17 Two visual pathways in monkey cortex. The lower (ventral) pathway goes from occipital cortex to the temporal lobe and is believed to be specialized for object recognition (the "what" system). The upper (dorsal) pathway goes from occipital cortex to parietal cortex and is believed to be specialized for object location (the "where" system). Parts B and C illustrate experiments that support this division. (See text for details.) (After Goldstein, 1989.)

system seem to be involved in *locating objects*. These two pathways are often called the **"what" system** and the **"where" system**, respectively. The evidence for this claim comes from experiments in which monkeys were required to perform two different kinds of tasks after one or the other area of cortex had been surgically removed (Ungerleider & Mishkin, 1982; Mishkin, Ungerleider, & Macko, 1983).

One task was an *object discrimination* problem, as illustrated in Figure 1.3.17B. After being familiarized with a particular object, the monkey has to select the familiar object over a novel one to receive a food reward. This is an easy task for a normal monkey. It turns out also to be

---

[4]This topological transformation actually takes place in a series of less radical stages. There is some magnification of the central regions in going from receptor to ganglion cells, more going from ganglion to LGN cells, and still more going from LGN to striate cells.

easy for a monkey with a portion of its parietal lobe removed. However, it is extremely difficult for the monkeys that are missing their inferior temporal cortex. The second task, called a *landmark discrimination* problem, is illustrated in Figure 1.3.17C. It also required the monkey to make a choice between two objects, but this time the two objects were identical in shape, differing only in their spatial proximity to a third, landmark object. This is also an easy task for normal monkeys, but this time it is the parietally lesioned monkeys that have trouble and the temporally lesioned ones that are unaffected.

The results of this and several other experiments support Ungerleider and Mishkin's (1982) hypothesis that the temporal pathway processes the shape information required to identify objects and that the parietal pathway processes the location information required to determine where objects are. More recently, other investigators have suggested that the parietal pathway is more accurately described as subserving spatially guided motor behavior (the "how" system), such as reaching and grasping (Goodale, 1995; Milner & Goodale, 1995). In any case, it seems almost inevitable that these two different kinds of information must get together somewhere in the brain so that the "what-where" connection can be made, but it is not yet known where this happens. One likely candidate is the frontal lobes, since they receive projections from both the parietal and temporal areas. The information processing might take a more circuitous route, however, and go through several intermediate cortical regions before linking up in some as-yet-unidentified place.

The distinction between these two visual pathways appears to be important in humans as well as monkeys. People who have damage in certain areas of their temporal cortex exhibit **visual agnosia**: a deficit in identifying certain kinds of objects by sight. One form of visual agnosia is specific to faces. The patient cannot recognize anybody by sight—even a spouse, parent, or child—but can immediately do so by hearing them speak. This disability is not due to the lack of visual experiences, for such patients are able to describe the faces they see quite precisely, including the presence of freckles, glasses, and so on. They just cannot tell whose face it is. This is easy to understand in terms of a breakdown in the ventral "what" pathway that leads to the temporal lobe.

Some patients with brain damage in the parietal lobe suffer from a syndrome known as **unilateral neglect**. Neglect is a complex pattern of symptoms that we will discuss more fully in Chapter 11; one of its main features is the apparent inability to attend to objects in the half of the visual field opposite to their brain damage. A person with a lesion in the right parietal lobe, for example, will eat only the food on the right side of the plate and draw only the right half of a picture he or she is asked to copy. It is as though objects in the left visual field were not there at all. Although many features of neglect are not yet well understood, it seems consistent with the possibility that some aspect of the "where" system is damaged.

These lesion results are particularly useful for understanding the overall function of gross regions of the brain, but they do not address more specific issues concerning the precise neural processing that underlies complex abilities like these. Doing so requires more detailed physiological studies using a variety of other techniques, including anatomical tracing of neural projections from one area to another and recording from individual cells in specific brain areas to find out what kinds of information they process. We do not yet understand this level of functioning in detail for areas outside primary visual cortex, but we will now briefly consider some of what is known at the present time.

Mapping Visual Cortex. Much of visual cortex in humans and closely related primates is hidden within the folds of the cortex. Figure 1.3.18 shows an anatomically correct depiction of the location and arrangement of some of the principle areas of visual cortex (areas V1 through V5) in the brain of macaque monkeys. Notice that these areas are part of the highly convoluted sheet of cortical neurons, much of which is not visible on the exterior surface of the brain. These are only a few of the visual areas, however, many of which lie quite far from primary visual cortex.

An anatomically distorted map of the currently known visual areas in the macaque monkey's cortex is shown in Figure 1.3.19. It is a strange view of a brain because the convoluted surface of the cortex has been "unfolded" so that areas hidden within the cortical folds (called *sulci*) can be seen in approximately correct spatial relations to visible areas. A side view of a normal macaque brain is given in the inset so that you can see

An Introduction to Vision Science

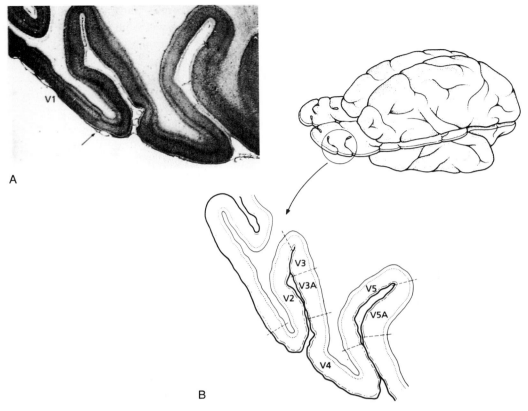

A

B

Figure 1.3.18 The location of primary visual cortex in macaque monkeys. The anatomical positions of striate cortex (area V1) and several prestriate areas (V2 through V5) are shown in a (displaced) horizontal slice through the brain. The cellular struc-ture of these areas is shown in the inset (A) with the transition between V1 and prestriate areas indicated by an arrow. (From Zeki, 1993.)

how the visible areas are arranged in an intact (properly "folded") brain. It shows that visual processing takes up almost the entire back half of the cortex. Notice that in the flattened map, the border between areas V1 and V2 has been cut so that the sizes of the different areas do not become too distorted.

The first cortical stage of visual processing—called *striate cortex,* **primary visual cortex**, or area **V1**—is the largest and is located at the very back of the occipital lobe. It receives the majority of ascending projections from the LGN and is responsible for the first few operations of visual processing. We know a great deal about the precise anatomy and physiology of this area, perhaps more than for any other area in the brain. In Chapter 4, when we consider spatial processing in detail, we will explore the architecture of this part of visual cortex. For now, we will just describe its gross anatomical connections to other areas of visual cortex.

It was originally thought that there might be a strict serial ordering of visual processing, each area projecting to the next in a linear sequence. That simple hypothesis was quickly laid to rest as researchers found more and more anatomical connections among visual areas. It is now abundantly clear that a great deal of processing takes place in parallel across different areas, each region projecting fibers to several other areas but by no means to all of them. A schematic diagram of some of the currently known direct connections is given in Figure 1.3.20. Although simplified for clarity, it indicates the interconnections between some of the best known and most studied visual areas. The connections are generally bidirectional; that is, if area X projects to area Y, then Y projects back to X as well. It turns out that the projections in the two different directions are not completely symmetrical, however, in that they originate and terminate in different layers of the cortex.

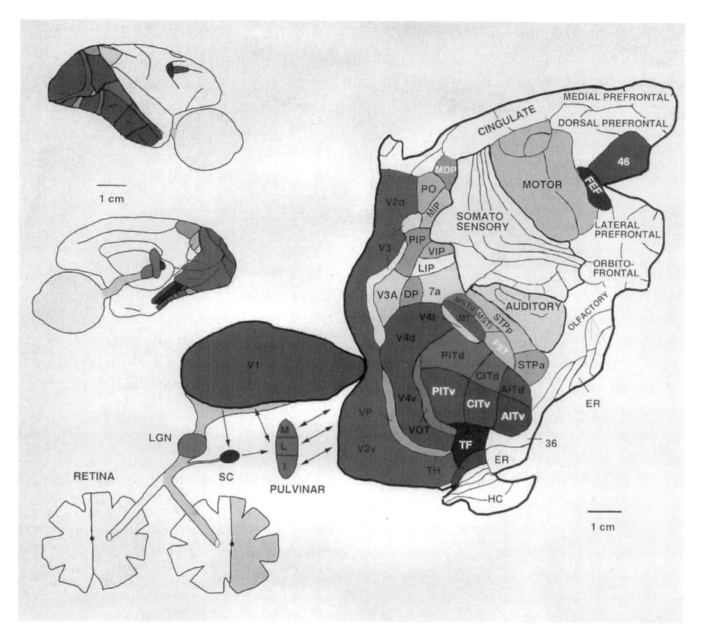

Figure 1.3.19 A flattened map of visual areas in monkey cortex. The principle areas of cortex currently known to be involved in vision are shown in three views of a macaque brain. The top left diagram shows a lateral (side) view of a normal brain (facing right), and the one below it shows a medial (central) view (facing left). The large diagram to the right and below shows a more detailed view of the visual system after the cortex has been flattened. Note that the border between V1 and V2 has been cut to minimize size distortions. (From Van Essen, Anderson, & Felleman, 1992.)

41   An Introduction to Vision Science

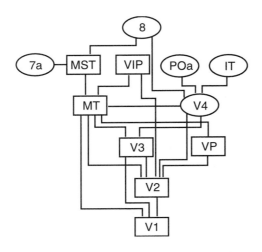

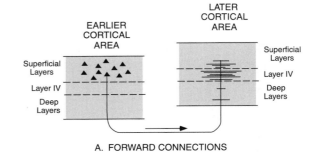

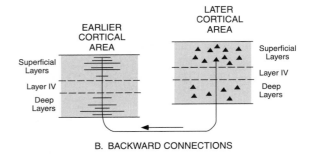

Figure 1.3.20 Interconnections between cortical areas. This diagram summarizes just a few of the known connections between visual areas of monkey cortex. (From Van Essen & Maunsell, 1983.)

Figure 1.3.21 Interconnections between cortical layers. Forward connections originate in upper layers of cortex and terminate in central layers, primarily in layer 4. Feedback connections originate and terminate outside of this central region. (From Van Essen & Maunsell, 1983.)

The cerebral cortex has a **laminar structure**, in that it is constructed in layers. Visual cortex has six major anatomically defined layers, with several more sublayers being defined by physiological evidence. Of these, the fourth seems to be the input layer for "forward" or "ascending" projections from lower parts of the nervous system. This is certainly true in area V1, where the ascending fibers from the LGN are known to synapse mainly in layer 4. For other cortical areas, it is somewhat less clear which projections are "forward" and which are "backward" or "descending." In one direction, the projections systematically originate in the superficial layers of cortex and terminate primarily in layer 4 (Figure 1.3.21A). These are called *forward projections* by analogy with those from the LGN. Projections in the opposite direction—called *feedback* or *backward connections*—typically originate and terminate outside of layer 4 (Figure 1.3.21B). This distinction between forward and backward connections has been used to define the hierarchy diagrammed in Figure 1.3.20. Each area is located at a level in the hierarchy just above the highest area from which it receives forward projections. As you can see, the many different visual centers have complex interconnections, few of which are yet well understood. In later chapters, we will discuss what is known about the function (or physiology) of some of the better understood of these cortical areas.

Do these purely anatomical facts bear any useful relation to cortical function? One clear correlation is between the level of a cell in the anatomical hierarchy of Figure 1.3.20 and size of the region of the retina from which it receives information. Cells from lower levels in the cortical hierarchy receive input from small retinal areas, and cells from higher levels receive input from larger retinal areas. For example, the cells in area V1 can be activated by stimulation within foveal retinal areas 0.1–0.5 degrees of visual angle wide; in V2, they are typically 0.5–1.0°; in V4, they are 1–4°; and in IT, they are often 25° or more (Desimone, Moran, & Spitzer, 1988). The increase in receptive field size from lower to higher visual areas in cortex is thus 100-fold or more.

The Physiological Pathways Hypothesis. A further possible relation between anatomical structure and physiological function has begun to emerge during the last decade or so. The hypothesis is that there are separate neural **pathways** for processing information about different visual properties such as color, shape, depth,

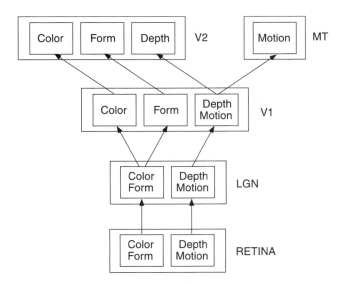

Figure 1.3.22 Schematic diagram of the visual pathways hypothesis. Some theorists believe that color, shape, motion, and depth are processed independently in the visual system. This diagram summarizes a simplified form of the theory.

and motion. This idea arose from studies suggesting that different areas of cortex were specialized for processing different properties (e.g., Zeki, 1978, 1980). It later became increasingly apparent that this specialization had roots earlier in the visual system. Livingstone and Hubel (1987, 1988) summarized much of this anatomical, physiological, and perceptual evidence and proposed that these four types of information are processed in different neural pathways from the retina onward. They traced these differences from two classes of retinal ganglion cells (one for color and form, the other for depth and motion) to the LGN and from there to different regions of V1, V2, and beyond.

They report evidence from single cell recordings that color, form, motion, and stereoscopic depth information are processed in distinct subregions of V1 and V2, as indicated schematically in Figure 1.3.22. These areas then project to distinct higher-level areas of cortex: movement and stereoscopic depth information to area **V5** (also called **MT**, <u>M</u>edial <u>T</u>emporal cortex), color to area **V4**, and form through several intermediate centers (including V4) to area **IT** (<u>Infero</u><u>T</u>emporal cortex). From these areas, the form and color pathways may project to the ventral "what" system for object identification and the depth and motion pathways to the dorsal "where" system for object localization. We will review this theory

in Chapter 4 when we describe the physiology of visual cortex in greater detail.

The nature of visual processing in higher level areas of cortex is much less clear than in area V1. For example, some cells in cortical area IT have been found to be strongly activated by the sight of a monkey's hand and other cells to a monkey's face (Gross, Rocha-Miranda, & Bender, 1972). The nature of the spatial processing that occurs between V1 and IT remains mysterious, however. The motion analysis in area MT provides output to area **MST** (<u>M</u>edial <u>S</u>uperior <u>T</u>emporal cortex) and several other parietal areas. But again, very little is known about what specific processing occurs in these later centers.

As vague as this story is for monkey cortex—and parts of it are fairly controversial—the understanding of visual areas in human cortex is even less clear. Researchers in human neuropsychology have begun to discover some interesting correlations between locations of strokes and tumors and the visual deficits that they produce, but the evidence is complex and often difficult to evaluate. The use of brain-imaging techniques such as PET and fMRI (see Section 2.2.3) is just beginning to provide useful information about localization of visual function in humans, but their promise is enormous. We will mention some of the clinically significant findings at various points later in this book when we discuss the relevant subject matter. Some of the most interesting neurological phenomena will arise in the last chapter when we discuss the complex but fascinating topic of visual awareness.

An Introduction to Vision Science

Suggestions for Further Reading

The Nature of Vision

There are many excellent books about the phenomena of visual perception. The ones that I find most readable and broadly compatible with the views presented in this book are the following:

Gregory, R. L. (1970). *The intelligent eye.* New York: McGraw-Hill.

Rock, I. (1984). *Perception.* New York: Scientific American Books

Optical Information

The classic discussions of the relations among the world, optical information, and visual perception are found in the three principal works of James J. Gibson:

Gibson, J. J. (1950). *The visual world.* Boston: Houghton Mifflin.

Gibson, J. J. (1966). *The senses considered as perceptual systems.* Boston: Houghton Mifflin.

Gibson, J. J. (1979). *The ecological approach to visual perception.* Boston: Houghton Mifflin.

Visual Systems

There are many good treatments of the physiology of vision. Among the most informative and readable are the books by Nobel laureate David Hubel and by Semir Zeki.

Hubel, D. (1995). *Eye, brain, and vision.* New York: Scientific American Books.

Zeki, S. (1993). *A vision of the brain.* Oxford: Blackwell.

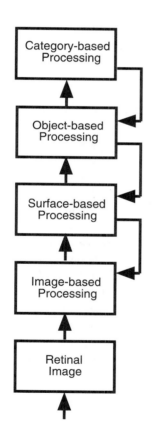

Theoretical Approaches to Vision

Vision scientists seek to understand how knowledge of the environment can arise from light entering the eyes. You might think that such a question could be answered simply by discovering all the relevant facts. But scientific understanding of a complex domain such as visual perception requires more than just knowing facts; it requires a **theory**. A theory is an integrated set of statements (called **hypotheses**) about underlying mechanisms or principles that not only organizes and explains known facts, but also makes predictions about new ones.

We will examine many theories in the course of this book. All of them have one thing in common: They will ultimately be proved inadequate. The reason is simple: For any given domain, there is but one "correct" theory. The idea of studying incomplete and imperfect theories upsets many students, who are understandably impatient with their deficiencies. But discovering that theories are wrong and trying to improve them is an essential component of the scientific enterprise. Even incorrect theories often contain important elements of truth or lead to new and illuminating ways of thinking. Because one cannot understand any scientific enterprise properly without learning about its theories as well as its facts, the present chapter will be devoted to a discussion of visual theory and its historical development.

Why do scientists rely so heavily on theories? One of the most persuasive arguments was offered by pioneering cognitive scientist Allen Newell in an address to a conference of prominent visual psychologists (Newell, 1973). His talk was titled "You Can't Play 20 Questions with Nature and Win." Its point was to remind his distinguished audience of the crucial role played by integrated theories in science. "Twenty questions" is a game in which one person thinks of an object and others try to guess what it is by asking a series of yes/no questions: "Is it alive?," "Is it bigger than a breadbox?," "Is there one in this house?" and so on. The game is won by correctly guessing the target object.

Newell drew an interesting analogy between this game and the scientific method. Doing an experiment is like asking a yes/no question of nature, and getting the results is like nature giving the answer. His point was that even the answers to all possible experimental questions would not lead to a proper scientific understanding of the subject matter because they would never comprise more than a very long list of facts. Knowing the facts does not constitute scientific understanding, any more than knowing the answers to a long list of yes/no questions constitutes winning at 20 questions. At some point, one must make a qualitative leap from facts to theories. Only then, Newell claimed, could one win the 20 questions game with nature.

A theory is an internally consistent set of hypotheses or assumptions from which one can derive explanations of known facts and testable predictions of new facts. Because of its dual role as *integrator of old facts* and *predictor of new facts*, a theory is more economical than a simple list of facts. The theory relates facts to one another and allows them to be derived from a smaller set of underlying assumptions. For example, the biologist Gregor Mendel proposed the existence of genes that carry hereditary traits to account for the regularities he discovered in experiments concerning the inheritance of characteristics in offspring. Once he formulated the theory of genetic combination, his huge tables of probabilities were no longer needed to predict heritability. Rather, the probabilities could be derived from the few basic assumptions of genetic theory.

One important consequence of the fact that theories are *integrated* sets of assumptions or hypotheses is the requirement that these assumptions and their logical consequences be *internally consistent*. Theories that have internal contradictions are intrinsically flawed and can be rejected out of hand. Philosophers have always been particularly concerned with finding such logical flaws. Logical consistency is not the only criterion for a good theory, however. It must also be consistent with a large number of known facts about the domain—ideally, all of them. To determine the empirical adequacy of the theory, scientists test its predictions against observations from reality. Only if the theory both is logically sound and has substantial empirical support will it be taken seriously.

It might seem that these two criteria—logical consistency and empirical adequacy—would jointly be sufficient to identify the "correct" theory for a scientific domain. Unfortunately, one can show that, logically speaking, if there is *any* internally consistent theory that fits a set of data, there are *many* such theories. Sometimes, two or more genuinely different theories can account for the same data. How is one to decide which theory is best? Scientists rely on a principle called **Ockham's razor**. It states that the best theory is the most **parsimonious** one: the theory that can account for the empirical results with the fewest assumptions. Parsimony must therefore be added to logical consistency and empirical adequacy as a criterion for evaluating scientific theories.

2.1 Classical Theories of Vision

The distinguished Gestalt psychologist Kurt Koffka (1935) framed the problem for theories of visual perception perhaps better than anyone else. He asked the single deceptively simple question "Why do things look as they do?" Many different answers have been proposed, as we will see, but underlying all of them are three "classical" issues that form the core of psychological theories of visual perception:

1. *Environment versus organism.* One possible answer to Koffka's question would be "Because the *world* is the way it is." It advocates analyzing external stimulus conditions as the proper way to understand perception. In particular, it suggests that one should examine the kinds of information in the proximal stimulus that correspond to the perceived information in the distal stimulus. An alternative answer would be "Because *we* are the way we are" or, more precisely, "Because our *visual nervous systems* are the way they are." It advocates an internal approach to perceptual structure, emphasizing the nature of the organism rather than the external nature of the world around it. Intermediate positions are possible, such as the sensible compromise that both external stimulus structure and internal organismic structure are important.

2. *Empiricism versus nativism.* A second kind of answer to Koffka's question about why things look as they do would be "Because we have *learned* to see them that way." This is the **empiricist** view, according to which we see the way we do because of knowledge accumulated through personal interactions with the world. An alternative response would be, "Because we were *born* to see them that way." This is the **nativist** view, according to which we do not need specific knowledge acquired during our lifetime because evolution has supplied us with the necessary neural mechanisms. The nativist view holds that, in effect, the whole species has learned by experience through evolution, so each individual organism does not have to start from scratch as a *tabula rasa* ("blank slate") waiting for experience to etch its impressions.[1] The organism need not actually be born with an ability for nativists to claim it as innate, because later development may be genetically programmed rather than learned. Explanations in terms of **maturation** can therefore still be considered nativistic.

3. *Atomism versus holism.* Another possible response to Koffka's question about why things look as they do would be "Because of the way in which each small piece of the visual field appears." According to this *atomistic* idea, perception of the whole visual field can be predicted simply by putting together the bits of visual experience in each local region. This approach contrasts with the answer "Because of the way in which the whole visual field is organized." This *holistic* view suggests that how one part of the field appears perceptually will be strongly affected by other parts of the field. Local bits cannot simply be put together; they must be globally integrated. According to this alternative approach, the visual system organizes stimuli so that the properties of whole objects or even whole scenes supersede those of local regions of the visual field.

The fourth critical issue related to theories of perception is methodological. It is relevant to how Koffka posed his question, for he presupposed one view rather than the other.

---

[1] This evolutionary view of nativism does not diminish the importance of the learned/innate distinction, however, because the mechanisms of learning by individuals versus species are presumably very different. The associative mechanisms of learning that we will discuss are relevant only to learning by individuals. Evolutionary learning through survival of the fit-test applies to the species as a whole, although it might be metaphorically applied at the level of individuals by talking about competition and survival among alternative perceptions or their biological substrates (e.g., Edelman, 1987).

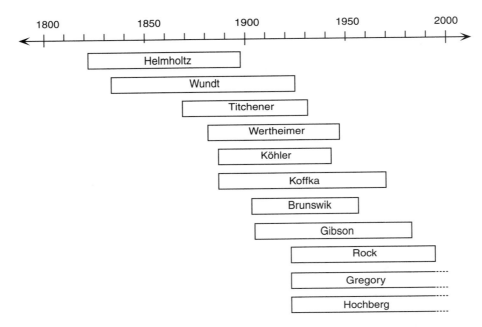

Figure 2.1.1 A timeline of visual theorists. The life spans of some of the most important psychological theorists of vision are represented over the past two centuries. Wundt and Titchener were structuralists; Wertheimer, Köhler, and Koffka were Gestaltists; Brunswick and Gibson were ecologists; and Helmholtz, Rock, Gregory, and Hochberg were constructivists.

4. *Introspection versus behavior*. This controversy concerns whether perceptual theory should be derived from phenomenological observations of one's own conscious experience (introspection) or from objective measurements of human performance (behavior). Koffka presupposes an introspective approach by asking, "Why do things *look* as they do?" because how they look concerns conscious experience. A behaviorist might have asked, "What does vision enable us to *do*?" This is a legitimate question, to be sure, but it is quite different from Koffka's.

With these four issues in mind, we will now consider four psychological theories of visual perception and the theorists who championed them (see Figure 2.1.1). Three of the theories—known as structuralism, Gestaltism, and ecological optics—are easily identified by the strong stands they take on the four key issues (see Figure 2.1.2). They also differ in the theoretical analogies to which they appeal. The fourth psychological theory of perception—often called constructivism—is something of a mixture of the other three. It represents the currently dominant approach to perceptual theory within psychology and leads directly into the modern

information processing view that will be presented in the rest of the chapter and in the remainder of this book.

2.1.1 Structuralism

The earliest psychological approach to perceptual theory is known as **structuralism**. Its roots lie in the views of a philosophical school called **British empiricism**, particularly in the writings of Locke, Berkeley, and Hume. These ideas were introduced into the new field of psychology by its founding father, Wilhelm Wundt, in Germany (see Figure 2.1.3) and were later brought to the United States by one of his disciples, Edward Titchener.

The structuralist view was that perception arises from a process in which basic **sensory atoms**—primitive, indivisible elements of experience in a given sense modality—evoke memories of other sensory atoms that have been associated (linked together) in memory through repeated prior joint occurrences. Such associations were thought to occur whenever sensory experiences were close enough in space and time over a sufficient number of presentations. In the case of vision,

THEORY	NATIVISM vs. EMPIRICISM	ATOMISM vs. HOLISM	ORGANISM vs. ENVIRONMENT	PRINCIPAL ANALOGY	METHOD
Structuralism	Empiricism	Atomism	Organism	Chemistry	Trained Introspection
Gestaltism	Nativism	Holism	Organism	Physical Field Theory	Naive Introspection
Ecological Optics	Nativism	Holism	Environment	Mechanical Resonance	Stimulus Analysis

Figure 2.1.2 Three psychological theories of visual perception. Structuralism, Gestaltism, and ecological optics are characterized by their different stands on five important issues: nativism vs. empiricism, atomism vs. holism, organism vs. environment, the principal theoretical analogy, and the principal scientific method they used.

Figure 2.1.3 Wilhelm Wundt. Wundt is generally acknowledged as the founder of scientific psychology and one of the main advocates of Structuralism. (From Gleitman, 1981.)

the sensory atoms were thought to be visual experiences of color in each tiny localized region of the visual field, presumably resulting from the activity of individual photoreceptors in the retina. These local sensations were assumed to combine in perceptions by simple *concatenation*, that is, merely by putting them together as one would create a picture by overlaying many transparencies, each of which contained a small spot of color at a single location.

Visual experiences were also thought to arouse memories from other sensory modalities by association. The memory of how a dog looks would be associated with how it sounds, smells, and so forth. And how one part of a dog looks, such as its head, would be associated in the observer's mind with the appearance of its other parts, such as its legs, body, and tail. Thus, perception was thought to occur by very rapid and unconscious associative processes that accessed memories acquired through extensive experience with the world. According to structuralism, as observers learn more and more about the world through associations, their perceptions become richer, more accurate, and more complex.

As the above reference to "atoms" of sensory experience suggests, structuralist theory relied heavily on a theoretical analogy to chemistry—namely, that the relation between simple sensations (such as the experience of redness in a particular location of the visual field) and complex perceptions (such as the perception of an apple) is the same as the relation between primitive atoms and

Theoretical Approaches to Vision

more complex molecules in chemistry.[2] The "glue" that holds sensations together in more complex percepts was thought to be associations resulting from their spatial and temporal contiguity in past experiences. As this description of structuralism implies, both atomism and empiricism lie at the heart of structuralist theory.

Another foundation upon which the structuralist approach to perception was built is the method of **trained introspection**. Structuralists claimed that one could discover the elementary units of perception by turning one's mind inward (introspecting) and carefully observing one's own experiences. However, structuralists thought that a person could achieve this goal only if he or she was first trained in the method of introspection by a qualified expert. Unfortunately, the nature of this training often had remarkably strong influences on the results obtained (Boring, 1953). On the topic of imagery, for example, one group of introspectionists claimed that human thought was nothing but a stream of sensory images, while an opposing group claimed that human thought was totally devoid of such images! Inconsistencies like this seriously undermined the credibility of trained introspection, and it was eventually replaced by more reliable behavioral techniques, such as the psychophysical methods described in Appendix A.

Structuralism can perhaps best be viewed as a transitional phase between an early philosophical period in the history of perceptual theory to a more sophisticated psychological period. Without the benefit of new scientific insights, structuralists attempted to translate the philosophical views of the British empiricists more or less directly into the emerging discipline of psychology.

2.1.2 Gestaltism

Historically, the Gestalt movement arose as a reaction against structuralism. Its leaders—Max Wertheimer (Figure 2.1.4), Wolfgang Köhler, and Kurt Koffka—rejected nearly everything about structuralism: its theoretical assumptions of atomism and empiricism, its chemical analogy, and its method of trained introspection. The Gestaltists were largely successful in arguing

Figure 2.1.4 Max Wertheimer. Wertheimer was one of the founders of the Gestalt school of psychology and made several key contributions to the understanding of perceptual organization. (From Goldstein, 1989.)

against their predecessors' ideas but were less successful in promoting their own.

Holism. Gestalt (pronounced *geh-schtalt'*) is a German word that means, roughly, "whole form" or "configuration." As this name suggests, the structuralist idea that the Gestaltists rejected most vehemently was that perceptions were built out of local sensory atoms by simple concatenation. Their well-known rallying cry, "The whole is *different* from the sum of its parts," conveyed their belief that perceptions had their own intrinsic structure as wholes that could not be reduced to parts or even to piecewise relations among parts.

---

[2] The fact that later results in physics required the modification of atomic theory when subatomic particles (electrons, protons, etc.) were discovered does not diminish the force of the atomistic approach. In fact, it reinforced it, because the later theories achieved their success by analyzing atoms in terms of even smaller components. Today, still smaller constituent parts (called *quarks*) are envisioned as the most elementary building block of matter, but the basic assumptions of the atomic approach are clearly still in force.

Figure 2.1.5 Emergent properties of a configuration. The arrangement of several dots in a line gives rise to emergent properties, such as length, orientation, and curvature, that are different from the properties of the dots that compose it.

A   B   C

Figure 2.1.6 Effects of perceptual organization. The letters M and W are obvious in part A, less so in part B, and fully camouflaged in part C as a result of different spatial relations among their parts. Gestalt psychologists studied many such phenomena.

As evidence of holism, Gestaltists pointed to examples in which configurations have **emergent properties** that are not shared by any of their local parts. This idea can be illustrated simply by a line made up of many separate dots (Figure 2.1.5). By itself, each dot has just three perceptual properties: color, size, and position. But when many such dots are arranged in a line, the whole configuration has additional properties such as length, orientation, and curvature. These properties emerge from the configuration only when the points are arranged in a line, because they do not reside in the individual parts at all.

Examples like this led Gestaltists to reject structuralism because the simple concatenation of parts can seldom capture the perceived structure of the whole. Gestaltists therefore studied and theorized primarily about those aspects of perception that depend on qualities of whole figures or configurations. They were particularly interested in the way in which the structure of a whole figure organizes its subparts, a topic that we will discuss more fully in Chapter 6. For example, why is it that you immediately and automatically perceive the letters M and W in Figure 2.1.6A, do so only with difficulty in Figure 2.1.6B, and can scarcely manage to find them at all in Figure 2.1.6C? Exactly the same letters are physically present in all three cases; they are just structured in part B so that the two letters overlap and in part C so that they align precisely to form an integrated whole in which parts of the M and W are continuous with each other. Gestalt psychologists were the first to realize that perceptual organization was an important problem and the first to analyze the properties that govern it.

Not surprisingly, the Gestaltists also rejected the classical chemical analogy of structuralism as too atomistic. They preferred to think of mental processes as analogous to force fields in physics, such as magnetic or elec-

trical fields. A crucial aspect of physical fields that appealed to Gestaltists was their holistic nature. For example, a single positively charged particle defines an electrical field that extends over space, as shown in Figure 2.1.7A. But if a second charged particle is added, the structure of the entire field changes, and it changes in a way that depends on the relation between the two charged particles, as illustrated in Figures 2.1.7B and 2.1.7C. This idea appealed to the Gestaltists because of their emphasis on the structure of configurations as wholes rather than as concatenations of parts.

As a further reaction against structuralism, Gestalt theorists rejected empiricism as the basis for much of perception. For example, they believed that the mechanisms of perceptual organization (such as those responding to the continuity of line segments in Figure 2.1.6C) did not require learning from experience, but arose from the interaction of the brain structure with stimulus structure. Even so, their nativistic stance was less central to Gestalt theory than their position on holism. Perhaps the best way of stating the Gestalt view on the nativism/empiricism issue is that they rejected the structuralist view that experience played the dominant role in perception, claiming instead that unlearned processes were more important.

Psychophysiological Isomorphism. Although Gestaltists were centrally concerned with the structure of the stimulus image, they appealed heavily to explanations based on brain mechanisms inside organisms. Gestaltists formulated their position on the relation between mind and brain in their doctrine of **psychophysiological isomorphism**. It stated that one's (psychological) perceptual experiences are structurally

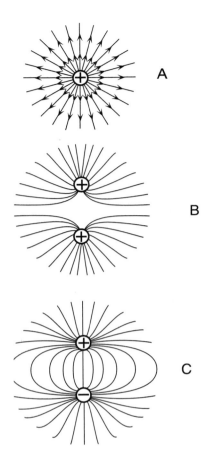

A

B

C

Figure 2.1.7 Holism in physical force fields. A single, positively charged particle has the force field in part A. Adding a second charged particle (parts B and C) changes the entire field in a way that depends on the relation between the two particles.

the same as (isomorphic to) the underlying (physiological) brain events (Wertheimer, 1912; Köhler, 1947).[3]

A useful example of the doctrine of psychophysiological isomorphism is the **opponent process theory** of color perception (Hering, 1878/1964). It states that there are six psychologically primary colors structured into three pairs of opposites: red versus green, blue versus yellow, and black versus white. This analysis was based on insightful observations about the nature of color experiences. To illustrate one such phenomenon, stare at Color Plate 2.1 for at least 30 seconds, fixating

your eyes on the dot as steadily as possible, then quickly shift your eyes to the white rectangle beside it. You should see an afterimage of an American flag in red, white, and blue instead of green, black, and yellow. Together with many other phenomena that point to the same conclusion (see Section 3.2.1), this red/green, blue/yellow, black/white opposition in color afterimages supports Hering's opponent process theory.

Given that color experience has this opponent structure, the Gestalt doctrine of psychophysiological isomorphism suggests that there should be some corresponding opponent structure in the neural events that underlie color perception. In fact, there is now good evidence that this is the case. As we will discuss in Section 3.2.3, there are indeed three types of neurons within the human visual system that code color into the opposing pairs of red/green, blue/yellow, and black/white, just as Hering's analysis of color experiences suggested (De Valois & Jacobs, 1968). This correspondence between opponent color experiences and opponent neural events thus supports the Gestalt doctrine of psychophysiological isomorphism.

Psychophysiological isomorphism alone is not a sufficiently strong constraint to define a neurological theory of brain function, however. Wolfgang Köhler (1920/1950) explored further connections between Gestalt theoretical ideas and underlying brain mechanisms. First, he proposed that the brain was an example of what he called a **physical Gestalt**: a dynamic physical system that converged toward an equilibrium state of minimum energy. Gestaltists often used soap bubbles to illustrate this concept. Free-floating soap bubbles have the intriguing property that, no matter what their initial shape, they inevitably evolve over time into a perfect sphere. The changes occur because the distribution of local stresses and strains in the surface of the bubble are propagated so that they are eventually spread uniformly over the entire surface. Ultimately, the soap bubble achieves a state of global stability in which the forces on its surface reach minimum physical energy. There are many other physical Gestalten defined by this abstract

---

[3] Prior hypotheses along this line were proposed by Mach (1865/1965), Hering (1878/1964), and Müller (1896), but their ideas were less comprehensive that those of Gestalt theorists.

dynamic property, and the Gestaltists believed that the brain was among them.

Köhler's second, more specific proposal was that the causal mechanisms underlying perception in the brain were electromagnetic fields generated by electrical events in millions of neurons. Such electrical brain fields had all the important properties of a physical Gestalt and were deemed physiologically plausible in Köhler's day. Experiments to test this idea later showed that, contrary to Köhler's predictions, disrupting electrical brain fields did not seriously affect perceptual abilities. Neither covering the cortex with highly conductive gold foil (Lashley, Chow, & Semmes, 1951) nor inserting electrically insulating mica strips into the cortex (Sperry & Miner, 1955) had the devastating effects that were predicted by the theory of electrical brain fields. Köhler objected to these experiments on a number of grounds, but they were generally taken as decisive by the scientific community. Largely because of the failure of these physiological proposals, Gestalt theory quickly lost favor. However, Gestalt ideas are making a comeback in the guise of dynamic connectionist theories, as we shall see later in this book.

2.1.3 Ecological Optics

The next classical theory of visual perception that we will consider was primarily the work of one man: James J. Gibson of Cornell University (see Figure 2.1.8). Like the Gestaltists, Gibson vigorously opposed structuralism. Indeed, Gibson was strongly influenced by the Gestalt movement, particularly by its emphasis on holism, which also characterizes much of his own work. Gibson's rejection of structuralism went even further, however. Unlike the Gestaltists, he took the radical step of rejecting the idea that organismic structure should be the basis for perceptual theory. Instead, he proposed that perception could be better understood by analyzing the structure of the organism's environment, called its **ecology**. As one writer put it, Gibson's approach was "Ask not what's inside your head, but what your head's inside of" (Mace, 1977). In effect, Gibson's theory of **ecological optics** is a theory about the *informational basis* of perception in the environment rather than about its *mechanistic basis* in the brain. This approach marked a drastic departure from previous theories and

Figure 2.1.8 James J. Gibson. Gibson developed the ecological school of visual perception. His work on identifying sources of information in image structure foreshadowed modern research in computer vision. (From Gleitman, 1981.)

foreshadowed a great deal of modern work in computational vision.

Analyzing Stimulus Structure. The goal of Gibson's ecological theory of perception was to specify how the world structures light in the ambient optic array (or AOA, as discussed in Section 1.2.1) such that people are able to perceive the environment by sampling that information. In somewhat different terms, Gibson was proposing to discover what characteristics of the *proximal* stimulus provide information about the *distal* stimulus. He contended that the whole pattern of proximal stimulation provided much more information about the distal stimulus than was previously suspected. For example, Gibson noticed that when a surface of uniform texture (the distal stimulus) is slanted in depth, its image on the retina (the proximal stimulus) forms a **texture gradient** in which the texture elements in the image gradually diminish in size, increase in density, and change in projected 2-D shape as the real-world elements to which they correspond recede in the distance (see Figure 2.1.9). Many surfaces in the world have approximately uniform textures that project texture gradients onto the retina when viewed at a slant: grassy meadows, stone walls, textured ceilings, and tiled floors, to name just a few. Gibson identified texture gradients as sources of information about the depth, slant, and size of objects in the environment and further showed that people could perceive these properties when presented with such gradients (Gibson, 1950).

Figure 2.1.9 Texture gradients. When a surface consisting of many similar objects is slanted in depth, they form an image texture whose elements gradually gets smaller, denser, and more foreshortened as the surface recedes in distance.

Gibson's theory of ecological optics is also important because it emphasized perceiving as the active exploration of the environment and the informational consequences of this fact. When the observer moves about in the world, the spatial pattern of stimulation on the retina constantly changes over time. Gibson stressed the richness of this *optic flow* on the retina in understanding perception and invented the concept of the dynamic AOA (see Section 1.2.1) to refer to it. Much of the earlier work on perception was based on studying subjects who sat with their heads immobilized while viewing stationary stimuli under highly restricted and artificial conditions. But Gibson and his followers argued forcefully that perceptual systems evolved in organisms on the move: seeking food, water, mates, and shelter. The theory of ecological optics therefore tries to specify what information about the environment is available to the eyes of a moving observer.

One of Gibson's most important and original insights in studying the information available in the dynamic AOA is that the same optical information that specifies the nature of the environment also specifies the trajectory of the observer through it. The sequence of views shown in Figure 2.1.10, for example, not only indicates the presence of a doorway leading to a different room, but also specifies the observer's direction of approach. Perception of the environment and of the moving station point are thus codetermined by the nature of the optical information reaching the eye.

Gibson believed that sufficient information was available in retinal stimulation to allow an actively exploring organism to perceive the environment unambiguously. He called the process by which the brain accomplished this feat **information pickup**. Although he was less concerned with the biological mechanisms of perception than he was with their informational support in the stimulus, he suggested a **resonance metaphor** for how this process of information pickup might occur. Gibson likened the brain to a system of tuning forks and suggested that whatever the brain might be doing in detail, it was analogous to a process of mechanical resonance (Gibson, 1966, 1979). Information in the stimulus simply causes the appropriate neural structures in the brain to fire, much as mechanical vibration of a specific frequency in the air causes a tuning fork of the same characteristic frequency to vibrate. Unfortunately, Gibson never developed this analogy much further. It is an interesting idea, not unrelated to Köhler's idea of a physical Gestalt, but needs much more elaboration to be testable in any meaningful way.

Direct Perception. By far the most controversial aspect of Gibson's theory was his proposal of **direct perception**: the idea that visual perception of the environment is fully specified by the optical information available at the retina of a moving, actively exploring organism without any mediating processes or internal representations. (The degree of disagreement over this idea is well represented by Ullman's (1980) critique "Against Direct Perception" and the 27 commentaries that follow it.) In trying to understand Gibson's idea of direct perception, it is helpful to realize that he was reacting against earlier proposals that perception is possible only by making "unconscious inferences" that go beyond the information strictly given in the sensory stimulation (see Section 2.1.4 on constructivism). He categorically rejected this influential account of perception, claiming instead that inferences are not needed if one takes into account the many sources of optical information that were not considered in the traditional analysis of static retinal images, particularly those available in optic flow as the organism explores the environment.

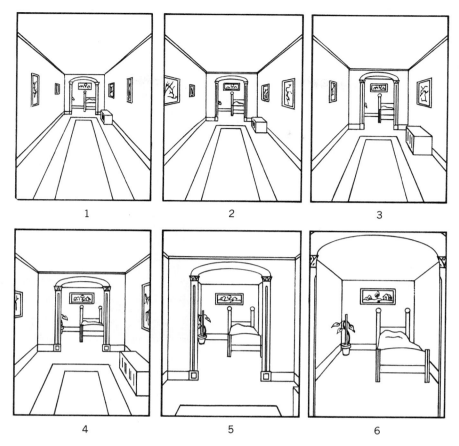

Figure 2.1.10 Codetermination of environment and stationpoint in the dynamic optic array. The optic flow sampled by these pictures determines both the layout of environmental surfaces and the observer's trajectory with respect to them. (From Gibson, 1966.)

Unfortunately, even Gibson's brilliant analyses of the information available in the dynamic AOA have difficulty dealing with the fundamental indeterminacy of recovering real-world (3-D) information from flat (2-D) retinal images—the inverse problem that we discussed in Section 1.2.3. Gibson's emphasis on an actively exploring observer can be seen as an attempt to solve the inverse problem by adding the temporal dimension to the proximal stimulus. Doing so does indeed add greatly to the observer's information, but it does not provide enough leverage to allow direct perception in the sense of unique determination of the environment purely from optical information.

The problem is that time is also a dimension of the environment. The additional information in the dynamic AOA is therefore still insufficient to uniquely recover environmental events that are effectively four-dimensional (three spatial dimensions plus one temporal dimension) because the information in the dynamic AOA is only three-dimensional (two spatial dimensions plus one temporal dimension), even when both eyes are used. The additional information made available by the temporal dimension constrains the inverse problem more tightly and in important ways that other theorists failed to consider, but it still does not present a unique solution, as Gibson claimed.

2.1.4 Constructivism

Surely one of the most important facts about vision is that despite the logically certain conclusion that optical information is insufficient to solve the inverse problem uniquely, our visual systems manage to arrive at the

Theoretical Approaches to Vision

right solutions with remarkable regularity. How is this possible? Most perceptual theorists have concluded that there must be some additional source of information beyond retinal images that is used in the process of seeing. In one way or another, our visual system must be contributing information to that contained in retinal images—even dynamic ones—to arrive at the single most likely possibility from among the logically infinite number of solutions to the inverse problem. This is the position advocated by constructivism.

Constructivism, which is the dominant classical approach to visual theory, combines many of the best aspects of the three approaches just discussed. Because it is such an eclectic approach, it is not easily characterized by strong stands on the four major issues that we have used to characterize other psychological theories. Modern constructivism is intended to be primarily a theory about internal mechanisms of perception rather than one about the external environment. Nevertheless, the internal mechanisms of constructivist theories are often based on extracting environmental information from the patterns of retinal stimulation that Gibson described in his theory of ecological optics. Constructivism is committed to the idea that global percepts are *constructed* from local information. However, it also acknowledges the importance of emergent properties of lines, edges, angles, and even whole figures, as argued by Gestalt theorists. With respect to the controversy over nativism versus empiricism, modern constructivism is neutral. Some aspects of perceptual processing must certainly be innate, but others are undoubtedly learned through interaction with the world. Which ones are which is an empirical question to be settled by careful investigation of infant development. Finally, most modern-day constructivists are methodological behaviorists. That is, they draw inferences about perceptual processes by studying quantitative measures of human or animal behavior rather than (or in addition to) introspecting about the contents of perceptual consciousness. In this, they contrast with both structuralists and Gestaltists, who tended to make extensive use of phenomenological observations. There can be no doubt, however, that introspective analysis is an important first step of much constructivist theorizing. The difference is that constructivists then proceed to collect behavioral measures to test their ideas objectively.

Figure 2.1.11 Hermann von Helmholtz. Helmholtz was a physicist, mathematician, and physiologist whose ideas about vision laid the foundation for constructivism and modern computational theories. (From Goldstein, 1989.)

Unconscious Inference. The father of constructivist theory was Hermann von Helmholtz (see Figure 2.1.11), a brilliant German physicist, mathematician, and physiologist who was a contemporary of Wundt and the structuralists. Many of his basic ideas, originally published in his 1867 book *Treatise on Physiological Optics*, have survived surprisingly intact into modern times.

Although Helmholtz made many significant contributions to the understanding of visual perception, one of the most enduring and the one that is most central to constructivist theory is his proposal that perception depends on a process of **unconscious inference**. Unlike Gibson, Helmholtz acknowledged the logical gap that exists between the optical information available directly from retinal stimulation and the perceptual knowledge derived from it. (This gap, the reader will recall, is due to the indeterminate nature of the inverse problem discussed in Section 1.2.3.) Helmholtz advocated the idea that the gap could be bridged by using hidden "assumptions" in conjunction with retinal images to reach perceptual "conclusions" about the environment. He therefore claimed that vision requires a process of "inference"—or something very much like it—to transform insufficient 2-D optical information into a perceptual interpretation of the 3-D environment. The process of perceptual inference is unconscious because, unlike normal inferential processes involved in thinking and problem solving, people have no awareness of how or when or why or even that they are making visual inferences. More recently, other constructivists, such as Richard Gregory (1970), Julian Hochberg (1964), and Irvin Rock (1983), have modernized and elaborated Helmholtz's ideas.

If the visual system is making inferences about the nature of the environment from optical information in retinal stimulation, it is important to know the basis on which these inferences are made. Helmholtz took the position that vision arrives at the interpretation that is the most likely state of affairs in the external world that could have caused the retinal stimulation. This proposal is usually called the **likelihood principle**. It is a probabilistic view of perception in which the visual system is hypothesized to compute the interpretation with the highest probability given the retinal stimulation.[4]

The likelihood principle is often contrasted with the Gestalt **principle of Prägnanz** (also sometimes called the **minimum principle**), which effectively states that the basis for selecting among possible interpretations is the "goodness" or "simplicity" of the alternatives. (See Pomerantz & Kubovy, 1986, for a contrastive analysis of these two positions.) For example, the fact that people perceive Figure 2.1.12A as a circle behind a square (interpretation B) rather than as a square next to a three-quarter circle (interpretation C) would be explained by the constructivist likelihood principle as resulting from the fact that it is much more probable that a whole circle would be partly occluded by a square than that the straight sides of a three-quarter circle would be exactly

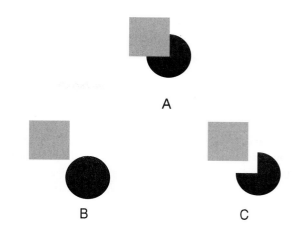

Figure 2.1.12 Two possible interpretations of a simple image. Image A can be interpreted either as a circle behind a square (interpretation B) or as a three-quarter circle next to a square (interpretation C). The fact that the visual system strongly prefers interpretation B to C can be explained by the principles of likelihood and/or Prägnanz.

aligned with those of a square. The same perception would be explained by the Gestalt principle of Prägnanz as resulting from the fact that whole circles are much "better" figures than three-quarter circles in the sense of being simpler, more regular, and more symmetrical (see Section 8.3). It seems as though it should be easy to distinguish between these two rather different theoretical positions, but it is not. One of the difficulties is that there is a very high correlation between what is likely and what is simple. The kinds of objects and events that are most likely to produce observed patterns of stimulation also tend to be simpler than the alternative objects and events that might have produced the same optical image.

Heuristic Interpretation. The theoretical perspective that is taken in this book is broadly consistent with

---

[4] Stated in this way, the likelihood principle suggests a Bayesian approach to vision. In the Bayesian framework, the visual system arrives at the most likely interpretation by computing the conditional probability of each of many different possible 3-D scenes (S_i) given the particular sensory evidence (E) from other probabilities that are usually simpler to obtain. Bayesian probability theory is derived from Bayes' theorem, which states

$$P(S_i|E) = \frac{P(E|S_i)P(S_i)}{P(E)},$$

where $P(S_i|E)$ is the probability of a particular scene S_i (among N possible scenes) given the evidence, $P(E|S_i)$ is the probability of the evidence given the scene, $P(S_i)$ is the prior probability of the scene, and $P(E)$ is the prior probability of the evidence. If the quantities on the right-hand side of the equation are known or can be computed from prior experience in viewing the world, then the crucial probability on the left side (of a particular 3-D scene given the current sensory evidence) can be calculated. One difficulty with this approach is that it implies a finite set of possible 3-D scenes and a finite set of possible patterns of sensory evidence. Neither assumption is easily justified in the case of an active observer exploring natural environments, for both sets seem to be quite open ended.

Theoretical Approaches to Vision

Helmholtz's notion of unconscious inference. We will develop the idea that the visual system transcends the available optical information by implicitly making a number of highly plausible assumptions about the nature of the environment and the conditions under which it is viewed. When these assumptions are coupled with the sensory data in the incoming image, they result in a **heuristic interpretation process** in which the visual system makes inferences about the most likely environmental condition that could have produced the image. The process is heuristic because it makes use of probabilistic rules of thumb that are usually, but not always, true. If these underlying assumptions are false, they will lead to erroneous conclusions in the form of visual illusions (see Section 2.3.5). Under most everyday circumstances, however, the assumptions are true, in which case perception is approximately veridical.

The likelihood principle is closely related to the constructivist notion that perception involves heuristic assumptions. As I have just argued, perception will be veridical when the assumptions on which it rests are true of the current situation and will be illusory when they are false. This means that the more likely the assumptions are to hold true, the more likely the perception is to be correct. Thus, the evolutionary utility of vision will be maximized by using the most probable assumptions to arrive at an interpretation. We will point out these heuristic assumptions throughout the rest of this book. They will allow us to understand in precisely what sense the visual system goes beyond the information given to solve seemingly insoluble inverse problems in plausible and effective ways.

The hidden assumptions made by the visual system are many and varied. One example is the assumption that certain large-scale edges of indoor visual environments, such as those of ceilings, floors, walls, and the like, are either aligned with gravitational vertical or perpendicular to it. By and large, this assumption is true, so it normally serves us well in accurately perceiving the orientation of other objects around us. But when it is false, as it is in the tilted room of an amusement park fun house, our perceptions go strikingly awry. Within such a room, we not only perceive the truly vertical chandelier as hanging askew, but also feel our own bodies to be tilted precariously in the same direction (see Figure 2.1.13). Such illusory perceptions usually occur under

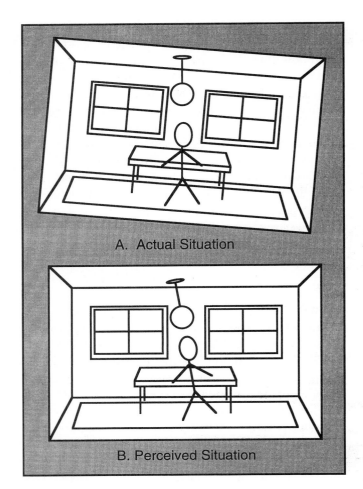

A. Actual Situation

B. Perceived Situation

Figure 2.1.13 An illusion caused by an erroneous hidden assumption. The tilted room in a fun house (part A) seems upright because the visual system assumes that the floor, ceiling, and walls are gravitationally horizontal and vertical. Because they are not, observers perceive themselves and the chandelier to be tilted instead (part B).

highly artificial circumstances for the very good reason that these assumptions tend to be true under normal viewing conditions. When they are false, however, as in the case of the tilted room, illusory perceptions reveal the existence of the assumptions. This close interdependency between reality, illusion, and hidden assumptions will be discussed in greater detail in Chapter 7.

A literal or strict interpretation of unconscious inference would be that perception is accomplished by sequentially applying the rules of symbolic logic or by solving mathematical equations. Indeed, these are the kind of processes Helmholtz seemed to have had in mind when he proposed his notion of unconscious inference. It was also this strict interpretation of unconscious inference to which Gibson objected so emphatically in his doctrine of direct perception. Fortunately, there are now more plausible interpretations within the computational framework we will employ that still fit the general inferential scheme advocated by constructivists. We will see, for example, that connectionist networks can reach perceptual conclusions based partly on incoming sensory data and partly on additional assumptions that are embodied in the pattern of interconnections among its neuronlike elements (see Sections 5.3.3 and 6.4 for two examples). Such networks are able to "make inferences" on the basis of heuristic assumptions (or "soft constraints," as they are sometimes called by connectionist theorists) without using either symbolic logic or mathematical equations. In this book, we will interpret the concept of "unconscious inference" broadly enough to encompass such computational formalisms as well. In fairness to the Gestaltists and Gibson, however, we should also note that the behavior of such networks is closely related to the dynamic behavior of Köhler's physical Gestalts and to Gibson's metaphor of mechanical resonance for information pickup.

2.2 A Brief History of Information Processing

The modern era in vision science began in the 1950s and 1960s when three important developments fundamentally changed the way scientists understood vision: the use of computer simulations to model cognitive processes of various kinds, the application of information processing ideas to psychology, and the emergence of the idea that the brain is a biological processor of information. All three developments have exerted major influences on the evolution of vision science as an interdisciplinary field.

2.2.1 Computer Vision

A breakthrough of immense importance in the development of vision science was the idea that modern digital computers could be used to simulate complex perceptual processing. Vision and other forms of perception and cognition had previously been considered the exclusive province of living organisms. Scientists were there-

Figure 2.2.1 Alan Turing. Turing was the brilliant British mathematician who invented the digital computer. He also conceived of the idea of artificial intelligence and proposed a behavioral test, now called Turing's test, for its success. (From Turing, 1959.)

fore in the position of investigating a working system by constructing theories and testing them experimentally on living beings, which is an expensive and difficult enterprise. The emergence of computer simulation techniques changed the situation dramatically, however. It allowed vision scientists to build synthetic systems whose principles of operation were known quite explicitly in advance, since the computer had been programmed by the theorist, and then to compare their behavior with that of sighted organisms. We will now consider a brief history of how this breakthrough came to pass.

The Invention of Computers. The modern computer age was born in the 1930s when the brilliant English mathematician Alan Turing (see Figure 2.2.1) defined a class of hypothetical machines, now known as universal **Turing machines** (Turing, 1937). These machines could be programmed to process information automatically in a theoretically infinite variety of ways. The machine Turing described was indeed hypothetical in the sense that it was a mathematical abstraction, but it did not take long for engineers to begin building such machines. Mathematician John von Neumann led the team that built the first general-purpose digital computer, a giant vacuum-tubed behemoth named ENIAC, in 1946 at the University of Pennsylvania. Since then, modern digital computers have improved enormously in speed, power, size, and sophistication, but they are all examples of universal Turing machines, carrying out the ever-increasing variety of procedures that programmers have devised for them.

As early as the 1940s, Turing himself understood the incredible possibilities of his computing machine for simulating intelligent thought (Turing, 1950). This idea gave rise to the field of **artificial intelligence** (or **AI**), the branch of computer science in which computer programs are written to simulate intelligent behavior. Originally, AI theorists focused on trying to simulate difficult intellectual tasks such as playing chess and proving mathematical theorems (e.g., Newell, Shaw, & Simon, 1958; Newell & Simon, 1963). Only later was it realized that programming computers to perceive the environment visually would be a challenging and useful goal. This endeavor gave rise to the field now known as **computer vision**: the study of how computers can be programmed to extract useful information about the environment from optical images.

Computer vision promoted two important developments that changed the theoretical branch of vision science dramatically and forever:

1. *Real images.* Theories of vision simulated on computers can be applied to gray-scale images that have been obtained from video cameras recording real-world scenes. Classical theories of visual perception were generally designed to account for stimulus conditions that never exist in real situations: perfect, noiseless, line drawings of ideal objects. Computer vision changed this by allowing theories to be tested on real images of real objects, warts and all.

2. *Explicit theories.* Before computer simulations, theories of visual perception were vague, informal, and incomplete, stressing large conceptual issues at the expense of important details. This is clearly the case for the four classical theories of vision we considered in Section 2.1, for example. Computer simulations changed this because one hallmark of computer programming is that it forces the theorist to make everything explicit.

The first insight derived from these two developments was the realization that *vision is extremely difficult.* It turns out to be unbelievably hard to get computers to "see" even the simplest things. Processes that had previously been taken for granted by psychological theorists (for example, detecting edges, finding regions, and determining which regions are part of the same three-dimensional object) have required heroic computational efforts. These are all tasks that the human visual system accomplishes with incredible speed and accuracy yet without any apparent effort. In comparison, even state-of-the-art computer programs running on the fastest, most powerful computers that have yet been devised fail to achieve the speed, accuracy, and flexibility of human perceivers on even such simple and basic visual tasks as these.

Blocks World. The goal of early computer vision theories was to understand scenes from **blocks world**: a "microworld" in which all of the to-be-perceived objects were simple, uniformly colored, geometrical solids on a flat tabletop, like a child's set of blocks. The limited number and types of objects simplified the task enough that computers attained some degree of success. But if a coffee cup or, even worse, a piece of crumpled paper appeared in the scene, the computer program would fail miserably.

One of the first significant simulations of blocks world vision was a program by Roberts (1965). It is a good example both because it set the agenda for decades of computer vision research and because it illustrates just how restricted the conditions had to be for early computer vision programs to work. It could recognize visual scenes from gray-scale images, but only if they contained nonoverlapping polyhedral blocks that were constructed from a limited set of known prototypes (see Figure 2.2.2A). The program was divided into two main stages. The goal of the first stage was to construct a clean line drawing from the video image (see Figure 2.2.2E). This was done by finding local **luminance edges**: changes in the amount of light falling in two adjacent regions of the image. Edges were detected at just four orientations at 45° intervals (see Figure 2.2.2C), and were then linked together to produce smooth lines at the contours (see Figure 2.2.2D). The goal of the second phase was to fit a model of the known set of volumetric primitives to the line drawing in order to construct a geometrical description of its shape (see Figure 2.2.2F). This was done by using shapes of planar regions in the line drawing to suggest which 3-D primitives

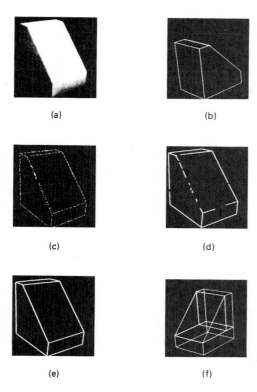

(a) (b)

(c) (d)

(e) (f)

Figure 2.2.2 Roberts's "blocks world" computer vision program. A video image of a configuration of blocks (part a) was processed for local edges (part c) that were then linked into smooth contours (parts d and e). Such line drawings were then matched to find primitive volumes that would fit together to produce the correct shape (part f) and predict its appearance from another perspective (part b). (From Roberts, 1965.)

might be present and then selecting the shapes that fit together to produce a coherent description of the blocks.

Computational Approaches to Ecological Optics.

More recent advances in computer vision have resulted from formal analyses of the information available in optical images under less restrictive conditions. This approach was strongly advocated by Gibson's earlier writing on ecological optics (Gibson, 1950, 1966, 1979). It led to a new emphasis on the mathematical analysis of how environmental structure of various sorts is reflected in image structure. The upshot of this development was that theorists began spending a great deal of time trying to figure out ways of recovering more complete information about the visual scene directly from the image,

Figure 2.2.3 David Marr. Marr was a brilliant vision scientist whose computational theories of vision and conjectures about their relation to visual physiology helped to define the interdisciplinary field of vision science. (From Vaina, 1991.)

particularly about the depth and slant of surfaces in the 3-D environment.

In many respects, the pioneers of this approach were the Dutch psychophysicists Jan Koenderink and Andrea Van Doorn. They applied sophisticated mathematical techniques from differential geometry to problems such as motion perception from optical flow (Koenderink & Van Doorn, 1976a), depth perception from stereoscopic information (Koenderink & Van Doorn, 1976b), the 3-D orientation of surfaces from shading information (Koenderink, Van Doorn, & Kappers, 1992), and related topics. They themselves did not create computer vision programs, but their work inspired others who did.

The mathematical approach to creating working computer vision programs was most clearly and effectively articulated at the Massachusetts Institute of Technology (M.I.T.), particularly by David Marr (see Figure 2.2.3) and his many talented colleagues. This research is characterized by mathematical analyses of how the luminance structure in two-dimensional images provides information about the structure of surfaces and objects in three-dimensional space (Marr, 1982), an endeavor that is very much in line with Gibson's ecological approach. A great deal of progress has been made on

Theoretical Approaches to Vision

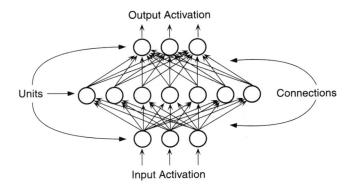

Output Activation

Units →

Connections

Input Activation

Figure 2.2.4 A three-layer feedforward connectionist network used in back propagation learning. The first layer of units represents the input, the last layer represents the output, and the middle "hidden" layer accomplishes the transformation from input to output. Learning occurs by adjusting the weights of the connections to minimize errors. (See Appendix B for details.)

this project, and it dominated computer vision research for much of the past two decades. We will have a great deal to say about the results that have been achieved within this general computational framework during the course of this book.

Connectionism and Neural Networks. The most recent development in computer simulations of vision is the explosion of interest in **connectionist network** or **neural network** models (e.g., Feldman, 1981; Feldman & Ballard, 1982; Grossberg, 1982; Hinton & Anderson, 1981). These models are based on the assumption that human vision depends heavily on the massively parallel structure of neural circuits in the brain. As their name implies, such models are complex networks of many densely interconnected computing *elements* (or *units*), each of which works like a simplified neuron. The element's current state is characterized by an **activation level** that corresponds roughly to the firing rate of a neuron. Activation is spread throughout the network by **connections** that are either excitatory or inhibitory, much like the synapses through which neurons communicate (see Figure 2.2.4). Although these connectionist models can be specified mathematically, their behavior generally depends on nonlinear equations

that are not easily solved analytically. (The reader is referred to Appendix B for a brief primer on connectionist theory.) This means that to determine how a given network will behave, its operation must be simulated on computers.[5]

The historical precursors to modern connectionist theories of perception came from the study of **perceptrons**, a particular class of neuronlike network models that were studied intensively by Frank Rosenblatt (1962) and his colleagues. What made perceptrons especially interesting and important was that they were able to learn how to identify examples of new categories by adjusting the weights on their connections according to explicit rules. Rosenblatt was able to prove that a simple learning rule was sufficient to allow the network to learn to make any categorical discrimination that was possible for it to make. At about the same time, psychologist Donald O. Hebb was able to synthesize a large body of behavioral and physiological research on human and animal learning within a neural network framework in which associations were formed within and between complex "cell assemblies" that fired at the same time (Hebb, 1964). Despite these advances, research on neural networks suffered a severe blow when computer scientists Marvin Minsky and Seymour Papert (1969) exposed serious limitations of Rosenblatt's perceptrons. Their critique brought neural network research to a virtual halt for over a decade.

A few persistent researchers around the world kept neural network theory alive, however, and in the early 1980s, a group of cognitive scientists working in the psychology department at the University of California at San Diego achieved several important results that revitalized the approach. Calling their theories **parallel distributed processing (PDP) models**, David Rumelhart, James McClelland, Geoffrey Hinton, Paul Smolensky, Michael Jordan, and their colleagues demonstrated that neural networks models have several important advantages over more traditional programs in computer science (see McClelland & Rumelhart, 1986, 1988; Rumelhart & McClelland, 1986). We will discuss examples of such models at several points later in this book.

---

[5] The fact that modern digital computers are generally serial, whereas the models are highly parallel, does not affect the solution, though it does slow down the simulation. Parallel processes can always be simulated on serial machines simply by stringing out the processes that are supposed to be happening at the same time so that they are actually computed sequentially.

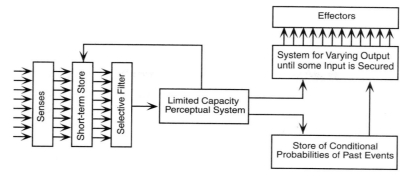

Figure 2.2.5 Broadbent's filter theory of auditory attention. Proposed in 1958, this was one of the first perceptual theories to be cast in terms of information processing operations and flow diagrams. The selective filter acts as a switch that allows information from only one sensory channel to reach the higher level perceptual system with limited capacity. (From Broadbent, 1958.)

2.2.2 Information Processing Psychology

Another important historical development in the evolution of modern vision science was the rise of the information processing approach in psychology. From the 1920s onward, most of psychology was dominated by **behaviorism**. Behaviorists believed that the proper approach to psychology was to deal only with directly observable behavior. Methodologically, this meant banishing introspective methods such as those used by structuralists and Gestaltists. Theoretically, it meant purging psychological theories of any internal processes that smacked of "mentalism" or "consciousness." In its purest and most extreme form, this would require removing any reference to perception from psychological theories, because perception is fundamentally a kind of internal experience of the external world. Perhaps this is why theoretical behaviorism never really gained much of a foothold within the perceptual community.

The dominance of behaviorism persisted during the 1940s and 1950s, especially in areas related to learning. But toward the end of the 1950s, a new approach began to emerge that rejected the behaviorist dogma against positing internal states and processes. The idea that launched this movement was that mental processes could be understood as information processing events, on the basis of new concepts that were developed in the fields of electrical engineering, computer science, and information theory. This allowed psychological researchers to state their theories of vision within a new, more precise language that was closely related to the programs computer scientists were beginning to write. New experimental methods were also developed in the service of testing these information processing theories, especially ones using response time as the objective measure of performance (e.g., Sternberg, 1966, 1969). Within a decade, the information processing approach was firmly established in cognitive psychology, and it soon became the dominant framework for understanding visual perception and many other kinds of mental activity.

One of the ground-breaking publications of this era was Donald Broadbent's 1958 book *Perception and Communication*, in which he analyzed the process of attending to auditory information coming in one ear versus the other. Broadbent suggested that attention operated as a kind of switch that selected among several information processing channels after an initial analysis of gross sensory features had been done (see Figure 2.2.5). Although the particular theory that he advanced has since been superseded by a series of more sophisticated information processing theories of perception and attention, Broadbent was among the first to propose a psychological theory in the form of a flowchart that specifies the temporal structure of information processing events (see Section 2.3).

A landmark development in the history of visual information processing was the discovery of a very brief form of visual memory by psychologist George Sperling, then at the Bell Telephone Laboratories. By devising a clever technique to avoid overloading the observer's ability to respond to very brief visual displays (less than a tenth of a second), Sperling (1960) discovered a previously unknown form of visual memory, called **iconic memory**, that generally lasts for less than half a second. His elegant experiments revealed many fascinating properties of this memory system and spawned hundreds of further studies into its mechanisms (see Section 12.1). This work encouraged many other psychologists to begin exploring vision within the emerging framework of information processing that Sperling and his colleagues employed so successfully.

These and subsequent developments within psychology began to turn the tide against behaviorism as the dominant approach to understanding human cognition. A watershed event was the publication of Ulric Neisser's influential book *Cognitive Psychology* in 1967. The information processing approach that Neisser advocated diverted psychologists from the behaviorist preoccupation with general theories of learning and toward specific models of particular subdomains of cognition, particularly perception and attention. There have been many noteworthy successes of this approach in understanding the human mind, including a large number in vision, as will be documented in the coming chapters.

2.2.3 Biological Information Processing

The third important development that influenced the emergence of the information processing paradigm was the invention of physiological techniques for studying neural activity in the visual system. These new methods allowed scientists to ask and answer detailed questions about how visual information is processed in the retina and visual centers of the brain. This was important because the neuron was taken to be the appropriate unit of analysis in the visual system in the sense that vision was assumed to be explicable in terms of the firing pattern that emerged from the interactions among many individual neurons (Barlow, 1972). In principle, then, the existence of methods for studying the activity of individual neurons meant that scientists could trace out a functional wiring diagram of the entire visual system, neuron by neuron, specifying what operation each neuron accomplished.

This development marked the beginning of research into biological information processing, a field in which vision has played a leading role. The more recent development of a variety of techniques for imaging the structure and function of living brains has greatly expanded the possibilities for physiological research into visual perception, especially in normal human observers.

Early Developments. Before the 1950s, the brain was not generally viewed as an information processing device, but simply as a biological organ whose mechanisms were opaque. Indeed, it took many years of study and debate before biologists realized that neurons were not directly connected to each other, but separate entities that had to communicate through chemical transmissions across synaptic clefts. Even so, the idea that brains were processing information did not gain wide acceptance until the analogy between brains and computers began to take hold. Mathematician John von Neumann (1951) made the analogy explicit, going so far as to suggest that the neural spikes that travel along axons are essentially a digital code, similar to the binary 1s and 0s processed by digital computers. Few neuroscientists take this simple analogy seriously anymore, for there are many striking differences between brains and modern digital computers. But the idea that the brain is doing some kind of information processing is now almost universally held, and the results of most modern physiological studies of brain function are interpreted within this context.

The first studies of brain function were **lesion experiments** in which areas of animals' brains were surgically removed or otherwise destroyed. Such experiments led to many fascinating discoveries about the gross localization of function in the brain, as was mentioned briefly in Section 1.3. The same can be said for **electrical brain stimulation** techniques, in which an electrode is inserted into the brain and mild electrical current is delivered to the neurons surrounding its tip to see what behavior (or, in the case of human surgical patients, what reportable conscious experience) is elicited. Both of these techniques have been important in understanding the large-scale structure of visual centers in the brain, but neither is really an adequate technique for studying information processing events as they take place in a normally functioning brain because they do not measure the electrochemical behavior of individual neurons.

Single-Cell Recording. During the 1950s, a physiological technique called **single-cell recording** was developed to explore the information processing carried

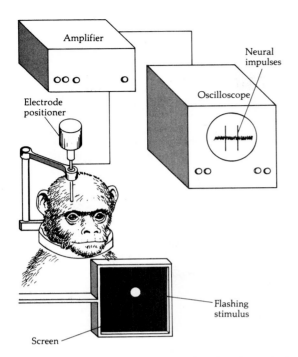

Figure 2.2.6 Single-cell recording. A microelectrode is inserted into an animal's visual system while patterns of light are presented to the retina. Electrical activity from neural impulses is registered by the electrode and monitored by the researcher. (From Sekuler & Blake, 1985.)

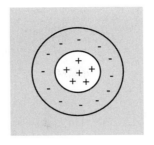 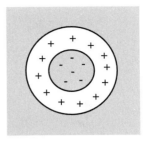

A. On-center, Off-surround
Receptive Field

B. Off-center, On-surround
Receptive Field

Figure 2.2.7 Receptive fields in retinal ganglion cells. The firing rate of on-center, off-surround cells (part A) increases when light stimulates the central region, decreases when it stimulates the surround, and is unaffected by light outside the surround. The firing rate of off-center, on-surround cells (part B) is affected in the opposite way.

out by individual neurons. Extremely thin electrodes are positioned close to a neuron's axon so that they can register the small changes in electrical potential that occur each time a spike of neural activity passes along the axon (see Figure 2.2.6). The output of the electrode can then be recorded and analyzed to determine the stimulus conditions that activate the neuron. In the case of vision, this usually is discovered by projecting specific patterns of light onto the animal's retina to find out whether their presence makes the neuron fire more or less than it does in their absence.

The groundbreaking work in the 1950s and 1960s that inspired the surge of interest in biological information processing was done on mammalian visual systems, particularly those of cat and monkey. The most important early discoveries were made by Stephen Kuffler, David Hubel, and Torsten Wiesel at Harvard University. Kuffler (1953) used single-cell recording techniques to determine the **receptive field** of retinal ganglion cells: the region of the retina that influences the firing rate of the target neuron by increasing it (excitation) or

decreasing it (inhibition). (Similar pioneering studies were carried out at the same time by Barlow (1953) in the frog retina.) It turned out that the optimal stimulus pattern for making ganglion cells fire vigorously was either a bright spot in the center of the receptive field with a dark disk surrounding it or the reverse pattern (see Figure 2.2.7). From this knowledge, theories were constructed in terms of neural wiring diagrams that would account for the observed results. Such theories specified what information was carried by the firing rate of retinal ganglion cells and how it was processed to produce a given output.

Nobel laureates Hubel and Wiesel (Figure 2.2.8) used similar techniques to map out the more complex receptive fields of cells in the visual cortex (Hubel & Wiesel, 1959, 1962). They found elongated receptive fields that carry information about orientation as well as position (see Figure 2.2.9). Their discoveries produced an explosion of research into neural mechanisms of visual information processing. As a result, portions of visual cortex are now perhaps the best understood area of the entire cerebral cortex. We will have a great deal more to say about the properties of these cells when we discuss the neural processing of spatial information in Chapter 4.

Single-cell recording techniques have some significant limitations, however. They are, by definition, confined to the study of individual cells. Many electrodes must therefore be used to find out what many different cells are doing at the same time. There are currently severe

Theoretical Approaches to Vision

Figure 2.2.8 David Hubel and Torsten Wiesel. Nobel laureates Hubel and Wiesel pioneered the study of visual cortex by discovering many properties of receptive fields for cells in primary visual cortex. Their discoveries spawned thousands of studies of the physiology of visual cortex using single cell recording techniques. (From Goldstein, 1989.)

technical limits on the number of cells from which simultaneous recordings can be made. Such constraints make mapping the overall structure (or **architecture**) of cortical areas with single-cell techniques cumbersome and laborious.

Autoradiography. Fortunately, new physiological methods have been developed that are more efficient than single-cell recording techniques at studying the overall architecture of cortex. One of the first techniques to be explored was **autoradiography**. To construct an autoradiogram, an animal is injected with a dose of a radioactively labeled substance—usually some form of sugar, such as 2-deoxyglucose—that is taken up by active neurons and accumulates within them because it is not metabolized. After the chemical is injected, the animal is shown a visual stimulus bearing specific prop-

erties of interest, such as lines of a single orientation. Radioactive sugar then accumulates most rapidly in the cells that fire most strongly to lines of that orientation. The animal is then sacrificed, and thin slices of brain tissue are placed in contact with photographic paper sensitive to the amount of radioactivity. The resulting picture thus displays the spatial distribution of the thousands of cells activated by the image. Figure 2.2.10 shows the cells activated by many lines in a particular orientation (see Figure 2.2.10). Together with single-cell recording techniques, autoradiographic methods have proved quite valuable in understanding the architecture of visual cortex.

Brain Imaging Techniques. The most exciting new tools for studying the neural mechanisms underlying vision are noninvasive methods for constructing images

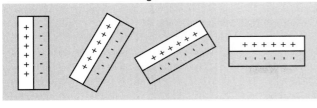

Edge Detectors

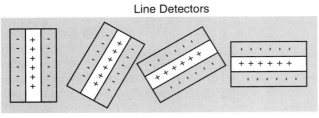

Line Detectors

Figure 2.2.9 Receptive fields in cortical cells. Cells in the first area of visual cortex have elongated receptive fields that respond most vigorously if stimulated by an edge or line at a particular orientation and position.

of the human brain: **computer tomography (CT)**, **positron emission tomography (PET)**, and **magnetic resonance imagery (MRI)**. These amazing techniques were developed in the 1970s and have literally revolutionized modern medicine by enabling physicians to examine bodily tissues, including the brain, without breaking the skin.

The first imaging technique to be developed was X-ray computer tomography. To make a CT image of the brain, a highly focussed beam of X-rays is directed at a thin cross section of the brain from one side, and the intensity of the X-rays that have passed through it is measured on the other side (see Figure 2.2.11B). Because brain tissues of different densities affect the beam in different but lawful ways, the strength of the beam passing through the various tissues carries information about their density, but only the *average* density of all the tissue it goes through. Measuring X-ray intensity from beams in a single direction is therefore insufficient to determine the densities of the tissues at different locations along the X-ray's path.

It turns out, however, that measuring the X-rays from many different directions allows a complete map of tissue density to be determined. The same procedure is therefore followed repeatedly from many different angles. The masses of resulting data are then processed by a powerful computer using sophisticated modeling

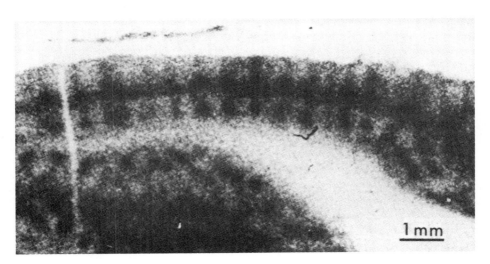

Figure 2.2.10 An autoradiograph of orientation columns in visual cortex. Cortical cells are darkly stained if they were highly active while vertical stripes were being presented. The dark vertical bands are orientation columns in the upper and lower layers of cortex. The dark horizontal band is layer 4, which receives input from the lateral geniculate nucleus and responds to all orientations. (From Hubel, Wiesel, & Stryker, 1977.)

Theoretical Approaches to Vision

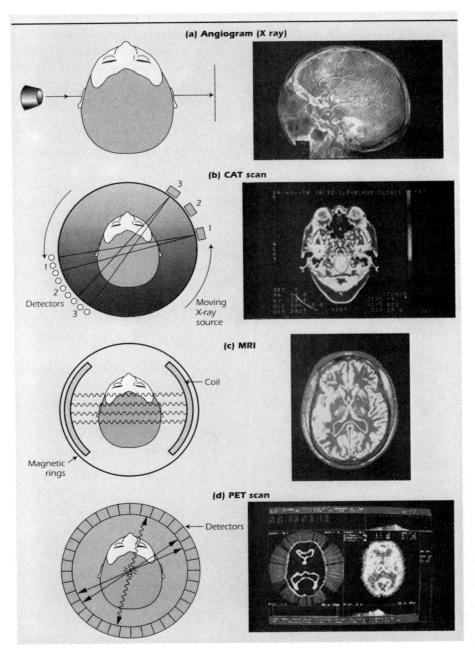

Figure 2.2.11 Brain imaging techniques. The human brain can be examined noninvasively by (a) standard X-rays, (b) computer-aided tomography (CT or CAT) scans, (c) magnetic resonance imaging (MRI) scans, and (d) positron emission tomography (PET) scans. (From Sternberg, 1995.)

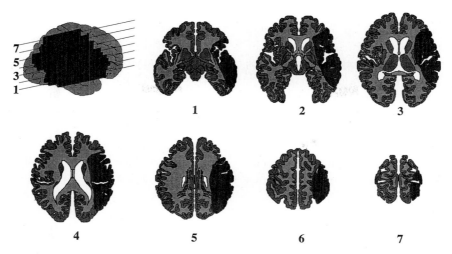

Figure 2.2.12 Multiple imaging slices through a human brain. These diagrams show computerized maps of a brain containing a large lesion in the right parietal lobe. The scans were taken at the levels indicated on the side view of the human head, with the lesion area blackened. (From Ro & Rafal, 1996.)

algorithms that enable the measurements to be turned into a map of the tissue densities at each point in the cross section. This map constitutes a single "slice" through the brain. Many different slices can be taken at different levels to achieve a relatively complete image of the anatomical structure of the brain, as illustrated in Figure 2.2.12.

After CT scans were developed, biophysicists realized that similar computer techniques could be used to reconstruct brain images by using measurements other than X-ray intensity. MRI was the second form of brain imaging to be developed. It is accomplished by placing the brain in a strong magnetic field (see Figure 2.2.11C), which polarizes the molecules within the brain, like a needle in a compass, so that their magnetic poles all line up with the magnetic field (and with each other). When tissue in this state is pulsed with radio waves, the molecules emit detectable radio signals that carry information about their chemical properties. This information is recovered by detectors placed around the head. Their measurements are processed by computer tomography algorithms, similar to those used in CT scans, which construct a map of the brain tissue. MRI produces much more detailed brain images than CT technology and has the added advantage of not exposing the brain to the adverse effects of X-rays.

PET scans are created by yet another procedure. Subjects are given a small dose of a radioactive sub-stance that enters their bloodstreams. It works its way into brain tissues, just as in the autoradiographic techniques describe earlier. The radioactive isotope then emits positrons spontaneously as it decays, and these emissions can be detected outside the head, as illustrated in Figure 2.2.11D.

By measuring the positron emissions coming from the brain in many directions and processing them with computer tomography algorithms, PET images can be constructed that reflect the distribution of radioactivity in the brain. Because the amount of radioactivity at each point is closely related to the amount of neural activity that has occurred there since administration of the radioactive tracer, the resulting PET scan reflects the degree to which that part of the brain is involved in the mental activity in which the person is engaging. PET measures activity not directly, but indirectly through blood flow. When an area of the brain is active, it receives an increased supply of blood, and this increase is detected through positron emissions.

Even though PET images are less detailed than MRI images, they represent an important advance because they provide *functional*, rather than just structural, measures. That is, they enable scientists to measure ongoing activity in the brain rather than just its anatomy. For example, if PET scans are made when a person is engaged in a highly visual task, the occipital cortex "lights up," reflecting the high level of neural activity there. In an

Theoretical Approaches to Vision

auditory task, this area of cortex will show little activity, but part of the temporal lobe lights up. PET techniques can therefore be used to discover which portions of the brain are active during a variety of complex visual tasks, such as reading, visual imagery, attention, and memory.

One difficulty with PET techniques is that they require at least 40 seconds to collect the necessary data. They are therefore not quick enough to examine ongoing processing at the finer-grained time scale of seconds and fractions of seconds at which neural activity seems to occur. Another drawback is that their spatial resolution is rather coarse in comparison with MRI images.

One of the most promising recent developments in brain imaging techniques has been the modification of MRI methods to provide functional measurements of brain activity as well as structural ones. This form of brain imaging is now usually referred to as *fMRI*, which stands for "functional MRI." Like PET methods, fMRI ultimately depends on the fact that blood flow increases to areas of the brain that are highly active, although the relevant measurements for fMRI are related to the concentration of oxygen in the blood in different parts of the brain. It improves on PET methods in both spatial and temporal resolution. Moreover, it does not require injecting any radioactive substances and has no known harmful side effects. fMRI research is still in its infancy, however, and it will probably take several years before neuroscientists know the full potential of this new method. With further improvements and refinements, it may prove to be the "microscope" of human neuroscience: the breakthrough technology that will change forever the way scientists study how brains work.

2.3 Information Processing Theory

In the remainder of this chapter, we will lay the theoretical groundwork for the rest of the book. First, we will examine the theoretical foundations of the information processing paradigm within which modern theories of vision are cast. Next, we will discuss the central concepts of information processing theories—representations and processes—and examine some important issues surrounding them. At the end of the chapter, we will preview the general theoretical framework that will structure much of our discussion of visual perception. It is based on four information processing stages that lead from the retinal image to object recognition. In later chapters, we will clarify and elaborate the concepts introduced in this section.

The reader is forewarned that the material in this section is abstract and theoretical. It is perhaps especially difficult because it appears so early in the book, before we have examined any specific examples. Still, it is important to tackle the basic concepts of information processing as early as possible so that they can be used in explaining the material to follow.

The **information processing** paradigm is a way of theorizing about the nature of the human mind as a computational process. It has been applied with considerable success not only to visual perception, but also to a wide range of cognitive phenomena in auditory perception, memory, language, judgment, thinking, and problem solving. In fact, the information processing approach so dominates these topics that several writers have suggested that it constitutes a "Kuhnian paradigm" for cognition (Lachman, Lachman, & Butterfield, 1979; Palmer & Kimchi, 1986).

The noted philosopher of science Thomas Kuhn (1962) defined a **scientific paradigm** as a set of working assumptions that a community of scientists shares (often implicitly) in conducting research on a given topic. The assumptions of a paradigm usually involve pretheoretical or metatheoretical ways of conceptualizing the major issues and sensible ways of approaching them theoretically. Kuhn describes the Newtonian view of physics as a paradigm that survived largely intact from the seventeenth century until the early part of the twentieth century. Although there had been many important theoretical developments since Newton's day—such as Maxwell's equations describing electromagnetic fields—none of them required rejecting the fundamental assumptions that underlay Newton's ideas about the nature of the physical world. For example, Newton and his successors implicitly or explicitly assumed that there is a qualitative distinction between mass and energy, that time is absolute, and that causality is deterministic. Quantum mechanics and Einstein's theory of relativity eventually brought about the demise of this Newtonian paradigm and ushered in a new paradigm that incorporated a new set of assumptions, including the ideas that mass and energy are equivalent, that time is relative, and that causation is inherently probabilistic.

The claim that information processing constitutes a paradigm for the cognitive sciences—including vision science—is based on the widely held belief that the nature of mental processes can be captured by theories that specify them in terms of information processing events (see below). Although there remains a small but vocal subset of vision scientists who do not view visual perception as information processing—most notably proponents of Gibson's theory of ecological optics—it is certainly the framework within which most current theories of visual perception are cast.

2.3.1 The Computer Metaphor

The historical development of visual theories has been strongly shaped by available research techniques. In the case of information processing theories, the most significant force has surely been the invention of electronic computers. Their influence has been felt in two distinct but related ways. First, they have become the preferred tool for testing new theories of visual processing to find out whether they actually work on real images. As we discussed in Section 2.2, this approach gave rise to computer vision as a specialty field within computer science. Its goal is to program computers so that they can understand the world around them in much the same way people do.

The second influence of computers has been even more profound: They have served as the primary theoretical analogy for mental processes within the information processing paradigm. In a nutshell, the analogy is that mental processes (such as visual perception) bear the same relation to the brain as programs do to the computer on which they run. In other words, minds are like programs that run on machines called brains; minds are the "software" of biological computation, and brains are the "hardware." Because of this analogy, many perceptual theories over the past 20 to 30 years have actually been implemented as computer programs, and many more have been described within the framework of information processing without having actually been implemented in programs. In this chapter, we will take a closer look at what form this theorizing takes and why it has become so popular.

The computer analogy has largely replaced the theoretical analogies that we discussed in Section 2.1: the chemical analogy underlying structuralist theory, the field theoretical analogy underlying Gestalt theory, and the resonance analogy underlying Gibson's theory of information pickup. The computer analogy is quite com-

patible with the inferential analogy of constructivism because making inferences is, in effect, what computers do when they execute programs. Many cognitive theorists believe that the similarities between brains and computers run deeper than mere analogy, however, and that the brain is literally a biological computer. If this is true, a properly programmed computer may be able to perceive its environment in the same sense that a person does.

Some theorists even believe that the similarities between mind/brain and program/computer are extensive enough that a properly programmed "seeing" computer would actually have conscious visual experiences. This view of the relation between the computer programs and mental events is sometimes called "**strong AI**" (Searle, 1980) to indicate that the strong claim for artificial intelligence (AI) is being made: namely, that a properly programmed machine actually has mental processes, including conscious experiences. This position is to be contrasted with so-called "**weak AI**," in which the claim is that such a machine is only simulating mental events, conscious or otherwise. Whether the claims of strong AI are valid or not is open to serious debate, with heated arguments on both sides (see Searle, 1980, and the many commentaries that follow it).

Regardless of the more extreme claims that have been made, if mental events occurring in the human brain are indeed analogous to programs running on computers, then it will be useful to examine what is known about information processing on devices such as computers for potential insights into how the mind might work and how it might be studied most fruitfully.

2.3.2 Three Levels of Information Processing

In his influential book *Vision*, David Marr (1982) distinguished three different levels of description involved in understanding complex information processing systems: the *computational*, *algorithmic*, and *implementational* levels. In so doing, he provided a metatheoretical analysis of the information processing paradigm. A **metatheory** is a theory about theories, a theory that attempts not to analyze vision itself, but to analyze the nature of theories about vision. Marr argued that there are important conceptual distinctions among these three levels and that all of them are essential for understanding vision—or anything else—as information processing.

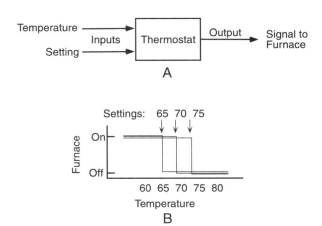

Settings: 65 70 75

COMPUTATIONAL LEVEL

Figure 2.3.1 Computational-level description of a thermostat. (A) The box diagram shows the inputs and output of a thermostat. (B) The graph plots the input/output behavior of the thermostat for three particular settings as a function of temperature.

The Computational Level. The most abstract description that Marr proposed was the **computational level**. He defined it as the informational constraints available for mapping input information to output information. This level of theorizing specifies what computation needs to be performed and on what information it should be based, without specifying how it is accomplished.

To illustrate this concept, we will consider a very simple information processing system: a household thermostat. The "computation" that a thermostat must perform is to map both the current temperature of the air and the user's setting of preferred temperature (the input information) into an on/off signal for the furnace (the output information), depending on whether the air temperature is lower or higher than the set-point (see Figure 2.3.1A). Figure 2.3.1B graphs this binary (two-valued) mapping as a function of air temperature for three different set-points: if the temperature is below the set-point, the furnace should be on, and if it is equal to or above the set point, the furnace should be off. We can summarize this computational level description in mathematical form as a binary function in two variables,

$$O(T, S) = \begin{cases} 1 \text{ if and only if } T < S \\ 0 \text{ if and only if } T \geq S, \end{cases}$$

where O is the output function, T is the temperature, and S is the set-point. Notice that we have not yet said anything about how this mathematical function is to be

achieved; we have merely defined what the inputs are and how they are formally related to the outputs. This is a computational-level description of a thermostat.

The Algorithmic Level. At the middle level in Marr's hierarchy is the **algorithmic level** of description for an information processing system. Algorithmic descriptions are more specific than computational descriptions in that they specify how a computation is executed in terms of information processing operations. There are, in principle, many different ways in which a given computational-level mapping of input to output might be accomplished, in the same sense that there are many different computer programs that would accomplish the same computational task. Thus, the algorithmic level corresponds most closely to the concept of a program as it is understood in computer science.

To construct an algorithm for a given computationally defined task, one must decide upon a *representation* for the input and output information and construct a set of *processes* that will transform the input representation into the output representation in a well-defined manner. The concepts of representation and processing will be discussed in depth shortly, but for now, you can think of a representation as a way of encoding information about something and a process as a way of changing one representation into another. In the case of our thermostat example, the most obvious algorithm is to use one continuous variable to encode the temperature and another to encode the set-point and then to perform a comparison operation between these two magnitudes to determine whether the temperature is higher or lower than the set-point. A flowchart diagram corresponding to this algorithm is given in Figure 2.3.2.

This is the standard algorithm for most thermostats, but others are also possible. One alternative would be to represent the temperature as a series of binary (two-valued) variables—say, above 60° versus below 60°, above 61° versus below 61°, and so on—and then to have the set-point select which of these temperature variables controls the output. (Note that the representation of temperature and set-point would be discrete in this case, in contrast to their continuous representations in the previous algorithm.) Still other algorithms are possible even for this simple information processing system, but the important point is that more than one algorithm can satisfy a given computational description.

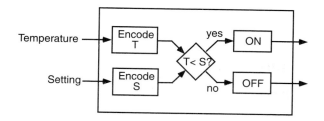

ALGORITHMIC LEVEL

Figure 2.3.2 Algorithmic-level description of a thermostat. The black box diagram shows a decomposition of the computational diagram in Figure 2.3.1 into encoding, comparison, and output operations.

The Implementational Level. The lowest level description is at the **implementational level**. It specifies how an algorithm actually is embodied as a physical process within a physical system. Just as the same program can be run on many computers that differ in their physical construction, so the same algorithm can be implemented using many physically different devices. We should stress here that by "different devices," we mean to include the possibility that the same algorithm might be implemented on brains as well as various different kinds of computers.

To illustrate the implementational level concretely, Figure 2.3.3 shows one way to construct a physical thermostat using the first algorithm that we described. The double curved line depicts a bimetallic strip, made by putting together two strips of metal that have different thermal expansion rates. The differential expansion of the two metals at different temperatures causes the strip to bend more or less as the temperature changes. The free end of this strip is part of a contact switch that completes an electrical circuit when it touches the contact. The vertical position of the contact is changed by a user adjusting the setting of the thermostat; raising the contact increases the set-point and lowering it decreases the set-point. Whether or not the switch closes thus depends on two factors: the height of the end of the bimetallic strip (as determined by the temperature) and the height of the contact (as determined by the setting).

This device implements the first thermostat algorithm (see Figure 2.3.2) as follows: The continuous temperature variable is implemented by the vertical position of the end of the strip. The continuous setting variable is

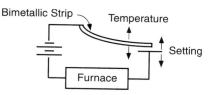

IMPLEMENTATION LEVEL

Figure 2.3.3 Implementational-level description of a thermostat. A schematic diagram shows a physical device that carries out the operations indicated in the algorithmic-level flowchart in Figure 2.3.2. (See text for details.)

implemented by the vertical position of the contact. The comparison of temperature and setting is made directly by the relative positions of the end of the strip and the contact. If they are touching, the circuit is completed, switching the furnace on. If they are not touching, the circuit is broken, switching the furnace off. This device does the job, but it is just one of many ways to build a thermostat based on this algorithm. There are countless alternative ways to implement continuous temperature and setting variables so that they can be compared by a simple physical process, all of which employ the same algorithm specified in the flowchart of Figure 2.3.2.

2.3.3 Three Assumptions of Information Processing

Palmer and Kimchi (1986) provided a different metatheoretical analysis of the information processing paradigm from a psychological perspective. Although their analysis at first appears quite different from Marr's, we will see that it is closely related.

Informational Description. Palmer and Kimchi (1986) analyzed the implicit assumptions that underlie information processing theories in cognitive psychology. The three most important are listed in this and the following sections.

1. *Informational description.* Mental events can be functionally described as **informational events**, each of which consists of three parts: the **input information** (what it starts with), the **operation** performed on the input (what gets done to the input), and the **output information** (what it ends up with).

Theoretical Approaches to Vision

Figure 2.3.4 A black box diagram. Mental events can be described as an informational event defined by the input information, output information, and the operation that maps input to output.

The first assumption states that mental events, including visual perception, can be specified as an operation that transforms an initial ensemble of input information into output information. Such an informational event can be diagrammed as a black box in an **information flow diagram**, as illustrated in Figure 2.3.4. If the input/output mapping is well defined, there will be a way of specifying the operation such that knowing the input and the operation determines the output. A cognitive theory at this level of abstraction corresponds to Marr's computational level because it specifies what information is mapped from input to output but without specifying how this transformation might be accomplished. A mathematical function relating input to output is the ideal way of specifying the operation, as we did for the thermostat example above, but any well-defined description will do.

Recursive Decomposition. Although informational description is a necessary condition for an information processing theory, it is not sufficient, for there are theories that invoke the assumption of informational description that are nevertheless *not* information processing theories. Gibson's theory of information pickup, for example, specifies informational correspondences between input (the dynamic ambient optic array) and output (perception of the environment) and therefore satisfies the assumption of informational description. But Gibson's theory is not an information processing theory because it explicitly denies the necessity of analyzing internal representations or processes to accomplish the mapping. Palmer and Kimchi (1986) specify this crucial further requirement of information processing theories as the assumption of **recursive decomposition**. It is used to generate more complete descriptions of what goes on inside the black box.

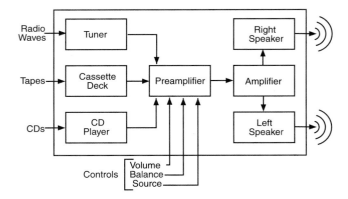

Figure 2.3.5 Flow diagram of a stereo system. Functional decomposition of a typical stereo system separates it into several components (the black boxes) and their information processing interrelations (the arrows between them).

2. *Recursive decomposition.* Any complex (nonprimitive) informational event at one level can be specified more fully at a lower level by decomposing it into a number of component informational events and a flow diagram that specifies the temporal ordering relations among the components.

The important concept introduced by this assumption is that one can define a black box in terms of a number of smaller black boxes inside it, plus a specification of how they are interconnected. These smaller black boxes are often called **stages**, each of which is assumed to be independent of other stages to some degree. A simple example of decomposition is the analysis of a stereo system into its functional components: a tuner, CD player, cassette deck, preamplifier, amplifier, and speakers (see Figure 2.3.5). In many cases, all of these components are housed within a single cabinet (e.g., a "boombox"), but in other cases, each has its own separate enclosure, with wires between them that correspond to the information flow arrows in Figure 2.3.5.

Saying that decomposition is *recursive* means that it can be performed again on the results of previous decompositions. Thus, each component of the stereo system example could in principle be further decomposed into its internal circuits in an *iterative* (repeating) process of further decomposition. Repeated decomposition would eventually lead to a flow diagram in which the boxes correspond to the functions performed by individual

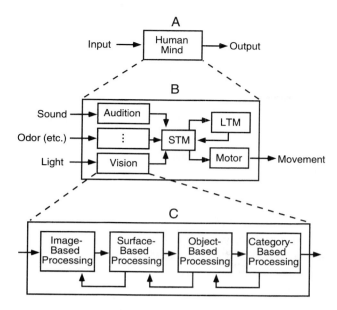

Figure 2.3.6 Recursive decomposition of human cognition. The mind can be described as an informational event at several levels of detail. Each flow diagram shows a functional decomposition of the black box above it (connected by dashed lines) into a set of simpler operations and the flow of information among them.

electrical components, such as resistors, capacitors, and transistors.

These decomposed flow diagrams of an information processing system correspond roughly to what Marr called the algorithmic level, because in breaking down a system into a flow diagram of simpler components, one begins to specify the algorithm through which the higher-level computation is accomplished. The main difference is that Marr viewed his algorithmic level as a single, unitary entity, whereas Palmer and Kimchi conceive of it as composed of many hierarchically nested levels. A computer program can also be viewed either as a single entity or as a hierarchy of embedded flow charts of routines, subroutines, sub-subroutines, and so on.

Palmer and Kimchi (1986) argue that recursive decomposition lies at the heart of the information processing approach for psychologists because it reflects how they typically work: by trying to specify and test successively more detailed flow diagrams. Figure 2.3.6 illustrates an example of recursive decomposition as applied to human cognition. The mind as a whole is represented by the single black box in Figure 2.3.6A. Psychologists typically decompose it into the relatively small number

of basic components illustrated in Figure 2.3.6B and their interconnections. Notice that the topic of this book—visual perception—is represented as a single process in this flow diagram. Because decomposition is recursive, any stage can be further decomposed into a flowchart of lower-level stages and the ordering relations among them. One such decomposition is indicated for the stage of visual perception. It is broken into the sequence of four component processes shown in Figure 2.3.6C, which will be described more fully at the end of this chapter. In later chapters, we will see that these four stages can be decomposed further into more detailed flow diagrams of more specific and simpler processes.

Recursive decomposition allows the complexity of an information processing system to be understood little by little. Each successive decomposition removes some of the complexity that is *implicit* within a single black box and makes it *explicit* through the connections among the operations at the next lower level of analysis. As a result, the operations performed within boxes at successively lower levels become correspondingly simpler. It is important to remember, however, that informational events at the lower (decomposed) level must also have an informational description that specifies *what* they do in terms of mapping input to output but need not specify *how* they do it. The "how" question is answered by going down another level in the hierarchy via further decomposition.

This enterprise of recursively decomposing a system into a hierarchy of components will be successful only to the extent that the system is actually structured as a hierarchy. Nobel laureate Herbert Simon (1969) has advanced several arguments that the human information processing system is structured in this way, at least approximately. He characterizes human cognition as "nearly decomposable" to distinguish it from certain human-made systems, such as the stereo in our previous example, which are fully decomposable. Simon's distinction compares the interactions that occur *within* components (i.e., within a single black box) with those that occur *between* components (i.e., between two or more boxes). A **decomposable system** is one in which the interactions among components are negligible in comparison with those within components. In more recent terminology, such systems are called **modular**, meaning that they are decomposable into a set of independent processes, as philosopher Jerry Fodor (1983) has

Theoretical Approaches to Vision

claimed is generally true of human cognition in his **modularity hypothesis**. A **nearly decomposable system** is one in which the interactions among components are weak but not negligible, and an **undecomposable system** is one in which the interactions among components are as strong as those within components.

Some perceptual theorists—particularly within the Gestalt, ecological, and connectionist schools of thought—are considerably less optimistic than Simon (1969) and Fodor (1983) about the extent to which human cognition is even "nearly" decomposable into modules. Most Gestaltists believed that mental events should be understood in terms of complex, holistic, fieldlike interactions that take place in the brain. This conception does not fit well with the idea that cognitive processes constitute a nearly decomposable system, characterized by recursively decomposable flow diagrams. More recently, some connectionist theorists have also questioned the validity of recursive decomposition by endorsing neural-level explanations of perception and cognition. They argue that any higher-level description—such as are typically proposed in flow diagrams—is only a crude approximation of the proper description at the neural level (Smolensky, 1988). Gibson and some of his followers take the opposite stance, focusing primarily on the informational description of perception at the highest computational level without attempting to analyze it into internal processes at all.

The idea that decomposition can be applied recursively to informational descriptions raises the important question of when to stop. The obvious answer is to stop when some sort of primitive informational event is reached. But this raises the further question of how to define "primitive" events. Palmer and Kimchi (1986) distinguish two different approaches to this problem, one based on **software primitives** and the other on **hardware primitives**.

The software approach is to take as primitive some computationally plausible set of operations that is sufficient to perform the task. For example, Newell and Simon (1972) have proposed a set of primitive information processing operations for human cognition that they have proven to be equivalent in power to a universal Turing machine (or general-purpose digital computer). They are called "software" primitives because the operations they perform are inspired by the requirements of the "programs" that are written in this proposed "information processing language of the mind" rather than by the operations performed by the primitive physical components of the machine on which they run. Software primitives have proven useful in modeling a wide variety of high-level cognitive processes, such as thinking and problem solving, but have not had as much impact on perceptual models.

The hardware approach is to take as primitive those operations that are thought to be performed by the basic physical components of the system. In the case of mental events, the usual supposition is that the basic units of the brain are neurons, and so one stops decomposing when the operations are functionally equivalent to information processing that can be carried out by individual neurons. Neural modeling is a more common approach to primitives in perceptual theory, particularly in early processing, about which vision scientists now know many details of neural structure. Modeling based on neuronlike primitives is also strongly advocated by connectionist theorists.

It is important to realize that even if one decomposes to the descriptive level of hardware primitives, one never actually reaches the physical system itself. The decomposed description remains within the informational domain no matter how finely it is dissected into simpler black boxes. This is because information is a fundamentally different commodity than physical matter or energy, even though its existence requires embodiment in matter and energy. Information therefore cannot be completely reduced to its particular physical implementation.

Perhaps the clearest way to illustrate this point is to imagine that one had decomposed the stereo system of our previous example (Figure 2.3.5) all the way down to hardware primitives. Each black box would then perform a function equivalent to that of a resistor, transistor, capacitor, or whatever. Even this description, however, makes no reference to what actual physical device performs it. It would apply as well to standard electrical resistors and transistors as to some high-technology optical equivalent or any other device that implements the same input/output function. This observation is closely related to Marr's distinction between the algorithmic and implementational levels. In both cases, the physical system is seen to be a fundamentally distinct domain.

Physical Embodiment. Palmer and Kimchi (1986) specify the connection between the informational and physical levels in their third assumption of *physical embodiment*.

3. *Physical embodiment.* In the physical system whose behavior is being described as informational events, information is carried by states of the system (called *representations*), while operations that use this information are carried out by changes in state (called *processes*).

This third assumption bridges the gap between the abstract functional level of disembodied information and operations and the actual workings of a real physical system (or *implementation*, in Marr's terms). According to this view, information and operations are, technically speaking, entities in the abstract domain of information processing descriptions, whereas representations and processes are entities in the physical world when viewed as embodiments of information and operations. This is a fine distinction, however, and one that is not commonly made in the literature. Many theorists appear to use the term "representation" to refer to informational entities and "processes" to refer to changes in information content.

The three levels that we have discussed—computational, algorithmic, and implementational—will frame our discussion of visual theory throughout this book. Much of the work at a computational level is currently being done by researchers in computer vision. These theorists attempt to identify the optical information available in retinal images that allows perception of the external environment. In doing so, they are implicitly following Gibson's program of ecological optics, studying perception through careful analyses of the mathematical relations between the proximal and the distal stimulus. At the functional, algorithmic level, both computer scientists and psychologists are actively exploring how complex computational problems can be decomposed into sets of simpler components and the flow of information among them. Computer scientists are generally more interested in determining how well the algorithm works in producing useful perception; psychologists are generally more concerned with determining how well the algorithm models human performance in well-controlled experiments. At the implementational level, computer scientists sometimes embody their algorithms in actual electronic devices; physiologists and psychologists try to determine how

brains actually process visual information neurally. One of the central tenets of the present interdisciplinary point of view is that only by approaching the problem of vision at all three levels simultaneously are we likely to reach an adequate understanding.

2.3.4 Representation

We have claimed that the fundamental components of an information processing system are *representations* and *processes*. We have further defined a representation as a physical entity that carries information about something and processing as physical transformations that change one representation into the next. But what kind of information does a visual representation carry, and how does it manage to accomplish this? And what type of processes are performed by a visual information processing system? These are basic questions about the nature of information processing theories that we will now consider.

As the term will be used throughout this book, a **representation** refers to a state of the visual system that stands for an environmental property, object, or event: it is a *model* of what it represents (Palmer, 1978). In this way of thinking, a representation occurs only as part of a larger **representational system** that includes two related but distinct worlds: the **represented world** outside the information processing system (usually called the *external world* or *environment*) and the **representing world** within the information processing system (usually called *the internal representation* or simply *the representation*).

What enables an internal world to represent an external world? One possibility is that the internal representation preserves information about the structure of the external world by virtue of having a similar structure. For this to happen, the structure of the two worlds must be the same to some extent. More formally, a representational system can be analyzed as a **homomorphism**: a mapping from objects in one domain (the external world) to objects in another domain (the internal representation) such that relations among objects in the external world are mirrored by corresponding relations among corresponding objects in the representation (Tarski, 1954). This homomorphic mapping is diagrammed schematically in Figure 2.3.7. If such a mapping exists, then the internal objects can function as a representation of certain aspects of the external environment.

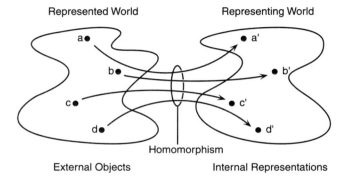

Figure 2.3.7 Representation as a homomorphic mapping. External (represented) objects are mapped to internal (representing) objects such that relations among external objects are reflected by corresponding relations among internal objects.

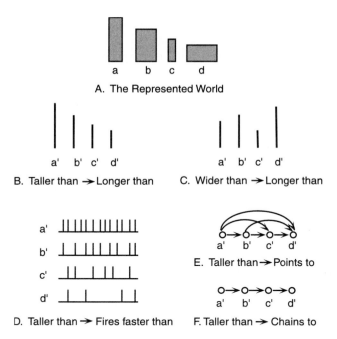

Figure 2.3.8 Examples of representational systems. Each representational system (parts B–F) represents the specified relations among properties of the rectangles in part A by different relations among the corresponding internal objects: line lengths in parts B and C, neural firing rates in part D, and network connections among nodes in parts E and F. (See text for details.)

We encountered some simple examples of representations in our discussion of thermostats. We said, for example, that temperature was represented by the height of the free end of the bimetallic strip. We can now see what this means more precisely. As the temperature in the external world increases, it causes the vertical position of the strip's end to rise correspondingly. As a result, relations between external temperatures (*colder than* and *warmer than*) are paralleled by relations between heights of the strip's end (*lower than* and *higher than*, respectively). The strip's height thus preserves information about external temperature by virtue of this causally driven homomorphism and thereby represents external temperature.

The causal factor underlying the homomorphism is important for two reasons. One is that for the representation to be current, as a perceptual representation must be, it requires constant updating. A causal chain from events in the external world to events in the internal representation is an ideal way (though not the only way) to achieve this. The other is that for the representation to be authentic, rather than accidental, there must be some linkage to the world it represents. Again, a causal connection seems to be the ideal solution.

Causally driven structural similarity between a model and its object may be a necessary condition for something to function as a representation, but it is not sufficient. A further requirement is that there be processes that use it as a representation in the sense of taking it as a surrogate of the world to which it corresponds. For

example, air temperature has many causal consequences that might be used to represent it—such as the amount of water vapor it can hold or the temperature of objects it surrounds—but unless these properties are used by a system (such as a thermostat) to influence its behavior (such as controlling a furnace), it would not be considered to be a representation.

Figure 2.3.8 shows several examples that illustrate some other aspects of this notion of representation (Palmer, 1978). No claim is made that they are realistic representations for a neural information processing system; they are intended merely to further illustrate what it means for representations to be homomorphic mappings. In all cases, the "external world" being represented is the set of four rectangles shown in Figure 2.3.8A. Despite their simplicity, these objects contain many different aspects that could be modeled or encoded in a representation, such as their height, width, and area. Figures 2.3.8B and 2.3.8C show how two different aspects of this miniature world could be represented by the same internal relation: *longer than*. In Figure 2.3.8B, the length of the lines in the representation reflect the relative height of the rectangles in the external world: that is, the fact that a' *is longer than* b' in world B reflects the fact (preserves the information) that a *is taller than* b in world A. Similar statements can be made for any pair of rectangles in A and their corresponding lines in B. Given this state of affairs, we can say that the relative length of lines in B preserves the information about the relative height of rectangles in A. Any question that could be answered about the height of rectangles in A could equally well be answered by considering the relative length of lines in B. It is in this sense that relative line length in world B *represents* relative height in world A. Line length is also used in Figure 2.3.8C to represent facts about the rectangles in A, but this time, it is the relative width of rectangles that is represented. Exactly the same analysis holds as in Figure 2.3.8B.

Figure 2.3.8D depicts a physiologically plausible representation of rectangle height in terms of the firing rate of neurons, in which each vertical line indicates a spike discharge and the horizontal line corresponds to time. These hypothetical neurons fire at a rate proportional to the height of the corresponding rectangles such that taller rectangles cause higher firing rates. Note that rectangle height could legitimately have been coded in the opposite way: Firing rate might be *inversely* related to rectangle height, in which case greater firing rates would correspond to shorter rectangles. Despite the obvious differences between the firing rate representations and the line length encodings in Figure 2.3.8B, they are **informationally equivalent** in the sense that they reflect the same facts about the external world (Palmer, 1978) and therefore carry identical information about the rectangles.

A fundamentally different way to encode *taller than* relations about the rectangles is illustrated in Figures 2.3.8E and 2.3.8F. Each rectangle corresponds to a specific node (circle) in these directed graphs (or networks), and the relative height relations are encoded by the arrows between them. In Figure 2.3.8E, the arrows are interpreted directly as *taller than* relations. Thus, the fact that a *is taller than* b in part A is reflected by the fact that a' *points directly to* b' via one of the arrows in part E. In this case, all of the required arrows are present in the

representation, so no relations need to be "inferred" by additional processing.

Figure 2.3.8F, in contrast, illustrates a more economical representation of the same information. *Taller than* relations in part A are encoded by *chains to* relations in part F, where "x *chains to* y" means that there exists a chain of arrows that starts at x and goes to y. This definition of the *chains to* relation is an economical representation in the sense that fewer arrows are required to express all the potential relations. This economy comes at a cost, however, because additional processing is required to retrieve the "indirectly" coded information, such as the fact that a' *chains to* c'. The required information can be inferred from the facts that a' *chains to* b' and that b' *chains to* c'. This is a standard tradeoff in representing information: The more information is stored directly, the less must be inferred by additional processing; the less information is stored directly, the more must be inferred by additional processing.

There are many controversies about the nature of visual representations: whether the representation of a given fact is *localized* in a particular representing element or *distributed* over many such elements, whether visual presentations are *analog* (i.e., continuous and "picture-like") or *propositional* (i.e., discrete and "languagelike"), whether a certain fact is represented *explicitly* or *implicitly*, whether all visual representations can be reduced to a *finite set of primitive atoms* or constitute an *open-ended system*. These and other issues will arise at various points in the chapters to come as we consider the wide range of representations that theorists have suggested to underlie various visual abilities.

Before we leave the topic of representation, it is worth mentioning that although we have generally spoken of the represented and representing entities as being objects, both are more correctly considered as *events*. Internal representations in the brain constitute temporally extended neural activity of some kind, which is surely an event rather than an object. And the environmental entities that they represent are more appropriately considered temporally extended events than timeless objects. Even an unmoving object can (and should) be viewed as an event, albeit an unchanging one. We have avoided the temporal structure of events because it complicates the situation considerably and because the underlying issues are mainly the same, whether time is included or not.

Theoretical Approaches to Vision

2.3.5 Processes

We have said that representations are the physical entities in an information processing system and that they carry information. But where do these representations come from? And how is one representation derived from another? To answer such questions, we must examine the other half of information processing systems: namely, *processes*.

Processes are the active components in an information processing system that transform or operate on information by changing one representation into the next. In other words, processes are the dynamic aspect of the information processing system that actually cause informational transformations to occur. It should now be easy to see why both representations and processes are needed. Without representations, processes would have nothing to work on; without processes, no work would get done. In the present section, we will consider what processes do and how they do it.

Implicit versus Explicit Information. One of the most important aspects of what processes do is to make information that was *implicit* in the input representation *explicit* in the output (and vice versa). Processes cannot create information about the environment out of thin air; they can merely transform it by moving it around, in effect, and changing its form. All the information must be available either in the optical structure that is projected from the environment onto the retina or from internal sources within the observer. Processes collect and combine information in appropriate ways to construct new representations in which the next process will have easy access to the information it requires.

The initially explicit information for vision is the light intensity that is registered by each photoreceptor in the two-dimensional retinal mosaic. Unfortunately, this information is nearly useless to an organism in this form because very little of what it needs to know about its environment is explicitly represented. What *are* important are much more complex facts such as where the boundaries lie between retinal regions projected from different surfaces, where in three-dimensional space those surfaces are located, how surfaces are configured to form meaningful objects, and to what use those objects might be put. None of this information is explicitly represented in the retina's response to optical images. Still,

there is a sense in which all of it must be implicitly present in the retinal image plus whatever additional internal knowledge the perceiver brings to bear in processing the image. The job of visual perception is to combine external and internal information to make meaningful facts about the environment available to the organism. The complex processes that are responsible for doing so are the primary focus of this book.

Processing as Inference. According to the information processing view as considered thus far, implicit information can be made explicit by mapping one representation into another. Processes that accomplish such transformations can be understood as **inferences**, as Helmholtz suggested, albeit unconscious ones. To illustrate the nature of inference, consider a classic logical syllogism. The initially explicit information is given in the form of the **premises** (e.g., "All people are mortal," and "John is a person"), and logic provides the rules by which information that is only implicit in the premises can be made explicit in the **conclusion** ("Therefore, John is mortal"). There is a sense in which the premises contain the conclusion from the start, but only implicitly. It is the application of logical operations that makes the conclusion explicit.

Extending this inferential view of information processing metaphorically to vision, we might take the "premises" to consist of the retinal image plus whatever stored knowledge or prior assumptions the perceiver brings to bear in the course of perceptual processing. For example, given a retinal image in which a set of lines converge toward a vanishing point (see Figure 2.3.9), plus the convergence assumption of linear perspective (that lines converging to a point on the horizon in a projected image are actually parallel and receding in depth in the external world), the visual system concludes that the converging lines in the image are, in fact, parallel lines receding into the distance in the three-dimensional environment. This is a simple example in which we might conceive of perceptual processing as some form of inference, as Helmholtz (1867/1925) proposed and as Gregory (1970) and Rock (1983) have elaborated.

Despite the formal similarity between logical inferences and visual processing, there are several differences. The "real" logical inferences that people make in solving syllogisms are usually quite deliberate, slow, verbal, and conscious, whereas visual inferences are

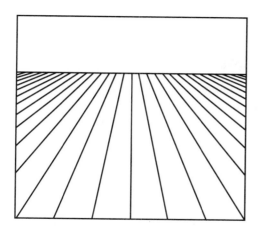

Figure 2.3.9 An example of convergence of parallel lines. Parallel lines on a slanted depth plane in the environment converge toward a vanishing point in its image as defined by perspective projection.

generally effortless, rapid, nonverbal, and unconscious. Indeed, few people are aware that parallel lines in the world project converging lines onto their retinas, and even the few who are, such as artists and photographers, do not consciously consider such facts when they perceive the world. In what sense, then, can visual processes be considered mechanisms of inference? To find out, let us consider more carefully what perceptual inference is about and how it might occur within an information processing system.

There are two general types of inference: **deductive inference** and **inductive inference**. Both are ways of combining information to reach conclusions, but they differ in important ways. We have already considered a classic example of deductive inference in the "John is mortal" syllogism. Other forms of symbolic logic also fall into the class of deductive inference, and so do standard mathematical operations. If you have two apples and you are given two more, deduction supports the conclusion that you now have a total of four apples. One of the key features of deductive inference is that its conclusions are *certain* as long as its premises are true. If the premises are false, any deductive inferences that are based on them cannot be trusted. If all people are not mortal, then John might not be mortal (although he certainly might be), and if you had three apples initially, you might not have four apples (although you still might, if the second batch of apples contained only one).

In contrast, inductive inferences are inherently *uncertain* and *probabilistic* even if the statements on which they are based are true. A classic example of inductive inference is the conclusion that all people are mortal. You probably did not think of this statement as a conclusion because we used it as a premise in the syllogism, but what is the basis for believing it? It cannot be deduced from the set of facts from which it was presumably derived about people having died (e.g., that person A died, that person B died, that person C died, and so forth) because there may be some person now living or as yet unborn who will, in fact, never die. Therefore, all past experience with people dying does not ensure the truth of the generalization that all people are mortal. Inductive inferences have this uncertain character because they are based on incomplete or probabilistic evidence.

Most inferences in visual processing are inductive in the sense that they are not guaranteed to be true, largely because of the underconstrained and probabilistic nature of the inverse problem that they attempt to solve. For example, the convergence assumption that we used to deduce the parallelism of converging lines in Figure 2.3.9 is not universally true, but only probabilistically so. Many converging lines are indeed projections of parallel lines receding in depth, but the nonparallel sides of a trapezoid and other polygons also converge in their projected images, even when they are not parallel in the environment. The perceiver therefore cannot be certain that the converging lines in Figure 2.3.9 are images of parallel lines receding into the distance; they may actually be converging lines in the frontal plane, as indeed they are in Figure 2.3.9 itself.

Hidden Assumptions. The foregoing discussion suggests a general strategy for visual inference. Although many key processes in vision are effectively inductive rather than deductive inferences, they can be treated as deductive inferences by making **hidden assumptions** (Cutting, 1991). This is actually what we did in the example of converging/parallel lines. The explicitly given premise of converging lines in the image does not, by itself, allow the inference of parallelism except in the probabilistic sense of induction (i.e., in previous experience, lines that converged toward a vanishing point have usually turned out to be parallel in the world). However, by assuming the truth of the additional premise of the convergence assumption, the conclusion of parallel lines

Theoretical Approaches to Vision

Figure 2.3.10 The Ponzo illusion as unconscious inference. If the converging lines are (unconsciously) interpreted as parallel lines in depth, the upper (farther) horizontal line would actually be longer than the lower (closer) one, even though they are actually the same in length on the page.

can be drawn deductively from the image plus the hidden convergence assumption of linear perspective.

If the additional assumptions turn out to be untrue of the current situation, the conclusion will not necessarily be valid. In fact, this is the case in the example of Figure 2.3.9, because the lines actually *do* converge in the picture plane rather than being parallel in depth. This is how inferential theories of vision account for the existence and nature of many illusions, as we will discuss in detail in Chapter 7. For example, many theorists believe the Ponzo illusion shown in Figure 2.3.10 to be due to the unconscious misapplication of the convergence assumption of linear perspective that we have just discussed (e.g., Gregory, 1970; Rock, 1975, 1983). If the converging lines are actually parallel in a receding depth plane and the horizontal lines lie on this plane, then the upper horizontal line would indeed be longer than the lower one. Because all lines actually lie in the picture plane, however, the difference in length is illusory.

By framing the problem of visual processing in terms of deductive versus inductive inferences, Cutting (1991) has reformulated the debate between direct (Gibsonian) and indirect (Helmholtzian) theories of perception. He identifies Gibson's position that perception is direct with the claim that perception is deductively based on information that is present in the image alone and therefore certain. He identifies Helmholtz's position of unconscious inference with the claim that perception is inductively based on the image and can be accomplished only with the addition of further assumptions, some of which will be violated in unusual situations and there-

fore produce illusions. According to "indirect" theorists such as Rock (1983, 1997) and Gregory (1970), an important function of perceptual learning is to incorporate the most appropriate hidden assumptions so that veridical perception will be achieved as often as possible.

Many information processing theorists view some of the processes that change one representation into another as involving inductive inference in the sense that something akin to hidden assumptions must be used. This does not necessarily mean that languagelike logical rules are involved, however, since many visual processes seem to operate on continuous rather than discrete representations, and the processes through which inference takes place often seem more like numerical calculation than application of symbolic logic. Still, there is no reason to restrict the processes that operate on representations to those of symbolic logic, since mathematical operations are also examples of deductive inference. In fact, quantitative processes that transform analog representations are extremely common in modern computational theories of vision, as we will see in later chapters.

Many different hidden assumptions are usually involved in perceiving the same visual scene. This is fine as long as they all point to the same conclusion, as they often do. But what if they do not? In the case of Figure 2.3.9, for example, the visual system might invoke the "equidistance assumption" that, all else being equal, objects are perceived to lie at the same distance from the observer (Gogel, 1965, 1978). If this were true of Figure 2.3.9, it would support the conclusion that the converging lines are not parallel in depth, but converging in the picture plane (as they actually are). How can the visual system determine which inference is correct in the face of conflicting assumptions?

This difficulty points out a problem with taking standard logical inference as the process by which vision arrives at conclusions about the environment. If different assumptions lead to different conclusions, one cannot conclude anything using both assumptions. Rather, one assumption (or a set of consistent assumptions) must be selected to the exclusion of the other assumptions. This is a possible solution, but not a particularly satisfying one because then rules must be proposed to determine which assumption will dominate. However, there are alternative frameworks that seem more compatible with the probabilistic nature of visual inference.

One possibility is to model hidden assumptions as **soft constraints**: informational restrictions that should be taken into account but may be overridden by other considerations. Soft constraints can vary from weak to strong, and many potentially conflicting ones can be integrated in arriving at a visual inference. The perspective convergence assumption, for example, appears to be stronger than the equidistance assumption because it overcomes the equidistance tendency in perceiving the lines in Figure 2.3.9 as parallel in depth. Certain kinds of connectionist models (see Appendix B) can be viewed as mechanisms that maximize the satisfaction of many conflicting soft constraints. Another alternative is to use **fuzzy logic** rather than standard logic to model visual inferences. Fuzzy logic allows statements to have different degrees of truth instead of the standard two values of true and false. Such a logic has been formulated by computer scientist Lotfi Zadeh (1965) and employed in a number of interesting visual processing models (e.g., Kay & McDaniel, 1978; Massaro, 1987). Yet another approach is to cast the problem in terms of **probabilistic inference** using Bayes' theorem (e.g., Geman & Geman, 1984; Yuille & Bülthoff, 1995). The advantages of working within this framework are that it is inherently probabilistic and that many different pieces of evidence can be integrated within a single mathematical framework. Certain formulations of fuzzy logical models have been shown to be mathematically equivalent to Bayesian decision rules (Massaro & Friedman, 1990), so these alternatives are not mutually exclusive.

Heuristic Processes. Regardless of exactly how one models inferential processes in vision, procedures that solve a given problem by making use of uncertain, probabilistic information are called **heuristic processes**. As we mentioned before, heuristics are procedures that usually, but not always, provide the correct solution.

To understand the heuristic nature of visual processes, consider again the converging/parallel lines example in Figure 2.3.9. The initial problem was to interpret the three-dimensional environmental orientation of a set of lines that converge in the image. Because of the information that is lost in projecting the three spatial dimensions of the environment to the two spatial dimensions of the image, this problem cannot be uniquely solved without further constraints. The assumption of converging lines being parallel in linear perspective was thus invoked as a heuristic assumption that is usually, but not always, true. An inference process of some sort was then hypothesized that would combine this assumption with information from the retinal image and yield the conclusion (or "interpretation") that the converging lines are actually parallel on a receding depth plane.

Bringing further constraints to bear appears to be the only way in which visual perception can be accomplished—Gibson's claims of direct perception notwithstanding. The additional information does not need to be stated explicitly as logical rules in propositional format, as in a syllogism, however. It could be embedded in the pattern of interconnections within a complex neural network, for example. Using the term "inference" to describe such a process may seem to be somewhat metaphorical and thus to undercut the force of the claim that perception works by unconscious inference. But, as we said at the outset, unconscious inference must be at least somewhat metaphorical, since normal inference is quite clearly slow, laborious, and conscious, whereas perception is fast, easy, and unconscious. The important point for present purposes is that perception relies on processes that can be usefully viewed as inferences that require heuristic assumptions. We will take the broadest possible interpretation of what biological processes might implement those inferencelike processes.

Hidden Assumptions versus Ecological Validity. As we mentioned in Section 2.1.3, Gibson vehemently opposed the idea that perception involves inference or anything like it, championing instead the idea that perception is direct. It is therefore worthwhile to consider how a brilliant theorist like Gibson responded to claims by other theorists that certain perceptual phenomena involve inference based on heuristic assumptions (e.g., Gregory, 1966, 1970). As we have indicated, much of the evidence for heuristic inference comes from illusions in which the hidden assumptions are wrong, as in the case of the converging lines of the Ponzo illusion being taken as parallel lines receding in depth.

Gibson's general tactic in answering such arguments was to rule out the evidence by invoking boundary conditions on direct perception. He claimed that such illusions occur only under conditions that are **ecologically**

Theoretical Approaches to Vision

invalid, that is, conditions that are seldom or never present in normal everyday living conditions.[6] He maintained that his theory of direct perception was correct but that it held only for unrestrained observers who were able to actively explore a natural environment. He argued, quite persuasively, that when psychologists require subjects to view a scene from a single static viewpoint, force them to wear unusual glasses to view strange computer-generated displays, or show them two-dimensional pictures that simulate the optical structure of a three-dimensional scene, they violate the conditions under which humankind evolved the ability to perceive in the first place. Perception under such artificial conditions, he therefore claimed, could not be used as evidence against his theory, which was a theory of *ecological* perception.

Taken on its own terms, Gibson's defense of his position is both reasonable and persuasive. The conditions under which vision scientists often study perception are undeniably odd and unnatural in many ways. Yet the phenomena *do* occur and seem to require an explanation of some sort. What is most interesting about Gibson's defense for the present discussion, however, is the close relation that exists between the boundary conditions for ecological perception and the heuristic assumptions of computational theories.

Generally speaking, what Gibson calls ecological conditions are those in which the heuristic assumptions of inference-based theories are true: for example, that observers are not looking from some special vantage point, that both eyes are looking at the same environmental scene, that the environment is a three-dimensional world populated with objects rather than a two-dimensional projection composed of light and dark regions, and so forth. Notice that if the boundary conditions of ecological perception are exactly the situations in which the heuristic assumptions of inference theories are true, ecological perception *will* always be veridical. Thus,

Gibson was able to defend his theory of direct perception against evidence of nonveridicality by claiming that such situations were not ecological. This is why Gibson was so effective at deflecting criticisms based on the existence of illusions; he did not deny that illusions existed, but only that they occurred under natural ecological conditions.[7]

The view that will be taken in this book is that perceptual theory must account for *all* phenomena of visual perception, whether ecologically valid or not. From this perspective, an approach based on heuristic computational inference is preferable to one based on direct perception because it can potentially give an explanation for both ecological and nonecological phenomena. We will therefore adopt the stance that perception involves some form of inductive inference and that it is carried out by performing computations in neural networks of some sort. In the course of our explorations of visual perception, we will attempt to identify the heuristic assumptions that underlie it, the processes that carry it out, and the neural mechanisms through which it occurs.

Top-Down versus Bottom-Up Processes. Another important distinction in the processing of perceptual information is its metaphorical "direction": whether it is **bottom-up** or **top-down**. The spatial metaphor underlying the naming of this distinction can be understood in terms of a flowchart of visual processing in which the retinal image is depicted at the bottom and temporally subsequent interpretations farther along the visual pathway are located at higher and higher levels (see Figure 2.3.11). "Bottom-up" processing—more descriptively called **data-driven processing**—refers to processes that take a "lower-level" representation as input and create or modify a "higher-level" representation as output. Top-down processing—also called **hypothesis-driven** or **expectation-driven processing**—refers to processes that operate in the

---

[6] Arguments about ecological validity were previously employed by Egon Brunswik (1956) to undermine the importance of results based on improbable stimulus situations. Gibson and his followers broadened the meaning of this concept in important ways, however, using it to rule out certain "everyday conditions" in which the stimulus is artificial, such as 2-D photographs and movies that portray 3-D scenes and events. Even though we may encounter such conditions frequently in our modern high-technology society, they do not correspond to the conditions under which human vision evolved.

[7] Many simple geometric illusions are present even under natural, unrestricted viewing conditions, however. DeLucia and Hochberg (1991) report that the Muller-Lyer illusion (see Figure 1.1.4A) persists under "gallery" conditions when observers can walk around models of the inward and outward arrows and view it from any angle.

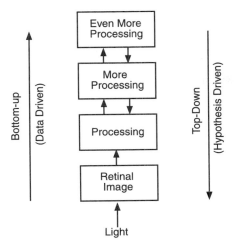

Figure 2.3.11 Bottom-up versus top-down processing. The two directions of processing are referred to as *bottom-up* (or *data driven*) from lower to higher levels of processing and *top-down* (or *hypothesis driven*) from higher to lower levels of processing.

opposite direction, taking a "higher-level" representation as input and producing or modifying a "lower-level" representation as output.

Many people's naive intuition is that vision is essentially a bottom-up process. It begins with the sensory information in the retinal images and goes "upward" to perceptual and then conceptual interpretations. Most theorists concur that the early stages of visual processing are indeed strictly bottom-up. But there are good reasons to think that this cannot be true for the entire process of visual perception. I argued in Section 1.1, for example, that perception of the present state of affairs produces expectations about the future. These expectations imply a top-down component to visual processing, because they suggest that prior higher-level interpretations influence current processing at lower levels. For example, it turns out that how people identify letters depends strongly on whether those letters are part of known words or meaningless letter strings. For this to occur, there must be top-down feedback from some higher-level representation of known words to the lower-level representation of letters. When we examine theories of perceptual categorization in Chapter 9, we will encounter further examples of the idea that top-down processing is involved in fitting stored models of familiar objects and scenes to incoming sensory data. The point at which top-down processes begin to aug-

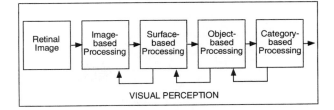

Figure 2.4.1 Four stages of visual processing. Visual processing can be divided into four main stages beyond the retinal image itself: image-based, surface-based, object-based, and category-based processing. (See text for details.)

ment bottom-up processes is currently a controversial issue, however. Some theorists believe that it happens early in visual processing; others believe that it happens late.

2.4 Four Stages of Visual Perception

With this general background in the information processing approach, we will now apply some of these concepts to vision. We will begin by decomposing visual perception at the algorithmic level into four major stages beyond the retinal image itself, as illustrated in Figure 2.4.1. Because we will be using this theoretical framework throughout the rest of the book, it will be useful to consider it at the outset.

Each stage is defined by a different kind of output representation and the processes that are required to compute it from the input representation. Although different theorists refer to these stages by different names, we will use a generic labeling scheme in which each stage is named for the kind of information it represents explicitly: the *image-based*, *surface-based*, *object-based*, and *category-based* stages of perception. Much of the rationale for this theoretical framework came from the influential writings of David Marr (1982) and his colleagues at M.I.T. Other schemes have been and continue to be considered, but these four stages provide a fairly general and robust framework for understanding vision as a computational process.

2.4.1 The Retinal Image

The proximal stimulus for vision is the pair of 2-D images projected from the environment to the viewpoint of the observer's eyes. Figure 2.4.2 shows one such image

       Theoretical Approaches to Vision

Figure 2.4.2 An image of a simple scene. People effortlessly perceive a ceramic cup resting on a table top, but all that is present to the visual system is an array of light whose intensity varies continuously over space.

of an extremely simple scene consisting of a ceramic cup resting on a flat, white surface in front of a dark wall. The optical image that strikes the retina is completely continuous, but its registration by the mosaic of retinal receptors is discrete. The complete set of firing rates in all receptors of both eyes therefore constitutes the first representation of optical information within the visual system. This retinal representation is complicated by the distribution of receptors. Receptors are more densely packed in the fovea than in the periphery (see Figure 1.3.9), and the four different kinds of receptors (the three cone types plus the rods) have different spatial distributions over the retina (see Section 1.3).

In formal and computational theories of vision, the retinal representation is almost always simplified and regularized by approximating it as a homogeneous, two-dimensional array of receptors. The spatial locations of these idealized receptors can be identified uniquely by their coordinates, denoted (x, y), in an integer plane whose center is in the middle of the fovea and whose x and y axes are aligned with retinally defined horizontal and vertical, respectively.[8] These square image elements—called **pixels**, a shortened form of "picture elements"—are taken as the primitive, indivisible, explicitly represented visual unit of information in the input image. The value of a given pixel in a gray-scale image is usually denoted $I(x, y)$ for the image "intensity" (or luminance) at the given location. These aspects of the image representation are illustrated in Figure 2.4.3 for a small portion of the scene in Figure 2.4.2. Figure 2.4.3A displays an enlargement of the small region inside the white box in Figure 2.4.2 to show the gray-scale levels of individual pixels. Figure 2.4.3B displays the numerical intensity values (from a potential range of 0 to 25) of the individual pixels shown in Figure 2.4.3A.

Regardless of whether such simplifying assumptions are made, the coordinate system of the retinal image is presumed to be explicitly tied to the intrinsic structure of the retina. The center of the retinal coordinate system is identified with the center of the fovea, and its axes are identified with retinally defined horizontal and vertical. Receptor positions are specified relative to this retinal frame of reference.

To appreciate just how difficult the problem of interpreting the raw output of such an array of sensors or receptors is, consider again the display in Figure 2.4.3B. It indicates the light intensity falling on each receptor as a two-digit number. All of the spatial information of the gray-scale image in Figure 2.4.3A is present but in a numerical form that your visual system cannot interpret in terms of edges, regions, surfaces, objects, and so forth. It appears completely meaningless and uninterpretable. This is not so when you look at Figure 2.4.2, however, which shows the whole image in gray-scale shadings from which these numbers were derived. Immediately, you perceive edges, regions, surfaces, and objects, the important aspects of the visual scene that were missing when you examined the numerical array.

The reason the numerical version is so difficult to comprehend is that your visual system is finely tuned to pro-

---

[8] In older theories of vision, the information that specified the location of a receptor was called its *local sign*.

04	04	04	04	04	04	04	04	04	04	04	04	04	04	04	04	04
04	04	04	04	04	04	04	04	04	04	04	04	04	04	04	04	04
04	04	04	04	04	04	04	04	04	04	04	04	04	04	04	04	04
04	04	04	04	04	04	04	04	04	04	04	04	04	04	04	04	04
04	04	04	04	04	04	04	04	04	04	04	04	04	04	04	04	04
04	04	04	04	04	04	04	04	04	04	04	04	04	04	04	04	04
04	04	04	04	04	04	04	04	04	04	04	04	04	04	04	04	04
04	04	04	04	04	04	04	04	04	04	04	04	04	04	04	04	04
04	04	04	04	04	04	04	04	04	04	04	04	04	04	04	04	04
04	04	04	04	04	04	04	04	04	04	04	05	08	09	11	13	15
04	04	05	09	12	15	16	17	18	17	17	17	17	16	16	17	16
18	17	16	15	15	14	12	14	13	13	13	13	13	14	14	14	14
09	07	07	07	07	07	07	07	09	09	10	10	11	13	13	13	13
04	04	04	04	04	05	05	05	08	08	09	09	10	12	13	13	13
04	04	04	04	04	04	05	07	08	08	10	11	11	13	13	13	13
04	04	04	04	04	05	06	07	08	09	10	11	11	12	13	13	13
04	04	04	04	04	05	06	07	08	08	10	11	11	12	12	13	13
04	04	04	04	04	05	05	05	08	08	09	10	11	12	12	13	13
04	04	04	04	04	04	04	05	06	08	08	10	11	12	12	13	13
04	10	04	04	04	04	05	07	08	08	09	10	11	12	12	13	13
04	04	04	04	04	04	05	07	08	08	10	10	11	11	13	13	13
04	04	04	04	04	04	04	05	07	08	08	10	11	11	12	13	13
04	04	04	04	04	04	04	05	07	07	08	09	11	11	12	13	13
04	04	04	04	04	04	04	04	06	07	08	09	10	11	12	12	13

A

B

Figure 2.4.3 A portion of the cup scene and its corresponding numerical intensity array. (A) The enlargement of the boxed portion of Figure 2.4.2 shows the individual pixels that correspond to the output of light sensors in a video camera around the edge of the cup. (B) The numerical array shows the intensity of the light falling on each square pixel element in the video image shown in part A.

cess information contained in intensity images and not at all well equipped to process numerical ones. Therefore, all of your edge detection, region-finding, surface location, and object interpretation processes were useless—except in reading the numbers themselves—and you were forced to search laboriously for every scrap of information you could find to get some notion of what might be depicted. When you consider the problem of trying to specify what information processes might be required for visual perception to occur, you should remember how difficult it was to interpret this numerical image, for this is the challenge that all perceptual theories ultimately face: perceiving objects arrayed in the three-dimensional environment just on the basis of a two-dimensional array of numbers. It is a daunting task indeed.

2.4.2 The Image-Based Stage

Most theorists currently agree that the initial registration of images in the two eyes is not the only representation based on a two-dimensional retinal organization. We call these additional representations and processes the **image-based stage**. It includes image-processing operations such as detecting local edges and lines, linking local edges and lines together more globally, matching up corresponding images in the left and right eyes, defining two-dimensional regions in the image, and detecting other image-based features, such as line terminations and "blobs." These two-dimensional features of images characterize their structure and organization before being interpreted as properties of three-dimensional scenes. For example, Figure 2.4.4A

Theoretical Approaches to Vision

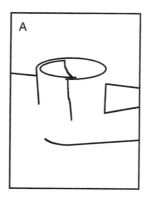 

Figure 2.4.4 Edges in the cup image. Local intensity edges can be detected using computerized edge-finding algorithms, as illustrated in part A. The set of edges thus identified are not the same as those in a clean line drawing of the image (part B), however.

indicates the locations of local edges that would constitute part of the image-based representation for the cup image shown in Figure 2.4.2.

Notice that the luminance edges that have been detected in Figure 2.4.4A are not exactly the same as the edges most people readily identify in the same image, as shown in Figure 2.4.4B. Many of the edges represented in part A are ones that people typically do not notice, either because they are faint or because they are due to differences in illumination (shadows and shading) rather than surface edges. Equally interesting is the fact that some of the most obvious edges that everyone perceives in the image are actually missing in the edge map of Figure 2.4.4A. The light side of the cup shades smoothly into the light table top on the left, and its dark side shades into the dark background and shadow on the right, with no discernible edge in the image to indicate their presence. Pieces of the top edges of the cup are similarly missing in the luminance edges. These simple demonstrations are dramatic proof that the set of luminance edges detected in an image (Figure 2.4.4A) are not the same as a clean line drawing of the objects people typically perceive (Figure 2.4.4B). Would that it were so simple!

Marr (1982) called the representations that resulted from such image-based processes **primal sketches** and suggested that there are two of them. The first he called the **raw primal sketch**, which includes just the results of elementary detection processes that locate edges, bars, blobs, and line terminations. The second he termed the **full primal sketch**, which also includes global grouping and organization among the local image features present in the raw primal sketch.

Marr's particular proposals about image-based processing may be incorrect—indeed, we will suggest a rather different conception at the end of Chapter 4—but the general idea of constructing an image-based representation of some sort is a useful one. Whatever it might be in detail, the common underlying structure of such an image-based representation is defined by the following properties:

1. *Image-based primitives.* The primitive elements represent information about the 2-D structure of the luminance image (such as edges and lines defined by differences in light intensity) rather than information about the physical objects in the external world that produced the image (such as surface edges or shadow edges). The two kinds of information are correlated, of course, but this correlation can only be used after the image features have been made explicit in the image-based representation.

2. *Two-dimensional geometry.* The geometry of spatial information in image-based representations is inherently two-dimensional and can be represented in the analog format of two-dimensional arrays.

3. *Retinal reference frame.* The coordinate system within which the 2-D features are located is specified relative to the retina in the sense that the principle axes are aligned with the eye (rather than the body, gravity, or the environment).

We will have a great deal more to say about how such image-based representations might be constructed in Chapter 4 when we discuss this topic in detail.

2.4.3 The Surface-Based Stage

The second stage of visual processing, which we will call the **surface-based stage**, is concerned with recovering the intrinsic properties of visible surfaces in the external world that might have produced the features that were discovered in the image-based stage. The fundamental difference is that the surface-based stage represents information about the external world in terms of the spatial layout of visible surfaces in three dimensions, whereas the image-based stage refers to image features in the two-dimensional pattern of light falling on the retina.

The notion that the visual system is fundamentally concerned with perceiving the **surface layout**—the spatial distribution of visible surfaces within the three-dimensional environment—was first proposed and strongly advocated by Gibson (1950). While almost every other theorist was talking about perceiving 3-D objects, Gibson realized that perceiving visible surfaces was a more basic task. His idea did not gain wide acceptance, however, until computer vision theorists began to advocate it fairly recently (e.g., Marr, 1978; Marr & Nishihara, 1978). Part of the difficulty was that Gibson never suggested a specific representation for this surface layout or a set of processes that could construct it from retinal images. This is not terribly surprising because he was not an information processing theorist and therefore did not believe in either representations or processing. Still, he recognized more clearly than anyone else that surface perception was basic and crucial.

The concept of an explicit surface-based representation as an intermediate stage in vision became popular when it was formulated quantitatively by computer vision theorists and implemented in working computer simulations. Marr (1978) and Barrow and Tennenbaum (1978) proposed surface-based representations at about the same time and sketched algorithms that might be able to construct them from actual gray-scale images. Marr (1978) named his surface-based representation the **2.5-D sketch** to emphasize the fact that it lies somewhere between the true 2-D structure of image-based representations and the true 3-D structure of object-based representations (see below). Barrow and Tennenbaum (1978) called their surface-based representations **intrinsic images** to emphasize the fact that they represent intrinsic properties of surfaces in the external world rather than properties of the input image.

Constructing a surface-based representation is the first step in recovering the third spatial dimension from two-dimensional images. It does not contain information about *all* the surfaces that are present in the environment, only about those that are visible from the current viewpoint. As we will see in Chapter 5, visible surfaces provide a great deal of sensory information about their distance from the viewer and their slant. They cannot be computed from the retinal images without additional assumptions because doing so is an underconstrained inverse problem. But the additional assumptions that are required to infer the properties of visible surfaces are relatively few and almost always true, especially compared with those needed to infer the same properties of surfaces that are hidden from view.

Because the surface-based representation includes only the visible portions of surfaces, it can be conceived as a single, extremely flexible rubber sheet that has been "shrink wrapped" to just those surfaces in the environment that reflect light into the perceiver's eyes. Most current visual theories treat surfaces in this representation as being composed of many small, locally flat pieces. This is possible because even a strongly curved surface is nearly flat over a sufficiently small region, just as the spherical earth seems flat on the scale at which people experience it. This simplification allows the surface-based representation to be specified completely by just information about the color, slant, and distance from the viewer of each locally flat patch of surface in each direction radially outward from the viewer's position. Figure 2.4.5 illustrates what such a surface-based representation would look like for the ceramic cup in Figure 2.4.2 by showing circles lying on the local surface patches and vectors sticking perpendicularly out of them at a sampling of locations, as though needles were sticking perpendicularly out of the small patches of surface.

Again, Marr's particular conception of the 2.5-D sketch may be flawed, but some kind of surface-based representation seems necessary. Among the crucial properties of such a representation are the following:

1. *Surface primitives.* The primitive elements of the surface-based representation are local patches of 2-D surface at some particular slant located at some distance from the viewer within 3-D space. Each such patch of surface can be further specified by its color and texture.

2. *Three-dimensional geometry.* Although the surfaces themselves are locally only 2-D, their spatial distribution is represented within a 3-D space.

3. **Viewer-centered reference frame**. The coordinate system within which the 3-D layout of surfaces is represented is specified in terms of the direction and distance from the observer's stationpoint to the surface rather than in terms of the retina.

The flow diagram in Figure 2.4.6 indicates that the representation of surfaces is constructed from several

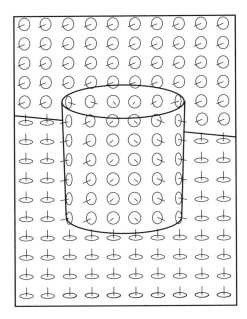

Figure 2.4.5 A surface-based representation of the cup scene. The surfaces visible in Figure 2.4.2 are represented as a set of local estimates of surface orientation (slant and tilt) and depth with respect to the viewer. Surface orientation is depicted by a set of imaginary circles on the surface and "needles" pointing perpendicularly out of them at a sampling of image locations.

different sources: stereopsis (the small difference between the lateral position of objects in the images of the left and right eyes), motion parallax (differences in velocity of points at various distances due to motion of the observer or object), shading and shadows, and various other pictorial properties such as texture, size, shape, and occlusion. We will have a great deal more to say about these factors in Chapter 5, which is concerned primarily with how the surface-based representation might be constructed.

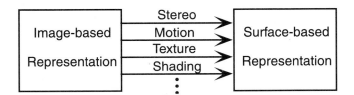

Figure 2.4.6 A flowchart showing how the surface-based representation might be derived from the image-based representation. These sources of information about depth and surface orientation are discussed in detail in Chapter 5.

Figure 2.4.7 An example of an object-based representation. The cup of Figure 2.4.2 is shown with its occluded edges represented by dashed lines, indicating how people typically perceive this scene as being composed of 3-D volumes.

2.4.4 The Object-Based Stage

Visual perception clearly does not end with a representation of just the surfaces that are visible. If it did, we should not be surprised were a change in viewpoint to reveal that the lower back side of the cup in Figure 2.4.2 simply did not exist or that it had some quite different shape from the smooth cylindrical one everyone perceives so effortlessly. But, as I argued in Chapter 1, either of these revelations would surprise us greatly. The fact that we have such expectations about partly and completely hidden surfaces suggests that there is some form of true three-dimensional representation that includes at least some occluded surfaces in the visual world. It is in this **object-based stage** that the visual representation includes truly three-dimensional information. For the visual system to manage this, further hidden assumptions about the nature of the visual world are required, because now the inferences include information about unseen surfaces or parts of surfaces. We call this stage of processing *object-based* because the inclusion of these unseen surfaces implies that they involve explicit representations of whole objects in the environment. Figure 2.4.7 shows as dashed lines the hidden edges that everyone perceives in Figure 2.4.2. The table edge is occluded by the cup, and the back, inner sides, and bottom of the cup are occluded by the parts of the cup that we can actually see. Recovering the 3-D structure of these environmental objects is the goal of object-based processing.

There are at least two ways in which such an object-based representation might be constructed. One is simply to extend the surface-based representation to include unseen surfaces within a fully three-dimensional space. This might be called a boundary approach to object-based representation. The other is to conceive of objects as intrinsically three-dimensional entities, represented as arrangements of some set of primitive 3-D shapes. This might be called the volumetric approach, since it represents objects explicitly as volumes of a particular shape in three-dimensional space.

Figure 2.4.8 illustrates how a human body might be approximated by a hierarchy of parts, each of which is represented in terms of shape primitives based on cylindrical volumes. Influential work on 3-D shape primitives in computer vision by Agin and Binford (1976) and Marr and Nishihara (1978) caused the volumetric approach to dominate theories of object-based processing for many years. It is possible, of course, that some filling-in of occluded surfaces can take place in an intermediate stage before construction of a full volumetric representation. We will discuss in Chapters 6, 7, and 8 how object-based representations might be derived.

Once again, it is important to separate the details of Marr's particular version of an object-based representation in terms of generalized cylinders from the more abstract theoretical concept of a volumetric description. In this case, however, even the general nature of the representation is far from clear. In addition to the issue of whether the primitive elements are surfaces or volumes, there is much debate over the precise nature of the relevant reference frame and geometry. The current best guess is as follows:

1. **Volumetric primitives**. The primitive elements of the object-based representation may be descriptions of truly three-dimensional volumes, thereby including information about unseen surfaces of the object.

2. *Three-dimensional geometry*. The space within which the volumetric primitives are located is also fully three-dimensional.

3. *Object-based reference frames*. The coordinate system within which the spatial relations among the volumetric primitives are represented may be defined in terms of the intrinsic structure of the volumes themselves. (The concept of intrinsic, object-based reference frames is complex and will be discussed in detail in Chapter 8.)

2.4.5 The Category-Based Stage

I argued in Chapter 1 that the ultimate goal of perception is to provide the perceiving organism with accurate information about the environment to aid in its survival and reproduction. This strongly implies that the final stage of perception must be concerned with recovering the functional properties of objects: what they afford the organism, given its current beliefs, desires, goals, and motives. We call this processing the **category-based stage** because it is widely believed that functional properties are accessed through a process of categorization. The perception of Figure 2.4.2 as showing a cup is thus the result of category-based processing of some type. But what type?

The categorization (or pattern recognition) approach to perceiving evolutionarily relevant function proposes that two operations are involved. First, the visual system classifies an object as being a member of one of a large number of known categories according to its visible properties, such as its shape, size, color, and location. Second, this identification allows access to a large body of stored information about this type of object, including its function and various forms of expectations about its future behavior. The object in Figure 2.4.2 is then known to be useful for containing liquids and for drinking out of them. This two-step scheme has the advantage that any functional property can be associated with any object, because the relation between the form of an object and the information stored about its function, history, and use can be purely arbitrary, owing to its mediation by the process of categorization.

There is also a very different way in which the visual system might be able to perceive an object's function, and that is by registering functional properties of objects more or less directly from their visible characteristics without first categorizing them. Gestalt theorists first suggested this approach, calling them **physiognomic characters**. Koffka put it this way: "To primitive man, each thing says what it is and what he ought to do with it: a fruit says, 'Eat me'; water says, 'Drink me'; thunder says, 'Fear me'; and woman says, 'Love me'" (Koffka, 1935, p. 7). Gibson (1979) later advocated a similar approach, expanding his claim of direct perception to include function. He referred to the visible functions of an object as its **affordances** for the perceiver. Examples of affordances would be whether an object affords

Theoretical Approaches to Vision

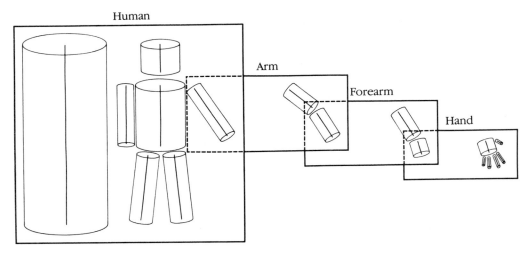

Figure 2.4.8 Using shape primitives in an object-based representation. The shape of a person's body as a 3-D volume is roughly represented here as a set of cylinders of the appropriate size, shape, orientation, and connectedness. Each box shows a perceptual object at a coarse, global level as a single cylinder and at a finer, more local level as a configuration of several cylinders. (From Marr & Nishihara, 1978.)

grasping by the observer's hand or whether it affords sitting upon by the observer's body. According to this view, one does not first have to classify something as a member of the category "chair" to know that one can sit on it because this affordance is directly perceivable without categorization.

It is possible—indeed, even likely—that people employ both types of processes (direct and indirect) in perceiving function. Some objects such as chairs and cups have functional properties that are so intimately tied to their visible structure that one might not need to categorize them to know what they can be used for. Other objects, such as computers and telephones, have functions that are so removed from their obvious visual characteristics that they almost certainly need to be categorized first. The extent to which people use each of these strategies to perceive functionally relevant information about objects is currently unknown. We will explore these and other issues involved in perceiving function more fully in Chapter 9.

These four proposed stages of visual processing—image-based, surface-based, object-based, and category-based—represent the current best guess about the overall structure of visual perception. We have listed them in the particular order in which they must logically be initiated, but that does not necessarily mean that each is completed before the next begins. The arrows going backward in Figure 2.4.1 indicate that later processes may feed back to influence earlier ones. In the coming chapters, we will use this four-stage framework to structure our discussion of each of the main topics that we consider: perception of color (Chapter 3), spatial properties (Chapters 4–9) and motion (Chapter 10). In the final three chapters, we will examine three related topics that surround this core of visual processing: visual selection by eye movements and attention in Chapter 11, visual memory and imagery in Chapter 12, and visual awareness in Chapter 13.

Suggestions for Further Reading

Classical Perceptual Theories

Koffka, K. (1935). *Principles of Gestalt psychology.* New York: Harcourt Brace. This is the most comprehensive statement of the Gestalt view of psychology. The vast majority of it concerns vision, but other topics are covered as well.

Gibson, J. J. (1950). *The perception of the visual world.* Boston: Houghton-Mifflin. Gibson's first book—many say his best— lays the foundation for his ecological approach.

Rock, I. (1983). *The logic of perception.* Cambridge: MIT Press. This is the definitive modern statement of a neo-Helmholtzian constructivist position. In Rock's hands, perception is likened to a problem-solving process in which the visual system must figure out what environmental situation gave rise to the optical image registered on the retina.

History of Information Processing

Gardner, H. (1985). *The mind's new science: A history of the cognitive revolution.* New York: Basic Books. This is a very engaging and readable presentation of the emergence of cognitive science in a historical context.

Information Processing Theory

Pylyshyn, Z. (1984). *Computation and cognition.* Cambridge, MA: MIT Press. This is a rather dense but comprehensive exposition of the computational view of mind from an interdisciplinary perspective.

Nalwa, V. S. (1993). *A guided tour of computer vision.* Reading, MA: Addison-Wesley. This is an excellent, general-purpose introduction to the field of computer vision.

Four Stages of Vision

Marr, D. (1982). *Vision.* New York: Freeman. One of the most influential books on vision ever written, this volume describes Marr's particular conception of image-based, surface-based, object-based, and category-based stages of visual perception.

Color Vision:
A Microcosm of Vision Science

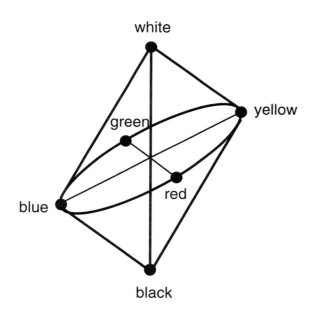

One of the most fascinating and distinctive aspects of vision is the experience of color. It provides a variety of experiences that are qualitatively unlike those of any other property and are unavailable in any other sensory modality. Physical objects and light sources have the almost miraculous property of appearing to be colored. It is not obvious why this should be; it simply *is*. People universally believe that objects *look* colored because they *are* colored, just as we experience them: The sky looks blue because it *is* blue, grass looks green because it *is* green, and blood looks red because it *is* red.

As surprising as it may seem, these beliefs are fundamentally mistaken. Neither objects nor lights are actually "colored" in anything like the way we experience them. Rather, color is a *psychological* property of our visual experiences when we look at objects and lights, not a *physical* property of those objects or lights. The colors we see are based on physical properties of objects and lights that cause us to see them as colored, to be sure, but these physical properties are different in important ways from the colors we perceive. Color is more accurately understood as the result of complex interactions between physical light in the environment and our visual nervous systems. Understanding how this happens will require a fair amount of explaining. It is worth the effort, though, because certain aspects of color perception are among the best-understood topics in vision science, perhaps in all of cognitive science. We now know a great deal about how color perception occurs, from the physics of light and how retinal receptors respond to it to how people in different cultures name the color of surfaces.

This is not to say that we now know everything about color perception, for certainly we do not. But we know enough more about it than about other domains that it will serve us well as a model system for understanding why an interdisciplinary approach to other aspects of vision is useful. Important pieces of the color puzzle have come from physics, psychology, physiology, computer science, linguistics, genetics, and anthropology. If color perception and naming provide a good model of what is required to understand a cognitive domain, it must be a very broad and integrative enterprise.

The story of how vision scientists came to understand color perception is also instructive from a historical standpoint. It nicely illustrates the way scientific discoveries have unfolded in time to produce a coherent theory of a complex perceptual domain. A body of basic facts were discovered that required explanation. A theory was proposed to account for certain of these facts, an alternative theory was proposed to account for others, and a heated debate arose between advocates of the two theories. Ultimately these disputes were resolved through a theoretical integration, and further tests supported the integrated theory. We will therefore tell much of the "color story" in chronological order to trace the interesting history of how our understanding has progressed.

The present chapter is structured according to the metatheoretical principles described in Chapter 2. We begin with an analysis of the computational problem of color perception. First, we consider the nature of the input information, which is *light* as a physicist would describe it. Next, we consider the output information, which is the *experience of color* as a psychologist would describe it. Then we examine the nature of the relation between the two: how the physical domain of light maps onto the psychological domain of color experience.

After completing this computational analysis, we turn to the algorithmic level: how the mapping of light energy onto color experiences might be accomplished in terms of information and operations. We define three major stages of color processing that will be discussed in the remainder of the chapter: an image-based stage, a surface-based stage, and a category-based stage. An object-based stage is not necessary because color is a perceived property of surfaces rather than of volumes.

Within these stages we will analyze the algorithms of color processing by recursive decomposition, searching for lower-level descriptions of the operations involved. In some cases we reach the point at which we see in detail how this functional analysis relates to the implementation of the algorithm: the underlying physiology of color processing in the neural structures of the eye and brain. This is mainly true of image-based processing as described in Section 3.2. By the time we get to surface-based and category-based processing in Sections

Color Vision

3.3 and 3.4, our understanding of the visual nervous system is not yet complete enough to make contact with the more abstract information processing analyses we consider. Making those connections will require a great deal of further research.

3.1 The Computational Description of Color Perception

Marr (1982) proposed that the best place to start in understanding any complex information processing system is at the computational level, describing the input, the output, and the principles underlying the mapping from input to output. In the case of color perception, the input is light reflected into the eye by surfaces in the environment, the output is color experiences that arise when an observer views those surfaces, and the mapping is the psychophysical correspondence between the two. In the present section we will provide a simplified computational description of these aspects of color perception. In later sections we will examine the algorithmic and implementational aspects.

3.1.1 The Physical Description of Light

The first great stride toward understanding color vision was made in 1666 by the great English physicist Sir Isaac Newton, when he discovered that "white" (uncolored) light from the sun is actually made up of many separate components that individually produce different color experiences. Newton made a small hole in his laboratory shade and placed a triangular glass prism behind it. When a shaft of light passed through the prism and onto a white surface, a rainbow of different colors appeared, as illustrated in Figure 3.1.1. Newton then focused the rainbow of light back into a single shaft using additional prisms and observed that the recombination again produced white light. On the basis of these and other systematic observations, Newton theorized that sunlight was actually composed of many different "colors" of light rather than just one. He also realized that the "colors" were not in the light itself, but in the effect of the light on the visual system, as the following quotation eloquently states:

[T]he Rays to speak properly are not coloured. In them there is nothing else than a certain Power and Disposition to stir up a

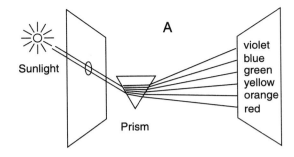

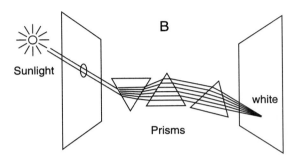

Figure 3.1.1 Newton's experiment. (A) A single glass prism separates uncolored (white) sunlight into its component wavelengths of radiant energy, which people perceive as a rainbow of colors. (B) Additional prisms recombine the different wavelengths into uncolored (white) sunlight again.

Sensation of this or that Colour.... So Colours in the object are nothing but a Disposition to reflect this or that sort of Rays more copiously than the rest.

Newton's discoveries were the first fundamental insights into the physical properties of light that produce color vision, but there have been many advances since then. As we said in Chapter 1, visible light is now known to come in tiny, indivisible units called photons that behave like particles in some respects and like waves in others. In most other parts of this book, it is the particle behavior of photons that is most important, but for the topic of color vision, it is their wave behavior that matters most. A **photon** is a tiny packet of vibrating **electromagnetic energy** that can be characterized by one of its wave properties: the **wavelength** of its vibration. The wavelengths of photons are measured in units of distance, varying from extremely small (10^{-14} meters) to extremely large (thousands of kilometers). The photons that we experience as visible light cover just a small portion of this **electromagnetic spec-**

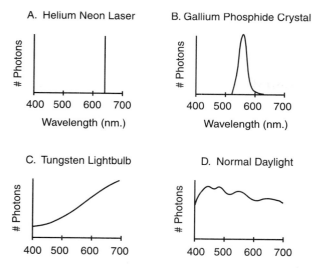

Figure 3.1.2 Physical spectra of various lights. The number of photons per unit of time is graphed as a function of wavelength over the visible range of the electromagnetic spectrum for four light sources: (A) a monochromatic helium neon laser, (B) a gallium phosphide crystal, (C) a tungsten lightbulb, and (D) normal daylight.

trum, as illustrated in Color Plate 3.1. In fact, the human visual system is sensitive only to photons with wavelengths between about 400 and 700 nanometers (1 nm = 10^{-9} meters). X-rays, microwaves, radio, and TV waves are also part of this spectrum, as indicated in Color Plate 3.1, but none of our sensory organs respond to photons outside this range. As a result, we cannot perceive them without the aid of complex devices— such as X-ray cameras, televisions, and radios—that convert them into visible light or audible sound.

Given these facts, a physicist can completely describe any uniform patch of visible light in terms of the number of photons it contains (per unit of time) at each wavelength from 400 to 700 nanometers. This description, called the spectrum of a light, can be graphed succinctly as shown in Figure 3.1.2; the graph is called its **spectral diagram**. Light that has a spectrum containing only one wavelength (Figure 3.1.2A) is called **monochromatic light** (from *mono*, meaning "one," and *chroma*, meaning "color"). All other lights are **polychromatic** (from *poly*, meaning "many"), and their spectra can vary from having just a narrow band of component wavelengths (Figure 3.1.2B) to having some photons at all visible wavelengths (as in Figure 3.1.2C). Natural sun-

light contains roughly equal numbers of photons at all visible wavelengths (Figure 3.1.2D), just as Newton claimed.

3.1.2 The Psychological Description of Color

Notice that in the physical description of light there was no mention of *color* at all. This is because, as Newton said, "the Rays to speak properly are not coloured." Color becomes relevant only when light enters the eyes of an observer who is equipped with the proper sort of visual nervous system to experience it. The situation is reminiscent of the old puzzle about whether a tree that falls in the forest makes a sound if nobody is there to hear it. There may be *light* of different wavelengths independent of an observer, but there is no *color* independent of an observer, because color is a psychological phenomenon that arises only within an observer.

Although we sometimes see colored light emitted directly by a luminous object or surface, such as a TV or computer screen, we normally experience color as a property of surfaces. This occurs because some of the light emitted by luminous objects, such as the sun or light bulbs, is reflected by surfaces into our eyes (see Section 1.2). It is this reflected light that enables us to see nonluminous surfaces and their properties. They appear differently colored because different surfaces reflect different proportions of light at different wavelengths.

Color Space. The subjective experience of surface color has a very different structure from that of physical light. All the surface colors experienced by a person with normal color vision can be described in terms of just three dimensions: *hue*, *saturation*, and *lightness*. Together these dimensions define **color space**: a three-dimensional coordinate system within which each possible color experience can be represented as a single point with a unique position (see Color Plate 3.2). The complete set of colors that people with normal color vision actually perceive occupies a subset of color space, called the **color solid** or the **color spindle**, which looks rather like a lopsided child's top (see Color Plate 3.2). Every experience of surface color can be located at a specific point within this region of color space.

Notice that there is an enormous reduction in complexity from the physical description of light to the

Color Vision

psychological description of color. In principle, a physicist needs to specify an infinite number of values to describe the spectrum of a given *light*, one for each wavelength in the continuum between 400 and 700 nm. A psychologist, however, can specify a *color* with just three values: one for hue, a second for saturation, and a third for lightness. This implies that color experiences lose much (but not all) of the information that is carried in the full spectrum of a light. It also implies that many physically different lights (that is, lights having different spectra) will produce exactly the same color experience. This latter fact turns out to be an important property of color vision, one to which we will return when we consider color mixture.

A color space that is defined by subjectively equal steps in hue, saturation (sometimes called *chroma*), and lightness (sometimes called *value*) was originally devised in 1905 by the artist and art teacher Albert Munsell. A standardized color atlas based on his analysis, called the *Munsell Book of Color*, is published in a two-volume set containing 1600 glossy samples of carefully controlled paint chips. Any surface color can be specified by finding the Munsell chip that most closely approximates the sample and giving its three coordinate values according to Munsell's system.

The conditions under which colored chips are viewed for color analysis must be strictly regulated. For meaningful comparison, the colors should be observed under carefully controlled illumination conditions and either on a uniform, medium gray background or through an opening in a uniform neutral gray mask. Otherwise, differences in the background color and/or the lighting conditions will alter the perceived color of the test sample. Most people have experienced the frustration of buying an article of clothing whose color looked quite acceptable under the fluorescent lights in the store, only to find that it looks appreciably different when viewed in sunlight or incandescent lighting. Such complexities are important for a full understanding of color perception, but we will put them aside for the moment to simplify our task. We will return to them later in this chapter.

Hue. The dimension we normally associate with the basic "color" of a surface is **hue**. In color space, hue corresponds to the direction from the central axis to the location of the point representing a given color. If we examine the hue of monochromatic lights (those containing just one wavelength) arrayed from shortest to longest wavelengths as in the rainbow, there is a smooth progression from violets, through blues, greens, yellows, oranges, and reds. Thus, it might appear that the psychological dimension of hue is the same as the physical dimension of wavelength. There are some important differences, however.

If lights are arranged according to their physical similarity in terms of wavelength, they lie along a straight line, as indicated in Color Plate 3.1. Lights at the shortest and longest visible wavelengths are therefore the least similar in physical terms. If monochromatic lights are arranged according to their *perceived* similarity, however, they lie along the circumference of a **color circle** (see Color Plate 3.3). Here the hue dimension is curved, so the shortest wavelengths (which appear violet) and longest wavelengths (which appear orangish red) are rather close together, reflecting their psychological similarity due to their shared reddishness. Thus, the psychological dimension of hue and the physical dimension of wavelength for monochromatic lights are related, but they are not the same. Between the violets and orangish reds on the hue circle lie the **nonspectral hues** from purples through magentas to deep reds. They are called "nonspectral" because there is no single wavelength in the visible spectrum (that is, no monochromatic light) that produces them. These hues can be created only by combining two or more wavelengths of light.

Saturation. The second dimension of color, called **saturation**, captures the "purity" and "vividness" of color experiences. In color space, it corresponds to the distance outward from the central axis to the position of the point representing a given color. For example, all the vivid, monochromatic colors of the rainbow lie along the outside edge, at the highest saturation levels. All the grays lie along the central axis and have zero saturation. The muted, pastel colors in between have intermediate levels of saturation.

Lightness. The third dimension of surface color is **lightness**. In the coordinates of color space, lightness refers to the "height" of a color's position as it is drawn in Color Plate 3.2. All surface colors have some value on the lightness dimension, although it is perhaps most obvious for the **achromatic colors** (grays) that lie along the central axis, with white at the top and black at the bottom.

Color Plate 3.3 displays an oblique slice through color space that shows in more detail how hue and saturation combine to form the 2-D color circle. Gray is at the center, and the most vivid (highly saturated) colors are located around the edges. This section through the color spindle is oblique because the most saturated yellows are very light, whereas the most saturated blues and violets are quite dark, the most saturated reds and greens being at intermediate lightness values. Hues on opposite sides of the color circle are called **complementary colors**. If lights of complementary color are mixed in the proper proportions, they produce achromatic (un-colored) light that will appear as some shade of gray.

Color Plate 3.4 shows a vertical slice through the color solid that illustrates how the saturation and light-ness dimensions combine to form **color triangles** for yellow and blue hues. Notice that grays from black to white form a vertical strip along one side, corresponding to the central axis of color space. Notice also that the colors that we call "browns" are actually dark members of yellow hues.

Lightness versus Brightness. The dimension of lightness concerns the perception of surfaces that reflect light rather than emit it. This is the usual case in vi-sual perception, since only a few objects—for example, the sun, stars, various kinds of light bulbs, TVs, and computer monitors—actually emit light. And except for color TVs and computer monitors, the light they emit is generally fairly neutral in color. In analyzing the color of luminous objects, the dimension of **brightness** takes the place of lightness.[1] This is because luminous surfaces appear brighter or dimmer, rather than lighter or darker, as reflective surfaces do. Otherwise, the shape of the color space for emitted and reflected light is essen-tially the same.

The perceived dimensions of lightness and brightness are both due largely to the contrast of one region with a surrounding region. If two surfaces reflect the same number of photons per unit time, the one surrounded by a darker region will look lighter, and the one sur-rounded by a lighter region will look darker. If two sur-faces emit the same amount of light, the same contrasts hold for their brightnesses. You can easily convince yourself of this fact by considering your television set. When it is off (that is, when it is merely reflecting light from other sources rather than emitting any light of its own), it looks a dull medium gray. After you turn it on, however, you see both good whites and good blacks. The whites are easy enough to understand, because those regions are now emitting photons. But how do black regions of the TV screen appear darker than they did when it is off? It cannot be because of emitting fewer photons than before, because the TV was not emitting any photons when it was off, and it cannot emit "negative photons" to reduce the amount of light. The enhanced blackness when the TV is on must therefore result from contrast with the increased brightness from other parts of the TV image.

The importance of contrast holds not just for black and white, but for all other dark and light colors as well. Brown is an important case, for it is a dark version of orange and yellow. This means, for example, that a brown region on your color TV set or computer screen will look orange or yellow if you look just at it through a black piece of construction paper rolled into a tube. We will return to such contrast effects later in this chapter.

3.1.3 The Psychophysical Correspondence

Now that we have a basic understanding of the input and output information for color perception, we can ask how they are related. Specifying how physical descrip-tions map onto psychological ones is called a **psycho-physical correspondence**, and it is generally what is specified in a computational analysis. It would be con-venient if there were a clear and simple correspondence between physical light and color experience, but there is

---

[1] Unfortunately, there is ambiguity in the use of the term "brightness," because reflective surfaces are often discussed as having different levels of brightness as well as lightness. This usage refers to the raw appearance of a surface's color before variations in illumination are taken into account (see Section 3.3). A uniform region that lies partly in sunlight and partly in shadow, for example, would have constant perceived lightness after the differential illumination has been perceived but would have higher bright-ness in sunlight than in shadow. In the terminology we developed in Sec-tion 2.4.1, brightness is the name used for the intensity dimension of all regions in the image-based stage, whereas at the surface-based stage, sur-faces that reflect light have the property of lightness, whereas those that emit light have the property of brightness.

not. Understanding how reflected light maps onto experiences of colored surfaces is enormously complex and requires a great deal more information than we have yet considered. We do have enough to make a start, but only if we simplify things a bit.

We have already simplified the perceptual situation in certain ways, such as viewing color chips under standardized conditions, using a constant neutral source of illumination, and viewing the chips against a neutral gray background. The further simplification we will now make is to consider only surfaces that reflect light whose spectrum is approximately the shape of a normal distribution (that is, bell-shaped), as illustrated in Figure 3.1.3. This includes only a tiny fraction of possible surfaces, few of which exist in nature. The attractive property of such distributions is that they are defined by just three parameters: their *central value* (the "mean" or "mode"), their *area*, and their *width* (or "variance"). These parameters turn out to have a particularly simple relation to the three dimensions of perceived color.

For spectra with approximately normal distributions, there are three simple psychophysical correspondences between properties of the light spectrum and properties of the perceived color:

1. *Mean wavelength determines hue* (see Figure 3.1.3A). We have already considered the relation between hue and wavelength briefly in the case of monochromatic lights. With a normally distributed polychromatic spectrum, the hue will be essentially the same as that of a monochromatic spectrum at the peak (modal) wavelength. Saying that monochromatic light will have the same hue as the polychromatic light does not imply that they will look identical, because there may be differences in lightness (or brightness) and saturation as well. It is also important to realize that not all hues can be produced by normally distributed spectra—particularly the nonspectral purples—for reasons that we will consider later.

2. *Spectral area determines lightness* (see Figure 3.1.3B). This should not be too surprising, because the area under the spectral curve corresponds to the total number of photons (per unit of time) that strike the retina. Large areas

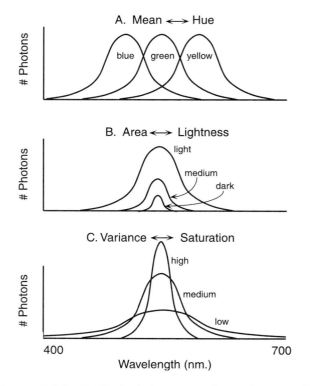

Figure 3.1.3 Psychophysical correspondences for normally distributed spectra. (A) Differences in spectral mean produce differences in hue perception. (B) Differences in spectral area and height produce differences in lightness perception. (C) Differences in spectral variance (width) cause differences in saturation perception.

under the spectral curve thus correspond to bright lights and light surfaces, and small areas correspond to dim lights and dark surfaces.[2]

3. *Variance (width) determines saturation* (see Figure 3.1.3C). This makes sense too, because we have already mentioned that monochromatic lights, which have zero variance in their spectrum, are the most saturated ones and that "white" sunlight, which has maximal variance (that is, a nearly flat spectrum) is the least saturated. The same relation between saturation and spectral variance holds for reflected light.

<hr />

[2] In fact, it is not the absolute number of photons that matters, but the number relative to those coming from the surrounding region. This is because of the importance of contrast in producing the brightness/lightness dimension, as we mentioned earlier. But if all the color chips are viewed against the same background, surfaces reflecting less light will look darker and those reflecting more light will look lighter.

Thus, under the restriction that the light reflected from a surface has a roughly normally distributed spectrum, the psychophysical correspondence is quite orderly. Once the restriction of normal wavelength distributions is relaxed, however, things get very complicated very quickly. To predict the hue, saturation, and lightness of a surface with an arbitrary spectrum would require a much more complex analysis than can be provided here.

Even more complications are introduced when we consider the perceived color of real objects under real viewing conditions. As we will see in Section 3.3, one cannot predict the perceived color of a surface simply by knowing the spectrum of the light being reflected from it into the eye. Other factors that come into play include the nature of the surrounding surfaces, the lighting conditions, the orientation of the surface relative to the illuminating light, the perceived spatial layout of surfaces in depth, and shadows cast by other objects. Each of these can have a substantial effect on color perception. However, we will postpone discussing them until Section 3.3.

3.2 Image-Based Color Processing

In discussing the image-based stage of color processing, we will analyze the representation of color at the level of a two-dimensional image. To be truthful, it is not clear exactly what this means, because people may well not have color experiences at the image-based level. It seems far more likely that conscious color experiences arise only at some later stage of processing when the colors of surfaces arrayed in 3-D space are perceived. If so, the color representation in the image-based stage can be inferred only with the help of some additional assumptions. For instance, it is generally assumed that if the stimulus is unambiguously and veridically perceived as two-dimensional, perpendicular to the line of sight, and uniformly illuminated, the massively complicating factors that enter into surface-based perception will not affect color processing. If this is true, the color experience arising from such a two-dimensional display will reflect processing that has taken place at the image-based stage.

The optimal conditions for achieving this sort of perception are viewing homogeneous patches of colored light (or paint chips) through a neutrally colored **reduction tube** or **reduction screen** that blocks out everything in the visual field except the test color (or colors). Such conditions produce a phenomenon called **aperture color** (or **film color**) because the color has a filmy appearance behind the aperture of the reduction screen. The reduction screen thus removes all complicating depth and contextual information from the stimulus. For purposes of this discussion, then, we will presume that color perception under these reduction conditions reflects essentially image-based processing.

3.2.1 Basic Phenomena

Our understanding of image-based color vision rests on a number of basic facts about two-dimensional color perception. Many of them were discovered more than a century ago by scientists using behavioral methods such as discrimination tasks and introspective descriptions. They include the rules of color mixture, the types of color blindness, the nature of color afterimages, the existence of induced colors, and the nature of chromatic adaptation. These phenomena were especially important for early theories of color vision because they represented the primary observations that needed to be explained. Once we have described them, we can proceed to ask how they might be understood within a theory of image-based color processing.

Light Mixture. As we mentioned previously, only a small portion of the colors in color space correspond to monochromatic lights. To see nonspectral colors such as purples and desaturated colors such as pastels and grays, two or more different wavelengths must be mixed. This raises the important question of how colors combine. It turns out that the answer depends very much on whether one mixes lights or paints. Light mixture is rather simple to understand in terms of color space, so we will examine it first. Paint mixture—with which most people are more familiar in practical terms—is more complicated and is described in Appendix B, which explains it in the context of a variety of different color technologies.

There is a simple rule for predicting the color produced by mixing two lights, A and B: The resulting color lies on the line connecting A and B in color space (see

A. Mixing Two Lights

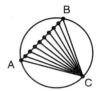

B. Mixing Three Lights

Figure 3.2.1 Light mixture in color space. (A) Mixing two lights in varying proportions produces colors that lie along the straight line between them in color space. (B) Mixing three lights in varying proportions produces colors that lie within the triangle they define in color space.

Figure 3.2.1A).[3] If the two lights are mixed in equal proportions, their combination lies midway between them. If the mixture contains a lot of A and a little of B, then the combination lies closer to A but still along the line between A and B. Now it should be clear why lights of complementary colors mix to produce achromatic (white) light: They are on opposite sides of the color circle, so the chromatically neutral center point lies on the line connecting them.

If a third color, C, is also included in the mixture, the result will lie somewhere within the triangle in color space whose vertices are at A, B, and C. You can see that this must be true by the following logic: If the mixture of A and B lies somewhere along the line AB (depending on the relative amounts of A and B) and if each of these possible results is then mixed with variable amounts of C, the final results will lie somewhere along the lines connecting each point of AB with C (see Figure 3.2.1B). This set of alternatives defines the triangle ABC in color space. Precisely where the mixture will be located depends on the relative proportions of the three lights.

From what we have said so far, you can see that if the three colors A, B, and C are in the color circle of maximum saturation (see Color Plate 3.3) and are chosen to be sufficiently far apart in this plane—say, at some appropriately chosen red, blue, and green—then their mixture will produce most of the rest of the colors in the plane just by varying the relative amounts.[4] This means that any color within the triangle formed by A, B, and C can be matched exactly by some combination of these three lights. The colors that will be missed in this mixing scheme are highly saturated yellows, purples, and blue-greens, although these hues can be produced in less saturated form. By varying the absolute amounts of the A, B, and C lights so that brightness varies as well as hue and saturation, most of the colors in the whole of the color solid can be produced. This fact about human color vision was discovered in 1855 by James Clerk Maxwell, the famous Scottish physicist who formulated (Maxwell's) equations governing the behavior of electromagnetic fields.

These observations can be generalized into the following law of color mixture: People with normal color vision can match any given color by some combination of three appropriately chosen lights. ("Appropriately chosen" means that the three lights cannot fall along a straight line in color space.) This law holds for color mixture experiments in which subjects are given a region containing a colored light to be matched (the test region) and an adjacent region composed of some number of other colored lights in variable proportion (the mixture region), as illustrated in Figure 3.2.2A. They then adjust the proportion of components in the mixture region until it looks exactly the same as the test region with no visible boundary between them. Note that the two regions will be physically different in the sense that they will contain different amounts of different wavelengths. Pairs of lights (or surfaces) that look the same but have different physical spectra are called **metamers**.

---

[3] Technically, this is true in a color space called the C.I.E. chromaticity diagram, which is explained in Appendix C. In many other color spaces, the lines representing mixtures of two colors are not necessarily straight.

[4] By "relative amounts" of lights in a mixture, we mean that the overall sum of the intensities of the three lights is constant, so the colors produced by mixing them will remain the same plane of color space. What varies is the balance of the three different lights.

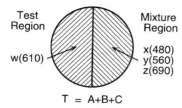

A. Standard Mixture Task

Test Region — w(610)

Mixture Region — x(480) y(560) z(690)

T = A+B+C

B. Adding "Negative" Colors

Test Region — w(500) z(690)

Mixture Region — x(440) y(560)

T+C = A+B

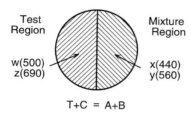

Figure 3.2.2 Metameric matches of light mixtures. (A) In the standard matching task, a test light (*w* units of a monochromatic light at 610 nm) is matched by mixing variable amounts of three fixed wavelengths in the mixture patch (*x* units of 480 nm, *y* units of 560 nm, and *z* units of 690 nm). (B) If the test light falls outside the triangle formed by the mixture lights in color space, "negative" amounts of a mixture color (here, 690 nm) can be produced by adding a corresponding "positive" amount to the test patch instead.

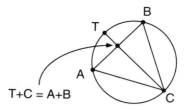

T+C = A+B

Figure 3.2.3 Color matching in color space using "negative" amounts of light. Because the test light (T) lies outside the triangle formed by the mixture lights (A, B, and C), it can be matched only by using the "negative color" procedure, producing a particular mixture of T and C that matches a particular mixture of A and B, as indicated at the intersection of lines AB and TC.

The reader may object to the law of color mixture as stated above because, as we have already seen, certain highly saturated colors cannot be matched by simple mixtures of three lights—namely, the ones that lie outside the triangle formed by the three mixture colors. The reason that simple mixtures of three lights will not cover the whole of color space is that the mixture procedure described above does not allow for adding negative colors (in the sense that one can add negative vectors in spanning a standard geometrical vector space). As it turns out, however, there is a methodological trick in color mixture that makes it all work out nicely. A "negative" amount of a mixing color can be added to the mixture region, in effect, simply by adding a "positive" amount of it to the test region instead, as illustrated in Figure 3.2.2B.

Figure 3.2.3 shows how a color that lies outside the triangle defined by the three mixture lights can be matched by using negative color mixture. The color not adjacent to the test color among the three mixture

colors—in this case, color C—is added to the test patch instead of the mixture patch by using the "negative color" trick. This combination can produce any color along the line between T and C. Because one of these points also lies along the line between the other two mixture colors, A and B, T can be matched by a combination of positive amounts of A and B plus a "negative" amount of C. By allowing mixture of negative colors in this sense, colors outside the mixture triangle can be matched, making the law of color mixture valid for all test colors.

The fact that just three lights are needed to mix any hue is of enormous practical importance, because it is the basis of some very important forms of color technology. For instance, all the colors you see on your color TV and computer screens are combinations of just three lights: highly saturated shades of red, green, and blue. You may have noticed this on large, projection TVs because the red, green, and blue lights that project onto the screen are often in plain view. Other color TVs work in pretty much the same way, except that the electron beams are inside the picture tube so you cannot see them. If you examine the screen from a very short distance, however, you can see that white areas of the picture are not actually white but are composed of tiny red, green, and blue dots or rectangles. (This is easiest to do on a color computer terminal because you can generate a highly stable image with an abundance of white in it. If you can find a magnifying glass, take a closer look.) When you adjust the color control knobs of your color TV, you are actually changing the relative intensities of these three colors, matching colors on the screen to your

Color Vision

knowledge of characteristic colors, such as skin tones. All forms of color technology—paints, dyes, color photography, TV, video, and computer images—make use of additive color mixture (as just explained), subtractive color mixture (as explained in Appendix B), or some combination of both. How they achieve their effects is described more fully in Appendix B.

Color Blindness. When we stated that any color can be matched by a mixture of three appropriately chosen lights, we qualified it by saying "for a person with normal color vision." As this caveat suggests, not everyone perceives colors in the same way. In fact, about 8% of males and fewer than 1% of females have some form of **color blindness**: They cannot discriminate among all the colors in the color solid. The discrepancy between the incidence rates in men and women reflects the fact that deficits in color vision are sex-linked, hereditary conditions. To find out whether you have a major color deficit, look at Color Plate 3.5. If you can discern the numbers 57 and 15 in the dot patterns, your color vision is probably normal. If you see something else, you are probably at least partially color blind.

There are several distinct varieties of color blindness and many degrees of severity. People with "normal" color vision are called **trichromats** (*tri*, meaning "three" + *chroma*, meaning "color") because, as we have seen, they can match any color with some mixture of three others. Full trichromats experience all the colors in the color solid. Most people who are "color blind" are some form of **dichromat** (*di* means "two") because they can match any color with some mixture of just two others. A few people experience the world only as variations in lightness, much as you do when you look at a black-and-white movie or photograph. They are called **monochromats** (*mono* means "one"), and as you might guess, they can match any color with some intensity level of any other color. For them, the whole volume of trichromatic color space projects onto the single central axis of achromatic colors.

There are three distinct types of dichromats. Two types fail to experience red and green hues, both of which are presumably seen as grays. As a result, the world appears to them in various shades of blues, yellows, and grays, as though the red/green dimension of the color solid had been eliminated (see Color Plate 3.6). These two forms of so-called red/green color blindness—more

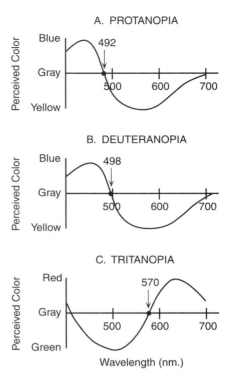

Figure 3.2.4 Neutral points in color blindness. There is one wavelength of monochromatic light that appears uncolored to dichromats. The specific wavelength at which this occurs is characteristic of the type of color blindness, as shown by the point at which the curve crosses the *x* axis.

formally known as **protanopia** (*pro*, meaning "first" + *anopia*, meaning "inability to see") and **deuteranopia** (*deuter* means "second")—are qualitatively very similar. However, they can be distinguished by carefully measuring the observer's monochromatic **neutral point**: the specific wavelength at which a monochromatic light looks uncolored (gray). For both groups, short wavelengths appear bluish and long wavelengths appear yellowish, but somewhere in between is a wavelength that is perceived as neutral gray, appearing neither blue nor yellow. (Normal trichromats have no such neutral point, since all monochromatic lights, as in the rainbow, produce vivid hue experiences.) For protanopes, this neutral point occurs as 492 nm, and for deuteranopes, it occurs at 498 nm. (see Figure 3.2.4). Despite their obvious similarities, the distinction between these two varieties of color blindness has important physiological implications, which we will examine shortly.

The red/green forms of color blindness are by far the most common, each one affecting about 1% of males and 0.02% of females. The third type of dichromatism, **tritanopia** (*tri* means "third"), is much rarer, occurring in only 0.02% of males and 0.01% of females. Tritanopes fail to discriminate blues and yellows, so their subjective experience of their world presumably consists only of shades of red, green, and gray (see Color Plate 3.6), as though the blue/yellow dimension of the color solid had been eliminated. As Figure 3.2.4 indicates, short wavelengths appear green to them and long wavelengths look red, with the neutral (gray) point occurring at 570 nm.

There are also corresponding forms of **color weakness** in which the color solid is affected in less extreme ways. These **anomalous trichromats** constitute the remainder of the population with color deficiencies. They are able to match any color with some mixture of three others, but they mix them in different proportions than normal trichromats. For someone who is red/green weak, the color solid would look like a flattened version of the normal one, compressed along the red/green dimension but still three-dimensional. For someone who is blue/yellow weak, it would be compressed along the blue/yellow dimension. The distinction between "normal" and "anomalous" trichromats is not a sharp one, however, and different degrees of deviation from normalcy are present among the population of anomalous trichromats.

Once we explain the physiology underlying the color vision system, it will become clear why these particular forms of color deficiencies, and no others, exist. The basic behavioral facts about color deficiencies were well known long before the underlying physiology was understood, however, and one of the tasks of early perceptual theories of color vision was to explain them. As we will see, the phenomena of color blindness play an especially important role in the history of color theory.

Before leaving the topic of color deficiency, it is worth asking how normal trichromats could know—or think they know—what the world looks like to dichromats or monochromats. The problem is an old philosophical one concerning the private nature of conscious experiences. How do you know that my experience of redness is the same as yours? The fact that we call the same things "red" does not prove it, for I might have red experiences that are just like your green experiences, only I

would call them "red." (There is nothing deceitful going on here; I would simply be using the label "red" as I had been taught, just as you would, but our sensory experiences would be reversed.) Indeed, it is logically possible that my experiences of color are simply the inverse of yours, as if the rainbow were reversed for me. (See Section 13.1.2 for a more detailed discussion of this possibility.)

Given such problems, how could trichromats know what the world looks like to dichromats? There are two answers. One comes from those extremely rare individuals who are color blind in only one eye (MacLeod & Lennie, 1976; Sloan & Wollach, 1948). Such people can tell us what a dichromatic image looks like to a trichromat simply by looking one eye at a time, because the same person experiences both images. This seems to be a satisfactory answer until one begins to wonder whether the fact that one eye is trichromatic might not have some effect on what experiences arise from the dichromatic eye. That is, perhaps it is only when the brain has the full range of trichromatic color experiences from a normal eye that the color-deficient experiences of a red/green blind eye appear blue and yellow. Perhaps standard two-eyed dichromats experience radically different colors from anything normal trichromats do. This more circumspect view leads to the second answer, which is simply that we do not really know. Indeed, there may be no way to know with complete certainty, as we will argue in Chapter 13 when we turn to the problem of visual awareness.

Color Afterimages. Another important class of phenomena in understanding color vision comes from **color afterimages**: the aftereffects of viewing highly saturated colors for prolonged period of time. Almost everyone has experienced simple achromatic afterimages following brief exposure to an intense light, such as a flashbulb or the sun. With steady, prolonged viewing of a brightly colored stimulus, however, you can also experience afterimages in very convincing color, as you did with the green, black, and yellow flag in Chapter 2. Use Color Plate 2.1 again to remind yourself just how dramatic the effect can be. Stare at the dot in the center of the flag for at least 30 seconds, moving your eyes as little as possible. Then stare at the dot in the white rectangle until an afterimage forms.

You see an American flag in red, white, and blue (albeit in desaturated shades) because each hue produces its *complementary hue* in the afterimage. The complement of a hue is the one located in the opposite direction with respect to the central point of color space. Thus, green's complement is red, black's is white, and yellow's is blue.[5] In fact, this is a simple way to determine what the complement is for a given hue: Just stare at a highly saturated patch of it while fixating on a dot in the center, then look at a sheet of white paper. Your visual system gives you the answer automatically.

Simultaneous Color Contrast. Complementary hues are also important in the phenomenon of **simultaneous color contrast**—sometimes called **induced color**—but the effect of the complementary hue is perceived over space rather than over time. Simultaneous contrast effects are classically demonstrated by displaying two regions with identical spectra that result in different color perceptions owing to the spectra of surrounding regions. In other words, when a target figure is surrounded by a strongly colored background, the background color can visibly affect the perceived color of the target. An example is shown in Color Plate 3.7. Notice that the different quadrants of the uniform neutral gray ring, which are physically identical, look subtly colored. It is greenish against the red background, reddish against the green background, bluish against the yellow background, and yellowish against the blue background. The induced color is thus complementary to the background if the target is achromatic. If the target is chromatic, its perceived color will be shifted toward the complementary hue to a degree determined by its saturation and the viewing duration.

Simultaneous contrast affects achromatic perception as well. An example of **simultaneous lightness contrast** is shown in Figure 3.2.5. It is analogous to the color contrast demonstration except that here the background regions are achromatic. Notice that the different quadrants of the gray ring have different perceived lightnesses, depending on their backgrounds. The section within the black square appears lightest, and that

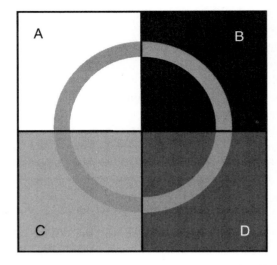

Figure 3.2.5 Lightness contrast. A gray ring of uniform reflectance appears darkest against a white background (A), lightest against a black background (B), and intermediate lightnesses against intermediate backgrounds (C and D).

within the white square appears darkest, with the others in between. If you were to cut out the ring and examine it against a uniform background, you would see that it is exactly the same shade of gray in all four quadrants.

Another well-known achromatic contrast effect is the existence of **Mach bands**, named for the nineteenth century physicist and psychologist Ernst Mach, who discovered them. Mach bands are illusory variations in perceived lightness (or brightness) that occur at certain types of edges. In Figure 3.2.6, for instance, an extra-light band is perceived on the light side of the edge, and an extra-dark band is perceived on the dark side. The nature of the illusion is indicated in the graph below the demonstration. The gray line in the graph shows the actual luminance profile of the display, whereas the black line indicates the lightness profile that is typically perceived. Mach bands constitute a contrast effect because the extra-dark and extra-light bands are believed to be caused by the contrasting regions on the opposite side of the edge. Later in this chapter we will consider

---

[5] Specifying complementary colors by verbal labels is sometimes misleading because they are so vague. "Red" and "green" each cover a multitude of colors, but for any particular red, there is but one particular green that is its complement. The complement of orangish red is a bluish green (cyan), whereas the complement of purplish red (magenta) is a more neutral green. The fact that complementary colors lie on opposite sides of color space (at least in C.I.E. color space; see Appendix B) means that when two lights of those colors are mixed, they will produce white light.

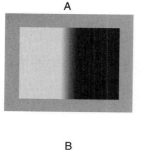

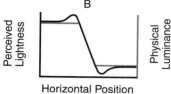

Figure 3.2.6 Mach bands. (A) Illusory lighter and darker bands are perceived on opposite sides of the graded edge. (B) A graph comparing physical light intensity (gray curve) with perceived lightness (black curve) as a function of horizontal position shows the nature of the illusory Mach bands.

how contrast phenomena such as Mach bands might arise from neural processing.

Chromatic Adaptation. In Section 1.1.3 we mentioned the well-known phenomenon of dark adaptation: the fact that the visual system becomes more sensitive to light after extended periods in darkness. Its opposite, light adaptation, refers to the visual system's temporary loss of sensitivity to light after prolonged exposure to bright light. Given these forms of adaptation, it should not be too surprising that the visual system also undergoes **chromatic adaptation**. That is, prolonged exposure to light that is perceived as a specific color reduces the visual system's sensitivity to that color immediately afterward. To demonstrate chromatic adaptation, look at the red-green square in Color Plate 3.8A under bright illumination with just your left eye, fixating on the dot in the center. After about 30 seconds of adaptation, switch to your right eye and notice how much more saturated the red and green regions appear with this unadapted eye. Then adapt your left eye to the red-green square again for a bit and look at Color Plate 3.8B, first with your left eye and then with your right. With your left eye, the red stripe will appear less saturated at the bottom and more saturated at the top. The opposite happens to the green stripe, which appears

more saturated at the bottom and less saturated at the top. The yellow stripe undergoes a rather dramatic chromatic shift because of adaptation, looking distinctly reddish on the top and greenish on the bottom. The same differences are evident in the blue stripe as well. Notice that none of these differences are present with your unadapted right eye, however.

Chromatic adaptation is especially dramatic if the entire visual field is stimulated for an extended period of time by a homogeneous expanse of color. A completely uniform stimulus over the entire visual field is called a **Ganzfeld** (pronounced *"Gahnts'-felt"*), which is German for "whole field." Regardless of its initial color, any Ganzfeld is eventually experienced as neutral gray because of chromatic adaptation. You can experience this effect by cutting a yellow Ping-Pong ball into two hemispheres and placing them over your eyes. After a few minutes, you will perceive a colorless gray fog with a filmy appearance rather than a solid yellow surface.

When you remove the yellow Ping-Pong balls after complete chromatic adaptation, the world will initially appear slightly bluish. This is a chromatic aftereffect. It occurs because there exists a close relation between adaptation and aftereffects: Chromatic adaptation causes chromatic aftereffects of the complementary hue. They are not the same phenomenon, however. Adaptation refers to the lowering of sensitivity to a given type of stimulation after prolonged exposure to it (or similar stimulation). Aftereffects involve the tendency to experience an "opposite" perception afterward, particularly in response to a neutral stimulus, such as a white surface in the case of chromatic adaptation.

3.2.2 Theories of Color Vision

We have now described several important phenomena of color perception. As we remarked in Chapter 2, facts are important, but they are not sufficient to achieve scientific understanding. For this we need a theory of color vision that will coherently relate these facts to each other and make new predictions that can then be tested. Let us see how perceptual theorists dealt with the behavioral facts about color perception that we have just reviewed.

Trichromatic Theory. The first scientific theory of color vision was initially proposed in 1777 by George Palmer and independently rediscovered in 1802 by the

Color Vision

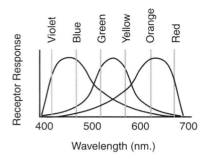

Figure 3.2.7 Trichromatic theory of color vision. Trichromatic theory assumes that color experiences arise from the activity of three hypothetical types of receptors with overlapping, but different, responses to different wavelengths of light. According to this theory, different patterns of activation correspond to the perception of different colors.

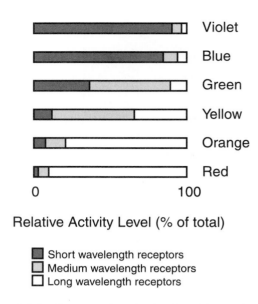

Figure 3.2.8 Patterns of activation in trichromatic theory. Different color perceptions were proposed to result from different balances of activity in the three receptor systems, as illustrated here for six basic colors.

British philosopher, Sir Thomas Young. The theory proposed that there are three types of color receptors in the human eye. These elements were hypothesized to produce the psychologically primary color sensations of red, green, and blue. All other colors were explained as combinations of these primaries. This theory was later refined and extended by Maxwell (1855) and Helmholtz (1867/1925), and it has since come to be known as the Young-Helmholtz **trichromatic theory**.

According to Helmholtz, the three kinds of color receptors respond differently as a function of the wavelength of photons falling on them, as shown in Figure 3.2.7. One receptor type was thought to produce peak activation in the short-wavelength region of the spectrum, where light appears blue, one in the medium-wavelength region, where light appears green, and the third in the long-wavelength region, where light appears red. Each of the receptor types is, in itself, "color blind" in the sense that no single receptor could distinguish between different wavelengths of light. But because the three receptor functions overlap, any given wavelength would stimulate the three receptor systems to different degrees. Helmholtz proposed that the pattern of activation across the three receptor types determined the perceived color (see Figure 3.2.8).

This three-receptor theory is able to account for many important phenomena of color vision. The fact that there are three dimensions in color space is explained by the existence of the three types of receptors. The fact that three colors are sufficient to match any

perceived color can also be explained by the existence of the three receptor types, plus the pattern-of-activation hypothesis. Metamers arise simply because exactly the same pattern of activation across the three receptor types can be produced by many physically distinct combinations of wavelengths.

Trichromatic theory is also able to explain the basic varieties of color blindness. The three categories of dichromacy arise through the absence of one of the three receptor types. Protanopes lack the long wavelength receptors, deuteranopes the medium wavelength receptors, and tritanopes the short wavelength receptors. Monochromats would arise through the absence of any two of the three receptor types. Trichromatic theory was successful because it was able to explain many facts from a few relatively simple underlying assumptions. As a result, it dominated the field of color perception for over a century.

Opponent Process Theory. Despite the considerable successes of trichromatic theory, there were some facts and observations that it did *not* explain very well, particularly those concerning the *phenomenology* of color perception: the nature of people's subjective color experiences. Many of these facts were marshalled

Figure 3.2.9 Ewald Hering. Hering proposed the opponent process theory to account for subjective aspects of color vision (From Goldstein, 1989.)

against trichromatic theory by Ewald Hering (see Figure 3.2.9), who used them as the cornerstones of his competing **opponent process theory** (Hering, 1878/1964).

Perhaps the most striking phenomenological shortcoming of trichromatic theory is that, although it is brilliantly successful at accounting for the existence of the three forms of dichromatic color blindness, it provides no explanation of why color experiences are always lost in certain pairs: Either red and green or blue and yellow always disappear together. Colors are never lost singly (just red or just blue or just green), as one would expect from standard trichromatic theory, nor are they lost in other pairings, such as red and blue or green and yellow. These certainly seem to be important facts, yet trichromatic theory fails to provide an adequate explanation.

Another puzzle for trichromatic theory concerns the phenomenology of primary colors. Young and Helmholtz hypothesized just three primary colors—red, green, and blue—corresponding to the peaks in the proposed receptor activity functions. These colors seem to be subjectively "pure" in the sense that none looks like a combination or mixture of other colors, in the way orange looks like the mixture of red and yellow or the way purple looks like the mixture of red and blue.[6] In trichromatic theory, yellow is not a primary color but is analyzed as the additive mixture of red and green primaries.

The trouble with this explanation of yellow is that it simply does not square with the phenomenological facts. The subjective experience of yellow does not appear to be a mixture of red and green in anything like the sense that the subjective experience of purple looks like the mixture of red and blue. Rather, yellow seems to be psychologically just as "primary" as red, green, and blue. This fact about color experience is hard to deny, yet trichromatic theory again fails to provide an adequate explanation.

A related observation concerns the phenomenology of color mixture. Even though trichromatic theory can explain the mixtures people use to match colors, it cannot account for the absence of particular "mixture experiences." As we just mentioned, there are colors that appear to be both red and blue (purples), both red and yellow (oranges), both blue and green (blue-greens), and both yellow and green (yellow-greens). This covers all pairings of these four colors except for two: There is no color that is subjectively the combination of red and green, nor is there any that is subjectively the combination of blue and yellow (assuming that we discount experience based on knowing that green paint results from mixing blue and yellow paint). Like the pairwise loss of color experiences in color blindness, this observation suggests some kind of pairwise polarity between red and green and between blue and yellow. Further evidence for polar opposites among colors comes from color

---

[6] Some people think that green looks like a mixture of blue and yellow, but this belief almost certainly comes from experience mixing paints. Although there are surely yellow-greens and blue-greens, there is also a pure green that appears to contain neither yellowness nor blueness to people who are inexperienced in mixing paints.

Color Vision

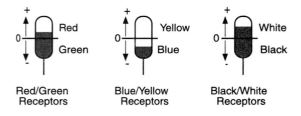

Figure 3.2.10 Hering's opponent process theory of color vision. Hering suggested that three types of receptors could respond in two opposite directions (+ versus −) from a neutral point (0) to signal red versus green, blue versus yellow, and black versus white.

afterimages and induced colors. Again, trichromatic theory does not provide a convincing explanation of these phenomena.

On the basis of these and other observations, Hering became convinced that there are *four* chromatic primaries rather than three and that they are structured into pairs of polar opposites: red versus green and blue versus yellow. He therefore formulated his opponent process theory of color vision with these ideas at its center.

Hering agreed with Helmholtz that the color processing system was based on three primitive mechanisms but disagreed on nearly everything else. Hering's three components are *opponent* mechanisms.[7] One responds oppositely to red and green, the second responds oppositely to yellow and blue, and the third (the achromatic system) responds oppositely to white and black (see Figure 3.2.10). Hering believed that this form of color processing occurred at the receptor level and that the polarity was caused by the buildup and breakdown of retinal chemicals. For example, a chemical might build up in the retina to cause a red experience, and that same chemical might be broken down to cause a green experience.

Hering's opponent process theory neatly accounts for the phenomenological facts from which he started. It explains the psychologically primary status of red, green, blue, and yellow because these are indeed the four chromatic primaries in this theory. It likewise ac-

counts for the simultaneous disappearance of red/green and blue/yellow in color blindness because each pair is part of a single mechanism. Hering theorized that colors produce complementary aftereffects because sustained activity in one element of the system (for example, red) depleted its underlying biological mechanism and thus shifted the balance in favor of its opponent element (green). Induced colors due to simultaneous contrast can be explained by analogous mechanisms operating across space rather than across time. Thus, Hering's theory explained many phenomena that trichromatic theory could not, and it did so in an economical and elegant fashion.

Dual Process Theory. For many decades there were heated debates between two warring factions. Helmholtz's advocates cited the importance of the objective behavioral evidence their theory could predict and criticized the subjectivity of Hering's approach. Hering's advocates retaliated by citing the deficiencies of Helmholtz's theory. The solution to this theoretical impasse came with the development of a two-stage theory of color vision—often called **dual process theory**—that resolved the Helmholtz/Hering controversy in an elegant but unexpected way: Both theories were correct, but for different stages of visual processing. This idea was foreshadowed by von Kries (1905) and was developed more fully in the 1920s by Müller and Schrödinger. But the complete theoretical synthesis did not occur until 1957, when psychologists Leo Hurvich and Dorthea Jameson proposed a precise, testable formulation of a theory based on two sequential stages of color processing.

Hurvich and Jameson began by measuring Hering-type opponent processes quantitatively. They reasoned that the amount of "blueness" in any given light could be measured by mixing it with enough of its opposite (yellow) that the resulting color appeared neither blue nor yellow. Beginning with the shortest wavelength, they determined how much yellow light was required to cancel (or neutralize or "null") the blueness of that light.

---

[7] Although red/green and blue/yellow are truly opponent pairs of colors, black/white is less clearly so. One important difference is that although there are no colors that simultaneously appear both red and green or blue

and yellow, grays simultaneously appear to contain both black and white. There is thus something qualitatively different about the achromatic dimension.

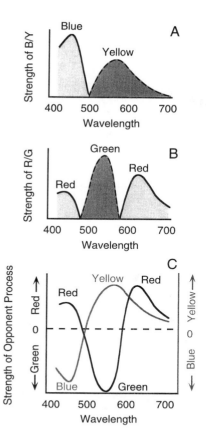

Figure 3.2.11 Results from Hurvich and Jameson's hue cancellation experiments. Graph A shows the amount of red or green required to cancel the perception of greenness or redness (respectively) in colored lights, and graph B shows the amount of blue or yellow required to cancel the perception of yellowness or blueness (respectively). Graph C shows the two curves together as opponent processes. (After Hurvich & Jameson, 1957.)

When this procedure is applied to successively longer wavelengths, it generates quantitative measures of the "blueness" at each wavelength (see Figure 3.2.11A). At about 500 nm, light appears pure green, and no yellow needs to be added at all. Above 500 nm, lights look yellowish, so they measured the amount of blue light that was needed to neutralize their yellowness.

Hurvich and Jameson also used this procedure with red and green light to cancel the greenness and redness, respectively, in lights of varying wavelength with the results indicated in Figure 3.2.11B. Notice that wavelengths at both ends of the spectrum are considerably reddish. This reflects the fact that these two ends are bent toward each other in the psychological representa-

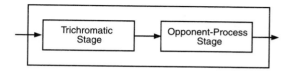

Figure 3.2.12 Hurvich and Jameson's dual process theory of color vision. An initial trichromatic stage (à la Helmholtz) provides the input for a second opponent process stage (à la Hering).

tion of color space. Both sets of results can be summarized in the single graph shown in Figure 3.2.11C. Here the opponency of the red/green and blue/yellow mechanisms is explicitly represented by making the y axis bipolar and arbitrarily assigning one of each pair to the positive direction.

In working with quantitative formulations of opponent process theory and their relation to trichromatic theory, Hurvich and Jameson realized that Helmholtz's and Hering's theories are not necessarily in conflict— provided one disregards Hering's claim that the opponent process mechanism resides in the receptors. In an elegant theoretical synthesis, they determined how two different stages of color processing might be able to account for a wide variety of findings. A version of Helmholtz's trichromatic theory formed the first stage of this dual process theory. Its output became the input to the second stage, which was a version of Hering's opponent process theory. Hurvich and Jameson's theory is diagrammed in Figure 3.2.12. It explains not only both sets of phenomena, but also Hurvich and Jameson's own quantitative measurements of the opponent structure of color experiences as described above.

Both stages of this dual process theory are now known to be performed in the retina itself. But it is important to realize that the crucial theorizing by Helmholtz, Hering, Hurvich, and Jameson about the mechanisms of color vision all transpired *before* the relevant physiology was known. This has often been the case in perceptual research. Theories that are based on strictly behavioral analyses have frequently (but not always) preceded knowledge of the underlying physiological mechanisms. One critical factor in this sequence of events is obviously the order in which the required technologies became available. A behavioral analysis can be accomplished with psychophysical and phenomenological techniques,

Color Vision

both of which have been around for more than a century. By contrast, the physiological techniques needed for studying biological mechanisms have existed for a few decades at most, with new methods being developed all the time.

But there may be a second factor at work, one that is related to Marr's (1982) three levels and Palmer and Kimchi's (1986) assumption of recursive decomposition discussed in Chapter 2. It is generally easier to work from the more abstract functional level downward toward the physical implementation than to work in the reverse direction. With an algorithmic theory in hand that has been decomposed to a quasi-neural level, physiologists know what to look for in their studies and how to interpret their results when they get them. Without such a functional theory as a guide, biological data can be accumulated, but their theoretical meaning is unclear. (We will encounter a fascinating example of this situation in Chapter 4 when we discuss the cortical cells in area V1 studied by Hubel and Wiesel.) In the case of color vision, functional theories came first, so once physiologists had the requisite tools, they knew what to look for.

3.2.3 Physiological Mechanisms

Anatomical and physiological techniques that are capable of revealing the selective processing of wavelength information in the eye and brain were developed in the 1950s, and researchers immediately began to look for evidence of the Helmholtzian trichromatic theory in the retina. Despite the cogency of Hering's arguments for his opponent process theory and despite the elegance of Hurvich and Jameson's synthesis of the two opposing theories, the Zeitgeist was such that few researchers expected to find compelling evidence of opponent mechanisms in the color vision system, much less in the retina itself. One of the great virtues of science, however, is that experimental results can defy expectations, forcing researchers to change their minds about theories.

Three Cone Systems. In Chapter 1, we briefly remarked that the photoreceptors that are responsible for color vision are the cones rather than the rods. It turns out that there are, as G. Palmer, Young, and Helmholtz predicted, three types of cones in the normal trichromat's retina, each of which contains a different light-

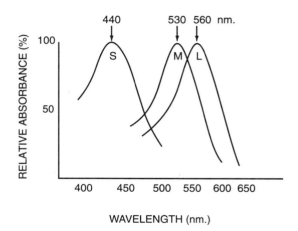

Figure 3.2.13 Neural response curves for the three types of cones. Short- (S), medium- (M), and long- (L) wavelength cones provide overlapping but differential responses to light of different wavelengths, as predicted by trichromatic theory. These curves are defined by the absorption spectra of the three pigments found in normal cones. (After Schnapf, Kraft, & Baylor, 1987.)

absorbing pigment. Using several techniques, measurements have been made of the **absorption spectra** of these three cone types to determine the percentage of light absorbed for each wavelength of light over the visible spectrum (Brown & Wald, 1964; Marks, Dobelle, & MacNichol, 1964). The results converge on the three overlapping functions graphed in Figure 3.2.13. The *short-wavelength* (or *S*) *cones* absorb maximally at about 440 nm, the *medium-wavelength* (or *M*) *cones* at about 530 nm, and the *long-wavelength* (or *L*) *cones* at about 560 nm (Schnapf, Kraft, & Baylor, 1987). The number of each type and their spatial distribution over the retina are not uniform, however. The S cones account for only about 5–10% of the population, and psychophysical data suggest that there are about twice as many L cones as M cones. The ratio of L to M to S cones therefore appears to be decidedly nonuniform: about 10 : 5 : 1 (De Valois & De Valois, 1993). Moreover, the receptors in the central 0.1° of the fovea are almost exclusively M and L cones, the proportion of S cones increasing to about 6% at 1.0° from the center.

These three cone types—sometimes misleadingly called blue, green, and red cones—work very much the way Helmholtz envisioned; only the details of the absorption spectra are different. As Helmholtz also predicted, people who are color blind lack one or more of these three cone types. Protanopes are missing the L cones, deuteranopes the M cones, and tritanopes the S cones.[8] Anomalous trichromats have three functioning cone systems, but the pigments in either the M or L cones (or both) appear to be different from those in so-called "normal" trichromats. Sometimes, the spectral absorption function of the M cone pigment is shifted toward that of the L cone pigment, and sometimes the reverse happens (Neitz, Neitz, & Jacobs, 1993). The result is a functioning trichromat whose color mixture matches are different from those of normal trichromats to a degree that depends on the particular pigments they have.

Color Opponent Cells. The discovery of cone types that corresponded to Helmholtz's trichromatic theory was not the final word in the debate over the mechanisms of color vision, however. Physiological psychologist Russell De Valois (1965) and his colleagues (De Valois, Abramov, & Jacobs, 1966) measured responses in the LGN of macaque monkeys and discovered color-selective cells whose responses to wavelengths of light were incompatible with trichromatic theory but conformed roughly to the pattern predicted by Hering's opponent process theory. Some were excited by red light and inhibited by green (R^+G^- *cells*), as illustrated in Figure 3.2.14A. Others responded in the opposite way, exciting to green and inhibiting to red (G^+R^- *cells*). In addition, they found cells that were excited by yellow and inhibited by blue (Y^+B^- *cells*) as well as ones showing the reverse pattern of responses (B^+Y^- *cells*), as shown in Figure 3.2.14B. Still other cells were not spectrally opponent at all, some being excited by all wavelengths of light and inhibited by their absence (Wh^+Bl^- *cells*) and others being excited by the absence of light and inhibited by its presence (Bl^+Wh^- *cells*), as graphed in Figure 3.2.14C. Together, these LGN cells can reasonably be interpreted as a neural implementation of Hering's opponent process theory. Further research has shown that these patterns of response are also present in the bipolar and ganglion cells of the retina.

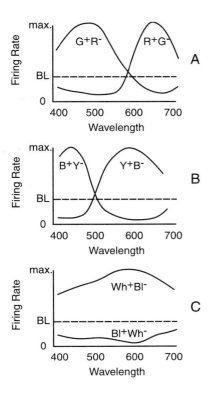

Figure 3.2.14 Neural response curves of opponent process cells. The relative firing rates for R^+G^-, G^+R^-, B^+Y^-, Y^+B^-, Wh^+Bk^-, and Bk^+Wh^- cells in macaque monkey LGN are plotted as a function of wavelength. (After De Valois, et al., 1966.)

Given the opponent responses of these cells, one can ask how they are derived from the outputs of the three cone systems. Somewhat surprisingly, this is not yet known with certainty, but a number of similar theories have been proposed that match the physiological data reasonably well. One neural network theory that specifies the recombination of cone outputs is diagrammed in Figure 3.2.15 (De Valois, 1965; De Valois, Abramov, & Jacobs, 1968). It shows that the output of R^+G^- opponent cells can be derived by combining excitatory input from the L cones and the inhibitory input from M cones, essentially computing the difference between the output of these two cone systems (L − M). The output of the

---

[8] Dichromats do not actually have fewer receptors, as they would if one class of cones were completely absent. Studies show that protanopes and deuteranopes have as many foveal cones as normal trichromats (Cicerone & Nerger, 1989), but the pigment that is normally associated with the L or M cone type is replaced by the pigment appropriate to the other cone type.

Color Vision

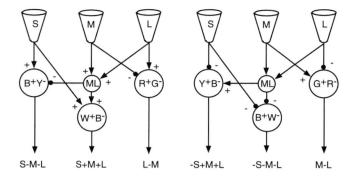

S-M-L   S+M+L   L-M   -S+M+L   -S-M-L   M-L

Figure 3.2.15 Possible neural circuits for dual process theory. Opponent responses are derived from S, M, and L cone outputs by excitatory connections (arrows) and inhibitory connections (solid dots). The ML units encode the sum of activities in the M and L cones.

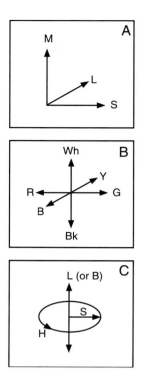

Figure 3.2.16 Reparameterizing color space. (A) The initial trichromatic representation of color is based on dimensions that are defined by the outputs of the short- (S), medium- (M), and long- (L) wavelength cones. (B) The opponent process representation is based on the three opponent dimensions of red/green, blue/yellow, and black/white. (C) The third representation is based on the three dimensions of hue (H), saturation (S), and lightness (L) or brightness (B).

opposite G^+R^- cells can be derived by combining the excitatory input from the M cones with the inhibitory input from the L cones $(M - L)$. The B^+Y^- opponent cells can likewise be derived from the excitatory output of S cones and the inhibitory sum of the M and L cone outputs $(S - (M + L) = S - M - L)$, and the Y^+B^- opponent cells can be derived from the excitatory sum of the M and L cones and the inhibitory output of the S cones $((M + L) - S = M + L - S)$. The Wh^+Bl^- cells can be derived by summing the excitation from all three cone types $(S + M + L)$, and the Bl^+Wh^- cells can be derived from summing the inhibitory output from all three cone types $(-S - M - L)$.

This two-stage model of color vision is an elegant synthesis that accounts for many facts with few assumptions. Even so, there are residual problems, suggesting that further modifications will be required. Most of them concern the short-wavelength (blue) end of the spectrum, where the response of opponent cells does not agree very well with corresponding perceptual data. It is not clear, for example, why the shortest wavelengths of the spectrum (in the violet range) should appear reddish if the red/green channel is defined exclusively by the difference between M and L cones (e.g., compare the red/green data in Figure 3.2.11C with the R^+G^- firing rates in Figure 3.2.14A). De Valois and De Valois (1993) have recently proposed a four-stage model of color vision that attempts to explain some of the discrepancies with a more complex system of transformations that extend into visual cortex.

Reparameterization in Color Processing. The two initial steps in color processing we have just considered constitute a very simple example of how an information processing system begins with one representation and then transforms it into another representation, as we discussed in Chapter 2. The initial representation is the trichromatic one in which each physical combination of wavelengths gets mapped into a three-dimensional color space whose axes are defined by the outputs of S, M, and L cones, as shown in Figure 3.2.16A. The simple algebraic sums and differences in Figure 3.2.15 produce an opponent representation that transforms the color space by redefining its axes in terms of the responses of the black/white, red/green, and blue/yellow cells, as indicated in Figure 3.2.16B. Assuming that there is also a later cortical representation in terms of hue, saturation, and lightness—as the phenomenology of color perception suggests—then the red/green and blue/yellow axes must be further transformed into hue and saturation, as diagrammed in Figure 3.2.16C.

The effect of these transformations is to **reparameterize** the three-dimensional color space so that different—and evolutionarily more useful—information is made explicit in successively higher levels of representation. Reparameterization is the process of changing the variables that directly control a system's behavior. Its long name makes it sounds like a complicated and esoteric concept, but you are already familiar with several everyday examples.

The plumbing system in your house carries hot and cold water to your sink in separate pipes. In the simplest arrangement, the flow of hot and cold water is controlled independently by two separate faucets. However, many modern faucets transform this two-dimensional control system into a different one that is more convenient for normal use. One control function (say, forward versus backward position of a single lever) regulates the overall volume of water (hot + cold), and the other (say, left versus right) regulates its temperature balance (hot − cold). A similar kind of reparameterization occurs in your stereo system. The magnitude of the signals in the left and right speaker channels are processed independently inside your stereo, but instead of separate knobs for each channel, there is one knob for overall volume (left + right) and another knob for balance (left − right). The transformation from the output of the three cone systems (S, M, and L) to the output of the three ganglion systems (R/G, B/Y, and Bl/Wh) constitutes a similar reparameterization. The Bl/Wh system represents the overall "volume" of light, while the R/G and B/Y systems represent two dimensions of the "chromatic balance" of light.

Why might the visual system contain three different color representations? The answer is that different representations provide information that is useful for different purposes. The trichromatic representation is useful because it is an efficient and effective way to extract information about the spectral composition of light in physical receptor systems. Unfortunately, it is not very useful to the perceiving organism. The opponent representation is more useful because it helps determine which differences between adjacent retinal regions result

from changes in the level of illumination (such as when a shadow falls across a surface) and which result from changes in spectral reflectance (such as when a surface is painted two different colors). Changes in the amount of illumination will generally just raise or lower the overall amount of light (that is, change the output of the Bl/Wh system) while the chromatic balance remains constant (that is, the outputs of the R/G and B/Y systems are invariant). Changes in the spectral reflectance of a surface, however, will generally change the output of at least one of the two chromatic systems substantially and may or may not change the overall amount of light as well. It is not entirely clear what advantage the hue/saturation representation might have over the red/green, blue/yellow opponent process representation, although it would be useful for determining which chromatic changes result merely from variations in the density of the same pigments in surfaces and which from changes in the pigments themselves.

Lateral Inhibition. The physiological mechanisms discussed thus far are capable of explaining many of the phenomena we have considered, but something more is needed to understand brightness contrast and simultaneous color contrast effects. These can be understood only by positing some kind of spatial interaction between neighboring regions of the retina. A possible mechanism for such effects is **lateral inhibition**, one of the most pervasive architectures in the visual nervous system. It is encountered in the first few layers of the retina and is thought by many to be responsible for Mach bands and simultaneous color contrast (e.g., Ratliff, 1965).

Lateral inhibition refers to an architecture for neural networks in which neurons inhibit spatially neighboring neurons. Figure 3.2.17 illustrates a simplified model of lateral inhibition in a one-dimensional neural network. Lateral inhibition occurs in a two-layer network when each neuron in the first layer excites a corresponding neuron (or set of neurons) in the second layer but inhibits the second-layer neurons lateral to the excitatory connection. In this diagram, excitatory connections (arrowheads) between layers are indicated by positive numbers, and inhibitory connections (black dots) are indicated by negative numbers. As with most neural network models, the output of a target neuron is calculated

Color Vision

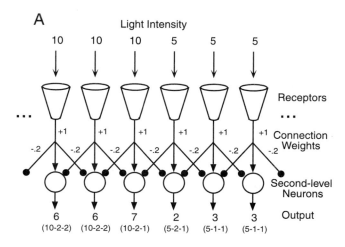

A

Light Intensity

10 10 10 5 5 5

Receptors

Connection Weights

+1 +1 +1 +1 +1 +1
-.2 -.2 -.2 -.2 -.2 -.2 -.2

Second-level Neurons

Output

6 6 7 2 3 3
(10-2-2) (10-2-2) (10-2-1) (5-2-1) (5-1-1) (5-1-1)

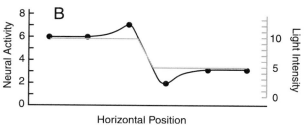

B

Figure 3.2.17 A lateral inhibitory network exhibiting contrast effects. (A) Each receptor excites a spatially corresponding neuron in the second layer (the +1 arrow connection) and inhibits its nearest neighbor on both sides (the −.2 dot connections). (B) A graph of stimulus intensity (gray curve) and neural activity from this network (black curve) is plotted as a function of horizontal position. Notice the enhanced response on both sides of the intensity transition, similar to Mach bands (see Figure 3.2.6).

by multiplying the activation of each of its input neurons by the weight of its connection to the target neuron and summing these products over all inputs. When you do this for the lateral inhibitory network shown here, using the input luminances given above the "receptor" neurons, the resulting pattern of outputs from the second layer show a Mach band phenomenon. Thus, this neural network simulates the perception of Mach bands under appropriate conditions.

Because the lateral inhibition network we have just considered is only one-dimensional, it is unrealistic as a model of retinal processing. Lateral inhibition can be implemented in a two-dimensional structure, however, simply by rotating the one-dimensional structure through a second spatial dimension, as indicated in

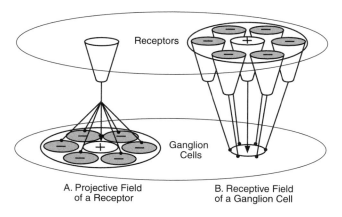

Figure 3.2.18 Projective and receptive fields of 2-D lateral inhibitory networks. (A) A single receptor projects to many ganglion cells in a center/surround organization. (B) Each ganglion cell receiving such connections therefore has a center/surround receptive field. The illustrated network exhibits an excitatory center and inhibitory surround, but the opposite organization (inhibitory center and excitatory surround) also exists in the retina.

Figure 3.2.18A. The result is a rotationally symmetric network in which the lateral inhibition emanating from a given receptor cell spreads out in all directions from the excitatory center. We will call this pattern of connections its **projective field** (cf. Lehky & Sejnowski, 1988).

If we now examine the connections in the opposite direction, from all receptors to a given cell—called its **receptive field**—we can determine the spatial pattern to which it will be maximally responsive. In the case of a two-dimensional lateral inhibitory network, we find that it has what is called a **center-surround organization**, as depicted in Figure 3.2.18B. That is, cells in the second layer will respond most vigorously to a pattern in which there is a bright spot activating its excitatory center and a dark ring surrounding the spot. Notice that if the whole receptive field were stimulated equally by a homogeneous field of light, the inhibitory surround would *reduce* the response of the second-layer cells. It turns out that the ganglion cells of many mammalian retinas have a center-surround organization just like this. In Chapter 4 we will discuss the receptive field structure of retinal ganglion cells in more detail.

Many theorists believe that such a lateral inhibitory architecture can account for simultaneous lightness contrast effects as well as Mach bands. If the conditions

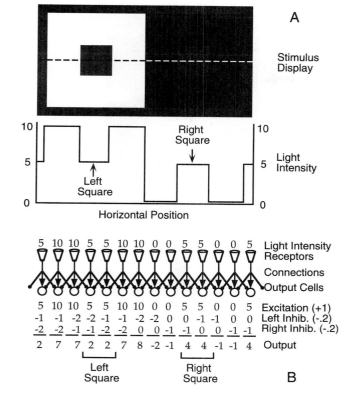

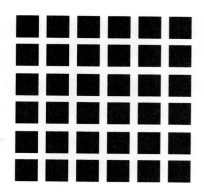

Figure 3.2.20 The Hermann grid illusion. Illusory dark spots appear at all intersections of the white stripes except the one on which you are currently fixated.

Figure 3.2.19 Lateral inhibition and lightness contrast. (A) A lightness contrast stimulus is shown above its luminance profile through the center (dashed line). Notice that the two central squares have the same physical intensity even though they appear different in lightness. (B) A lateral inhibitory network whose output predicts that the left square will look darker than the right square.

of lightness contrast are simulated by using a one-dimensional luminance profile of the appropriate shape, a contrastlike effect due to lateral inhibition is obtained, as shown in Figure 3.2.19. The test area inside the light surround is strongly inhibited because of the high luminance from the lateral surround. This causes inhibition of the test area, and it is therefore perceived as darker. No similar effect occurs for the test area in the dark surround, because the luminance from the dark surround is so low that it does not inhibit the test area. Thus, this lateral inhibitory network predicts that the test square in the light surround should appear darker than the one in the dark surround. This is consistent with the phenomenon of lightness contrast illustrated in Figure 3.2.5.

A major problem for this theory is that it is unclear whether lateral inhibition actually operates over distances as large as those for which simultaneous contrast effects are found. Lateral inhibition in the retina typically extends over only small fractions of a degree of visual angle, whereas simultaneous contrast effects can span $10°$ or more. One possibility is that lateral inhibition at higher levels of the visual system extends over much larger distances. Another is that there may be contrast effects only near the edges but some additional mechanism may extend this effect into the center of the region.

There are other contrast phenomena that might also be explained by this lateral inhibitory architecture. One is the fascinating Hermann grid illusion (see Figure 3.2.20), in which illusory dark spots seem to occupy the light intersections. You can convince yourself that the dark spots are indeed illusory because when you look directly at an intersection, the spot disappears. That is, dark spots appear at every intersection except the one on which you are fixated.

The perception of the dark spots can be simulated by a lateral inhibitory network because the amount of inhibition at the light intersections is appreciably greater than that in other light regions. Each intersection is surrounded by light regions on *four* sides, in contrast to just *two* in other places (see Figure 3.2.21). The fact that dark spots do not appear when you look at them directly can be explained if there is less lateral inhibition in the fovea than in the periphery. "Less" could mean either inhibitory weights closer to zero or less lateral spread of

Color Vision

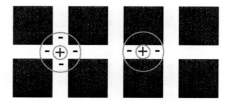

Figure 3.2.21 Applying lateral inhibitory networks to the Hermann grid illusion. An excitatory-center, inhibitory-surround cell at the intersections will receive more inhibition than similar cells at other places along the white stripes.

inhibition, or both. The degree of lateral spread of inhibition thus turns out to be an important issue in accounting for contrast effect and is currently a matter of some controversy.

There are also contrast effects for which accounts based on lateral inhibition at retinal levels are highly implausible, however. Figure 3.2.22 shows one compelling example (Todorovic, 1997). The upper circle appears a good deal darker than the lower circle, even though they are exactly the same in lightness. At first glance, it seems to be just another example of simultaneous lightness contrast. But notice that the circle that looks darker is bordered mainly by the four *black* squares, and the one that appears lighter is bordered mainly by the four *white* squares. This is exactly the opposite of what would be predicted from lateral inhibition mechanisms working on this image. The obtained effect suggests that a more sophisticated mechanism underlies lightness contrast, one that is based on complex organizational factors such as those studied by Gestalt psychologists (e.g., Benary, 1924). The contrast with the four surrounding squares seems to be irrelevant because they are perceived to lie in a depth plane in front of that containing the circle and its ground. The relevant contrast is that between the circle and its coplanar background: The upper circle looks darker because it is seen in contrast to the white background, and the lower circle looks lighter because it is seen in contrast to the black background. Lateral inhibition may play some role in the neural mechanisms underlying this contrast effect, but it cannot operate at on a flat, image-based representation as implied above.

An even more surprising example of organizationally induced contrast effects has recently been reported by Agostini and Proffitt (1993). Subjects were shown a field

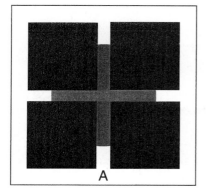

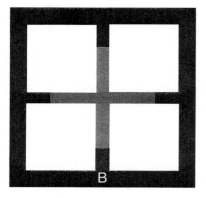

Figure 3.2.22 A lightness illusion. Two circles of equal lightness are shown with four large squares occluding them. The circle on the light background (A) looks darker than the one on the dark background (B) even though contrast effects due to the large occluding squares predict the opposite result. (After Todorovic, 1997.)

of many black dots and one gray dot moving in one direction and a field of many white dots and one gray dot moving in another direction. The two gray dots were the same shade of gray and appeared equally dark when the dots were stationary. But when the dots began to move, the gray dot that moved with the white dots was perceived to be darker than the gray dot that moved with the black dots. Because all the dots were seen against the same background and because the effect arose only when the dots were in motion, standard theories based on lateral inhibition cannot explain this effect. Rather, it appears to depend on whether the gray dots are perceived as belonging with the white dots or the black ones because of their common motion. (We will return to this topic of perceptual organization and grouping by common properties in Chapter 6.) Such organizational effects may someday be integrated into a theory that employs lateral inhibition as a mechanism for lightness and brightness contrast, but they cannot be explained by the simple neural networks that have been proposed thus far.

Adaptation and Aftereffects. Chromatic adaptation is very much like achromatic light adaptation. Both produce reduced sensitivity to light after prolonged exposure to an unchanging stimulus by temporarily depleting resources in the visual system. The biological processes underlying light adaptation are just the reverse of those involved in dark adaptation (see Section 1.3.2). When you come out of a darkened theater or room into bright sunlight, you initially experience blinding brightness because the long period of dark adaptation has put most of the photosensitive pigment molecules in both rods and cones into their maximally sensitive state, ready to be bleached by photons. When you first step out into the sun, therefore, receptors fire much more strongly than usual because of their hypersensitive state, and many more of them begin firing. Continued exposure to the bright sunlight then causes light adaptation, during which a huge number of the photopigment molecules are bleached. This massive bleaching puts the receptors into a less sensitive state and greatly reduces their response to light. Light adaptation thus allows you to see normally in brightly lighted conditions.

In the case of chromatic adaptation, a vividly colored stimulus reduces sensitivity to different degrees in the three cone systems. In response to the yellow Ping-Pong ball, for example, the greatest reduction would be in the M and L cones, with little adaptation in the S cones. This occurs by selective bleaching of the photopigment molecules that are most likely to absorb the photons coming from the adapting stimulus. Further adaptation takes place in later cells of the visual system as well (Mollon & Polden, 1979). The result is that, over time, the activity in the chromatic system shifts away from the perception of the adapting stimulus. In the case of a Ganzfeld, it eventually reaches equilibrium at firing rates that normally signal neutral gray. That is why the yellow Ping-Pong ball looks gray after extended chromatic adaptation.

Chromatic afterimages are closely related to chromatic adaptation. Viewing any highly saturated color for a long time with fixed gaze causes a tendency to per-

ceive the opposite (complementary) hue in the corresponding retinal region in response to a neutral (white) test field. Thus, adaptation to the green, black, and yellow flag (see Color Plate 2.1) produces an afterimage of a desaturated red, white, and blue flag when viewed against a white background. Color afterimages demonstrate the essential features of all aftereffects as well as their relation to adaptation. Prolonged exposure to an intense stimulus causes adaptation to that specific form of stimulation, selectively and temporarily lowering visual sensitivity to that stimulus. During this period of lowered sensitivity, the opposite of the adapted stimulus tends to be perceived in response to objectively neutral stimuli, such as the white test field in the case of chromatic afterimages.

How do chromatic afterimages arise physiologically? Not surprisingly, they appear to result from temporal changes in the response of color-sensitive neurons following prolonged stimulation. To illustrate, consider the situation in which the retina is being stimulated with a circle of highly saturated red for a long time. After an extended period of intense firing, the R^+G^- opponent cells for this region of the retina will temporarily become less responsive. In addition, the corresponding G^+R^- cells will be somewhat *more* responsive after a long period of constant inhibition. These changes are illustrated schematically in Figure 3.2.23.

During the time of altered sensitivity, chromatic afterimages will be experienced under suitable conditions. If the red circle is replaced by neutral white stimulation, for example, the greatly fatigued R^+G^- cells will fire less strongly to the white light than usual, and the G^+R^- cells will be somewhat more active because of their release from inhibition. The net result is that the balance between the R^+G^- and G^+R^- cells will be decidedly different from neutral in those cells that code color in the adapted region of the retina. In particular, there will be relatively more activity in the G^+R^- system than in the R^+G^- system. Normally, these two outputs are balanced in response to neutral white light. The pattern of activity that occurs after adaptation, however, normally signals the presence of light green, so that is what you experience as the aftereffect of prolonged viewing of the saturated red patch.

Double Opponent Cells. Chromatic color contrast is generally thought to result from the operation of so-

Color Vision

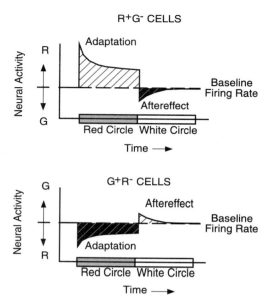

Figure 3.2.23 A neural theory of chromatic adaptation and aftereffects. Opponent process cells show diminished activation and inhibition (adaptation) after prolonged exposure to a red circle. When a white circle is then presented, a negative aftereffect in neural activity produces chromatic afterimages of the complementary hue that diminish over time as equilibrium is restored.

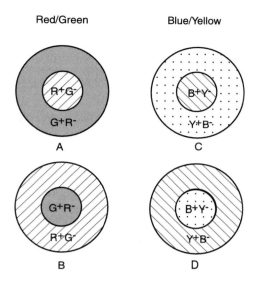

Figure 3.2.24 Receptive fields of double opponent cells. Some cells in area V1 of cortex show spatial opponency in their center/surround organization as well as chromatic opponency in their bipolar response to red/green or blue/yellow in their center and surround.

called **double opponent cells** found in visual cortex (Michael, 1978). Double opponent cells have a spatially opponent center-surround organization similar to those just described in accounting for brightness and lightness contrast, but they also have a chromatically opponent structure, as illustrated in Figure 3.2.24. In other words, the centers and the surrounds both have color opponent coding, and the surround colors are opponent to the center colors. Thus, a red/green double opponent cell would be excitatory to red and inhibitory to green (R^+G^-) in the center and excitatory to green and inhibitory to red (G^+R^-) in the surround, or vice versa. A blue/yellow double opponent cell would be excitatory to blue and inhibitory to yellow (B^+Y^-) in the center and excitatory to yellow and inhibitory to blue (Y^+B^-) in the surround, or vice versa. If you add to these the achromatic center-surround cells—excitatory to white and inhibitory to black (Wh^+Bl^-) in the center and excitatory to black and inhibitory to white (Bl^+Wh^-) in the surround (or vice versa)—there are spatially opponent cells for all opponent pairs in Hering's opponent process theory. These may well provide the basis for simultaneous color contrast effects.

To see how such double opponent cells might account for chromatic color contrast, consider why the part of a gray circle that is surrounded by a highly saturated green might appear pinkish (see Color Plate 3.7). First consider the output of the red-center/green-surround cells centered on the gray region. They will tend to fire much more vigorously than they would to a more extended gray region because the green from the surrounding region will fall on their surround. This extra activity in the cells with an R^+G^- center and G^+R^- surround (Figure 3.2.24A) should cause the central gray region to appear pinkish, as it does. The greenish appearance of the part of the gray circle within a saturated red surround can be explained in an analogous fashion, appealing to activation of the cells with a G^+R^- center and R^+G^- surround (Figure 3.2.24B) owing to the intense red surround. The same theory can account for blue/yellow contrast effects in the same way. Other chromatic color contrasts can be explained as appropriate mixtures of these basic effects.

Higher Cortical Mechanisms. As we hinted above, it is plausible to suppose that there is a third neural stage somewhere in the brain that recombines the output of the red/green and blue/yellow opponent systems into dimensions that correspond to hue and saturation. (Brightness or lightness is already represented by the black/white system.) This is currently mere speculation because nobody has yet found cortical cells that represent color according to this scheme. However, the fact that hue, saturation, and lightness dominate the subjective experience of color perception suggests that a corresponding neural structure will eventually be found.

Present knowledge of higher cortical processing comes mainly from neuropsychological observations. Damage to certain areas of cerebral cortex in humans produces different kinds of deficits in color processing, all of which are distinct from normal color blindness. One kind of color perception impairment, called **achromatopsia**, results in a syndrome in which patients complain of not being able to see colors, as though they were looking at the world on a black-and-white TV, or report that colors have lost their vividness (Meadows, 1974). The deficit may affect the entire visual field or just a part of it. The correlated neural damage is located in an area of prestriate cortex, just in front of primary visual cortex, perhaps corresponding to the color processing areas that have been identified in prestriate cortex of monkeys (Zeki, 1980).

Achromatopsia is quite different from color blindness caused by lack of one or more cone types. In one particularly revealing case, an achromatopsic patient demonstrated normal spectral sensitivities in threshold tasks that measured the functioning of the three cone systems but was still unable to match, sort, or name colors that were presented at levels well above threshold (Mollon, Newcombe, Polden, & Ratcliff, 1980). Such patients typically can name the characteristic colors of objects from memory (for example, "the sky is blue" and "bananas are yellow") but cannot color them correctly in an outline drawing because they cannot select the appropriate crayon. Therefore, the problem seems to be that cortical damage has affected a part of the brain that makes use of the color information that is initially registered in the retinal cones, while leaving intact cognitive knowledge about the characteristic color of objects.

A second form of high-level perceptual dysfunction resulting from cortical lesions are deficits in color knowledge (Kinsbourne & Warrington, 1964). Although such patients can identify colors, they do not know what colors objects should be. They may also be unable to color a line drawing properly, but the reason is that they simply do not know which colors are appropriate for which objects. If told the correct color, they can select the right crayon and color the drawing correctly. This problem is often accompanied by linguistic difficulties, a feature suggesting that its locus may be near linguistic rather than perceptual centers of the brain.

A third cortical defect related to color processing is **color anomia**, the inability to produce linguistic labels for colors (Geschwind & Fusillo, 1966). Not only do color anomics fail to name colors correctly, but they typically are unable to interpret color names properly. For example, they cannot point to the correct color when given its name. Such patients can color a line drawing appropriately if they are doing it from knowledge of characteristic object colors but cannot follow explicit verbal instructions to use specific colors by name. Color anomics can *see* colors perfectly well, as indicated by their ability to discriminate and to match them, and they also know an object's characteristic color from memory. Their impairment seems to be specific to the association between perceived colors and their linguistic labels. However, there is one documented case in which a color anomic patient was able to point correctly to colors when given their names (Davidoff & Ostergaard, 1984), a finding suggesting that there may be two related abilities located in nearby, but distinct, areas within the brain. We will consider color naming phenomena in normal perceivers at the end of this chapter when we discuss color categorization.

These cortical deficits are quite distinct from classical color deficiencies, not only because primary color processing seems to be intact, but also because they are *acquired* deficits. They usually appear suddenly after the patient has suffered a stroke or some other trauma to the brain. By contrast, classical color blindness is invariably present from birth and is clearly hereditary (Nathans, 1987, 1989).

3.2.4 Development of Color Vision

Given that color vision is genetically determined, the principal developmental questions concern how early babies begin to perceive color. What does the world look like when they open their eyes for the first time? Does it immediately appear in vivid "Technicolor," or is it a drab black-and-white affair, with color appearing only slowly after days, weeks, or months of maturation and development?

Although we still do not have final answers to these questions, it is fairly certain that two-month-old babies have fairly normal trichromatic vision. You might wonder how we know this, since babies cannot tell us how the world appears to them. They cannot tell us in words, but it turns out that they *can* tell us by their behavior in cleverly designed experiments. Over the past two decades a number of ingenious methods have been developed for discovering what babies see and hear in early infancy. One of them, the **preferential looking paradigm** (Fantz, 1958, 1965), has been used effectively to investigate color vision in very young infants.

The basic question is whether an infant can tell the difference between two colors. To find out, using the preferential looking paradigm, the infant is shown two displays, with one color on the left and the other on the right, as illustrated in Figure 3.2.25. The predominant direction of the baby's gaze during the fixed time period of a trial is judged by a hidden observer who does not know which stimulus is on which side. On half the trials, the left/right positions of the stimuli are reversed to be sure that the baby's looking preference is not merely to a particular side. The rationale for this procedure is that if the baby looks preferentially to one color or the other— it makes no difference which one—the baby must be able to see some difference between them. Otherwise, he or she would have no basis for looking at one longer than the other.

The color vision of very young infants has been studied by using this and similar methods to determine whether or not babies can discriminate particular pairs of colors. The results indicate that by two months of age, all three cone systems seem to be functioning. Even one-month-olds clearly have some degree of color vision, but it is as yet unclear whether they are full trichromats. They seem unable to discriminate yellow-greens or mid-purples from white (Teller, Peeples, & Sekel, 1978). This finding suggests that babies may have a weakness in their short-wavelength (S) cone system very early in life, but other interpretations cannot yet be ruled out. In any case, it is clear from the results of such experiments that babies do have some color perception

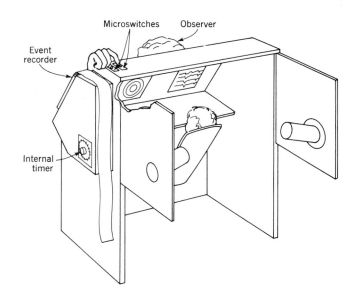

Figure 3.2.25 Experimental apparatus for preferential looking studies with infants. The direction of the baby's gaze is judged by a hidden observer. (From Fantz, 1961.)

at a very young age and that it is at least qualitatively similar to adult color vision.

3.3 Surface-Based Color Processing

The preceding description of image-based color processing provides no more than the rudimentary beginnings of an explanation of real-world color perception. Indeed, if the principles described there were applied directly to the projected retinal image of a complex environmental scene, the predictions would differ dramatically from the colors people would actually perceive. Consider the perception of grays in the picture shown in Figure 3.3.1 as an example. Virtually everyone would agree that this clapboard church is a uniform shade of white with dark gray roof shingles. Yet, if one were to calculate what shades of gray people should perceive strictly on the basis of the amount of light reflected into the eye from each region of the picture, the sides of the church would be perceived as white with gray stripes instead of uniformly colored clapboard whose overlapping arrangement causes shadows. Similarly, the regions near the corners should be perceived to be various darker shades of gray than other regions instead of being white

Figure 3.3.1 A demonstration of lightness constancy. People perceive the white siding of the church to be lighter than the dark gray shingles even when the siding is in deep shadow and the shingles are in bright sunlight. These facts cannot be explained by simple 2-D image-based color processing; they require further processing of surface orientation and illumination. (From Rock, 1984.)

but in shadow. In fact, parts of the white siding in deep shadow on the left side of the picture reflect less light than the nearly black shingles in direct sunlight, the opposite of what one would expect from the fact that the siding is white and the shingles are dark gray. This example reveals that there is a great deal more to the perception of surface color—even for simple grays—than there is to the perception of 2-D color patches as discussed in Section 3.2. The slant, texture, and illumination of surfaces in the three-dimensional world combine to produce profound effects on how we perceive surface color in real-world scenes.

When we speak about the "color" of a surface, we are talking about a psychological property attributed to an external object. Physically, surfaces are not "colored" any more than light is. The physical attribute that primarily determines the perceived color of a surface is its **reflectance spectrum**: the percentage of incident light it reflects at each wavelength. This reflectance spectrum can be graphed in much the same way as the illumination spectrum of a light, except that the y axis represents the percentage of photons reflected by the surface instead of the number of photons emitted. For opaque surfaces, the nonreflected light is absorbed by the material of which it is made. For translucent surfaces, a significant fraction of the incident light is transmitted through the material.

The reflectance spectrum (or simply the *reflectance*) of a surface is an invariant property in the sense that it does not change under different lighting or viewing conditions: It always reflects the same proportion of light at each wavelength, independent of the illumination. The reflectance spectrum of a surface is therefore a useful property for an organism to perceive if it must discriminate objects for which this is a diagnostic property, such as ripe from unripe fruit, cardinals from bluejays, redheads from brunettes, and so forth.

The problem that the visual system faces in perceiving surface color is that the light that falls on the retina—the **luminance spectrum**—is jointly determined by the reflectance spectrum of the surface and the illumination spectrum of the light that strikes the surface. You can convince yourself of this fact by considering what happens when a given surface with a constant re-

123

Color Vision

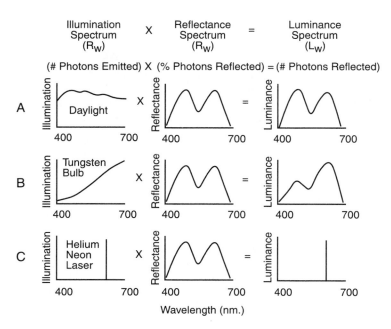

Illumination Spectrum (R_W)	X	Reflectance Spectrum (R_W)	=	Luminance Spectrum (L_W)
(# Photons Emitted)	X	(% Photons Reflected)	=	(# Photons Reflected)

Figure 3.3.2 The problem of color constancy. The same surface with the same reflectance spectrum (center column) can project greatly different luminance spectra to the eye (right column) under different kinds of illumination (left column). Color constancy requires the visual system to recover the invariant reflectance properties of surfaces despite differences in illumination.

flectance is illuminated by radically different lights, as shown in Figure 3.3.2. To compute the luminance spectrum of light in the retinal image for a given region (L_w), the number of photons in the incident light at each wavelength (I_w) must be multiplied by the percentage of light reflected by the surface at that wavelength (R_w):

$$L_w = I_w \times R_w,$$

where w represents the wavelength of light over the visible range from 400 to 700 nm. Thus, if the incident light is "white" sunlight with a flat spectrum (Figure 3.3.2A), then the luminance spectrum will mirror almost exactly the reflectance spectrum of the surface, depending only on the overall level of illumination. In this sense, the color of a surface in normal daylight is the best approximation to its "true color" (that is, its actual reflectance properties). Under the somewhat different illumination spectrum of an incandescent light bulb, the luminance spectrum of the same surface is different from its luminance spectrum in sunlight, but at least it is qualitatively similar (see Figure 3.3.2B).

Now consider what happens when the same surface is placed under a radically different light source, such as monochromatic light from a laser. Multiplying the same reflectance spectrum times the monochromatic illumination spectrum produces a grossly different luminance spectrum (Figure 3.3.2C). The projected image contains only one wavelength of light because the incident light contains only one wavelength, and nonluminous surfaces cannot add light, but only remove it by absorbing photons. This example is far more extreme than one normally encounters in the real world because monochromatic lights are exceedingly rare and never used for general purpose illumination—for reasons that should now be obvious. The same general principle holds true in real situations, however. When viewing a given surface, the luminance spectrum that reaches your eye depends not only on a surface's reflectance, but also on the illumination spectrum of light that bathes it. You can now understand why it is so important for color researchers to use very carefully controlled light sources in studying the perception of colored surfaces.

The task that the visual system faces in recovering surface reflectance is somehow to disentangle the effects of reflectance and illumination so that the invariant property of surface reflectance can be perceived despite differences due to illumination. This is another example of an inverse problem, as discussed in Chapter 1. The visual system is faced with the task of "undoing" the interaction between the illuminating light and the reflective surface to recover the intrinsic properties of the surface itself. Once again, the problem is underconstrained because the eye receives information about only one proximal variable (luminance), which is determined jointly by two distal variables (reflectance and illumination). It seems logically impossible to recover both distal variables, but we know that it can be done, at least to some approximation, because the human visual system can do it under a fairly wide range of natural conditions. Once again, we infer that the visual system must be using some additional source of information, probably in the form of clever heuristics, to accomplish this feat.

The ability to perceive the reflectance properties of surfaces despite changes in illumination and other viewing conditions is called **color constancy**. We will discuss it in two parts, considering first the simpler case of achromatic *lightness constancy* and then the additional complexities of full-blown *chromatic color constancy*. Both are examples of the general construct of **perceptual constancy**: the ability to perceive the properties of environmental objects, which are largely constant over different viewing conditions, rather than the properties of their projected retinal images, which vary greatly with viewing conditions. We will discuss many other examples of constancy in Chapter 7 when we consider spatial properties such as size, orientation, position, and shape.

3.3.1 Lightness Constancy

Lightness constancy is the perception of a given achromatic surface (one that is perceived as some shade of gray from white to black) as having the same surface lightness regardless of differences in the illumination or viewing conditions. You can demonstrate lightness constancy to yourself by looking at this page indoors under artificial lighting conditions and then taking it outdoors into bright sunlight. In both cases, the paper looks white and the ink looks black. Although this might not seem surprising, consider how much light the white and black parts of the page are reflecting into your eye under these two different conditions (see Figure 3.3.3). Let us say that in an average, artificially illuminated room, 100

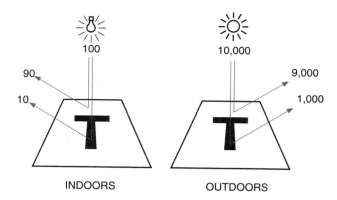

Figure 3.3.3 Lightness constancy under different illumination levels. White paper looks white and black ink looks black regardless of whether the page is viewed indoors under low illumination or outdoors under high illumination.

units of light are incident on the paper per unit of time and that the white paper reflects 90% of them into your eye whereas the black ink reflects only 10%. Thus, 90 units of light are coming from the white part of the page and 10 from the black part. In normal outdoor sunlight there will be at least 100 times more light (say, 10,000 units of light), so 9,000 units will now be reflecting from the white part and 1,000 units will be reflecting from the black part. Notice that the amount of light coming from the black regions in high illumination is actually more than ten times greater than the amount coming from the white regions in low illumination. Yet you still perceive the white page under low illumination as being much lighter than the black ink under high illumination. How is this possible?

Adaptational Theories. One kind of explanation of lightness (and color) constancy is that the visual system simply adapts to the overall change in illumination by becoming less sensitive in bright light and more sensitive in dim light (e.g., Hurvich, 1981; von Kries, 1905). The basic idea is that if adaptation to different levels of illumination causes the visual system to adjust its level of neural activity to some neutral range, lightness constancy would occur automatically. Illumination level would simply be factored out by adaptation, leaving reflectance as the main determinant of neural activity. Since adaptation takes place to a large extent right in the retina, this would be a very low-level mechanism for achieving lightness constancy.

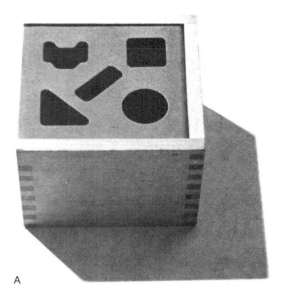

A

B

Figure 3.3.4 Perceiving shadows. (A) Normal shadows are perceived as being due to differences in the illumination falling on a surface rather than to being painted or stained in that region.

(B) Outlining the same shadow causes the surface to appear painted or stained rather than differently illuminated. (From Goldstein, 1989.)

Although adaptational processes are undoubtedly involved in adjustments to different levels of overall illumination, they just as clearly cannot account for all the phenomena of lightness constancy. One problem is that adaptation to changes in illumination typically requires a relatively long time (on the order of minutes), whereas lightness constancy is virtually immediate. If you turn off your reading light, for example, and there is some distant source of illumination in the room, the page appears to remain white despite the precipitous drop in overall luminance. It does not look as though it turns gray and then lightens progressively over the period of many minutes it takes for dark adaptation to occur (see Section 1.3.2, Figure 1.3.12). Rather, it looks as though there is suddenly much less light falling on the same white page and everything else around it. But even if adaptation were instantaneous, it could not explain our perception in such a situation because adaptation solves the constancy problem by eliminating information about changes in illumination. In fact, if adaptation were instantaneous, we would not even notice that the light had been turned off. Rather, we seem to perceive illumination separately from surface reflectance, as illustrated by turning off the reading lamp.

Another problem for adaptational theories of lightness constancy is that some form of constancy clearly occurs within a single visual scene under constant illumination. When an object on a table casts a shadow, as shown in Figure 3.3.4A, the surface of the table does not appear darker there, as though it were stained or painted, it simply looks as though there is less light falling on it because of the object's shadow. This form of lightness constancy cannot be explained by adaptation because classical light and dark adaptation is a much more global phenomenon, affecting the whole visual field. Interestingly, if the shadow on the table is outlined by a darker border, as shown in Figure 3.3.4B, the tabletop *does* appear darker within the border (Hering, 1905). No known adaptational mechanism could account for the dramatic difference between the perception of a shadow and an outlined shadow. Thus, although adaptation mechanisms may indeed influence long-term changes in the visual response to changing light levels, it is certainly insufficient as a general explanation of lightness constancy. We must therefore look elsewhere.

Unconscious Inference versus Relational Theories. Two classical theories of lightness constancy were developed by the same theorists who sparred over theories of color vision: Hermann von Helmholtz and Ewald Hering. Helmholtz tried to explain lightness constancy by applying his general principle of unconscious inference (see Section 2.1.4). He proposed that the visual system unconsciously "knows" (from prior experience) the relation between surface reflectance (R), incident illumination (I), and the resulting luminance (L) of the retinal image, namely,

$$L = R \times I.$$

He further proposed that the visual system can "undo" this operation by taking illumination into account in the proper way. If both the incident illumination (I) and the luminance in the retinal image (L) are known, then surface reflectance (R) can be calculated by the appropriate division ($R = L/I$). The uncertain proposition in Helmholtz's theory is that the visual system actually has information about incident illumination (I). If it does, then this equation could indeed be solved, at least in principle. The problem is that because of light adaptation, people are quite insensitive to absolute levels of illumination under normal viewing conditions, although they can detect slow changes in illumination under optimal conditions (Schubert & Gilchrist, 1992).

Hering proposed a very different explanation for lightness constancy. He thought it was directly determined from information in the image itself, with no mediating "inference" in which level of illumination was explicitly taken into account. Hering's insight was that although the *absolute* amounts of light being reflected into the eye from different regions of a given surface change drastically under different illumination conditions, the *relative* amounts of light reflected from one region with respect to another stay very much the same. Therefore, Hering proposed that perceived lightness depends on the *relative luminance* (or **contrast**) between neighboring regions.

A more recent and specific version of this theory was proposed by Hans Wallach (1948). Wallach suggested that perceived lightness was determined by *luminance ratios*. To illustrate how this might produce lightness constancy, recall our previous example of black ink on white paper (see Figure 3.3.3), and notice that the ratio of light from the white versus black regions is the same (9 : 1) in both dim light (90 : 10) and bright light (9000 : 1000). Therefore, taking ratios of image luminances from different regions can potentially explain lightness constancy without requiring the visual system

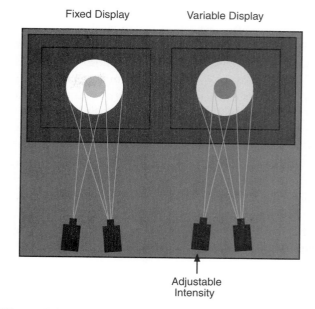

Figure 3.3.5 Wallach's lightness constancy experiment. Subjects were shown a fixed and a variable center/surround display. They were instructed to adjust the center of the variable display to match the center of the fixed display in perceived lightness.

to have any direct information about the level of illumination. Notice also the fundamental difference between unconscious inference and relational theories: Relational theories factor out illumination (that is, use measures that are invariant over changes in illumination) to achieve constancy, whereas unconscious inference theories take illumination into account to actively correct for luminance information.

Wallach tested his ratio theory in a very simple, but clever, experiment. He shone incident light of two different intensities on two adjacent regions of a uniform white screen. The central circular region was illuminated with one projector and the surrounding region with a second projector, both of which were hidden from view (see Figure 3.3.5). By independently manipulating the illumination of the two light sources, he was able to vary both the relative and absolute amounts of light in the center and surround. In his experiment, Wallach used two such displays. Both center and surround in the fixed display were set at predetermined levels, and the surround in the second display was set at a level different from that in the first display. The subject's task was to adjust the level of the central circle in the variable display until its perceived lightness matched that of the central circle in the fixed display.

The results strongly supported Wallach's ratio formulation. The intensity level of the central circle in the variable display was set so that its luminance ratio with respect to its surround was the same as that of the fixed circle with respect to its surround. Notice that, strictly speaking, lightness constancy actually *fails* quite dramatically in this experiment because the reflectance of the surface is actually a uniform white screen. The differences in perceived lightness are produced solely by differences in incident illumination from the four projectors. They are perceived as differences in reflectance rather than illumination, however, for reasons we will consider later.

The Importance of Edges. If luminance ratios determine perceived lightness, as Wallach proposed, then a ratio-based theory must specify how such ratios are computed. One important issue is whether luminance ratios are computed globally across large distances or locally at luminance edges (discontinuities in light intensity).

Somewhat surprisingly, research suggests that only local luminance ratios at edges matter. Figure 3.3.6 provides a simple, but compelling, demonstration known as the Craik-O'Brian illusion. The luminance profile of the display at the bottom shows that the central and surrounding regions actually have the same luminance except very near the inner border, where local changes in luminance create a clearly detectable edge. The crucial observation is that the central disk looks noticeably darker than the surrounding ring, even in the disk's interior, where the luminance is the same as in the outer region. If you wish to demonstrate to yourself that the edge is responsible, you can cut out a ring of opaque paper that occludes the edge. You will find that the difference in lightness between the inner and outer regions disappears. This confirms that local edge information determines the perceived relative lightness of the two regions, which is then propagated across the entire region.

Retinex Theory. If lightness is determined by local luminance ratios at edges, the visual system must somehow manage to integrate these values across all the edges in an entire image. How is this accomplished? An

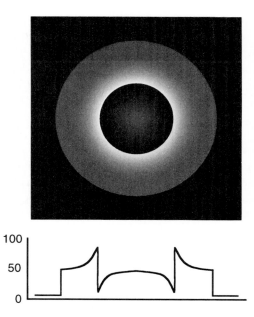

Reflectance — Horizontal Position

Figure 3.3.6 The Craik-O'Brian illusion. The middle of the inner circle appears darker than the outer region of the surrounding ring even though they have the same reflectance. The differences in reflectance are localized entirely near the edge between them, as indicated by the reflectance profile graphed below.

interesting answer to this question was formulated by Edwin Land (of Polaroid-Land camera fame) and John McCann (1971) in their **retinex theory** of color constancy. Retinex theory was actually developed to explain full color constancy, but because it is complex and applies to lightness constancy as well, we will examine the simpler case.

Land and McCann tried to understand how the human visual system could perceive the lightnesses of complex two-dimensional displays that they called **Mondrians** (see Figure 3.3.7A) after the artist Piet Mondrian, whose abstract paintings they resemble. In a series of informal experiments, they argued that lightness constancy holds for such displays under a wide variety of different lighting conditions. In the condition shown in Figure 3.3.7B, an artificial light source is located at the bottom of the display, creating a gradient of illumination across the simplified Mondrian, with less light incident at the top than at the bottom. Because the luminance of each region is the mathematical product of the gradually increasing illumination and its

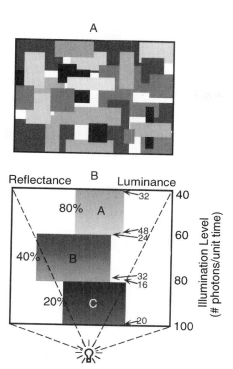

$$\frac{48}{24} \times \frac{32}{16} = \frac{1536}{384} = \frac{4}{1}$$

Luminance Edge Calculation of A to C

Figure 3.3.7 Black-and-white Mondrians. (A) A complex Mondrian like those used by Land and McCann (1971). (B) A simplified Mondrian with an illumination gradient increasing from top to bottom, as indicated by the scale along the right margin. Reflectances of the three regions are indicated to the left of each region as percentages. Luminances (= Illumination × Reflectance) are given to the right of each region at the edges. Despite the gradual change in illumination, luminance ratios at the edges are the same as the corresponding reflectance ratios for those regions. The calculation at the bottom shows how to compute global reflectance ratios by multiplying edge ratios.

own reflectance, the task of the visual system is to recover the reflectance of each region given only the luminance information. This is an underconstrained inverse problem because the only factor given in the retinal image is luminance, yet it is determined by both illumination and reflectance.

Retinex theory proposes that lightness depends on the global integration of locally determined luminance ratios at edges. Figure 3.3.7B illustrates how this can be done for the set of three regions whose reflectances are given in this simplified Mondrian. The relative reflectance of region A to region C is 4:1 (80%/20%).

The same answer can be calculated by sequential multiplication of the luminance ratios at the edges between them. The luminance ratio of A to C can thus be found by multiplying the luminance ratio from A to B (48/24) by that from B to C (32/16). As indicated, this calculation also yields a ratio of 4:1. This demonstrates that local luminance information at edges is sufficient to recover the relative reflectances of all regions. The absolute reflectances of the regions cannot be recovered, however, because the illumination of the display is simply factored out by the ratio computation. Notice also that the gradual reduction in illumination level from bottom to top (100 to 40 photons per unit time) due to the Mondrian being lighted from below does not disrupt the analysis. The reason is that the luminance ratios are taken only locally at the edges, which are so narrow that illumination changes are negligible.

Land and McCann suggested that the human visual system contains densely connected retinex systems that work by this sequential multiplication scheme or its functional equivalent. A 2-D version of this computational scheme was devised by Horn (1974) that works in parallel over the entire visual field. The relative reflectances of all regions in the Mondrian can thus be recovered in a way that will not be affected either by overall changes in incident illumination (such as bright sunlight versus dim room light) or by slow variations in illumination (due to distance from a nearby light source).

The Scaling Problem. Lightness perception requires more than just computing luminance ratios, however. When people look at surfaces, they perceive each as having a determinate lightness along the scale from white to black. The problem with luminance ratios is that they only specify the *relative* lightness of adjacent pairs of regions. If a given region is reflecting five times as much light as its background region, we do not know whether the lighter region is white and its background is gray or the lighter region is gray and its background is black. Luminance ratios alone cannot tell us. This is the **scaling problem** of lightness perception: How are luminance ratios mapped onto the white-to-black scale of achromatic lightness?

In many circumstances, the visual system appears to use a very simple **anchoring heuristic**: It assumes that the region of highest luminance is white and then scales

Color Vision

all other regions relative to it (Land & McCann, 1971; Wallach, 1948). Dramatic experimental evidence for this rule has recently been reported when subjects viewed Mondrians whose reflectances varied only from darkish gray to black. When subjects viewed these surfaces under conditions in which nothing else was visible, they perceived the lightest region (which was actually darkish gray) as white and the darkest region (which was actually black) as middle gray (Cataliotti & Gilchrist, 1995).

Despite the success of the highest luminance rule in this and many other experiments, it cannot be the whole story. The problem is that it requires that the region of highest luminance to be perceived as *white*, yet people perceive certain objects as *luminous*. The moon is a good example. Its surface is actually medium gray. It does not emit light but merely reflects light from the sun. Yet when it is seen against a dark night sky, it looks as though it is self-luminous. The factors that influence such perceptions of luminosity are complex, depending on the spatial configuration of the regions as well as their luminances (Li & Gilchrist, in press). A small light region completely surrounded by a large dark region— as in the case of the moon—are optimal for the perception of luminosity.

Illumination versus Reflectance Edges. We have now discovered that local luminance ratios at edges appear to determine perceived lightness, that these edge ratios can be integrated globally over a complex scene, and that the highest luminance region is usually perceived as white. Are we now in a position to explain lightness constancy? Unfortunately, we are not, for there is still a major problem to be solved.

The problem is that luminance edges in the retinal image can arise from two very different kinds of edges in the environment:

1. **Reflectance edges** are changes in image luminance caused by changes in the reflectance of two retinally adjacent surfaces. Reflectance edges can occur when the surfaces are made of different materials or are painted different colors.

2. **Illumination edges** are changes in image luminance caused by different amounts of light falling on a single surface of homogeneous reflectance. Illumination edges can be caused by cast shadows, reflected highlights

on glossy surfaces, restricted spotlights (as in theater lighting), or changes in surface orientation.

Retinex theory is accurate at integrating over multiple reflectance edges in a flat display, but it is grossly inaccurate whenever it encounters an illumination edge. The reason is not hard to identify: Retinex theory assumes that any changes in illumination are gradual and therefore are eliminated by computing edge-based luminance ratios. Retinex theory therefore achieves lightness constancy only if all the abrupt luminance edges that are present in the image are caused by reflectance edges in the world.

The critical importance of illumination versus reflectance edges in lightness perception has been elegantly demonstrated by psychologist Alan Gilchrist of Rutgers University. In one of his experiments, Gilchrist (1988) placed observers in a situation in which they viewed a display created by clever placement of lights and shadows, as illustrated in Figure 3.3.8A. He created two viewing situations that had identical luminance patterns in the central region but different surrounding contexts. Figure 3.3.8B shows the illumination edge display, and Figure 3.3.8C shows the reflectance edge display. In both cases, the darker left region contains a target square whose perceived lightness was measured by matching it to the most similar element in a 4×4 array of 16 squares in the lighter right region. In both cases, subjects were asked to indicate which of the 16 squares on the right matched the one on the left in terms of its perceived shade of gray, so that if the left square were physically moved onto the array, the two squares would look the same.

In the illumination edge condition (Figure 3.3.8B), subjects could see that the darker background of the target on the left was caused by a shadow cast over the left part of the display. They were therefore likely to perceive the central edge between the dark and light halves as an illumination edge. In the reflectance edge condition (Figure 3.3.8C), a masking screen removed all information that the central edge was due to a shadow. In the absence of evidence of a shadow, subjects perceived the central edge as being due to a difference in reflectance. Thus, the primary difference between the two conditions was that the central edge was perceived as an illumination edge in one case (B) and as a reflectance edge in the other (C). The question of interest

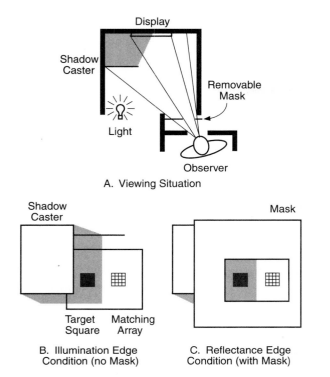

A. Viewing Situation

B. Illumination Edge Condition (no Mask)

C. Reflectance Edge Condition (with Mask)

Figure 3.3.8 Gilchrist's experiment on illumination versus reflectance edges. (A) The observer viewed a half-shadowed display either through a mask that occluded information about the shadow or without the mask. (B) In the illumination edge condition (without the mask), observers perceived the central edge between the target square and matching array as a shadow. (C) In the reflectance edge condition (with the mask in place), observers perceived the central edge as being due to a difference in surface reflectance. (After Gilchrist, 1988.)

is whether this difference had any effect on the observer's lightness judgments.

Gilchrist found a huge difference between subjects' lightness matches in the two conditions, as indicated in Figure 3.3.9. In the reflectance edge condition (Figure 3.3.9B), subjects picked grays that were only slightly lighter than an exact luminance match of the target square on the left (that is, one that delivered slightly more photons to the eye). Thus, they came very close to achieving lightness constancy, assuming that the central edge was due solely to a difference in reflectance with equal illumination on both sides. These subjects apparently integrated lightness information over the whole display, as Land and McCann's retinex theory would predict. In the illumination edge condition (Figure 3.3.9A), however, subjects picked grays that were dra-

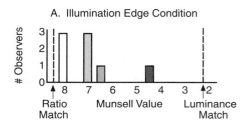

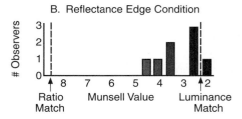

Figure 3.3.9 Results of Gilchrist's experiment. Histograms show the number of observers who chose different shades of gray Munsell chips in the matching array as looking the same as the target square in the two conditions. (A) In the illumination edge condition, most subjects chose a light gray chip close to the value that represented constancy if the central edge were due to a difference in illumination. (B) In the reflectance edge condition, most subjects chose a dark gray chip close to the value that represented constancy if the central edge were due to a difference in reflectance (even though it was not). (After Gilchrist, 1988.)

matically lighter than a luminance match. In fact, their choices came very close to lightness constancy, assuming that the central edge was due solely to a difference in illumination. These matches appear to have been based on equal luminance ratios of the target regions to their immediate surrounds without integrating over the central edge at all.

The difference between the results for these two conditions cannot be explained by local luminance information alone because the luminances of corresponding regions in the center of the displays were identical. The most satisfactory interpretation is that in the illumination condition, subjects perceived the central edge as a change in illumination and therefore suppressed the process of determining relative lightness by integrating luminance ratios over this edge. Instead, they assumed that the reflectances on both sides of the central edge were the same and that all the difference was due to the shadow. In the reflectance condition, however, the luminance ratios across the central edge were computed in

Color Vision

a retinexlike manner, thus providing near-perfect luminance matches.

This interpretation suggests that the computation of lightness values over a complex display containing both illumination and reflectance edges probably requires two separate representations: an **illumination map** of regions that differ in the amount of light striking them and a **reflectance map** of regions that differ in the percentage of light they reflect. Relative brightnesses of illumination in regions of the illumination map can be integrated across illumination edges, ignoring reflectance edges. Similarly, relative lightnesses of reflective surfaces of the reflectance map can be integrated across reflectance edges, ignoring illumination edges. These two computations must be kept separate, however.

Distinguishing Illumination from Reflectance Edges. An important piece of the puzzle is still missing: How does the visual system determine which edges are due to differences in illumination and which are due to differences in reflectance? Several heuristics are available for making this critical discrimination, including *fuzziness*, *planarity*, and *ratio magnitude*.

One factor is whether the edge is fuzzy or sharp. Illumination edges due to shadows or spotlights tend to be fuzzy and somewhat graded, whereas reflectance edges tend to be sharp. In the absence of information to the contrary, the visual system tends to assume that a sharp edge between coplanar regions is a reflectance edge. For example, if a stationary, sharp-edged spotlight is shone onto a surface of constant reflectance, the visual system automatically interprets it as a region of higher reflectance on a background of lower reflectance. This is why Wallach's center-surround stimuli (Figure 3.3.5) were perceived as differing in reflectance rather than illumination, even though they were produced by differences in the intensity of projector lights.

A second factor is planarity. If depth information (see Chapter 5) indicates that two regions are not coplanar, the edge between them tends to be perceived as an illumination edge rather than a reflectance edge, even if it is sharp rather than fuzzy. The reason is that surfaces at different depths and/or orientations usually receive different amounts of illumination because of the physical behavioral of light.

A third factor is the magnitude of the luminance ratios at the edge: Illumination edges can produce much greater changes in luminance than reflectance edges. A good white surface typically reflects no more than about 90% of the incident photons, and a good black surface reflects no less than about 10%. Reflectance ratios are therefore unlikely to be greater than about 10:1. But illumination ratios can be 1000:1 or more. Therefore, if a luminance ratio is 10:1 or more, a good heuristic is to assume that it is due to a difference in illumination.

Color provides additional information for distinguishing between illumination and reflectance edges, as we will discover shortly when we discuss chromatic color constancy. Intuitively, the crucial fact is that differences in illumination will almost always produce similar hue and saturation values on opposite sides of an edge, whereas differences in reflectance almost never will. For example, if a shadow falls over a blue window shutter next to the yellow wall of a house, the shutter will be some shade of blue on both sides of the shadow edge, and the wall will be some shade of yellow. The reflectance edge between the shutter and wall will have quite different hues on its opposite sides: blue on one side and yellow on the other. Generally speaking, if hue or saturation varies across an edge, it is probably a reflectance edge. If only brightness varies, it is probably an illumination edge.

Before leaving the topic of lightness constancy, let us return to the Helmholtz/Hering controversy we discussed earlier. Recall that Helmholtz argued for lightness constancy resulting from unconscious inference based on illumination information, and Hering argued for lightness constancy based on "direct" relational perception of contrast at edges. At first it seemed that Hering's contrast approach was clearly preferable, at least as modified in Wallach's ratio formulation and as extended in Land and McCann's retinex theory of edge integration. However, Gilchrist's experiment revealed a critical problem that arises for such simple edge-based schemes in the presence of changes in illumination: Different kinds of edges require different kinds of computations in arriving at lightness perceptions.

The picture that is now emerging includes a Helmholtzian component in the sense that the effects of illumination must be taken into account in computing perceived lightness. It is not the process of unconscious inference based on absolute levels of illumination that Helmholtz envisioned, to be sure, but it does require a process that classifies (or "interprets") edges as being due to changes in illumination versus reflectance, and different computations (or "inferences") are carried out as a result of this classification. Therefore, it appears that both Hering and Helmholtz may again turn out to be right, each in his own way, and that an adequate theory of lightness perception may require synthesizing aspects of both approaches. This theoretical synthesis is not yet in hand, but it does seem to be within reach.

3.3.2 Chromatic Color Constancy

We have just discussed facts and theories about constancy for achromatic color perception along the black/white axis of color space. We will now consider how it might be extended into the chromatic domain. As you might imagine from the fact that two more dimensions of color space are being included, these topics are correspondingly more complex and less well understood. This does not mean that chromatic color constancy is necessarily more difficult for the visual system to achieve, for chromatic information often provides additional constraints that make constancy easier.

Chromatic color constancy is the perception of invariant properties of a surface's spectral reflectance despite changes in illumination and viewing conditions. You have probably never thought of this as a problem because objects seem to have approximately the same color when differently illuminated: under cloudy versus cloudless skies, morning versus noon versus afternoon light, and tungsten versus fluorescent versus halogen light bulbs. Roses look red, violets look blue, and they do not seem to change color when the lighting changes. But the fact is that different light sources can have substantially different illumination spectra and can therefore cause the same surface to present different luminance spectra to the eye, as illustrated in Figure 3.3.2.

One mechanism that is generally believed to be important in color constancy is chromatic adaptation. If the receptors in the eye—and farther along in the neural chain of processing—become fatigued owing to the constant presence of, say, a green component that is introduced by green-tinted sunglasses, for example, the M cones will soon begin to fire less, effectively discounting the additional green component from the glasses. This change in the appearance of colors due to chromatic adaptation is in the direction that would aid color constancy. Even so, adaptation is not the only mechanism

involved—or even the main one—for the same reasons we considered in our discussion of adaptational effects in lightness constancy.

Constraining the Problem. Human color constancy, although not perfect, is remarkably good. The perceived color of each region of a chromatic Mondrian is determined largely by its reflectance spectrum, even though the light entering the eye (the luminance spectrum) is actually the product of its reflectance spectrum times the spectrum of the illuminating light. Thus, the visual system is somehow able to separate out the wavelength information in the illuminating light from the wavelength information in the surface reflectance. Theoretically, this is another inverse problem with no unique solution. But the performance of the visual system proves that this problem must be largely soluble by virtue of the fact that people manage to achieve approximate color constancy under normal conditions. By making heuristic assumptions that are generally (but not always) true, the visual system apparently adds information. We really do not yet know the full story of how color constancy is achieved, but we are beginning to understand some of its workings.

The problem in color constancy is that, logically speaking, there are six unknown parameters for each region (three for the illuminating light and three for the surface reflectance), but only three observations are available in the image (the outputs of the three cone types) resulting from the combined effect of both the incident light and the surface reflectance. This is a theoretically insoluble problem because there are more unknowns than knowns. But the situation an observer faces under natural viewing conditions is not quite this underdetermined for at least three reasons: (1) consistencies in the illuminating light within a single scene, (2) a restricted range of illumination spectra for normal illuminants, and (3) a restricted range of reflectance spectra. Let us consider each of these constraints in turn.

1. *Consistency of illumination.* The first helpful reduction in the number of free parameters is that the chromatic properties of the light source (its hue and saturation) are likely to be the same (or very similar) for all regions, even though the intensity of the light may vary owing to shadows, distance from the light, surface orientation, and the like.

Color Vision

For parts of the image in which the intensity of the light is also constant, the number of free parameters is cut almost in half. For example, if there are 10 coplanar regions of different reflectance in a Mondrian that are equally illuminated by a single light source, there are not 60 independently varying parameters in the image (six for each of the 10 regions), but only 33 (three for the reflectances of each of the 10 regions plus three more for the constant illuminant) and 30 known observations. Notice that even under this most restrictive condition, the problem does not have a unique solution, but the gap is closing quickly. Notice also, however, that to make this scheme work, the visual system must somehow be able to discriminate between edges that are due to illumination changes and those that are due to reflectance changes (see below).

2. *Restricted illuminants.* The second useful constraint is that we do not encounter all possible light sources under normal viewing conditions, but a severely restricted range.

Natural illumination differs somewhat in various conditions (cloudy versus sunny, morning versus afternoon), and the most frequently used artificial lights (incandescent and fluorescent) differ from each other more noticeably (see Figure 3.3.2). But these illuminants are not wildly different from each another. Strongly chromatic light sources are rarely encountered—except in stage lighting and perceptual experiments—and color constancy tends to falter under these conditions. The restricted range of standard illuminants means that the visual system is not required to contend with anywhere near the full range of possible color constancy problems to do a credible job, as long as it somehow makes use of this reduction (Judd, McAdam, & Wyszecki, 1964).

3. *Restricted reflectances.* A third useful constraint is that not all possible surface reflectance spectra are encountered in the natural world either, and the ones that are encountered tend to be smooth rather than jagged and decomposable into a small number of simple reflectance functions (Cohen, 1964).

Maloney and Wandell (1986) devised an algorithm for achieving approximate chromatic color constancy by taking advantage of all three types of constraints. Their algorithm assumes a single, common illuminant and models different light sources and different surface re-

flectances as linear combinations of just two or three different underlying illumination and reflectance spectra. Under these conditions, it displays approximate color constancy that is similar to that achieved by humans (Brainard & Wandell, 1991, 1992).

Shepard (1992) has speculated on an evolutionary explanation for the tridimensional basis of color vision and its opponent structure that is based on arguments concerning color constancy. He proposes that human color vision is three-dimensional because it evolved to provide people with color constancy under normal variations of daylight, which have essentially three degrees of freedom (Judd et al., 1964). The statement that "variations in daylight have three degrees of freedom" means that the different spectra of daylight that an organism typically encounters can be approximated by adjusting only three parameters that have the following physical interpretations:

1. *Light/dark level:* the overall amount of light present, varying from midday sunlight to deep shade or moonlight;

2. *Blue/yellow balance:* the relative amount of short (blue) versus other wavelengths (centered on yellow), as determined by the selective scattering of short wavelength light by the air molecules themselves; and

3. *Red/green balance:* the relative amount of long (red) versus other wavelengths (centered on green), as determined by the angle of the sun in the sky and the amount of water vapor present in the air (because water vapor selectively absorbs long wavelength light).

If the evolutionary role of color vision is to allow organisms to perceive the reflectance of surfaces as approximately constant over variations in normal daylight, then one way to accomplish this is for the visual system to effectively remove these variations by a compensatory internal process. The black/white, red/green, blue/yellow structure of color vision may therefore be an evolutionary adaptation to compensate for the structure of changes in normal daylight. Shepard's intriguing conjecture is highly speculative, however, and does not yet have solid empirical support.

Illumination Versus Reflectance Edges Revisited. The ultimate solution to the color constancy problem will certainly require the same types of information as lightness constancy does. Among the most im-

A. Illumination Edge

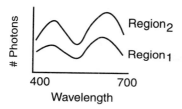

B. Reflectance Edge

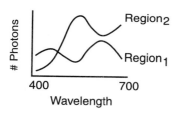

Figure 3.3.10 Chromatic aspects of illumination versus reflectance edges. (A) Edges due to changes in illumination produce luminance spectra that are qualitatively similar. (B) Edges due to changes in reflectance produce luminance spectra that can be arbitrarily different. (After Rubin & Richards, 1982.)

SPECTRAL CROSSPOINTS

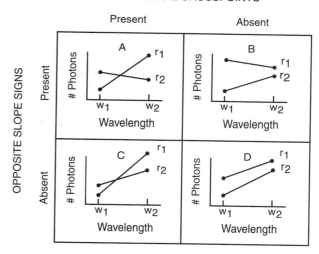

Figure 3.3.11 Rubin and Richards's chromatic heuristics for discriminating between reflectance and illumination edges. Adjacent regions (r_1 and r_2) are sampled at two wavelengths (w_1 and w_2) and classified according to whether their graphs cross (A and C) or not (B and D) and whether they have slopes of opposite sign (A and B) or not (C and D). Only condition D is likely to be due to a difference in illumination. (After Rubin & Richards, 1982.)

portant is distinguishing between illumination and reflectance edges. Because some of the most useful information for distinguishing between such edges depends on chromatic properties of the image, we will now consider how this might be accomplished.

Rubin and Richards (1982) realized that reflectance edges usually present quite different luminance spectra than do illumination edges. The important fact is that a simple change in illumination—such as that caused by a shadow or a change in surface orientation—will generally produce luminance spectra on different sides of the edge that are qualitatively very similar, as illustrated in Figure 3.3.10A. However, a change in surface reflectance—such as that caused by different materials or pigments—will generally produce qualitatively distinct luminance spectra, as illustrated in Figure 3.3.10B. If the visual system can discriminate these similar versus different spectra, then it can distinguish between illumination and reflectance edges using chromatic information. As we remarked in discussing lightness constancy, this information would be enormously useful in recovering the reflectance of visible surfaces.

Rubin and Richards proposed two conditions that signify changes in the spectral reflectance of surfaces: **spectral crosspoints** and **opposite slope signs**. These conditions are defined by relations between the light reflected from the two regions of interest as sampled at two different wavelengths. They are most easily understood in terms of the graphs showing the amount of light reflected from each region at both wavelengths. The spectral crosspoint condition is illustrated in Figures 3.3.11A and 3.3.11C (Rubin & Richards, 1982). It holds when the measurements in the two regions produce opposite differences in the amount of light at the two wavelengths, resulting in the "crossed" spectral graphs of 3.3.11A and 3.3.11C. The opposite slope sign condition is illustrated in Figure 3.3.11A and 3.3.11B (Rubin & Richards, 1989). It holds when the slopes of the graphs of the two regions have different signs: One goes up and the other down. The fact that these two conditions are independent is demonstrated by the four graphs in Figure 3.3.11, each of which shows a different pairing of presence versus absence of the two conditions. Only the last condition (Figure 3.3.11D), showing the absence of both, indicates a case in which the

Color Vision

spectral difference between the two regions is likely to be due to an illumination edge.

Whether the visual system actually uses something like Rubin and Richards's computational scheme to discriminate reflectance from illumination edges is not yet known. The human chromatic system does not have access to the complete spectrum of light coming from surfaces, for reasons that we discussed at length in the previous chapter. However, it does have two distinct chromatic channels—the red/green and blue/yellow opponent systems—and these may be the biological mechanism that implements some version of Rubin and Richards's scheme. In fact, it is quite possible that the conditions for discriminating illumination from reflectance edges are computed by using the double opponent color cells mentioned briefly in Section 3.2.3. These have roughly the right computational characteristics, since their output represents the difference between redness and greenness (or blueness and yellowness) across adjacent spatial regions.

Development of Color Constancy. Perceived constancy of surface lightness and chromatic color does not seem to be an inborn ability. Although this problem is only beginning to be studied in selective looking and adaptation experiments, the results thus far show that both chromatic and achromatic color constancy are absent at birth and develop over the first few months of life.

The development of color constancy in infants has been studied most effectively by using an adaptation paradigm (e.g., Dannemiller, 1989). In this procedure, infants are initially adapted to a given stimulus until they become tired of looking at the same thing. They are then shown either the same stimulus again or a different one, and the amount of time they spend looking at the test stimulus is measured. The standard result is that infants look more often at the novel stimulus than at the familiar one. In this way, one can find out whether or not an infant can tell the difference between two sets of stimulus conditions.

Dannemiller (1989) used this technique to study color constancy in infants between two and four months of age. The babies were initially adapted to a surface containing regions of two different colors (i.e., regions having two different reflectance spectra) that was illuminated by a particular daylight spectrum, as indicated in

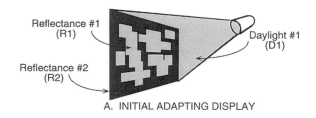

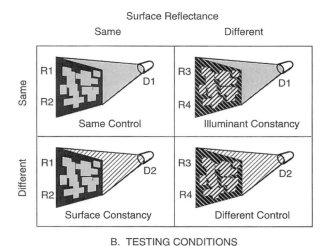

Figure 3.3.12 Development of color constancy. Infants were adapted to an initial display (A) consisting of a surface with two different reflectance spectra (R1 and R2) illuminated by a particular daylight spectrum (D1). After adaptation, they were tested on one of the four displays shown in part B. Different textures are used to indicate spectral differences in surface reflectances (R3 and R4) and in the illuminant (D2).

Figure 3.3.12A. They were then shown one of four test displays illustrated in Figure 3.3.12B: the same surface under the same illuminant (the "same control" stimulus), the same surface under a different illuminant (the "surface constancy" stimulus), a different surface under the same illuminant (the "illuminant constancy" stimulus), or a different surface under a different illuminant (the "different control" stimulus).

The two-month-olds looked significantly longer at the surface constancy test display than at the same control test display. Indeed, they looked at the surface constancy display just as long as they did at the different control display. This pattern of responses indicates that they do not have color constancy. The four-month-olds showed a different pattern. They looked at the surface constancy display no longer than they did at the same control display, but they did look longer at both the illuminant constancy display and the different control display. This is exactly what one would expect if the four-month-olds have chromatic color constancy under the two different daylight spectra used in the experiment. Dannemiller thus concluded that color constancy is not present from birth but develops sometime between two and four months of age.

3.4 The Category-Based Stage

Once the intrinsic character of a colored surface or light has been perceived and represented internally, one might think that color processing is complete. At some level, this is true. But a ubiquitous fact about human cognition is that people go beyond the purely perceptual experience to classify things as members of categories and often to attach linguistic labels to them. Color is no exception. Fresh blood, ripe tomatoes, and certain kinds of apples are all classified as red, even though they produce their own particular hues, saturations, and lightnesses. Grassy fields, tree leaves, and other kinds of apples are analogously classified as green, despite the differences in their perceived colors. These are just two examples of how people divide the continuous three-dimensional space of colors into discrete color categories.

That color categories are perceptually significant can be demonstrated by the striped or banded appearance of the rainbow, as shown in Color Plate 3.9A. Why do we perceive these bands? In physical terms, the rainbow is just a smooth continuum of light wavelengths from 400 to 700 nm. If the perception of hue were similarly smooth and undifferentiated, it should look like the unstriped "lightness rainbow" shown in Color Plate 3.9B. Clearly, it does not. The unmistakable stripes in the hue rainbow result from the articulation of this continuum into qualitatively different categories. Although they blend into each other, so that the boundaries are fuzzy, we see clear and distinct bands of color. This phenomenon suggests an experiential basis for the articulation of colors into at least some categories.

Another important fact about color categories is that we have simple names for at least some of them: *red*, *green*, *blue*, *yellow*, and so forth. It is unlikely that this is accidental. Perhaps it is unclear which came first, however: the division of colors into categories or the labels with which we refer to them. Do we categorize colors in the way we do because we have these labels, or do we label them in this way because of how the visual system categorizes them? In this section, we will consider a variety of evidence that supports the view that the most fundamental color categories are psychologically prior to color names. Indeed, there are excellent reasons to believe that these color categories are largely determined by the physiology of the human visual system. We will also present current ideas about how color categories are structured internally and how they relate to one another. But because the study of color categorization is so strongly tied to the study of color naming, we will begin by considering how colors are named.

3.4.1 Color Naming

Understanding how people describe colors linguistically seems a daunting task. Just think of all the words we have in English that refer to colors: *red, green, black, white, pink, brown, blue-green, reddish-brown, gold, silver, lime, persimmon, mauve, chartreuse,* and *magenta*, to name just a tiny fraction. Consider the dozens of color names in a large box of assorted crayons or the hundreds given to paint chips in a paint store. Is there any order to be found in this seeming chaos?

The first breakthrough in the current understanding of color categorization came from cross-cultural research on color naming: how people in different cultures who speak different languages apply linguistic labels to colors. Cognitive anthropologists Brent Berlin and Paul Kay of the University of California at Berkeley published the landmark study on this problem in 1969.

Before Berlin and Kay's work, color naming was thought to be a clear example of **cultural relativism**: the idea that each culture (and language) imposes its own idiosyncratic structure on the individual's kaleidoscopic flux of chromatic experiences. In linguistics, this idea is known as the **Sapir-Whorf hypothesis**, named after two of its strongest advocates, Edward Sapir and Benjamin Lee Whorf. One well-known example of this idea is the notion that Eskimos have more than a dozen different words that refer to ice and snow. According to cultural relativism, each culture creates its own words to refer to categories as the need for them arises, and Eskimos are thought to have a greater need to distinguish among different kinds of ice and snow than, say, Australian aborigines who have never seen the stuff. Cultural relativists not only affirm the role of culture in dictating the structure of human color categories, but also reject the possibility that physical, psychological, or biological structure had a hand in determining it. As one prominent textbook author put it:

There is a continuous gradation of color from one end of the spectrum to the other. Yet an American describing it will list the hues such as red, orange, yellow, green, blue, purple—or something of the kind. There is nothing inherent either in the spectrum or in the human perception of it which would compel its division in this way. (Gleason, 1961)

Such claims were severely undercut by Berlin and Kay's findings. They began their assault on the relativistic view of color categories by focusing their study on a small subset of color words. They defined the concept of **basic color terms** as linguistic descriptions of color that meet the following criteria:

1. *Monolexemic.* Basic color terms must be single lexical items such as *red*, *pink*, and *brown*. This criterion rules out color descriptions such as *blue-green*, *off-white*, and *light-blue* as basic color terms.

2. *Primary chromatic reference.* Basic color terms must refer primarily to the color of objects or materials rather than the objects or materials themselves. This criterion rules out *gold*, *silver*, *lime*, *persimmon*, and similar examples. (It seems to rule out *orange* as well, but Berlin and Kay allowed this exception because there are cultures that have a basic color term for *orange* (the color) without a corresponding term for oranges (the objects) or any similarly colored object.)

3. *General purpose.* Basic color terms must be widely applicable to all kinds of objects. This rules out color terms that apply only to narrow ranges of objects, such as *blond* (for hair color) or *roan* (for horses).

4. *High frequency.* Basic color terms must be used frequently in the language. This rules out esoteric color terms that fit all of the above criteria, such as *mauve*, *puce*, and *taupe*. (These terms are useful for professionals who deal extensively with subtle shades of color, such as interior decorators, but most people are uncertain about their meaning.)

In English, these four criteria reduce the set of basic color terms to just 11: *red*, *green*, *blue*, *yellow*, *black*, *white*, *gray*, *orange*, *purple*, *brown*, and *pink*. There are a few mar-

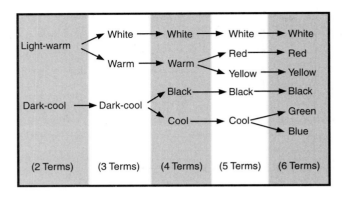

Figure 3.4.1 A simplified ordering rule for the first six basic color terms. This sequence of sets of basic color terms captures many of the regularities in which specific subsets of basic color terms are found in natural languages having up to six terms, although there are a number of exceptions.

ginal cases, such as *beige* and *tan*, but we will follow Berlin and Kay in identifying these 11 as the basic color terms of English.

When Berlin and Kay examined 20 languages experimentally and another 78 through literature reviews, they discovered two remarkable regularities.

1. *Sixteen basic color terms.* Initially, Berlin and Kay (1969) found only 12 basic color terms across all the languages they examined: the 11 in English plus one more that refers to light blue (analogous to the English word *pink* for light red). Later studies raised the number to 16 by adding four color terms that encompass more than one basic color term in English: *warm* (red or yellow), *cool* (blue or green), *light-warm* (white or red or yellow), and *dark-cool* (black or blue or green) (Kay & McDaniel, 1978).

2. *Twenty-two subsets.* Berlin and Kay found just 22 different subsets of the 16 basic color terms from among over a million logical possibilities ($2^{16} - 1$). Moreover, the ones that they did find were by no means drawn at random but exhibited the kind of striking regularities captured by the rule diagrammed in Figure 3.4.1.

The rule relating the 22 subsets of basic color terms can be interpreted as a developmental ordering for the acquisition of color terms. The one illustrated in Figure 3.4.1 specifies that if a language has only two basic color terms, they are always *light-warm* and *dark-cool*; if it has three, they are always *white*, *warm*, and *dark-cool*; and so on, each time adding the next basic color term to the

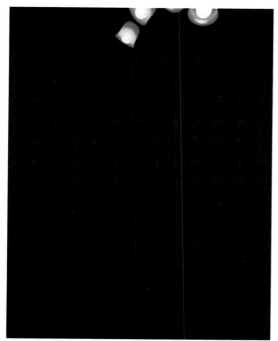

A

B

C

D

Plate 1.1 Effects of emitted and reflected light on the appearance of a scene. Image A shows a computer-generated scene that includes only direct illumination from the lamps. Images B–D show the same scene with the addition of (B) primary, (C) secondary, and (D) higher-order reflections from surfaces. (Images courtesy of Greg Ward Larson of Silicon Graphics, Inc.; visit radsite.lbl.gov/radiance/ for further information.)

 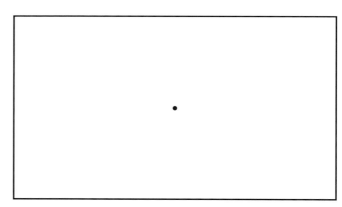

Plate 2.1 A demonstration of color afterimages. Stare at the dot in the middle of the green, black, and yellow flag for about a minute, and then fixate on the dot in the plain white rectangle. You should experience a vivid illusion of a red, white, and blue flag inside the rectangle.

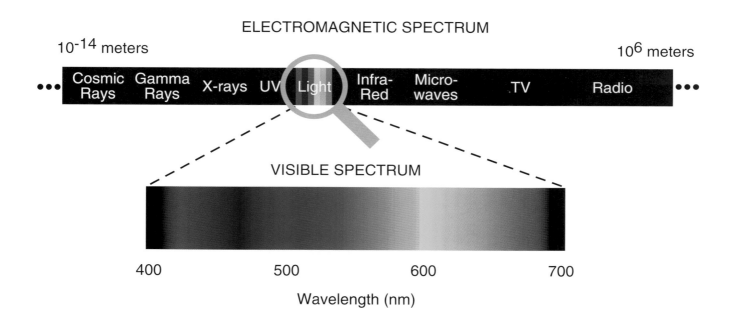

ELECTROMAGNETIC SPECTRUM

10^{-14} meters

10^6 meters

Cosmic Rays · Gamma Rays · X-rays · UV · Light · Infra-Red · Micro-waves · TV · Radio

VISIBLE SPECTRUM

400 · 500 · 600 · 700

Wavelength (nm)

Plate 3.1 The electromagnetic spectrum. Radiant energy is characterized by its wavelength, which varies continuously from very small to very large. Visible light occupies the limited range from 400 to 700 nanometers (10^{-9} meters) and is the only form of electromagnetic radiation that people can sense directly.

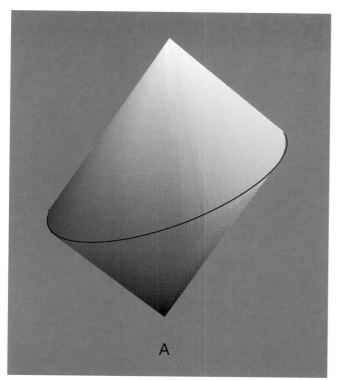

A

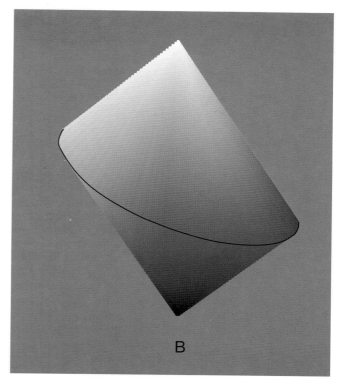

B

Plate 3.2 The color solid within color space. Each color is represented as a point within a three-dimensional space defined by the dimensions of hue, saturation, and lightness.

This figure shows the outer surface of the color solid separately for the red side (A) and the green side (B). Sections through the interior are given in color plates 3.3 and 3.4.

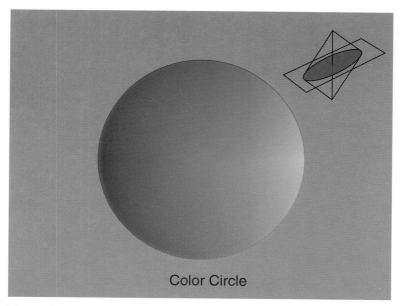

Color Circle

Plate 3.3 The color circle. This oblique section through the color solid shows the color circle, including the most saturated colors around its outer edge. Neutral gray is at the center, and the colors at various intermediate levels of saturation are located at intermediate positions.

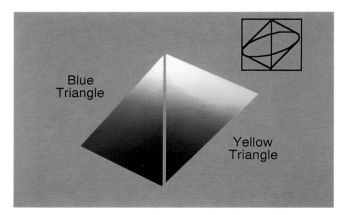

Plate 3.4 Two color triangles. A vertical section through the color solid reveals the blue and yellow color triangles that contain all the colors having these particular hues. Grays from white to black lie along the central axis, intermediate colors being light mixtures of the most saturated color with the grays along the central axis.

A   B

C   D

Plate 3.6 A simulation of color blindness. This picture shows what the world might look like to people with the three main forms of dichromacy. Part A shows a full color version of the scene, and parts B, C, and D show how it might appear to a protanope, a deuteranope, and a tritanope, respectively. (From *Sensation and Perception, An Integrated Approach, third edition* by H.R. Schiffman, 1990. New York, John Wiley.)

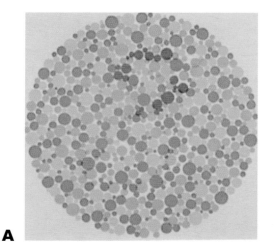

A

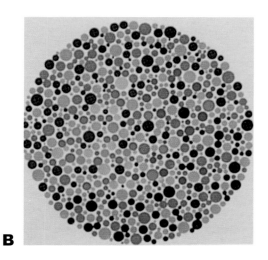

B

Plate 3.5 A test for color blindness. People with normal color vision see the number 3 in A and 42 in B, whereas protanopes see no number in A and a 2 in B, and deuteranopes see no number in A and a 4 in B. (Courtesy of Graham-Field Surgical Company.)

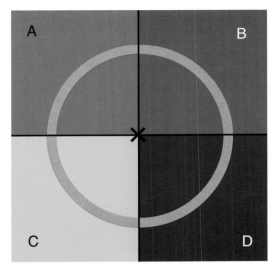

Plate 3.7 Simultaneous color contrast (or induced color). The gray circle is actually the same neutral gray throughout, but it appears greenish where it is surrounded by red, reddish where surrounded by green, yellowish where surrounded by blue, and bluish where surrounded by yellow.

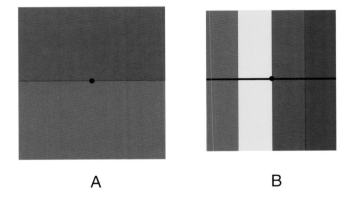

Plate 3.8 Chromatic adaptation. Staring at the green and red square (A) for 60 seconds will cause color–specific adaptation when the test stripes (B) are fixated at the black dot in the center. Adaptation to the red region at the bottom will make the red stripe appear less saturated in the lower half than in the upper half. Adaptation to the green region at the top will make the green stripe appear less saturated in the upper half than in the lower half. Such chromatic adaptation also affects the appearance of other colors.

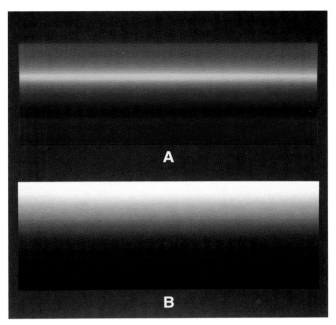

Plate 3.9 A comparison of rainbows defined by wavelength versus intensity. Both figures show a rainbow defined by a single physical continuum: wavelength in A and intensity in B. Nevertheless, the wavelength rainbow has a distinctly banded appearance that is not present in the intensity rainbow. These bands may reflect the categorical structure of perceived color.

Plate 4.1 A demonstration of the effects of equiluminance on perception. The same photograph is displayed in a black-and-white version (left) that contains normal luminance differences and an equiluminant version (right) in which the dark-to light gradient has been replaced with a red-to-green gradient. (Original image courtesy of Jeff Jacobson.)

Control	Conflicting	Compatible
XXXXX	BLUE	YELLOW
XXXXX	GREEN	BLUE
XXXXX	RED	GREEN
XXXXX	YELLOW	RED
XXXXX	BLUE	YELLOW
XXXXX	RED	GREEN
XXXXX	GREEN	BLUE
XXXXX	BLUE	YELLOW
XXXXX	YELLOW	RED
XXXXX	RED	GREEN

Plate 11.1 A demonstration of the Stroop effect. Name the color of the ink as quickly as possible for each letter string in a given column. This should be hardest and slowest in the conflicting conditions, intermediate in the control condition, and easiest and fastest in the consistent condition.

Plate 5.1 Aerial perspective. The reduced contrast and increased bluish cast of the farther mountains are due to the effects of the additional atmosphere through which their light must travel before reaching the observer (or camera). These factors add to the impression of depth in this picture.

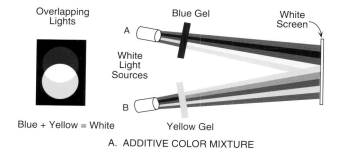

Overlapping
Lights

Blue Gel

White
Screen

A

White
Light
Sources

B

Yellow Gel

Blue + Yellow = White

A. ADDITIVE COLOR MIXTURE

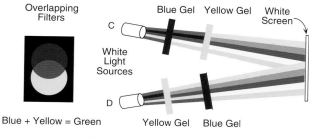

Overlapping
Filters

Blue Gel   Yellow Gel   White
Screen

C

White
Light
Sources

D

Yellow Gel   Blue Gel

Blue + Yellow = Green

B. SUBTRACTIVE COLOR MIXTURE

Plate C.1 Additive versus subtractive color mixture using spotlights and colored gels. In additive color mixture (A), full-spectrum white light (represented here by a set of rainbow stripes) is passed through blue and yellow gels and combined by superimposing the light on the screen. The blue gel removes wavelengths in the red and yellow regions and the yellow gel removes those in the blue and violet regions, but their light mixture contains light at all wavelengths, resulting in white light. In subtractive color mixture (B), the gels are superimposed in the same beam of light, removing all wavelengths except those in the middle of the spectrum, which appear green. (See text for details.)

Plate C.2 Additive mixture of paints and inks by spatial adjacency. When small blue and yellow regions are juxtaposed and viewed from far enough away that they cannot be resolved, their combined effect is the same as the additive mixture of these two colors, as shown on the right.

Plate C.3 An example of a pointillist painting. Paul Signac's *The Dining Room* shows how paints can be applied in small nonoverlapping dabs to create an additive combination of the components.

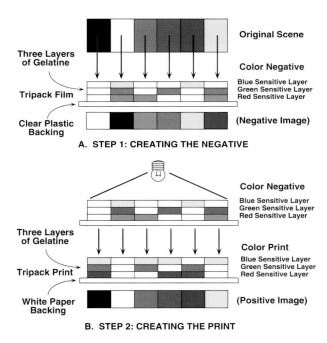

Plate C.4 The two-step process for making color prints. After the scene is photographed onto color tripack film, the exposed film is processed to create three negative images of the scene (A): one in yellow, one in magenta, and one in cyan. This color negative is then turned into a positive image by producing negatives of these three negatives on the tripack print paper (B). (See text for details.)

right. Additional evidence supports the further hypothesis that this logical ordering represents the temporal sequence according to which developing languages add new terms.

Both of these regularities undermine the credibility of the cultural relativity hypothesis because it simply cannot account for them. Indeed, pure cultural relativism leads one to predict no regularities at all. The facts obviously contradict this view, supporting instead the alternative hypothesis of **linguistic universality**: the idea that language is determined either by invariant physical characteristics in the structure of the environment or by invariant biological features in the structure of the organism (or both). On this score, the evidence strongly favors biological determination. Notice, for example, that the first six terms correspond to the polar opposites in Hering's opponent process (black/white, red/green, and blue/yellow). Given the strong physiological evidence that cells corresponding to these three systems exist in trichromatic visual systems, their primacy in color naming can be explained quite simply in terms of this universal biological structure. Why the color terms should appear in this particular sequence is not yet entirely clear, but there may be physiological reasons for this as well. The compelling conclusion of Berlin and Kay's work, then, is that the most basic and fundamental structure of color naming is fixed by genetically determined physiology. This conclusion does not deny that there are also additional aspects of color naming that are determined by culture. For example, object names, such as *turquoise*, *rust*, *gold*, and *pumpkin*, could not be used to refer to colors unless the objects were present in the culture.

3.4.2 Focal Colors and Prototypes

One of the key problems Berlin and Kay faced in their research on basic color terms was how to define color categories. The classical view can be traced to Aristotle, who proposed that membership in categories was defined by the presence of a set of necessary and sufficient conditions. This view implies that all instances of a category are equally "good" (that is, equally representative), since each has all the required features. The view that emerged from Berlin and Kay's research on color categories is quite different in that the "best" or "most representative" examples, called **prototypes**, play a

special role in structuring color categories. Let us now examine the evidence for this claim.

In the 20 languages that Berlin and Kay studied experimentally, they had to determine which colors could be described by which basic color terms. They tried two methods. In the *boundary colors method*, they showed their informants an ordered array of 329 Munsell color chips (from the outer surface of the color spindle) and asked them to pick out the boundaries of each category by pointing to all of the chips to which the basic color term would apply. In the *focal color method*, they showed the same color chips but asked the informants to pick out the "best example" of each basic color term. Interestingly, they found that informants were able to choose the best examples much more quickly and reliably than the boundary examples. Berlin and Kay called these best examples **focal colors** and suggested that color categories were structured around them rather than around boundary conditions.

This idea that color categories are based on prototypical examples received striking support from a number of classic studies by Eleanor Rosch (formerly Eleanor Heider), a cognitive psychologist at the University of California, Berkeley. Rosch studied several aspects of color categorization in the Dani tribe in New Guinea. The Dani have the minimal set of just two basic color terms: *mola* and *mili*, corresponding roughly to *light-warm* and *dark-cool*, respectively. Rosch studied the Dani's memory for colors by showing them a series of Munsell color chips and asking them to pick from memory the previously presented colors out of a large array of colors chips. Consistent with the prototype notion, she found that the Dani performed better—that is, they made fewer and smaller errors—with focal colors than with boundary colors (Heider, 1972).

Rosch also studied the role of focal versus boundary colors in how the Dani learned new color terms. She found that they learned new categories more easily when the colors to which they referred were centered on the focal colors found in other languages—for instance, the best examples of *red*, *green*, *blue*, and *yellow*—than when they were centered on boundary colors between focal ones. These results indicated that, in accord with the prototype view, learning new categories was indeed easier in the conditions structured around focal colors (Rosch, 1973a).

Rosch has confirmed several further predictions of the prototype theory for color categories in a variety of experimental tasks. For example, in one study, she had American college students indicate as quickly as possible on each trial whether or not a color was an instance of the category name presented just before it. The results showed that subjects were much faster at responding "yes" for focal colors than for nonfocal ones (Rosch, 1975a). More specifically, she found that the latency of these responses increased systematically as a function of the color's distance from the prototype in color space.

In another study, Rosch (1975b) had college students rate the similarity of one color to another. She found that subjects perceive nonfocal colors as being more similar to focal ones than vice versa. Further studies have shown that children learn the names of focal colors first and those of more peripheral colors later (Mervis, Catlin, & Rosch, 1975). On the basis of these and other results, Rosch (1975b) has proposed that focal colors serve as **cognitive reference points** for color categories, relative to which other colors are learned, categorized, and encoded in memory.

All of these results indicate that prototypical colors play a crucial role in the internal representation of color categories. Membership in color categories does not seem to be defined in terms of necessary and sufficient conditions, as the Aristotelian view predicts. Rather, they seem to be represented relative to prototypes. As we will see in Chapter 9, this conception of color categories generalizes to a wide variety of other natural categories and has now replaced the Aristotelian view as the standard theoretical conception of the internal structure of natural categories in the human mind.

3.4.3 A Fuzzy-Logical Model of Color Naming

Many of the known findings about basic color categories and naming can be understood in terms of a model of color classification proposed by Paul Kay and Chad McDaniel (1978), both then at the University of California, Berkeley. In their model, membership in color categories is formalized in terms of *fuzzy set theory*, a modification and extension of the concepts in classical set theory developed by computer scientist Lotfi Zadeh (1965, 1976), also of the University of California, Berkeley. To understand this theory, we will have to make a brief digression into the nature of classical versus fuzzy sets.

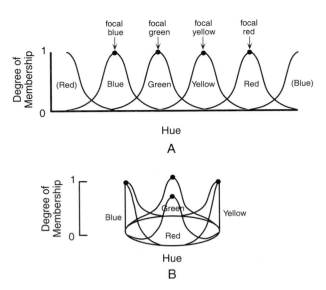

Figure 3.4.2 A fuzzy set representation of primary color categories. Focal colors have a membership degree of 1.0, and nonfocal colors have membership degrees that decline monotonically with dissimilarity to the focal color along the hue dimension. All hues except the focal colors thus belong to two primary color categories to some degree. (The graph in part A shows the hue dimension as linear for simplicity, depicting an unwrapped version of the more accurate circular graph shown in part B.)

Fuzzy Set Theory. Classical set theory is compatible with the Aristotelian notion of category membership in the sense that each object either is a member of a given set or is not; there is no middle ground. Classical set membership can thus be conceived as a function that assigns to each object a value of 1 if it meets the necessary and sufficient conditions for set membership or 0 if it does not. Zadeh's **fuzzy set theory** modifies classical set theory by allowing objects to be members of a given set *to some degree*. The degree of membership is specified by a function that assigns to each object a variable ranging continuously between 0 (certainly not a member) and 1 (a prototypical member). Fuzzy set theory can therefore naturally represent intermediate degrees of membership in a set, unlike classical set theory.

In terms of color categories, this means that a focal or prototypical color will be represented as having a membership degree of 1 for its category. Other, nonfocal colors will have membership degrees that decrease systematically with distance from the focal color in color space. This notion is illustrated in idealized form in Figure 3.4.2 for the basic color categories of blue, green, yellow, and red. Notice that colors between the prototypes have some intermediate degree of membership in more than one category, reflecting the fact that blue-greens are "sort of" members of both the blue and the green category to a degree that depends on their relative proximity to the blue and green focal colors. This seems natural within the fuzzy set formulation but quite unnatural in standard set theory. If the amount of time it takes to decide whether a given color is a member of a given category is inversely proportional to its fuzzy membership value for that category—with high membership values producing short reaction times—then Rosch's results showing that focal colors are classified more quickly than nonfocal colors can be explained very simply and elegantly by this fuzzy set model. Classical set theory, however, has no obvious way to account for Rosch's results.

Primary, Derived, and Composite Color Categories. Kay and McDaniel (1978) proposed that there are actually three different kinds of color categories underlying the 16 basic color terms. The six **primary color categories** are based directly on the six biological primitives of the visual system: black, white, red, green, blue, and yellow. (Recall that these are exactly the polar opposites in Hering's opponent process theory.) They further propose that other basic color terms can be analyzed by applying operations of fuzzy logic to primary color categories. These operations are fuzzy versions of standard logical operations such as AND and OR.

If X and Y are two fuzzy sets, X AND Y is defined by their **fuzzy intersection**. The fuzzy intersection of two fuzzy color categories is defined by their overlap, as illustrated in Figure 3.4.3A. In Kay and McDaniel's theory, the fuzzy intersection is modified as indicated in Figure 3.4.3B. It has a maximum of 1 at the point where the two membership functions cross and falls off regularly on both sides until it reaches zero where each individual membership function is zero. Thus, all members of the fuzzy category of orange, which they define as red AND yellow, are necessarily both red and yellow to some degree, but many of the central members are "better" members of the orange category than of either the red or yellow category. According to Kay and McDaniel's analysis, then, orange is the fuzzy intersection of red AND yellow, gray is the fuzzy intersection of

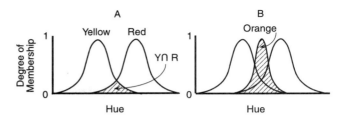

Figure 3.4.3 A fuzzy logical representation of derived color categories. Color categories that are smaller than primary color categories (such as orange) are analyzed as being similar to the fuzzy intersection of primary categories (such as the overlap of red and yellow as indicated in graph A) except that they are scaled to have a maximum value and a shape like that of the component membership functions (as indicated in graph B).

black AND white, purple of red AND blue, pink of red AND white, and brown of yellow AND black (since brown is actually a dark, desaturated yellow or orange). Kay and McDaniel call these **derived color categories** because they are derived from the primary categories by fuzzy intersection.

The only basic color terms that are left to be defined in terms of fuzzy sets are those from less developed color naming systems—*warm, cool, light-warm,* and *dark-cool*—which Kay and McDaniel call **composite color categories**. They are defined by the OR operation of fuzzy logic, which, in turn, is defined as the **fuzzy union** of two primary color membership functions. The fuzzy union of two fuzzy sets is simply the maximum of the two component membership functions, as illustrated in Figure 3.4.4. Thus, warm is the fuzzy union of red OR yellow, cool of blue OR green, light-warm of white OR red OR yellow, and dark-cool of black OR blue OR green. Their multimodal form in fuzzy set theory actually accords well with the fact that such composite terms produce greater variability in the choice of best examples than for either the primary or the derived color categories. For example, some informants faced with the task of picking the best example of warm would pick a focal red, and others would pick a focal yellow, but few would pick intermediate orange examples.

This fuzzy logical model of color categories is consistent with a large number of findings in human color naming and color categorization research. Moreover, it links these high-level cognitive functions closely with what is known about the underlying physiology of the human color processing system in an elegant and sys-

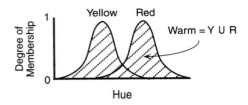

Figure 3.4.4 A fuzzy logical representation of composite color categories. Color categories that are larger than primary color categories (such as warm) are analyzed as the fuzzy union of primary categories (such as the combined membership functions of red and yellow).

tematic way.[9] It is for this reason that I suggested at the outset of our discussion of color perception that this topic provides an excellent example of the benefits to be derived from an interdisciplinary approach. In the course of this chapter we have relied on important contributions from physics, psychology, physiology, computer science, linguistics, and cognitive anthropology. Integrating the results from these diverse fields has added significantly to the breadth and depth of our understanding of color perception. The topics we will consider in the rest of this book are not yet as well developed in this sense, but the success of the interdisciplinary approach to color perception suggests that it will bear fruit in other areas as well. It is already making a significant impact, as we shall see.

Suggestions for Further Reading

Image-Based Color Processing

Kaiser, P. K., & Boynton, R. M. (1996). *Human color vision.* Washington, DC: Optical Society of America. This up-to-date revision of Boynton's 1979 classic book of the same title is a standard reference on all aspects of color vision, with especially thorough and deep coverage of low-level (image-based) color vision.

Surface-Based Color Processing

Gilchrist, A. L. (in press). *Seeing in black and white.* Cambridge: MIT Press. A leading researcher on perception of surface lightness, Gilchrist presents a detailed description of lightness perception, particularly the processes involved in lightness constancy, and a historical view of the field.

Category-Based Color Processing

Berlin, B., & Kay, P. (1969). *Basic color terms; Their universality and evolution.* Berkeley: University of California Press. This is the classic, groundbreaking work on the cognitive anthropology of color categorization and naming that began the line of research described in Section 3.4.

Kay, P., & McDaniel, C. K. (1978). The linguisitc significance of the meanings of basic color terms. *Language, 54,* 610–646. This article contains the original statement of the fuzzy logical theory of color naming.

A Collection of Original Papers

Byrne, A., & Hilbert, D. R. (Eds.). (1997). *Readings on color: Vol. 2. The science of color.* Cambridge: MIT Press. This collection includes reprints of many classic papers in color science. It is an excellent resource for students interested in reading original source materials.

---

[9] The correspondence between color naming phenomena and the biological mechanisms discussed is not as close as it appears in Kay and McDaniel's theory. They claim, for example, that the six primary basic color terms correspond to the operation of the opponent process cells in the retina and LGN. However, it is highly unlikely that people's color experiences arise this early in the visual system, for reasons we will consider in Chapter 13 on visual awareness. Conscious experiences must come much later in the visual system, after lightness and color constancy have been achieved. Even so, the structure of the color representation at that higher level, wherever it might be, seems likely to be similar to the red/green, blue/yellow, black/white opponent structure apparent in these early cells.

Spatial Vision

Processing Image Structure

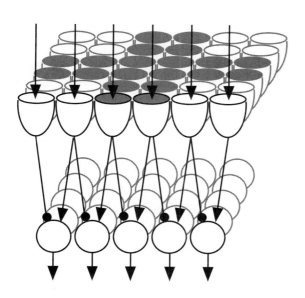

The perception of color as described in Chapter 3 is only one of our many visual abilities. Indeed, from an evolutionary perspective, it may be among the least important. Many animals, especially nocturnal ones, such as cats and rats, appear to have little color vision yet manage to survive quite well within their environments. Far more important is the ability to perceive spatial structure: the shapes, locations, sizes, and orientations of objects in space. These are the topics we will begin to examine in this chapter.

Our discussion of spatial vision will again be framed by the four stages of visual processing we described briefly at the end of Chapter 2: image-based, surface-based, object-based, and category-based processing. But there is so much material about the perception of spatial information that it will be divided into six chapters. This chapter concerns image-based spatial processing: those visual processes that primarily concern computing spatial features of the two-dimensional retinal image rather than features of external surfaces and objects. Vision scientists generally agree that a fair amount of preliminary processing is required to represent two-dimensional features of images themselves before they can be interpreted in terms of environmental entities such as surfaces and objects.

There have been three principal approaches to the study of image-based spatial processing within vision science: computational, psychophysical, and physiological. They use fundamentally different methods, as discussed in Chapter 2, but have closely related goals. According to Marr's analysis of the three levels of information processing (see Section 2.3), the ideal procedure for covering these topics would be to begin with a general description at the computational level, continue with a discussion of psychophysical findings that constrain algorithms for image processing, and end by explaining the physiological implementation of these algorithms in neural hardware. This is essentially the agenda we followed in discussing color vision, and it worked well in that domain because that is how the understanding of color vision actually unfolded over time.

In this chapter, however, we will start with the physiological story of spatial image processing because that came first historically, resulting from the application of recently developed single-cell recording techniques in the 1950s and 1960s. As astonishing as it sounds, it is still not clear, more than 40 years later, exactly what func-

tion is served by these intensively studied cells! Indeed, this lack of understanding was partly responsible for Marr's suggestion that the computational analysis ought to come first. There are now several competing theories about the function of these enigmatic little cells. The bulk of this chapter chronicles the long, arduous journey toward understanding their role in vision. It is not yet clear that we know the complete answer, but enormous progress has been made. The pieces of the puzzle seem to be coming together into a coherent picture, and, as in the case of color vision, different pieces have come from different approaches.

This chapter concludes with a discussion of more recent research into the global architecture of image-based processing. In Section 2.3.3 we briefly mentioned Fodor's (1983) modularity hypothesis that cognition can be divided into independent (or nearly independent) subsystems that are specialized for processing different kinds of information. Within the visual system, this hypothesis can be linked to the proposal that image-based processing of color, form, motion, and depth are carried out in different pathways within the visual nervous system (e.g., Livingstone & Hubel, 1987). The physiological substrates of the proposed pathways are intricate, and the psychophysical evidence for them is controversial, but the possibility that there may be such specialized pathways provides a provocative perspective on the global structure of image-based processing.

4.1 Physiological Mechanisms

As we mentioned in Chapter 1, the first knowledge of the biological underpinnings of vision emerged from studies of impaired perception due to large-scale brain damage from strokes, tumors, and gunshot wounds (e.g., Ferrier, 1878; see Glickstein, 1988, for a recent review). This established that the brain areas that are dedicated to visual abilities are in or near the occipital cortex at the back of the head. Despite this important advance, very little was known about the specific neural events that resulted in vision until the development of single-cell recording techniques in the 1950s (see Section 2.2.3). This gave vision scientists their first glimpses of neural information processing and opened a whole new scientific enterprise: that of exploring the mechanisms of vision neuron by neuron. We will now examine what has been learned about image-level processing from such physiological investigations.

4.1.1 Retinal and Geniculate Cells

The first chapter of the physiological story concerns how spatial processing occurs in the retina. In Chapter 1 we briefly mentioned several different layers of retinal cells that did some spatial and temporal processing before the neural signals left the eye. Now it is time to examine them in detail. They are important not only because of what they revealed about the earliest operations of visual processing, but also because their discovery set the stage historically for Hubel and Wiesel's landmark studies of cortical mechanisms of spatial vision.

Ganglion Cells. The first retinal cells whose spatial properties yielded to scientific analysis were the ganglion cells. At about the same time, Stephen Kuffler (1953) and Horace Barlow (1953) began recording the firing rates from individual ganglion cells using a **microelectrode**: an extremely thin glass or metal shaft with a tip diameter of about 0.001 cm. These **extracellular recordings** were made from outside a neuron but near enough to pick up its spike discharges. While the cell's activity was being recorded, different images were presented to the animal's retina to determine which ones made the cell fire and which ones did not. Kuffler recorded from ganglion cells in cats, and Barlow from those in rabbits, but they found essentially the same thing: The firing rate was highest for a spot of light of a particular size at a particular position on the retina. If the size of the spot was either increased or decreased, the firing rate diminished (see Figure 4.1.1). This pattern of results suggested some sort of antagonism between an inner circle and a surrounding ring (or *annulus*).

In further studies, researchers mapped the complete receptive fields of these ganglion cells and found two distinct types. **On-center cells** caused spike discharges when the light at the center of the receptive field was turned on (Figure 4.1.2A). **Off-center cells** caused discharges when the light at the center was turned off (Figure 4.1.2B). Another way of describing the difference between these two cell types is that on-center cells respond excitatorily to light at the center (meaning that light there makes them fire more vigorously), whereas off-center cells respond inhibitorily to light at the center

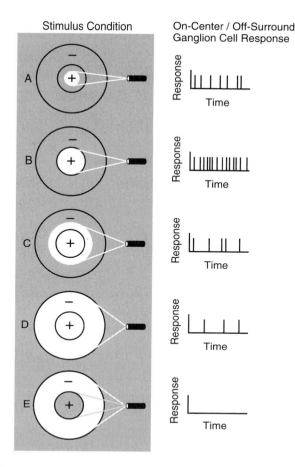

Stimulus Condition

On-Center / Off-Surround Ganglion Cell Response

Figure 4.1.1 Responses of on-center, off-surround ganglion cells. As the size of a spot of light increases, the response of an on-center, off-surround ganglion cell first increases (A), reaching a maximum when it covers just the excitatory center (B), and then decreases as the spot falls on the inhibitory surround (C and D). Minimum response (E) occurs when light falls only on the inhibitory surround.

(meaning that light there makes them fire less vigorously). The area surrounding the central region always has the opposite characteristic, as illustrated in Figure 4.1.2. That is, on-center cells have off-surrounds, and off-center cells have on-surrounds, leading to the center/surround organization we mentioned in Chapter 3 in connection with lateral inhibition and Mach band effects (see Figure 3.2.6). Careful study of receptive fields reveals the characteristic structure of on-center cells shown in Figure 4.1.2A. Here the excitation/inhibition of the cell to light within its receptive field is plotted as the height of the graph. This type of receptive field is

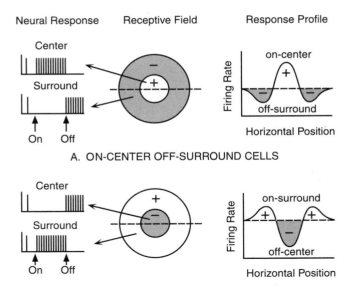

Neural Response   Receptive Field   Response Profile

A. ON-CENTER OFF-SURROUND CELLS

B. OFF-CENTER ON-SURROUND CELLS

Figure 4.1.2 Receptive field structure of ganglion cells. On-center, off-surround cells (A) fire to light onset and stop at offset in their excitatory center, but they stop firing to light onset and begin firing at offset in their inhibitory surround. Their 2-D receptive field is shown in the center. The "Mexican hat" response profile graphed at the right results when firing rate is plotted as a function of horizontal position through the center of the receptive field (as shown by the dashed line in the middle diagram). Off-center, on-surround cells (B) exhibit the opposite characteristics.

often referred to as a "Mexican hat" because its three-dimensional structure, formed by rotating the graph in depth around its central axis, resembles such a hat. Off-center cells (Figure 4.1.2B) have an "inverted Mexican hat" receptive field structure.

Bipolar Cells. Although bipolar cells come before ganglion cells in the neural anatomy of the visual pathway, they were studied later for technical reasons. Ganglion cells are the first cells in the visual system to produce spike discharges. Receptors and bipolar cells respond by producing **graded potentials**—continuous (rather than discrete) changes in electrical potential—which travel much more slowly and are practical only for cells with short axons, such as those in the retina. Ganglion cells were studied first because spike potentials can be recorded from outside the cell, whereas graded potentials must be recorded from inside the cell (**intracellular recording**), and it is not easy to posi-

tion an electrode inside a cell or to keep it there long enough to make useful recordings. Nevertheless, later studies using intracellular methods showed that bipolar cells, like ganglion cells, have circularly symmetric receptive fields with antagonistic relations between center and surround (Dacey, 1996; Werblin, 1969).

The precise neural architecture underlying the receptive fields of bipolar cells is now well understood, as illustrated in Figure 4.1.3A. Retinal receptor cells synapse directly onto both bipolar cells and horizontal cells. The horizontal cells, in turn, synapse onto bipolar cells, thus completing an indirect pathway from receptors to bipolar cells in addition to the direct one. The direct pathway from receptors to a given bipolar cell can be either excitatory or inhibitory, but whatever it is, the indirect pathway is always the opposite. In the example shown in Figure 4.1.3, there is a smaller central excitatory region from the direct pathway and a broader (but weaker) inhibitory region from the indirect ones. These two regions of excitation and inhibition are summed by the bipolar cell to produce the Mexican hat receptive field structure, as shown in Figure 4.1.3B.

Lateral Geniculate Nucleus. Axons from the ganglion cells exit the eye through the optic nerve, pass through the optic chiasm, where some of them cross to the opposite side, and finally synapse onto cell bodies in the lateral geniculate nuclei (LGN) of the thalamus (see Figure 1.3.15). LGN cells have center/surround receptive fields that are much like those of retinal ganglion cells but somewhat larger and with a stronger inhibitory surround.

The major difference between the last retinal layer and the LGN lies in their cellular architecture. The ganglion cells form a two-dimensional sheet parallel to the receptor surface of the retina and receive input just from nearby cells in their own eye. In contrast, the LGN is a three-dimensional structure and receives input from both eyes. Each individual LGN cell is monocular, however, firing in response to stimulation from just one eye. **Binocular cells**, ones that receive input from both eyes, are not present until visual cortex.

The internal architecture of the LGN is interesting and has provided researchers with important clues about a crucial functional distinction in the visual system. As with many neural structures in the brain, the

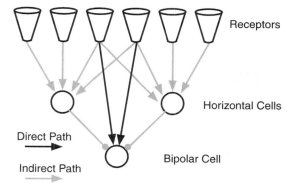

A. WIRING DIAGRAM

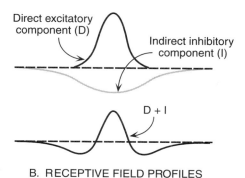

B. RECEPTIVE FIELD PROFILES

Figure 4.1.3 Neural inputs to an on-center, off-surround bipolar cell. The direct path (black connections) comes from receptors in the center of the receptive field. The indirect path of opposite polarity (gray connections) comes from receptors throughout the receptive field via horizontal cells.

LGN turns out to be *laminar* (or layered), consisting of many 2-D sheets of neurons. Each LGN is constructed of six distinct layers of cells that are then folded as shown in Figure 4.1.4. The lower two layers are called the **magnocellular layers** (from the Latin *magnus,* meaning "large") because they contain large cell bodies; the upper four layers are called **parvocellular** (from the Latin *parvus,* meaning "small") because they contain small cell bodies. These cells differ in their physiology as well as their anatomy, however. The magnocellular cells are quite sensitive to differences in contrast, are not very selective to color, have relatively large receptive fields, and exhibit a transient response to appropriate changes in retinal stimulation that both begins and ends quickly.

The parvocellular cells are relatively insensitive to contrast, are highly selective to color, have relatively small receptive fields (typically half the size of magnocellular fields), and exhibit a more sustained response to changes in retinal stimulation.

These differences in function between "magno" and "parvo" cells in LGN are summarized in Table 4.1.1. It is worth noting that most of these distinctions are not clear-cut but are statistical in the sense that there is substantial overlap between magno and parvo cells. Nevertheless, this specialization of function has led some investigators to speculate that the magno cells constitute a specialized neural pathway for processing motion and depth information, whereas the parvo cells constitute a separate pathway for processing color and shape (e.g., DeYoe & Van Essen, 1988; Livingstone and Hubel, 1988). We will discuss this controversial claim in detail at the end of this chapter.

Subsequent studies have shown that there are two different kinds of ganglion cells in the monkey retina that project selectively to the magnocellular and parvocellular cells in LGN. They are called **M ganglion cells** and **P ganglion cells** by analogy to the LGN cells to which they project (Shapley & Perry, 1986). Like parvocellular LGN cells, P ganglion cells are more sensitive to color than to black and white, whereas the reverse is true for M ganglion cells and magnocellular LGN cells. It is evident from their different responses to color that the M and P ganglion cells differ in their patterns of connectivity to receptors. P cells receive input just from cones, and M cells receive input from both rods and cones. Later in this chapter we will see how this division between the M and P pathways propagates to higher levels of the visual system in the cortex via the magno and parvo layers of the LGN.

Although the LGN as a whole receives input from both eyes, each layer gets signals from only one eye. The four parvocellular layers alternate between left and right eye input, as do the two magnocellular layers, with both the top and bottom layers receiving input from the eye on the opposite side of the head (see Figure 4.1.5). Each layer is laid out spatially like the retina of the eye from which it receives input. This is called **retinotopic mapping** or **topographic mapping** because it preserves the relative location of cells from retina to LGN: Nearby regions on the retina project to adjacent regions

Processing Image Structure

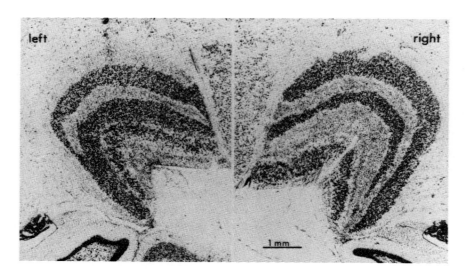

Figure 4.1.4 Cross section through the lateral geniculate nucleus (LGN) of a macaque monkey. The dark layers receive input from the intact left eye; the light layers receive input from the blind right eye. The output of these LGN cells goes to visual cortext (area V1) via the axons in the optic radiations, as illustrated in Figure 1.3.1. (From Hubel & Wiesel, 1977.)

Table 4.1.1
Functional Differences between Magno and Parvo LGN Cells

	Parvo	Magno
Color sensitivity	High	Low
Contrast sensitivity	Low	High
Spatial resolution	High	Low
Temporal resolution	Slow	Fast
Receptive field size	Small	Large

of the LGN, thus preserving qualitative (but not quantitative) spatial relations in the retinotopic map. This kind of spatial mapping is a common feature of higher levels of the visual nervous system, having been found in many areas of the visual cortex, as we will soon discover. The retinotopic maps in the different layers of the LGN are aligned so that corresponding locations are above and below one another, but there appear to be no interactions between layers. Each map represents only the half of the retina on the ipsilateral (same) side of the fovea, which corresponds to the contralateral (opposite) side of the visual field. This occurs because of the way the axons in the optic chiasm cross (see Figure 1.3.15). The same hemifield projection is maintained as the LGN axons make their way to the striate cortex through the **optic radiations**.

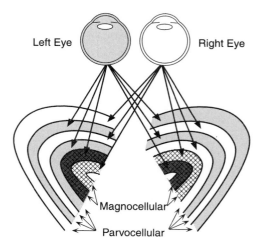

Figure 4.1.5 Diagram of the mapping from eyes to layers of the LGN. The upper four layers are parvocellular, and the bottom two (hatched regions) are magnocellular. Layers receiving input from the left eye are gray, and those receiving light from the right eye are white. The topmost layer receives input from the contralateral (opposite) eye, with successive parvocellular layers alternating the eye of origin. In the magnocellular layers, the upper layer receives input from the ipsilateral eye and the lower layer from the contralateral eye.

4.1.2 Striate Cortex

Striate cortex is a thin sheet of neurons only about 2 mm thick and a few square inches in surface area, yet it is the single largest cortical area in primates, containing some 200 million cells. This is more than 100 times larger than the number of LGN cells (about 1.5 million) or retinal ganglion cells (about 1 million), so it seems likely that much more complex visual processing occurs there. Although it was known to be the primary cortical region for vision from early lesion studies, no details of its function were known until the late 1950s when researchers began using single-cell recording techniques.

Hubel and Wiesel's Discovery. Hubel and Wiesel were the first to successfully apply the receptive field mapping techniques pioneered by Kuffler and Barlow to striate cortex. Others had tried before them but were unable to find stimuli that made the cells fire. Actually, Hubel and Wiesel made their discovery in an interesting way (Hubel, 1995). They were trying to make a cell fire using a small spot that they mounted on a microscope slide and moved around in front of a projector, thus producing a dark moving spot on the screen in front of an anesthetized cat. Sometimes while they were moving the slide around, the cell produced a vigorous burst of activity. They had finally succeeded in "talking" to a cortical cell but did not know what they had done to make it respond. It took a while to figure this out, because they naturally supposed that something about the *spot* on the slide was the crucial factor. After much experimentation, however, they finally realized that the cell's response had nothing to do with the spot. It was actually caused by the shadow of the slide's edge moving in a particular direction across the retina in a particular position. Further tests confirmed that the orientation and direction of movement of this edge were indeed the crucial variables. Thus the study of cortical receptive fields was launched from the edge of a microscope slide. Hubel and Wiesel's (1959) subsequent investigations quickly revealed that there were several different kinds of cortical cells that had different receptive field characteristics. They classified them into three types, which they called *simple cells*, *complex cells*, and *hypercomplex cells*.

Simple Cells. Hubel and Wiesel named certain neurons **simple cells** because their responses to complex stimuli can be predicted from their responses to individual spots of light. A simple cell's receptive field can therefore be mapped just by determining its response to a small spot of light at each position on the retina. Within an excitatory region, turning on the spot will cause the cell to fire more vigorously than its spontaneous background firing rate. Within an inhibitory region, a spot of light will cause the cell to fire at less than its spontaneous rate. A simple cell's response to a larger, more complex pattern of stimulation can be roughly predicted by summing its responses to the set of small spots of light that compose it. This approximate linearity of response is one of the central characteristics of simple cells.

Using such techniques to map receptive fields, Hubel and Wiesel identified several different subtypes of simple cells. The vast majority have an elongated structure, firing most vigorously to a line or an edge at a specific retinal position and orientation. Examples of the receptive field types that they reported for simple cells are shown in Figure 4.1.6. Some have an area of excitation on one side and an area of inhibition on the other. Because such cells respond most vigorously to a luminance edge in the proper orientation and of the proper polarity (light-to-dark or dark-to-light), they are often called **edge detectors**. Other simple cells have receptive fields with a central elongated region that is either excitatory or inhibitory, with an antagonistic field on both sides of it. Because these respond maximally to bright or dark lines, they are often called **line detectors** or **bar detectors**. Hubel and Wiesel speculated that such edge and line detector units could be constructed from the output of several properly aligned center/surround units from the LGN, as illustrated in Figure 4.1.7.

The view of image processing that has emerged from these findings is that an early step in spatial image processing is to find the lines and edges in the image. In this sense, the line and edge detector theory is very much in keeping with the atomistic view of vision we discussed in Chapter 2, except that the atoms out of which the rest of spatial vision is constructed are lines and edges at particular positions, orientations, and contrasts. Higher-level properties, such as shapes and orientations of objects, might then be constructed by putting together the many local edges and lines that have been identified by their detector cells in V1. Whether or not this is the correct view is still an open question, but it has dominated

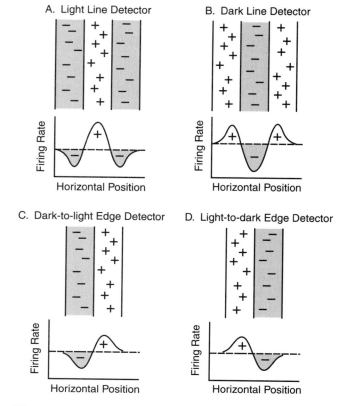

Figure 4.1.6 shows the receptive fields (diagrams) and response profiles (graphs) for four types of simple cells:

A. Light Line Detector

Firing Rate / Horizontal Position

B. Dark Line Detector

Firing Rate / Horizontal Position

C. Dark-to-light Edge Detector

Firing Rate / Horizontal Position

D. Light-to-dark Edge Detector

Firing Rate / Horizontal Position

Figure 4.1.6 Receptive fields and response profiles of vertically oriented simple cells in area V1. The receptive fields (diagrams) and response profiles (graphs) for four types of simple cells are illustrated: light line detectors (A), dark line detectors (B), dark-to-light edge detectors (C), and light-to-dark edge detectors (D). Area V1 also contains similar cells that are tuned to other orientations (not shown here).

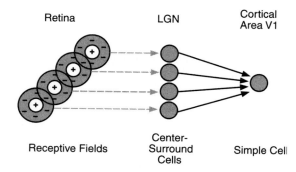

Figure 4.1.7 Possible neural wiring of cortical simple cells from LGN cells. Simple cells are proposed to receive input from several LGN cells that have receptive fields whose centers are aligned along the preferred orientation.

thinking about the initial stages of visual processing for several decades.

More recent quantitative studies have shown that the receptive fields of simple cells are somewhat more complicated than Hubel and Wiesel believed. For example, many simple cells have additional smaller lobes of excitation and inhibition to the side of the primary ones, as shown in Figure 4.1.8 (De Valois & De Valois, 1988). A wide variety of different receptive field sizes have also been found, large ones responding to coarse spatial structure and small ones responding to fine spatial structure. Moreover, there seems to be a correlation between these two aspects of receptive fields: Simple cells with smaller receptive fields tend to have more lobes and those with larger receptive fields to have fewer lobes

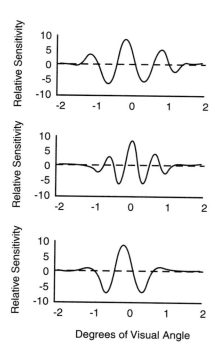

Figure 4.1.8 Quantitative response profiles for receptive fields of three simple cells. Each graph plots the firing rate relative to baseline (*y* axis) to a narrow bar in the preferred orientation at different positions across its receptive field (*x* axis). Notice the presence of additional lobes of excitation and inhibition in the upper two graphs. (After De Valois & De Valois, 1988, p. 122.)

(De Valois & De Valois, 1988). These differences might seem like minor variants of the receptive fields originally reported by Hubel and Wiesel, but they are not what one would expect if the cells were simply detecting lines and edges. Russell De Valois and Karen De Valois (1980, 1988) have advanced a substantially different interpretation of the functional role of these cells based on these differences. We will postpone detailed consideration of their views until the next section after we have discussed psychophysical theories of image processing, because their alternative theory is based centrally on those ideas.

Complex Cells. The single most common cell type in striate cortex is **complex cells**. Although they also have elongated receptive fields, they differ from simple cells in several important respects:

1. *Nonlinearity.* Complex cells are highly nonlinear, scarcely responding to small stationary spots at all. As a result, the orientation tuning of their receptive fields cannot be mapped by the technique of measuring their response to individual spots in each retinal location.

2. *Motion sensitivity.* Complex cells tend to be highly responsive to *moving* lines or edges anywhere within their receptive field. Often the motion sensitivity is specific to a particular direction of movement, as illustrated in Figure 4.1.9.

3. *Position insensitivity.* Complex cells are not very sensitive to the position of certain stimuli. Small differences in the location of a bar or grating, for example, will not affect their response rates much, if at all.

4. *Spatial extension.* Complex cells tend to have somewhat larger receptive fields, on average, than simple cells.

The first cortical cell that Hubel and Wiesel "talked to" with the edge of their slide was, in fact, a complex cell. Given that about 75% of the cells in striate cortex are complex, it is easy to see why previous investigators did not get vigorous responses from cortical cells using diffuse light, stationary spots, or even moving spots. To make these cells fire strongly, an elongated contour moving in the proper direction at the proper retinal position is needed, and that is just what the moving edge of Hubel and Wiesel's slide provided. As it turned out, they were lucky to be using a "low-tech" microscope slide to present their stimuli. If they had been using a more so-

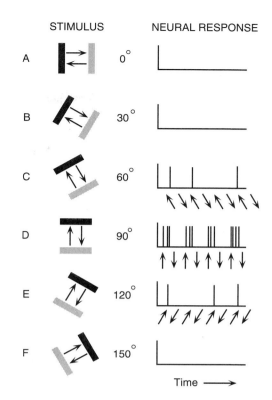

Figure 4.1.9 Response of a complex cell in visual cortex of a cat to moving bars. Stimulus bars are moved back and forth perpendicular to their orientation (left column) while neural responses are recorded (right column). This cell responds optimally to a horizontal bar moving upward (D and somewhat in C and E) but not in the opposite directions or in any other directions shown. (After Hubel & Wiesel, 1959.)

phisticated optical display, the study of cortical receptive fields might have taken many more years to get off the ground!

Hubel and Wiesel proposed that complex cells were constructed by integrating the responses of many simple cells, as illustrated in Figure 4.1.10. This appears generally to be the case, although some complex cells receive input directly from the LGN. This architecture explains why complex cells fire strongly to properly oriented bars or edges throughout their receptive fields.

Hypercomplex Cells. Hubel and Wiesel identified a third type of striate cell that they called **hypercomplex** because they seemed to have even more selective receptive fields than complex cells. The most striking characteristic of hypercomplex cells is that extending a line or edge beyond a certain length causes them to fire *less*

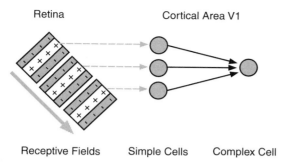

Retina   Cortical Area V1

Receptive Fields   Simple Cells   Complex Cell

Figure 4.1.10 Possible neural wiring of a complex cell from simple cells. Complex cells are thought to receive input from several simple cells whose receptive fields have the same orientation but different positions. When connected with appropriate time delays, this circuit produces motion-sensitive receptive fields like those of complex cells.

vigorously than they do to a shorter line or edge (see Figure 4.1.11). For this reason, they are often called **end-stopped cells**. Researchers now believe that hypercomplex cells are actually end-stopped simple or complex cells, rather than constituting a single qualitatively different cell type. Recent quantitative studies suggest further that the degree of "end-stopping" is a continuum rather than an all-or-none phenomenon (De Angelis, Freeman, & Ohzawa, 1995). Indeed, it may arise via lateral inhibition from nearby cortical cells, much as the sort of lateral inhibition we discussed in Section 3.2.3. Figure 4.1.12 shows a possible wiring diagram that would account for the properties of end-stopped cells by combining the outputs of two complex cells.

4.1.3 Striate Architecture

Receptive fields specify how individual cells respond to patterns of retinal stimulation. Extensive studies in which many different features of stimulation have been varied show that cells in visual cortex respond selectively to a rather limited set of spatial features: the orientation, position, size, color, and motion of a stimulus plus the eye (left or right) to which it was presented. Given that all these factors affect the response of cortical neurons, the question arises of how the cells that respond to them are arranged or organized in cortex. This is the question of the **architecture** of striate cortex: What are the spatial layout and pattern of interconnection among cells that are tuned to different values of these stimulus variables? Are they all intermixed in a crazy-quilt

STIMULUS   NEURAL RESPONSE

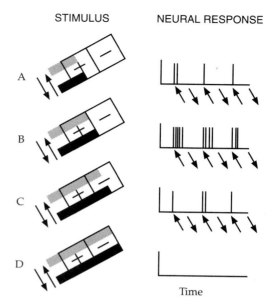

Time

Figure 4.1.11 Response of a hypercomplex (end-stopped) cell in visual cortex of a cat to moving bars of different lengths. This cell responds increasingly to motion upward and leftward when a dark diagonal bar falls in the lower-left portion of its receptive field. The firing rate then decreases as the bar is extended so that it falls in the upper-right portion of its receptive field as well.

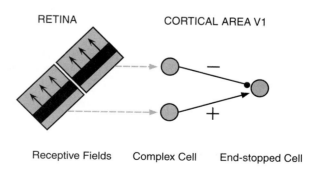

RETINA   CORTICAL AREA V1

Receptive Fields   Complex Cell   End-stopped Cell

Figure 4.1.12 Possible wiring of hypercomplex (end-stopped) cells from complex cells. Hypercomplex cells are proposed to receive input from two or more complex cells, including inhibition from one end. (After Kuffler & Nichols, 1976.)

pattern with no discernable structure, or are they regularly arranged in the cortex according to a systematic scheme?

Early studies to answer these questions were conducted laboriously in marathon recording sessions using single-cell techniques. Researchers would find a cell and record from it until they could determine the optimal location, orientation, size, and eye dominance of its receptive field. The microelectrode was then pushed just a bit further until another cell was found. The same procedure was then followed for the second cell. The microelectrode was advanced a bit further until a third cell was found, and so forth. After the entire session, the animal was sacrificed, and its brain was examined microscopically to find out precisely where the electrode had penetrated. The critical issue was whether there were any regularities in the progression of parameters that characterized the sequence of cells that had been studied. Indeed, truly remarkable regularities were discovered, as we will see shortly.

The study of cortical architecture was greatly advanced by the development of autoradiographic techniques. As described in Section 2.2.3, these methods rely on the uptake of radioactive sugar into highly active cells and provide a visual picture of the spatial distribution of the resulting radioactivity across large areas of striate cortex. The results of autoradiographic studies have generally corroborated prior results from single-cell recording sessions but in a more convincing way and over a much larger spatial extent.

The Retinotopic Map. The layered sheets of neurons that make up striate cortex within each hemisphere are laid out in a retinotopic map of exactly half the visual field. This cortical map preserves retinal topography, in the sense that areas adjacent to each other on the retina are also adjacent in the cortex. The metric properties of the map are distorted, much as a rubber sheet can be distorted by stretching it in certain ways, but adjacent regions of the retina still map to adjacent regions of the cortex. The primary distortion is due to **cortical magnification** of central areas relative to peripheral ones. This magnification, depicted by an artist in Figure 1.3.15, can actually be seen in the results of an elegant experiment by Tootell, Silverman, Switkes, and De Valois (1982).

Figure 4.1.13 shows an autoradiographic demonstration of both the retinotopic mapping in V1 and the distortion caused by cortical magnification. It was produced as follows: A monkey was shown the stippled, wheel-shaped pattern consisting of random black and white rectangles shown in Figure 4.1.13A. It flickered in time while radioactive sugar was being taken up by active cells. After the animal was sacrificed, the radioactive cortex was flattened, sliced very thinly parallel to the cortical surface, and placed on X-ray–sensitive film. The cortical image from one hemisphere—which receives information from only half the wheel—clearly shows all five radial lines and all three semicircular lines connected with the appropriate topographic relationships (Figure 4.1.13B). Notice, however, that the logarithmically spaced semicircular lines in the stimulus are about equally spaced on the cortical projection. This indicates that the small portion of the retina near the center occupies a disproportionately large area of cortex and that more peripheral regions are less fully represented. This is partly a consequence of the dense packing of receptor cells in the central region of the retina (see Figure 1.3.9) and partly a consequence of the more detailed analysis cortex performs on this small but important region of the visual field.

Ocular Dominance Slabs. We have two eyes, and the fact that both eyes project to both hemispheres raises the question of whether there are two separate retinotopic maps in the cortex, one for each eye, or a single integrated one. The answer lies somewhere in between: There is one global map for each cortex, within which cells that are dominated by one versus the other eye are interleaved (LeVay, Hubel, & Wiesel, 1975). Figure 4.1.14 shows a diagram of what we will call **ocular dominance slabs**[1] in a slice of tissue from layer 4

---

[1] What I am calling ocular dominance *slabs* are more standardly referred to as ocular dominance *columns*. I have chosen the "slab" terminology (following De Valois & De Valois, 1988) to distinguish this aspect of cortical architecture from the hypercolumns discussed in the following section. The term "slab" also seems to convey more effectively the two-dimensional quasi-planar form of ocular dominance structure.

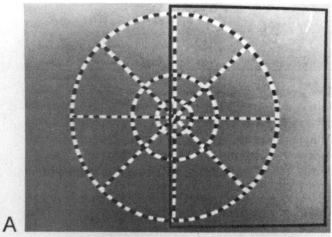

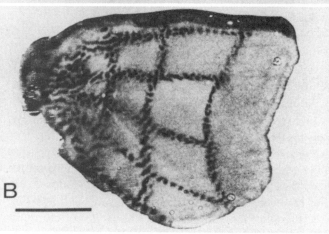

Figure 4.1.13 An autoradiograph showing the retinotopic map in area V1 of a macaque monkey. The monkey viewed the stimulus shown in part A centered on the fovea while radioactive 2-deoxyglucose was injected into the bloodstream. The pattern of radioactive uptake in area V1 is shown in part B. Its spatial distribution reflects the retinotopic map of the right half of the wheel-like stimulus. The foveal projection is on the left, the hemicircles correspond to the vertical lines (with the outer one on the right), and the radial stimulus lines correspond to the horizontal lines. (From Tootell, Silverman, Switkes, & De Valois, 1982.)

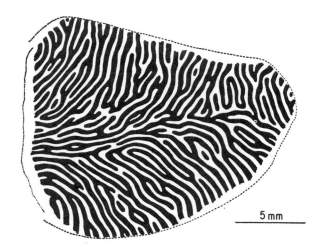

Figure 4.1.14 Ocular dominance slabs in area V1 of monkey cortex. The section was made tangent to the surface of the cortex by using a reduced silver staining technique. (From LeVay, Hubel, & Wiesel, 1977.)

(where the cells are monocular), parallel to the cortical surface. (The "slabs" therefore run perpendicular to the cortical surface.) Clearly, the pattern of light (right eye) and dark (left eye) is not random, since there are very clear stripes. But the stripes are not as regular as they could be. Even though there is a strong tendency for cells that are dominated by the same eye to be clustered, there is some latitude in exactly how this aspect of cortical architecture is realized, resulting in complex interleaving patterns like the one shown.

Columnar Structure. At a finer grain, the overall retinotopic map is composed of many smaller cortical units called **hypercolumns**. Hypercolumns are long, thin columns of cortical tissue about 1 mm by 1 mm on the surface of the cortex that run perpendicularly through all six cortical layers. One such hypercolumn is shown in detail in Figure 4.1.15 for both the left-eye–dominant and the right-eye–dominant cells. Within each hypercolumn there is a regular progression along one dimension that represents the tuning of cells for orientation (Hubel & Wiesel, 1968). Studies using both single-cell recording and autoradiographic techniques converge in supporting this aspect of cortical architecture.

More controversial is the claim that there is another functional dimension of each hypercolumn perpendicu-

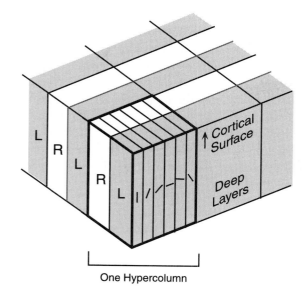

One Hypercolumn

Figure 4.1.15 The organization of hypercolumns in striate cortex. Along one dimension, the optimal orientation varies systematically within a hypercolumn. Along the other dimension, right versus left eye dominance alternates. The left-eye regions are shaded gray to indicate how the ocular dominance slabs (see Figure 4.1.14) relate to this hypercolumnar structure.

lar to the orientation dimension that represents a regular progression of size-scale values, from small to large. This idea has been proposed by Russell De Valois and Karen De Valois (1988) on the basis of considerable physiological evidence from their laboratory. Because of this additional dimension of cortical processing, an entirely different interpretation has been made for the function of the same cortical cells that Hubel and Wiesel claim to be line and edge detectors. We will consider their theory in some detail later in this chapter.

4.1.4 Development of Receptive Fields

The existence of all these different types of cortical cells in adult monkeys immediately raises a developmental question: Are such cells present and differentiated at birth, or do they develop as the organism interacts with its environment? This is, of course, the nativism/empiricism controversy we considered in Section 2.1, but at a cellular rather than an organismic level. Because the biological basis of this aspect of vision is known, it has been possible to obtain very detailed answers to the developmental question.

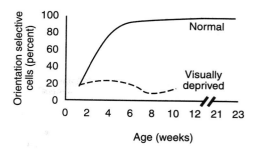

Figure 4.1.16 Development of cortical orientation cells in normal versus visually deprived cats. In normal kittens (solid curve), most cortical cells become highly selective for orientation between one and five weeks of age. When kittens are deprived of visual stimulation in both eyes until testing (dashed curve), the percentage of orientationally selective cells does not increase over this period. (After Blakemore & Van Sluyters, 1975.)

Hubel and Wiesel (1963) studied newborn kittens and found orientationally selective cells even in the youngest animals. This clearly implies an innate component. But there also appears to be further development after birth because the receptive fields of the newborn kittens were less orientation specific and less responsive to stationary bars and edges than those in adult cats. The crucial question is whether the additional development arises from preprogrammed maturation or from learning as the organism is exposed to visual stimulation after birth. This question has been studied in a number of different ways.

In early experiments, animals that were raised without any visual stimulation for a period of time were compared to those raised with normal stimulation. Visual deprivation was achieved either by sewing the animals' eyelids shut at birth or by raising them in a completely dark environment. In a pioneering study, Wiesel and Hubel (1963) found that cortical cells in deprived kittens were still orientation selective, but they were not nearly as selective to edge orientation or direction of movement as those of normally reared kittens. A more quantitative study later showed that the difference between light- and dark-reared kittens increases dramatically in the first five weeks of life in terms of the number of oriented cells, as shown in Figure 4.1.16 (Blakemore & Van Sluyters, 1975). Autoradiographs measuring uptake of 2-deoxyglucose also show evidence of a marked increase in orientation selectivity up to an age of five weeks (Thompson, Kossut, & Blakemore, 1983).

Processing Image Structure

These and other studies indicate that the visual system exhibits a **critical period**: an interval of time during which it undergoes rapid development owing to the effects of environmental stimulation. Both before and after the critical period, few effects of experience are found. This means that the effects of visual deprivation during the critical period are particularly debilitating. Normal gains in visual function are not made because of lack of stimulation, and the resulting deficits cannot be overcome because later stimulation has little or no effect. This is true of visual development in humans as well as animals. For example, the effects of **cataracts**—the clouding of the eye's lenses—depends on when they develop and when they are removed. Cataracts that develop after the eighth year of life have almost no lasting effects once they are removed because the critical periods of visual development are over. But cataracts that are present from birth have devastating effects on vision if they are not removed surgically during the first few months of life, a fact that was discovered when effective medical procedures were first developed to remove such cataracts.

Once perfected, cataract removal operations were performed on many adults who had had cataracts from birth, thus giving them vivid visual experiences for the first time. It was hoped that their restored vision would be normal, allowing them to live fully sighted lives. The results of these operations were generally less effective than had been hoped because patients were not able to perceive the environment as normally sighted people do and appeared to be unable to learn to do so. As the literature on visual development now makes plain, normal vision includes important components of maturation and learning that can take place only in the presence of normal stimulation. Patients whose vision was restored as adults sometimes became depressed after the operation, and some even chose to live much of their lives in darkness rather than having to deal with the confusing and chaotic visual experiences that intruded into their lives (Gregory, 1970; Von Senden, 1960).

There is no single critical period in visual development for all visual properties, but there are different critical periods for different properties. The critical period for orientation selectivity, for example, appears to be from one to five weeks of age in cats (Blakemore, Van Sluyters, & Movshon, 1976). That for ocular dominance occurs somewhat later, at five to ten weeks (Daw &

Wyatt, 1976). In general, it appears that the critical period for a given type of cortical cells depends on its level in the visual system: Those of lower-level cells occur sooner than those of higher-level cells. This hypothesis fits the current data because orientation selectivity is a property of cells in the input layer of cortex, whereas ocular dominance is characteristic of the output layers (Shatz & Stryker, 1978). This pattern of development makes sense because higher-level cells can develop their response properties only after lower-level cells have developed theirs.

4.2 Psychophysical Channels

Surely one of the most interesting facts about image-based spatial processing is that the functional interpretation of the cells that Hubel and Wiesel discovered over 30 years ago is still very much in dispute. There are some relatively minor disagreements about the precise shapes of the receptive fields and some of the variables that are important in specifying them, but these are completely overshadowed by the controversy that rages over their functional significance: What are these cells *doing*? Thus far, we have considered only one of the contenders in detail—namely, the line and edge detector hypothesis. We briefly mentioned that there is an alternative hypothesis but have not yet explained it. We will now take a closer look at this theory, how it evolved from behavioral research in human visual psychophysics, and how it suggests a different view of spatial processing in area V1.

This second approach to image-based processing arose within a branch of sensory psychology known as **psychophysics**. As explained briefly in Chapter 2 and more thoroughly in Appendix A, psychophysics is the study of quantitative relations between people's conscious experiences (their psyche) and properties of the physical world (physics) using behavioral methods. Calling the methods "behavioral" indicates that psychophysicists, unlike physiologists, do not record electrical events in neurons or directly measure any other aspects of neural activity. Instead, they measure people's performance in specific perceptual tasks and try to infer something about underlying mechanisms from behavioral measurements. For instance, a psychophysicist might be interested in studying how bright a spot has to be within a darker surrounding field for it to produce a just barely perceptible experience. This is called the *threshold* for detecting the spot. A psychophysicist might study how this threshold depends on factors such as the size of the spot, the darkness of the surrounding field, or the length of time the subject has been sitting in the dark before testing. Appendix A explains the standard psychophysical methods for measuring various kinds of thresholds.

From the answers to questions about sensory thresholds and how they are affected by other variables, psychophysicists try to understand the mechanisms underlying people's performance. Since these mechanisms must ultimately be implemented physiologically, there should be a great deal of overlap in the subject matter of psychophysical and physiological approaches to vision. Often there is. For example, in the study of color vision, there has been a satisfying convergence of insights from these two domains that have mutually reinforced each other, as we discovered in Chapter 3. In the study of spatial vision, however, there has been less convergence than one might expect. Indeed, we will see that psychophysical theories of image processing have developed in quite a different direction from physiological theories of line and edge detectors.

For nearly 30 years the psychophysical community has been working within a theoretical framework called the *spatial frequency theory*. It dominates psychophysical theories of spatial vision because it is able to explain a large number of important and surprising results from psychophysical experiments. Unfortunately, it is also a rather complex and technical theory, so we will have to cover a fair amount of background material to understand it. Once we have done so, however, a very different conception will emerge of what the cells that Hubel and Wiesel discovered in striate cortex might be doing.

4.2.1 Spatial Frequency Theory

Like the line and edge detector theory of image processing, the **spatial frequency theory** of image processing is based on an atomistic assumption: that the representation of any image, no matter how complex, is an assemblage of many primitive spatial "atoms." The primitives of spatial frequency theory, however, are quite different from the lines and edges that we considered in the previous section. Rather, they are spatially

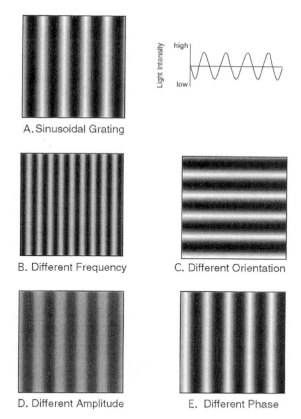

A. Sinusoidal Grating

B. Different Frequency

C. Different Orientation

D. Different Amplitude

E. Different Phase

Figure 4.2.1 Sinusoidal gratings. Sinusoidal gratings are shown for (A) a standard grating and four comparison gratings of (B) a lower spatial frequency, (C) a different orientation, (D) a different amplitude, and (E) a different phase. A graph of grating A is shown to its right.

extended patterns called **sinusoidal gratings**: two-dimensional patterns whose luminance varies according to a sine wave over one spatial dimension and is constant over the perpendicular dimension. Figure 4.2.1 shows examples of various sinusoidal gratings. The graph (top right) shows the luminance profile of the sinusoidal grating. This graph plots the reading of a tiny light meter that traverses the grating perpendicular to the orientation of the stripes. Notice that the light and dark bars look fuzzy or "out of focus." This is because the changes in luminance over space are smooth and gradual instead of sharp, as indicated by the smooth continuous curve of the sinusoidal graph.

Each primitive sinusoidal grating can be characterized completely by just four parameters: its *spatial frequency*, *orientation*, *amplitude*, and *phase*. Figure 4.2.1 shows

Processing Image Structure

how these parameters change the appearance of the grating.

1. The **spatial frequency** of the grating refers to the width of the fuzzy light and dark bars: Low-frequency gratings have thick bars, and high-frequency gratings have thin ones. Spatial frequency is usually specified in terms of the number of light/dark cycles per degree of visual angle, a quantity that varies inversely with stripe width. In Figure 4.2.1, grating B differs from all the others in having a higher spatial frequency.

2. The **orientation** of the grating refers to the angle of its light and dark bars as specified in degrees counter-clockwise from vertical. In Figure 4.2.1, grating C differs from all the others in having a horizontal orientation.

3. The **amplitude** (or **contrast**) of the grating refers to the difference in luminance between the lightest and darkest parts, which corresponds to the difference in height between the peaks and the valleys in its lumi-nance profile. Contrast is specified as a percentage of the maximum possible amplitude difference, so 0% con-trast is a uniform gray field (since there is zero difference between the lightest and darkest parts), and 100% con-trast varies from the brightest white to the darkest black. In Figure 4.2.1, grating D differs from all the others in having a lower amplitude.

4. The **phase** of a grating refers to the position of the sinusoid relative to some reference point. Phase is speci-fied in degrees, such that a grating whose positive-going inflection point is at the reference point is said to have a phase of 0° (called *sine phase*), one whose peak is at the reference point has a phase of 90° (*cosine phase*), one whose negative-going inflection point is at the reference point has a phase of 180° (*anti-sine phase*), and one whose valley is at the reference point has a phase of 270° (*anti-cosine phase*). In Figure 4.2.1, grating E differs from all the others in its phase.

Fourier Analysis. It might seem odd to consider sin-usoidal gratings as primitives or atomic elements for spatial vision. After all, we don't consciously experience anything like sinusoidal gratings when we look at natu-rally occurring scenes. If conscious perception of visual elements were a necessary condition for their having primitive status, the case would be far stronger for bars and edges than for sinusoidal gratings. At least we see

bars and edges in natural scenes. There is no reason to suppose that primitive elements in early spatial vision need to be conscious, however. We do not experience tiny points of color that are presumably signaled by the output of the three cone types, for example, yet they are surely the initial set of primitives in the visual system.

There is actually a good theoretical reason for choos-ing sinusoidal gratings as primitives, but it is a formal mathematical reason rather than an experiential one. The rationale is based on a well-known and widely used mathematical result called *Fourier's theorem*, after the French physicist and mathematician Baron Jean Fourier, who proved it in 1822. As applied to the 2-D image pro-cessing problem, **Fourier analysis** is a method, based on Fourier's theorem, by which any two-dimensional luminance image can be analyzed into the sum of a set of sinusoidal gratings that differ in spatial frequency, orientation, amplitude, and phase. Two very simple examples of how sinusoidal gratings can be combined to form more complex images are shown in Figures 4.2.2 and 4.2.3. In Figure 4.2.2 a series of sinusoidal gratings of the same orientation at spatial frequencies of f, $3f$, $5f$, ... are added together in the proper amplitude and phase relationships to obtain a square wave that has sharp edges rather than fuzzy ones. Figure 4.2.3 shows how two such square waves at different orientations can then be added together to produce a plaid pattern.

Fourier analysis is not limited to these simple, regu-larly repeating patterns, however. It can be applied to complex images of objects, people, and even whole scenes. Although we cannot demonstrate how to con-struct such complicated images from individual sinus-oidal components—far too many gratings would be required—we *can* demonstrate what kind of spatial in-formation is carried by different ranges of spatial fre-quencies. Figure 4.2.4 shows a picture of Groucho Marx together with two different versions of it that contain only low and high spatial frequencies, respectively. You can see that low spatial frequencies in the middle picture carry the coarse spatial structure of the image (that is, the large black and white areas), whereas the high spa-tial frequencies in the right picture carry the fine spatial structure (that is, the sharp edges and small details).

The Fourier analysis of an image consists of two parts: the power spectrum and the phase spectrum. The **power spectrum** specifies the amplitude of each

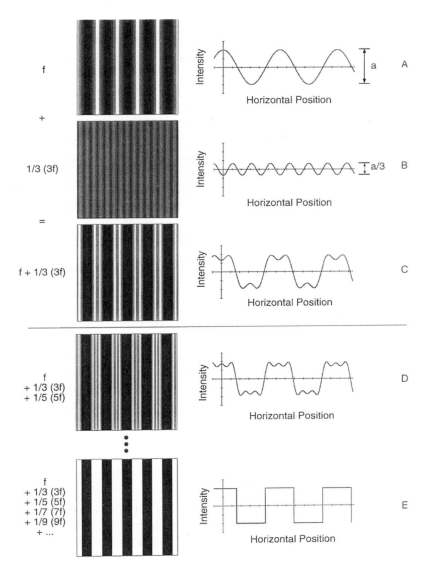

Figure 4.2.2 Constructing a square wave by adding sinusoidal components. (A) A grating at the fundamental frequency (f) of the square wave together with its luminance profile. (B) A grating at the third harmonic ($3f$) with one-third the amplitude. Adding these two gratings results in the grating and luminance profile in part C. Adding the fifth harmonic ($5f$) at one-fifth the amplitude gives the result shown in part D. Adding all the odd harmonics in the proper amplitudes and phases gives the square wave shown in part E.

Processing Image Structure

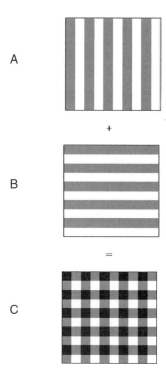

A

+

B

=

C

Figure 4.2.3 Constructing a plaid grating by adding square wave gratings at different orientations. The plaid grating at the bottom is formed by adding square wave gratings at vertical and horizontal orientations as shown.

constituent grating at a particular spatial frequency and orientation, whereas the **phase spectrum** specifies the phase of each grating at a particular spatial frequency and orientation. If all of these gratings at the proper phases and amplitudes were added up, they would exactly recreate the original image. Thus, Fourier analysis provides a very general method of decomposing complex images into primitive components, since it has been proven to work for any image. Fourier analysis is also capable of being "inverted" through a process called **Fourier synthesis** so that the original image can be reconstructed from its power and phase spectra. The invertibility of Fourier analysis shows that these spectra contain all the information in the original image.

It is unclear whether the same claims are true for analyzing an image into sets of line and edge primitives or for resynthesizing an image from them, however, because no general theorems like Fourier's have ever been proven that use lines and edges as spatial primitives. Be that as it may, mathematical power and elegance alone

are not convincing arguments that the visual system does anything like a Fourier analysis. Empirical evidence must be brought to bear—and so it has been. We will now examine some of these findings.

Spatial Frequency Channels. The spatial frequency theory of image-based vision proposes that early visual processing can be understood in terms of a large number of overlapping **psychophysical channels** at different spatial frequencies and orientations. The concept of a psychophysical channel will require some explaining because it is a fairly technical construct. It can be understood intuitively, however, by analogy with channels with which you are already familiar: the channels in your TV set.

The signals from all TV stations are simultaneously present in the air around us. They are broadcast in the form of electromagnetic energy, which, as you may remember from Chapter 3, lies within a band of wavelengths far outside the visible region of the spectrum (see Color Plate 3.1). Different TV stations broadcast their signals in different subranges so that their signals do not interfere with each other. An important part of what your TV set does is to select the proper subrange of wavelengths from all the others for the particular channel you have tuned. When you tune your TV to channel 4, for example, you are actually tuning it to select just the range of wavelengths on which your local "channel 4" station is broadcasting. Thus, you can think of your TV's channel selector as controlling internal mechanisms that allow it to receive signals selectively from only a small subrange of wavelengths.

The concept of a psychophysical channel is a hypothetical mechanism in the visual system—whose actual physiological substrate is not specified—that is selectively tuned to a limited range of values within some continuum. In the domain of color vision, for example, Helmholtz proposed that there were three channels defined by the wavelength sensitivity curves of three classes of hypothetical elements in the retina (see Figure 3.2.7). In the case of the spatial frequency theory of vision, each channel is defined by the spatial frequency and orientation of the gratings to which it is maximally sensitive.

The spatial frequency approach to image processing asserts that the visual system can be understood as consisting of many overlapping channels that are selectively

Figure 4.2.4 Spatial frequency content of a complex image. The picture of Groucho Marx on the left has been analyzed into its low-frequency information (middle) and high-frequency infor- mation (right). Low frequencies carry the global pattern of light and dark; high frequencies carry the local contrast information at the edges of objects. (From Frisby, 1979.)

tuned to different ranges of spatial frequencies and orientations. There is now a great deal of evidence to support this view. One of the landmark papers that launched the spatial frequency theory of vision was published in 1969 by British psychophysicists Colin Blakemore and Fergus Campbell. In it, they reported the results of an experiment that provided striking evidence for the existence of spatial frequency channels in vision. The point of the experiment was to show that when people viewed a sinusoidal grating for a long time, their visual systems adapt selectively to gratings at the presented orientation and frequency but not others, as measured by psychophysical techniques. Because of its historical and conceptual importance to the spatial frequency theory of vision, we will now examine this experiment in some detail.

Contrast Sensitivity Functions. The basic idea behind Blakemore and Campbell's (1969) experiment was to determine the effects of adapting an observer to a particular spatial frequency grating by measuring their sensitivity to such gratings both before and after adaptation. The standard measurement of how sensitive observers are to gratings at different frequencies is called the **contrast sensitivity function (CSF)**. It is determined by finding the lowest contrast at which the observer can just barely detect the difference between a sinusoidal grating and a uniform gray field, that is, the threshold at which a very low-contrast grating stops looking like a uniform gray field and starts to look

striped. This threshold is measured for gratings at many different spatial frequencies from low (wide fuzzy stripes) to high (narrow fuzzy stripes).

The fastest and easiest procedure for measuring contrast thresholds is using the method of adjustment. Each subject adjusts a knob that controls the contrast of the grating at a particular spatial frequency on a TV monitor to the point at which he or she can just barely detect its striped appearance. (Other, more complex methods are also available, as explained in Appendix A.) This adjustment procedure is repeated for many gratings at different spatial frequencies. The results of such an experiment can be summarized in a graph in which the contrast at threshold is plotted as a function of spatial frequency, as shown in Figure 4.2.5A. The reciprocal of this graph—made by flipping it upside down—defines the contrast sensitivity function over the spatial frequency continuum, since threshold is high when sensitivity is low and vice versa. The CSF produced by this procedure typically looks like the one shown in Figure 4.2.5B.

You can observe the overall shape of your own CSF by looking at Figure 4.2.6. It shows sinusoidal stripes of increasing spatial frequency along the horizontal axis and of decreasing contrast along the vertical axis. At threshold contrast, your ability to detect the grating disappears, and so the height at which you no longer see the stripes but just a gray background indicates your sensitivity to gratings at the given spatial frequency. If you hold the book about 30 inches from your eyes, the

Processing Image Structure

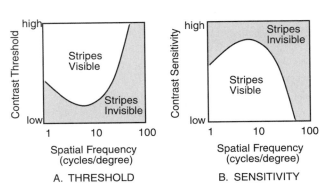

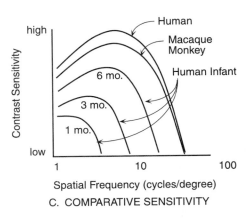

A. THRESHOLD

B. SENSITIVITY

C. COMPARATIVE SENSITIVITY

Figure 4.2.5 Contrast sensitivity functions. (A) Minimum contrast at threshold plotted as a function of spatial frequency. (B) Contrast sensitivity plotted as a function of spatial frequency, the inverse of graph A. (C) Contrast sensitivity functions for adult humans, macaque monkeys, and infants at several ages.

Figure 4.2.6 Demonstration of the shape of the contrast sensitivity function for luminance gratings. Spatial frequency increases continuously from left to right, and contrast increases from top to bottom. The envelope of the striped region should approximate the curve shown in Figure 4.2.5B.

outline of the striped portion of Figure 4.2.6 should look very much like the CSF plotted in Figure 4.2.5B.

The CSF shows that people are most sensitive to intermediate spatial frequencies at about 4–5 cycles per degree of visual angle. Some other CSFs are shown in Figure 4.2.5C for comparison. Notice that babies are much less sensitive at birth, especially at high frequencies (Atkinson, Braddick, & Moar, 1977). As for other species, the macaque monkey's CSF is almost identical to that of humans, a fact that makes macaques an almost ideal animal model for studying the physiology of human spatial vision. If the CSF is measured under low-light (scotopic) conditions in humans, sensitivity to all frequencies drops dramatically, especially at the highest frequencies. This means that at night, when just the rods are operating, human vision lacks the high acuity that it has in daylight. This is primarily because there are no rods in the fovea, the area of greatest visual acuity under photopic (high light) conditions.

Selective Adaptation of Channels. Now let us return to Blakemore and Campbell's experiment. After measuring each subject's CSF, they had the subject adapt to a grating of a particular spatial frequency by having him or her scan back and forth over it for a few minutes. Then they remeasured thresholds at each spatial frequency. The extended exposure to the grating caused the subject's visual system to *adapt*, that is, to become less sensitive after the prolonged viewing experience (see Section 1.1.3), but only near the particular spatial frequency and orientation of the adapting grating. The postadaptation CSF, shown as the dotted function in Figure 4.2.7A, indicates just how selective the change in sensitivity is for the spatial frequency of the adapting grating. Test gratings with much lower or higher frequencies were not affected at all by adapting to the grating. The extent of the adaptation can be measured by plotting the difference between the original CSF and the adapted CSF, as shown in the graph in Figure 4.2.7B. This property of selective adaptation is one of the signatures of a psychophysical channel: Each channel adapts to a degree that reflects how sensitive it is to the adapting stimulus. Adaptation therefore results in lowered sensitivity for just a small portion of the spatial frequency continuum rather than equally throughout the whole range.

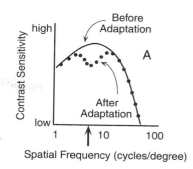

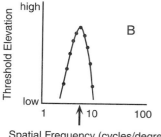

Figure 4.2.7 Contrast sensitivity before and after adaptation to a sinusoidal grating. The solid curve in the top graph shows the normal contrast sensitivity function before adaptation. The data points show it after adaptation to a grating at about 8 cycles per degree (see arrow). The lower graph shows the difference between these two measurements (data points) and a smooth-fitting curve that approximates the reduction in sensitivity (or elevation in threshold).

The results of this experiment can be explained rather simply by a theory based on spatial frequency channels. The theory states that the broad-band CSF that was originally measured actually represents the combined contribution of many overlapping narrow-band channels, each of which is sensitive to a different range of spatial frequencies, as illustrated in the upper graph in Figure 4.2.8. When the adapting grating is presented for an extended period, the channels that are sensitive to that spatial frequency *fatigue*, that is, they "get tired" and respond less vigorously. This fatigue is represented in the lower graph in Figure 4.2.8 as lowered sensitivity in channels near the frequency of the adapting grating. The overall CSF after adaptation thus has a "notch" or "dip" around the adapting grating because, after adaptation, the specific channels that are responsible for perception of the gratings in this frequency range are less sensitive to the same or similar stimuli. It is worth noting that this adaptation effect cannot be

Processing Image Structure

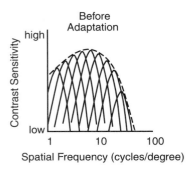

Before
Adaptation

high

Contrast Sensitivity

low

1   10   100

Spatial Frequency (cycles/degree)

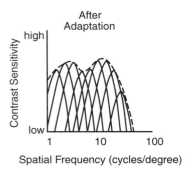

After
Adaptation

high

Contrast Sensitivity

low

1   10   100

Spatial Frequency (cycles/degree)

Figure 4.2.8 The multiple spatial frequency channels hypothesis. The contrast sensitivity function (dashed curve in the upper graph) is hypothesized to be the overall envelope of many overlapping spatial frequency channels (solid curves). The dip in contrast sensitivity following adaptation (dashed curve in the lower graph) is hypothesized to be due to selective adaptation by channels near the adapting frequency.

attributed to simple afterimages because observers moved their eyes back and forth over the grating during adaptation, thus thoroughly smearing any afterimage.

Selective adaptation has similar effects on the orientation of gratings (Blakemore & Campbell, 1969; Blakemore & Nachmias, 1971). We demonstrated the aftereffect of such adaptation effects in Chapter 1 (Figure 1.1.3). To measure their effect on thresholds, one must first determine each subject's sensitivity to sinusoidal gratings of a specific spatial frequency at many different orientations. Once this is established, subjects adapt to a single grating at one particular orientation. Sensitivity at each orientation is then redetermined by measuring postadaptation thresholds to gratings of the same spatial frequency but different orientations. The results, shown in Figure 4.2.9 for a relatively low spatial frequency, clearly indicate reduced sensitivity for orientations close to the adapting grating, analogous to the "notch" found in the CSF as a function of spatial frequency.

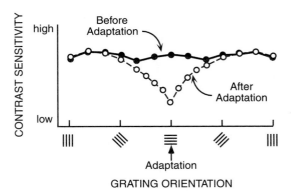

Figure 4.2.9 Selective adaptation to orientation of gratings. Measured sensitivity to sinusoidal gratings is shown as a function of orientation before adaptation (solid circles) and after adapting to a horizontal grating (open circles). (After Bradley, Switkes, & De Valois, 1988.)

Spatial Frequency Aftereffects. Just as gratings of a particular spatial frequency and orientation produce specific adaptation effects, they also produce specific aftereffects. Figure 4.2.10 will allow you to experience the spatial frequency aftereffect for yourself. First, look at the two gratings on the right side and convince yourself that they are identical. Then stare at the gratings on the left for about a minute, moving your eyes back and forth along the horizontal bar in the middle so that the high-frequency grating always stimulates the upper half of your retina and the low-frequency grating always stimulates the lower half. After doing this for a full minute, change your fixation to the bar in the center of the right two gratings. Do they still look the same? If you have adapted for long enough, the upper grating will look as though it has decidedly narrower stripes (that is, higher spatial frequency) than the lower one, even though the two gratings are actually identical. This perception is therefore due to the differential aftereffects of viewing the two adapting gratings.

The standard explanation of this spatial frequency aftereffect is closely related to the one proposed for color afterimages, except that the cells involved are tuned selectively to different spatial frequency bands. Prolonged viewing of the wide grating fatigues the cells that respond selectively to low spatial frequencies in the upper half of the visual field. Similarly, prolonged viewing of the narrow grating fatigues the cells that respond selectively to high spatial frequencies in the lower half of the visual field. The two identical gratings on the right

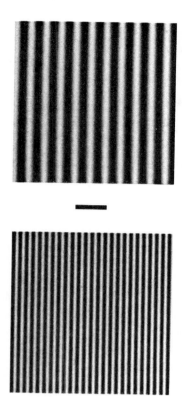

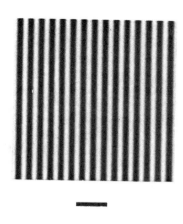

Figure 4.2.10 A demonstration of aftereffects of spatial frequency adaptation. After checking to be sure the two gratings on the right are identical, adapt to the gratings on the left by running your eyes back and forth along the central part for about a minute. Then fixate on the central bar between the gratings on the right and compare their stripe widths. (From De Valois & De Valois, 1988.)

look different because the high-frequency cells are relatively more sensitive on top after adaptation to the low-frequency grating, and the low-frequency cells are relatively more sensitive on bottom after adaptation to the high-frequency grating. These altered sensitivities thus shift the pattern of activity in opposite directions for the upper and lower gratings on the right, producing the experience of narrower stripes in the upper grating and wider stripes in the lower grating.

The reader will recall an analogous demonstration for orientation specific aftereffects—often called *tilt aftereffects*—in Chapter 1 using gratings that differed in orientation (Figure 1.1.3). The explanation in terms of neural fatigue changing the pattern of firing to the identical gratings will also work here, except that the cells in question are ones that are selectively tuned to different orientations rather than to different spatial frequencies.

Thresholds for Sine Wave versus Square Wave Gratings. Further support for the spatial frequency theory of image-based processing has come from many other psychophysical studies of people's detection and discrimination of grating stimuli. The experiments that psychophysicists Norma Graham and Jacob Nachmias (1971) performed to study the difference between detecting gratings made from sine waves versus square waves are particularly elegant. They made several precise, counterintuitive predictions based on spatial frequency theory and found them to be exactly correct.

The basis of their predictions was the hypothesis that a square wave grating would be represented in the early visual system not as a unitary stimulus, but as a collection of many sine wave gratings at different spatial frequencies and amplitudes. Specifically, spatial frequency theory asserts that a square wave grating of frequency f with amplitude a is decomposed into a sine wave grating of frequency f with amplitude a, plus another sine wave

Processing Image Structure

grating of frequency $3f$ with amplitude $a/3$, plus a third sine wave grating of frequency $5f$ with amplitude $a/5$, and so on (see Figure 4.2.2). The first prediction that Graham and Nachmias tested was that the threshold for detecting the presence of a square wave grating would be exactly the same as that for detecting a sine wave grating with the same spatial frequency as the fundamental (f) of the square wave. The rationale is simply that the threshold for detecting the square wave grating will be crossed whenever any of its sine wave components crosses its own independent threshold. The component at the fundamental frequency will be crossed first because its amplitude is much greater than that of any of the higher harmonics of the square wave ($3f$, $5f$, $7f$,...).

Graham and Nachmias tested this prediction by determining the contrast threshold (i.e., the lowest amplitude) at which a square wave grating can be discriminated from a uniform gray field whose luminance is the same as the average luminance of the grating. (See Appendix A for a description of methods for determining thresholds.) From the subject's point of view, the task was to determine whether the test stimulus has any hint of periodic light-dark striping that distinguishes it from a uniform gray field. Graham and Nachmias found that the threshold for performing this task with a square wave grating was exactly the same as the threshold for a sine wave grating whose spatial frequency was the same as the fundamental frequency of the square wave. This finding is surprising because a square wave grating has a much steeper luminance gradient (i.e., a more rapid change over space from light to dark; see Figure 4.2.2E) than does a sine wave grating (Figure 4.2.2A), and the threshold task can sensibly be considered one of detecting whether the luminance gradient of the test stimulus is greater than zero (the luminance gradient for a uniform field). From this viewpoint, the most obvious prediction is that the square wave grating would have a lower threshold than the sine wave grating because its luminance gradient is steeper. But no such difference was found, just as spatial frequency theory predicted.

Graham and Nachmias also examined the contrast threshold at which subjects could discriminate between a sine wave grating and a square wave grating of the same spatial frequency. In this task, the subject must discriminate between these two different striping patterns rather than just whether or not striping is present.

Here again, spatial frequency theory makes a precise, nonintuitive prediction: The contrast threshold for discriminating between a sine wave grating and a square wave grating should be the same as the contrast threshold for discriminating between a uniform field and a sine wave grating whose spatial frequency is the third harmonic ($3f$) of the square wave. This prediction is also based on the hypothesis that the visual system decomposes a square wave grating into a series of sinusoidal components, including its fundamental (f) and all its odd harmonics ($3f$, $5f$, $7f$,...). If so, the difference between a square wave grating and a sine wave grating at its fundamental frequency is only in the presence of the odd harmonics, and for this difference to be detected, one of these harmonics must cross its independent threshold. Because the third harmonic of the square wave grating has the greatest amplitude ($a/3$) of all the odd harmonics, it is the one that should cross its threshold first, and this threshold should be crossed at the same contrast at which the third harmonic can be discriminated from a uniform field.

The results of this experiment again showed remarkably close agreement with the predictions of spatial frequency theory. The fit is all the more remarkable because nobody would have made such predictions from any other existing theory. Many additional experiments have confirmed further tests of spatial frequency theory, making it the dominant psychophysical theory of early spatial vision for the past several decades. It revolutionized the study of visual psychophysics, not only in adult vision, but in infant vision as well.

Development of Spatial Frequency Channels. Psychophysical studies of infant perception have shown that babies see the world quite differently from adults, at least in some respects. These studies are typically conducted by using the preferential looking paradigm discussed in Section 3.2.4 (Fantz, 1958, 1965) with sinusoidal gratings as stimuli. An infant is typically shown a sine wave grating on one side and a homogeneous field on the other side. The two displays are matched for average luminance, so the only difference between them is the degree of modulation into light and dark stripes. If the baby cannot tell the difference, he or she will spend equal amounts of time looking at each. If the grating looks different in any way, the baby will spend more time looking at the grating, presumably be-

A   B

Figure 4.2.11   A simulation of adult versus infant perception of a face. The woman's face in part A would look to an infant like the filtered version in part B, in which the high spatial frequencies have been removed. (Courtesy Sheryl Ehrlich.)

cause it is visually more interesting. By varying the contrast between the light and dark stripes and measuring looking times, researchers can measure the infant's contrast sensitivity function (CSF).

The CSFs for infants at several ages are plotted in Figure 4.2.5C (Atkinson et al., 1977). It shows that infants are less sensitive overall to the gratings and that the biggest difference occurs at high spatial frequencies. The perceptual consequences of this fact are illustrated in Figure 4.2.11. Part A shows a picture of a woman's face as it appears to an adult, and part B shows how it (presumably) appears to infants, given the limited range of spatial frequencies to which they are sensitive. The fuzzy contours result from infants' insensitivity to high-frequency information.

4.2.2 Physiology of Spatial Frequency Channels

Psychophysical channels are hypothetical mechanisms inferred from behavioral measures rather than directly observed biological mechanisms of the nervous system. Thus, psychophysical channels are information processing constructs at Marr's algorithmic level of de-

scription rather than at his implementational level. If these channels are real, however, they must be implemented somewhere in the visual nervous system. The questions to which we now turn are how and where.

The answers to these questions provide the second theory about the function of the cells that Hubel and Wiesel discovered in striate cortex. There is now substantial evidence that these cells may be performing a **local spatial frequency analysis** of incoming images. The analysis that they perform is "local" because the receptive fields of striate cells are spatially limited to a few degrees of visual angle (or even less in the fovea). This is obviously quite restricted in comparison with the theoretically infinite extent of the sinusoidal gratings on which classic Fourier analysis is based. It is even much more restricted than the large grating stimuli (10° or more) normally used in psychophysical studies. However, a local, piecewise, spatial frequency analysis can be accomplished through many small patches of sinusoidal gratings that "fade out" with distance from the center of the receptive field, as illustrated in Figure 4.2.12. This sort of receptive field structure—called a **Gabor function** (or **wavelet**[2])—is constructed by multiplying a global sinusoidal grating by a bell-shaped Gaussian envelope. The one-dimensional luminance profile of this function is shown in Figure 4.2.12A together with a full two-dimensional display that shows how light intensity varies over space according to a Gabor function.

As described in Section 4.1.2, Russell De Valois, Karen De Valois, and their colleagues have mapped the receptive fields of V1 cells carefully and have found evidence for multiple lobes of excitation and inhibition (see Figure 4.1.8). Such receptive fields clearly look a great deal like profiles of Gabor functions (Figure 4.2.12A). To strengthen the connection between these cells and local spatial frequency theory, De Valois, Albrecht and Thorell (1982) measured the spatial frequency tuning of both simple and complex cells. They found many to be quite sharply tuned to small frequency ranges, as would be expected if they were the biological

---

[2] Formal distinctions can be drawn between Gabor and wavelet functions (see Field, 1994). If Gabor functions are taken to be all functions derived from a Gaussian modulated sinusoid, then wavelet functions are a particular kind of Gabor function in which the variance of the Gaussian is a constant number of cycles of the sinusoid. That is, wavelets are Gabor

functions that are "self-similar" in the sense that they differ only by dilations, translations, and rotations of a single underlying function. We will not make this distinction in the text of this book, however, and refer generically to wavelets as Gabor functions.

Processing Image Structure

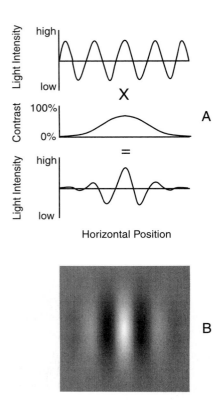

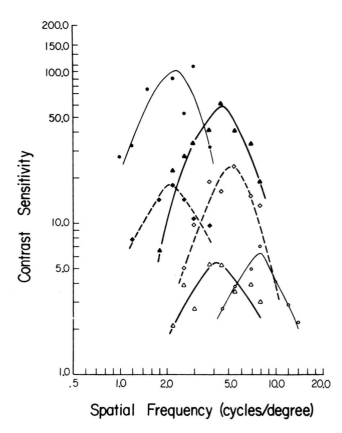

Figure 4.2.12 Gabor functions. A Gabor function is constructed by multiplying a sinusoidal function by a Gaussian function as indicated in part A. The resulting luminance pattern is shown in part B.

Figure 4.2.13 Contrast sensitivity functions for six cells in macaque striate cortex. Each cell shows fairly sharp tuning in spatial frequency, much as is predicted by the multiple spatial frequency channels hypothesis illustrated in Figure 4.2.8. (From De Valois, Albrecht, & Thorell, 1982.)

implementations of local spatial frequency channels in the brain. Figure 4.2.13 shows a sampling of the frequency tuning characteristics of cells in macaque monkey cortex.

The degree of tuning in cortical cells seems to fall along a continuum; some are very sharply tuned and others quite broadly tuned (De Valois et al., 1982). In general, cells that are tuned to high spatial frequencies have narrower tuning than do cells that are tuned to low spatial frequencies. Simple cells also tend to be more narrowly tuned than complex cells, although the difference is not large. There is a similar continuum in the degree of orientation tuning; some cells respond only to gratings that are very close to their "favorite" orientation, whereas others respond almost equally to gratings in any orientation. As it turns out, the frequency and orientation tuning characteristics of cortical cells are correlated: Cells that are broadly tuned for spatial frequency are also broadly tuned for orientation, and cells that are narrowly tuned for spatial frequency are also narrowly tuned for orientation (De Valois & De Valois, 1988).

Further physiological studies have shown that the cortical layout of cells that are tuned to different spatial frequencies is quite systematic. In particular, they appear to be ordered along a dimension perpendicular to that of orientation selectivity within each hypercolumn (De Valois & De Valois 1988). Spatial frequency and orientation thus define a literal two-dimensional space within hypercolumns. In cats, De Valois and De Valois propose that the spatial frequency dimension is laid out in a Cartesian coordinate system as indicated in Figure 4.2.14A. In monkeys, they believe that the architecture is slightly different, orientation and spatial frequency being arranged as dimensions in polar coordinate space, as illustrated in Figure 4.2.14B. Orientation is represented by direction from the center of a hypercolumn; spatial frequency is represented by distance from the center.

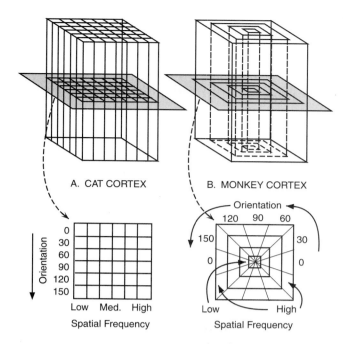

Figure 4.2.14 Models of cortical hypercolumn architecture in cats and monkeys including a spatial frequency dimension. In cats, the spatial frequency dimension is hypothesized to be orthogonal to the orientation dimension in a Cartesian structure, whereas in monkeys it is hypothesized to be radially organized in a polar structure. (After De Valois & De Valois, 1988.)

Although the evidence that simple and complex cells in area V1 may be doing a local spatial frequency analysis of input images is impressive, this conclusion is not universally held. Nevertheless, local spatial frequency theory has led to several interesting and important discoveries about the properties of V1 cells and so must be counted a very serious alternative to the line and edge detector theory suggested by Hubel and Wiesel.

It is interesting to examine the relation between these two theories. They compete because their functional implications are quite different. Spatial frequency theory suggests that these cells are not "detectors" of naturalistic image features, such as lines and edges, but are general purpose analyzers (often called **filters**) that decompose the image into a useful set of primitives that can describe any possible image succinctly. This view does not preclude the existence of line and edge detector cells in the visual system, however. Rather, it simply locates them at a higher level, where the appropriate Gabor filters could be combined to specify the line or edge. Thus, the local spatial frequency theory is poten-

tially compatible with line and edge detector theory but not with the further claim that these detectors are implemented in the cells of area V1. We will return to this controversy later in the chapter, after we have considered the further insights provided by computational approaches to image processing.

4.3 Computational Approaches

Computational theorists have investigated the nature of image processing from a number of different perspectives. The majority have attacked the problem in terms of effective techniques for detecting naturalistic image features such as edges and lines in gray-scale images. Many of the best known practitioners of this so-called traditional approach have worked in the vision group at M.I.T., including David Marr, Tomasso Poggio, Ellen Hildreth, Shimon Ullman, and their colleagues. Much of their research has been aimed at producing a computer implementation of Marr's raw primal sketch that we mentioned briefly at the end of Chapter 2. This group has produced some important results concerning the computational and algorithmic descriptions (in Marr's sense) of edge and line detection problems. This work is closely related to Hubel and Wiesel's conjecture that striate cortical cells are detecting edges and lines.

Despite the relative dominance of this approach, alternative computational views have arisen. One advocates taking a filtering approach to vision, which is based largely on the spatial frequency theory of early vision described in the previous section. Filtering theorists such as Adelson and Bergen (1985), Heeger (1988), Koenderink and Van Doorn (1976a), and Malik (Jones & Malik, 1992; Malik & Perona, 1990) are exploring the computational advantages of using a set of multiorientation, multiscale filters (such as the Gabor functions mentioned in the previous section) as the spatial primitives on which higher level processes operate.

Yet another group of computational theorists is the emerging camp of connectionists who are taking a very different approach to the problem of determining how image processing might work. They are using powerful computational learning techniques (e.g., back propagation, described in Appendix B) that enable neural networks to "program themselves" to perform a well-defined perceptual task. Once the network has learned to perform the task adequately, the researchers examine how the network has accomplished it. One of the networks that emerged from this enterprise contains neuronlike units with "receptive fields" that are surprisingly similar to the cells Hubel and Wiesel discovered in striate cortex. This result suggests some new and unexpected possibilities for the function of these cells beyond the line and edge detector theory and the local spatial frequency theory we have already considered. We will discuss this connectionist research after describing Marr's proposals within the more traditional computer vision framework.

4.3.1 Marr's Primal Sketches

Unlike visual physiologists, who discovered what they took to be edge and line detectors rather unexpectedly, computer vision researchers knew almost from the start that finding edges and lines would figure critically in image processing. (This is not really very surprising, given that computational theorists design vision systems from scratch, so they know the function of the mechanisms they construct beforehand, whereas physiologists have the very different task of figuring out how an existing system works from experimental results.) From the computer vision perspective, almost the first thing that needs to be done with a real image of a scene or even a page of text is to find the lines and edges that are present. These elements, which seem so perfectly obvious when human perceivers look at a gray-scale image (e.g., the cup in Figure 2.4.2), are quite obscure when the image is considered as an array of luminance values registered by a video camera (Figure 2.4.3B). Even in Roberts's (1965) early computer vision program, the first step was to detect local edges and lines.

The computational view of image processing was dominated for many years by David Marr's (1982) proposals about the structure of his primal sketches. Although he was hardly the first computer scientist to recognize the importance of image-based processing, he articulated the outlines of an integrated theory more compellingly than anyone before him. Marr actually suggested that there are two primal sketches: the *raw primal sketch* and the *full primal sketch*. Marr's specific proposals about the nature of an image-based representation in terms of these primal sketches are no longer

widely held, and we will consider an alternative view at the end of this section. Even so, Marr's formulation of the primal sketch played an important role in the development of computational theories of low-level spatial vision and is worth describing for historical as well as theoretical reasons.

Marr's raw primal sketch accomplishes the first step in the transition from the fully analog, gray-scale image to a largely symbolic representation of image-based features. Marr suggested that vision must "go symbolic" almost immediately. To accomplish this task, he proposed four qualitatively different types of image features in the primal sketch: edges, lines (or bars), blobs, and terminations. These primitives are called "symbolic" because they constitute discrete classes of image-based features. The raw primal sketch also has important analogue aspects, however, in that it represents essentially continuous information about several parameters for each image symbol (edge, bar, blob, or termination): its position, size, orientation, and contrast. Although Marr didn't talk about motion or color as parameters of image symbols explicitly, they could also be added to the raw primal sketch by including direction of motion, speed of motion, and color contrast in the list of analog values that define each symbolic image feature.

The full primal sketch is a more elaborately organized version of the raw primal sketch. It includes the results of operations such as linking short line segments and edges together into longer ones, grouping similar elements together, and perhaps characterizing the texture of areas within the visual field. Much less computational research has been done on these problems of perceptual organization at the image level than on edge and line detection, but we will consider some of it in Chapter 6.

4.3.2 Edge Detection

The spatial primitives of Marr's first stage of image-level processing are edges, lines, blobs, and terminations. Of these, by far the most work has been done on the processes required to detect luminance edges. We will examine it in some detail as an example of how such low-level image features can be extracted from a gray-scale image. As we will see, the issues involved are surprisingly complex.

When a three-dimensional scene of objects reflects light onto a two-dimensional surface such as the retina or an array of sensors in a video camera, the changes in luminance that take place along a uniformly colored smooth surface tend to be gradual, owing to subtle changes in illumination. The changes that take place across a transition from one surface to another, however, are generally much more abrupt, and they tend to form luminance edges. These abrupt edges are particularly important because they signify either a change in the reflectance of the surface (e.g., from one material to another), a change in the amount of light falling on it (e.g., due to a shadow), or a change in surface orientation relative to the light source (since most surfaces at different angles to the source reflect different amounts of light into the eye). For these and other reasons, luminance edges are almost universally agreed to be important image-based features.

Edge Operators and Convolution. Early attempts at detecting luminance edges automatically by computer algorithms were relatively unsystematic. Researchers took a purely empirical approach, trying a variety of different **edge operators** on a variety of images to determine which ones worked best. An edge operator is a computational scheme for integrating the gray-scale values over some neighborhood of adjacent pixels in an image to come up with a single number that represents the likelihood that there is a luminance edge at that location in the image. Figure 4.3.1 shows several simple edge operators that might be used to detect vertical and horizontal edges.

In the language of computer vision, edges are detected by performing the **convolution** of an edge operator with an image. As we will see shortly, "convolution" is just the mathematical name for what a sheet of retinotopically organized cortical cells does to an incoming image if their receptive fields have the structure of the edge operator. Each cell computes the sum of its excitatory inputs plus the sum of its inhibitory inputs (which are negative, so inhibition subtracts from excitation) and produces the final result as its output. The output for the whole sheet of cells responding to the image is essentially the convolution of the cell's receptive field (that is, the edge operator) with the image.

To understand how edge operators and convolution work in detail, consider Figure 4.3.2. It shows a simple noiseless image of a cross in gray-scale form (A) and numerical form (B) together with the results of convolving

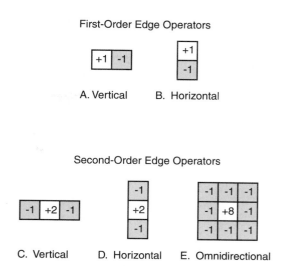

Figure 4.3.1 Five simple edge operators. Weighting schemes for integrating local neighborhoods of pixels to represent the likelihood of a luminance edge. First-order operators for vertical (A) and horizontal (B) edges simply compute the difference between adjacent pixels. Second-order operators for vertical (C), horizontal (D), and omnidirectional (E) edges effectively compute differences of differences. Note that in all cases, the sum of the weights is zero.

the image with a vertical (C) and a horizontal (D) edge operator. To compute the convolution of the vertical edge operator (C) with the numerical image (B), begin at the upper left of the numerical image (B) and apply the weighting scheme of the vertical edge operator to the top-left pixel and the pixel immediately to its right. To do so, simply multiply the top-leftmost pixel value (10) times -1 ($= -10$) and the one to its right (10) times $+1$ ($= +10$), and then add these two values ($-10 + 10 = 0$). The result is zero because the gray-scale value of these two pixels is the same, and so we enter this value in the upper left pixel of the output (E). Note that whenever the values of two adjacent pixels are the same (or nearly so) the output of this operator will be zero (or nearly so). Therefore, this operator will not respond at all to regions of uniform luminance and will respond very little to ones with gradual changes in luminance. Its output will be greatest for the abrupt changes in luminance that occur at edges.

The next step in calculating the convolution of the image with this edge operator is to "slide" the edge operator one pixel to the right and compute the output in the same way for the next two pixels in this row (i.e., the second and third in the top row). Here, the left pixel is

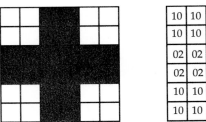

A. Grayscale Image

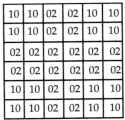

B. Image Intensities

C. Vertical Edge Operator

D. Horizontal Edge Operator

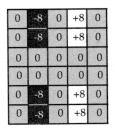

E. Convolution of Image with Vertical Edge Operator

F. Convolution of Image with Horizontal Edge Operator

Figure 4.3.2 Convolving an image with edge operators. A gray-scale image (A) can be convolved with a variety of edge operators (e.g., C and D) by multiplying their weights times the numerical values of each pixel in the image (B) according to a computational scheme called convolution (see text). The vertical edge operator (C) gives the results shown in part E, and the horizontal edge operator (D) gives those shown in part F. (Dark pixels in parts E and F represent large negative values, and light pixels represent large positive values.)

much brighter (10) than the one just to its right (2), and so the output of the edge operator will be a large negative value $(-10 + 2 = -8)$, indicating a light-to-dark luminance edge at that position. Continue this procedure for the rest of the pixels in the top row by sliding the edge operator one pixel to the right each time and summing the product of the edge operator's weights with the pixel intensity values. There will be some more zeros as the operator computes its output over the dark part of the vertical bar and then a large positive value where the change from dark to light occurs. Large positive values indicate the presence of dark-to-light luminance edges. Continue this procedure for each pair of pixels in each row of the image, and you will have computed the convolution of this local edge operator with

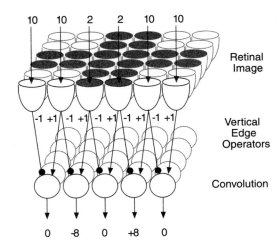

Figure 4.3.3 A neural network for convolving an image with a vertical edge operator. A simple first-order edge operator (see Figure 4.3.2C) is implemented in a neural network via excitatory and inhibitory connections between the layer of retinal receptors and the layer of units representing the convolution of the image with the edge operator. The output for this image (Figure 4.3.2A) will be the same as shown in Figure 4.3.2E.

the image. The result is shown in numerical form in Figure 4.3.2E. It can be represented in gray-scale form (as superimposed on the numerical array in E) by mapping 0 to neutral gray pixels, positive values to lighter gray pixels, and negative values to darker gray pixels. Note that the vertical edge operator has responded strongly to the vertical edges in the original image and nowhere else.

This procedure for computing convolutions of an image with an edge operator is just a sequential version of what a sheet of cells would compute in parallel if their receptive fields corresponded to the weighting scheme of the edge operator. Figure 4.3.3 shows how this vertical edge operator could be implemented in a neural network. The weightings from input layer to output layer indicate an inhibitory connection from the left input (-1) and an excitatory connection from the right input $(+1)$, which are then summed by the output cell. Thus, the output of this network is the convolution of the image (represented by the activation of the input layer) with the operator represented by the connection weighting scheme. Convolution is thus not inherently sequential, as might have been assumed from the stepwise procedure we initially carried out, but it is implemented this way on serial computers. The visual system does convolutions much faster by implementing them in parallel hardware, using the connections between layers of neurons to compute the value of the convolution at each location.

Everywhere there is a vertical edge in the image, the value of the convolution is either highly positive or highly negative. Thus, the presence of extreme values for this edge operator indicates the likely presence of a vertical edge. If you perform the same convolution operation between the image and the horizontal edge operator (Figure 4.3.2D), you will find that horizontal edges produce extreme output values in the appropriate locations (Figure 4.3.2F). An example of using such edge operators on a real image is given in Figure 2.2.2B, which depicts the result of Roberts's (1965) pioneering program finding edges at vertical, horizontal, right diagonal, and left diagonal orientations.

These particular local edge operators are called **first-order differential operators** because they take the simple difference between adjacent pixels. They are essentially computing the slope of the luminance function along a particular direction because the slope of this function is just the difference between adjacent values. More complicated local edge operators can be constructed by computing the difference between adjacent first-order operators to produce **second-order differential operators**, as shown in Figures 4.3.1C, 4.3.1D, and 4.3.1E. Second-order edge operators work differently from first-order ones in the sense that edges are indicated not by extreme values, but by zero values with extreme values flanking them for reasons we will examine in detail shortly. Figure 4.3.1E shows a second-order edge operator that will detect vertical, horizontal, left-diagonal, and right-diagonal edges simultaneously. This is possible because the positive-negative-positive cross-sectional profile is present in all four of these orientations through the center of the edge operator. With these pieces in place, we can now understand an influential computational theory of edge detection and how it might relate to structures in the visual nervous system.

The Marr-Hildreth Zero-Crossing Algorithm. Marr and Hildreth (1980) formulated an interesting theory of edge detection within the framework of Marr's three levels of description of an information processing system. It is no longer a serious contender for state-of-the-art edge detection algorithms, having been supplanted by Canny's (1986) algorithm and its successors (e.g., Deriche, 1987; Spacek, 1985), but it is of historical interest as one of the first edge detection schemes in which a serious attempt was made to match its computational structure with the physiology of the mammalian visual system. We will therefore examine it in some detail.

For the computational description, Marr and Hildreth (1980) began by characterizing an idealized one-dimensional luminance edge of the sort they would like their edge detection scheme to find (see Figure 4.3.4A). They reasoned that such an edge could be located by finding the position of maximum slope in its luminance function (a graph of the luminance value as a function of space). Thus, the luminance profile of a one-dimensional luminance edge can be graphed as a curve in which the x axis is the spatial dimension and the y axis corresponds to the luminance (or light intensity), as illustrated in Figure 4.3.4B.

First-order differential operators compute the slope of such luminance functions. The slope of the luminance function is represented in Figure 4.3.4B at seven positions by the orientation of the gray rectangles that follow the curve. Figure 4.3.4C plots this slope function, called its **first derivative**, in terms of the change in intensity as a function of position. The position of the luminance edge can thus be found by detecting the maximum (highest value) in the first derivative of the luminance function, which would correspond to the maximum of a first-order edge operator. Marr and Hildreth criticized this scheme because first-order edge operators must be computed at every possible orientation, and they felt that this process was computationally wasteful in terms of the number of edge operators needed, particularly compared with the alternative they envisioned.

Marr and Hildreth reasoned that a more economical algorithm for finding edges would be to detect **zero-crossings of the second derivative** of the luminance function. The **second derivative** of a luminance function is just the slope of the first derivative of the luminance function. To see what this looks like, we can simply repeat the procedure that we just followed but use the first derivative as the basic function. The second derivative thus computes the "slope of the slope" of the original luminance function, as indicated in Figures 4.3.4D and 4.3.4E. Notice that in this second derivative function, the position of the luminance edge corresponds to the zero value in between a highly positive

Processing Image Structure

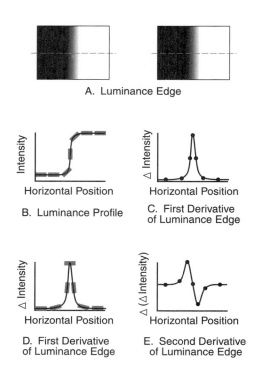

A. Luminance Edge

B. Luminance Profile

C. First Derivative
of Luminance Edge

D. First Derivative
of Luminance Edge

E. Second Derivative
of Luminance Edge

Figure 4.3.4 First and second derivatives of luminance edges. A luminance edge (A) can be represented by a graph (called its luminance profile) that plots light intensity (luminance) as a function of spatial position (B). The first derivative (or slope) of this function (C) has a peak at the center of the luminance edge. The second derivative (E), which is the slope of the first derivative function, has a zero crossing at the center of the luminance edge with a positive value on one side and a negative value on the other.

and a highly negative value. The local operators that compute the second derivative are the second-order differential operators we mentioned earlier (Figure 4.3.1C, 4.3.1D, and 4.3.1E).

The zero-crossing of the second derivative (Figure 4.3.4E) is formally equivalent to the maximum of the first derivative (Figure 4.3.4C), but it offers the potentially important computational advantage mentioned above: Because the second-order operators are symmetrical about their midpoint (see Figure 4.3.1C and 4.3.1D), the second derivative of a two-dimensional image can be computed in all orientations simultaneously by the single two-dimensional operator shown in Figure 4.3.1E and 4.3.5A. This edge operator is essentially the simultaneous combination of second-order operators at vertical, horizontal, left-diagonal, and right-diagonal orientations. In a continuous space, the same two-

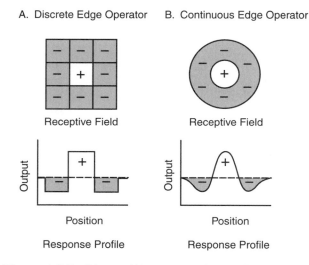

A. Discrete Edge Operator B. Continuous Edge Operator

Receptive Field

Receptive Field

Response Profile

Response Profile

Figure 4.3.5 Discrete (A) versus continuous (B) versions of a second-order omnidirectional edge operator. The upper diagram shows the receptive field of the operators on the imaging surface. The lower graph shows its response profile across the horizontal dimension.

dimensional second-order operator would be as shown in Figure 4.3.5B, and its cross-sectional response profile would be as shown below it. The fact that the second derivative for all orientations can be collapsed into a single operator means that this scheme would be much more efficient computationally. This edge operator should look familiar, for its center/surround (Mexican hat) receptive field structure is essentially the same as that of retinal ganglion and LGN cells that we discussed in Section 4.1.1.

Figure 4.3.6 shows the application of this zero-crossing algorithm in somewhat greater detail to the image of a plant behind a chain-link fence. Figure 4.3.6A shows the gray-scale image. Figure 4.3.6B shows the convolution of image A with the second-order operator in gray-scale form, so zero values are neutral gray, positive values are lighter, and negative values are darker. Figure 4.3.6C shows the same thing in binary form, so zero-crossings are represented as black/white edges. Figure 4.3.6D shows the actual zero-crossings that were identified by the zero-crossing algorithm.

One complication in computational theories of edge detection is that luminance edges occur at different size scales, some being slow changes in intensity over broad regions of space and others being rapid changes over tiny regions. Marr and Hildreth dealt with this problem

A

B

C

D

Figure 4.3.6 Finding edges by detecting zero-crossings. The gray-scale image (part A) is first convolved with a second-order omnidirectional edge operator (e.g., Figure 4.3.5B) to produce the image shown in part B, where zero is represented as neutral gray, positive values as lighter gray and negative values as darker gray. Part C shows positive values as white and negative values as black. The zero-crossings in B have been detected in part D to show the locations of the edges found by this algorithm. (From Marr, 1982.)

by employing second-order edge operators of three different sizes: large ones to detect low-resolution (coarse) edges, medium ones to detect medium-resolution edges, and small ones to detect high-resolution (fine) edges. To appreciate just how different the edges at these levels of spatial resolution can be, consider Figure 4.3.7A, which shows a discretely sampled digital approximation of the face of Abraham Lincoln (Harmon & Julesz, 1973). The zero-crossings detected by Marr and Hildreth's edge operator at fine (part B), medium (part C), and coarse (part D) levels of resolution show that the edges that allow the viewer to see Lincoln's face are located primarily at low resolution levels. You can see these low-resolution edges selectively by squinting your eyes to blur the original picture, by viewing it from far enough away that the

high-resolution edges are too fine for your visual system to discriminate, or by taking off your glasses if you wear any.

In this rather artificial case, few edges at high and low levels of resolution are the same. In natural images, however, most real edges that can be found at low levels of resolution will also be found in the same general location at higher levels of resolution. Moreover, finding edges at multiple levels of resolution in the same location increases the likelihood that a real edge (rather than just noise) is present. Figure 4.3.8 shows the zero-crossings that are detected at the three different size scales Marr and Hildreth proposed when applied to the image shown in part A. Notice that many more edges are present at the finer-grained size but that the most important edges are present at all three levels of resolution.

Processing Image Structure

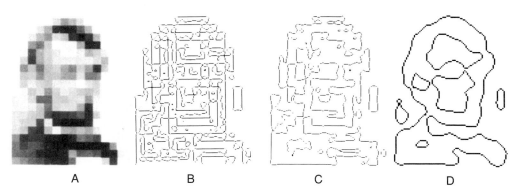

A   B   C   D

Figure 4.3.7 Edge detection at different spatial scales. The quantized image of Lincoln's face (A) has been analyzed for edges at fine (B), medium (C), and coarse (D) levels of resolution by using the Marr-Hildreth zero-crossing algorithm. Note that the outlines of Lincoln's face are most apparent in the edges found by the coarse operator. (From Marr, 1982.)

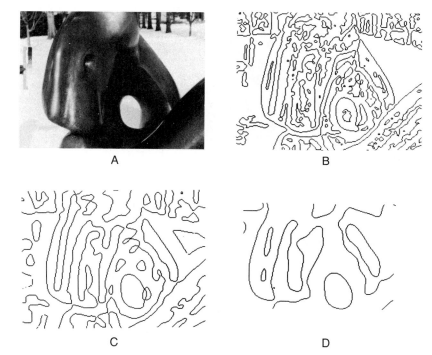

Figure 4.3.8 Zero-crossings at different spatial scales in a natural image. The gray-scale image of a sculpture by Henry Moore (A) has been analyzed for edges at fine (B), medium (C), and coarse (D) levels of resolution by using the Marr-Hildreth algorithm. Such different outputs must somehow be integrated into a single representation. (From Marr & Hildreth, 1980.)

It is noteworthy that Marr and Hildreth did not invent their theory of edge detection out of thin air. Virtually every component was known from the work of previous investigators in computer vision: convolution with bar and edge operators (Duda & Hart, 1973), detecting zero-crossings of second-order differential operators (Horn, 1971), and working on the image at several levels of resolution (Rosenfeld, Thurston, & Lee, 1972). What Marr and Hildreth did was to bring all these elements together in a single, well-integrated algorithm.

Neural Implementation. Marr and Hildreth also did something else that was equally important. They paid careful attention to how their edge and line detection algorithm might be implemented in neural hardware by performing a fairly detailed analysis of correspondences between their algorithm and the types of cells that are known to exist early in the mammalian visual nervous system. As you might have guessed, they proposed that the convolution of the image with the second-order edge operator was accomplished by ganglion and LGN cells whose receptive fields have a rotationally symmetric center/surround organization with the Mexican hat shape. The result of this neural information processing—presumably at the output of the LGN cells—would be analogous to Figure 4.3.6B. In this representation, zero crossings of the second-order differential operator are present but have not yet been explicitly detected. Finding the zero-crossings must therefore be carried out by some further process.

To understand how these zero-crossings might be detected by neural processing, recall that zero-crossings in the output of the second-order operator are found between highly positive values on one side and highly negative values on the other. Marr and Hildreth therefore proposed that zero-crossings could be explicitly detected by looking for these positive-to-negative (or negative-to-positive) changes in the output of center/surround receptive fields. This can be accomplished by constructing an operator that performs a logical AND operation on adjacent on-center and off-center geniculate cells. Such an edge detector unit will fire vigorously only if both LGN cells are highly active, as illustrated in Figure 4.3.9A. Edge detectors sharply tuned to specific orientations can then be constructed by combining the output of many aligned zero-crossing detectors, as illustrated in Figure 4.3.9B.

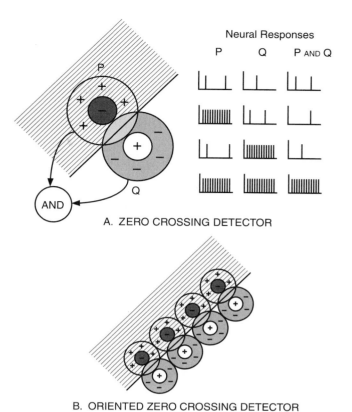

Figure 4.3.9 A neural model of the Marr-Hildreth zero-crossing algorithm. A zero-crossing detector (A) can be constructed by taking the logical AND of the outputs of an on-center and an off-center receptive field. Several such units arranged in tandem (B) will be highly selective to edges at a specific orientation. (Adapted from Marr & Hildreth, 1980.)

This proposal may sound familiar, because it is very similar to Hubel and Wiesel's conjecture about how "edge detector" simple cells in striate cortex could be constructed by summing the outputs of LGN cells. Thus, Marr and Hildreth suggest that oriented "edge detector" simple cells in striate cortex are actually **zero-crossing detectors**. In effect, their theory proposes that simple cells are indeed detecting edges but not quite as Hubel and Wiesel proposed. Rather, they are the detection process in an edge algorithm that computes explicit zero-crossings in the output of second-order difference operators.

More recently, Canny (1986) devised a "more effective" edge detection algorithm for computer vision using sophisticated analyses to maximize performance in edge detection under certain conditions. Canny departs from

Marr and Hildreth's approach by using first-order differential operators at several different orientations rather than the single second-order differential operator they proposed. Through a series of complex mathematical arguments, Canny derived an optimal detector for two-dimensional luminance "step edges," which turned out to be a very close approximation to an idealized Hubel-Wiesel edge detector, as shown in Figure 4.3.10. The excellent performance of this operator is illustrated in Figure 4.3.11. Other effective edge detection algorithms have since been devised by Deriche (1987) and Spacek (1985) using maximization techniques similar to Canny's.

Scale Integration. At first blush it would seem that once zero-crossings have been detected in Marr and Hildreth's algorithm, the edge-finding algorithm has done its job. But there is some unfinished business, namely, integrating the edge information from different sizes or scales. This has proven to be a problematic aspect of the theory, and Marr and Hildreth never implemented a reliable simulation of it. Canny's edge algorithm also requires integration over different sizes (widths) of edge operators. To the extent that scale integration is necessary for accurate edge detection, further processes are required to accomplish it.

The problem of **scale integration**, as it has come to be known, is that the visual system needs to determine how the different edges at different scales match up: Which ones are due to the same edge and which ones are not? The problem is illustrated in Figure 4.3.12. The jagged curve at the bottom is the one-dimensional luminance profile from an image, and the tick marks on the four lines above it mark the locations of edges detected at four different scale sizes. The scale integration problem comes in trying to put the ticks together: Which edge goes with which? The most obvious strategy is to base the correspondence on the location and orientation of the edges. The problem is that the location and even the orientation of a given edge may differ somewhat from one scale to another, spoiling the possibility of a clean solution.

The problem of integrating edge information across different size scales has been addressed with some success by Witkin's (1983) *scale space algorithm*. Witkin replaces the Marr-Hildreth assumption of three discrete scales with the idea of a continuous **scale space** that ranges from very small edge operators to very large

ones. If there is a virtual continuum of scale sizes, edge information can be followed throughout this dimension to determine which edges go with which. It is illustrated in Figure 4.3.13. Notice that, going from top (coarse) to bottom (fine), new edges appear at many different levels and that some of them appear alone, whereas others appear in pairs that begin together and end up farther apart.

One of the most important features of Witkin's scale space algorithm is that it presupposes a continuous representation of sizes. This means that if the human visual system uses such a system, it would require a more complete representation of sizes than many theorists have supposed. However, the notion of a continuous scale space is highly compatible with results showing that the receptive fields of cortical cells include a fairly dense representation of sizes in the spatial frequency dimension (e.g., De Valois & De Valois, 1988). Perhaps one function of this dimension in cortical cells is to implement some form of Witkin's scale space algorithm for edge integration.

The Raw Primal Sketch. Marr includes not only edges, but also bars, blobs, and terminators as primitive elements in his concept of the **raw primal sketch**. Figure 4.3.14 illustrates these components for the chain-link fence image shown in Figure 4.3.6A. Figures 4.3.14A and 4.3.14B show the zero-crossings at two different scale sizes, and Figures 4.3.14C, 4.3.14D, and 4.3.14E show the blobs, edges, and bars that were found by automatic detection programs. Bars are defined as short line segments whose terminators lie outside the receptive field, terminators are defined as ends of edges or bars, and blobs are defined as short bars with terminators at both ends. As was the case for edge detector units, there are fairly obvious physiological analogs of detectors for these features in visual cortex: Bars can be found by simple cells and terminators by end-stopped (hypercomplex) cells. Indeed, Hubel and Wiesel's physiological findings undoubtedly figured heavily in Marr's decision to include them in his primal sketch, which can easily be interpreted as a computational view of what information processing the cells in area V1 might be doing.

The idea of including line and edge terminations in the primal sketch might seem surprising at first, since they are not "things," like edges, bars, and blobs, but

A. Cross Section Parallel to Edge

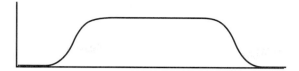

B. Cross Section Perpendicular to Edge

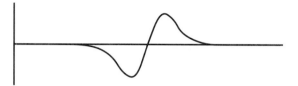

C. Examples of Edge Operators at 8 Orientations

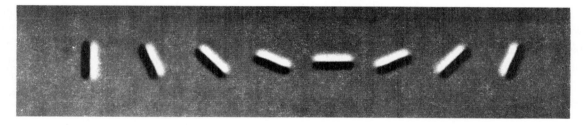

Figure 4.3.10 Edge operators for Canny's algorithm. The edge operators are defined by the cross sections parallel to the edge (A) and perpendicular to the edge (B). Several oriented edge operators of this form at different orientations are shown in part C. (From Canny, 1986.)

Figure 4.3.11 An application of Canny's edge algorithm. A gray-scale image (A) is shown together with the edges detected by Canny's algorithm (B). (From Canny, 1986.)

Processing Image Structure

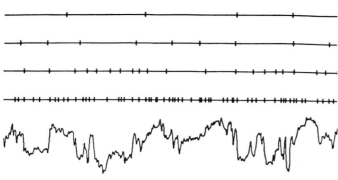

Figure 4.3.12 The problem of scale integration of edge information at discrete levels of resolution. A noisy 1-D waveform (bottom) is analyzed for zero-crossings at four discrete scales of resolution, resulting in the detection of many edges at each level (ticks on the four upper lines). The scale integration problem is how to determine which edges at different scales correspond to each other. (From Witkin, 1983.)

"endings of things." There are several striking perceptual phenomena that seem to depend importantly on the presence of terminations, however. Figure 4.3.15 shows two cases in which aligned terminations of lines have clear perceptual consequences. Part of the importance of terminations is that they often signal occlusion of a line or edge by a closer edge. This is probably what gives the strong impression of **illusory contours** in Figures 4.3.15A and 4.3.15B. Illusory contours are visual experiences of edges where there is no physical luminance edge present in the image. If a figure is defined by these aligned edges, as in Figure 4.3.15B, it often seems to be lighter than the surrounding background as well. We will return to the topic of illusory contours in Chapter 6 when we discuss perceptual organization.

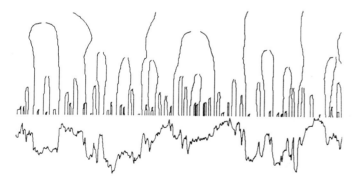

Figure 4.3.13 Witkin's scale space algorithm for edge integration. Witkin solved the scale integration problem by proposing a continuum of scales that automatically links edges across spatial scales. (From Witkin, 1983.)

The raw primal sketch is the first symbolic representation in Marr's theory of visual information processing in that it is the point at which aspects of the analog grayscale image get transformed into a discrete set of edges, bars, blobs, and terminators. These four categories of image features are referred to as **types** in the symbolic representation, and each particular edge, bar, blob, or terminator in the visual field is called a **token** of the corresponding type. Each token is **instantiated**—specified as a particular instance of the type—by several parameters that distinguish among possible tokens: a particular bar's position (x and y coordinates), orientation, luminance contrast (light-on-dark or dark-on-light), length, and width.

Notice that x and y position are represented in Figure 4.3.14 as retinotopic maps. Many further computations that need to be done on the primal sketch within a local region are easy to accomplish by searching neighboring locations in a retinotopic map in which neighboring locations are, by definition, close together. Because much of the processing that is required to get to the next level representation—the full primal sketch—requires exactly this kind of local search, Marr kept the 2-D structure of the spatial image intact in the primal sketch. Also, when later stages must integrate results across different sets of features, retinotopic structure makes it easy to access features at corresponding locations. This will figure importantly in attentional theories of feature integration, which we will examine in Chapter 11.

Marr's full primal sketch is derived from the raw primal sketch by the operation of organizational processes. These operations are hypothesized to link short line segments into long ones, group image elements into aggregates, and segment regions that differ from each other in texture. We will postpone a full discussion of such processes until Chapter 6 when we explore the topic of perceptual organization in detail.

4.3.3 Alternative Computational Theories

Detection of image-based features such as edges, bars, and blobs is not the only computational theory that has been advanced to explain the function of the cells Hubel and Wiesel discovered. We have already seen that local spatial frequency analysis is a serious contender, but still other functions have been proposed. One alternative is that these cells are a crucial link in the analysis of

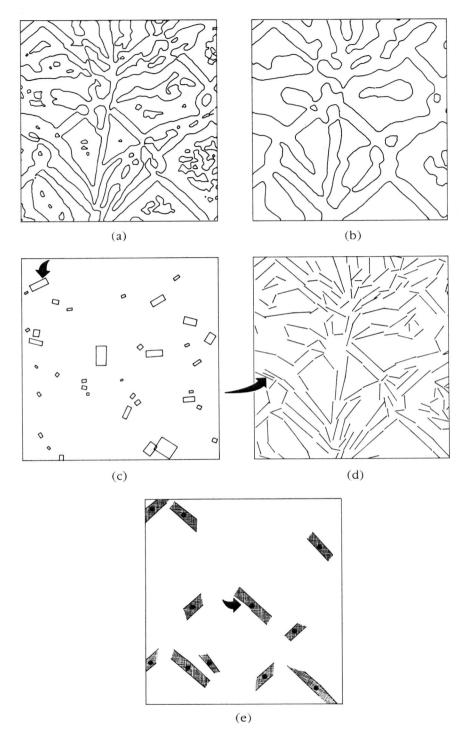

(a)

(b)

(c)

(d)

(e)

Figure 4.3.14 Marr's raw primal sketch. The gray-scale image of a chain-link fence (Figure 4.3.6A) is analyzed for zero-crossings at fine (A) and coarse (B) spatial scales, and the results are integrated to form a symbolic map of oriented edges (D). Other analyses detect the presence of "blobs" (C) and "bars" (E) at different locations. (From Marr & Hildreth, 1980.)

Processing Image Structure

A   B

Figure 4.3.15 Examples of illusory contours defined by line terminations. Marr suggests that such illusory contours are constructed by joining termination points in the primal sketch.

texture information. Another is that they mediate the recovery of the curvature of a surface from shading information. We will briefly examine these hypotheses and then evaluate their implications for theories of what these enigmatic cells might be doing.

Texture Analysis. Another computational theory that has implications for the possible function of the cells Hubel and Wiesel discovered in visual cortex comes from Malik and Perona's (1990) theory of **texture analysis**: the process by which the visual system defines regions that differ in the statistical properties of spatial structure. They make a persuasive argument that V1 cells provide an initial stage in the segregation of regions according to texture information. Figure 4.3.16 demonstrates texture segregation because the difference between the concentric squares lies in their textural properties rather than in their color or overall luminance. We will describe Malik and Perona's theory in detail in Chapter 6 when we discuss the problem of texture segregation, but the gist of their proposal is that

Figure 4.3.16 Demonstration of texture analysis. The different regions in this image have the same average luminance but can be defined by their different textures. Malik and Perona's (1990) theory of texture segregation is based on the output of receptive fields like those found in area V1 of visual cortex.

many of the results on texture perception can be parsimoniously explained by a theory that assumes an initial stage in which the visual image is convolved with receptive fields like those measured in area V1. Differences in both the orientation and scale (spatial frequency) of receptive fields are crucial in their analysis.

This idea might not at first seem too different from the notion that the corresponding cells are detecting luminance edges, for one would expect that the edges of the texture elements would play a significant role in texture perception. The important difference is that Malik and Perona's algorithm does not explicitly detect luminance edges at all. Rather, it simply uses the output of the multiorientation multiscale cells as input to a process that detects large-scale discontinuities in texture, not luminance. If this is true, and if the same cells are also involved in edge detection, it suggests that they may be fulfilling several different functions, a possibility to which we will return shortly.

Structure from Shading. A radically different computational theory about the possible role of the cells in area V1 has been advanced by Lehky and Sejnowski (1988, 1990) on the basis of neural network research. The problem they studied was **structure from shading**: how information about the curvature of surfaces can be extracted from changes in luminance due to depth structure in the image. Figure 4.3.17 demonstrates the importance of shading information. The unshaded 2-D version in Figure 4.3.17A looks quite flat and is virtually unrecognizable as anything except an oddly shaped blob. When shading information is added in Figure 4.3.17B, however, the object takes on a strikingly 3-D quality and is immediately recognizable. Obviously, shading information is quite important in how you perceive this figure.

The approach that Lehky and Sejnowski took to the problem of perceiving surface curvature from shading was to investigate how a three-layer connectionist network, such as that depicted in Figure 4.3.18, might learn to be able to compute the curvature of surfaces from image luminance. They used a learning procedure called **back propagation** to automatically change the connection weights so that the middle "hidden" layer

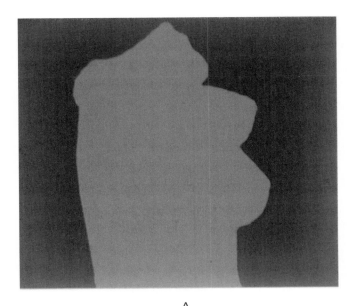

A

Figure 4.3.17 Demonstration of shading analysis. The striking difference between perception of the outline version (part A) and the shaded version (part B) on the next page is due entirely to information about relative depth from gray-scale shading. (After Koenderink, Kappers, Pollick, & Kawato, 1997.)

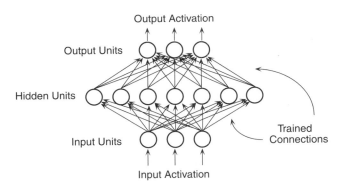

Figure 4.3.18 The architecture of a three-layer feedforward network used to learn shading analysis. There were 122 input units simulating LGN cells with center/surround receptive fields (61 on-center and 61 off-center units), 27 hidden units, and 24 output units to represent surface curvature information. Learning was accomplished by an automatic procedure that adjusted the weights on the connections between units.

was able to map the input representation to the shape-from-shading representation. Lehky and Sejnowski gave the input layer the Mexican hat–shaped center/surround receptive fields of LGN cells (see Figure 4.1.2), and they gave the output layer the characteristics needed to code the curvature of local surface regions. Then they let the back propagation algorithm adjust the weights of the connections to and from the middle layer as necessary to map the LGN input representation to the output representation of surface curvature.

We will not describe the back propagation algorithm by which the network learned (see Appendix B), nor the details of exactly how the researchers determined the receptive fields of the hidden middle layer of units. The interesting result was that after the network had learned to extract surface curvature, many of the hidden layer "neurons" had constructed receptive fields that looked strikingly similar to those of cells in cortical area V1. That is, many of them had elongated receptive fields with two or more lobes of excitation and inhibition, as shown in Figure 4.3.19. Although the analysis of the similarity between these receptive fields and those of real cells is quite subjective, it is nevertheless suggestive. It is not immediately clear why these simulated cells have this computational structure, but it is related to the kinds of shadows and shading one finds on various sorts of curved surfaces. Perhaps most importantly, this analysis has awakened researchers to the wide variety of possible uses to which such elongated receptive field structures might be put.

A formal mathematical analysis of structure from shading by Pentland (1989) has further shown that under certain restricted conditions, a set of Gabor filters is sufficient to recover the approximate shape of the surface in depth from its projected image. The set of filters included a sampling of different spatial frequencies and orientations in both sine and cosine phase at many different positions. This is precisely the set of receptive fields some researchers have postulated to compose the cells in area V1 (e.g., Daugman, 1980; De Valois & De Valois, 1988). It can therefore be assumed that the output of these cells could be used as the basis of a later process that recovers shape from shading, at least for small regions of the retinal image, as Lehky and Sejnowski's results suggested. Whether they are so used or not remains an unanswered question.

Processing Image Structure

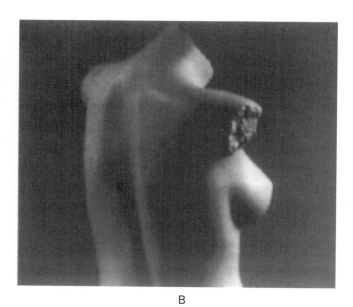

B

Figure 4.3.17 (continued)

4.3.4 A Theoretical Synthesis

We have just reviewed several theories about the function of the cortical cells that Hubel and Wiesel discovered more than 40 years ago. They are generally assumed to be doing image-level processing of some sort, but of what particular sort? Can any conclusions be drawn or lessons be learned from the enormous amount of work that has been directed at understanding them?

Local Spatial Frequency Filters. From the psychophysical perspective, these cells appear to be the physiological implementation of the spatial frequency channels that Campbell and Robson first postulated in 1968. The primary difference is that each cell's receptive field is localized in a small region of the retina rather than being distributed globally over the whole visual field. Still, each hypercolumn in V1 may be capable of performing a local spatial frequency analysis of the small patch of the retinal image to which its cells are sensitive. Simple cells have the right properties in that they are tuned to different ranges of spatial frequency and orientation at a particular retinal position, just as one would expect from local spatial frequency theory.

The functional significance of these observations about the spatial frequency tuning of cortical cells is not yet entirely clear, however. The psychophysical view is that these cells describe images in a piecewise, local Fourier analysis. However, computational theorists such as Marr and Hildreth have claimed with equal conviction that these same cells are actually the physiological implementation of edge detection mechanisms at different spatial scales. In a related vein, Witkin could identify the so-called spatial frequency dimension of cortical cells as the neural implementation of the scale dimension in his scale space analysis. Add to this Malik and Perona's suggestion that these cells are involved in texture analysis and Lehky and Sejnowski's conjecture that these same cells may be doing some intermediate shape-from-shading analysis, and we have the makings of a real theoretical morass. How can we tell what the real function of these cells might be?

The first important point is that these different views are not as incompatible as they initially appear. Like Helmholtz's and Hering's supposedly conflicting views about color processing, these descriptions of spatial processing may be appropriate for different levels of the visual system, as diagrammed in Figure 4.3.20. In particular, the psychophysical view that these cells are performing a local spatial frequency analysis is quite general, specifying only that the cells' receptive fields

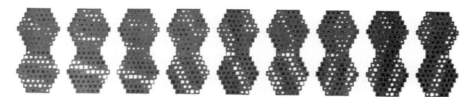

Figure 4.3.19 Examples of receptive fields of hidden units after learning shading analysis. Each hexagon shows the strength of the connections from the on-center input units at the specified location. Excitatory weights are represented by white squares, and inhibitory weights are represented by black squares, the size of the square representing the magnitude of the connection weight. Notice that the receptive fields are strongly oriented in a variety of different orientations. (From Lehky & Sejnowski, 1990.)

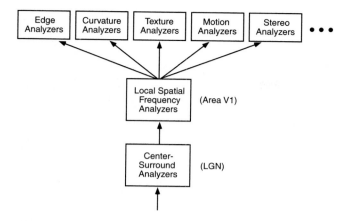

Figure 4.3.20 A theoretical hypothesis about the architecture of image processing. Center/surround cells in retina and LGN provide input to local spatial frequency analyzers in area V1 of cortex, which then project their output to a variety of different modules that compute edges, surface curvatures, textures, stereopsis, and so on, at later stages.

have a spatial luminance structure that is characteristic of Gabor functions—that is, local patches of sinusoidal grating that decrease in contrast with distance from the center of the receptive field. It is therefore compatible with the possibility that the outputs of these cells could then be integrated by later processes to detect edges, compute shape from shading, segregate textures, or perhaps all three. Indeed, their outputs could be used for any number of further operations that theorists have not yet imagined.

According to this view, edge detectors would then be constructed from the output of local spatial frequency analyzers by coding for the output pattern that is characteristic of luminance edges. True edge detectors would then be located at least one level beyond the cells in V1, after the results at different spatial scales have been integrated. Very much the same can be said of Pentland's and Lehky and Sejnowski's interesting results on describing surface curvature from shading information. The units that are actually sensitive to the curvature of surfaces would have to exist at the level beyond the "Hubel-Wiesel" cells, which would just be an intermediate representation from which higher-level surface curvature analyzers integrate the appropriate patterns of activity. This view also makes the edge and surface curvature processing algorithms compatible with each other, since there is nothing to preclude the same inter-

mediate representation (constructed in terms of local spatial frequency components) from being used in different ways by different higher-level processes. Indeed, it seems fairly likely that this would be the case, given that virtually all of the cortical processing of visual information in primates goes through area V1 and then fans out to a variety of other cortical areas. Exactly what additional visual properties might be computed from the output of these cells in extrastriate areas remains to be seen. Recent theoretical investigations by Malik and his colleagues, for example, have suggested that the output of cells tuned to such local spatial frequency components are useful and efficient in solving computationally difficult problems such as the perception of motion (Weber & Malik, 1995) and stereoscopic depth (Jones & Malik, 1992).

The present view suggests that the representation of image structure in V1 may well be a kind of unified image-based representation as suggested by Marr, although its specific structure now appears to be quite different from his primal sketch proposal. Whereas Marr suggested that the primal sketch was a symbolic representation constructed of bars, edges, blobs, and terminators, V1 appears to represent the visual image in terms of the continuous output of analyzers (or filters) at a variety of different positions, orientations, spatial scales, and phases. The cellular machinery in each cortical hypercolumn appears capable of representing something very like the Fourier decomposition of a small patch of image, a representation that is both general and efficient.

If this is indeed the case, it suggests that Marr's proposal that the visual system "goes symbolic" very early in visual processing is wrong. No categorical types of naturalistic image features would be detected this early. Indeed, it makes a certain amount of sense to avoid this kind of commitment to edges, lines, blobs, and terminators because restricting the image-based representation in this way could eliminate the gradual changes in luminance that reflect shading due to surface curvature and are necessary for certain kinds of depth and texture perception. A representation that essentially preserves all the structure in the image in a more efficient form would be preferable. This is especially important in V1 because nearly all further cortical processing depends on its output. If information were lost at this crucial stage,

Processing Image Structure

it could not be recovered subsequently. Local spatial frequency analysis using Gabor or wavelet filters has the advantage of preserving all the information (up to some level of resolution) without committing the visual system prematurely to a specific set of symbolic primitives.

Exploiting the Structure of Natural Images. If the visual system does represent image-based information in this fashion, why might it do so? It is certainly not because it corresponds to what we consciously perceive when we view the environment, for any visual representation in terms of Gabor filters appears to be completely and utterly unconscious. Perhaps the most plausible explanation is that such a representation arises to exploit structure in natural images that are projected onto our retinae (Barlow, 1961, 1983). The term "natural images" refers to retinal images that arise from natural environments under natural viewing conditions (e.g., Figure 4.3.21A). The term "exploiting structure" refers to eliminating redundancies so that the information from such natural images can be represented more efficiently. This would be true, for example, if recoding images in terms of the outputs of Gabor filters were more efficient, in some well-defined sense, than the outputs of other types of receptive field structures. Computational investigations of the statistical structure of natural images suggest that this is so (Field, 1993, 1994) and that the receptive fields of V1 cells may be optimized for extracting this information according to particular computational principles (Olshausen & Field, 1996).

To understand the idea of statistical structure in natural images and how it might be exploited to create an efficient representation, it will help first to explain the concept of the **state space** of a receptor array. Given an array composed of n receptors, each of which can represent any value within a range of luminances, every possible image that can be represented in that array corresponds to a single point in an n-dimensional space, called its *state space*. Each dimension of the state space corresponds to the output of one receptor (or, equivalently, the luminance of the corresponding pixel). The complete set of luminance values for every pixel in an image therefore specifies a single point in this space, and that point corresponds to a particular image that has that particular pattern of luminance values for its pixels. The state space therefore represents any image that can be registered by that receptor array as a single point,

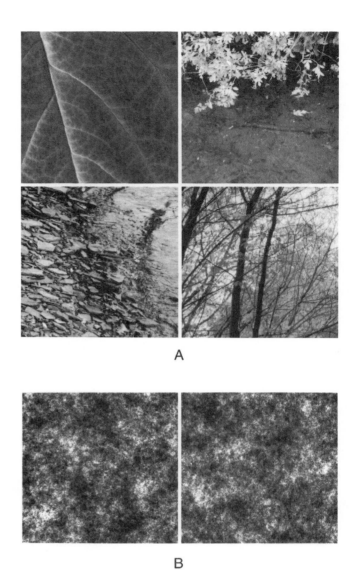

Figure 4.3.21 Natural versus unnatural images. The images shown in part A are sampled from the domain of natural environments. They have a remarkably different structure from those shown in part B, which are highly unlikely to be encountered in a natural environment. (From Field, 1994.)

and the entire state space represents the set of all possible images that the array can encode. If the array consists of 1024×1024 receptors, each of which could register one of 256 distinct gray levels, then the state space would be able to represent $1024 \times 1024 \times 256 = 268,435,456$ (or 10^{18}) distinct gray-scale images. When one considers retinal images with more than a hundred million receptors and a nearly continuous range of luminance levels—not to mention the three types of color receptors—the number of possible images in the state space literally boggles the mind.

What does such a state space have to do with the statistical structure of natural images? The first important fact is that the set of natural images constitutes only a small fraction of the set of logically possible images. Figure 4.3.21B shows a few unnatural images for contrast with the natural images in Figure 4.3.21A. It seems clear that one would be quite unlikely to encounter such images in natural environments. Because the set of natural images is but a small subset of all possible images, it will necessarily occupy only a very restricted set of locations in the state space. The key question is how these natural images are distributed within the state space. Are they more or less randomly located over the whole space, or are they clumped together in systematic ways?

To illustrate these concepts in a concrete but simplified case, consider the state space for two-pixel images consisting of luminance values of pixels A and B, as diagrammed in Figure 4.3.22A. The luminance of A, denoted $L(A)$, is represented along the x axis, and the luminance of B, denoted $L(B)$, is represented along the y axis. A few examples of two-pixel images are shown at their appropriate locations within the state space for reference. Within this state space, we will represent the set of natural images as a subset of images indicated by black dots, as shown in Figures 4.3.22B and 4.3.22C. If the subset of natural images occupies completely random locations, as do the black dots in Figure 4.3.22B, then there would be no statistical structure in natural images for the visual system to exploit. However, if natural images tend to occupy restricted regions of the state space, as do the black dots in Figure 4.3.22C, then the visual system could take advantage of this structure to increase efficiency. In this simple example, the structure consists of a high correlation between the luminances of pixels A and B, which means that these adjacent pixels tend to have very similar values. Although the examples

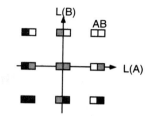

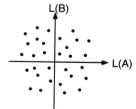

A. State Space of 2-pixel Images

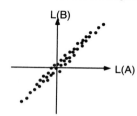

B. Random Subset of Images

C. Structured Subset of Images

Figure 4.3.22 The state space of representable images in a two-pixel array. The luminance of pixel A, $L(A)$, specifies the x coordinate of an image, and that of pixel B, $L(B)$, specifies the y coordinate, such that the two-pixel images shown in part A are located in the indicated positions of state space. Part B shows a random distribution of a subset of images within state space. Part C shows a structured distribution of a subset of images in which the values of pixels A and B are highly correlated.

that we are considering are highly artificial in many ways, natural images do, in fact, have a great deal of statistical structure, although it is much more complex than is shown in these examples. Differences in statistical structure are part of the reason the images in Figure 4.3.21B look so obviously different from those of Figure 4.3.21A and so much less natural.

The next question is how the visual system might exploit such structure. Two possibilities have recently been investigated computationally: *compact coding* and *sparse distributed coding*. **Compact coding** assumes that the output of the receptor array should be recoded so that the number of units needed to represent the image is minimized, as illustrated in Figure 4.3.23A. **Sparse distributed coding** assumes that the receptor output

Processing Image Structure

A. COMPACT CODING

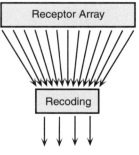

Represents data with the
minimum number of units

B. SPARSE DISTRIBUTED CODING

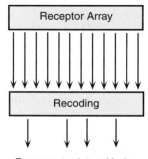

Represents data with the
minimum number of **active** units

Figure 4.3.23 Compact versus sparse coding. Compact coding (part A) represents the image in terms of the minimum number of neural units, whereas sparse coding (part B) represents it in terms of the minimum number of active units.

should be recoded so that the number of *active* units is minimized, as illustrated in Figure 4.3.23B. It turns out that these two methods of capturing statistical structure in images have different implications for the kinds of receptive fields the visual system might use to recode images.

One method for achieving compact coding is **principle components analysis** (**PCA**) (e.g., Linsker, 1988; Sanger, 1989). Principle components analysis is a procedure that identifies a reduced set of orthogonal vectors

(also called **basis functions**) that capture the maximum variance of the subset of points corresponding to the set of natural images within the state space. Images can then be recoded by using these vectors as the dimensional axes. In our simplified example of a structured subset of images (Figure 4.3.22C), the axis along the positive diagonal is by far the most informative vector. Coding the designated subset of images in terms of the single value along this axis would therefore capture an enormous amount of the statistical structure in these images. Representing the images in this way provides a very efficient representation because the dimensionality of the subset of correlated images is reduced by half (from two to one) without degrading the structure of the image much at all. Notice that this particular recoding method would not do a very good job of providing an accurate representation of random images (Figure 4.3.22B) because the images of points lying far from the positive diagonal would be seriously distorted.

To the extent that natural images have the kind of nonrandom statistical structure that PCA can exploit, it can be used to derive more compact encodings of natural images. Because natural images have such structure, theorists conjectured that the receptive fields of V1 cells might be learned from extensive viewing of natural images using the compact coding principle of PCA. This hypothesis was tested by using unsupervised neural network learning algorithms[3] that determined optimal receptive fields according to this principle. The learning procedure makes small adjustments in the weights of the connections from the receptor array to the recoding units in such a way that the recoding increases its compactness as learning progresses. Figure 4.3.24 shows the set of receptive fields produced by PCA on small patches (8 × 8 pixels) of natural images. Notice that some of the receptive fields resemble those of simple cells, but only at the lowest spatial frequencies. Another problem is that the receptive fields that are learned via PCA fail to simulate the local nature of receptive fields of V1 cells, spanning instead the entire image patch with strong connections to all receptors. Although the results appear to be on the right track, they do not correspond closely

---

[3] Like the supervised learning algorithms described in Appendix B, unsupervised learning uses gradient descent procedures, but it does not require explicit feedback.

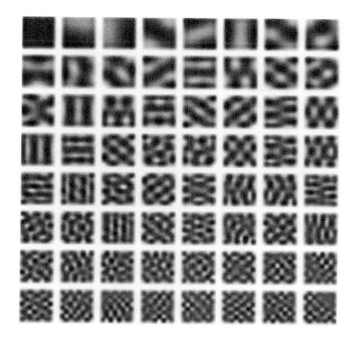

Figure 4.3.24 Receptive fields learned from exposure to natural images via principle components analysis. Each 8 × 8 pixel square represents the strength of connections to the receptor array, light pixels corresponding to excitatory connections and dark pixels to inhibitory connections. Few of these receptive fields have the structure found in V1 simple cells. (From Olshausen & Field, 1996.)

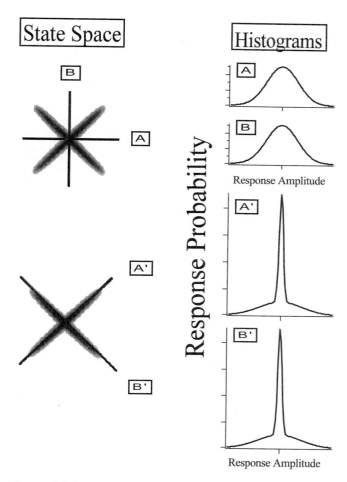

Figure 4.3.25 A more complex example of state space structure for two-pixel images. The upper half shows the state space and dimensional histograms for the coding in terms of luminance of pixels *A* and *B*. The lower half shows the state space and histograms for the same subset of images recoded in terms of axes rotated 45°. Notice how much more peaked the response histograms are after rotating the axes. (From Field, 1994.)

enough to actual receptive fields in V1 cells to provide a convincing explanation.

Another method that has been employed in recoding natural images to exploit their statistical structure is sparse coding (Field, 1993, 1994). In the sparse coding framework, efficient representation is achieved by minimizing the number of *active* units rather than the number of *available* units. Figure 4.3.25 gives an example. The upper state space in this figure shows a statistical structure for the designated subset of images that is different from (and more complex than) the one shown in Figure 4.3.22C: there is no simple correlation between pixels *A* and *B*, but there is obviously a strong relation of some sort. If the pixels are coded in terms of their raw luminances, $L(A)$ and $L(B)$, the histograms of their values are shown in the graphs to the right of the state space. These diagrams show the distribution of luminance values for pixels *A* and *B* plotted independently. Both dimensions have an expected value at the mean luminance (neutral gray) but relatively high probabilities

of both higher (brighter) and lower (darker) values. But suppose these images were recoded in terms of dimensional axes rotated 45°, as illustrated in the lower state space of Figure 4.3.25. These new axes have the histograms shown to their right, both of which are much more peaked than those of the unrotated codings. This peakedness (called high **kurtosis**) of a probability distribution is characteristic of sparse codings. It means that sparse recodings will have relatively few active units (in which the response is far from the highly peaked mean value for the designated subset of images) and rel-

Processing Image Structure

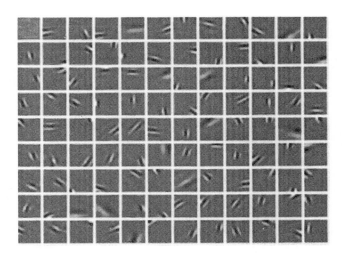

Figure 4.3.26 Receptive fields learned from exposure to natural images using sparse coding constraints. Each 16 × 16 pixel square represents the strength of connections to the receptor array, light pixels corresponding to excitatory connections and dark pixels to inhibitory connections. These receptive fields have the same kind of local, oriented structure as is found in V1 simple cells. (From Olshausen & Field, 1996.)

atively many inactive units (in which the response is at or near the mean value).

Recent experiments using unsupervised learning algorithms to shape the receptive fields of units to produce sparse coding have shown very promising results (Olshausen & Field, 1996). Many natural image patches (16 × 16 pixels) like those shown in Figure 4.3.21 were presented to a network of 192 recoding units. The learning procedure then adjusted the connection weights from the receptor units to the recoding units in a way that penalized dense (nonsparse) representations. The resulting receptive fields for the recoding units are shown in Figure 4.3.26. Notice that these receptive fields show localized, oriented structure at a variety of different spatial scales. Indeed, they are very much like the Gabor/wavelet functions that characterize V1 simple cells. As Figure 4.3.27A shows, these receptive fields include many small and few large receptive fields, much as Field (1993) has theorized that a system based on wavelet filters should (see Figure 4.3.27B).

These results show that receptive fields very much like those found in area V1 can be generated by learning algorithms that incorporate just two theoretical constraints. The first is that the information in the image

be preserved by the output of the recoding units. This means that the output is sufficient to recover the original image with a high degree of accuracy. The rationale for this is obvious: The recoding should lose as little information as possible. This can occur because the redundancies in natural images are not informative and can therefore be removed in the recoding without seriously distorting the image. The second constraint is that the recoding be sparse. This means that the structure of any particular image is represented by activity in relatively few of the units. The rationale for this is not so obvious. It embodies economy of a sort, for only a few cells are active, but a sparse coding may require many more cells than compact coding. Field (1994) has made three suggestions about why sparse codings might be desirable in the visual system:

1. *Signal-to-noise ratios.* Sparse codings increase signal-to-noise ratios because only a few cells will be active with many more inactive, and the active ones will tend to be more active than those that are active in dense codings of the same images. Sparse coding effectively concentrates activation in a relatively few cells.

2. *Feature detection.* Sparse codings should assist later recognition processes based on the detection of specific features because relatively few feature detectors will be active, and they will be more active than those in dense codings.

3. *Storage and retrieval from associative memory.* Research into associative connectionist memories has shown that sparse codings allow networks to store more memories and to retrieve them more effectively than dense codings (Palm, 1980).

While research on methods of capturing the statistical structure of natural images is highly suggestive and fits well with many current beliefs about the neural coding of images in simple cells of area V1, it is important to recognize that these investigations are still in their infancy. We do not yet know how to find the optimal sparse code for a given subset of images, for example, and much work remains to be done in specifying a neurally plausible learning mechanism that implements sparse coding. Even so, the research that has been done reinforces the conjecture that the structure of the visual system is designed to take advantage of the structure in natural images.

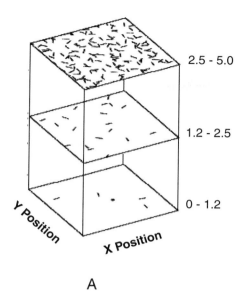

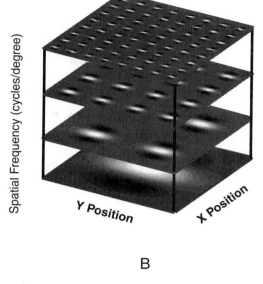

A

B

Figure 4.3.27 Representing image structure via a pyramid of local oriented filters at different spatial frequencies. Part A shows the distribution of positions and orientations of receptive fields at different spatial frequency ranges (high, medium, and low). Part B shows a similar theoretical representation in terms of wavelet filters at different positions and spatial frequencies, but only for a single orientation. (Part A from Olshausen & Field, 1996; part B from Field, 1993.)

4.4 Visual Pathways

Fairly recently, a new aspect of the overall architecture of early visual processing has been proposed and studied intensively. The idea is that the visual system is structured into several different pathways for concurrent processing of different visual properties such as form, color, motion, and stereoscopic depth. These pathways are often called "channels," but we will avoid this term because of possible confusion with its use in designating different subregions of the spatial frequency and orientation continua in psychophysics. The pathways for color, form, motion, and depth are much larger neural structures, embodied in whole populations of many interconnected cells. We mentioned this idea briefly at the end of Chapter 1; now we will consider the evidence for it in more detail.

4.4.1 Physiological Evidence

The idea that there might be identifiable neural representations for different visual properties began to accumulate in the results of studies of higher visual areas. As we mentioned in Section 1.3.3, early studies suggested that area MT was specialized for processing motion information (Zeki, 1974) and area V4 for color information (Zeki, 1980). Since the receptors carry all kinds of information, albeit extremely local and restricted parts of it, the visual system must separate out different kinds of information somewhere along the way to the higher cortical areas. But where?

A number of researchers have reported anatomical and physiological evidence of functional differences between cells in the retina that are maintained in magnocellular and parvocellular layers of the LGN and then are further divided into different substructures in area V1 (e.g., Ungerleider & Mishkin, 1982; Van Essen & Maunsell, 1983). Livingstone and Hubel (1987) followed these processing streams through pathways in higher cortical visual centers and made some interesting speculations about their functional role in perception.

The overall structure of Livingstone and Hubel's proposal is illustrated schematically in Figure 4.4.1. The first important distinction is between the M ganglion cells (solid circles) and the P ganglion cells (open circles) in the retina. Livingstone and Hubel conjectured that the M cells carry information about motion and stereoscopic depth, whereas the P cells carry information

Processing Image Structure

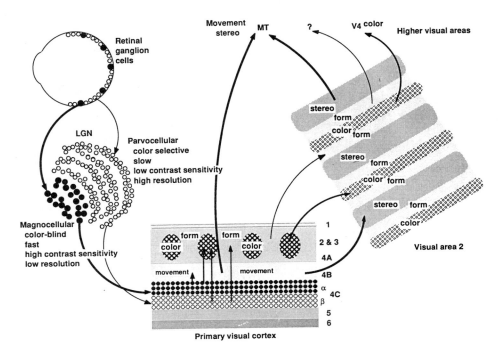

Figure 4.4.1 A theory of separate functional pathways in the primate visual system. Livingstone and Hubel suggested that form, color, motion, and stereo information become increasingly differentiated from retina to extrastriate visual cortex. (LGN = lateral geniculate nucleus; MT = medial temporal lobe; V4 = visual area 4.) (From Livingstone & Hubel, 1988.)

about color and form. The M and P cells project selectively to the magno and parvo cells in the LGN, which, they argue, continue the functional separation between motion and depth versus color and form. Livingstone and Hubel then suggested that a further differentiation occurs in area V1. First, they observed that the magno and parvo cells in the LGN terminate in different regions of layer 4 in cortical area V1 (see Figure 4.4.1). The magno cells synapse on neurons in layer $4C\alpha$, and the parvo cells synapse on neurons in layer $4C\beta$. These sublayers, in turn, project to different higher-level layers of V1: the magno-$4C\alpha$ cells to layer 4B and the parvo-$4C\beta$ cells to layers 2 and 3.

To complicate the story somewhat, it turns out that there are two distinct subregions within layers 2 and 3 in each hypercolumn of V1: the **blob region** in the center of the hypercolumn and the **interblob region** around it. These regions are defined anatomically by the fact that the blob regions are rich in the enzyme **cytochrome oxidase** and the interblob regions are not. As a result, the upper layers of V1 have a characteristic spotted appearance after being stained for the presence of cytochrome oxidase, as shown in the upper portion of Figure 4.4.2 (Tootell et al., 1983). The dark spots are the blobs, and the light regions are the interblobs.

Area V2 also produces a distinctive pattern when stained for cytochrome oxidase, causing alternating thick and thin stripes interleaved with pale stripes, as illustrated in the lower regions of Figure 4.4.2. Livingstone and Hubel (1984) reported that layer 4B in V1 projects to the thick stripes in V2, the blobs in layers 2 and 3 of V1 project to the thin stripes in V2, and the interblobs in layers 2 and 3 of V1 project to the pale interstripe areas of V2. The other major pathway in their analysis goes directly from layer 4B in V1 to area MT.

This rather complex anatomical arrangement is potentially important because it defines four pathways that may have different perceptual functions. Livingstone and Hubel (1988) trace the properties of cells in each pathway and argue that they constitute four functional subsystems: the thick stripes in V2 for binocular depth perception, the thin stripes in V2 for color perception, the pale stripes in V2 for form perception, and the direct projection to MT for motion perception (see also DeYoe & Van Essen, 1988). The division is by no means clean, for any given area typically contains

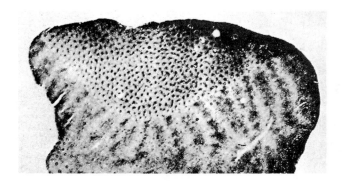

Figure 4.4.2 Tangential section through monkey cortex stained for cytochrome oxidase. Primary visual cortex (V1) is dotted with cytochrome oxidase blobs. Area V2, adjacent to V1, shows a characteristic pattern of alternating thin, thick, and pale stripes. (From Tootell et al., 1983.)

several different types of cells. But there appears to be a relative preponderance of binocular cells in the thick stripes, of color cells in the thin stripes, of end-stopped cells (which are useful in form perception) in the pale stripes, and of motion cells in MT.

Thus, Livingstone and Hubel argue that there are four functionally distinct pathways to higher levels of visual cortex, defined as follows:

1. *Color pathway:*

retinal P cells → LGN-parvo → V1-4Cβ → V1-blobs

→ V2-thin stripes → V4 → . . .

2. *Form pathway:*

retinal P cells → LGN-parvo → V1-4Cβ

→ V1-interblobs → V2-pale stripes → V4 → IT . . .

3. *Binocular pathway:*

retinal M cells → LGN-magno → V1-4Cα → V1-4B

→ V2-thick stripes → MT, → . . .

4. *Motion pathway:*

retinal M cells → LGN-magno → V1-4Cα → V1-4B

→ MT → MST . . .

The hypothesis that there are four functional pathways in the visual system is controversial, especially in its strong form. It is clear that the functional separation of

the pathways is not complete, as there is significant cross-talk among them (Van Essen & DeYoe, 1995). But even if Livingstone and Hubel's ideas turn out to be wrong in detail, they constitute the sort of bold, integrative hypothesis that is bound to generate interesting research findings and ultimately to advance our understanding of the functional architecture of the visual nervous system, if only to show exactly how their theory is in error.

Even if the functional separation of the visual system into four pathways is basically correct, it is far from clear how the required perceptual analyses are carried out in neural circuitry, especially at the higher levels. The form pathway, for example, leads from V1 to V2 to V4 and eventually to inferotemporal cortex (IT), where cells have been found that respond selectively to faces, hands, and other highly complex stimuli (Desimone, Albright, Gross, & Bruce, 1984). But we have no clear idea how the various local oriented spatial frequency filters of V1 are processed to arrive at detection of faces and hands. Studies of area V4, for example, have found cells that are highly selective to patterns other than spatial frequency gratings, including the concentric, radial, spiral, and hyperbolic gratings shown in Figure 4.4.3, but the functional significance of such cells is far from clear (Gallant, Braun, & Van Essen, 1993).

4.4.2 Perceptual Evidence

From one point of view, the idea that information about form, color, motion, and depth might be processed quite separately in the visual nervous system seems odd, perhaps even absurd, because our visual experience of objects normally appears to be so completely integrated. If I see a red car coming toward me, for example, I do not have separate experiences of disembodied redness, car shape, and motion toward myself. But from another point of view, it seems quite natural. If people are asked to list different aspects of visual experience, they would most likely mention color, form, and motion as being quite distinct. These are also features to which people appear to be able to attend selectively.

Both viewpoints can be accommodated by assuming that these different attributes are initially processed independently but are normally united at some later stage by a further perceptual process. In Chapter 11 we will consider an influential theory based on the idea that this

Processing Image Structure

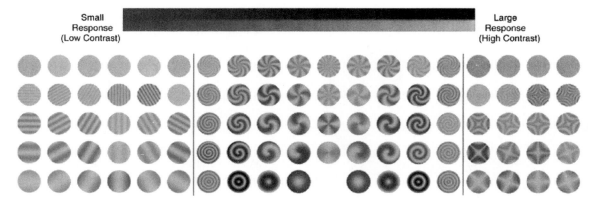

Small
Response
(Low Contrast)

Large
Response
(High Contrast)

Figure 4.4.3 Cartesian and non-Cartesian gratings. This diagram indicates the response of a single cell in area V4 to a variety of stimulus patterns. Magnitude of response is coded in terms of the degree of contrast of the patterns. This cell responds most strongly to concentric patterns. (Image courtesy of Jack Gallant; data from Gallant, Braun, & Van Essen, 1993.)

unification occurs through the action of selective visual attention to a given location. In this theory, attention forms a kind of metaphorical perceptual glue that binds independent features into coherent objects (Treisman & Gelade, 1980). This rather surprising idea has a great deal of support from perceptual experiments.

If these streams of processing are really separate in the visual system, even if only for a restricted subset of neural processing, there ought to be clear and measurable effects on perceptual experience. Indeed, a number of phenomena suggest that the neural separation of the color, form, depth, and motion systems is perceptually important, at least under certain restricted circumstances.

One important source of evidence comes from property-specific deficits in visual perception that have been discovered in patients with brain damage in visual areas of the brain. One neurological patient lost her ability to perceive motion almost completely but without any noticeable disturbance in her perception of color, depth, or form (Zihl, Von Cramon, & Mai, 1983). Other patients have lost their ability to perceive color following brain trauma but without reporting loss of motion, form, or depth perception (Damasio, 1985). Such selective loss of function can be explained quite easily if there are separate brain centers for processing these properties. Otherwise, it is mysterious.

Another kind of evidence comes from psychophysical effects that would be predicted from the separate pathways hypothesis. For example, Ramachandran and Gregory (1978) reasoned that if motion information is processed in the magnocellular pathway and color information in the parvocellular pathway, there might be conditions under which people would be unable to see motion in stimuli defined only by differences in color. They found that when randomly positioned red and green dots of equal luminance were alternately presented in slightly different positions under conditions that would normally produce motion perception, observers could not detect motion. When luminance-defined black and white dots were presented in exactly the same way, however, observers easily detected motion. This is just what one would predict if motion and color were processed in different pathways.

Related effects are found for continuous motion of low spatial frequency gratings. Equiluminant gratings that contain no luminance information can be constructed by varying sinusoidally between red and green instead of black and white. When such gratings are drifted across the visual field, their perceived speed is much slower than that of corresponding black-to-white luminance gratings (Cavanagh, Tyler, & Favreau, 1984). Indeed, the color-defined gratings sometimes appear to stop, even when the bars themselves are clearly visible. This seemingly paradoxical perception can be explained if the color system is indeed "motion blind."

Similar claims have been made about the separation of color and depth information. Certain kinds of depth information surely depend on luminance rather than color. As we will discover in Section 5.5.8, shadows and shading are important for perceiving depth, and both are normally carried in luminance pathways rather than color pathways. When light-to-dark gradations in a photograph with normal shading are changed to equiluminant chromatic differences (for example, red-to-green gradations), the perception of depth due to shading is greatly diminished or disappears entirely, as illustrated in Color Plate 4.1. More surprisingly, another kind of depth information that depends on differences between the two retinal images (called binocular disparity or stereopsis; see Section 5.3) has also been reported to disappear under equiluminance conditions (Lu & Fender, 1972), although this may be partly due to reductions in the effective contrast of equiluminant stimuli.

Further studies have shown that the separation is far from complete, however. Color seems to contribute to the perception of motion (Cavanagh & Anstis, 1991) and depth can be achieved with binocular disparity when the images are defined by purely chromatic boundaries (DeWeert & Sadza, 1983). It appears that the perceptual situation may be much like the physiological situation: The segregation of information from different properties into separate pathways is not complete, and there is cross-talk among them. This leads to reduction of motion and depth perception under conditions of equiluminant stimulation, but seldom their complete absence.

Livingstone and Hubel (1987) have argued that a number of other perceptual effects reflect the underlying separation of color, form, depth, and motion information in different physiological pathways. Much of the evidence is suggestive of their claim, but little of it is definitive. Many of their observations concern phenomena that occur with stimuli defined by color rather than luminance differences. A major difficulty in evaluating claims about such matters is that it is not easy to achieve absolute equiluminance. As a result, failures to find complete separation effects may reflect either incomplete segregation of pathways or failure to achieve equiluminance. Given that even the physiological separation appears to be incomplete, it seems unlikely that clean perceptual effects are likely to be obtained. Indeed, this appears to be the case.

Another difficulty for Livingstone and Hubel's conjectures is that the state of physiological knowledge about the anatomy and physiology of neural pathways is constantly changing. For example, they identify V4 as part of the color pathway but not of the form pathway. This hypothesis was based mainly on Zeki's (1983) early results, but more recent studies provide evidence against this conclusion. Selective lesions of V4 in the macaque monkey, for example, produce greater deficits in pattern discrimination than in color discrimination (Schiller & Lee, 1991). Moreover, single-cell recordings in V4 have shown large numbers of cells that are selective for complex aspects of form (Desimone & Schein, 1987; Gallant et al., 1993). Given such findings, perhaps the most accurate statement that can be made at present is that the "four pathways" conjecture is a vast simplification, at best. Whether a modified version of it will survive further experimental tests is unclear. Perhaps a whole new conceptualization of how cortical architecture relates to perceptual function will be required. In the meantime, however, the idea that there are distinct pathways in the visual system that correspond to different kinds of perceptual information is an interesting one that bears further exploration and no doubt will receive it.

Processing Image Structure

Suggestions for Further Reading

Physiological Approaches

Hubel, D. (1995). *Eye, brain, and vision.* New York: Scientific
American Books. Written for a wide nontechnical audience,
this book presents an engaging description of the classical view
of functions performed in visual cortex.

Psychophysical Approaches

De Valois, R. L., & De Valois, K. K. (1988). *Spatial vision.*
New York: Oxford University Press. This book presents both
a good summary of the psychophysical background on spatial
frequency theory and a compelling case for the hypothesis
that V1 cells perform a local spatial frequency analysis of the
image.

Computational Approaches

Marr, D. (1982). *Vision.* San Francisco: Freeman. This is the
classic statement of Marr's computational approach to vision
science. Though dated, it contains the fullest presentation of
Marr's theoretical ideas about vision.

Nalwa, V. S. (1993). *A guided tour of computer vision.* Reading,
MA: Addison-Wesley. An excellent, general-purpose
introduction to the field of computer vision.

Visual Pathways

Livingstone, M. S., & Hubel, D. H. (1987). Psychophysical
evidence for separate channels for the perception of form,
color, motion, and depth. *Journal of Neuroscience, 7,* 3416–3468.

Perceiving Surfaces Oriented in Depth

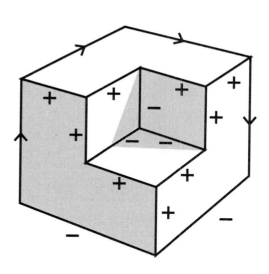

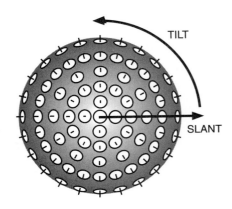

Figure 5.0.1 Slant and tilt of local surface patches on a sphere. The 3-D orientation of any local surface patch can be specified by two parameters: slant and tilt. Slant refers to the angle between the line of sight to the surface patch and its surface normal (the direction perpendicular to the surface), as indicated by the degree of elongation of the ellipses and length of the line segments in this figure. Tilt refers to the direction of the surface's depth gradient, as indicated by the orientation of the ellipses and line segments in the figure.

The naturally occurring 2-D image features we discussed in Chapter 4, such as edges, lines, and texture elements, are important for vision because they convey information about the world around us. But they must be interpreted in terms of 3-D structure to make the inferential leap from image to environment. This leap is required because perceiving organisms aren't interested in edges between regions of different retinal luminance, color, or texture; they are interested in edges between different environmental surfaces of objects. The interpretation of image structure in terms of visible surfaces in 3-D space is therefore one of the most crucial steps in trying to solve the inverse problem discussed in Section 1.2.3. It is a difficult and complex process that is not yet fully understood, but vision scientists have made enormous strides in understanding how it might happen.

Two of the three spatial dimensions of the environment are explicitly present in the 2-D images on the two retinae. These two dimensions can be conceived as jointly specifying the direction from the observer to the surface. But the third dimension—the distance of the surface from the observer, which is often called *depth*—is lost in the process of optical projection from surfaces in a 3-D world to the 2-D retinae. Once this information is lost, it can never be regained with absolute certainty for the reasons that we considered in Section 1.2. But the fact that people are very good at perceiving their 3-D environment demonstrates that surfaces in depth can indeed be accurately recovered from 2-D images under the vast majority of naturally occurring circumstances. How is this possible?

There are actually two closely related problems that must be solved in perceiving the spatial arrangement of surfaces with respect to the observer. One is determining **depth**: the distance of the surface from the observer in the 3-D environment. The other is perceiving **surface orientation**: the slant and tilt of the surface with respect to the viewer's line of sight. Slant and tilt, although often used as synonyms, technically refer to two different parameters of surface orientation in depth. **Slant** refers to the size of the angle between the observer's line of sight and the surface normal (the virtual line sticking perpendicularly out of the surface at that point). The larger this angle, the greater the surface slant. In the circular *gauge figures* illustrated in Figure 5.0.1, slant corresponds to the elongation of the projected ellipses, greater elongation resulting from greater slant relative to the frontal plane (which is zero slant). Slant also corresponds to the length of the projection of the unit surface normal (the surface normal of unit length) onto the frontal plane, longer projections resulting from greater slants. **Tilt** refers to the direction of the depth gradient relative to the frontal plane. In Figure 5.0.1, tilt corresponds to the orientation of the projected ellipse in the frontal plane and to the direction of the surface normal projected onto the frontal plane.

It makes sense that depth and surface orientation are recovered together because they are intrinsically interdependent. The 3-D orientation of a surface determines how far away its various parts are from the observer, and the distance of its various parts likewise determines its 3-D orientation. One way to formulate the problem is to say that the visual system must compute, for each

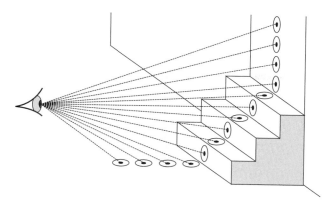

Figure 5.0.2 Orientation at a distance. The layout of visible surfaces in the environment can be represented by small patches of (locally) flat surface in each direction from the viewer's eye. Each patch can be characterized by its distance from the observer's eye and its orientation relative to the line of sight to it.

direction outward from the viewer's stationpoint, the orientation and distance (or depth) of the surface that has reflected light in that particular direction (see Figure 5.0.2). This conception of surface perception as determined by its distance and orientation (or **orientation at a distance**) was originally formulated by J. J. Gibson (1950), who placed great emphasis on the importance of surface perception long before anyone else. He called it perceiving the **surface layout**. The idea of recovering orientation at a distance was later reformulated more precisely in computational terms by Marr and Nishihara (1978). As we mentioned at the end of Chapter 2, Marr called this surface-based representation the *2.5-D sketch*. We will take a somewhat broader view of the surface-based representation than Marr's concept of the 2.5-D sketch, however. Regardless of what it is called and exactly how it is defined, a representation of oriented surfaces in depth is indispensable to vision and is required to understand many higher-level perceptual phenomena (Nakayama, He, & Shimojo, 1995).

Why might the first step toward perceiving the spatial structure of the environment be to extract information about the nature of visible surfaces? Perhaps the best answer is that visible surfaces are the environmental entities that actually interact with light to determine the optical information that is projected onto the retina (see Section 1.2). Because most surfaces are opaque, we get no visible information about what lies beyond them or

inside them, if the surfaces bound a three-dimensional solid. This means that surfaces occupy the privileged status of being the source of all directly visible information about the 3-D structure of the environment. After perceiving the structure of visible surfaces, perceivers may make further inferences—such as the nature of partly or completely occluded surfaces—but anything beyond visible surfaces is at least one step further removed from the retinally available information.

5.1 The Problem of Depth Perception

The perceptual problem of recovering the distance to a surface is that depth perception from 2-D images is inherently ambiguous. The reason for this ambiguity is that the optical processes of surface reflection and image formation project light from a 3-D world onto a 2-D surface at the back of the eye, and, as we discussed in Section 1.2, such projections can be inverted in an infinite number of ways. Depth perception is thus the paradigm example of logical ambiguity in perception. Figure 5.1.1 illustrates the basic dilemma. Suppose light is reflected into the eye from point A so that it stimulates the retinal receptor at point A'. The question is: How does the observer know that the light didn't come from point A_1, A_2, or A_3 instead of A? Indeed, it seems that it could have come from anywhere along the ray from A' through A. In other words, because all points on this ray project to the same retinal point A', the inverse projection of the retinal point A' could be any point along the same ray.

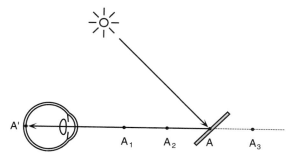

Figure 5.1.1 The problem of depth ambiguity. Photons reflected by a surface at point A strike the retina at point A', but they could also have come from A_1, A_2, or anywhere along the ray from A' through A.

Perceiving Surfaces Oriented in Depth

5.1.1 Heuristic Assumptions

This analysis of depth perception seems to lead to the conclusion that veridical depth perception is impossible. But how does this seemingly inescapable conclusion square with the fact that people consistently achieve accurate depth perception every minute of every day? The answer is that only infallible depth perception under all possible circumstances is logically impossible. Since human depth perception is hardly infallible under all possible circumstances, there is no logical contradiction. As we will see, there are many conditions under which people are fooled into seeing depth inaccurately. You are already familiar with examples from everyday life, although you probably don't think about them as fooling you: Flat photographs portray depth relations quite convincingly, motion pictures do so even more compellingly, and so-called 3-D movies (such as the *Captain Io* film at Disneyland) and virtual reality displays create depth perception of uncanny realism. All four are examples of your visual system being fooled because the resulting perception of depth is illusory; the depth that you so readily perceive arises from looking at images that are completely and utterly flat.

Normal everyday depth perception is possible because, as we said in the first three chapters, the visual system implicitly makes certain heuristic assumptions about both the nature of the external world and the conditions of visual observation. Together with the specific information available in the two retinal images, these assumptions are sufficient to recover depth information far more accurately than one would expect from the logical analysis given above. The logical ambiguity of depth information is important, however, for it helps to define the conditions under which the depth processing system can be deceived, and these conditions provide crucial information about the nature of the assumptions it makes. For example, our visual systems are fooled by 3-D movies because the visual system implicitly assumes that both eyes are looking at the same scene. The 3-D effect arises because the special glasses that the viewer wears allow different images to be presented to each eye. The visual system interprets the differences as resulting from depth that is not actually present in the stimulus. Under normal circumstances, which occur 99.99% of the time, this assumption serves us well, allowing us to perceive depth that is actually

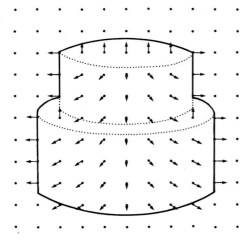

Figure 5.1.2 Marr's 2.5-D sketch. At each position in the visual field, a vector is shown (called the surface normal) that is perpendicular to the local patch of surface at that point and looks like a needle sticking out of the surface. The 2.5-D sketch also includes information about the distance along the line of sight. (From Marr & Nishihara, 1978.)

present in the environment on the basis of the slightly different images present in the two eyes.

You might think from the fact that the visual system can be fooled by visual technology that retinal stimulation must not contain much depth information. In fact, there is an enormous amount of it. Under normal viewing conditions—that is, an observer moving with both eyes open through a largely stationary world of opaque surfaces bathed in ambient light—there is an astonishing amount, as Gibson was fond of pointing out. Equally important, however, is the fact that different depth cues generally converge on the same depth interpretation. It is this convergence of multiple sources of information that allows depth perception to be as accurate as it is. Only in the vision scientist's laboratory or under other conditions designed specifically to deceive the visual system do we regularly fail to apprehend the actual distance to environmental surfaces.

5.1.2 Marr's 2.5-D Sketch

How might visual information about the layout of surfaces in depth be represented? The most influential proposal to date has been David Marr's conception of the 2.5-D sketch (see Figure 5.1.2). As the name implies, the 2.5-D sketch is somewhere between the 2-D properties of an image-based representation and the 3-D proper-

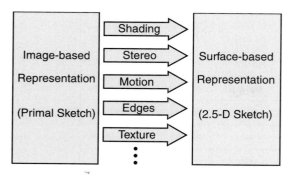

Figure 5.1.3 Flowchart of depth-processing modules. A 2.5-D surface-based representation is thought to be computed from a 2-D image-based representation by a set of parallel and quasi-independent processes that extract information about surface orientation and depth from a variety of sources, such as shading, stereo, and motion.

ties of a true object-based representation. It summarizes the many converging outputs of different processes that recover information about the depth and orientation of local surface patches in the environment into a convenient representation of orientation at a distance, much as Gibson suggested many years earlier. Marr's theorizing went beyond Gibson's contribution, however, by proposing how such a representation might actually be computed from real images.

The view of surface recovery and depth processing that underlies the 2.5-D sketch is that there are many independent (or nearly independent) processing modules computing depth information from separate sources, as indicated in Figure 5.1.3. Each module processes a different kind of information, which then provides different constraints on the final common depth interpretation in the 2.5-D sketch. In the computer vision community, these processes are frequently referred to as the "shape-from-X modules," where X is the source of depth information, as in "shape-from-shading" or "shape-from-motion." Although this terminology is catchy, it is seriously misleading because shape is not explicitly represented in the output of such modules at all. What *is* represented is either depth or surface orientation, so it seems more appropriate to call them "depth-from-X" or "orientation-from-X" modules. The representation of shape is a great deal more complicated, as we will discover in Chapter 8.

There are many different sources of depth information that can be classified in many different ways, as

indicated in Figure 5.1.4. One distinction is whether the information in question concerns the state of the eyes themselves (**ocular information**) or the structure of the light entering the eyes (**optical information**). A second is whether the information requires both eyes (**binocular information**) or is available from just one eye (**monocular information**). A third is whether the information is available in a motionless image (**static information**) or requires movement of the observer and/or the object (**dynamic information**). A fourth is whether the source determines the actual distance to objects (**absolute information**) or merely specifies how far objects are relative to each other (**relative information**). A fifth concerns whether the information specifies numerical distance relations (**quantitative information**) or merely the ordinal relations of closer/farther (**qualitative information**). I have organized the present discussion of sources of depth information in terms of four categories: ocular information (accommodation and convergence), stereoscopic information (binocular disparity and Da Vinci stereopsis), dynamic information (motion parallax and accretion/deletion of texture), and pictorial information (all the rest). There is nothing sacred about this division, however.

5.2 Ocular Information

Ocular information about the distance to a fixated surface arises from factors that depend on the state of the eyes themselves and their various components. Of particular importance for depth perception are the focus of the lens (*accommodation*) and the angle of between the two eyes' lines of sight (*convergence*). Analogous information could be made available to a computer vision system from whatever mechanical and/or electronic apparatus controls similar functions for a pair of video cameras.

5.2.1 Accommodation

Accommodation is the process through which the ciliary muscles in the eye control the optical focus of the lens by temporarily changing its shape. It is a monocular depth cue because it is available from a single eye, even though it is also present when both eyes are used. As we mentioned in Section 1.3, the lens of the human eye has a variable focusing capability, becoming thin to focus

Perceiving Surfaces Oriented in Depth

INFORMATION SOURCE	Ocular/ Optical	Binocular/ Monocular	Static/ Dynamic	Relative/ Absolute	Qualitative/ Quantitative
Accommodation	ocular	monocular	static	absolute	quantitative
Convergence	ocular	binocular	static	absolute	quantitative
Binocular Disparity	optical	binocular	static	relative	quantitative
Motion Parallax	optical	monocular	dynamic	relative	quantitative
Texture Accretion/Deletion	optical	monocular	dyanmic	relative	qualitative
Convergence of Parallels	optical	monocular	static	relative	quantitative
Position relative to Horizon	optical	monocular	static	relative	quantitative
Relative Size	optical	monocular	static	relative	quantitative
Familiar Size	optical	monocular	static	absolute	quantitative
Texture Gradients	optical	monocular	static	relative	quantitative
Edge Interpretation	optical	monocular	static	relative	qualitative
Shading and Shadows	optical	monocular	static	relative	qualitative
Aerial Perspective	optical	monocular	static	relative	qualitative

Figure 5.1.4 Sources of information about depth. This chart specifies five important characteristics of depth information: ocular versus optical, binocular versus monocular, static versus dynamic, relative versus absolute, and qualitative versus quantitative. (See text for explanation of the distinctions.)

light from faraway objects on the retina and thick to focus light from nearby ones (see Figure 5.2.1). If the visual system has information about the tension of the muscles that control the lens's shape, then it has information about the distance to the focused object.

Although accommodation is generally considered to be a weak source of depth information (Hochberg, 1971), experimental results indicate that people use it at close distances. Observers are notoriously poor at using it to make direct judgments about distance, but they do rely on it to judge the size of objects (Wallach & Floor, 1971). That is, they compute the perceived size of an object at close range by taking accommodation information into account. Beyond 6–8 feet, however, accommodation provides little or no depth information. At this distance the muscles that control the shape of the lens are already in their most relaxed state, so the lens cannot get any thinner.

Accommodation provides information about absolute depth. That is, it can specify the actual distance to the

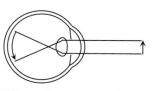

Thick Lens → Close

Thin Lens → Far

Figure 5.2.1 Depth information from lens accommodation. The lens of a human eye changes shape to focus the light from objects at different distances: thin for objects far away and thick for ones nearby.

fixated object, provided the visual system is properly calibrated. As Figure 5.1.4 shows, most optical depth cues merely provide information about *relative* distance, indicating which of two things is closer or the ratio of the distances of two objects. Such relative depth information is quite important, of course, but absolute depth information is required for people to estimate actual distances to environmental objects. If we couldn't determine actual distances, especially at close ranges, we would constantly stumble into things that were closer than we thought and reach for things that were out of range.

For accommodation to provide accurate depth information, the object must be in proper focus on the retina. This implies that the visual system must somehow "know" when an object is in focus. The best indication of proper focus is the presence of sharp edges rather than blurry ones. Thus, image blur is the effective stimulus that drives accommodation. As we discussed in Section 4.3, information about the blurriness/sharpness of edges is carried in high spatial frequencies: Sharp edges contain more energy in high spatial frequencies than do blurry ones. It is therefore likely that the visual system controls accommodation by adjusting the tension of the ciliary muscles so that the output of high spatial frequency channels is maximized.

Because of its restricted range, accommodation is rarely a crucial source of depth information in humans. In the African chameleon, however, it is of paramount importance, for it controls this organism's ability to feed itself (Harkness, 1977). A chameleon catches its prey by flicking its sticky tongue out just the right distance to catch an insect and pop it into its mouth. When chameleons were outfitted with prisms and spectacles that manipulated the accommodation and convergence of their eyes, the distance they flicked their tongues was governed exclusively by accommodation information. Notice that this is possible because of the close range of distances relevant for chameleons catching flies.

5.2.2 Convergence

The other ocular source of information about depth comes from eye **convergence**: the extent to which the two eyes are turned inward (toward each other) to fixate an object. The eyes **fixate** a given point in external space when both of them are aimed directly at the point

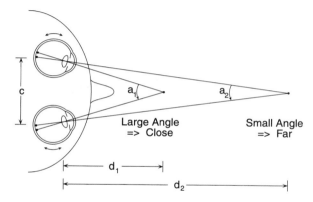

Figure 5.2.2 Depth information from eye convergence. The angle of convergence between the two eyes (a) varies with the distance to the object they fixate: smaller angles for objects far away (a_2) and larger angles for objects nearby (a_1).

so that light coming from it falls on the centers of both foveae simultaneously. Since each fovea has only one center, only one point can be precisely fixated at any moment (see Figure 5.2.2). The crucial fact about convergence that provides information about fixation depth is that the angle formed by the two lines of sight varies systematically with the distance between the observer and the fixated point. Fixating a close object results in a large convergence angle, and fixating a far object results in a small one, as illustrated in Figure 5.2.2. Because convergence depends on the observer using both eyes, it is a *binocular* source of depth information, unlike accommodation. Like accommodation, however, convergence provides information about the absolute distance to the fixated object.

The geometry of binocular fixation and convergence is illustrated in Figure 5.2.2. The equation relating distance to the angle of convergence is given in Figure 5.2.3, based on the trigonometry of right triangles. This equation shows that if the distance between the two eyes is known, the angle of eye convergence could be used by the human visual system to determine distance to the fixated point. But is it? Controlled experiments have shown that it is (e.g., Hofsten, 1976), but only up to a distance of a few meters. The reason for this limitation becomes apparent when the angle of convergence is plotted as a function of distance to the fixated object, as shown in Figure 5.2.3. At close distances the convergence angle changes rapidly for points that are only slightly different in depth, but at distances beyond about

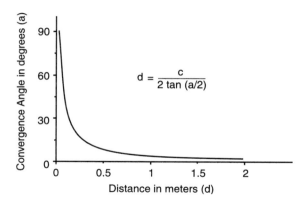

Figure 5.2.3 Convergence as a function of distance. The angle of convergence changes rapidly with distances up to a meter or two but very little after that.

$$d = \frac{c}{2 \tan (a/2)}$$

6–8 feet, convergence changes very little as it approaches an *asymptote* (or limiting value) of zero degrees when the eyes are directed straight ahead to converge on a point at infinite distance.

Convergence and accommodation normally covary; as the distance of the fixated object changes, both accommodation and convergence change in lockstep. Indeed, if a fixated object is moved closer and farther when one of the eyes is covered, the (binocular) convergence of the eyes will change appropriately, driven by the (monocular) accommodation of the lens of the uncovered eye. This fact makes it difficult to tease apart the independent contributions of accommodation and convergence to depth perception. They are important sources of depth information, however, especially at close distances, for they are among the few that specify the absolute distance to objects.

5.3 Stereoscopic Information

Perhaps the most compelling experience of depth comes from **stereopsis**: the process of perceiving the relative distance to objects based on their lateral displacement in the two retinal images. Stereopsis is possible because we have two laterally separated eyes whose visual fields overlap in the central region of vision. Because the positions of the eyes differ by a few inches, the two retinal images of most objects in the overlapping portion are slightly different. That is, the same point in the environment projects to locations on the left and right retinae

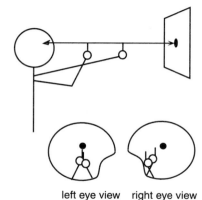

left eye view   right eye view

Figure 5.3.1 Demonstration of binocular disparity. The fact that the two eyes register somewhat different views of the world can be demonstrated by performing the finger experiments described in the text.

that are displaced in a way that depends on how much closer or farther the point is from the fixation point. This relative lateral displacement is called **binocular disparity**.

5.3.1 Binocular Disparity

The two retinal images are sufficiently similar that you are unlikely to notice any difference if you compare them simply by closing first one eye and then the other. You can experience the lateral disparity of corresponding points rather dramatically, however, in the following demonstration. First, hold up your left index finger at full arm's length and your right index finger at half arm's length. Then close your right eye, and align your two fingers using your left eye so that they both coincide with some distant point in the environment, as illustrated in Figure 5.3.1. Now, keeping your fingers in the same place and continuing to focus on the distant object, close your left eye and open your right. What happens to the images of your two fingers? They are no longer aligned either with the distant fixated point or with each other but are displaced markedly to the left. These differences occur because the few inches of separation between your eyes provide two slightly different views of the world.

The lateral displacement of your fingers relative to the distant object in this situation is a clear demonstration that binocular disparity exists. When such disparity is registered by your visual system in two simultaneously present retinal images, it is interpreted as your two fingers and the distant object being at different depths. What you normally experience as a result of binocular disparity is not lateral image displacement at all but objects positioned at different distances from you.

The information that binocular disparity provides is actually much more precise than we have yet suggested. The *direction* of disparity provides information about which points are closer and which are farther than the fixated point. The *magnitude* of this disparity provides information about how much closer or farther they are. To demonstrate the quantitative relation between amount of disparity and depth in the present situation, repeat the finger experiment exactly as before, but this time notice how far the images of your fingers are displaced to the left of the fixated distant object. Because of the geometry of binocular disparity, the closer finger ends up much farther to the left than the more distant finger. Making the close finger even closer to your face will displace it even farther to the side. The quantitative nature of binocular disparity is perceptually important because, even though it provides only relative depth information, it specifies *ratios* of distances to objects rather than simply which is farther and which is closer.

To demonstrate the relation between direction of disparity and depth, repeat the finger experiment exactly as before, except this time fixate the close finger instead of the distant object, first with your left eye and then with your right. (This is a bit harder, but you can do it if you concentrate.) You will see that the images of the far finger and the distant object now displace to the right of the fixated object (the close finger) rather than to the left, the distant object moving the greater distance. Therefore, when switching eyes from left to right, leftward displacement of objects is interpreted as their being closer than the fixated point, and rightward displacement is interpreted as objects being farther than the fixated point. This demonstrates the relation between direction of disparity and depth relative to fixation. By examining the geometry of binocular disparity, we can understand why these relationships hold and what information the visual system is using to interpret image displacements as depth.

Corresponding Retinal Positions. The first step in understanding the geometry of binocular disparity is to define **corresponding positions** on the two retinae:

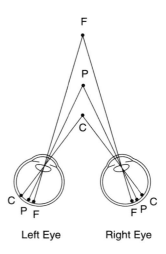

Figure 5.3.2 Crossed versus uncrossed binocular disparity. When a point P is fixated, closer points (such as C) are displaced outwardly in crossed disparity, whereas farther points (such as F) are displaced inwardly in uncrossed disparity.

positions that would coincide if the two foveae were superimposed by simple lateral displacement. To understand this concept, imagine each retina as half an eggshell with the fovea at the center. Then imagine superimposing the two retinae by placing one eggshell inside the other so that their centers coincide. Now imagine making a pinhole through both eggshells at some position, separating the shells, and putting them back in their original locations at the back of the two eyes. The two holes are located at what would be geometrically corresponding positions on the two retinae.

Binocular disparity arises when a given point in the external world does *not* project to corresponding positions on the left and right retinae. For example, consider the diagram of two eyes fixated on a point, P, shown in Figure 5.3.2. By definition, point P falls on the foveae of both eyes and thus stimulates corresponding points. Now consider the projections of a closer point C while the eyes are still fixated on point P. As indicated in Figure 5.3.2, they do *not* fall on corresponding retinal points, since the one on the right retina is to the right of the fovea and the one on the left retina is to the left of the fovea. This outward direction is called **crossed disparity** (which you can remember because it begins with "c" just like "close"). Crossed disparity for the two images of a point (C) indicates that it is closer than the fixated point (P). How much closer it is depends on how far apart the disparate points are in the crossed direc-

Perceiving Surfaces Oriented in Depth

tion. You can probably imagine from looking at Figure 5.3.2 that the closer point C is to the eyes, the greater will be the crossed disparity between its position on the two retinal images (that is, the farther apart will be its left and right images).

Now consider the retinal projections of a point, F, that is farther than the fixated point, P. As shown in Figure 5.3.2, this point also falls on disparate retinal points, but this time the one on the right image is to the left of the fovea and the one on the left image is to the right of the fovea. This inward (or nasal) direction is called **uncrossed disparity**. It indicates that the point that gave rise to it (in this case, F) is farther away than the fixated point (P). Again, how much farther away it is depends on the amount of uncrossed disparity.

The Horopter. Not all points in the environment produce disparate images on the left and right retinae, however. The most obvious example is the fixation point, which falls on the center of both foveae. The set of environmental points that stimulate corresponding points on the two retinae is called the **horopter**. There are two ways of defining the horopter: theoretically by geometrical means and empirically by experimental means. The *theoretical horopter* can be defined geometrically by projecting pairs of corresponding retinal points outward through the nodal point of the eye. Some of these pairs of lines intersect at a point in the environment, which, by definition, projects to corresponding retinal positions. The set of all such points constitutes the horopter. In the horizontal plane of the eye, the theoretical horopter is a circle, called the **Vieth-Muller circle**, which passes through the fixation point and the nodal points of both eyes, as shown in Figure 5.3.3. The disparity of every point on this circle is therefore (theoretically) zero. In the vertical plane, the environmental locations that project to corresponding points on the two retinae lie along a straight line perpendicular to the line of sight, as illustrated in Figure 5.3.4. (Note that the horizontal and vertical planes referred to here are specified relative to the orientation of the eyes rather than to the environment. The horizontal horopter will actually lie in a vertical plane of the environment if the observer is looking straight down.)

The *empirical horopter* is defined by the results of psychophysical experiments. Such studies can be done in several ways, but they generally indicate that the empir-

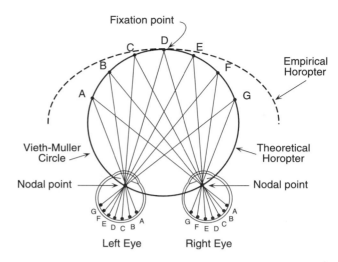

Figure 5.3.3 The horopter in the horizontal plane. The set of environmental positions that project to corresponding retinal positions in the two eyes is called the horopter. The theoretical horopter in the horizontal plane of the eyes is a circle—called the Vieth-Muller circle—that passes through the nodal points of both eyes and the fixation point (D). The empirical horopter (dashed curve) is slightly behind the theoretical horopter as indicated.

ical horopter in the horizontal plane lies slightly behind the theoretical horopter, as depicted in Figure 5.3.3 (Ogle, 1950). The empirical horopter in the vertical plane is systematically slanted away from the observer above the fixation point and toward the observer below it, as indicated in Figure 5.3.4 (Nakayama, 1977). It is not known with certainty why the empirically measured horopter differs from the theoretically defined horopter, but the differences are relatively small and can usually be ignored for practical purposes.

Stereoscopic depth perception thus arises from different directions and degrees of retinal disparity for environmental points that lie in front of and behind the horopter. When you think about the implications of this fact, it becomes clear that binocular disparity is a relative rather than an absolute source of depth information. The direction and amount of disparity specify how much closer or farther a given point is relative to the horopter. The absolute distance to points along the horopter varies with the distance of the fixated point. Therefore, to get absolute depth information from binocular disparity, it must be coupled with some source of absolute depth information about the distance to some object in the field of view, such as from binocular convergence or accommodation. Once the absolute dis-

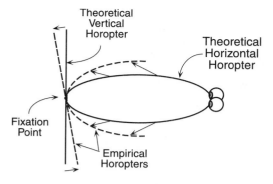

Figure 5.3.4 The theoretical versus empirical horopter in the vertical plane. The theoretical horopter in the vertical plane is a straight line perpendicular to the line of sight that passes through the fixation point. The empirical horopter in the vertical plane (dashed line) is slanted backward in depth as indicated.

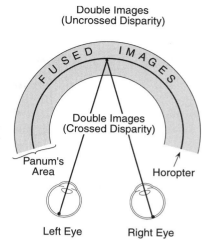

Figure 5.3.5 Panum's fusional area. Environmental points within Panum's area are fused perceptually into a single image. Points that are closer or farther produce double images of crossed or uncrossed disparity.

tance to one object is known, the relative distances to all other objects can be scaled to arrive at their absolute distances.

One question that naturally arises from all this talk about disparity between the two retinal images is why we don't normally experience double images (**diplopia**). After all, every point in the external world that falls within the binocular portion of the visual field produces two retinal images, yet we seldom experience double vision. The answer has at least two parts. One is that points on or near the horopter are fused perceptually into a single experienced image. The region around the horopter within which disparate images are perceptually fused is called **Panum's fusional area**, as indicated in Figure 5.3.5. The second part of the answer is that for points that lie outside Panum's area, the disparity is normally experienced as depth. You *can* experience double images if you attend to disparity as "doubleness," however, or if the amount of disparity is great enough, as when you cross your eyes by focusing on your nose.

To demonstrate double vision due to binocular disparity, repeat the initial finger experiment—one finger at arm's length and the other at half arm's length—but this time with both eyes open. If you fixate on the distant object, you will see double images of both your fingers because they lie outside Panum's area when you fixate on the distant object. If you now repeat the experiment with the distant object less than an inch beyond your farther finger, you will see a double image of your closer

finger but not of the farther one. That is because the farther finger is now close enough to the horopter defined by the distant object that it lies within Panum's fusional area. The close finger is perceived as double because it still lies outside Panum's area.

Stereoscopic vision is exquisitely sensitive to binocular disparity. Most people can detect differences of just a few seconds of angle (1/360 of a degree, because one second of angle is 1/60 of a minute and one minute is 1/60 of a degree). Its only major drawback is that its effectiveness is limited to a range of less than about 30 meters (100 feet). Beyond this range, disparities become too small to detect reliably. Stereoscopic vision is also necessarily limited to the central region of the visual field where the two retinal images overlap.

Not everyone who can see with both eyes has stereoscopic depth perception. **Stereoblindness**, as it is called, is relatively common, affecting from 5% to 10% of the general population (Richards, 1970) and is usually caused by visual disorders during childhood. The single most common cause is **strabismus**, the misalignment of the two eyes. If this condition is corrected surgically at an early age, stereoscopic vision can develop normally (Banks, Aslin, & Letson, 1975). Stereopsis also fails to develop in children who have good vision in only one eye because of either monocular nearsightedness or a cataract. Stereoblind individuals can still perceive

Perceiving Surfaces Oriented in Depth

depth, of course—just as people with normal stereo vision can perceive depth if they simply close one eye—but they must use sources of depth information other than binocular disparity.

Stereograms. Perhaps the most powerful demonstration that binocular disparity can produce the experience of surfaces at different depths comes from **stereograms**: pairs of images that differ in the relative lateral displacement of elements such that, when viewed stereoscopically, they produce compelling illusions of depth from a completely flat page. Stereograms were invented by Charles Wheatstone when he analyzed the geometry of binocular disparity in 1838. Wheatstone realized that if the left and right eyes could be presented with images that differed only by the appropriate lateral displacement of otherwise identical objects, they should be experienced as located at different depths. Simple optical devices for viewing stereograms became fashionable in the late nineteenth century, and more sophisticated versions continue to be popular as children's toys. Stereograms can also be perceived in depth without any such apparatus, however, as we will now demonstrate.

The key feature of a stereogram is that corresponding objects in the left and right images are laterally displaced, producing binocular disparity. The direction of disparity (crossed or uncrossed) and the amount of disparity determine the depth that is perceived. Figure 5.3.6A shows one such stereo pair. Notice that, relative to the square borders, the circles are displaced somewhat toward the outside, and the squares even more so. When these two images are stereoscopically fused by crossing the eyes, as described below, this lateral disparity produces a percept in depth like the display shown in Figure 5.3.6B. Figure 5.3.6C shows a pair with the reverse disparity, which produces the same percept, except reversed in depth, as depicted in Figure 5.3.6D. This result is precisely what we would predict given our previous discussion of crossed versus uncrossed disparity.

To experience these stereograms in depth, you must get your two eyes to register different images that your brain can fuse into a single image. There are two ways to do this: the *crossed convergence method* and the *uncrossed convergence method*. The images in Figure 5.3.6A and 5.3.6C have been constructed to produce the percepts illustrated below them using the crossed convergence method, which we will describe first. Viewing them

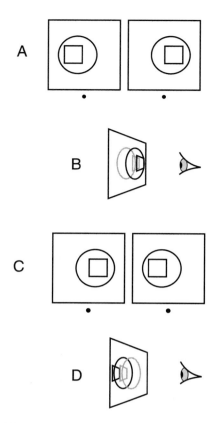

Figure 5.3.6 Binocular disparity and stereograms. If the two images in part A are stereoscopically fused with crossed convergence (see text for instructions), the circle and square will appear above the page as indicated in part B. If the two images in part C are cross-fused, the circle and square will appear behind the page, as indicated in part D.

using the uncrossed convergence method will reverse perceived depth, so that Figure 5.3.6A will look like Figure 5.3.6D, and Figure 5.3.6C will look like Figure 5.3.6B.

To achieve stereoscopic fusion of a stereo pair by the crossed convergence method, you need to cross your eyes by just the right amount to bring the left image in your right eye into registration with the right image in your left eye. Because there are two physical images registered in each eye, you will generally experience four images once you misalign them by crossing your eyes. The goal in crossed convergence fusion is to adjust this misalignment so that there are exactly three images, the middle one of which is the alignment of two images that together produce the perception of depth.

Misaligning your eyes in just the right way is not easy to do without practice, but here is a useful trick. Focus your gaze on a pencil point positioned on the page midway between the two black dots below the two images. Then move the pencil toward your eyes, focusing continually on its tip. As you do so, you will experience diplopia (double images) for each half of the stereogram, producing a total of four images and four dots. At some distance above the page, the borders of two of the four images will overlap exactly, and this is the point at which you should stop moving the pencil, whose point should now be aligned with the middle dot of three dots below the stereo images.[1] (If your eyes are not horizontally aligned with the images on the page, they will not line up exactly, so you may need to tilt either your head or the book slightly as a final adjustment.) Once the images are exactly aligned, without moving your eyes, focus your attention on the middle image and look for the square and circle to float magically above the background border. This may take a few moments, but once you have achieved it, you will experience a vivid sense of depth.

To fuse stereograms using the uncrossed convergence method, begin by bringing the book very close to your face, with your nose touching the page. Relax your eyes—that is, do not try to focus on the page by crossing your eyes—and slowly move the book away from your face. Again you will see four images and four dots most of the time, but at some distance from the page, you will see exactly three images and three dots. Stop at this point and attend to the middle image, which will eventually appear in depth—if you have stereoscopic vision. Notice that the depth you perceive this way is the reverse of what you saw when you used the crossed convergence method.

In both methods, your eyes are misconverged for the distance to the page. In the crossed method, your eyes are overconverged, and in the uncrossed method, they are underconverged. These deviations from normal viewing convergence are what allow such stereograms to produce the illusion of depth.

5.3.2 The Correspondence Problem

Thus far we have talked about stereoscopic vision as though the only problem it poses for the visual system is to measure the direction and amount of disparity between corresponding image features in the two retinal images. But we have not yet come to grips with the far more difficult problem of determining which features in one retinal image correspond to which features in the other. This is called the **correspondence problem** for obvious reasons. We avoided it in our previous discussion because we followed light into the eyes from the environment, starting with a single environmental point and following its projections to distinct points in the left and right retinal images. In doing so, we assumed the proper correspondence of images in the two eyes. But the visual system faces the much more taxing inverse problem: It starts with two images and has to discover which features in the left image correspond to which features in the right one. How our visual systems determine this correspondence requires an explanation.

For many years, theorists assumed that this problem was solved by some sort of shape analysis that occurred before stereopsis. Figure 5.3.7A shows a flowchart indicating how depth and shape analyses were thought to be ordered. Shape was assumed to be analyzed first, separately for the left and right images, so that the results could be used to solve the correspondence problem. The rationale was that although it would be difficult to determine which point of light among thousands in one retinal image went with which point among thousands in the other, it would be easy to determine that, say, the tip of a German shepherd's nose in one retinal image went with the tip of a German shepherd's nose in the other. Ambiguity in the correspondence problem would therefore be enormously reduced if shape analysis came first. But does it? The alternative possibility, shown in Figure 5.3.7B, is that stereopsis might actually come first and occur without the benefit of monocular shape information.

---

[1] If you have trouble finding the right spot for the pencil point with both of your eyes open at once, try looking alternately with your left and right eyes. That is, without moving your head or the book, adjust the position of the pencil point closer or farther from the page (*not* left or right) until it lines up with the dot under the right image when you look with your right eye and with the dot under the left image when you look with your left eye. Then open both eyes and fixate the pencil point. You should now see three dots and three images, the middle one of which can be stereoscopically fused to perceive depth.

Perceiving Surfaces Oriented in Depth

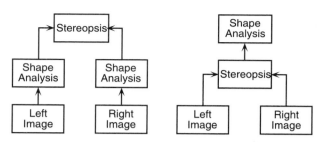

A. Shape-First Theory
B. Stereopsis-First Theory

Figure 5.3.7 Flowcharts for two theories of stereopsis. (A) The shape-first theory assumes that images in the two eyes are matched by comparing the results of two separate shape analyses. (B) The stereopsis-first theory assumes that stereopsis occurs before shape analysis. Perception of random dot stereograms supports the stereopsis-first theory (part B).

Random Dot Stereograms. Bela Julesz (1971), then working at Bell Telephone Laboratories, realized that he could test the shape-first theory of the correspondence problem by constructing what he called **random dot stereograms**. A random dot stereogram is a pair of images consisting of thousands of randomly placed dots whose lateral displacements produce convincing perception of depth when viewed stereoscopically so that one image stimulates one eye and the other image stimulates the other eye. Figure 5.3.8 shows an example of such a stereo pair that encodes a square floating above the page.

When each image of a random-dot stereogram is viewed by itself, the dots look random in the sense that no global shape information is present in either image alone. The shape-first theory of stereoscopic correspondence therefore predicts that it should be impossible to perceive depth by fusing random-dot images stereoscopically because it assumes that the correspondence must be based on recognized monocular shape information.

To test this prediction yourself, use the crossed convergence method described above to fuse them. It may take a while for the square to emerge in depth because random dot stereograms are quite a bit harder to see than standard stereograms, such as those in Figure 5.3.6. But once you succeed, a randomly speckled square will stand out clearly against a speckled background. (If you fuse Figure 5.3.8 using the uncrossed convergence method, the square will be perceived behind the page through a square hole in the background.)

Since there are no monocular shapes to be matched in the two retinal images, the appropriate conclusion is that the shape-first theory is *incorrect*. The stereoscopic system seems to be able to solve the correspondence problem without monocular shape information because Julesz's random dot stereograms contain little, if any, such information. Another stereogram is shown in Figure 5.3.9 for your enjoyment. Be forewarned that it is a good bit more difficult to perceive than the simple square, but the results are well worth the extra effort. It depicts a spiral surface coming out of the page.

It is important not to overstate the conclusion reached from the perception of random dot stereograms. The fact that people can perceive stereoscopic depth in random dot stereograms does not prove that there is no shape analysis prior to stereopsis. It shows only that stereoscopic depth can be perceived without monocular shape information. There may well be some primitive shape or contour analysis before stereopsis that aids in solving the correspondence problem when monocular shape information is present. The orientation of local lines and edges is one example of further information that would be useful in solving the correspondence problem, for only lines or edges of similar orientation would be potential matches. Such orientation information is available relatively early in the visual system in the output of simple cells in area V1 (Hubel & Wiesel, 1962). In fact, the difficulty of achieving depth perception in random dot stereograms compared to stereo pairs of normal photographs suggests that monocular shape information is indeed useful. Even so, random dot stereograms show that in the absence of such information, binocular depth perception is possible.

To understand how the visual system might be able to solve the correspondence problem for random dot stereograms, we first have to understand how they are constructed. It is really a very simple process, which you can carry out yourself. The first image of the pair is constructed by placing a large number of dots at completely random locations. (You can just photocopy one of the two images in Figure 5.3.8.) The second image of the pair can then be generated from the first one by the following procedure (see Figure 5.3.10):

1. Photocopy the first image.

2. Cut out the shape of the region you want to appear in a different depth plane and slide it to the right by a

Figure 5.3.8 A random dot stereogram. These two images are derived from a single array of randomly placed squares by laterally displacing a region of them as described in the text. When they are viewed with crossed disparity (by crossing the eyes) so that the right eye's view of the left image is combined with the left eye's view of the right image, a square will be perceived to float above the page. (See pages 210–211 for instructions on fusing stereograms.)

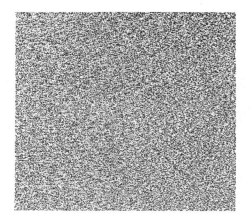 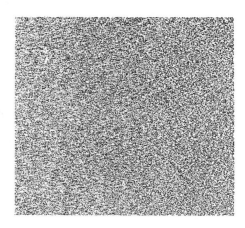

Figure 5.3.9 A random dot stereogram of a spiral surface. If these two images are fused with crossed convergence (see text on pages 210–211 for instructions), they can be perceived as a spiral ramp coming out of the page toward your face. This perception arises from the small lateral displacements of thousands of tiny dots. (From Julesz, 1971.)

quarter of an inch or so, as illustrated in Figure 5.3.10. The amount of displacement will determine the difference in depth.

3. In sliding the cut-out portion sideways, you will have covered up some of the texture on the right of the cut-out shape and will have uncovered a hole on the left side. Fill up this hole with a new pattern of random dots by photocopying another replica of the original random dot image and placing some of it behind the hole.

4. Now place the two images side-by-side (as in Figure 5.3.8) with the original on the left.

Voilà! You have just made a random dot stereogram. If you now view it stereoscopically, there will be disparity between the points within the region you moved sideways. The distance you moved it corresponds to the amount of disparity and therefore determines the amount of depth that will be perceived between the planes of the figure and its background: greater disparity produces greater perceived depth. The direction in which you moved them will make the shape you cut out float in front or behind a background plane of random dots.

Perceiving Surfaces Oriented in Depth

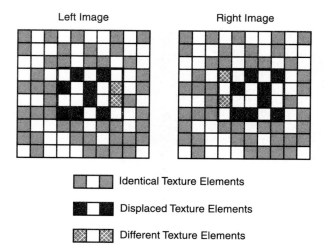

Left Image   Right Image

▨□▨ Identical Texture Elements

■□■ Displaced Texture Elements

▧□▧ Different Texture Elements

Figure 5.3.10 Constructing a random dot stereogram. The left and right images are identical (light gray and white squares) except for a region that has been laterally displaced (dark gray and white squares) and the unique regions (hatched gray and white squares) revealed by the displacement. (All texture elements are black and white in the actual stereogram, as in Figure 5.3.8.)

Here is an experiment you can try with stereogram 5.3.8 that demonstrates an interesting property of the stereoscopic depth system. Move your head back and forth slightly relative to the stereogram while you look at it. If you can do this while maintaining the depth illusion—it is difficult and may take several tries—the square will miraculously appear to slide laterally back and forth to follow your own movements. This curious phenomenon results from the difference between the actual structure of the stereogram and what would be the physical structure of the 3-D surfaces you are perceiving. For instance, consider what would happen if the square were really in front of the background surface when you moved your head to the right, illustrated in Figure 5.3.11A. As you move rightward, additional random dots would appear along the right edge of the square as they are disoccluded by the square, and other dots would disappear along the left edge as they are occluded by the square. But in the stereogram, the square is actually coplanar with the surrounding field, so neither occlusion nor disocclusion of texture occurs when you move your head. Similarly, if the square were actually in front of the background, moving your head would generate motion parallax. No motion parallax occurs, so the stimulus information seems inconsistent

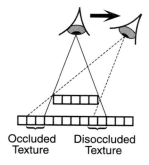

Occluded   Disoccluded
Texture   Texture

A. STATIC SQUARE

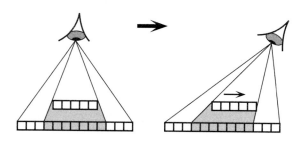

B. MOVING SQUARE

Figure 5.3.11 Phenomenal movement in random dot stereograms. When the observer moves while viewing a random dot stereogram, the closer surface moves in the same direction (part B) because no texture elements are occluded or disoccluded during the motion, as would occur in real depth if both surfaces were stationary (part A).

with the perception of depth. Why then does the square not flatten into the background as soon as you move your head?

The reason is that there is an alternative explanation for the lack of dynamic depth information that nevertheless allows the observer to maintain the illusion of a square floating in front of the background. If the square were moving rightward along with you as your head moved rightward, as illustrated in Figure 5.3.11B, it would exactly cancel the effects of moving your head: that is, there would be no occlusion or disocclusion of texture elements and no motion parallax. Because this state of affairs is consistent with the proximal stimulus, it is an alternative perception that allows you to maintain the illusion of stereoscopic depth.

Autostereograms. Another kind of stereogram has become popular in the past few years that does not require special glasses or viewing apparatus. They were

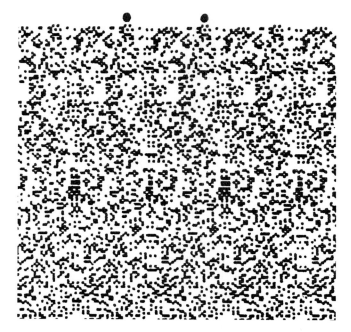

Figure 5.3.12 An autostereogram. When this image is viewed as directed in the text, a square can be seen floating in front of the rest of the figure, without the aid of special glasses. (From Tyler, 1980.)

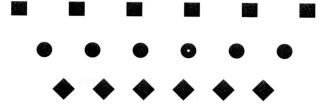

Figure 5.3.13 A simplified autostereogram. To experience a depth illusion with this figure, follow the instructions in the text to achieve crossed convergence. The rows of figures should begin to appear in different depth planes. The squares will appear closer than the circles, and the diamonds will appear farther away than the circles.

initially called **autostereograms** by Tyler and Chang (1977), but they are now more widely known as **magic-eye stereograms**. Figure 5.3.12 shows an example. When viewed normally, it looks like what it is: a flat picture with a repetitious horizontal structure. When viewed somewhat differently, however, it creates a compelling illusion of stereoscopic depth. To experience this illusion, hold the book in the frontal plane and cross your eyes somewhat so that the two black circles at the top appear as three dots in a line. When you have accomplished this, the elements in the autostereogram will start to fuse, and you will begin to get the impression of objects at different depths. Eventually, you will see a checkerboard of random dot squares floating above an underlying plane of random dot background texture.

To understand how such patterns manage to create the perception of depth, consider the much simpler autostereogram shown in Figure 5.3.13. View it using the crossed convergence method, and when you see two adjacent circles with white dots inside them, the different rows of shapes will appear to be located at different distances away from you: squares closest, diamonds

farthest, and circles in the middle. If you view this autostereogram with uncrossed convergence, the depth of the shapes will reverse.

The illusion of depth is created when the two eyes fixate on two *different* objects and fuse them as though they were the *same* object. (You can verify that this must be the case because there is actually only one circle with a white dot in it, yet you see two such circles whenever you perceive illusory depth.) By crossing your eyes, you can induce the visual system to fixate different objects with your two eyes. The objects in the same row are identical in shape to enable this fusion error to occur. When this happens, the two fixated objects appear to be a single object in the depth plane on which the eyes are converged. This plane lies in front of the actual depth plane, as illustrated in Figure 5.3.14. Once this happens, the other objects in that row can also be fused. If their spacing is even, wrongly matched pairs will be perceived to be located in the same plane as the illusion of the fused fixation objects.

Figure 5.3.13 is a very simple autostereogram compared to the complex, computer-generated example in Figure 5.3.12 and the much more complex ones available in recent commercial books (e.g., *Magic Eye: A New Way of Looking at the World*, by N. E. Thing Enterprises, 1993), but the basic principles are the same. More complex surfaces can be constructed by using dense textures of random elements, more subtle and complex spacings among the elements to be fused, and color to enhance the matching process (Tyler, 1990). In each case, the stereoscopic depth effect depends on managing to fool the visual system into matching up elements in the two retinal images that are actually different from each other

Perceiving Surfaces Oriented in Depth

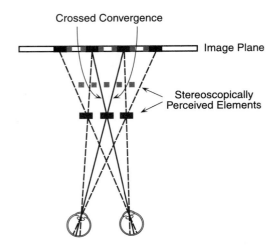

Figure 5.3.14 Autostereograms explained. Illusions of depth occur in viewing autostereograms when the eyes are misconverged such that different elements in the repetitive pattern are fused. (See text for details.)

and making their horizontal disparities in the stimulus correspond to the intended depth relations.

Binocular Rivalry. In our discussion of the correspondence problem thus far we have been assuming that there are corresponding points because that is the normal state of affairs. But what happens if quite different images are presented to the two eyes, such as a grating of horizontal stripes to the left eye and a grating of vertical stripes to the right eye?

Grossly mismatched images in the two eyes result in the observer seeing only one image at a time, a phenomenon known as **binocular rivalry** or **binocular suppression** (Levelt, 1968). With small patterns subtending 1° of visual angle or less, rivalry tends to be holistic, the two entire images alternating in perceptual experience over cycles lasting about 1–4 seconds. With larger images, rivalry tends to lead to piecemeal perception of different parts of the two images at once. You can experience binocular rivalry by viewing Figure 5.3.15 using either the crossed or uncrossed convergence method. Fusing it into a single, stable percept is almost impossible, but if you look at it for a while you will see how your experience changes in different areas of the square at different times. The alternation in appearance over time presumably occurs because the

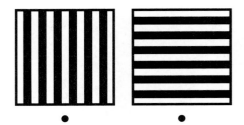

Figure 5.3.15 Binocular rivalry. Fuse the two squares using either the crossed or uncrossed convergence method, and you will experience rivalry between the vertical and horizontal stripes. In any given region, the stripes will sometimes appear vertical and sometimes horizontal.

neurons that are responsible for one perception become fatigued after prolonged firing, leading to the perception of the nonfatigued alternative.

Binocular suppression seems like an unnatural phenomenon because the eyes are usually viewing the same environment in which there are veridical correspondences. But there are many cases in which normal conditions produce different images on corresponding points of the retina, particularly when large disparities exist between corresponding points in the images. Since we seldom experience double images, one explanation is that binocular suppression is at work, leading to the perception of a single image under conditions that ought to result in two displaced images.

5.3.3 Computational Theories

We will now return to our earlier question: How does the visual system solve the correspondence problem in random dot stereograms when there is no global shape information? To appreciate the difficulty of this problem, consider precisely what must be done. Most (but not all) dots in the left image have some corresponding dot in the right image that came from the same environmental location. The visual system must somehow figure out which pairs go together. To simplify the problem somewhat, we will consider only the pairs of points that lie along the orientation of binocular displacement, which is horizontal if the head is upright. If there are 100 points along a given horizontal line in one image, then the number of logically possible pairings is 100! (read "one hundred factorial," which equals $100 \times 99 \times 98 \times \cdots \times 2 \times 1$). This is a very large number indeed, and it is just for one of a hundred or more horizontal rows of points.[2]

A number of different computational approaches to the correspondence problem have been explored. Some match individual points (pixels), others match lines and edges, and still others match local regions in one form or another. We will now consider a small sampling of these theories.

The First Marr-Poggio Algorithm. One interesting and well-known algorithm was devised by David Marr and Tomasso Poggio of M.I.T. in 1977. It is neither the latest nor the best theory of human stereopsis, but it is an interesting—and historically important—example of how a dynamic neural network can be constructed to solve a computationally difficult visual task. It is also a good example of how heuristic assumptions or constraints can be implemented in such networks. We will therefore examine it in some detail.

The basic idea behind the Marr-Poggio (1977) algorithm is to solve the correspondence problem by matching individual pixels in the left and right images. The starting point for understanding how this is done is the concept of an **inverse projection** from the two retinal images back into the world, as illustrated in Figure 5.3.16. This diagram depicts a top view of two black-and-white striped surfaces in the environment, a small one situated in front of a larger one, as shown at the top. Light reflected from these surfaces registers on the left and right retinal images—which have been flattened here for simplicity—as shown in the middle of the diagram. To form an inverse projection, each pixel of these images is then projected back into the "mirror-image environment" shown below. The shaded cells in this matrix represent positions at which there are color matches between pixels in the two images. The points match (and are shaded) if both pixels are black or both

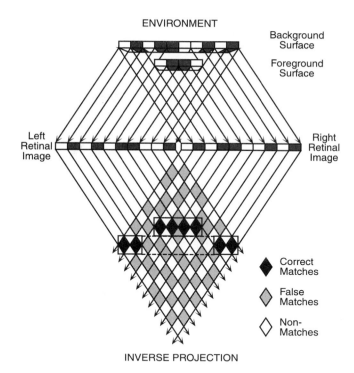

Figure 5.3.16 Inverse projection of two surfaces in depth. The upper half of the figure shows a top view of how two surfaces project to (flattened) left and right retinal images. The lower half shows how these images can be used to form an inverse projection in which there are many same-color matches, some of which correspond to the correct depth solution (dark elements) and many of which are false matches (gray elements).

are white; they do not match (and are unshaded) if one is black and one is white. If you trace the projections from a shaded cell back to their pixels in the left and right retinal images, you will find that both have the same color. Among these numerous matches are the correct ones that correspond to the visible portions of the actual surfaces in the real world. These correct matches are shaded more darkly in Figure 5.3.16 to differentiate them from the false matches that also arise.[3]

---

[2] This number is computed as follows. Pick a single dot in one row of the right image, and call it dot A. If there are 100 dots in the corresponding row of the left image, there are 100 possible ways of pairing dot A with one in its row of the left image. Then pick a different dot in the same row of the right image, and call it dot B. There are 99 ways of pairing dot B with one of the remaining dots in the left image because one dot has already been paired with A. Thus, there are 100×99 ways of pairing dots A and B in the right image with dots in the same row of the left image. A third dot in the right image (dot C) can then be paired with any of the 98

remaining dots in the left image, yielding $100 \times 99 \times 98$ possible pairings of dots A, B, and C. Continuing in this way for all 100 dots in that row of the right image thus yields $100 \times 99 \times 98 \times \cdots \times 1$ possible pairings.

[3] Notice that no correct matches arise for the farther surface where it is occluded by the nearer one. This results from the fact that neither eye receives optical information from these points owing to occlusion. This is why Marr restricted the 2.5-D sketch to *visible* portions of surfaces.

Perceiving Surfaces Oriented in Depth

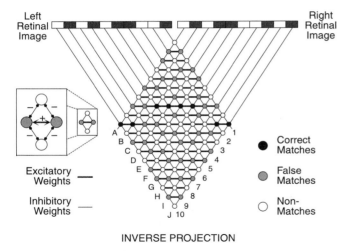

Left
Retinal
Image

Right
Retinal
Image

Excitatory
Weights ——

Inhibitory
Weights ——

● Correct
Matches

● False
Matches

○ Non-
Matches

INVERSE PROJECTION

Figure 5.3.17 The first Marr-Poggio stereo algorithm. A neural network performs an inverse projection of the two retinal images, activating nodes corresponding to positions where the left and right images are the same color. Inhibitory connections (see inset) implement the surface opacity constraint, and excitatory connections implement the surface continuity constraint. (See text for further details.)

The fact that there are false matches as well as true ones reflects the fact that this is an underconstrained inverse problem, one that has many possible solutions. The problem for the visual system is how to determine which matches are correct and which are false.

Marr and Poggio (1977) proposed that this could be accomplished by the dynamic neural network diagrammed in Figure 5.3.17. It shows the left and right images from Figure 5.3.16 activating internal nodes in a neural network that represent the set of all possible correspondences. That is, each node represents a potential match between two pixels: the one from the left image that projects to it and the one from the right image that projects to it. Only the intersections that come from pixels of the same color are possible matches because pixels that are projected from the same point in the environment must have the same color (both white or both black). These color matches, illustrated as shaded nodes, therefore constitute a major constraint on solving the correspondence problem because all the white nodes can be eliminated from consideration.

Matching by color does not produce a unique solution to the correspondence problem, however, because there are still many color matches for each point in the

left and right images. This is why random dot stereograms pose such a difficult problem for the visual system. The question is: What further heuristic constraints might be brought to bear on this formulation of the problem that would produce a unique, correct solution most of the time? Marr and Poggio (1977) employed two such further constraints:

1. *Surface opacity*: The opacity constraint states that because most surfaces in the world are opaque, only the nearest one can be seen. Thus, if correspondence A10 is correct in Figure 5.3.17 (that is, if pixel A in the right image actually corresponds to pixel 10 in the left image), then correspondences B10, C10, D10, and so forth *cannot* be correct, and neither can A9, A8, A7, and so forth.

2. *Surface continuity*: The continuity constraint states that because surfaces in the world tend to be locally continuous in depth (except at occluding edges), the correct solution will tend to be one in which matches are "close together" in depth, as they would be on locally continuous surfaces.

Note that both constraints are heuristic assumptions that are usually true but not always. If they are true, the solution the algorithm finds will generally be correct. If they are not—that is, if one or more of the surfaces are transparent and/or if the surfaces are not locally continuous—the solutions that it finds will tend to be incorrect.

Marr and Poggio implemented these two constraints in the connections between nodes of the neural network in Figure 5.3.17. The model works by first activating all of the nodes in the "intersection network" that represent like-colored pixels in the left and right images. These are just the shaded nodes in Figure 5.3.17, indicating that they have been activated in the initial phase of the algorithm. This set of possible correspondences is then subjected to the opacity and continuity constraints by the nature of the connections between nodes in the network as illustrated in the enlarged four-node inset at the left of the figure. Opacity is implemented by having mutual inhibition among all nodes along the same line of sight in the network. This part of the architecture, denoted by the diagonal connections in Figure 5.3.17, is called a **winner-take-all network** because it allows

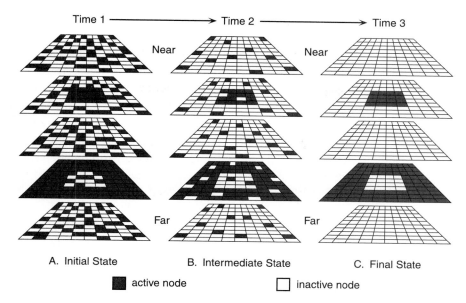

Figure 5.3.18 Dynamic behavior of the Marr-Poggio stereo network. Active nodes corresponding to different depth planes are represented by black squares. (A) Initially, all positions where there are same-color matches are activated, including both true and false correspondences. (B) As excitatory and inhibitory interactions occur, false matches diminish, but so do some true ones. (C) Further interactions leave only the true matches.

only one node in each diagonal line to remain active after activation has settled into a stable state.[4]

The continuity constraint is implemented in the network by having mutual excitation between pixels in the same or nearby depth planes. These interactions between nodes are indicated in Figure 5.3.17 by the thicker horizontal connections. They have the effect that possible correspondences in the same environmental depth plane tend to "help each other out" by activating each other through mutual facilitation. This will cause solutions to tend toward coplanarity as the continuity constraint implies.

The joint effect of these two constraints is to progressively reduce the complete set of possible matches to the single set most compatible with (1) the disparity information available in the sensory images, (2) the opacity constraint, and (3) the continuity constraint. The network churns away, sending activation and inhibition back and forth through the excitatory and inhibitory connections, until it eventually settles into a stable state.

This final state of the network usually—but not always—corresponds to the actual state of affairs in the environment. Figure 5.3.18 shows how activation in the intersection network changes over time for the simple case of a square figure in front of a background plane, as in the stereogram in Figure 5.3.8. The initial pattern of activation is completely determined by the set of pixel pairs whose colors match. As the nodes begin to interact via the excitatory and inhibitory connections, the opacity and continuity constraints begin to take effect. Eventually, the initial correspondences are reduced to just the set representing a square in front of a background.

Marr and Poggio's first algorithm is an interesting example of how a process of unconscious inference can be implemented in a neural network. A deductively insoluble inverse problem has been solved by introducing heuristic assumptions that provide correct solutions when the assumptions are true. The "problem" in this case is finding the correct correspondences in a random dot stereogram. It is "solved" by making certain "as-

---

[4] Winner-take-all networks have this effect because whichever node has the most activation will inhibit the other nodes more than they will inhibit it. As the interactions among nodes in the network continue over time, mutual inhibition causes this disparity in activation to increase—the most active node becomes more active and the others become less active—until a stable state is reached in which only one node is active.

Perceiving Surfaces Oriented in Depth

sumptions" about the structure of surfaces in the world, such as that they are opaque and continuous. These assumptions are "heuristic" because they are only probabilistically (rather than strictly) true of real-world situations. As a result, this algorithm is generally able to solve the problem when these assumptions are met. Thus, the algorithm is an example of how unconscious inference might be accomplished in perception without invoking deductions based on either numerical calculations or the sequential application of symbolic logical rules. Instead, the assumptions are built into the connection strengths within the network, and they work simply by having a favorable effect on its behavior with respect to achieving veridical perception.

Marr and Poggio's (1977) stereo algorithm is also an interesting example of dynamic neural networks as physical Gestalten. Recall from Section 2.1.2 that Köhler described physical Gestalten as dynamic physical systems that converge to a minimum energy state. In the case of the brain arriving at perceptions, the Gestaltists believed that the minimum energy state reflected the principle of Prägnanz: that the percept would be as "good" or "simple" as the prevailing conditions allow. Marr and Poggio's network similarly converges to a state that can be shown to be the minimum in an energy-like function (Hopfield, 1982). Moreover, the solution emerges from ambiguous stimulus conditions (the "prevailing conditions") plus further conditions within the network that embody constraints arising from certain kinds of simplicity (e.g., that surfaces are opaque and continuous). The argument that continuous surfaces are simpler than discontinuous ones is straightforward. That opaque ones are simpler than translucent ones could also be defended on the grounds that their optical properties are less complicated.

Edge-Based Algorithms. A few years after publishing their first stereo algorithm, Marr and Poggio (1979) suggested a second one that differs from their first in a number of important respects:

1. *Edge-based matching.* The second Marr-Poggio algorithm finds stereoscopic correspondences by matching edges in the right and left images rather than individual pixels. This is more efficient because it allows the process to take information into account that simply is not available in matching individual pixels, such as the ori-

entation of the edges and their polarity (light to dark versus dark to light). Edges that do not match in orientation and polarity can be eliminated from consideration, thus adding further constraints on the solution.

2. *Multiple scales.* The second algorithm exploits the multiple size (or scale, or spatial frequency) channels in the visual system (see Chapter 4) by first looking for corresponding edges at a large spatial scale (that is, at low spatial frequencies) and only later at smaller scales (that is, at high spatial frequencies). In terms of solving random dot stereograms, this means that the early, large-scale process works not on individual dots, as their first algorithm did, but on larger regions of the image. Only after possible edge matches are found at this global level is a more detailed matching attempted at the finer-grained level of individual dot contours.

3. *Single-pass operation.* The edge-based algorithm is a noniterative process, meaning that it does not require many cycles of interaction to converge, as did the first Marr-Poggio algorithm. Instead, it simply finds the best edge-based correspondence in a single pass through a multistage operation. Because iteration is a time-consuming process, computer implementations of the second algorithm are much faster than those of the first.

Many of the benefits of the second Marr-Poggio algorithm derive from the fact that the matching operation is performed on the output of edge detectors rather than individual pixels. This is more plausible biologically because binocular processing begins in area V1 of the cortex, after the outputs of individual receptors have been recombined into the more complex elongated receptive fields of the cortex. If these cells are indeed doing edge detection, as Marr (1982) claimed, then solving the correspondence problem by matching edges is a sensible approach. It also has distinct computational advantages because edge detectors carry information about more complex features of the image (that is, oriented edges of a given polarity) than do individual receptors, and this complexity enables many potential matches to be rejected. The second Marr-Poggio algorithm also agrees more closely with the results of psychophysical experiments using human subjects (Marr, 1982). It is thus a better model of human stereo vision than their first algorithm. Unfortunately, there are important findings that neither algorithm can explain, as we will discover shortly.

There are also disadvantages to the edge-based approach. One significant problem is that the resulting depth information is sparse, because edge-based algorithms specify the correspondences only at edges. This is not the case for pixel-based approaches, which specify a dense correspondence for nearly every pixel in the image. In Marr and Poggio's second algorithm, depth information about the spaces between edges must therefore be filled in by some additional process of interpolation.

Filtering Algorithms. More recently, Jones and Malik (1992) have proposed an algorithm that, in effect, matches local regions around the point in question. It doesn't match local image regions directly, however, as this would be computationally too costly. Rather, their algorithm is based on matching the output of a set of biologically inspired spatial filters that differ in their orientation and size tuning, as described at length in Section 4.2. Recall that the results of both psychophysical and physiological experiments strongly suggest that the visual system performs something like a local spatial frequency analysis in which cells respond selectively to gratings at specific orientations and size scales (De Valois & De Valois, 1988). Jones and Malik argue that the output of such local **multi-orientation, multiscale (MOMS) filters** actually provides a much more efficient starting point for stereo matching than either individual pixels or oriented edges do. They do not take a strong stand on the exact nature of the receptive fields, which could be Gabor functions, wavelet functions, differences-of-Gaussian functions, or many other similar possibilities, all of which are defined by a variety of positions, orientations, and scales.

The starting point of their theory is the fact that there are many cells in a single cortical hypercolumn whose receptive fields are centered on the same retinal position, each cell being tuned to a different orientation and scale. The pattern of activity in such a hypercolumn of cells can be modeled mathematically as a vector: an ordered set of numbers corresponding to the firing rates of each of the cells. This vector contains a surprisingly rich representation of the spatial structure within a region centered at that position. Figure 5.3.19 shows two examples in which the central position is the center of the left images. The right images show the reconstruction of the spatial information in the vector representing

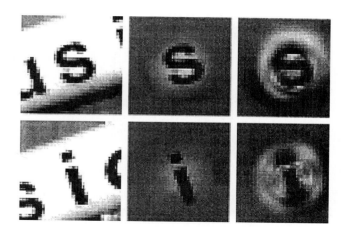

Figure 5.3.19 Reconstructing an image from Jones and Malik's MOMS filters. The two images on the left were reconstructed from the responses of multiorientation, multiscale spatial filters positioned at the center of these images. The results, shown at right, demonstrate that the outputs of such filters contain a great deal of local spatial information. The original images, masked by a Gaussian, are shown in the center for comparison. (From Jones & Malik, 1992.)

the output of about 60 cells in a hypothetical hypercolumn. Clearly, these cells are capturing a good deal of information about the spatial structure of the image in the neighborhood of the central position.

The heart of Jones and Malik's MOMS model is the process of matching the vector representing a given position in one eye to each of the vectors representing laterally displaced positions in the other eye. The mathematical details of this comparison will not concern us here. The important thing is that the laterally displaced position in the other eye that has the most similar vector specifies the most likely correspondence for that position. When the same comparison is performed for all positions at all possible disparities, the result gives a well-defined solution to the correspondence problem. The matches that such an algorithm finds are usually better and more robust than those found by pixel-based or edge-based algorithms because the MOMS vectors carry a great deal more spatial information about local image structure than the outputs of single receptors or edge detectors. This allows the matches to be more selective and accurate.

Like both of the Marr-Poggio algorithms, Jones and Malik's theory makes use of something akin to the continuity constraint, based on the assumption that surfaces

Perceiving Surfaces Oriented in Depth

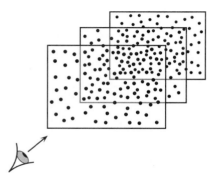

Figure 5.3.20 Prazdny's sparse, transparent stereo display. Human subjects can solve a random dot stereogram that depicts a scene like this, with sparsely distributed dots on transparent surfaces, even though it fails to conform to either the surface opacity or surface continuity constraint.

are locally continuous. As a result, all the theories we have discussed have difficulty solving random dot stereograms depicting surfaces that are locally discontinuous.

It turns out that people *can* solve such random dot stereograms, however. Prazdny (1984) constructed stereograms depicting dots randomly scattered on several transparent surfaces separated in depth (see Figure 5.3.20). Notice that in these displays neither the assumption of surface opacity nor that of local surface continuity is met; the "surfaces" containing the dots are largely transparent, and adjacent dots in the stereo images often come from widely different depth planes. The human visual system is able to span the spaces between the dots on the surfaces, however, as long as the distance in depth among them is great enough.

Another interesting fact that causes problems for current computational theories of the correspondence problem is that the human visual system is able to achieve stereoscopic perception by fusing luminance boundaries in one eye with texture or chromatic boundaries in the other eye (Ramachandran, Rao, & Vidyasagar, 1973). This finding implies that mechanisms for solving the stereo correspondence problem exist at a higher level than has generally been supposed. Any algorithm that is based on matching similar luminance based features—be they pixels, edges, local regions, or whatever—is incapable of explaining how stereopsis can be achieved from such mixed pairs of images. Such matches require correspondence of image features at some more abstract level at which different types of

edges are represented independently of the specific domain of image structure on which they are based. This does not mean that the correspondence problem is solved only at this abstract level, but that the kinds of within-feature schemes that have been devised will need to be augmented by some additional later mechanism.

5.3.4 Physiological Mechanisms

The fact that human vision is much better than any existing computational scheme for stereopsis leads inevitably to the question of how the human brain does it. Unfortunately, the answer is not known at the level of detail we have been considering in these computational models, but some interesting facts have been discovered.

The first binocularly sensitive cells were discovered by Hubel and Wiesel (1962) while recording in area V1 of cat cortex. They found cells that responded much more strongly when stimulated with the same bar or edge in both eyes simultaneously than when that feature stimulated just the left eye or just the right eye. However, the cells they found in V1 seemed to be tuned to features that appeared in corresponding retinal locations of the two eyes rather than to binocularly different locations. Thus, although the cells were binocular, they did not seem to be sensitive to binocular disparity.

Several years later Barlow, Blakemore, and Pettigrew (1967) disputed this claim, reporting that some binocular cells in area V1 responded optimally to stimulation in disparate locations of the two retinae. Further research by Hubel and Wiesel (1970)—this time on monkeys—supported their prior claim that V1 cells were sensitive to zero or near-zero disparity (that is, they responded to stimulation in corresponding or almost-corresponding retinal locations). They also reported new evidence that cells in area V2 were tuned to respond optimally in the presence of the same image features in locations at relatively large disparities. Figure 5.3.21 shows a typical pattern of response for a cell sensitive to binocular disparity in area V2 of monkey cortex. The diagrams on the left side show the relative positions and orientations of the two stimulus bars, one in the left eye and one in the right eye. The firing records on the right show how the cell responded to motion of the bars in opposite directions as indicated by the arrows above each trace. Figure 5.3.21C reveals that this cell is tuned to provide maximal response to disparities around 30

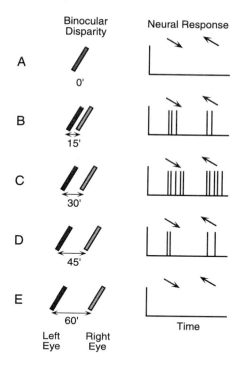

Binocular Disparity

A   0'

B   15'

C   30'

D   45'

E   60'

Left Eye   Right Eye

Neural Response

Time

Figure 5.3.21 Neural responses of a binocular depth cell in monkey cortex. This cell responds maximally to moving bars (in either direction) separated by 30 minutes of arc as indicated in part C, somewhat less when separated by 15 or 45 minutes of arc (parts B and D), and not at all when the same moving bars stimulate corresponding retinal locations in both eyes (part A) or when they are separated by 60 minutes of arc (1°) or more (part E).

minutes of visual angle. Other records show that this cell responds less to nearby disparities (parts B and D), that it fails to respond when the disparity is either much less (part A) or much greater (part E) than this or when the same moving bar is presented monocularly to the right or left eye alone.

The dispute among these researchers about the disparity tuning of binocular cells turned out to be the result of serious methodological difficulties. Primary among them is the problem of establishing which retinal positions correspond at any given moment in time. This can be determined reasonably well if the animal is fixating a particular location, but most single-cell recording

studies are performed on anesthetized animals that are not even awake, much less fixating on anything in particular. This problem was overcome by Poggio and Fischer (1977), who recorded from cortical cells in alert monkeys that had been trained to fixate on a particular spot.[5] By using this technique to maintain precise alignment of the two eyes during recording sessions, V1 cells were found that were sensitive to nonzero disparities as Barlow, Blakemore, and Pettigrew had claimed, but the disparities were quite small, as Hubel and Wiesel had maintained. Also consistent with Hubel and Wiesel's results, cells in area V2 were found that were tuned to much wider disparities, some of which were sensitive to crossed disparity and others to uncrossed disparity.

Perhaps the most intriguing interpretation of these results is that two separate physiological systems are involved in stereoscopic depth perception. One, located in area V1, is highly sensitive to small or zero disparities. The other, located in area V2, is sensitive to large disparities in both crossed and uncrossed direction. This division of function suggests that cells in V1 may be responsible for binocular fusion within Panum's area around the horopter and cells in V2 for depth perception in front of and behind this region where double images can be experienced.

Despite the substantial progress that has been made through such physiological studies of stereoscopic vision, no light has yet been shed on the specific algorithms through which the visual system solves the correspondence problem. The answer must await a more detailed analysis of the neural information processing that occurs within binocular cells in visual cortex than is yet available. Computational theories of binocular correspondence using biologically plausible representations, such as Jones and Malik's (1992) MOMS filter model (see Section 5.3.3), should provide physiologists with clearer notions of what kinds of mechanisms they are likely to find and how they are likely to work. We have not yet reached the point at which such models have been tested, however.

---

[5] Recording from brain cells of awake monkeys does not cause them pain because, strangely enough, there are no pain receptors inside the brain itself.

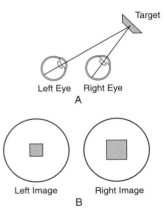

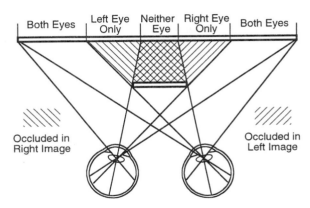

Figure 5.3.22 Vertical binocular disparity. When a target object is closer to one eye than the other (part A), differences in the size of corresponding images produced vertical as well as horizontal disparity (part B).

Figure 5.3.23 Da Vinci stereopsis. Depth information also arises from the fact that certain parts of one retinal image have no corresponding parts in the other image. (See text for details.)

5.3.5 Vertical Disparity

Thus far we have been talking about binocular disparity as though it were purely horizontal. Vertical binocular disparity also exists, although it has not received nearly as much attention from vision scientists until quite recently. It is perhaps easiest to understand why vertical disparity is present in binocular images by considering differences in size that can exist between the images of the same object in the left and right eyes. Figure 5.3.22A illustrates the viewing geometry of the situation for a target object that is on the right side of the observer. If both eyes are fixated on the center of the target object (say, a square), the image in the right eye will be larger than that in the left eye because the right eye is closer. This difference in size results in vertical disparity between corresponding points in the square in the two eyes, as illustrated in Figure 5.3.22B. There will be distance-induced disparity in the horizontal dimension as well, because the difference in size scaling due to variable distance from the two eyes is present in all directions.

5.3.6 Da Vinci Stereopsis

There is one further source of stereoscopic information. It concerns the fact that in binocular viewing of surfaces at different depths, there is usually a portion of the farther surface that is seen by just one eye (e.g., Nakayama & Shimojo, 1990). Figure 5.3.23 shows an example.

Notice that there is a portion of the farther surface to the right of the closer surface that is seen by the right eye but not the left. Similarly, there is a portion to the left of the closer surface that is seen by the left eye but not the right. This means that for these regions, there is no proper solution to the correspondence problem simply because there are no corresponding points in the other eye's image.

Nevertheless, these regions of monocular stimulation provide important binocular information about the relative distance of surfaces. Nakayama and Shimojo (1990) call this form of depth information **da Vinci stereopsis** in honor of the famous artist Leonardo da Vinci, who first commented upon it. The depth information arises from the viewing geometry adjacent to occluding depth edges: The monocularly viewed region is always part of the *farther* surface. If this monocularly viewed region is present in the right image, it will necessarily lie just to the right of the occluding edge; if it is in the left image, it will necessarily lie to the left of the occluding edge. Nakayama and Shimojo have demonstrated the efficacy of da Vinci stereopsis experimentally. They found that it produces the predicted perception of relative depth when properly presented (as just described) but not when the geometrical relations are artificially reversed (that is, when the monocular region in the right image is just to the left of the occluding edge or when the monocular region in the left image is just to the right of the edge). Since their rediscovery of this form of stereopsis, it has been incorporated into some computational models of binocular disparity processing (e.g., Jones & Malik, 1992).

5.4 Dynamic Information

Dynamic visual information refers to changes in visual structure that occur over time because of certain kinds of image motion, or "optic flow," as Gibson called it. When an observer moves with respect to the environment, the direction and rate at which different objects are retinally displaced depends not only on the observer's motion, but on how far away the objects are and on where the observer is fixated. Depth-from-motion information arises from **motion parallax**: the differential motion of pairs of points due to their different depths relative to the fixation point. Although we will not provide a detailed discussion of the perception of motion until Chapter 10, we briefly consider it now because it is an important source of information about depth.

5.4.1 Motion Parallax

You can demonstrate the existence and nature of motion parallax by carrying out some finger experiments very much like the ones we used for binocular disparity. Here's how:

1. Hold your two index fingers in front of your face, one at arm's length and the other halfway to your nose.

2. Close your right eye and align your two fingers with some distant object, focusing on the distant object.

3. Keeping your fingers as still as possible, slowly move your head to the right. Notice that both of your fingers move leftward relative to the distant object, but the closer finger moves farther and faster.

4. Now move your head to the left and notice that your fingers move rightward, the closer one again moving farther and faster.

The differential motion of your fingers in this demonstration illustrates the nature of motion parallax: The images of points at different distances from the observer move at different retinal velocities as the observer's stationpoint changes.

The close informational kinship between motion parallax and binocular disparity can be appreciated by comparing the corresponding finger experiments that you performed. In the case of binocular disparity, you kept your head still and compared the left retinal image with the right one, both of which are normally available at the same time. In the case of motion parallax, you moved your head over time and compared an earlier image with a later one. Thus, binocular disparity involves the difference between a pair of displaced *simultaneous* retinal images, and motion parallax involves the difference between a pair of displaced *sequential* retinal images. If you had moved your head laterally in the motion parallax demonstration by exactly the distance between your eyes, then the difference between the first and last retinal images would have been the same as the difference between your left and right images in the corresponding binocular disparity demonstration.

Controlled experiments have shown that motion parallax is sufficient for depth perception when no other sources of depth information are present, but only when the spatial information is sufficiently rich and complex. If two luminous disks at different distances are viewed monocularly in a dark room, for example, while the viewer moves his or her head left and right, the perception is often of one object moving relative to another instead of two stationary objects at different distances (Rock, personal communication). More complex arrays of luminous points, however, can produce compelling perceptions of depth. For example, random dot displays containing thousands of points moving as though they lay on corrugated surfaces with different spatial structures, as illustrated in Figure 5.4.1, yield strong perceptions of appropriate depth when either the observer moves or the display is moved to produce motion parallax on a computer screen (Rogers & Graham, 1979).

As was the case for binocular disparity, the nature of retinal motion parallax depends not only on the distance to objects in the environment but also on the observer's fixation point. To see the difference, repeat the finger experiment described above, but this time try focusing first on the distant object and then on the closer finger. When you move your head to the right while focusing on the far object, your fingers move laterally to the left—opposite the direction in which you moved your head—the closer one moving faster. Now move your head to the right again, but this time keep your eye focused on the *closer* finger. (Be careful; it's a bit harder to do.) Notice that this time, both your farther finger

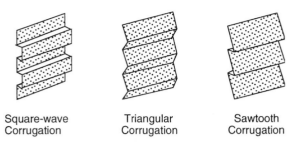

| Square-wave Corrugation | Triangular Corrugation | Sawtooth Corrugation |

Figure 5.4.1 Motion parallax displays. Rogers and Graham (1979) used corrugated surfaces covered by random dots to demonstrate that motion parallax is effective in producing depth perception. These perspective drawings depict some of the surfaces they used, but there were no visible edges in the actual displays except those defined by the relative motion of the otherwise random dots.

and the distant object move to the *right*—in the same direction as you moved your head—the farther object moving faster. Thus, the pattern of retinal motion parallax actually reverses for different depths relative to fixation. These differences in direction and speed of motion parallax are exactly analogous to the amount of crossed versus uncrossed disparity in stereoscopic vision.

It is also worth mentioning that, analogous to binocular disparity, what you normally experience from motion parallax is objects at different distances from you rather than objects moving at different speeds over the retina. You experienced differential motion in the finger experiments because you explicitly attended to this aspect of visual stimulation as motion (rather than as depth) and because the situation made the motion particularly obvious. But when you walk around normally in the environment, it is difficult to experience motion parallax as such, even if you try. Environmentally stationary objects are perceived as stationary, even though their retinal images move whenever your eyes move with respect to them. This tendency toward perceiving the actual position of objects in the environment in spite of changes in their retinal position is called *position constancy*, and it plays an important role in depth perception from motion parallax. We will consider this and other forms of perceptual constancy in Chapter 7 when we focus on the perception of object properties in more detail.

Motion parallax is also like binocular disparity in that it provides only relative information about depth. That is, it does not specify the actual distance to an object, but only how much closer or farther it is than the fixated

one. Unlike binocular disparity, however, motion parallax can provide effective depth information at great distances. If you were to drive past two hills, for example, one of which was 2 miles away and the other 4 miles away, you would be able to determine which one was closer from relative motion parallax. Binocular disparity would provide no information in such a case because the distances between the two eyes is too small in comparison with the distance of the mountains. With motion parallax, however, the separation that is achieved from successive views can be much greater—particularly in a speeding car—thus affording much greater parallax.

5.4.2 Optic Flow Caused by a Moving Observer

In naturally occurring perception, relative motion parallax of two isolated points is seldom, if ever, encountered. As Gibson (1966) emphasized in his influential writings, observers are usually moving about and actively exploring cluttered environments, engaging in activities that cause complex patterns of optic flow. He argued, quite forcefully and correctly, that the image motion resulting from observer motion is not chaotic, but highly structured in a way that depends precisely on both the layout of surfaces in the 3-D environment and the observer's motion. He further realized that this global pattern of optic flow can be used to perceive the spatial layout of surfaces. The systematic changes in image motion that occur over extended regions of the optic array he called **motion gradients** to emphasize that they were often gradual changes in speed and direction. He analyzed the nature of these motion gradients for certain ecologically important situations.

Figure 5.4.2 shows some examples of Gibson's motion gradients. The diagrams indicate how a sample of image points changes over time as the observer moves, as though tracing their paths in a time-lapse photograph. Part A indicates the pattern of optic flow when the observer moves smoothly in the direction indicated by the large arrow below the figure and fixates the point indicated in the center of the scene. It is the pattern of optic flow that would occur on your retina if you were riding past a flat field in a car and looking directly at a cow (the fixation point) standing along a straight fence (the diagonal line). The fixated point does not move on the retina, of course, because the observer tracks it with head

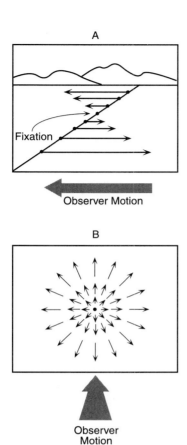

A

Fixation

Observer Motion

B

Observer
Motion

Figure 5.4.2 Motion gradients. Gibson discussed patterns of relative motion produced by a moving observer. (A) The optic flow created by an observer moving leftward (large arrow) while fixating the point in the middle of the line. (B) The optical expansion pattern that results from an observer moving toward a fixation point straight ahead, as in walking toward a wall.

and eye movements, so it stays on the fovea. The rest of the visual field moves at a speed and in a direction that depend on the depth relation between it and the fixated object. All points closer to the observer than the fixation point flow in the direction opposite the observer's motion, and all points farther than the fixation point flow in the same direction as the observer's motion. In both cases, the speed of optic flow depends on the difference in depth: It is maximal for points that are maximally different in depth from the fixation point and minimal for points that are minimally different in depth. Thus, the arrows in Figure 5.4.2A show how a sample of positions along the fence would flow while you fixated on the cow as you traveled leftward. If you think back to

the finger experiments, you will recall that these motion gradients are consistent with what you observed then.

Another common pattern of optic flow that Gibson discussed is **optic expansion** or **looming**, as illustrated in Figure 5.4.2B. It occurs when an observer moves directly toward a surface in the frontal plane, fixating on the point toward which he or she is heading. Ocular expansion results, for example, when you walk toward a wall while looking straight ahead. The fixated point is, as always, stationary on the retina, and other points on the surface flow outward from it at a rate that increases with their distance from the fixation point in the frontal plane. As you might imagine, moving directly away from a surface in the frontal plane produces the opposite pattern of optic flow, in which all points on the surface move toward a center of optic contraction.

These motion gradients are just a few special cases of very simple optic flow patterns that arise from very simple motions with respect to a single environmental surface. Optic flow patterns become exceedingly complex as the situation begins to approximate naturally occurring conditions. More complicated flow patterns result from changes in the direction of gaze (due to head and eye movements), up-and-down movements of walking, curved paths of motion, and complex environments consisting of many surfaces at different orientations, distances, and degrees of curvature. Realistic optic flow patterns produced in the course of normal activities in normal environments are so complex that they could not possibly be cataloged in terms of a few simple types. Their structure can be discerned only through sophisticated mathematical analysis.

A general computational analysis shows that the relative depth of each pair of points on a curved, rigid, textured surface can be recovered from a moving monocular point of view and that the path of observer motion can be recovered from the same sensory data (Longuet-Higgens & Prazdny, 1980; Prazdny, 1980). This effectively proves Gibson's original conjecture that optic flow contains important information about both the distance to surfaces and the observer's motion. But the mathematical analysis of this information requires three cubic equations of 20 terms each and involves both the first and second derivatives of the flow field (that is, both the velocity and acceleration of flow). Restricting the surfaces to planar ones considerably reduces the complexity of the analysis (Prazdny, 1982),

Perceiving Surfaces Oriented in Depth

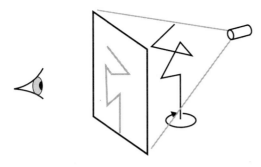

Figure 5.4.3 The kinetic depth effect. A 3-D bent-wire object is illuminated from behind, and its shadow is cast onto a translucent screen viewed by an observer. When stationary, it looks like a flat 2-D figure; but when rotated, it pops into a compellingly 3-D rotating object.

and other simplifications can be made by imposing further restrictions. We will return to the computational problems involved in motion perception—for there are many, including a version of the correspondence problem—in Chapter 10 when we discuss this topic in more detail.

5.4.3 Optic Flow Caused by Moving Objects

Depth information about a specific object becomes available not only when the observer moves with respect to it, but also when it moves with respect to the observer. If different parts of the object are positioned at different distances from the observer (that is, if there is differential depth to be perceived) and if these parts change their relative distances from the observer during the motion—as when an object rotates in place about an axis—then there will be relative motion among points on the object's surface when it moves. This relative movement provides information about which points of the surface are closer and which are farther. The net result is that the relative depth of the entire visible surface can be recovered from object motion so that its shape can be perceived.

This ability to perceive depth from object motion was first demonstrated by Wallach and O'Connell (1953) in a phenomenon called the **kinetic depth effect** (**KDE**). As indicated in Figure 5.4.3, they constructed a three-dimensional bent-wire figure and back-projected its shadow onto a translucent screen. When the wire is stationary, no depth is perceived; only a bent linelike shape is seen on the flat 2-D screen. But when the wire

figure is rotated about its vertical axis, the figure immediately pops into a three-dimensional shape. When the angular wire figure stops rotating, the previously 3-D percept flattens into a 2-D line in the plane of the screen. This demonstration shows that depth information is clearly available from such dynamic displays, at least under certain circumstances. But where does it come from and how might the visual system make use of it?

First, we must understand why recovering depth from object rotation, like recovering all depth information, is geometrically underdetermined and therefore logically ambiguous. In this case, the 2-D retinal motion that arises from a 3-D object's rigid motion *could* be perceived as exactly what it is: a 2-D figure that deforms nonrigidly over time. In the case of the KDE, the stimulus is quite literally a deforming 2-D image, since it is just a shadow on a rear-projection screen. This is only one possibility, however, for there are many other deforming 3-D objects that would also project the same moving image on the shadow screen. Instead, however, people perceive the only possible interpretation of a rigid object that is consistent with the moving image: an object of the proper shape rotating in depth.

As always in the case of logically underdetermined stimulus conditions, the visual system must implicitly or explicitly make additional assumptions to reach a single interpretation. In this case, the visual system appears to use a **rigidity heuristic**: a bias toward perceiving rigid motions rather than plastic deformations, provided the sensory stimulation is consistent with such an interpretation. It would be an extremely improbable natural event, for example, if a two-dimensional figure were to deform in just the way that would correspond to a rigid object undergoing a rigid transformation such as rotation—unless a rigid transformation is actually causing the 2-D deformation, as in the case of Wallach and O'Connell's experiment. (In Chapter 10, however, we will see that there are some circumstances in which rigid rotations are perceived as plastic deformations, but the general tendency is still toward perceiving rigid motions.)

Why might the visual system be selectively "tuned" to perceive rigid rather than plastic motions? The most obvious answer is the empiricist's: Rigid motions are much more probable than corresponding plastic ones if the image motion is consistent with a rigid motion. A

Gestalt theorist, however, would claim that the same outcome actually resulted from applying the principle of Prägnanz: The visual system prefers the simplest interpretation, given the prevailing conditions of stimulation. The rigid interpretation can be counted as simpler because it does not involve changes in the object's shape over time and so could be more economically represented and processed. This is another example of the fact that the principles of likelihood and Prägnanz often predict the same outcome for very different reasons.

There is a great deal more to say about how the visual system processes motion to extract depth, including what is known about the physiology of the motion perception system. Rather than going into these detailed issues here, however, we will save them for Chapter 10 when we return to the problem of motion perception for a more general and comprehensive treatment.

5.4.4 Accretion/Deletion of Texture

One further source of depth information arises from image motion events: the appearance (**accretion**) and disappearance (**deletion**) of texture behind a moving edge (Gibson, Kaplan, Reynolds, & Wheeler, 1969). The edge necessarily belongs to the closer surface, and the appearing/disappearing texture to the farther surface. You can demonstrate this source of depth information as follows. First photocopy the random dot stereogram in Figure 5.3.8. Next cut out a small square of the random texture and place it on Figure 5.3.8. If the copy is accurate and its edges lie flat on the page, it will be difficult to see the square at all. Then place your finger on the square and move it around. The perception immediately changes from a flat homogeneous texture to that of a textured square moving around in front of a textured background. The information for the depth aspects of this perception comes from the accretion and deletion of texture elements at the edges of the square. Stop moving it, and within seconds the square disappears into the textured background.

Accretion and deletion of texture due to a moving observer are related to da Vinci stereopsis in the same way that motion parallax is related to binocular disparity. That is, accretion and deletion of texture are a dynamic source of depth information revealed over time that is conceptually the same as the static information revealed binocularly across space (between the views of

Figure 5.5.1 A demonstration of pictorial sources of depth information. This photograph contains a great deal of optical information about depth that arises from stationary, monocular structure in the image.

the left and right eyes) in da Vinci stereopsis. They are also related to static occlusion information, which will be discussed in the next section. The major difference is that information from accretion and deletion of texture is inherently dynamic and therefore requires integration over time.

5.5 Pictorial Information

Although stereopsis and motion produce particularly compelling experiences of depth, they are by no means the only sources of depth information. The most obvious argument in favor of this conclusion is that if you close one eye and keep your head still, the world continues to look quite three-dimensional. Another is that photographs and certain kinds of realistic drawings and paintings can produce compelling impressions of depth. This is obvious from even a brief glance at Figure 5.5.1, which shows a simple photograph of a 3-D scene. The remaining sources of depth information are known collectively as **pictorial information** because they are all potentially available in static, monocularly viewed pictures. Pictorial information can be very powerful, for it often leads to good depth perception in 2-D pictures when both stereo and motion information indicate that they are quite flat. Indeed, it can even overcome stereo depth information that is reversed by an optical device that switches the images going to the left and right eyes,

Perceiving Surfaces Oriented in Depth

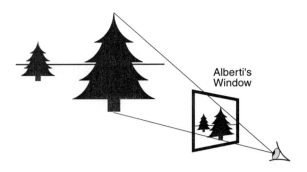

Figure 5.5.2 Alberti's window. Perspective depth information from a 3-D scene can be captured on a 2-D surface by tracing the contours of objects onto a pane of glass while viewing the scene through the glass from a fixed vantage point.

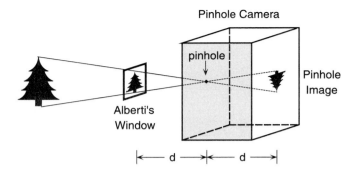

Figure 5.5.3 The relation between pinhole cameras and Alberti's window. The image on Alberti's window is a nonreversed version of the image that would be focused by a pinhole camera of the same scene. The aperture of the pinhole camera is at the vantage point, and its image plane is the same distance from the aperture as Alberti's window is from the vantage point. (See Section 1.2 for a discussion of pinhole cameras.)

as we will see in Section 5.5.10 when we discuss the integration of depth information.

5.5.1 Perspective Projection

In Chapter 1 we discussed the fact that light travels in straight lines and is reflected onto the retina by environmental surfaces. The geometry most applicable to this process is called **perspective projection**, and it produces profound differences between real-world objects and their optical images. The most obvious of these differences is in dimensionality: Three-dimensional objects and scenes produce images that are only two-dimensional. The lost dimension is depth. Fortunately, it turns out that 2-D images formed by perspective projection actually contain a great deal of information about this "lost" dimension that allows it to be recovered, albeit imperfectly.

The importance of perspective projection in depth perception was recognized centuries ago when artists tried to depict depth realistically on flat canvas. In 1436, an artist named Alberti described a method for drawing pictures in proper perspective that revolutionized the artistic representation of depth.

The basic idea is quite simple, as illustrated in Figure 5.5.2. To paint a 3-D scene accurately on a 2-D canvas, one merely needs to recreate the image that would pass through a flat window in place of the canvas. Taking this idea quite literally, one could recreate a realistic line drawing of a scene by viewing it through a pane of glass with one eye in a fixed position and tracing all the contours directly onto the glass with a grease pencil. If the

glass were then placed over a uniform white surface and viewed monocularly from the same relative position, the line drawing would recreate the pictorial depth information in the contours of the scene perfectly. This technique for achieving proper perspective in drawing is called **Alberti's window**. Leonardo da Vinci, who is sometimes credited with the invention of perspective drawing, advocated similar ideas more than a half century later.

The most interesting implication of the facts about perspective projection is that one can create convincing illusions of depth by employing Alberti's window. It is quite similar, in fact, to what a pinhole camera does when it captures an image on a flat sheet of film, as illustrated in Figure 5.5.3. The scene in Alberti's window is just a right-side-up version of the upside-down image that would be formed in a pinhole camera whose image plane is as far from the pinhole as the observer's eye is from Alberti's window. This means that if the painter captured the image on Alberti's window perfectly, it would be equivalent to the (upside-down and backward) photographic image from a pinhole camera. Under the proper viewing conditions, then, the illusion of (monocular) depth should be essentially perfect. And it will be, provided that (1) the photographic quality is excellent, (2) the eye remains fixed at the proper viewing position so that there is no motion information, (3) the edges of the photograph are occluded so that one cannot see its boundaries occluding the world behind the picture, and

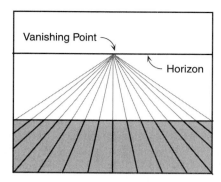

Figure 5.5.4 Convergence of parallel lines. In perspective projections of a 3-D scene onto a flat 2-D surface, parallel lines on the ground plane project to lines that converge to a vanishing point on the horizon.

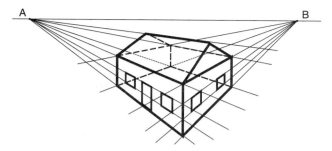

Figure 5.5.5 A draftsman's drawing in two-point perspective projection. A simple house is portrayed at an orientation in which its parallel edges converge to two vanishing points on the horizon (A and B).

(4) the picture is more than 6–8 feet away so that monocular accommodation information does not spoil the illusion of depth (Pirenne, 1970). The sense of depth will never be as compelling as that provided by stereoscopic vision, or even as compelling as mobile vision with complete motion information, but it can be just as convincing as viewing the real scene through a window with one eye in a fixed position.

The perspective projection that a perfect photograph achieves actually incorporates all of the pictorial depth cues we will discuss below because it captures all the information available in light falling on a single stationary retina. In the next few sections we will unpack some of the most important pictorial sources of depth information to see what they are and how they work. Before we do, however, it is important to note that all of these sources of depth information are essentially heuristics that can lead to depth illusions. As we have mentioned before, perceiving depth in pictures is a form of illusion because pictures are actually quite flat.

5.5.2 Convergence of Parallel Lines

One important fact about perspective projection is that parallel lines in the 3-D environment do not generally project as parallel lines in the 2-D image, but as lines converging toward a *vanishing point* on the horizon line. Figure 5.5.4 illustrates this fact and shows further that all parallel lines in any plane converge to the same vanishing point. Parallel lines in depth converge toward a point in the image plane because the constant environmental distance between them (due to their parallelism)

maps to increasingly large image distances where the lines are close to the observer and increasingly small distances farther away.

This aspect of perspective projection is often referred to as **linear perspective**, but we will call it **convergence of parallels** to be more specific about the nature of the information. It is perhaps most noticeable in the convergence of the parallel rails of train tracks or the parallel sides of a straight road as they recede into the distance. Look carefully at the draftsman's sketch in Figure 5.5.5 and notice the use of vanishing points to produce realistic depth. There are two vanishing points in this drawing because there are two different sets of parallel lines that lie in the ground plane. Although it is easiest to appreciate the existence of vanishing points along the horizon line of the ground plane, there are infinitely many vanishing points that lie on the "horizon lines" of other planes in 3-D space. A vertical line through vanishing point B in Figure 5.5.5, for example, is the horizon line for the vertical plane that contains the right front surface of the object depicted. All parallel lines in this plane will converge to a vanishing point somewhere along this horizon line, just as in the case of the "true" horizon for the special case of the ground plane.

5.5.3 Position Relative to the Horizon of a Surface

Another pictorial source of depth information that arises from perspective projection is the height of objects in the picture plane relative to the horizon. Figure 5.5.6 shows a simple scene in which there are no parallel lines

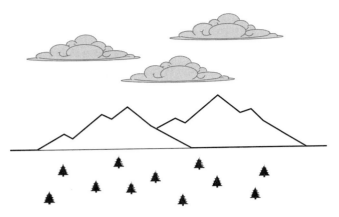

Figure 5.5.6 Position relative to the horizon. In perspective projection of a 3-D scene, objects on a level plane that are closer to the horizon are perceived as being farther from the observer.

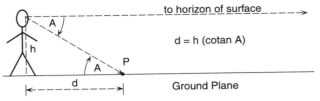

Figure 5.5.7 Distance as a function of the horizon angle to a point on a surface. The distance (d) to a point on a surface (in this case, the ground plane) is the product of the perpendicular distance to the surface (h) times the cotangent of the angle (A) between the line of sight to the horizon and that to the point.

converging to a vanishing point, yet there is a strong impression of depth. The trees toward the bottom appear closer than the ones farther up, and the clouds toward the top may also look closer than the ones farther down. The reason for these perceptions is the placement of objects on a plane relative to its horizon line.

Consider first the case of objects resting on a level ground plane, such as stones strewn upon the earth and viewed obliquely from about 5–6 feet above it, as is usually the case. The objects located higher in the picture plane—that is, closer to the horizon—are farther away from the observation point. Now suppose that the same stones were scattered on a level transparent surface above your head. In this case the stones located lower in the picture plane—but still closer to the horizon—are farther from the observation point. The general rule, then, is that for all objects on a level plane, the ones closer to the horizon in the picture plane are perceived as being farther away.

This description makes it sound as though position relative to the horizon on the ground plane is merely ordinal depth information. In fact, quantitative information is available if the horizon is visible or can be determined from visible information (Sedgwick, 1986). It can then be proven geometrically that the distance, d, from the observer to any point, P, on the surface can be determined from the horizon angle, A (the angle between the line of sight to the horizon and the line of sight to the point on the plane), and the perpendicular distance to the surface, h (see Figure 5.5.7). Because

observers generally have good information about the height of their own eyes above the ground plane from their bodily height and current posture, they can, in principle, determine the egocentric distance to the bottom of objects on that plane. Because the same geometrical relations hold for any surface whose horizon line is visible, the distance to locations on other surfaces can also be determined as long as their horizon lines are specified in the optical image and the perpendicular distance from the eye to the surface is known. Perpendicular distances to surfaces other than the ground plane are less likely to be known, but even without this parameter, the relative distance to two objects on the same surface can be determined from their horizon angles. This is possible because the perpendicular distance to the surface (h) cancels out in taking the ratio of the distances to two objects on the same plane. Angular distance to the horizon of a plane thus provides a good deal of quantitative information about distances to objects along it.

5.5.4 Relative Size

Something about the trees and clouds in Figure 5.5.6 strikes most people as rather strange, namely, that the nearer objects are not bigger in the image. This feeling arises from another of the more obvious facts about depth in perspective projection: All else being equal, more distant objects project smaller images onto the retina. Figure 5.5.8 illustrates why this is so. When light from two identical objects at different distances is reflected into the eye, the visual angle subtended by the closer object will necessarily be larger than that subtended by the farther object.

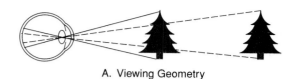

A. Viewing Geometry

B. Retinal Image

Figure 5.5.8   Relative size. If two otherwise identical objects are viewed at different distances, the farther object projects a smaller image onto the retina. The relative size of such objects can therefore provide information about relative depth.

A little trigonometry is sufficient to determine the function relating the distance of an object to the retinal size of its image, as measured in degrees of visual angle. As Figure 5.5.9 shows, the triangle subtended by the lines of sight to the top and bottom of an upright object at eye level is a right triangle. If the height of the object is h and the visual angle that it subtends is a, then the right triangle has a height of h and an angle of a. The distance to the object, d, can then be expressed in terms of the tangent of the angle,

$$\tan(a) = \frac{h}{d},$$

or, if we solve the equation for d,

$$d = \frac{h}{\tan a}.$$

This **size-distance relation** tells us that the size of an

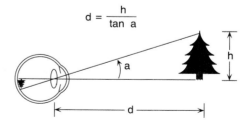

$$d = \frac{h}{\tan\ a}$$

Figure 5.5.9   The size-distance relation. The viewing geometry of perspective projection shows that the distance to an object can be determined from its size (h) and the tangent of its visual angle (a).

object's retinal image (a) provides important information about its distance from the observer (d).

But there is a problem. To solve this equation for distance, the actual size of the object (h) must be known as well, and this information cannot be obtained in any simple way from the retinal image because the object's size and distance jointly determine its projected image size. You therefore can't tell from a given image size whether you are looking at a smaller object nearby or a larger one farther away, as was illustrated in Figure 1.2.9. In fact, there is an infinite number of logically possible object sizes for an image of a particular retinal size. If you saw two objects that you somehow knew were identical in size, you could tell which one was closer just by comparing their relative image sizes. But for this rule to apply, the objects must actually be the same size, and you can't know whether this is true without knowing how far away they are—a visual version of Catch-22. A heuristic that the visual system uses to break this vicious circle of indeterminacy is to assume that two otherwise identical objects have the same objective size so that their relative distances can then be determined from relative image sizes.

This situation is another example of how unconscious inference might be used in perception of depth from relative size. The stimulus information is logically underdetermined, but by making an additional heuristic assumption—in this case, that two retinal images, similar except for retinal size, are actually the same size in the environment—depth information can be computed. To the extent that the objects are actually the same size, depth perception based on retinal size will be veridical. To the extent that they are not, illusions of distance will occur.

An example of image size as a source of information about depth is shown in Figure 5.5.10. The young women in this photograph are all about the same size, but their images decrease in size because they are positioned at increasing distances from the stationpoint. Your visual system interprets them as being the same size, and so you perceive the progressively smaller images as being progressively farther away. Other compelling examples of the visual system making use of relative size to indicate relative distance come from *texture gradients*, a topic we will turn to shortly.

233

Figure 5.5.10 Relative size as a cue to depth. The cheerleaders in this line are all about the same size, but their projected images become smaller as their distances from the camera increase. If one assumes that they are actually about the same size, their relative distances can be recovered from their image sizes by using the size-distance relation given in Figure 5.5.9.

5.5.5 Familiar Size

The depth cue of relative size is independent of the identity of the objects involved. But many objects—perhaps even most—tend to have a characteristic size or range of sizes with which experienced perceivers are familiar. Adult men vary somewhat in height, but the vast majority are between 5 feet 6 inches and 6 feet 2 inches. Similarly, tables are about 2 feet 6 inches off the floor, cars are about 5 feet high; ceilings are about 8 feet above the floor, and so on. The importance of these facts is that if the size of an object is known to the perceiver, then the size-distance equation can be solved for its actual distance from the observer. The knowledge involved here is not conscious knowledge, nor is solving the equation deliberate symbolic manipulation. Rather, they are rapid, unconscious processes that occur automatically, without our even thinking about them.

The effect of familiar size on depth perception was first demonstrated in an experiment by Ittleson (1951). He showed that people could give reasonably accurate judgments of the distance to a playing card, whose actual height is presumably known by the visual system—although probably not consciously—to be about 3.5 inches. Another convincing experimental result was obtained by Epstein (1965), who showed his subjects

high-quality photographs of a dime, a quarter, and a half-dollar under monocular viewing conditions in a darkened room where spotlights precisely illuminated just the images of the coins. Subjects had to judge the distance to each coin. The display was constructed so that all three coin images actually had the same photographed diameter and were located in the same depth plane. Nevertheless, observers perceived the dime to be closest and the half-dollar to be farthest because of their knowledge of the sizes of the real objects.

5.5.6 Texture Gradients

Another important manifestation of the structure of perspective projection in depth perception is what Gibson (1950) called **texture gradients**: systematic changes in the size and shape of small texture elements that occur on many environmental surfaces. Examples of naturally occurring texture include the blades of grass in a lawn, the pebbles in a driveway, the strands of yarn in a carpet, the warp and woof of a woven fabric, the tiles in a bathroom floor, and so forth. Two examples are shown in Figure 5.5.11. In addition to providing information about depth, texture gradients also can inform observers about the orientation of a surface in depth and about its curvature. Quite complex surface shapes can be realistically depicted by textural variations, as the example in Figure 5.5.12 shows.

Stevens (1979) demonstrated that two aspects of textural variation—element size and shape—provide independent sources of information about surface orientation. The overall size of texture elements diminishes with distance because all dimensions decrease as the distance to the stationpoint increases. Element size can therefore be used to estimate the relative distance to different parts of the surface and thus to recover the orientation of the textured surface. But notice that this will be true only if the texture elements are actually about the same size.

This is another example of heuristic assumptions in depth perception, since the perceptual conclusion about the distance to texture elements based on their image-size will be accurate only if the objects forming the texture *are* similar in size. If they are not, then illusions of depth and surface orientation will result. The depth and changes in surface orientation you perceive in the tex-

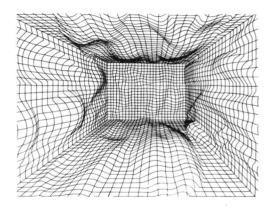

Figure 5.5.12 Artificial texture gradients. Artificial surfaces of arbitrarily complex shapes can be rendered by using identical texture elements in computer graphic displays. (From Marr, 1982.)

Figure 5.5.11 Natural texture gradients. Many natural surfaces are defined by texture elements of about the same size and shape so that surface depth and orientation can be recovered from systematic changes in their projected sizes and shapes.

ture gradients of Figures 5.5.11 and 5.5.12, for example, are actually illusory, because the texture elements in the picture itself have quite different sizes. If you were viewing the real scenes of which the pictures were taken, of course, this same assumption—that all the texture elements are roughly the same size—would generally lead you to perceive depth veridically. In the case of the picture, however, it leads you to perceive depth where it does not actually exist. Thus, the fact that we perceive depth in pictures of textured surfaces results from the fact that, although the equal-size assumption is false for the picture itself, it is generally true of the environmental scene represented in the picture.

The projected shape of texture elements can also carry information about the orientation of the surface, as illustrated in Figure 5.5.12. Again, however, this information can be recovered from the image only if additional assumptions are made about the actual shapes of the texture elements in the environment. Stevens (1979) used the *aspect ratio* (the ratio of the longest to the shortest dimension) of texture elements to estimate the orientation of the elements themselves and the surface on which they lie. His analysis rested on the assumption that the dimensions of real-world texture elements are approximately uniform over different orientations. Kender (1979) developed other algorithms for estimating surface orientation from textural shape by making slightly different assumptions: that the texture elements are maximally regular, homogeneous, and symmetrical. Witkin (1981) proposed yet another algorithm based on the assumption that the edges of texture elements tend to be distributed *isotropically*, meaning that the amount of contour at different orientations will be approximately the same, or at least equally distributed over orientations. This is a useful heuristic because when isotropic texture elements are viewed at a slant, their edges will not be isotropic in the image plane. Rather, they will be biased toward orientations that are perpendicular to the direction of tilt owing to foreshortening along the axis of tilt, as illustrated in Figure 5.5.13.

Making use of heuristic assumptions like these is a double-edged sword, however, because algorithms based

Perceiving Surfaces Oriented in Depth

(a)

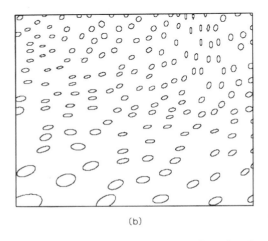

(b)

Figure 5.5.13 Estimating local surface orientation from texture. Panel A shows a natural scene that includes significant texture information, and panel B shows the output of Witkin's program in which the shape and size of the ellipses convey the estimated depth and orientation of the local regions of surface. (From Witkin, 1981.)

on them fail when their underlying assumptions are untrue. As a result, the computer programs by Stevens, Kender, and Witkin tend to fail in simulating perception of surfaces with elongated textures such as grass or wood grain. They assume that the elongated structure of the image elements arises from their being slanted in depth rather than the possibility that the objects themselves might simply be elongated. If the human visual system characteristically made this same mistake, it would be strong evidence in favor of the theory, but people seldom make this error.

Figure 5.5.14 Partial occlusion as depth information. When one object partly occludes another, the occluding object is perceived as closer and the occluded object as farther.

Malik and Rosenholtz (1994) have recently proposed a better computational solution to the texture problem. They have devised an algorithm for recovering the slant and tilt of small patches of surface texture based only on the weaker assumption that the texture elements are approximately invariant over small translations along the surface. That is, they assume that all the texture elements have approximately the same size and shape, differing only by translations within the textured plane. This assumption enables the algorithm to take advantage of all the information that is available in the texture without further restrictions such as isotropy, symmetry, and the like. It works by finding the best-fitting parameters of surface orientation and curvature to account for the transformations in shape and size between nearby texture elements. This procedure does a good job of recovering the surface in situations in which the algorithms mentioned above typically fail.

5.5.7 Edge Interpretation

One very important class of pictorial information about depth comes from the interpretation of edges or contours. A simple example we considered in Chapter 1 is **occlusion** or **interposition**: the blocking of light from an object by an opaque object nearer the viewer. In Figure 5.5.14, for example, people invariably perceive a square behind and partially occluded by a circle. All that is actually present, of course, is a 2-D configuration of regions bounded by edges, yet we perceive these edges as indicating a depth relation: The circle is in front of the square.

As a source of depth information, edges have both strong and weak points. On the weak side, edge information is relative rather than absolute and qualitative rather than quantitative. That is, edge information specifies only ordinal depth relations; it can tell us that the square is farther than the circle but not how much farther. On the strong side, however, edge information is available from virtually unlimited distances. The only requirements are that the objects be within visible range and that the closer (occluding) one be opaque. The questions we will address in this section concern how depth information arises from edges in 2-D images and how our visual systems might extract it.

A sophisticated theory of edge interpretation has evolved within computer vision in the *blocks world* environment we mentioned in Chapter 2. The goal of this theory is to determine the best interpretation for all edges in a line drawing of a blocks-world scene. Edges can arise in an image in several different ways, and the output of an edge interpretation program is a classification of the edges in terms of their environmental sources. Some arise from one surface occluding another, others arise from two surfaces meeting along a common border, still others arise from a shadow being cast over a single surface, and so on. Such distinctions are important for pictorial depth information because some edge interpretations imply specific depth relations. For example, if edge A partly occludes edge B, then A is necessarily closer to the observer than B is.

Vertex Classification. The computational theory of edge interpretation began with Guzman's (1968, 1969) program SEE, which attempted to interpret line drawings of simple configurations of blocks, such as shown in Figure 5.5.15. Guzman realized, as had others before him, that the intersections of edges were crucial to determining what edges were occluded by what others. He developed a standard classification scheme for edge intersections (or **vertices** or **junctions**): T's, Y's, K's, X's, L's, and so forth. T-junctions are the ones that are most obviously related to occlusion situations. The top of the T corresponds to the occluding edge, and the stem of the T to the occluded edge. Other types of junctions have different depth interpretations, as we will discover shortly.

Guzman's SEE program was a clever bundle of heuristics for interpreting edge information. It worked remarkable well, given its modest theoretical foundations. The beginnings of a formal analysis for a simplified case were later provided independently by Huffman (1971)

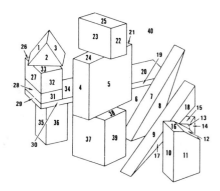

Figure 5.5.15 A line drawing of a blocks-world scene. Guzman's SEE program grouped regions together into likely objects by using information about lines and vertices. The results generally agreed with human perception (e.g., regions 26, 27, 32, and 33 were grouped into one object, and regions 19, 20, 29, 30, and 34 into another). (From Guzman, 1968.)

and Clowes (1971). They developed a complete catalog of the vertex types that arise in viewing simple trihedral angles (solid angles bounded by three planar faces) from all possible viewpoints. They also were able to show how local constraints at each vertex and their interrelations reduced the number of possible interpretations of each edge. Waltz (1972) then extended these results to include shadow edges, and Malik (1987) generalized them further to apply to curved objects. The net result is that the most sophisticated programs are able to correctly interpret edges in almost any line drawing of simple geometrical solids. We will now examine this computational theory of edge interpretation to find out how it reveals information about the relative depth of surfaces from their bounding edges.

Four Types of Edges. We begin by assuming that earlier processes have produced an image in which the edges—meaning discontinuities in image luminance, as discussed in Chapter 4—have been accurately identified. Thus, the input to this edge interpretation algorithm is an essentially perfect line drawing of all the edges in the scene. The task is to interpret them in terms of the environmental situation that produced them. To begin, we distinguish among four types of edge interpretations:

1. *Orientation edges.* Orientation edges refer to places in the environment in which there are discontinuities in surface orientation. These occur when two surfaces at

Perceiving Surfaces Oriented in Depth

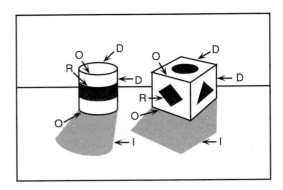

Figure 5.5.16 Four kinds of edges. This scene contains four different kinds of luminance edges: orientation edges (O) due to abrupt changes in surface orientation, depth edges (D) due to gaps between surfaces at different distances, reflectance edges (R) due to different surface pigments or materials, and illumination edges (I) due to shadows.

different orientations meet along an edge in the 3-D world. They usually arise at internal edges within a single object (e.g., a cube) or where one object abuts another, such as a block sitting on a table. Examples of orientation edges in Figure 5.5.16 are labeled with O's.

2. *Depth edges.* Depth edges refer to places where there is a spatial discontinuity in depth between surfaces, that is, places in the image where one surface occludes another that extends behind it, with space between the two surfaces. If they actually touch along the edge, then it is classified as an orientation edge. Examples of depth edges in Figure 5.5.16 are labeled with D's.[6]

3. *Illumination edges.* Illumination edges are formed where there is a difference in the amount of light falling on a homogeneous surface, such as the edge of a shadow, highlight, or spotlight. Examples of illumination edges in Figure 5.5.16 are labeled with I's.

4. *Reflectance edges.* Reflectance edges result where there is a change in the light-reflecting properties of the surface material. The most obvious examples are when designs are painted on an otherwise homogeneous surface. Examples of reflectance edges in Figure 5.5.16 are labeled with R's.

We discussed illumination and reflectance edges at some length in Chapter 3 when we talked about color and lightness constancy. Now we will focus on orientation and depth edges because these edges provide the strongest constraints on depth interpretations of the scene. We therefore begin with a line drawing that contains only orientation and depth edges.

Edge Labels. Orientation and depth edges in objects with flat surfaces are mutually exclusive. If an edge in the image is caused by two differently oriented surfaces meeting, it is an orientation edge; if it is caused by one surface occluding another with space between, it is a depth edge. Each edge in the line drawing is therefore either an orientation edge or a depth edge and can be unambiguously labeled as one or the other. The goal of a theory of edge interpretation is to discover a process that labels every edge in the way that corresponds to people's perception of the same scene.

We need to further differentiate the labeling system so that there is a unique label for each qualitatively different type of orientation and depth edge. Two kinds of orientation edges and two kinds of depth edges are required. The two types of orientation edges are called *convex* and *concave*, and they carry important information about the depth of the edge relative to the surfaces.

1. **Convex orientation edges** occur when two surfaces meet along an edge and enclose a filled volume corresponding to a dihedral (two-faced) angle of less than 180°. Convex edges indicate that the edge's angle points toward the observer, as do the external edges of a cube seen from the outside. Convex edges are illustrated in Figure 5.5.17 by the lines labeled with a "+."

2. **Concave orientation edges** occur when two surfaces meet along an edge and enclose a filled volume corresponding to a dihedral angle of more than 180°. Concave edges indicate that the edge's angle points away from the observer, as do the internal edges of a hollow cube seen from within. Concave edges are illustrated in Figure 5.5.17 by the lines labeled with a "−."

---

[6] Note that the edge between the side of the box and the surface on which it rests is an orientation edge rather than a depth edge, even though both surfaces belong to different objects and the table is occluded by and extends behind the side of the box. The reason is that there is no space between these two surfaces: They meet at the edge.

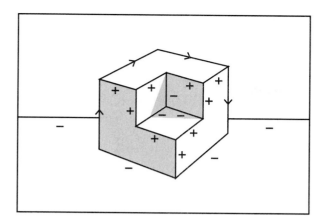

Figure 5.5.17 Convex versus concave orientation edges. Convex edges, labeled by a "+," arise when two surfaces meet at an interior angle of less than 180°. Concave edges, labeled by a "−," arise when two surfaces meet at an interior angle of more than 180°. Arrows indicate that the closer surface along a depth edge is on the right.

In the simple trihedral planar objects analyzed by Huffman and Clowes, each orientation edge is either convex or concave, never both.

There are also two cases of depth edges that need to be distinguished: one in which the occluding surface is on one side of the edge and another in which it is on the other side. Depth edges are labeled by single arrowheads running along the edge, and the convention for its direction is a right-hand rule: The arrow is placed facing in the direction along which the closer, occluding surface is on the right side of the edge in the image (and the farther, occluded surface is on the left). In other words, if you imagine yourself moving forward along the edge in the direction of the arrow, the closer surface is always on your right. These two possible labels for each depth edge—an arrow in one or the other direction along the edge—are mutually exclusive, since the occluding edge can be on only one side. The correct labeling carries important depth information because it designates which surface is closer to the observer.

Thus far we have four possible labels for each edge in a line drawing containing only orientation and depth edges, all of which contain significant depth information. This means that if there are n edges in the drawing, there are 4^n logically possible labelings for it, corresponding to 4^n qualitatively different depth interpretations. (Each edge has four interpretations, so if there

were just one edge, there would be four possible labelings; if there were two edges, there would be 16 possible labelings; and so forth.) This is an astronomically large number even for very simple scenes. For example, although there are only 20 edges in Figure 5.5.17, this simple line drawing allows for 1,048,576 logically possible edge labelings! In this case, however—and in most other cases—people generally perceive just one. How can the set of logically possible interpretations be reduced to a manageable number, much less just one?

Physical Constraints. Huffman and Clowes based their analyses on the crucial insight that not all *logically* possible labelings are *physically* possible. They examined local constraints at vertices of trihedral objects—objects whose corners are formed by the meeting of exactly three faces—and found that only a small fraction of logically possible labelings could be physically realized. Consider, for example, the set of possible "arrow" junctions, in which three edges meet at an angle in the image plane of less than 180°. Because each edge could be labeled in any of the four ways described above—as a concave or convex orientation edge or as a right-handed or left-handed occluding edge—there are $4^3 (= 64)$ logically possible labelings for an arrow junction. However, Huffman and Clowes proved that only *three* of them are physically possible. The same reduction of 64 to 3 possibilities is achieved for "Y" junctions. Huffman's catalog of all physically possible realizations of trihedral angles is given in Figure 5.5.18.

Huffman and Clowes also pointed out that there are further constraints on edge interpretation that operate at a more global level. They result from the fact that within the constraints of the objects in blocks world—polyhedra with planar surfaces—each edge has a constant interpretation along its entire length. Convex edges cannot become concave and right-handed occluding edges cannot become left-handed unless there are vertices between the edges that allow the change in interpretation. By making sure that the interpretations assigned to the same edge at adjacent vertices are consistent in this way, the number of logically possible labelings can be further reduced. Figure 5.5.19 gives a simple example of how this global consistency constraint works for a tetrahedron:

Perceiving Surfaces Oriented in Depth

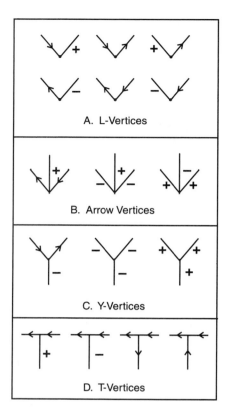

Figure 5.5.18 The catalog of vertex types for trihedral angles. All physically possible interpretations of vertices from trihedral angles are shown for "L," "arrow," "Y," and "T" vertices.

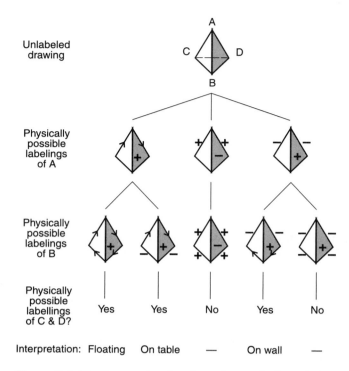

Figure 5.5.19 Interpreting the edges of a tetrahedron. A simple tetrahedron (top) can be interpreted by first labeling vertex A in all physically possible ways, then labeling vertex B in all physically possible ways, and finally eliminating impossible labelings of vertices C and D. Only three physically possible interpretations remain.

1. Consider all physically possible labelings of the arrow vertex A. From the catalog shown in Figure 5.5.18, we know that there are just the three shown.

2. Next, consider how these possibilities interact with all physically possible labelings of the arrow vertex B. Of the nine logical possibilities, four are eliminated by physical constraints because they would require two different labels for the central edge.

3. Finally, consider whether the resulting five labelings of vertices A and B provide physically possible labelings for the "L" junctions at vertices C and D. This constraint eliminates two more, leaving only three physically possible interpretations.

What are these three interpretations? The perceptually preferred one has concave orientation edges at the bottom, as would be found if the tetrahedron were sitting with its lower surface (BCD) on a table. The alternative with concave orientation edges at the top corresponds to

the percept of the tetrahedron attached to a wall by its back surface (ACD). And the one with occluding depth edges all along the perimeter corresponds to a tetrahedron floating unsupported in the air.

Notice how drastically the set of possible labelings was reduced by imposing physical constraints. We began with a five-line drawing that could have 4^5 ($= 1024$) logically possible labelings. After analyzing purely physical constraints, only three remained! Notice that this edge analysis does not provide any way to decide among these three alternatives, and so further constraints must be introduced to settle on a single solution.

Notice also that there might actually have been no possible interpretations! This usually occurs for so-called impossible objects such as the images that we mentioned in Section 1.1. These drawings seem to depict real objects, but they are physically impossible (Penrose & Penrose, 1958). The "blivit" shown in Figure 5.5.20A, for example, cannot be consistently labeled, because it

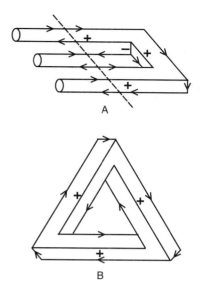

Figure 5.5.20 Labeling edges of impossible objects. (A) A "blivit" has no internally consistent labelings, but (B) a Penrose triangle does.

requires that occluding edges on one side be orientation edges at the other side. There are some impossible objects that do have consistent labelings, however, such as the Penrose triangle shown in Figure 5.5.20B.

Extensions and Generalizations. The Huffman-Clowes analysis of physical constraints was a major conceptual breakthrough in the theory of edge interpretation. David Waltz (1975), then a graduate student at M.I.T., extended the Huffman-Clowes analysis to include 11 types of edges, including shadows and "cracks" (lines that result from the exact alignment of coplanar edges: essentially, orientation edges at 180° angles). This expansion of edge types proliferated the catalog of physically possible vertices to thousands of entries, but as you might guess by extrapolating the conclusions of the Huffman-Clowes analysis, it turned out to reduce even further the number of possible interpretations that could be assigned to a given shaded line drawing. For example, the complex drawing shown in Figure 5.5.21 yields only one physically possible labeling, which is the one people always perceive. As it turns out, the strongest additional constraints in Waltz's analysis come from corners that cast a shadow.

The success of Waltz's algorithm for assigning edge interpretations does not even approach human levels of competence, however, because its application is limited

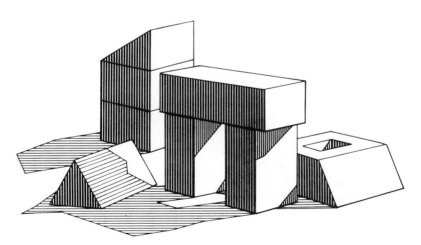

Figure 5.5.21 A blocks world scene with shadows. Waltz's algorithm for edge interpretation produces just one interpretation for this scene, which is the one people always perceive. Adding shadows makes the interpretation process more accurate because it provides further constraints. (From Waltz, 1975.)

Perceiving Surfaces Oriented in Depth

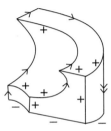

Figure 5.5.22 Edge interpretation of curved objects. Malik's algorithm for labeling curved objects is able to interpret a much larger class of line drawings by including extremal edges or limbs (double arrowheads) that occur when a curved surface partly occludes itself because of its own curvature.

Figure 5.5.23 A line drawing of a potted plant. Although human perceivers have no difficulty perceiving the shape of the leaves of this plant from the drawing, blocks-world edge algorithms cannot interpret it correctly. (From Barrow & Tennenbaum, 1981.)

to planar polyhedra. It does not work for curved surfaces or for objects that contain thin sheets (such as folded paper) rather than volumes. Neither of these pose serious problems for human observers, who can interpret line drawings of scenes involving quite complex objects of either type. On the other hand, within its own domain Waltz's program is uncanny in its ability to arrive at physically possible interpretations, some of which people seldom, if ever, perceive without explicit guidance.

The analysis of edge labeling was extended to curved objects by Jitendra Malik, a cognitive scientist at the University of California, Berkeley. Malik's analysis requires differentiating a new kind of depth edge called an **extremal edge**, or **limb**, which results when a surface curves smoothly around to partly occlude itself. Limbs are labeled by double arrowheads running along the edge in the direction for which the occluding surface is to the right. Curved objects raise an important complication in edge-labeling algorithms because the same physical edge can have different interpretations at different points along its extent. A convex edge, for example, can change to a depth edge, as illustrated by the top edges of the object in Figure 5.5.22.

Even Malik's analysis of curved surfaces is outstripped by human performance in interpreting depth information from line drawings, however. People easily perceive the leaves of the potted plant depicted in Figure 5.5.23 as having a relatively specific shape in 3-D space, much more so than is available from the constraints we have discussed thus far. How might this information be recovered from such an image?

Barrow and Tennenbaum (1978) pointed out the important fact that where an occluding edge is formed by a smooth, self-occluding surface—that is, a limb or extremal edge—the surface orientation along the edge can be recovered precisely. At every point along the extremal edge, the surface is perpendicular both to the line of sight and to the tangent of the self-occluding curve, as illustrated in Figure 5.5.24. These two constraints specify the orientation of the surface along the extremal edges as indicated by the surface normals (the vectors pointing perpendicular to the surface along the extremal edge).

At other occluding edges the constraints are weaker, and so further assumptions must be made to yield a unique solution. The additional constraints brought to

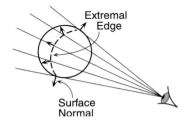

Figure 5.5.24 Recovering surface orientation at an extremal edge. The surface normal along an extremal edge must be perpendicular to the line of sight as well as to the tangent of the surface. This uniquely specifies the orientation of the surface normal along extremal edges.

bear in Barrow and Tennenbaum's analysis of this problem are *smoothness* and *general viewpoint*.

1. *The smoothness assumption* is that if an occluding edge in the image is smooth, then so is the contour of the surface that produced it. This is not universally true—that is, it is a heuristic assumption—because a surface with edge discontinuities might happen to be viewed from the precise angle at which its projected edge would be smooth in the image plane.

2. *The general viewpoint assumption* requires the stationpoint to be general in the sense that small changes in viewpoint will not cause qualitative differences in the image, such as introducing hidden discontinuities. Thus, the assumption of general viewpoint blocks the possibility of discontinuities being disguised by a particular perspective as mentioned above.

Under these conditions, Barrow and Tennenbaum showed that it is possible to recover the 3-D shape of the occluding surface with the most uniform curvature and the least torsion (or twist).

Extremal and other occluding edges can thus provide quite specific information about the orientation of curved surfaces at their contours, but what about the parts of the surface in between? Here theorists postulate a process of interpolation by the "best-fitting" surface that passes through the known points and that minimizes some energylike quantity. Such interpolation processes appeal to a metaphor of finding a thin plate or membrane that goes through the known points at the proper orientation and requires minimal force to hold it in that shape. Again, the assumptions that are made in such computational theories tend to bear close relationships both with the most likely state of affairs in the world (as Helmholtz and the Constructivists proposed) and with the "best" or simplest possibility in some well-defined sense (as the Gestaltists proposed).

These computational analyses by computer vision scientists identify the information available in 2-D images for interpreting edges in the 3-D world, but they do not show that this is how people actually arrive at such interpretations. Surprisingly little effort has been directed at testing the predictions of this line of computational theory in human vision. At this point, its main strength lies in its formal development and power. As a *computational* description of the information on which edge interpretation must be based, it is a giant step forward. As

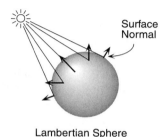

Figure 5.5.25 Recovering surface orientation from shading. The pattern of luminances reflected from a matte surface provides information about the local slant and tilt of the surface.

an *algorithmic* description of the actual processes involved in human vision, it has not yet been evaluated.

5.5.8 Shading Information

Yet another useful and effective source of information about the shape of surfaces curved in depth comes from **shading**: variations in the amount of light reflected from the surface as a result of variations in the orientation of the surface relative to a light source. To appreciate the nature of this information intuitively, consider the sphere shown in Figure 5.5.25. It is made of a homogeneous matte material that diffuses light uniformly in all directions—called a **Lambertian surface**—and is illuminated by a single distant point source. Under these conditions you can see that the brightest part of its surface is where the surface normal—the direction perpendicular to the surface—points directly back to the light source. As the angle between the surface normal and the incident light increases, the amount of light reflected into the eye decreases, producing a shading pattern that reveals structure in the illuminated surface.

Perceiving Surface Orientation from Shading. The ability of human observers to recover surface orientation and depth from shaded objects and pictures has been studied experimentally by Koenderink, Van Doorn, and Kappers (1992, 1996). They showed observers pictures of the human torso shown in Figure 5.5.26 and had them indicate the perceived orientation of a fairly dense sampling of positions on the surface. They made their measurements by giving the subjects control over a small computer-generated display, called a *gauge figure*, consisting of an oval surrounding a short line segment, as indicated for several positions in Figure

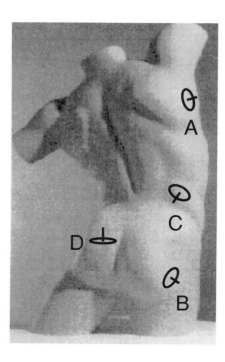

Figure 5.5.26 Studying the perception of surface orientation from shading. Subjects saw this picture of a male torso and adjusted the shape and orientation of oval test figures so that they looked like circles lying flat on the surface (A and B) rather than askew (C and D). (Courtesy of J. J. Koenderink.)

5.5.26. These gauge figures were used to probe surface orientation because they can easily and accurately be perceived as circles oriented in depth, at a particular slant and tilt, with short lines sticking perpendicularly out of their centers. (Gauge figures were used in Figure 5.0.1 to demonstrate the difference between slant and tilt, for example.) Subjects were instructed to adjust each gauge figure so that it appeared to be a circle lying flat on the surface of the object with the line sticking perpendicularly out of the surface, as illustrated by ovals A and B in Figure 5.5.26. For contrast, ovals C and D show examples in which they do not appear to be circles lying flat on the surface.

Figure 5.5.27 shows the results from one subject averaged over several sessions. Notice that this representation of the data approximates the appearance of the original torso in the texture gradient of many circles on its surface. Such findings allowed the experimenters to reconstruct people's perception of surface depth and orientation using minimal assumptions. They found that

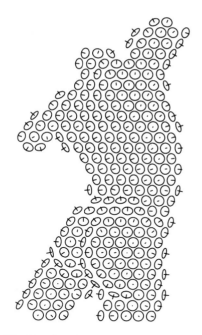

Figure 5.5.27 Local surface orientations reported by one subject. The average ovals produced by one subject for every point tested on the surface of the male torso shown in Figure 5.5.26. (From Koenderink, van Doorn, & Kappers, 1996.)

different subjects were remarkably similar in their qualitative perception of these surfaces but that they differed quantitatively in the amount of depth they perceived. Another important conclusion they reached was that observers were not using strictly local information in making their responses, but were integrating over a substantial region of the object's surface. These conclusions were not dependent on the surface depicting a familiar object such as a torso because they obtained similar results using unfamiliar abstract sculptures. Exactly what perceptual process might have produced these global effects is not yet clear.

Like many other aspects of depth and surface perception, the visual analysis of shading often rests on heuristic assumptions. Perhaps the most striking is that our brains implicitly assume that illumination comes from above. Figure 5.5.28 shows an example of a surface with two rows of indentations. The top ones typically appear to be convex bumps, bulging outward toward the viewer, and the bottom ones appear to be concave dents, curving inward away from the viewer. In fact, this perception is veridical only if the illumination comes

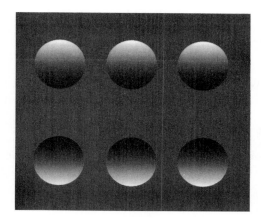

Figure 5.5.28 Direction of illumination and perceived convexity. The top row looks like convex bumps and the lower row like concave dents because the visual system assumes that illumination comes from above. If you turn the book upside down, the perceived convexity of these elements reverses.

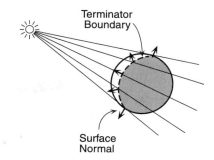

Figure 5.5.29 Recovering surface orientation from shadow boundaries. Horn's analysis shows that the surface normal can be uniquely recovered along a terminator boundary because its points are known to be perpendicular to the direction of the incident light.

from above in the depicted scene. You can demonstrate this simply by turning the book upside down. This reverses the assumed direction of illumination (relative to the rows) and thus reverses the perceived covexity/ concavity of the dimples. The ones at the top of the page (now the lower ones) appear concave, and the others (now the upper ones) appear convex. The assumption of illumination from above makes a great deal of sense because our visual environment almost always *is* illuminated from above. It is therefore another example of using plausible hidden assumptions to determine how we solve an underconstrained inverse problem.

Horn's Computational Analysis. Although the relation between shading and surface orientation had been known qualitatively for many years and has been exploited for centuries by artists in their paintings, Berthold Horn (1975, 1977) of M.I.T. was the first to mine its implications for computational vision. He showed that percentage changes in image luminance are directly proportional to percentage changes in the orientation of the surface. (More precisely, percentage changes in luminance are proportional to percentage changes in the cosine of surface orientation.) This information is not sufficient to recover the orientation of the surface, but only to compute the angle between the incident light and the surface normal. To determine the absolute orientation of the surface, there must be some points of known orientation to anchor the computation.

We have already discussed one condition under which absolute surface orientation can be determined: at points along extremal edges, as in the case of a sphere's boundary, where the orientation of the surface is perpendicular both to the line of sight and to the tangent of the surface. A second condition arises along **terminator boundaries** between illuminated and shadowed regions, as shown in Figure 5.5.29. Here, the surface normal is known to be perpendicular to the direction of incident light. Horn showed that, by using such additional constraints, the orientation of Lambertian surfaces can be recovered. Pentland (1989) later showed that this can be accomplished by using biologically plausible receptive fields such as those found in cells in area V1 (see Section 4.3.3).

Current shading algorithms are well suited to certain restricted types of situations, such as viewing Lambertian surfaces under a single point source of illumination. Their abilities are again completely overshadowed by human abilities to perceive surface orientation and depth from shading. The main reason is that people are able to perform well under a much wider variety of conditions than Horn's algorithms. For example, normal lighting conditions have multiple illumination sources, including reflections from other nearby surfaces, that complicate the mathematical analysis enormously. People are also able to deal with surfaces that are not Lambertian but have significantly specular characteristics, such as glossy or semigloss surfaces that reflect light more coherently than matte surfaces do. Theorists do not yet know how people are able to make use of this complex information to perceive the shape of surfaces

Perceiving Surfaces Oriented in Depth

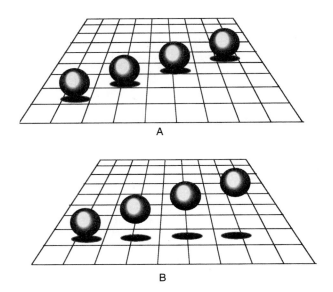

A

B

Figure 5.5.30 A demonstration of the role of cast shadows in depth perception. The perceived distance of the spheres from the viewer changes importantly with changes in the positions of their cast shadows.

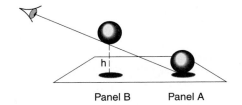

Panel B   Panel A

Figure 5.5.31 Viewing geometry of the scene depicted in Figure 5.5.30. The height (h) of the sphere above its shadow provides information about its height above the surface onto which its shadow is cast, thereby specifying where it lies in depth along the line of sight.

from the pattern of shading, but clearly they can, as Koenderink and van Doorn's data demonstrate.

Cast Shadows. Further information relevant to recovering depth information comes from **cast shadows**: shadows of one object that fall on the surface of another object. Figure 5.5.30 shows an example. The positions of the four balls and textured surface are identical in the two displays; the only things that differ are the positions of the shadows cast by the balls onto the surface (Kersten, Knill, Mamassian, & Bulthoff, 1996). In part A, the shadows are attached to the balls at the bottom, indicating that they are resting on the surface. They therefore appear to be positioned diagonally in depth, the right ball being considerably farther away than the left one. In part B, however, the shadows are increasingly distant from the bottom of the balls, indicating that they are positioned at different heights above the surface. They therefore appear to be arrayed diagonally in height within the frontal plane, the right one being considerably higher than the left one.

Cast shadows can thus provide information about the distance to an object. The retinal position of a particular ball gives its direction from the viewer, as indicated by the line of sight in Figure 5.5.31. The distance between the ball and its shadow cast on the surface gives the height of its bottom above the surface, which is zero when the shadow is attached to it in part A and greater than zero in part B. Together, these two sources of information are sufficient to locate the balls at quite different distances from the viewer in the two situations shown in Figure 5.5.30.

5.5.9 Aerial Perspective

Aerial (or **atmospheric**) **perspective** refers to certain systematic differences in the contrast and color of objects that occur when they are viewed from great distances. You may have noticed that buildings and other large objects appear "fuzzier" and more "washed out" when they are viewed from far away. Their contrast is reduced by the additional atmosphere through which they are viewed, because it contains particles of either dust, water (from fog, mist, or humidity) or pollutants (from smog produced by industry or automobiles) that scatter light. These particles add noise to the imaging process by scattering light, effectively smearing the image so that its contours appear less distinct ("fuzzier") and have lower contrast (are more "washed out"). A photographic example is provided in Color Plate 5.1.

You may also have noticed that mountains often look somewhat bluish or purplish when viewed from far away. When you think about it, this is somewhat surprising because the same tree-covered mountains look quite green when viewed from a closer vantage point. The additional atmosphere through which it is seen when far away gives it this bluish cast and makes it appear farther away, as illustrated in Color Plate 5.1. The reason for this bluish tint is that the particles in the atmosphere scatter longer wavelengths of light more

(a)

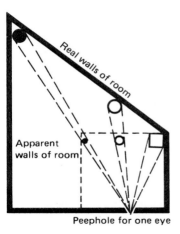

- ● real place and size of "smallest" man
- • apparent place and size of "smallest" man
- ○ real place and size of "medium" man
- ○ apparent place and size of "medium" man
- ☐ "largest" man

(b)

Figure 5.5.32 Conflicting information in an Ames room. Perspective information and familiar size information conflict when people are seen in an Ames room, a distorted room that appears to be rectangular from a single viewpoint. Perspective information dominates, so the people are perceived as greatly different in size. (Photograph by William Vandivert.)

than shorter wavelengths. This means that relatively more of the short wavelengths, which are in the range we see as blue, will come through a large amount of atmosphere, producing a systematic spectral shift toward blue.

Artists have long used atmospheric perspective in portraying distant landscapes in their work. The differences in contrast, resolution, and color that result from it are not terribly effective depth information in isolation, but when they are used in conjunction with others, they give an added sense of depth.

5.5.10 Integrating Information Sources

We have now examined a large number of widely different information sources for perceiving depth in a scene. Since all these sources bear on the same perceptual interpretation of surfaces oriented in depth, they must somehow be put together into a coherent consistent representation. How does the visual system accomplish this integration?

Under normal viewing conditions, integrating different sources of depth information is largely unproblematic because they are very highly correlated. They therefore converge naturally on a single, coherent, and accurate representation of the distance and orientation of surfaces relative to the viewer. In the laboratory, however, different factors can be manipulated independently so that cues come into conflict. What happens in such cases, and what do the results imply about the rules for integrating different information? We will consider three different possibilities: that one source *dominates* a conflicting source, that a *compromise* is achieved between two conflicting sources, and that the two sources *interact* to arrive at an optimal solution.

Dominance. Perhaps the simplest possibility is that one information source will dominate some other conflicting source with the result that the latter is completely ignored. This form of integration implies a hierarchy of depth sources such that those higher in the ordering dominate those lower down, although it is not clear what might happen in this hierarchy if several sources "gang up" on one outlier.

A well-known example of what appears to be dominance between depth cues is the **Ames room**, which pits perspective information against familiar size of objects. The Ames room is a greatly distorted room that looks normal from one particular viewpoint. Figure 5.5.32 shows an Ames room together with its floor plan. Even though it is not rectangular, it looks rectangular from the designated viewpoint. When objects known to be approximately equal in size are placed along the back wall of the room, such as the three people in Figure 5.5.32, observers at the special viewpoint invariably re-

Perceiving Surfaces Oriented in Depth

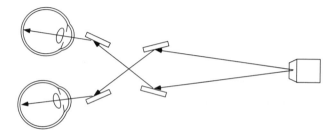

Figure 5.5.33 A pseudoscope. The projection of light to the left and right eyes is optically reversed by a pseudoscope, thus reversing stereoscopic depth information. Normal depth is perceived in complex real-world scenes, however, because monocular pictorial information is not changed and usually wins out.

port two illusions: (1) the people are seen as equally distant and (2) they are seen as differing greatly in size. The perspective information about depth in the 2-D image of the Ames room at the special viewpoint leads to the perception of a normal rectangular room, with corners at equal distances. If this were actually true, the people would have to be enormously different in actual size to account for their differences in retinal size, and this is what is perceived. Familiar size information suggests that the men are about the same size, but this possibility is overwhelmed by the evidence from perspective, which appears to completely dominate perception in this case.

A somewhat surprising example of dominance in depth perception shows that even a source as important and compelling as binocular disparity can be overridden. An optical device called a **pseudoscope** (Figure 5.5.33) reverses binocular disparity simply by reversing the images that are projected to the left and right eyes. Because this instrument reverses the horizontal disparities of everything in the image, objects that are closer should appear farther (and vice versa), and convex objects should appear concave (and vice versa). But if a complex normal scene is viewed through a pseudoscope, its depth does *not* reverse as binocular disparity predicts. The reason is that disparity information can be overridden by monocular pictorial information, such as occluding edges, texture gradients, perspective, and prior knowledge of object convexity, none of which is altered by the pseudoscope. Conflicts are therefore present between disparity and these other sources of depth information at many places in the scene, and the pictorial sources almost always win out.

Compromise. A second possibility for dealing with conflicts between depth cues is that the visual system may integrate information from different sources by finding compromise solutions that are consistent with neither source alone but fall somewhere in between. The most obvious way of doing this is for the visual system to make independent estimates of depth from each source alone and then to integrate the results according to some mathematical rule. Bruno and Cutting (1988), for example, constructed stimuli in which four depth sources varied independently: relative size, position relative to the horizon, occlusion, and motion parallax. They asked their subjects to rate perceived depth on a scale from 0 (no depth) to 99 (maximum depth) for displays in which different combinations of factors conflicted with others. They reported convincing evidence that subjects integrated multiple information sources in their depth judgments rather than simply relying on one of them, as would be expected from dominance within a hierarchy. They also found that the rule of information integration was additive. Subjects were, in effect, simply summing the independent effects of the four factors, so more sources of depth information resulted in subjects perceiving more depth. Massaro (1988) reanalyzed the same data and suggested that a multiplicative model of integration provides a better account, and others have also found multiplicative integration functions (e.g., Dosher, Sperling, & Wurst, 1986). Still other mathematical rules are possible, and the exact form that the visual system uses remains to be established.

This theoretical position has been called **weak fusion** (Clark & Yuille, 1990; Landy, Maloney, Johnston, & Young, 1995) because it assumes no interaction between different information sources. (Fusion of multiple sources of depth information should not be confused with stereoscopic fusion of left and right images; they are entirely unrelated concepts.) Weak fusion is compatible with the strongly modular position we discussed briefly in Section 2.3.3 and again early in this chapter (Section 5.1.2). The basic idea is that many different estimates of depth may be computed independently and in parallel, each producing a different estimate of depth at each point in a *depth map*. These multiple depth maps are then integrated by averaging, adding, multiplying, or some other mathematical rule of combination at each location in the depth map. The result is usually a compromise between the different depth estimates produced by the various depth-from-X modules.

Interaction. Although this description of weak fusion sounds plausible enough on the surface, it glosses over many important problems that become apparent on deeper reflection. Notice first that only absolute depth sources are capable of producing metric depth maps that can be numerically combined to obtain meaningful results. Even highly quantitative sources of relative depth (e.g., binocular disparity and motion parallax) require further information to produce absolute depth information, and it is not clear how purely qualitative sources (e.g., occlusion and accretion/deletion of texture) could enter into such a theoretical framework at all. Furthermore, it seems quite likely on a priori grounds that different kinds of depth information from different "modules" are not kept separate, but interact, at least to some degree, in arriving at a single coherent representation of the distance to visible surfaces.

Consider, for example, the synergistic interaction between binocular disparity and convergence. By itself, binocular disparity does not specify absolute distances to surfaces, but only ratios of distances, for the reasons we discussed above. Convergence *does* specify absolute depth, but only for the single fixated object. Together, however, they determine the absolute distance to every object in the field of view. If convergence provides the absolute distance to the one fixated object, this measurement can then be used to scale the disparity ratios of relative depth to provide absolute distances to all other objects. Thus a complete depth map can be computed if these two sources of depth information interact. The same is true for interactions between binocular disparity and any other absolute sources of depth information, such as familiar size and accommodation: Knowing any one absolute distance determines the distances to every object in the scene.

Such interactions between different sources of depth information are so useful that it is almost unthinkable that they fail to occur. Theoretically, however, they are complex and messy in comparison to the modular simplicity of weak fusion. Landy et al. (1995) have therefore formulated a version of weak fusion, which they call **modified weak fusion**, that allows for certain limited kinds of interactions among depth sources. One of the

most important is the kind we just described between binocular disparity and any absolute depth source, in which one source provides information that is sufficient to upgrade another to the level of absolute depth for the whole visual field. Landy et al. (1995) call this metric representation a "depth map," and they call the process of upgrading information from a depth source to the level of a metric depth map "promotion." Thus, convergence, accommodation, or familiar size can be used to promote binocular disparity information to a depth map via scaling. These promoted depth maps can then be combined by numerical integration as proposed in the weak fusion framework.

The question of how different sources of depth information are combined into a single coherent representation of the 3-D layout of visible surfaces (such as Marr's 2.5-D sketch) is a complex and difficult one. The perceptual evidence is generally scant and unsystematic, computational investigations are just beginning, and there is no systematic physiological evidence at all. Everyone acknowledges that some form of integration must occur, but no one yet knows precisely how. This is one of the least understood topics in the perception of surface layout.

5.6 Development of Depth Perception

As adults we perceive the distance to surfaces and their orientations in space with no apparent effort. Is this because we were born with the ability, because it matured autonomously after birth, or because we learned it and have become so well practiced that it has become automatic? Experiments with young children have begun to provide answers to this intriguing question.

Some of the earliest and most dramatic studies demonstrating that infants have functional depth perception early in life employed an apparatus called a **visual cliff** (E. Gibson & Walk, 1960). The visual cliff consists of a glass-topped table with a central board across the middle, as illustrated in Figure 5.6.1. Textured surfaces can be placed below the glass on either side of the central board at varying distances beneath it, and the lighting can be arranged so that the glass is essentially invisible. In the classic visual cliff experiment, Walk and Gibson placed a textured checkerboard surface directly below the glass on the "shallow" side and an identical

Perceiving Surfaces Oriented in Depth

Figure 5.6.1 An infant on the visual cliff. Infants are placed on the central board over a thick sheet of glass that covers a textured surface on each side, one of which is shallow, lying just beneath the glass and the other of which is deep. When beckoned by their mothers, most infants will cross the shallow side, but few will cross the deep side. (From Gibson & Walk, 1960.)

texture on the floor, 40 inches below the glass on the "deep" side.

The experimenters then asked the baby's mother to put her child on the central board and to try to entice the baby to crawl across either the shallow side or the deep side. If the baby is able to perceive the distance to the two textured surfaces, it should be willing to crawl to its mother over the shallow side but not over the visual cliff. Of the 36 children tested from ages 6 to 14 months, 27 could be persuaded by their mothers to leave the central board. Of these, all 27 crawled across the shallow side at least once, whereas only three attempted to negotiate the visual cliff. This result shows that by the time babies can crawl at age 6 to 12 months, they have functional depth perception.

To find out whether babies who are too young to crawl perceive depth, Campos, Langer, and Krowitz (1970) recorded the heart rates of infants as young as two months old on a visual cliff apparatus. They found that when two- to five-month-old infants were placed on the shallow side, there was a small but not statistically reliable change in heart rate. When they were placed over the deep side, however, their heart rates slowed significantly. The fact that heart rate decreased rather than increased suggests that the infants were not afraid on the deep side—for that would have increased their heart rates—but were studiously attending to the depth information. Consistent with this interpretation, they cried and fussed less on the deep side than on the shallow side. It therefore appears that children as young as two months old are already able to perceive depth but have not yet learned to be afraid in the cliff situation.

One difficulty with the classic visual cliff studies is that they do not specify which specific sources of depth information babies are using. Ocular, stereoscopic, motion, and pictorial information might all develop at about the same time and contribute to their responses, or they might develop at different times and contribute selectively, depending on the child's age and experience. To tease apart such questions, more refined techniques are required that can isolate different sources of information. We will now consider some later studies that have shed light on these issues.

5.6.1 Ocular Information

Ocular information about depth comes from the control of muscles, an ability that newborn infants have only in rudimentary form. It is not too surprising, therefore, that both accommodation and convergence take some time to develop. Banks (1980) studied accommodation in babies between one and three months of age using a **retinoscope**: a device that allows the examiner to determine how well the eye focuses light. He found that one-month-old babies can accommodate slightly and that three-month-olds can accommodate nearly as well as adults. This does not necessarily mean that they use accommodation information to perceive depth, however; this requires the additional assumption that accommodation is an effective source of depth information in these infants. Proper accommodation is also needed for good stereopsis and perception of detail, both of which play important roles in depth perception as well.

Whether binocular convergence is present at birth or not seems to depend on how it is studied. Richard Aslin (1977) directly measured the eye movements of infants as a visual target was moved from near to far positions. When they are able to converge binocularly, their eyes should rotate outward as the target recedes and inward as it approaches. Aslin found that although there seemed to be some ability to converge appropriately quite early, accurate tracking with binocular fixation does not occur until three months of age. Again, these measurements of ocular performance cannot assess whether the infant gets useful depth information from this ability, but only whether they *could*. Hofsten (1977) showed that five-month-olds perceive depth on the basis of convergence by fitting them with glasses that alter convergence and finding that the distance babies reach for an object is altered in corresponding ways.

Indirect methods suggest that convergence information may be present at birth, however. Studies of newborns show that tendencies toward size and shape constancy (see Sections 7.1.1 and 7.2.1) are measurable in the first week of life (Slater, Mattlock, & Brown, 1990; Slater & Morison, 1985). For this to be true, the newborns must have some information about depth, and although it is not certain, binocular convergence appears to be the most likely possibility. We will describe these findings in more detail in Chapter 7 when we discuss the development of constancy.

5.6.2 Stereoscopic Information

Once infants are able to converge their eyes, they can develop stereoscopic vision. Several different procedures indicate that depth perception based on binocular disparity develops at about 3.5 months of age, slightly after direct methods indicate that the ability to converge properly develops.

One approach to studying this issue is to find out how early infants are able to perceive depth in random dot stereograms. As the reader will recall from Section 5.3.2, random dot stereograms contain no monocular information about either form or depth, but when they are viewed binocularly, an observer with normal stereoscopic vision perceives a distinct shape in front of or behind the background plane of dots. In experiments by Fox, Aslin, Shea, and Dumais (1980), infants between 2.5 and 6 months of age were shown random dot stereograms using special glasses. The figure in depth was a rectangle that moved either rightward or leftward, and the experimenters assessed the presence of depth per-

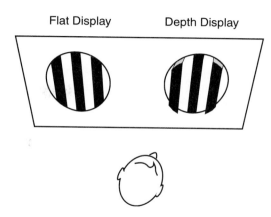

Figure 5.6.2 Depth displays in selective looking studies of visual development. Infants were shown a flat grating display and one with depth from binocular disparity. Babies younger than about 3.5 months showed no preference, whereas older ones preferred looking at the depth display (Held, Birch, & Gwiazda, 1980).

ception by scoring the extent to which the infant tracked the rectangle in the proper direction. They found that three-month-old babies would not track it but 3.5-month-olds would. Notice that the results of this experiment indicate that the infants are actually perceiving depth, not just that they might be, for if they were not, there would be nothing for them to track.

The ability to perceive depth in random dot stereograms is a rather stringent criterion for the presence of stereoscopic depth perception, however. Other methods might show earlier stereo perception. Held, Birch, and Gwiazda (1980) used the preference paradigm to find **stereoacuity thresholds**: the smallest disparity that babies are able to resolve. They used the stereoscopic display shown in Figure 5.6.2. On one side of the display was a flat grating pattern (with no disparity); on the other was an analogous display in which the bars would be perceived at different depths (because of the presence of disparity) for an observer with stereo vision. Prior results with real displays indicated that babies prefer to look at a 3-D display rather than a 2-D display (Fantz, 1965). The experimenters therefore reasoned that a preference for the stereoscopic display would emerge when the babies could perceive the depth. Using special stereoscopic glasses to present slightly different displays to the left and right eyes, Held and his colleagues found a reliable preference for the depth grating at about 3.5 months of age for disparities of about 1° of visual angle.

Perceiving Surfaces Oriented in Depth

Preferences at disparities as low as 1 minute of angle (1/60°) were found by 5 months of age. This is considerably less than the adult ability to detect binocular disparity, which is visible at just a few seconds of angle (1/60 minute), but it clearly indicates that by 3.5 months of age, babies have reasonably good stereo vision.

5.6.3 Dynamic Information

As noted earlier in this chapter, there are a variety of dynamic sources of information about depth: motion parallax, motion gradients, looming, the kinetic depth effect, and accretion/deletion of texture. Are any of these depth cues found early enough in life to be considered present at birth, or do they all develop later?

Perhaps the best candidate for inborn dynamic depth information is *looming* (the motion gradient of an approaching surface) because it applies to objects coming toward a stationary observer. Newborns cannot really move themselves enough to produce extensive self-generated optic flow, but biologically significant objects—such as Mom and their own limbs—do move toward and away from babies as soon as they are born. Human babies one to two months old respond to looming (that is, visually expanding) objects with appropriate defensive reactions (Bower, Broughton, & Moore, 1970, 1971). They push back with their heads and lift their arms in front of their faces when contours expand in their field of view. These researchers interpreted such findings as indicating that depth information from a looming object is present very early in life, perhaps even at birth (Bower, 1974).

Bower's interpretation of these results is open to question, however. Perhaps the babies push their heads back and lift their arms simply because they are tracking the upper contour of the looming image, for example, which moves upward. In support of this possibility, other researchers have found that babies gave the same responses to a single contour moving upward as to an expanding contour (Yonas et al., 1977). Interestingly, however, babies as young as one month old blink their eyes more frequently to a looming object (Yonas, 1981). Thus, optical expansion may be an innate source of depth information, and even if it is not, it arises very early.

Other dynamic sources of information—motion gradients, accretion/deletion of texture, and kinetic depth

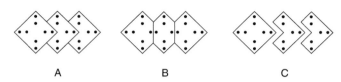

Figure 5.6.3 Stimuli for studying development of occlusion and depth information. Babies older than 7 months reached more often for display A, which portrays depth due to occlusion, than for displays B and C, which do not. (After Granrud & Yonas, 1984.)

effects—have also been found to affect infants' behavior when they are quite young (see Kellman, 1995, 1996, for recent reviews). For example, Kellman (1984) found that after three months of age, infants are sensitive to the shape of objects as revealed by kinetic depth effects. Babies were first habituated to one object rotating in depth about two different axes. Then they were tested with a rotating object that was either the same or different in shape from the habituated one. Three-month-old infants dishabituated only to the different object, indicating that they perceived its shape. Further conditions showed that this behavior was not based on static perception of the object's shape, because it failed to occur when the objects were presented in sequences of static views.

5.6.4 Pictorial Information

There are many pictorial sources of depth information, and not all of them have yet been studied from a developmental perspective. The available evidence suggests that size, occlusion (or interposition), shading, linear perspective, and texture gradients all develop sometime between five and seven months of age. It makes a certain amount of sense that these would develop later than seemingly more basic kinds of depth information, such as ocular, stereoscopic, and motion information.

Rather than trying to give a complete review of the studies that have been done on these topics (for a review, see Yonas, Arterberry, & Granrud, 1987), we will describe just one of them as an example. Granrud and Yonas (1984) examined the age at which infants become sensitive to occlusion information. They were allowed to view displays such as those illustrated in Figure 5.6.3 with just one eye so that binocular disparity information would not reveal their two dimensionality. Displays like that in Figure 5.6.3A used T-junctions to indicate occluding and occluded edges, providing good information about the relative depth of the different objects. Displays such as those shown in Figures 5.6.3B and 5.6.3C were used as superficially similar control conditions in which depth information is not present and so is not perceived, even by adults. The results showed that seven-month-olds reached significantly more often for the display in part A than for those in part B or part C, but the five-month-olds did not. Granrud and Yonas therefore concluded that occlusion information about depth becomes available somewhere between five and seven months of age.

The results of ingenious developmental experiments such as the ones just described have shown that most sources of depth information are not present at birth but develop at different times during the first year of life. It is possible that even more sensitive measures will reveal still earlier depth capabilities, however, so the final answers to the question of nature versus nurture in depth perception are not yet in hand.

Suggestions for Further Reading

Perceiving Space and Depth

Sedgwick, H. A. (1986). Space perception. In K. R. Boff, L. Kaufman, & J. P. Thomas (Eds.), *Handbook of perception and human performance: Vol. 1. Sensory processes and perception* (pp. 21-1–21-57). New York: Wiley. This chapter is an excellent review of findings and theories of spatial perception.

Stereoscopic Vision

Julesz, B. (1971). *Foundations of cyclopian vision*. Chicago: Chicago University Press. This book presents much of Julesz's classic work on random dot stereograms and contains some truly spectacular images.

Computer Vision

Marr, D. (1982). *Vision*. San Francisco: Freeman. Much of Marr's book is devoted to his ideas about how to construct the 2.5-D sketch from modules that process stereo, motion, shading, and so forth.

Winston, P. H. (Ed.). (1975). *The psychology of computer vision*. New York: McGraw-Hill. This edited volume contains several classic papers in computer vision, including contributions by Waltz on edge labeling, Horn on structure from shading, Winston on learning by example, and Minsky on "frames."

Visual Development

Kellman, P. J. (1995). Ontogenesis of space and motion perception. In W. Epstein & S. Rogers (Eds.), *Handbook of perception and cognition: Perception of space and motion* (pp. 327–364). New York: Academic Press. This chapter reviews the literature on the development of spatial perception.

Perceiving Surfaces Oriented in Depth

Organizing Objects and Scenes

The world we perceive consciously is populated with large-scale objects such as people, trees, houses, and cars, not with the edges, bars, and blobs we discussed in Chapter 4 or even with the local pieces of oriented surface we considered in Chapter 5. What is missing thus far in our inquiry into spatial vision is any discussion of large-scale **perceptual organization**: how all the bits and pieces of visual information are structured into the larger units of perceived objects and their interrelations.

Perceptual organization is so pervasive and deeply ingrained in visual experience that it is often hard to appreciate its importance, much less the immense difficulties involved in achieving it. When we look at the environment, we almost invariably perceive whole connected objects arranged in three-dimensional space. We do this so automatically and effortlessly that it is hard to imagine that anything terribly complex is going on. But think for a moment what it might be like if perception had no organization at all—no large-scale structure into extended surfaces and objects. The very idea is so foreign that one can scarcely conjure up an appropriate image of visual experience without organization. Perhaps the best description is that visual experience without any organization would be like watching a snowstorm of swirling, multicolored confetti resulting from the output of millions of unrelated retinal receptors.

Perceptual theorists in the empiricist tradition typically suppose that this must be what a newborn infant experiences. Because empiricists believe that all visual structure is learned from experience, it follows that a newborn's world must be completely unstructured. The noted philosopher/psychologist William James called it "a blooming, buzzing confusion." In fact, we don't really know what the visual experience of a newborn infant is like, because babies can't tell us about their visual experiences—at least not directly. Recently, however, a number of fascinating and imaginative techniques have been developed that have begun to allow us to infer what the visual world of infants might be like. The more we find out, the more it appears that even newborns have certain kinds of perceptual organization. The rest seems to develop during the first six to eight months of life as the infant learns from its interactions with the world. Thus, perceptual organization depends on both innate mechanisms and subsequent learning, as we shall argue at the end of this chapter.

One can get some notion of the importance of perceptual organization from the following description by a man whose vision was disorganized—or at least wrongly organized—as a result of brain damage. The problems he describes are not nearly as radical as experiencing confetti storms, for his perceptual organization appears to have been impaired only at a fairly high level. Even so, his problems give some insight into what it might be like if perceptual organization were to go awry. His description gains special authority from the fact that before the onset of his neurological problems, he was a psychologist trained in introspective reporting of his conscious experiences.

If I saw a complex object, such as a person, and there were several people in my field of view, I sometimes saw the different parts of the people as not, in a sense, belonging together, although ... if a given person moved so that all the parts of him went in one direction, that would ... tend to make him into a single object. Otherwise there was this confusion of lots of things, all of which were there, but did not seem to belong together.... Several of these cases of things not belonging together gave quite absurd results. For instance, I do remember one case where there was what seemed to me to be one object which was partly motor car, partly tree and partly a man in a cricket shirt. They seemed somehow to belong together. More frequently, however, a lot of things which to any ordinary viewer would be parts of the same thing were parts of different things. (Quoted by Marcel, 1983a)

The Problem of Perceptual Organization. The concept of perceptual organization originated with Gestalt psychologists early in this century. It was one of the central concepts in their attack on the atomistic assumption of Structuralism. As we discussed in Chapter 2, the Structuralists conceived of visual perception as a simple concatenation of sensory "atoms" consisting of pointlike color sensations. This view of visual perception is extremely local in the sense that each atom was defined by a particular retinal position and thought to be independent of all other atoms, at least until they were bound together into larger spatial complexes by the process of associative learning. The Gestaltists, in contrast, believed that visual perception arose from global interactions within the visual nervous system and resulted from the overall structure of visual stimulation itself. "Perceptual organization" was the name they used to refer both to this theoretical idea and to the set of phenomena they discovered in support of it.

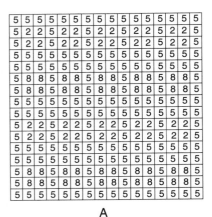

5	5	5	5	5	5	5	5	5	5	5	5	5	5	5
5	2	2	5	2	2	5	2	2	5	2	2	5	2	2	5
5	2	2	5	2	2	5	2	2	5	2	2	5	2	2	5
5	5	5	5	5	5	5	5	5	5	5	5	5	5	5
5	5	5	5	5	5	5	5	5	5	5	5	5	5	5
5	8	8	5	8	8	5	8	8	5	8	8	5	8	8	5
5	8	8	5	8	8	5	8	8	5	8	8	5	8	8	5
5	5	5	5	5	5	5	5	5	5	5	5	5	5	5
5	5	5	5	5	5	5	5	5	5	5	5	5	5	5
5	2	2	5	2	2	5	2	2	5	2	2	5	2	2	5
5	2	2	5	2	2	5	2	2	5	2	2	5	2	2	5
5	5	5	5	5	5	5	5	5	5	5	5	5	5	5
5	5	5	5	5	5	5	5	5	5	5	5	5	5	5
5	8	8	5	8	8	5	8	8	5	8	8	5	8	8	5
5	8	8	5	8	8	5	8	8	5	8	8	5	8	8	5
5	5	5	5	5	5	5	5	5	5	5	5	5	5	5

A

B

Figure 6.1.1 The problem of perceptual organization. When an optical image is registered on the retina, the visual system is faced with trying to find structure in the pattern of receptor outputs, depicted in part A by a numerical array in which high numbers correspond to light regions and low numbers to dark regions. When observers view the corresponding gray-scale image (B), they immediately and effortlessly organize it into four rows of light and dark squares against a gray background.

Max Wertheimer, one of the founding fathers of Gestalt psychology, first posed the problem of perceptual organization. He asked how people are able to perceive a coherent visual world that is organized into meaningful objects rather than the chaotic juxtaposition of different colors that stimulate the individual retinal receptors. His point can perhaps be most easily understood by considering what the output of the retinal mosaic would be for a simple but highly structured image. Figure 6.1.1A illustrates such an output as a numerical array, in which each number represents the neural response of a single retinal receptor. In this numerical

form, it is nearly impossible to grasp the structure and organization of the image without extensive scrutiny. This situation is a lot like the one the visual system faces in trying to organize visual input, because the structure we perceive so effortlessly is not explicitly given in the stimulus image but must be discovered by the visual nervous system. In fact, there is a potentially limitless number of possible organizations in an image, only one of which we typically perceive. Which one we experience and why we perceive it rather than others are thus questions that require explanations.

The structure of the numerical image becomes completely obvious when you see these same values as luminance levels, as illustrated in Figure 6.1.1B. It is a picture of several black and white squares that are organized into four horizontal rows on a gray background. But why is this simple structure so obvious when we view the image and so obscure when we look at the array of numbers? The reason is that the human visual system has evolved to learn how to detect edges, regions, objects, groups, and patterns from the structure of luminance and color in optical images. The gray-scale image in Figure 6.1.1B engages these mechanisms fully, whereas the numerical image scarcely does at all. The same information is present in both images, of course, but the numerical image comes in a form that the visual system cannot discern directly. A theorist who is trying to explain visual perception is in much the same position as you are in trying to find structure in the numerical image: None of the organization that the visual system picks up so automatically and effortlessly can be presupposed, since that is the very structure that must be explained.

Why does visual experience have the organization it does? The most obvious answer is that it simply reflects the structure of the external world. By this account, the physical environment actually consists of things like surfaces and objects arranged in space rather than points of color, and this is why perception is organized as it is. This is the naive realist's answer, and there is undoubtedly something to it. Surely evolutionary utility requires that perceptual organization reflect structure in the organism's environment, or at least the part of it that is relevant to the organism's survival. Imagine, for example, how much less useful vision would be if it characteristically misorganized the world, as in the case of the brain-damaged patient described earlier. But although the naive realist's answer might help explain perceptual organization in an evolutionary sense—*why* perceptual experience has the structure it does—it does not explain the mechanisms of organization: *how* it unfolds in time during acts of perception. The goal of this chapter is to shed light on these mechanisms and the stimulus factors that engage them.

The Experience Error. The major difficulty with the view of naive realism is that the visual system does not have direct access to facts about the environment; it has access only to facts about the image projected onto the retina. That is, an organism cannot be presumed to know how the environment is structured except through sensory information. The Gestaltists referred to the naive realist's approach to the problem of perceptual organization as the **experience error** because it arises from the false (and usually implicit) assumption that the structure of perceptual experience is somehow directly given in the array of light that falls on the retinal mosaic (Köhler, 1947). This optic array actually contains an infinite variety of possible organizations, however, only one of which the visual system usually achieves.

The confusion that underlies the experience error is typically to suppose that the starting point for vision is the distal stimulus rather than the proximal stimulus. This is an easy trap to fall into, since the distal stimulus is an essential component in the causal chain of events that normally produces visual experiences. It also corresponds to the interpretation the visual system strives to achieve. Taking the distal stimulus as the starting point for vision, however, seriously underestimates the difficulty of visual perception because it presupposes that certain useful and important information comes "for free." But the structure of the environment is more accurately regarded as the *result* of visual perception rather than its starting point. As obvious and fundamental as this point might seem, now that we are acquainted with the difficulties in trying to make computers that can "see," the magnitude of problem of perceptual organization was not fully understood until Wertheimer raised it in his seminal paper in 1923. Indeed, although significant progress has been made in the intervening years, vision scientists are still uncovering new layers of this important and pervasive problem.

6.1 Perceptual Grouping

Wertheimer's initial assault on the problem of perceptual organization was to study the stimulus factors that affect **perceptual grouping**: how the various elements in a complex display are perceived as "going together" in one's perceptual experience. He approached this problem by constructing very simple arrays of geometric elements and then varying the stimulus relations among them to determine which ones caused certain elements to be grouped together perceptually.

Logically, a set of elements can be partitioned in a number of different ways, corresponding to the number of possible ways of dividing them into mutually exclusive subsets. This number becomes very large very quickly: For 10 elements, there are 42 possible groupings; but for 100 elements, there are 190,569,292. The number of logically possible groupings is even larger than the number of partitions if one considers hierarchical embedding of subsets and/or overlap among their members. Psychologically, however, only one of these groupings is perceived at one time, and the first one is usually the only one. How does this happen? And what properties of the stimulus image determine which grouping people perceive?

6.1.1 The Classical Principles of Grouping

In his investigations, Wertheimer started with a single line of equally spaced dots as shown in Figure 6.1.2A. These dots do not group together into any larger perceptual units—except the line of dots as a whole. He then noted that when he altered the spacing between adjacent dots so that some pairs were closer together and others were farther apart, as in Figure 6.1.2B, the closer ones grouped strongly together into pairs. This factor of relative closeness, which Wertheimer called **proximity**, was the first of his famous **laws of grouping**. (From now on, we will refer to them as "principles" or "factors" of grouping because, as we will see, they are considerably weaker than one would expect of scientific laws.) The evidence that he offered for the potency of proximity as a factor in grouping was purely phenomenological. He simply presented the array in Figure 6.1.2B to his readers and appealed directly to their experiences of which dots they saw as "going together." Since nobody has ever seriously disputed Wertheimer's

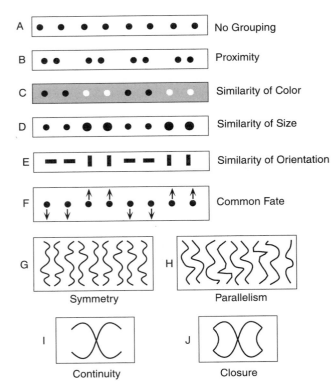

A	● ● ● ● ● ● ● ●	No Grouping
B	●● ●● ●● ●●	Proximity
C	● ● ○ ○ ● ● ○ ○	Similarity of Color
D	● ● ⬤ ⬤ ● ● ⬤ ⬤	Similarity of Size
E	▬ ▬ ❘ ❘ ▬ ▬ ❘ ❘	Similarity of Orientation
F	● ● ● ● ● ● ● ●	Common Fate

G Symmetry H Parallelism

I Continuity J Closure

Figure 6.1.2 Classical principles of grouping. Gestalt psychologists identified many different factors that govern which visual elements are perceived as going together in larger groups. (See text for details.)

claim that the closer dots group perceptually, the principle of proximity was thereby firmly established simply by demonstration, without any formal experiment.

It is perhaps worth making a brief digression here concerning the phenomenological methods employed by Gestalt psychologists. Their demonstrations have often been criticized because they lack the rigorous experimental procedures adhered to by behaviorally oriented researchers (e.g., Pomerantz & Kubovy, 1986). In actuality, however, the Gestaltists were often able to bypass formal experiments simply because the phenomena that they discovered were so powerful that no experiment was needed. If hundreds or even thousands of people viewing their displays agree with their claims about the resulting phenomenological impression, why bother with a formal experiment? As Irvin Rock often remarked, the demonstrations of Gestalt psychologists, such as those in Figure 6.1.2, can actually be viewed as ongoing experiments with an indefinitely large number

of subjects—of which you are now one—virtually all of whom "show the effect." In cases for which the facts were less clear, Gestalt psychologists often performed perfectly reasonable experiments and recorded objective data, such as the number of observers who reported one percept versus another (e.g., Goldmeier, 1936/1972). Thus, their phenomenological methods are not as far removed from modern behavioral ones as is often suggested.

After demonstrating the effect of proximity, Wertheimer went on to illustrate many of the other principles of grouping portrayed in Figure 6.1.2. Figures 6.1.2C, 6.1.2D, and 6.1.2E, for example, demonstrate the principle of **similarity**: All else being equal, the most similar elements (in color, size, and orientation in these examples) tend to be grouped together. Similarity can thus be considered a very general principle of grouping because it covers many different properties.

Another powerful factor is what Wertheimer called **common fate**: All else being equal, elements that move in the same way tend to be grouped together. Although this cannot be demonstrated in a static display, grouping by common fate is indicated symbolically by the arrows in Figure 6.1.2F. Notice that common fate can actually be considered a special case of similarity grouping in which the similar property is velocity of movement. It has even been claimed that proximity can be considered a special case of similarity grouping in which the underlying dimension of similarity is the position of the elements.

Not all possible similarities are equally effective, however, and some do not produce much grouping at all. Consider the row of V's in Figure 6.1.3A, for example. Adjacent pairs differ by 180° in orientation, yet there is very little spontaneous grouping by similarity in this display. Figure 6.1.3B shows the same figures in pairs that differ by only 45° in orientation, and now the pairwise grouping is immediately apparent. The visual system thus seems to be much more sensitive to certain kinds of differences than to others. Even subtle differences like those in Figure 6.1.3A can be perceived by deliberate scrutiny involving focused attention, but such processes appear to be different from normal effortless grouping such as occurs in viewing Figure 6.1.3B. Later in this chapter, we will consider why this might be the case.

Gestalt psychologists also described several further factors that influence perceptual grouping of linelike

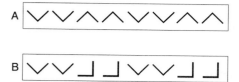

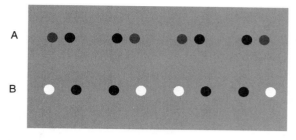

Figure 6.1.3 Degrees of grouping. Not all factors are equally effective in producing grouping. In part A, elements that differ by 180° in orientation are not strongly grouped, whereas those in part B that differ by only 45° produce strong grouping.

Figure 6.1.4 Tradeoffs between grouping by color and proximity. Large differences in proximity and small differences in color lead to grouping by proximity, whereas large differences in color and small differences in proximity lead to grouping by color.

elements. Symmetry (Figure 6.1.2G) and parallelism (Figure 6.1.2H), for example, are factors that influence the grouping of individual lines and curves. Figure 6.1.2I illustrates the important factor of **good continuation** (or **continuity**) of lines or edges: All else being equal, elements that can be seen as smooth continuations of each other tend to be grouped together. Its effect is manifest in this figure because observers perceive it as containing two continuous intersecting lines rather than as two angles whose vertices meet at a point. Figure 6.1.2J illustrates the further factor of **closure**: All else being equal, elements forming a closed figure tend to be grouped together. Note that this display shows that closure can overcome continuity because the very same lines that were organized as two intersecting lines in part I are organized as two angles meeting at a point in part J. According to Wertheimer's analysis, this is because the noncontinuous segments now constitute parts of the same closed figure.

The demonstrations of continuity and closedness in Figure 6.1.2I and 6.1.2J illustrate an important limitation in current knowledge about grouping principles. As formulated by Gestalt psychologists, they are **ceteris paribus rules**, which means that they can predict the outcome of grouping with certainty only *when everything else is equal*—that is, when there is no other grouping factor influencing the outcome. We saw, for example, that continuity governs grouping when the elements do not form a closed figure, but it can be overcome by closure when they do.

The difficulty with ceteris paribus rules is that they provide no general purpose scheme for integrating several potentially conflicting factors into an overall outcome—that is, for predicting the strength of their combined influences. The same problem arises for all the previously mentioned principles of grouping. If

proximity influences grouping toward one outcome and similarity in color toward another, the grouping that will be perceived depends heavily on the particular example. Figure 6.1.4A shows a case in which proximity is strong enough to overcome color similarity, whereas Figure 6.1.4B shows one in which color similarity dominates. The visual system clearly integrates over many grouping factors, but we do not yet understand how it does so. Later in this chapter we will describe a recent theory that is able to integrate several different aspects of similarity grouping in the process of texture segregation, but it cannot yet handle other grouping principles such as common fate, continuity, and closure.

6.1.2 New Principles of Grouping

There has been surprisingly little modern work on principles of perceptual grouping in vision. Recently, however, three new grouping factors have been proposed: *synchrony* (Palmer & Levitin, in preparation), *common region* (Palmer, 1992) and *element connectedness* (Palmer & Rock, 1994a).

The principle of **synchrony** states that, all else being equal, visual events that occur at the same time will tend to be perceived as going together. Although this factor has previously been acknowledged as important in auditory perception (e.g., Bregman, 1978), it has not been systematically studied in vision until recently (Palmer & Levitin, in preparation). Figure 6.1.5 depicts an example. Each element in an equally spaced row of black and white dots flickers at a given rate between black and white. The arrows indicate that half the circles change from black to white or from white to black at one time and the other half at a different time. When the alterna-

Organizing Objects and Scenes

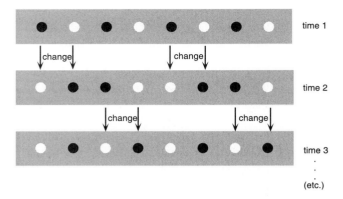

Figure 6.1.5 Grouping by synchrony. All else being equal, elements that change their properties at the same time (as indicated by the arrows) are grouped together.

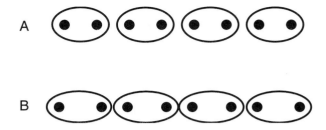

Figure 6.1.6 Grouping by common region. All else being equal, elements within the same region of space are grouped together (A), even when they are farther apart than elements in different regions (B). (After Palmer, 1992.)

tion rate is about 25 changes per second or less, observers see the dots as strongly grouped into pairs based on synchrony. At faster rates, there is no grouping in what appears to be chaotic flickering of the dots. At very slow rates there is momentary grouping into pairs at the moment of change, but it dissipates during the constant interval between flickers. Synchrony is related to the classical principle of common fate in the sense that it is a dynamic factor, but as this example shows, the "fate" of the elements does not have to be common—some dots get brighter, and others get dimmer—as long as the change occurs at the same time.

Another recently identified principle of grouping is common region (Palmer, 1992). **Common region** refers to the fact that, all else being equal (ceteris paribus), elements that are located within the same closed region of space will be grouped together. Figure 6.1.6A shows an example that is analogous to Wertheimer's classic demonstrations (Figures 6.1.2B—6.1.2E): A line of otherwise equivalent, equally spaced dots is strongly organized into pairs when they are enclosed within the same surrounding contour. Figure 6.1.6B shows that grouping by common region is powerful enough to overcome proximity that would, in itself, produce the opposite grouping structure.

A third newly proposed principle of grouping is **element connectedness**: All else being equal, elements that are connected by other elements tend to be grouped together. Palmer and Rock (1994) provide a number of demonstrations of its potency in grouping. An example that is analogous to Wertheimer's classic demonstrations

is shown in Figure 6.1.7A. The line of equally spaced dots is strongly grouped when subsets of the dots are connected by additional elements, such as the short horizontal line segments of this example. Figure 6.1.7B demonstrates that element connectedness can overcome even the powerful effect of proximity.

Wertheimer may not have considered element connectedness as a separate principle because it could be considered as the limiting case of maximal proximity. However, Palmer and Rock argue for distinguishing connectedness from proximity for several reasons. First, there is an important qualitative distinction between actual connectedness and mere proximity. Indeed, this distinction is a cornerstone of the mathematical field of topology. Second, they note that what "goes together" in the strongest physical sense are those pieces of matter that are actually connected, not those that are merely close together. Parts of objects that are connected are much more closely coupled in their physical behavior than are two nearby objects, no matter how close they may be. Therefore, it makes sense for the visual system

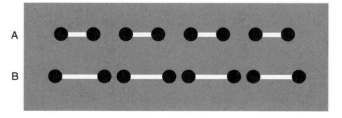

Figure 6.1.7 Grouping by element connectedness. All else being equal, elements that are connected to each other via additional elements are grouped together (A), even when they are farther apart than elements in different regions (B). (After Palmer & Rock, 1994a.)

to be especially sensitive to connectedness as an indication of how to predict what will happen in the world. Third, there is an important phenomenological difference between connected and merely nearby objects. Element connectedness usually results in the perception of a single, unified object consisting of different parts, whereas mere proximity results in the perception of a looser aggregation of several separate but related objects. For these reasons, Palmer and Rock argued that proximity should be viewed as derivative from connectedness rather than the other way around.

The difference between the effects of mere proximity and those of actual connectedness suggests that the principles of grouping may not be a homogeneous set. In some cases, they result in **element aggregations**: loose confederations of objects that result from perceptual grouping operations. Proximity, similarity, common region, and certain cases of common fate often produce element aggregations in which the elements retain a high degree of perceptual independence despite their interrelation within the group. Other principles of grouping can produce **unit formation**: perception of a single, perceptually connected object from multiple underlying elements. Element connectedness, good continuation, and other cases of common fate frequently produce this more coherent organization into single unified objects.

One might think from the discussion of grouping principles that they are mere textbook curiosities, only distantly related to anything that occurs in normal perception. Wertheimer claimed, however, that they pervade virtually all perceptual experience because they are responsible for determining the objects and parts we perceive in the environment. Some dramatic examples of where perceptual organization goes wrong can be identified in natural camouflage, as illustrated in Figure 6.1.8.

The goal of camouflage is to foil grouping processes that would normally make the creature stand out from its environment as a separate object. The successfully camouflaged organism is grouped with its surroundings instead, primarily because of the operation of similarity in various guises. If the animal's coloration and markings are sufficiently similar to its environment in color, orientation, size, and shape, it will be grouped with the background, thus rendering it virtually invisible in the proper context. The effect can be nearly perfect as long

Figure 6.1.8 An example of natural camouflage. Many animals, birds, and insects exhibit a remarkable ability to blend into their habitual surroundings by foiling many Gestalt principles of grouping. The camouflage is invariably broken when the animal moves relative to the background, however. (Photograph by David C. Rentz.)

as the organism remains stationary, but even perfect camouflage is undone by the principle of common fate once it moves. The common motion of its markings and contours against the background causes them to be strongly grouped together, providing any nearby observer with enough information to perceive it as a separate object.

6.1.3 Measuring Grouping Effects Quantitatively

Gestalt demonstrations of grouping are adequate for establishing the existence of ceteris paribus rules, but they are *not* adequate to support quantitative theories that specify how multiple factors might be integrated. For this purpose, quantitative methods are needed to enable measurement of the amount or degree of grouping. Two such methods have recently been devised, one based directly on reports of grouping and the other based on an indirect but objectively defined task.

Kubovy and Wagemans (1995) measured the relative strength of different groupings by showing observers dot lattices like the one shown in Figure 6.1.9A and measuring the probability with which they reported seeing them organized in various different ways. Such lattices are ambiguous in that they can be seen as being grouped

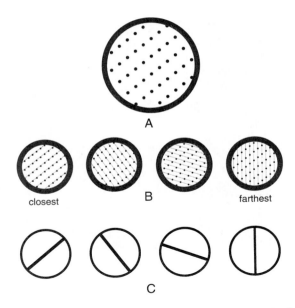

Figure 6.1.9 Ambiguity in the grouping of dot lattices. Lattices of dots, such as that shown in part A, can be seen as grouped into lines of different orientations as illustrated in part B by the thin gray lines connecting the dots. Kubovy and Wagemans (1995) had subjects indicate the orientation of dot-lines that they saw by choosing the corresponding response symbol shown in part C. (After Kubovy & Wagemans, 1995.)

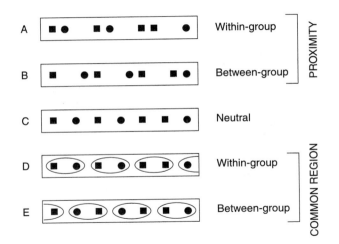

Figure 6.1.10 Examples of stimuli used in the repetition discrimination task. Subjects must detect whether the adjacent repeated pair are squares or circles. In within-group trials (parts A and D), the repeated elements are within groups defined by a given grouping factor (proximity in part A and common region in part D). In between-group trials (B and E), they are in different groups. In neutral trials (C), no other grouping factor is present.

into lines in one of four orientations as indicated in Figure 6.1.9B. Observers were shown a particular lattice for 300 milliseconds (ms) and then were asked to indicate which organization they saw by choosing one among four response symbols representing the possible orientations for that lattice. After many trials, the probabilities of perceiving each grouping could be calculated. Consistent with the Gestalt principle of proximity, their results showed that the most likely organization is the one in which the dots are closest together, other organizations being less likely as the spacing between the dots in that orientation increased. Moreover, the data were fit well by a mathematical model in which the attraction between dots decreases exponentially as a function of distance (see also Kubovy, Holcombe, & Wagemans, in press).

Another quantitative method for studying grouping, called the *repetition discrimination task*, has recently been devised by Palmer and Beck (in preparation). Unlike Kubovy and Wagemans's procedure, this method relies on a task in which there is an objectively correct answer for each response. Subjects are presented with displays

like the ones shown in Figure 6.1.10. Each consists of a row of squares and circles that alternate except for a single adjacent pair in which the same shape is repeated. The subject's task on each trial is to determine whether the adjacent repeated pair is composed of squares or circles. They indicate the answer by pressing one button for squares or another for circles as quickly as they can. Response times are measured in three different conditions. In the *within-group* trials, a grouping factor (proximity in Figure 6.1.10A) biases the target pair to be organized into the same group. In the *between-group* trials, the same factor biases the target pair to be organized as part of two different groups (Figure 6.1.10B). In the *neutral* trials, the factor does not bias the pair one way or the other (Figure 6.1.10C). The expectation is that the target pair will be detected more quickly when it is part of the same group than when it is part of different groups.

The results showed substantial effects of grouping factors on reaction times. Responses were much faster in the within-group trials (719 ms) than in the between-group trials (1144 ms) for the proximity stimuli (Figure 6.1.10A versus Figure 6.1.10B). Responses in the within-group trials were about as fast as those in the neutral trials (730 ms), presumably because the shape similarity of the target pair caused them to be grouped together even in the absence of other grouping factors. Similar results were obtained for detecting adjacent pairs of squares or circles when they were grouped by color similarity, common region, and element connectedness. Figures 6.1.10C, 6.1.10D, and 6.1.10E show neutral, within-group, and between-group displays for the common region experiment. Similar results were obtained, despite the fact that there are no differences in distance between the elements in the target pair. Such findings confirm the importance of grouping factors on this objective perceptual task.

An important advantage of quantitative methods such as these is that they allow precise measurement of grouping effects when phenomenology is unclear. For example, Palmer and Beck used the repetition detection task to determine whether small or large ovals have the greater effect in grouping by common region when they conflict within the same display. Palmer (1992) had previously suggested that smaller regions dominate perception on the basis of the demonstration displays shown in Figure 6.1.11A and 6.1.11B but admitted that this claim pushed the limits of introspective observations. Using the repetition discrimination task and several stimulus manipulations, Palmer and Beck were able to show that small ovals have a much greater effect than large ovals on response times in this task and that this difference is due primarily to the size of the ovals rather than their orientation. Somewhat surprisingly, the dominance of the small ovals persisted even when "smiles" were added to the large ovals to make them into faces, as illustrated in Figure 6.1.11C. This finding suggests that grouping in this particular task is not influenced by the familiarity and meaningfulness of faces, which presumably affect perception fairly late in visual processing.

6.1.4 Is Grouping an Early or Late Process?

The question of where in visual processing grouping occurs is an important one. Is it an early process that works at the level of image structure, or does it work later, after depth information has been extracted and perceptual constancy has been achieved? (Recall from Section 3.3 that perceptual constancy refers to the ability to perceive the unchanging properties of distal environmental objects despite variation in the proximal retinal images

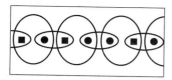

A. Pair within Small Ovals

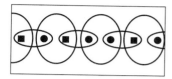

B. Pair within Large Ovals

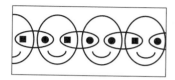

C. Pair within Smiling Faces

Figure 6.1.11 Effects of size in common region. Results from the repetition discrimination task showed that repeated pairs within small regions (A) are detected more quickly than are the same pairs within large regions (B). This is true even when the large regions were made salient and meaningful by adding "smiles" to form "happy faces."

caused by differences in viewing conditions. This topic will be pursued in detail in Chapter 7.)

Wertheimer (1923/1950) discussed grouping as though it occurred at a very low level, presumably corresponding to what we have called image-based processing. He presented no empirical evidence for this position, but the generally accepted view since his seminal paper has been that organization must occur early to provide higher-level processes with the perceptual units they require as input. Indeed, this early view has seldom been seriously questioned, at least until recently.

As sensible as the early view of grouping appears a priori, however, there is little empirical evidence to support it. The usual Gestalt demonstrations of grouping do not address this issue because they employ displays in which depth and constancy are irrelevant: two-dimensional displays viewed in the frontal plane with homogeneous illumination. Under these simple conditions it cannot be determined whether the critical grouping factors operate at the level of 2-D image structure or that of 3-D perceptual structure. The reason is that in the Gestalt demonstrations grouping at these two levels—2-D retinal images versus 3-D percepts—lead to the same predictions.

The first well-controlled experiment to explicitly separate the predictions of organization at these two levels concerned grouping by proximity (Rock & Brosgole, 1964). The question was whether the distances that govern proximity grouping are defined in the 2-D image plane or in perceived 3-D space. Rock and Brosgole used a 2-D rectangular array of luminous beads that could be presented to the observer in a dark room either in the frontal plane (perpendicular to the line of sight) or slanted in depth so that the horizontal dimension was foreshortened to a degree that depended on the angle of slant, as illustrated in Figure 6.1.12. The beads in Figure 6.1.12A were actually closer together vertically, so when they were viewed in the frontal plane, as illustrated in Figure 6.1.12B, observers always reported them as grouped vertically into columns rather than horizontally into rows.

The crucial question was what would happen when the same lattice of beads was presented to the observer slanted in depth so that the beads were closer together horizontally when measured in the retinal image, as depicted in Figure 6.1.12C. (Notice that they are still closer together vertically when measured in the 3-D world.) Not surprisingly, when observers viewed this slanted display with just one eye, so that no binocular depth information was available, they reported the beads to be organized into rows as predicted by retinal proximity. This presumably occurs because they mistakenly perceived the lattice as lying in the frontal plane, even when it was slanted more than 40° in depth. When observers achieved veridical depth perception by viewing the same display binocularly, however, they reported seeing the slanted array of beads as organized into vertical *columns*, just as they did in the frontal viewing condition. This result supports the hypothesis that grouping occurs after stereoscopic depth perception.

Rock, Nijhawan, Palmer, and Tudor (1992) addressed a similar issue in lightness perception: Is similarity grouping by achromatic color based on the retinally measured *luminance* of elements or their phenomenally perceived *lightness* after lightness constancy has been achieved? (See Section 3.3 for a discussion of lightness

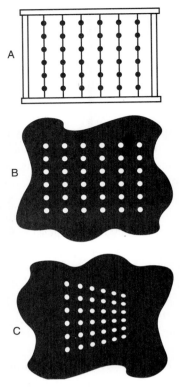

Figure 6.1.12 Retinal versus perceived distance in proximity grouping. Luminous beads spaced as shown in part A appear to be organized in columns when viewed in the frontal plane (B), because of proximity. When slanted in depth (C) and viewed with both eyes, they are still seen as organized into columns, even when they are closer together horizontally on the retina. This result shows that proximity grouping is influenced by stereoscopic depth processing.

constancy.) The first experiment used cast shadows to decouple luminance and lightness. Observers were shown displays similar to the one illustrated in Figure 6.1.13 and were asked to indicate whether the central column of elements grouped with the ones on the left or on the right.

The structure of the display in the critical constancy condition is illustrated in Figure 6.1.13. It was carefully constructed so that the central squares were identical in reflectance to the ones on the left (that is, they were made of the same shade of gray paper) but were seen under a shadow cast by an opaque vertical strip hanging nearby. As a result, their luminance—the amount of light reaching the observer's eye after being reflected by the central squares—was identical to the luminance of the squares on the right. Therefore, if grouping

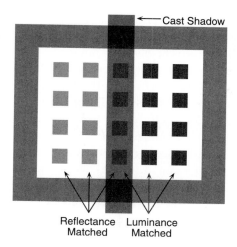

Reflectance Matched   Luminance Matched

Figure 6.1.13 Grouping and lightness constancy. When the central column of squares was seen as being in shadow, they were grouped with those of the same reflectance (on the left) rather than those of the same retinal luminance (on the right). This result shows that grouping by achromatic color similarity is influenced by lightness constancy. (After Rock, Nijhawan, Palmer, & Tudor, 1992.)

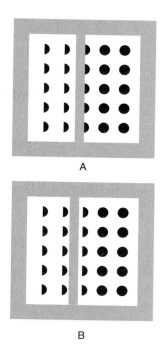

A

B

Figure 6.1.14 Grouping and visual completion. The central column of half circles was grouped more often with the complete ones to their right than with the half-circles to the left when they were seen as partly occluded (A) than when they were seen in their entirety (B). (After Palmer, Neff, & Beck, 1996.)

were based on relatively early processing of image structure, the central squares would be grouped with the luminance-matched ones on the right. If it were based on relatively late processing after perception of shadows had been achieved, they would group with the reflectance-matched ones on the left. The results showed that grouping followed the predictions of the post-constancy grouping hypothesis: Similarity grouping was governed by the perceived lightness of the squares rather than by their retinal luminance. Other conditions ruled out the possibility that this result was due to simple luminance ratios of the squares to their backgrounds.

Perceptual grouping is also affected by visual completion (Palmer, Neff, & Beck, 1996). As mentioned in Chapter 1, visual completion refers to the fact that when observers see an object partly occluded by another, there is a strong tendency to perceive its shape as being completed behind the occluder. Many theorists believe that this process is relatively late, occurring after perceptual objects and depth relations have already been defined. If grouping by shape similarity is determined by completed shape, this would then be further evidence that it is a relatively late process.

Palmer, Neff, and Beck (1996) investigated whether grouping by shape similarity was determined by the

retinal shape of the incomplete elements or by the perceived shape of completed elements. Using the same type of displays as Rock et al. (1992), they constructed a display in which half-circles in the center column were generally perceived as whole circles partly occluded by a vertical strip, as shown in Figure 6.1.14A. An early view of grouping predicts that the central elements will be seen to group with the half-circles on the left because they have the retinal shape of a half-circle. A late view of grouping predicts that they will group with the full circles on the right because they are perceived as being completed behind the occluding strip.

As the reader can see, the central figures group to the right with the completed circles, indicating that grouping is based on similarity of completed shape rather than on retinal shape. The possibility that this outcome was determined by the presence of the occluding strip that divides the elements into two regions according to common region was ruled out by the control condition illustrated in Figure 6.1.14B. Here the occluding strip is

Organizing Objects and Scenes

simply moved a little further to the side to reveal the entire contour of the central elements, allowing their half-circular shape to be perceived unambiguously. Although common region had a measurable effect in their experiment, most subjects now perceived the central elements as being grouped with the half-circles on the left. These findings provide further evidence that grouping is a relatively complex and late process in vision.

Such results show that grouping cannot be attributed entirely to early, preconstancy visual processing. However, they are also compatible with the possibility that grouping is a temporally extended process that includes components at both early and later levels of processing. A provisional grouping might be determined at an early, preconstancy stage of image processing but might be overridden if later, object-based information (from depth, lighting conditions, occlusion, and the like) requires it. Evidence that this might be the case could come from cases in which early grouping can be shown to affect constancy operations, in which case grouping must precede constancy processing. Evidence of this sort has not been reported as such in the literature, but this may be because it has not yet been examined rather than because it does not exist. Another sort of evidence for both early and late grouping comes from experiments in which early and late grouping factors combine to produce intermediate results (e.g., Beck, 1975; Olson & Attneave, 1970).

6.1.5 Past Experience

Before we leave the topic of grouping, it is worth pointing out that Wertheimer (1923/1950) discussed one further factor in perceptual grouping that is seldom mentioned: **past experience**. The idea is that if elements have been previously associated in prior viewings, they will tend to be seen as grouped in present situations. Figure 6.1.15 illustrates the point. Initially, you will probably see this picture as a nearly random array of black regions on a white background. Once you are able to see it as a Dalmatian with its head down, sniffing along a street, the picture becomes dramatically reorganized with certain of the dots going together because they are part of the dog and others going together because they are part of the street. The interesting fact is that once you have seen the Dalmatian in this picture, you will continue to see it that way for the rest of your

life. Past experience can thus have a dramatic effect on grouping and organization, especially if the organization of the image is highly ambiguous.

The principle of past experience is fundamentally different from the other factors Wertheimer discussed in that it concerns not geometrical properties of the stimulus configuration itself, but rather the viewer's history with respect to the configuration. Perhaps partly for this reason, it has largely been ignored in subsequent presentations of Gestalt principles of grouping. Another reason may be that it is rather easy to show that other grouping factors can block recognition of even the most frequently seen objects (e.g., Gottschaldt, 1929). Figure 6.1.16 shows an example in which the very simple, common shape of a rectangular prism (Figure 6.1.16A) is completely hidden in a configuration (Figure 6.1.16B) in which good continuation, symmetry, and other intrinsic factors make the embedded prism nearly impossible to perceive. In fairness to past experience, it is important to realize that, unlike the Dalmatian example, in which the dots initially appear unorganized, the deck is stacked strongly against seeing the familiar embedded figure by the intrinsic principles of grouping.

One of the reasons the effects of familiarity and object recognition on grouping are theoretically interesting is because they suggest that grouping effects occur as late as object recognition. This should not be too surprising, because the stored representation of the object itself presumably includes information about how its various parts are grouped and related. If part of the object (say, the Dalmatian's head) is identified first, prior knowledge of the shapes of dogs' bodies and legs can be exploited in reorganizing the rest of the image to correspond to these structures. This further process of reorganization suggests that organization is probably occurring *throughout* perception, first at the image-based stage, later at the surface- and object-based stages, and finally at the category-based stage, each result superseding the ones before.

6.2 Region Analysis

The observant reader may have noticed an important gap in the story of perceptual organization as told by the Gestaltists: They neglected to explain how the "elements" of their analysis arise in the first place. Wer-

Figure 6.1.15 Effects of past experience on grouping. Once you see the Dalmatian in the center, it will forever change the grouping you perceive when viewing this picture. This change can only be attributed to past experience, which can have a dramatic effect on perceived organization of ambiguous images. (Photograph by R. C. James.)

theimer appears simply to have assumed the existence of such elements, as though it were so phenomenologically obvious that no analysis was required. If so, this is an example of the very experience error for which the Gestaltists often criticized others. The elements of Wertheimer's displays are not directly given by the structure of the stimulus array, but require an explanation, including an analysis of the factors that govern their existence as perceptual objects.

The obvious basis for the elements of perceptual experience that Wertheimer presupposed in his principles of grouping is an analysis of **regions**: bounded, 2-D areas that constitute spatial subsets of the image. As basic as the concept of a region is to image processing, we have not yet discussed it explicitly, having concentrated mainly on the essentially one-dimensional constructs of lines and edges. In Chapter 4, for example, we discussed at great length how 1-D edges might be located but said very little about why edges might be important. In Chapter 5 we found that edges were involved in several crucial aspects of depth perception, such as edge interpretation and perspective information. Now we will consider another important aspect of their perceptual function: as boundaries that define 2-D regions. Bounded regions are central to perceptual organization because they may well define the first level of fully 2-D units on which subsequent visual processing is based.

Organizing Objects and Scenes

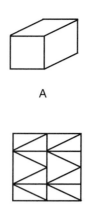

A

B

Figure 6.1.16 Intrinsic grouping factors can overcome past experience. Perception of the familiar shape of a rectangular prism (A) can be blocked by other grouping factors when it is embedded in the context shown in part B.

6.2.1 Uniform Connectedness

Palmer and Rock (1994a) provide an explicit analysis of how Wertheimer's presupposed elements might be formed in terms of an organizational principle they call **uniform connectedness**: the tendency to perceive connected regions of uniform image properties—e.g., luminance, color, texture, motion, and disparity—as the initial units of perceptual organization.[1] As we will see, the principle of uniform connectedness also forms a crucial link between the literature on edge detection discussed in Chapter 4 and that on perceptual organization and grouping discussed in this chapter.

Let us consider the elements in Wertheimer's original displays as examples of how organization into regions by uniform connectedness might occur as an initial stage in perceptual organization. The dots, lines, and rectangles in Figures 6.1.2A–6.1.2F are all connected regions of uniform luminance, and they correspond to the elements to which Wertheimer appealed in his analysis of grouping. The V's in Figure 6.1.3A, the lines in Figures 6.1.2G and 6.1.2H, the X-shaped drawing in Figure 6.1.2I, and the hourglass-shaped contour in Figure 6.1.2J are also uniform connected regions according to Palmer and Rock's analysis, but their relation to Wertheimer's "elements" is slightly more complex and will be considered more fully later.

The powerful effect of uniform connectedness on perceptual organization can be demonstrated in simple displays of dots like those used by Wertheimer, as illustrated in Figure 6.2.1. Part A shows that a row of uniformly spaced dots of different luminance are seen as unitary entities, and part B shows that the same is true for regions that are defined by differently oriented texture elements. Parts C and D show that such regions merge into larger, more complex unitary elements when they are connected by regions defined by the same property, whereas parts E and F show that when they are connected by regions of different properties, they are no longer perceived as fully unitary elements.

One might at first think that uniform connectedness is nothing more than the principle of similarity operating on the basis of luminance and color. For example, if the tiny patch of light falling on each retinal receptor were taken as an element, could uniform connected regions not be explained by grouping these elements according to similarity of luminance and color? Perhaps this is how Wertheimer himself thought about the organization of elements. But sameness of color is not sufficient to explain the perceptual unity of uniform connected regions because it does not account for the difference between *connected* regions of homogeneous color and *disconnected* ones. That is, without the additional constraint of connectedness, there is no basis for predicting that two black areas within the same dot or bar are any more closely related than comparable black areas within two different dots or bars.[2] Phenomenologically speaking, there is no doubt that each individual dot is more tightly organized as a perceptual object than is any pair of separate dots. This observation suggests the hypothesis that uniform connectedness is an important principle of perceptual organization.

---

[1] Koffka (1935) foreshadowed the idea of uniform connectedness in his discussion of perceptual organization, but he did not examine the implications of his observations, and his brief remarks appear not to have influenced subsequent theories until the rediscovery of the concept by Palmer and Rock (1994a).

[2] One other way of accounting for this fact is to appeal to associative grouping (Geisler, in press). The idea of associative grouping is that if A is grouped with B and B is grouped with C, then A will be grouped with C. This hypothesis can be used to explain why the points within a uniform connected region are grouped more strongly with each other than with those of points in other regions.

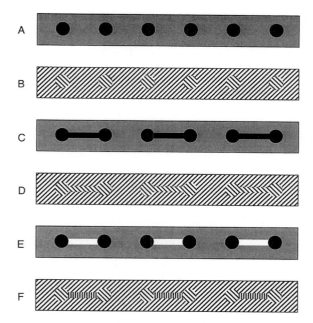

Figure 6.2.1 Uniform connectedness. Observers perceive connected regions of uniform visual properties as unitary elements whether they are defined by luminance (A and C), texture (parts B and D), or other simple visual properties. Similar elements defined by different properties (E and F) do not have the same unitary nature as those defined by uniform connectedness.

Palmer and Rock (1994a, 1994b) argue that uniform connectedness cannot be reduced to any principle of grouping because uniform connectedness is not a principle of grouping at all.[3] Their reasoning is that grouping principles presuppose the existence of independent elements that are to be grouped together, whereas uniform connectedness is defined on an unsegregated image. For this reason, uniform connectedness must logically operate *before* any principles of grouping can take effect. This is just another way of saying that because uniform connectedness is the process responsible for forming elements in the first place, it must occur before any process that operates on such elements.

If uniform connectedness is so fundamental in perceptual organization, it is important to understand why. Palmer and Rock argue that it is because of its informational value for designating connected objects (or parts of objects) in the world. As a general rule, if an area of the retinal image constitutes a homogeneous connected region, it almost certainly comes from the light reflected from a single connected object in the environment. This is not invariably true, of course, for the pattern on a camouflaged animal sometimes merges with identically colored regions of the background in its natural habitat, as illustrated in Figure 6.1.8. This is yet another example of a case in which perception goes astray whenever the heuristic assumptions underlying a perceptual process fail to hold. Even so, such situations are quite rare, and uniform connectedness is indeed an excellent heuristic for finding image regions corresponding to parts of connected objects in the environment. It therefore makes good sense for the visual system to make a first pass at organizing an image into objects by segregating it into uniform connected regions.

On the basis of this reasoning, Palmer and Rock suggest that uniform connectedness is the first principle of 2-D perceptual organization to operate and the foundation on which all later organization rests. The goal of this initial analysis is to divide the image into a set of mutually exclusive regions—called a **partition** of the image—much like a stained-glass window or a paint-by-numbers template. The regions thus identified can then be further organized by other processes such as discriminating figure from ground, grouping two or more regions together, and parsing a single region into two or more subregions. A flowchart capturing Palmer and Rock's (1994a) view of the relations among these organizational processes is shown in Figure 6.2.2. Later in this chapter we will consider the additional organizational process of figure/ground determination, and in the next chapter, we will consider parsing. But before we do, we must examine in more detail how an image might be partitioned into uniform connected regions.

6.2.2 Region Segmentation

The process of dividing an image into mutually exclusive areas based on uniformity of an image-based property, such as luminance, chromatic color, texture,

---

[3] Note that *element* connectedness is a principle of grouping, but *uniform* connectedness is not. These are two different factors of perceptual organization in Palmer and Rock's (1994a) theory that have quite different interpretations.

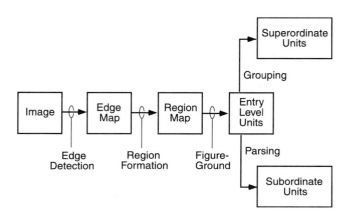

Figure 6.2.2 A flowchart of Palmer and Rock's (1994a) theory of perceptual organization. After edges are detected, regions are formed, and figure/ground principles operate to form entry-level units. Grouping and parsing can then occur in any order to form higher and lower units in the part/whole hierarchy. (After Palmer & Rock, 1994a.)

motion, or binocular disparity, is called **region segmentation**. It is the process that underlies the principle of uniform connectedness. There are two obvious ways of approaching this task. One is to explicitly detect the sameness (or similarity) of adjacent portions of the image. Although this is a logical possibility to which we will return shortly, there are good reasons to believe that the visual system actually detects differences (or gradients) in local visual properties that divide one region from another and that this is the basis of region segmentation.

Boundary-Based Approaches. At least indirectly, we have already discussed a possible mechanism for the boundary-based approach to region segmentation: edge-detection algorithms (see Section 4.3.2). Whenever luminance edges form a closed contour, they necessarily define two regions: the fully bounded inside and the partly bounded outside. An image can therefore be segmented into a set of connected regions by using an edge detection algorithm to locate closed contours. This idea forms an effective theoretical bridge between the well-known physiological and computational work on edge detection and the Gestalt work on perceptual organiza-

tion. Specifically, it suggests that 1-D edge detection may be the first step in perceptual organization, occurring as part of the process of 2-D region segmentation whose purpose is to find regions of roughly uniform connected areas in the image.

We described Marr and Hildreth's (1980) zero-crossing algorithm for edge detection in some detail in Section 4.3. There are other algorithms that produce similar results, such as Canny's (1986) edge detector, because they all work by explicitly locating a gradient (or graded change) in luminance. In the Marr-Hildreth algorithm, this is accomplished by convolving the image with a set of second-order edge operators and detecting zero-crossings in the output. One advantage of the Marr-Hildreth scheme from the current perspective is that edges defined by zero-crossings necessarily form closed contours. They therefore implicitly define a partition of the image, as illustrated in Figure 6.2.3.[4] Given these edges, each pixel can be assigned to one and only one image region.

Algorithms for detecting luminance edges can thus be used to partition the image into connected regions of approximately uniform luminance. For some exceedingly simple, noise-free geometrical displays—such as the ones used to demonstrate the classical principles of grouping in Figure 6.1.2—luminance edge algorithms would be sufficient to segment the image into the same objects people perceive in viewing them. In most naturally occurring images, however, many other factors must be taken into consideration to determine the regions that a human observer might identify as such. Consider more carefully the example shown in Figure 6.2.3. Part A shows the original image, and part B shows its segmentation into regions by zero-crossings. Notice that this edge operator has located many regions that seem perceptually spurious. Some of them result from relatively small differences in luminance that can be eliminated simply by merging adjacent regions between which there is a sufficiently low-contrast edge (Yakimovsky, 1976).

More importantly, however, there are also distinct regions defined by relatively large luminance differences

---

[4] Not all edge detection algorithms have this convenient property of forming closed contours, however. For those that do not (e.g., Canny, 1986), complex additional processing can be required to group the piecewise

edges into extended contours and to use these contours to define 2-D regions.

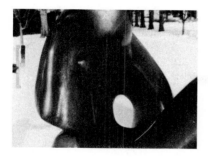

A

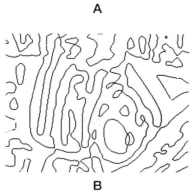

B

Figure 6.2.3 An example of a local edge-based approach to partitioning an image. The Marr-Hildreth edge algorithm has been used to divide the image of a glossy sculpture (A) into connected regions of approximately uniform luminance (B). Some regions correspond to significant parts of the object; others correspond to highlights, shadows, or spurious factors. (From Marr & Hildreth, 1980.)

that correspond to different regions of the same perceived object. Many cases result from the interaction of lighting and surface conditions, such as shadows and reflective highlights. Such regions must eventually be unified by lightness constancy processes. For example, there are quite large regions of high luminance in Figure 6.2.3 that are grouped together with adjacent dark regions, all of which constitute the sculpture's dark surface. This perception of a uniformly dark, glossy surface results from the light regions being interpreted as highlights arising from reflected light.

Other examples of distinct regions in the image belonging to the same perceived object arise from occlusion. When one object is in front of another, blocking part of it from view, two or more distinct regions can be present in the image that we see as part of the same object. Grouping processes must then be used to put them together again. Phenomena such as shadows, highlights,

and occlusion indicate that many processes beyond region segmentation are required to determine the final organization of a realistic image into the objects that people perceive. We will consider some of these issues later in this chapter.

Region-Based Approaches. It is perhaps worth mentioning that boundary-based algorithms for region segmentation are quite different from the sort of processes that Gestalt theorists envisioned when they talked about grouping phenomena. Wertheimer's demonstrations and discussion of grouping by similarity suggest a more global process that "puts together" a set of discrete elements, perhaps by some process of "mutual attraction" due to common properties. This is quite unlike the boundary-finding approach to region segmentation that occurs as a by-product of edge detection. Gestalt ideas suggest that there may be other approaches to region segmentation that do not depend on a prior process of local edge detection but find regions much more directly. Indeed, it is even possible that edge detection is a result of region segmentation rather than its cause. That is, if a process finds uniform connected regions by some more global process of attraction, edges are defined implicitly by the boundaries between the regions. This is quite the opposite of an edge-based approach.

Although virtually all the algorithms for finding boundaries between regions that have been devised to date are essentially local processes, it may be preferable for them to be determined more globally. The edge operators defined by Marr and Hildreth, Canny, and others all find luminance gradients by performing computations over very restricted patches of the image. These local edges must then be integrated into a set of closed contours to find the regions into which the image will be segmented. This process can be computationally difficult and seldom produces intuitively satisfying segmentations of the scene into regions (e.g., Figure 6.2.4D, which shows the output of a Canny edge detector on the penguin image of Figure 6.2.4A).

A more global region-based procedure has recently been devised by Malik and his colleagues (Leung & Malik, 1998; Shi and Malik, 1997). Their graph theoretic approach does not start by finding edges or lines at all. Rather, it directly partitions the image into regions by finding the set of pixels that are simultaneously most similar within a given region and most dissimilar be-

Organizing Objects and Scenes

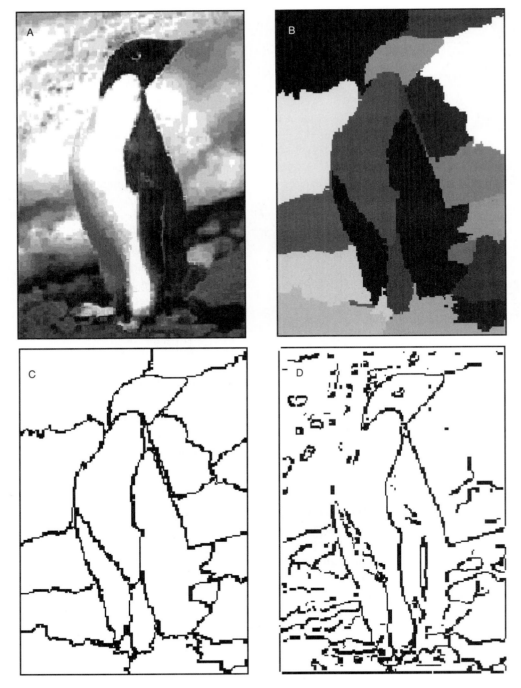

Figure 6.2.4 An example of a region-based approach to partitioning an image. Malik's "normalized cuts" algorithm identifies plausible uniformly connected regions (B) in this image of a penguin (A) using a global graph-theoretic approach based on maximizing similarities within regions and differences between them. Part C shows the boundaries of the regions in B, to be contrasted with the output of a Canny edge detector (D) on the same image. Notice that the edges in part D do not produce a coherent partition into closed regions without considerable further processing. (Parts A, B, and C from Leung & Malik, 1998; part D courtesy of Thomas Leung.)

tween regions. Similarity is defined in their algorithm by the integration of a number of Gestaltlike factors, such as similarity of luminance, color, texture, and motion.

Figure 6.2.4 shows an example of an image of a penguin (part A) and the regions into which their algorithm partitions it (part B). The boundaries of these regions, which are shown in part C, are quite different from the kinds of local edges found by standard edge detectors (part D). Notice, for example, that the output of the Canny edge detector seldom produces connected regions at all, whereas the region-based approach of Malik and his colleagues does so by design. Its regional parsing, while not perfect, is quite plausible and finds the important regions first, with minimal presence of the inconsequential disconnected edges that plague most other methods. Although it is not yet clear how such a graph-theoretic approach might be implemented in the brain, this work is an important reminder that the local edge-based approach to region segmentation is not the only way, much less the best way, to partition an image into uniform connected regions.

Evidence from Stabilized Images. We have suggested that edge detection, however it might actually be computed, is a likely mechanism for segmenting the image into different regions, but we have not yet provided any evidence for this claim. As it turns out, there is some striking support for it from experiments on the perception of **stabilized images**: images presented so that they are completely stationary on the retina (see Section 11.1). Strange as it may seem, the visual system actually stops responding (or adapts) to optical structure in the retinal image if there is no change over time. (Recall from Chapter 1 that this is why we don't perceive the blind spot or the blood vessels in our retina.) The startling result of the experiments on stabilized images is that after viewing one for more than a few seconds, it fades away completely!

The relevance of stabilized images to the claim that edge detection is the basis of region segmentation is that it supports the conclusion that people experience the shape and color of regions solely on the basis of edge information. Perhaps the most striking demonstration comes from a simple but elegant experiment by Krauskopf (1963). He presented observers with a central red circle surrounded by a green annulus (ring). Under normal viewing conditions, it looks like a red circle inside a

Figure 6.2.5 Simulation of stabilized contours. Stare at the black dot at the center for 30–60 seconds, and the fuzzy inner circle will disappear and be filled in by the surrounding gray. (See text for details.)

green ring. But Krauskopf stabilized the inner contour between the red and green portions of the visual field without stabilizing the outer one. The astonishing result is that the inner red disk disappears and is filled in by green to create the perception of a single large green circle!

You can experience a closely related phenomenon by staring at the dot in the middle of Figure 6.2.5 for a minute or so. Because you cannot hold your eyes steady enough to stabilize the inner edge completely, it has been made "fuzzy" so that the small movements your eyes make involuntarily have only small effects on your visual system. As a result, after staring at the black dot for long enough that your visual system adapts to the fuzzy inner contour, the light center region disappears and is filled in by the darker surrounding gray. If you then make a large eye movement, the inner region will reappear because the fuzzy edge is once again perceived.

Krauskopf's results are just what one would expect if the perceived color and boundaries of regions were determined exclusively by edge information. Once adaptation to the inner edge is complete (because of its stabilization on the retina), only the outer edge has any effect on the visual system. Thus, the situation is the same as when only a large green circle is present: the presence of an outer green edge with no further edges inside it. That is precisely what people perceive when

Organizing Objects and Scenes

the interior edge is stabilized, despite the continued physical presence of the inner red circle on the retina.

This remarkable phenomenon might seem like a mere laboratory curiosity, but it actually occurs all the time in normal everyday vision. As we mentioned in Section 1.3.2, there are two kinds of filling-in phenomena that produce visual experience: in the blind spot and where the shadows of blood vessels fall over receptors. These are naturally stabilized images, since they move with the retina at all times. As a result, we are quite literally blind to them under normal viewing conditions.

Parts and Parsing. We have now discussed two fundamental processes of perceptual organization: region segmentation and grouping. We have further hypothesized that region segmentation must be the earlier, more primitive process because it defines the elements on which grouping processes operate. But another important process is involved in the organization of perceptual objects that we have not yet considered: dividing a single element into parts. This process is called **parsing**.

Parsing is an important aspect of perceptual organization because it determines what subregions of a perceptual unit are perceived as "going together" most coherently. To illustrate, consider again the uniform connected regions of Figure 6.2.1C. The principle of uniform connectedness defines each as a single region, and this conforms to our experience of them as single objects. But we also experience them as having clear and obvious parts: namely, two circular parts connected by a bar. Also consider the X-shaped figure in Figure 6.1.2I. Despite its global unity, the analysis of its organization into two intersecting lines according to good continuation requires that it be analyzed into four segments, as Wertheimer claimed, pairs of which are then grouped together. According to the analysis by Palmer and Rock (1994a), however, unity of the whole figure arises first, followed by parsing into the four segments. The four segments can then be grouped by good continuation as Wertheimer suggested.

How does parsing divide objects into parts? First, notice that it clearly depends on the shape of the object. A filled circle or a straight line, for instance, has no natural parsings, whereas two overlapping circles or two intersecting lines do, as illustrated in Figure 6.2.6. If we examine the places at which it is natural to divide such figures, it turns out that they divide at **deep con-**

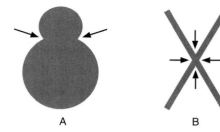

Figure 6.2.6 Parsing at concave discontinuities. Arrows indicate the location of concave discontinuities in the contours of these uniform connected regions. They can be divided into parts at pairs of such discontinuities.

cavities: points at which the contour undergoes a sharp bend toward the interior of the region (Hoffman & Richards, 1984). In Figure 6.2.6, arrows point to all the concave discontinuities. It shows that parsing occurs where there are pairs of such discontinuities. We will have a great deal more to say about parts and parsing in Chapters 7 and 8 when we discuss object shape in detail. For now, the important question is how parsing relates to the region segregation and grouping processes about which we have already spoken.

Like grouping, parsing must logically come after region segregation, for parsing also presupposes the existence of an element to be divided, and we have claimed that region segregation forms such elements. Notice that parsing is essentially the opposite of grouping, since it takes a single perceptual unit and divides it into two or more units, rather than taking two or more units and putting them together into a single one. But there is no constraint on the order in which parsing and grouping must occur relative to each other; they could very well occur simultaneously. This is why the flowchart of Palmer and Rock's theory (Figure 6.2.2) shows grouping and parsing taking place at the same time after regions have been defined.

Figure 6.2.7 gives an example due to Palmer and Rock (1994a) of how these three organizational processes— region segregation, grouping, and parsing—relate to each other in arriving at a complex perceptual organization. The stimulus array whose organization will be considered is shown at the top of the figure. In natural language, one might describe it as a row consisting of three pairs of double-lobed figures. Notice first that this description implies a hierarchy of levels. At the highest level, there is the whole figure: the "row." At the next

Image

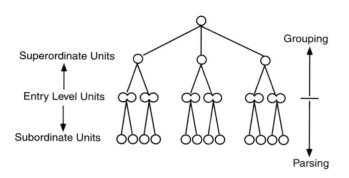

Grouping

Superordinate Units

Entry Level Units

Subordinate Units

Parsing

Figure 6.2.7 Constructing a part/whole hierarchy according to Palmer and Rock's theory. The image at the top shows the input array. The graph below shows the various levels of organization that exist in this simple example and how they might be derived from entry-level units consisting of uniform connected elements. (From Palmer & Rock, 1994b.)

lower level, there are the "three pairs" of figures. Just below that, there are the "figures" themselves. And at the bottom, there are the "lobes" into which the figures can be seen as divided. How might this sort of hierarchical organization be achieved by organizational processes?

According to Palmer and Rock's theoretical account, region segregation must operate first because it is the only organizational process that works on unorganized images. Region formation processes of some sort partition the image into a set of nonoverlapping, uniform, connected regions. At this point, another organizational process, called "figure/ground organization" must operate, but we will defer its discussion until a bit later in this chapter. Figure/ground organization designates which regions are to be taken as objects (or figures) and which as background (or ground) by assigning each contour as belonging to one side or the other (the figural side). The regions designated as figures then constitute the first units of perceptual organization and provide the initial entry into the part/whole hierarchy, as indicated in Figure 6.2.7. Palmer and Rock call the units at this level **entry-level units**.

Once the entry-level units are in place, the rest of the part/whole hierarchy can be constructed by the appli-

cation of grouping and parsing processes. That is, entry-level units can be either aggregated into superordinate units at a higher level by the operation of grouping processes or divided into subordinate units at a lower level by the operation of parsing processes. Logic does not dictate the order in which these two processes are applied. Indeed, they may operate simultaneously to extend the part/whole hierarchy in both directions at once. In the present example, grouping unifies pairs of entry-level figures into two-unit groups and then unifies the three pairs into the whole row of figures. The level subordinate to the entry level is constructed by parsing each uniformly connected figure into two circular parts at the pair of concave discontinuities in the center of each entry-level unit.

Palmer and Rock's (1994a) theoretical analysis attempts to bridge the gap between classical Gestalt ideas about perceptual organization and modern computational theories in vision science. Although it fulfills this function reasonably well, there are certainly other possibilities (e.g., Geissler, in press; Rensink & Enns, 1995). The fact that there is as yet no evidence that entry-level units are processed before other levels in the part/whole hierarchy suggests that Palmer and Rock's proposals should be viewed with caution.

6.2.3 Texture Segregation

Palmer and Rock (1994a) claimed that uniform connected regions could be defined by higher-order properties than luminance and color. This claim is based largely on the extensive literature on **texture segregation** showing that regions can be perceived solely on the basis of texture information. At this point, it would be appropriate to give a clear, unambiguous definition of "texture," but this is not an easy matter, as we shall see.

Texture segregation is usually studied in images composed of many discrete elements, such as the display shown in Figure 6.2.8. The lower-right quadrant is effortlessly perceived as different from the rest of the circle, even without consciously perceiving the shapes of the individual elements that comprise it. Texture segregation seems closely related both to classical grouping and to region segmentation, but in different ways. Its connection to classical grouping is that it can be considered the result of grouping texture elements according to the Gestalt principle of similarity. As we noted earlier, however, not all similarities are equally

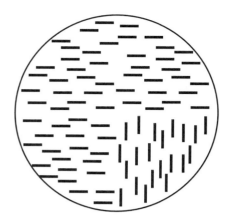

Figure 6.2.8 *Texture segregation. The visual system easily divides this image into two different regions based on the orientation of the texture elements. (After Beck, 1966.)*

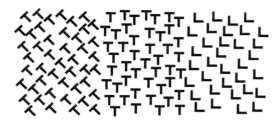

A. Texture Segregation

B. Shape Similarity

Figure 6.2.9 *Texture segregation versus shape similarity. Textures segregate more strongly on the basis of the orientation of component line segments than on pattern identity (A), whereas configural properties dominate line orientation in perception of similarity among whole figures (B).*

effective in grouping (see Figure 6.1.3), and Wertheimer didn't study the salience of different similarities. Texture segregation can also be understood as a special case of region segmentation, one in which edge operators detect spatial gradients in some as-yet-undefined dimensions of texture, analogous to detecting the abrupt changes in luminance we discussed in Chapter 4. As we will see, recent theoretical advances in understanding texture segregation have been made through the latter approach, extending region segmentation techniques to textural properties.

Discovering the Features of Texture. The first major discoveries about the nature of texture perception were made by Jacob Beck, a perceptual psychologist at the University of Oregon. He had subjects perform tasks such as detecting which region in a display of many discrete texture elements look most different from the rest, as illustrated in Figure 6.2.9A. For example, you probably perceive the tilted T's in the leftmost region of Figure 6.2.9A as being different from the upright T's in the center region more quickly and easily than you perceive the upright L's in the rightmost region as being different from the upright T's in the center.

In exploring people's performance in this task, Beck began with the hypothesis that displays containing a large number of elements would be grouped on the basis of their shape similarity, as one would predict from the Gestalt principle of similarity. But he soon dis-

covered that the factors governing texture segregation are not necessarily the same as those that determine the shape similarity of the very same elements when they are perceived as individual figures. For instance, the texture segregation evident in Figure 6.2.9A is the opposite of what would be predicted from simple shape similarity ratings. When subjects judged these same elements for similarity in shape as individual figures (see Figure 6.2.9B), a tilted T was judged to be more similar to an upright T than was an upright L. From the results of many such experiments, Beck (1972, 1982) concluded that texture segregation resulted from detecting differences in the feature density—meaning the number of features per unit of area—of certain simple attributes, such as line orientation, overall brightness, color, size, and movement.

Texture Segregation as a Parallel Process. Other important ideas about texture segregation were introduced by Bela Julesz, the inventor of random dot stereograms. He pointed out that textures could be discriminated in either of two ways: through "normal" texture segregation, which takes place effortlessly and simultaneously over the whole visual field, or through what he called "conscious scrutiny." According to Julesz, scrutiny involves sequentially focusing attention on different parts of the display in an attempt to find shape

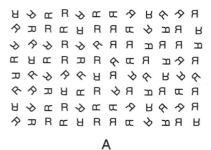

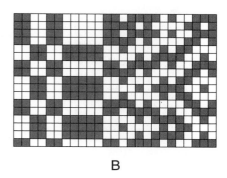

A

B

Figure 6.2.10 Examples of Julesz's texture discrimination stimuli. (A) Physically different textures (normal versus mirror-reversed R's) that do not segregate without scrutiny. (B) A counter-example to Julesz's early theory that texture discrimination is based on dipole statistics. (See text for details.) (After Julesz, 1981.)

differences between individual elements. He therefore claimed that normal texture segregation was a *preattentive* process, one that occurs before the operation of focused attention. (In Section 11.2.5 we will argue that although such processing operates before *focused* attention to individual objects, it does not happen before attentional processing in general.)

In his research on texture segregation, Julesz also discovered many cleverly constructed textures that could not be segregated in parallel, despite well-defined physical differences in the elements of which they were comprised. Figure 6.2.10A shows an example: Normal R's on the left side cannot be discriminated from mirror-reflected R's on the right if they are randomly oriented. He conjectured that physically different textures could be segregated if and only if they had different statistical properties based on the lightness of pairs of points—called the **dipole statistics** of the image—and many experiments seemed to support his hypothesis (see Julesz, 1975). Eventually, he discovered patterns like the

one shown in Figure 6.2.10B, which have the same second-order and even third-order statistics yet are nevertheless easily discriminable as textures. Such examples forced Julesz to give up his analysis based on statistical properties and to move toward a theory like Beck's. He eventually proposed that textures are segregated by detecting changes in the density of certain simple, local textural features that he called **textons** (Julesz, 1981).

According to Julesz (1981), there are three types of textons: (1) elongated blobs defined by their color, length, width, orientation, binocular disparity, and flicker rate; (2) line terminators; and (3) line crossings or intersections. He further suggested that there are detectors in the visual system that are sensitive to these textons and that texture segregation takes place through the differential activation of these texton detectors. Notice that Julesz's textons sound similar to the critical features ascribed to cortical cells in V1 by Hubel and Wiesel (1968) and like some of the primitive elements of Marr's (1982) primal sketch, as described in Chapter 4.

This work on texture segregation by both Julesz and Beck was important because it began to forge theoretical links among three interrelated topics: perceptual findings on texture segregation, the physiology of visual cortex, and computational theories of vision. From these beginnings, new theories have emerged that attempt to present a unified account of their interrelations.

A Theory of Texture Segregation. Vision scientists Jitendra Malik and Pietro Perona (1990) have proposed a biologically plausible, computational theory of texture segregation based on detecting edges in the output of known cortical cell types. Their theory—which we mentioned very briefly in Section 4.3.3—consists of the three stages illustrated in Figure 6.2.11: a filtering stage, a lateral inhibition stage, and a gradient computation (or edge detection) stage. We will consider this model in some detail for two reasons. First, it is among the most successful theories of texture segregation to date. Second, it is a good example of the value of an interdisciplinary approach to vision. Contributions from perceptual, biological, and computational science were combined to produce a significant advance over what would have been achieved within any of the individual approaches alone.

        Organizing Objects and Scenes

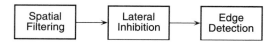

Figure 6.2.11 The overall structure of Malik and Perona's three-stage theory of texture segregation. (See text for details.)

The initial filtering stage models the output of V1 cells as described in Section 4.1. The filters used by Malik and Perona include center/surround receptive fields (Figures 6.2.12A and 6.2.12B) and variously oriented bar detector fields (Figure 6.2.12C). Each of these filter types represents a textural dimension that the visual system can use to segregate regions on the basis of texture. Many filters of each type are distributed densely over the visual field so that the output of a complete set at every position approximates the convolution of the image with the receptive field of that filter type. (See Section 4.3 for an explanation of convolution.)

Figure 6.2.13A shows a texture of elongated blobs at different orientations. Figure 6.2.13B shows the output at every position for this image of the set of dark-bar filters whose receptive field is shown in the bottom right corners. Figure 6.2.13C shows the output at every posi-

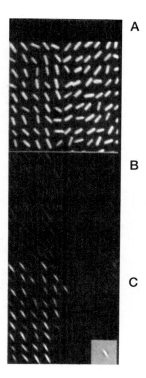

Figure 6.2.13 Examples of the output of the filtering stage of Malik and Perona's theory. Part A shows an input image, part B shows the output for dark-bar filters at the left-oblique orientation (shown at bottom right) for a sample of positions in the visual field, and part C shows the output for a similar set of light-bar filters. The output of the light-bar filters provides good information for discriminating between the left and right halves of the image. (From Malik & Perona, 1990.)

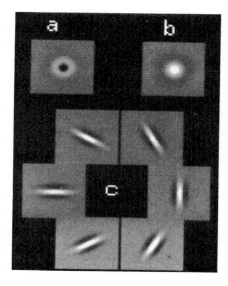

Figure 6.2.12 Examples of filters in the first stage of Malik and Perona's theory of texture segregation. Some have rotationally symmetric center/surround receptive fields (A and B); others have oriented bar detector (or Gabor filter) receptive fields (C). All are similar to receptive fields found in cortical V1 neurons. (From Malik & Perona, 1990.)

tion for the light-bar filters at this orientation. These output images represent the convolution of the input image (part A) with the appropriate filter type. In a neurophysiological implementation of the model, the brightness at each position in this output image indicates the amount of neural activity that would result in a cell with the given receptive field at the corresponding position in the visual field. The output image therefore corresponds roughly to a retinotopic map of the activation of a sheet of cells that have the specified receptive field.

Notice that the bright-bar filter (at the bottom of Figure 6.2.13) produces a much larger output to the left side of the texture than to the right side. This is because the bright-bar filter is tuned to an orientation very similar to that of the blobs on the left and quite different from that of the blobs on the right. Thus, there is a large difference (or *gradient*) between the left and right halves of the visual field for this filter. In the output image this difference is represented by the large difference in the overall brightness of the left and right sides. (Notice that although this difference exists *implicitly* in the output of the filtering stage, it is not detected *explicitly* until the final stage of the model.) In contrast, the dark-bar filters at the same orientation (Figure 6.2.13B) produce only a weak response to the left side and therefore only a very slight gradient for the same input image.

The second stage of the Malik-Perona model imposes lateral inhibition between spatially nearby cells that have different receptive fields. The purpose of this lateral inhibition is to suppress or reduce spurious weak responses. Through this mechanism, for example, the weak responses of the dark-bar filters (in Figure 6.2.13B) would be suppressed by the strong responses of the light-bar filters (in Figure 6.2.13C).[5] Although it is not yet known exactly what inhibitory interconnections exist in visual cortex, Malik and Perona's model does not contradict any known biological facts and is plausible, given current knowledge of visual cortex.

The third and final stage of the model explicitly computes the strength of texture gradients. It takes the output of the inhibitory interaction stage for each filter type and analyzes it through a set of very coarse (low-resolution) edge detection operators at different orientations and positions, much as we discussed in Section 4.3.2 when we considered computational theories of edge detection. Malik and Perona's edge operator is large enough relative to the texture elements that it averages over the output of many individual filters with the same receptive fields. Separate analyses of this type are performed for each set of receptive-field filters. The final texture gradient is defined as the maximum gradient over all filter types. Texture boundaries are then located at local maxima of the output of this gradient computation stage.

Malik and Perona's theory has many desirable attributes:

1. Unlike Beck's feature theory and Julesz's texton theory, it is completely specified in explicit computational

Figure 6.2.14 Texture boundaries in part of a painting by Gustav Klimt. The Malik and Perona algorithm found the boundaries indicated on the right when given the image shown on the left. (From Malik & Perona, 1990.)

terms. This means that it can be—and indeed has been—implemented as a computer program that actually performs texture segregation on images.

2. Also unlike Beck's and Julesz's theories, it applies to any sort of image, not just ones composed of discrete elements. To illustrate this fact, Malik and Perona used their computer implementation to find texture boundaries from a portion of a painting by Gustav Klimt, as shown in Figure 6.2.14. Although one might quibble about small deviations from what people typically perceive, the model does a credible job of capturing the essential texture boundaries in this complex image.

3. A measure of how strongly various textures are discriminated by the model corresponds closely to human performance on the same textures. Figure 6.2.15 compares human and computer performance on 10 widely different textures. It shows data from human performance in a texture segregation task (Kröse, 1986, 1987) and the predictions of the model in units that are scaled to correspond to the human data. There is some room for improvement, but the overall agreement is impressive.

4. Malik and Perona's model of texture segregation integrates several different factors into an overall prediction for any arbitrary stimulus image. It is true that it concerns only a very small subset of Wertheimer's classic principles of grouping—namely, similarities related to shape and perhaps color—but it is nevertheless an important first step.

5. Finally, the textural dimensions of their model correspond more closely to the receptive field structure of the

---

[5] The reasons for believing that this process might occur are based on analyzing people's ability to segregate certain critical texture displays rather than on physiological knowledge. The logic underlying this inference is too complex to explain here, however.

Organizing Objects and Scenes

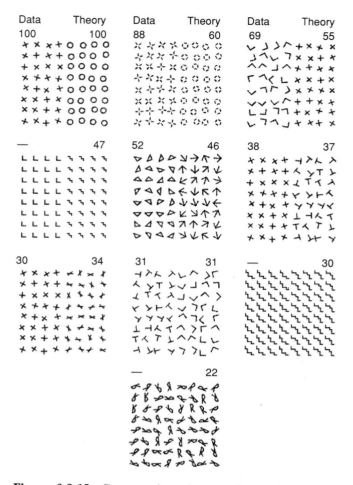

Data	Theory	Data	Theory	Data	Theory
100	100	88	60	69	55

| — | 47 | 52 | 46 | 38 | 37 |

| 30 | 34 | 31 | 31 | — | 30 |

| — | 22 |

Figure 6.2.15 Correspondence between data and theory in texture segregation. Ten textures are shown together with two empirical measures of their discriminability by human observers and corresponding predictions by Malik and Perona's theory of texture segregation. (After Malik & Perona, 1990.)

cells that they model than to naturalistic features of the environment. Thus, the model suggests that the texture processing system may be one of many different modules based on the output of early cortical cells, as suggested in Figure 4.3.20.

It is currently an open question whether texture segregation algorithms such as Malik and Perona's can also account for cases of classical grouping by similarity as discussed by Wertheimer. We have taken the view here that texture segregation may be more usefully viewed as an instance of region segmentation based on textural properties than as an instance of classical similarity grouping,

but this distinction may be unfounded. If so, algorithms like Malik and Perona's may be extendable to account for both sorts of phenomena, as suggested by Nothdurft (1992). Still, it is clear that other grouping phenomena, particularly those of unit formation based on closure, continuity, and certain cases of common fate, are of a different sort altogether and require a different kind of theory. We will consider one attempt in this direction later in this chapter.

6.3 Figure/Ground Organization

If the goal of perceptual organization is to construct a hierarchy consisting of parts, objects, and groups, region segmentation can be no more than a very early step, because image-based regions seldom correspond directly to environmental objects in naturally occurring images. Even in the simplest artificial visual displays, such as the one shown in Figure 6.3.1A, this is not the case. Region segmentation will partition this image into two uniform connected regions, one white and the other black; but when you look at it, you will almost certainly see either a white object on a black background or a black object on a white background. This particular display is highly ambiguous, so sometimes you see a black thing with "pointed claws" and other times a white thing with "rounded fingers," as illustrated in the two unambiguous drawings below it (Figure 6.3.1B and Figure 6.3.1C, respectively).

This further aspect of perceptual organization, known as **figure/ground organization**, was discovered by Danish psychologist Edgar Rubin (1921). The "thing-like" region is referred to as the **figure**, and the "background-like" region as the **ground**. Rubin based his distinction on a phenomenological analysis of the differences between the subjective experiences for figures and grounds (see Table 6.3.1). Most importantly, the figure appears closer to the observer and has the shape imparted by the contour (that is, the contour "belongs to" or "is assigned to" the figural region rather than the ground). In contrast, the ground appears farther away and extends behind the contour. He also proposed that the figure looks denser than the same color would as ground, but this is a less important and more debatable claim.

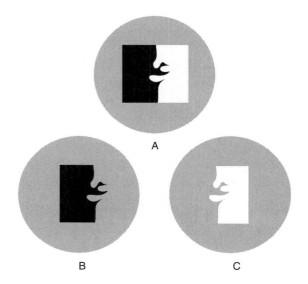

Figure 6.3.1 Ambiguous figure/ground organization. The black/white contour in the center of part A is usually assigned to either the left or the right region. The perception of a black, clawlike object (B) results from assigning the contour to the left region, and that of a white, fingerlike object (C) results from assigning it to the right region. (After Rock, 1975.)

Experimental results support Rubin's claim that people tend to perceive only one side of a contour as a thinglike figure. His own initial study (Rubin, 1921) was methodologically improved upon by Rock (1983) using the following recognition memory paradigm. Subjects were presented with a series of ambiguous figure/ground stimuli such as those shown in Figure 6.3.1A. Half of the subjects were asked to attend to the white figures, and the other half were asked to attend to the black figures. After the whole series was presented, subjects were shown a series of unambiguous gray test figures consisting of just one region. Some were regions they had originally seen as figures, some were ones they had originally seen as grounds, and some were ones they had never seen before. They were told to respond "old"

Table 6.3.1
Properties of figures versus grounds

Figure	Ground
Thinglike	Not thinglike
Closer to observer	Farther from observer
Bounded by contour	Extends behind contour
Shape defined by contour	No shape at contour

for any region that had appeared in the initial sequence. The results showed that subjects remembered the figural test shapes quite well but remembered the ground test shapes no better than chance. This striking difference in memory for the shape of figures versus grounds suggests either that subjects had never perceived the grounds as having shape in the first place or that they had selectively forgotten the shape of the grounds. Because the latter possibility seems highly unlikely, Rock endorsed the former interpretation, which was consistent with Rubin's initial analysis.

Such results show that the visual system has a strong preference to ascribe the contour to just one of its bordering regions and to perceive the other side as part of a surface extending behind it. The fact that the figure is always perceived as lying in front of the ground region further suggests that figure/ground organization is intimately related to depth perception, particularly to pictorial information from occlusion. In support of this idea, notice that all the distinctions between figure and ground listed in Table 6.3.1 are consistent with such a depth hypothesis. Indeed, figure/ground organization can be interpreted as part of the edge interpretation processes that we considered in Section 5.5.7, particularly those involved in labeling depth edges.

Figure 6.3.1 is highly ambiguous in its figure/ground organization in the sense that it is about equally easy to see the black and white regions as figure, but this is not always—or even usually—the case. Consider Figure 6.3.2, for instance. You immediately see a white bloblike figure on a gray background. Notice that it is also possible to see it as a gray rectangle with an irregular hole in it that reveals a white surface in the background, but that is almost never one's first perception. The fact that you see the "white blob" interpretation first and that it is much harder to achieve the "gray hole" interpretation shows that the visual system has distinct preferences for perceiving certain kinds of regions as figure. We will now consider what stimulus factors govern the assignment of figure and ground and how they relate to relevant ecological information about environmental scenes.

6.3.1 Principles of Figure/Ground Organization

Analogous to the Gestalt principles of perceptual grouping, the principles of figure/ground organization

Organizing Objects and Scenes

Figure 6.3.2 Unambiguous figure/ground organization. The white region in the center is always perceived as figure initially because it is surrounded by, smaller than, and more convex than the gray region. It is almost never seen as background through a hole in a square gray figure, at least unless this possibility is explicitly suggested.

are ceteris paribus rules, that is, rules in which a given factor has a stated effect if all other factors are eliminated or neutralized. Among the most important factors are the following:

1. *Surroundedness.* If one region is completely surrounded by another, the surrounded region is perceived as figure and the surrounding region as ground. This principle is illustrated in Figure 6.3.2 by the fact that it is much easier to see a white blob on a gray background than a hole in a gray surface revealing a white ground. Surroundedness is a very potent factor.

2. *Size.* All else being equal, the smaller region is perceived as the figure. This principle is also at work in Figure 6.3.2 because the white region is decidedly smaller than the surrounding gray one. But "all else" is not equal in this example because surroundedness is also at work. A purer example is the pinwheel pattern shown in Figure 6.3.3B, in which the black blades are usually seen as figure on a white ground because of their smaller size. Compare this version with the one in Figure 6.3.3A, in which the blades are equal in size and therefore maximally ambiguous as to which blades are figural.

3. *Orientation.* If the orientation of the equal-sized pinwheel blades is changed as illustrated in Figure 6.3.3C, the set that is vertical and horizontal tends to be perceived more frequently as figure than does the oblique set. Thus, orientation is another factor that affects figure/ground organization.

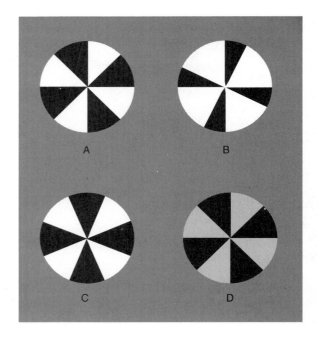

Figure 6.3.3 Principles of figure/ground organization. Part A is highly ambiguous as to whether the black or white pinwheel is seen as figure. In parts B, C, and D, the black pinwheel tends to be seen as figure owing to its smaller size (B), horizontal/vertical orientation (C), and higher contrast to the background (D).

4. *Contrast.* The white and black pinwheel displays have been presented on a gray background to eliminate the factor of contrast in figure/ground selection. All else being equal, the regions with greatest contrast to the surrounding area are taken as figural. This principle is exemplified in Figure 6.3.3D, in which the white blades have been darkened to reduce their contrast to the gray background, thus increasing the probability of the black blades being seen as figure.

5. *Symmetry.* A further property that Rubin found to influence figure/ground perception is symmetry: All else being equal, symmetrical regions tend to be perceived as figure. Its effect is illustrated in Figure 6.3.4A because one tends to see the symmetrical black regions as figure against a white ground.

6. *Convexity.* Another factor that operates in such displays is convexity: All else being equal, convex regions tend to be perceived as figure and concave ones as ground. This factor was called the "law of the inside" by Metzger (1953) and was later discussed as convexity by Kanizsa and Gerbino (1976), who showed that con-

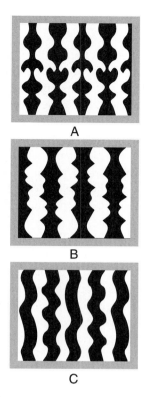

Figure 6.3.4 Symmetry, convexity, and parallelism in figure/ground organization. Part A demonstrates that symmetrical regions tend to be seen as figure rather than ground. Part B shows that convexity can override symmetry. Part C shows the importance of parallel contours. (Parts A and B after Kanizsa & Gerbino, 1976; part C after Metzger, 1953.)

vexity can overcome symmetry. In Figure 6.3.4B, for example, one tends to perceive the asymmetrical white regions as figure, even though the black regions are symmetrical, because the white ones are more convex than the black ones.

7. *Parallelism.* Yet another feature that favors figural status for a region is that its contours are parallel. Figure 6.3.4C shows an example due to Metzger (1953) in which the regions with parallel sides are usually perceived as figure rather than ground.

As qualitative, ceteris paribus rules, these principles of figure/ground organization have the same weaknesses as the principles of grouping, including the inability to predict the outcome when several conflicting factors are at work in the same display. Unfortunately, there has been little progress on this problem theoreti-

cally since Rubin made his initial discoveries. Kienker, Sejnowski, Hinton, and Schumacher (1986) have proposed a simple neural network architecture that produces some interesting figure/ground-like organization, but it has not been systematically evaluated against human perception in terms of known principles of figure/ground organization or their various combinations.

While we are comparing figure/ground organization with grouping, let us consider why we claimed earlier that figure/ground organization must operate before both grouping and parsing processes. The reason in the case of grouping is that the entry-level elements on which grouping operates must already have been differentiated from ground because, if they were not, each region would be grouped with its immediately adjacent regions by the principle of element connectedness (or proximity, if you prefer). However, if entry-level elements are identified only after figure/ground organization has operated, they will tend to be separated from each other by ground and can be sensibly grouped by the principles described earlier.

Parsing objects into parts (see Section 7.6.2) also requires prior organization into figure and ground for logical reasons. If parsing is based on dividing figures at deep concavities, as Hoffman and Richards (1984) have claimed, one must know which side of the contour constitutes the figure because concavity (versus convexity) can be defined only relative to the interior of a figure. The same curved contour, for example, is convex with respect to one side being the interior and concave with respect to the other side being the interior. Another telling fact is that the ground is not parsed into parts at its concavities; only the figure is. Thus figure/ground organization must operate initially before either parsing or grouping can sensibly take place.

6.3.2 Ecological Considerations

There is an almost unavoidable tendency to think that figure/ground organization might be determined simply by attending to one region rather than another. In looking at Figure 6.3.1, for instance, whichever region one first attends is usually seen as figure. The relation of attention to figure/ground organization is not so simple, however, for one can easily attend to a region as ground without its necessarily becoming figure.

Organizing Objects and Scenes

The ability to attend selectively to the perceptual ground suggests that figure/ground organization probably comes *before* attentional selection. Thus, the more likely dependency is that attention is drawn to the figure rather than that attention determines the figure. In other words, attention tends to be driven by figure/ground organization rather than the other way around. It actually makes a great deal of sense ecologically that people would attend to figures rather than grounds, because the figure is closer and therefore of more immediate interest and concern. Attention cannot be completely determined by figure/ground organization, however, for if it were, we would be unable to attend to the ground even if we tried. It thus seems clear that attention can be flexibly allocated to either figure or ground, depending on the goals and intentions of the observer, but that there is a strong bias to attend to figures.

Ecological considerations also lead to a functional hypothesis about why the visual system imposes figure/ground organization and why it is affected by the particular factors identified by Rubin and others. The functional role of figure/ground organization appears to be determining which 2-D image regions correspond to objects and which to spaces between objects. The link to attention is then that it makes sense to deploy attention to analyzing objects rather than the spaces between them, whose properties are largely accidental. This preference is adaptive for a variety of reasons, not the least of which is that objects are the primary entities of ecological importance.

Objects are also the entities that have stable properties either when the observer's viewpoint is changed or when one of the objects moves. After all, the shape of the ground region in the image is essentially an accident of the viewer's stationpoint and the particular objects that happen to be occluding it (Rock, 1983). Thus, in attending to figures rather than grounds, the perceiver is selectively processing the *nonaccidental features* of the visual field. (We will return to this concept of nonaccidentalness at the end of this chapter as a possible unifying principle for perceptual organization.) The contour seems to belong to the figure rather than the ground because, if the figure is closer, it actually *does*. Thus, the principles of figure/ground organization operate in the service of veridical perception of the environment.

From this viewpoint, the factors that influence figure/ground organization can be interpreted as relevant to distinguishing objects from the spaces between objects. Smaller size and surroundedness may be relevant because it is more likely that there is a small object in front of a larger one than that there is a hole in the larger object. Orientation may have its effect because most objects in the real world tend to be more gravitationally stable in either a horizontal or a vertical orientation than in oblique ones. Real-world objects also tend to be more convex than concave, and the regions of empty space around them tend to be correspondingly more concave than convex. Finally, objects are much more likely to have symmetrical or parallel sides than are the empty spaces between the objects, where such properties would arise only by accident. Thus the factors in figure/ground organization are systematically related to properties that distinguish 2-D regions that correspond to environmental objects from those that correspond to spaces between objects. They are therefore useful heuristics for distinguishing the regions that correspond to objects from those that correspond to their backgrounds.

6.3.3 Effects of Meaningfulness

We have just argued that the processes underlying figure/ground organization may be viewed as the way in which the visual system decides which regions correspond to objects (or significant parts of objects) and which ones are partly occluded surfaces of objects farther away. If this is the case, then it seems plausible that figure/ground processing might be influenced by whether the shape of a region corresponds to that of a known, meaningful object. Recent experiments by psychologist Mary Peterson and her colleagues have shown that figure/ground organization is indeed affected by this form of past experiences (e.g., Peterson & Gibson, 1991, 1993, 1994; Peterson, Harvey, & Weidenbacher, 1991).

In Peterson's experiments, subjects are shown ambiguous figure/ground images such as the ones depicted in Figure 6.3.5. Notice that in each case, one side is meaningful (the silhouette of a pineapple, a seahorse, and a woman's body) and the other is not. The two regions are roughly equal in terms of standard figure/ground principles, such as area, surroundedness, and convexity. Subjects are instructed to view a given display and to press one button while they perceive the white region as a figure on a black background and another button

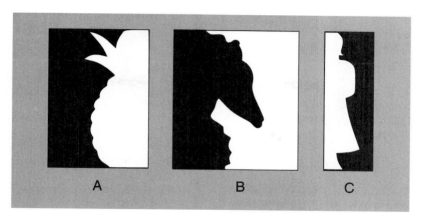

Figure 6.3.5 Meaningfulness in figure/ground organization. Ambiguous figure/ground displays were constructed in which one region was meaningful and the other was not. Subjects perceived the meaningful regions as figures for longer periods of time than the nonmeaningful regions. (After Peterson, Harvey, & Weidenbacher, 1991.)

while they perceive the black region as a figure on a white background. The results showed that the region corresponding to the meaningful object was perceived as figure substantially more of the time than the non-meaningful region. Subjects were also more likely to perceive the meaningful region as figure initially.

Even though care was taken to match meaningful versus nonmeaningful regions for classical figure/ground factors, it is difficult to be sure that stimulus differences other than meaningfulness are not responsible for these effects. Peterson et al. (1991) therefore compared the duration of figural perception for meaningful and meaningless regions when the same figures were presented upside-down versus rightside-up. (Just turn the book upside-down to see what they look like this way.) They reasoned that the meaningful objects they used were familiar only in their upright orientation, so whatever differences they found for upright figures should disappear when they were upside-down. This is exactly what they found.

The results of Peterson's experiments indicate that figure/ground processing is influenced by knowledge of specific object shapes. Note that this conclusion is entirely consistent with our speculation that the goal of figure/ground processing is to determine which regions correspond to objects and which to spaces between objects. If a region is identified as having the shape of a known object type, that region is almost certainly an object rather than a space between objects.

Peterson's results raise an interesting problem, however. The classical view has always been that figure/ground organization must precede object recognition because it requires a candidate object (namely, the figure) on which to work. Peterson (1994; Peterson & Gibson, 1994) interprets her results as contradicting this view, arguing instead for the existence of a "prefigural" recognition process that operates on *both* sides of each contour before any figure/ground processing. Palmer and Rock (1994b) argued that the logical priority of figure/ground can be maintained as long as the results of later object recognition processes feed back to figure/ground processes. This would allow ambiguous figure/ground stimuli such as Peterson's to be disambiguated by the later recognition process rather than requiring that object recognition precede figure/ground processing. A recent neural network simulation models has demonstrated that this sort of feedback architecture can, in fact, produce many of the differences that Peterson has reported (Vecera & O'Reilly, 1998). Which interpretation of these results is correct is currently an unsettled issue, but there is no doubt about the fact that figure/ground processes are influenced by object recognition processes.

6.3.4 The Problem of Holes

We mentioned above that a surrounded region can be perceived either as a convex figure against a ground that extends behind it or as a hole in a surrounding surface that reveals another surface behind the hole. This ambi-

Organizing Objects and Scenes

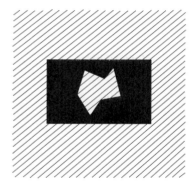

Figure 6.3.6 The problem of holes in figure/ground organization. The interior of a hole is perceived as background, but it is also perceived as having shape. This raises a problem for the cardinal feature of figure/ground organization: that the boundary imparts shape only to the figural region.

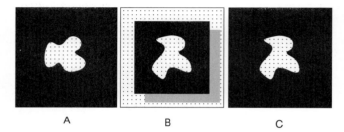

A   B   C

Figure 6.3.7 Stimuli for an experiment on perception of holes. Half the stimuli were amorphous shapes pasted onto black square backgrounds (A), and half were correspondingly shaped holes cut in a black square figure through which the background was visible (B). Memory for the shapes of figures and holes was tested by using objects whose shapes were identical to the objects and holes previously presented (e.g., A and C) plus distractor shapes that were different from any of those presented.

guity is only one interesting fact about the perception of holes. Another is that it produces an anomaly in the standard analysis of figure/ground relations.

By definition, holes are interior regions of objects or surfaces that do not contain matter. In the cases of primary interest for figure/ground organization, the hole goes all the way through the object, so the background surface is visible through it, as shown in Figure 6.3.6. The problems this raises for figure/ground perception concern the quasi-figural status of holes. They appear to be distinct phenomenological entities that have a shape of their own, even though they are actually just an empty space through which the background surface can be seen. (See Casati & Varzi, 1993, for a discussion of philosophical issues in the perception of holes.)

Recent experiments by Rock, Palmer, and Hume (in preparation) provide good evidence that holes are indeed perceived as having shape. They showed subjects a series of 2-D objects, half of which were amorphous green cardboard shapes pasted onto a square black background (Figure 6.3.7A) and half of which were objects containing similarly shaped holes cut out of a black cardboard square and presented several inches in front of a spotted green background (Figure 6.3.7B). (The background was spotted to give good stereoscopic depth information that the green surface was indeed behind the hole.) After seeing the objects, which all subjects perceived veridically as either solid or containing holes, subjects were shown a series of solid test objects (not holes) and asked to say which were shapes they had seen

in the original series. Some of the test objects were the same as the initially presented blobs (part A), some had the same shape as the initially presented holes (that is, the cut-out parts of the squares containing holes as in part C), and others were shapes that had never been seen before.

Rock, Palmer, and Hume (in preparation) found that, unlike what would be expected from classical ideas about figure and ground, recognition memory was just as good for the holes as for the blobs. They therefore argued that subjects perceived the holes as having shape rather than being perceived as shapeless ground extending behind the figure. Several other experiments supported this interpretation.

Within the standard conception of figure/ground organization, the fact that holes are perceived to have shape involves a paradox. It arises from the fact that if the contour of the hole is assigned to the surrounding object, as it surely must be for an observer to perceive it as a hole in the first place, then it is the *surrounding* object that should acquire shape as a result. But how can observers then see the hole itself as having a shape? The inner contour seems to be doing double duty by imparting shape to regions on *both* sides.

One possible answer is that the simple perception of a region as figural—and therefore as having a determinate shape—may be quite different from the process of actually representing the shape of that region. People may perceive the shapes of objects with holes in terms of a "holeless" object plus a hole of a particular shape at a

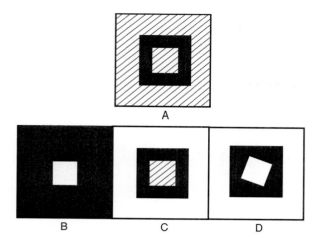

Figure 6.3.8 Factors influencing perception of holes. Holes tend to be perceived when there is a surrounding region that can be seen as figural, good evidence of continuity with the background, and nonaccidental relations to the outer contour (A). Holes are perceived less frequently when these conditions are not met (B, C, and D).

particular position. According to this view, there is no ambiguity about which region is the figure (versus the ground); it is the region surrounding the hole. This figure is also perceived as having a shape defined by both the inner side of its outer contour and the outer side of its inner contour. But its shape is still, at this point, implicit. It must be made explicit by some further process of shape description (see Chapter 8), one that may well describe objects with holes in terms of a holeless object plus a hole. It would then be this higher-level descriptive process that changes the status of the hole so that its shape can be described in terms of its outer contour, one which also happens to be the inner contour of the actual object. Thus, the hole is ground for purposes of defining depth relations and what is material versus open space, but it is figure for purposes of describing shape.

Other perceptually interesting issues concern the conditions under which holes are perceived as such, as illustrated in Figure 6.3.8A. The fact that needs to be explained is why the hole isn't perceived simply as a smaller object in front of a separate, larger object that surrounds it. Indeed, when there is only weak evidence to support the hole interpretation, the inner region will be perceived in exactly this way, as illustrated in Figures 6.3.8B, 6.3.8C, and 6.3.8D. Some of the factors that

support the perception that a hole is present are the following:

1. *Surrounding figure.* For a hole to be perceived, the surrounding region must have an outer boundary that is perceived as figural, since there can be a hole only in a figural region. Figure 6.3.8B shows a case in which the surround is usually perceived as ground and a hole is not generally perceived to be present.

2. *Ground continuity.* There must be some evidence that the region within the hole is the same surface as that behind the object's outer boundary. Many factors are potentially relevant here, some of the most important being whether they have the same color, have the same texture, or exhibit good continuation of elements perceived to be on the ground. Figure 6.3.8C shows an example in which a hole is seldom perceived because the inner region does not match the outer one.

3. *Nonaccidental relation to the outer boundary.* Evidence that the inner boundary is nonaccidentally related to the outer boundary also supports the perception of the inner region as a hole. Parallel contours are particularly effective. This fact is illustrated in Figure 6.3.8D, where the slight change in orientation of the inner square usually results in the perception of a white object in front of the black one rather than a hole in the black object (Bozzi, 1975).

In general, the stronger the evidence is for each of these features, the more likely the inner contour is to be perceived as a hole. Notice that these are again ceteris paribus rules that cannot yet be integrated when they conflict.

6.4 Visual Interpolation

Even after regions of similar visual properties have been segmented and figures have been discriminated from grounds, the visual system is far from finished in organizing the visual field into the objects that populate our visual experience. One of the main complicating factors in achieving the proper organization is that most surfaces are opaque, routinely hiding portions of objects from view. As we move around in the three-dimensional world, surfaces therefore continually undergo further occlusion and disocclusion by edges of closer surfaces (see Section 5.4.4). What is needed to cope with this incomplete, piecewise, and changeable montage of visible surfaces is some way to infer the nature of hidden parts from visible ones. The visual system has evolved mechanisms to do this, which we will call processes of **visual interpolation**. They have limitations, of course, primarily because all they can do is make a best guess about something that cannot be seen. For example, totally occluded objects are seldom interpolated even if they are present, because there is no evidence from which to do so,[6] and even partly visible objects are sometimes completed incorrectly. Even so, we are remarkably adept at perceiving the nature of things that are only partly seen. Take a look at the world around you right now and try to count the number of objects that are partly occluded. Chances are that you will not be able to do so because there are so many, yet you probably were unaware of this fact until you paid attention to it.

Before we begin describing the phenomena of visual interpolation, a distinction must be made between the kind of perceptual completion that occurs when parts of a surface are occluded and the kind of literal filling-in that occurs in the blind spot. Filling-in refers to cases in which the observer has full visual experiences of appropriate sensory qualities in the missing region of the image. Visual interpolation does not include visual experiences of the completed surface, but only perceptual knowledge—or, more accurately, beliefs—about its properties.

6.4.1 Visual Completion

The phenomenon of **visual completion** (also known as **amodal completion**) is that the visual system often automatically perceives partly occluded surfaces and objects as whole and complete, usually including their shape, texture, and color. A simple example is provided in Figure 6.4.1A. One spontaneously perceives a full circle behind a square, as indicated in Figure 6.4.1B, even though one quarter of its area is not visible. Although the modifiers "amodal" and "visual" might seem contradictory, both are appropriate for different aspects of the completion phenomenon. Completion

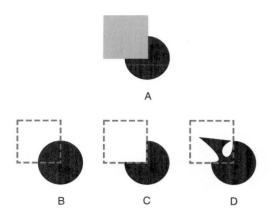

Figure 6.4.1 Visual completion. Partly occluded objects (e.g., the circle in part A) are usually perceived as completed behind other objects (B). Logically, however, many other perceptions are possible, including a mosaic organization (C) or an infinite number of other possible completions (such as part D).

can rightly be called amodal because the completed portion is not supported by local stimulation or sensory experience in any modality. It can also rightly be called visual because the completed portion is supported indirectly by visible information elsewhere in the image.

There is also a curious phenomenological ambiguity about amodal completion: There is a sense in which you see the circle as complete (rather than just knowing that it is), even though you do not experience all of it directly. It seems, appropriately enough, to fall midway between full sensory experience of visible objects and purely cognitive knowledge of the existence of completely unseen objects, say, in the next room. If the occluded portion of the contour is relatively small, the experience of its completed shape, although still not visual, can be nearly as certain as if it were viewed in its entirety.

As we noted in Chapter 1, visual completion is logically underdetermined. The real state of affairs corresponding to Figure 6.4.1A might be a square covering a whole circle (Figure 6.4.1B), a mosaic of a square abutting a three-quarter circle (or "Pac Man") (Figure 6.4.1C), a square in front of a circle with odd protrusions (Figure 6.4.1D), or an infinite number of other possibilities. The visual system therefore appears to have

---

[6] Interestingly, completely occluded *surfaces* of visible objects—such as the back and bottom of a cube—are visually completed, because other parts of the object are clearly perceived. The other case in which fully occluded objects are completed are those in which the object in question is part of a larger familiar object. A partly occluded face, for example, will lead to completion of an eye that is fully occluded.

Figure 6.4.2 Familiarity and visual completion. Partly occluded figures need not be familiar in shape to be completed (A), but familiarity and context can affect the perceptual outcome (part B).

strong preferences about how to complete partly occluded objects, and these preferences are clearly aimed at achieving veridical perception of whole objects in the world. How might it happen?

Several different theories have been advanced to account for amodal completion phenomena. We will consider three of the most important types: those based on *figural familiarity*, on *figural simplicity*, and on *ecological constraints*.

Figural Familiarity Theories. One possibility that may have already occurred to you is that we complete the circle behind the square because of prior experience in seeing whole circles. We have also had experiences of seeing three-quarter circles, of course, but most people see a good many more full circles. This line of thinking leads to the familiarity hypothesis: People complete partly occluded figures according to the most frequently encountered shape that is compatible with the visible stimulus information. One problem with this theory is that we seem able to complete objects that we have never seen before just as easily as quite familiar ones. An example of an amodally completed novel figure is shown in Figure 6.4.2A. We seem to have no more uncertainty about the shape of the occluded figure in this figure than the circle in Figure 6.4.1A.

This argument does not prove that familiarity has no effect on amodal completion; it merely indicates that something more than familiarity must be involved. In fact, there are some compelling examples of familiarity

effects on completion. Figure 6.4.2B shows a partly occluded letter in a context of other letters. Most people complete it as an R even though it could logically be perceived as a P, a B, or some other geometrical pattern that does not form a letter at all. The facts that R, P, and B are familiar letters and that WORD is a familiar English word—whereas WOPD and WOBD are not—seem to be important factors in this example. Familiarity at the level of the completed figure cannot be the whole story, however, so we must look for other kinds of explanations as well.

Figural Simplicity Theories. A second possibility is that partly occluded figures are completed in the way that results in the "simplest" perceived figures. For example, a square occluding a complete circle in Figure 6.4.1A is intuitively simpler than any of the alternatives in this set of figures, and the same could be true for completion of quite novel shapes. The idea of explaining phenomena of perceptual organization in terms of maximizing simplicity—or, equivalently, minimizing complexity—was the theoretical approach favored by Gestalt psychologists (see Section 2.1.2). It seems to fit particularly well with many completion phenomena.

The Gestaltists called their hypothesis that the visual system perceives the simplest possibility the **principle of Prägnanz**, although others later dubbed it the **minimum principle** (Hochberg & McAlister, 1953). It states that the percept will be as good as the prevailing conditions allow. The term "good" refers to the degree of figural simplicity or regularity, and the prevailing conditions refer to the structure of the current stimulus image. The problem is that for such a hypothesis to generate testable predictions about what will be perceived, one needs a definition of "goodness." This is a difficulty with which the Gestaltists never fully came to grips, but other theorists have since offered explicit theories. We will discuss this problem more fully in Chapter 8 when we consider the problem of figural goodness directly, but for now, we can illustrate the basic idea with a single intuitive rule.

Suppose that the goodness of a figure can be measured just by counting the number of axes of bilateral symmetry, such that more axes correspond to greater figural goodness. The matter is actually much more complex, but this definition will do for purposes of illustration. By this account, the perception of a square

Organizing Objects and Scenes

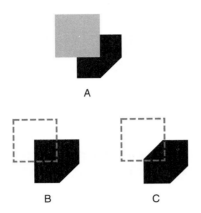

Figure 6.4.3 A problem for simplicity theories of completion. The black figure in part A is generally perceived to have the shape indicated in part B rather than the more symmetrical version in part C.

occluding a circle is the simplest alternative shown in Figure 6.4.1 because the circle is bilaterally symmetric about all axes passing through its center. The mosaic interpretation by contrast has only one axis of symmetry (about a left-diagonal line through its center), and the irregularly completed circle has no symmetries at all. Perceiving a square in front of a circle turns out to the simplest possible interpretation, given this definition of goodness and simplicity. As we will see in Chapter 8, it is too simple a definition to work in general, but it does illustrate the kind of theoretical account that one can construct of amodal completion within the general framework of the Gestalt principle of Prägnanz.

One problem with such theories of completion is that although they can account for many examples, there are others for which they do not seem to give correct predictions. One counterexample is shown in Figure 6.4.3A. The usual perception is of a square in front of another square that is missing its lower right corner (Figure 6.4.3B). According to the symmetry-based definition, however, the simplest completion would be the hexagon shown in Figure 6.4.3C because it has two axes of symmetry (about both diagonals), whereas the cornerless square has only one (about the left diagonal).

This counterexample is not definitive; it may merely point out a flaw in the definition of figural goodness.

For example, the number of sides may be a crucial factor in figural goodness. Indeed, defining goodness solely in terms of the number of sides gives the correct answer in this case: The preferred cornerless square has only five sides, whereas the hexagon has six. It is also possible that many factors jointly determine figural goodness. This example therefore reveals a general problem with theories of completion based on the principle of Prägnanz: They are only as good as the measure of simplicity on which they are based. Failures to account for experimental results can thus easily be dismissed on the grounds that a better measure would bring the predictions into line with the results. This may be true, of course, but it makes the theory difficult to falsify.

Ecological Constraint Theories. Theories in the third class try to explain visual completion by appealing directly to ecological evidence of occluded contours. For example, when a contour of one object is occluded by that of another, they typically form intersections known as a T-junction. The continuous contour (the top of the T) is interpreted as the closer edge whose surface occludes the other edge (the stem of the T). The further assumption that is required to account for visual completion is that the occluded edge (and the surface attached to it) somehow connects with another occluded edge in the scene.

One such theory of completion is Kellman and Shipley's (1991) **relatability theory**. It can be understood as a more complete and well-specified extension of the classic grouping principle of good continuation. Relatability theory is based on the following four proposals.

1. Edge discontinuities are necessary, but not sufficient, conditions for visual interpolation of amodal contours.

Intuitively, an **edge discontinuity** is an abrupt change in the direction of a contour.[7] Edge discontinuities thus occur at all contour intersections, including ones that are not completed, such as the corners of a square. To give a more concrete understanding of discontinuities, Figure 6.4.4A shows a completion display with all its edge discontinuities circled. Discontinuities alone are not sufficient to produce amodal

---

[7] Formally, an edge discontinuity is defined as a discontinuity in the first derivative of the mathematical function that describes the edge over space.

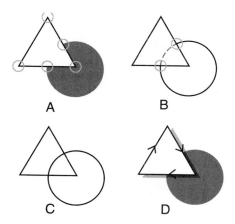

Figure 6.4.4 Stages of completion according to Kellman and Shipley's relatability theory. First, edge discontinuities are identified (part A), then relatable pairs are completed (B). Closed figures defined by completed edges then form new perceptual units (C), after which depth relations are determined (D).

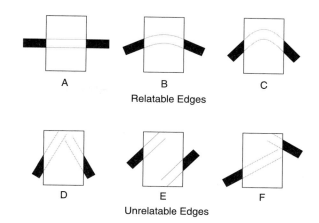

Figure 6.4.5 Conditions for edge relatability. Because edge pairs in parts A, B, and C are relatable, the figures of which they are part are completed behind the occluding rectangle. The edges in parts D, E, and F are not relatable and therefore are not completed. (See text for details.) (After Kellman & Shipley, 1991.)

completion because completion depends on whether or not the discontinuities can be related to other discontinuities in the image—hence the name of the theory.

2. Amodally completed contours are perceived when the edges leading into discontinuities are relatable to others (see Figure 6.4.4B).

According to Kellman and Shipley, two edges are relatable if and only if (a) their extensions intersect at an angle of no less than 90° and (b) they can be smoothly connected to each other, as illustrated in Figure 6.4.4B. To make this concept clearer, Figure 6.4.5 shows three cases of relatable edges and three cases of unrelatable ones. When the edges are collinear (part A)—meaning that their extensions meet at an angle of 180°—relatability is very strong. It declines as the angle between the extensions decreases (parts B and C) and drops rapidly to zero or near zero below 90° (part D). Edges can also fail to relate if their extensions do not intersect at all, either because they are parallel and displaced (part E) or because the extension of one intersects the other edge rather than its extension (part F).

Notice that this definition determines whether a given pair of edges are relatable, but it does not specify how the visual system determines which edges are actually perceived as related to which. This correspondence is

important because a given edge may be relatable to many other edges, yet only one will be perceived as its extension. Presumably the visual system tries to find the "best" matches by finding the correspondences that have the strongest overall relatability.

3. A new perceptual unit is formed when amodally completed edges form an enclosed area (see Figure 6.4.4C).

This proposal simply means that after the edges leading to discontinuities have been related to each other, another process is required to determine which sets of connected edges form a closed contour, as illustrated in Figure 6.4.4C. Typically the new unit that is formed when this process succeeds will correspond to a connected environmental object, but it might also be a hole, as we will see shortly when we consider the relation between illusory contours and amodal completion.

4. Units are assigned positions in depth based on available depth information (see Figure 6.4.4D).

In completion, for example, depth information from occlusion (or interposition) specifies that the amodally completed edges are behind the object at whose borders they terminate. This is illustrated in Figure 6.4.4D, where arrows and the right-hand rule (see Section 5.5.7) specify which surface is in front of which. The process

Organizing Objects and Scenes

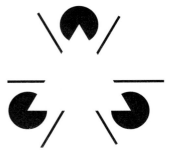

Figure 6.4.6 Illusory contours. Observers perceive an illusory white triangle on a background of partly occluded circles and lines. The interior of the triangle generally appears whiter than the ground, even though it is not.

of depth assignment is actually separate from the unit formation process itself, but it is included in the theory because it enables the same underlying processes to account for other phenomena of unit formation, such as illusory contours, transparency, and figural scission, as we will see shortly.

It might seem unlikely that such a complex process could be required to perceive something as simple as the completed circle in Figure 6.4.4. Experiments have shown, however, that the process of completing simple geometrical shapes such as squares and circles takes about 400 ms (Sekuler & Palmer, 1992). Whether the processes that are occurring during this time correspond to those proposed by relatability theory is not yet known.

6.4.2 Illusory Contours

The next form of visual interpolation that we will consider produces a fascinating illusion in which contours are seen that do not actually exist in the stimulus image. This phenomenon of **illusory contours** (also called **subjective contours**) has been known for some time (Schumann, 1904), but the modern resurgence of interest in it was sparked by the striking demonstrations of Kanizsa (1955, 1979). One of the best known examples is the so-called **Kanizsa triangle** shown in Figure 6.4.6. The white triangle that is so readily perceived in this display is an illusory figure defined by illusory contours because the stimulus image consists solely of the three black Pac Men and three line segments arranged

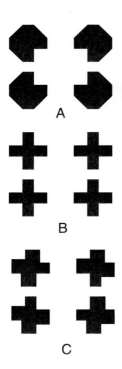

Figure 6.4.7 Conditions for perceiving illusory figures. A white rectangle occluding four hexagons is perceived in part A, but no such rectangle is perceived in part B or part C, despite the presence of the same local contours. Factors such as symmetry and parallel edges in parts B and C appear to block the perception of illusory contours.

in this particular way. Most observers report actually seeing well-defined luminance edges where the contours of the triangle should be, the interior region of the triangle appearing slightly brighter than the surrounding region. These edges simply are not present in the image.

The perception of illusory contours is generally accompanied by amodal completion of the inducing elements. For example, when you perceive the illusory triangle in Figure 6.4.6, you simultaneously perceive the Pac Men as partly occluded circles and the lines as extending behind the triangle. In fact, if the inducing elements are not perceived as incomplete, no illusory contours or figures are seen, as illustrated in Figure 6.4.7. In part A, an illusory rectangle is perceived because the inducing elements are seen as incomplete octagons. In part B, however, no illusory rectangle is seen, even though the same cut-out corners are present as in part A.

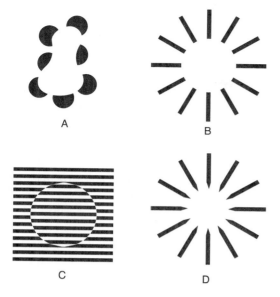

Figure 6.4.8 Further demonstrations of illusory figures. Illusory figures can be novel (A) or induced only by line terminations (B and C). Line terminations must be consistent with occlusion by a smooth contour, ruling out tapered (D) line endings. (Parts B and D after Kennedy, 1988.)

The difference is that in Figure 6.4.7B, the cut-out corners are perceived as integral parts of the crosses, which are visible in their entirety. The inner notches therefore require no perceptual "explanation" in terms of occluding objects blocking them. One factor that may be partly responsible for this is the symmetry of the crosses. To be perceived as partly occluded by a white rectangle, the crosses' symmetry would have to be perceived as accidentally arising from the specific alignment of the occluding white rectangle and the inducing elements. Even so, symmetry is not necessary to block the formation of illusory contours. Figure 6.4.7C shows that asymmetrical crosslike figures also fail to produce illusory contours as long as their sides are parallel. Again, the explanation may lie in the fact that it is very unlikely that the sides of an occluding rectangle would turn out to be parallel to the sides of the inducing figures (Albert, 1993). In any case, this contrast shows quite clearly that illusory figures and contours are a relatively complex phenomenon that depends on more than local conditions of stimulation. It is a good example of the Gestalt claim that what is perceived depends impor-

tantly on the structure of the whole configuration and cannot easily be predicted from the structure of local parts.

Figure 6.4.8A demonstrates that illusory figures, like amodally completed ones, do not have to be familiar shapes such as triangles or circles, for novel shapes can be perceived just as easily (Gregory, 1972). Other compelling examples of illusory contours can be produced by line segments that terminate as though they were occluded, as in Figure 6.4.8B, where an illusory white circle is perceived as covering the radial pattern of line segments. Illusory contours can also be perceived when line segments are merely displaced inside and outside the illusory boundary so that their ends align along its contour (Figure 6.4.8C).

Kennedy (1988) has shown that these line-induced illusory contours depend on the precise nature of the line terminations. As illustrated in Figure 6.4.8D, the perception of illusory contours weakens or disappears if the ends of the lines are tapered to points. Similar weakening occurs with rounded line terminations. These facts are consistent with the general claim that illusory contours depend on the perception of occlusion, for lines that are occluded by a closer edge terminate abruptly along the occluding contour (as in Figure 6.4.8B) rather than tapering to a point (as in Figure 6.4.8D) or being rounded at the end.

Relation to Visual Completion. We have already hinted at one way in which subjective contours and illusory figures are related to amodal completion: The inducing elements are amodally completed behind the illusory figure. Kellman and his associates have argued persuasively, however, that the connection between these two phenomena goes much deeper (Kellman & Loukides, 1987; Kellman & Shipley, 1991). They claim that both result from the very same set of underlying processes of unit formation and that both can be described in terms of relatability theory.

Kellman and his colleagues first noticed that many illusory figures can take on an alternative appearance that produces amodal completion instead of illusory contours. The Kanizsa triangle in Figure 6.4.9A, for example, can also be seen (albeit with some difficulty) as a white triangle on a homogeneous black background as viewed through three circular holes in an occluding white surface. Figure 6.4.9B produces this perception

Organizing Objects and Scenes

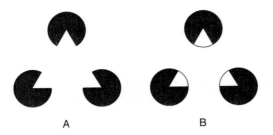

A   B

Figure 6.4.9   Illusory contours, amodal completion, and depth relations. The illusory sides of the triangle in part A are eliminated when it is seen as an occluded triangle seen through holes, as indicated in part B. Rather, the circles produce illusory contours, and the triangle's sides are perceived as amodally completed. (After Kellman & Shipley, 1991.)

more clearly by including the missing portions of the holes' edges. The key observation here is that in this interpretation, illusory contours of the triangle are *not* seen. Rather, the sides of the triangle are amodally completed behind the occluding white surface. Illusory contours *are* seen at the edge of the circular holes, however, where the extra arcs have been added in Figure 6.4.9B.

Kellman and Shipley (1991) pointed out another important relation between amodal completion and illusory contours: Many illusory contour configurations can be converted into examples of amodal completion. The simple three-step procedure for doing this is illustrated in Figure 6.4.10:

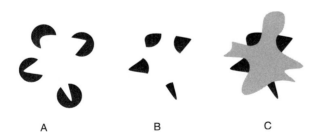

A   B   C

Figure 6.4.10   A procedure for converting illusory figures into amodal completion. Beginning with an illusory figure (A), take the complement of the inducing elements (B) and add an occluding figure whose contours smoothly follow the interior contours of the complements (C).

1. Begin with an illusory figure such as the one shown in Figure 6.4.10A.

2. Take the complement of the inducing elements as shown in Figure 6.4.10B.

3. Add an occluding figure whose contours smoothly follow the interior contours of the complements, as shown by the gray shape in Figure 6.4.10C.

The result is an example of amodal completion in which the missing contours of the completed figure—previously the illusory contours—are now perceived as being occluded by the new figure.

Such close connections between these two phenomena led Kellman to propose that illusory contours and amodal completion are actually just two different manifestations of the same underlying unit formation processes, as implied by relatability theory. But if a single process is at work in both cases, why do examples of the two phenomena look so different? The answer lies in the fourth proposal concerning depth assignment. That is, whether the observer perceives illusory contours or amodally completed contours depends on the perceived depth relations between the figures in question. If the missing contours are part of the closer occluding figure, then illusory contours are perceived. If the missing contours are part of the farther occluded figure, then they are amodally completed behind the closer figure.

Physiological Basis of Illusory Contours.   Recent research in cortical physiology has identified cells in area V2 that appear to respond to the presence of illusory contours. V2 cells have receptive fields that do not initially appear much different from those in V1 (see Section 4.1.2). Careful testing by von der Heyt and his colleagues, however, has shown that about 40% of the orientation selective cells in V2 fire when presented with stimuli that induce illusory contours in human perception (Peterhans & von der Heydt, 1989, 1991; von der Heyt, Peterhans, & Baumgartner, 1984; von der Heyt & Peterhans, 1989).

Figure 6.4.11 shows examples of the kind of stimuli they used in one of their experiments. They first recorded the firing of each cell to a white bar (Figure 6.4.11A) at 16 different orientations. If the response was

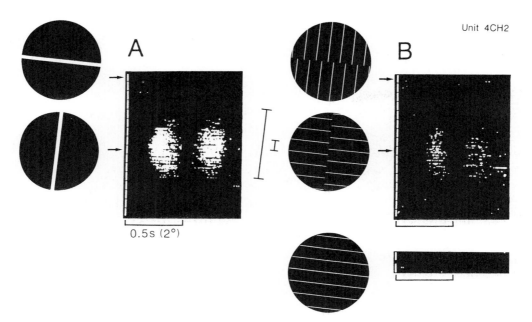

0.5 s (2°)

Figure 6.4.11 Stimuli and responses of a V2 neuron to real and illusory contours. This V2 cell showed selective responding to real moving lines at a nearly vertical orientation as indicated by the high density of white spots along the middle rows of the spike record (A). The same cell also showed selectivity to an illusory contour in the same orientation but not to the same inducing lines without an illusory contour (B). (From von der Heydt and Peterhans, 1989a.)

selective to orientation—as shown by sharp peaks in the solid curves in Figure 6.4.12—they also recorded the response of that cell to illusory contour stimuli shown in Figure 6.4.11B. They found that many V2 cells also showed sharp orientation tuning functions for the illusory contours, as shown in the dashed curves in Figure 6.4.12. Figure 6.4.12C shows the tuning curves for cells in which the responses to real and illusory contours were nearly the same. Figures 6.4.12A and 6.4.12B show cases in which the cells were tuned to the same orientation but had different sensitivities to real and illusory contours. Figure 6.4.12D shows an example in which the best orientation for real contours differed from that of illusory contours by 45°. Note that the cell shown in Figure 6.4.12A responds to the orientation of the real lines in the illusory contour stimulus but that the other cells do not. Both types of cells were commonly found in V2.

How might these cells produce responses to such illusory contours? There are many possibilities, but one theory is that these so-called **contour cells** integrate

the output of a number of oriented cells in V1, as shown in Figure 6.4.13. One type of input comes from simple or complex V1 cells that are aligned with the favored contour orientation of the V2 cell. The other type of input comes from a set of orthogonally oriented end-stopped V1 cells whose inhibitory ends are aligned along the favored contour orientation. Such a cell would exhibit a tuning function like the one shown in Figure 6.4.12A, with responses to both real and illusory contours at orientations that differ by 90°. The lower part of Figure 6.4.13 shows how the end-stopped receptive fields would be aligned to respond appropriately to a nonexistent contour in an illusory rectangle.

Notice that this theory of contour cells in V2 does not provide a full explanation of illusory contours, but just a plausible mechanism for how the response of such V2 contour cells might be derived from the output of V1 cells. In particular, it does not provide an explanation of why the illusory figure appears in front of the inducing elements, and it cannot explain why Figure 6.4.7A produces illusory contours and Figure 6.4.7B does not. A

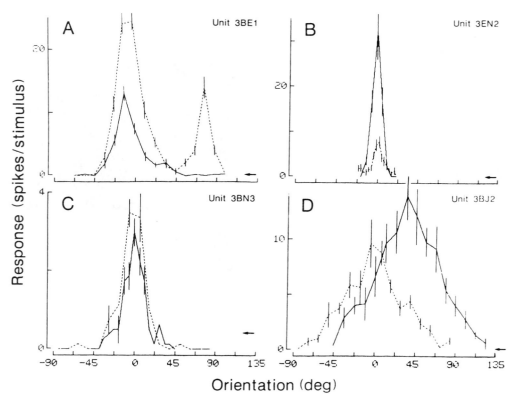

Figure 6.4.12 Tuning functions for cells in area V2 to real and illusory contours at different orientations. Neural firing rates for four contour cells in V2 in response to light bars (solid curves) and illusory contours (dashed curves), which are quite similar for some cells and quite different for others. (From von der Heydt and Peterhans, 1989a.)

much more complex theory is required to account for such subtle but important phenomena.[8]

6.4.3 Perceived Transparency

Another phenomenon of perceptual organization that is closely related to amodal completion and illusory contours is that of **perceived transparency**: the perception of an object as being viewed through a closer, translucent object. A translucent object is one that transmits some portion of the light reflected from farther objects rather than reflecting or absorbing all of it. Under conditions of translucency, the light striking the retina at a given position provides information about at least two different external points in the same direction from the observer's viewpoint: one on the translucent surface itself and the other on the opaque surface visible through it (see Figure 6.4.14A). I say "at least" two points because there can be more than one intervening translucent surface. For simplicity, we will consider only the case of a single translucent layer, however.

Perception of transparency depends on both spatial and color conditions. Violating the proper relations of either sort is sufficient to block it. For example, transparency will be perceived if the translucent surface is

---

[8] Grossberg and Mingolla (1985) provide a more complex computationally derived neural network theory that attempts to explain illusory contours and related phenomena. It is based not on known physiology but on how neuronlike processors might be wired together to produce similar phenomena. Because their theory is too complicated to describe here, the interested reader is referred to their original paper.

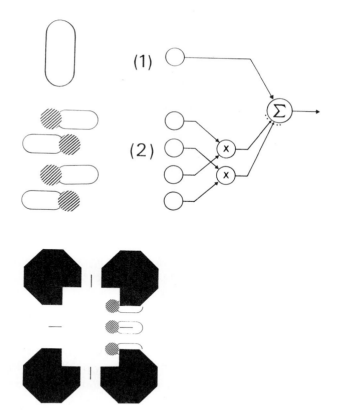

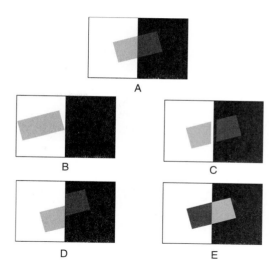

Figure 6.4.14 Conditions for perceiving transparency. Observers will perceive transparency if the color and spatial relations among four (or more) regions are all compatible with a single translucent surface in front of two (or more) overlapping regions, as illustrated in part A. If any of these relations is incompatible (B, C, D, and E), transparency is not perceived.

Figure 6.4.13 A neural theory of the wiring diagram for contour cells in V2. The contour cell (Σ) sums the signals in two parallel pathways: (1) an edge detection path from simple or complex cells in V1 and (2) a grouping path from perpendicular end-stopped cells. (From von der Heydt and Peterhans, 1989b.)

positioned so that reflectance edges on the opaque surface behind it can be seen both through the translucent surface and outside it, as illustrated in Figure 6.4.14A. When this happens, a phenomenon called **color scission** or **color splitting** occurs, and the image colors in the regions of the translucent surface are perceived as a combination of two other colors, one belonging to the background and the other to the translucent surface.

Color scission will not occur if either the spatial or the color relations are violated. If the translucent surface lies completely within a single reflectance region, as illustrated in Figure 6.4.14B, the display is perceived as a single opaque surface containing regions of different reflectances, with no trace of transparency. The percep-

tion of transparency can also be blocked by destroying the unity of the translucent region, as shown in Figure 6.4.14C, or merely weakening it, as shown in Figure 6.4.14D. Color scission in transparency perception is thus a good example of the importance of spatial organization in that the effect does not occur unless the organization of the regions is appropriate (Metelli, 1974). Proper spatial conditions alone are not sufficient, however, because improper color relations will block transparency perception in the very same spatial configuration that produces perception of transparency with appropriate color relations (see Figure 6.4.14E versus Figure 6.4.14A).

We will now briefly examine the color conditions that are required for perception of transparency. In simple two-surface displays like the ones we have been examining, there are four spatial regions whose color relations need to be considered, as illustrated in Figure 6.4.15. Two of these regions (A and B) show the two different reflectances of the underlying, opaque surfaces. The other two (C and D) show these same underlying reflectances as filtered through the translucent surface. The problem that color scission presents to the visual

Organizing Objects and Scenes

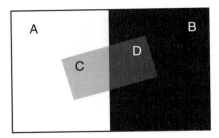

Figure 6.4.15 Color relations in perceived transparency. The luminance of the regions of overlap (C and D) must be intermediate between those of the directly visible regions (A and B) and a single, partly transparent surface in front of them.

Figure 6.4.16 Figural scission. A single homogeneous region is sometimes perceptually divided into two overlapping objects, one of which partly occludes the other. The depth relation between them is ambiguous.

system is that only one image color is actually present in each of the two regions of overlap (C and D), but two environmental surface colors are present in each region: one for the background and one for the transparent layer.

This is yet another example of an underconstrained inverse problem because there are more unknowns (the surface lightnesses of the transparent layer and both of the opaque regions) than there are knowns (the luminance in each region of overlap). The additional information that is required to solve the problem comes from heuristic assumptions concerning the relations among the colors in the surrounding spatial contexts. The critical role of context can be demonstrated simply by viewing the two overlapping regions through a reduction tube or screen, in which case no scission or transparency will be perceived. Therefore, the reduction screen must somehow remove crucial information that enables color scission to occur.

Qualitatively, we can say that the perceived color in each region of overlap is split into a component from the transparent layer and a component from the opaque layer. If they can be split such that the components due to the transparent layer are the same, then color scission will be experienced, and transparency will be perceived. Metelli (1974) and Gerbino (1994) have formulated quantitative analyses of these conditions, but for now, we will simply observe that transparency requires the region of overlap to be intermediate between the lightness of the opaque layer and that of the translucent layer. If the opaque layer is black and the translucent layer is medium gray, for example, the combined result in the region of overlap will be a dark gray. If the opa-

que layer is white and the translucent layer is medium gray, the overlap region will be light gray.

6.4.4 Figural Scission

The final phenomenon that we will discuss as an example of visual interpolation is called **figural scission** by analogy to color scission in transparency perception. In figural scission, a single homogeneous region is split perceptually into two figures of the same color with one in front of and occluding the other, as illustrated in Figure 6.4.16. This phenomenon has several interesting aspects:

1. *Underdetermination.* There is no local sensory information that requires the uniform connected region to be split at all. That is, there are no luminance or color edges in the interior of the region where they would be if two figures were actually present.

2. *Illusory contours.* The visual system constructs the missing contours where it expects to find them. Thus, when figural scission occurs, illusory contours appear in the interior of the region where the closer figure occludes the farther one.

3. *Completion.* Once illusory contours of the closer figure have formed, the visual system also completes the portions of the farther figure that are occluded by the closer one.

4. *Ambiguity.* The stimulus conditions do not determine which figure is in front and which is behind, so either possibility can often be perceived.

5. *Multistability.* After you stare at such displays for awhile, the depth relations of the two parts sponta-

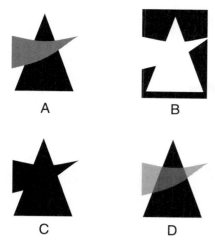

Figure 6.4.17 An example of relations among several organization phenomena. The same two figures are used to highlight commonalities among visual completion (A), illusory contours (B), figural scission (C), and perceived transparency (D). (After Kellman & Shipley, 1991.)

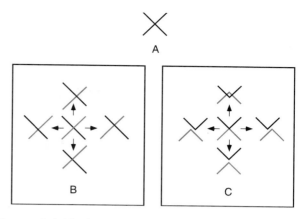

Figure 6.4.18 Nonaccidentalness and good continuation. Slight changes in the position of the elements in part A lead to minor changes in image geometry if it consists of two continuous lines at different depths (B). The same changes in position lead to much more drastic changes if the scene consists of two angles that accidentally align at their vertices (C).

neously reverse. When this happens, the subjective contour switches, so you see the edges of what used to be the farther figure, which is now the nearer one.

The close relations among the four organizational phenomena we have been discussing—amodal completion, illusory contours, perceived transparency, and figural scission—are illustrated in Figure 6.4.17. It shows each of the four phenomena for a single spatial configuration of edges in which different colors have been appropriately assigned to the component regions. There are several more phenomena that fall within the range of Kellman's theory of visual interpolation, but because the rest involve motion, we will postpone discussing them until Chapter 10 when we focus on the perception of dynamic events.

6.4.5 The Principle of Nonaccidentalness

Many of the phenomena of perceptual organization can be understood within a general framework of **nonaccidentalness** (sometimes also called **genericity**): the hypothesis that the visual system avoids interpreting structural regularities as arising from unlikely accidents of viewing, usually from violations of the assumption of general viewpoint. In the psychological literature, this idea was first discussed by Irvin Rock (1983) as the rejection-of-coincidence principle. He pointed out that many phenomena of perceptual organization can be explained by assuming that the visual system rejects interpretations in which the properties of the retinal image arise from coincidences of any sort. Similar ideas were independently proposed within a computational framework by Lowe (1985) and extended by others (for example, Albert & Hoffman, 1995).

Grouping phenomena provide many good examples of the principle of nonaccidentalness. It might be the case, for example, that two regions moving in the same direction and at the same rate belong to two different objects that coincidentally happen to be moving the same way, but it is far more likely that they do so because they are parts of a single object. If they are parts of two separate objects, the similarity of their motion might be accidental; if they are parts of the same object, it is not. The visual system prefers the nonaccidental interpretation that they are parts of the same object.

The same is true of good continuation. We perceive that the segments in the X of Figure 6.4.18A consist of two intersecting straight lines (Figure 6.4.18B) rather than two angles that just happen to align at their vertices (Figure 6.4.18C) because the latter arrangement is a rather unlikely coincidence compared to the former.

One way of assessing which interpretation is less coincidental is to examine the consequences of slight changes in the position of the objects or in the viewpoint of the observer. Notice in this case that moving the two segments slightly in any direction changes only minor details of the resulting figure (Figure 6.4.18B), but moving the two angles slightly in any direction changes it greatly (Figure 6.4.18C). It is logically possible that the continuity of the segments is an accident of alignment of the two angles, but it is far more likely that they are aligned because they are continuations of the same environmental object.

The analysis I gave of the principles of figure/ground organization is also consistent with the principle of non-accidentalness. I claimed, for example, that symmetrical regions tend to be seen as figural because objects are far more likely to be symmetrical than are the spaces between objects. Spaces between objects are symmetrical only under extraordinarily coincidental circumstances, and small changes in their positions relative to each other or to the observer are likely to destroy any accidental symmetry that might exist. Moving a symmetrical object, however, does not affect its symmetry. The same is true of parallelism because many objects have parallel contours, but spaces between objects are bounded by parallel contours mainly by coincidence.

Similar analyses can be given of visual completion, perceived transparency, and illusory figures. It is logically possible that the visible regions of the two regions in Figure 6.4.19A constitute a mosaic of precisely aligned shapes, but this would require a much more accidental arrangement than would occur if it were one object occluded by another. Again, moving the two mosaic objects in any direction produces qualitative changes in the configuration (Figure 6.4.19C), thus indicating that the alignment is highly coincidental. Moving the two overlapping shapes, in contrast, produces only minor quantitative changes (Figure 6.4.19B). Thus, the accidental configuration requires much more precision of alignment than the nonaccidental one. The same can be said of the arrangement of regions in transparency and illusory contour phenomena. In both cases, the perceptually preferred interpretation requires far fewer accidents of alignment than the alternatives.

The principle of nonaccidentalness provides a very general explanation of many key phenomena of percep-

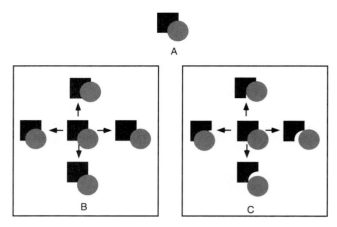

Figure 6.4.19 Nonaccidentalness in visual completion. Slight changes in the position from which part A is viewed lead to minor changes in image geometry if it consists of a circle in front of a square (B). The same changes in viewing position lead to much more drastic changes if the scene consists of a circle in front of a notched square (C).

tual organization. It can be viewed as a particular instance of Helmholtz's likelihood principle that the visual system perceives the situation that is most likely to have given rise to the particular stimulus pattern on the retina. The main alternative explanation is the Gestalt principle of Prägnanz: that perception will be as "good" as the prevailing conditions allow, maximizing simplicity and regularity rather than likelihood. We considered this Gestalt idea briefly above with respect to completion, and we will return to it in Chapter 8 when we discuss theories of shape representation.

6.5 Multistability

In most naturally occurring scenes, there is a single organization that is rock-solid and completely dominates perception. That may be one reason why the problem of perceptual organization was not recognized until 1923 when Wertheimer raised it. But carefully chosen examples illustrate the possibility of arriving at different organizations for the same image, organizations that can profoundly change our perceptual experiences. We first demonstrated such ambiguities in Chapter 1 with examples such as the Necker cube, the vase/faces, and the duck/rabbit (see Figure 1.1.5). Not only do these figures allow for more than one perception, but they are **mul-**

tistable perceptions: perceptions that spontaneously alternate among two or three different interpretations, once they have been seen.

One of the most interesting questions about multistability is why it occurs. The most widely accepted theory is the **neural fatigue hypothesis** proposed many years ago by the Gestalt psychologist Wolfgang Köhler (1940). He claimed that perception of ambiguous figures alternates among different interpretations owing to different sets of neurons getting "tired" of firing after they have done so for a long time. The underlying theoretical assumptions are that:

1. different interpretations are represented by different patterns of neural activity,

2. perception corresponds to whichever pattern is most active in the brain at the time, and

3. neural fatigue causes different patterns of activation to dominate at different times.

6.5.1 Connectionist Network Models

To make the neural fatigue hypothesis more concrete, let us suppose that the different patterns of neural activity can be identified as the firing rates in two different neural networks. Let us suppose further that when one network becomes more active than the other, the corresponding interpretation arises in conscious perception. According to the neural fatigue hypothesis, extended perception of a given interpretation causes the neurons within that network to become fatigued—that is, their activity level decreases because they have depleted their biochemical resources for continued firing. Eventually, the activation level in the network of the first interpretation falls below that of the second network. At this time conscious perception switches from the first to the second alternative.

Figure 6.5.1 shows a connectionist model for perception of a Necker cube that has this general structure (Rumelhart, Smolensky, McClelland, & Hinton, 1986). The network representations of the two interpretations of the cube are two subnetworks embedded within the larger interconnected network. These two subnetworks are shown in the top-left and top-right regions of Figure 6.5.1 next to unambiguous cubes illustrating the perceptions to which they correspond. The left subnetwork

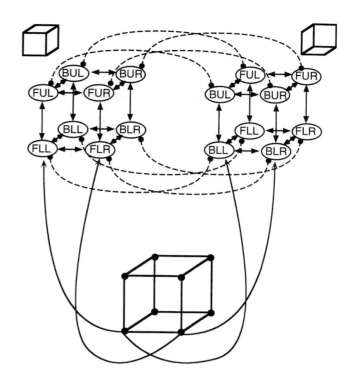

Figure 6.5.1 A connectionist network model of perceiving a Necker cube. The left and right subnetworks at the top correspond to perceiving the two ambiguous organizations of this reversible, multistable figure. Solid lines represent excitatory connections, and dashed lines represent inhibitory connections. (See text for details.) (After Rumelhart, Smolensky, McClelland, & Hinton, 1986b.)

represents the perception of the cube viewed from above, and the right subnetwork represents it viewed from below. Each node in each subnetwork represents the interpretation of a particular vertex in the image as a particular corner of a 3-D cube. The nodes are labeled according to their 3-D interpretation: front or back (F or B), upper or lower (U or L), and left or right (L or R). "BUL," for example, indicates the back upper-left corner of a cube, and "FLR" indicates the front lower-right corner.

The two different perceptual interpretations of the cube arise because of ambiguity in the depth interpretations of the vertices. This ambiguity is reflected in the different labeling of corresponding nodes in the two subnetworks as front or back—F or B in the first position. These pairs of corresponding corner nodes in the two subnetworks are connected to the same vertex in the

Organizing Objects and Scenes

ambiguous Necker cube, as shown at the bottom of Figure 6.5.1, to indicate that they are both activated by the same sensory information coming from the appropriate vertex. (The excitatory connections coming from the sensory image are shown only for the two bottom vertices for clarity; all vertices activate each corresponding unit in the two subnetworks.)

The behavior of this network exemplifies bistability: Activation spreads dynamically throughout the network, and it eventually settles into one of two stable states. Sometimes, all the nodes in the left network end up active, whereas those in the right network are not, and sometimes the reverse happens. The bistability of this network arises from its **architecture**: the pattern of connections among its nodes. In this case, the architecture is such that some connections produce *cooperation* between pairs of nodes (via mutual excitation) whereas others produce *competition* (via mutual inhibition).

Cooperation arises when two nodes are connected by mutually excitatory links. As a result, activation in one node tends to increase activation in the other. In the Necker cube example, such mutually excitatory connections (solid lines with arrows at both ends) are present between adjacent nodes within the same subnetwork. This means that when one node of a given interpretation is activated, this activation spreads first to its nearest neighbors and eventually to all the nodes within its subnetwork. These cooperative connections therefore make each subnetwork function as a cohesive unit, tending to settle into a state in which either all its units are active or none of them are.

Competition arises when two nodes are connected by mutually inhibitory links. As a result, activation in one tends to decrease activation in the other. This is the architecture of a so-called winner-take-all network. In the Necker cube network, such mutually inhibitory connections (dashed lines with filled dots at both ends) are present between corresponding nodes in different subnetworks. This means that the more active node of such a pair reduces the activation of the other node of the pair more than the other inhibits it, so that eventually only the more active unit is firing. Mutual inhibition between corresponding nodes thus produces competition between mutually exclusive interpretations of the same vertex as being either in front or in back, but not both.

Together, the mutually excitatory and inhibitory connections in this example produce a complete network in which activation tends to settle into one of two stable states: Either all the nodes in the left subnetwork are activated and all the nodes in the right network are inactive or vice versa. This mutual exclusivity in the behavior of the network thus mimics an important aspect of the perception of Necker cubes: One interpretation or the other is experienced at any given time, never both.

The network shown in Figure 6.5.1 thus accounts for the fact that the Necker cube can give rise to two different and mutually exclusive interpretations: Some presentations will activate one subnetwork, and other presentations will activate the other subnetwork. Without some additional factor, however, the network will not exhibit true multistability, for once it settles into one of these two stable perceptions, it will stay in that state until the stimulus changes. For it to alternate between these two interpretations of the same stimulus, the additional mechanism of neural fatigue is needed.

6.5.2 Neural Fatigue

Neurons tend to fire less vigorously after a period of prolonged stimulation. This happens because the biochemical resources that the cell needs to continue firing begin to become depleted over a matter of seconds, thus lowering its firing rate to the same stimulus. To understand how this aspect of neural behavior might bring about multistability, consider what happens to the two mutually inhibitory (that is, competitive) units in the simplified network shown in Figure 6.5.2A. The graph below it (Figure 6.5.2B) illustrates how the activations in the nodes change over time.

Let us suppose that unit X is initially slightly more active than unit Y because of its slightly higher input activation from the unit that is driving it. Unit X therefore inhibits unit Y more than Y inhibits X, so unit X becomes relatively more active, and Y becomes relatively less active. This domination by unit X becomes more pronounced over time until its activation reaches a maximum and unit Y's activation reaches a minimum, as indicated in Figure 6.5.2B. This behavior is due to the mutually inhibitory connections between the nodes, quite independent of fatigue. After unit X has been firing for an extended period of time, however, it begins

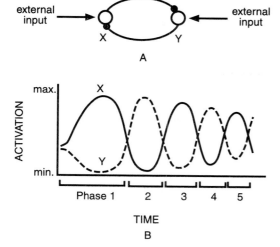

external input → ○ ● ― ● ○ ← external input
X   Y

A

max.

ACTIVATION

min.

Phase 1   2   3   4   5

TIME

B

Figure 6.5.2 Dynamics of mutual inhibition and neural fatigue. In a connectionist network with two mutually inhibitory units (A), when one unit is initially slightly more active than the other, the more active unit (X) will increase to a maximum and the less active (Y) to a minimum (B, phase 1). Neural fatigue will eventually cause the pattern of firing to reverse (B, phases 2, 3, 4, etc.). (See text for details.)

to fire more slowly as neural fatigue takes effect. This lowered activation then reduces X's inhibition of Y, causing Y's activation to rise as X's falls. Eventually, X's activation drops below Y's, at which time Y begins to inhibit X more than X inhibits Y. This situation causes Y's activation to rise to its maximum and X's activation to fall to its minimum, just the reverse of what happened previously. It is easy to see that this alternation between the dominance of X and Y could continue indefinitely, at least in theory.

The same alternation behavior occurs in the far more complex network for the Necker cube when neural fatigue is present. The eight pairs of corresponding nodes within the component subnetworks in Figure 6.5.1 are related by mutual inhibition, just as the two nodes are in Figure 6.5.2A. As a result, one subnetwork initially gains the upper hand and moves to its maximum activation, owing to mutual excitation within it causing it to act as a cohesive unit. Neural fatigue then begins to set in and reduces the domination of the one subnetwork until the other subnetwork takes over and climbs to its maximum activation. The details of the interactions are more complicated because of the larger number of nodes involved, but its globally multistable

behavior is qualitatively very similar to that of the simple two-unit network in Figure 6.5.2A.

Neural networks of this general type can simulate multistability in the perception of ambiguous figures. The critical ingredients are as follows:

1. *mutual excitation* within each of the subnetworks representing the alternative interpretations to produce cooperation within subnetworks,

2. *mutual inhibition* between the subnetworks for alternative interpretations to produce competition between them, and

3. *neural fatigue* that decreases the activation of highly active units over time.

Other ambiguous figures would require quite different subnetwork representations, of course, but whatever the neural network representations might be, if the subnetworks have these three properties, they should exhibit multistability.

Data from experiments on the perception of ambiguous figures support several predictions derived from neural fatigue theories. One is that if subjects view an unambiguous version for an extended period of time, they should then tend to see the other interpretation when they are finally exposed to the ambiguous version (Hochberg, 1950). Such effects have been reported with a variety of different ambiguous stimuli (e.g., Carlson, 1953).

Another prediction of the neural fatigue hypothesis that has been supported by experimental evidence is that the rate of alternation between the two interpretations should accelerate over time (Köhler, 1940). This acceleration should occur if the fatigue that has built up during extended perception of one interpretation (call it "A") does not completely dissipate during the perception of the other interpretation (call it "B"). Then, when interpretation A is perceived for the second time, its neural representation will already be partially fatigued. As a result, the level of activation in the neural representation of A will decrease more quickly the second time than it did the first. By the same logic, similar reductions in duration will occur for the third perceptions of A and B, and the fourth, and so on. The behavior of the two-unit inhibitory network (Figure 6.5.2B) shows this kind of increase in the rate of alternation as a result of cumulative depletion of resources.

303   *Organizing Objects and Scenes*

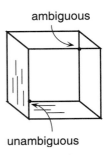

ambiguous

unambiguous

Figure 6.5.3 The stimulus for a study of multistability. Subjects were shown this stimulus and instructed to try to see either the horizontal or the vertical line in front while they fixated on the ambiguous or the unambiguous vertex. Both factors produced large effects on subjects' reported perceptions. (See text for details.) (After Peterson & Hochberg, 1983.)

6.5.3 Eye Fixations

Despite these successes, the neural fatigue hypothesis has not gone unchallenged. One alternative idea is that reversals are caused by eye movements to different fixation points. You may have noticed, for example, that if you fixate on the upper central Y-vertex of the Necker cube, you tend to perceive the cube-from-above interpretation. Fixating the lower Y-vertex similarly biases the cube-from-below interpretation. In general, the fixated vertex tends to be perceived as nearer, as Necker himself noticed. Further studies have shown that this cannot be the whole story, however, because afterimages and even stabilized images of a Necker cube have been found to reverse (Gregory, 1970; Pritchard, 1958). Moreover, there is evidence that the causal relation between eye fixations and reversals may run in the opposite direction: Eye movements may be the result of perceptual reversals rather than their cause (Noton & Stark, 1971a; Woodworth, 1938).

More recent research by Peterson and Hochberg (1983), however, has confirmed that local information around the position at which the eye is fixated *does* exert a disproportionately strong influence on what is perceived. It also showed the effect of the subject's intention to perceive a given interpretation and how such intentions interact with the position of fixation. Their subjects were presented with a modified version of the Necker cube that had one ambiguous central vertex and one unambiguous one, as illustrated in Figure 6.5.3. Subjects were instructed to fixate on the ambiguous or the unambiguous vertex during each 30-second trial. They were also told to try to achieve and hold a given interpretation, seeing either the horizontal or the vertical line in front at the fixated vertex. The total amount of time during which the subject reported each interpretation was measured.

Peterson and Hochberg found that subjects were influenced by both the vertex of fixation and the instruction to hold a particular interpretation. They were more successful at perceiving the instructed interpretation when fixating the unambiguous vertex consistent with that instruction (26 out of 30 seconds) than when fixating the ambiguous vertex (20 seconds). Correspondingly, they were less successful at achieving the instructed interpretation when fixating the vertex that was inconsistent with that instruction (13 seconds) than when fixating the ambiguous vertex (20 seconds). Both results show that local information around the fixated vertex is more powerful than local information around the other vertex. A strong effect of intention was clearly evident as well. When fixating the ambiguous vertex, subjects reported seeing the instructed interpretation for much longer than the uninstructed interpretation (20 versus 10 seconds), and the same was true for the unambiguous vertex (19 versus 11 seconds).

6.5.4 The Role of Instructions

Another challenge to the neural fatigue hypothesis has come from Irvin Rock and his colleagues, who have questioned whether this simple mechanism is indeed sufficient to explain multistability of ambiguous figures (Girgus, Rock, & Egatz, 1977; Rock, Gopnik, & Hall, 1994; Rock & Mitchener, 1992). Rock pointed out that in virtually all previous research on ambiguous figures, the experimenter has informed subjects about the two alternative perceptions beforehand. But what happens if a naive subject is *not* instructed about the nature of the two different interpretations before viewing the ambiguous figure? Will both be perceived and will they alternate back and forth as the neural fatigue hypothesis implies, or will they simply perceive whatever interpretation they achieve first?

Rock and Mitchener (1992) showed 18 subjects three ambiguous figures like the one illustrated in Figure 6.5.4A. Their only instructions before viewing the figures were, "Tell me what you see. Continue to look at

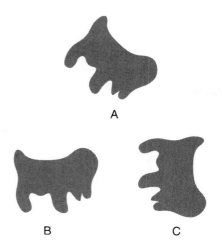

A

B   C

Figure 6.5.4 Ambiguous figures used to study the effects of instructions on multistability. When subjects were shown the ambiguous figure in part A for 30 seconds with no instructions about reversibility, many reported seeing no reversals, even when explicitly probed with unambiguous versions of the same figure (e.g., the dog in part B and the chef in part C). Once informed of the ambiguity, all subjects reported many reversals.

the picture, since I am going to ask you some questions about it later.'' After viewing the three figures sequentially for 30 seconds each, they were interviewed to determine whether they had perceived any interpretation other than the one they had reported initially. To aid in eliciting reports of perceptual change in the interview phase, the experimenter showed subjects unambiguous versions of each stimulus figure, such as those illustrated in Figures 6.5.4B and 6.5.4C. By their own report, fully one third of the subjects reported *never* seeing any of the three figures reverse. Once they were given the standard instructions, however, all of them reported seeing frequent reversals.

Such results challenge the idea that neural fatigue alone is sufficient to explain multistability. But recall that in the network theory of the Necker cube described above, two additional conditions were required for a network to be multistable: (1) The alternative interpretations had to be represented within different internally cooperative subnetworks, and (2) these subnetworks had to compete with each other through mutual inhibition. The implications of the these conditions in network architecture for eliciting multistability in human observers are (1) that subjects must have perceived the two alternative interpretations previously for both alternative subnetworks to be available in the first

place and (2) that the subjects must realize (at a perceptual level) the competitive, mutually exclusive relation between the alternative interpretations. These conditions are just what the standard experimental instructions ensure, of course, and just what are (purposely) missing in Rock's experiments.

In light of the network-based theory of multistability, then, it is not too surprising that Rock and Mitchener (1992) found many subjects who failed to report spontaneous reversals. Indeed, the surprising thing is that *any* subjects experienced reversals under these conditions. Perhaps they were not truly naive about ambiguous figures. After all, science museums and television programs—as well as perception textbooks—often include material on ambiguous figures, making it difficult to find adults who are truly naive. Rock, Gopnik, and Hall (1994) therefore reasoned that young children were far more likely to be naive than adults were. They found that without explicit instructions about the alternative interpretations, three- to four-year-old children *never* report spontaneous reversals during extended viewing of three ambiguous figures (including the vase/faces and the duck/rabbit shown in Figure 1.1.5). These children also showed slower reversal rates than adults once they were given instructions about the alternative perceptions.

Another possible explanation of spontaneous reversal in naive adult subjects is that the instruction to stare at the same figure for 30 seconds may well make some subjects suspicious that something might be odd about these particular figures. This might then lead them to search for an alternative interpretation in a way that does not occur in normal perception. In any case, it is not yet clear the conditions under which the visual system might spontaneously achieve alternative interpretations of an image for which it already has a fully viable one. This is a difficult and deep question that has received little serious attention.

6.6 Development of Perceptual Organization

We said at the beginning of this chapter that empiricist theorists asserted that the visual world of a newborn baby is completely unorganized and that all organization has to arise from experience with the world. Gestalt

Organizing Objects and Scenes

theorists, in contrast, suggested that most, if not all, of the basic organizational processes operate from birth and therefore do not need to be learned. There is a third alternative, however, which is that organizational processes are not present at birth but develop in a predetermined way as the infant matures. Now that we know something about what kinds of organization are present in adults, we can ask which of these three developmental views applies to the processes underlying perceptual organization.

6.6.1 The Habituation Paradigm

Answering this question is not as easy as it might seem, because newborn babies cannot describe their visual experiences—at least, not directly. Determining what their visual experience might be like therefore requires nonverbal behavioral techniques. Several revealing methods are now available and have told us a great deal about the visual world of infants.

The problem of grouping in infant vision has been studied extensively by Philip Kellman, Elizabeth Spelke, and their associates, using the **habituation paradigm**. In this procedure, which has unlocked a number of previously inaccessible secrets of infant perception, babies are exposed to an initially novel stimulus and allowed to look at it as much as they want. For example, they might be shown a big red square. The amount of time they spend looking at this figure is measured over a series of trials. As you might expect, the time they spend looking at the object decreases with successive blocks of trials as they **habituate**; that is, they look at it for less time over blocks as its novelty wears off. Once their looking time has decreased by some criterial amount— say, 80%—they are shown one of two displays. One is the same as the habituated display (the big red square), and the other is new (for example, a little green circle). Even very young infants will spend more time looking at the novel display than at the old one, a phenomenon known as **dishabituation**.

This technique was applied to the problem of grouping in infants by Kellman and Spelke (1983) as follows. The initial display to which infants were habituated was ambiguous because its center was occluded by a surface in front of it, as shown in Figure 6.6.1. The question was whether the infants perceived the two ends of this display as being connected behind the occluder into a sin-

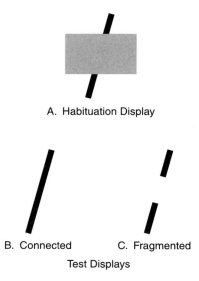

A. Habituation Display

B. Connected   C. Fragmented

Test Displays

Figure 6.6.1 The habituation paradigm for studying development of organization. Infants were initially adapted to an ambiguous stimulus (A) in which two regions were partially occluded by another. Following habituation, they were shown an unoccluded test stimulus that revealed either a single connected object (B) or two disconnected ones (C), and dishabituation was measured. (After Kellman & Spelke, 1983.)

gle perceptual object. To find out, Kellman and Spelke tested them with two disoccluded displays, one revealing a single connected object and the other revealing two disconnected objects with a gap where the occluder had been. If the infants had perceived the center-occluded display as covering a single connected object, they should spend more time looking at the fragmented test display because it is different from what they perceived in the occluded display. But if they had perceived the center-occluded display as covering two disconnected objects, they should spend more time looking at the connected test display.

6.6.2 The Development of Grouping

There is an interesting developmental story to be told about what babies do in this situation. Which test display they look at longer depends critically on both the particular grouping factors that are present in the habituation display and the age of the infant. If four-month-old infants are shown the static display depicted in Figure 6.6.1, they do not spend much time looking at it to begin with—it's sort of boring—and show no particular preference for looking at the fragmented rod when

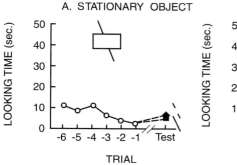

A. STATIONARY OBJECT

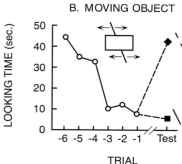

B. MOVING OBJECT

Figure 6.6.2 Grouping by good continuation and common fate. When the two occluded regions are stationary, four-month-old infants do not dishabituate to either test stimulus. When the regions move together, infants dishabituate to the two discon-nected objects but not to the one connected object. This result implies that they perceive the moving stimulus as a single connected object, but not the stationary stimulus. (From Kellman & Spelke, 1983.)

they are tested after habituation. The looking time data for this display are plotted in the left graph in Figure 6.6.2. However, if four-month-olds are shown a *moving* display in which the two ends of the rod oscillate back and forth in common motion, they show the dramatically different pattern of responses plotted in the right graph in Figure 6.6.2. They spend much more time looking at the habituation display in the first place—moving objects are much more interesting—and after they have habituated, they show a very strong preference for looking at the fragmented test display.

From this pattern of responses, we conclude that the infants perceived the occluded habituation display as a single, connected object in the moving-object condition but not in the stationary-object condition. Interestingly, any uniform translatory motion produced this result, and it occurred even if the two occluded parts of the display were quite dissimilar in shape, color, size, and texture (see Figure 6.6.3). Thus, what Wertheimer (1923/1950) called "common fate" seems to be a very important principle of perceptual organization for four-month-olds. This does not prove that grouping by common fate is innate, however, since it could have been learned some time during the previous four months. Even so, it is clearly present very early in infancy, much earlier than most researchers expected.

Other classical grouping factors do not produce this pattern of results with such young infants, however. If the habituation display contains two stationary parts that are similar in color, size, orientation, and texture and have good continuation of edges across the oc-cluded contour (see Figure 6.6.4), they show no measurable preference for the separated over the connected display. This indicates that four-month-old infants do not use these static grouping factors to complete the two visible ends in the display. Contrary to the beliefs of Gestalt theorists, then, it appears that static similarity grouping is not an innate ability, but one that either is learned through experience by interacting with the world or develops spontaneously as the infant develops.

When do these static factors in grouping become effective in governing object perception? Spelke (1990) reports that when five-month-old infants were presented with the two habituation displays shown in Figure 6.6.4,

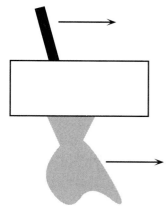

Figure 6.6.3 Common fate overcomes static grouping factors. The pattern of results for moving stimuli in Figure 6.6.2 was obtained even when the two regions differed dramatically in their static properties, such as color, shape, and continuity. (After Kellman & Spelke, 1983.)

Habituation Displays

(a)

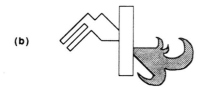

(b)

Test Displays

Figure 6.6.4 Static grouping factors emerge later in development. Four-month-old infants fail to show dishabituation to two disconnected regions following habituation to occluded regions that were similar in color, size, orientation, texture, and continuity. Seven-month-olds, however, did show dishabituation, indicating that they initially perceived a single object behind the occluder. (From Spelke, 1990.)

they dishabituated equally to the two test displays shown beneath them. At seven months, however, infants who were habituated to the display with homogeneous color and aligned edges dishabituated more to the fragmented test display than to the unitary one. Thus, the ability to use good continuation and similarity of color as information influencing unit formation appears to develop between five and seven months of age. These results cannot be explained by an inability to discriminate such properties because other studies have shown that young infants *can* detect the presence of homogeneous versus heterogeneous surface coloration (Fantz, Fagan, & Miranda, 1975), good continuation of contours (Van Giffen & Haith, 1984), and even symmetry (Bornstein, Ferdinandsen, & Gross, 1981). Younger infants therefore must not yet realize that these properties are relevant to perceiving the unity of partly occluded objects.

Given the early emergence of common fate as an effective factor in unit formation, one can ask whether it is based on motion in the retinal image or motion of an object in the world. Kellman, Gleitman, and Spelke (1987) designed a clever experiment to answer this question for center-occluded displays like the ones shown in Figure 6.6.5. They placed the infant in a seat that could either be stationary or be moved to control observer motion as well as object motion. Figure 6.6.5 shows the four conditions in the experiment: stationary object with stationary observer (part A), moving object with stationary observer (part B), stationary object with moving observer (part C), and moving object with moving observer (part D). The results showed that babies dishabituated to the fragmented display only when the occluded object was in motion (parts B and D). They showed virtually no dishabituation when the object was stationary, even when their own motion in the chair produced considerable movement in the retinal image (part C). Thus, it appears that even at four months of age, grouping by common fate is based on relatively sophisticated analysis of object motion rather than simply on movement within the retinal image.

From these and other findings, Spelke (1990) argues that neither the strict empiricist nor the strict nativist view is correct for infant perception of object unity. Rather, she suggests that babies are born with a primi-

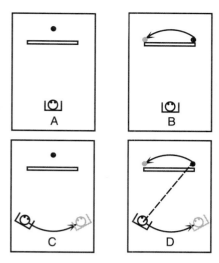

Figure 6.6.5 Retinal versus object motion in infant perception of unified objects. Infants dishabituated only when the common motion of the habituation display was caused by object motion (B and D) and not by observer motion (C). (After Kellman, Gleitman, & Spelke, 1987.)

made in studying the development of perceptual organization, how infants acquire the ability to perceive objects as being unified behind an occluder remains something of a mystery. We now know that organizational processes are present much earlier than most empiricists would have supposed, but they do not appear to be innate. Perhaps some sort of maturational explanation will turn out to be correct after all.

tive mechanism for grouping disconnected pieces of objects that depends almost exclusively on how they move in the world, that is, on the principle of common fate. This enables them to correctly organize their visual experiences into objects, at least under favorable circumstances. As a result of their properly organized experiences with moving objects, they come to learn that the objects that are so defined tend to have other correlated properties that are also useful in defining their unity, such as smooth, continuous contours, homogeneous color and texture, symmetry, and the like. This knowledge then forms the basis for extending the conditions that lead to veridical organization into objects until the baby eventually acquires the competence that defines adult performance.

As simple and elegant as this theory is, it is probably not sufficient to explain early development of grouping. When newborns were tested with motion displays like ones shown in Figure 6.6.1, they looked more at the complete rod than at the broken one, which is the opposite of what one would predict if Spelke's theory were correct (Slater, Johnson, Brown, & Badenoch, 1996). By two months of age, however, infants reliably prefer the broken rod after habituation to a moving display, provided the occluding rectangle is not too wide (Johnson & Aslin, 1995). Despite the great advances that have been

Organizing Objects and Scenes

Suggestions for Further Reading

Koffka, K. (1935). *Principles of Gestalt psychology*. New York: Harcourt Brace. The first portion of this classic work presents a Gestalt treatment of perceptual organization.

Palmer, S. E., & Rock, I. (1994). Rethinking perceptual organization: The role of uniform connectedness. *Psychological Bulletin and Review, 1,* 29–55. This review article presents a revisionist view of Gestalt principles of organization that attempts to integrate them into a modern computational framework.

Kellman, P. K., & Shipley, T. F. (1991). A theory of visual interpolation in object perception. *Cognitive Psychology, 23,* 141–221. Kellman and Shipley present a computational theory that unifies many superficially diverse phenomena into a coherent framework.

Pomerantz, J. R., & Kubovy, M. (1986). Theoretical approaches to perceptual organization: Simplicity and likelihood principles. In K. R. Boff, L. Kaufman, & J. P. Thomas (Eds.), *Handbook of perception and human performance: Vol. 2. Cognitive processes and performance.* New York: Wiley. These authors review many phenomena of perceptual organization to shed light on whether the Gestalt (simplicity-based) or Helmholtzian (likelihood-based) approach to selection among alternative organizations provides the best account of known phenomena.

Kanizsa, G. (1979). *Organization in vision: Essays on Gestalt perception.* New York: Praeger. This volume contains a collection of papers on visual organization by one of the most important modern Gestalt psychologists.

Perceiving Object Properties and Parts

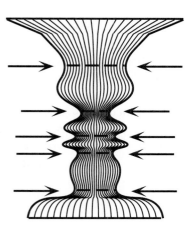

Meaningful 3-D objects are the most fundamental units of visual experience. What we generally perceive as a result of looking at the environment is not the 2-D array of colored patches that stimulate the retina, nor a "primal sketch" of primitive edges, lines, and blobs, nor even a "2.5-D sketch" of surfaces at various depths and orientations. Rather, we experience what seems to be an array of solid objects, composed of various parts and positioned relative to us and to each other in 3-D gravitational space. In the next three chapters we will examine some of the further processes required to experience the properties and parts of 3-D objects in a way that will ultimately yield information about what kind of objects they are and of what use they might be to us in pursuing our everyday plans and goals.

The environmental objects we perceive differ in many ways that can readily be seen. Among the most important properties are their color, texture, size, position, orientation, shape, motion, and parts. Most of these properties are themselves complex entities having further internal structure. For example, the perceived color of an object's surface can be decomposed into the three dimensions of hue, saturation, and lightness, as we discussed at length in Chapter 3. The spatial properties of an object likewise require analysis into a set of more basic components. Its perceived position and orientation, for example, must each contain at least three dimensions to fully represent the object's physical position and orientation in the 3-D environment. Moreover, its physical extension can usually be decomposed into a configuration of different parts in a particular spatial arrangement. In this chapter we will begin to discuss the visual perception of environmental objects by considering how observers recover the intrinsic properties of external objects from the properties of their projected retinal images under the given viewing conditions. We will then consider how such perceived objects might be analyzed perceptually into an arrangement of component parts.

Constancy and Illusion. Perhaps the most fundamental and important fact about our conscious experi-ence of object properties is that they are more closely correlated with the intrinsic properties of the *distal stimulus* (objects in the environment) than they are with the properties of the *proximal stimulus* (the image on the retina). This is perhaps so obvious that it is easily overlooked. How it happens is not so easy to explain, however.

Right now, I perceive my cat's location in terms of his position in the world, curled up on the end of the sofa. I do not perceive his position in terms of his location within my retinal image, although he is currently occupying a region in the upper left quadrant of my visual field as I type this sentence. Similarly, I perceive his size in terms of his actual physical extension (about 18 inches long) rather than the dimensions of his retinal image (about $4°$ of visual angle from where I currently sit). Therefore, the first issue that must be addressed in understanding the perception of object properties is how this is possible. After all, the light that is reflected from objects is projected into my eyes as a pair of 2-D images that constitute the starting point for all visual perception. How do people manage to recover the intrinsic properties of environmental objects from these retinal images?

As we said in Chapter 1, the fact that people veridically perceive the constant, unchanging properties of external objects rather than the more transient properties of their retinal images is called *perceptual constancy*. We examined one example in some detail in Chapter 3 when we discussed color constancy. The gist of that discussion was that a variety of complex processes are required to explain how people recover information about surface reflectance despite differences in illumination that change the physical spectrum of light stimulating the retina. Analogous problems arise in understanding how we perceive virtually all spatial properties as well, including an object's size, shape, orientation, and position, as we will soon see. In each case, approximately veridical perception of intrinsic object properties is achieved through a variety of processes that include both automatic and attentional components (Epstein & Broota, 1986; Epstein & Lovitts, 1985).

There have been two major theoretical approaches to perceptual constancy. The classic view due to Helmholtz, which is sometimes called the *indirect approach*, hypothesizes the computational integration of the retinal properties of an object's image with other sources of information that are relevant to determining the object's intrinsic properties in the environment. For example, an object's size can be computed from the size of its retinal image and its distance from the observer. Any information about the distance to the object can be used, including both the optical and nonoptical sources discussed in Chapter 5. This approach to constancy is called indirect partly because it hypothesizes that constancy is mediated by other aspects of perception (such as distance, in the case of size) and partly because it contrasts with the direct approach advocated by Gibson (1950, 1966).

As we mentioned in Chapter 5, Gibson pointed out that the properties of objects that are constant over different viewing conditions are often correlated with higher-order invariants of optical structure in the image. When an object is seen resting on a coplanar textured ground plane, for instance, the number of texture elements it occludes is invariant over different viewing distances and perspectives. This higher-order variable is therefore sufficient to support perceived size constancy without resorting to nonoptical sources of information. We will return to this controversy over the proper theoretical treatment of constancy later in the chapter.

Somewhat surprisingly, the same processes that usually result in constancy—that is, veridical perception—sometimes produce illusions. The reason is that, as we suggested in Chapters 1 and 2, veridical perception of the environment often requires heuristic processes based on assumptions that are usually, but not always, true. When they are true, all is well, and we see more or less what is actually there. When these assumptions are false, however, we perceive a situation that differs systematically from reality: that is, an illusion. In several cases we will find that in the perception of object properties, constancy and illusion are therefore opposite sides of the same perceptual coin.

Modes of Perception: Proximal and Distal. We have just claimed that perceptual constancy refers to perceptions that correspond to the intrinsic properties of environmental objects rather than those of their pro-

Figure 7.0.1 Lightness constancy. The sides of the church appear to be the same white color (i.e., have the same reflectance) despite fairly dramatic differences in their luminance values due to differential illumination in shadows and direct light.

jected images. This makes it sound as if the experience of object-based (distal) versus image-based (proximal) properties is an either/or proposition. Although this is often the case, it is nevertheless true that we can sometimes be aware of both simultaneously. In the case of lightness perception, for example, we can see the region of a wall on which a shadow is cast as being darker than surrounding regions at the same time as it appears to have the same surface color (reflectance) as the rest of the wall. An example of such a situation is shown in Figure 7.0.1. Similarly, in shape perception we can see the top of the dining room table as being rectangular in shape at the same time as we realize that its retinal image is trapezoidal, as illustrated in Figure 7.0.2. How are we to understand such seemingly contradictory perceptions?

An interesting approach to this problem that has been taken by a number of different theorists is to posit the existence of two different modes of visual perception. What we will call the **proximal mode** reflects mainly the properties of the retinal image, or proximal stimulus. What we will call the **distal mode** reflects mainly the properties of the environmental object, or distal stimulus.[1]

---

[1] Gibson (1950) referred to them as the "visual field" and the "visual world," respectively; Mack (1978) called them the "proximal" and "constancy" modes; and Rock (1983) called them the "proximal" and "world" modes. In this chapter, we call them the "proximal" and "distal" modes to make their contrastive meanings as clear and unambiguous as possible.

Figure 7.0.2 Shape constancy. The table is perceived as rectangular even though its image is trapezoidal on the retina.

Perceptual experience can often be considered a blend of these two aspects. One aspect can dominate the other in different situations, depending on the task and the observer's intentions. Perceptual constancy is, by definition, the hallmark of distal mode perception because it is the properties of the distal stimulus that remain constant despite variable viewing conditions. Indeed, perception is dominated by the distal mode under most ordinary circumstances, such as locomotion in the world, coordinating bodily interactions with objects, and making standard comparisons among objects. It makes sense to be strongly in the distal mode, for example, in trying to choose the largest piece of cake on the dessert tray. Otherwise you might erroneously choose the smallest piece simply because it is closest, thereby causing its retinal image to be the largest. But it is the biggest piece of cake we are after, not the biggest retinal image, so the distal mode is appropriate.

There are other activities for which proximal mode perception is more useful. Suppose you were trying to paint a realistic picture of a scene. To do this as accurately as possible, you need to create an image on the canvas that will stimulate the viewer's retina in the same way as the original scene would. Therefore, you need to paint what is essentially a large-scale (and uninverted) version of the optical image that falls on your retina. In this situation, it is the size of objects' images that would be important for you to perceive and reproduce on the canvas. The same would be true for painting other

properties of objects in the picture, such as their shape, color, orientation, and position. Representational painters are actually trained in what we are calling proximal mode perception so that they can realistically and accurately recreate the properties of optical images on painted canvas. When viewers then look at such paintings, their visual systems enable them to perceive the painted scene as containing objects of the proper size, shape, color, and so forth.

Which perceptual mode you are in can be strongly influenced by explicit instructions (Carlson, 1960, 1977). If you were shown two identical disks at different distances in an experiment, for example, and were asked to compare the "apparent sizes of the two objects," you would probably settle into the distal mode and report them as being about the same in size. If you were then shown the same display and were asked to compare the "sizes of the objects' images as they appear from where you are standing," you would probably shift to proximal mode and report that the closer one appeared bigger.

The existence of proximal and distal modes of perception can complicate the study of perceptual constancy considerably. If there are indeed two aspects of conscious perception that correspond to the proximal and distal modes, perceptual judgments can easily go one way or the other, depending on the instructions and the task. Perhaps for this reason perceptual constancy is seldom complete. Indeed, most experiments show systematic deviations from accurate perception of objective properties in the direction of proximal image matches. This phenomenon of a perceptual compromise between true proximal and distal matches is called **under-constancy**. We will encounter several instances of it later in this chapter.

7.1 Size

The first constancy problem we will tackle is how the size of an environmental object can be perceived from its retinal image. At first, one might think that an object's size could be determined simply from its retinal size: All else being equal, larger objects project larger images onto the retina. We already know from Chapter 4 that visual cortex contains cells that are sensitive to a range of different sizes or scales—the so-called spatial frequency dimension of hypercolumns in area V1—so perhaps differential activity in these cells might be the basic mechanism of size perception.

A moment's reflection reveals that retinal size cannot be the sole determinant of perceived object size, however, because retinal size depends critically on the distance of the object from the observer as well as its physical size. That is, all else being equal, closer objects project larger images onto the retina than farther ones. If you hold your hand just a few inches from your face, for example, it fills almost your entire visual field, but if you move it to arm's length, it covers a much smaller area. The visual system must therefore disentangle the effects of object size and object distance in interpreting retinal size. How might this be accomplished?

7.1.1 Size Constancy

Size constancy refers to the ability to correctly perceive the constant intrinsic size of an object despite its variable retinal size due to differences in the distance from which it is viewed. Everyday experience shows that we are able to achieve this form of constancy reasonably well for most objects over a wide range of viewing distances. We seldom mistake the closer piece of cake for the bigger one, for example, despite considerable differences in retinal size due to distance. In other cases, however, size constancy breaks down rather dramatically. Cars traveling along a distant highway look no bigger than ants, and houses seen from the window of a landing plane look like tiny toy models. How can such facts about the perception of size be understood and explained?

The Size-Distance Relation. Let us first consider a computational-level description of how an observer might perceive the size of an object. As we have just argued, the fundamental fact of size perception is that two different factors determine the size of the image an object projects onto the retina: its objective size and its distance from the observer. The nature of this relation among objective size, retinal size, and distance is expressed mathematically in terms of the **size-distance relation**, which we discussed at some length in Section 5.5.4. There we focused on its implications for depth perception, concentrating on the fact that knowing something about image sizes and making some assumptions about object sizes can provide information about

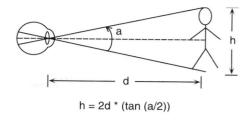

$$h = 2d * (\tan (a/2))$$

Figure 7.1.1 The size-distance relation. The size of an object can be computed from knowing the size of its retinal image (a) and the distance to the object (d).

the distance of objects from the observer. In the present context of perceiving object size, the key observation is the "flip side" of this relation: If the distance to an object is known, it can be used in conjunction with its retinal size to determine its objective size.

The equation specifying the size-distance relation is the same as that stated in Chapter 5, although it has a slightly different form:

$$h = 2d * \tan\left(\frac{a}{2}\right) \tag{7.1}$$

where h is the linear height of the environmental object, d is the distance to the object, and a is the retinal size of its image expressed in degrees of visual angle (see Figure 7.1.1). Here we have written it to express object size in terms of the relation between distance and retinal angle, whereas in Chapter 5 we wrote it to express object distance in terms of the relation between object size and image size. Equation 7.1 shows that if you know the actual distance (d) to an object—say, from binocular convergence information—then its actual size (h) can be determined from this value together with its retinal size (a).

Demonstrations of Size Constancy. You can demonstrate size constancy using the same kind of finger exercises we employed in Chapter 5. Put one index finger at arm's length with the other at half that distance, but this time move your closer finger out to the side by at least a few feet so that you can see only one finger at a time. Now with both eyes open so that you have good binocular information about the distance to the finger you are fixating, look back and forth between them and compare their sizes as objects. Not too surprisingly, they will appear to be approximately the same size, as indeed they are.

Perceiving Object Properties and Parts

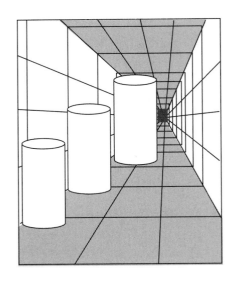

A

B

Figure 7.1.2 The hallway illusion. Although the farthest cylinder in part A appears somewhat smaller than the closest cylinder, most people are astonished that the difference is as large as it actually is: The image size of the black cylinder is identical to that of the farthest white cylinder. All three cylinders in part B are identical in image size, although the farthest looks much bigger.

This is an example of size constancy because your fingers look about the same size even though their retinal sizes differ greatly. You may simultaneously be aware of some difference in retinal size—due to proximal mode perception—but even so, you are likely to be surprised by the actual magnitude of the difference. To see how great it is, close one eye and line up the tops of your two fingers without changing their distances from your eye. The image of your closer finger will be about twice as big as that of your farther one, the image of the far finger extending only to about the knuckle of the near one.

This demonstration illustrates some of the conditions under which proximal mode perception is most likely to intrude into or even dominate awareness. You are most conscious of the difference in image sizes of two identical objects at different viewing distances when (1) the difference in retinal size is large, (2) the two images are close together, (3) you reduce the information about depth (e.g., by closing one eye), and (4) you consciously try to attend to image-based (i.e., proximal mode) differences.

Size constancy is also at work, at least to some degree, when the information about depth comes purely from pictorial depth cues. An example is given in Figure 7.1.2. In part A, perspective information gives the strong impression of depth in a receding corridor. Within this context, the three white cylinders appear to be the same environmental size, the largest cylinder appearing closest and the smallest one appearing farthest. Despite the differences in depth, you are (or can become) aware that there are differences in image sizes among the cylinders. Even so, the actual magnitudes of the differences are quite surprising. For comparison, the black cylinder next to the closest white one is actually the same retinal size as the farthest white cylinder. This demonstrates that the farthest cylinder is actually only one-third the retinal size of the closest cylinder. Part B shows an illusion based on the same basic phenomenon. Here the cylinders are all exactly the same in retinal size, yet the farthest one appears enormously larger. This illusion is similar in many respects to the Ponzo illusion (see Figure 7.1.10) but with much stronger depth information.

Most people find that, no matter how hard they try, they cannot see the retinal sizes of objects accurately in the presence of large differences in depth. This demonstrates that size constancy mechanisms operate even when we try to inhibit them by attending specifically to image size in the proximal mode. That is why artists are often trained to gauge the size of an object in their

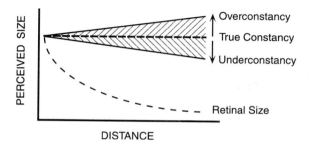

Figure 7.1.3 Approximations to constancy. With perfect constancy, perceived object size would not change with distance (flat dashed line). Actual performance deviates somewhat from perfect constancy depending on the instructions, but it never corresponds to retinal size (curved dashed line).

painting by closing one eye and measuring the object's projected size against their thumb or paintbrush held at arm's length. This provides an objective measure of image size, one that is uncontaminated by the visual system's tendency to take distance into account when perceiving objective size.

Departures from Constancy. The reader may have noticed that many of the statements we have made about size constancy contain some form of hedge, such as saying that it is "approximate" or that it occurs only under "certain conditions." This is because controlled experiments show that size constancy is not perfect.

In experiments on size constancy, subjects are typically shown a standard object of a particular size at a particular distance—say, a line 12 inches tall at a distance of 6 feet from the observer—and are then asked to pick out the comparison object that looks the same size at some different distance, say, 10 feet away. This procedure is repeated at many different distances for each standard. If subjects always chose the comparison object that was objectively the same size as the standard—that is, if size constancy were perfect—the graph of their choices would be the flat line labeled "True Constancy" in Figure 7.1.3. If they always chose the comparison object that projected the same sized image as the standard, the graph of their choices would fall along the lower curve labeled "Retinal Size."

Typically, the results lie somewhere between these two extremes but closer to true constancy. Subjects come very close to matching objective size when (1) there is good distance information from binocular view-

ing conditions and (2) they are instructed to judge how big the object looks. As the depth information available to the subject becomes weaker—for example, when the subject views the scene with only one eye and/or through a small peephole—subjects tend to choose objects that are closer to retinal size matches (Holway & Boring, 1941). It is as though subjects are making a compromise between constancy (distal mode perception) and the size of the retinal image (proximal mode perception). This phenomenon of size underconstancy may arise from perceiving objects as closer than they really are.

Size constancy can also be affected in complex ways by different instructions about how to perform the size-matching task. When subjects are told to judge how big an object *looks*, they usually exhibit approximate constancy, often with a small degree of underconstancy. However, if they are instructed to judge how big an object actually *is*—so-called objective instructions—they often exhibit **overconstancy**: the tendency to match the standard with a farther comparison object that is larger (Carlson, 1960; Gilinsky, 1955). It is as though subjects know that apparent size diminishes with distance, and so they overcompensate for this relation by choosing an object that looks somewhat bigger. Because an object looks about as big as it actually is, choosing one that looks somewhat bigger than that will result in overconstancy.

Most examples of underconstancy and overconstancy are relatively minor departures from veridical perception. But size constancy can break down quite dramatically in extreme situations. The most familiar examples occur in observing people, cars, and houses at large distances, such as from the top of a tall building or from a low-flying airplane. If size constancy were perfect, everything would appear to be normal in size—ideally, just as big as if you were standing next to them. But they don't. Indeed, they don't even appear slightly smaller, as would be expected from underconstancy. Rather, they appear *much* smaller, like tiny toy versions of themselves. Why does this happen? How can we explain both the successes and failures of size constancy?

Taking Account of Distance. A number of different theories of size constancy have been proposed. The classic explanation is in the tradition of Helmholtz's notion of unconscious inference. It proposes that the visual

Perceiving Object Properties and Parts

system effectively computes object size from retinal size and perceived distance using something like Equation 7.1. This indirect theory of size constancy is often referred to as **taking account of distance** (e.g., Epstein, 1973; Rock, 1975). It is appealing in large part because of its generality: It applies to any situation in which the observer has information about how far away an object is. It therefore does not depend crucially on the presence of other contextual objects that are necessary components for the direct theories of constancy discussed below.

When based on the correct size-distance relation (Equation 7.1), the unconscious inference theory of size perception seems to predict perfect size constancy. How then can it also explain departures from constancy? The answer is simplicity itself: Inaccuracies in size perception should result from inaccuracies in distance perception. Specifically, underconstancy will occur when large distances are perceived as smaller than they actually are. If the observer perceives the object in question to be closer than it really is, computing the object's size from the size-distance equation with this underestimate will necessarily result in perceiving the object as smaller than it actually is. Overconstancy can also be predicted by the theory. If the object appears to be farther than it actually is, it would be perceived as bigger than it actually is. Thus, the unconscious inference explanation of deviations from size constancy is that they result from systematic misperception of the distance to the target object.

This is an elegant theory, but is it true? Unfortunately, the answer is neither clear nor simple. Although much supporting evidence has been reported, there is also conflicting evidence. Most disconcertingly, cases have been reported in which size has been systematically *overestimated* at the same time as distance has been systematically *underestimated* (Gruber, 1954). This is exactly the opposite of what is predicted by taking distance into account. Perhaps the safest summary statement is that more is involved in size constancy experiments than just taking perceived distance into account. The nature of the viewing conditions, the instructions given to subjects, the kinds of judgments required, and individual differences among subjects all seem to affect the results (see Epstein, Park, and Casey, 1961, for a review).

Texture Occlusion. A fundamentally different theoretical account of size perception was offered by Gibson

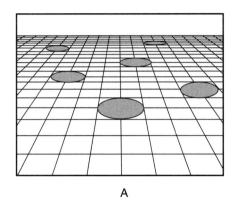

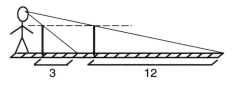

Figure 7.1.4 Textural cues to size constancy. Objects that are the same size cover the same number of textural elements under certain conditions (A). If the objects are elevated from the textured plane, however, this relation does not hold (B). (See text for details.)

(1950) within his framework of direct perception (see Section 2.1.3). He proposed that texture provided a potentially important source of information about object size because the texture elements occluded by an object could effectively provide a uniform size scale relative to which the object's size could be perceived. As illustrated in Figure 7.1.4A, if two flat objects rest on the same textured surface at different distances from the observer, the number of texture elements they occlude provides an indication of their relative sizes. If they cover the same number of elements, for example, they must be the same size. This explanation is compatible with the tenets of direct perception because it identifies perceived size with a higher-order stimulus property: the number of texture elements occluded. It does not invoke any mediating perceptions, such as the perceived distance to the object.

Although it is true that texture occlusion can provide some information about relative object size, it is important to realize that its generality is restricted by the conditions that must be met for it to be a meaningful indicator of object size:

1. The objects whose sizes are to be compared must be seen against the same textured surface. If the objects are seen against different textured surfaces or even against a single untextured surface, nothing meaningful can be said about their relative sizes based on texture occlusion.

2. The texture elements on the background surface must be of approximately the same size. If they vary so that the texture elements covered by one object are systematically larger or smaller than those covered by another, the amount of texture occluded is not a valid measure of object size.[2]

3. The objects whose sizes are being judged must be coplanar with the textured plane (Gillam, 1981). If the objects protrude from the textured surface—as a tree does from a field of grass or as a ball does from a tiled floor—this simple relation does not hold, as illustrated in Figure 7.1.4B.

These restrictions mean that texture occlusion is a less useful indicator of object size in natural scenes than one might expect. Moreover, unlike unconscious inference theory, texture occlusion cannot provide a general explanation of size perception, because it provides information only about the relative sizes of objects. The texture elements effectively provide a size scale relative to which the size of any coplanar object can be measured, but this will not tell the observer how big any object is in absolute terms unless the absolute size of the texture elements is known. Since we are able to perceive absolute sizes in many circumstances, some additional factor must be at work.

It is worth pointing out that texture may figure importantly in size perception in ways other than the number of texture elements occluded. As discussed in Chapter 5, for instance, texture gradients can provide quantitative information about depth. It can therefore serve a useful function in determining object size via unconscious inference using perceived distance. However,

this function is quite different from the texture occlusion proposal made by Gibson because it postulates that the effect on perceived size is mediated by the perception of distance rather than being used directly, as Gibson suggested.

Relative Size. Another explanation that is compatible with direct theories of size perception and constancy can be constructed from the invariance of the relative sizes of adjacent objects. According to this **proportionality hypothesis**, size constancy is not really a problem because the ratios between image heights of objects at the same distance will be the same, whether they are observed from near or far (Rock & Ebenholtz, 1959). If a man is four times taller than the dog he is walking, for example, that ratio will be the same whether they are 10 feet away or 20 feet away, as illustrated in Figure 7.1.5.

This account of size perception is precisely analogous to the ratio theory of lightness constancy described in Chapter 3. It is also similar to Gibson's theory of size perception based on texture occlusion, because that proposal ultimately rests on the constant size ratio between the occluding object and the texture elements. It differs from the unconscious inference theory because it does not require that distance be taken into account in any way. Distance is simply irrelevant, provided the objects whose size ratios are in question happen to be located at the same distance from the viewer. Note that this is a significant constraint, however, one that severely limits the conditions under which the proportionality principle is relevant. If the dog suddenly runs away from its master and toward the observer, for instance, the 4:1 size ratio will no longer hold.

The influence of relative size on size perception was studied by Rock and Ebenholz (1959) under controlled conditions. They showed subjects a luminous line inside a luminous frame within a dark room, as illustrated in Figure 7.1.6A. The line was 3 inches tall inside a rectangle that was 4 inches tall. Subjects then turned around to view a second display at the same distance as the first. The second rectangle was 12 inches tall, as shown in

---

[2] Unless the visual system has information about the distance to the texture elements that can be used to verify their uniformity in size, it must assume that the texture elements are of equal size. As a result, this explanation of size constancy actually presupposes size constancy in terms of the uniform size of the texture elements themselves. It is therefore circular as an explanation of size constancy, although it still can be used effectively as a valid method for estimating relative object sizes under appropriate circumstances.

Perceiving Object Properties and Parts

Figure 7.1.5 Relative size is invariant with distance. This man is about four times taller than his dog regardless of how far they are from the observer. This relation holds only if they are next to each other, however. If the dog were to run toward the observer, the ratio would change.

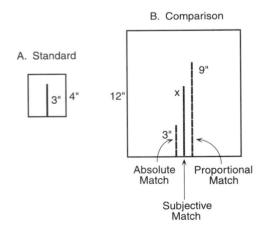

Figure 7.1.6 Effects of relative size on size perception. Subjects were shown a standard line inside a standard frame (A) and asked to set a variable line (x) inside a second frame (B) to match the standard line. People set the line closer to the same relative size (9 inches) than to the same absolute size (3 inches).

Figure 7.1.6B, and subjects were told to adjust the length of the line inside it to exactly match the length of the previously viewed line, without looking back and forth. If size perception were based exclusively on actual lengths in the environment, subjects should have adjusted the second line to a 3-inch length. If it were based exclusively on relative size, they should have set it to 9 inches, because the height ratio of the second display (9:12) should be the same as that of the first (3:4). In fact, subjects set the second line to a length of almost 7 inches, which is between the two predictions but closer to the one based on proportional size. Therefore, it appears that relative size has a substantial effect on size perception.

It is important to realize, however, that relative size cannot explain the full range of size perception phenomena. Like texture occlusion, it provides information only up to a scaling factor, so it alone cannot determine the absolute size of objects. Under normal conditions, however, relationally determined size perception converges with distance-based size perception to produce normal size constancy (Rock & Ebenholtz, 1959). The proportionality hypothesis also has difficulty explaining why constancy fails as distance increases. This is a problem because size ratios remain constant no matter how far away objects are. For example, the size ratio of cars to houses is the same when viewed from a distant hill as from across the street.

Results that are often cited as evidence against direct accounts of size perception concern the effects of ocular depth information on perceiving the size of a single object. The reader will recall from Chapter 5 that ocular depth information refers to facts about the state of the eyes—accommodation (the variable shape of the lens) and binocular convergence (the angle between the left and right eye's lines of sight when fixating an object)—rather than facts about the optical images that stimulate them. If subjects are shown a single circle stereoscopically at different convergence angles, so that they have the same retinal size and same retinal position in all cases, for example, the circle's perceived size will change dramatically from small (when converged for a close distance) to large (when converged for a far distance).

Such changes in size are taken as evidence against direct theories of size perception because there are no differences in optical structure that could produce a higher-order invariant to account for the differences in perceived size. While this is true, it shows only that direct theories cannot account for size perception under all possible conditions. They may still be useful in explaining many other phenomena in which complex optical relations are available. It seems likely that the visual system uses whatever information it can get about the distance to an object to compute its intrinsic size. In many cases, this includes both ocular and optical information.

The Horizon Ratio. Another source of information about the size of an object on a plane comes from its relation to the horizon of that plane. As illustrated for the ground plane in Figure 7.1.7, if the horizon of a surface is visible (or can be derived from visible information) and the perpendicular distance from the observation point to the surface is known, the size of an object on that plane can be determined geometrically (Sedgwick, 1986). (This fact is closely related to depth information from a position relative to the horizon of a surface, discussed in Section 5.5.3.) Even if the perpendicular dis-

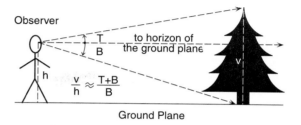

Figure 7.1.7 The horizon ratio relation. The perpendicular height (v) of an object resting on a surface (here, the ground plane) can be determined from the visual angles of its top (T) and bottom (B) relative to the line of sight to the horizon and the perpendicular distance to the surface (h). When the angles T and B are relatively small, this relation is well approximated by the simple horizon ratio relation: $v/h = (T + B)/B$.

tance to the surface is not known, the relative heights of two objects resting on the same surface can be determined.

Development of Size Constancy. The foregoing discussion argues that people can perceive the intrinsic size of an object by performing a computation that reflects both the retinal size of the target object and its distance from the observer. Is this ability learned by interaction with the world (e.g., by correlating visual features with information from touch), or is it prewired in each person's visual nervous system at birth?

Recent evidence suggests that size constancy is innate. Slater, Mattock, and Brown (1990) studied this issue using a habituation paradigm (see Section 6.6.1). In the habituation phase of the experiment, each infant was presented with either a large or a small cube at different distances over many trials. They were then tested with either the same cube they had just seen or one that was identical except for its size, and their looking behavior was measured. The test trials were cleverly constructed so that the retinal sizes of the two cubes on the two test trials were identical, that is, the large cube was presented at a greater distance than the small one. The newborns exhibited a significant preference for looking at the novel cube, indicating that they could reliably detect the difference in intrinsic size. Other research using somewhat different procedures leads to the same conclusion (e.g., Granrud, 1987).

Because these studies did not control the kind of depth information that was available to the infants, it is not clear what mechanisms they have at birth. Some

Perceiving Object Properties and Parts

possibilities can be ruled out by the nature of the experimental situation, such as projective size (which was equal), texture occlusion (because there was no background texture), and various relational features (because a single object was presented), but several possibilities remain. Perhaps the most likely source of depth information is binocular convergence. Regardless of which source is innate, its existence would then allow infants to learn about other indicators of intrinsic object size by correlating them with whatever mechanism is available at birth.

7.1.2 Size Illusions

Interestingly, the same mechanisms that account for size constancy under normal conditions predict the existence of certain kinds of size illusions. This makes sense because size perception should be systematically incorrect whenever distance perception is systematically incorrect. Failure of constancy at great distances is one likely example. Another is the illusion that occurs in the perception of object sizes in the Ames room (see Section 5.5.10). Recall that the geometry of the Ames room is such that it looks perfectly rectangular from one special vantage point, but one side of the room is actually much closer than the other, as illustrated in Figure 5.5.32. Thus, there is a discrepancy between the perceived distances to the two objects and their actual distances. Consistent with the hypothesis that the visual system computes object sizes from retinal sizes and perceived distances, the closer person appears much larger than the far one, even though they are actually the same size, as illustrated in Figure 5.5.32.

The Moon Illusion. Systematic misperception of the distance to an object is also an integral part of the most influential explanation for perhaps the oldest of all visual illusions: the **moon illusion**. The moon illusion is the universal perception of the moon as being larger when it is located low in the sky (near the horizon) than when it is high in the night sky. This illusion is powerful and pervasive, but it has puzzled scientists from ancient times. Indeed, most people never suspect that it results from an error in perception at all, but assume that there must be a physical explanation for it. Although most people realize that the moon does not actually get smaller as it rises in the sky, many people assume that

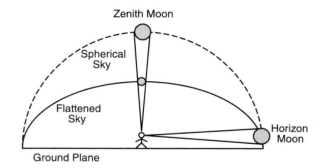

Figure 7.1.8 The apparent distance theory of the moon illusion. The moon should appear larger when it is located at the horizon than when it is high in the sky because it is perceived as farther away along the horizon than higher in the sky, as though the sky were flattened rather than hemispherical.

it appears to do so either because it is getting farther away or because there is some sort of optical distortion caused by the earth's atmosphere. Neither explanation is correct, however, for photographic images of the moon reveal that its image remains exactly the same size throughout its trajectory. The explanation for this gross misperception of the moon's size must therefore be sought in how the situation is perceived.

According to the most widely accepted theory, the moon illusion is caused by an error in distance perception. This **apparent distance theory**, originally proposed in antiquity by Ptolemy and more recently championed by Lloyd Kaufman and Irvin Rock (1962; Rock & Kaufman, 1962), suggests that the moon looks bigger near the horizon because it is perceived as farther away, as illustrated in Figure 7.1.8. The moon is actually more than 200,000 miles from the earth. This is much too far for us to get accurate visual information about its absolute distance. (If we did, size constancy would theoretically obtain, and the moon illusion would not occur, because we would always perceive it veridically as being 2160 miles in diameter!) Instead, we must settle for the relative depth information that is available from the surrounding spatial context. This somehow leads us astray.

According to the apparent distance theory, the relevant factor in misperceiving the size of the moon is pictorial depth information derived from its spatial context. When the moon is on the horizon, it is seen in the context of the ground terrain extending into the distance. When it is at its zenith, it is seen only in the context of stars and empty space. The apparent distance theory

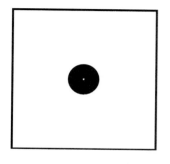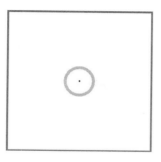

Figure 7.1.9 Emmert's law. Stare at the black dot in the left panel for at least 30 seconds to form an afterimage, then look at its afterimage against a distant white wall versus against the white square to the right. It will look much bigger against the far wall, even though its retinal size is identical in both cases.

hypothesizes that the impression of great distance caused by the textured ground terrain makes the moon appear farther away at the horizon than at its zenith, as though the sky were flattened rather than spherical. The size-distance relation tells us that when the same-sized retinal image is seen as farther away (on the horizon), it will be perceived as larger than when it is seen as closer (high in the sky). This is exactly what happens in the moon illusion.

The fact that two identically sized retinal images—such as the moon in its two positions—are perceived as having different sizes when they are perceived at different distances is an example of **Emmert's law**. Emmert's law states that the perceived size of a constant retinal image is proportional to its perceived distance. This relation, which is implicit in Equation 7.1, can be demonstrated most directly with a visual afterimage. To see how, stare at the dot in the center of the black circle on the left side of Figure 7.1.9 for 30–60 seconds under bright illumination. This will cause a light afterimage of the circle on your retina that is fixed in retinal size. You can then see (literally) how its size changes with distance simply by "projecting" it onto surfaces at different distances.

First, look at a distant wall. The light afterimage will look as though it is positioned on the wall and will be quite large in comparison to the small circle on the page, perhaps several feet across if the wall is far enough away. (Blinking your eyes often helps to refresh the afterimage.) Then look at the book page in the square to the right. Notice that the spot now appears much smaller than it did on the wall, about the same size as

the original circle. (Should the afterimage fade while you are carrying out these instructions, you can reestablish it by looking back at the dot from the same distance as you did initially.) These changes in the perception of size demonstrate Emmert's law because the very same retinal afterimage is producing the different impressions of size when it is perceived at different distances.

The major stumbling block for the apparent distance theory of the moon illusion is that if observers are asked in which position the moon looks *closer*, they typically choose the horizon moon, which the theory hypothesizes to be registered as *farther*. This conflict is sometimes called the **size-distance paradox**. Rock and Kaufman explain this seeming anomaly by suggesting that people answer this question by consciously judging the moon's distance from its apparent size, the reverse of what they claim happens to produce the size illusion in the first place. If true, this implies a two-stage process based on two different kinds of distance perception: an initial unconscious one and a later conscious one.

1. Distance information from texture gradients at the horizon is registered unconsciously and causes the horizon moon to appear farther from the observer than the zenith moon, thereby producing an illusion in perceiving its size consistent with Emmert's law.

2. When explicit judgments of apparent distance are required, the perceived sizes of the moon in its two positions are taken as evidence of their relative distances (the "relative size" cue to distance discussed in Chapter 5). This results in the impression that the seemingly larger horizon moon is closer than the seemingly smaller zenith moon.

Although this theory might sound a bit complex and confusing, Kaufman and Rock collected a substantial body of evidence supporting it. Four of their most important findings are the following:

1. When observers were asked to scan the sky on a moonless night and to see it as a surface, they judged an imaginary point at the horizon to be farther away than one at the zenith of the sky. This supports the proposition that the sky appears flattened, with the horizon sky seeming farther away than the zenith sky.

2. When observers viewed artificial moons (whose size could be precisely controlled by optical means) through a screen that occluded the ground terrain, the standard

Perceiving Object Properties and Parts

moon illusion disappeared. The same occurred when observers judged the size of artificial moons inside a completely darkened planetarium. Both results support the proposal that it is the ground terrain that causes the difference in apparent distance to the horizon versus the zenith sky.

3. Using optical tricks, Kaufman and Rock were able to reverse the visual context of the two moons, projecting the horizon moon with its contextual ground terrain upward into the zenith position and the zenith moon with its surrounding empty sky down into the horizon position. As the apparent distance theory predicts, the moon illusion then reversed.

4. Kaufman and Rock showed that observers always reported a smaller-appearing artificial moon as being farther away, regardless of whether it was at the horizon or zenith, thus supporting the proposal that the moon's apparent size governs the answer to questions about its distance.

Although the apparent distance theory has a great deal of experimental support, it is by no means universally accepted. An entire book was recently published about the moon illusion, in which the authors of numerous chapters advanced many different theories (Hershenson, 1989). The correct explanation of the moon illusion is still far from settled, although the apparent distance theory has been the favorite for many years.

The Ponzo Illusion. Size illusions also occur when people appear to have perfectly accurate information about the distance of objects from binocular depth sources. There are several examples among the classic geometrical illusions that we encountered in Chapter 1 (see Figure 1.1.4). One is the **Ponzo illusion**, which is reproduced in Figure 7.1.10. The lower horizontal line appears shorter than the upper one despite their actual equivalence in length and the observer's excellent information about their absolute distance in depth from accommodation and convergence information: Both lines appear to lie solidly on the plane of the page. How can this size illusion be explained in the absence of a systematic misperception of depth?

One of the best-known and most influential theories of this illusion actually invokes a form of the incorrect depth explanation, despite the lack of a true illusion of depth (e.g., Gregory, 1966). The theory assumes that even when no depth is explicitly perceived in this dis-

Figure 7.1.10 The Ponzo illusion. The two horizontal lines are actually the same length, but the converging lines make the upper one appear longer.

play, the converging lines activate the depth perception system that is responsible for interpreting pictorial perspective information (see Section 5.5). There is no illusion that the upper line is actually behind the picture plane because the converging lines do not engage depth mechanisms fully enough to bring its results into consciousness. Rather, the converging lines are unconsciously interpreted as parallel lines receding into the distance (like the rails of railroad tracks) and the horizontal lines as lying in the same receding ground plane as the converging lines (like the ties of railroad tracks). The unconscious perception of differential depth leads to the conscious perception of differential size: The upper line would have to be longer because it nearly connects the receding parallel lines, whereas the lower one is not even close. Thus, some size illusions may arise due to depth processing that occurs automatically and unconsciously in cases in which there is no conscious illusion of depth.

As intriguing as this "unconscious depth" account of the Ponzo illusion may be, it does not square fully with the facts. One problem is that it makes some incorrect predictions. If the two test lines are unconsciously processed as though they were at different distances from the observer, it should not matter how they are oriented with respect to the inducing lines. In fact, however, rotating the lines by 90° destroys the illusion, as illustrated in Figure 7.1.11 (Gillam, 1973). The unconscious depth theory requires important modifications to explain this difference.

There are other theories of the Ponzo illusion that fare better with this effect of line orientation, however. One is the claim that the visual system determines the perceived length of the test lines primarily from the low-

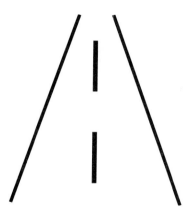

Figure 7.1.11 The Ponzo illusion with rotated test lines. Rotating the test lines 90° makes the illusion disappear.

spatial-frequency information in the display. As Figure 7.1.12A shows, a filtered version of this illusion with only low-spatial-frequency information effectively blurs the image so that the upper test line merges with the side bars and makes it appear longer (Ginsberg, 1986). Since the lower test line does not do this, it looks shorter than the upper one. This hypothesis could account both for the existence of the classic Ponzo illusion (Figure 7.1.12A) and for the fact that it disappears when the test lines are rotated (Figure 7.1.12B). But it does not square with all the facts either. For example, when the low-spatial-frequency information is selectively removed, as illustrated in Figure 7.1.13, the illusion is still present.

Illusions of Relative Size. Another kind of explanation of the Ponzo illusion is couched in terms of differences in relative size. One can rightly claim that the upper line is perceived as longer because it actually *is* longer—at least when each test line's length is expressed relative to the distance between the converging lines. Another way of saying this is that the upper line fills up proportionally more of the space between the converging lines than does the lower line. This explanation of the illusion is based on *relative size*: the ratio of an object's extent to that of other nearby objects or spaces between objects. It is therefore an illusion of the sort that would be predicted from the proportionality explanation for size constancy mentioned earlier in this chapter.

Another classical geometric size illusion is the Ebbinghaus illusion shown in Figure 7.1.14. The illusion is that the central circle on the right looks smaller than the one on the left, even though they are actually the

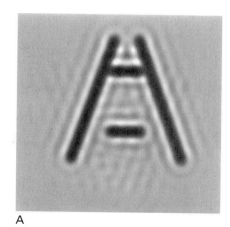

A

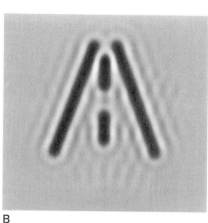

B

Figure 7.1.12 The low-spatial-frequency Ponzo illusion. Filtering out the high spatial frequencies creates a blurred version of the Ponzo illusion in which the upper test line actually becomes longer because it merges with the inducing lines (part A). When the test lines are rotated, as in part B, the blurring does not affect their length.

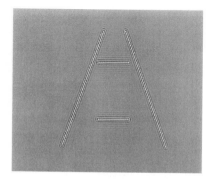

Figure 7.1.13 The high-pass-filtered Ponzo illusion. When the low-spatial-frequency information is removed from the classic Ponzo illusion, the illusion does not disappear, contrary to the prediction of the low-spatial-frequency hypothesis.

Perceiving Object Properties and Parts

same size. One could, in principle, invoke a distance-based explanation here, saying that the circle on the left looks larger because its surrounding context of small circles causes it to be perceived as farther away than the one surrounded by larger circles. It seems more plausible and natural, however, to say simply that the one on the left looks larger because it is perceived relative to the smaller circles around it, and the one on the right looks smaller because it is perceived relative to the larger circles around it. This is obviously an explanation based on the size of objects relative to surrounding objects, much as is the proportionality explanation of size constancy.

There are still other theories about why this seemingly simple geometrical illusion occurs, but none proposed to date gives a satisfactory account of all the conditions under which it diminishes or disappears. This is generally true of the classical illusions like the ones shown in Figure 1.1.4. There are many different theories of why they arise, but no theory is fully satisfactory.

Occlusion Illusions. Before leaving the topic of size illusions, it is worth mentioning a different class that arises in perceiving objects that are visually completed behind an occluding object. Two illusions are simultaneously present that alter size perception in opposite directions:

1. There is an apparent increase in the size of the visible portion of the occluded object (Kanisza, 1979).

As illustrated in Figure 7.1.15A the visible portion of the

Figure 7.1.15 Occlusion illusions. Although the two half-circles in part A are identical, the occluded one looks considerably larger. And although the two black squares in part B are identical, the occluded one looks smaller.

visually completed black circle on the left appears to be substantially larger than the physically identical black hemicircle that is fully visible on the right. This illusion seems to arise from the expansion of the visible portion of the completed object along the occluding border, as though the visual system were filling in a thin strip of surface behind the occluder that is not actually visible.

2. There is an apparent decrease in the size of the invisible (amodally completed) portion of the occluded object.

This second part is not apparent in Figure 7.1.15A because the rest of the circle is occluded. But consider Figure 7.1.15B. Here, both sides of an occluded square are visible behind an occluding strip. The size of the occluded square is physically identical to the unoccluded square next to it, yet the occluded square looks noticeably narrower (Kanisza, 1979). This finding indicates that the amodally completed portion of the occluded object phenomenally shrinks.

These occlusion illusions have several interesting aspects. First, note that although the two effects are in opposite directions—increasing the perceived size of the visible portion and decreasing the perceived size of the occluded portion—they do not cancel each other out. If

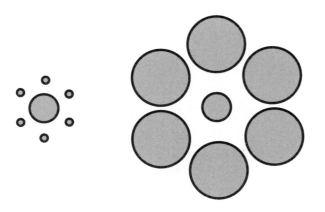

Figure 7.1.14 The Ebbinghaus illusion. The two central circles are the same size, although the left one looks larger because of the smaller size of the circles around it.

they did, the square in Figure 7.1.15B would presumably appear to be square, identical in width to the unoccluded square next to it. More puzzling, however, is the fact that although the occluded portion of the square behind the rectangle is perceptually narrowed, the occluding rectangle itself does not appear to be narrowed, as shown by comparing it with the physically identical rectangle next to it. These size illusions do not fit any distance-based theories of size perception and therefore require a different kind of explanation. There is not yet any satisfactory theory that accounts for all aspects of these illusions. The most likely explanation is that they arise from a filling-in process that partly completes the occluded region with sensory experience and partly with amodal knowledge (see Section 6.4.1).

7.2 Shape

Shape is by far the most complex of all visually perceivable properties. It is complex because it is a combination of many different attributes. Indeed, the shape of an object seems implicitly to include information about all the other spatial properties we consider in this chapter: size, orientation, and position. The reason is that shape depends critically on the part structure of objects and how its various parts are related to one another in terms of their relative positions, relative orientations, relative sizes, and so forth. In fact, the nature of shape perception is so complex and enigmatic that there is as yet no accepted theory of what shape is or how shape perception occurs. We will consider some of the possibilities in detail in Chapter 8. For now, however, we will consider shape perception from the restricted viewpoint of shape constancy.

7.2.1 Shape Constancy

Like size, shape is a property of objects that people usually perceive as constant despite changes in viewing perspective. The obvious starting point for a theory of shape perception is the shape of its retinal image. In the case of a 2-D object presented in the frontal plane, the shape of this image will accurately reflect that of the environmental object. But for all other cases—either 2-D objects viewed at a slant, as illustrated in Figure 7.2.1, or almost any 3-D object—optical projection results in significant differences between the object's actual shape and that of its projected image. The fact that we per-

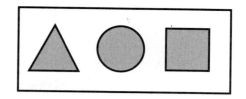

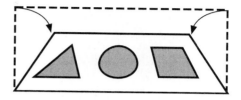

Figure 7.2.1 Shape constancy. With good depth information available, shapes at a slant look the same as they do in the frontal plane, at least under many viewing conditions.

ceive the same object as having the same shape when observed from different viewpoints is therefore called **shape constancy**. As with all forms of constancy, it is a perceptual achievement that requires explanation.

Perspective Changes. The major challenge to shape constancy occurs when the position of the observer changes so that he or she views the object from a different perspective. In most cases, this change in viewing geometry causes a transformation in the shape of its projected image. If the object is either a flat planar shape or an object made of thin wire, the transformation can be characterized mathematically as a simple projection from three to two dimensions because all parts of the object are visible. Figure 7.2.2 gives some indication of how projective transformations change the

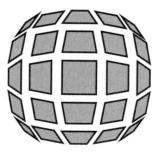

Figure 7.2.2 Perspective views of a square. An ordinary square takes on a wide variety of different projected shapes at different perspectives: trapezoids, parallelograms, rhombuses, and irregular quadrilaterals.

A   B   C

Figure 7.2.3 Projective views of a solid 3-D object. Several different views of a solid 3-D sculpture are shown to illustrate the complex changes in the shape of its projected image that occur when it is viewed from different stationpoints. Indeed, no two views of this object will be identical.

shape of an object's image by showing a sample of the projections of a square. If the object is solid and three-dimensional, however, changing the perspective from which it is viewed transforms its retinal shape far more radically, since new portions of its surface come into view as other portions go out of view. Figure 7.2.3 shows several projections of a solid object that undergoes complex self-occlusion as the viewing perspective is changed.

How might we expect changes in perspective to affect shape constancy? First, consider the special case of objects that do not substantially occlude themselves: all 2-D planar figures and objects made of thin wire. In these cases, shape can be accurately recovered, at least in principle, if the distance to every point on the object is known. We will not derive this result formally, but its intuitive basis is easy to understand. Imagine that each retinal point on the object is projected outward from the eye along the direction from which it came for a distance equal to the perceived distance of that point from the eye. (This is precisely the kind of information that is represented in the 2.5-D sketch.) If the perceived distance to each point is accurate and if all points are visible, this set of points will exactly reconstruct the object in the 3-D environment. If accurate depth information is available from *absolute* sources (e.g., accommodation and/or convergence), both the object's shape and its size can be completely recovered. If accurate relative depth is available from *quantitative* sources (e.g., binocular disparity, motion parallax, or many of the metric sources of perspective information), its shape will be recoverable, but not its size, since it might be at any absolute distance. If only *qualitative* depth information (e.g., from edge interpretation) is available, however, neither its precise shape nor its size can be unambiguously recovered without invoking additional assumptions. Reasonable approximations to shape constancy may still be possible, however.

Two-Dimensional Figures. How does this computational analysis compare with people's actual shape constancy under comparable circumstances? The vast majority of studies on shape constancy have been performed with 2-D shapes presented at varying slants. When such objects are close enough to provide accurate depth information, shape constancy is quite good (Lappin & Preble, 1975; Thouless, 1931). There is the usual tendency toward underconstancy—meaning that the apparent shape is something of a compromise between its actual shape and that of its 2-D image—but we generally perceive the shapes of 2-D figures with reasonable accuracy. Shape constancy declines, however, as the degree of slant increases, even with binocular presentation (Massaro, 1973; Thouless, 1931). At extreme slants, observers begin to perceive shapes that are clear compromises between the actual distal stimulus and its retinal projection. They also exhibit a strong bias toward perceiving symmetrical shapes such as circles and squares rather than ellipses and trapezoids (King, Meyer, Tangney, & Biederman, 1976).

At large viewing distances, for which depth perception is poor, the degree of shape constancy depends heavily on pictorial depth information. In the absence of any depth information, there is a strong tendency to perceive the shape of an object as though it were located in the frontal plane (Gogel, 1965, 1978). However, there is also a tendency to perceive the figure as the most symmetrical shape that is consistent with its retinal projection. Thus, shape constancy for circles presented in various slants is rather good, even at large distances. When they are presented so that they project various ellipses onto the retina, they tend to be correctly perceived as circles at a slant. This may occur either because circles are more symmetrical than ellipses, because circles are more familiar shapes, or both.

On the other hand, shape constancy is quite poor for figures whose projections are consistent with being perceived as being more symmetrical and/or familiar than they actually are, especially in the absence of good depth information. At large distances or when viewed monocularly, for example, an ellipse that is presented at a particular slant tends to be perceived as a circle at a different slant. This phenomenon is particularly compelling when an ellipse is presented at the particular slant at which it projects a circle onto the retina. In this case, the tendencies toward perceiving shapes as symmetrical and lying in the frontal plane converge, leading invariably to the perception of a circle in the frontal plane rather than an ellipse at a slant. This is another example in which the same processes that normally lead to shape constancy fail. Instead, they produce the illusion of circles where actually there are ellipses.

The tendency to perceive 2-D figures at large distances as the most symmetrical figure that is consistent with its retinal projection is a reasonable paraphrase of the Gestalt principle of Prägnanz, which states that the percept will be as "good" as prevailing conditions allow. We have not yet said exactly what makes one shape "better" or "simpler" than another, but symmetry is among the most important factors. The Gestalt concept of Prägnanz is complex, however, and requires a deeper analysis than this. We will consider this problem more fully in Section 8.3.1 when we consider shape perception in greater detail.

Three-Dimensional Objects. Shape constancy for wire objects viewed binocularly at close distances should theoretically be nearly as good as that for two-dimensional figures. As we argued above, the reason is that if both the distance and the direction from the viewer to each point are known, the entire wire object in the 3-D environment can be reconstructed. In fact, however, perceiving the shape of 3-D wire objects appears to be substantially more difficult than perceiving the shape of 2-D figures. Irvin Rock and his colleagues have shown that even at fairly close distances with good depth information from binocular viewing, observers have surprisingly poor shape constancy for wire objects (Rock & DiVita, 1987; Rock, DiVita, & Barbeito, 1981).

Rock and DiVita (1987) showed their subjects a series of wire objects, such as the one depicted in Figure 7.2.4A. Their memory for these shapes was later tested under conditions in which the object was seen either from the same viewpoint (i.e., having the same retinal projection) or from a different viewpoint. Figure 7.2.4B shows what the wire object in part A looked like from the different viewpoint. When the retinal views were changed from presentation to test, subjects' recognition rates dropped from 70–75% correct to 39% correct. If shape constancy had been fully achieved in this situation, recognition performance would have been equal for both viewpoints.

Rock and DiVita (1987) speculated that their results were probably because subjects' perception of (and memory for) shape is strongly influenced by the qualitative changes in the retinally projected shape. This does

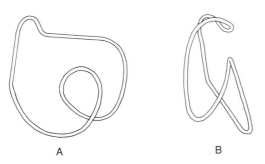

A
B

Figure 7.2.4 Wire stimuli in an experiment on shape constancy. Subjects who initially viewed wire objects like this from one perspective and were later tested from another perspective performed much worse on a memory test than subjects who saw them from the same perspective both times. (After Rock, DiVita, & Barbeito, 1981.)

not mean that depth perception failed to operate, but only that the wire object's phenomenal appearance may depend heavily on its particular retinal projection. This may be yet another example of the influence of proximal mode perception in a situation for which distal mode perception is optimal, since proximal mode perception corresponds to the retinal image of the object. In any case, the results of this study show that shape constancy for such figures is not nearly as good as one might expect from everyday experience.

It is tempting to think that these results are an artifact of the unusual wire figures that were used as stimuli. But the situation is even worse for opaque 3-D objects because the surfaces closest to the viewer actually occlude their other surfaces. Figure 7.2.5, for example, shows the same clay object from two different viewpoints. Clearly they look quite different, and it is very likely because

their retinal projections are so different. Unpublished experiments by Rock, Pinna, and Costa using such figures bear out this intuition, showing that shape constancy is poor for solid objects as well as wire ones. Other investigators have reported that shape constancy is better for "potato chip" objects (formed by creating curved surfaces on wire loops) than it is for the plain wire loops themselves (Farah, Rochlin, & Klein, 1994). Clearly there is a need for further research to clarify the relation between shape constancy for 3-D wire objects versus that for solid objects.

Finally, we must consider shape constancy for 3-D objects under distant viewing conditions when only pictorial information is available about depth. If anything, shape constancy should be worse than in near viewing conditions because important quantitative depth information from convergence and binocular disparity is missing. Amorphous shapes such as Rock and DiVita's bent wire objects are not generally perceived veridically with just pictorial information, and so shape constancy should be correspondingly worse than it is when there is good depth information.

In spite of all the evidence that shape constancy is poor, everyday experience nevertheless gives the distinct impression that shape constancy is good, even in viewing distant objects. We typically see objects from many different perspectives and manage to recognize them reasonably well despite the variations in appearance. The sample of perspective views shown in Figure 7.2.6 provides some informal evidence for this claim. Why should Rock and DiVita's experiment have turned out so differently?

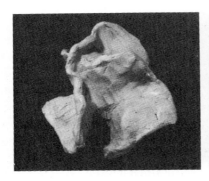 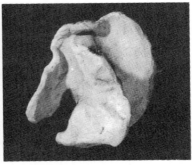

Figure 7.2.5 A solid 3-D stimulus in an experiment on shape constancy. Clay objects similar to this were used in a shape constancy experiment similar to the one by Rock and DiVita (1987) using wire figures (see Figure 7.2.4). The results also showed poor shape constancy when viewpoint was varied. (From Rock & DiVita, 1987.)

Figure 7.2.6 Multiple perspectives of a familiar object. Despite differences in ordinary viewing perspectives, this object is fairly easily recognized as the same tape dispenser. This fact does not fit well with Rock and DiVita's results showing poor shape constancy from different viewpoints.

There are several possibilities. One is that our intuitions about shape constancy are based primarily on situations in which we perceive the same object from different stationpoints by continuously moving from one view to another. Under these conditions, the perspective changes from moment to moment are quite gradual and easily perceived as shape preserving, especially when the object is being viewed continuously. Thus, these "normal" conditions are quite different from those in Rock and DiVita's experiment, in which two views were presented discretely, with a substantial time lag between them.

Another possibility is that much of the time our perception of an object's shape is closely correlated with its identity. That is, we may believe that shape constancy occurs simply because we are able to recognize the same object from different perspective views by using different features. For example, you may be able to recognize a friend's face both from a front view and from a profile view of his or her head. If you recognize it as the same person, its shape must also be the same. Even so, we might not be nearly as good at performing the same task on two different perspective views of a complete stranger's face or of some novel object.

A final possibility for why shape constancy appears to be good in everyday situations is that most objects we see have features that distinguish some particular parts of them as the "front" and "back," whereas Rock's wire and clay objects do not. The presence of axes of symmetry or elongation might allow the object's shape to be perceived relative to such distinctive axes, allowing it to remain constant despite different viewpoints. Amorphous, asymmetric objects, however, lack axes or planes of symmetry, and so their shape might be perceived differently from different viewpoints. We will pursue this line of thinking further in Chapter 8 when we consider the concept of object-centered frames of reference.

It is important to realize that these different hypotheses are not mutually exclusive, and all might therefore be true simultaneously. Although it is not yet clear how completely the visual system is able to overcome perspective differences in perceiving the 3-D shapes of objects, there is no doubt that it attempts to do so and frequently succeeds. Otherwise, we would see the same object from different perspectives as completely different objects, and that very seldom happens in everyday life.

Development of Shape Constancy. Not only do people have approximate shape constancy, but current evidence suggests that it is innate. Slater and Morison (1985) found reliable perception of planar shapes despite variations in surface slant with infants who were no more than a few days old. They first habituated each newborn to a particular shape (either square or trapezoid) by presenting it at a number of different orientations in depth. They then tested the infants' looking preferences in the presence of both the old shape and the new shape. Every baby looked longer at the novel

Perceiving Object Properties and Parts

shape than at the habituated one, leading the researchers to conclude that shape constancy is present at birth. As with the experiments demonstrating innate size constancy, there is as yet little information about just what depth information these newborn infants are using to achieve shape constancy, however. Eye convergence appears to be the most likely candidate, but this hypothesis has not yet been confirmed by adequate tests.

7.2.2 Shape Illusions

The fact that the visual system automatically interprets depth from appropriate 2-D structure in retinal images leads to some interesting illusions in the perceived shape of objects. We have already mentioned that if an ellipse is viewed monocularly or from far enough away that good depth information is lacking, observers generally see it as a circle slanted in depth. A number of similar shape illusions based on trapezoids were discovered by psychologist Adelbert Ames (1951). The simplest is analogous to the ellipse/circle illusion: When a luminous trapezoid in the frontal plane is viewed monocularly in an otherwise dark room, it appears to be a square or rectangle at a particular slant. These are examples of shape illusions resulting from the use of the same heuristic assumptions that normally produce shape constancy under ambiguous conditions lacking sufficient depth information.

Ames used the illusion of trapezoids appearing to be rectangles as the basis of one of the most celebrated of all illusions: the **Ames room**. As discussed in Section 5.5.10, the Ames room is a trapezoidal room that appears rectangular when it is viewed from a particular stationpoint (see Figure 5.5.32). The rear wall is trapezoidal, since one side is much taller than the other, but it appears rectangular from the special vantage point because the taller side is actually much farther away. This produces a 3-D illusion of shape. It has the interesting consequence of being powerful enough to produce illusions of distance and size as well, as discussed at some length in Chapter 5. It is a particularly compelling example of the tendency to perceive the shapes of objects—in this case, the room itself—in accord with simple, regular, and frequently encountered alternatives.

Another powerful shape illusion related to depth perception was discovered by Roger Shepard (1981) and is

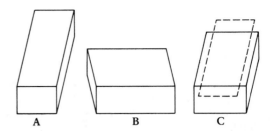

Figure 7.2.7 The Shepard illusion. The parallelogram that forms the top surface in object B appears most similar to the top of object C, but its retinal shape is actually identical to the top of object A following a rotation. The dashed outline superimposed on C shows the actual shape of B's top rotated. (From Shepard, 1981.)

illustrated in Figure 7.2.7. The question is whether the object on the right or the one on the left has a top surface that has the same 2-D (projected) shape as the top of the center one. (Decide which one you think looks the same before you continue reading.) Almost everybody sees the right object as having the same top, but it is actually the left one! As surprising as it may seem, the dashed outline superimposed on the right object shows the actual shape of the top of the center object after being rotated in the picture plane.

This compelling illusion results from the same mechanisms that normally produce shape constancy from pictorial depth information. The 2-D shapes of the tops are not accurately perceived, even when we try to do so. Rather, we perceive something much closer to the actual shape of the tops in 3-D space because depth processing occurs more or less automatically, and we make our choice on the basis of this perception. The illusion occurs because this perception isn't the one required by the task. If you had been asked to pick the object whose top surface is most similar in shape to the center one in terms of environmental surfaces, your answer would have been correct.

Another illusion of shape that may be related to depth interpretation and shape constancy mechanisms is shown in Figure 7.2.8. It is actually a variant of the Ponzo illusion shown in Figure 7.1.10. The quadrilateral is actually a perfect square, but it tends to look like a trapezoid that is larger at the top. The depth-based explanation of this illusion is essentially the same as that of the classic Ponzo illusion: If the converging lines are perceived as parallel lines receding on a ground plane, the top side of

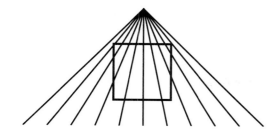

Figure 7.2.8 An illusion of shape. The central figure is a perfect square, but it looks like a trapezoid that is bigger at the top than at the bottom because of the converging diagonal lines.

the square should be perceived as longer than the bottom one. Consistent with this hypothesis, the illusion is especially pronounced when the lines are perceived as defining a slanted ground plane and the quadrilateral is seen as lying in the same plane. If the quadrilateral is seen as standing up, perpendicular to the ground plane, it looks considerably more like a true square.

7.3 Orientation

Another important property of objects that we generally perceive veridically despite changes in viewing conditions is their orientations with respect to the environment. Lines and edges that are aligned with gravity are usually perceived as vertical, for example, and ones that are parallel to the horizon are usually perceived as horizontal. This fact is evolutionarily important because of the ubiquitous and portentous effects of gravity on survival. The usefulness of being able to tell the difference between gravitationally upright objects and tilted ones is difficult to overestimate. Upright objects tend to be relatively stable in gravity, whereas tilted ones are likely to fall over. How can we explain this ability to perceive the orientation of objects in the environment from visual information?

7.3.1 Orientation Constancy

Again, the obvious starting point for a theory of how an object's orientation is perceived is the orientation of its image on the retina. In Chapter 4 we discussed the fact that retinal orientation is well represented by cortical cells in area V1 that are selectively tuned to lines and edges (or local spatial frequency patches) in different orientations. Perhaps the firing of these neurons can

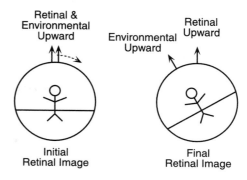

Figure 7.3.1 Orientation constancy. The perceived orientation of objects in the environment does not appear to change when we tilt our heads, even though their retinal images rotate in the opposite direction.

account for the perception of an object's orientation via the orientation of its component lines and edges.

Unfortunately, the firing of orientationally tuned neurons in V1 would correlate with the perceived orientation of lines and edges only if the observer's head is gravitationally vertical and if the lines and edges lie in the frontal plane. The problem is that the retinal orientation of a line or edge is determined not only by the orientation of the object in the world, but also by the orientation of the head and by the orientation of the line in depth. To simplify matters, we will restrict our attention to lines lying in the frontal plane so that we have to worry only about the effects of head orientation.

Head orientation can vary over a surprising range during normal activities. We typically tilt our head when we are perplexed, peek around a corner, rest it on one hand, or lie sideways on the couch. If you tilt your head 30° clockwise, the images of all objects in your field of view rotate 30° counterclockwise on your retina, as illustrated in Figure 7.3.1. The surprising thing is that we don't perceive the orientations of objects to change when we do this. Rather, objects in the environment appear to retain their original orientations. How might this happen?

These are examples of **orientation constancy**: people's tendency to perceive the gravitational orientation of objects veridically despite changes in head orientation. If orientation constancy did not hold and orientation perception were simply determined by retinal orientation, then the world would appear to tilt back and forth as we tilted our heads forth and back. This would be perceptually unsatisfactory for innumerable

Perceiving Object Properties and Parts

reasons. Instead, the visual system seems to determine the environmental orientation of objects by taking both head orientation and the object's retinal orientation into account.

In general, the relation between an object's environmental orientation (O_{object}), its image orientation with respect to the long axis of the head (O_{image}), and the observer's head orientation with respect to gravity (O_{head}) can be expressed by the equation

$$O_{object} = O_{image} + O_{head}. \qquad (7.2)$$

This means that the environmental orientation of the object relative to gravity (O_{object}) can be determined by adding the angle of the long axis of the head relative to gravity (O_{head}) to the angle of the object's image on the retina relative to the long axis of the head (O_{image}). Because the orientation of the image relative to the head can be computed from the output of orientationally tuned line and edge detectors, the remaining problem is how the visual system determines the gravitational orientation of the head.

The primary source of information about gravitational vertical and head orientation comes from the **proprioceptive system**: the biological structures responsible for (among other things) the sense of upright and balance within the gravitational field of the earth.

The **vestibular system** is the principle organ of balance. It is located in the middle ear and contains the anatomical structures illustrated in Figure 7.3.2A: three interconnected fluid-filled tubes, called the **semicircular canals**, and two fluid-filled sacs, called the **utricle** and the **saccule**. All three organs send information about head orientation to your brain, although they differ in the kinds of information to which they are most sensitive. This vestibular output is capable of producing orientation constancy if it is properly combined with orientation information about images on the retina. The appropriate combination is given by Equation 7.2 for computing the environmental orientation of objects from head orientation and their retinal orientation.

The utricle and saccule provide information about the orientation of the head with respect to gravity. They are both small chambers filled with fluid and lined with tiny hair cells. The hairs protrude into a gelatinous mass that has many heavy particles attached to its upper side. Gravity acts on the heavy particles so that when the head is tilted, the hairs are bent to a degree that depends on the angle of tilt. The bending of the hairs causes nerve cells to fire, sending information about head tilt to the brain.

The semicircular canals also respond when the head is tilted, but they mainly signal *changes* in head orientation rather than absolute gravitational orientation. Each canal is a fluid-filled tube with a single pliable receptor organ attached to its side. As the head rotates, the tube moves with respect to the fluid, causing the receptor organ to bend. This bending causes nerve cells attached to the receptor organ to fire. When the head is at rest—even if it is not upright—the relative motion of the fluid within the tube ceases, stopping the output to the brain. The semicircular canals thus encode information about dynamic rotations of the head rather than about its static orientation.

If the vestibular system worked perfectly and if its output were perfectly integrated with retinal orientation, position constancy would also be perfect. As usual, however, this is not quite the case. When the angle of head tilt is too great, for example, people tend to perceive a gravitationally upright line as being tilted somewhat in the direction of their head. An observer whose head is at an orientation of 90° in a dark room, for example, will see a luminous rod tilted about 8° toward their head orientation as being vertical. By the same token, a truly vertical luminous rod will be seen as tilted about 8° in the opposite direction (Aubert, 1861). These failures of complete orientation constancy can be easily explained, however, if a head orientation of 90° is underestimated by about 8°—that is, if head orientation is registered at 82° instead of 90°. The implication of this underestimation of head tilt for orientation constancy is that extreme head tilts disrupt constancy, at least in a dark room when only a luminous rod is visible.

When you tilt your head by 90° in a fully lighted room, however, orientation constancy doesn't break down in this way, as you can easily verify for yourself. It may be a bit difficult to tell whether objects are exactly vertical under these viewing conditions, but the world generally looks pretty much upright rather than leaning decidedly in the opposite direction, as would be predicted from Aubert's (1861) study using a luminous rod in a dark room. The reason is that the visual system doesn't rely entirely on vestibular information but augments it with converging visual information that we will consider shortly.

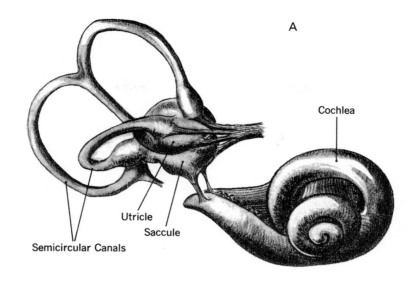

A

Cochlea

Semicircular Canals

Utricle

Saccule

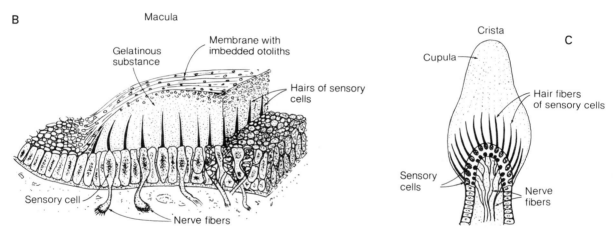

B

Macula

Gelatinous
substance

Membrane with
imbedded otoliths

Hairs of sensory
cells

Sensory cell

Nerve fibers

Crista

Cupula

C

Hair fibers
of sensory cells

Sensory
cells

Nerve
fibers

Figure 7.3.2   The vestibular system. The inner ear (A) contains three organs that respond to changes in head orientation: the utricle, the saccule, and the tripartite semicircular canals. The receptor in the utricle and saccule (B) consists of hair cells embedded in a gelatinous mass that is covered by heavy particles. The receptor in the semicircular canals (C) consists of hair cells embedded in a jellylike substance that moves with the flow of fluid within the tubular canals. (Part A from Gibson, 1966. Parts B and C from Geldard, 1972.)

Another proprioceptive source of information about gravitational vertical comes from its effects on your body, specifically the pressure exerted on your skin where your body is supported against the force of gravity. Notice, for example, that if you tilt your whole body to the right when you are standing, there is a fairly dramatic increase in the amount of pressure you feel on your right foot, accompanied by a corresponding decrease on your left foot. The same is true of the pressure on your buttocks when you tilt your body while seated. Most of the time, these bodily sensations are quite unconscious, but they are still registered and constantly monitored by your brain in maintaining your sense of balance.

These sensations of skin pressure constitute a source of information about gravity independent of the vestibular system. To be useful for orientation constancy, they must be augmented by information about how your head is aligned with respect to the proprioceptively informative parts of your body. This information is available via **kinesthetic feedback** from your joints about their relative orientations. Together, proprioceptive information and kinesthetic feedback allow the orientation of the head to be determined relative to the gravitational field.

7.3.2 Orientation Illusions

As we noted briefly above, visual information also affects orientation perception. Such effects are surprisingly potent, often being strong enough to overpower proprioceptive information and cause striking perceptual illusions.

One of the most compelling demonstrations of the powerful effects of visual information on orientation perception occurs when you enter a room that is somewhat tilted, like those in a fun house or mystery house of an amusement park. Although you may notice the slant of the floor as you first enter the room, you rapidly come to perceive the walls of the room as gravitationally upright. Once this misperception occurs, all sorts of orientation illusions follow. You perceive the chandelier as hanging at a strange angle from the ceiling, for example, rather than straight down. Even more disconcertingly, you perceive yourself as leaning precariously to one side, despite the fact that you are standing perfectly upright with respect to gravity. If you try to correct your posture to align yourself with the orientation of the room, you may even lose your balance and fall.

Frames of Reference. What happens in the tilted room is that your sense of gravitational uprightness is captured by the erroneous **frame of reference** provided by the visual structure of the room. A frame of reference in visual perception is a set of reference standards with respect to which the properties of objects are perceived. Among the most important aspects of the visual frame of reference is its orientation. When you are upright in a normal environment, the vertical orientation of your reference frame coincides with gravitational vertical because the dominant orientation in the visual environment—due to walls, tree trunks, standing people, and so forth—is either aligned with or perpendicular to gravity.

The heuristic assumption that the walls, floor, and ceiling of a room are vertical and horizontal is generally true and serves us well in perceiving the orientations of objects veridically within such contexts. When you walk

Figure 7.3.3 The tilted room illusion. Upright observers inside a gravitationally tilted room (A) perceive the room as upright and themselves as tilted (B).

into a tilted room, however, this assumption is violated, giving rise to illusions of orientation. The visual reference frame of the room, which is out of alignment with gravity, captures your sense of upright, as illustrated in Figure 7.3.3. You then perceive yourself as tilted because your own bodily orientation is not aligned with your perception of uprightness. As we will see, the concept of a frame of reference can be invoked in many different situations to explain illusory perceptions resulting from visual context effects.

One particularly well known contextual effect due to a surrounding rectangular frame is the **rod-and-frame effect**, which was studied extensively by psychologists Asch and Witkin (1948a, 1948b). They presented a luminous rod within a large, tilted, luminous rectangle and asked their subjects to set a luminous rod inside it to gravitational vertical, as indicated at the top of Figure 7.3.4. They found that subjects made systematic errors of the sort shown in Figure 7.3.4B, setting the rod to an orientation that was somewhere between true vertical

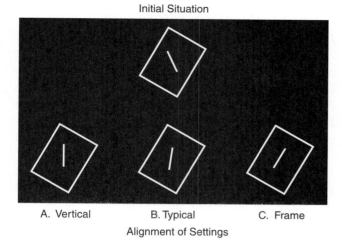

Initial Situation

A. Vertical   B. Typical   C. Frame

Alignment of Settings

Figure 7.3.4 The rod-and-frame effect. When observers are presented with a luminous rod inside a large, luminous, tilted frame in an otherwise dark environement and are told to set the rod to gravitational vertical, they orient the rod toward the frame orientation (B) rather than at true vertical (A).

(Figure 7.3.4A) and complete alignment with the frame's most nearly vertical sides (Figure 7.3.4C).

Like the failure of orientation constancy in the tilted room, the rod-and-frame effect can be explained by assuming that the rectangle influences people's perception of uprightness in the direction of its own orientation. Unlike the case of the tilted room, however, the influence of the frame orientation is less than complete. That is, subjects seldom set the rod parallel to the most nearly vertical sides of the frame, but rather set it in a compromise orientation, somewhere between true vertical and the orientation of the sides.

Several experiments show that the effect of the frame is greatest when the rectangle is large and that small frames just surrounding the line have little effect (Ebenholtz, 1977; Wenderoth, 1974). Other studies have shown that when two frames are present, one inside the other, it is the larger frame that dominates perception (DiLorenzo & Rock, 1982). These facts are consistent with the interpretation that the rectangle in a rod-and-frame task induces a visual frame of reference that is essentially a "world surrogate" for the visual environment (Rock, 1990). By this account, a visual structure will be more likely to induce a frame of reference when it is large, surrounding, and stable over time, like the tilted room in the previous example.

Figure 7.3.5 The Zöllner illusion. The vertical lines appear to converge and diverge but are fully parallel.

Geometric Illusions. There are also geometric orientation illusions that appear to be quite independent of errors in perceiving gravitational upright. One of the best known is the Zöllner illusion, in which parallel lines are perceived as being tilted because of the influence of a background of many obliquely oriented line segments, as shown in Figure 7.3.5.

Although the explanation of this illusion is uncertain, one possibility is related to the idea of contrast already mentioned with respect to size illusions. In this case, the orientation of the long vertical lines may be perceived in relational contrast to the orientation of the many short oblique ones. The leftmost line, for example, is seen as tilted slightly clockwise because it is clockwise relative to the orientation of all the short segments touching it (which are oriented counterclockwise relative to vertical). The next line to the right is seen as tilted counterclockwise in contrast to its inducing lines, which are oriented clockwise; and so forth.

Contrast illusions in orientation perception are well known. In Figure 7.3.6, for example, the two circular gratings in the middle are actually both vertical and parallel but are perceived as slightly oblique and nonparallel because of the contextual influence of the surrounding background gratings. Exactly how such

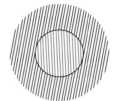 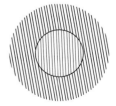

Figure 7.3.6 Simultaneous orientation contrast. The central circular gratings are both vertical but appear tilted because of the surrounding context of tilted lines.

     Perceiving Object Properties and Parts

illusions arise is less clear, however. One kind of explanation is based on the hypothesis that there are inhibitory interactions among orientation selective neurons (e.g., Blakemore, Carpenter & Georgeson, 1970; Tyler & Nakayama, 1984).

Another possible explanation for the Zöllner illusion is that the visual system overestimates small angles and underestimates large ones due to lateral inhibition between the lines comprising the angle (e.g., Békésey, 1967). This would tend to make the acute angles between the vertical line and cross-hatch lines appear larger than they actually are. To account for the illusory tilt of the vertical line, one must further assume that the change in orientation accrues more to the single long line than to the many short ones. Exactly why this should be true is not clear, however. Perhaps it is because, although the entire vertical line is longer than the hatch marks, the short vertical segments between each pair of hatch marks are shorter and therefore more susceptible to change in their perceived orientation.

7.4 Position

Another crucial global property of real-world objects is their position in the environment. There are at least two different ways in which objects' positions can be perceived: relative to the observer's body and relative to various other objects in the environment. In this section we will focus on the perception of an object's position relative to the observer, often called its **egocentric position**. In Chapter 8 we will consider other schemes for perceiving positional information that depend on relations to other objects (or parts) in the environment.

The egocentric position of an object is most appropriately specified in terms of its **polar coordinates**: the *radial direction* from observer to object and the *distance* from observer to object. All visible objects can be described by these two kinds of coordinates. More precisely, the radial direction of an object with respect to the observer is the direction from a point midway between the observer's two eyes (the center of the so-called **Cyclopian eye**) to the center of the object. How this direction is perceived will be the main focus of this section. We will not discuss the factors that govern perception of the object's distance here, as we covered this topic in Chapter 5.

7.4.1 Perception of Direction

Perception of an object's radial (or egocentric) direction begins with information about the position of its image on the retina. An object's position on the retina relative to the center of the retina specifies its direction relative to the observer's direction of gaze because each retinal receptor signals light coming into the eye from one particular direction. We already know that information about retinal position is preserved in the early stages of visual processing via the many retinotopic maps that preserve relative position in the 2-D sheets of cortical cells. Can this physiological structure therefore account for the perception of an object's egocentric direction?

Unfortunately, it cannot, at least not by itself. A computational-level analysis reveals that the direction of an object depends not only on its retinal position, but also on the direction in which the observer's eyes are pointed. When you look straight ahead, for example, a point that stimulates the center of the retina is perceived as being straight ahead. But when your eyes are directed, say, 10° to the right, the point that is now stimulating your fovea is perceived as being about 10° to the right of straight ahead. A point that is actually straight ahead will now stimulate a position that is 10° to the right of your fovea (which is 10° to the left of the center of your visual field). Thus, the direction in which you perceive an object to be located is not affected by the direction in which the eyes are pointed (Hill, 1972). This fact strongly implies that your visual system determines the radial direction of an object by integrating eye direction and retinal position.

Each of the quantities in question can be expressed as a vector: the environmental position of the object with respect to egocentric "straight ahead" (P_{object}), the image position of the object's projection with respect to the center of the retina (P_{image}), and the position of the eye with respect to the egocentric straight ahead (P_{eye}). Figure 7.4.1 shows the relation among these quantities, which can be expressed as the following vector equation:

$$P_{\text{object}} = P_{\text{image}} + P_{\text{eye}}. \tag{7.3}$$

If the head is pointed straight ahead, the egocentric direction of gaze is given directly by the eye's position relative to the head. But if the head is turned as well, eye position must be computed by adding the vector posi-

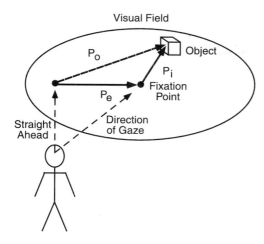

Figure 7.4.1 Position constancy. The egocentric position of an object (P_o) depends on both the direction of gaze relative to egocentric straight ahead (P_e) and the direction to the object's image within the visual field (P_i).

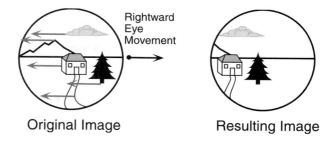

Figure 7.4.2 Eye movements and position constancy. When the eyes move in any direction, the images of stationary objects are displaced by an equal amount in the opposite direction.

tion of the eye with respect to the head plus the vector position of the head with respect to the body. If such equations can be solved by the visual system, position constancy can be accomplished.

7.4.2 Position Constancy

It seems almost absurd to claim that the visual system's ability to perceive unmoving objects as stationary is an accomplishment, but when you think about it, it is. We typically move our eyes dozens of times each minute, and every one of these eye movements causes the images of all stationary objects to sweep across the retina to a new position. For example, every rightward movement of the eye causes the images of all stationary objects to shift leftward relative to the visual field,[3] as illustrated in Figure 7.4.2. Yet in spite of their zigzagging retinal trajectories, stationary objects appear rock-solid in their environmental position, an achievement known as **egocentric position constancy**. The question is how the visual system is able to do this.

A computational-level analysis of the situation shows that constancy in perceived egocentric direction of environmental objects can be computed by the vector addition of displacements of the object's image on the retina

and displacements of the eye relative to the body, as shown in Figure 7.4.3. Each vector represents a *change* in the position (denoted by ΔP) of the eye, an environmental object, or its projected image relative to its previous position. Thus, the null vector ($\Delta P = 0$, as indicated by a dot in Figure 7.4.3) represents no change in position, and all other vectors represent a positional change consisting of a *distance* along a particular *direction*. If we represent the change in environmental direction of an object after an eye movement as a vector, ΔP_{object}, the change in its image position on the retinal as a vector, ΔP_{image}, and the change in direction of the eye as a third vector, ΔP_{eye}, then the relationship among them can be expressed as

$$\Delta P_{\text{object}} = \Delta P_{\text{image}} + \Delta P_{\text{eye}}. \tag{7.4}$$

For example, if the object is stationary and an eye movement to the right is made, its image will be displaced to the left by an equal but opposite amount. Thus, its perceived environmental displacement (the null vector: 0° of visual angle) is the sum of the eye movement (say, 30° rightward) and its resultant image displacement (30° leftward). Thus, direction constancy following an eye movement will be indicated by a zero-change vector for the direction of the environmental object. This will occur whenever the eye movement and retinal displacement exactly cancel each other. (Note that Equation 7.4 is essentially identical to Equation 7.3 except that here we are representing *changes* in direction rather than simple directions.)

---

[3] Because the image on the retina is left-right reversed, images of objects actually move rightward on the retina during a rightward eye movement. We will not consider this fact in our analysis, as it is an essentially irrelevant complication for the points of interest.

Perceiving Object Properties and Parts

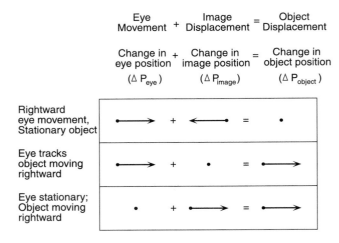

Eye Movement +	Image Displacement =	Object Displacement
Change in + eye position (ΔP_{eye})	Change in image position (ΔP_{image}) =	Change in object position (ΔP_{object})

Figure 7.4.3 Vector addition of eye movements and image displacements. The perceived change in the position of an object after an eye movement is the vector sum of the eye movement and the displacement of the object's image.

Indirect Theories of Position Constancy. The obvious question at this point is how position constancy might be achieved in the human visual system during eye movements. The classical theory, due to Helmholtz, is one of unconscious inference based on the vector equation just discussed. If the observer knows the image displacement directly from sensory information and somehow knows the displacement the eye has undergone, then the displacement of the environmental object can be computed simply by adding the vectors according to Equation 7.3.

But where does the information about eye displacement come from? Helmholtz considered two distinct possibilities:

1. **Afferent theory** (also called **input theory** or **feedback theory**) proposes that after the brain tells the eye to move to a particular position, sensors in the eye muscles register information about muscular tension, which is then sent to the brain to provide feedback about the actual positions of the eyes. The brain then combines this incoming (or *afferent*) information with that from the retinal position of the object's image to compute the direction of the object according to Equation 7.3.

2. **Efferent copy theory** (also called **output theory** or **command theory**) proposes that whenever the brain sends an outgoing (or *efferent*) command to move the eye, it also sends a copy of that command to the brain centers that compute new positions of environmental objects. This signal is sometimes called the **corollary discharge**. It is then combined with the retinal position vector to compute object position according to Equation 7.3.

Both theories assume that eye movement information is used in computing object position, but they differ in the source of that information. In the efferent theory, it is a copy of the initial outgoing command signal; in the afferent theory, it is an incoming feedback signal resulting from the execution of the command. Figure 7.4.4 provides a flowchart for each theory.

Helmholtz (1867/1925) realized that one way to discriminate between the two theories experimentally was to move the eye passively by an external force rather than by issuing a central command from the brain. If the mechanism of position constancy were an afferent signal from the tension in the muscles, it would accu-

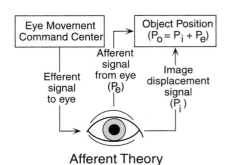

Afferent Theory

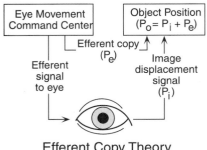

Efferent Copy Theory

Figure 7.4.4 The afferent theory and efferent copy theory of position constancy during eye movements. The afferent theory proposes that a feedback signal from the eye is combined with the retinal displacement signal to compute the change in the position of an object. The efferent theory proposes that a copy of the eye movement command is combined with the retinal displacement signal.

rately reflect the passive eye displacement, and position constancy would be maintained. If it were an efferent copy of the command signal, however, constancy should not occur, because the eye's movement would cause changes in retinal position without any command signal to counteract it. The whole environment would therefore appear to move when the external force was applied to the eye.

The experiment is so simple that you can try it yourself right now: Close one eye and push (gently!) on the outside corner of the open eye with your finger. When the finger moves your eye, the world wiggles noticeably back and forth, indicating that position constancy has failed. This movement is an illusion, of course, because the world has not actually moved. The results of this experiment thus support the efferent copy theory. Various objections to this simple demonstration have been raised, but a more rigorous version of this experiment using forceps to move the eye passively—under anesthesia, of course—gave essentially the same results (Brindley & Merten, 1960).

Another experimental test between these two theories was devised by Ernst Mach (1914/1959), who explored the converse of Helmholtz's prediction. Mach reasoned that the efferent copy theory predicted that if an eye movement command were issued but were not carried out for some reason, the world should appear to move even though the eye had not. In contrast, the afferent theory predicts no perception of movement because the eyes would not move, so there would be no change in the feedback from the muscle sensors. Mach carried out the experiment on himself by wedging putty into the corners of his eye to keep its position fixed. Then, when he tried to make an eye movement, he perceived the world to move. This result provides further support for the efferent copy theory.

A much more rigorous—and dangerous—version of this experiment was performed by psychologist J. Stevens to rule out any possible slippage of the eye when the eye movement was attempted. Stevens had doctors give him an injection of curare, a poison that paralyzed his muscles temporarily (Stevens et al., 1976). In addition to paralyzing the eye muscles, curare paralyzes the muscles required for breathing, so an artificial respirator had to be used to keep him alive. But because his eye muscles were totally paralyzed, Stevens could not possibly have moved his eyes as a result of any efferent

command, thus providing a critical test of Mach's prediction. One more problem had to be overcome, however: Stevens needed some way to signal to his associates—while his muscles were paralyzed—whether or not the world appeared to move when he tried to make an eye movement. The solution was to apply a tourniquet to one arm so that the curare would not affect those muscles. This allowed him to use that hand to signal whether or not the world appeared to move. It did, confirming Mach's earlier finding with the low-tech putty.

The conclusion from all these tests thus appears to be that position constancy during eye movements is maintained by the brain sending a copy of the efferent eye movement command to the center where image displacements are corrected for eye displacements. This system works perfectly well as long as the command causes the corresponding eye movement. If the command causes no eye movement (as in Mach's and Stevens's experiments) or an eye movement is caused by something other than the efferent command (as in Helmholtz's experiment), the same mechanisms that normally produce constancy produce an illusion of movement instead.

Direct Theories of Position Constancy. The efferent copy theory of position constancy is an indirect theory of the "taking-into-account" variety: Changes in egocentric object position are derived from displacements in the retinal image by taking eye movements into account. However, there is an alternative, direct account of position constancy due to Gibson (1966) that is based entirely on the structure of optical flow.

When you make an eye rotation in a static environment, without moving your head at all, the entire image is displaced in the opposite direction. A rightward eye movement therefore produces a uniform optic flow field like the one illustrated in Figure 7.4.5A. The same pattern of retinal motion could logically result from the leftward displacement of the whole environment by rotating about an axis through the observer's eye, but the likelihood of this occurring is exceedingly small. A uniform optic flow field is thus evidence that the eye has rotated in the opposite direction by a corresponding amount. Position constancy during eye movements can therefore be explained by assuming that the visual system simply subtracts out any common motion vector

Perceiving Object Properties and Parts

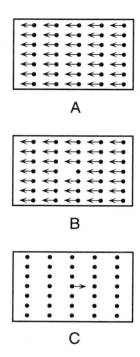

A

B

C

Figure 7.4.5 Optic flow in position constancy. When making a rightward eye movement, retinal images undergo a uniform flow to the left (A). If an object moving rightward is tracked, its image is stationary, whereas the images of all other objects are uniformly displaced to the left (B). Subtracting the common motion vector field from (B) yields the true state of affairs: a rightward moving object against a stationary background (C).

in the flow field. Figure 7.4.5B shows the flow field generated by an observer tracking a rightward moving object. The fixated object is stationary, and the rest of the field flows in the opposite direction. If this common motion component is subtracted at every point, the resulting flow field reveals the true state of affairs: a single object moving in the rightward direction of the eye movement and a static background, as indicated in Figure 7.4.5C.

There are other more complex circumstances in which the retinal positions of stationary objects change yet we correctly perceive them as stationary. These include movements of the head and entire body as well as those of the eye. If eye position remains fixed with respect to the head, rotating the head produces image displacements in the opposite direction, as in the case of eye movements. To the extent that accurate information is available about head rotations, the image displacements they cause can also be discounted. When both

the head and eye are moved simultaneously, these vectors must be added together to cancel the resulting image displacement. Again, however, there is sufficient information in the optic flow field to compute such transformations and achieve position constancy (Longuet-Higgins & Prazdny, 1980).

Movements of the whole body through space as an observer locomotes around the environment also cause image displacements of stationary objects without producing perception of object motion. Consider what happens when you simply walk forward, for example, fixating on an object directly ahead of you. As illustrated in Figure 7.4.6, the images of other objects are displaced radially outward in the image. Even so, we do not perceive these objects as changing their position but as stationary. The nature of the complex transformations induced by observer motion cannot be counteracted by updating the previous image with a simple compensatory displacement as in the case of head and eye movements, however. Rather, the visual system must compute both the positions of objects and the motion of observer from the entire pattern of optical flow. We will defer the consideration of this more complex topic until Chapter 10 when we discuss the perception of motion and events.

7.4.3 Position Illusions

As we have seen, the perception of egocentric position and direction is quite good: Objects appear to be pretty much where they are with respect to the viewer. This is evolutionarily important, of course, because for active, mobile organisms, it is the positions of objects in the world relative to them that matters, not where the images of the objects are on the retina. Even so, perception of egocentric position is not foolproof.

One position illusion arises from the contextual influence of a surrounding object, as illustrated in Figure 7.4.7. Roelofs (1935) showed subjects a luminous rectangular frame in an otherwise dark environment and asked them to indicate which direction was straight ahead. He found that when the frame was presented directly in front of observers, they were extremely accurate in perceiving this direction. When the rectangle was presented slightly to one side of straight ahead, subjects systematically perceived egocentric straight ahead to be displaced by a few degrees toward the center of the frame, a phenomenon known as **Roelofs' effect**.

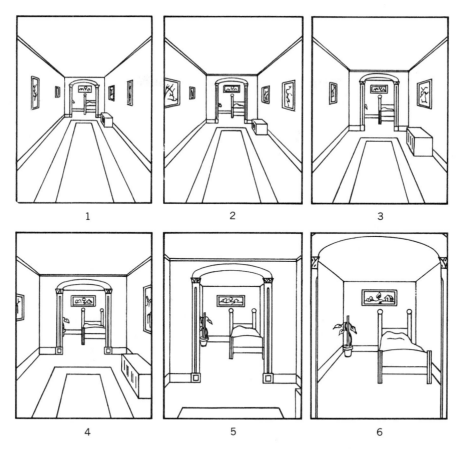

Figure 7.4.6 Position constancy while walking into a room. As we move around within our environment, the structure of optic flow informs us not only about where environmental objects are located relative to us, but also about how we are moving relative to the (generally stationary) environment. The computational processes required to do this are complex and will be discussed in Chapter 10. (From Gibson, 1966.)

This illusion of egocentric straight ahead is a contextual effect, analogous in many ways to the rod-and-frame effect, but not nearly as strong. In Section 7.3 we discussed the fact that people sometimes make systematic errors in judging gravitational vertical if they are shown a large rectangular frame that is misaligned with vertical and horizontal, as illustrated in Figure 7.3.4. In the case of Roelofs' effect, people have difficulty judging the direction of straight ahead relative to themselves when they are shown an object that is off-center.

In summary, we see that in the case of each of the global properties we have considered—size, shape, orientation, and position—the visual system is able to achieve veridical perception of object properties under many, but by no means all, viewing conditions. In some ecologically unusual cases, the same mechanisms that normally lead to veridical perception cause substantial illusions. This happens because the mechanisms underlying perceptual constancy are heuristic, being based on assumptions that are usually, but not always, true. When the assumptions are true, constancy results. When they are false, we experience various sorts of illusions.

7.5 Perceptual Adaptation

It is beyond question that we have roughly accurate perception of object properties such as size, shape, position, and orientation under a wide range of normal viewing conditions. The foregoing discussion of how these intrinsic properties are perceived supports the hypothesis

Perceiving Object Properties and Parts

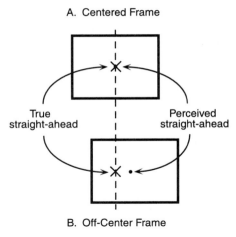

A. Centered Frame

True
straight-ahead

Perceived
straight-ahead

B. Off-Center Frame

Figure 7.4.7 Roelofs' effect. When a rectangular frame is centered on egocentric straight ahead, perceived straight ahead is accurate. When it is displaced to one side, perceived straight ahead is shifted toward the center of the frame.

that they are computed from corresponding properties of their retinal projections plus a variety of other relevant factors. The perceived size of an object thus depends on both its retinal size and its distance from the observer, for example, and the perceived orientation of an object depends on both its retinal orientation and the orientation of the head relative to gravity. These are clear examples of how the visual system is able to use collateral information that varies over normal viewing conditions, such as object distance and head orientation, to recover intrinsic properties of objects from retinal information. The result of these compensatory processes is what we have called perceptual constancy. The visual system is able to take these transformations of the retinal image into account.

The question we now address is whether the visual system is also able to compensate for changes in conditions of viewing that normally do not vary but can be artificially manipulated by optical transformations. The optics of the eye, for example, inverts the retinal image relative to the environment, so light from above the direction of gaze projects to the lower half of the retina and light from below the direction of gaze projects to the upper half of the retina. Corresponding inversions occur in all directions owing to the projection of light through the pupil of the eye (see Figure 1.2.6). This optical inversion *always* takes place and therefore never has to be corrected or reinterpreted during the life of a nor-

mal perceiver. The organism either has the appropriate mapping from birth or learns it once and for all shortly thereafter. It seems logically possible, however, that a transformation in this optical projection could be eliminated by a compensatory inversion in the map between retinal direction and perceived direction. What would the world look like, for example, if retinal images were somehow transformed so that they were *not* inverted? And would we be able to learn to perceive them accurately after a period of practice with this dramatic transformation?

Questions like these about the effects of various image transformations on the perceived properties of objects in the world have been studied extensively in research on **perceptual adaptation**. Perceptual adaptation refers to semipermanent changes in perception or perceptual-motor coordination that reduce sensory discrepancies that have been caused by stimulus transformations (Welch, 1986). It differs from *sensory adaptation* (see Section 1.1) mainly in that sensory adaptation is a short-term change in perception that occurs automatically from normal but prolonged stimulation in a single sensory modality.

Helmholtz (1867/1925) was among the first to investigate perceptual adaptation systematically. He wore spectacles containing prisms that shifted the image of the visible world about 11° to the side. This modest lateral displacement is not at all obvious when you merely observe the world through such prisms; everything looks just fine. But if you shut your eyes and try to reach for an object you just looked at, your hand will miss it by the prism's angle of displacement, as illustrated in Figure 7.5.1A. This error is caused by the discrepancy between the visually perceived position of the object and its actual position. Helmholtz noticed that he could quickly overcome such reaching errors by practicing reaching for objects, provided he received feedback by seeing his hands as well as the objects (Figure 7.5.1B). This reduction in motor errors is one hallmark of perceptual adaptation. Helmholtz also found that once adaptation to the displaced image had occurred, subjects made errors in the *opposite* direction immediately after the prisms were removed from their eyes. This *negative aftereffect*, illustrated in Figure 7.5.1D, is the other main indicant of perceptual adaptation. It is especially important because it appears to rule out the possibility that adaptation is the result of a conscious correction

POINTING WITH PRISM

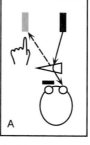 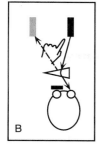

Before Adaptation   After Adaptation

POINTING WITHOUT PRISM

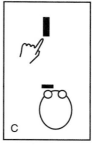 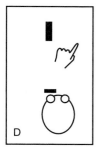

Before Adaptation   After Adaptation

Figure 7.5.1 Adaptation to optical displacement. Before adaptation, people point accurately to a target without prisms that optically displace it (C) and inaccurately with such prisms (A). After experience with feedback, adaptation occurs, and people point accurately to a target with the prisms in place (B) and inaccurately without them (D).

by the observer. If it were, the subject would immediately revert to normal (and accurate) reaching behavior once the prisms were removed.

One of the earliest and most famous studies of adaptation to transformed images examined the effects of "uninverting" the retinal image, as mentioned above. Despite the optically upside-down images on our retinas, we experience the world as fully and completely upright. George Malcolm Stratton (1896) studied perceptual adaptation to image inversion by viewing the world through a prism that uninverted the retinal image. Every waking moment for a period of eight days he wore goggles that allowed him to see the world only through a prism mounted inside a tube in front of his right eye, causing his retinal image to be upright with respect to the world. His left eye was completely covered so that the only visual information he received

was from the uninverted image on his retina. At night, he covered both eyes so that he would not inadvertently expose himself to inverted retinal stimulation when he awakened.

Not surprisingly, the world initially looked completely and utterly upside-down through the goggles. During the eight days of the experiment, Stratton went about his daily activities to the degree that he was able, attempting to walk, dress himself, eat, read, write, and so forth. Almost all tasks that required visual-motor coordination were nearly impossible at first. The difficulties were so severe that he at first found that he could usually do better by closing his eyes and using visual imagery of a rightside-up world to guide his actions in the absence of visual input. But after he had worn the goggles continuously for several days, he began to adapt to the transformed visual world. Eventually he was able to read, write, and carry out standard activities while wearing the prisms. It is clear from his reports that there were many tasks on which his performance began to approach normal levels of proficiency by the end of eight days, such as reaching accurately for objects and getting around adequately in his environment. This indicates that he adapted motorically to the transformation, but did he adapt perceptually as well? That is, did he eventually come to *experience* the world as upright?

As straightforward as this question sounds, its answer is not so simple. Stratton reported that on a number of occasions, especially when he didn't think about it explicitly, he came to be unaware of the world's being upside-down. Toward the end of the experiment he even reported experiencing things as rightside-up. This was not always (or even usually) a simple all-or-none affair, however. Sometimes only part of the world appeared rightside-up while the rest appeared upside-down. At other times, Stratton experienced the world as rightside-up but himself as upside-down, as though he were hanging from the ceiling! He appears never to have really achieved complete adaptation of visual experience in the sense of perceiving the world as wholly and convincingly upright for extended periods of time, more or less as he did before beginning to wear the inverting lens. Moreover, when he removed the goggles at the end of eight days, he reported no negative aftereffect: The world did not appear upside-down. Such negative aftereffects are generally taken as a litmus test for true perceptual adaptation.

Still, it can be objected that he did not wear the goggles for long enough or that his restricted field of view hindered full adaptation in some way. Other psychologists have therefore repeated Stratton's experiment for longer periods of time and used improved methods for inverting the image (e.g., Kohler, 1962). Their findings have generally corroborated Stratton's in terms of demonstrating impressive motor adaptation. Indeed, Kohler was able to ride a bicycle and ski while wearing the optical inversion apparatus. Unlike Stratton, however, Kohler claims to occasionally have had complete and convincing experiences of an upright world for extended periods of time.

Another major phenomenon that Stratton discovered when he wore the inverting lens was the loss of position constancy. He described it as "the swinging of the field" when he rotated his head. This visual motion results from the optical inversion for the following reason. When one rotates one's head rightward, there is normally optic flow leftward in the visual field. This retinal motion can be canceled by adding the eye displacement and visual displacement vectors, resulting in position constancy as described in Section 7.4.2 for the case of eye rotations rather than head rotations, but the logic is the same. Because the lens inverts left and right, however, leftward optic flow is transformed into rightward optic flow. When this rightward visual displacement vector is added to the rightward head displacement vector, the result is rightward motion of environmental objects at twice the speed of the optic flow. The result is thus a far cry from normal position constancy and explains why Stratton experienced the visual field as "swinging" when he turned his head.

Unlike the upside-down phenomenon induced by the inverting goggles, Stratton (1896) found that the swinging-field effect adapted completely. After several days of practice, position constancy was virtually normal, with no noticeable swinging of the field when he turned his head. At the end of the experiment, when he removed the goggles, he noted the reinstatement of the swinging-field effect, even though the optical projection was now completely normal. It is not clear why this adaptation to image inversion should be so much easier and more complete than orientation adaptation.

Later research on perceptual adaptation has investigated other optically induced transformations, such as rotations, enlargements and reductions, left-right reversals, lateral displacements, changes in curvature, and so forth (see Rock, 1966, and Welch, 1978, 1986, for reviews). The findings show that the degree of adaptation and its time course vary substantially for different transformations. Perceptual-motor integration is initially abysmal in the visually transformed world, but within some period of time—ranging from minutes to weeks of practice with only the transformed images—it improves to the point of proficiency. In some cases, such as with modest lateral displacements of the image, subjects often report that they experience the world as completely normal following adaptation. Indeed, subjects usually say that their hand *feels* as if it is located where they see it, rather than where it actually is. This phenomenon, in which vision dominates other sensory modalities with which it is discrepant, is known as **visual capture**.

The mere fact of adaptation does not reveal what exactly adapts in such situations, however. Is it the visual experience or the motor movements? Further experiments have shown that the answer depends on the specific transformation being studied, but both the motor and visual systems are often implicated, their effects being additive (Hamilton, 1964; Harris, 1965).

One of the most striking findings of adaptation research is that the amount of adaptation depends on the type of activities in which the subject is allowed to engage. Psychologist Richard Held of M.I.T. has argued that active exploration of the environment is crucial in producing adaptation to spatial transformations. His clever experiments investigated adaptation in active versus passive observers (Held & Freedman, 1963). Human observers were first fitted with goggles that made straight lines look curved, and the amount of distortion they produced was measured. Then half the subjects actively walked around in a large cylinder whose interior was speckled with random dots, whereas the other half were moved passively on a wheeled cart (see Figure 7.5.2). Later measurements of distortion showed that the active observers had adapted more fully to the transforming effects of the goggles than the passive observers.

Held's findings suggest that attempts to control one's own bodily movements under conditions of optical transformation play an important role in adaptation. This makes a good deal of sense, for without controlling one's own movements, discrepancies in visual stimulation would be much harder to detect. The observer that knows how he or she is trying to move can tell that the

Figure 7.5.2 Adaptation during active versus passive movement. Some observers were allowed to actively explore their environment while wearing distorting goggles whereas others received similar stimulation during passive movement as shown here. The active observers adapted more fully to the optical transformation produced by the goggles than the passive observers did. (From Held, 1965.)

Perceiving Object Properties and Parts

visual input is transformed (and how it is transformed) much more effectively than the observer that is just being taken for a ride and has no intentional control of his or her movements.

7.6 Parts

Perceived objects have an important aspect that cannot be captured by veridical perception of global properties such as their size, shape, orientation, and position: the fact that most complex objects are perceived as being composed of distinct **parts**. As we will use the term, a part is a restricted portion of an object that has semi-autonomous, objectlike status in visual perception. A human body, for example, is perceived as being composed of a head, a torso, two arms, and two legs; a standard wooden desk chair is perceived as containing a seat, a back, and four legs; a tree is perceived as consisting of a trunk, numerous limbs, and masses of individual leaves. In addition to these parts, object perceptions include the spatial relations among the parts, for a disassembled pile of chair legs, seat, and back does not look even remotely the same as a properly constructed chair.

7.6.1 Evidence for Perception of Parts

Phenomenal experience strongly suggests that perceiving complex objects gives rise to the spontaneous perception of parts. We also have the distinct impression that the parts that we perceive are stable and nonarbitrary. We further believe that other people perceive them in pretty much the same way we do. Normal observers, for example, never see the lower half of a human head and the upper half of a human torso as a single natural body part, nor do they see the seat and one leg of a chair as a single natural chair part. Convincing evidence for the assertion that we perceive most objects as composed of parts comes from a number of sources: the language we have for talking about the world, demonstrations employing cleverly constructed examples, and behavioral results from psychological experiments. We will consider each of these in turn.

Linguistic Evidence. One of the most obvious kinds of evidence for the perceptual reality of object parts comes from the language we have for talking about

them. The perception of parts is so important and ubiquitous that we have separate words to refer to the salient parts of many familiar objects—words such as *head* and *torso* for bodies, *legs* and *seat* for chairs, and *trunk* and *limbs* for trees—even though we seldom see these parts separately from the object of which they are a subset. The structure of language thus seems to reflect the underlying structure of perception.

But we must also consider the possibility that the perception of part structure might be determined by the linguistic conventions of our culture rather than by perception itself. This idea is another version of the Sapir-Whorf hypothesis that we discussed in Chapter 3 with respect to color categories: the idea that perception and thought are determined by language rather than the other way around.

There are two sorts of evidence against this idea. One is that the way objects are divided into parts by language, although not completely universal, is quite similar across languages. Virtually all languages have single words that refer to heads, arms, and legs, and none have words that refer to things like the combination of the lower half of the head and the upper half of the torso (Fillmore, personal communication). This is what one would expect if perceived part structure were universal and if the cultural conventions of language were determined by perception rather than vice versa. This is not to say that how object parts are lexicalized is completely systematic or universal across languages. In English, for example, we have single lexical entries that refer to the hand and to the forearm but not to the upper arm. With regard to legs, we have different words to refer to the front (*shin*) and back (*calf*) of the lower leg but no single word for that whole lower portion of the leg. Other languages name these subparts of limbs somewhat differently, but the linguistic structures for referring to objects with well-articulated parts are still relatively stable across languages, much more so than one would expect if part structure were arbitrarily designated by different languages.

The other sort of evidence against a strong Whorfian hypothesis about the perception of part structure is that people spontaneously perceive part structure in objects they have never seen before and have no words to use in referring to them. If the parts we perceive were determined by the language we learn to describe them, we wouldn't know how to divide a novel object into parts or

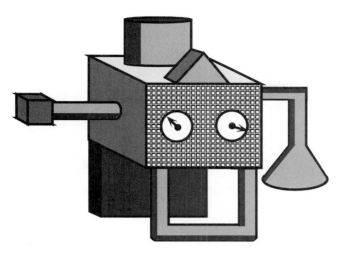

Figure 7.6.1 A novel object. Even though you have never seen this object before, it is still perceived as having clearly defined parts.

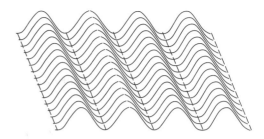

Figure 7.6.2 A wavy surface. Despite the smoothness of this surface, it is usually perceived as being composed of parallel ridges (rather than troughs) as indicated by the fact that the dashed lines divide it between parts (as long as the surface is perceived as viewed from above).

be able to do it with any consistency. A quick look at the nonsense object depicted in Figure 7.6.1 shows that this is not the case. Not only do observers immediately perceive this object as containing parts, but they are quite consistent in what parts they see. This ability can be explained only if perceiving parts within complex objects is a natural function of perception itself, largely independent of language. Linguistic structure may indeed have *some* effect on perception, but the major influence appears to be in the other direction: Perception (together with use) specifies the parts, for which language then provides names.

Phenomenological Demonstrations. Further evidence of part structure in perception comes from several compelling phenomenological demonstrations. Hoffman and Richards (1984) have provided a number of examples in which even seemingly unitary and well-integrated object perceptions have a highly stable part structure.

Consider first the wavy surface depicted in Figure 7.6.2. Although entirely smooth and continuous, this surface seems to be composed of many parallel ridges, as indicated by the dashed lines that lie along the perceived boundaries between these parts. When this figure is turned upside down, the organization into parts changes with respect to the image, so the dashed lines are now seen as lying in the middle of the perceived parts. In either case, the figure could logically be seen as

composed of parallel "troughs" or "valleys" rather than "ridges" or "mountains," but it almost never is. This demonstration shows not only that this surface is perceived as being made up of parts, but also something about how the parts are determined, as we will discuss shortly.

Another of Hoffman and Richards's (1984) demonstrations comes from the reversible staircase shown in Figure 7.6.3. The two dots in this image are typically seen as lying on the same part, corresponding to what we call a "step." This figure is perceptually reversible, however, and when it reverses to look like an upside-down staircase, the same two dots appear to lie on different parts (the flat part of one step and the rise of the next). If you have trouble reversing the staircase perceptually, you can try turning the figure upside-down as you did for the wavy surface of Figure 7.6.2. The reversed staircase will now look rightside-up, but the dots will be on two different steps rather than one. The important

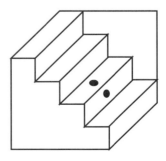

Figure 7.6.3 The Schroder reversible staircase. The two dots initially appear to be located on the same step, but when the figure undergoes depth reversal—turning it upside-down helps—the same dots appear to be located on two different steps.

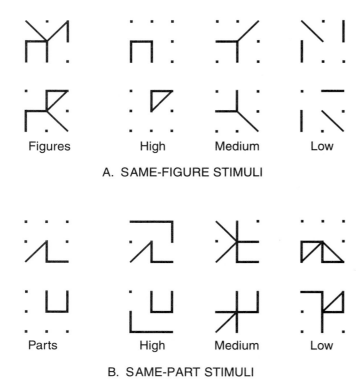

A. SAME-FIGURE STIMULI

B. SAME-PART STIMULI

Figure 7.6.4 Stimuli for experiments on part detection. Subjects had to rate the "goodness" of three-segment parts within six-segment whole figures in one task and to verify the presence of parts within wholes in another task. The goodness of parts within wholes was varied from high to low for two sets of stimuli. (After Palmer, 1977.)

observation is how strong the phenomenological impression is that the dots lie on the same part in one case and on two different parts in the other.

Perceptual Experiments. Further evidence about the nature of part perception comes from psychological experiments. For example, Palmer (1977) performed several studies using converging operations to investigate the perception of part structure in simple 2-D nonsense figures. The results show that certain subsets of figures are perceived as parts whereas others are not.

The stimuli were simple planar figures containing six line segments, as depicted in Figure 7.6.4. In one experiment subjects were asked simply to divide figures like the ones on the left in Figure 7.6.4A into their natural parts. In a second experiment they were asked to rate the "goodness" or "naturalness" of several different subsets of each figure. In a third experiment they were

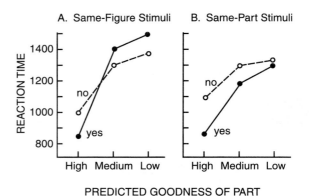

PREDICTED GOODNESS OF PART

Figure 7.6.5 Results of an experiment on part detection. Time to verify the presence of parts within wholes increased as the goodness of the part within the whole decreased for both same-figure stimuli (part A) and same-part stimuli (part B) (see Figure 7.6.4). (After Palmer, 1977.)

required to decide as quickly as possible whether or not various three-segment parts—constituting "good," "medium," or "bad" parts—were contained within a given six-segment figure. The results of all three kinds of experiments supported the hypothesis that even these novel figures are spontaneously perceived as having well-defined part structures.

Figure 7.6.5A shows the results that Palmer (1977) obtained from the part verification experiment when several different parts were tested within the same figure: "Good" parts were found much more quickly and accurately than "medium" or "bad" parts. This result strongly suggests that "good" parts are spontaneously perceived in such figures and that "bad" parts are not (see also Reed & Johnson, 1975). It is possible, however, that the results from this "same figure" condition were due to intrinsic differences between good and bad parts—for example, the fact that good parts are connected and compact whereas bad ones tend to be disconnected and dispersed. To rule out such an interpretation of the results, and to show that the perception of parts is strongly context dependent, other stimuli (the "same part" conditions) were included in which the very same three segment parts were embedded in different figures to produce good, medium, and bad parts (Figure 7.6.4B). The results for part verification time in this condition also showed much faster responses to the good parts than to either the medium or bad parts, even though they were, in some sense, the very same parts

(Figure 7.6.5B). These data agreed with those of the parsing task and the part-rating task, leading to the conclusion that these novel figures are spontaneously perceived as containing certain parts to the exclusion of others.[4]

7.6.2 Part Segmentation

Given that perception of complex objects and surfaces is characteristically structured into distinct parts, how does the visual system determine what the parts are? From the evidence just reviewed, part structure cannot be considered arbitrary, because it is highly regular and stable across both objects and observers. How might the parts of an object be determined from the structural characteristics of the object itself?

At the most general level, there are two ways to go about dividing an object into parts (a process often called **parsing**): using shape primitives or boundary rules. Once a set of parts has been identified by either method, higher-level parts can then be constructed by using the grouping principles described in Section 6.1.

The **shape primitive** approach to part segmentation requires a set of simple, indivisible shapes that constitute the complete set of the most basic parts. More complex objects are then analyzed as configurations of these primitive parts. Thus, any object can be divided into the primitives of which it is composed by specifying the segmentation of that object. This approach can be thought of as analogous to dividing words written in cursive into parts by knowing the cursive alphabet and finding the component letters by visual search. The unbroken line of a word is divided at points between the letters that have been identified. This works well only as long as there is a relatively small set of primitive components, however, and it is far from obvious what these primitives might be in the case of standard everyday 3-D objects.

The **boundary rules** approach assumes that objects can be divided into parts by applying a set of rules that specify where part boundaries are located. It does not require any fixed set of primitive shapes but works directly on the whole object by dividing it into whatever parts result from the application of the boundary rules. This would be like trying to parse a cursively written word by using rules such as "divide the line at upward, U-shaped curves" without first trying to find the letters. We will now consider these two approaches in more detail.

Shape Primitives. The underlying idea of parsing by shape primitives is both attractive and familiar. It is essentially the structuralist idea of atomism applied to object and part perception. The basic proposal is that all perceptions of object shape can be decomposed into configurations of a relatively small set of *atomic shapes*. We have already implicitly considered this idea in discussing Marr's notion of a raw primal sketch, in which the primitive elements are line segments, edge segments, blobs, and terminators (see Chapter 4). But as attractive as such primitives may be for 2-D images, they are hard to justify as 3-D object-based primitives. Rather, it seems natural that the shape primitives for 3-D object perception should be **volumetric**, meaning that they are based on 3-D volumes rather than on 2-D surfaces or 1-D edges and lines.

Marr's (1982) influential book popularized Binford's (1971) proposal that complex shapes can be analyzed into primitives consisting of generalized cylinders. Although we will defer a full discussion of this idea until the next chapter on shape perception, the reader may recall that we mentioned it briefly at the end of Chapter 2 when we first described Marr's computational framework for vision. Roughly speaking, Binford's idea is that shapes can be represented as constructions of appropriately sized and shaped cylinders, as illustrated in Figure 2.4.8. Obviously, standard cylinders do a pretty crude job, but their extension to generalized cylinders improves their capabilities a great deal. Figure 7.6.6 shows some examples of generalized cylinders (part A) and how they can be combined to form common objects in an everyday scene (part B). The important point for

---

[4]Palmer (1977) modeled the results of his experiments using a linear weighted average of several Gestalt grouping principles such as connectedness, continuity, and proximity (see Section 6.1), which he quantified using simple mathematical definitions. This approach has been extended by Shimaya (1997) to much more complex stimuli, including cases that involved occlusion and visual completion. Shimaya's model was able to predict the parts observers reported in viewing such figures using a linear weighted combination of seven different factors, many of which are closely related to Gestalt principles of grouping.

Perceiving Object Properties and Parts

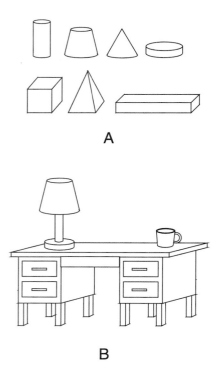

A

B

Figure 7.6.6 Generalized cylinders. Several current theories suggest that everyday objects, such as those depicted in part B, can be analyzed into shape primitives consisting of generalized cylinders, examples of which are shown in part A. Generalized cylinders are a generalization of standard cylinders that allow variations in several different parameters. (See Section 8.2.4.)

present purposes is that if one has a set of shape primitives and some way of detecting them in images, complex 3-D objects can be segmented into parts consisting of these primitives. Provided the primitives are sufficiently general, part segmentation will be possible, even for novel objects such as the one in Figure 7.6.1, which is readily decomposed into generalized cylinders.

The shape primitives approach to part segmentation has several potential problems, however. One is the existence of contextual effects in part segmentation. Experiments such as Palmer's (1977) have shown that the same part will be easily detected in one figural context and not in another (see Figure 7.6.4B). If part segmentation occurs by finding shape primitives, why is the same part harder to recognize in some cases than in others? One possible answer is that there may be a preference ordering among primitives such that the visual system tends to detect certain primitives before others. Then, if several primitives were present in an object in compet-

ing organizations, the preferred one would be detected first, and the others would be "hidden" by the part structural organization that resulted from detecting the preferred one. Such preferences have not yet been worked out, however, and remain a promissory note in primitive-based accounts of part segmentation.

Another potential difficulty with the shape primitive approach is that we not only perceive objects as containing parts, but also often perceive those parts as having subparts. A head is part of a person, but the head itself is composed of eyes, nose, ears, mouth, and so forth. Even these subparts can have further part structure, as eyes do, being composed of lids, lashes, pupils, irises, and so on. This means that a theory of part segmentation will have to be capable of generating a potentially complex and elaborate **part/whole hierarchy**. This is a potential problem for shape primitives because if there is only one set of primitives, it seems to define just one level of part structure, whereas more levels are required.

This difficulty may be overcome in either of two ways. One is by assuming that there are **multiple scales** of description at which the primitives can be detected. We have already seen an example of this idea in Marr's analysis of body parts into cylinders at different levels of resolution (see Figure 2.4.8). The body as a whole is represented as a cylinder of certain dimensions, but so is the hand at a higher level of resolution, and so are the individual fingers at a still higher level of resolution. Thus, different primitive parts could be identified at different levels of resolution or scale, potentially resulting in a hierarchy of parts. A second way to generate a hierarchy of parts is by using grouping principles to unite different subsets of primitives into higher level parts.

Another problem for a primitive-based theory of part segmentation is that there must be some well-defined process that will find or recognize those primitives. This might not seem like much of a problem in perfect hand-crafted line drawings, such as in Figure 7.6.6, but it is a very hard problem in real-world images, which are noisy, messy arrays of gray levels. Without a set of processes capable of finding the presumed primitives, part segmentation by primitives is just an elegant fiction.

The most difficult problem for a primitive-based theory of part segmentation, however, is perhaps the most obvious one: What set of primitives will do justice to the huge diversity and immense subtlety of shapes that must be described? Simple geometric primitives, such as cylinders, cones, ellipsoids, and prisms, seem to fall short of the mark, especially in capturing smooth, subtle, organic shapes such as faces. This does not mean that there are no primitives underlying perception of parts and wholes, but only that figuring out what they might be is a difficult problem. Until it is solved, the shape primitive approach rests on the promissory note that an adequate set can eventually be identified.

Boundary Rules. The other major approach to part segmentation is to define a set of general rules that specify where the boundaries lie between parts. This approach does not require a set of primitive shapes because it finds part boundaries—and thereby divides the object into parts—without specifying the precise nature of the resulting parts beforehand. In the shape primitives approach, parts are primary and boundaries are by-products of finding parts. In the boundary rules approach, boundaries are primary and parts are by-products.

The best known theory of the boundary rule type was developed by vision scientists Donald Hoffman and Whitman Richards (1984). They based their analysis on a geometric property of multipart objects formed by one object penetrating another. The key property, called the **transversality regularity**, refers to the fact that when one object penetrates another, as illustrated in Figure 7.6.7, they meet in **concave discontinuities**: places where their composite surface is not smooth but angles sharply inward toward the interior of the composite object. Concave discontinuities of this sort are formed, for example, when you stick your finger into a

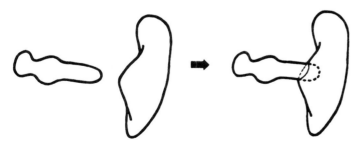

Figure 7.6.7   The transversality regularity. When any two surfaces interpenetrate, they meet in concave discontinuities. These discontinuities are used to divide an object into parts in Hoffman and Richards's (1984) theory of visual parsing. (From Hoffman & Richards, 1984.)

ball of clay or push a candle into the icing of a birthday cake.

As a first step toward a theory of part segmentation, Hoffman and Richards (1984) proposed the **concave discontinuity rule**: The visual system divides objects into parts where they have abrupt changes in surface orientation toward the interior of the object (i.e., concave surface discontinuities). This would explain why the two dots on the ambiguous staircase (see Figure 7.6.3) look as though they are on the same part in one interpretation and on different parts in the other. The staircase would be divided into parts along the sharply concave edges between steps rather than along the convex corner of the steps themselves or the flat parts in between. When this figure undergoes figure/ground reversal, the concavity/convexity of each edge reverses, and so, therefore, does the part structure.

Strictly speaking, however, the transversality regularity does not apply to most of the cases in which people perceive parts. The problem is that many objects, including the human body and the wavy surface of Figure 7.6.2, have smooth transitions between parts. Hoffman and Richards therefore generalized their transversality regularity into a weaker—and thus more widely applicable—principle of part segmentation by analyzing what would happen if the composite surface were smoothed at the junction, as by stretching a taut skin over it. The resulting analysis led to the **deep concavity rule**. Roughly speaking, it states that a surface should be divided at places where its surface is maximally curved inward (concave), even if these curves are smooth and continuous rather than discontinuous, as required by the concave discontinuity rule.

An example in which the deep concavity rule has been applied to smooth surfaces is given in Figure 7.6.8A. It seems to parse this object in the way that people usually do when they perceive it. The same rule also allows the wavy surface in Figure 7.6.2 to be divided along the dashed lines because these are the places in which the surface has the deepest concavities, assuming that the observer is looking down so that the "object" lies below the surface. Again, the theory predicts that reversing concavity and convexity should reverse the part structure, as it does when the figure is turned upside down.

More needs to be said about both of these rules, however, because, as stated, they apply to the actual surfaces

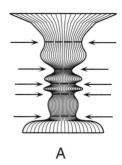

A

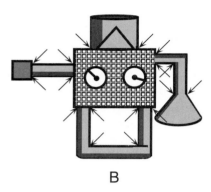

B

Figure 7.6.8 Parsing objects by boundary rules. Hoffman and Richards (1984) proposed that objects can be divided into parts at minima of curvature on smooth surfaces (part A) or at concave discontinuities (part B), as indicated by the arrows.

of 3-D objects rather than to their 2-D projections on the retina. Because the visual system does not have access to the objects themselves, but only to their projected images, we must ask how these rules about object concavities can be translated into heuristics that work directly on images. Hoffman and Richards proposed that a good rule of thumb is to divide silhouettes of objects into parts at **maximal concavities**, which, mathematically speaking, are local negative minima of curvature.

A further difficulty for Hoffman and Richards's original theory is that it merely identifies the points at which cuts should be made to divide an object into parts; it does not say which pairs of these points should be the endpoints of the cuts. Their examples are well chosen to avoid problematic cases, but many real-world cases are not nearly as clear. This gap has recently been filled by an analysis of rules for matching up concavities accord-

ing to further sets of rules, one of which is to make cuts between the nearest dividing points (Singh, Seyranian, & Hoffman, in preparation).

7.6.3 Global and Local Processing

Given that objects are perceived as being structured into parts, subparts, and so on, the question naturally arises of which level has priority in perceptual processing. The issue, to put it somewhat crudely, is whether parts are perceived before wholes or wholes before parts. Although the Gestaltists never actually posed the question in precisely this form, their doctrine of holism suggests that perception of wholes should dominate that of parts. This in turn suggests that wholes may be processed first, for this is one way in which the whole might dominate perceptual experience. Nearly all other approaches to perception oppose this idea, however, implying that wholes are constructed by integrating smaller parts into increasingly larger aggregations. Such theories therefore predict that parts should be processed first. Which view is correct?

Like many theoretical issues, the answer depends on precisely how the question is posed. Within a physiological framework, the answer almost certainly is that local parts are processed before global wholes. As we noted in Section 1.3, retinal receptors respond to exceedingly tiny regions of stimulation, and as one traces the path of neural information processing, neuron by neuron, deeper into the brain, the receptive fields become ever larger and responsive to ever more complex stimulus configurations. From this physiological perspective, then, there seems to be little doubt that processing proceeds from local stimulation to global structure.

There are grave problems in accepting this line of argument as settling anything about perceptual experience, however. First, the order in which processing is *initiated* may not be nearly as relevant for determining perceptual experience as the order in which it is *completed*. And it is by no means clear that neural processing is completed in a local-to-global order. Indeed, it is highly unlikely that the flow of neural information processing is unidirectional from the sensory surface of the eye to higher centers of the brain. Anatomical evidence shows that massive backward projections exist from higher to lower centers of the visual system. This fact suggests that a great deal of feedback may be occurring, although nobody yet knows precisely what form it takes or even what function it serves.

Another problem with using physiological evidence to draw conclusions about perceptual experience is that it is questionable whether a simple equation can be made between the order of neural response and the order of perceptual experience. Does the fact that the pattern of firing on the retina is the first neural activity in the visual system imply that this information is first to be experienced? Quite the contrary. Compelling arguments can be made that we have no direct perceptual experience of this retinal information at all, as explained at the beginning of Chapter 13. Unlike any form of perceptual experience, the response of retinal receptors is almost totally unorganized and occurs before any form of perceptual constancy has taken place.

Just where conscious experience occurs within the human visual system in terms of neural processing mechanisms is an open question, but it is quite possible that perceptual experience follows a very different time course from the sequence of neural information processing, much of which is probably not conscious at all. Conscious perception might even run in the opposite direction from the order in which neural processing seems to occur, that is, from larger wholes to smaller parts, as the Gestaltists implied long ago in their doctrine of holism. We will now examine some evidence from psychological experiments suggesting that we take seriously the possibility that the experience of global objects precedes that of local parts.

Global Precedence. Given the hierarchial nature of part structure—whole objects being composed of parts, subparts, and so on—we can pose the question about the priority of wholes versus parts in a well-formed way. If the stimulus object is structured in a clear, two-level hierarchy, we can ask whether the whole (at the global level) is perceived before its parts (at the local level) or vice versa. Psychologist David Navon at the University of Haifa examined this question using stimuli in which the global and local levels contained essentially the same information. He did this by constructing large letters of many appropriately positioned small letters, as illustrated in Figure 7.6.9.

Navon (1977) presented subjects with these hierarchically constructed letters in two kinds of configurations. In *consistent configurations*, the global and local letters were

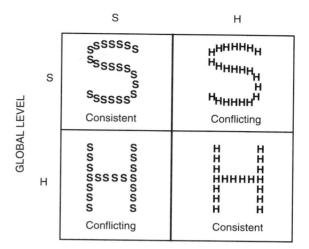

Figure 7.6.9 Hierarchical stimuli. Large, global S's and H's are composed of small, local S's and H's for experiments in which subjects are instructed to report the identity of the letter present at either the global or the local level. (After Navon, 1977.)

the same, such as a large H made of small H's or a large S made of small S's. In *inconsistent configurations*, the global and local letters conflicted, such as a large H made of small S's or a large S made of small H's. Subjects were cued on each trial whether to report the identity of the letter represented at the global or the local level. Response times and accuracies were measured for the four conditions shown in Figure 7.6.9.

If **global precedence** holds—that is, if the global level is perceived first—three predictions follow:

1. **Global advantage**: Responses to global letters should be faster than those to local letters.

2. **Global-to-local interference**: Inconsistent global letters should slow responses when subjects attend to the local level, because the local level is perceived only after the global one.

3. **Lack of local-to-global interference**: Inconsistent local letters should not slow responses when subjects attend to the global level because the global level is perceived first.

If the local level is perceived first, however, the opposite results are predicted: (1) faster responses to the local level (local advantage), (2) slower responses to inconsistent conditions in the global attention condition (local-

Perceiving Object Properties and Parts

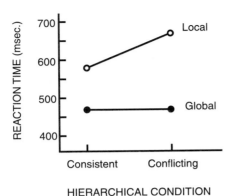

Figure 7.6.10 Results of an experiment on perception of hierarchical stimuli. Identification of global letters (solid circles) is fast and not affected by local letters. Identification of local letters (open circles) is slower, especially when the identity of the global letter conflicts with that of the local letter. (After Navon, 1977.)

to-global interference), and (3) no slower responses to inconsistent conditions in the local condition (lack of global-to-local interference).

The results of Navon's experiment are shown in Figure 7.6.10. They support the predictions of global precedence on all three counts: Response times are faster to global than to local letters, and inconsistent conditions are slower only when subjects were attending to the local level. The data thus appear to indicate that perceptual processes proceed from global processing toward more and more fine-grained analysis.

Further investigations showed global precedence to be a real and replicable phenomenon but not as robust as it first appeared. Under somewhat different stimulus conditions, other experimenters have reported other patterns of results. Kinchla and Wolfe (1979), for example, found that the speed of naming local versus global forms depended on their retinal sizes. Identifying global letters was faster than identifying local ones when the global stimuli were smaller than about 8–10° of visual angle, but identifying local letters was faster than identifying global ones when the stimuli were larger than this.

Kinchla and Wolfe argued that the visual system followed a "middle-out" order of processing, beginning with structure at intermediate sizes and working "outward" toward both smaller and larger levels. This possibility seems consistent with the contrast sensitivity function of the visual system (see Section 4.2), since it shows that people are most sensitive to intermediate

spatial frequencies and less sensitive to both high and low ones. Still, global precedence for figures up to 8–10°—about the size of your fist held at arm's length—is a fairly surprising result when one considers that receptive fields of simple cells in area V1 of visual cortex are seldom more than 1° in size.

Other experiments suggest that global and local levels of information may be processed simultaneously rather than sequentially. For example, when subjects are monitoring for a target letter at *both* the global and the local levels, their responses are faster when a target letter is present at both global and local levels than when a target letter is present at either level alone (Miller, 1981). Careful analysis of response times in this experiment supports the hypothesis that both levels are being processed in parallel, the results of both processes being pooled in making the response. If this is true, the findings on global versus local precedence may best be understood as the result of parallel processing in different size (or spatial frequency) channels, some being processed slightly faster than others. The claim that the visual system sequentially processes first one level and then the other may therefore be misguided. Thus, global precedence is a finding that supports the primacy of global information in conscious perception—at least under certain conditions—but its interpretation is not as straightforward as it first appeared.

Experiments by neuropsychologist Lynn Robertson and her colleagues studying brain-damaged patients have shown that global and local information is processed differently in the two cerebral hemispheres. Several lines of evidence show that there is an advantage for global processing in the right temporal-parietal lobe, whereas there is an advantage for local processing in the left temporal-parietal lobe (Robertson, Lamb, & Knight, 1988). Figure 7.6.11 shows how patients with lesions in the left versus right temporal-parietal region copied the same hierarchical target stimulus shown on the left side (Delis, Robertson, & Efron, 1986). Patients with right hemisphere damage, who suffer deficits in global processing, are able to reproduce the small letters making up the global letter but are unable to reproduce their global structure (middle column of Figure 7.6.11). Patients with left hemisphere damage, who suffer deficits in local processing, are able to reproduce the global letter but not the small letters that compose it (right column of Figure 7.6.11).

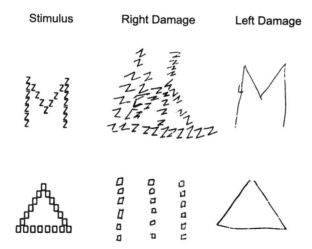

Stimulus **Right Damage** **Left Damage**

Figure 7.6.11 Drawings of hierarchical stimuli from brain-damaged patients. Patients with lesions in the right hemisphere (central column) accurately reproduce the local elements but not the global configuration. Those with lesions in the left hemisphere (right column) reproduce the global configuration but not the local elements. (From Delis, Robertson, & Efron, 1986.)

As you might guess from these drawings, patients with damage to the right temporal-parietal lobe show a strong local advantage in Navon's identification task, whereas patients with damage to the left temporal-parietal lobe show a strong global advantage (Robertson et al., 1988). Studies with normal subjects using special techniques to measure hemispheric asymmetries support the same general conclusion: Global information is processed more effectively in the right hemisphere, and local information is processed more effectively in the left hemisphere (Sergent, 1982). Surprisingly, however, neither of the brain-damaged groups shows any interference effects whatsoever (Lamb, Robertson, & Knight, 1989). This suggests that quite different neural mechanisms may underlie global versus local advantage effects (i.e., which level is identified faster) and global-to-local versus local-to-global interference effects (i.e., which level inhibits the other).

Additional studies with patients whose corpus callosum has been surgically severed have shed some light on this unexpected finding. Specifically, it appears that processing in the left versus right temporal-parietal cortex is critical in producing global/local advantage effects, whereas the transfer of information between these two cortical areas in the left and right hemispheres

via the corpus callosum is critical in producing interference effects (Robertson & Lamb, 1991). There are obviously many more questions that need to be answered before we understand in detail the neural mechanisms underlying these complex effects, but interesting and unexpected discoveries have already arisen from neuropsychological studies such as these.

Configural Orientation Effects. Other findings that indicate important influences of global structure on local perception come from a series of experiments by Palmer on what he calls **configural orientation effects**: the fact that perception of local spatial orientation is influenced by more global orientational structure (e.g., Palmer 1980, 1989). The basic phenomenon comes from an observation by Attneave (1968) that equilateral triangles are directionally ambiguous figures: They can be seen as pointing in any of three directions but in only one of them at once. For example, in Figure 7.6.12A, the triangle can look like it is pointing toward 3, 7, or 11 o'clock. The interesting fact for the present issue of global influences on local perception is that when several triangles are aligned in particular ways, the configuration can strongly affect the direction in which the individual triangles are perceived to point. If the triangles are aligned along an axis of symmetry (Figure 7.6.12B), observers tend to see them point along the configural line. If they are aligned along one of their sides (Figure 7.6.12C), observers tend to see them point perpendicular to the configural line.

Palmer and Bucher (1981) investigated how global these configural influences were. Could they be affected by configural structure anywhere on the retina, or are they restricted to some more limited region of stimulation? To answer this question, they needed a way to measure the strength of the configural effect. They devised a speeded discrimination task in which subjects were shown several triangles at once, all of which could be seen as pointing either directly left (toward 9 o'clock) or directly right (toward 3 o'clock), as shown in Figure 7.6.12. Subjects were instructed to press the left response button for left-pointing triangles and the right one for right-pointing triangles as quickly as possible without making errors. On some trials, the triangles were aligned to facilitate perceiving the triangles point in the correct direction (upper rows of Figure 7.6.12B

Perceiving Object Properties and Parts

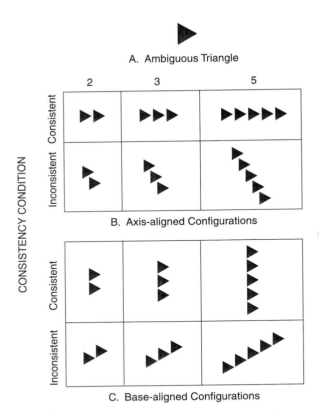

A. Ambiguous Triangle

CONSISTENCY CONDITION

B. Axis-aligned Configurations

C. Base-aligned Configurations

Figure 7.6.12 Perceived pointing of ambiguous triangles. A single equilateral triangle is ambiguous in that it can be seen to point in any of three directions (A). Several triangles aligned along their axes of symmetry (B) or sides (C) strongly affect how the component triangles are seen to point. (See text for details.)

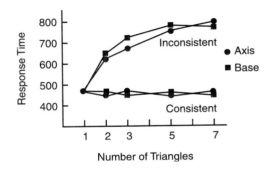

Figure 7.6.13 Results of an experiment on perceived pointing of ambiguous triangles. Response time to determine the direction in which equilateral triangles point depends strongly on the orientation of the configuration of which they are part. The difference between consistent and inconsistent configurations increases with the number of triangles but levels off at about five triangles. (After Palmer & Bucher, 1981.)

and 7.6.12C). These trials were called *consistent conditions*, and response times on them were expected to be fast. On other trials, they were aligned to interfere with the perception of the appropriate direction of pointing (lower rows of Figures 7.6.12B and 7.6.12C). These trials were called *inconsistent conditions*, and response times on them were expected to be slow. The difference in response times between these two conditions thus provides a measure of how strongly the orientation of the configuration affects the perception of pointing in the individual triangles.

Palmer and Bucher addressed the question of how global these configural orientation effects are by conducting a series of experiments. In the first, they measured the amount of configural influence as a function of the number of triangles in the configuration. They used stimuli containing one, two, three, five, or seven tri-

angles, examples of which are illustrated in Figures 7.6.12B and 7.6.12C. They reasoned that if these configural effects were truly global, adding more triangles would continue to increase the size of the effect. If they were restricted in spatial scope, however, the effect would level off when additional triangles were added beyond the critical region of interaction. The results, shown in Figure 7.6.13, indicate that response times to the inconsistent conditions increase rapidly with increasing numbers but level off at about five triangles. This supports the view that this configural effect arises from limited spatial interaction over a region that is nevertheless quite large.

In a second experiment, Palmer and Bucher varied the spacing between the triangles in three-triangle configurations as shown in Figure 7.6.14. They reasoned that if there were a limited region of interaction among the triangles, the configural orientation effect would disappear when the distance between triangles increased beyond a critical value. The results showed that the configural orientation effect did indeed diminish rapidly as the spacing increased, vanishing when the triangles were more than two side-lengths apart. A third experiment showed further that this spacing effect was governed by the spacing relative to the size of the triangles rather than by absolute distance on the retina as measured in degrees of visual angle. Taken together, these findings indicate that configural orientation indeed has robust effects on the perception of the individual tri-

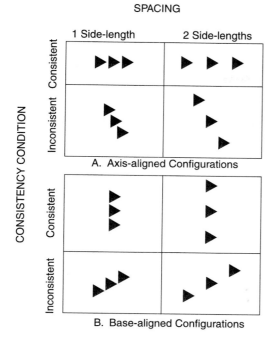

SPACING

1 Side-length   2 Side-lengths

CONSISTENCY CONDITION

Consistent

Inconsistent

A. Axis-aligned Configurations

Consistent

Inconsistent

B. Base-aligned Configurations

Figure 7.6.14 Spacing effects on perceived pointing of ambiguous triangles. The configural orientation effect shown in Figure 7.6.13 diminishes as the distance between the triangles increases. The effect is negligible when the centers of the triangles are more than two side-lengths apart.

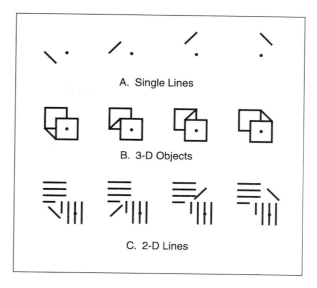

A. Single Lines

B. 3-D Objects

C. 2-D Lines

Figure 7.6.15 The object superiority effect. Subjects must discriminate the four orientations of diagonal lines in brief presentations either alone (A), in 3-D object configurations (B) or in 2-D line configurations (C). Performance is almost 20% worse in the 2-D control condition than in the 3-D object condition.

Word, Object, and Configural Superiority Effects. Other psychological evidence that global properties may be primary in human perception comes from experiments in which discrimination of parts is found to be superior when they are embedded within meaningful or well-structured wholes. Not only is performance better than that in comparable control conditions in which the same parts must be discriminated within meaningless or ill-structured contexts, but it is also better in comparison with discriminating the same parts in isolation. This evidence comes from several different but related kinds of experiments.

The first evidence of improved perceptual performance within meaningful wholes was reported by Reicher (1969), who discovered a phenomenon that has come to be known as the **word superiority effect**: Subjects are better able to perceive single letters when they are presented as part of meaningful words than when they are presented alone or in meaningless strings. Somehow, the presence of the additional letters in the word actually improves performance. We will discuss this effect and how it might be explained theoretically in Chapter 9 when we consider models of letter and word identification.

Weisstein and Harris (1974) reported a similar contextual effect, called the **object superiority effect**. Subjects were required to determine which target among a certain set of line segments was contained within displays consisting of many line segments. Some displays were drawings of simple 3-D objects; others were merely collections of line segments. Figure 7.6.15 shows some examples. Subjects were required to discriminate among the four diagonal lines, which were presented either alone (part A), within a possible 3-D object (part B), or in a number of other 2-D configurations in which the line segments of the object context were rearranged (part C). Notice that the contextual lines are identical for the different target segments and that all four of them form a coherent 3-D object in the "object" condition. Weisstein and Harris found that subjects were more accurate in the 3-D object condition than in either of the other two conditions.

359

Perceiving Object Properties and Parts

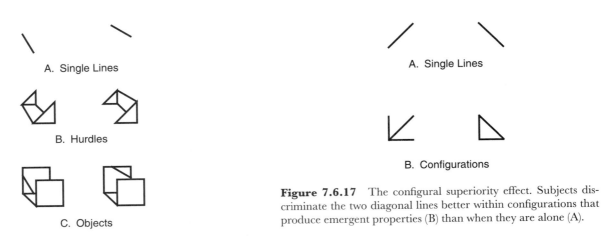

A. Single Lines

B. Hurdles

C. Objects

Figure 7.6.16 Structural relevance in the object superiority effect. Subjects discriminate the diagonal targets better when they are structurally relevant in the hurdles condition (B) than when they are presented alone (A) or in the objects condition (C).

A. Single Lines

B. Configurations

Figure 7.6.17 The configural superiority effect. Subjects discriminate the two diagonal lines better within configurations that produce emergent properties (B) than when they are alone (A).

Later experiments showed that the object superiority effect is not due merely to the three dimensionality of the stimuli, for it occurs only if the target lines have structural relevance for the 3-D interpretation of the whole. Stimuli from an experiment that supported this conclusion are illustrated in Figure 7.6.16 (McClelland & Miller, 1979). Subjects were able to discriminate the lines better only in the condition in which they change the percept from an upright hurdle to one that is knocked over (Figure 7.6.16B). The other 3-D condition in which they formed essentially meaningless marks on another object (Figure 7.6.16C) did not produce an object superiority effect.

Yet another example of superior discrimination performance for parts within larger wholes is the **configural superiority effect** illustrated in Figure 7.6.17 (Pomerantz, Sager, & Stover, 1977). Again, subjects were instructed to discriminate simple elements that were presented either alone (part A) or as part of a configuration (part B). To be sure that the extra configural elements themselves could not be used to perform the discrimination task, exactly the same elements were added to both targets in the configural condition. In the case illustrated in Figure 7.6.17, a right angle is added to the target diagonal line segments, forming an arrow vertex in one case and a triangle in the other. Response time measurements showed that subjects were much faster at discriminating the configurations than the isolated parts.

The most likely explanation of these results is that the diagonal line segments combine with the contextual lines to form emergent features such as closed versus open figures. If these emergent features are more quickly and easily discriminated than left versus right diagonality in the isolated segments, the configural superiority effect can be explained. The evidence thus indicates that at least some global, emergent properties can be processed more quickly than at least some local properties. Exactly why certain emergent features might be so much easier to detect than one of its components is by no means clear, however.

The word, object, and configural superiority effects seem to indicate that perceptual performance on these simple discrimination tasks does not occur in the local-to-global order that would be predicted from what is currently known about the order of physiological processing. It seems highly unlikely, for example, that the physiological processing of configurations such as triangles and arrows precedes that of the individual lines that compose them, particularly given that receptive field sizes generally increase as one moves from the retina to more central mechanisms. It seems even more unlikely from what we know of visual physiology that the analysis of whether 3-D hurdles are "tipped over" or "standing up," as in the experiment by McClelland and Miller (1979), takes place before the analysis of retinal line segment orientation, since the latter probably occurs in cortical area V1 or only a few synapses beyond it.

Exactly how these contextual effects should be interpreted is open to debate. One possibility is that neural processing proceeds from local parts to global wholes, but feedback from the holistic level to the earlier part levels then facilitates processing of local elements if they are part of coherent patterns at the global level. In Chapter 9 we will examine a connectionist model that embodies this general idea to account for the word superiority effect. Another possibility is that although neural processing proceeds from local parts to global wholes, people may gain conscious access to the results in the opposite order, from global wholes to local parts (Marcel, 1983b). Regardless of what mechanism is ultimately found to be responsible, the experiments described above clearly rule out the possibility that the perception of local structure necessarily precedes that of global structure. The truth, as usual, is much more complex and interesting.

Suggestions for Further Reading

Rock, I. (1983). *The logic of perception*. Cambridge, MA: MIT Press. This book is a modern classic in which Rock, one of the major advocates of a constructivist approach to visual perception, assesses the evidence for the claim that perception is a thoughtlike problem-solving process aimed at discovering the most likely distal stimulus that could have given rise to the retinal image.

Epstein, W. (1977). *Stability and constancy in visual perception: Mechanisms and processes*. New York: Wiley. This edited volume contains a number of excellent chapters related to the problem of perceptual constancy, written by some of the most important researchers in the field.

Welch, R. B. (1986). Adaptation of space perception. In K. R. Boff, L. Kaufman, & J. P. Thomas (Eds.), *Handbook of perception and human performance* (Vol. 1, pp. 24-1–24-45). New York: Wiley. This review chapter integrates and evaluates the substantial literature on adaptation to various spatial transformations of visual input.

Coren, S., & Girgus, J. S. (1978). *Seeing is deceiving: The psychology of visual illusions*. Hillsdale NJ: Erlbaum. This book gives a thorough introduction to all sorts of visual illusions and a variety of different kinds of explanations for their existence.

http://www.illusionworks.com   This site on the World Wide Web provides a comprehensive playground of illusions for your amusement and delight, interlaced with facts, artifacts, history, speculations, and references.

Representing Shape and Structure

Of all the properties we perceive about objects, shape is probably the most important. Its significance derives from the fact that it is the most informative visible property in the following sense: Shape allows a perceiver to predict more facts about an object than any other property. Suppose, for example, you knew the color of an object but nothing else. What could you predict from the knowledge that it was, say, a certain shade of red? Most likely, almost nothing. But suppose you knew its shape and nothing else. From knowledge that it was the shape of, say, an apple, you would be able to predict a great deal about it, such as how big it is, what color it might be, what it is used for, how it might taste, where it might be found, and so forth. In this sense, at least, shape is the single most significant property we perceive about objects.

It is also the most complex. Although it is tempting to think of shape as a unitary property, it is surely made up of many different components, just as other seemingly unitary properties have turned out to be. In Chapter 3, for example, we discovered that surface color can be analyzed into the three-dimensional components of hue, saturation, and lightness. This more detailed analysis has significant advantages over the unitary view. For example, the similarity of two colors can be modeled by their proximity within three-dimensional color space. Similar colors, such as two different shades of red, are located near each other in color space, whereas dissimilar colors, such as red and green, are far apart.

Is it possible to perform a similar analysis of shape into simpler components? If so, what are the components into which it should be analyzed? If not, might shape somehow be represented holistically? In either case, how might the similarity between two shapes be determined? These are some of the questions that we will address in this chapter. Many of them are closely related to topics we will discuss in the next chapter on perceptual categorization. The reason is that the most important property for determining the category to which an object belongs is its shape. Many important theories of object categorization, therefore, depend on the position they take with respect to their representation of shape.

Another simplistic temptation in thinking about shape perception is to believe that the representation of object shape can be identified with the surface-based 2.5-D sketch. Indeed, the terms that were initially used in the

computer vision literature to refer to the processes by which the 2.5-D sketch is derived imply that this is the case. The modules leading from 2-D to 2.5-D representations are often called "shape-from-shading," "shape-from-motion," and so forth, as though the 2.5-D sketch contained representations of object shape. Unfortunately, it does not.

Although it is true that the 2.5-D sketch contains information about shape, it does so only *implicitly* and *locally*. Recall from Chapter 5 that what is actually represented in the 2.5-D sketch is the distance to and orientation of local surface patches. Recall also that the 2.5-D sketch is organizationally undifferentiated: It does not explicitly represent the division of visible surfaces into separate objects, much less their parts and interrelations. And it contains no information at all about the back surfaces of objects that are occluded by their front surfaces. For all of these reasons, it is safe to say that the 2.5-D sketch does not contain an explicit representation of 3-D object shape. Something much more global and complex is required to represent 3-D shape.

As we saw at the end of Chapter 7, the representation of objects often involves dividing them into parts, such as the eyes, nose, and mouth of a human face, as well as representing various global features. The parts into which objects are divided, the spatial interrelations among those parts, and the global features that define them are all important aspects of their shape. Again, none of this complex information is directly available in the 2.5-D sketch. In perceiving an object's shape, local bits and pieces of information must somehow be organized into the representation of objects, features, parts, and their complex interrelations within a coherent overall structure. Understanding how this might be accomplished is the primary goal of a theory of shape perception. In this chapter we will explore the problems and prospects for such a theory.

8.1 Shape Equivalence

We will begin our discussion of perceiving object shape by tackling a simpler problem: the perception of **shape equivalence**. The problem of shape equivalence involves understanding the conditions under which people perceive two distinct objects as having the same shape. The phenomenon of perceived shape equivalence is closely related to classical shape constancy. Recall from Section 7.2 that shape constancy is defined in terms of perceiving the *same* object as having the same shape despite differences in viewing conditions. In contrast, shape equivalence is concerned with the question of whether two *different* objects are seen as having the same shape, despite other spatial differences between them. A full-sized car appears to have the same shape as a miniature scale model of it, despite their obvious difference in size, for instance. And an upright chair appears to have the same shape as an otherwise identical one that has been knocked over, despite their obvious difference in orientation.

8.1.1 Defining Objective Shape

We will approach the problem of shape equivalence by considering which transformations can be applied to an object without changing its *objective shape* (Palmer, 1989). Given that shape is a property of our perceptions of objects, it might seem strange to talk about shape as an "objective" property. Still, the notion of objective shape can be defined in a meaningful way that provides an important toehold in our assault on the problem of shape perception. In fact, the idea that each object has an objective shape is no different in principle from the well-established belief that each object has an objectively definable size, position, orientation, and the like.

Consider the simple geometric figure shown in Figure 8.1.1, for instance. Everyone would agree that the figures in the right column have the same shape as the ones in the left, despite the differences in their position, orientation, size, and reflection (as in mirror images). This fact leads us to define **objective shape** as the spatial structure of an object that does not change when the following spatial transformations are applied to it:[1]

1. **translations**, which change only an object's position,

2. **rotations**, which change only its orientation,

3. **dilations** (expansions and contractions), which change only its size,

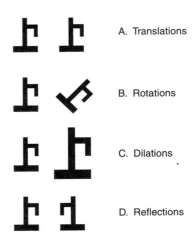

Figure 8.1.1 Shape invariance over similarity transformations. Pairs of figures that are related by these four types of transformation, or any combination of them, have the same objective shape.

4. **reflections**, which change only its handedness or sense, and

5. any combination of these transformations.

In mathematics, this particular set of transformations is called the **similarity group**. ("Similarity" is just the name of this mathematical set of transformations; it should not be taken to indicate anything about the perceptual similarity of the figures it relates.) You probably first encountered similarity transformations in geometry class when you had to prove that two triangles were "similar"—for example, by showing that all three corresponding angles were equal.

Although we have given an example of the shape-preserving nature of these transformations using 2-D figures, the objective shapes of 3-D objects are also preserved by 3-D versions of the same set of transformations: translations, rotations, dilations, reflections, and their various combinations. They preserve objective shape in the well-defined sense that any pair of objects that can be brought into exact correspondence by applying some sequence of these transformations can be said to have the same objective shape. Thus, the similarity transformations provide an objective test of whether or not any given pair of objects have the same shape. If

---

[1] Shape is also invariant over nonspatial transformations, such as changes in color and texture. We do not consider any such nonspatial transformations here simply because they appear to be irrelevant to shape perception. We will return to them briefly later when we consider the problems they pose for certain theories of shape representation.

any other spatial transformations are required to bring the objects into exact spatial correspondence—such as squashing, stretching, or deforming them in any way—they have different objective shapes according to this definition, even though their shapes may be perceived as extremely similar.

The fact that people perceive all the various objects in Figure 8.1.1 as having the same shape leads to the obvious hypothesis that perception of shape equivalence is generally veridical—that is, two objects are perceived as having the same shape whenever they have the same objective shape. One might think that this is always the case, but as we will see shortly, there are important exceptions. Thus, we will take this definition of shape equivalence as an objective standard and examine how well human shape perception conforms to it. The situation is not unlike defining a line's objective orientation with respect to gravity and examining how well people's perception of it conforms to this standard. Perception may produce various illusions and distortions, but these can be usefully understood in relation to objectively defined orientation. So it should be with shape.

The definition of perceived shape equivalence based on invariance (lack of change) over the similarity transformations is a computational-level theory of shape equivalence. It does not make any pretense of specifying what processes are involved in determining shape equivalence in the sense defined in Chapter 2. At an algorithmic level, however, the question arises of what information and operations are involved in determining that two objects have the same shape. There are at least three possibilities:

1. **Invariant features hypothesis**. This hypothesis assumes that shape equivalence is determined by comparing some set of "shape features" of two objects for equivalence. If these two sets (or lists) of features are identical, the objects have the same perceived shape. For this scheme to work, the features must be invariant over the set of transformations for which shape is invariant.

2. **Transformational alignment hypothesis**. This hypothesis assumes that shape equivalence is analyzed by determining whether two objects can be brought into exact correspondence by one of an allowable set of transformations, such as the similarity group. If they can, their shape is perceived as identical; if not, their shapes differ.

3. **Object-centered reference frames hypothesis**. This hypothesis assumes that shape equivalence is assessed by comparing objects within a reference frame defined by the intrinsic properties of the object. If the objects are the same with respect to their own reference frames, they are perceived to have the same shape.

There can be intermediate, hybrid approaches as well, but for simplicity, we will now consider just the pure versions of these hypotheses in detail.

8.1.2 Invariant Features

The invariant features hypothesis assumes that shape perception depends on encoding those properties of objects that do not change (are invariant) when it is transformed in particular ways. Let us examine what this means and how it might account for the perception of shape equivalence.

Any given set of transformations divides the set of all possible object properties into two mutually exclusive subsets: those that do not change as a result of the transformation (called **invariant features**) and those that do (called **variant features**). As an example, consider the effect of 2-D translations on the set of properties of 2-D figures listed in Figure 8.1.2. Changing the position

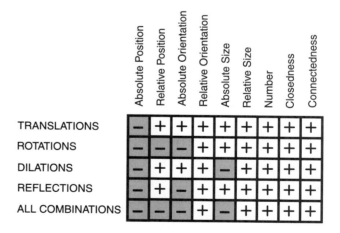

	Absolute Position	Relative Position	Absolute Orientation	Relative Orientation	Absolute Size	Relative Size	Number	Closedness	Connectedness
TRANSLATIONS	−	+	+	+	+	+	+	+	+
ROTATIONS	−	−	−	+	+	+	+	+	+
DILATIONS	−	+	+	+	−	+	+	+	+
REFLECTIONS	−	+	−	+	+	+	+	+	+
ALL COMBINATIONS	−	−	−	+	−	+	+	+	+

FEATURE CHANGE

(− = variant feature, + = invariant feature)

Figure 8.1.2 The invariant features approach to shape equivalence. Each type of transformation leaves certain features invariant and changes others. This table shows which features vary (−) and which are invariant (+) with respect to transformations in the similarity group.

Representing Shape and Structure

of an object alters the absolute position of its component lines, angles, and so forth, which are therefore translationally variant features, as indicated by the shaded "−" entry in the first column of the first row. It does not affect the relative positions of pairs of these components, however, nor does it alter any of the other properties listed, such as the number of lines and angles the figure contains or the orientations and sizes of those lines and angles. These are therefore among its translationally invariant features, as indicated by the "+" in the remaining columns of this row.

Now consider what happens when the orientation of an object is changed. Rotations alter not only the absolute and relative positions of the components, but also their absolute orientations, which are therefore rotationally variant features. Rotations do not change the relative orientations of components (that is, the angular differences in orientation between them), nor properties such as the number or size of the lines and angles, which are therefore rotationally invariant features.

Taken together with our previous definition of objective shape equivalence in terms of the action of the similarity group of transformations, the invariant features hypothesis suggests that shape might be represented by the set of properties that are invariant over the similarity group: translations, rotations, reflections, dilations, and their various combinations. This is the basic claim of a "pure" invariant features hypothesis. The bottom row of Figure 8.1.2 thus indicates that the candidate features for shape according to this hypothesis are things like the number of lines, angles, and various other components, their relative orientations, sizes, plus their closedness and connectedness. The reason is that none of these features are changed by any of the similarity transformations.

Notice that this list includes few absolute metric properties but many relative ones. This is in accord with the early observations of Gestalt psychologists, who stressed the idea of **relational determination**: that perception is dominated by configural relations among properties and parts rather than by absolute properties.

The very definition of the set of invariant features as those properties that do not change despite the action of transformations guarantees that any two figures that can be superimposed by a similarity transformation will have identical shape representations in terms of these properties. Therefore, to the extent that *perceived* shape

equivalence is the same as *objective* shape equivalence—that is, as defined by the action of similarity transformations—representing shape in terms of the similarity-invariant features is guaranteed to solve the perceptual problem of shape equivalence.

In one form or another, the invariant features hypothesis has dominated theories of shape perception from the classic statement by Pitts and McCullough (1947) until relatively recently. Explicitly or implicitly, its assumptions underlie Gestalt theories of shape perception, J. J. Gibson's theory of shape constancy, and classical "feature list" theories of pattern recognition such as the Pandemonium theory (Selfridge, 1957; Selfridge & Neisser, 1960).

Theories based on invariant features are attractive, at least in part, because of their simplicity: Shape can be represented as a simple set or list of attributes. The properties within this set can be differentially weighted according to their perceptual salience or importance, but the basic idea is that the list of invariant features is sufficient to explain why some pairs of distinct objects are perceived as having the same shape whereas other pairs are not.

Unfortunately, there is persuasive evidence that the invariant features approach is seriously flawed as a theory of perceived shape equivalence. The problem arises from important differences between perceived and objective shape equivalence. The most damaging phenomenon is the well-documented relation between perceived orientation and perceived shape to which we alluded briefly in Chapter 7. One of the earliest, simplest, and most elegant demonstrations of this relation was Mach's (1914/1959) observation that when a square is rotated 45°, people generally perceive it as an upright diamond rather than as a tilted square (see Figure 8.1.3). You *can* see this figure as a tilted square, of course, if you take the flat side at 45° to be its top. But if the upper vertex is perceived as the top, the shape of the figure is seen as diamondlike and quite distinct from that of an upright square.

Mach's square/diamond poses a serious problem for the invariant features hypothesis. If perceived shapes were defined solely by attributes that are invariant over rotations, then any two figures that are rotations of each other—such as Mach's square and diamond—must be perceived as having the same shape. But they are not. This simple fact seriously undermines the invariant fea-

Square   Diamond

Figure 8.1.3 The ambiguous square/diamond. The same figure is perceived as a square when its sides are vertical and horizontal but as a diamond when its sides are diagonal. The diamond's perceived shape can easily be changed by imagining that it has been rotated 45°. The same is possible for the square but is more difficult.

tures hypothesis as an algorithmic-level theory of perceived shape equivalence.

One might think such problems could be solved simply by eliminating rotations from the set of transformations that preserve perceived shape. This solution throws the baby out with the bathwater, however, because there are many cases in which two figures related by rotations are spontaneously perceived as having the same shape. One such pair is illustrated in Figure 8.1.1B. Examples like this effectively block any attempt to "patch up" the invariant features hypothesis simply by dropping rotations. Some other account must be constructed on the basis of different perceptual processes.

8.1.3 Transformational Alignment

A second way to assess whether two objects are equivalent in shape is to find a transformation that brings one into exact alignment with the other. If there is such a transformation and it comes from the allowable set—that is, the similarity group—then objects have the same shape. Otherwise, they do not.

This approach to shape equivalence is quite plausible, not only because it is so transparently similar to the objective definition of shape equivalence given above, but also because of its intimate connection with several other important visual phenomena. When we discuss motion perception in Chapter 10, for example, we will find out that the visual system has a strong tendency to perceive shape-preserving motions rather than shape-deforming ones. And in Chapter 12 we will discover the importance of performing imaginal transformations in comparing the shapes of two similar objects. Object transformation and alignment processes also figure im-

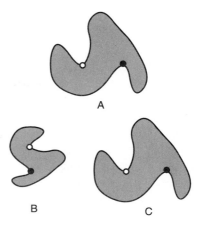

Figure 8.1.4 Determining shape equivalence by transformational alignment. The fact that objects A and B have the same shape can be determined by aligning the corresponding dots, identifying the transformation that equates the virtual lines connecting them, and then applying that transformation to the appropriate object. The result of applying this transformation to object B (namely, object C) can then be matched directly to object A.

portantly in certain theories of object recognition that will be described in Chapter 9.

To illustrate how such a process would work, imagine that there are two identically shaped 2-D objects that differ in position, orientation, and size, as shown in Figures 8.1.4A and 8.1.4B. Both objects have two salient points on them in the same object-relative positions, such as the black dot and the white dot in Figure 8.1.4. The two objects (A and B) can then be compared for shape equivalence by the following procedure:

1. Find the correspondence between dots: black to black and white to white.

2. Determine the translation, rotation, reflection, and dilation required to exactly align the dots of B with the corresponding dots of A.

3. Apply the same transformation to figure B in its entirety, including all points rather than just the black and white ones.

4. Determine whether the transformed version of figure B (figure C) is identical to figure A. If it is, figures A and B have the same shape; otherwise, they do not. This conclusion is guaranteed because the transformations that are used to bring the figures into alignment come from the similarity group.

Using such an alignment procedure on real figures is more complicated than this example for a variety of reasons. One of the most important is that objects don't come conveniently marked with black and white dots. Rather, a small number of salient points, sometimes called **anchor points**, must be identified from the structure of the figure itself. Points of maximum concavity along the contour—which is where the black and white dots are located in Figure 8.1.4—are good anchor points, as are points of maximum convexity and the center of a figure (Huttenlocher & Ullman, 1987). Although two anchor points are sufficient for aligning 2-D figures in the frontal plane, at least three noncollinear points are required for 3-D cases. Since naturally occurring anchor points are not colored, however, it is not initially obvious which points of one object correspond to which of the other. Labeling them by type (convexity, concavity, center, etc.) will help, since a convexity in one figure can correspond only to a convexity in the other. Even so, the example in Figure 8.1.4 is ambiguous because both anchor points are at concavities. The procedure must therefore try both possible correspondences and determine whether either results in identical figures.

Despite its virtues, the transformational alignment hypothesis faces several difficulties. One is that if the figures are complex and contain numerous potential anchor points, either some principled way must be found to eliminate all but a few possibilities or many different correspondences must be tried. Without labels to help, n anchor points on each object allow $n!$ ($= n \times (n - 1) \times (n - 2) \times \cdots \times 1$) possible correspondences, and this can be a very large number. For example, with five undifferentiated anchor points, there are 120 possible correspondences, and with ten anchor points, there are 3,628,800. The set of possible correspondences must be searched until either an acceptable alignment is achieved or all correspondences have been exhausted.

A second problem is that the same set of anchor points must be visible in the two figures. This is not a problem for the 2-D figures we considered in Figure 8.1.4 or for certain classes of 3-D objects (such as wire objects for which occlusion does not arise), but it is a significant problem with most 3-D objects, for which anchor points that are visible in one object may not be visible in the other, owing to self-occlusion.

A third problem is that there are certain objects that are typically seen as having different shapes yet can be brought into exact alignment by a similarity transformation. Mach's square/diamond demonstration provides one example (see Figure 8.1.3), because the square and diamond are 45° rotations of one another. The transformational alignment hypothesis implies that such figures should always be seen as equivalent in shape, but as we have already noted, sometimes they are not.

To account for this discrepancy, a transformational alignment theory would have to provide an explanation for why the rotational alignment is missed for Mach's square/diamond, when the same alignment—for example, between an upright R and one rotated 45°—is always perceived. To do so, the visual system would have to either choose different anchor points for the square and the rotated square or make different correspondences between them yet choose the same anchor points and make the correct correspondences for the upright R and the rotated R. The kinds of anchor points mentioned above—centers of mass and maximum concavities or convexities —are rotationally invariant and so do not provide a plausible account of this phenomenon. Other kinds of anchor points and/or orientationally biased schemes for establishing correspondences between anchor points could be devised that would do the trick, however. If the alignment were defined by an axis of symmetry, for example, and if the visual system were biased toward using vertical axes of symmetry, then Mach's square and diamond would be orientationally aligned as they appear in Figure 8.1.3 and would therefore be perceived to have different shapes.

8.1.4 Object-Centered Reference Frames

A third alternative to solving the problem of shape equivalence is to define shape relative to object-centered reference frames. In many ways, this idea is similar to the transformational alignment process that we just discussed, but it is different enough to require a separate description.

The notion that shape perception might involve reference frames at all is suggested by the observation that one can see Mach's diamond as a tilted square if one perceives a diagonal side as its top. What does this mean? It means that Mach's figure can be perceived as having one shape (diamond) relative to gravitational vertical and another shape (square) relative to a diagonal orientation that redefines the figure's perceived top, bottom, and sides. Notice that these alternatives are mutually exclusive in that the figure cannot be perceived to have both shapes simultaneously. Irvin Rock (1973) was among the first to suggest that this relation between shape and orientation arose because perceived shape is a description relative to a perceptual frame of reference, although the idea of reference frames had previously been used by Gestalt theorists in explaining other phenomena of orientation perception (e.g., the rod-and-frame effect discovered by Asch & Witkin, 1948a, 1948b). Rock proposed this idea specifically to handle the case of orientation, but other theorists (e.g., Marr & Nishihara, 1978; Palmer, 1975b, 1989) later generalized it to other properties, such as position and size, by analogy with geometric reference frames (see below).

In its most general form, the object-centered reference frame hypothesis provides an alternative to the invariant features and transformational alignment hypotheses as an account of perceived shape equivalence. It is based on the idea that the effects of similarity transformations on shape perception can be removed by imposing an intrinsic reference frame that effectively insulates the shape representation from the action of the transformations. To understand how this is possible, we will examine the analogous situation in analytic geometry, in which coordinate systems play the role of reference frames in the description of geometric objects.

Geometric Coordinate Systems. In analytic geometry, geometric objects, such as lines, curves, circles, and ellipses, are mapped into symbolic descriptions in the form of equations. What makes this possible is a **coordinate system**: a formal structure, devised by the great French philosopher and mathematician René Descartes, that allows each point in an *n*-dimensional space to be represented as an ordered set of *n* numbers, called its **coordinates**. The set of points that make up the to-be-described geometric object (line, circle, or whatever) can then be specified by an equation that expresses the relation among the numerical coordinates of points that are part of the object.

Consider a standard Cartesian coordinate system in 2-D space, for example. It works by establishing a structured set of reference standards for mapping positions

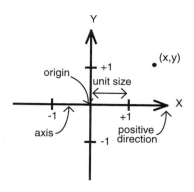

Figure 8.1.5 The Euclidean coordinate system of analytic geometry. Geometric points in a 2-D space can be converted to pairs of numbers by establishing an axis for each dimension, a position shared by both axes (the origin, which defines "0"), a direction along each axis (which defines "+" versus "−"), and a unit size (which defines the value of "1"). (After Palmer, 1983.)

into coordinates, usually denoted as (x, y). The standards for each dimension of a Cartesian coordinate system include:

1. a reference *location* that defines its **origin**,

2. a reference *orientation* that defines its **axis**,

3. a reference *distance* that defines the **unit size**, and

4. a reference *sense* along the orientation that defines the **positive direction** along the axis.

These reference standards for two spatial dimensions turn out to be sufficient to assign a unique pair of numbers, (x, y), to every point in a 2-D plane, as illustrated in Figure 8.1.5.

As a concrete example of how a coordinate system can produce a symbolic description, consider the circle labeled *a* in the left panel of Figure 8.1.6. Within the Cartesian coordinated system shown, it can be described by the equation

$$x^2 + y^2 = 1.$$

For this particular equation to describe the circle, the center of the coordinate system must be at the center of the circle, and its unit size must be equal to the radius of the circle. (The orientation and direction along the axes actually do not matter for circles because circles are invariant—that is, symmetric—over all central rotations and reflections.) This particular reference frame allows this particular circle to be described symbolically by this particular equation.

Representing Shape and Structure

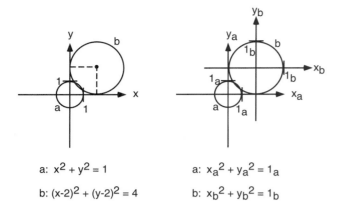

a: $x^2 + y^2 = 1$

b: $(x-2)^2 + (y-2)^2 = 4$

a: $x_a^2 + y_a^2 = 1_a$

b: $x_b^2 + y_b^2 = 1_b$

Figure 8.1.6 Object-centered coordinate systems. The left panel shows that when two different circles are described by equations within a single coordinate system, each circle has a different description. The right panel shows that when a different coordinate system is chosen for each circle, they have the same description relative to their own object-centered reference frame. (After Palmer, 1983.)

Could this equation be used to represent the shape of all circles? To find out, consider how other circles, such as the one labeled *b* in the left panel of Figure 8.1.6, would be described within the same coordinate system. Although similar in certain important respects, *b*'s equation is actually somewhat different:

$$(x - 2)^2 + (y - 2)^2 = 4.$$

The differences arise because the position and size of circle *b* are different from those of circle *a*, and using the same coordinate system to describe both requires that the equations be different in these particular ways.

The key observation for understanding object-centered reference frames in perception is that instead of using the *same* coordinate system to describe circles *a* and *b*, we could have used a *different* coordinate system for each. If the center of the coordinate system for circle *b* were at its own center, and if the unit size of the coordinate system for *b* were equal to its own radius, then *b*'s equation within this second coordinate system would be exactly the same as *a*'s within the first coordinate system. This possibility is illustrated in the right panel of Figure 8.1.6, which shows the same two circles described within two different coordinate systems. The important insight from this example is that, relative to their own intrinsically defined coordinate systems, the two circles now have identical equations. Thus, by choosing the "right"

coordinate systems, variations in the circle's position and size can be eliminated from their equations. They are, in effect, absorbed by the different coordinate systems so that their equations are invariant across all circles.

Perceptual Reference Frames. A reference frame in perception is hypothesized to be analogous to a coordinate system in analytic geometry in the sense that it can be used to map a spatial object into a symbolic perceptual description. One way in which this could be done is in terms of a **viewer-centered reference frame**: a single coordinate system whose reference standards are chosen relative to the viewer, with its center at the point of fixation, its orientation and positive direction aligned with the vertical orientation and rightward direction of the retina, and its scale (unit size) defined by some arbitrary visual angle on the retina. In a viewer-centered reference frame, it is as though the retina had a Cartesian grid painted on it, relative to which all objects could be described. This is perhaps the most obvious way of assigning a perceptual reference frame, but it is not the only way.

An alternative is to assign each perceptual object its own **object-centered reference frame**, a perceptual reference frame that is chosen on the basis of the intrinsic properties of the to-be-described object. The object-centered reference frame hypothesis suggests that the coordinate system used in describing each object is somehow "made to order" for that particular object. Indeed, we will later suggest that different coordinate systems may even be used to describe different *parts* of the same object.

Roughly speaking, object-centered reference frames tend to produce identical descriptions for shape-equivalent objects because most (but not all) shapes are sufficiently well structured to induce the visual system to describe them within the same object-centered reference frame. For example, if the orientations of two otherwise identical objects are different, such as an upright chair and a tipped-over chair, the orientation of their object-centered frames will be defined such that both will have the same shape description *relative to their object-centered frames*. Similarly, if the sizes of two otherwise identical objects are different, such as a full-sized and a miniature car, the sizes of their object-centered reference frames will differ correspondingly. As long as the differences in the reference frames compensate for transformational differences between the objects, shape equivalence will be veridically perceived over the entire group of similarity transformations. However, if different frames are chosen for some reason—as when different axes of symmetry are aligned with gravity in Mach's square/diamond example—objects with the same objective shape may be perceived as having different shapes. This is the key observation that makes reference frames such an appealing hypothesis in accounting for perceived shape equivalence.

"Object-centered" frames are so named because the perceptual reference standards for describing each object are chosen to fit its own structure, just as the centers and unit sizes of the coordinate systems in the right panel of Figure 8.1.6 were chosen to correspond to the circles' centers and radii. The general proposal is that shape equivalence is perceived whenever two objects have the same symbolic description—whatever that might be—within their own object-centered reference frames. Such perceptual frames can compensate for differences in the orientation of two objects in the same way as for differences in position and size. If the orientations of two otherwise identical objects differ, then the objects will be perceived as having the same shape as long as the orientations of their object-centered frames are assigned in the same way relative to the object. The net result is that if the same intrinsic frame were used for the same shape in all situations, shape equivalence would be perfect over all transformations in the similarity group.

Accounting for Failures of Shape Equivalence.
Both the weakness and the strength of the intrinsic reference frames proposal lie in the conditional clause "*if the same intrinsic frame were used for the same shape in all situations.*" It is a weakness because it may not be computationally possible to meet this condition. How can frame choice be so closely coupled to the properties of the object that the same frame will always be chosen? The problem turns out to be difficult enough that it seems quite likely that "wrong" frames will sometimes be chosen, resulting in occasional failures to perceive objective shape equivalence. As a theory of human perception, however, this difficulty can ultimately be a strength, provided people fail in the same ways, such as with Mach's square and diamond.

How might these failures to perceive shape equivalence be explained by the object-centered reference frames hypothesis? Palmer (1985) proposed three important assumptions for the case of differences in orientation:

1. *Relative description.* Shape is perceived relative to a reference frame in which a specific orientation is taken as the descriptive standard.

This assumption implies that shape equivalence is determined by comparing the symbolic descriptions of objects rather than by matching the objects directly, as in the transformational alignment approach.

2. *Intrinsic biases.* The perceptual system uses heuristics (rules of thumb) that are based on the intrinsic structure of the object itself for assigning an object-centered reference frame to an object.

We will consider what these heuristics might be shortly, but some possibilities are that the reference orientation might be established along an axis of symmetry or elongation. Such heuristics allow veridical perception of shape equivalence in most cases because the same rules applied to the same object will generally produce the same outcome. Because heuristics are imperfect, however, there will be certain circumstances—such as objects with multiple symmetry axes (e.g., Mach's square/diamond)—in which different orientations can be chosen, leading to the possibility of errors in perceived shape equivalence.

3. *Extrinsic biases.* In addition to object-based biases in orientation selection, there are also biases toward picking salient orientations with respect to other reference objects or directions, such as gravitational vertical, the orientation of the observer's body, or the top-bottom axis of the retina.

For an upright observer, these are all consistent with one another, but they can be placed in conflict when the observer's head and/or body are tilted with respect to gravity. Extrinsic biases are sometimes strong enough to cause errors in the perception of shape equivalence.

These three assumptions together imply that the perceived reference orientation for a given object will be a joint function of its intrinsic structure, its orientation relative to the observer, and its orientation relative to the environment. For instance, if a figure has two or more good intrinsic axes for the object-based reference orientation and one of them happens to be aligned with gravitational vertical, then the vertical axis will tend to be chosen, resulting in some particular shape description. If an otherwise identical figure is then seen in a different orientation such that a different intrinsic axis aligns with vertical, that axis will then be chosen as the reference orientation. The same object in different environmental orientations can therefore produce different shape descriptions.

In fact, this is how object-centered reference frames explain the failure of shape equivalence in the case of Mach's ambiguous square/diamond. It can be given two different shape descriptions depending on which symmetry axes are aligned with environmental horizontal and vertical—its *side bisectors* or its *angle bisectors*. When the side bisectors are aligned with horizontal and vertical, people perceive it under the description that corresponds to the "square" perception; when the angle bisectors are aligned with vertical, people perceive it under the description that corresponds to the "diamond" perception. Thus, this violation of objective shape equivalence may result from the same reference frame mechanisms that usually produce veridical perception of shape equivalence.

Why might different reference frames result in different shape descriptions for the same object? Palmer (1983) suggests that different reference frames make different relational properties available to perception, as illustrated in Figure 8.1.7. In the square/diamond case, for example, the square perception makes plain the fact that its sides are parallel to the axes of the frame and to each other as well as certain properties that arise from reflectional symmetry about the frame axes—for example, that opposite sides are equal in length and that adjacent angles are equal in size (Figure 8.1.7A). This further implies that a square should be seen as more similar in shape to a rectangle (which has this same structure) than to a rhombus (whose sides are oblique relative to the frame axes and whose adjacent angles are not equal). This comparison is illustrated in Figure 8.1.8A, based on a demonstration by Goldmeier (1936/1972).

The diamond percept, in contrast, makes plain that the sides are oblique relative to the axes, that opposite angles are equal in size, and that adjacent sides are equal in length (Figure 8.1.7B). This implies that the

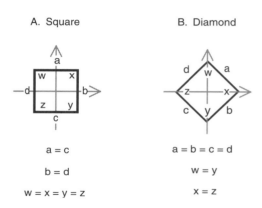

$$a = c$$

$$b = d$$

$$w = x = y = z$$

$$a = b = c = d$$

$$w = y$$

$$x = z$$

Figure 8.1.7 Explaining the shape ambiguity of the square/diamond via reference frames. Different equivalences are evident in the square versus diamond perceptions of the same figure. In squares, the equality of opposite sides and adjacent angles dominate perception. In diamonds, the equality of adjacent sides and opposite angles dominate perception. (After Palmer, 1983.)

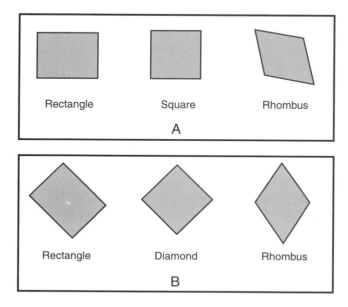

Figure 8.1.8 Different shape similarities of squares versus diamonds. A square is perceived as being more similar to a rectangle than to a rhombus, whereas a diamond is perceived as being more similar to a rhombus than to a rectangle. These facts are consistent with the equivalences noted in Figure 8.1.7.

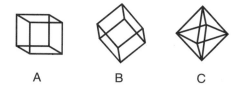

Figure 8.1.9 Reference frame effects in visual imagery. When Hinton (1979) asked subjects to imagine rotating a standard cube (part A) so that it was standing on a vertex, most were unable to correctly point to its other vertices (as in part B), pointing instead to those indicated in part C, which is not a cube at all. (After Palmer, 1983.)

diamond should look more like a rhombus than like a rectangle, reversing the similarity relations in the square example (see Figure 8.1.8B). This is true, even though all three of these figures are just 45° rotations of the objects shown above them in Figure 8.1.8A.

Hinton (1979, 1981) has made some related observations about failures in shape equivalence due to the use of different reference frames. He studied a mental imagery task employing a three-dimensional cube. He first asked his subjects to imagine a cube sitting flat on a table in front of them (see Figure 8.1.9A). He then asked them to imagine rotating this cube so that two opposite vertices were vertically aligned, as though balancing the cube on one of its corners (see Figure 8.1.9B). Once they had accomplished this mental transformation, he asked them to point to the locations of the (imaginary) additional vertices. Nearly everyone pointed to four points in a square configuration, lying in the horizontal plane that bisects the line between the vertically aligned vertices. In fact, this does not define a cube at all, but a double pyramid, as illustrated in Figure 8.1.9C. The correct answer is much more complicated: There are actually six vertices that lie alternately on two parallel planes connected by edges that go back and forth between them, as shown in Figure 8.1.9B.

What these analyses and demonstrations suggest is that the ultimate effect of selecting a perceptual reference frame is to afford the observer different sets of geometric relations contained in the structure of the figure. Since it would be impossible to extract all the possible relations in the figure—there being indefinitely many— and since many of them are highly redundant, the visual system picks the most stable and useful set it can find. It is this set of potentially perceivable relations that Palmer (1983) has suggested constitute the structure of a per-

ceptual reference frame. It remains to be determined precisely what these relations might be or whether this is actually the best way to characterize perceptual reference frames.

Orientation and Shape. It may seem unreasonable to make such a fuss over Mach's square/diamond demonstration, which might be just an interesting anomaly. In fact, however, Rock (1973) has shown this phenomenon to be far more pervasive than one would have guessed from everyday experience. The importance of his findings lies in their implication that object-centered reference frames are routinely involved in perceiving shape equivalence. As is often pointed out, the failures of a system sometimes turn out to be more illuminating about its underlying mechanisms than its successes. Still, we should not lose sight of the fact that correct perception of shape equivalence is the rule, and failure is the exception. In terms of the reference frame hypothesis, this means that the frame is usually established in the same way relative to the object; only rarely is it aligned differently.

Rock (1973) demonstrated that under some conditions, the perception of shape equivalence following picture plane rotations is quite difficult to achieve. He showed subjects a sequence of several amorphous, novel shapes in a particular orientation during an initial presentation phase and then tested them for recognition memory for the figures in the same versus a different orientation (see Figure 8.1.10A). The results showed that people are far less likely to recognize the shapes if they were tested in a different orientation than in the same orientation. Their poor recognition performance, which approached chance for 90° rotations, indicates that subjects often fail to perceive shape equivalence of the presented and tested figures.

In a series of further studies, Rock showed that the primary factors determining the reference orientation for these poorly structured figures are not retinal, but environmental and/or gravitational. For instance, when observers tilted their heads by 90° between presentation and test without changing the figure's orientation in the world, recognition performance was much better than when the orientation of the figures was changed by 90° without tilting the observer's head. Rock took these and related results as evidence that shape is perceived relative to an environmental frame of reference in which

Representing Shape and Structure

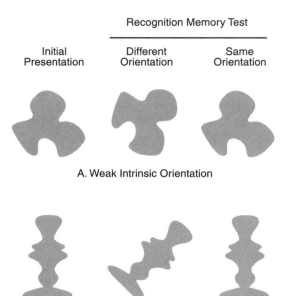

Recognition Memory Test

Initial
Presentation

Different
Orientation

Same
Orientation

A. Weak Intrinsic Orientation

B. Strong Intrinsic Orientation

Figure 8.1.10 Effects of orientation on perceived shape. When subjects were shown figures with poor intrinsic axes (A) in one orientation and tested for recognition memory with figures in the same versus different orientations, they were much better at remembering when the figure's orientation was the same. Figures with good intrinsic axes (B) showed no such difference when orientation was changed at testing.

gravity defines the reference orientation, at least in the absence of intrinsic axes in the object itself. If the environmental orientation of the figure changes from the initial presentation to the later testing, the description of the test figure will not match the description stored in memory, and the observer will therefore often fail to perceive the equivalence of two figures.

Rock's classic finding of failure to perceive shape equivalence pertains to amorphous shapes of the sort he used. But what happens when figures with "good" intrinsic axes are used, ones that should lead to the choice of appropriate object-centered reference frames? Wiser (1981) examined precisely this question and found that figures with good intrinsic axes are recognized as well when they are presented and tested in different orientations as when they are presented and tested in the same orientation (Figure 8.1.10B). Using amorphous figures like Rock's, however, Wiser replicated Rock's finding of poor recognition (Figure 8.1.10A). These results are fully consistent with Rock's (1973) theoretical

analysis, although he was more interested in explaining the failures of perceived shape equivalence than the successes.

In further experiments Wiser (1981) showed that when a well-structured figure is presented initially so that its axis is not aligned with gravitational vertical, subsequent recognition is actually fastest when the figure is tested in its *vertical* orientation. She interpreted this result to mean that the shape is stored in memory as though it were upright relative to its own object-centered reference frame. This result is especially important because it disproves the simple hypothesis that shape recognition is always best when figures are presented and tested in the same orientation. It is still consistent with an account in terms of reference frames, however. One merely needs to assume that the figures' object-centered reference frame is established by its own internal structure when that structure is sufficiently strong. Wiser's results, then, imply that the process of recognition operates most efficiently and effectively when the object-centered frame of the figure is aligned with the gravitational frame of its environment.

Notice that Wiser's results for figures with good intrinsic axes demonstrate successful perception of shape equivalence. The figure is recognized best in a different orientation because it is perceived as having the same shape. However, this happens only when the figure has a good intrinsic axis that drives the reference orientation to the same axis both times. If the figure has more than one good axis (as Mach's square/diamond does) or lacks any good axes (as Rock's stimuli do), shape equivalence can fail to be perceived when different axes align with a salient extrinsic orientation at presentation and testing. Thus, the results of both Rock's and Wiser's experiments support the object-centered reference frame hypothesis.

Heuristics in Reference Frame Selection. If the account of perceived shape equivalence in terms of object-centered reference frames is correct, then it is important to consider what factors might govern selection of appropriate frames. For some properties the answer is fairly obvious; for others it is surprisingly elusive. The reference position of the frame—corresponding to the center of a geometric coordinate system—could be identified with the object's center of mass. This is an easily computed property of the object itself that could be used to define the center of its object-centered reference frame. The reference size scale—corresponding to the unit distance in a geometric coordinate system—could be identified with the extent of the object along its longest dimension. This is also an easily computed property of the object that therefore could be used to define the size of an object-centered reference frame. Thus, absolute position and absolute size are two properties that could easily be factored out in the perception of object shape with little or no ambiguity.[2]

As you might guess from the previous discussion of the interdependence between orientation and shape, selecting the reference orientation for the intrinsic reference frame of an object is a good deal more complex. A number of stimulus factors seem to be important in determining it:

1. *Gravitational orientation.* Because gravity is such an important factor in determining the orientational structure of the environment, it is important for defining object-centered reference frames as well. Gravitational vertical seems to function as the **default value** for orientation: the orientation that will be selected for an object-centered frame in the absence of strong orientational structure in the object itself (Rock, 1983). Horizontal is another salient environmental orientation that affects frame selection.

2. *Axes of reflectional symmetry.* One type of object-based structure that is particularly useful for defining the orientation of an internal reference frame is an axis of reflectional (or bilateral) symmetry (Palmer, 1983, 1985). If there is just one, then it can be used unambiguously to define the orientation of the frame, as in Figure 8.1.10B. If there is more than one—as in Mach's ambiguous square/diamond (Figure 8.1.3)—then the orientation of the frame is potentially ambiguous.

3. *Axes of elongation.* Another type of figural structure that is quite useful for defining the orientation of an internal reference frame is an axis of elongation (Marr & Nishihara, 1978; Palmer, 1975b; Rock, 1973). Again, to the extent that there is one clear axis of elongation, it could be used to specify the frame unambiguously, as

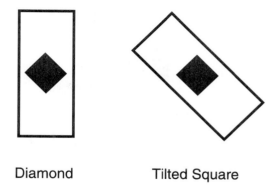

Diamond   Tilted Square

Figure 8.1.11 Effects of frame orientation on perceived shape. When an ambiguous square/diamond is presented with its sides diagonally oriented inside a rectangular frame, it looks like a diamond if the frame is upright and like a tilted square if the frame is diagonal. (After Kopferman, 1930.)

in Figure 8.1.10B. But if more than one possibility is present, ambiguity will result.

4. *Contour orientation.* Another factor in defining the orientation of an object-centered reference frame is the orientation of an object's contours, especially if they are straight. A horizontal bottom edge is particularly important because it suggests gravitational stability, an ecologically important property that is unlikely to be accidental. Contours at other orientations can also produce substantial reference frame effects, especially if they are long and/or occur in parallel pairs.

5. *Textural orientation.* The orientation of textural elements within a figure, such as stripes, can be important in defining the orientation of a reference frame, especially if the elements are relatively large and thick in comparison to the figure (Palmer & Bucher, 1982).

6. *Contextual orientation.* The orientation of nearby objects can also affect the orientation of a reference frame, especially if they are themselves strongly oriented and bear a close structural relation to the figure in question. A particularly powerful contextual influence is exerted by a surrounding rectangle. For example, Figure 8.1.11 shows that a rectangle that is tilted by 45° can cause Mach's upright "diamond" to be perceived as a tilted

---

[2] This is true only for 2-D objects in the frontal plane. If 3-D perception is involved, then the longest dimension can change substantially depending on the viewing perspective.

Representing Shape and Structure

Figure 8.1.12 An ambiguous figure. This shape usually looks like an asymmetrical polygon resting on its flat bottom side. However, it can also be seen as a symmetrical figure if one takes its upper right side as the top (or bottom) of the figure and its orientation as tilted 45° clockwise from vertical.

square (Kopferman, 1930; Palmer, Simone, & Kube, 1988). The orientation of textural stripes on the ground around the figure can also affect the orientation of the perceived reference frame (Palmer & Bucher, 1982).

7. *Motion.* The direction of an object's motion can also strongly influence its perceived orientation and shape (Bucher & Palmer, 1985). Presumably, this occurs because motion distinguishes the orientation aligned with its path from all others. The part of the object that faces in the direction of motion is generally taken to be the front or top of the object with one of the frame's axes aligned along the direction of motion.

These principles of frame selection are like the Gestalt principles of grouping in the sense that they are ceteris paribus rules. That is, they are potentially independent biases that can be used to predict frame selection only in pure cases or in ones for which several factors converge to bias the same orientation. In many situations, however, different factors conflict with each other, as shown in Figure 8.1.12. Most people perceive this figure as an upright, asymmetrical polygon. There is nothing surprising in this until one realizes that there is actually an axis of symmetry along an oblique orientation. The most likely reason that this figure is initially perceived as upright rather than tilted is the horizontal orientation of the bottom contour. The resulting perception of gravitational stability thus reinforces the natural bias toward selecting vertical as the reference orientation.

Figure 8.1.13A shows the same figure greatly elongated along its axis of symmetry. Now it is much more easily seen as a tilted, symmetrical, arrowlike figure pointing downward and to the left. Figure 8.1.13B

shows the same figure as in Figure 8.1.12 but rotated 180 degrees. In this orientation it is more likely to be perceived as a tilted symmetrical figure pointing upward and to the right because it is not gravitationally stable. That is, it looks like it would tip counterclockwise so that the longest side would end up being horizontal and its axis of symmetry vertical. Figure 8.1.13C shows the same figure with thick textural stripes inside it that bias perception toward an oblique reference frame. Figure 8.1.13D shows the same figure again but inside a surrounding rectangle that strongly biases frame orientation to align with its sides. And Figure 8.1.13E depicts the influence of moving the same figure along its axis of symmetry which creates a very strong bias toward perceiving it as a tilted symmetrical shape. Unfortunately, there is not yet any unified theory of frame selection that

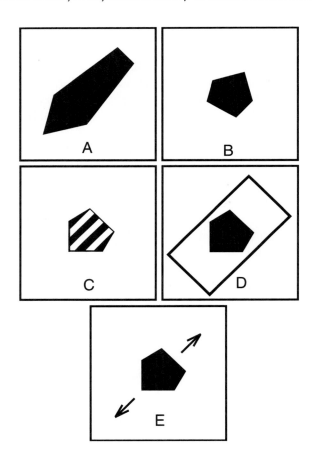

Figure 8.1.13 Examples of reference frame effects on perceived shape. The perceived orientation of the pentagon can be influenced by elongation (A), gravitational stability (B), textural orientation (C), a surrounding frame (D), and motion (E).

specifies how multiple factors are combined into a single measure that predicts the resulting orientation of an object-centered reference frame.

It is worth noting that theories of shape equivalence that are based on object-centered reference frames bear a close relation to those based on transformational alignment. The reason is that in both cases one is using a set of transformations to absorb, cancel, or factor out differences between the two objects. In alignment theories, one of the objects is transformed into exact correspondence with the other, whereas in reference frame theories, the reference frame is transformed into correspondence with the structure of the object. This is not to say that the two theories are the same. Transformational alignment is based on matching two images, whereas reference frame comparisons are based on symbolic descriptions of shape within the reference frame. In addition, alignment theories are often based on anchor point computations (e.g., Huttenlocher & Ullman, 1987), whereas reference frame theories are usually based on finding an intrinsic orientation, via symmetries, axes of elongation, texture, and so forth, as just described (e.g., Palmer, 1983, 1985). It is not yet clear which approach conforms more closely with human perception of shape.

8.2 Theories of Shape Representation

Shape equivalence is just one aspect of shape perception. It deals with the problem of deciding when two objects are *identical* in shape but does not address the crucial problem of *similarity* in shape between objects that are not identical. Shape similarity is a much more difficult problem because it requires a theory specifying how to represent shape in a way that will provide a graded measure corresponding to perceived similarity. Notice that we did not have to say much about shape representation in our discussion of shape equivalence because it required only a binary decision: Do two objects have the same shape or not? This simplification allowed us to define the conditions under which two objects have the same shape without ever having to propose a complete theory of shape perception. In this section we will consider various theoretical proposals about how the shape of objects and their parts might actually be represented within the human visual system

and how two such representations might be compared for similarity.

The reader is forewarned that all of the theories we are about to consider are inadequate to capture the astonishing power, versatility, and subtlety of human shape perception. How people perceive shape is certainly among the most difficult problems in visual perception, so difficult that no satisfactory solution has yet been proposed. Still, significant progress has been made, and much can be learned by considering the theories that have been considered to date. Because there is no agreed-upon solution, our focus will be on learning as much as possible by analyzing both the strengths and the weaknesses of each major theory.

8.2.1 Templates

The idea behind **templates** is simply to represent shape as shape, pretty much as an unreformed structuralist might do. In template representations, shape is specified by the concatenation of receptor cells on which the image of a particular object would fall. A template of a square can be formed, for example, by associating together all the receptors that it would stimulate plus the receptors around it that it would not stimulate. The most obvious way to implement this idea is to construct a "square detector cell" whose receptive field structure embodies the shape in question—in this case, that of a square against its immediate ground. As illustrated in Figure 8.2.1, this means that the central square region of the receptive field would be excitatorily connected to the square detector. The ground region around the square would be inhibitorily connected to the square detector to penalize departures from squareness, much as known cortical receptive fields have inhibitory surrounds. Thus, a white square on a black ground will maximally excite such a square detector cell because its spatial structure corresponds optimally to that of the receptive field. We will call such representations **standard templates** to differentiate them from more complex alternatives that we will later suggest in response to certain problems.

The atomic elements of which templates are composed are typically represented as binary features corresponding to whether particular receptors are firing or not. This means that each element in the template's field is either excitatory (i.e., responds positively to the pres-

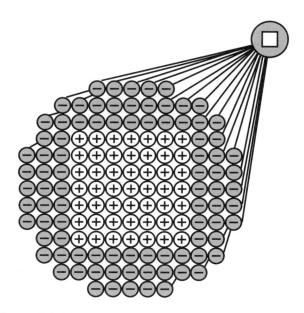

Figure 8.2.1 A template representation of a square. The square detector (upper right) is excited by the receptors in the central region (white circles containing a "+") and inhibited by receptors in the surrounding region (dark circles containing a "−"). Such a cell will be maximally excited by a light square on a dark surround and maximally inhibited by a dark square on a light surround.

of their pointwise correspondence or degree of fit. A particularly simple scheme for templates is to compute the correlation between the input image and the template. This measure ranges from +1.0 for maximal positive correspondence (between two identical images) to −1.0 for maximal negative correspondence (between an image and its black-white reversed version). The expected value for two unrelated images is zero. This comparison measure can be used for both binary and gray-scale templates.

Strengths. Templates are typically ridiculed in textbooks and research articles as grossly inadequate for representing shape. In fact, however, they have a very powerful argument in their favor: Templates *must* be used at some point in visual processing to convert spatially structured images into symbolic representations. Templates are always the starting point for discussions of shape representation for the simple reason that they are the most obvious mechanism for performing this conversion. Line and edge detector theories of simple cells in area V1 are template representations, albeit very simple ones. Each line detector cell, for example, responds maximally to a line at a specific position, orientation, and contrast (light on dark versus dark on light). The firing rate decreases as any of these parameters is changed from its optimal value, thus providing a measure of the degree of similarity between the local structure of the image that falls within its field and the spatial structure of its receptive field. The minimum firing rate occurs for the opposite distribution of light within its receptive field.

The same is true of the local spatial frequency approach to the function of V1 cells that we discussed in Section 4.2.2. Each cell is effectively computing a measure of the similarity between the local spatial structure of the input image and the Gabor function encoded in its receptive field. In this case the conversion is being made from images to local spatial frequency components rather than to lines and edges, but the basic representation can still be accurately characterized as a form of template matching. The major difference is that local spatial frequency components are not taken to be meaningful aspects of the object's shape, whereas edges and lines are.

We know with a fair degree of certainty, then, that the visual system makes use of templates to represent

ence of light) or inhibitory (i.e., responds negatively to the presence of light). This two-valued system is not the only possibility, however. One can easily construct "grayscale" templates by converting the representation of each spatial element from a binary feature (white versus black at a particular receptor) into a continuous grayscale dimension by varying the strength of the connections continuously from +1 (excitatory links) to −1 (inhibitory links). Thus, one could build a set of templates for local sine wave gratings as the basis for a local spatial frequency theory of shape perception. One could even build a "grandmother detector" template that would respond maximally to the image of your grandmother's face under some particular viewing conditions: from a particular viewing angle and distance with light sources at particular environmental locations. The fact that gray-scale templates are possible does not necessarily mean that they will solve the problems of shape perception, however, as we shall see.

To determine the similarity between two shapes, one needs a method to compare representations. Two templates can be compared simply by computing a measure very simple "shapes," such as lines and edges or local patches of sinusoidal gratings. The question is whether there are any principled reasons why this approach cannot be extended to encode more complex shapes of real objects, such as squares, Volkswagens, or your grandmother's face.

Weaknesses. Having now given templates their due as a necessary first step in creating a symbolic shape representation, it must be acknowledged that their weaknesses as a general theory of shape representation are many and profound. We will now consider several of the most important objections in some detail, because these will also serve as benchmarks against which other theories can be evaluated.

1. *The problem of multiple sensory channels.* A number of visual factors have little, if any, impact on perceived shape yet strongly influence the correlation between two template representations. Perhaps the most obvious factor is differences in color. A green square on a yellow ground is seen as having the same shape as a blue square on a red ground or any other combination of colors. This poses a problem for standard template representations because they are defined in terms of specific receptor outputs. A template representing a green square on a yellow background will not match an otherwise identical template for a blue square on a red ground because the underlying color elements are different. The general problem is that retinally based template representations are not invariant with respect to color, whereas shape perception is.

As it turns out, the color problem is just the tip of a very large iceberg. There are many other differences in the visual channels within which a square can be presented that would profoundly affect any standard template representation yet have little or no effect on perceived squareness. Consider the fact that squares can be perceived via illusory contours, misaligned line segments, and different textures, as illustrated in Figure 8.2.2. Even these do not exhaust the possible channels through which a square can be presented and still give rise to the perception of squareness. Common fate can cause a square group of moving dots to be seen against either a static background or one that moves in a different direction. Binocular disparity can cause a square region of dots to stand out in depth against a background of dots in a random dot stereogram, as we have seen in

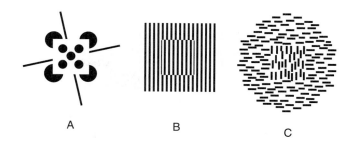

Figure 8.2.2 The problem of visual channels for a square template. People perceive squares defined by illusory contours (A and B) and texture edges (C), even though none of these patterns will cause high levels of activation in the luminance-based square template depicted in Figure 8.2.1.

Chapter 5 (see Figure 5.3.8). The contours of a square can also be revealed over time through a small aperture that reveals its sides over time (see Section 10.2.4), and so forth. The general problem is that there are many different visual channels through which the contours of a square can be presented, making use of radically different modes of sensory stimulation. The notion that shape templates can be wired up by putting together a set of peripheral input units is therefore problematic.

There are two ways of overcoming this difficulty. One is to construct a separate template for each sensory channel. The problem is that there would then be a multiplicity of square templates instead of just one. The second way to overcome the sensory channels problem is to define templates for shape representation at some more abstract level in the visual system, after all the contour extraction channels (e.g., color, texture, binocular disparity, motion, illusory contours) have had their effects. What is needed is a template that somehow represents differences between figure (the square) and ground (its background) regardless of which sensory channel carries the information about the contours. Such a template representation would be suitably general with respect to sensory channels.

2. *The problem of spatial transformations.* In the first section of this chapter, we discussed the important fact that shape is largely invariant over the similarity transformations: translations, rotations, dilations, reflections, and their various combinations. One of the major problems with standard template schemes is that comparing the template representations of two objects with the same shape does not generally result in a good fit if they differ only with respect to one of these transformations.

Representing Shape and Structure

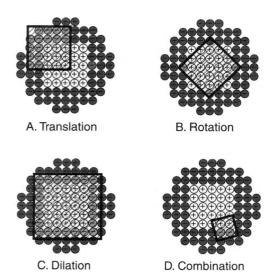

A. Translation   B. Rotation

C. Dilation   D. Combination

Figure 8.2.3 The problem of spatial transformations for a square template. People perceive the shaded areas in parts A, C, and D as square, despite the fact that they overlap poorly with the template. Moreover, people do not perceive the diamond in part B as square, despite the fact that its overlap with the template is reasonably good.

Figure 8.2.3, for example, shows that if a second square template is compared with the initial one, changing its position, orientation, and size has devastating effects on the correlations. Since these objects all have the same objective shape, as we defined it in Section 8.1.1, simply computing the correlation between two templates does not give a reasonable measure of shape similarity.

There are two ways to solve this problem for template representations: *replication* and *normalization*. **Replication** is the strategy of constructing a different template for each shape in every possible position, orientation, size, and sense (reflection). Then the template with the best match to the target will be a reasonable approximation to their "true" similarity within this shape similarity scheme. This is the approach the visual system appears to take for lines and edges (and/or for local spatial frequency components) in area V1, repeating the same receptive field structure over and over for all possible retinal positions, orientations, sizes, and senses. As you might imagine, this approach is feasible only if the set of template shapes is very small. Lines and edges (or Gabor functions in cosine and sine phase) are indeed a very small set. But if all possible shapes people can dis-

Standard   Plastic Deformations

Figure 8.2.4 Plastic deformations and shape similarity. The shapes of the three variants on the right are very similar to the standard on the left even though they would not match a template for the standard figure very well.

criminate had to be repeated in every position, orientation, size, and sense, the proliferation of templates that would result—called a **combinatorial explosion**—boggles the mind. Replication of templates therefore is not a tractable solution to the general problem of shape representation, although it may indeed suffice for a minimal set of very simple templates such as lines and edges.

Normalization is quite a different approach to solving the problem of spatial transformations, one that is closely related to two ideas that we have already discussed: transformational alignment and intrinsic reference frames. The assumption is that a reasonable theory of template-based shape similarity can be constructed without replicating templates if the input image can first be transformed or "normalized" to conform to a set of reference standards. For example, the position of a figure could be normalized relative to its center of mass, its orientation relative to its longest dimension, and so forth, much as we discussed at some length in Section 8.1.4 when we considered object-centered reference frames. Inserting such a normalizing process into the system before comparing templates for similarity would solve the spatial transformation problem for the similarity transformations. It is unlikely to provide a general solution to the problem of shape similarity, however, because of the further problems that other spatial transformations introduce.

The similarity transformations seem to be sufficient to define the basis of what we have called objective shape equivalence, but other spatial transformations must be included if we are to address the more general problem of shape *similarity*. Consider plastic deformations such as stretching, squashing, or shearing. As Figure 8.2.4 shows, these transformations can alter the "quantitative" shape of a figure while preserving many aspects of its "qualitative" shape. Simple comparisons between such transformed figures using standard template representations will not generally produce a large enough overlap to conform to the high perceived similarity between such figures. Good matches could be obtained by using templates that are normalized with respect to these further transformations, but doing so causes new and unforseen problems.

An example of the kind of problem that extended normalization introduces is that certain plastic transformations, such as stretching, can change important properties of the figure, such as its longest dimension. This will change the orientation that is chosen as the reference orientation; that, in turn, will change the orientational normalization process. For example, if the longest dimension of the objects in Figure 8.2.4 were used to normalize orientation, the first (squashed) version would not match the standard because its longest dimension is horizontal rather than vertical. One could avoid this problem by trying all possible normalizing transformations, but this solution avoids the proliferation of templates only by trading it for enormous complexity in processing transformations. In fact, no completely general normalization scheme has yet been devised for template representations that will produce reasonable predictions of perceived shape similarity without some sort of combinatorial explosion. More sophisticated systems based on transforming images to align with each other have been devised, as we mentioned in describing transformational alignment (see Section 8.1.3), but the matching processes are based on salient features, such as contour concavities and convexities, rather than undifferentiated templates. We will consider such systems in more detail in Chapter 9 when we explore view-based approaches to object recognition (e.g., Huttenlocher & Ullman, 1987; Lowe, 1985; Ullman, 1996).

3. *The problem of part structure.* At the end of Chapter 7 we reviewed some of the evidence that people perceive most objects as having a hierarchical structure of parts. Where, one might reasonably ask, is this part structure in a template representation? The answer is quite simply that standard templates have none. There are just two levels in template representations—that of the whole template and that of the atomic elements (receptors or pixels) that are associated within the template—with nothing in between. It is therefore difficult to see how a template representation of shape could possibly predict

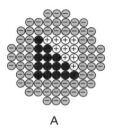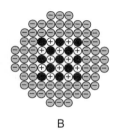

A   B

Figure 8.2.5 The problem of partial matches. Both figures depict overlap of about half the elements of a square template, yet the dark figure in part A is perceived as a triangle rather than a square, whereas that in part B is perceived as a square made of loosely spaced dots. Templates cannot make such distinctions based on different kinds of partial matches.

performance in Palmer's (1977) part verification task, in which part structure is crucial (see Section 7.6.1).

The lack of part structure in standard templates also becomes problematic in considering the nature of partial matches. For instance, consider two different ways in which half the elements of a square template can match those of another template. The triangle in Figure 8.2.5A matches about half of the elements of the square template, and so does the "dotted square" of Figure 8.2.5B. But no sighted person would claim that these two figures were equally similar in shape to the square represented by the original template. The shape of the triangle is very different, whereas that of the dotted square is virtually identical. This problem arises from the lack of appropriate part structure in the square template. The only thing that matters is the number of matching elements, and this is essentially the same for the two cases illustrated in Figure 8.2.5.

What is needed is some general way of building explicit part structure into template representations. This can be done by constructing **hierarchical templates**: complex templates that are constructed by concatenating simpler templates rather than elementary units. A square, for instance, could be represented by combining the outputs of four separate edge templates in the appropriate spatial arrangement, as illustrated in Figure 8.2.6. Given current theories about the structure of the visual nervous system, hierarchical templates seem to be the only viable version of the template proposal. Only a very limited number of spatial templates appear to be represented in area V1 of cortex, and most further spatial processing seems to occur on the output from this

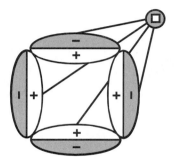

Figure 8.2.6 A hierarchical template for a square. The square detector at the upper right receives input from other templates (here, edge detectors of the indicated orientation and polarity) rather than from individual receptors.

region. As was described in detail in Chapter 4, the receptive field structure of cells in area V1 is generally thought to be either line and edge templates or local spatial frequency templates. If so, other, more complex shape analyzers at higher cortical levels are likely to be constructed from these primitives. Studies of area V4 have found cells that are highly selective to patterns other than simple lines, edges, and spatial frequency gratings, for example, including concentric, radial, spiral, and hyperbolic gratings (see Figure 4.4.3), but it is not yet clear how such receptive fields are derived from the output of V1 cells (Gallant, Braun, & Van Essen, 1993).

Hierarchical templates have a number of attractive features. First, they are physiologically plausible in that they are consistent with the fact that the early visual nervous system is largely hierarchical. More complex receptive fields seem to be constructed by putting together receptive fields from the next lower level. Standard templates are not consistent with visual physiology because they presume that all shapes can be represented directly by concatenating atomic retinal elements. Second, if only a few simple parts were required—for example, straight lines, edges, and their terminations, as in Marr's (1982) primal sketch—it seems that hierarchical templates could potentially solve the problem of similarity transformations by allowing replication of the required parts in all possible positions, orientations, sizes, and senses. As we mentioned, this seems to be what the visual nervous system does in area V1 by repeating the same receptive field structures throughout the visual field. Third, hierarchical templates can be extended to

account for part structures of arbitrary complexity simply by allowing additional levels of hierarchical embedding. Angles can be composed of lines or edges, simple shapes like squares and triangles out of lines and angles, more complex shapes out of squares and triangles, and so forth, ad infinitum. For these and other reasons, physiologistis often assumed that something like a hierarchical template scheme was how the visual system encoded the shape of complex objects.

It is important to realize, however, that these benefits come at the cost of considerable additional complexity in shape representation. We are no longer dealing with simple "shape-as-shape" encodings, but with a piecewise version of it. This has important consequences. For instance, the simple measure of shape similarity we discussed at the outset in terms of correlation is no longer appropriate. It can still be used at the lowest level where the standard templates reside, but matches at higher levels require some more complex integration of the component inputs that it receives from lower-level units. Further, some principled way is needed for specifying the "appropriate arrangement" of lower-level templates. If the basic edge and line templates are simply hard-wired to the higher level units, the same problem of generalizing shape over the similarity transformations will arise, for there still would need to be a different higher-level template for every shape in every position, orientation, size, and so forth. To avoid this problem, some way must be found to specify the arrangement of basic templates more generally. One possibility is to locate the low-level templates by their coordinates within a single object-centered reference frame. Another solution is to specify the locations of parts relative to each other. The most useful schemes for doing this will take us well beyond the domain of template representations, however. We will describe one approach later when we consider the class of shape representations known as structural descriptions.

4. *The problem of three-dimensionality.* As problematic as templates might be in representing the shapes of simple squares and triangles, they are even less satisfactory for representing the shapes of chairs, dogs, and human bodies. The important new problem raised by these examples is that templates are two-dimensional whereas most object shapes are three-dimensional. Templates take the seemingly straightforward approach of representing shape as shape, but this simple idea be-

comes less appealing when the shape representations have lower dimensionality than the shapes they represent.

There are just two ways to make the dimensionality of templates match 3-D objects, and neither is particularly satisfactory. One is to make the templates themselves three-dimensional like the objects. This would make the dimensionality of the objects and templates the same, but unfortunately, the matching process must be mediated through the retina, which is only two-dimensional. This means that 3-D templates would have to be constructed by some complex process that integrates many different 2-D views into a single 3-D representation. The other solution is to make the internal representations of 3-D objects two-dimensional by representing 2-D projections of their shapes. The apparent difficulty here is that many different templates would be needed—in the extreme, one for each distinct perspective view. This would lead to a proliferation of templates for complex 3-D objects, requiring perhaps hundreds or even thousands of templates for a single, reasonably complex 3-D object.

Despite such problems, the value of view-specific templatelike representations has been explored recently by computational theorists who have demonstrated that fewer templates can be stored if there are processes that enable intermediate views to be derived from the nearest stored ones (e.g., Poggio & Edelman, 1990; Ullman & Basri, 1991; see Section 9.3.3). Unfortunately, this solution succeeds only at the expense of considerable increases in processing complexity, and it does nothing to solve the other problems with templatelike representations mentioned above, such as their lack of part structure (see Hummel, in press) or their sensitivity to different input modes or sensory channels. We will return to the problem of three-dimensionality many times, because it is a stumbling block for all theories of shape representation, not just for templates.

8.2.2 Fourier Spectra

A second representational scheme that has been proposed for shape representation is based on the spatial frequency content of images, or their **Fourier spectrum** (e.g., Ginsburg, 1971, 1986; Kabrisky, 1966). The idea behind this approach is that if the early stages of visual analysis perform a Fourierlike analysis of the image into its spatial frequency components (see Section 4.2), a good bet for representing shape and other higher-level properties of visual perception would be to describe them in terms of their spatial frequency content.

The global Fourier analysis of an image consists of two spectra: the **power** (or **amplitude**) **spectrum** and the **phase spectrum**. The power spectrum specifies the amplitude (light-to-dark contrast) of the component sinusoidal gratings at each spatial frequency and orientation, as described in Section 4.2. The phase spectrum specifies the phase (spatial position) of the component gratings at each spatial frequency and orientation. Early psychophysical studies showed that human observers are almost completely blind to phase information when gratings are presented at threshold (e.g., Graham & Nachmias, 1971). Most Fourier approaches to shape perception have therefore focused on the power spectrum.

One of the attractions of using the power spectrum as the basis for shape perception is that it automatically solves the problem of shape equivalence over changes in position. Because positional information is carried entirely in the phase spectrum, the power spectrum is invariant over locational differences. In most other regards, however, power spectra are not much better than standard templates for representing shape. Without significant modifications, they cannot handle the other transformational aspects of shape equivalence, such as changes in size, orientation, and reflection. The Fourier power spectrum of a big square and that of a little one, for example, are not identical in the same way that those of two otherwise identical squares at different positions would be.

The problem with standard Fourier power spectra in this regard is that they represent the *absolute* amplitude of the sinusoidal components at *absolute* spatial frequencies and absolute orientations (i.e., as defined with respect to the retina). As we discussed earlier, shape seems to depend more on the *relative* properties of figures. This suggests that these problems with standard Fourier spectra due to differences in the size, orientation, and reflection of shapes might be overcome by encoding *relative* amplitudes, *relative* spatial frequencies, and *relative* orientations in a representation. Let us call such a representation the **object-relative power spectrum**.

Object-relative encoding can be accomplished by applying the basic idea behind object-centered reference frames once again: Simply encode the amplitudes,

Representing Shape and Structure

spatial frequencies, and orientations of the components relative to some reference standard that is defined by intrinsic properties of the figure. For example, an obvious heuristic would be to code them relative to the component with the lowest (or fundamental) spatial frequency that is present in the pattern. We have already encountered this scheme in Chapter 4 when we described a square wave as the sum of an infinite series of sine waves:

$$F + 1/3(3F) + 1/5(5F) + 1/7(7F) + \cdots,$$

where F represents the amplitude of the fundamental spatial frequency of the square wave, $1/3(3F)$ represents its component at 3 times the frequency of the fundamental with an amplitude $\frac{1}{3}$ as great as that of the fundamental, and so on. Notice that all the frequencies and amplitudes are specified in object-relative terms: Frequency is coded as multiples of the fundamental frequency, and amplitude is coded as fractions of the amplitude at the fundamental frequency. Using this representational scheme, all square waves have the same object-relative power spectrum. Similar tactics can be used for other dimensions. For example, orientation information can be coded in relation to the orientation at which there is maximum power (Jañez, 1983). By encoding the spectra of images in relative terms, it seems plausible that a reasonable measure of shape similarity could be computed from the correspondence between the relative power spectra of two patterns.

Strengths. The Fourier approach has several noteworthy factors in its favor. First, it not only is consistent with, but was actually derived from, a prominent theory of low-level vision. We discussed some of the evidence supporting the spatial frequency theory of image processing in Section 4.2. As we mentioned in that discussion, there is also a good deal of physiological support for the proposal that some form of local spatial frequency analysis is performed in area V1 of visual cortex. Therefore, the Fourier approach to form perception has a good deal of plausibility from low-level image-processing considerations.

Another attractive feature of the Fourier approach to shape is its formal mathematical status. Fourier analysis is a well-known and fully developed analytical technique that can be applied to image processing with all the mathematical knowledge that has accumulated since

Fourier proved his important theorem in 1822. This mathematical rigor stands in contrast to virtually all other theories of shape representation, whose formal foundations might charitably be called "uncertain." The status of the local Fourier approach—based on the Gabor and wavelet functions we described in Chapter 4—is less well understood but still fully formalized. This allows the power of standard mathematical techniques to be brought to bear on the problem of shape similarity in a way that is better developed than for other theories of shape representation.

A more tangible advantage is that relative power spectra appear to solve the problem of shape equivalence over the similarity transformations. In other words, 2-D figures with the same objective shape necessarily have identical object-relative power spectra under equivalent viewing conditions. Relative power spectra are also invariant over differences in luminance contrast because all amplitudes are reduced or increased proportionally. Even texture differences can potentially be eliminated by filtering out high spatial frequencies, because overall shape information is carried in low-frequency channels and texture information in high-frequency ones.

Weaknesses. Despite these significant strengths, object-relative power spectra have a number of drawbacks that seriously undermine their plausibility as a viable basis for shape representation. One of the most important is that a global Fourier analysis represents an entire, uninterpreted image rather than individual objects. For example, the relative power spectrum of a scene does not separate the representation of a figure from the background against which it is seen. This means that the representation of the shape of a figure will be inextricably intertwined with that of the background on which it appears. This is a fatal flaw, because the same object on different backgrounds can have dramatically different power spectra.

Object-relative power spectra also fail to solve, or even to provide insight into, the problems of part structure and three-dimensionality. Because they describe an uninterpreted image holistically, they do not include any explicit representation of naturally perceived parts. Indeed, the way in which spatial information is represented in Fourier spectra makes this problem particularly intractable, since, unlike templates, there are not even identifiable subsets of the power spectrum that constitute explicit representation of its parts. They fail to solve the problems introduced by three-dimensionality because, like templates, they are representations of 2-D images rather than 3-D objects. Many different views of the same object would therefore have to be encoded as distinct power spectra, leading to a very large number of different representations for the shape of a single complex 3-D object.

Finally, relative power spectra have a fairly serious empirical shortcoming: They do not seem to be very good predictors of perceived shape. Piotrowski and Campbell (1982) reported an interesting demonstration. They performed global Fourier analyses of the two images shown along the positive diagonal of Figure 8.2.7: one of a woman's face (part A) and the other of a tank (part D). When the power and phase spectrum of the same image are used together to synthesize an image, they combine to produce the original images from which they were derived, as indicated in the upper left and lower right quadrants of Figure 8.2.7.

Piotrowski and Campbell (1982) also recombined the power and phase spectra in the opposite ways. One image was synthesized using the face's power spectrum and the tank's phase spectrum (part B), and the other using the tank's power spectrum and the face's phase spectrum (part C). As you can see for yourself in Figure 8.2.7, it is the phase spectrum that dominates perception of these hybrid images rather than the power spectrum. This demonstration does not show that Fourier approaches to shape representation are wrong, but only that the power spectrum may be less important for perception than the phase spectrum. Previous results showing that human observers are insensitive to phase information at threshold (e.g., Graham & Nachmias, 1971) clearly do not generalize to suprathreshold contrast levels. Interestingly, newborn babies differ from adults in this respect, since experiments show that they spend more time looking at a hybrid image that has the same power spectrum as a face until the age of two months, at which time they begin to prefer looking at the image with the same phase spectrum as a face (Kleiner & Banks, 1987).

The phase spectrum encodes information about the relative positions of the component gratings at different spatial frequencies and orientations—essentially, how the components "line up" with each other spatially. The

fact that this information dominates shape perception in the tank/face demonstration suggests that advocates of a Fourierlike approach to shape representation must rethink the initial assumption that phase information is irrelevant. Its importance for shape information is now being recognized, although it is not yet clear exactly how it is used.

The idea of a local Fourier analysis—which is most compatible with the known physiology of the visual system—may provide an interesting alternative way to encode positional information. Whether or not it will lead to interesting solutions to the problem of shape representation remains to be seen, however, for it must still come to grips with the other problems mentioned above, especially that of three-dimensionality.

8.2.3 Features and Dimensions

For several decades, the most popular class of shape representation was **feature lists**: a symbolic description consisting of a simple set of attributes. According to this view, an object's perceived shape is defined by the set of its spatial features, and the degree of similarity between two shapes can be measured by the degree of correspondence between the two feature sets. We encountered the concept of features in the beginning of this chapter when we discussed the invariant features approach to shape equivalence. There we considered the possibility that shape equivalence could be captured by features such as the number of lines and angles the object contained and their relative orientations and lengths.

In general, the features that have typically been proposed for representing shape are of two types: **global properties**, such as symmetry, closedness, and connectedness, and **local parts**, such as containing a straight line, a curved line, or an acute angle. Both types of properties are most often represented as binary features: Symmetry is either present or absent, the figure is either connected or not, and a horizontal line is either present or absent. Nevertheless, feature theories can be modified to allow variations in the *degree* to which different features are present. Therefore, a figure need not be either symmetrical or asymmetrical but can have different degrees of symmetry. Likewise, a figure needn't simply contain a vertical line or not but can have a line whose orientation approximates verticality to some degree.

Representing Shape and Structure

Phase Spectrum

Face   Tank

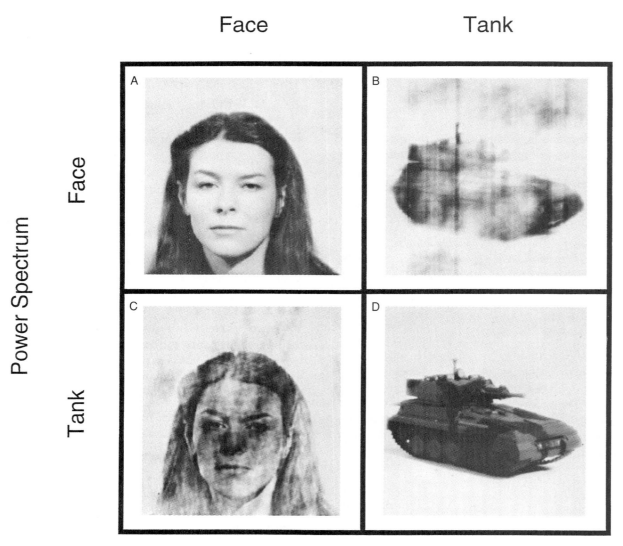

Figure 8.2.7 Power spectra versus phase spectra in shape perception. Each quadrant of the matrix represents the combination of power and phase information from a woman's face and a tank. When properly combined (upper left and lower right), the original pictures are reproduced. When mismatched (upper right and lower left), phase information clearly dominates perception. (After Piotrowski & Campbell, 1982.)

Theories that are based on representations consisting of several continuous dimensions are technically referred to as **multidimensional representations**, but because their strengths and weaknesses as shape representations are closely related to those of standard discrete featural representations, we will discuss them together in this section. One important type of continuous feature theory has been formalized in terms of **fuzzy set theory** (e.g., Massaro & Hary, 1986; Oden & Massaro, 1978). As we mentioned in Chapter 3 when we talked about the fuzzy logical model of color naming, fuzzy set theory is an extension of classical set theory (Zadeh, 1965). The main advantage of fuzzy feature theories is their ability to represent features as quantitative dimensions, more or less as one might expect the brain to do if the presence of features were encoded in the firing rate of neurons. The firing rate of edge and line detectors in visual cortex, for example, does not seem to be all-or-none, as standard binary feature theories suppose, but graded. Fuzzy features allow for such gradations in terms of features being present to varying degrees.

One of the critical questions for the multifeatural and multidimensional approaches to shape representation is how one might determine what features should be included in a given shape representation. Perhaps the most obvious possibility is the one we discussed in considering the problem of shape equivalence: Include in the list all those features that are invariant over the transformations that preserve shape. We have seen that this approach can overcome the problem of similarity transformations—although it is perhaps a little too good in this respect, as we mentioned in Section 8.1—so perhaps it can solve the other problems of shape perception as well. The problem is that it has not been possible to identify a set of transformations that underlie shape similarity in the same way that it has for shape equivalence.

In the absence of a compelling rationale for defining a set of appropriate features a priori, clever methods have been devised for constructing feature-based representations from empirical measures of similarity. There are two rather different methods: one for constructing standard binary feature representations and another for constructing multidimensional (i.e., continuous) feature representations. We will consider the continuous case first.

Multidimensional Representations. A natural way of representing a set of objects that are defined by values along two or more continuous dimensions is as a set of points in a **multidimensional space**. The feature dimensions define the axes of the space, so each object can be represented as a point within the space at the particular position whose coordinates correspond to its values for each featural dimension. We have already considered an example of multidimensional representations in Chapter 3 when we described color experiences as points within color space. Each possible surface color was represented as a point in the three-dimensional color space defined by hue, saturation, and lightness, as illustrated in Color Plate 3.2. The idea behind multidimensional representations of shape is that perhaps the same kind of model can be used to understand the internal representation of shape for complex perceptual objects.

A simple example related to shape perception would be representing the set of possible rectangles within a two-dimensional space, as illustrated in Figure 8.2.8A. Each rectangle can be defined by its height and its width. These two numbers can be used to define each rectangle's coordinates within a two-dimensional space, as illustrated in Figure 8.2.8B, where the letters' positions in the space indicate height and width. There is an alternative dimensional structure for this same set of stimuli, however, consisting of the rectangle's overall size and aspect ratio (height-to-width ratio), as shown in Figure 8.2.8C. Notice that the configuration of points in this space is the same as that in Figure 8.2.8B, but with the axes rescaled and rotated by 45° because the dimensional axes are different.

Multidimensional representations would not be very useful or interesting if they applied only to figures that could easily be defined by obvious physical dimensions such as rectangle height and width. However, there are computer algorithms—called **multidimensional scaling (MDS) programs**—that are able to construct representations within a multidimensional space automatically from appropriate data concerning the similarity (or dissimilarity) between pairs of objects. Such programs promise the possibility that a researcher can discover the psychologically relevant dimensions for a given set of objects without knowing them in advance. Thus, MDS programs are a potentially powerful tool

Representing Shape and Structure

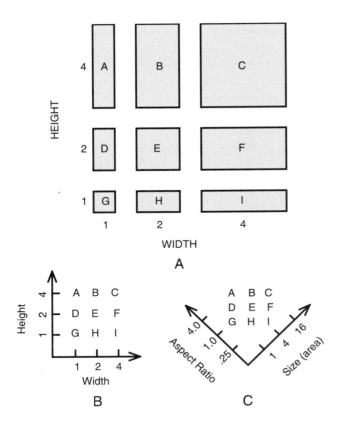

Figure 8.2.8 Representing the shape of rectangles in multi-dimensional spaces. A set of nine rectangles is defined by three values of height and width (A). These rectangles can therefore be represented in a multidimensional space defined by orthogonal axes of height and width (B) or axes of aspect ratio and size (C).

	Violet	Blue	Green	Yellow	Red
Violet (434 nm.)	99	85	40	25	70
Blue (472 nm.)	85	99	70	25	25
Green (504 nm.)	40	70	99	55	10
Yellow (584 nm.)	25	25	55	99	55
Red (674 nm.)	70	25	10	55	99

Figure 8.2.9 Proximity matrix of perceived similarities of five colors. Each entry represents the average judged similarity of the stimulus pair defined by its row and column colors on a scale of 0 to 99 (where 99 means identical). Such proximity matrices are used as input to multidimensional scaling (MDS) programs.

for determining what features might underlie people's internal representations of perceived shapes.

The best-known MDS techniques derive from a method initially formulated by psychologist Roger Shepard, then working at the Bell Telephone Laboratories and now at Stanford University. They are based on the general idea that the perceived similarity between two objects can be modeled as the distance between their corresponding points in a multidimensional space, as measured by some appropriate distance metric. To construct a multidimensional representation of *n* objects, the MDS program takes as input an *n* × *n* **proximity matrix**: a table consisting of *n* rows and *n* columns in which each entry of the table is a number that represents the similarity (or dissimilarity) of the item in that row to the item in that column. Figure 8.2.9 illustrates an example of such a matrix for patches of

color. The entries in the proximity matrix are usually obtained by presenting subjects with a pair of objects and having them rate the subjective similarity (or dissimilarity) of that pair on some numerical scale, in this case from 0 (maximally different) to 99 (identical). The average rating over many subjects is the entry for the row and column corresponding to those two items. Repeating this procedure for every possible pair of items defines the complete proximity matrix, which provides the input for the scaling program.

The MDS program works by trying to find the set of locations for the objects within a multidimensional space that provides the best fit between two measures: (a) the rated similarity of pairs of objects in the proximity matrix and (b) the distance between corresponding pairs of points in the multidimensional space. The program begins by placing the objects at random locations in the space. It then computes a measure, usually called **stress**, of how badly the distances between pairs of points in that spatial configuration fit the rated similarity of corresponding objects in the proximity matrix. If the configuration of points fits the similarity data well, high similarity ratings for object pairs should correspond to small interpoint distances, and low similarity ratings should correspond to large interpoint distances. To the extent that this is true for the current configuration of points, stress measures will be low, indicating a good solution. To the extent that it is not true, stress measures will be high, indicating a poor solution.

The heart of an MDS program is a method for adjusting the locations of the objects within the space according to a formula that systematically decreases stress with each successive adjustment. After many iterations in which small adjustments are made in the locations of

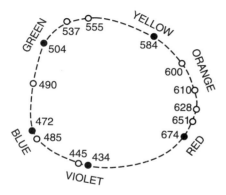

Figure 8.2.10 A reconstruction of the color circle using multidimensional scaling. By using a 14 × 14 proximity matrix like that shown in Figure 8.2.9, Shepard's original MDS algorithm recovered the nearly circular configuration shown here. Black dots correspond to the subset of five colors shown in Figure 8.2.9. (After Shepard, 1962b.)

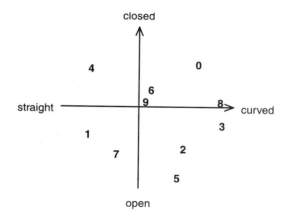

Figure 8.2.11 A multidimensional scaling solution for the shape of single numerals. An MDS algorithm recovered this 2-D solution for rated similarities of the numerals 0–9. The two dimensions were interpreted as straightness/curvature and open/closed. (After Shepard, Kilpatric, & Cunningham, 1975.)

the points within the space, the program finally outputs the best-fitting configuration of points that it can find as the "solution" in the specified dimensionality. Shepard's (1962a, 1962b) original method was later reformulated by Kruskal (1964) in a way that takes advantage of gradient descent procedures (see Appendix B) to ensure that stress is reduced by each small adjustment of point locations.

An example of a solution found by an MDS program is given in Figure 8.2.10 for judgments of similarity among highly saturated patches of color. (The solid circles show the subset of stimuli whose rated similarities are presented in the proximity matrix of Figure 8.2.9.) In this case, we already know that the representation should be a two-dimensional configuration of highly saturated hues lying around the edge of the color circle, and that is essentially the configuration of points recovered by the MDS program. Thus, the program has correctly reconstructed the two-dimensional representation of the color circle.

A second example of MDS is shown in Figure 8.2.11 for objects consisting of the single-digit numerals 0 through 9 (Shepard, Kilpatric, & Cunningham, 1975). Here, the dimensions of perceptual similarity were not known in advance but were discovered by using the MDS program. It recovered the configuration of points shown here as the best-fitting solution in two dimensions to the initial similarity matrix, but it does not specify the

dimensional axes of the space. In most MDS applications, the axes can be in any orientation and therefore must be determined by the researcher. Usually, he or she simply inspects the configuration of points in the MDS solution and finds a set of orthogonal axes along which the stimuli are properly ordered. In the present case, the two dimensions seem to be (1) curvedness versus straightness and (2) openness versus closedness, as indicated by the regular ordering of the stimuli according to these dimensions. Extensions of MDS techniques that specify the axes uniquely—but do not identify or name them—have also been developed (e.g., INDSCAL; see Carroll & Chang, 1970).

Virtually any set of visual stimuli can be represented in a multidimensional space using such a program. When given a proximity matrix as input, it simply cranks through its procedures to find the best-fitting solution under the assumptions of the multidimensional representation scheme within a specified number of dimensions.

Despite their popularity as models for the structure of complex stimuli, MDS representations have two major limitations. First, their usefulness is pragmatically limited to solutions in three dimensions or fewer. The reason is that for MDS solutions to be useful, researchers must be able to inspect the configuration of objects within the space, and doing so with physical models is possible only for solutions with three or fewer dimen-

Representing Shape and Structure

sions. Techniques exist for recovering the structure of high-dimensional solutions (e.g., Wish, Deutsch, & Biener, 1970), but they are complex and difficult to use. Note that this limitation has no serious theoretical drawbacks. MDS representations might still be excellent candidates as psychological theories of shape representation. The only problem is that high-dimensional solutions from the output of MDS programs are difficult to interpret.

The second problem is theoretically more damaging. It is that serious questions have been raised about whether the assumptions underlying MDS models are true of human similarity judgments. For instance, Tversky (1977) pointed out that for proximity between points in space to be a good model of judged similarity between objects, similarity judgments must be symmetrical: *A* must be as similar to *B* as *B* is to *A*. This is true by definition of distances in a multidimensional space, but is it equally true of similarity judgments?

Despite the a priori plausibility of this assumption, it turns out to be false for at least some perceptually judged similarities. For example, people systematically rate an off-red as more similar to focal red than they rate focal red as similar to the same off-red (Rosch, 1975a). Tversky and Gati (1982) have demonstrated a number of such violations of the assumptions underlying the distance model in multidimensional spaces, although most of them were more conceptual than perceptual in nature. Unlike the first problem, this one has potentially negative implications for the viability of MDS models. Some theorists have attempted to make interpoint distances in multidimensional spaces asymmetrical (e.g., Krumhansl, 1978), but the ad hoc flavor of such proposals makes them less than compelling. Even so, the asymmetry effects in similarity judgments that have been reported are small enough that it is difficult to justify abandoning MDS representations on their account.

Multifeatural Representations. Another approach to representing complex perceptual objects that overcomes both objections to MDS representations assumes that objects can be analyzed into a structure of discrete features rather than continuous dimensions. The representation of an object within a multifeatural approach is typically conceived as a set (unordered list) of its features. A square, for example, might be represented by the following set of discrete features:

SQUARE:

- closed
- four sides
- four right angles
- vertical symmetry
- horizontal symmetry

(etc.)

Just as multidimensional representations can be viewed as mapping objects to points in a dimensional space, multifeatural representations can be viewed as mapping objects to terminal nodes in a tree structure. Figure 8.2.12 shows an example of a **hierarchical tree** representing the features of some uppercase letters of the alphabet. In a hierarchical tree, there is always a single **root node** at the top representing the set of all objects. It then branches via links representing the presence or absence of various features to **nonterminal nodes** representing different levels of nonoverlapping subsets of objects. This branching continues until the **terminal nodes** at the bottom are reached, which represent individual objects. Each object is thus defined by the set of featural links between its terminal node and the root node. In the particular tree shown in Figure 8.2.12, for example, the letter C is represented by the features of containing curved lines, being open, and being symmetrical. More features would be required to distinguish it from other letters—such as U, which is also curved, open, and symmetrical—but there is no reason why additional nodes and links cannot be added to the tree to expand its representational capabilities.

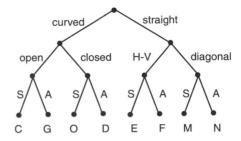

Figure 8.2.12 Hierarchical clustering of perceived shape similarities among some uppercase letters of the alphabet. Terminal nodes at the bottom represent individual letters, and higher nodes represent groups of letters with similar shape features. (H-V = horizontal and vertical lines, S = symmetrical, A = asymmetrical.)

Using different links for vertical versus horizontal symmetry, for instance, would be sufficient to define different terminal nodes for C and U.

As was the case with MDS representations, multifeatural theories are useful only if reasonable sets of features can be identified with which to represent the objects in question. To aid in this process, **hierarchical clustering programs**, analogous to MDS programs, exist for converting an $n \times n$ matrix of proximity (similarity) data into the best-fitting tree structure of a particular type. The underlying assumption of such programs is that the distance between object nodes in the tree diagram corresponds to the similarity of the two corresponding objects. Distance between two nodes in a tree is measured as the length of the shortest path between the nodes along the links connecting them.

The earliest clustering programs constructed hierarchical tree structures of the type illustrated in Figure 8.2.12. A hierarchial clustering program produces as output the hierarchical tree that best fits the input similarity data, but the program does not specify the interpretation of the features that characterize the links in the tree. The user must then determine the best feature interpretation for the links, given the nature of the objects and his/her ingenuity. This interpretation of features is analogous to the interpretation of dimensions in the output of MDS programs.

Multifeatural representations avoid some of the problems of multidimensional space representations. For example, unlike the practical limit in MDS representations that only three dimensions can easily be grasped by the user in inspecting the whole structure, multifeatural trees representing a very large number of features can easily be comprehended by the user of a clustering program. Also unlike the inherently symmetric spatial representations in MDS, certain types of multifeatural trees—namely, ones with separate links for each direction between a pair of nodes—can represent asymmetric similarity relations. Even so, it is difficult to deny the intuitive appeal of the graded, quantitative differences that dimensional representations are so good at capturing.[3]

Strengths. One reason for the popularity of feature representations is that they do not fall prey to the very simple and basic objections that so cripple template and Fourier approaches. Although it is not yet clear whether feature theories can actually solve all of them in practice, they seem promising in principle.

Feature representations for shape can solve the problem of sensory channels simply by postulating features that are already abstract and symbolic. That is, feature representations avoid the specific sensory input mode of the shape by not including any features that refer directly to the type of peripheral stimulation that defines the edges or lines in question. The feature list that we suggested for a square earlier in this section, for example, made no reference to its color, texture, position, or size. It is an abstract, symbolic description of all kinds of squares.

Features also seem to be able to solve the problem of part structure simply by including the different parts of an object in its feature list. The feature list for squares, for example, included "having four sides" and "having four angles" as features. Similarly, a feature representation of a human body might include the part-based features of "having a head," "having a torso," "having two legs," and so forth. The features of a head would likewise include "having two eyes," "having a nose," "having a mouth," and so on. Part structure thus seems to be much less of a problem for featural representations than for template or Fourier representations.

Features also seem capable of solving the problems resulting from three-dimensionality, at least in principle. The difficulty of intrinsic dimensionality that defeats inherently 2-D representations, such as templates and Fourier approaches, is simply not a problem for a featural approach. The kinds of features that are included in a shape representation can refer to intrinsically 3-D qualities and parts as well as 2-D ones and so can be used to capture the shape of 3-D as well as 2-D objects. For instance, the shape of an object can be described as having the feature "spherical" as easily as "circular" and "contains a pyramid" as easily as "contains a triangle." Therefore, there is nothing in the feature list

---

[3] Graded structure can be captured in fuzzy multifeatural representations, but doing so makes them formally equivalent to multidimensional representations.

approach that is limited to 2-D features. Indeed, postulating features that have 3-D structure is as easy as postulating ones that have 2-D structure.

Weaknesses. Despite these considerable strengths, feature theories do have several important weaknesses. We have already mentioned one of them: that invariant feature theories of shape equivalence are not able to cope well with cases in which human perception deviates from objective shape equivalence. For example, they typically cannot account for the difference Mach noted between the perceived shape of an upright square and one tilted by 45°. If orientationally specific features are added, then these two figures will have different feature lists, but so will many other figures that people see as having the same shape despite changes in orientation, as illustrated in Figure 8.1.1B.

A very different problem with feature list theories is that it is often unclear how to determine computationally whether a given object has the features that are proposed to make up its shape representation. Simple part features of 2-D images, such as lines, edges, and blobs, can be computed from an underlying template system as we discussed previously, but even these must somehow be abstracted from the specific peripheral channels that have found the lines, edges, and blobs. Moreover, these simple image-based features are just the tip of another very large iceberg. They do not cover the plethora of different attributes that feature theorists might (and do) propose in their representations of shape. For example, simply asserting that aspects of 3-D shape can be represented as features is a snap compared with the difficulty of actually computing them. Features such as "containing a cylinder" or "having a nose," for instance, are not easy to compute from an image, and there is no known template scheme that will do the trick. Until such feature extraction routines are available to back up the features proposed for the representations, feature-based theories are incomplete in a very important sense. This is not a fundamental theoretical problem with the feature list proposal—unless, of course, the features were found to be incapable of being computed for some reason—but it is a practical problem of enormous proportions.

Assuming that the computational difficulties of extracting features can be overcome, there is still the very difficult problem of specifying what the proper features for a shape representation might be. It is one thing to

- 1 horizontal line
- 2 diagonal lines
- 3 acute angles
- 2 obtuse angles
- 2 free ends
- vertical symmetry
- fully connected
- closed portion

A

B

Figure 8.2.13 Features of an A. Part A shows a feature list for the shape of a prototypical A containing many of the standard features for alphanumeric symbols. Part B shows a figure that has every feature listed in part A yet has a very different shape.

propose that some appropriate set of shape features can, in principle, account for shape perception but quite another to say exactly what those features are. Computer-based methods such as multidimensional scaling and hierarchical clustering can help in limited domains, but they have not yet succeeded in suggesting viable schemes for the general problem of representing shape in terms of a list of properties. Let us see why this is such a difficult problem by examining a specific example.

Consider a reasonable list of features that might be used to characterize the shape of the letter A, as shown in Figure 8.2.13A. We include both global features, such as symmetry, connectedness, and closedness, as well as part features, such as having three straight lines, having three acute angles, and having two obtuse angles. It seems like a pretty good shape representation—until we discover that other figures with quite different shapes have exactly the same features. One of these is shown in Figure 8.2.13B. It has all of the same features as those listed in the representation of the A, yet its shape is significantly different from that of an A. This is of concern because if two figures have the same feature list representation, they should be perceived as having the same

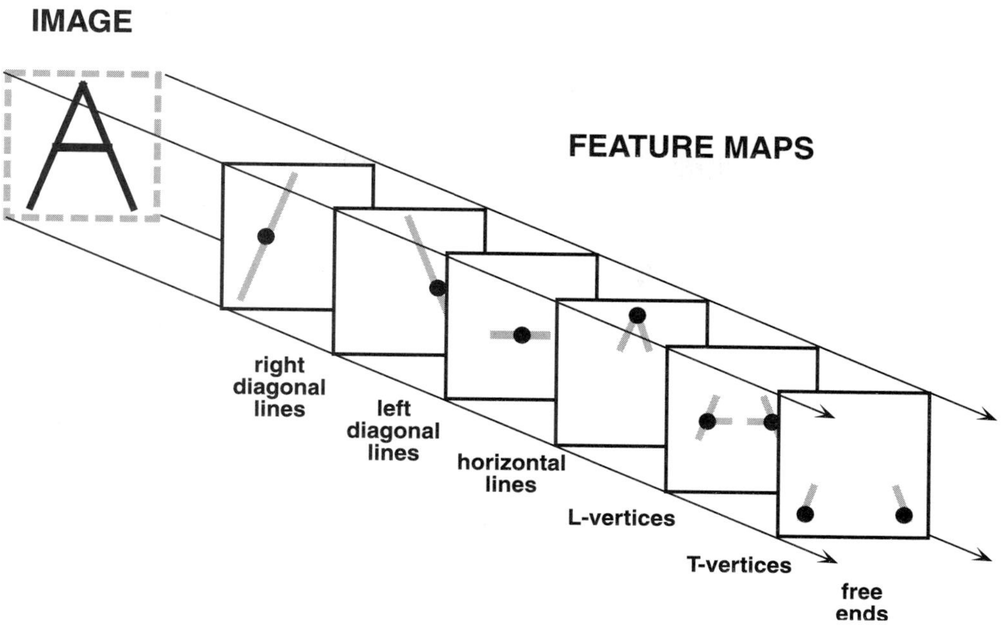

IMAGE

FEATURE MAPS

right diagonal lines

left diagonal lines

horizontal lines

L-vertices

T-vertices

free ends

Figure 8.2.14 A feature map representation of an A. The various features of an A, consisting of its component lines, vertices, and free ends, are associated with their locations in a set of spa-

tially defined feature maps. The locations of these features place further constraints on shape descriptions, reducing the problem of underdetermination by simple feature lists.

shape. This is not the case in this example, despite the use of a relatively complete and obvious set of features.

At least two solutions are open to feature theorists in overcoming this problem. One is to enrich the representation by pairing features with their positional coordinates in the image, as illustrated in Figure 8.2.14. Whereas two different objects might have the same set of features, it is most unlikely that they would have them in the same locations. In the present case, for example, specifying the positions of the two free ends in the image would be sufficient to distinguish between the two figures shown in Figures 8.2.13A and 8.2.13B. Such location-specific feature representations, which we will call **feature maps** to distinguish them from simple feature lists, provide additional constraints on shape because positional information is completely unspecified in standard feature lists. Important decisions have to be made about how one defines the location of different kinds of features—for example, lines by their center point, angles by their vertex, and global properties by the center of the object as a whole—but it is clear that this can be done in systematic ways that will succeed in discriminating different shapes. It is also important that

the locations be specified in object-relative coordinates —that is, within an intrinsic reference frame for the object—or else feature map representations will suffer from the same problems as templates and Fourier spectra: Changing the position, size, orientation, and reflection of the object within the image will derail the comparison process.

The idea that object shape might be represented as maps (rather than simple lists) of features also has some degree of physiological plausibility because many areas of visual cortex appear to contain maps organized by retinal location (see Section 1.3.3). If different features are coded in different cortical maps, as many theorists suppose, the composite firing pattern over these maps in visual cortex can be considered functionally equivalent to what we are calling a feature map representation. As we will see in Chapters 9 and 11, such feature map representations have recently become popular in theories of object recognition based on alignment of different views of the same object (e.g., Lowe, 1985; Ullman, 1989, 1996) and in theories of attention based on binding features by retinal location (e.g., Treisman & Gelade, 1980).

Representing Shape and Structure

Another avenue that is open to feature theorists is simply to propose additional features that would discriminate between two nonidentical shapes that have the same feature list representations. For example, one could add a feature such as requiring that the horizontal line be shorter than the oblique lines or that the ends of the horizontal line be connected to the middle of the two oblique sides. Although these are, in fact, discriminating features, they are disturbingly ad hoc and specific to this particular pair of objects. Even if "having a horizontal line that is shorter than an oblique line" were a generally useful feature for shape representation—and this seems unlikely—the number of such ad hoc features would soon grow astronomically large. Even more problematic, such features would constitute a new class because they specify the relation between several other part features—in this case, the three component lines.

This strategy points out a general underlying problem with feature list representations: Describing the shape of an object adequately often requires specifying not only its component parts and global properties, but also the spatial relations that hold among its parts. These part-relational features do not fit with the conception of feature lists as a simple set of independently specifiable attributes because they inherently depend on the features that represent the parts. This way of describing the problem suggests a more complex form of representation that directly encodes relational information among explicitly represented parts. It is the primary rationale for structural descriptions, the theory of shape representation to which we now turn.

8.2.4 Structural Descriptions

Structural descriptions are representations that contain explicit information about parts and about relations between parts. They are usually depicted as networks in which nodes represent the whole object and its various parts and labeled links (or arcs) between nodes represent the relations between parts. To illustrate how this kind of structure can represent shape in a way that solves at least some of the problems that feature list theories encounter, consider the structural description of the shape of an A presented in Figure 8.2.15. The highest node represents the entire figure, and the lower nodes represent its component parts: the line segments and vertices that compose it. The relational features we

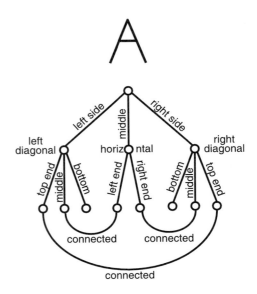

Figure 8.2.15 Structural description of an A. The network shown represents the various parts of an A (its component lines and their ends) together with structural relations among them. (See text for details.)

proposed earlier to discriminate between the A and the non-A are economically represented by labeled arcs between nodes. For example, the fact that the ends of the central line attach to the middles of the oblique ones is explicitly represented by creating nodes for the ends and middles of the lines (as parts of the lines) plus links between the appropriate nodes specifying the appropriate connections. (That the oblique lines are longer than the central one could also be represented by a "longer than" arc between the relevant nodes, but such arcs are not shown in this example.)

Such a representation of relational information is far more economical than corresponding representations in feature theories because one does not need a different feature for all possible combinations of relations among parts. Rather, the network structure allows for the relations to be separate entities (the arcs) that connect the nodes to each other. The tradeoff is that the structure of the network is considerably more complex than that of a simple feature list.

Basic structural descriptions bear important similarities to the hierarchical template scheme we mentioned earlier in this chapter, mainly because both represent parts in a hierarchy. Structural descriptions are more

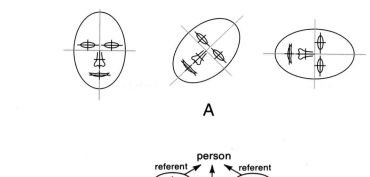

A

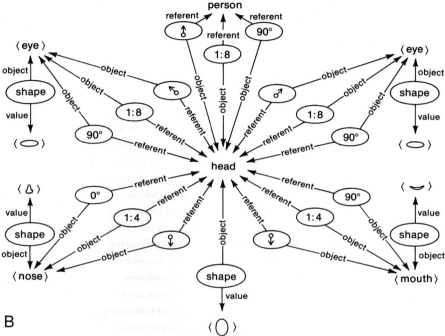

B

Figure 8.2.16 Using structural descriptions and reference frames to represent a schematic face. Part A illustrates the invariance of the relation between the intrinsic frame of the head and those of eyes, nose, and mouth over rotations. Part B shows a structural description that encodes such invariant relations by specifying the translation (arrow symbol), rotation (angle size), and dilation (size ratio) that relate the reference frames for each component of the description (head, eyes, nose, and mouth). (After Palmer, 1975b.)

powerful, however, in allowing relational information among the parts to be explicitly encoded. Moreover, structural description networks can be elaborated in a number of ways. For instance, global features of any component can be represented simply by attaching feature nodes for the relevant information. This allows structural descriptions to explicitly encode information that is only implicitly available in their components: symmetry, openness, aspect ratio, and so on.

Of special importance for representing shape is information about the intrinsic reference frame for each component. Figure 8.2.16 shows how Palmer (1975b) incorporated this idea into his representation for a schematic face via feature nodes. The head as a whole is represented as an oval whose intrinsic frame is defined by the position of its center, the orientation of its long axis, and the length of its axis of elongation. The eyes are similarly represented as ovals with their own intrinsic frames defined by their positions, orientations, and axes of elongation. The relations among these frames can then be economically encoded by specifying the similarity transformation that relates one frame to another (i.e., the combination of translations, rotations, dilations, and reflections that bring the frames into com-

Representing Shape and Structure

plete correspondence). The result is an encoding scheme that represents the spatial relations among parts in a way that is largely invariant over changes in absolute position, orientation, size, and sense, because frame relations are encoded relative to one another. For example, the position, orientation, and size of the eyes relative to the head do not change when the whole head is moved, tilted, or enlarged. This allows the relational structure of object-centered frames within the network to remain invariant over the similarity transformations, as discussed at the beginning of this chapter.

There is nothing to prevent variant features from being represented in structural descriptions as well. One can simply represent relations that change over transformations, such as encoding orientation in gravitational frame of reference rather than in an object-relative one (e.g., Hummel & Biederman, 1992). In this case, the structural description of the same object will be different when it is viewed in different orientations, as Rock's (1973) classic studies showed for figures with poor intrinsic axes. Such descriptions can still be invariant over different positions, sizes, and reflections, however.

Shape Primitives. One serious issue with structural descriptions is how to represent the global shapes of the components. One particularly attractive solution is to postulate shape primitives that can be used to encode the global shape of every object or part, at least approximately. As you will recall from the end of Chapter 7 when we discussed part segmentation, the idea underlying shape primitives is that everything can be analyzed as one element of a basic vocabulary of shapes. For two-dimensional patterns such as Palmer's (1975b) schematic faces, ovals might be one primitive and curved lines another. For three-dimensional objects, such as real faces, the shape primitives would have to be three-dimensional volumes, such as ellipsoids, cylinders, and cones.

There are a number of different theoretical proposals about how to define a set of volumetric shape primitives. We have already described in Section 2.4.4 how Marr (1982) represented complex shapes by combinations of generalized cylinders (see Figure 2.4.8), following Binford's (1971) pioneering work. As the name implies, generalized cylinders are a generalization of standard geometric cylinders. A standard cylinder can be constructed by taking a circle of some diameter as the base and sweeping it along a straight axis for some distance.

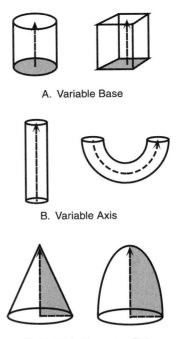

A. Variable Base

B. Variable Axis

C. Variable Sweeping Rule

Figure 8.2.17 Generalized cylinders as 3-D shape primitives. Generalized cylinders are produced by sweeping a base of a specified cross-sectional shape (A) along a particular axis (B), during which the radius of the base can change in different ways (C).

The only variable parameters in this description of a standard cylinder are its diameter and its length. A generalized cylinder, however, allows several of the *fixed* parameters of a standard cylinder to become *variable*:

1. *Variable base.* The 2-D shape of the base of the volume (also called its *cross section*) that is swept along the axis, for example, need not be a circle but could be an ellipse, a rectangle, a triangle, or any other closed 2-D figure, as illustrated in Figure 8.2.17A. Square prisms, for example, are generalized cylinders whose bases are squares, and triangular prisms are generalized cylinders whose bases are triangles.

2. *Variable axis.* Similarly, the axis along which the base is swept need not be straight but can be curved in a potentially infinite variety of ways. The U-shaped tube in Figure 8.2.17B, for example, is a generalized cylinder with a circular base whose axis is bent into a U.

3. *Variable sweeping rule.* Finally, the shape need not remain entirely fixed as it is swept along the axis but can change in size, as illustrated in Figure 8.2.17C. A cone,

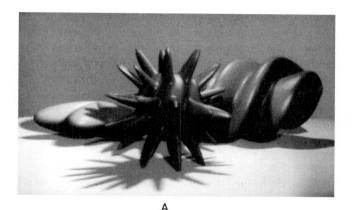

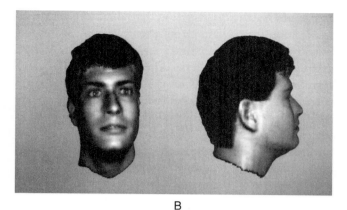

A

B

Figure 8.2.18 Two images of complex shapes constructed from superquadric primitives. Pentland (1986) proposed superquadrics as an alternative to generalized cylinders as 3-D shape primitives. When rendered with appropriate smoothing, highlights, shading, and cast shadows, they can produce convincingly natural images of organic shapes. (Courtesy of Alex Pentland.)

for example, is a generalized cylinder in which the diameter of the circular cross section decreases linearly as it is swept along its axis.

The examples just mentioned change only one parameter at a time for the sake of clarity, but all three may be different from their standard values in a classic cylinder and still produce examples of generalized cylinders.

There are many other possibilities for a set of primitive 3-D shapes from which structural descriptions can be built. Some of them are very closely related to generalized cylinders, such as Biederman's (1987) "geons," which we will discuss at length in Chapter 9, and some are rather different. As one example, Figure 8.2.18 shows two images of more "organically shaped" objects that were synthesized from primitives called *superquadrics* (Pentland, 1986). Despite many years of work on different sets of volumetric shape primitives, however, it is not yet clear whether building descriptions out of such primitive shapes—regardless of their specific nature—is the best way to construct shape representations. No set of 3-D shape primitives has yet been devised that seems fully up to the task of representing the shape of all the complex objects people are able to recognize.

Strengths. Structural descriptions overcome many of the difficulties with templates, Fourier spectra, and features. They are invariant over different sensory channels—such as edges defined by luminance, texture, and motion—because the primitives of which they are com-

posed can be abstracted from these specific dimensions. They can account for the effects of spatial transformations on shape perception by absorbing them within object-centered reference frames. They deal explicitly with the problem of part structure by having quasi-independent representations of parts and spatial relations among them. And they are able to represent 3-D shape by using volumetric primitives and 3-D spatial relations in representing 3-D objects.

Weaknesses. There is a price to be paid for these desirable features, however, some of which have already been mentioned in passing. One is that the representations become quite complicated, so matching two graph structures constitutes a difficult problem by itself (Grimson & Lozano-Perez, 1987). Another is that a sufficiently powerful set of primitives and relations must be identified. Given the subtlety of many shape-dependent perceptions, such as recognizing known faces, this is not an easy task. A third is that the shape primitives and their relations must be computable from real images. It is one thing to suppose that all objects can be represented by a given set of primitives, but quite another to specify algorithms that can detect them. Even so, structural descriptions at least seem to be in the right ballpark and to have some hope of serving as an adequate basis of shape perception.

The last theory of shape representation we will consider is another type of structural description that is

Representing Shape and Structure

based on neither shape primitives nor boundary rules and is not formalized in terms of networks of nodes and links. Instead of specifying an "alphabet" of primitive shapes, it determines the parts in a context-sensitive way as it attempts to find the "best" description in the sense suggested by Gestalt psychologists many years ago. To understand this theory, we will first have to make a digression to explain two concepts that are important contributions of Gestalt psychology to the understanding of shape perception: figural goodness and Prägnanz.

8.3 Figural Goodness and Prägnanz

Gestalt psychologists identified an aspect of perceptual experience arising from object shape that they called "gute Gestalt" (pronounced *goo'-teh ge-shtalt'*)— literally, "good shape" or "good form." In modern perceptual literature, the more usual term for this idea is **figural goodness**. Figural goodness is the aspect of perceptual experience that is perhaps best described as a composite of (at least) the simplicity, order, and regularity of an object. Certain shapes, like the circle in Figure 8.3.1A, seem highly simple, regular, and orderly. Virtually any change one might make in a circle reduces the experience of "goodness" in viewing it. In contrast, the chaotic jumble of lines in Figure 8.3.1B seems complex, irregular, and random.

Before giving a detailed analysis of the nature of figural goodness, let us consider why figural goodness might be important for perception of shape, aside from its phenomenological component. One possibility is that "good" figures might be processed more efficiently by the visual system than "bad" figures. Psychologist Wendell Garner (1974) of Yale University has marshalled strong support for this view in his studies of how people perceive, describe, and remember simple visual pat-

terns. He performed many elegant experiments demonstrating that human performance on several tasks is closely related to people's ratings of the subjective "goodness" of the figures. For example, he found that people can:

1. match pairs of "good" figures more quickly for physical identity than pairs of "bad" ones,

2. remember "good" figures more accurately than "bad" ones,

3. describe "good" figures in fewer words than "bad" ones, and

4. learn "good" figures more quickly than "bad" ones.

All these findings fit together nicely if "good" patterns can be more easily and economically represented and processed. It appears that the visual system is particularly sensitive to the kind of structure that "good" patterns have and makes use of it in processing shape information. We will soon consider just what sort of structure makes some patterns "better" than others.

As important as processing efficiency may be, Gestalt theorists placed much greater theoretical significance than this on figural goodness in their theories of visual perception. As mentioned in Section 2.1.2, they believed that it determines the way in which all of perception is organized. This view was expressed concisely in their **principle of Prägnanz**: Perception will be as "good" as the prevailing conditions allow. In effect, they proposed that many different perceptions are possible for any given figure and that figural goodness determines which one is actually perceived. This was a radical notion when it was proposed, one that was probably well ahead of its time. Unfortunately, Gestalt theorists never managed to formulate an explicit theory of shape perception based on it. Later theorists, particularly the Dutch psychologist Emanuel Leeuwenberg (1971) and his colleagues (Buffart & Leeuwenberg, 1981; Van der Helm & Leeuwenberg, 1991), have done so, however.

We will consider two questions about the concept of figural goodness in the remainder of this chapter. First, what factors determine how "good" a given shape appears to be? Second, how can figural goodness be related to people's perception of shape? The latter question will lead us back to structural descriptions of shape via Leeuwenberg's structural information theory.

A   B

Figure 8.3.1 Figural goodness. People generally find figure A far simpler, more regular, and orderly than figure B.

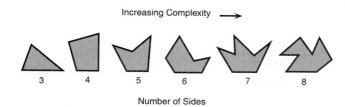

Increasing Complexity ⟶

Number of Sides

Figure 8.3.2 A demonstration of how increasing complexity affects figural goodness. All else being equal, figures with fewer sides tend to be perceived as "better" than figures with more sides.

8.3.1 Theories of Figural Goodness

One obvious factor that influences figural goodness is the number of component parts an object has. Figure 8.3.2 shows that as the number of sides of a figure increases, so does the complexity of its perceived shape. As we mentioned briefly in Chapter 6, however, the number of parts is not the whole story, since objects can differ in figural goodness even if they have the same number of physical parts. For example, consider the set of four-sided figures shown in Figure 8.3.3. Observers generally agree that there is an ordering from simple, regular ones on the left to more complex and irregular ones on the right. These differences in figural goodness cannot depend solely on the number of physical parts the figure contains, since all of them have exactly four sides. Rather, the differences stem from the way in

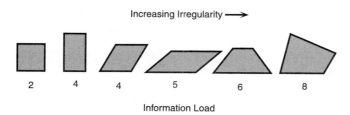

Increasing Irregularity ⟶

Information Load

Figure 8.3.3 A demonstration of how increasing irregularity affects figural goodness. Although all these figures have exactly four sides, people generally agree that there is a progression from simpler shapes on the left to more complex ones on the right. (The numbers shown below the figures correspond to their information load according to structural information theory, explained in Section 8.3.2.)

which the lines are arranged or configured. It is the influence of this global structuring on shape perception that we now seek to understand.

As discussed by Gestalt psychologists, figural goodness is an aspect of perceptual experience. They identified it as roughly corresponding to the subjective simplicity/complexity of perceived objects. Unfortunately, they failed to relate this psychological phenomenon to physical measures of the objective simplicity/complexity of the corresponding objects. For them, "goodness" was an undefined quality of perceptual experience arising from whole figures. They believed that it was fundamentally irreducible to piecewise properties such as the number of components or their interrelations. If figural goodness was to be analyzed at all, they felt it should be in terms of global properties such as bilateral symmetry. They did not believe that symmetry was sufficient to account for all of figural goodness, but to them, it had the right holistic flavor. Little further progress was made on the objective analysis of goodness by Gestalt theorists themselves, but later work by Garner (1974) and Palmer (1991), to be discussed shortly, follows in their footsteps.

Classical Information Theory. The first significant advance in objective theories of figural goodness came from applying basic concepts from Claude Shannon's **information theory**. Information theory is a mathematical theory of communication that measures a commodity (in "bits") that depends on the degree of predictability or certainty associated with a given signal in a particular communication context (Shannon, 1948; Shannon & Weaver, 1949).[4] Shannon called this commodity "information," although its relation to the everyday, commonsense notion of information is perhaps less obvious than it might be.

Relations between information theory and the Gestalt concept of figural goodness were formulated independently by Attneave (1954) and Hochberg and McAlister (1953) at about the same time. They realized that if the perceptual system codes figures optimally by eliminating all redundancies—for example, symmetries and repetitions—"good" figures can be encoded and stored more

---

[4] "Bit" is actually a shortened form of "binary digit," defined as the amount of information required to reduce the number of equally probable alternatives by half. Because the content of the alternative doesn't matter, knowing whether a tossed coin lands on heads or tails is one bit of information, and so is knowing whether the roll of a die produces an odd- or even-numbered outcome (six equally likely alternatives are thus reduced to three). More generally, there are $\log_2(N)$ bits of information in N equally likely alternatives.

Representing Shape and Structure

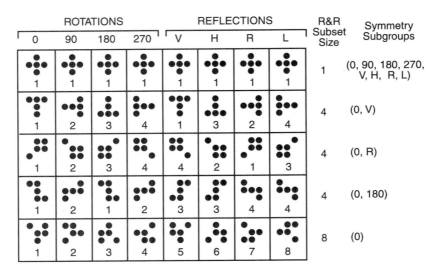

Figure 8.3.4 Stimuli used to study figural goodness. The figural goodness of each of the five patterns in the leftmost column can be predicted from the size of its rotation and reflection (R & R) subset, as proposed by Garner and Clement (1963), and from the transformations in its symmetry subgroup, as proposed by Palmer (1983). (See text for details.) (From Palmer, 1983.)

efficiently than "bad" ones. The term "efficiency" here refers to coding the shape of a figure in fewer "bits" of information. In effect, they proposed that good figures could be described in fewer bits than bad figures.

The informational analysis of figural goodness was based on breaking figures down into local components such as angles and lines and analyzing them for structural regularities, such as the sameness of angle sizes or line lengths within the same figure. A square and an irregular quadrilateral, such as are illustrated in Figure 8.3.3, both consist of four lines and four angles, but the square is "better" than the irregular quadrilateral because all of its sides are the same length and all of its angles are 90°. Such regularities mean that fewer bits of information are required to describe it, although information theorists were never very clear about what the descriptions might be like or how many bits of information a given figure contained. Still, these informational analyses were generally applauded as an advance over Gestalt ideas because they showed that "good" figures were objectively simpler than "bad" ones in a well-defined sense.

Rotation and Reflection Subsets. Although information theorists sought to explain the Gestalt construct of figural goodness in objective terms, their ideas do not fit well into the Gestalt style of explanation which generally opposed piecewise theories of perception (Wert-

heimer, 1924/1950). A formulation that is more in keeping with the holistic approach of Gestalt theory was provided by Garner (1974). He proposed that figures are "good" to the extent that they are the same as transformed versions of themselves. He formalized this notion in his theory of **rotation and reflection (R & R) subsets**.

When a set of spatial transformations is applied to a figure, it produces a set of transformational variants of that figure, as we discussed at the outset of this chapter. The key observation for Garner's theory of figural goodness is that "better" figures produce fewer transformational variants than "poorer" figures do. In the original formulation of this theory, Garner and Clement (1963) used simple patterns consisting of five dots within a square 3 × 3 matrix and applied a set of eight possible transformations to them: four central rotations (through angles of 0°, 90°, 180°, and 270°) and four central reflections (about vertical, horizontal, left-diagonal, and right-diagonal axes). Applying these transformations to a given figure defines its *rotation and reflection set*, some examples of which are illustrated in Figure 8.3.4. Within this set, there is a subset of distinguishably different figures called the *R & R subset* (rotation and reflection subset), enumerated in Figure 8.3.4 by the numbers below the transformational variants. Garner and Clement (1963) found that patterns rated as "good" (such as the top one in Figure 8.3.4) had few transformational variants, whereas those rated as "bad" (such as the bottom one) had many transformational variants. Therefore, they proposed that the goodness of a figure was an inverse function of the size of its R & R subset.

This analysis is particularly appealing from the Gestalt point of view because it applies to whole figures. There is no sense in which patterns need to be broken into piecewise components to apply it. In fact, patterns that are the same as themselves after being reflected about a line through their centers are just those patterns that have bilateral symmetry, the Gestalt prototype for goodness. Even so, Garner did not couch his theory in terms of symmetry because he found that rotational invariance was also important, and this did not seem to fit with the idea of symmetry, at least in its everyday, commonsense form. However, rotational invariance actually conforms precisely to the modern mathematical definition of symmetry, a fact that forms the cornerstone of Palmer's (1991) subsequent reanalysis of figural goodness in terms of symmetry subgroups, to which we now turn.

Symmetry Subgroups. Garner's theory based on R & R subset size is able to account for a large portion of the differences that arise in the goodness ratings of these dot patterns. But notice that this measure lumps together several kinds of qualitatively different structures. For example, consider the three middle rows in Figure 8.3.4. All have exactly four different figures in their R & R subsets, but the first is bilaterally symmetrical about a vertical axis, the second is bilaterally symmetrical about a left diagonal axis, and the third is not bilaterally symmetrical at all. Most people find the vertically symmetrical figure "better" than the other two, and many experimental findings support this fact (e.g., Chipman, 1977; Palmer, 1991; Palmer & Hemenway, 1978; Royer, 1981). Such differences cannot be explained in terms of R & R subsets because such figures have the same number of transformational variants.

A possible solution is suggested by the analysis we just carried out in terms of symmetry structure, however. Each figure can be characterized by the kind of symmetry it possesses, thus differentiating between bilateral symmetry about vertical, horizontal, and diagonal axes. But what about the pattern in the fourth row of Figure 8.3.4, which has no bilateral symmetry? It turns out that such figures have symmetry too, but of a different kind.

In modern mathematics, the analysis of **symmetry** is given in terms of **transformational invariance** (Weyl, 1952). Intuitively, a figure is symmetrical with respect to a given transformation if applying that transformation leaves the figure unchanged. For the standard example of bilateral (or mirror-image) symmetry, the underlying transformation is reflection of the figure about the axis of symmetry. Thus, a vertically symmetric pattern—such as an upright A or T—is the same before and after being reflected about a vertical line through its center. Similarly, a horizontally symmetric pattern—such as an upright C or B—remains the same after being reflected about a horizontal line through its center.

Within this general framework, rotational symmetry has exactly the same form as bilateral symmetry, except that the transformation involved is a central rotation through some specified angle. Thus, patterns that have 180° rotational symmetry (e.g., S, N, and Z) remain the same after being rotated 180° about their centers. This is the symmetry possessed by the dot pattern shown in the fourth row of Figure 8.3.4. Patterns with 90° rotational symmetry—such as a swastika—remain unchanged after being rotated 90° about their centers. (Notice that patterns with two symmetries of reflection (such as H, O, and X) always have 180° rotational symmetry as well.)

The **symmetry subgroup** of a given figure can therefore be characterized as the subset of spatial transformations that leave it invariant. Simply apply each transformation to the figure and include in its symmetry subgroup just the ones that leave it unchanged.[5] The

---

[5] It turns out that the subsets so constructed have some special structural properties whose effect is that not all logically possible subsets of transformations can be symmetry subsets. For instance, a pattern cannot have both vertical and horizontal reflectional symmetry (e.g., an H or an X) without also having 180° rotational symmetry. Similarly, a pattern cannot have 90° rotational symmetry (e.g., a swastika) without also having 180°

and 270° rotational symmetry. This additional structure of symmetry subsets qualifies them as instances of mathematical *groups* and *subgroups* rather than sets and subsets. (Technical descriptions of these properties of groups and subgroups can be found in Weyl (1952) or any textbook on abstract algebra.)

Representing Shape and Structure

rightmost column of Figure 8.3.4 shows the symmetry subgroups for Garner's five-dot patterns. Notice that the "better" patterns have more symmetries (i.e., more transformations in their symmetry subgroups) than the "poorer" ones. For this reason, Palmer (1991) proposed that the goodness of a figure be identified with its symmetry subgroup.

Given the close relation between Garner's R & R subsets and Palmer's symmetry subgroups, it is not surprising that their quantitative structure is also closely related. In fact, the number of transformations in a pattern's symmetry subgroup is just the inverse of its R & R subset size with respect to the full set of transformations:

$$R * S = T,$$

where R is the size of the R & R subset, S is the size of the symmetry subgroup, and T is the size of the total group of transformations. This relation makes sense because the two theories differ only by something like a theoretical figure/ground reversal: Garner's focuses on the *patterns* generated by the group of transformations, whereas Palmer's focuses on the *transformations* over which the patterns are invariant.

Despite this close relation, there are important advantages to the analysis in terms of symmetry subgroups. The crucial difference is that the elements in symmetry subgroups come from a fixed set of transformations, which are the same for all possible figures. Symmetry subgroups can therefore be compared directly across different figures for possible effects of the identity of transformations in the subgroup. This is not possible with R & R subsets because the elements of the subsets are figures, which cannot be meaningfully compared across different figures. Only the number of figures in R & R subsets can be compared across figures. That is why the three middle patterns in Figure 8.3.4 have the same R & R subset size—and the same number of symmetries—but different transformations in their symmetry subgroups. Because differential weightings for different forms of symmetry are needed to account for ratings of goodness, Palmer (1991) argues that symmetry subgroups are preferable to R & R subsets as a theory of figural goodness.

8.3.2 Structural Information Theory

With this background, we can now examine the theory of shape representation that relies most heavily on the Gestalt concepts of figural goodness and Prägnanz. This theory—initially called **coding theory** and later **structural information theory**—was formulated by the Dutch psychologist Emanuel Leeuwenberg (1971) and later extended in collaboration with his colleagues, Hans Buffart and others (e.g., Buffart & Leeuwenberg, 1981; Van der Helm & Leeuwenberg, 1991). It provides a method for constructing different shape descriptions of the same object and for relating them to perception via the Gestalt principle of Prägnanz. In this respect it is quite unlike any of the other theories of shape representation that we have considered thus far.

Shape descriptions are derived in structural information theory by generating and then simplifying perceptual descriptions called **codes** that are sufficient to generate the figure. Figural goodness and Prägnanz are then introduced into the theory through a measure called information load. **Information load** is a measure of descriptive complexity that is used to identify the "best" possible code, more or less as advocated in the Gestalt principle of Prägnanz. Leeuwenberg argues that the alternative most observers perceive is the one that has the simplest code (or shape representation) as measured by the lowest information load. Not only does the theory account well for judgments of figural goodness, but it has successfully explained a number of interesting organizational effects discussed in Chapter 6, such as perception of partly occluded objects and transparent objects. The general outline of structural information theory is as follows:

1. Construct a **primitive code** by tracing the contour of the figure and describing it symbolically as a sequence of line segment lengths and the angles between them. (This description is much like generating the figure in the "turtle geometry" computer language, LOGO.)

2. Use a set of **semantic operators** (or **rewrite rules**) to simplify the primitive code by removing as many structural redundancies as possible. The resulting simplified codes are called **reduced codes**.

3. Compute the **information load** of each reduced code by counting the number of parameters (numerical values) it contains. This value corresponds roughly to the figural goodness of the perception that contains the structure specified in the reduced code.

4. The reduced code with the lowest information load, called the **minimum code**, is the one that structural

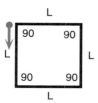

Primitive code: L 90 L 90 L 90 L 90

Reduced code: 4 * (L 90)

Figure 8.3.5 Coding a square in structural information theory. Beginning at the upper left vertex and moving downward, the primitive code is generated by specifying the distance to move directly ahead followed by the angle through which to rotate before the next segment. Reduced codes can then be derived by applying rules to eliminate redundancies.

information theory predicts will be perceived most often. Others may also be perceived with a probability that depends on their information load.

Although these procedures might sound like steps in a computer program, structural information theory is not intended to be a model of the actual processes the visual system carries out in perception. In Marr's terms, it is a computational theory, not an algorithmic one, because it merely describes the relation between input patterns and their possible shape representations, rather than the process by which these outcomes are reached.

Primitive Codes. To understand how structural information theory generates shape descriptions, we will run through the example of coding a square. The square is first converted into a symbol string by selecting a starting position and direction along its contour, as indicated in Figure 8.3.5 by the dot and arrowhead. The symbol string of the primitive *code* then consists of a sequence of numbers representing (1) the length of the line to be drawn in the present direction and (2) the angular adjustments to be made after the previous line segment is drawn. (We will indicate the difference between these two entities by italicizing the length symbols but not the angle symbols.) Thus, the primitive code for a square of side-length *L*, starting from the upper-left corner and heading downward, would be the symbol string:

$L\ 90\ L\ 90\ L\ 90\ L\ 90.$

This code would "draw" the square, ending at the initial position and direction. This code is a special case of the general description for any arbitrary quadrilateral, which can be expressed as

$W\ \text{a}\ X\ \text{b}\ Y\ \text{c}\ Z\ \text{d},$

where W, X, Y, and Z represent the lengths of the four sides and a, b, c, and d represent the sizes of the four angles. By replacing these variables with the appropriate numbers, any of the quadrilaterals in Figure 8.3.3 could be described.

Removing Redundancies. The simpler and more regular quadrilaterals receive simpler descriptions in structural information theory by removing redundancies in the primitive code. For example, the code for the square contains four repetitions of the sequence (L 90). This regularity can be eliminated from the string by applying the *iteration operator*, a rewrite rule that reduces the primitive code to a shorter, simpler string of symbols. The iteration operator replaces a symbol string, S, that consists of n repetitions of a subsequence, X, with the symbol string, $n * X$. The iteration rewrite rule can be specified as follows:

$S \rightarrow n * (X),$

where the arrow symbol, $\rightarrow$, is read "is rewritten as." In the case of the description of the square, this means that the primitive code can be rewritten as the reduced code

$L\ 90\ L\ 90\ L\ 90\ L\ 90 \rightarrow 4 * (L\ 90).$

This code corresponds to perceiving the 90° rotational symmetry of the square, but not its bilateral symmetries.

There are several different semantic operators (or rewrite rules) in structural information theory that allow complexity in symbol-strings to be reduced. The three most important are as follows:

1. *Iteration*: The iteration operator eliminates repeated sequences and replaces them with a parameter, n, that indicates the number of iterations and a specification of the repeated substring:

$S \rightarrow n * (X).$

An example of its application would be the following:

$a\ b\ c\ a\ b\ c\ a\ b\ c \rightarrow 3 * (a\ b\ c).$

2. *Symmetry*: The symmetry operator eliminates mirror-image symmetry in sequences and replaces it by a

Representing Shape and Structure

symbol, *SYM*, indicating the symmetry operation and the substring to which it is applied:

$$S \rightarrow SYM \, (X).$$

Its use can be illustrated in the following example:

$$a \, b \, c \, c \, b \, a \rightarrow SYM \, (a \, b \, c).$$

3. *Distribution:* The distribution operator eliminates the alternation between one substring and a series of other substrings and replaces it with a pair of substrings in angle brackets indicating the two substrings to be interleaved:

$$S \rightarrow \langle X \rangle \langle Y \rangle.$$

An example would be the following reduction:

$$a \, b \, a \, c \, a \, d \rightarrow \langle a \rangle \langle b \, c \, d \rangle.$$

The rules are actually a bit more complex than this, and further operators can be introduced, but these provide the most basic set (Van der Helm & Leeuwenberg, 1991). Using them, one can understand how structural information theory eliminates the most frequently occurring forms of redundancy in primitive codes.

Information Load. Intuitively, the simplicity or "goodness" of a reduced code corresponds to the informational compactness of its description, since the rewrite rules allow very long strings to be rewritten as much shorter ones. Formally, goodness can be defined in terms of structural information theory's measure of the information load of a particular code string, denoted $I(S)$, which is the number of parameters the description contains. In the case of the primitive code for the square, the information load is 8, one unit for each length and one unit for each angle encountered in its description. In the case of the reduced code, $4 * (L \, 90)$, the information load is 3: one for the number of iterations (4), one for the length (L), and one for the angle size (90). Thus, this reduced code is much simpler than the primitive code, and it corresponds to a "better" percept in the Gestalt sense because it reflects the perception of regularity in the form of rotational symmetry. But is this reduced code the simplest of all possible codings for the square? This is an important question because, consistent with the Gestalt principle of Prägnanz, structural information theory proposes that the percept that is most likely to be perceived is the one with the lowest information load.[6]

There are many other codings for a square that correspond to seeing different aspects of its structure. As we noted earlier, the code $(4 * (L \, 90))$ explicitly encodes the 90° rotational symmetry of a square, but it does not capture the most salient of its global properties: its fourfold reflectional symmetries. These can be captured by a different coding, however. To see how such a description can be generated, begin at the center of one side and code the sides as two adjacent segments of length $L/2$ and the angles as two adjacent rotations of 45°. This primitive code would then be

$$L/2 \, 45 \, 45 \, L/2 \, L/2 \, 45 \, 45 \, L/2 \, L/2 \, 45 \, 45$$
$$L/2 \, L/2 \, 45 \, 45 \, L/2.$$

Although this primitive code is actually longer than the one we considered initially, it can be recoded into an even simpler reduced code by three embedded applications of the symmetry operator:

$$(SYM \, (SYM \, (SYM \, (L/2 \, 45)))).$$

This description has an information load of just 2: one for the length parameter, $L/2$, and other for the angle parameter, 45°. (The symmetry operator itself, *SYM*, does not count in the information load because there is no parameter associated with it. The iteration operator, in contrast, requires an extra parameter for the number of iterations to be performed.) In fact, the reduced code specifying the reflectional symmetries of a square is its minimum code, and it corresponds well with the bilateral symmetries most people perceive in a square.

Structural information theory can be applied to the different quadrilaterals in Figure 8.3.3 to predict the figural goodness of each. The information load of the minimum code for each of the figures is shown below it. The square has the lowest information load (2), followed by the rectangle and rhombus (4), followed by the parallelogram (5), the trapezoid (6), and finally the irregular

---

[6] Actually, structural information theory is slightly more complex, suggesting that the probability of perceiving any particular interpretation is a function of the ratio between that information load and those of alternative interpretations. We will not be concerned with this added complexity here, although it can be important in predicting quantitative patterns of empirical results.

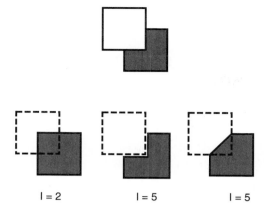

Figure 8.3.6 Explaining visual completion within structural information theory. The figure at the top is generally perceived as a dark square behind a light one. Structural information theory explains the shape of the completed square because it has the lowest information load of any alternative consistent with the stimulus.

quadrilateral (8). This ordering of information load thus corresponds well with the ordering of perceived goodness for these figures.

Applications to Perceptual Organization. Structural information theory has been used not only to account for perceived figural goodness of shapes, but also to explain perceptual organization in a number of potentially ambiguous situations, such as completion of partly occluded figures and transparency (e.g., Buffart, Leeuwenberg, & Restle, 1981). We will examine the case of one square partly occluding another (see Figure 8.3.6) to illustrate how it accounts for visual completion. First, we will consider three of the possible perceptual interpretations of this image: the usual one consisting of one square behind another, the mosaic interpretation consisting of a square abutting a backward L-shaped figure, and a third interpretation of a square with a corner cut off, as illustrated in Figure 8.3.6. The code for the white square in the upper left position is the same in all three cases, so we can safely ignore it and concentrate on the codes for the alternative completions of the dark figure in the lower right position.

As shown in Figure 8.3.6, the minimum code for the square has a lower information load than that for either the L shape or the cornerless square. Thus, structural information theory is able to predict the fact that people

perceive this image as a partly occluded square rather than either of the other two alternatives. It does so because the square is a "better" figure (i.e., has a lower information load) than the mosaic shape as well as all possible alternative completions. Interestingly, structural information theory is also able to predict that people will tend to complete the octagons in Figure 6.4.7A but will *not* complete the crosses in Figure 6.4.7B. The reason is that the symmetries of the cross are sufficient to make its minimal code simpler than that of its completed alternative.

Structural information theory is closely related to the three theories of figural goodness mentioned above. Like the information theoretical analysis of Attneave (1953) and Hochberg and McAlister (1953), it identifies "good" figures with efficient descriptions that have had all the redundancies removed. And like both Garner's (1974) R & R subset theory and Palmer's (1991) symmetry subgroup theory, the redundancies it removes from the codes are related to rotational and reflectional symmetries. But structural information theory goes significantly beyond these other theories because it also specifies an actual representation of shape and uses it to predict what people perceive in ambiguous situations.

Strengths. Structural information theory can easily deal with the problem of similarity transformations because the minimum code is independent of the position, size, orientation, and reflection of the figure. These variables are effectively factored out in the starting position, direction, and variable side lengths used in generating the code. Additional strengths are its close connection to figural goodness and its ingenious way of explaining a number of important perceptual phenomena by analyzing the codability of different shape interpretations.

Weaknesses. Despite these virtues, structural information theory faces a number of serious difficulties. Some of the most troublesome are the following:

1. Structural information theory cannot be applied directly to gray-scale images. Like many psychological theories, it works on idealized outline drawings. It therefore requires a front end or preprocessor that reduces gray-scale images to images containing only clean contours, thus eliminating the problem of different input channels.

Representing Shape and Structure

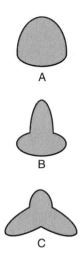

Figure 8.3.7 Part structure. People generally perceive these figures as containing one (A), two (B), and three (C) parts, yet their minimal codes in structural information theory would not reflect this fact.

2. It does not contain any explicit encoding of parts other than simple lines or curves. Concavities and convexities are treated in essentially the same way, for instance, and despite all the structure represented in minimal codes, none of it is related to parts. Figure 8.3.7 illustrates three figures whose different numbers of parts would not be reflected in their minimal codes.

3. It is easy to see how to apply structural information theory to 2-D figures but more difficult for 3-D volumes. The latter can be generated by sweeping 2-D figures along an axis, much as in generalized cylinders, but this kind of algorithm generates a description of the 3-D volume without explaining how the perception of this volume is achieved from a 2-D projection of it.

In addition to these problems, common to most of the shape representations we have discussed, there are several others that are specific to structural information theory. They include the following:

4. The only way to guarantee that the perceived interpretation is the one with the lowest information load is to compare all possible codes. This is seldom easy and in most cases impossible. For example, in the case of the partly occluded square, there are an infinite number of logically possible completions for the square, and they obviously cannot all be computed and compared.

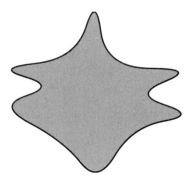

Figure 8.3.8 Approximate symmetry. People spontaneously perceive this figure as being roughly symmetrical about a vertical axis, but this is a difficult fact to explain in structural information theory because of how precisely it codes the shapes of figures.

5. The codes it generates are highly sensitive to noise. Shape is represented very precisely but at the expense of its more perceptually obvious large-scale structure. The approximate symmetry of the shape shown in Figure 8.3.8, for example, cannot be captured by structural information theory using the symmetry operator because its symmetry is imprecise. Even so, most people spontaneously perceive it as being approximately symmetric about its vertical axis.

6. As we mentioned before, structural information theory is not a process theory. That is, it does not specify the actual processes or algorithm the visual system might use to derive the reduced code with the lowest information load. Even more problematic, however, is the fact that there is no known computational method for constructing minimum codes except under very restricted conditions (Van der Helm & Leeuwenberg, 1991). This limits the applicability of the theory rather dramatically.

Even so, structural information theory is the best-defined and most successful extension of Gestalt ideas about figural goodness and Prägnanz to the representation of shape. It is not yet clear whether the problems listed above have good solutions or not. If they do, structural information theory may turn out to be a serious contender as a theory of shape representation.

We have now surveyed a sampling of major theories of shape representation and found none to be without difficulties. Perhaps not surprisingly, the most promising approach appears to be the most complex: encoding shape in terms of hierarchically nested structural descriptions based on some set of shape primitives and object-centered reference frames. But even this scheme has serious problems. In the next chapter we will encounter some of these kinds of shape representations again as part of theories of visual categorization. There is currently a great deal of debate about which approach is most promising for visual recognition of objects, with serious advocates of some variant of almost all the approaches we have just considered.

Suggestions for Further Reading

Palmer, S. E. (1992). Reference frames in the perception of spatial structure. In H. Geissler, S. Link, & J. Townsend (Eds.), *Cognition, information processing, and psychophysics: Basic issues*. Hillsdale, NJ: Erlbaum. This chapter describes the transformational approach to shape equivalence, with particular emphasis on the problem of reference frames and the factors that influence their establishment.

Goldmeier, E. (1936/1972). Similarity in visually perceived forms. *Psychological Issues, 8*, 1–134. This monograph is a beautiful example of a Gestalt inquiry into the difficult problem of shape similarity. Despite its age, it is perhaps the most extensive and best study of the topic.

Pinker, S. (1985). Visual cognition: An introduction. In S. Pinker (Ed.), *Visual cognition*. Cambridge, MA: MIT Press. This chapter reviews several theories of object recognition, with emphasis on different representations of shape.

Garner, W. R. (1974). *The processing of information and structure*. Hillsdale, NJ: Erlbaum. This is a classic monograph in which Garner describes his approach to the perception of structure. The first part of the book explains his theory of figural goodness in terms of rotation and reflection (R & R) subsets. Later parts describe his equally famous work on integral and separable dimensions, discussed in Chapter 11.

Leeuwenberg, E. L. J. (1978). Quantification of certain visual pattern properties: Salience, transparency, and similarity. In E. L. J. Leeuwenberg & H. F. J. M. Buffart (Eds.), *Formal theories of visual perception*. New York: Wiley. This chapter describes the basic idea of structural information theory and applies it to several important perceptual problems.

Perceiving Function and Category

Let us pause for a moment to take stock of what we have learned about spatial vision thus far. First, we considered how spatial information is initially extracted from the 2-D images that have been projected from the environment onto the two retinae (Chapter 4). Next, we examined how these images might be interpreted as arising from surfaces arrayed in 3-D space (Chapter 5). Then we considered how image regions can be organized into hierarchies of parts, objects, and groups (Chapter 6). Finally, we investigated how such objects can be analyzed into their intrinsic properties and parts (Chapter 7), culminating in the representation of the shape of an object (Chapter 8).

In doing so, we have covered a great deal of ground and learned a lot about spatial perception. But we have not yet examined how perception achieves the important goal we attributed to it in Chapter 1: providing the observer with information about the personal utility of objects in its environment. What is still missing from our analysis is any serious consideration of how vision assesses the *function* of the objects being perceived. The goal of this chapter is to consider how that might be achieved.

9.1 The Perception of Function

Visual perception of function enables you to know, simply by looking, what objects in the environment might be useful in reaching your current goals. If you could perceive everything that we have discussed to this point but you were unable to determine the function of the objects around you, you would be in much the same position as if you had suddenly been transported to an alien planet populated with totally unfamiliar objects and organisms. You would be able to perceive their shapes, positions, orientations, colors, and other physical properties perfectly well, so you would be able to navigate through the 3-D environment without falling over or bumping into them. If required, you could even make 3-D models of them, given the requisite materials and sculptural skills. But without some further information, you wouldn't know what to do with them. Which objects are edible, for instance, and which ones are not? Are there any that could be used for or made into clothing? Which would provide effective shelter from the elements? Without perceiving such functional information, even such seemingly basic information as whether you could or should sit on an object would be unclear.

There is an important sense in which all the processes we have discussed thus far are ultimately in the service of perceiving the function of objects, for therein lies the evolutionary utility of vision. In the case of humans, of course, the utility of objects is an enormously complex subject that encompasses the daunting cultural and interpersonal structure of modern society. We will make no attempt to analyze the sociocultural basis of the staggering amount of functional information people learn about familiar objects, but will merely assume its existence. Instead, we will focus on the more perceptually relevant question of how sighted people manage to perceive an object's functional significance by looking.

It is worth mentioning that many classical treatments of perception exclude the apprehension of function from perception proper, discussing it instead as some later process involving associative memory (e.g., Rock, 1975). The reason is that whereas perception of the physical properties of objects has generally been considered possible without prior experience with specific objects, apprehension of function has not. There is undeniably something to this argument, but ignoring the functional component of vision constitutes a serious hole in the explanation of perceptual experience, as the reader can readily appreciate from the alien planet thought experiment. We therefore include the perception of function as a proper—indeed, crucial—subject for vision science.

There are two major theoretical approaches to the visual perception of function, which are schematically diagrammed in Figure 9.1.1.

1. **Affordances.** One is the *direct* or *unmediated* approach advocated by James J. Gibson. He proposed that at least some of the opportunities for action that environmental objects provide to an exploring observer can be perceived directly from their visible structure

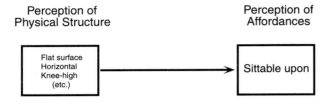

A. DIRECT PERCEPTION OF FUNCTION

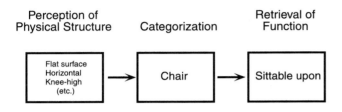

B. MEDIATED PERCEPTION OF FUNCTION

Figure 9.1.1 Direct versus mediated perception of function. Gibson's notion of affordances asserts that certain functions can be perceived directly from visible properties of the object. In the alternative categorization approach, function is retrieved from memory after the object has been categorized.

in the dynamic optic array. He called such functional properties *affordances*.

2. **Categorization.** The other is the *indirect* or *mediated* approach advocated by almost all other perceptual theorists. It assumes that function is perceived by matching the perceived structure of the object with internal representations of known categories of objects. Function is then determined by retrieving associations between the object category and its known uses.[1]

We will first consider Gibson's direct approach to perception of function via affordances because it is the simpler and more basic approach. Very little is known about the perception of affordances, however, largely because almost no effort has been made to study it. There are several reasons for this gap. One is that Gibson died shortly after he began to develop his theory

and therefore had little time to pursue his ideas. Another is that his analysis was unclear in certain respects to be discussed shortly. A third is that the field has been dominated for so long by the categorization approach that the possibility of perceiving affordances has not been given the attention it deserves. Following the brief discussion of affordances, the rest of the chapter will be devoted to an extended examination of object categorization, which forms the backbone of nearly all modern research related to how we perceive function from optical information.

9.1.1 Direct Perception of Affordances

Historically, the traditional approach to the perception of function was categorization in the guise of associationism and unconscious inference. That is, the meaning of an object was thought to be accessed by its visual appearance's activating a category representation that was linked to known uses via associations in memory. This process can be viewed as a kind of inference: This object is a chair; chairs are for sitting upon; therefore, this object is for sitting upon. This view originated with British empiricist philosophers and was later promoted by Helmholtz, Wundt, and their contemporaries.

The first dissenting voice, as usual, came from Gestalt psychologists. They raised the possibility that certain aspects of an object's function could be perceived directly. Kurt Koffka, in one of his more poetic moments, put it like this: "To primitive man, each objects says what it is and what he ought to do with it: a fruit says, 'Eat me'; water says, 'Drink me', thunder says, 'Fear me,' and woman says, 'Love me' " (Koffka, 1935, p. 7). Gestaltists called this idea that certain objects reveal their significance to an observer in a particularly immediate way the **physiognomic character** of perception. Unfortunately, they did not elaborate on this idea, and it lay dormant for decades until Gibson (1979) revived and extended it in the guise of his doctrine of affordances.

Affordances can be understood as opportunities for action or interaction provided by objects to an organism

---

[1] Logically speaking, perception of function and categorization are independent of one another. One can perceive that an object is throwable, for instance, without knowing that it is a widget. Conversely, one can know that an object is a widget without necessarily knowing what it is for. In practice, however, knowing how to categorize an object generally implies knowing what it is for, as well as where it is likely to be found and a host of other things.

that can perceive them directly.[2] Gibson claimed, for example, that one can see whether an object affords being grasped, sat upon, walked upon, or used for cutting without first categorizing it as, say, a baseball, a chair, a floor, or a knife. Indeed, despite the importance of such functional properties for active creatures like us, we don't even have standard categories or simple linguistic expressions for objects defined by most affordances. They can be referred to only by phrases such as "things that can be grasped," "things that can be sat upon," and so on. Chairs can be sat upon, of course, but so can lots of other things that are not chairs, including logs, beds, stumps, low tables, and a host of other relatively sturdy objects that have the appropriate functional features: an approximately level surface at about knee height that will comfortably accommodate the perceiver's buttocks and support his or her weight.

Two important conditions underlie direct perception of most Gibsonian affordances:

1. *Functional form.* The relation between an object's form and its affordance (the function it offers) must be "transparent" enough that the relevant properties are visible. That is, some combination of visible properties should be sufficient to determine whether it has a given affordance, such as the height, stability, and level top for the affordance of being "sittable-upon." Affordances, therefore, cannot be arbitrarily related to object structure: Function must follow from form.

2. *Observer relativity.* Affordances are functional properties of objects in relation to the observer: They are the opportunities for interaction that the object affords to the perceiving organism. The same stump that affords sitting to an adult, for example, would not afford sitting to a small child, although it might afford climbing to the child and not to the adult.

Following Neisser (1989), we will call functional properties that conform to both these conditions **physical affordances** to convey the fit between their physical structure and their functional utility. It is because of this fit that their function can potentially be perceived di-

Figure 9.1.2 Objects with similar structure but different functions. Mailboxes afford letter mailing, whereas trash cans do not, even though they have many similar physical features, such as size, location, and presence of an opening large enough to insert letters and medium-sized packages.

rectly from information in the optic array, for it is the object's physical structure that enables these functions.

Not all the affordances Gibson discussed conform to this mold, however. He also claimed that apples afford eating, that pencils afford writing, and that mailboxes afford mailing letters (Gibson, 1979). None of these functions appears to be available solely from visible information, however. Consider the mailbox example. Although mailboxes might be perceived as having the complex physical affordance of allowing envelopes and small packages to be inserted into them, much more than this is required for such actions to result in letter mailing. Many trash cans, for instance, are the right size and have openings that are appropriately shaped for depositing envelopes and small packages (see Figure 9.1.2), but inserting such items into trash cans does not result

---

[2] In this case, "directly" means without mediation by activating an association or by unconscious inference through the intermediary of a category representation. It does not necessarily mean through *direct perception* as dis-

cussed in Section 2.1.3, although the two meanings are certainly related in that both come from Gibson's ecological theory.

in mailing for reasons having little to do with the cans' visible structure. For mailboxes to afford mailing, postal service employees must remove objects from the box and deliver them to the post office on a regular basis—rather than to the dump, as is typically the case for the contents of trash cans. This property of mailboxes cannot possibly be perceived from their projected optical structure without the mediation of associations stored in memory, at least to the present author's way of thinking. Such functions may indeed be perceived via associations, but they are not physical affordances as defined above.

The perception of physical affordances can be direct in the precise sense that they do not require mediation through categorization. An observer can determine whether an object is sittable-upon without first classifying it as a chair or sofa, for example. Calling it "direct," however, does not mean that it is error-free. Affordances can be misperceived whenever nonvisual information carries information that is at odds with the visual information. A wooden bench or log might *look* eminently sittable-upon, but if it is sufficiently rotten, it will not afford sitting to a normal adult. Similarly, a baseball might look as though it affords throwing, but if it has been super-glued to the table, it will not, in fact, be throwable.

Physical affordances are the only ones for which a sensible case can be made that perception of function is direct in the sense of not requiring mediation by categorization. They would therefore be the only functions that were perceivable in novel objects on an alien planet. You would probably not have too much difficulty perceiving which surfaces were walk-on-able, which objects were throwable, and which ones were sit-on-able even though you had never seen them before. They are unquestionably important for an organism's survival, because many of them concern critical behavioral possibilities for locomotion, support, manipulation, and other forms of basic physical interaction with the immediate environment.

Neisser (1989) has gone beyond Gibson's analysis of function by suggesting that affordances and categorization are such fundamentally different modes of perceiving that they are accomplished by different neural systems in the brain. Recall that in Chapter 1 we made a distinction between the "what" and "where" systems in visual cortex. Ungerleider and Mishkin (1982) suggested

that that the ventral "what" system leads from visual cortex toward the infratemporal cortex and the dorsal "where" system leads from visual cortex toward the posterior parietal cortex. Neisser (1989) has conjectured that the dorsal system underlies Gibsonian ecological perception: the pickup of information about surface layout and object affordances in an organism that is actively exploring its environment. The "what" system, he believes, underlies recognition and categorization, both of which require accessing internal representations of categories in memory. The "where" system, he suggests, is a system for direct perception, unmediated by memory for known categories of objects.

Neisser's suggestion is consonant with Goodale and Milner's recent reinterpretation of the two-visual-systems hypothesis in terms of "what" versus "how" systems (Goodale, 1995; Milner & Goodale, 1995). They identify the ventral system as the neural substrate of conscious visual perception, aimed at identifying objects for the purpose of high-level planning of voluntary actions. The dorsal system, they claim, is a parallel visual system for executing voluntary actions on-line, such as grasping, moving, and releasing objects in well-practiced visually guided tasks. They further claim that this action-oriented system is not necessarily conscious and can function even if the ventral perceptual system is damaged.

As evidence for their view, Milner and Goodale (1995) report the case of a patient, D.F., whose ventral system was damaged but whose dorsal system was intact. She performed nearly at chance in simple perceptual tasks such as matching two rectangles for shape, reporting the orientation of lines, and indicating the size of objects. The surprising fact is that despite these seemingly debilitating deficits in conscious, reportable perceptions, she was able to perform simple visually guided motor tasks with precision and ease. For example, she could insert a letter-shaped object into a slot at any particular orientation as well as normal controls and could smoothly and accurately adjust the separation of her fingers while reaching to grasp objects of different sizes. Patients with damage to the dorsal action-based system typically have the opposite pattern of abilities. They can make accurate perceptual judgments but have problems controlling actions that require visual feedback. Such observations are broadly consistent with the possibility that the dorsal system may be involved with perceiving simple physical affordances of objects and carrying out appropriate actions under visual control.

However useful and important the perception of affordances may be, it cannot account for all the functional information that we perceive about objects. In particular, the first condition of functional form excludes objects whose function cannot be determined directly from their physical properties without additional information from past experience. This includes some of the cases Gibson discussed in terms of affordances (e.g., eating via apples, writing via pencils, and mailing via mailboxes) as well as many human artifacts whose functions are visually obscure. Video cassette recorders (VCRs), compact disk players, and stereo receivers, for instance, have shapes that are about as unrevealing of their function as they could possibly be. The same problem arises, although less compellingly, for many other human-made objects, such as lamps, clocks, musical instruments, books, stoves, and refrigerators. Although we might be able to figure out their functions after extended viewing and interaction if we didn't know them already, vision enables us to short-circuit this process of exploration and discovery via accessing associations stored in memory. It is for this reason that the categorization approach to perceiving function is both necessary and important.

9.1.2 Indirect Perception of Function by Categorization

As mentioned above, categorization requires first perceiving the intrinsic properties of an object to determine that it is a member of a certain class of objects and then retrieving the function of that class from memory. Notice that there are virtually no constraints on what functional information about an object can be apprehended in this way. Anything is possible because the link between the object's category and its function is potentially arbitrary, depending only on associations established by prior experiences.

One can ask whether affordances or categorization provides the better account of human perception of function. In all likelihood, both are used, but for somewhat different purposes in complex tasks that include perceiving, planning, and acting. It seems exceedingly unlikely (though logically possible) that we categorize everything in our visual fields. Even so, much of what we need to know about our immediate environment for purposes of locomotion and basic motor control is contained in their affordances: whether the ground plane is flat enough to walk on, whether something needs to be avoided in getting from here to there, and whether a given object can be manipulated manually or by other bodily movements. For more complex goal-directed tasks, such as beating an egg as part of making a cake, attended objects are categorized almost effortlessly, incorporated in plans for voluntary action, and then used in the prescribed fashion, quite possibly in ways that involve the on-line assessment of simpler affordances, such as how to grasp the bowl and fork in beating the egg. In practice, the distinction between affordances and categorization is further blurred because the relation between form and function of objects can vary from very strong (e.g., sittable objects) to very weak (e.g., VCRs), with many intermediate gradations. Both affordances and categorization are thus likely to be important in everyday perception.

Four Components of Categorization. Given that one often categorizes objects into known, functional classes, how might that goal be accomplished? There are a very large number of possibilities, but all of them require the following four basic components:

1. *Object representations.* The relevant characteristics of the to-be-categorized object must be perceived and represented within the visual system.

2. *Category representations.* Each of the set of possible categories must be represented in memory in a way that is accessible to the visual system.

3. *Comparison processes.* There must be some way in which the object representation is matched or compared against possible category representations.

4. *Decision processes.* There must be some method for deciding, on the basis of results of comparison processes, to which category a given object belongs.

We have already discussed the problem of representing object properties extensively in Chapters 7 and 8. Shape is the single most important type of information for categorization (Biederman & Ju, 1988), although other properties such as texture, color, size, and orientation are also relevant. As discussed in Chapter 8, templates, Fourier spectra, feature lists, and structural descriptions are the main classes of shape representations, various hybrids also being possible. Next we will consider a few possibilities concerning the nature of the comparison and decision processes involved. Together with the kinds of shape representations, these considerations will give us some idea of the scope of possible theories of object categorization.

Comparison Processes. The comparison process requires matching the object representation to the category representation. For this to happen, the object and category representations must be of the same *type*, although their specific content may (and usually does) differ. In other words, the object representation might be a template, a feature list, a structural description, or some as-yet-unknown alternative, but whatever it is, the category representation must be of the same kind so they can be matched. Trying to compare a template and a feature list, for instance, is futile. The only ways it could be accomplished is by processes that essentially convert the template into a feature list that can then be compared with the other feature list, convert the feature list into a template that can then be compared with the other template, or convert both representations into a third possibility that can then be compared with each other. In every case, however, the comparison is between two representations of the same kind.

One major issue concerning the comparison process is whether it takes place serially (sequentially) or in parallel (simultaneously). This question arises in two quite different forms:

1. *Comparing representations across categories.* The first question is whether the process of matching a given object representation to the set of all category representations takes place serially or in parallel.

The relevant question here is whether the object representation is matched to just one category representation at a time or is matched simultaneously to all possible categories. Given the large number of object categories people know about—estimated by one theorist to be about 30,000 (Biederman, 1987)—it seems virtually certain that categories are matched in parallel. Otherwise, categorization would take too long to be useful; the lion would have eaten you long before you figured out that it was a lion.

2. *Comparing elements within a representation.* Assuming that each object representation consists of multiple elements (features, dimensions, parts, or whatever), the second question concerns whether these elements are matched to a given category representation one at a time (serially) or all at once (in parallel).

Consider a feature list representation, for example. If the representation of the category in question contains, say, 20 features, does it take twice as long to match to the object as another category that has only 10 features, as would be predicted by a serial comparison process? Or do they take the same amount of time, as would be predicted by a parallel comparison process? Or is there some other outcome? The answers to these questions are far from obvious.

Decision Processes. The final step in categorization is making a decision about the category to which the current object belongs. This decision is based, explicitly or implicitly, on the outcome of the comparison process between the object representation and one or more category representations. Let us assume that each comparison can be specified in terms of a single number that represents the degree of fit or similarity of the object representation to the category representation. There will be one number for each category that indicates how well the object representation matches the category representation. Once these values have been determined, the decision process can be cast in terms of how these numbers can be used to choose the right category.

There are two important problems that must be considered in choosing an appropriate decision process:

1. *Novelty.* The novelty problem is that we sometimes see objects that are not members of any known category. They are simply instances of unknown categories and are usually perceived as such. Figure 9.1.3 shows one example. The decision rule should be able, in principle, to recognize that an object is novel so that a new category can be established for it rather than incorrectly assigning it to a known category.

2. *Uniqueness.* The problem of uniqueness is that because many object categories are mutually exclusive (i.e., have no members in common), each object is a member of just one of them. Something can't simultaneously be a dog and a cat, for example, or a chair and a sofa. Ideally, the decision process should allow this fact

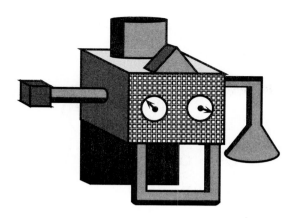

Figure 9.1.3 An unfamiliar object that illustrates the novelty problem. Sometimes we perceive an object that we do not recognize as belonging to any known category.

about object categories to be reflected in categorization performance.

It should be noted that an object can be correctly identified as a member of several different categories, such as a particular car being a Corvette, a sports car, a car, a vehicle, a machine, and a human artifact. These are not failures of categorical uniqueness as we have defined it, however, because these are not mutually exclusive categories, but nested or overlapping ones. We will have more to say about the hierarchical structure of categories shortly.

Assuming for the sake of argument that we have measures of how well the to-be-categorized object fits each known category, there are two classical approaches to making decisions about which category it belongs to: *threshold rules* and *maximum (or best-fit) rules*. They turn out to have complementary virtues and drawbacks with respect to the problems of novelty and uniqueness.

1. **Threshold rules.** The threshold approach is to set a criterial value on the outcome of the comparison process and to assign the currently processed object to whatever category, if any, exceeds that value.

Threshold rules are, in principle, able to recognize novelty, for if no category exceeds the threshold, the system can decide that the object represents a new type and act accordingly. Its major drawback is the potential failure of uniqueness, since more than one category may exceed the threshold at the same time. Threshold rules can therefore result in multiple classifications among

mutually exclusive categories. For example, there is no way to ensure that something won't be perceived as both a dog and a wolf at the same time.

2. **Maximum (best-fit) rules.** The maximum approach is to choose whatever category has the highest value (best fit) among all possible categories.

Maximum rules necessarily assign objects to categories uniquely, for it is nearly impossible that more than one category will have the same maximum value at any given time. They cannot recognize novelty, however, because there is, by definition, always one category that has the highest similarity to the incoming object. A maximum rule therefore always assigns the object to the best-fitting category, no matter how bad the fit may be.

The virtues of both decision rules can be combined—with the drawbacks of neither—by using a hybrid decision rule that we will call the *maximum-over-threshold rule*.

3. **Maximum-over-threshold rule.** This approach is to set a threshold below which objects will be perceived as novel but above which the category with the highest value is chosen. This combination allows for the possibility of identifying objects as novel without resulting in ambiguity when many categories exceed the threshold.

It is worth mentioning that the decision process need not be a little "man-in-the-head" (or **homunculus**) who examines the output of comparison processes and "decides" whether a given value is over the threshold or which one is the maximum. It is quite possible—indeed, desirable—that the decision is an entirely mechanistic process. For example, a winner-take-all connectionist network, consisting of units that all mutually inhibit each other, is one algorithm for achieving a maximum rule. The unit with the highest activation will inhibit all the other units more than they inhibit it and thereby eventually become the only unit with a substantial amount of activation (see Section 6.5). The inhibitory interactions among the units effectively "decide" which unit is the most active without the help of any sort of homunculus.

We have now examined a number of possible kinds of theories of object categorization: different representational aspects in Chapter 8 and different comparison and decision aspects in this chapter. Within these bounds lie a huge number of possible theories whose

Perceiving Function and Category

characteristics need to be explored in terms of their ability to account for the phenomena of human perceptual categorization. Toward this end, we will now consider some of the most important of these phenomena. We will then consider a small sample of theories of object categorization and explore how they might explain such phenomena.

9.2 Phenomena of Perceptual Categorization

Theories are intended to explain a set of facts. By comparing the predictions of various theories with these facts, one can identify their inadequacies and revise them in ways that, it is hoped, will improve their explanatory power. In the case of perceptual categorization, some of the facts that require explanation arise from the structure of human categories themselves, and others arise from measuring aspects of human performance in categorization tasks. Both are important in arriving at a viable theory of visual categorization.

9.2.1 Categorical Hierarchies

The first fact that must be considered about categorizing objects is that although we typically think of objects as belonging to just one category—something is either a dog or a house or a tree or a book—objects *can* be members of more than one category. Lassie is a dog, to be sure, but also a collie, a mammal, an animal, a living thing, a pet, a TV star, and so on. The categories of human perception and cognition are complex entities with various structural relations among them. Careful analysis of these relations provides important information for understanding perceptual categorization.

Perhaps the most basic fact about categorical structure is that it is largely hierarchical. One way of representing hierarchical structure is by trees, as indicated in Figure 9.2.1A. Nodes in the tree stand for classes of objects. Higher nodes stand for larger classes, and lower nodes stand for smaller classes, with individual objects at the terminal nodes at the bottom. The "vertical" structure of the tree indicates, for example, that all collies are dogs and that all dogs are animals. The "horizontal" structure of the tree indicates that there may be many different subcategories within a given category. Dogs include beagles, boxers, dachshunds, golden retrievers, and

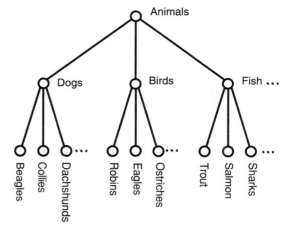

A. Hierarchical Tree Representation

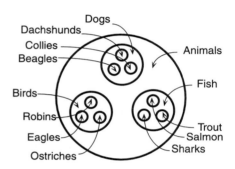

B. Venn Diagram Representation

Figure 9.2.1 Two representations of hierarchical structure in categories. Tree representations of categories (A) represent hierarchy in terms of nodes in a network, in which higher nodes encompass all lower nodes to which they are connected. Venn diagrams (B) represent hierarchies by the nesting of bounded areas of space, such that circles encompass all smaller circles that lie completely inside them.

so forth, in addition to collies; and animals include cats, monkeys, birds, fish, and so forth, in addition to dogs.

Another way of representing hierarchical category structure is in terms of **Venn diagrams** of their relations as sets of exemplars, as shown in Figure 9.2.1B. Venn diagrams depict categories as bounded areas, as though the boundaries enclosed all members of that category. The fact that all dogs are animals is represented by the fact that the circle corresponding to dogs is completely contained within the circle corresponding to animals. The hierarchical structure of categories is therefore captured by the nesting of regions. Either

Venn diagrams or tree structures can thus be used to capture the hierarchical structure of object categories.

Prototypes. One of the most fundamental questions about the nature of human categorization concerns the status of different exemplars with respect to the category. Not all dogs look alike, nor do all birds, nor all cars. How should the variation among exemplars of a given category be understood? This issue goes to the very heart of object classification for it is fundamentally concerned with how categories are defined in terms of perceptual representations.

The classical answer to the question of how categories are defined came from Aristotle's influential analysis. He suggested that a category was designated by a set of rules that specified the **necessary and sufficient conditions** for membership in that category, that is, a list of properties that an object must have to be counted as a member of that category. The geometrical category of triangles provides a good example. To be a triangle, a figure must be a closed polygon with exactly three straight lines as sides. Each of these two properties alone is a *necessary* condition for something to be a triangle because all triangles have them. Each feature alone is not *sufficient*, however, because there are other figures that are closed polygons (e.g., squares) or that have three straight lines (e.g., an arrow) that are not triangles. Together, however, they are sufficient conditions because any object that has both of them must be a triangle.

If a category can be defined by a set of necessary and sufficient conditions, it implies a simple binary conception of category membership. In the case of triangles, for example, either something is a triangle or it is not; there is no middle ground. This aspect of the classical view of categories can be illustrated by using Venn diagrams. All triangles can be represented by the shaded region labeled "triangles" in Figure 9.2.2 because containment within a closed boundary is a binary relation: Each point is either inside or outside a given boundary. Relations among categories can then be represented by the overlap of areas in a Venn diagram. Figure 9.2.2 shows how the category of triangles relates to the category of closed polygons and that of figures containing three lines. As required by the definition in terms of necessary and sufficient conditions, triangles are the intersection of these two larger sets.

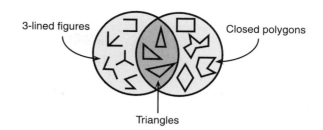

Figure 9.2.2 Defining categories in terms of necessary and sufficient conditions. Triangles are the intersection of the set of all three-lined figures and the set of all closed polygons, as indicated by the darker region of overlap in this Venn diagram.

From a logical, mathematical point of view, the Aristotelian approach to categories is unassailable. Indeed, it is the foundation of formal reasoning about logical classes. But is it a good theory about how natural perceptual categories—in contrast to logical, mathematical ones such as triangles—are represented in people's minds? Can dogs, fish, chairs, trees, and the like be characterized in terms of lists of necessary and sufficient conditions and binary category membership?

For many years, the answer to this question was assumed to be "yes," mainly because there seemed to be no obvious alternative. But the celebrated philosopher Ludwig Wittgenstein (1953) criticized this view and showed that it was fatally flawed for real-world categories. What, he asked, are the necessary and sufficient features common to all games? He argued persuasively that there is no such set of features and that the same arguments apply to most natural categories. As a more appropriate alternative, Wittgenstein pointed to the notion of family resemblances. The faces of members of the same family are often recognizable as such, not because they all have any set of particular features in common, but because they are globally similar in ways that cannot be captured by simple logical rules.

Following Wittgenstein's lead, psychologist Eleanor Rosch of the University of California at Berkeley demonstrated the problems with the Aristotelian approach in a series of elegant and influential studies published in the 1970s (e.g., Rosch, 1973b, 1975a, 1975b; Rosch & Merris, 1975). Her findings radically changed the way cognitive scientists think about the nature of human categorization in many domains, including vision. In Chapter 3, we discussed her early studies of the structure of color categories. They demonstrated the impor-

Perceiving Function and Category

tance of ideal examples in color categorization, called *focal colors* in Berlin and Kay's (1969) seminal study of basic color terms. Further studies by Rosch in other domains led her to suggest that *all* natural categories might be structured in a similar way, that is, in terms of a central or ideal example, which she called a **prototype**.

The basic idea underlying prototype theories of categorization is that prototypes represent each category in terms of a best example. In most cases, the prototype for a category is an "average" member. The prototypical dog, for example, would be the "doggiest" possible dog: probably a "mutt" rather than a pure-bred dog, about average in size, having standard coloring, and the usual doggy sort of shape. In other cases, the prototype is an "ideal" example, such are found in focal colors. The prototypical red is the purest, most saturated, reddest possible red rather than the average of all red examples. In both cases, the prototype plays a privileged role in categorization.

The prototype view of category structure that emerged from Rosch's work differs from the classical Aristotelian view in two crucial respects:

1. *Rule-based versus instance-based representation.* Prototype theories of category representation are defined in terms of a relatively specific instance within each category (the prototype) rather than in terms of a set of logical rules based on lists of necessary and sufficient conditions.

2. *Binary versus graded membership.* Prototype theories allow for continuous gradations (or degrees) of membership in a category rather than the binary distinction between membership and nonmembership in the Aristotelian conception.

We encountered the binary versus graded membership issue in Chapter 3 when we discussed color categories. There we described the difference between classical set theory, which assumes a strictly binary distinction between members and nonmembers of a set, and fuzzy set theory, which assumes the existence of continuous gradations of set membership (Zadeh, 1965). Prototype theories of categorization are thus closely allied with fuzzy set formulations of perceptual categorization.

Rosch tested several implications of her theory of prototype structure for natural categories (Rosch, 1975b). She reasoned, for example, that objects should vary systematically in their "goodness" as examples of a category. When subjects were asked to rate various members of a category, such as dogs, in terms of how "good" or "typical" they were as examples, they rated beagles quite high and Saint Bernards and chihuahuas quite low. Similarly, subjects strongly agreed that robins and sparrows are good examples of birds and that ostriches and penguins are bad ones. These **typicality** (or **goodness-of-example**) **ratings** turned out to predict how quickly subjects were able to respond "true" or "false" to verbal statements such as "A robin is a bird" versus "A penguin is a bird." Later experiments showed that pictures of good examples of categories can similarly be perceptually categorized more quickly than bad ones (Ober-Thompkins, 1982). That is, it takes longer to verify that a picture of a penguin depicts an example of a bird than that a picture of a robin does. Therefore, the time required to classify an object as a member of a category depends on how "good" it is as an example of that category.

Basic-Level Categories. Rosch's discovery of prototypes and their importance for human categorization showed for the first time that there is significant structure in the categorical hierarchy that is not captured by classical Aristotelian ideas. Within the hierarchical tree representation of categories, typicality concerns what we have called the "horizontal" dimension of categorization. Rosch's findings about prototypes and typicality then led her to investigate the "vertical" dimension as well. For example, when a given object (say, Lassie) is categorized, at which vertical level of the hierarchy does this process occur? At the lowest, most specific level, as a collie, or perhaps even as Lassie? At the highest, most general level, as a living thing or perhaps even as a concrete physical object? Or at some intermediate level, as a dog?

The answer appears to be that most people recognize objects first at an intermediate level in the categorical hierarchy. Lassie, for instance, would first be categorized as a dog by most people, rather than as an animal or as a collie. Rosch called categories at this level of abstraction **basic-level categories**. She called categories above the basic level **superordinate categories** and those below the basic level **subordinate categories**.

Rosch originally defined basic-level categories in terms of three different criteria: shape similarity, similar motor interactions, and common attributes (Rosch, Mervis, Gray, Johnson, & Boyes-Braem, 1976).

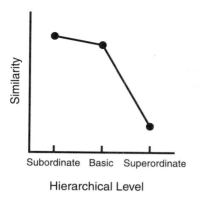

Figure 9.2.3 Defining basic-level categories by similarity. Similarity declines only slightly going from subordinate to basic-level categories (e.g., from collies to dogs) and then drops dramatically from basic-level to superordinate-level categories (e.g., from dogs to animals).

1. *Similar shape.* Basic-level categories are the highest-level categories for which their members have similar shapes.

All dogs, for example, have roughly the same shape; the same is true within the categories of fish, birds, horses, and so forth. Members of subordinate categories (such as collies, poodles, trout, bass, robins, and pigeons) have even more similar shapes, of course, but members of the superordinate category (animals) have a very wide variety of different shapes. Thus, if one plots the degree of shape similarity within a category as a function of its level in the categorical hierarchy, as shown in Figure 9.2.3, there would be a dramatic decrease between the basic and the superordinate levels.

Rosch and her colleagues tested an interesting implication of this claim. They reasoned that if the shapes of members of basic-level categories were "averaged" by finding the average outline of many different dogs—as seen from a canonical viewpoint, in a canonical size, orientation, and so on—the resulting shape would still be recognizable as a member of the category. However, if the average shape were derived in the same way from members of a superordinate category (e.g., many different kinds of animals), the resulting outline shape would be unrecognizable. The results confirmed this prediction.

2. *Similar motor interactions.* Basic-level categories are the highest-level categories for which people interact with its members using similar motor sequences.

Consider the movements you would make in playing a piano, for instance, versus a clarinet or a guitar, each of which is a basic-level category within the superordinate category of musical instruments. There are a few common movements at the superordinate level, such as moving the fingers on particular parts of the instruments, but by far the majority of similarities in motor interaction occur at the basic level. You play an upright piano the same way you do a grand piano, for instance, but very differently from how you play a guitar. The similarity is even greater in how people interact with different members of subordinate categories, but only by a slim margin, such as how the top is raised on upright versus grand pianos. If one were to plot the degree of similarity in motor interactions as a function of level in the categorical hierarchy, there would be a rapid drop between the basic and superordinate levels, as indicated in Figure 9.2.3.

3. *Common attributes.* Basic-level categories are the highest categories for which there are significant numbers of attributes in common between pairs of members.

The first two criteria (similar shapes and similar motor interactions) can actually be considered special cases of the more general criterion of common attributes, since shape and motor interactions are just two very important attributes of objects and how we use them. The same general pattern holds when any possible attributes of members are listed, including high-level conceptual ones: There is a steep decline in the number of common attributes between the basic and superordinate levels, as illustrated in Figure 9.2.3.

Of these definitions of basic-level categories, the one in terms of shape similarity is clearly the most relevant to the problem of perceptual classification. Rosch and her colleagues initially found that most objects were initially recognized as instances of their basic-level category (Rosch et al., 1976). Later research, however, has shown the matter to be somewhat more complex.

Entry-Level Categories. Jolicoeur, Gluck, and Kosslyn (1984) performed a series of experiments aimed at studying perceptual classification at basic, subordinate, and superordinate levels. In one experiment, they simply had subjects name a wide variety of pictures with the first verbal label that came to mind. They found strong support for the idea that *typical* members of basic-level

Perceiving Function and Category

categories are indeed named at the basic level, as expected from Rosch's theory. However, *atypical* members tend to be classified at a subordinate level. For instance, most people who are faced with naming a robin would call it a bird rather than a robin. But when shown an ostrich, they tend to call it an ostrich rather than a bird.

This pattern of naming was not universal for all atypical category members, however. It occurs mainly for members of basic level categories that are relatively diverse. Consider some basic level categories from the superordinate categories of fruit (e.g., apples, bananas, and grapes) versus animals (dogs, birds, and monkeys). Most people would agree that the shape variation within the categories of apples, for instance, is more constrained than that within the categories of dogs. Indeed, most people would be hard-pressed to distinguish between two different kinds of apples, bananas, or grapes from shape alone, but consider how different dachshunds are from greyhounds, penguins are from ostriches, and goldfish are from sharks. Not surprisingly, the atypical exemplars from diverse basic-level categories are the ones that tend to be named according to their subordinate category.

Because the categories into which objects are initially classified is sometimes different from the basic level, Jolicoeur et al. (1984) called them **entry-level categories**. At first, one might think that they just redefined the basic level, but this is not true. Their results pose an insurmountable problem for the simpler basic-level hypothesis. The problem is that Rosch's construct of basic-level categories is defined for an entire category. However, the data show that some members of a category are first identified at the basic level, while others in the same category are first identified at the subordinate level. By Rosch's criteria, the basic-level category must be either birds or all its various subcategories. The concept of an entry-level category for a given object is not subject to this constraint and so can describe the results. Unlike basic-level categories, however, entry-level categories are not independently defined by results other than the level at which given objects are identified. For this reason, the term "entry-level category" is just a name for that level.

Perceptual classification into entry-level categories is often called **object recognition** or **object identification**, as well as **object categorization** or **object classification**. We will avoid the "object recognition" terminology for this process, reserving that for the more specific task of realizing that one has seen a given object before, regardless of whether one knows what kind of object it is. For example, now that you have seen the nonsense object in Figure 9.1.3, you would be able to recognize it in this sense if you saw it again, even though you would still not be able to categorize it in terms of some known class of objects. Similarly, object identification is better reserved for recognizing a particular known object rather than a member of a category. Recognizing an object as my own particular cat, Motor, is technically object identification rather than object classification or categorization, but these are rather fine distinctions that are not universally acknowledged. Object identification can be related to object categorization by noting that individual objects are the smallest categories (consisting of just one object), but the two are not necessarily accomplished by the same perceptual process.

It is worth noting that, as in the case of basic-level categories, the entry-level category of an object can vary over different observers and perhaps over different contexts. To an ornithologist or even to an avid bird watcher, for instance, bird may be the entry-level category for very few, if any, species of bird. Through a lifetime of experience at discriminating different kinds of birds, their perceptual systems may become so finely tuned to the distinctive characteristics of birds that they first perceive robins as robins and sparrows as sparrows rather than just as birds (Tanaka & Taylor, 1991).

9.2.2 Perspective Viewing Conditions

One of the seemingly obvious facts about categorizing 3-D objects is that they can be identified from almost any viewpoint. The living room chair, for example, seems to be easily perceived as such regardless of whether one is looking at it from the front, side, back, top, or any combination of these views. Therefore, one of the important phenomena that must be explained by any theory of object classification is how this is possible. We have already seen in Chapter 8 that it is difficult to represent perceived 3-D shape, so it should come as no great surprise that 3-D object categorization, which is based primarily on shape information, is also a difficult theoretical problem.

Given the fact that we *can* categorize objects from various perspective views, it is all too easy to jump to the conclusion that object categorization is invariant over perspective views. Closer study indicates that this is not quite true. One might say that the ability to recognize 3-D objects despite wide variations in perspective is a "first-order" fact about the influence of viewpoint on perceptual categorization. The often overlooked "second-order" fact, however, is that the particular perspective view influences the speed and accuracy with which objects can be classified and recognized. When you examine the series of perspective views of the horse shown in Figure 9.2.4, it becomes fairly obvious that some views are more representative of how horses look to us than others. Indeed, several are quite unusual, and a few are even a bit bizarre.

Canonical Perspective. Palmer, Rosch, and Chase (1981) systematically investigated and documented perspective effects in object categorization. They began by having subjects view many pictures of the same object—such as the horse series in Figure 9.2.4—and make subjective ratings of how much each one looked like the objects they depict using a scale from 1 (very much like) to 7 (very unlike). Subjects found this to be a sensible task and, as a group, made the average ratings indicated below the horse pictures in Figure 9.2.4. The particular views that received the best (lowest) average rating for each object in this study are shown in Figure 9.2.5.

Palmer et al. (1981) then had other subjects name the entry-level categories of the objects shown, as quickly as possible, using several different perspectives for each of the objects illustrated in Figure 9.2.5. As indicated in Figure 9.2.6, the results showed that the pictures that were rated as the best views were named fastest and that naming latencies gradually increased as the "goodness" of the views declined, the ones rated "worst" being named much more slowly than the "best." Palmer et al. called the best, most easily identified view for each object its **canonical perspective**. The existence of canonical perspective and perspective effects in general shows the error in the intuition that we can recognize objects equally well from all possible perspective views. There are clear and systematic variations in naming latencies that must be explained by an adequate theory of human object categorization.

Such perspective effects can be explained in a number of different ways. The two most obvious are the *frequency hypothesis* and the *maximal information hypothesis*.

1. **Frequency hypothesis.** One possibility is that the speed of naming is simply a function of the number of times we see the objects from those viewpoints. By itself, this explanation is unlikely because there are several cases in which it gives the wrong predictions. Cups, for example, are very often seen from directly above, especially as we guide them to our mouths in the act of drinking, yet this view was rated as quite a poor view and was slow to be identified. Conversely, horses are probably seldom seen in a pure side view—there is usually some of the front, back, or top visible too—yet this view received high ratings and was identified very quickly.

2. **Maximal information hypothesis.** A second possibility is that perspective effects simply reflect the amount of information different views reveal about the shape and use of the object. This may account for the fact that the best views tend to show multiple sides of the object, such as their front, side, and top, rather than just one. It seems to be contradicted, however, by the fact that there are some objects for which the view of a single surface is the best view, such as the purely frontal view of the clock.

It is likely that both hypotheses contain some measure of truth and that the perspective effects Palmer et al. reported depend jointly on both. Canonical views appear to provide the perceiver with what might be called the most *diagnostic* information about the object: the information that best discriminates it from other objects, given what the perceiver knows, derived from the views from which it is most often seen. This would account for the fact that the front view of the clock is canonical, since virtually all the information about a clock that differentiates it from other objects is on its front. There may even be cases in which certain surfaces of an object contain *negative* diagnostic information. This would mean that such a surface looks more like a view of some other object than it does like itself.

The diagnosticity of different pieces of visual information about an object will also be affected by their familiarity, however. Since most people see houses from the ground and seldom get the opportunity to see them from above, views from the ground are rated as better and recognized more quickly than views of the roof. This pattern of results might well reverse for birds, however, which probably see houses from above a great deal more frequently than they do from ground level.

Perceiving Function and Category

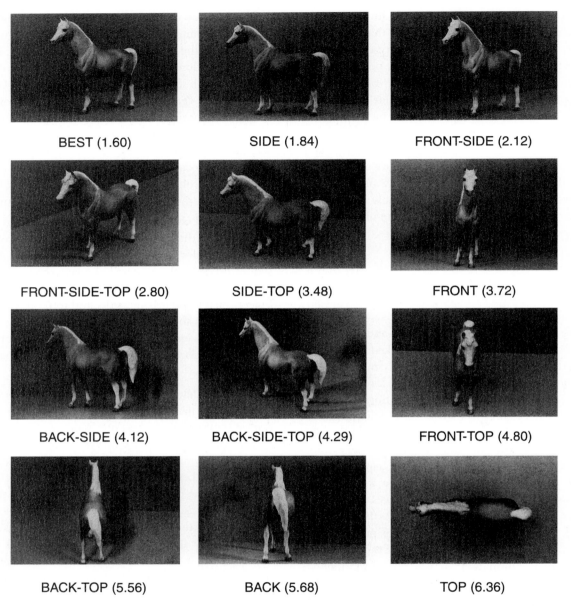

BEST (1.60)   SIDE (1.84)   FRONT-SIDE (2.12)

FRONT-SIDE-TOP (2.80)   SIDE-TOP (3.48)   FRONT (3.72)

BACK-SIDE (4.12)   BACK-SIDE-TOP (4.29)   FRONT-TOP (4.80)

BACK-TOP (5.56)   BACK (5.68)   TOP (6.36)

Figure 9.2.4 Canonical perspective. Perspective views of a horse differ significantly in how much they look like the object they depict. Numbers represent average ratings by subjects on a scale from 1 (looks very much like the object) to 7 (looks very unlike the object). Verbal labels indicate the viewpoint from which the pictures were taken. (From Palmer, Rosch, & Chase, 1981.)

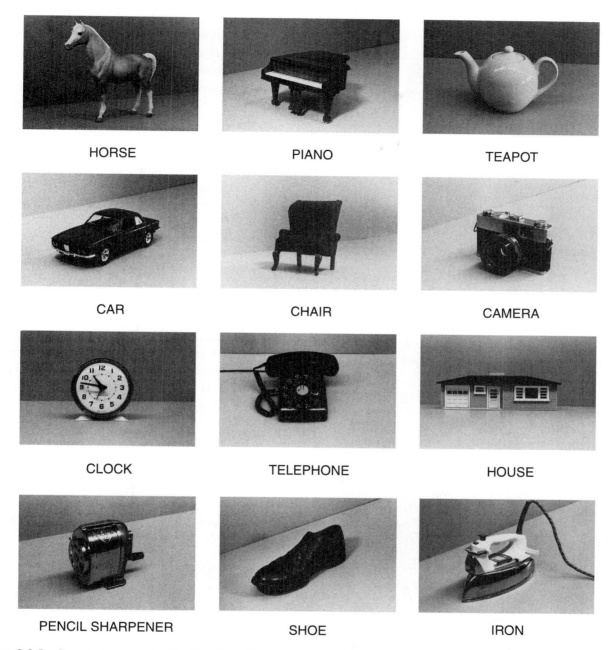

HORSE PIANO TEAPOT

CAR CHAIR CAMERA

CLOCK TELEPHONE HOUSE

PENCIL SHARPENER SHOE IRON

Figure 9.2.5 Canonical perspective for 12 objects. The perspective view receiving the best rating is shown for each of the 12 objects in the study by Palmer, Rosch and Chase (1981). In subsequent studies, subjects named these views more quickly than views from other perspectives, as indicated in Figure 9.2.6. (From Palmer, Rosch, & Chase, 1981.)

Perceiving Function and Category

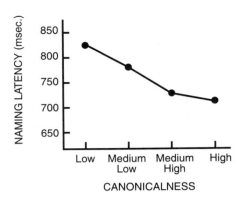

Figure 9.2.6 Perspective effects on naming latencies. The average time subjects took to name the objects shown in Figure 9.2.5 is graphed for four levels of canonicalness, as measured by subjective ratings.

Recent studies have examined perspective effects more carefully using novel objects so that frequency effects can be studied independently of other factors. Edelman and Bülthoff (1992) found canonical viewpoint effects in recognition time for novel bent paper clip objects (Figure 9.2.7) that were initially presented to subjects in a sequence of static views that produced apparent rotation of the object in depth. Each single view was presented exactly once in this motion sequence, so familiarity effects should not be present. Even so, recog-

Figure 9.2.7 Examples of stimuli used in an experiment on object recognition from different viewpoints. Subjects had to recognize which of several objects was depicted by particular views of paper clip objects like the one shown here from five perspectives. (From Bülthoff & Edelman, 1992.)

nition performance varied significantly over viewpoints, replicating the canonical perspective effects reported by Palmer et al. (1981). Such effects are therefore not solely a function of familiarity.

Further studies showed that familiarity does have an effect, however. When only a small subset of views were displayed in the initial apparent motion sequence of the training session, later recognition performance was best for views from the training sequence and decreased with angular distance from these training views, even when stereoscopic, shading, and motion information were included to maximize perceived depth information (Bülthoff & Edelman, 1992; Edelman & Bülthoff, 1992). These results suggest that subjects may be storing specific 2-D views of the objects and matching novel views to them via processes that deteriorate with increasing disparity between the novel and stored views.

Further experiments demonstrated that when multiple views of the same objects were used in the training session, recognition performance improved, but the improvement was specific to the relation between the presented views (Bülthoff & Edelman, 1992). In particular, if the views that subjects saw initially were related by rotations about a particular axis, recognition improved for novel views that were rotations about that same axis much more than they did for novel views that were rotations about an orthogonal axis. For example, if subjects saw the middle and right views of the bent paper clip object in Figure 9.2.7 initially, they were better at recognizing the left view as being the same object than the top or bottom views. This suggests that people may be interpolating between and extrapolating beyond specific 2-D views in recognizing 3-D objects. We will return to this possibility later in the chapter when we consider theories of object categorization based on aligning and matching 2-D views (e.g., Poggio & Edelman, 1990; Ullman, 1996; Ullman & Basri, 1991).

Priming Effects. Another method that has produced interesting but somewhat different results concerning the effects of perspective views is a priming paradigm used by Irving Biederman and his colleagues. The basic idea behind the **priming paradigm**, originally developed by Bartram (1974), is that categorizing a particular picture of an object will be faster and more accurate if the same picture is presented a second time, because the processes that accomplish it are in a state of heightened readiness. Measurable **priming effects** persist for a relatively long time—several hours or more—so the usual procedure is to ask subjects to name (as quickly as possible) a series of many different objects in one block of trials and then show them a second block containing repetitions of items from the first set to find out how much faster they can name them the second time. The difference between the two reaction times measures the magnitude of the priming effect.

What makes priming experiments informative about object categorization is that the repetitions in the second block of trials do not have to be *exact* repetitions of pictures in the first set but can differ from the initial presentation in different ways. For example, repetitions can be of the same object but with changes in its position within the visual field (e.g., left versus right half), its retinal size (large versus small), or its mirror-image reflection (as presented initially or left-right reversed). Of particular interest is what happens when changes are introduced in the perspective from which the object is viewed, as illustrated in Figure 9.2.8. The question of interest in each case is whether the priming effect for the modified repetitions is the same as or smaller than the priming effect for exact repetitions. If it is the same, then that type of modification has no apparent effect on object categorization. If the priming effect is smaller for the modified repetitions, however, then that type of modification *does* affect object categorization. Any theory of object categorization must then be able to account for which factors diminish priming effects and which do not.

The results of such studies show that the magnitude of the object priming effect does not diminish when the second presentation shows the same object in a different position or reflection (Biederman & Cooper, 1991a) or even at a different size (Biederman & Cooper, 1992).[3] Showing the same object from a different perspective, however, has been found to reduce the amount of prim-

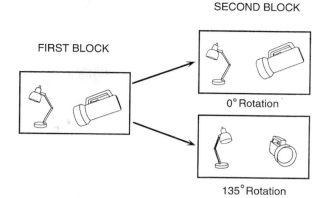

Figure 9.2.8 Stimuli for a priming experiment. Naming latencies were measured to pictures of objects in the first block of trials. In the second block, the same objects were presented again from either the same perspective or a different one, and reductions in naming latency relative to the first block were measured. (After Biederman & Gerhardstein, 1993.)

ing (Bartram, 1974). This perspective effect is thus consistent with the naming latency results reported by Palmer et al. (1981) and the recognition results by Edelman and Bülthoff (1992) and Bülthoff and Edelman (1992).

Later studies on priming with different perspective views of the same object by Biederman and Gerhardstein (1993), however, showed *no* significant decrease in priming effects due to depth rotations. Biederman and Gerhardstein then went on to show that the conditions under which priming effects did not diminish were that the same parts had to be visible in the different perspective conditions. Note that this same-part visibility condition is not necessarily met by the views used by Palmer et al., which often included examples in which different parts were visible from different perspectives. Visibility of the same versus different parts may thus explain why perspective effects have been found in some experiments but not in others.[4]

---

[3]It turns out that the magnitude of these priming effects depends importantly on whether subjects are attending to the initial presentation, as in the studies by Biederman, or not (Stankiewicz, Hummel, & Cooper, 1998). Although there is some priming over different positions and sizes even when the initial presentations are unattended, these effects are much greater and last longer when the object is attended than when it is not.

[4]This condition does not apply to the studies by Edelman and Bülthoff (1992) and Bülthoff and Edelman (1992), however, because they used bent

paper clip objects in which all parts were visible in all perspective views. Biederman and Gerhardstein (1995) claim that these studies do not show perspective invariance because the objects used cannot be discriminated by their geon structural descriptions (see Section 9.3.1), since they differed only in the angles between their segments. The interpretation of these studies is currently a matter of fierce debate (Biederman & Gerhardstein, 1995; Tarr & Bülthoff, 1995).

Perceiving Function and Category

One possible objection to Biederman's conclusion that priming effects show object categorization to be insensitive to changes in size, position, reflection, and perspective is that the discrepant information was simply never registered in the first place. That is, if subjects never noticed the size, position, reflection, or perspective of the initially presented object, it would not be surprising that changing these factors did not diminish the priming effect. However, Biederman also tested subjects for their specific memory of the first presentation of each object by means of a same/different recognition memory test when shown the second presentation. In these control conditions, subjects were asked whether each picture in the second (test) set was exactly the same as a picture they had seen in the first set or whether it differed in some way. The results indicated that the different sizes, positions, reflections, and perspectives were indeed perceived, encoded, and remembered; they just do not appear to affect categorization performance.

The results of these experiments on perspective effects suggest care in distinguishing two different kinds of changes in perspective: those that do not change the set of parts that can be perceived and those that do. Other effects due to different viewing conditions cannot be explained in this way, however, because the same parts are visible in all cases. This is true not only for experiments using bent paper clip objects (Bülthoff & Edelman, 1992; Edelman & Bülthoff, 1992), but also for orientation effects, which we will now consider.

Orientation Effects. Changes in perspective can be produced either by changing the observer's viewpoint around a stationary object or by rotating the object relative to a stationary observer. Depth rotations of the object often change the visibility of different parts of the object, as just discussed, but rotating the object about the line of sight does not. Exactly the same parts and object-relative spatial relations are present in all such rotations within the picture plane. The question is whether changes in object orientation produce systematic effects on object categorization.

For many years, most vision scientists assumed that they did not, but this belief was based more on untested intuition than on well-controlled experimental data. Studies by Canadian psychologist Pierre Jolicoeur (1985) have shown that subjects are indeed faster at

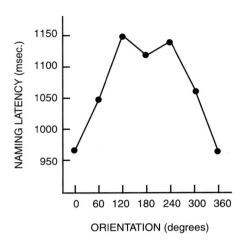

Figure 9.2.9 Orientation effects in object categorization. Subjects are fastest at naming objects in their upright orientation (0° and 360°) than in other orientations. (After Jolicoeur, 1985.)

categorizing pictures of objects in their normal, upright orientation than when they are misoriented by rotating them about the line of sight. Naming latencies increase with angular deviation from their upright orientation, as though subjects were mentally rotating the objects to upright before making their response. (See Chapter 12 for a discussion of mental rotation.) Figure 9.2.9 shows the orientation effect for the first exposure of each object in one of Jolicoeur's experiments. With repeated presentations, however, these orientation effects diminish considerably.

Further experiments by Tarr and Pinker (1989, 1990, 1991) examined why orientation effects diminish with practice. They used novel objects rather than familiar ones so that the orientations at which subjects saw the objects could be precisely controlled. When subjects learned a novel figure at a particular orientation, naming latencies were fastest at the learned orientation and increased with angular distance from it, much as in Jolicoeur's (1985) study. When subjects received extensive practice with the objects at several orientations, however, naming latencies were fast at *all* the learned orientations, and response times at other orientations generally increased with distance from the nearest familiar orientation. Such findings suggest that people may actually store multiple representations of the same object at different orientations rather than either a single representation at one canonical orientation or an orientation-invariant representation. We will return to this possibility later in this chapter when we consider view-specific theories of categorization.

Although object categorization initially seemed like an orientation- and view-invariant process, effects of these variables have turned out to be both interesting and complex. The results of such experiments are important because they provide clues about how the process of perceptual categorization may take place. They show conclusively, for example, that it cannot be an orientation- and view-invariant process. Exactly how such effects might arise within different theories will be discussed in Section 9.3 when we consider theories of object categorization.

9.2.3 Part Structure

In Chapter 7 we first examined the question of whether objects are structured into parts and, if so, how they are determined. One of the arguments we considered was the fact that most familiar natural objects have salient parts. Human bodies have heads, arms, legs, and a torso; tables have a flat top surface and legs; an airplane has a fuselage, two main wings, and several smaller tail fins. The important question for theories of object categorization is whether these parts play a significant role in how objects are classified into entry-level categories.

The most revealing studies of this question were performed by Biederman and Cooper (1991b) using a version of the priming paradigm discussed earlier in this chapter. The clever manipulation that enabled them to study this issue was to use line drawings of an object in which portions of its contours had been deleted. They studied the importance of parts by manipulating the relation between the deletions made in the first and second presentations as described below.

In the first experiment, Biederman and Cooper constructed two versions of line drawings of common objects by deleting half of the contours in each. The two versions were complementary halves, such that superimposing them would reconstruct the whole original drawing, as shown in Figure 9.2.10B. In the first block of trials, subjects saw one set of pictures, each depicting a different object with half of its contour deleted. Then, in the second block, they saw another set of drawings that were related to those in the first set in particular ways. The question of interest was how much the prior presentation of the same or a different drawing would

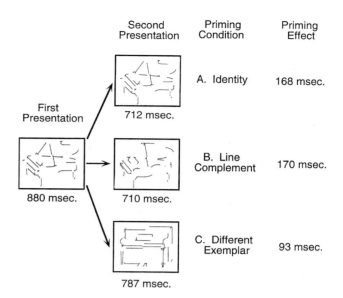

Figure 9.2.10 A line-complement priming experiment. In the first block of trials, naming latencies were measured to pictures of objects containing half the component lines. In the second block, the same objects were presented again using the same set of lines (A), the complementary set (B), or those of a different exemplar (C). (After Biederman & Cooper, 1992b.)

facilitate (that is, prime) the classification of the object in the second set. Three conditions were studied:

1. *Identity priming.* In the identity repetition condition, exactly the same contours were presented in the first and the second presentations for the same object, as illustrated in Figure 9.2.10A. This serves as a baseline to define the maximum amount of priming possible in this task.

2. *Line-complement priming.* In the line-complement priming condition, the second presentation was of the same object but contained just the contours that were deleted in the first presentation, as illustrated in Figure 9.2.10B.

3. *Different-exemplar priming.* In the different-exemplar priming condition, the second presentation was a drawing of an object that was a member of the same entry-level category but was either a different object or a radically different perspective view showing different parts of the same object. For example, in the first set of pictures, a grand piano might have been presented, and in the second set it would be changed to an upright piano, as illustrated in Figure 9.2.10C. Or a side view of an elephant might have been presented first and then a front view of the elephant.

Biederman and Cooper argued that the segments in the line-complement condition were sufficient in each case to identify all of the component parts of the objects. If so, this condition effectively measures priming due to component parts, uncontaminated by priming due to specific image features in the contour. They also argued that the different-exemplar condition defines the amount of priming one would expect from general practice effects and from repeating the category name.

The results of this experiment were very clear, as shown in the reaction times below the stimuli in Figure 9.2.10. Repeating the parts (without repeating any of the individual segments) in the line-complement priming condition produced almost exactly the same amount of priming as repeating the identical segments in the identity priming condition: about 170 ms. Merely repeating the same category, however, produced much less priming: only 93 ms. From these results, Biederman and Cooper concluded that object categorization was based on the perception of parts rather than on the individual line segments and vertices that compose them.

This interpretation has a potential problem, however. The strong priming in the line-complement condition could have been due to the fact that the same view of the same object was presented in the second set rather than because the same parts were perceived. Thus, the priming might have been at the level of perspective views of whole objects rather than at the level of parts. The crucial question is what would happen if the same view of the same object were presented in the second block via different parts.

This question was answered in a second experiment by deleting half of the parts, as illustrated in Figure 9.2.11, instead of half of the lines. The corresponding three conditions were examined again, but in this part-deletion experiment, the part-complement priming condition does not repeat the same parts, but only the same view of the same object. Therefore, if it is repetition of the particular perspective view of the object that produces priming, the results of the second experiment should be the same as the first, with part-complement priming being as strong as identity priming. If it is repeating the component parts that produces priming, however, the part-complement priming condition should produce much less priming than the identity condition because it does not repeat the parts.

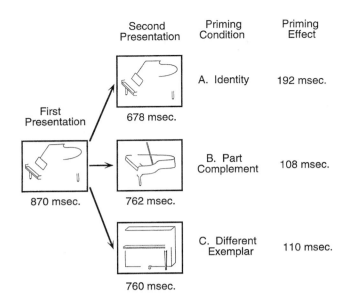

Figure 9.2.11 A part-complement priming experiment. In the first block of trials, naming latencies were measured to pictures of objects containing half the component parts. In the second block, the same objects were presented again using the same set of parts (A), the complementary set of parts (B), or those of a different exemplar (C). (After Biederman & Cooper, 1992b.)

Again, the results were very clear, as shown in the reaction times in Figure 9.2.11. Complement priming of part-deleted images resulted in a much smaller priming effect than identity priming. In fact, it produced about the same decrease as the different-exemplar priming condition. Taken together, the results of these two experiments provide convincing evidence that perception of parts plays a crucial role in object categorization in these studies. Later in this chapter we will present Biederman's theory of object categorization, a theory that is specifically based on the assumption that objects are categorized by perception of their component parts and their spatial interrelations.

9.2.4 Contextual Effects

All the phenomena of object categorization that we have considered thus far directly concern the target object itself: How typical it is of its entry-level category, the perspective from which it is viewed, its size, position, orientation, and parts. But these factors do not exhaust the influences on object categorization, for there are also **contextual effects** on object categorization: changes

TAE CAT

Figure 9.2.12 Contextual determination of an ambiguous stimulus. The H and A that observers perceive so readily are physically identical but are perceived differently because of contextual constraints.

in categorization performance due to the spatial array of objects surrounding the target object.

One simple demonstration of this phenomenon is shown in Figure 9.2.12, in which the perceived identity of the letters is strongly influenced by the letters surrounding it. Everyone perceives THE CAT, and nobody perceives TAE CHT, THE CHT, or TAE CAT, even though the stimulus is equally compatible with all four interpretations. The central letters of both words are actually identical and ambiguous—being halfway between an H and an A in each case—but the first is seen as an H in the context of T_E and the second as an A in the context of C_T. The phenomenon is so strong that almost nobody ever notices the ambiguity of the letters, much less that they have the same physical form.

Figure 9.2.13 shows another demonstration of the importance of context in object categorization (Palmer, 1975b). It also illustrates that a tradeoff exists between the amount of part-structural detail that is needed for object categorization versus the amount of context that is provided. A given object, such as a nose, eye, or mouth, can be depicted with only its approximate global shape

when it appears in the proper context. When seen alone, however, its own part structure must be articulated more fully and accurately to achieve the same level of categorization. It is as though the visual system needs to perceive two levels of part structure to categorize an object, and either the one below (its parts) or the one above (its context) will be sufficient in conjunction with the target level itself.

Perhaps a more striking demonstration of the same contextual influence is the "fruit face" shown in Figure 9.2.14 (Palmer, 1975b). Here the specific shapes of the "facial features" can be easily identified as pieces of fruit. Yet because their spatial arrangement corresponds to that of eyes, nose, and mouth, the global configuration of a face is spontaneously perceived. Indeed, it dominates perception, as is indicated by the fact that observers experience it as a distinctly weird face rather than as an unusual arrangement of fruit. The analysis we have provided thus far is based on purely subjective evidence, however. Are there any objective findings to support the conclusion that context affects object categorization?

Several well-controlled experiments have documented the effects of context in categorizing objects. As one might expect, they show that appropriate context facilitates categorization, whereas inappropriate context hinders it. In one study, Palmer (1975a) presented subjects briefly with line drawings of common objects following presentation of a contextual scene, as illustrated in Figure 9.2.15. The contextual relation between the

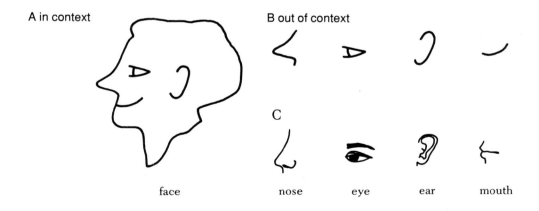

Figure 9.2.13 An illustration of part/whole context. Facial features that are easily recognizable in the context of a profile face (A) are not recognizable out of context (B). When the internal part structure of the features is articulated, however, they become recognizable out of context (C). (From Palmer, 1975b.)

Perceiving Function and Category

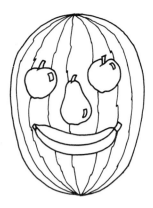

Figure 9.2.14 A fruit face. Configural information allows immediate global recognition of a face despite local features consisting of pieces of fruit. (From Palmer, 1975b.)

scene and the target object was varied. In the case of the kitchen counter scene, for example, the subsequently presented object could be either *appropriate* to the scene (a loaf of bread), *inappropriate* (a bass drum), or *misleading* in the sense that the target object was visually similar to the appropriate object (a mailbox). For the no-context control condition, the objects were presented following a blank field instead of a contextual scene. By recombining the objects and scenes in different ways, all objects were presented in all four contextual conditions.

The results of this experiment are graphed in Figure 9.2.16. They show that appropriate contexts facilitate correct categorization relative to the no-context control

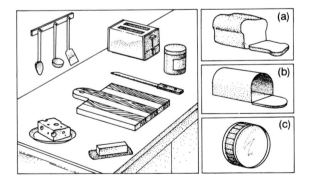

Figure 9.2.15 Stimuli from an experiment on contextual effects on object categorization. A contextual scene was presented briefly prior to a single to-be-identified object that was either appropriate to the context (A), visually similar to an appropriate object (B), or inappropriate to the context (C). (From Palmer, 1975a.)

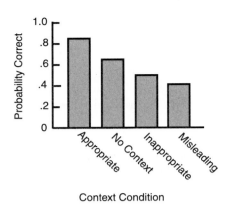

Figure 9.2.16 Results from an experiment on contextual effects on object categorization. The probability of correctly categorizing the target object was highest for the appropriate context and lowest for inappropriate and misleading contexts. (Replotted from Palmer, 1975a.)

condition and that inappropriate contexts inhibit it. Performance is worst in the misleading context condition, in which subjects were likely to name the visually similar object appropriate to the scene. These differences demonstrate that recognition accuracy can be substantially affected by the nature of the surrounding objects in a simple categorization task. This is an important fact for which theories of object categorization must provide an account.

Biederman (1972; Biederman, Glass & Stacy, 1973) used a different method to study context effects. He had subjects search for the presence of a given target object in a scene and measured their reaction times. In his initial study, he manipulated context by presenting either the normal photograph or a randomly rearranged version. Subjects took substantially longer to find the target object in the rearranged pictures than in the normal ones. In further experiments he investigated several different types of relations that could be violated between the target object and its surrounding context. The factors he studied included (1) how likely the objects were to appear in the given scene, (2) whether they occupied a likely position (e.g., a hydrant on the sidewalk) or an unlikely one (e.g., a hydrant on top of a mailbox, as illustrated in Figure 9.2.17), (3) whether the object was bigger or smaller than normal in comparison with other objects in the scene, (4) whether the object was visibly supported or not, and (5) whether it conformed to proper occlusion relations or appeared partially trans-

Figure 9.2.17 An example of a stimulus from an experiment on contextual effects on object search. In this case, the hydrant violates positional constraints, leading to longer times to detect its presence in the scene. Increases in visual search response times also occur when the target object is unlikely to appear in the scene, when it is the wrong size, and when it appears partially transparent. (From Biederman, 1981.)

parent. He found that each factor that violated contextual relations made detecting the target more difficult.

These contextual effects indicate that relations among objects in a scene are both complex and important for normal visual categorization. Obviously, people can manage to categorize objects correctly even in bizarre contexts. A fire hydrant on top of a mailbox might take longer to identify—and cause a major double-take once it has been—but people recognize it even so. Rather, context appears to affect the *efficiency* of categorization. The visual system seems able to use contextual information to facilitate perception when the usual relations among objects hold. In each case, the "normal" situation is processed quickly and with few errors, whereas "abnormal" situations take longer to process and are more likely to produce errors. Since normal situations are, by definition, encountered more frequently than "abnormal" ones, such contextual effects are generally beneficial to the organism in its usual environment and serve an evolutionarily useful function.

9.2.5 Visual Agnosia

A very different kind of phenomenon that constrains theories of object categorization is **visual agnosia**, a perceptual deficit due to brain damage in which patients are unable to correctly categorize common objects with which they were previously familiar. ("Agnosia" is a term derived from Greek that means "not knowing.") There are many different forms of visual agnosia, and the relations among them are not well understood. Some appear to be due primarily to damage to the later stages of sensory processing (termed **apperceptive agnosia** by Lissauer, 1890/1988). Such patients appear unable to recognize objects because they do not see them normally. Other patients have fully intact perceptual abilities yet cannot identify the objects they see, a condition Lissauer called **associative agnosia**. Teuber (1968) described their condition as involving "a normal percept stripped of its meaning" due to an inability to categorize it correctly.

The case of a patient whom we shall refer to as "GL" is a good example of associative agnosia (Ellis & Young, 1988). He suffered a blow to his head when he was 80 years old, after which he complained that he could not see as well as before the accident. The problem was not that he was blind or even impaired in basic visual function, for he could see the physical properties of objects quite well indeed; he just could not identify them as familiar and meaningful objects. He mistook pictures for

Figure 9.2.18 Examples of drawings by an agnosic patient. Despite their inability to name objects, agnosics can copy pictures well, a fact that rules out sensory deficits as the basis for their inability to identify objects. (From Rubens & Benson, 1971.)

boxes and his jacket for a pair of trousers. Generally speaking, he could not categorize even the simplest everyday objects correctly.

GL's abilities were studied extensively to determine the precise nature of his problem. Several simple tests confirmed that his problem was specifically in visual object recognition:

1. *Lack of sensory deficits.* His impairment was not of sensory origin, for his visual acuity and other basic visual functions were normal. He could even copy pictures of objects that he could not identify. (See Figure 9.2.18 for some representative drawings from similar patients.)

2. *Lack of conceptual deficits.* His problem was not conceptual, for he could define objects verbally and talk about their structure and use quite normally.

3. *Lack of deficits in other sensory modalities.* His problem was not that he was unable to categorize objects in general, for he could do so quite normally by touching them.

4. *Lack of linguistic deficits.* His problem was not simply an inability to retrieve the verbal label of objects that he

could categorize but not name, for he also *behaved* inappropriately with respect to objects he could not name and was unable to mime their correct use.

With all of these alternative explanations eliminated, the unavoidable conclusion is that GL could not categorize objects that are presented visually. His case is rather pure in this sense, for there are many patients who cannot categorize objects visually yet are also impaired in one or more of these other abilities. But the existence of even one such pure case is important evidence that object classification is a separate physiological process that can be selectively impaired.

Patients with visual agnosia suffer from a variety of different symptoms. Some have deficits specific to particular classes of objects or properties. One classic example is **prosopagnosia**: the inability to recognize faces visually. Prosopagnosic patients can describe in detail the facial features of someone they are looking at yet can be completely unable to recognize the person, even if it is their spouse or child. Such patients will typically react to a relative as though to a complete stranger—until the person speaks, at which time the patient can recognize his or her voice. Just how severe this form of agnosia can be is revealed in the following quotation from Pallis (1955): "At the club I saw someone strange staring at me, and asked the steward who it was. You'll laugh at me. I'd been looking at myself in a mirror" (p. 219).

Other agnosic patients have been studied who have problems with object categories such as living things. Patient JBR, for example, was able to identify 90% of the pictures depicting inanimate objects but only 6% of those depicting plants and animals (Warrington & Shallice, 1984). Even more selective deficits have been reported, including those confined to body parts, objects found indoors, and fruits and vegetables, although some of these deficits may be linguistic rather than perceptual (Farah, 1990).

One problem for many visual agnosics that has been studied experimentally is their particular inability to categorize objects presented in "unusual" perspective views. Warrington and Taylor (1973, 1978) found that many agnosics who are able to categorize pictures of common objects taken from a usual perspective are unable to do so for an unusual view, as illustrated in Figure 9.2.19. This phenomenon in agnosics bears a striking

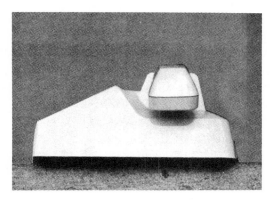

Figure 9.2.19 Unusual perspectives stimuli. Agnosic patients can sometimes correctly categorize objects from standard views but seldom from unusual views. (From Goldstein, 1989.)

resemblance to perspective effects found in normals (Palmer, Rosch & Chase, 1981), except that instead of simply taking longer to arrive at the correct answer, these patients are unable to identify them even in unrestricted viewing conditions. These phenomena may have the same origin; agnosics may simply be unable to overcome the difficulties presented by poor perspective views whereas normals are merely impeded.

The views that prove most troublesome for these agnosic patients are ones in which the long axis of the object is foreshortened. This finding has suggested to some theorists that they have difficulty deriving the appropriate object-centered frame of reference (e.g., Marr, 1982). Choosing the wrong reference frame would cause the wrong structural description to be constructed; this, in turn, would block correct categorization. Patients with this specific problem tend to have damage to the right posterior cortex, typically in the parietal lobe (Ellis & Young, 1988).

There are many other visual disorders due to brain damage that are related to visual agnosia. They exhibit a bewildering array of complex symptoms, are caused by a wide variety of underlying brain pathologies, and are not generally well understood. Still, their case histories and phenomenological descriptions make for fascinating reading, such as that of the patient whose agnosia led neurologist Oliver Sacks (1985) to title one of his books *The Man Who Mistook His Wife for a Hat*. The interested reader is referred to Farah (1990) for a thorough discussion of these and related disorders.

9.3 Theories of Object Categorization

The preceding section described a number of important phenomena in visual object categorization. Now we turn to the difficult question of explaining how objects might be identified within the human visual system and how these facts can be understood within a computational theory of visual recognition and categorization.

Perhaps the single most influential theoretical approach to object categorization over the past several decades is extension of ideas behind structural description theories of shape representation presented in Chapter 8. Versions of it have been developed by a number of computer scientists and computationally oriented psychologists, including Binford (1971), Biederman (1987), Marr and Nishihara (1978), and Palmer (1975a). Indeed, there is a sense in which the four-stage theory of vision (image-based, surface-based, object-based, and category-based processing) was devised as a plausible sequence of stages that would lead to volumetric structural descriptions of 3-D objects for categorization.

Of the many specific theories that have been advanced within this general framework, we will consider only one in detail: Irving Biederman's (1985, 1987) recognition by components theory of object categorization. It is not radically different from several others but is somewhat easier to describe and has been developed with more attention to the results of experimental evidence. It is presented as representative of this class of models rather than as the "correct" one or even the "best" one. After describing it in detail, we will consider some alternative approaches to the problem of object

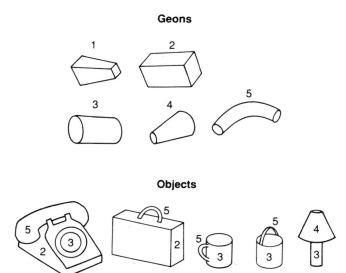

Geons

1 2

3 4 5

Objects

5 5 5 4

5 2 3 2 5 3 3 3

Figure 9.3.1 Examples of geons and their presence in objects. Five simple geons are shown together with several common objects that can be analyzed into configurations of geons. (From Biederman, 1987.)

recognition based on matching of specific 2-D views rather than 3-D structural descriptions (e.g., Koenderink & van Doorn, 1979; Poggio & Edelman, 1990; Ullman, 1996; Ullman & Basri, 1991).

9.3.1 Recognition by Components Theory

Recognition by components (RBC) theory, sometimes also called **geon theory**, is an attempt to integrate many of the visual processes that we have been considering into a single, psychologically meaningful theory of how people classify objects as members of entry-level categories. It is based on the idea that objects can be specified as spatial arrangements of primitive volumetric components, which Biederman (1985, 1987) called **geons**. Object categorization then occurs by matching a geon description of the target object with corresponding geon descriptions of object categories.

Geons. The first important assumption of RBC theory is that both the stored representations of categories and the representation of a currently attended object are volumetric structural descriptions. This means that RBC representations are essentially hierarchical networks whose nodes correspond to 3-D parts and whose links

correspond to relations among these parts. Biederman calls the primitive 3-D parts *geons*, which is a shortened form of *geometric ions*. Geons are generalized cylinders whose inherently continuous parameters have been divided into a few discrete ranges that are fairly easy to distinguish from most vantage points. This produces a relatively small set of distinct primitive volumes from which a huge number of object representations can be constructed by putting two or more together, much as letters serve as a small set of primitives from which an enormous number of words can be constructed. A small set of geons is illustrated in Figure 9.3.1 along with some common objects that can be constructed by putting several geons together to form spatial configurations that are fairly recognizable.

As the reader will recall from Chapter 8, generalized cylinders (also called generalized cones) are volumes constructed by sweeping a 2-D shape along an axis, as illustrated in Figure 8.2.17). Different shapes are obtained by varying the 2-D cross-sectional shape, the shape of the axis along which the cross section is swept, the sweeping rule that changes the size of the cross section, and the aspect ratio of axis to base. Biederman defines a set of 36 qualitatively different geons by making the following distinctions in these variable dimensions.

1. *Cross-sectional curvature.* The cross section of the geon can be either *straight* (as in the square base of Figure 9.3.2A) or *curved* (as in the circular base of Figure 9.3.2B).

2. *Symmetry.* The cross section can either be *asymmetrical* (Figure 9.3.2D) or possess one of two kinds of symmetry: *reflectional symmetry* alone (Figure 9.3.2C) or both *reflectional and rotational symmetry* (Figure 9.3.2A).

3. *Axis curvature.* The sweeping axis can be either *straight* (Figure 9.3.2A) or *curved* (Figure 9.3.2E).

4. *Size variation.* The size of the cross section as it is swept along the axis can be either *constant*, resulting in parallel geon sides (Figure 9.3.2A), *expanding and contracting*, resulting in nonparallel sides with a point of maximum convexity (Figure 9.3.2F), or just *expanding*, resulting in nonparallel sides that converge toward one end (Figure 9.3.2G).

The nature of each of these variables is illustrated in Figure 9.3.2 by showing how a single geon (the cube in the center) can be changed into other geons by changing

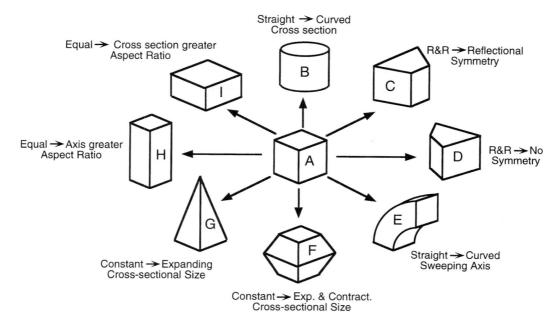

Figure 9.3.2 Illustrations of five variables in constructing generalized cylinders. The central cube (A) can be modified to construct the eight other geons shown by changing just one of five parameters: curvature of cross-sectional edges (B), cross-sectional symmetry (C and D), curvature of sweeping axis (E), diameter of sweeping rule (or cross-sectional size) (F and G), and aspect ratio (H and I).

its value on each of these features (plus one more, to be discussed shortly).

The rationale for making these four kinds of distinctions among geons is that they are qualitative (rather than merely quantitative) differences that result in qualitatively different retinal projections. The image features that characterize different geons are therefore relatively insensitive to changes in viewpoint. Straight lines project to straight lines in the retinal image from every vantage point, for example, and curved lines project to curved ones from almost every vantage point. (A curved line can project to a straight line if it lies entirely within a 2-D plane that includes the line of sight.) Because of the qualitative nature of the distinctions among the 36 qualitatively different geons (2 values of cross-sectional curvature × 3 values of symmetry × 3 values of size variation × 2 values of axis curvature = 36 geons), they are relatively easy to identify despite differences in perspective viewpoint.

Biederman proposes a further feature of geons, one that leads to quantitatively (rather than qualitatively) distinct geons, which he quantizes to produce three different values:

5. *Aspect ratio*. The ratio of the length of the sweeping axis to that of the largest dimension of the cross-sectional area is called the aspect ratio, which can be either *approximately equal* (1 : 1), as in Figure 9.3.2A, *axis greater* (a long, thin volume) as in Figure 9.3.2H, or *cross section greater* (a short, fat volume) as in Figure 9.3.2I.

The three aspect ratios bring the number of possible geons to 108, since each of the 36 qualitatively different geon can be constructed in all three aspect ratios.

Nonaccidental Features. Although geons are themselves volumetric entities, RBC theory proposes that geons are identified directly from image-based features such as edges and vertices. Featural differences between the image of a "brick" geon and a "cylinder" geon are illustrated in Figure 9.3.3. The properties from which geons are proposed to be identified are called **nonaccidental features**, following Lowe's (1985) distinction, because they are aspects of image structure that do not depend on rare "accidents" of viewpoint. A brick, for instance, that is viewed purely from the side will project a rectangular image, missing the crucial Y-vertex and reducing the three sets of three parallel edges

Perceiving Function and Category

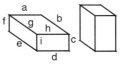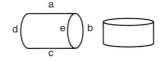

"BRICKS"

- 3 sets of 3 parallel edges:
  (a, h, d) (b, e, g) (c, f, i)
- 1 inner Y-vertex:
  (ghi)
- 3 outer arrow vertices:
  (afg) (bch) (dei)

"CYLINDERS"

- 2 parallel straight edges:
  (a, c)
- 2 parallel curved edges:
  (d, e)
- 2 tangent Y-vertices:
  (abe) (bce)

Figure 9.3.3 Nonaccidental properties of two geons. A brick and a cylinder can be distinguished by many properties that are present from all but a few specific viewpoints.

to two pairs of two parallel edges. This fairly unlikely and nonrepresentative perspective from which to view a brick-shaped object will therefore cause problems for RBC theory in correctly identifying the geons of which an object is composed.

This seeming weakness may actually be a strength in disguise, however, at least as a theory of how people categorize objects. Remember that human categorization is known to result in several perspective phenomena that we mentioned previously: canonical perspective effects in normal perceivers (Palmer et al., 1981) and "unusual view" effects in visual agnosic patients (Humphreys & Riddoch, 1984; Warrington & Taylor, 1973). If RBC theory exhibits the same kinds of difficulties as human perceivers, these "defects" actually support RBC as a theory of human perception. Some perspective effects will certainly occur in RBC theory when the 2-D edge-based features are mapped into 3-D geons because "unusual views" tend to be degenerative cases in which accidental features are likely to be found. Although this argument is suggestive, whether RBC theory can account for these perspective effects in detail has not yet been determined.

Geon Relations. Because complex objects are conceived in RBC theory as configurations of two or more geons in particular spatial arrangements, they are encoded as structural descriptions that specify both the geons present and their spatial relations. If geons are the alphabet of complex 3-D objects, then spatial relations among geons are analogous to the order of letters in

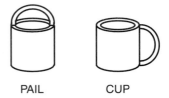

PAIL   CUP

Figure 9.3.4 The importance of geon relations. Different objects can be formed from the same geons by putting them together in different relations. (After Biederman, 1987.)

words. Just as it is possible to construct different words by arranging the same letters differently (e.g., BAT versus TAB), so is it possible to construct different object types by arranging the same geons differently. The cup and pail shown in Figure 9.3.4 are but one example.

To represent the structure of complex objects consisting of two or more geons, RBC uses structural descriptions in which 108 qualitatively different relations can be represented between two geons. Some of these relations concern how they are attached (e.g., SIDE-CONNECTED and TOP-CONNECTED); others concern their relational properties, such as relative size (e.g., LARGER-THAN and SMALLER-THAN). With these 108 geon relations and 108 geons, it is logically possible to construct more than a million different two-geon objects. Adding a third geon and its relations to the other two geons pushes the number of combinations into the trillions. Clearly, geons are capable of generating a rich vocabulary of different complex shapes. Whether it is sufficient to capture the power and versatility of visual categorization is an open question at this point, one to which we will return shortly.

Once the shape of an object has been represented via its component geons and their spatial relations, the problem of object categorization within RBC theory reduces to the process of matching the structural description of an incoming object with the set of structural descriptions for known entry-level categories. Biederman (1987) has estimated that most people know about 30,000 different object categories, indicating that there are far more possible combinations of geons than there are actual objects. This is important if the visual system is to be able to realize that a novel object is not a member of any known category (e.g., the one in Figure 9.1.3), for there must be arrangements of geons that do not correspond to known categories.

Stages of Object Categorization in RBC. RBC theory proposes that object categorization takes place in several stages, some of which have already been discussed in previous chapters. In the original formulation (Biederman, 1985, 1987), the overall flow of information was proposed to be as depicted in the flowchart of Figure 9.3.5.

1. *Edge extraction.* Edges are detected initially as luminance gradients, as described in Chapter 4. No particular claims are made in RBC theory about exactly how this occurs. The result is presumed to be a clean line drawing of the edges present in the visual scene.

2. *Feature detection.* Next, the image-based, nonaccidental properties that are needed to identify geons are extracted from the edge information. The crucial features are the nature of the edges (e.g., curved versus straight), the nature of the vertices (e.g., Y-vertices, K-vertices, L-vertices), parallelism (parallel versus nonparallel), and

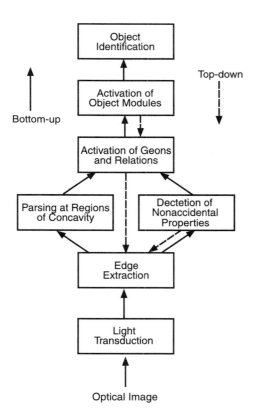

Figure 9.3.5 Processing stages in RBC theory. Bottom-up processes are shown as solid arrows, and top-down ones as dashed arrows. (See text for details.) (From Biederman, 1987.)

symmetry (symmetric versus asymmetric). The goal of this process is to provide the feature-based information required to identify the different kinds of geons (see stage 4).

3. *Object parsing.* At the same time as these features are being extracted, the system attempts to parse objects at regions of deep concavity, as suggested by Hoffman and Richards (1984) and discussed at the end of Chapter 7. The goal of this parsing process is to divide the object into component geons without having to match them explicitly on the basis of edge and vertex features.

4. *Geon categorization.* The combined results of feature detection (stage 2) and object parsing (stage 3) are used to identify which specific geons are present at different positions in the scene and what spatial relations hold among them.

5. *Category matching.* Once the geon description of the input object is constructed, it automatically activates similar geon descriptions that are stored in memory. Matching is accomplished by activation spreading through a network from geon nodes and relation nodes that are present in the representation of the target object to similar geon nodes and relation nodes in the category representations. This comparison is a fully parallel process, matching the geon description of the input object against all category representations at once and using all geons and relations at once.

6. *Object categorization.* The target object is ultimately identified as an instance of the entry-level category that is most strongly activated by the comparison process, provided that it exceeds some threshold value.

Although the general flow of information within RBC theory is bottom-up, it also allows for top-down processing. If sensory information is weak—because of noisy, brief, or otherwise degraded images, for example—top-down effects are likely to occur. There are two points in RBC at which they are most likely to happen: feedback from geons to geon features and feedback from category representations to geons.

1. *Feedback from geons to features.* Geon-level processing can affect feature-level processing because not all possible combinations of features constitute legal geons. This means that partial activation of a geon unit from certain of its features can generate expectations about which

Perceiving Function and Category

other features should also be present if that geon is actually at that location. Such expectation-based processing is a form of hypothesis testing in which the expectation plays the role of the hypothesis to be tested.

2. *Feedback from categories to geons.* Category-level processing can affect geon-level processing for similar reasons: Not all combinations of geons form representations of known category types. As a result, tentatively classifying an object as a member of some category generates expectations about what other geons should be present if the target object is actually a member of that category. Such expectations can thus be used to test hypotheses about what kind of object it is.

A Neural Network Implementation. The actual mechanisms of these processes were not fully specified in the original formulation of RBC (Biederman, 1985, 1987). They were supposed to be accomplished by spreading activation within a complex neural network but actual models of these processes were not specified. Since then, Hummel and Biederman (1992) have devised a neural network implementation of RBC (called JIM, for "John and Irv's model"). An overview of JIM's architecture is shown in Figure 9.3.6.

As Biederman originally proposed, the first two stages are extracting edges (in layer 1) and detecting features (in layer 2) of the neural network. Edges are extracted in layer 1 by straight and curved "segment cells" and straight and curved "termination cells" (i.e., end-stopped cells) at many orientations and positions. These units are thus similar to edge-based conceptions of the receptive fields of Hubel and Wiesel's cells in area V1 (see Section 4.1.2). Layer 2 detects three specific types of features: different kinds of vertices, axes of symmetry, and blobs. The vertices—including L's, T's, forks, arrows, and tangent-Y's—are useful in discriminating between different kinds of geons (e.g., bricks versus cylinders; see Figure 9.3.3), and axes and blobs help to further specify the geon attributes represented in layer 3.

Geon attributes are encoded by the firing pattern of units in layer 3 that respond to axis shape ("Axis" in Figure 9.3.6), which is straight (s) or curved (c); cross-sectional shape (X-Scn), which is straight (s) or curved (c); parallelism of sides (Sides), which are parallel (p) or nonparallel (n); coarse orientation (Orn.), which is vertical (v), diagonal (d), or horizontal (h); aspect ratio, which

varies from elongated (long) to flattened (flat); fine orientation (Orientation), which varies from vertical (v) through diagonal (d) to horizontal (h); horizontal position (Horiz. Pos.), which varies from left (l) to right (r); vertical position (Vert. Pos.), which varies from bottom (b) to top (t); and size, which varies from large to small. Each geon is thus defined by its values on all these attributes.

One of the key proposals in JIM is that many different attributes can be temporarily *bound* to a given geon (i.e., associated with that geon) by their units firing in synchrony. This mechanism, which is called **dynamic binding**, is an extremely useful and economical way to represent the association of different attributes that are part of the same component. It is also the mechanism that JIM uses to parse objects into geons. Different attributes are bound to different geons in the same representation by virtue of there being several different temporal patterns of activation present at the same time, one set of attribute units firing synchronously in one pattern of activation and another set of attributes firing synchronously in another pattern. These patterns of activation could be as simple as different temporal firing rates, provided the difference was large enough.

The idea that temporal synchrony could be used to solve the attribute-object binding problem was first proposed many years ago by Peter Milner (1974) and explored formally by von der Malsburg (1981, 1987) and others. The details of how this actually occurs in JIM's neural network are unfortunately too complex to describe here. We will simply assume that its dynamic binding mechanisms work and see how it can be used to parse a scene into geons that enable the model to achieve object categorization.

In Figure 9.3.6, different attribute-to-geon bindings in Layers 3 and above are represented by the large circles: white for the cone on top, black for the brick on bottom, shaded for either geon (the logical OR of the cone and brick geons), and X-ed for both geons (their logical AND). Thus, reading across the representations in layer 3, we can see that the upper, cone-shaped geon (white circles) has a straight axis, curved cross section, non-parallel sides, vertical orientation, and so on. The lower, brick-shaped geon (black circle) has a straight axis, straight cross section, parallel sides, horizontal orientation, and so on.

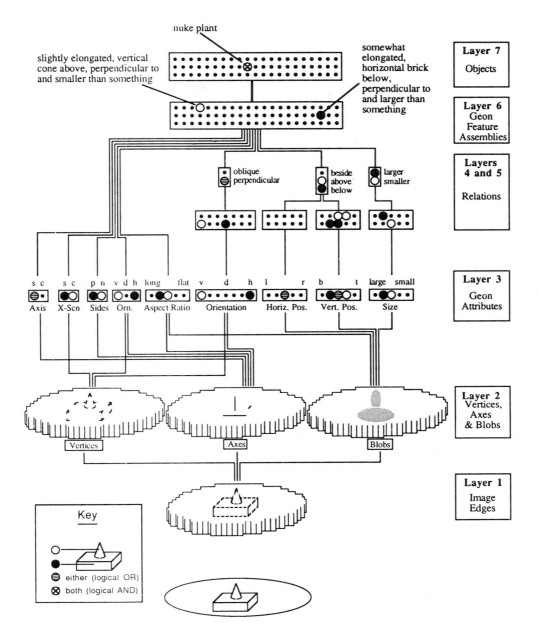

Figure 9.3.6 The overall architecture of JIM, a neural network model of RBC theory. The process of describing objects as structural descriptions of geons and geon relations occurs in layers 1–6, and the result is categorized by activating known category representations in layer 7. (See text for details.) (From Hummel & Biederman, 1992.)

In layers 4 and 5, relations between geons are extracted from the geon attributes for fine orientation, horizontal position, vertical position, and size. Units in these layers respond to relative attributes, such as the fact that the vertical cone and the horizontal brick are perpendicular, that the cone is above and the brick is below, and that the brick is larger and the cone is smaller. Together with the geon attributes in layer 3, these geon relations activate an appropriate geon "feature assembly unit" in layer 6, one for each geon present in the object. The activation of these units corresponds to the geon identification stage in Biederman's original RBC theory. The units in layer 6 represent the set of all possible geon descriptions, and the subset of them that are activated constitute a geon structural description in JIM. The set of all such active geon description units then activates entry-level category representations in layer 7 to a degree that depends on how closely the geons present in the image correspond to the geons encoded in the object category units. In this case, the geon structural description matches the "nuclear power plant" unit most strongly, and this is how the model categorizes this particular object.

Although many details of JIM's operation are well specified, some had not yet been worked out at the time Hummel and Biederman wrote their 1992 article. The model has since been fleshed out more fully and is capable of categorizing many simple objects at an entry level correctly from a clean line drawing (Hummel, personal communication). The model is not yet able to start with raw gray-scale images, but this is true of most theories of high-level perception and object identification.

9.3.2 Accounting for Empirical Phenomena

It is instructive to examine how the empirical observations mentioned earlier in this chapter might be explained within the RBC theory of object categorization. As we will see, some of them are quite central to RBC and easily explained. Others require further specification and elaboration.

Typicality Effects. Typicality effects in RBC theory correspond to differences in the degree of activation of a given category representation (such as bird) by different examples within that category (such as robin, sparrow,

penguin, and ostrich). Recall that activation of categorical representations is proposed to be a function of the similarity of their geon description to the geon description of the target object. Since geon descriptions are necessarily rather specific and concrete, a categorical representation in terms of geon structure defines a rough prototype—"rough" because geons and geon relations are only qualitatively specified. As just discussed, it follows that a prototypical instance (such as a robin) will activate the categorical representation (bird) more strongly than an atypical instance (such as an ostrich). Typicality effects thus arise naturally in RBC from gradations in category activation in the comparison process, at least for gross differences in typicality.

Explaining finer-grained typicality effects—say, the difference in typicality between robins and eagles for the category of birds—is more difficult within RBC theory, however. The problem is that the coarse, discrete categories of 108 geons and 108 geon relations does not seem to provide sufficient representational resolution to discriminate between subordinate-level category exemplars that are highly similar. If finer gradations of quantitative parameters were allowed in the geon descriptions of both the categorical prototype and the target object, however, there is no reason why typicality effects in general could not be accounted for in this way. Indeed, recent elaborations of RBC allow for this possibility (Hummel & Stankiewicz, 1998).

Entry-Level Categories. The entry-level categorization phenomenon is that typical members of basic-level categories are categorized initially at the basic level, whereas atypical members are more likely to be categorized initially at the subordinate level. How are we to understand this phenomenon within the RBC theory?

The entry level for a given object into the categorical hierarchy would be determined in RBC simply by which categorical representation is activated most strongly in the category matching stage. There is no reason to suppose, for example, that all members of the same basic-level category (e.g., all birds) would necessarily activate the bird representation equally strongly. Indeed, there is good reason to suppose that they will not, for the geon description of a robin would presumably activate the geon description of the bird category much more strongly than the geon description of a penguin or ostrich would. Thus, one expects that atypical examples of a given category will be the ones for which their subordinate category (e.g., penguin or ostrich) will provide a significantly better match than their basic-level category. Given the fineness of the discriminations that are required to distinguish a robin from a wren or sparrow (or some other typical bird) and the coarseness of qualitative geon specification, it is quite likely that RBC would not be able to make such discriminations at all, at least not without positing a more fine-grained quantitative representation of the basic geon parameters. Therefore, it makes good sense in RBC that robins would initially activate the geon description of birds, whereas penguins and ostriches would activate the geon descriptions of penguins and ostriches, respectively. How subordinate categorization could even be accomplished is an open question, however.

Viewing Conditions. Perspective effects can occur in at least two different stages of the RBC theory: geon categorization and/or category matching. As argued above, geon categorization might be hampered from some perspectives because the optimal set of edge-based features for the geon are simply not available owing to self-occlusion. A pure top view of a car, for example, shows only one surface of the geons that constitute its body and top, making their overall 3-D shape extremely difficult to determine from this perspective. The correct spatial relations between geons may also be more difficult to discern from some perspectives than others.

Even if all the visible geons are properly identified, further problems in categorization can arise from poor viewing perspectives because important geons may be completely occluded by visible ones. For example, the pure top view of a car does not show its wheels at all. This may severely impede the process of matching its geon description to the car representation in memory, because wheels are such salient parts of cars. Therefore, even though RBC theory is based on representations of 3-D volumetric structure that are as viewpoint invariant as possible, it is susceptible to perspective effects arising from occlusion.

Such perspective effects were not obtained in Biederman and Gerhardstein's (1993) study because care was taken to ensure that the same geons (and geon relations) were visible in the different views of the same object. Thus, they studied only a subset of perspective differences for which there were no differences in geon visibility, and for these views there were no measurable differences in priming. This result too is quite understandable within RBC theory, for it is geon visibility effects that should produce differences in categorization performance due to perspective.[5]

RBC theory must deal with orientation effects in a different way because the same geons are, by definition, visible in any picture-plane rotation of an object about the line of sight. They arise in RBC theory because some of the relations encoded between geons are not orientation invariant. For example, RBC theory defines the above/below relation in gravitational terms rather than intrinsic, object-relative terms (Hummel & Biederman, 1992). In the stored representation of a lamp, for example, the shade is represented as being *above* the base. If a 45°-tilted lamp is presented for identification, the shade will be both *above* and *beside* the base in JIM's encoding scheme (see Figure 9.3.6, Layer 5). Introducing the spurious *beside* relation will decrease the match between the presented picture and the stored representation, thus slowing recognition. Further rotation of the lamp will introduce further discrepancies between the picture and the stored representation. Interestingly, at 180° rotations, the match should improve somewhat because the spurious *beside* relation is not present, consistent with the small decrease that is often found in reaction times at this orientation (see Figure 9.2.9).

However, the data from several experiments suggest that subjects might rotate objects from their misoriented state to upright to identify them (Jolicoeur, 1985; Tarr & Pinker, 1989, 1990). It is unclear why this would occur within a theory like RBC. After all, if the object has already been matched to the category via orientation-invariant information, why bother to rotate it to upright? One possibility is that the rotation is essentially a verification procedure executed to be sure the match is

---

[5] The explanation of perspective effects is currently very controversial. A highly critical commentary of Biederman and Gerhardstein's (1993) article was published by Tarr and Bülthoff (1995), who argued that essentially all the available data support viewpoint-dependent recognition processes that do not require dividing objects into parts. Biederman and Gerhardstein (1995) vigorously rebutted these arguments and concluded just the opposite.

Perceiving Function and Category

complete (Corballis, 1988). Another possibility is that only one salient part of the object (e.g., its top) has been matched before rotation and that true categorization does not take place until the representation of the whole object is transformed into congruence with the category representation. Finally, the extra time might be consumed by the process of finding the top of the figure (Biederman, 1987). Unfortunately, we do not yet know which account is correct.

Part Structure. RBC theory is very successful in accounting for the part-structural effects obtained in Biederman and Cooper's (1991b) contour deletion experiments, as described above. This is not too surprising, since the cornerstone of RBC is the assumption that objects are recognized by matching their component parts (i.e., geons) to categorical representations rather than by matching them holistically. Indeed, it was Biederman's RBC theory that inspired the contour deletion experiments to begin with.

In the first contour deletion experiment described above, RBC accounts for the lack of any difference in priming effects between the identity and line-complement conditions because in RBC it is the component geons that activate the category representations, not the individual image-based features, such as lines and edges. These features serve only to activate the geons; once they are activated, the features play no further role. RBC accounts for the large difference in priming between the identity and part-complement conditions with the geon-deleted stimuli in the second experiment because in the complementary-part condition, a completely different set of geons have been activated in the second presentation. Thus, the results of these experiments constitute an important test of part-based theories of categorization, of which RBC is a prime example.

Contextual Effects. Contextual effects cannot be explained directly within RBC as described above because it is a theory of recognizing individual objects. It could be extended, however, in ways that would produce contextual effects of the appropriate kind. The missing ingredient is the representation of scene structure, that is, perceptual "objects" that are larger than individual objects. Representations containing multiobject structure

of whole scenes are typically called *schemas* (e.g., Palmer, 1975b) or *frames* (e.g., Minsky, 1975). (We avoid using the "frame" terminology here because of possible confusion with the concept of reference frames discussed in Chapters 7 and 8.) The important aspect of scene schemas is that they encode dependencies among objects that tend to occur together in meaningful environments. Thus, there might be a schema for kitchens that would contain geon descriptions of stoves, refrigerators, cabinets, counters, toasters, and so forth; a schema for playgrounds that would contain geon descriptions of slides, swings, sandboxes, merry-go-rounds, and so forth; and other schemas for the many different kinds of environments we experience frequently in daily life.

The idea of scene schemas is really just an extension of part-structural hierarchies for objects and parts (Palmer, 1975b). For example, a hubcap is part of a wheel, which, in turn, is part of a car. And a car can be part of numerous different scenes, many of which will have a different representational schema: garage schemas, city traffic schemas, parking lot schemas, freeway schemas, gas station schemas, automobile showroom schemas, and so on. The primary difference is that the component objects and spatial relations in scene schemas are inherently more variable and probabilistic than those in an object representation. Cars almost always have wheels, and they are almost always in the same places on the car. But gas stations may or may not contain cars at any given time; and when they do, the cars can be found in many different locations. Despite such differences, representations of individual objects and whole contextual scenes are so similar that both are often referred to as schemas: face schemas, person schemas, bird schemas, and so forth as well as gas station schemas and playground schemas. Calling all perceptual representations schemas emphasizes the essential unity and interconnectedness of all perceptual knowledge.

Given such hierarchical relations among parts, objects, and scenes, Figure 9.3.7 shows what a schema might look like for a kitchen scene, as coded in the form of a hierarchical network (Palmer, 1975b). Object schemas are the components of such scene schemas, just as geons are the components of object schemas. Such schema networks can explain contextual effects as follows: Suppose that the target object in the scene is the loaf of bread shown in inset A of Figure 9.2.15. The

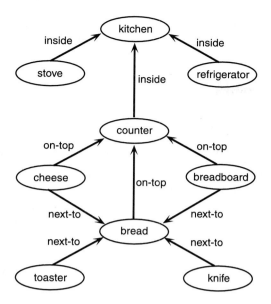

Figure 9.3.7 A partial schema for a kitchen scene such as shown in Figure 9.2.15. Locational relations are represented abstractly to illustrate the lack of specificity in generic scene knowledge. (After Palmer, 1975b.)

context shows a kitchen scene in which there is a counter, a cutting board, a toaster, a knife, and so on. Each of the nodes in the network corresponding to these objects will be activated by object categorization processes. Their activation, in turn, will spread to nearby nodes, priming them for recognition. Thus, the counter, toaster, cutting board, and knife will indirectly activate the internal representation for bread, corresponding to a perceptual expectation that bread may also be present in such a scene. Such priming by contextual activation makes it more likely that the visual system will interpret any loaf-shaped object in that context as bread. This is just what experimental results on the perception of such pictures have shown (Palmer, 1975b).

Visual Agnosia. There is probably no single explanation for visual agnosia, since there are many constellations of symptoms that fall within the general category (Farah, 1990). As we suggested earlier, the "unusual views" phenomenon of visual agnosia may be explained by the same processing difficulties required to explain perspective effects in normals. Another process that may be involved in the deficits manifest in visual agnosia is the selection of an appropriate object-cen-

tered reference frame along an axis of elongation (e.g., Humphreys & Riddoch, 1984, 1985). Not enough is yet known about visual agnosia to specify completely where categorization breaks down in these patients. Much current research is devoted to making a finer-grained analysis to determine how it might be accounted for within a theoretical framework like Marr's (1982) or Biederman's (1987) RBC theory.

Weaknesses. For all of the virtues of RBC as a theory of entry-level object categorization, it has some problems as well. One of the most serious was mentioned in Chapter 8 and again earlier in this chapter: the lack of representational power. Some of this comes from limitations of generalized cylinders as representational primitives for shape information. But these problems are aggravated by discretely classifying generalized cylinders into just 108 geons and reducing all possible geon relations to just 108 binary relations, because these restrictions further reduce the amount of visual detail geon descriptions can encode. Even the trillions of logically possible combinations are not sufficient to capture the subtle differences in shape that people normally and regularly detect in categorizing and identifying objects. They might suffice for much of entry-level categorization, but this is currently an open question. Differences between dogs and cats or between donkeys and horses, to pick just two examples, require relatively fine quantitative discriminations both in the shapes of their component parts and in the spatial relations among them. Such discriminations appear to be at or beyond the representational power of RBC theory as originally formulated.

Even more discriminative power is needed to distinguish among subordinate categories. The differences between different kinds of dogs, for instance, certainly require a good deal more quantitative information than geon structural descriptions provide. To take an even more difficult example, consider how 108 geons and 108 relations could possibly support the kind of categorization performance that people achieve in recognizing well-known individuals from their faces. Even if faces could be naturally analyzed into configurations of geons—and it is not clear that they can—human faces are so similar to one another that they all would have virtually identical geon descriptions.

Different responses to this criticism can be made. Hummel and Stankiewicz (1998) took the most direct route and proposed a revised theory that provides more finely graded quantitative representations that might be able to overcome such problems. Biederman's own response is that RBC is not meant to be a theory of face recognition, because he believes object categorization processes to be qualitatively different from face recognition processes. Findings that support this idea have been reported, including evidence that faces are processed in different areas of the brain (e.g., Tanaka & Farah, 1993; Wallace & Farah, 1992). These findings are subject to alternative interpretations, however, such as the possibility that this so-called "face area" is actually used whenever subtle visual discriminations are performed within a highly practiced domain (e.g., Gauthier & Tarr, 1997). In any case, it is too early to draw definite conclusions about just how "special" or "different" face perception might be from other forms of visual recognition.

Another potential problem with RBC as a theory of object categorization is that it is not yet clear that RBC will actually be able to categorize objects from images, much less perform as humans do. The proof must await a fully implemented computer simulation that is actually able to identify common objects from gray-scale images as people obviously can do. RBC sounds quite plausible as a conceptual theoretical framework in many respects, but one of the most important lessons that has been learned from research in computer vision is that even plausible theories often do not work as expected or do so only under very restricted conditions. Hummel and Biederman's (1992) neural network implementation of RBC theory avoids many difficult problems by starting with hand-coded feature descriptions rather than gray-scale images. It thus skips what has turned out to be one of the most difficult problems with theories based on volumetric structural descriptions: identifying the primitive volumetric components from gray-scale information. RBC theory will not rest on a firm foundation until it has solved this problem.

9.3.3 Viewpoint-Specific Theories

RBC theory is representative of the dominant trend in theorizing about object categorization processes in the 1970s and 1980s, being similar in many respects to prior structural description models by Binford (1971), Marr and Nishihara (1978), Palmer (1975b), and Winston (1975). Like Marr's approach in particular, RBC theory assumes that objects are represented by hierarchical structural descriptions of volumetric primitives based on generalized cylinders. Despite many years of effort at perfecting such models, computer implementations have not yet managed to achieve acceptable levels of performance starting with raw video images. In the wake of these disappointments, other computational theorists have pursued alternative approaches to object recognition and categorization. We will now consider three of these alternative theories: aspect graphs (Koenderink & Van Doorn, 1978), alignment with 3-D models (Huttenlocher & Ullman, 1987; Lowe, 1985; Ullman, 1989), and alignment with 2-D views (Poggio & Edelman, 1990; Ullman, 1996; Ullman & Basri, 1991).

The Case for Multiple Views. In many ways, the starting point for these alternative approaches is the existence of perspective effects that were described earlier in this chapter (e.g., Palmer et al., 1981). The fact that recognition and categorization performance is not invariant over different views raises the possibility that objects might be identified by matching 2-D input views directly to some kind of view-specific category representation. To begin with the most obvious possibility, the idea of canonical perspective suggests a particularly simple view-specific template-matching theory: Each object might be represented in memory by a single, canonical 2-D view, and 2-D input views might be matched directly against it. Canonical views would then be quickly and accurately categorized because they could be matched directly to the canonical 2-D representation in memory. Other input views would not match initially but would have to be rotated into alignment with the canonical view to achieve a successful 2-D match. (Alternatively, the canonical perspective view in memory might be rotated into alignment with the input image.) Performing such transformations would require more time and would increase the possibility of making errors, consistent with the general pattern of perspective effects reported by Palmer, Rosch, and Chase (1981), Edelman and Bülthoff (1992), and Bülthoff and Edelman (1992).

This single-view explanation of perspective effects runs afoul of at least three significant problems, however. First, it is logically insufficient for the task. No single 2-D view can support accurate 3-D object recognition or categorization from multiple perspectives without further information. There are many surfaces of the object that simply are not represented in a single view, even a canonical one, owing to self-occlusion. These occluded surfaces cannot be inferred from a single view except for special cases, such as symmetrical objects (Vetter, Poggio, & Bülthoff, 1994). Therefore, the complete 3-D shape of the object cannot be recovered from a single 2-D view in the general case.

Second, if one assumes that other views are recognized by being rotated into correspondence with the canonical one, there must be some representation or process in memory to support the rotation as previously occluded surfaces come into view. Therefore, the process of rotating into congruence with a canonical view presupposes the functional equivalent of the 3-D representation it was designed to eliminate. As we will see shortly, there are ways to use two or more views to accomplish this task, but no single view will suffice in the general case.

Third, the hypothesis of rotation from a single canonical view is inconsistent with the data from perspective experiments. Naming latencies are not a simple increasing function of the orientational difference between the input image and a single canonical view (Palmer et al., 1981; Edelman & Bülthoff, 1992). There are usually several good views of an object from a variety of different viewpoints, some widely separated from one another, with bad views in between.

A more realistic possibility is that there might be *multiple* 2-D representations from several different viewpoints that can be employed in recognizing objects. These multiple views are likely to be those perspectives from which the object has been seen most often in past experience. As mentioned in Section 9.2.2, Tarr and Pinker (1989, 1990) reported evidence for this possibility in a series of experiments that studied the identification of 2-D figures at different orientations in the frontal plane. After subjects had been shown unfamiliar letter-like figures several times in just a few orientations during an initial training phase, they were fastest at recognizing them in a later test phase at the particular orientations they had seen before, as though they had stored those specific images in memory. They were able to identify the same figures at orientations they had not seen

before, but it took longer, and response times increased as a function of the orientational difference between the tested image and the closest orientation at which it had been presented in the initial training phase. As subjects got more and more experience with different orientations, the effect of orientation on recognition time was gradually reduced. These findings suggest that recognition might actually be mediated by a fairly complete catalog of different view-specific 2-D representations. The same might be true for perspective effects, in which objects might be represented by a number of distinct view-specific 2-D representations.

This hypothesis may remind the reader of template representations of shape, which are also view specific. The difference is that multiple-view representations need not actually be templates but could be feature maps or even structural descriptions. The crucial thing is that they are representations of 2-D image-based (i.e., pictorial) structure rather than of 3-D object-based (i.e., volumetric) structure.

Aspect Graphs. We said in Chapter 8 that templates were not viable as representations of 3-D shape, at least in part, because an infinite number of templates would be required to account for recognizing different perspective views of the same object. This assertion is technically correct, but many views of the same object are actually very similar, differing only in metric details. Consider the views of the object shown in Figure 9.3.8, for example. None of them are exactly the same, but parts A and B show the same surfaces, edges, and vertices in essentially the same configurations of 2-D relationships. Part C, however, is qualitatively different in that it shows several surfaces that are not seen in either A or B and fails to show several other surfaces that A

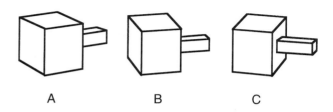

Figure 9.3.8 Qualitatively similar and different views of the same object. The views shown in parts A and B reveal the same surfaces of the object in the same qualitative relations, whereas that in part C reveals different surfaces.

Perceiving Function and Category

and B reveal. Perhaps the first two views could be recognized by being matched to a single view-specific representation stored in memory using some more abstract format than a template, with a different view-specific representation needed to recognize the third. If so, the crucial questions are how this can be accomplished and how many such qualitatively different views would be required to support object recognition from the variety of perspectives from which people can do so.

The idea of recognizing an object by matching its current perspective view to a set of qualitatively distinct representations from different viewpoints was pioneered by Dutch psychophysicists Koenderink and van Doorn (1979). They called the view-specific representations that they proposed **aspect graphs**. An aspect graph is a network of representations containing all topologically distinct 2-D views (or *aspects*) of the same object. Each aspect is represented by a structural description that defines its topology: the set of edges and vertices that mark the borders between visible and occluded surfaces in the projected image, as illustrated in Figure 9.3.9 for one aspect of a tetrahedron. Notice that because all three views at the top have the same topology—that is, the same edges and vertices are connected in qualitatively the same way, regardless of the specific edge orientations and edge lengths—they are represented by the same aspect description.

The representations of two different aspects are connected within the aspect graph of an object if there is a continuous change in viewpoint that takes the viewer

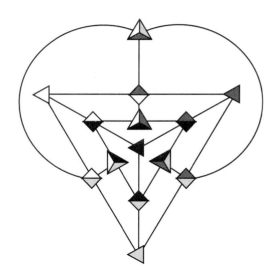

Figure 9.3.10 Fourteen aspects of a tetrahedron. All possible aspects of a simple tetrahedron are represented by this network. Either one, two, or three faces are visible simultaneously, and the lines between different aspects show physically possible transitions. Different faces are indicated by different shading. (After Koenderink & van Dorn, 1979.)

from one to the other. The connections among the set of 14 different topologically distinct views (aspects) of a tetrahedron are shown in Figure 9.3.10. Moving along any continuous path of viewpoints around this object thus corresponds to traversing a path over the links between aspects. In the graph, however, the shift from one aspect to another occurs at the moment the change in viewpoint causes the occlusion or disocclusion of edges and vertices. The graph traversal is thus discrete, even though the change in viewpoint is continuous because changes between its nodes occur at the instant the topological structure of the 2-D edges in the image changes.

Although a full and complete aspect graph representation with equal accessibility to all aspects would produce orientation invariant object recognition, perspective effects could arise naturally in a number of different ways. Perhaps the most obvious is that representations of aspects that are most frequently seen might be easier to access than those that are seldom seen. Speed of access might also depend on the number of edges and vertices a given aspect contains, the aspects that contain more edges being accessed more quickly. (Although this might seem counterintuitive at first, it makes sense if the matching of edges occurs in parallel because additional edges provide additional constraints

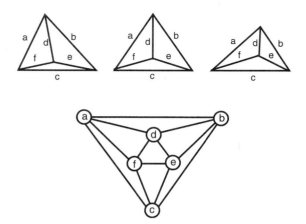

Figure 9.3.9 An aspect graph of a tetrahedron. The structure of all three views of this tetrahedron can be represented by a single aspect graph that shows the connectivity of the various edges by the links in the graph shown below.

that make the topological structure of that perspective less ambiguous.) Note that these two possibilities are essentially variations on the hypotheses mentioned previously to account for perspective effects—the frequency hypothesis and the maximal information hypothesis—stated in terms of the specific structure of aspect graphs.

Aspect graphs improve on template theories of object representation by greatly reducing the number of view-specific representations required to capture the shape of the object. They do so in part because, although they are view-specific representations, they are much more abstract than templates, being structural descriptions of the connectedness of edges and vertices and of the transitions between different views. Even so, the question remains of whether the reduction is great enough to make it a reasonable theory of human object recognition.

As one might imagine, the complexity of an aspect graph increases with the complexity of the object it represents. A sphere has a single aspect, but even an object as simple as a tetrahedron requires 14 different aspects to completely capture its structure (see Figure 9.3.10). The number of aspects for a reasonably complex object, such as the nonsense object shown in Figure 9.1.3, would be in the thousands. This is an improvement over the number of templates that would be required, but the numbers are still daunting.

A second difficulty with aspect graphs is that, because they are abstract, they cannot support discriminations among objects with different quantitative measurements that have the same 2-D topology of edges and vertices in their projected views. Figure 9.3.11 shows several objects that have the same aspect representation but different perceived shapes. This is not a problem for geon

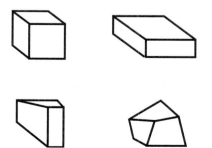

Figure 9.3.11 Topologically equivalent views of four distinct objects. Because the topology of edges and vertices is identical in these four drawings, they would match the same aspect representation despite their obvious metric differences.

representations because, despite their largely qualitative nature, they include features such as aspect ratio, symmetry, and edge parallelism that are sensitive to metric qualities. Standard aspect graphs contain no such quantitative information.

A third problem with aspect graphs is that even if observers have seen only a single representative view of an object, they typically appear to have some idea of its 3-D structure and are able to recognize it from many novel views. This is an ability that is not directly supported by aspect graphs for a truly novel object, since they are essentially just networks of topological descriptions of the 2-D views from which that object has been seen. Although it is computationally possible to recognize novel views from a relatively small number of suitably constrained 2-D views (Ullman & Basri, 1991), this ability is not supported by aspect graphs, which are good for recognizing objects only from the qualitative views represented in memory. A novel image of an object would be recognized by an aspect graph system only if it came from the same aspect as a previously seen view.

The second problem provides a clue to the direction view-specific theorists have taken to improve their theories. It suggests that there is more structure in the particular variations within the views of a single aspect than is captured by the topology of its edges. This becomes obvious when one realizes that all views within an aspect are related by being different 2-D projections of the same 3-D object. Because projective transformations are much more tightly constrained than topological transformations, a view-based theory could discriminate between the objects depicted in Figure 9.3.11 if some method could be devised to exploit this additional structure.

The third problem suggests that there must be some way to extrapolate from just a few views of an object to its 3-D structure—or at least to what the object would look like from other viewpoints. Such considerations have led several theorists to similar ideas about how objects can be recognized by matching incoming 2-D views with 2-D views that are either stored directly in memory as models or generated by a process that combines two or more of these 2-D models (e.g., Poggio & Edelman, 1990; Ullman, 1996; Ullman & Basri, 1991). Let us now see how these ideas have played out in developing more sophisticated view-specific theories of object recognition.

Alignment with 3-D Models. An important stepping stone for these view-specific theories was computational work on methods for matching 2-D images directly and holistically with 3-D models of objects stored in memory (Lowe, 1985; Huttenlocher & Ullman, 1987; Ullman, 1989). The basic idea was to solve this problem by transformational alignment in a sequence of processes analogous to the steps we mentioned in Section 8.1 with respect to the shape equivalence problem. In the present case, the key processes are as follows:

1. Find the correspondence between a few salient image features and model features.

2. Determine the viewpoint that best aligns these features of the image with the corresponding features of the 3-D model.

3. Compute the projection of the full 3-D model onto a 2-D image plane from the viewpoint determined in step 2, including all points rather than just the salient ones.

4. Determine the degree to which this projected image of the 3-D model matches the 2-D input image.

The model with the best match in step 4 that exceeds some minimum threshold is then identified as the object being viewed.

These 2-D to 3-D theories assume that all models of known objects are stored in memory as 3-D representations of spatial coordinates because this enables them to make use of all the structure of projective transformations. The mapping from salient pictorial features in the 2-D image to their corresponding features in the 3-D model and the mapping in the inverse direction are therefore both constrained by the laws of projective geometry. These constraints allow such theories to overcome the problem illustrated in Figure 9.3.11: These four images will now fit four different 3-D models, corresponding to the different 3-D shapes people perceive when they look at these drawings, rather than fitting the same aspect representation equally well. This improvement results directly from using projective constraints in the alignment and transformation processes.

Computer simulations by Lowe (1985) and Huttenlocher and Ullman (1987) demonstrated that this kind of approach could solve the object recognition problem from different perspectives, at least under certain restricted conditions. Figure 9.3.12 shows an example of the stages Lowe's model goes through in attempting to

interpret an image. Part A shows an input image depicting a bin full of disposable razors. The program's task was to identify individual razors in the image and determine their physical orientation in the bin. (This kind of task is of particular interest in computer vision because locating objects for industrial applications, such as robots picking objects out of bins, motivates a fair amount of research.) Part B shows the initial line segments that were identified using an algorithm based on Marr and Hildreth's (1980) method for finding luminance edges. These were then used to determine the best viewpoint from which this image fits the 3-D model. Part C exhibits the 3-D wire frame model of the razor category (shown here as a 2-D image viewed from one particular perspective) that was matched to the line segments depicted in part B. Part D shows the final correspondence between the input image and the internal model of the razor as seen from the variety of different perspectives. The dotted lines in part D indicate edges whose presence was predicted from the model but not located in the image by the low-level edge finder. Rather, they were found by top-down matching processes once the 3-D model was projected onto the 2-D image.

Alignment with 2-D View Combinations. Once the problem of matching 2-D views to 3-D models has been solved, solving the problem of 2-D to 2-D object recognition reduces to replacing the 3-D model's function by a small number of 2-D views. Progress on this front has been made recently by several computational theorists (e.g., Poggio & Edelman, 1990; Ullman, 1996; Ullman & Basri, 1991). The goal is to find a method that can derive new, unstored 2-D views of an object from a few stored ones, bypassing the need for a 3-D model in memory.

Ullman and Basri (1991) demonstrated that this goal can be achieved, at least under certain conditions, by proving that all possible views of an object can be reconstructed as a linear combination from just three suitably chosen orthographic projections of the same 3-D object. Figure 9.3.13 shows some rather striking examples based on this method. Two actual 2-D views of a human face (models M1 and M2) have been combined to produce other 2-D views of the same face. One is an intermediate view that has been interpolated *between* the two models (linear combination LC2), and the other two

A

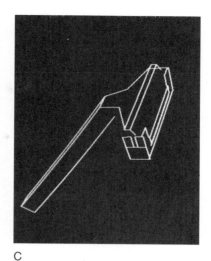

C

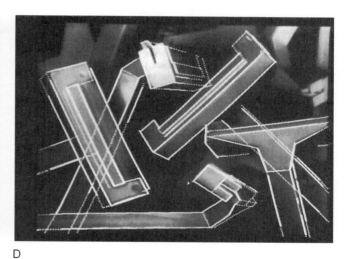

B

D

Figure 9.3.12 Lowe's viewpoint consistency model (SCERPO). Part A shows an image of a bin of many such razors. Part B displays the edges SCERPO derived from image A in a strictly bottom-up manner. Part C shows the 3-D wire model of a disposable razor. Part D shows the successful matches SCERPO found between image edges and different projections of its internal razor model, with the extrapolated model edges indicated by dotted lines. (From Lowe, 1985.)

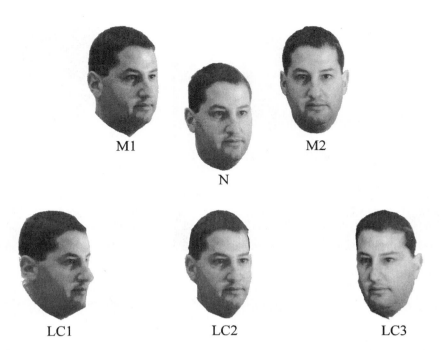

M1   N   M2

LC1   LC2   LC3

Figure 9.3.13 Novel views obtained by combination of gray-scale images. M1 and M2 show two model views of the same human face from different perspectives. N shows a novel intermediate view of the same face. LC1, LC2, and LC3 show novel views generated by a linear combination of M1 and M2 without any specific 3-D model of the face. LC2 matches the actual view from the same viewpoint (N) very well. (From Ullman, 1996.)

views have been extrapolated *beyond* them (linear combinations LC1 and LC3). Notice the close resemblance between the interpolated view (LC2) and the actual view from the corresponding viewpoint (novel view N).

This rather surprising result holds only under rather restricted conditions, however, some of which are ecologically unrealistic. Three key assumptions of Ullman and Basri's (1991) analysis are the following:

1. All points belonging to the object must be visible in each view.

2. The correct correspondence of all points between each pair of views must be known.

3. The views must differ only by rigid transformations and/or uniform size scaling (dilations).

The first assumption requires that none of the points on the object be occluded in any of the three views. This condition holds for wire objects, which are fully visible from any viewpoint, but is violated by almost all other 3-D objects for most sets of three viewpoints. The reason is simply that most objects are composed of opaque surfaces that occlude all points along lines of sight beyond them. The linear combinations of the face in Figure 9.3.13 are actually somewhat less impressive than they seem at first, because the method works only for points that are visible in both views. What is being generated is essentially just a mask of the facial surface itself rather than the whole head. The difference can be seen by looking carefully at the edges of the face where the head ends rather abruptly and unnaturally in LC1 and LC3. The linear combination method would not be able to derive a profile view of the same head, because the back of the head is not present in either of the model views (M1 and M2) used to extrapolate other views. For a linear combination of views to allow object recognition from all possible views, self-occluding objects would therefore have to have three different 2-D models for each set of views in which different points are visible. In comparison with aspect graph theory, this means that a full representation of a 3-D object via linear combinations would require three times as many 2-D views as there are aspects of the object. If the number of aspects in a complex object's aspect graph is daunting, then the number of 2-D views that it requires is three times more daunting.

The second assumption requires that the correspondence between points in stored 2-D views be known before the views can be combined. Although solving the correspondence problems is a nontrivial computation for complex objects, it can be derived "off-line" rather than during the process of recognizing an object. The third assumption means that the view combination process will fail to produce an accurate combination if the different 2-D views include plastic deformations of the object. If one view is of a person standing and the other is of the same person sitting, for instance, their combination will not necessarily be a possible view of the person. This restriction thus can cause problems for bodies and faces of animate creatures as well as inanimate objects made of pliant materials (e.g., clothing) or have a jointed structure (e.g., scissors). Computational theorists are currently exploring ways of solving these problems (see Ullman, 1996, for a wide-ranging discussion of such issues), but they are important limitations of the linear combinations approach.

The results obtained by Ullman and Basri (1991) prove that 2-D views can be combined to produce new views under the stated conditions, but they do not specify how these views can be used to recognize the object from an input image. Further techniques are required to find a best-fitting match between the input view and the linear combinations of the model views as part of the object recognition process. One approach is to use a small number of features to find the best combination of the model views, much as a small number of features can be used to align a view with a 3-D model. Other methods are also possible but are too technical to be described here. (The interested reader can consult Ullman's (1996) book for details.)

Poggio and Edelman (1990) employed a somewhat different method, called generalized radial basis functions (GRBF) to generate novel 2-D views from a set of stored ones. Their nonlinear method learns to approximate unknown views by using the known model views as constraints. The basic idea is analogous to other approximation methods, such as fitting a smooth curve to a set of data points. If one knows a set of points from an unknown function, computational methods exist for finding the smoothest curve that goes through (or near) all of them. In Poggio and Edelman's method, the

stored views are analogous to the data points, and the set of unknown novel views are analogous to the points along the curve that is fit to them. The novel views derived from the known ones might not be exactly right, but they are likely to be reasonable approximations, and the closer they lie to known views, the more accurate they are likely to be. The GRBF method can be viewed as a generalization of Ullman and Basri's (1991) linear combinations method, but it typically requires more than three views. On the other hand, it is also able to recover the pose of the object relative to the viewer, which the linear combination method does not do.

Weaknesses. Despite the elegance of some of the results that have been obtained by theorists working within the view-specific framework, such theories face serious problems as a general explanation of visual object recognition and categorization. Five of the most serious are the following:

1. *Three-dimensional structure.* Aspect graphs and alignment with 2-D view combinations have a problem in that they do not account well for people's perceptions of 3-D structure in objects. Just from looking at an object, we generally feel that we know a great deal about its 3-D structure, including how to shape our hands to grasp it and what it would feel like if we were to explore it manually. How can this occur if all we have access to is a structured set of 2-D views? One could appeal to depth maps based on stereoscopic or motion parallax information (as in Marr's 2.5-D sketch), but people also seem to have reasonably good perception of 3-D structure even for objects viewed with one stationary eye. In some sense it does not matter how many different 2-D interpolations or approximations can be generated from the stored 2-D views or whether they are sufficient for recognition; the problem is that they are still two-dimensional representations and therefore inadequate to represent 3-D structure.

2. *Novel objects.* Matching 2-D views to 3-D models in memory does not suffer from the problem of three-dimensionality in quite the same way because explicit 3-D models of known objects are stored in memory (e.g., Huttenlocher & Ullman, 1987; Lowe, 1985; Ullman, 1989). Once the object is recognized, its full 3-D structure is therefore accessible. But what if the object is novel, such as a piece of abstract sculpture or the nonsense

object in Figure 9.1.3? Surely people perceive such objects as having clear and obvious 3-D shapes even in the absence of a preexisting internal 3-D model that matches them. Such models must be constructed from visual input, but it is not clear how this is accomplished.

3. *Nonrigid objects*. All three of the view-specific theories that we have mentioned—aspect graphs, matching 2-D views to 3-D models, and matching 2-D views to 2-D view combinations—work in trying to recognize a rigid object. But what about trying to recognize a human body using this scheme, even the very same person's body? If one matches 2-D views to internal 3-D models, there would have to be hundreds of different 3-D models. For a dancer who needs to be represented in many different poses, the number may climb into the thousands. One can approximate many such deformations by locally rigid transformations of subsets of the object, as in the case of the body, but this introduces the functional equivalent of parts, a complication that view-specific theorists try to avoid.

4. *Part structure*. At the end of Chapter 7 we observed that most complex objects have a fairly clear perceived structure in terms of parts and subparts. The view-specific representations we have considered generally do not contain any explicit representation of such structure because they consist of sets of unarticulated points or low-level features, such as edges and vertices. It is not clear, then, how they could explain Biederman and Cooper's (1991b) experiments on the difference between line and part deletion conditions in priming experiments (see Section 9.2.3). Ullman (1996) has suggested that parts as well as whole objects may be represented separately in memory. This sensible idea should serve as a reminder that part-based recognition schemes, such as RBC, and view-based schemes are not mutually exclusive but can be combined into various hybrid approaches.

5. *Exemplar variation*. The situations to which view-specific theories have been successfully applied thus far are limited to identical objects that vary only in viewpoint—for example, Lowe's bin full of razors (Figure 9.3.12) or recognizing different views of the very same face. But what about classifying examples of more variable entry-level categories of objects, such as chairs, dogs, or houses? The large amount of metric variation across different exemplars in most categories makes viewpoint-specific theories unlikely to work for the general problem of visual categorization. To apply such techniques to entry-level categories, they would have to be represented in terms of concrete prototypes (e.g., Ullman, 1996). Even so, it seems unlikely that this would work. How well would different houses match the representation of a single instance, no matter how typical or representative it might be? Consider trying to match the specific image of a log cabin or Frank Lloyd Wright's "Fallingwater" with that of a prototypical house, whatever that might be. It just does not seem possible that the process of categorizing both as houses could be accomplished at the level of image matching.

A controversy is currently raging between advocates of part-based structural description theories and those of view-based pictorial alignment theories, as evidenced by the recent exchange between Tarr and Bülthoff (1995) and Biederman and Gerhardstein (1995) about the interpretation of Biederman and Gerhardstein's (1993) prior priming results from different viewpoints. The contrast between these approaches is often presented as an either/or proposition, but this need not be the case. One possible both/and resolution would be that both part-based and view-based processes may be used, but for different kinds of tasks (e.g., Farah, 1992; Tarr & Bülthoff, 1995). View-specific representations seem well suited to recognizing the very same object from different perspective views because in that situation, there is no variation in the structure of the object; all the differences between images can be explained by the variation in viewpoint. Recognizing specific objects is difficult for structural description theories because their representations are seldom specific enough to discriminate between different exemplars. In contrast, structural description theories such as RBC seem well suited to entry-level categorization because they have more abstract representations that are better able to encompass shape variations among different exemplars of the same category. This is exactly where view-specific theories have difficulty.

Another possibility is that both view-based and part-based schemes can be combined to achieve the best of both worlds. They are not mutually exclusive and could even be implemented in parallel (e.g., Hummel & Stankiewicz, 1996). This approach suggests that when the current view matches a view-based representation in memory, recognition will be fast and accurate; when it does not, categorization must rely on the slower, more complex process of matching against structural descriptions. Which, if any, of these possible resolutions of the current conflict will turn out to be most productive is not yet clear. The hope is that the controversy will generate interesting predictions that can be tested experimentally, for that is how scientific progress is made.

9.4 Identifying Letters and Words

Thus far we have considered how everyday 3-D objects might be categorized. Now we will turn to the much more restricted problem of how linguistic text, consisting mainly of letters and words, is identified. It is a significant special case of visual classification because of the immense importance of reading in modern culture. If we understood the visual processes that underlie how people read, we should be able to devise better techniques for teaching students to read, for helping people with reading problems, and for programming computers to "read" from images of text. The latter technology, under the name of **optical character recognition (OCR)** is already available, but it is far less proficient than human readers and typically relies on techniques that are unlikely to be involved in human reading.

We must begin by making an important distinction: Identifying letters and words in linguistic text is not the same as reading in the ordinary sense. Ordinary reading requires not only identifying words but also understanding their meanings in the specific context in which they appear. This process of language comprehension is an exceedingly complex mental ability that requires both knowing individual word meanings and being able to interpret them coherently within the context of the whole text. These are not perceptual problems, but conceptual ones, and exceedingly difficult ones at that. We therefore will consider only the front end of reading: the processes that are involved in identifying the letters and words that make up the text. As we will see, this is not a trivial task.

Significant progress on letter and word categorization was made earlier than that on object categorization, in part because of the more restricted nature of the problem. Important simplifications result from the following two properties of text:

1. *Two-dimensionality.* Normal linguistic text consists exclusively of markings on a flat 2-D surface. This means

that the structure of the proximal stimulus for text corresponds closely to the structure of the distal stimulus, provided that the surface is in or near the frontal plane. Most of the difficult problems involved in depth perception, achieving perceptual constancy, and completing partly occluded objects are thereby avoided.

2. *Combinatorial structure.* All Indo-European text consists of sequences of the same small set of characters. In English, these are the 52 letters (26 uppercase and 26 lowercase), 10 numerals, plus an assortment of punctuation marks and other symbols. (Languages such as Japanese and especially Chinese have much larger character sets, numbering into the thousands.) This means that these characters constitute a "natural" set of atomic primitives out of which all words, sentences, and written linguistic texts are constructed.

As important as these factors are in simplifying the problem of perceiving words and letters, they do not present anything close to a complete solution. Some constancylike problems remain, for example, in identifying letters in different positions, sizes, and orientations. The a priori status of characters as natural primitives appears to solve the problem that geons are intended to solve in RBC theory. Indeed, Biederman motivated the use of geons as a kind of alphabet for visual objects. Even so, the fact that letters are themselves complex entities that invite analysis into more basic properties or components means that the representation problem is not solved simply by the existence of the alphabet.

9.4.1 Identifying Letters

The obvious place to start is with an analysis of how letters are identified. To simplify the problem even further, we will consider only how the 26 uppercase letters of a typeset (not handwritten) font might be perceived.

The basic difficulties in representing the shapes of 2-D patterns have already been discussed in Chapter 8. Here, we simply recapitulate the conclusions we reached there:

• *Templates.* Standard templates are highly implausible because of the enormous number that would be required to recognize letters in all possible positions, sizes, and orientations, to say nothing of variations in type font. If the type font is known in advance—as it may be in certain real-world applications, such as automated systems for reading the numbers on bank checks—preprocessed templates can be used on text that has been normalized for size, position, and orientation. Templates cannot be taken too seriously as the basis of a general theory of human letter categorization, however, for people can read many fonts, including new ones they have never seen before.

• *Features.* Feature representations are, as always, an attractive possibility. Their major drawback is the lack of a set of features that will support categorization across different type fonts and the difficulty in identifying those features computationally.

• *Structural descriptions.* As in theories of object categorization, structural descriptions are also an attractive option. Significant drawbacks are that they are complex and difficult to match to one another.

The current state of affairs is that there is little agreement on what type of representation people employ in identifying letters, although templates have generally been considered a poor candidate until recently.

Feature theories have been proposed by many different researchers. Both part features and property features are usually included, although some theories manage with just part features (e.g., McClelland & Rumelhart, 1981). Figure 9.4.1 shows a representation of a possible set of features for capital letters of the alphabet. The entries in this table indicate the number of occurrences of each feature in each of the 26 letters. Note that no two letters have exactly the same set of features. This is necessary for the representation to be able to support correct categorization of all 26 letters. However, several letters have a great deal of overlap in their features, such as B and D or E and F. The overlap between the feature sets for a given pair of letters is a theoretical measure of their predicted perceptual similarity. It therefore should correlate well with empirical measures of how confusable the two letters are in categorization tasks: For example, how often do subjects perceive a B when a D was actually presented, and vice versa? Such measures of confusability can be (and have been) used to test theories of letter representation, although the results have not been conclusive in identifying the best or the correct set of features.

Other theories of letter representation allow continuous variation in the attributes that distinguish among them. Such theories can be derived from multidimensional scaling procedures, as described in Chapter 8. Empirical measures of the similarity between pairs of letter, such as their confusability, are transformed into a multidimensional space in which each letter is represented as a point within the space. The distance between points corresponds to the dissimilarity between the letters at those positions.

One kind of continuous dimensional representation that has been formulated for letters is the **fuzzy logical model of perception (FLMP)** (Massaro, 1989; Massaro & Hary, 1986; Oden & Massaro, 1978). One virtue of a fuzzy-set-based formulation is its ability to account for the effects of continuous variations in letter structure on their categorization. Analogous to the fuzzy logical model of color categorization we considered in Chapter 3, the continuous range of values possible for features in the FLMP corresponds to the degree to which a given letter has that feature. For example, Figure 9.4.2 shows a number of letterlike forms generated by continuously varying the orientation of the short segment and the openness of the oval portion. When the segment is clearly horizontal and the oval is quite open (at or near the top left of the array), everybody identifies the figure as a G. When the segment is clearly oblique and the oval is fully closed (at the lower right of the array), everybody identifies the figure as a Q. The rest of the array consists of ambiguous cases that can potentially be perceived either way. Figure 9.4.3 shows the data from a categorization experiment in which the experimenters measured the proportion of trials on which subjects responded that the figure was a Q as opposed to a G (Massaro & Hary, 1986). The data shows an orderly progression from G to Q responses, as expected from the FLMP.

It is difficult to explain such results within a binary feature approach. One possibility is to assume that intermediate feature values are registered unambiguously on each trial as one value or the other and that the probability of each value varies as a function of the stimulus parameters. While this predicts the same overall pattern of results as the fuzzy feature theory, it fails to capture the ambiguous appearance of the figures. If each oval were perceived as open or closed and each segment as horizontal or oblique, then each figure should appear to be unambiguously a G, a Q, or one of two nonletters (at the upper right and lower left corners of Figure 9.4.2) at any given moment, but this does not seem to be the case, at least under normal viewing con-

	Vertical Lines	Horizontal Lines	Oblique Lines	L-junctions	T-junctions	X-junctions	Free-Ends	Curved Portions	Closed Portions	Reflectional Symmetries
A	0	1	2	1	2	0	2	0	1	1
B	1	3	0	2	1	0	0	2	2	1
C	0	0	0	0	0	0	2	1	0	1
D	1	2	0	2	0	0	0	1	1	1
E	1	3	0	2	1	0	3	0	0	1
F	1	2	0	1	1	0	3	0	0	0
G	1	1	0	1	1	0	3	1	0	0
H	2	1	0	0	2	0	4	0	0	2
I	1	0	0	0	0	0	2	0	0	2
J	1	0	0	0	0	0	2	1	0	0
K	1	0	2	0	2	0	4	0	0	0
L	1	1	0	1	0	0	2	0	0	0
M	2	0	2	3	0	0	2	0	0	1
N	2	0	1	2	0	0	2	0	0	0
O	0	0	0	0	0	0	0	1	1	2
P	1	2	0	1	1	0	1	1	1	0
Q	0	0	1	0	0	1	2	1	1	0
R	1	1	1	1	2	0	2	1	1	0
S	0	0	0	0	0	0	2	2	0	0
T	1	1	0	0	1	0	3	0	0	1
U	2	0	0	0	0	0	2	1	0	1
V	0	0	2	1	0	0	2	0	0	1
W	0	0	4	3	0	0	2	0	0	1
X	0	0	2	0	0	1	4	0	0	2
Y	1	0	2	0	0	0	3	0	0	1
Z	0	2	1	2	0	0	2	0	0	0

Figure 9.4.1 A possible set of features for recognizing capital letters. The number of occurrences of each feature in a given letter is represented in the appropriate row and column. The particular features shown here are merely illustrative. Note that no two letters have the same set of feature values.

ditions. This lowers the plausibility of binary feature representations as adequate to capture the perception of these figures.

A problem with the fuzzy feature approach is that, like most other feature theories, it does not postulate a set of well-defined features sufficient to account for human performance in identifying letters. Rather, it defines an abstract framework for representing letters in terms of some to-be-identified features, with the details left to be filled in later. Although this is far from a satis-factory theoretical situation, it is where much current research on this problem stands.

9.4.2 Identifying Words and Letters Within Words

The combinatorial structure of textual material led us to suggest that letters are a natural primitive out of which larger units, such as words, can be constructed. Logically, this means that letters could serve as independent units in text categorization, each one being identified

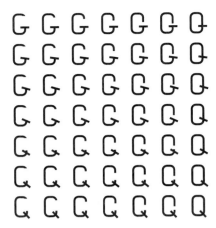

Figure 9.4.2 Ambiguous G/Q stimuli. Seven levels of obliqueness of the straight line segment (row variable) are combined with seven levels of gap size (column variable) to form 49 letterlike stimuli that vary from a prototypical G (upper left) to a prototypical Q (lower right). (From Massaro & Hary, 1986.)

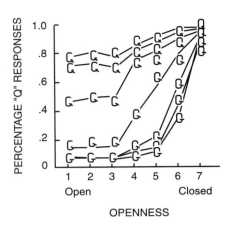

Figure 9.4.3 Results of the G/Q experiment. Percentages of subjects who identified the 49 stimuli in Figure 9.4.3 as a "Q" are plotted as a function of obliqueness of the line and openness of the gap. The lines in the figure show the average predictions of the fuzzy logical model of perception (FLMP). (Data from Massaro & Hary, 1986.)

separately from all others. Psychologically, however, this is not the case. Letter categorization actually depends on the context of other letters around them, just as object categorization has been shown to depend on the context provided by other objects around them. The example shown in Figure 9.2.12 ("THE CAT") is an excellent demonstration.

The fact that letters can be more quickly and easily reported when they appear within meaningful words than meaningless letter strings is easy to illustrate. Simply look at the top line of Figure 9.4.4 for about 5 seconds and report as many letters as you can. Then do the same for the bottom line. You will be able to report many more letters in the bottom line than the top one because they form meaningful words within a meaningful sentence. The letters that are present and the spaces between them are actually the same in the two cases, for the top line is just a scrambled version of the bottom one. The difference between the level of performance in reporting letters in words versus nonwords is known as the **word superiority effect**. It was first reported over a century ago by Cattell (1886), who compared the number of letters subjects could report in a 10-ms. presentation of random letter strings versus English words.

Unfortunately, there are difficulties in interpreting such experiments as showing that people actually *identify* letters better when they are located within known words. Instead, the difference might lie in the subject's ability to

remember the letters. That is, they might actually identify all letters in both cases but be able to group the letters into memorable units in the case of words yet be unable to remember them in the case of random strings. Another difficulty is that the word superiority effect might be due to effective guessing strategies based on incomplete perception rather than to efficient categorization. People have a well-documented tendency to guess that words (as opposed to random letter strings) have been presented under conditions of very brief exposure. One compelling piece of evidence is that subjects will guess words far more often than random letter strings when nothing but a smudge has actually been presented for a very brief duration (Goldiamond & Hawkins, 1958). If subjects have a tendency to guess words when they are unsure of the actual letter sequences, a word superiority effect can result.

HWO NMYA RSTELTE NCA OYU RPTERO NWO?

HOW MANY LETTERS CAN YOU REPORT NOW?

Figure 9.4.4 An informal demonstration of the word superiority effect. English speakers can report many more letters from the bottom row than from the top row, even though the letters are the same.

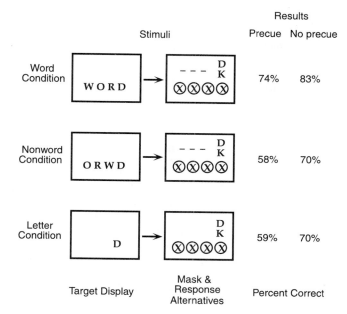

	Stimuli	Results	
		Precue	No precue
Word Condition	WORD → [--- D / K ⊗⊗⊗⊗]	74%	83%
Nonword Condition	ORWD → [--- D / K ⊗⊗⊗⊗]	58%	70%
Letter Condition	D → [D / K ⊗⊗⊗⊗]	59%	70%
	Target Display	Mask & Response Alternatives	Percent Correct

Figure 9.4.5 A controlled experiment demonstrating the word superiority effect. A word, nonword anagram, or single letter was presented briefly, followed by a mask and a two-alternative forced choice. Subjects were more accurate in the word condition than in either of the other two.

These problems in interpretation have been overcome by more sophisticated experimental procedures. The definitive study was performed by psychologist Gerald Reicher (1969) and has since been replicated and extended by many other researchers (e.g., Wheeler, 1970). In Reicher's experiment, subjects were presented with either a word (such as WORD) or a comparable random letter string (such as ORWD), as indicated in Figure 9.4.5. This target stimulus was presented very briefly (about 50 ms.), followed by a masking pattern over the area that had contained the crucial letters. Just above the mask was a pair of letters, *D* or *K*, shown one over the other, that might have been presented in the position indicated. The subject's task on each trial was to indicate which of the two letters in the test had actually been presented in the corresponding position. On half the trials, subjects were pre-cued with the two response alternatives before presentation of the target

stimulus. On the other half, the two alternatives were presented only in the test display, after the target was gone.

Notice that the memory requirements of the task are virtually nonexistent in the pre-cue condition. Subjects do not have to remember anything except the correct letter of the two pre-cued alternatives. Even in the post-cue condition, the memory load is minimal. Notice also that the design controls for guessing strategies based on words versus nonwords since both of the alternatives formed familiar words with the other three letters presented (WORD versus WORK). Even so, Reicher found a substantial advantage for word contexts over nonword contexts in both the pre-cue and post-cue conditions, as shown in Figure 9.4.5. The inescapable conclusion is that categorization of letters is indeed influenced by context: Letters in words are identified more accurately than letters in random strings. This effect is often called the **word-nonword effect**.

Reicher also included another condition in which only a single letter was presented as the target (Figure 9.4.5). The most plausible expectation is that a single letter would be perceived more accurately than any string of four letters, either words or nonwords, simply because there is only one character to be processed instead of four. The startling result was that the single target letter was perceived less accurately than when it appeared in a word. This finding is often referred to as the **word-letter effect**. It is quite puzzling, given the many results showing that the more letters are present in a random array, the worse is performance. Shortly, we will describe a connectionist theory of letter and word recognition that accounts for this word-letter effect as well as the word-nonword effect (McClelland & Rumelhart, 1981; Rumelhart & McClelland, 1982).[6]

Given Reicher's results, one can ask whether the advantage of perceiving letters in words is shared to any degree by nonwords that are nevertheless "wordlike." Some nonwords are easily pronounced (e.g., GRAP), whereas others are not (e.g., RPGA). It turns out that letters in pronounceable nonwords are also identified more accurately than those in unpronounceable non-

---

[6] There is some evidence that although the word-letter effect and the word-nonword effect are caused by some of the same mechanisms, others must be different. Prinzmetal and Silvers (1994) showed, for example, that the word-letter effect requires the presence of a mask to occur, whereas the word-nonword effect does not.

Perceiving Function and Category

words (McClelland & Johnston, 1977). This fact can also be explained by the connectionist model of letter and word perception, to which we now turn.

9.4.3 The Interactive Activation Model

One of the most ambitious and influential theories of letter and word perception is McClelland and Rumelhart's (1981) **interactive activation (IA) model**. The IA model postulates a multilayer connectionist network consisting of neuronlike nodes and synapselike connections between nodes. (See Appendix B for further information about connectionist networks.) Visual input activates the first layer of nodes—the input "feature" nodes—and this activation propagates throughout the network via the connections between nodes. Nodes become activated to a degree that depends both on the level of activation in all the nodes to which it is connected and on the strength (or weight) of these connections, which can be either excitatory or inhibitory. Excitatory connections increase the activation in the node to which they are connected, and inhibitory connections decrease the activation. Because the IA network contains feedback loops, the pattern of activation changes dynamically over time, eventually settling into a stable pattern in which some nodes are highly active and others are not. The goal of the IA model is to simulate perceptual processes that underlie letter and word categorization such that the pattern of activation in the stable state corresponds to what people perceive under comparable conditions.

To simulate categorization of letters and four-letter words, the IA network is structured into three distinct layers of nodes: a feature level, a letter level, and a word level, as indicated in Figure 9.4.6. We will now consider the architecture of the network: how its units are connected to each other, both within a given layer and across different layers.

Feature Level. The first layer consists of part-feature nodes, each of which represents a particular line segment at a particular position. The set of possible segments for the specific font simulated by the IA model is shown in Figure 9.4.7. All letters are composed of some subset of 12 possible segments. Thus, there are 12 nodes in the feature level for each of the four positions in which a letter can occur. The 48 resulting feature nodes

are activated by visual input when their corresponding segment is present in the target stimulus. They pass their activation to nodes in the second layer through either excitatory or inhibitory connections. Note that there is no feedback to the feature level from higher-level nodes: Features are processed in a strictly bottom-up direction.

Letter Level. The second layer consists of letter nodes, each of which represents the presence of one of 26 letters at one of the four possible positions. These 104 ($= 26 \times 4$) nodes receive excitatory connections from all feature nodes that represent segments present in that letter. For instance, the node for the top horizontal segment excites the nodes for all letters that include this feature in this type font: A, B, C, D, E, F, G, I, O, P, Q, R, S, T, and Z. The letter nodes also receive inhibitory connections from all feature nodes that represent segments not present in the letter. Thus, the node for the top horizontal segment inhibits the nodes for all other letters in this font (H, J, K, L, M, N, U, V, W, X, and Y). The net effect of these connections is that when just the segments of a given letter (say, an A) are present in the stimulus, the corresponding A-node in the letter level will be the most highly active. Other nodes will also be activated to a degree that depends on how many segments they share with an A. The H-node, for instance, will be quite active because it differs from an A (in this particular font) only in lacking the top segment (see Figure 9.4.7).

To sharpen the pattern of activation within the letter level so that only the correct letter node remains highly activated once the network settles into a stable state, all nodes representing letters in the same spatial position mutually inhibit each other. This mutual inhibition forms a winner-take-all network within each of the four 26-node sets. This aspect of the architecture thus ensures that once the activation pattern "settles down," the correct letter in each position will be the only one with substantial activation, having inhibited its 25 competitors more than they have inhibited it. (Errors can still occur within the model, however, especially when the presentation of letters is very brief or noisy.) The activation of letter nodes is actually more complex than we have described thus far, however, because they also receive feedback connections from the word level. We will consider this source of activation to the letter nodes

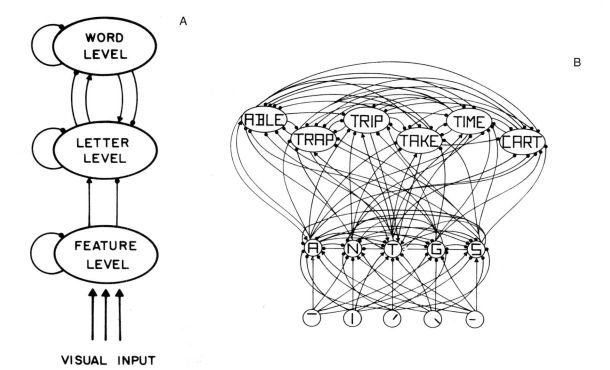

Figure 9.4.6 The architecture of the interactive activation model. Part A shows the overall architecture in terms of how units representing features, letters, and words are connected via excitation and inhibition. Part B shows a small subset of the individual units and connections in the network. (See text for details.) (Part A from McClelland & Rumelhart, 1981. Part B from Rumelhart & McClelland, 1986.)

Figure 9.4.7 The letter font used by the interactive activation model. Each letter is composed of a subset of the 12 possible segments shown at the bottom. (From McClelland & Rumelhart, 1981.)

after we have described the structure of the word level itself.

Word Level. The highest-level nodes represent whole four-letter words. There are over 1000 such nodes in the IA model, each of which corresponds to a different word in English. They receive excitatory connections from the nodes representing the four letters that it contains, one in each spatial position. The node for an A in the first position, for example, excites the word nodes for ABLE and ACTS (among many others), whereas the node for an A in the second position excites BACK and GAVE (among many others). Word nodes also receive inhibitory connections from the nodes representing the other 25 letters in each position. Thus, the node for A in the *first* position inhibits BACK and GAVE, whereas the one for an A in the *second* position inhibits ABLE and ACTS. These connections from letter nodes ensure that, given complete information, the correct word node will be more active than the others. Even so, many other nodes

Perceiving Function and Category

will be active to a lesser degree, depending on the number of letters they share with the presented word at corresponding positions.

Because some other word nodes may be very close to the activation of the correct word, even with complete information, a winner-take-all network of mutual inhibition is proposed to exist among all nodes in the word level network. This ensures that the correct word will be the only one with a high activation level in the final steady-state condition, having inhibited the other word nodes more than they have inhibited it.

Word-to-Letter Feedback. Because the three-layer network as described thus far treats the categorization of letters in different positions quite independently, it cannot predict contextual phenomena such as the word superiority effect or the word-letter effect. To enable the IA model to do this, McClelland and Rumelhart (1981) proposed that there are feedback connections from the word level to the letter level. In particular, they added excitatory connections from word nodes to the letter nodes that the word contains. The node for ABLE, for example, excites the letter nodes for A, B, L, and E in the first, second, third, and fourth positions, respectively. There are no inhibitory feedback connections from word to letter nodes, however.

With these excitatory feedback connections, the IA model is able to simulate a number of important contextual effects in letter perception. Consider first the word superiority effect: Letters are perceived more accurately within words than within random strings of letters. This occurs in the IA model because the node for the presented word is strongly activated and then feeds back its activation to the correct letter nodes, thereby increasing their activation. In a random string of letters, there is no corresponding word node to be activated, and so the letter nodes do not benefit from feedback from the word level. This difference in activation at the letter level allows the model to identify letters in words more quickly than it does in random strings.

Because the IA model contains nodes only for real four-letter words, one might think that it cannot predict the pseudo-word superiority effect in which letters in pronounceable nonwords (e.g., MAVE) can be perceived more accurately than letters in random strings (e.g., AEMV). After all, there is no word node for either MAVE or AEMV, so how could there be a difference? It

turns out, however, that the IA model produces a difference similar to that found in human perception: Performance with pronounceable nonwords is intermediate between real words and random letter strings. The reason is that even though there is no single node for MAVE, this letter string partially activates many word nodes that share three of the four letters (e.g., CAVE, HAVE, MATE, MAKE), and these partial activations also feed back to the letter level. Neither the activation nor the feedback is as strong as it is for a real word, such as CAVE, but the same kind of effect is present in its operation. Thus, it is able to simulate pseudo-word superiority effects as well as word superiority effects.

Word-to-letter feedback also enables the IA model to simulate the word-letter effect. A letter can be identified more accurately in a real word than when presented alone because the single letter does not benefit from feedback at the word level. Moreover, the model's simulated performance in the single-letter condition is comparable to that in the nonword condition because, in both cases, there is no appreciable feedback from the word level to influence letter activation. This result is also in accord with findings about human perception.

Problems. Despite its success in predicting these contextual effects, the IA model has not gone unchallenged. For example, Massaro (1989) has argued that it is incompatible with other experimental results. McClelland (1991) has disputed this claim. The focus of this controversy is whether context actually alters the sensory evidence for the presence of a given letter, as it does in the IA model through the word-to-letter feedback loop, or whether contextual information is merely combined with sensory information for the letter at some higher level. In Massaro's fuzzy logical model of perception (FLMP), which was described briefly above, sensory information about the target letter is initially quite separate from information about its context. These two independent sources of information are then combined at a later integration stage to provide an indication of how likely it is that a given letter was present on the basis of both contextual and sensory information. The crucial difference is that in FLMP the sensory information does not change as a result of context, as it does in the IA model.

This issue is not easy to resolve because we cannot look into the observer's head and inspect the level of activation in the letter representation—whatever that may be—to see whether it is affected by context or not. Rather, we must make inferences about what goes on in the observer's head from indirect behavioral measures, and such inferences are always based on assumptions of uncertain validity. The present situation is that although both sides agree that there is an important theoretical difference between these two types of theories, they do not agree on how to interpret the experimental evidence. Perhaps new experiments will produce definitive tests between the two theories.

Regardless of precisely how this theoretical debate is resolved, the existence of context effects in the process of categorizing letters within words and objects within scenes is an important and undeniable fact of perception. Such effects enable perception to make use of constraints imposed by the more global structure of visual input. Not all combinations of objects are equally likely to occur in a given scene, and not all combinations of letters are equally likely to occur in a given word. The visual system is clearly sensitive to this kind of information and uses it in categorizing visual input. The result is faster and more efficient processing of the kinds of scenes and words that have occurred frequently in the perceiver's experience, but at the expense of slower and less efficient processing of random collections of object and letters. This is an evolutionarily advantageous tradeoff, since normal scenes and words occur, by definition, more frequently than do random or abnormal collections.

Suggestions for Further Reading

Gibson, J. J. (1979). *An ecological approach to visual perception.* Boston: Houghton Mifflin. Chapter 8 of Gibson's last book provides the classic statement of his theory of affordances.

Mervis, C. B., & Rosch, E. (1981). Categorization of natural objects. *Annual Review of Psychology, 32,* 89–115. This chapter reviews much of Rosch's early work on natural categories. Most of it concerns cognitive rather than perceptual processes, but this work revolutionized cognitive scientists' views about the nature of human categorization.

Farah, M. (1990). *Visual agnosia: Disorders of object recognition and what they tell us about normal vision.* Cambridge, MA: MIT Press. Farah's book gives a broad review of neuropsychological syndromes that affect people's inability to recognize and categorize objects. It covers far more than classic visual agnosia and proposes a taxonomy of related disorders.

Biederman, I. (1987). Recognition by components: A theory of human image understanding. *Psychological Review, 94,* 115–147.

Hummel, J., & Biederman, I. (1992). Dynamic binding in a neural network for shape recognition. *Psychological Review, 99,* 480–517. The first article reports the original version of Biederman's RBC theory of entry-level image categorization. The second presents an extension and neural network simulation of RBC.

Ullman, S. (1996). *High-level vision.* Cambridge, MA: MIT Press. This recent book explores the possibility of visual object recognition and categorization via alignment with stored images of specific viewpoints. Some parts of it are quite technical, but readers with limited mathematical backgrounds can still find much that is useful and informative.

Visual Dynamics

Perceiving Motion and Events

Although the vast majority of objects in ordinary environments are stationary the vast majority of the time, ones that move are particularly important. They include the most significant of all objects—namely, ourselves—as well as other people, animals, certain classes of human artifacts (such as cars and other vehicles), and normally stationary objects (such as rocks and trees) that are falling or have otherwise been set in motion by the action of some force. Our very survival depends critically on being able to perceive the movement of such objects accurately and to act appropriately. The consequences of failing to perceive a falling tree or an approaching car can be dire indeed!

Considering the importance of perceiving movement, it is not too surprising that the visual system is particularly sensitive to it. Indeed, objects in motion grab our attention more forcefully than almost anything else. If there is a moving object in our peripheral vision, we usually turn our eyes rapidly to find out what it is and how it is moving. This much seems obvious, but like many other obvious facts about vision, explaining how it happens is not as easy as it seems.

10.1 Image Motion

The first issue with which we must come to grips is the difference between the motion of an object and the motion of its retinal image. When a moving object is viewed by an observer with eyes, head, and body fixed, its projected image moves across the retina. In this instance it is natural to equate object motion with image motion. But much of the time, our eyes, head, and body are in motion, and this fact invalidates any attempt to equate object motion directly with image motion.

Image motion depends on both eye movements and object motion. For example, eye movements produce image motion even in a completely stationary environment; as the eye moves in one direction, the image sweeps across the visual field in the opposite direction.[1] Here, there is image motion when there is no object motion at all. The opposite can also occur, as when a moving object is tracked by the eye: Its image on the retina will actually be stationary even though the object itself is in motion. For these reasons, it is important to distinguish clearly between image motion and object motion and to realize that perception of object motion always depends on eye, head, and body movements as well as image motion.

10.1.1 The Computational Problem of Motion

The computational problem of motion perception is how to get from the dynamic optical event on the retina to the veridical perception of moving objects within a generally stationary environment. This is not a trivial problem, particularly when the complications of eye, head, and bodily movements are considered. The visual system appears to solve it in at least two steps: an early process of motion analysis concerned with the registration of 2-D image motion and a later process concerned with interpreting image motion in terms of 3-D objects moving in 3-D space, independent of how the eyes are moving. We will consider each process in turn.

The starting point for motion and event perception—indeed, for *all* perception—is what Gibson called the dynamic ambient optical array: the flux of optical structure converging from all directions to a stationpoint (see Section 1.2.1, Figure 1.2.5). One useful way of conceptualizing the information in the dynamic ambient

---

[1] The image on the retina actually moves in the *same* direction as the eyes move because of inversion of the retinal image with respect to the world. We will ignore this complicating factor in our discussion by considering the motion of objects relative to the visual field as the observer experiences it. Within this frame of reference, images of stationary objects move in the direction *opposite* the eye movement.

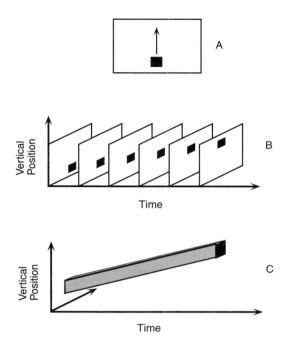

Figure 10.1.1 Space-time diagrams. The event of a square moving upward (A) can be sampled by a series of snapshots in which the position of the square changes discretely over time (B). This sequence approximates a representation of the continuous event in space-time (C) as the time between snapshots approaches zero.

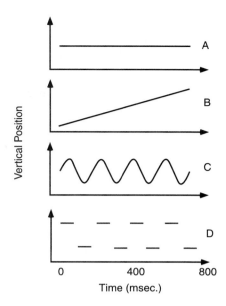

Figure 10.1.2 Space-time diagrams of four simple events. Each graph represents the motion of a single point along a vertical trajectory in the frontal plane: a stationary point (A), a point moving upward with uniform speed (B), a point moving continuously up and down in harmonic motion (C), and a point moving discretely up and down in a series of static snapshots, which produces the perception of apparent motion (D).

optical array is in terms of **space-time diagrams** of image motion.

Space-time diagrams represent image structure as it changes over time. Because the sample of the ambient optic array that strikes the retina at each moment in time is a two-dimensional luminance structure, the additional dimension of time makes space-time representations of image motion three-dimensional. Consider the space-time diagram of the simple visual event shown in Figure 10.1.1A: a square moving upward at uniform speed. In the space-time diagram, the two spatial dimensions of the image are preserved in the vertical (y axis) and depth (z axis) dimensions, so each "depth slice" constitutes the image—a square at some position—at a particular moment in time (Figure 10.1.1B). The temporal dimension is represented along the horizontal (x axis) dimension, with later times to the right of earlier ones. Thus, the square moving upward results in the space-time diagram of the square prism shown in Figure 10.1.1C. Space-time diagrams are therefore like a compilation of spatially aligned transparencies, with the most recent one at the end. The primary difference is that the transparencies would be discrete samples of image motion (as in Figure 10.1.1B), whereas the structure of real motion in space-time diagrams is continuous (as in Figure 10.1.1C).

To simplify things a bit, we will now consider space-time diagrams for some simple motions of a single dot. In Figure 10.1.2 the vertical position of the dot is plotted as a function of time. Because the horizontal dimension of space is now irrelevant, it can be dropped from the space-time diagram so that motions can be presented as simple 2-D graphs with time on the horizontal axis and vertical position of the dot on the vertical axis. Figure 10.1.2 shows a few representative examples of space-time diagrams for simple visual events.

1. *Stationary dot.* The simplest case of all is an unmoving dot. Since its position does not change over time, its space-time diagram is a flat horizontal line, as shown in Figure 10.1.2A.

2. *Constant velocity motion.* A dot moving upward at a constant speed corresponds to an oblique straight line in space-time, as shown in Figure 10.1.2B. The slope of the

line depends on the speed of the dot: The faster it moves, the greater is the slope of its line in space-time. A dot moving downward would correspond to a line with a negative slope.

3. *Harmonic motion.* The motion of a dot moving smoothly up and down is called *harmonic motion.* The space-time diagram of this event is a sinusoidally undulating line, as shown in Figure 10.1.2C. The wavelength of this sinusoid reflects the duration of one up/down cycle, and its amplitude reflects the distance between the highest and lowest positions.

4. *Apparent motion.* A dot can also be perceived as moving when it does not actually move at all. **Apparent motion** (also called **stroboscopic motion** when the frame rate is rapid, as in cinema) consists of a series of purely static frames in which an object is shown at different positions. When presented at the proper rate, the dot will be seen as moving continuously between the positions. The space-time diagrams of such stimulus events are discontinuous sequences of short horizontal line segments, each of which represents a single frame. In the case of Figure 10.1.2D, an unmoving dot alternates between a low and a high position but is nevertheless perceived as a dot moving alternately up and down.

The computational problem of motion perception is to convert information about image motion, all of which is preserved in a complete space-time diagram, into information about the velocity of objects moving about in the 3-D world. **Velocity** is a quantity that indicates simultaneously both the *speed* and the *direction* of motion. It is conveniently represented as a mathematical **vector**: a quantity that is completely specified by a direction and a magnitude, usually symbolized by an arrow whose direction corresponds to the direction of motion and whose length corresponds to the speed. If the velocity of an object is constant, it can be represented by a single vector. If it changes, as when the object accelerates, decelerates, or follows a curved path, a series of different vectors are needed to represent its motion. Figure 10.1.3 shows vector representations of image motion for two dots. The dot in part A is moving in a constant direction with a constant speed, and that in part B is moving in a circle with constant speed. Notice that although the direction of motion changes for object B, its speed remains constant, as reflected by the equal lengths of the motion vectors.

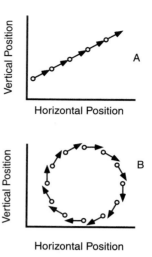

Figure 10.1.3 Vector representations of motion. The length of a vector represents the speed of motion and its direction represents the direction of motion. Both variables are constant in the uniform diagonal motion depicted in part A. Speed is constant in the circular motion depicted in part B, but direction changes constantly during the event.

The goal of perception, however, is to recover not the velocity of images on the retina, but the velocity of objects in the world. A necessary first step in this process is to determine how projected images are changing over time on the retina, and we will discuss how this might be accomplished. But, as in other cases involving spatial vision, this information about 2-D image motion must be interpreted in terms of objects in a 3-D environment to be useful to the organism. A baseball that is hurtling toward one's head is not just a rapidly expanding visual image, but a physical object that can really hurt if immediate action is not taken.

Once moving objects have been perceived and attended, they are usually classified. Much of this classification can take place on the basis of static shape information. But many moving objects have no single unique shape. The 3-D shape of a person, for instance, is quite different as it transforms from lying to sitting to standing to walking to running. It seems unlikely from a computational standpoint that our brains store all the different 3-D shapes of objects that move nonrigidly. A more viable option would be to store something about the ways in which such objects can move. If this were the case, it should be possible to identify objects purely on the basis of their motion, independent of their static shape. Indeed, this happens, as we will discover at the end of this chapter. The implication of this fact is that motion may play a role in object classification, although precisely how this might occur is not yet well understood.

Many phenomena of continuous motion perception are based on early sensory processes at the image-processing level. In this section we will describe some of the most important of these effects. Later we will consider phenomena that arise in the perception of apparent motion. Finally, we will examine recent developments in the theoretical explanation of these facts. The theories we will consider are based partly on computational models for extracting image motion and partly on what is known about the physiology of the motion-sensitive part of the visual system.

10.1.2 Continuous Motion

An environmental object is considered to be moving if its position changes over time. Because real objects do not disappear from one place and reappear in another, these changes in object position are continuous events. Not all such events produce visual experiences of motion, however; some occur too rapidly, and others too slowly. The blades of a window fan, for example, spin too quickly to be perceived as moving. Rather, they usually give the appearance of an unmoving, blurred, filmy surface. The moon, in contrast, moves too slowly to be experienced as moving. We realize that the moon has moved when its position has changed enough to be detected, but we do not have a direct experience of it as moving.[2] The movement of clock hands on an analog clock provide further examples of the distinction. We perceive the continuous motion of a second hand as moving smoothly, but the hour hands move too slowly to give rise to the experience of motion.

In terms of the space-time diagrams we have discussed, the boundary conditions for continuous motion perception are defined by the slope or orientation of space-time contours with respect to the temporal axis. As illustrated in Figure 10.1.4, a moving object is perceived as stationary if the slope of its space-time contour

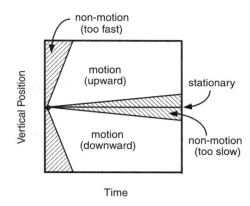

Figure 10.1.4 The limits of motion perception. Observers experience motion as long as the object's motion is neither too slow (too shallow in space-time) nor too fast (too steep in space-time).

is too shallow (that is, too close to the stationary case of zero slope). If the slope of its space-time contour is too steep (indicating very rapid motion), it is perceived not as moving, but as spatially smeared across its trajectory. In between is a wide range of velocities at which we can and do experience objects as moving.

Experiments show that the threshold for motion perception—the slowest motion that can be spontaneously perceived as such—depends on many factors, including the duration of the motion and whether the moving object is seen alone or against a background of stationary objects. If a single light is presented moving in the dark or against a completely homogeneous background for a long period of time, the threshold for motion perception is about one-sixth to one-third of a degree of visual angle per second (Aubert, 1886). At this *subject-relative motion threshold*, a spot would take about 10 s to travel the width of your thumb held at arm's length. If the same light moves against a textured background or one that contains stationary lines perpendicular to its trajectory, however, the threshold for perceiving it as moving is much lower: about 1/60 of a degree of visual angle per second. This lower threshold for object-relative motion indicates that the visual system is much more sensitive to the motion of one object relative to another than it is to the motion of the same object relative to the observer. With short-duration motion

---

[2] There are some cases in which we do perceive the moon as moving, but they are actually illusions arising when clouds move past the moon. We will consider this phenomenon later in this chapter when we discuss induced motion.

presentations (250 ms or less), motion thresholds are higher, and the presence of stationary referents do not change the motion threshold (Leibowitz, 1955).

Adaptation and Aftereffects. When an observer stares for a prolonged period at a field of image elements moving at a constant direction and speed, the visual system undergoes motion adaptation; that is, its response to the motion diminishes in intensity over time. This causes the motion itself to appear to slow down as adaptation occurs (Goldstein, 1957). It also changes subsequent perceptions, the most striking of which are **motion aftereffects**.

Motion aftereffects are phenomena caused by prolonged viewing of constant motion. After the motion has stopped (or changed), subsequent motion perception is significantly altered. A classic demonstration of motion aftereffects is that after watching a field in uniform motion for several minutes (e.g., a display of randomly positioned dots drifting downward), a stationary test field appears to move in the opposite direction. This phenomenon can readily be experienced after watching a waterfall. If you stare at a waterfall for a minute or more, keeping your eye fixed on some stationary object, such as a rock protruding through the water, and if you then move your eyes to an area in which the field is stationary, such as the landscape next to the waterfall, you will have a clear sensation of upward movement. Perhaps because waterfalls are so effective in producing this effect, it is often called the **waterfall illusion**.

Another situation in which you can experience powerful motion aftereffects is at the end of a movie or television show when a long list of credits is scrolled over the screen. Instead of tracking individual words so that you can read them, try to fixate something in the background that is not scrolling. Then, when the credits are done, you will experience motion in the opposite direction in any stationary object you happen to look at immediately afterward. The aftereffect you experience in such situations is **paradoxical motion** in the following sense: There is a clear perception of motion but no global change in the perceived position of the moving objects. These motion aftereffects suggest that the system for motion perception is separate from that for position perception, at least to some degree.

The **spiral aftereffect** is another motion aftereffect that you can experience using the spiral pattern on the inside front cover of this book. Photocopy it, and then cut it out along the dotted lines and place it on the turntable of a record player (if you can find one of these rapidly disappearing devices). Then "play" it at $33\frac{1}{3}$ rpm while you stare at the central spindle for about a minute. As the pattern rotates, you will see the spiral constantly expanding outward. After about 60 s of observation, look at a stationary pattern—a person's face is particularly interesting—and watch it spiral inward. Again, the motion aftereffect is paradoxical in that there is no global change in the positions of the objects relative to each other, yet the experience of motion is clear and unmistakable.

One interesting question about motion aftereffects is where in the visual system they occur. For example, are they localized in the early monocular system or in the later binocular system, after information from the two eyes has been integrated? This question has been studied by examining **interocular transfer effects**: the extent to which adaptation in one eye causes motion aftereffects in the other. Simple experiments of this form have shown that motion aftereffects can be produced in a test field viewed with one eye after adapting to motion in the other eye, although the duration of the effect is roughly half that produced after adapting the same eye (Wohlgemuth, 1911). Such results seem to support the hypothesis that motion aftereffects occur in the binocular nervous system, although there may be an additional contribution from the monocular system. However, more sophisticated experiments suggest that different motion aftereffects can occur in both systems independently. For example, Anstis and Duncan (1983) adapted the left eye to clockwise rotation, the right eye to the same clockwise rotation, and both eyes together to counterclockwise rotation. When a stationary test field was then presented to the left eye or the right eye alone, counterclockwise rotation was perceived. But when it was presented to both eyes at once, clockwise rotation was perceived! This surprising result indicates that separate monocular and binocular motion aftereffects can coexist in the visual system. From this we conclude that there must be both monocular and binocular components to the motion perception system.

Simultaneous Motion Contrast. Another way in which an illusion of motion can be perceived in a stationary image is through **simultaneous motion con-**

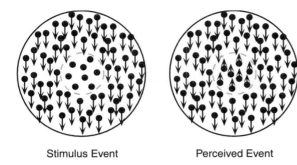

Stimulus Event   Perceived Event

Figure 10.1.5 Simultaneous motion contrast. If a region of stationary dots is surrounded by dots in motion (left panel), observers will perceive the stationary dots as moving in the opposite direction (right panel).

trast (Loomis & Nakayama, 1973). If a stationary patch of random dots is surrounded by a field of dots moving steadily downward, the central patch will appear to drift upward, as indicated in Figure 10.1.5. Motion contrast is analogous to the phenomenon of simultaneous lightness contrast in which the perceived lightness of a gray central patch is affected by the lightness of a surrounding region. It appears lighter when surrounded by a black region than when surrounded by a white region (see Figure 3.2.5).

As in the case of lightness contrast, motion contrast may be caused by lateral inhibition in the visual system. In this case, motion in the outer region would cause motion detectors that are sensitive to movement in that direction to fire rapidly. These motion detectors in the outer region would inhibit adjacent motion detectors that are tuned to the same direction in the central region. This inhibition would then reduce the firing rate in the central region below the baseline rate, a condition that normally indicates motion in the opposite direction. The central region would therefore appear to be moving in the direction opposite that in the outer region. Recent evidence suggests that lateral inhibition is unlikely to be the whole story and that relative motion detectors may also be involved.

The Autokinetic Effect. Another illusion of motion perception occurs, strangely enough, in the total absence of any moving object whatsoever. This phenomenon, called the **autokinetic effect**, refers to the perception of a stationary spot of light as moving when it is viewed for an extended period of time in total dark-

ness (Adams, 1912; Aubert, 1886). Observers are instructed to fixate the light throughout the viewing session, and measurements of eye movements suggest that they are largely successful in doing so. Nevertheless, after a minute or two, most people perceive the light to begin moving slowly in a consistent direction for up to several degrees of visual angle. This does not happen if any part of the environment is visible, for that provides clear evidence that the light is, in fact, stationary.

A variety of theories have been advanced to explain the autokinetic effect, none of which is wholly satisfactory. Most are based on the idea that eye movements are somehow involved. Gross eye movements can be ruled out because measurements show that subjects are successful at fixating the light (Guilford & Dallenbach, 1928). The influence of slight eye displacements due to tremor in the extraocular muscles is more difficult to disprove. Although there is some evidence supporting this hypothesis (Matin & MacKinnon, 1964), it is unclear how movements of tiny fractions of a degree of visual angle could result in perceived excursions of several degrees. Despite the attempts of many vision scientists to explain it, the autokinetic effect remains an enigma.

10.1.3 Apparent Motion

Perceiving motion in real objects is caused by physically continuous motion, but modern technology provides a host of situations in which realistic motion perception arises from the rapid presentation of completely static images. Movies, television, and video displays all rely on the fact that the human visual system can be fooled into perceiving continuous motion from a sequence of "snapshots" or "frames" presented at the proper rate. This general phenomenon is called *apparent motion*.

Apparent motion was first studied by Exner in 1875. His displays consisted of a regular alternation between two sparks at different positions in a dark room. At the optimal distance and rate of alternation, observers invariably reported that they saw clear and continuous motion of a single light that moved back and forth between the two positions, even though there was no corresponding physical or optical motion in the stimulus. Because this illusion of motion is so compelling and universal, the phenomenon of apparent motion has been of both theoretical and practical interest. Theoretically, it bears on how the visual system processes motion information. Practically, it is the basis for the technology of motion pictures.

Early Gestalt Investigations. Apparent motion received considerable attention from Gestalt psychologists who used it as a paradigmatic example of an *emergent property* (Wertheimer, 1912). The physical display in apparent motion consists of just two static lights, yet their alternation at the proper rate results in the seemingly direct perception of motion. Since there is no motion in the stimulus, where does it come from? The Gestaltists' answer was that it emerged from the interaction of the stimulus events within the observer's visual system. They proposed various theories about how it might occur physiologically from changes in electrical fields in the brain (Wertheimer, 1912), but their brain-based explanations are no longer taken seriously. The phenomena they investigated, however, are critical in understanding how the visual system perceives motion, and several of the effects they discovered are still being studied today.

The phenomenological impression created by two alternating lights depends on a number of factors. Perhaps the most powerful is the **alternation rate** of the two images: how rapidly they are interchanged. As this rate decreases from very fast to very slow, the perception of a display alternately presenting two lights across a fixed distance changes through the following sequence of different experiences:

1. *Simultaneous flickering.* When the rate of alternation is very rapid—faster than about 40 times per second (25 ms per presentation) in Wertheimer's original studies—motion is not perceived from one light to the other. Rather, two separate lights appear to be flickering on and off in two different positions, as depicted in Figure 10.1.6A.

2. *Phi motion.* When the rate of alternation is slowed slightly, motion is perceived between the two lights without the perception of intermediate positions (Figure 10.1.6B). Wertheimer placed great emphasis on this "pure" form of apparent motion because it seemed to be strong evidence for the existence of motion as a primitive component of visual perception: If no intermediate positions were perceived, motion could not be

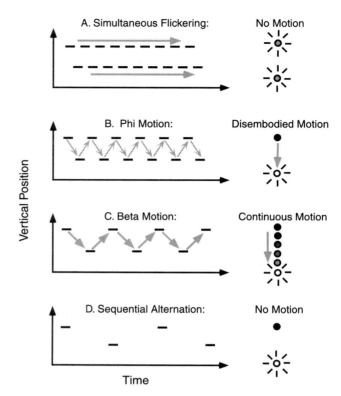

Figure 10.1.6 Phenomena of apparent motion. As the alternation rate between two stationary lights changes from very fast to very slow, observers perceive two simultaneously flickering lights (A), disembodied motion without intermediate positions, called *phi motion* (B), continuous motion with intermediate positions, called *beta motion* (C), and sequential alternation between two unmoving lights (D).

"inferred" from changes in position but must exist as an entity in its own right, distinct from the experience of changes in position.

3. *Beta motion.* When the rate is a bit slower—around 10 times per second (100 ms per presentation)—clear and distinct motion is perceived in which a single light appears to be moving continuously back and forth from one position to the other (Figure 10.1.6C). In beta motion, intermediate states of the light between the two end positions are phenomenally present as though the light were moving continuously.

4. *Sequential alternation.* When the rate of alternation is slowed even more—below about 2 times per second (500 ms)—apparent motion disappears (Figure 10.1.6D). It is replaced by the perception of two distinct lights that alternately flash on and off in two different positions.

Gestalt psychologists provided the first systematic studies of the relations among different parameters of simple, two-point apparent motion. Wertheimer's student Korte (1915) examined the quality of apparent motion as a function of the relations among three parameters: the alternation rate, the separation between the two points of light, and the intensity of the two lights. He summarized his results in what have become known as **Korte's laws**:

1. *Separation versus intensity.* With alternation rate held constant, intensity must increase as separation increases (and vice versa): Larger separations require higher intensities.

2. *Rate versus intensity.* With separation held constant, intensity must increase as alternation rate decreases (and vice versa): Slower rates require higher intensities.

3. *Separation versus rate.* With intensity held constant, alternation rate must decrease as separation increases (and vice versa): Larger separations require slower rates (i.e., more time).

The third law is perhaps the most interesting because it implies that there is a preferred speed of apparent motion. When two objects are moved farther apart, the time between their presentations must be lengthened to keep apparent motion intact. This increase in time is just what one would expect if the key to the relation between separation and rate were maintaining the object's speed at an optimal rate.

Although Korte's laws sound very precise and scientific, the visual system actually tolerates fairly wide departures from the stated relationships. Later studies have extended certain of Korte's laws and have refined the quantitative relations among them and other related parameters. We will consider some of this more recent research into apparent motion when we consider phenomena of apparent rotation later in this chapter.

Motion Picture Technology. Apparent motion lies at the heart of all motion picture technology, including film, TV, video tape, and computer graphics. All are capable of producing the perception of smooth, continuous motion, seemingly indistinguishable from real motion, yet they do so by presenting a rapid succession of discrete frames, each of which is entirely motionless. Movies, for example, are projected from a strip of film that contains a sequence of many static photographic images, each of which is slightly different because of the time at which it was exposed. After being developed, the frames on the film are flashed by a projector at a rate of 24 frames per second—the same rate at which they were originally taken—so each frame is presented for about 40 ms. This rate of presentation (for short distances) lies squarely within the range that produces beta motion, the most convincing perception of smooth continuous movement.

Motion is not the only perceptual phenomenon that is relevant to creating the illusion of a continuous event from a sequence of static images, however. To move the film past the projection light without its movement smearing the projected image, the light must be turned off and on rapidly. If this happens too slowly, it would be clearly perceived as flicker and would destroy the illusion of continuity. At a flicker rate of about 60 times per second or faster (i.e., 17 ms or less per flash), **flicker fusion** occurs, in which a flickering light appears to be on continuously. This is the case with fluorescent lights, for example, which actually flicker on and off 120 times per second. Because this rate is faster than the threshold for flicker fusion, they appear to be on continuously. Returning to movie technology, notice that the threshold for flicker fusion is greater than the presentation rate required for good beta motion. The most economical solution to this problem is simply to present each frame three times before moving to the next. This yields a flicker rate of 72 flashes per second, which is fast enough to produce full flicker fusion, and a frame rate of only 24 frames per second, which is fast enough to produce good perception of apparent motion.

Essentially the same problems arise in broadcast TV and videotape technologies. They are solved in much the same way, although the details are different. Motion is created by presenting a succession of static video images at a rate of 30 frames per second. Because this is too slow for flicker fusion, each video frame is effectively presented twice by interlacing the odd- and even-numbered lines of the video image. Appendix C describes how TV images are actually created by a scanning an electron beam across many discrete rows of pixels (see Figure C.2.1). If all the rows were presented in order, the beam would return to the same area of the screen only 30 times per second and would produce perceptible flicker. By presenting the odd rows on a first

Perceiving Motion and Events

sweep across the screen and the even rows on the second sweep, the video image is effectively presented twice, yielding a flicker rate of 60 times per second. Because this is about the threshold for flicker fusion, TV images are perceived as displaying unflickering images in continuous motion.

The Correspondence Problem of Apparent Motion. The existence of apparent motion implies that the visual system somehow determines which objects in one display go with which objects in the next display. If the alternation rate is appropriate, motion is then perceived between corresponding objects. But which objects are the "corresponding" ones? This is called the **correspondence problem of apparent motion**. It is very much analogous to the correspondence problem of stereoscopic vision (see Section 5.3.2), except that the relevant correspondence is between two successive images from the same viewpoint rather than two simultaneous images from slightly different viewpoints.

There is no problem in the simple, one-point apparent motion displays we have considered thus far, because each frame contains only a single object, making the correspondence unambiguous. But the correspondence problem arises whenever two or more objects are present in apparent motion displays, giving rise to two or more possible solutions. Figure 10.1.7 illustrates the problem in its simplest form with just two dots. Among the factors that affect which solution is perceived are the distance between the elements, the intrinsic properties of the elements (such as their color and orientation), and even the rate of alternation.

The most potent factor in solving the correspondence problem is proximity: the distance between potentially corresponding elements. All else being equal, the closest elements will be perceived as corresponding. This fact can be illustrated by the **wagon wheel illusion** that you may have noticed while watching Westerns at the movies and on TV. When a stagecoach or covered wagon with spoked wheels begins to move, the wheels initially are seen as turning forward. As the vehicle picks up speed, however, the wheels mysteriously appear to begin spinning backward. Why does this happen?

The first important fact is that both movies and TV broadcasts are actually made up of a series of static frames that are presented at a rate that produces good motion perception (beta motion). As a result, the visual

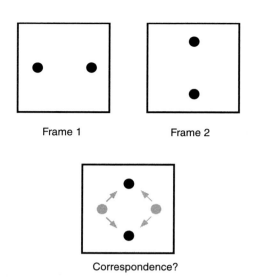

Figure 10.1.7 The correspondence problem of apparent motion. If more than one object is present in apparent motion displays, the visual system must determine which object in one frame goes with which object in the next.

system has to solve a correspondence problem like the one shown in Figure 10.1.8. The diagram is simplified in two ways: Only four spokes are shown, and the forward motion of the wheel is ignored. Neither simplification matters in understanding why the wagon wheel illusion occurs, however.

In each display, the gray lines indicate the positions of the spokes in the first frame, and the black lines indicate their positions in the second. Figure 10.1.8A shows an example of what happens when the wheel turns slowly. In the second frame (black lines), the spokes have turned only a short distance clockwise, as indicated by the black arrow. If the visual system solves the correspondence problem across frames in terms of pairing the closest spokes, it should produce clockwise apparent motion. And indeed it does, the speed of rotation increasing as the wagon wheel turns faster.

But there comes a rotation rate at which a dramatic change takes place. Figures 10.1.8B and 10.1.8C show why. In Figure 10.1.8B, the distance between the spokes in the first frame (gray lines) and those in the second (black lines) is the same when measured in the clockwise and counterclockwise directions. The correspondence based on distance is therefore maximally ambiguous, and the motion can be seen in either direction (gray arrows). As the wagon picks up still more speed (Figure

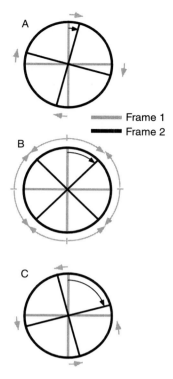

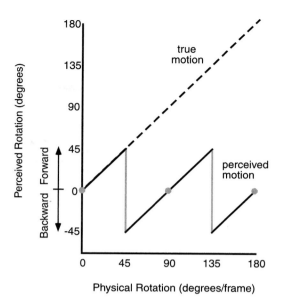

Figure 10.1.8 The wagon wheel illusion. At slow speeds (A), the wheel's actual motion (black arrow) is correctly perceived (gray arrows). At some speed (B), the wheel's perceived direction of motion becomes ambiguous (gray arrows). At higher speeds (C), it is perceived to turn backwards. (See text for details.)

Figure 10.1.9 Comparison of actual and perceived motion in the wagon wheel illusion. As a four-spoked wheel's actual rate of rotation increases linearly (dashed line), it is perceived to go through a cycle of forward and backward motion (solid line) with transition points of nonmotion (gray dots) and momentary ambiguity (vertical gray lines).

10.1.8C), the spokes have traveled even farther from one frame to the next (black arrow), so the closest spokes are clearly the ones in the counterclockwise direction (gray arrows). Solving the correspondence problem based on distance therefore predicts that the wheel will appear to turn backward. And so it does—even though the real-world wheel is still turning forward—as long as the motion is presented through a sequence of static frames.

Figure 10.1.9 shows a graph of the apparent direction and speed of rotation that should be perceived as the four-spoked wheel's speed increases from 0° to 180° per frame, assuming that the correspondence problem is solved strictly according to the closest-element principle. Note that the initial perception is veridical, the wheel appearing to turn forward at an increasing rate. The motion then becomes momentarily ambiguous at 45° (appearing either forward or backward), after which it switches to rapid backward rotation. Further increases in wheel speed cause this backward rotation to slow pro-

gressively until it comes momentarily to a standstill at 90°. Then it speeds up again, now appearing to turn in the correct direction but much more slowly than the rate at which it is actually turning (e.g., at 30° per s instead of 120°). This sequence continues repeatedly with further increases in the rate of rotation, as illustrated in Figure 10.1.9.

Do factors other than proximity affect the solution to the correspondence problem? For example, suppose that the elements in Figure 10.1.7 had different sizes, shapes, orientations, or colors. Is there any evidence that such factors also influence the solution to the correspondence problem? Logically, one would expect that they might, since these properties seem to define the identity of objects.

Surprisingly, however, several experiments indicated that these factors did not matter (e.g., Kolers, 1972; Navon, 1976). Red dots in apparent motion were perceived to move as easily to blue dots as to other red dots, changing color in midflight. Similarly, right-diagonal lines appeared to move as easily to left-diagonal lines as to other right-diagonal lines, changing orientation as they moved. These results were interesting

Perceiving Motion and Events

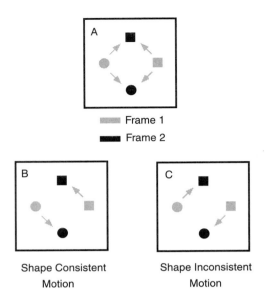

Figure 10.1.10 Using shape to solve the correspondence problem. If two elements in an ambiguous apparent motion display differ in shape (A), they might be perceived to move so that shape is preserved (B) or not (C).

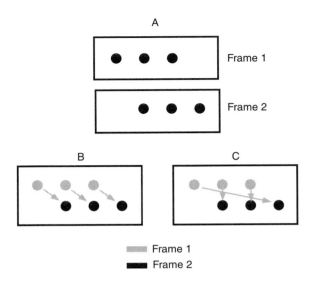

Figure 10.1.11 Ambiguity in the Ternus display. When three dots are presented in alternation so that two of them are the same (A), the correspondence problem can be solved either by seeing uniform motion of the whole group (B) or by seeing two of the dots as stationary and the third moving over a larger distance (C).

because they suggested that the visual system solved the correspondence problem almost exclusively according to distance criteria.

Later studies have shown that factors such as orientation, shape, and size do matter, provided they are properly isolated from confounding procedural variables (Mack, Hill, & Kahn, 1989). Two vertically arrayed elements were alternated with two horizontally arrayed elements so that apparent motion could occur along either the right or the left diagonal (see Figure 10.1.10). In the case shown, the motion along the right diagonal (Figure 10.1.10B) would occur more often than the motion along the left diagonal (Figure 10.1.10C) if shape mattered in solving the correspondence problem. If it did not, the two directions of motion would be equally likely. Navon (1976) found no preference for same-element motion using similar stimuli, but he did not consider the possibility that there might be strong dependencies from one trial to the next and so had tested subjects on many trials. When Mack and her colleagues gave subjects only a single 10-second trial, they found that subjects were 8–10 times more likely to see apparent motion between elements that had the same orientation, size, or shape than between ones that differed in these features.

The rate of alternation between apparent motion displays can also influence the solution to the correspondence problem. Consider, for example, the three-dot display studied by Ternus (1926/1955). As shown in Figure 10.1.11A, three identical dots are present in each frame. It is therefore unclear which dots in the first frame go with which dots in the second. One possibility is that *relative* positions are preserved, the leftmost dot in the first display corresponding to the leftmost dot in the second, the center dot to the center dot, and the rightmost dot to the rightmost dot, as indicated in Figure 10.1.11B. In this interpretation, all three dots would be seen sliding alternately right and left by the same distance. Another possible solution is that the middle and right dots in the first frame correspond to the left and middle dots in the second frame (because they are in the same absolute positions), and the leftmost dot of the first frame corresponds to the rightmost dot of the second frame, as indicated in Figure 10.1.11C. In this interpretation, the two central dots remain stationary while the outside dots move left and right around them. Other correspondences are logically possible, of course, but these are the most obvious alternatives. The question of interest is: Which one is actually perceived and under what conditions?

It turns out that there is no single answer to this question because what is perceived depends on the rate of alternation (Pantle & Picciano, 1976). When the alternation rate is slow, the uniform sliding motion of Figure 10.1.11B is perceived. When the alternation rate is fast, however, the interpretation of Figure 10.1.11C is perceived. More recent studies have shown that time and distance trade off against each other in solving the correspondence problem: At fast frame rates, correspondences over minimal distances are preferred, whereas at slow frame rates, correspondences over longer distances are preferred (Burt & Sperling, 1981).

Short-Range versus Long-Range Apparent Motion. Why might there be different outcomes for the same correspondence problem depending on the alternation rate? One possibility is that there might be more than one mechanism underlying the perception of apparent motion. In 1974 English psychophysicist Oliver Braddick suggested a dual process theory of motion perception that has been very influential. He called the two processes the *short-range* and *long-range motion systems* for reasons that will become clear shortly. This distinction has been a dominant theoretical framework in research on motion perception for many years, although it has recently come into question (e.g., Cavanagh, 1991; Cavanagh & Mather, 1989; Lu & Sperling, 1995).

Braddick proposed his dual process theory after he studied apparent motion using **random dot kinematograms**, which are motion stimuli composed of many randomly positioned elements. The first frame consisted of a completely random array of thousands of tiny black dots on a white background as shown in the gray dots of Figure 10.1.12A. Braddick generated the second display from the first by (1) displacing all of the dots within a central rectangular area by some particular distance and direction and (2) replacing the "background" dots by a completely new set of random dots, uncorrelated with the first frame (black dots in Figure 10.1.12A). These two displays were then presented to subjects by alternating back and forth at a specified rate. The subjects' task was to determine on each trial whether the long axis of the central rectangle of dots was oriented vertically or horizontally.

The critical question is for what alternation rates and displacements is the subject able to make the discrimination between the vertically and horizontally oriented

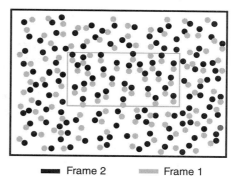

A. Random-dot Kinematogram

■ Frame 2   ▨ Frame 1

B. Classic (Long-range) Apparent Motion

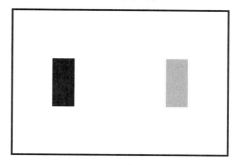

Figure 10.1.12 Random dot kinematograms. Many randomly positioned dots in the first frame (gray dots) are presented in the second frame (black dots) so that those in a central rectangle are uniformly displaced (here, upward), whereas those outside the rectangle are randomly repositioned (A). If observers are sensitive to the differential motion, they perceive a rectangular region of dots moving coherently (up and down) against a background of randomly moving dots. This stimulus is very different from those used in classic studies of apparent motion, which typically have only one large object per frame (B).

rectangular regions. If the visual system is sensitive to the systematic displacement of the dots within the rectangular area, the rectangle should be perceived to move coherently as a unit against a background of randomly moving dots, and the orientation of the rectangle should be easy to discriminate. If the correspondence cannot be detected, however, subjects should be unable to perceive the rectangle and therefore fail to determine its orientation.

Braddick found that for subjects to perform the orientation discrimination task accurately, the displacements had to be small (less than 0.25° of visual angle) and the alternation rate had to be rapid (less than 80 ms per

Perceiving Motion and Events

Table 10.1.1

Short-Range Motion	Long-Range Motion
Small displacements	Large displacements
Rapid alternation	Slow alternation
Monocular only	Monocular or Bincoular
Sensitive to masking	Resistant to masking
Insensitive at isoluminance	Responds at isoluminance

frame). He also found that subjects were unable to perform the task if the two random dot displays were presented to different eyes or if a bright uniform masking field was presented between the two displays. Subsequent findings with this task have also shown that it cannot be performed reliably when the dots are defined by purely chromatic differences, such as red dots on a green background of equal luminance (Ramachandran & Gregory, 1978). This pattern of results for perceiving random dot kinematograms is summarized in the left column of Table 10.1.1.

These findings are surprising because they differ dramatically from what has been found in classical studies of apparent motion (Anstis, 1980; Braddick, 1974). When two large-scale objects—such as filled circles, lines, polygons, or more complex objects—are presented in alternation against a homogeneous background, as illustrated in Figure 10.1.12B, smooth motion is perceived for displacements of many degrees of visual angle and for frame durations up to 300 ms (Neuhaus, 1930). This classical form of apparent motion is also perceived when the two displays are presented to different eyes, when a light masking field intervenes between them, and when the figures are defined by purely chromatic differences (see Braddick, 1974). Notice that this pattern of results for classical apparent motion, summarized in the right column of Table 10.1.1, is the opposite of what Braddick found with the random dot kinematograms for the same factors. Why should there be such marked differences in the two cases?

Braddick suggested that the differences result from the operation of two different motion processing systems. What he called the **short-range motion system** is responsible for performance on the random dot kinematograms. It is sensitive to relatively short displacements and rapid alternation rates and can be used to define perceptual units, such as the rectangle, on the

basis of detecting motion of regions within the 2-D image. Thus, the short-range motion system is thought to occur fairly early in visual processing, before information from the two eyes has been integrated and before shape and color have been extensively analyzed. Its operation is thought to be automatic, passive, and relatively "unintelligent," based on only a few low-level parameters such as luminance, distance, and time.

In contrast, the **long-range motion system** is thought to be responsible for classical phenomena of apparent motion with large-scale, individual figures. It is capable of detecting motion with relatively large displacements and slow alternation rates. The long-range system is thought to occur much later in processing than the short-range system, after information from the two eyes has been integrated, after perceptual units have been defined by figure/ground organization, after shape and color have been analyzed, and after constancy and depth have been achieved. It appears to be relatively sophisticated at solving the correspondence problem and at sorting out whether motion or some other situation is responsible for the alternation of the presented images. We will discuss this system in more detail later in this chapter when we talk about the analysis of object motion.

The two-stage (short-range/long-range) theory of motion perception has recently come under attack. One problem is that although Braddick's distinction is intended to contrast two different underlying *processes*, it is typically defined by differences in motion phenomena for dramatically different kinds of *stimuli* (Cavanagh & Mather, 1989; Chubb & Sperling, 1988). Short-range motion is almost always studied by using random dot kinematograms, whereas long-range motion is almost always studied by using apparent motion displays containing a small number of individuated objects, both of which are illustrated in Figure 10.1.12. Given such stimulus differences, how can one be sure that the differences between the phenomena are not due to differences between the way a single process responds to the different stimuli? For example, random dot kinematograms might produce coherent motion over smaller displacements than classic apparent motion displays simply because of differences in the difficulty of solving the correspondence problem. As the distance between correct matches becomes large relative to the distance between same-frame elements, the number of false matches that are closer than the correct match increases dramatically. The same correspondence process might therefore fail at a much shorter displacement in a random dot kinematogram than in a classic apparent motion display. Note that this account does not appeal to any difference in process at all.

Although the short-range/long-range distinction has been defended against such criticisms (e.g., Petersik, 1991), it has suffered further setbacks from recent psychophysical studies suggesting that the visual system conducts at least *three* different kinds of motion analyses. Lu and Sperling (1995) have proposed that two different motion detection analyses operate within the parameters of Braddick's short-range system: one based on luminance information (the *first-order system*) and another based on texture information (the *second-order system*). Both of these systems are believed to be strictly bottom-up processes that work by detecting motion energy using simple motion detection circuits (see Section 10.1.5). The third type of motion analysis, called the *feature tracking system*, appears to correspond to Braddick's long-range system. Rather than detecting raw motion energy, it is proposed to compute correspondences among features by using top-down attention-driven processes as well as bottom-up components. The development of such theories suggests that although the short-range/long-range distinction may have been a useful first step in analyzing the motion perception system, the truth is probably a good deal more complex.

The Aperture Problem. Thus far we have presented the correspondence problem as arising only in apparent motion. It seems unnecessary for real motion because when each point is displaced continuously, there would appear to be no ambiguity in the nature of the correspondence. But there is a particular version of the correspondence problem, known as the **aperture problem**, that arises in real motion as well. It is an important problem in motion perception not because we frequently perceive the world through apertures, but because the cells that code motion in the visual system typically have small receptive fields and therefore respond as though viewing a small portion of the visual field through an aperture.

The aperture problem refers to local ambiguity in the direction and speed of motion whenever the portion of the image that is visible within a restricted region—

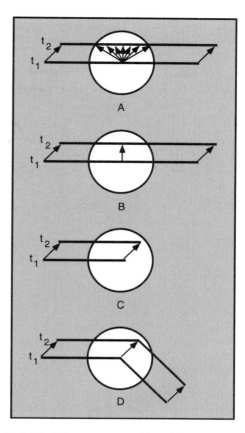

Figure 10.1.13 The aperture problem. The motion of a continuously moving straight line behind an aperture is ambiguous because any point along it at time t_1 can correspond to any point at time t_2 (A). In fact, observers perceive perpendicular motion (B) in the absence of any unique points. When unique points are visible (C and D), the actual motion will be perceived.

referred to as the *aperture*—lacks unique points whose correspondences can be unambiguously determined. Consider, for example, a straight horizontal line moving diagonally behind a circular aperture as shown in Figure 10.1.13A. An observer viewing such a display can know the direction and speed of motion only if the correspondence of points along the line is known. But because none of the points along the line are visually distinguishable, there are no unique points whose correspondences over time can be unambiguously determined. The center point at time t_1, for instance, could correspond to the center point at time t_2, but it could also correspond to any other point along the line at t_2, as indicated in Figure 10.1.13A. The line's motion is therefore ambiguous. It could be specified by *any* vector whose tail lies

Perceiving Motion and Events

along the visible line at t_1 and whose head lies along the line at time t_2. In fact, when people are shown a line moving behind such an aperture, they always perceive the line as moving perpendicular to its orientation (in this case, vertically, as shown in Figure 10.1.13B). This perception minimizes the speed and distance the line appears to move.

If one or both ends of a line are visible within the aperture, however, their correspondence is unambiguous and can therefore be used to determine the perceived motion of the whole line, as shown in Figure 10.1.13C. The unambiguous motion of the line terminators can then be attributed to the line as a whole, provided there is no conflicting information from other unique points. The same effect occurs with the vertex of an angle, as shown in Figure 10.1.13D. We will call this tendency to extrapolate the unambiguous motion of unique points to other parts of the same objects the **unique-point heuristic**.

A good example of the unique-point heuristic in solving the correspondence problem is provided by the **barberpole illusion**, illustrated in Figure 10.1.14A. A

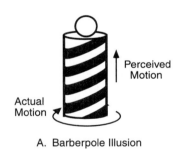

A. Barberpole Illusion

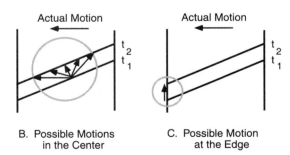

B. Possible Motions in the Center **C. Possible Motion at the Edge**

Figure 10.1.14 The barberpole illusion. The stripes on a barberpole are perceived to move upward even though the pole is actually turning laterally (A). This illusion arises because motion in the center of the stripes is ambiguous (B) and motion at the sides appears to be upward (C). (See text for details.)

barberpole consists of a cylinder painted with a helix of red stripes on a white background. It rotates continuously around its central vertical axis, so all points on its surface actually move laterally (leftward, in this case) at all times. Yet a rotating barberpole produces the illusion that the stripes move vertically up the pole. Why do we perceive this illusion rather than the actual sideways motion?

First, notice that along the middle of the stripes, there is directional ambiguity due to multiple solutions of the correspondence problem. Figure 10.1.14B shows the edge of just one stripe at two different times, labeled t_1 and t_2. From this midstripe information alone, the edges could be moving horizontally leftward (as they actually do), diagonally up and leftward, directly upward, upward and rightward, or any direction in between. But now consider the "ends" of the stripes. (They are not actually physical ends of the stripes, of course, but only the points at which the curvature of the cylinder occludes the continuation of the stripe on the other side of the pole.) These perceived ends appear to be unique points moving upward, and so their perceived upward motion specifies that the stripe as a whole is moving upward, as illustrated in Figure 10.1.14C.

This perception is illusory because the "endpoints" of the stripes are *not* actually the same from one time to another: They move laterally around the pole to locations that are occluded at time t_2. When the correspondence arrived at by the unique-point heuristic is erroneous, the motion that is perceived will be correspondingly erroneous. By this account, if the stripes had a clearly visible texture—for example, if they were made up of many red dots on a white background so that correspondences over time were unambiguous—the barberpole illusion should disappear. And indeed it does, provided that the texture is coarse enough.

Notice that the ends of the stripes at the bottom edge of the barberpole are actually moving leftward. Because they are true endpoints (rather than apparent ones, as are those along the sides), they specify the true motion of the pole. Why do these bottom endpoints not determine the perceived motion of the whole barberpole? The answer appears to be that they are simply overwhelmed by the larger number of ends along the sides. If barberpoles were very short and fat, the perceived motion of the stripes would indeed be horizontal. This interesting fact was discovered by psychologist Hans Wallach (1935) using a 2-D analog of the barberpole illusion in which diagonal stripes were moved behind a rectangular aperture. Regardless of the actual motion of the stripes, when they were moved behind a vertically oriented rectangular aperture, the stripes appeared to move upward. When the aperture was horizontally oriented, they appeared to move leftward.

There is a related phenomenon involving the perceived motion of "plaid" gratings created by superimposing two square wave gratings at different orientations (Adelson & Movshon, 1982). If a single grating is presented in motion, its perceived direction of movement is always perpendicular to the orientation of the stripes, as explained above in discussing the aperture problem. If a second moving grating of the same spatial frequency and contrast is added to the first so that it moves in a different direction (Figure 10.1.15A), the combined grating pattern is perceived to move in neither of the directions of the component gratings. Rather, it is seen to move in a direction midway between the two component motions. This result corresponds to the movement of the points where the gratings cross, as illustrated in Figure 10.1.15A. This is what would be expected from the above analysis of the aperture problem if the crosspoints are taken as unique points whose motion specifies the motion of the entire plaid pattern.

Interestingly, if the two component gratings have very different spatial frequencies (see Figure 10.1.15B) or very different contrasts, they are perceived as moving

quite independently in different directions, sliding past each other (Adelson & Movshon, 1982). That is, they do not form a single plaid grating that moves in the direction of the crosspoints, as would be expected from a simple analysis of unique points. In fact, the crosspoints do not affect motion perception in this case at all, as though the motion system doesn't even "see" them. This may actually be the case, since different populations of cells in area V1 would respond to the motion of the two different spatial frequencies. The existence of seemingly unique points in the stimulus thus cannot affect perceived motion unless the visual system responds to them as unique points. When such points arise from information processed in two different spatial channels, as when the difference in spatial frequency of components in a plaid grating is large, the motion system does not respond to them.

10.1.4 Physiological Mechanisms

Now that we know something about the basic phenomena of image-based motion processing, we can sensibly ask how they might arise in the visual nervous system. Our discussion will concern only the short-range motion system because virtually nothing is yet known about the physiology of the long range system. It is important to realize that the short-range system is thought to be involved in almost all motion perception, because it operates for all continuous motion as well as for apparent motion at short distances and rapid presentation rates, including movies and TV images. We will consider some more complex phenomena that are indicative of the long-range system and theories of those effects in a later section.

The physiological mechanisms underlying our perception of motion are not yet fully understood. Nevertheless, a number of well-established physiological facts strongly constrain current theories of the short-range motion system. We will now examine some of those findings.

The Magno and Parvo Systems. The reader may recall that we distinguished between two types of retinal ganglion cells in Chapter 4 that were called *M cells* and *P cells* because of their projections to the magnocellular and parvocellular layers of the LGN. In comparison to P cells, M cells respond rapidly to changes in stimula-

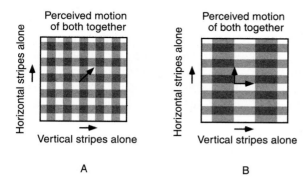

Figure 10.1.15 Moving plaid patterns. When the stripes of plaid patterns are similar in spatial frequency and contrast, they are seen to move as a single uniform pattern along the diagonal path of the intersections (A). When the gratings differ greatly in spatial frequency, they are seen to slide past each other, moving in two different directions (B).

Perceiving Motion and Events

tion, are highly sensitive to luminance contrast, have large receptive fields, and are low in spatial resolution. These general properties of the M cells match with those of global motion perception, leading several researchers to suggest that M cells are the first step in the visual system's analysis of image motion (e.g., Livingstone & Hubel, 1988), although this conclusion is by no means universally held (see Shapley, 1995).

A similar distinction holds for the properties to which magno and parvo cells in the lateral geniculate nucleus (LGN) are most sensitive. Of most relevance to the present discussion, magno cells respond more quickly than parvo cells, are more sensitive to small differences in luminance, have lower spatial acuity, and are less responsive to color. Moreover, the magno cells project to layers in V1 that, in turn, project to areas MT and MST in prestriate cortex, both of which appear to be heavily involved in processing visual motion information. All these facts are consistent with the suggestion by Livingstone and Hubel (1988) that the magno cells represent an early stage of processing in the motion system.

Cortical Analysis of Motion. The processing of image motion is greatly expanded in area V1 where the first cells that are specifically sensitive to directed motion are found. You may recall from Chapter 4 that Hubel and Wiesel were first able to produce responses in V1 cells when the edge of their microscope slide moved across a cell's receptive field in a particular direction. In retrospect, it is not surprising that the cell was motion-sensitive, for the majority of V1 cells are. The critical test for a cell's being sensitive to motion—as opposed to merely requiring some kind of change over time—is its selective response to different directions. Some cells, for example, will fire maximally to a luminance edge moving across its receptive field in a particular direction, less strongly to motion in increasingly different directions, and least strongly to motion in the opposite direction. The firing rate for a representative complex cell in visual cortex is shown in Figure 10.1.16 for several directions of motion. It is most sensitive to upward motion, as indicated in the polar plot summarizing its overall response. Such motion-sensitive cells in V1 send their output to other areas of visual cortex, most prominently to area MT in the medial temporal cortex. It is here that the piecemeal motion information from V1 appears

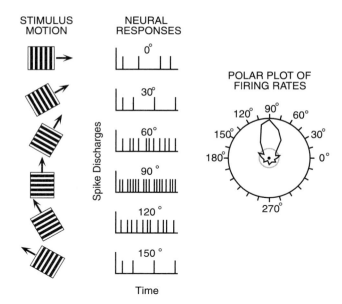

Figure 10.1.16 Neural response of a motion-sensitive complex cell. When a grating is drifted across the cell's receptive field, it fires most rapidly to motion within a small range of directions. Its directional selectivity can be plotted as a graph in polar coordinates, in which each point's distance from the center corresponds to the firing rate of the cell in each motion direction that is tested.

to be more globally integrated into useful information about the velocity of coherent objects.

One suggestive line of evidence about the integrative function of cells in MT concerns their response to plaid gratings, constructed by adding together two gratings that move in different directions (see Figure 10.1.15). As we mentioned earlier, people tend to see such stimuli as moving in the direction of their crosspoints rather than in the directions perpendicular to their component gratings, provided their spatial frequencies and contrasts are similar. Physiologist Anthony Movshon and his colleagues have studied how individual cortical cells respond to these stimuli (Movshon, Adelson, Gizzi, & Newsome, 1985). Do they respond to the motion of the component gratings or to that of the whole pattern?

Figures 10.1.17A and 10.1.17B show the firing rate of a cell that responds to the motion of the component gratings rather than the whole pattern. Panel A shows its response to a single grating moving in different directions. It fires most strongly to gratings that move downward and to the right. When shown plaid patterns whose component gratings are at a 90° angle, however, this

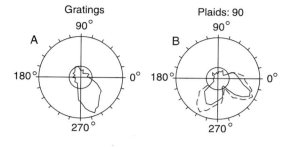

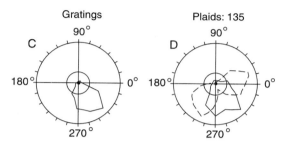

Figure 10.1.17 Directional selectivity of two neurons in area MT to single versus plaid gratings. Polar graph A shows the response of a component cell to a single grating moving in different directions. Graph B shows the response of the same cell to plaid gratings (solid lines) together with how it should behave if it was responding to the individual components in the plaid (dotted lines). Graphs C and D show the response of a pattern cell to similar stimuli. Note that this cell responds to the global motion of the whole plaid (solid line in part D) rather than its components (dashed lines in part D). (After Movshon et al., 1985.)

same cell fires most strongly when the plaid is oriented 45° to either side of its single-grating preference, precisely the direction at which the individual components would be seen to move (Figure 10.1.17B). This is what would be expected if the cell were responding solely to the motion of the component gratings of the plaid rather than the whole pattern. Movshon et al. (1985) classify cells with this type of response as **component cells**.

Figures 10.1.17C and 10.1.17D show the firing of what they call a **pattern cell**. Although somewhat more broadly tuned in orientation than the cell shown in part A, this cell also fires most strongly to a single grating that moves downward and to the right. In contrast with component cells, however, it gives its greatest response to plaids moving in the same direction as the single grating. This suggests that it may be coding the motion of the whole pattern rather than that of the components.

Virtually all directionally selective cells in V1 are classified as component cells when presented with plaid gratings, because they respond selectively to the motion of one of the component gratings, very much as though the other grating were not present. As we have noted, these responses are different from what people consciously experience when viewing such gratings, a finding that suggests that the neural activity underlying conscious motion perception must lie farther along the motion system. Although many cells in MT also respond to the component motions, Movshon and his colleagues found that about 25% of them (the so-called pattern cells) appear to respond in a manner corresponding to the perceived motion of the entire plaid. It is as yet unclear how the pattern cells might accomplish this feat. One intriguing suggestion is that the component cells respond to the best estimate of local image velocity, and the pattern cells evaluate the reliability of those local velocity estimates; that is, pattern cells determine which local estimates provide the best information about the movement of the object as a whole, putting particular weight on unique points (Nowlan & Sejnowski, 1995; Sejnowski & Nowlan, 1995). These different accounts of the operation of pattern cells in MT have not yet been resolved, however.

Neuropsychology of Motion Perception. Single-cell recording studies of motion processing have to be carried out on animal subjects for obvious reasons. Much less is known about the physiology of human motion perception as a result. Nevertheless, an intriguing neurological case has been reported of a highly specific deficit in human visual motion perception (Zihl, Von Cramon, & Mai, 1983). The patient was admitted to the hospital complaining of severe headaches, vertigo, nausea, and the inability to perceive motion. She reported that the world appeared to her as a series of frozen snapshots. She had difficulty pouring liquid into a cup, for example, because she could not experience its motion as the cup filled. First, she would see the empty cup, then some amount frozen and unmoving in the cup, and the next thing she saw, it had overflowed. She had similar problems in crossing the street. She would see an unmoving car at some distance from her, and then a moment later would see it almost upon her, without seeing it move between the two positions.

Perceiving Motion and Events

Psychophysical testing showed that she could perceive horizontal or vertical movement in the picture plane if it was slow enough but not rapid motion or any sort of movement in depth. Her perceptual problems were quite restricted to visual motion perception, however. Her ability to recognize objects was intact, as evidenced by identification of the car as a car and the cup as a cup. She was also able to perceive auditory motion events. She could comprehend speech—although this was somewhat more difficult because of her inability to see the person's face move—and she eventually learned to gauge the distance of approaching cars by attending to their increasing loudness.

Brain imaging tests indicated that the lesion in her brain was located in the border region between occipital and temporal cortex, clearly outside of primary visual cortex. The damaged area appears to be analogous to MT and MST in monkey cortex. The fact that primary visual cortex was intact may account for her very limited ability to perceive some motion in the frontal plane, given the existence of motion-selective cells in V1. Motion in depth, however, appears to be processed at a later stage where her cortex was damaged, probably in MT and MST.

10.1.5 Computational Theories

Directionally selective cells are clearly present in visual cortex, and they obviously play a crucial role in our ability to perceive motion. But why do they respond as they do? Somewhat surprisingly, the answer is not yet known with certainty, for it is difficult to determine the precise wiring of the visual system by using purely physiological and anatomical techniques. Computational theories of how motion-sensitive elements might be constructed have provided important additional insights. The behavior of these models can be compared with human performance and the results of physiological experiments with animals to find out whether they are plausible theories of how the visual system responds to motion.

Delay-and-Compare Networks. Most computational theories of image motion are based on some version of a **delay-and-compare scheme**: They compare what happens in one region of the retina with what happened shortly before in a nearby area, using

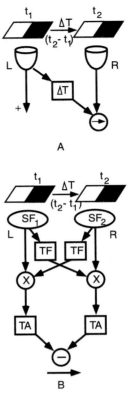

Figure 10.1.18 Two delay-and-compare theories of motion selectivity. The most basic scheme, diagrammed in part A, proposes that the output of two neurons that are sensitive to the same spatial properties in different retinal locations are combined by motion-sensitive neurons after a time delay (ΔT). The extended Reichard detector (Van Santen & Sperling, 1984), diagrammed in part B, also compares delayed and undelayed outputs over a delay (or temporal filter, TF), but with an additional temporal averaging process (TA). (See text for details.)

some form of time delay mechanism. The rationale is that if something is moving rightward (left to right) across the retina, the output of a cell responding to it in location L at time t_1 will be the same as (or similar to) the output of a corresponding cell in a location R (farther to the right) at some later time t_2, as illustrated in Figure 10.1.18A. If there is no motion or if the motion is in the other direction, the outputs will not be the same at the same time lag $(t_2 - t_1)$. The trick is to make the sameness of the input pattern at these two different locations and times sum to cause high activity in the motion-sensitive unit and differences in either the pattern or time lag to reduce activity.

This can be accomplished in a variety of ways, as reflected in several different versions of the same basic idea. One early formulation was Barlow and Levick's (1965) model of motion processing in the rabbit's retina, a version of which is shown in Figure 10.1.18A. Their proposal incorporates a temporal delay (ΔT) between the outputs of spatially separated receptors, thus causing the activity of both receptors to converge at the motion detector cell. This detector then sums the input of the delayed unit with that of the direct unit. The output will therefore be highest if the motion is in the preferred direction at the preferred time lag.

Another early delay-and-compare theory was devised by Reichard (1957, 1961) to model directional motion sensitivity in insects. He used temporal filtering operations to accomplish the time delay on one component and a multiplication of the two inputs to the motion detector to ensure its selectivity to motion in the proper direction. Figure 10.1.18B shows an "elaborated Reichard detector" that was recently proposed to account for human motion perception (Van Santen & Sperling, 1984). Although it is also a delay-and-compare scheme, it is more sophisticated than the theory shown in Figure 10.1.18A in several respects. One is that the input comes from local spatial frequency filters (SF_1 and SF_2) of the type that we considered in Section 4.2. The temporally delayed outputs (TF) of these filters are then multiplied ($\times$) with the direct output, after which the values are temporally averaged (TA) over a brief duration and finally subtracted from one another. The result produces a positive value for rightward motion and a negative value for leftward motion. A number of computationally equivalent models of this type were proposed by other theorists at about the same time (e.g., Adelson & Bergen, 1985; Watson & Ahumada, 1985).

Edge-Based Models. A different kind of motion detector circuit was proposed by Marr and Ullman (1981), based on the Marr-Hildreth (1980) edge detection algorithm that was described in Section 4.3.2. Marr and Ullman suggested that motion detectors could be constructed by analyzing the change in illumination over time in conjunction with an edge detector. To see how this computational scheme works, consider a vertical edge that is dark on the left and light on the right, as illustrated in Figure 10.1.19. In this case, rightward

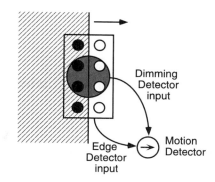

Figure 10.1.19 A computational theory of motion selectivity based on edge detectors. The output of an oriented edge detector is combined with that of a dimming detector to produce a directionally selective motion analyzer.

movement of the edge would produce darkening, and leftward movement would produce brightening. Thus, conjoining this edge detector with a cell that is excited by decreases in illumination at the same location would result in a detector for rightward-moving dark vertical edges, as illustrated. Conjoining it with a cell that is excited by increases in illumination would result in a detector for leftward-moving light vertical edges.

Spatial-Frequency-Based Models. One further type of model is based on the local spatial frequency theory that we considered in Section 4.2 for static patterns. The basic idea behind extending such models to motion (e.g., Adelson & Bergen, 1985; Watson & Ahumada, 1983) is essentially to build local filters for analyzing the structure of events in space-time. It is perhaps easiest to think about this in terms of the space-time diagrams we considered at the outset of this chapter (e.g., Figures 10.1.1 and 10.1.2). These motion filters can be tuned to different rates of motion, for example, by responding to different orientations of lines in space-time. Figure 10.1.20A shows a filter that responds to slow upward motion, and Figure 10.1.20B shows one that is tuned to faster upward motion. As indicated in these diagrams, each will respond most vigorously to the optimal speed of motion because of the excitatory and inhibitory regions of its receptive field in space-time. In addition to their tuning to different speeds, these motion filters are proposed to be tuned to different spatial frequencies and orientations, as in the static domain we considered in Section 4.2.

Perceiving Motion and Events

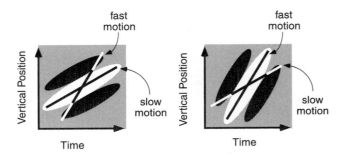

A: Slow motion detector   B: Fast motion detector

Figure 10.1.20 A computational theory of motion selectivity based on spatial frequency analysis. Motion analyzers respond selectively to the orientation of events in space-time, being activated maximally by motion at the favored direction and rate (slow upward motion in part A and fast upward motion in part B). White ellipses represent excitatory regions of the cell's receptive field in space-time, and black ellipses represent inhibitory regions. The lines represent motion events that fall either fully in the excitatory region (black lines) or in both excitatory and inhibitory regions (black and white lines). (See text for details.)

One might think that it should be easy to determine which theory of motion detection is correct simply by examining the corresponding neural circuitry. Such is not the case, however. In any animal whose visual system is similar to humans, the motion-sensitive cells are many synapses into the brain (area V1 or later), where it is not yet possible to trace out specific circuits, neuron by neuron and synapse by synapse, to test the theories. Rather, computational models are typically tested against psychophysical data obtained from human observers while they perform behavioral tasks. Many of the basic phenomena of motion perception, such as similar responses to apparent and continuous motion, are consistent with many models, making them difficult to discriminate without converging physiological evidence. Indeed, some of the models actually make identical predictions for all known psychophysical tests. This is the case, for example, with the extended Reicher detector model of Van Santen and Sperling (1985) and the spatial-frequency-based models of Watson and Ahumada (1983) and Adelson and Bergen (1985). This situation therefore requires physiological tests to discriminate between models. Unfortunately, the relevant data are not yet available.

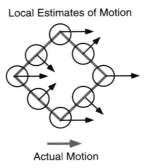

Figure 10.1.21 Local estimates of motion. Because of the aperture problem, a diamond moving rightward will produce local estimates of motion in different directions at different positions along its perimeter. Only the corners yield accurate information because of the unique points at the vertices.

Integrating Local Motion. The computational models considered thus far are concerned only with analyzing the motion of edges and lines within a local region defined by the cell's receptive field. Because of the aperture problem, however, estimates of local motion along the edges of an object may not provide the best interpretation of the object's motion as a whole. To illustrate, consider the rightward-moving diamond in Figure 10.1.21. Local motion analyses along the middle of the sides are ambiguous, because these motion analyzers are operating within the small aperture of their limited receptive fields and because there are no unique points within these regions. In the absence of unique points, their analysis alone would indicate motion perpendicular to the moving line. The local motion of vertices, in contrast, provides good local estimates of the figure's motion because of the presence of unique points. Somehow, these piecemeal analyses must be combined into a coherent perception of a unitary object moving rightward. How might this be accomplished computationally?

One simple and elegant theory specifies how to combine the constraints provided by all local motion analyses into a best estimate of the global motion (e.g., Adelson & Movshon, 1982). If a straight edge moves across an aperturelike local receptive field, its precise direction and speed are ambiguous because the actual motion might have been any vector that lies along the *constraint line* in velocity space, as shown in Figure 10.1.22A. The same ambiguity holds true for any other locally analyzed

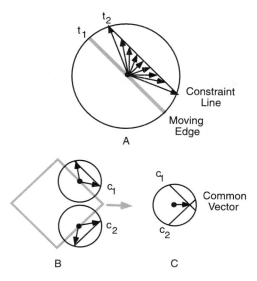

Figure 10.1.22 A computational theory of local motion integration. The vector representing the motion of each line or edge must lie somewhere along the constraint line, as illustrated in part A. Any object undergoing rigid translation will have a single common point for all its constraint lines when they are superimposed.

edge. If two edges are part of the same rigidly translating object, as illustrated in Figure 10.1.22B, however, they must both be moving in the same direction. This means that the constraint lines of two (nonparallel) edges, labeled c_1 and c_2 in Figure 10.1.22B, must contain exactly one vector in common, and this vector must represent the motion of the whole object. Locally analyzed motions from a single, rigid object can be integrated, therefore, by finding the vector that is common to all its constraint lines. That vector is the one where the constraint lines intersect when they are superimposed, as shown in Figure 10.1.22C.

Movshon and his colleagues (1985) suggest that the so-called pattern cells they discovered in MT may be implementing this function. That is, they speculate that pattern cells compute the motion of the whole plaid grating by integrating the joint constraints implied by the two component gratings. Whether this is true is not yet clear, but it is a stimulating example of how physiological and computational models of motion analysis can converge on a coherent, integrated account of an interesting phenomenon of motion perception.

10.2 Object Motion

The theories of motion that we have considered thus far are concerned with movement in the 2-D image: how changes in the retinal distribution of luminance can be detected over time. But this is only the first step in motion perception, for what is ultimately needed is information about how objects are moving in the 3-D environment. For a predator trying to catch its fleeing prey—and for the prey trying to escape its attacking predator—detecting motion in the 2-D retinal image is wholly inadequate. To be useful, image motion must be *interpreted* to provide information about the motion (or the lack of it) in environmental objects. This requires integrating image motion with information about how the eye is moving and the distance to moving objects to achieve **motion constancy**: veridical perception of the movement of physical objects in the environment despite variations in image motion due to viewing factors such as eye, head, and bodily movements. Only then does the observer have access to evolutionarily useful information about how objects are moving in the world.

We are considering motion as a separate topic in this chapter, but it is tightly woven into the fabric of spatial perception. As we mentioned in Chapter 5, relative motion provides important information about depth, including motion parallax, motion gradients, and the accretion and deletion of texture due to movement by observer, object, or both. Motion information also figures importantly in the organization of visual perception, particularly through the Gestalt principle of common fate, which strongly affects what regions of the image are seen as unified perceptual objects (see Section 6.1.1). In this section we will examine the related questions of how depth and organization affect the interpretation of objects in motion.

10.2.1 Perceiving Object Velocity

How is the speed of an object perceived? Is it determined by the proximal speed of its motion over the retinal image or by its distal speed in the environment? A simple demonstration will provide compelling evidence that it is not retinal speed. Hold up your index finger and move it in front of your face while you track it with your eyes. What you perceive is your finger (and hand) moving laterally in an otherwise stationary environment.

But this is not the event that occurs in the image on your retina. Because you tracked your finger by following it with your eyes, the image of your finger (and hand) on your retina is essentially motionless, and the rest of the visual world sweeps across the visual field in the direction opposite your eye movements. Notice that this retinal state of affairs is, in many respects, the opposite of what you perceived: The retinally stationary object (your finger) was perceived as moving, and the retinally moving objects (the background) were perceived as stationary.

The inescapable conclusion of this simple demonstration is that the perception of moving objects must be determined jointly by image motion and eye movements. The result is approximate motion constancy. It is achieved in very much the same way as position constancy, which we discussed at some length in Chapter 7. It should not be surprising that visual perception results in approximate motion constancy. To avoid being hit by a car, you need to know its direction and speed in the environment, not that of its image on your retina.

Naive experience supports the existence of at least approximate **velocity constancy**: Object speed, rather than image speed, is the major determinant of perceived velocity. If you watch the traffic on a freeway from a few hundred feet away, all the cars appear to be moving at about the same speed. The closest ones don't look as though they are moving appreciably faster than the farthest ones, even though this is what is happening in the 2-D images that are projected onto your retina.

Carefully controlled experiments have shown that velocity perception does indeed yield approximate constancy (Rock, Hill, & Fineman, 1968). Subjects viewed two vertically moving objects, one of which was four times farther away than the other. They were asked to adjust the speed of the farther one so that it appeared equal to that of the nearer one. When subjects viewed the display binocularly so that they had good depth information, they set the speed of the farther object at about the same real-world velocity as the closer object. This result thus exhibits velocity constancy. When subjects viewed the same objects without good depth information (by closing one eye), they set the real-world speed of the more distant object nearly four times faster than that of the closer object. This result would be predicted from matching retinal speeds directly, because when both objects move at the same real-world speed,

the farther object is moving only one-fourth as far across the retina as the nearer object in the same amount of time. Speeding up the farther object by a factor of 4 therefore equates their retinal speeds. The results of this experiment thus show that as long as the observer has good information about how far away an object is, he or she perceives its real-world velocity, presumably by taking into account the distance to the object.

As in size constancy, however, relational information is also available for velocity constancy. If a small object moves in front of a larger one—say, a car traveling past a house—the amount of time it takes to traverse the larger object does not change with viewing distance. Under controlled laboratory conditions, subjects match the speed of a test object traversing a rectangular aperture so that they take about the same time to cross the opening (Brown, 1931; Wallach, 1939). This result is entirely analogous to the proportionality (or relative size) account of size constancy described in Section 7.1.1. It is not incompatible with the taking-into-account explanation of velocity constancy but is complementary to it.

As in other forms of constancy, velocity constancy breaks down under extreme conditions. Cars moving along the freeway appear to be going much faster when viewed from a few yards away, for example, than when viewed from a few miles away. This discrepancy in velocity constancy might be explained by the same breakdown in size constancy that occurs at large distances, as discussed in Chapter 7. If the environmental distance the car moves during a given time interval is underestimated, for example, its speed will be correspondingly underestimated, and velocity constancy will suffer. Note that relative speed does not easily predict this breakdown in speed constancy, because it is invariant with distance.

10.2.2 Depth and Motion

In Chapter 5 we considered how the visual system is able to use information in the 2-D image to recover the third spatial dimension of depth. Many of these factors were quite independent of motion—for example, accommodation, convergence, binocular disparity, perspective projection, texture gradients, edge interpretation, shading, and so on—but several were derived directly from motion, including relative motion parallax, motion gradients, and accretion/deletion of texture. We will now consider more closely some of the factors that enable the visual system to interpret image motion in terms of objects in a 3-D spatial environment.

Rigid Motion in Depth. Velocity constancy typically concerns a situation in which static sources of depth information are independently available to specify how far away objects are. But what about cases in which this is not true, cases in which only motion information is present? Does the visual system interpret differential motion in terms of depth, and, if so, under what circumstances?

In studying the perception of motion in simple 2-D displays consisting of pairs of continuously moving points of light, Swedish psychologist Gunnar Johansson (1950) discovered some powerful depth effects in motion perception. In one display, two points moved back and forth in synchrony while they also moved closer together and farther apart, as shown in Figure 10.2.1A. You might expect that this simple pattern of retinal motion is what observers would perceive, but most did not. Instead, they saw the two dots moving forward and back-

ward in depth, as though they were lights attached to the ends of a rigid vertical rod (Figure 10.2.1B).

Other displays produced similar depth effects. Whenever the pattern of 2-D motion could be perceived as rigid motion in depth, it was. This included several rather surprising cases, such as the one shown in Figure 10.2.1C. The display consisted simply of two lights traversing the same rectangular path on opposite sides, but this is not what people perceived. Rather, they saw the lights moving as though attached to the ends of a rigid rod that rotated in 3-D space, producing the complex motion pattern in depth depicted in Figure 10.2.1D.

Such findings suggest that there is something quite special about rigidity in perceiving object motion: All else being equal, if there is an interpretation in which rigid motion can be perceived, it will be. We will call this the **rigidity heuristic**. We will see that it plays an important role in understanding the relation between depth and motion, although there are cases in which other factors override it.

The Kinetic Depth Effect. Johansson's results indicating perception of rigid motion in depth were obtained with a few simple points of light. Is this simplicity important in perceiving rigid motion in depth, or would similar preferences be evident with more complex visual displays of connected objects?

Wallach and O'Connell (1953) examined this question using a shadow-casting technique to present 2-D images of angular 3-D wire objects to observers, as illustrated in Figure 10.2.2A. When the object was stationary, observers reported seeing what was actually shown to them: a 2-D figure in the plane of the rear-projection screen. As soon as the wire object began to rotate, however, their perception changed dramatically to that of a 3-D wire object rotating in depth. This phenomenon, known as the **kinetic depth effect (KDE)**, demonstrates that human observers are indeed sensitive to the information that a complex object is rotating rigidly in depth. Indeed, the impression of depth and rigidity in the KDE is much more potent than in Johansson's simple displays of a few disconnected lights, which tend to produce ambiguous depth perception that varies from observer to observer.

Perception of rigid motion does not occur for all objects under these conditions, however. If the object is a smoothly curved wire, rather than one containing

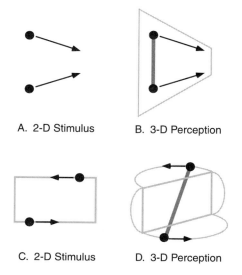

A. 2-D Stimulus   B. 3-D Perception

C. 2-D Stimulus   D. 3-D Perception

Figure 10.2.1 Depth effects in perceived motion of simple 2-D events. Two dots moving in phase as shown in part A are perceived as two dots moving in depth as though attached to the ends of a rigid rod (dashed line), as illustrated in part B. Two dots following each other around a rectangular path as shown in part C are also seen to move in depth as though attached to the ends of a rigid rod pivoting through the center, as illustrated in part D.

Perceiving Motion and Events

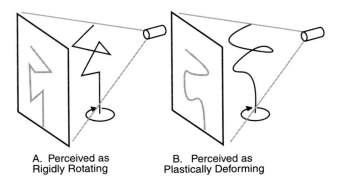

A. Perceived as Rigidly Rotating

B. Perceived as Plastically Deforming

Figure 10.2.2 The kinetic depth effect. The shadow of a stationary, sharply bent wire is perceived as a flat 2-D line, but if the wire is rotated as shown, it is perceived as a 3-D object rotating rigidly in depth (A). If a similar smoothly curved wire is rotated, it is usually perceived as plastically deforming rather than rigidly rotating (B).

sharp angles, rigid rotation in depth is frequently not perceived. Instead, observers report seeing plastically deforming 2-D curves in the plane of the projection screen (Figure 10.2.2B). This fact indicates that there are limits to the visual system's ability to utilize information about rigidity in perceiving motion in depth. Unique points, such as vertices and endpoints (but not crosspoints), appear to play an important role in the conditions required for veridical perception of rigid motion.

The Rigidity Heuristic and the Correspondence Problem. Computational analyses have been proposed to explain the KDE and related phenomena based on the rigidity heuristic. Vision scientist Shimon Ullman (1979) examined the geometry of rigidly moving objects from a series of discrete images. He proved mathematically that if one knows the correspondence of points from each view to the next and if one assumes that the object is rigid, then it is possible to recover both the 3-D location and the motion of the object from four noncoplanar points in three distinct orthographic projections. This **structure-from-motion theorem**, as it is called, thus provides an internal test for rigidity among the four non-coplanar points. A computational system based on it can therefore discriminate rigid from nonrigid motion for each possible set of four non-coplanar points from three different views, provided that the correspondences between the four points are accurately known.

Interestingly, human observers are able to recover depth and 3-D structure from just two views using apparent motion displays, and adding more views does little to change their perceptions (see Todd, 1995, for a review). How can this be so if three views are logically required? One possibility is that Ullman's three-view analysis does not yield the minimal conditions. Subsequent computational analyses, for example, have shown that with perspective projection (rather than orthographic projection; see Section 1.2), rigid structure can be deduced from five points in just two views, and adding a sixth point makes the recovered solution unique (Faugeras & Maybank, 1990). Only two views are needed with perspective projection because it provides additional constraints on structure in depth that are not available in orthographic projection. Human observers are able to perceive depth and structure from just two views of rigid motion *without* perspective information, however, so this analytical result does not explain optimal human performance. Another possibility is that the human visual system applies perceptual heuristics of some sort (Braunstein, 1976). We have encountered this kind of explanation many times in this book already, although in this case, there is no general agreement about what form these heuristics take. A third possibility is that the human visual system recovers only relative (rather than absolute) depth information, a possibility that is consistent with the geometrical information contained in just two views (Todd, 1995).

Regardless of how this controversy is resolved, it is important to realize that all mathematical analyses of structure from motion rest on the assumption that the correct correspondence of points across different views is known. This is a weighty assumption, because the proper correspondence is not directly given in the two discrete images on which the analysis is based. Rather, the visual system has to solve this correspondence problem for itself. If it is solved incorrectly, then the rigidity test may fail even when the stimulus is actually a rigid object in motion. This turns out to be important for understanding why the KDE occurs readily with wire objects having sharp angles but not with ones having smooth curves. The crucial difference, illustrated in Figure 10.2.3A, is that when a sharp angle rotates in depth, its vertex is a unique point in all its projections—except the two for which the angle degenerates into a straight line. This unique point can thus be accurately identified

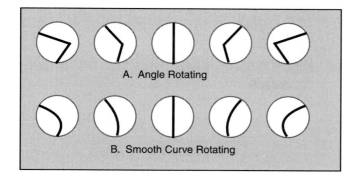

A. Angle Rotating

B. Smooth Curve Rotating

Figure 10.2.3 The unique point heuristic and the KDE. When an angle rotates (A), its vertex provides a unique point whose identity is preserved during rotation for all views except the degenerated case of a straight line. When a curve rotates (B), no such unique point can be recovered.

at almost every moment. When a smooth curve rotates, as shown in Figure 10.2.3B, there is no unambiguously unique point that can be recovered with such precision. Taking the points of maximum curvature of its various 2-D projections to be corresponding points in the 3-D object, for example, is often an incorrect solution to the correspondence problem. Any rigidity test that is based on an erroneous correspondence will fail, and the observer will perceive some sort of nonrigid motion.

The Stereo-Kinetic Effect. There are also cases in which observers perceive motion of an object in depth even when the actual display is rigidly rotating in the frontal plane. The best-known example is the **stereo-kinetic effect** (Musatti, 1924). You can experience it for yourself by photocopying the inside back cover of the book, cutting out the figure, and placing in on a turntable at $33\frac{1}{3}$ rpm. Watch it with one eye closed for a while, and you will begin to experience motion of a 3-D object. Two different depth perceptions are possible: a rotating cone protruding out of the turntable toward you or a rotating conical tunnel that recedes into the turntable. Both produce vivid impressions of depth from motion. This seems to be a puzzling phenomenon with respect to the rigidity hypothesis because the figure is actually undergoing rigid 2-D rotation. Why shouldn't the visual system prefer this veridical 2-D interpretation over an illusory one in depth?

Again, the crucial factor appears to be that whether a given motion is rigid or not depends critically on the

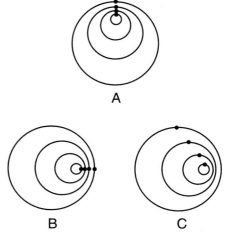

Figure 10.2.4 The stereo-kinetic effect. When rotated about its center, the configuration of circles shown in part A can be perceived either as a flat 2-D pattern rotating in the frontal plane (B) or as a 3-D cone pointing toward (or away from) the observer (C). Which is perceived depends on the solution to the correspondence problem, as explained in the text.

nature of the correspondence that is assigned during motion. Consider the correspondence problem that arises for the stereo-kinetic effect as depicted in Figure 10.2.4. Part A shows the initial stimulus display, and parts B and C show two alternative correspondences after the turntable has made a 90° rotation. The critical question is which points in the later display correspond to the points shown in the earlier one? The *actually* corresponding points are those shown in part B, because the whole display has rotated rigidly. But the circles in the display contain no unique points, and so there is no stimulus evidence supporting this particular correspondence over others. Another possibility is shown in part C. If the visual system interprets the circles as simply translating in circular paths (rather than as rotating around the central point), then the uppermost points of the circles correspond to each other at all times, as indicated in the A–C correspondence. This would be expected if the visual system prefers simple translations over rotations in the absence of specific evidence for rotation.

The crucial observation in understanding why the stereo-kinetic effect arises is that although the A–B correspondence is indeed rigid in the picture plane, the A–C correspondence is not. The mere fact that the points are farther apart in C than in A shows that this

Perceiving Motion and Events

correspondence does not reflect rigid motion in the frontal plane. It may be rigid, however, if these points are positioned at different depths, and this is what people usually perceive after viewing the motion for a short time. Thus, the particular way in which the visual system misperceives the rigid 2-D motion is oddly consistent with the rigidity heuristic. The perception is of an object in rigid motion, but in 3-D rather than 2-D.

If an erroneous solution to the correspondence problem is responsible for the stereo-kinetic effect, then it should be abolished by stimulus changes that allow the visual system to achieve unambiguous and correct correspondences. The evidence on this hypothesis is somewhat mixed. If the circles are replaced with other figures that have unique points—for example, hexagons or squares—the stereokinetic effect usually disappears and observers perceive a flat rotating display (Rock, personal communication). The vertices allow the correspondence problem to be solved correctly, yielding veridical perception of 2-D rotation. However, the same result was not found when the circles were constructed of dotted lines that should also have provided unique points (Musatti, 1975; Proffitt, Rock, Hecht, & Schubert, 1992). Instead of seeing the veridical picture-plane rotation of nested dotted circles, observers reported seeing a cone rotating in depth while the dots revolved around the contours! Although the explanation of this phenomenon is not certain, it is possible that the perception of global rotation and depth is governed by the low-spatial-frequency information (see Section 4.2) and the local revolution of the dots by the high-spatial-frequency information (Proffitt, Rock, Hecht, & Schubert, 1992).

Perception of Nonrigid Motion. There are other examples in which ambiguity in the solution of the correspondence problem leads to unexpected perception of nonrigid motion. The embedded ellipses on the inside back cover provide another demonstration for use on a turntable. When the turntable rotates, the ellipses rigidly rotate along with it. At first, you probably perceive this rigid rotation; but after you look at them for a while, your perception will probably change. They will begin to look as though they are ellipses undergoing plastic distortions (stretching and squashing) as they move rather than rigidly rotating ellipses (Wallach, Weisz, & Adams, 1956).

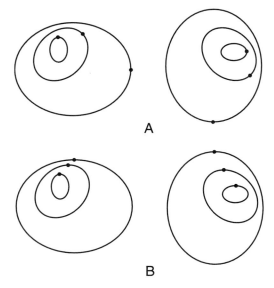

Figure 10.2.5 Nonrigid motion perception from a rigidly rotating display. If the correspondence problem is solved by using points of maximum curvature (A), rigid rotation should be perceived. If it is solved by using direction from the center of the figure (B), nonrigid deformations should be perceived. Both occur, but the nonrigid motion is preferred once it has been seen.

Again, these different perceptions can be explained through different solutions to the correspondence problem. If the points of maximum curvature are taken as corresponding across time, as illustrated in Figure 10.2.5A, the ellipses will be seen as rotating rigidly. However, if the correspondence is given instead by the direction of points from their figural center (e.g., the topmost point, as illustrated in Figure 10.2.5B), then the motion that will be perceived is decidedly nonrigid. Unlike the stereo-kinetic effect, there is no depth solution that preserves rigidity, and so plastic deformation in the frontal plane is perceived.

Support for this explanation again comes from discovering what happens with other shapes that have unambiguous unique points. If the ellipses are replaced with rectangles, for example, whose vertices are unique and perceived as corresponding over time, rigid rotation is experienced, with no hint of deformation. However, if rectangular figures are used in an apparent motion display, as shown in Figure 10.2.6, the ambiguity of motion returns. Without the information from the intermediate orientations of the rectangle, there is now ambiguity about the correspondence of vertices. In one possible

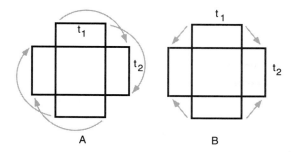

Figure 10.2.6 Ambiguous apparent motion of rectangles. Apparent motion between these two rectangles can be perceived either as a rigid 90° rotation (A) or as a plastic stretching and squashing without rotation (B). Which is perceived depends on factors such as the length-to-width ratio of the rectangle.

solution, apparent rotation is experienced (Figure 10.2.6A); in another, apparent squashing and stretching are experienced (Figure 10.2.6B). The dominant perception depends in part on the length-to-width ratio of the rectangle. As you might expect, the closer the rectangle is to the square, the stronger is the tendency to perceive deformation; the more elongated it is, the stronger is the tendency to see it rotate (Palmer, unpublished study).

It therefore appears that two important factors in understanding the perception of object motion are the rigidity of the object undergoing motion and the availability of unique points that can be used to determine the correct solution to the correspondence problem. When unique points, such as vertices or line ends, are continuously and unambiguously available, veridical rigid motion is almost always perceived. When unique points are not available (e.g., in smoothly curved lines) or are only intermittently available (e.g., in apparent motion displays), the solution to the correspondence problem is ambiguous, resulting in different perceptions of the same object engaging in different motions at different times.

10.2.3 Long-Range Apparent Motion

In discussing apparent motion earlier in this chapter, we made a distinction between short-range and long-range cases (Braddick, 1974). Whereas short-range apparent motion appears to coincide with image-level processing of motion, long-range apparent motion is more naturally associated with object-level processing, and so we will consider it now.

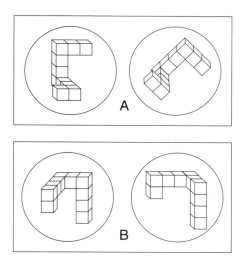

Figure 10.2.7 Apparent rotation displays. Pairs of perspective views of 3-D objects illustrate objects that differ by a rotation in the picture plane only (A) or in depth (B). (After Shepard & Judd, 1976.)

Apparent Rotation. Many fascinating phenomena concerning object-level apparent motion have come from experiments performed in the laboratory of psychologist Roger Shepard at Stanford University. One of the most interesting and well studied is the phenomenon of **apparent rotation**. Shepard and Judd's (1976) initial investigation demonstrated the basic phenomenon and showed that it is fundamentally a 3-D, object-based perception. Subjects were presented alternating views of the same 3-D object from different perspectives. As illustrated in Figure 10.2.7, the displays were line drawings of objects composed of a number of cubes stuck together. Some of the pairs were picture-plane rotations of the same object (Figure 10.2.7A), and others were 3-D rotations of such objects in depth (Figure 10.2.7B). When such pairs are presented alternately at an appropriate rate, they give rise to the clear and vivid perception of a single object rigidly rotating back and forth. When they are alternated too quickly, however, the perception of rigid rotation breaks down, either because the two views appear to be superimposed and flickering or because the shape of the object appears to distort as it moves rather than remaining rigid.

To study the processes underlying apparent rotation, Shepard and Judd (1976) determined the fastest alternation rate at which each observer reported smooth rigid motion of a single object. The results, averaged

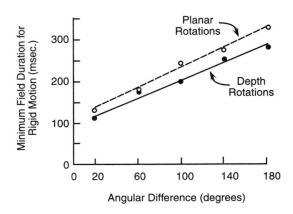

Figure 10.2.8 Results of an apparent rotation experiment. The minimum presentation duration for which rigid apparent rotation occurs is plotted as a function of the angular difference between the two perspective views for picture-plane rotations (dashed line) and depth rotations (solid line). (After Shepard & Judd, 1976.)

over subjects, are plotted in Figure 10.2.8. They show that the shortest frame duration for perceived rigid rotation increases linearly with the angular difference between the two perspective views. This result strongly suggests that the process underlying apparent rotation is an analog process, that is, a continuous process that requires time to go through intermediate orientations, just as real objects do when they rotate (see also Robins & Shepard, 1977). The results also showed that the linear increase was virtually identical for the pairs related by picture-plane rotations and depth rotations. This indicates that the motion that subjects perceived could not be adequately described in terms of transformations occurring in the 2-D image. Rather, the transformations must be taking place in an internal representation of three-dimensional space.

These findings of apparent rotation are strikingly reminiscent of Korte's third law for two-point apparent motion: As the separation between two lights increases, the alternation rate must slow correspondingly (i.e., the duration of each frame must increase). The only differences are that the perception is of apparent rotation rather than apparent translation and that the relevant stimulus variable is angular difference in orientation rather than linear difference in position. It appears, then, that the visual system is representing motion as it would occur in the external world and that there is some maximal rate at which such internal spatial trans-

formations can take place. In the case of apparent rotation, however, there is the interesting fact that the relation holds for rigid transformations that preserve object shape. Thus, Shepard and Judd's results provide further evidence for the importance of the rigidity heuristic: the visual system's preference for perceiving rigid motion rather than plastic deformations.

As we discovered in other cases of potentially rigid motion perception, however, this preference for rigid rotation is not absolute. At rapid alternation rates, Shepard and Judd's subjects reported substantial nonrigid motion. It appears, then, that the preference for rigid motion will be expressed perceptually only if there is sufficient time for the analog process underlying it to complete the appropriate transformation internally. Carlton and Shepard (1990a, 1990b) have formalized this relation in a geometrical model of apparent rotation based on the following three ideas that map object motions to geometrical paths in a high-dimensional space.

1. *Motion hyperspace.* Rigid rotations of an object in three dimensions can be modeled as a 3-D spherical surface (or **hypersphere**) within a higher-dimensional space (or **hyperspace**) of all possible motions. Any continuous motion can be represented as a continuous path within the higher-dimensional space, but the path will lie entirely on the surface of the rotational hypersphere only if the transformation is rigid rotation. Any portion of the path that lies off the surface of the hypersphere corresponds to nonrigid motion.

2. *Path impletion.* The two perspective views of the same object in an apparent rotation display correspond to two points within the higher-dimensional space, both of which lie on the hypersphere of rigid rotation. The visual system interprets apparent motion by traversing (*impleting*) one of many possible paths between these two points. Different paths correspond to different perceived motions.

3. *Maximum speed.* Rigid apparent motion will be perceived if and only if the alternation rate is sufficiently slow that the shortest path along the rigid-rotation surface can be traversed at or below a maximum speed in the time available between the onsets of the two displays. If this time is not long enough, a shorter path that does not lie on the surface will be followed, resulting in the perception of nonrigid motion.

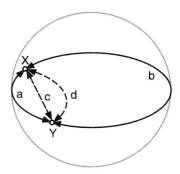

Figure 10.2.9 Shepard's path impletion model of apparent rotation. Rigid rotations between two views of the same object (*X* and *Y*) correspond to paths along the surface of a hypersphere (e.g., solid lines *a* and *b*), whereas nonrigid transformations correspond to paths that leave the surface (e.g., dashed lines *c* and *d*).

Figure 10.2.9 gives an impressionistic representation of these ideas. The two open dots represent two views of the same object located on the surface of the rotational hypersphere (gray circle). The solid lines labeled *a* and *b* are possible paths along the rigid-rotation surface, *a* being the shortest possible rigid rotation and *b* being the longest one. The dashed line *c* represents a nonrigid rotation over a shorter path that does not lie on the surface of the hypersphere. According to Shepard's (1981) theory, the preferred perception is of the rigid rotation along path *a*, provided that there is sufficient time to traverse it. If the rate of alternation is too rapid, however, the shorter, nonrigid motion of path *c* would be perceived.

Other spatial transformations also result in 3-D apparent motion, especially *dilations* (size changes). Using techniques similar to those of Shepard and Judd (1976), Bundesen, Farrell, and Larson (1983) showed that when figures that differ only in size are alternated in an apparent motion display, observers usually experience them as moving forward and backward in depth rather than as getting bigger and smaller. When the minimum time to achieve smooth depth motion was measured, it turned out to increase approximately linearly with distance in the third dimension. Thus, we have yet another generalization of Korte's third law, this time for motion in depth. In general, it seems that as transformational distance increases, the time between frames must increase correspondingly (i.e., the alternation rate must decrease).

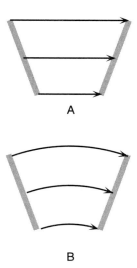

Figure 10.2.10 Curved motion in apparent rotation. When two lines are alternated in apparent motion displays, observers perceive the points on the line to undergo curved trajectories (B) rather than straight trajectories (A).

Curved Apparent Motion. In attempting to explain the examples of apparent motion discussed so far, the analogy to two-point apparent motion over the shortest (i.e., straight-line) path has played an important role. Other transformations have been analyzed as abstractly equivalent, and the shortest-path assumption has generally been made. The question we will now consider is whether apparent motion between two points necessarily follows a straight-line path or whether there are conditions that might induce the perception of curved motion.

We have already considered one phenomenon that implies curved apparent motion: apparent rotation. Consider, for example, an apparent motion display in which two lines at different orientations are alternated (Figure 10.2.10). One possible perception would be a translation along a straight-line path from left to right, with a concomitant clockwise rotation about the center of the line (Figure 10.2.10A). This trajectory would minimize the work required to move the object but would not produce curved trajectories of points. A second possibility would be a global rotation about a point below the two lines in which the points on the line follow curved paths (Figure 10.2.10B). This trajectory minimizes motion in kinematic geometry, as implied by Carlton and Shepard's theory described above. People

Perceiving Motion and Events

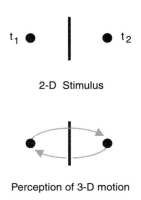

2-D Stimulus

Perception of 3-D motion

Figure 10.2.11 Barrier-induced curved apparent motion. When a barrier is introduced in the path between two points that are undergoing apparent motion, their path curves in depth to avoid the barrier.

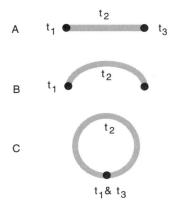

Figure 10.2.12 Path-guided apparent motion. When a gray path is briefly flashed between two points in an apparent motion display, the observer sees a single point moving along the path as long as the alternation rate is slow enough to provide sufficient time for the point to traverse the path.

perceive the second alternative with curved trajectories (Foster, 1975), a finding that demonstrates that curved apparent motion is indeed possible and that what is minimized in apparent motion is not work.

In this case the curved apparent motion was induced by rotation. But can it occur in pure translation? One way is when a "barrier," such as a line segment, is placed between two points that are in apparent motion in the picture plane (see Figure 10.2.11). Rather than perceive the dots as passing "through" the barrier in a straight line, the visual system prefers to see the dot as moving in depth around it (Kolers & Pomerantz, 1971). Here, the curved path is not in the picture plane, but in the third dimension.

Another way to induce a curved path of translation is through **path-guided apparent motion** (Shepard & Zare, 1983). In this phenomenon, a gray path is briefly flashed between the two alternated black dots, as illustrated in Figure 10.2.12A. The result is apparent motion between the two dots that follows the path induced by the gray region. If that path is curved, the dot follows the curved path (Figure 10.2.12B). Given Korte's third law, it is not surprising that the longer the path is, the more time is necessary to perceive smooth continuous motion along the path, even if the two dots are separated by a fixed, straight-line distance. The dots can even be induced to come full circle so that their initial and final positions are the same, provided that sufficient time is available for the visual system to traverse this longer path (Figure 10.2.12C).

Shepard (1984) interpreted the result of these studies on apparent motion as evidence that the visual system has internalized the structure of motions that objects undergo in the real world to a remarkable degree, allowing it to fill in the most likely motion in apparent motion displays. For example, it prefers rigid to nonrigid motion, presumably because it has learned through experience that the most likely motions are in fact rigid (or at least piecewise rigid) ones. By this way of thinking, the organism learns about the motion structure of its environment in much the same way that it learns to infer depth from evidence in 2-D retinal images. This is an example of a Helmholtzian likelihood approach to perceived apparent motion: The organism infers the most likely complete motion event that could have occurred given the two frames that are actually presented in alternation.

There is a competing interpretation of the findings in terms of the Gestalt principle of Prägnanz, however: The percept will be as simple as the prevailing conditions allow. It accounts for the preference for perception of rigid motion because rigid motions are simpler than nonrigid ones in the sense of requiring fewer parameters to describe them. The difficulty in distinguishing between these two hypotheses arises because the world in which we live tends to be informationally simple. Rigid motions, for example, are both frequent and simple. Evidence against the simplicity approach is the fact that apparent motion curves in depth around a barrier rather than just going straight through it. Intuitively, at least, this curved motion seems to be the more likely of the two possibilities rather than the simpler, although it is unclear what additional parameters a collision with the barrier would require.

Evidence against a strict likelihood approach is that some physical constraints on real motion, such as momentum, do not have much effect in apparent motion. For example, if a rectangle is presented first in a vertical orientation and then in a horizontal one, the apparent rotation that results is logically ambiguous: It could rotate either clockwise or counterclockwise about its center to reach the second frame. The interesting fact is that no matter which way it is perceived to rotate initially, it is invariably perceived to rotate back over the same path on presentation of the vertical rectangle again. This is a very unlikely event in the physical world, because the rectangle would be much more likely to continue rotating in the same direction owing to momentum.[3] If the visual system has indeed internalized ecological constraints on motion, it has not modeled all physical aspects of motion, but only the subset that can be perceived directly through vision. Shepard (1984) calls this domain **visual kinematics**.

Conditions for Long-Range Apparent Motion. In discussing physiological and computational models of short-range apparent motion, we considered the nature of so-called *motion detectors*: cells that respond selectively to motion in a particular direction. One important feature of such detectors is that stimulation of appropriate positions on the retina at an appropriate rate of alternation constitutes both necessary and sufficient conditions for them to fire. Is the same true for long-range apparent motion?

Although we do not yet know the physiological mechanisms underlying long-range motion, a classic experiment by Rock and Ebenholtz (1962) has shown that retinal displacement is actually *not* a necessary condition for long-range apparent motion. They had subjects view a standard apparent motion display in which two dots flashed on and off at a relatively slow alternation rate.

When viewed under normal conditions, this display produces a clear (although less than optimal) impression of apparent motion. But instead of asking subjects to keep their eyes still, as in the normal procedure for apparent motion, Rock and Ebenholtz had subjects move their eyes back and forth to the beat of a metronome so that the alternately flashed dots always stimulated the fovea. Thus, no retinal displacement took place when the dots alternated. Even so, all of the subjects who were able to move their eyes in the required fashion spontaneously perceived motion between the two dots.

How is it possible to see apparent motion when there is no retinal displacement? The answer comes from considering the role of eye movements and position constancy in this situation. Recall from Chapter 7 that the perceived position of an object is determined not by retinal position alone, but by integrating it with information about eye position. Therefore, although there was no *retinal* displacement of the dots under the conditions of Rock and Ebenholtz's (1962) experiment, there was still *phenomenal* displacement, because the mechanisms underlying position constancy integrate eye movements with retinal position. This result therefore shows that long-range apparent motion can occur after position constancy.

Rock and Ebenholtz's findings show that retinal displacement is not *necessary* for perception of apparent motion, but is it even *sufficient*? That is, if two different retinal positions are alternately stimulated at the appropriate rate, is apparent motion always perceived? Sigman and Rock (1974) performed an ingenious experiment to answer this question. They reasoned that alternating stimulation of two different retinal locations might produce apparent motion only if the appearance and disappearance of the dots were otherwise inexplicable. They therefore set up stimulus conditions in which there was a better explanation of the dots appearing and disappearing: A rectangle was shown moving continuously back and forth that alternately occluded the two dots as shown in Figure 10.2.13A. When subjects saw the dots alternating alone, they perceived clear apparent motion. But when the moving rectangle was

---

[3]There is a phenomenon known as representational momentum that occurs in visual memory for the positions of recently seen objects; it will be discussed in Section 12.1.5. The lack of momentum effects in apparent motion displays, however, must be counted against the hypothesis that the visual system has indeed internalized such physical constraints.

Perceiving Motion and Events

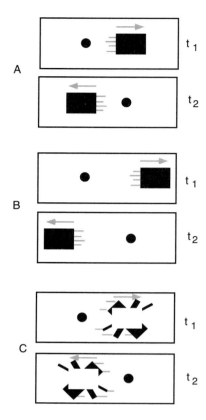

Figure 10.2.13 Apparent motion versus dynamic occlusion as explanations of the appearance/disappearance of objects. If the alternation of two points in an apparent motion display is occluded and disoccluded by a moving object (A), observers perceive that situation rather than apparent motion. If the occluding object moves too far (B), apparent motion is again perceived. Illusory occluding objects (C) also block apparent motion.

added, they saw no motion of the dots. Rather, they reported perceiving two spatially distinct dots being alternately covered and uncovered by the rectangle as it moved back and forth.

It might be objected that the edge of the rectangle moving back and forth over the dot positions was somehow responsible for blocking the apparent motion. Sigman and Rock (1974) countered this by using a display in which the same rectangle was moving back and forth in the same way, except that it moved too far, so that it should have uncovered the dot again as it moved past (see Figure 10.2.13B). Since it did not, the rectangle's motion no longer provided an explanation of the appearance and disappearance of the dots, and subjects reported seeing apparent motion between the dots

again. A further proof that the edge of the occluding rectangle was not responsible for blocking apparent motion was that the same effect was obtained with an illusory rectangle, as shown in Figure 10.2.13C. Here there is no luminance edge covering the alternating dots at all, yet the illusory rectangle succeeded in eliminating the perception of apparent motion.

Whatever mechanisms underlie long-range apparent motion, they must be a good deal more complex than the simple motion-sensitive circuits we discussed in connection with short-range apparent motion. To be consistent with the phenomena we have described here, the mechanisms of long-range apparent motion must be sensitive to seemingly high-level phenomena such as object rigidity, position constancy, and occlusion/disocclusion events. No one has yet devised a general-purpose theory of long-range apparent motion that can account for all these results.

10.2.4 Dynamic Perceptual Organization

Motion is often crucial in determining the organization we perceive in an object or scene. What regions are perceived to be part of the same object or group of objects and how they move with respect to each other can be strongly influenced by subtle factors in their dynamic behavior.

Grouping by Movement. An important dynamic factor in perceptual organization that we mentioned briefly in Chapter 6 was *common fate*: the tendency to group together units that move with the same velocity (direction and speed). A classic example of common fate is a region containing many dots, some of which move in one direction and the rest in another. The two sets of dots spontaneously separate into distinct groups. Flocks of birds, schools of fish, and dancers or swimmers following a choreographer's instructions can provide good examples, but such tightly synchronized movements of separate objects are rare events in the everyday world.

Much more common are cases in which two or more parts of a single moving object are separated in the retinal image by occluding objects so that the visual system must "put them back together." Looking at a moving car through gaps in foliage and a dog running behind a picket fence are good examples. As long as there is differential motion between the occluded object and the occluding one, common fate provides enough information to correctly perceive which regions are part of which objects. This differential motion can occur in several ways: (a) The occluded object could move while the occluder remained stationary, as when a dog walks behind a fence post; (b) both objects could be moving but at different rates, as when a dog walks behind a walking person; or (c) both objects could be stationary but positioned at different depths with respect to a moving observer. (The last case is an example of relative motion parallax as discussed in Chapter 5.) Because the images of rigid, connected objects in the environment tend to move in the same direction and at the same speed, common fate can destroy even the best natural camouflage. The moth or snake that was all but invisible against its color- and texture-matched background becomes clearly perceptible as soon as it moves.

Although common fate was originally discussed by Gestalt psychologists in terms of objects or regions moving in the same direction and at the same speed—that is, uniform rigid translations—these are not the only conditions that will produce the perception of moving unitary objects. In fact, any rigid motion will do. If a subset of dots in a random array begins to rotate rigidly clockwise about the central point in the display and the other half of the dots begin to rotate counterclockwise, they will spontaneously be perceived as belonging to two different groups. The same is true if one subset of dots begins to move radially outward (i.e., as though moving toward the observer in depth) while the other half moves radially inward (i.e., away from the observer in depth). Therefore, common fate may be generalized to include other types of rigid motion.

Configural Motion. Another outgrowth of common fate as an organizational principle in motion perception was discovered by Gunnar Johansson (1950). He was investigating the perceived organization of displays containing two or more moving dots when he realized that the displays sometimes caused different motions to be experienced than the ones he explicitly programmed into them.

A classic example is the L configuration shown in Figure 10.2.14A. The display consists of just two dots, one moving harmonically up and down and the other moving harmonically right and left. When each dot is viewed in isolation, this is precisely how they are per-

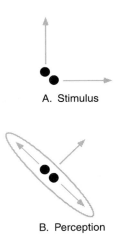

A. Stimulus

B. Perception

Figure 10.2.14 Dynamic organization of Johansson's L configuration. Two dots moving synchronously vertically and horizontally (A) are perceived as a group moving diagonally while they move apart and together within the group along the opposite diagonal (B).

ceived. When they are viewed moving together in synchrony, however, the perception changes in a surprising way. The two dots are experienced as a group moving in unison along a diagonal path while they simultaneously move toward and away from each other along the opposite diagonal, as depicted in Figure 10.2.14B. The **common motion component** of the group is represented by the arrow attached to the gray oval enclosing the group, and the **relative motion component** of the elements within the group by the arrows attached to the individual dots.

Notice that the grouped perception provides an alternative way in which the L stimulus might be created. To see how, imagine that the dots are disks that can only slide along a diagonal slot between them in a square board. Given this constraint, the original L motion could then be produced if the board is simultaneously moved along the perpendicular diagonal in phase with the dot motions. Thus, the two motions depicted in Figures 10.2.14A and 10.2.14B are different descriptions of the same motion event. Both are valid, but they correspond to different causal histories as physical events. In one case, the forces are acting along horizontal and vertical directions and are essentially independent; in the other, they are acting along diagonal directions and are tightly coupled by hierarchical organization.

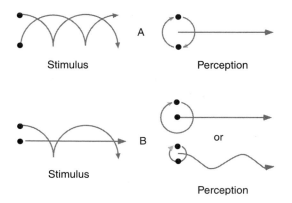

Figure 10.2.15 Dynamic organization of rolling wheel displays. Two dots following cycloidal paths (A) are perceived as positioned at opposite sides of the rim of a smoothly rolling wheel. The same rolling wheel perception can occur if one dot is on the rim and the other at the center (B), but this event can also be seen as a tumbling stick. (See text for details.)

Another example of configural motion is the rolling wheel phenomenon shown in Figure 10.2.15A (Duncker, 1929/1937). Each of the two dots follows a path called a *cycloid*, the two cycloidal paths being exactly opposite each other (i.e., 180° out of phase). When each dot is seen alone, its cycloidal path is clearly perceived, and nothing else. When these two cycloidal paths are seen together in the proper phase relation, however, the resulting perception is of a smoothly rolling wheel with two lights attached to its rim on opposite sides. The same perception of a rolling wheel often results if there is one light at the center and one on the rim (Figure 10.2.15B), although this display can also be perceived as a tumbling stick that bounces along a semicycloidal path as it rotates (Duncker, 1929/1937). Any other placement of the two dots along the rim of the wheel results in the tumbling stick perception (Cutting & Proffitt, 1982).

These phenomena are excellent examples of the Gestalt principle of holism. In each case, the perception of the motion configuration is strikingly different from the perception of the motion of each of its parts seen separately. But that doesn't answer the underlying theoretical question of why people perceive the combined motion not as the simple "sum" (or superposition) of the independent motions, but rather as complex, emergent, configural motions.

Johansson proposed a theory of configural motion perception based on a generalization of the idea of

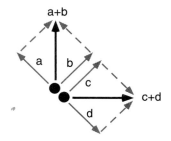

Figure 10.2.16 Vector decomposition of configural motion. The actual motion of both dots (black arrows) can be decomposed into two diagonal components ($a + b$ and $c + d$, as indicated by the gray arrows) so that both share a common motion component (b and c). The noncommon components (a and d) then constitute the relative motion of the system.

common fate. Specifically, he suggested that object motions can be represented as vectors and that these vectors can be decomposed by the visual system into two components:

1. *Common motion.* Common motion is a vector component that is shared by the motion of several different objects. These objects are grouped together by virtue of this common motion component, which is, by definition, the same for all objects in the group.

2. *Relative motion.* The relative motion vectors specify how each object is moving relative to the whole group (and relative to each other). Relative motion is the vector "left over" after the common motion vector has been removed.

To understand how this works, consider the analysis of the L configuration illustrated in Figure 10.2.16. The motion vector of the dot moving upward can be decomposed into the sum of two motion vectors: one diagonally upward and leftward (a), the other diagonally upward and rightward (b). When these two vectors are added head to tail, they combine to form the single upward motion vector of this dot ($a + b$). Similarly, the dot moving rightward can be decomposed into the sum of two diagonal motion vectors: one upward and rightward (c) and the other downward and rightward (d). When these two vectors are added head to tail, they combine to form the rightward vector of this dot ($c + d$). The crucial observation is that under this particular decomposition, both dots contain the same upward and rightward component, labeled b and c in Figure 10.2.16. This constitutes the common motion of the two dots moving as a group. The other two vectors, *a* and *d*, are the relative motions of the two dots with respect to the group. They specify opposite directions, so the dots are perceived to move toward and away from each other within the group. Note that this analysis corresponds to the motion organization that is perceived: two dots moving back and forth diagonally as a group while they move toward and away from each other within the group. Similar analyses into common and relative motion predict the perceptual outcomes of other examples of configural motion as well.

It appears, then, that the visual system somehow performs a vector analysis of the motion of objects moving synchronously. Exactly how is not yet known. Many different vector decompositions of each motion configuration are possible, yet only one is perceived. It is not yet clear how that one perception is determined. One possibility is that the common motion component might be extracted first, with the relative motion vector as the residual (e.g., Johansson, 1950). Another is that relative motion might be detected first, with the common motion vector as the residual (e.g., Cutting & Proffitt, 1982). A third is that they might be codetermined simultaneously.

However it is performed, Johansson's vector analysis of motion configurations into common and relative components is a good example of how hierarchical reference frames can be involved in motion perception. In the cases that we have just discussed, there are three frames of reference: the environment, the whole group of dots, and the individual dots. The stationary environment is the largest frame of reference, and the common motion of the whole group is perceived relative to it. The common motion of the group is the next largest frame of reference, and the motion of each individual dot is perceived relative to it. Further examples of the role of reference frames in motion perception come from the phenomenon of induced motion, which we will consider next.

Induced Motion. Have you ever noticed that when a large cloud passes in front of the moon, it often looks as though the moon is moving through the cloud? This is a good example of **induced motion**: an illusion in which a small stationary object is perceived as moving when it is surrounded by a larger moving object. The phenomenon of induced motion was known to ancient scientists (e.g., Euclid and Ptolemy) but was first studied systemat-

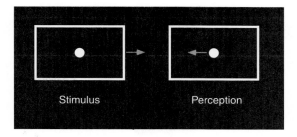

Figure 10.2.17 Induced motion. A stationary dot inside a slowly moving rectangle will be perceived as a moving dot inside a stationary rectangle as long as only these objects can be seen and the rectangle's motion is slow enough.

ically by the Gestalt psychologist Karl Duncker (1929/1937). In a completely dark room, he showed observers a small luminous dot inside a luminous rectangle. When the rectangle was moved slowly back and forth with respect to the stationary dot, they reported seeing the dot move inside a stationary rectangle, as illustrated in Figure 10.2.17. The dot's perceived motion was opposite that of the rectangle's actual motion, so the relative motion of dot and rectangle was the same in the stimulus and the perception.

Why does induced motion occur? The majority of facts fit an account based on the following two assumptions (Rock, 1983):

1. *Sensitivity to relative motion.* The visual system is more sensitive to relative motion between two objects than to absolute motion of a single object alone (Wallach, 1959).

2. *Stationarity of the surrounding object.* When the relative motion between two objects is above threshold and the absolute motion of each object is below threshold, the visual system uses the heuristic of assuming that the larger and/or surrounding object is stationary. It therefore assigns the registered relative motion to the smaller, enclosed object.

This account implies that any conditions that allow the observer to perceive the actual motion of the frame will destroy the illusion of motion in the stationary object because the motion will then be correctly attributed to the moving frame. This is generally true. If the room is not completely dark, for example, so the observer is able to see the frame's motion relative to its environment, induced motion does not occur. Also, if the frame moves fast enough that it is above the threshold for

Perceiving Motion and Events

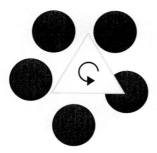

Figure 10.2.18 Kinetic illusory figures. When white wedges move through the five black circles at appropriate times, an illusory white triangle is perceived as rotating in front of the circles and alternately occluding and disoccluding them.

perception of absolute motion, pure induced motion of the stationary object does not generally occur. Sometimes both the frame and the central object are seen moving at the same time (Rock, 1983).

Why is induced motion perceived? The heuristic of attributing motion to the smaller object makes ecological sense because moving objects are generally smaller than their surrounding visual framework. The environment is largely stable and unmoving, so most of the time, assuming it to be stationary is correct and will produce veridical perception. In the unusual cases in which it is wrong, however, the illusion of induced motion results. As we will see later in the chapter, this can occur even when the smaller object is the observer's own body. That is, if the whole visual environment moves around us, we usually perceive ourselves as moving, even if we are actually stationary.

Kinetic Completion and Illusory Figures. Other organizational phenomena also involve motion and time. Kellman and Cohen (1984) have developed examples of dynamic illusory figures that are like classical illusory figures such as the Kanisza triangle (see Figure 6.4.6) but are defined dynamically as they unfold over time. An example of this **kinetic completion** effect is depicted in Figure 10.2.18. Note that any single image is insufficient to produce either illusory contours or an illusory figure: It is just four circles and a Pac Man. But when they are presented as part of a coherent motion sequence, the movement gives rise to the compelling perception of an illusory white triangle rotating in front of black circles on a white ground. It is revealed over

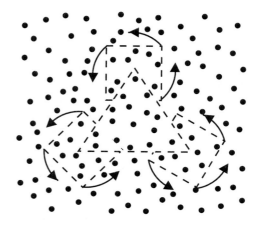

Figure 10.2.19 Illusory figures induced by kinetically specified elements. When the dots inside the dotted notched-square regions rotate as indicated, an illusory triangle is perceived in front of the rotating regions of texture.

time while rotating as its vertices occlude different black circles.

In this example, the elements that induce the illusory figure are defined by luminance edges: the dark circles against the white background and white illusory figure. But the same effect can also be achieved if the inducing elements are defined solely by movement (Kellman & Loukides, 1987). An example is shown in Figure 10.2.19. The three squares behind the illusory triangle are specified solely by the motion of their dots against the stationary dots of the background. Again, the shape of the triangle is revealed over time as its stationary dots occlude the moving dots of the inducing squares.

In Chapter 6 we mentioned Kellman and Shipley's proposal that the perception of illusory contours can be linked theoretically with that of amodal completion. We even discussed the rules for changing one into the other. Given this analysis plus the fact that kinetic illusory figures exist, it should be possible to define kinetic amodal completion: situations in which all but a small part of an object is occluded behind another object, but the shape of the entire object can be perceived over time owing to the motion of the object or of the occluder. An example of kinetic completion is revealed in Figure 10.2.20. A black triangle is shown behind a gray blob that slides back and forth in front of it.

Anorthoscopic Perception. We have just claimed that an object can be perceived over time as different

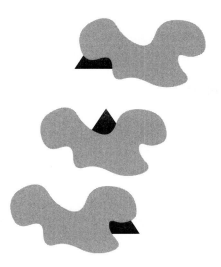

Figure 10.2.20 Kinetic completion behind an occluding object. If parts of a stationary figure are revealed over time by a moving occluder, observers perceive a complete triangle that is never seen in its entirety at any one time.

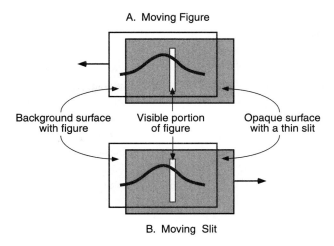

Figure 10.2.21 Anorthoscopic perception. If an object is seen moving behind a stationary slit such that only a small part is revealed at any time, observers perceive it in its entirety. The same is true if the object is stationary and the slit moves across the figure.

parts of it are occluded and disoccluded by another object. An everyday example is that of perceiving a person walking past a door that is open just a crack. You perceive the entire person passing by the door even though only a thin slice is actually present on your retina at any one time.

This phenomenon, called **anorthoscopic perception**, was first studied many years ago by Zöllner (1860) and Helmholtz (1867/1925) and was later rediscovered by Parks (1965). Anorthoscopic perception occurs under both moving figure and moving slit conditions. Moving figure conditions refer to a figure translating back and forth behind a stationary slit through which only a small portion of the figure is visible at any one time, as illustrated in Figure 10.2.21A. Moving slit conditions refer to a stationary figure situated behind a slit that translates back and forth, as illustrated in Figure 10.2.21B. In both cases, the object is revealed piecemeal through the slit, and the visual system must somehow integrate the results into a complete object. Thus, anorthoscopic perception is a special case of what we have just called kinetic amodal completion.

Anorthoscopic perception is a theoretically interesting phenomenon in part because of its implications for shape perception. Classically, shape perception is thought of as resulting from the simultaneous presentation of an object's contours spread out over space. But in anortho-

scopic perception, this is not the case. If the observer fixates on the slit, the object's contours are all presented in the same small region of the retina, but are spread out in time. The visual system appears to be able to extract the contour information and to integrate it over time to form a coherent object from the presented fragments.

What conditions are required for successful anorthoscopic perception? For one thing, the slit has to be wide enough. If it is too narrow, the observer does not perceive a coherent object behind the slit, but perceives just one or more points of light moving up and down in a temporal pattern. It also helps a great deal if the "ends" of the figure are shown and if the figure contains vertices and/or inflection points. These factors are important because perceiving contours behind a slit is an example of the aperture problem. As we discussed previously, the direction in which a straight line is moving behind an aperture is ambiguous unless unique points are visible to disambiguate the motion. Line ends, vertices, and points of inflection are all important in anorthoscopic perception because they are unique points.

How does anorthoscopic perception occur? One possibility is the *retinal painting hypothesis*: the theory that the shape of the completed object is actually "painted" onto the retina over time. If this were true, the only mechanism that would be required for anorthoscopic shape perception would be a visual memory to allow the retinal painting to be integrated over time. However, retinal painting would occur only if the observer were tracking the object behind the slit, and most subjects fixate the slit instead (Fendrich & Mack, 1980). Indeed, anorthoscopic perception occurs even when the slit is stabilized on the same retinal location by artificial means (Morgan, Findlay, & Watt, 1982). The retinal painting hypothesis is no longer a serious contender in accounting for this phenomenon. Rather, some more central form of visual memory must perform an integration over space and time. Just how this is accomplished remains unknown, but it indicates once again how clever the visual system is at figuring out what environmental event is most likely to have generated the optical event registered on the retina.

10.3 Self-Motion and Optic Flow

The optical events we have considered thus far concern the perception of moving objects. In most cases, we have assumed that the eyes and head were at rest during the perceptual event. But as we said at the outset of this chapter, retinal motion is produced every time we change the position of our eyes or head. This motion is global in the sense that it occurs over the entire visual field rather than differentially for selected objects. Figure 10.3.1 shows a very simple example in which the trajectories of a subset of points on visible surfaces have

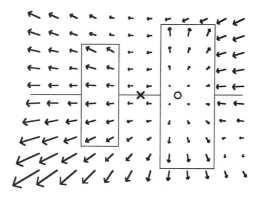

Figure 10.3.1 An example of optic flow. If an observer is moving toward the X while fixating his or her gaze on the O, the illustrated pattern of optic flow will result in an environment consisting of a ground plane, a distant wall, and two rectangular surfaces at different distances. (Courtesy of James Crowell.)

been tracked for a short period of time. As you can see, the visual stimulus is rich and complex.

Such global patterns of retinal motion were called "optic flow" by James J. Gibson and became a cornerstone of his theory of ecological optics (see Section 2.1.3). He rightly pointed out that because most people spend a large portion of their time in locomotion, actively exploring their environment by moving their bodies, heads, and eyes, the visual system must deal with global patterns of optic flow much of the time. Optic flow is thus not a laboratory curiosity, but the dominant proximal stimulus for normal everyday vision. The analysis of optic flow produces not only the perception of the surfaces that make up the visible environment, but also the perception of our own path through that environment. We thus use optic flow to navigate through the world and control our actions within it.

10.3.1 Induced Motion of the Self

In discussing the organization of object motion, we described the phenomenon of *induced motion*: the perception of a stationary object as moving because it is seen within a moving frame that is perceived as stationary. The most parsimonious account of this phenomenon, we concluded, is that the visual system tends to perceive the larger, surrounding object as stationary, provided there is no evidence to the contrary. The smaller enclosed object is then perceived as moving within the frame because the (clearly perceptible) relative motion between it and the frame is assigned to the smaller, enclosed object.

Position and Orientation. There is a very important kind of induced motion that plays a special role in specifying our relation to the environment. It is called **induced self-motion** and refers to an observer's experiencing himself or herself moving through the environment because of the pattern of optic flow on the retina. In most cases, it is veridical in the sense that the flow is caused by ourselves moving about within a stationary environment. In a few cases, it is illusory. You have probably experienced illusory induced self-motion on occasion while sitting in an unmoving train and looking out the window. When the train next to yours begins to pull slowly out of the station, you often vividly experience your own train as moving in the opposite direction instead. This is an example of induced motion

Figure 10.3.2 Induced motion of the self. A stationary person seated inside a drum that is rotating counterclockwise soon experiences himself or herself as rotating clockwise and the drum as stationary.

because your visual system registers the relative motion between your train and the other train but erroneously attributes the motion to your train (and you) rather than the other train. The other train does not literally enclose or surround your train, but if it is the only thing that is visible through the window, the visual system responds as though it is part of the stationary exterior world.

Even more powerful examples of induced motion of the self can be created in the laboratory. For instance, if you were seated inside a large, opaque, cylindrical drum with vertical stripes painted on it, as illustrated in Figure 10.3.2, and if the drum were rotating, you would soon perceive the drum as stationary and yourself as spinning in the opposite direction inside it. This experience of self-rotation is so compelling that many people become dizzy and nauseous, very much as they would if they were actually rotating. In fact, however, they are quite stationary; only the cylinder around them is moving.

This contrived situation makes induced self-motion seem like a sideshow trick. But when you stop to think about it, many everyday situations in which you do experience yourself as moving are similar. Consider driving a car as an example. Your eyes register a highly structured pattern of image motion, which you correctly interpret as indicating that you are moving forward in a stationary world. But how do you know that the world isn't streaming past you while you remain stationary, as in a high-tech video arcade game? When you accelerate in the car, your vestibular system in your inner ear provides information that you speed is increasing. But when you are cruising at a steady speed, this additional

information is not available, and visual information dominates your experience of motion. As in classical induced motion, the visual system assumes that the larger, surrounding world is stationary and that the smaller enclosed object (namely, you) is moving within it. In the driving example, this assumption is correct, so it produces veridical perception of self-motion through the world. In the cylinder example, however, the same assumption is erroneous, so it produces an illusion of self-motion.

Virtually all perception of self-motion within a visual environment can be thought of as visually induced self-motion. In most cases, there is other sensory information supporting the perception of self-motion, such as the vestibular input you get when you accelerate or decelerate and proprioceptive information available when you make yourself move via muscular movements of your legs as you walk or run. Despite these other sources of information about self-motion, visual information is sufficient, as Rock (1968) has shown by eliminating all other factors.

There are several differences between classical induced motion and induced self-motion that should be noted, however. One is that induced self-motion occurs when motion of the environment is well above the threshold of absolute motion. In the rotating drum demonstration, for example, the drum can be moving quite rapidly, and still you perceive yourself as spinning in the opposite direction. Second, there is an initial period of veridical perception: You first perceive the drum as rotating and yourself as stationary. Within a few seconds, however, the experience changes to one of self-rotation inside a stationary drum. One possible explanation is in terms of adaptational effects. Large-scale motion of the whole environment may adapt very quickly, resulting in the perception of a stationary environment, after which the alternative experience of self-rotation dominates. If this were true, however, it is somewhat peculiar that the perception of self-rotation does not also adapt, leading to the reemergence of world rotation. Another possibility is that the initial perception of external rotation arises because of the lack of vestibular input during visual acceleration. Once the drum is rotating at constant speed, the lack of vestibular input is consistent with either external rotation or self-rotation, and so the preferred perception of self-rotation dominates.

Perceiving Motion and Events

Balance and Posture. The importance of visual feedback in locomotion is perhaps self-evident, since we cannot get around very well with our eyes closed. Visual feedback is perhaps less obvious, but still crucial, in maintaining an upright posture and balance with respect to gravity. You can convince yourself of this by trying the following experiment. First balance on one foot for 30 seconds with your hands at your sides and your eyes open. Notice the level of difficulty of this task by monitoring the number and degree of adjustments you make with your foot and ankle. Now close your eyes and try it again. If you are like most people, maintaining balance with your eyes closed will be a great deal more difficult, causing larger and more frequent foot and ankle adjustments, if not outright loss of balance. The visual system is able to detect slight changes in head position and orientation with great speed and accuracy, enabling much tighter control of balance than is possible without visual input.

The importance of visual information in maintaining balance and upright posture was demonstrated most dramatically by Lee and Aronson (1974), who showed that visually induced self-motion can be powerful enough to make a young child fall down. They had children between the ages of 13 months and 16 months stand inside a **swinging room**: a large, bottomless box suspended from the ceiling of a larger room so that the floor was stationary, but the walls and ceiling could be moved forward and backward, as illustrated in Figure 10.3.3. When the experimenters moved the room toward the child, it induced the sensation of forward self-motion, as though the child were falling forward. In response to this purely visual motion information, fully one-third of the children fell backward, and the rest leaned, swayed, or staggered back in an attempt to compensate for the visually induced feeling of falling forward. When the room was moved away from them, they likewise felt themselves falling backward and compensated by falling, staggering, or leaning forward. Adults have the same experience of falling forward or backward within the swinging room and make postural adjustments in response, but they seldom actually lose their balance enough to fall down (Lee & Lishman, 1975).

10.3.2 Perceiving Self-Motion

Gibson (1950) proposed that the pattern of optic flow on the retina provides information about how you are

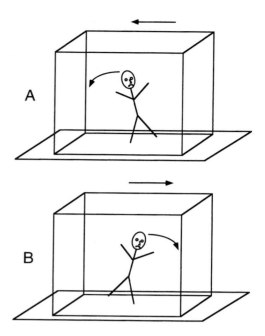

Figure 10.3.3 The swinging room. When a specially designed room moves toward a stationary observer, the observer experiences the sensation of falling forward (toward the approaching room) and compensates by shifting his or her weight backwards, causing the person to lose his or her balance (A). When the room moves away from the observer, the opposite phenomenon occurs (B).

moving within your environment. Two components are required to specify this motion: your direction and your speed. In this section, we will consider how information about the direction of self-motion can be computed from optic flow. In the next section, we will consider speed.

Direction of Self-Motion. Generally speaking, the direction of self-motion is determined by the pattern of optic flow. To take a particularly simple example, if you look directly forward and walk toward a textured wall in front of you, the pattern of optic flow is that of radial expansion outward from the fixation point, as illustrated in Figure 10.3.4A. If you back away from the fixation point instead, the flow field that is created is one of contraction toward the focal point, as illustrated in Figure 10.3.4B. (These same flow fields would be generated by the swinging room moving toward or away from the observer as he or she looked straight ahead.) Flow fields get more complex when the environment contains many different surfaces, but as long as we are moving forward,

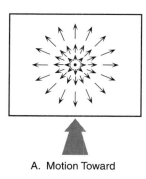

A. Motion Toward

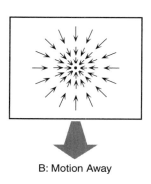

B: Motion Away

Figure 10.3.4 Optic expansion and contraction. If an observer moves closer to a surface (or the surface moves closer to the observer), its texture expands optically. Movement away results in the opposite pattern, optic contraction.

they will have some expansionlike pattern as surfaces get closer.

On the basis of such observations, Gibson (1950) suggested a simple invariant to specify the direction of self-motion: The observer is moving toward the **focus of optical expansion**. This is indeed true if you are fixating on the point toward which you are moving, as you often do. But when you look in a different direction, as you also frequently do, the situation becomes more complicated, because the pattern of optical flow changes every time you make an eye movement (Regan & Beverly, 1982). In the absence of other forms of image motion, an eye rotation in any particular direction causes optic flow in the opposite direction, as illustrated in Figure 10.3.5A. When a pursuit eye movement is made during self-motion—for example, to track a sign as it moves in the visual field while driving—this eye rotation component of motion is added to the flow field caused by the forward translation of the observer (Figure 10.3.5B), resulting in the complex combined optic flow

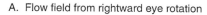

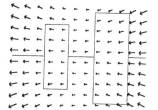

A. Flow field from rightward eye rotation

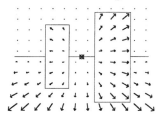

B. Flow field from moving toward X.

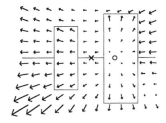

C. Flow field from moving toward X while tracking O.

Figure 10.3.5 Combined flow field from self-motion plus eye rotation. Part A shows the flow field generated by a rightward eye rotation without self-motion, part B shows the flow field generated by self-motion toward the X without eye rotation, and part C shows the flow field generated by self-motion toward the X while the observer makes a rightward eye movement to track the O. (Courtesy of James Crowell.)

depicted in Figure 10.3.5C. Here there is no true focus of expansion—X is the direction of heading and O is the tracked point—yet people are able to correctly perceive their heading (toward X) as being unchanged by the eye movements that produce fixation on O. How is this possible?

There are two different kinds of explanation about how people might be able to perceive their heading accurately in the face of eye movements. The **retinal image theory** assumes that the visual system itself is able to factor out the translational component that the eye movement produces from purely image-based information. Formal analyses have shown that optic flow on the retina contains sufficient information to do so (e.g.,

Perceiving Motion and Events

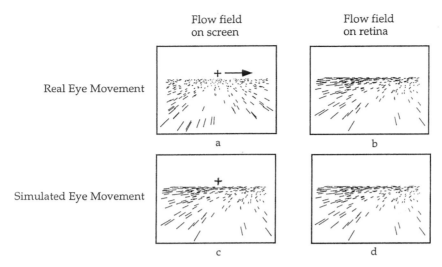

Flow field on screen   Flow field on retina

Real Eye Movement

a   b

Simulated Eye Movement

c   d

Figure 10.3.6 Experimental conditions to test retinal versus extraretinal theories of heading perception based on optic flow. In the real eye movement condition, subjects viewed a flow field while tracking a fixation cross with their eyes (A), resulting in the retinal flow field shown in part B. In the simulated eye movement condition, they fixated a stationary cross while the computer simulated the eye movement as well as the self-motion (C), resulting in the same retinal flow field as in the real eye movement condition (D).

Longuet-Higgins & Prazdny, 1980). The **extraretinal theory** assumes that information about the eye movement itself—either from the efferent copy of the eye command signal or from proprioceptive feedback (see Section 7.4.2)—is taken into account by effectively subtracting its contribution to the flow field (e.g., von Holst, 1954). Both theories thus posit that the translational component due to eye rotation is removed, but one does so by a computation based solely on retinal flow fields, whereas the other uses nonretinal information about the direction and speed of the eye movement.

Two experiments designed to distinguish between these theories have given seemingly contradictory results (Royden, Banks, & Crowell, 1992; Warren & Hannon, 1988). Both tested the theories by comparing how accurately people can determine their heading from computer-generated flow fields in two conditions. In the *real eye movement condition* (see Figure 10.3.6A), subjects viewed a simulation of the flow field that would be generated by moving forward on a textured ground plane. As this flow was displayed, subjects smoothly tracked a target circle in the scene by following it with their eyes. The resulting retinal flow is shown in Figure 10.3.6B. In the *simulated eye movement condition*, subjects viewed a simulation of the flow field that would be generated by

moving forward on the same textured ground plane, but this time, the effects of tracking the circle by eye movements were simulated in the display itself. Subjects viewed this display with their eyes fixated on a stationary circle while a flow field identical to the retinal flow field in the real eye movement condition was presented on the screen (Figure 10.3.6C). The only difference between these two conditions is whether or not the subject actually made an eye movement during the trial.

The retinal image theory predicts no differences between the real and simulated eye movement conditions because the only thing that matters is the retinal flow field, which is identical in both conditions. The extraretinal theory, however, predicts that performance will be highly accurate only in the real eye movement condition because that is the only condition in which the visual system should have all the information it requires to factor out the eye movement. Using slow speeds for the real and simulated eye movements (0.2–1.2° per second), Warren and Hannon (1988) found no difference between the two conditions, a result that supports the retinal image theory. Using faster eye movements (1–5° per second), Royden, Banks, and Crowell (1992) found that subjects were highly accurate only in the real eye movement condition, a result that supports the extraretinal theory. Since people frequently perform pursuit eye movements at speeds up to 5° per second, these results imply that the visual system uses ocular information in determining visual heading from optic flow fields at least some of the time. Further experiments with more complex, natural visual environments (e.g., scenes with trees that occlude each other and have varying sizes and heights in the visual field) and longer durations (about 4 s) show that optical information alone is sufficient to perceive heading accurately even with faster eye movements (Cutting, Vishton, Flückiger, Baumberger, & Gerndt, 1997). Clearly, the processes involved in the perception of heading from optic flow are complex and will require a great deal more study before they are fully understood.

Speed of Self-Motion. Given that the direction of self-motion can be determined visually, the other component that is required to specify one's motion through the environment is speed. Information about absolute speed is not available solely from optic flow because speed is defined as the rate of change in location over time, and this requires information about absolute distance. Absolute distance cannot be determined from purely optical information without additional assumptions because of the fundamental scaling indeterminacy discussed in Chapter 5: The same retinal events could result from environmental events in which all environmental distances were multiplied by a constant factor. Determining absolute speed from optic flow thus requires some scaling information from a nonoptical source, such as eye convergence or familiar size (see Chapter 5).

Although absolute speed cannot be computed solely from optic flow, a slightly different quantity, called time to contact, can be (Lee, 1976, 1980). The **time to contact** is the length of time it will take the observer to reach the surface toward which he or she is heading under present motion conditions. It is invariant over scale transformations because it affects distances and speeds in the same way. For instance, if the wall in front of you were twice as far as it actually is, you would have to be moving twice as fast to keep the optic flow field the same. But this would not change the time required for you to reach the wall because both the distance and the speed are twice as great. If distance scaling information can be determined from some nonoptical source, the time to contact can be used to compute speed simply by dividing it into the absolute distance to the object (because speed = distance/time).

David Lee analyzed optic flow information and claimed that the time to contact can be specified by the **tau function**, which is the ratio of any spatial variable (e.g., the position of a point relative to the focus of expansion) divided by its temporal derivative (e.g., the point's velocity relative to the focus of expansion). This function specifies, for example, that the time to contact will be proportional to the inverse of the rate of optical expansion (Lee & Young, 1985).[4] Qualitatively, this means that the more rapidly the image of the surface is expanding within your visual field, the shorter is the time until you will contact the surface. This makes sense because when you are far from the surface, its rate of optical expansion is very small, and when you are about to hit it, its expansion rate is very large. Although this will be precisely true only if the object or surface is approaching the observer at a constant velocity, Lee (1980) has suggested that tau may be used as an approximation of time to contact even when accelerations are present.

There are numerous examples in which time to contact plays an important role in controlling behavior. One of the most salient cases in modern daily life is stopping cars in time to avoid collision. A good driver will brake at an appropriate rate to stop the car before contact. If the brakes are applied too slowly or too late, the consequences can be dire indeed. If you are following another car at a safe distance and its image on your retina is constant in size, then you are getting neither closer nor farther, and you need make no adjustments to your speed. If its image begins to expand significantly, however, you are getting closer, and you must apply a braking force to maintain a safe distance. How great this force should be can be controlled from visual feedback by keeping the rate of change for the time to contact parameter within an acceptable range (Lee, 1976). As

---

[4]There is considerable controversy over the adequacy of the tau function in accounting for an organism's ability to anticipate contact with an object moving toward it. Despite many studies that appear to support Lee's theory, Tresilian (1991) and Wann (1996) have criticized it for its inability to account for all the available evidence.

Perceiving Motion and Events

long as you manage to do so, you will avoid colliding with the car in front of you. It is not clear, however, that people actually follow this strategy in their braking behavior (Kaiser & Phatak, 1993).

Virtual Reality and Ecological Perception. One of Gibson's greatest and most enduring contributions to vision science was his realization that a wealth of environmental information in the optic flow fields is available to a perceiver actively exploring its environment. It specifies not only the layout of surfaces in the environment, but also the viewpoint trajectory of the observer through that environment. Indeed, there is so much information that Gibson (1979) believed that it specified the layout of surfaces in the 3-D environment with sufficient precision to explain our perceptions. This led to his claim of *direct perception*: The observer's visual system does not need to add any extra information to arrive at an accurate perception of the world. All that is necessary is for the observer's visual system to resonate to the information contained within the optic flow fields. As we mentioned in Chapter 2, this is one of the most controversial claims in all of perceptual theory (see Ullman, 1980, and the many commentaries that follow it).

Whether or not Gibson was correct depends on whether one takes a logical or an ecological point of view. Logically, Gibson was wrong. Even two laterally displaced 2-D flow fields cannot uniquely specify a viewpoint trajectory through a 3-D environment without some kind of additional information or assumptions. This is simply a mathematical truism due to the loss of information in projecting from three spatial dimensions to two. If Gibson were correct, perception of a mobile, exploring observer would always be at least approximately veridical. Until recently, this claim was essentially untestable because the technology was not yet available for simulating an optical environment that could deal with a moving observer. But the recent development of so-called **virtual reality (VR) displays** has demonstrated the inaccuracy of Gibson's claim of direct perception (in its strongest form) by producing illusory perceptions of self-motion within a simulated 3-D environment. The best virtual reality displays consist of two small, flat, helmet-mounted video screens, yet the viewer perceives a 3-D environment consisting of 3-D objects that do not physically exist. The reason is

that the two flat screens display the same visual information that would have been produced had the observer actually moved in this simulated environment as he or she actually did move in the real environment. Such illusions amount to an existence proof of the inadequacy of visual information to correctly specify the nature of the true stimulus, because the virtual reality display causes us to experience self-motion through a 3-D environment that is quite different from the two miniature video screens before the observer's eyes that are actually causing the perceptions.

At the same time, however, VR displays also amount to an existence proof of the adequacy of visual information to specify a 3-D environment given the implicit assumptions the visual system makes in interpreting optical events. Viewers of VR displays perceive a 3-D environment of objects with startling realism, none of which exists except in the structure of the optical events generated on the flat video screens.

Ecologically, however, Gibson was correct about direct perception. Under natural viewing conditions in natural surroundings, people perceive their path through an optically rich 3-D environment with truly impressive accuracy. How can this be, if the optical information is logically insufficient to specify it? It can happen only if the assumptions that are logically required to recover the structure of the environment are actually true under "natural viewing conditions" in "natural surroundings." This is precisely the role of heuristic assumptions in inferential theories: to constrain perceptions in ways that conform to facts about natural viewing of natural surroundings. They yield correct solutions when true (i.e., perception is veridical under normal viewing conditions) and incorrect ones when false (i.e., perception can be illusory under various unusual/nonecological conditions, such as are found in laboratory experiments and VR displays). From an ecological perspective, this is not surprising, for vision evolved in organisms that were viewing natural surroundings under natural conditions, not in organisms that were viewing virtual reality displays connected to high-powered graphic workstations. It therefore makes perfect sense that the mechanisms of visual perception would evolve to work under the conditions in which they normally operate.

Thus, we can discern an important relation between two theories that were long held to be incommensurate: Helmholtz's theory of unconscious inference and

Gibson's theory of ecological optics. Helmholtz concentrated on a logical approach and emphasized the inadequacy of optical information to deal with all possible stimulus conditions, including VR displays. Because more information is required to specify the external world than is available in retinal events—even in a moving observer under unrestricted conditions—Helmholtz and his followers appeal to heuristic assumptions to fill the logical gap.

In contrast, Gibson concentrated on an ecological approach, emphasizing the adequacy of optical information to deal with normal viewing conditions. In these conditions, the heuristic assumptions that inference theorists discuss are almost universally true, and because of this, perception will almost always be veridical, just as Gibson claimed. Therefore, we see that the role played by heuristic assumptions in inferential theories is very closely related to the role played by boundary conditions of natural observation in ecological theories. Both theories are therefore able to explain why perception is veridical under natural viewing conditions, but they do so in radically different ways.

10.4 Understanding Events

Even after moving images have been organized into coherent objects and their motions have been interpreted within appropriate reference frames including movements of the observer through the environment, further processing is required to understand the event that gave rise to the pattern of retinal motion. Some of this processing is directed toward classifying the object as a member of some known category. This task is usually accomplished by processing static shape, as discussed in Chapter 9, but motion can bring additional constraints to bear.

Other research has addressed the question of how different physical events we perceive are related to one another. The ground-breaking studies of Belgian psychologist Albert Michotte (1946/1963) opened this area of inquiry by examining the conditions under which people perceive one event as causing another. Since then, there have been many further inquiries into how people understand the relations among events and the principles of physics that underlie them: how balls move when one collides with another, how objects be-

have under gravitational free-fall when dropped from a moving object, and so forth. Although early studies suggested that people know very little about such events (e.g., McCloskey, 1983; McCloskey, Caramazza, & Green, 1980), more sophisticated methods have revealed both strengths and weaknesses in people's understanding of physical events (e.g., Gilden & Proffitt, 1989; Proffitt & Gilden, 1989).

10.4.1 Biological Motion

The study of how moving organisms are perceived purely from motion information was pioneered by the Swedish psychologist Gunnar Johansson (1973, 1975). Recall that Johansson had previously discovered that when viewing simple two-point configurations (see Section 10.2.2) people have a strong propensity to interpret the moving points as though they were attached to a rigid rod moving in depth. This phenomenon led him to predict that people would be able to perceive the movement of a human body from just the motions of the joints. To test this hypothesis, he filmed an actor in the dark with small lights attached to his joints (ankles, knees, hips, shoulders, elbows, and wrists) so that nothing was visible except the lights (see Figure 10.4.1)

When the actor was seated motionless in a chair, observers perceived a meaningless configuration of points, rather like a constellation of stars. Nobody perceived the lights to be connected to a person. But within fractions of a second after the actor began to move, first standing up and then walking, he was immediately and unmistakably perceived as a person in motion. Different activities, such as walking versus jogging, were easily discriminated from one another, and two people dancing a lively folk dance, arm in arm, were effortlessly perceived as such. Unfortunately, it is not possible to demonstrate these striking phenomena in the static pictures of a book, but a trace of the lights over time is shown in Figure 10.4.1 for a walking person. The pattern is very complex, but in this static form it conveys none of the vivid meaningfulness perceived so spontaneously in Johansson's movies.

Later work on this topic has extended it in several directions. First, careful experimental work has shown that people are exquisitely sensitive to subtle differences in human gaits. For example, Johansson (1975) reported that observers had no difficulty discriminating between

Perceiving Motion and Events

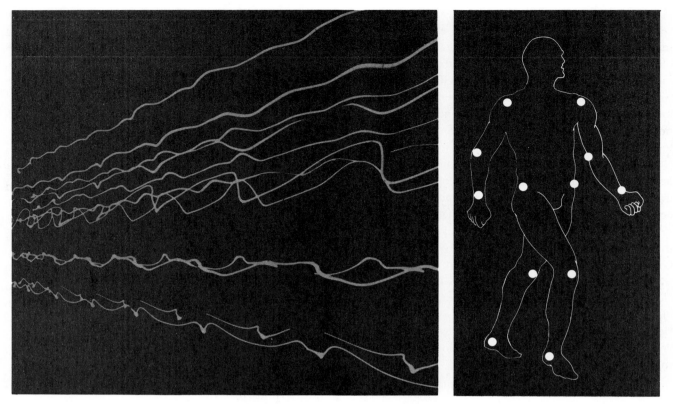

Figure 10.4.1 Biological motion. If lights are attached to the joints of a walking person (as shown at right) and recorded via time lapse photography (as shown at left), observers see nothing but meaningless wiggly lines. But if the same event is presented unfolding over time, observers vividly and spontaneously perceive a person walking. (From Johansson, 1975.)

an actor walking normally and the same actor walking with a simulated limp. Other researchers have found that observers are able to discriminate between male and female walkers who had lights placed just on their ankles, knees, and hips (Cutting, Proffitt, & Kozlowski, 1978). The probable bases of this gender discrimination are the slight changes in gait that result from the fact that women's hips are, on average, wider than men's and that men's shoulders are, on average, wider than women's (see Figure 10.4.2). As a result, the center of movement for male walkers is lower than that of female walkers, and this difference appears to be detected (Cutting, 1978). Observers can even identify specific individuals by their gaits when presented as the motion configuration of their joints. Curiously, subjects were better at identifying their own pattern of gait motion than that of others, even though people rarely see themselves walk (Beardsworth & Buckner, 1981).

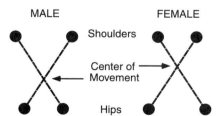

Figure 10.4.2 The relative location of the center of movements for walking male and female bodies. Such differences appear to be detected by observers while viewing lights on just the ankles, knees, and hips of walkers.

Another line of research has generalized people's ability to perceive the structure of an object in motion beyond Johansson's prototypical example of human gait perception. Cutting (1982) showed that people can perceive the structure of (simulated) trees and bushes as they are transformed by the force of a (simulated) wind. This is what one would expect from Johansson's (1950) initial experiments on the perception of rigid motion in depth from moving two-point configurations. It may not be the human body that is special, but rather the perception of the structure of a piecewise rigid object moving at flexible joints.

10.4.2 Perceiving Causation

Understanding motion events goes far beyond perceiving the physical structure of moving objects. As Gestalt psychologists emphasized, we do not see simple juxtapositions of elementary events; rather we see perceptually organized structures with important interrelations. One particularly important component of motion events is their causal structure: how the motion of one object appears to affect another when it strikes or otherwise interacts with it. A classic example is one billiard ball colliding with another. The first ball changes its trajectory abruptly on impact, and the second ball begins moving at the same time.

For many years, the dominant view of causality was the one advocated by British philosopher David Hume, who stated that causality must be inferred from accumulated experience with similar events rather than being directly perceived. Here is an example of his thinking:

It appears that, in single instances of the operation of bodies, we never can, by our utmost scrutiny, discover anything but one event following another. . . . All events seem entirely loose and separate. One event follows another, but we can never observe any tie between them. They seem conjoined, but never connected. (Hume, 1777/1966, pp. 79–80)

Michotte (1946/1963) opposed Hume's position, claiming instead that certain types of event sequences were directly and spontaneously perceived as causally connected. Moreover, he argued that such direct perception of causality could occur in a single event without the mediation of specific prior experiences.

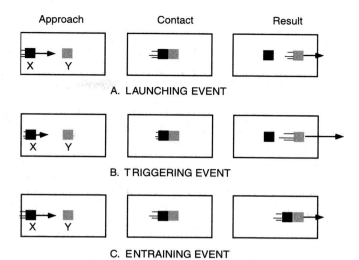

Figure 10.4.3 Perceiving causation. When a moving object strikes a second object and the second object moves in the same direction, observers spontaneously perceive that the motion of the first object caused the motion of the second. Subtle differences in the configuration of motion result in the perception of launching (A), triggering (B), or entraining (C) events.

Launching, Triggering, and Entraining Events. Michotte studied the perception of causality using variations on simple canonical events very much like billiard ball collisions. As indicated in Figure 10.4.3A, one square (X) would appear moving from left to right until its right edge touched the left edge of a stationary square (Y) in the center of the display, at which time square X stopped and square Y moved off to the right. When observers were shown such motion sequences, they were questioned about their perceptions. The vast majority spontaneously reported that the motion of X *caused* the subsequent motion of Y.

Michotte called this form of perceived causality the **launching effect**. He found that a number of stimulus conditions must hold for it to occur:

1. *Timing.* The motion of Y must begin within a fraction of a second after contact with X, not exceeding 200 ms.

2. *Direction.* The direction in which Y moves off must be approximately the same as the direction of X.

3. *Speed.* The speed at which Y moves must be slower or approximately the same as that of X.

If any of these conditions is not met, the perception of launching fails to arise. If Y moves off at right angles to

X's motion, for example, or if Y takes off at twice the speed of X, launching is not perceived. But Michotte described several other forms of perceived causality that are identified with other values of these three variables. What Michotte called the **triggering effect**, for example, occurs when the speed of Y exceeds that of X substantially, as though X's contact with Y caused some additional force to act upon Y to make it move so quickly (see Figure 10.4.3B). In the **entraining effect**, X does not stop moving upon contact with Y, but continues moving along with Y (see Figure 10.4.3C). Michotte claimed that all these forms of event perception contained causal relations between the motions of X and Y.

The phenomenological claim that Michotte was making is difficult to deny: We clearly see causality in the actions of objects upon one another under certain conditions. Whether this perceived causality is truly direct and unmediated by experience is a difficult matter to decide, however. Surely all adults have seen many events similar to the canonical events Michotte presented to his subjects, so experience effects cannot easily be ruled out. Still, it is difficult to understand how an infant or young child could actually learn causal relations among events without having some a priori notion of causality to begin with, as the philosopher Emanuel Kant (1781/1929) argued persuasively.

Perceiving Mass Relations. Runeson (1977) extended Michotte's investigations into the perception of collisions by examining the extent to which observers are sensitive to dynamic variables of colliding objects. One property that can often be perceived in a collision, for example, is the relative masses of the two objects. If one ball rolls into another and ricochets backward, as depicted in Figure 10.4.4A, it appears to be substantially lighter than the ball that it hits. If it hits the second ball and keeps rolling forward, as depicted in Figure 10.4.4B, it appears to be substantially heavier. Although this might not initially seem surprising, it is once you realize that the mass of an object is not a visible property. We cannot literally see whether one object is heavier than another when they are stationary, except possibly by categorizing them and retrieving information about the characteristic weight of such objects. When they collide, however, more information becomes available through the dynamics of their interaction.

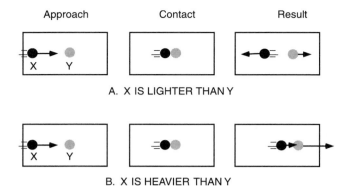

Figure 10.4.4 Perceiving mass relations. If the initially moving object ricochets backward after striking the second, the second object is perceived as being much heavier. If the first object keeps moving forward, it is perceived as being heavier.

Runeson (1977) showed how visually perceiving the relative mass of colliding objects is possible on the basis of an analysis of the underlying physics. Without going into the mathematical details, we can state the conclusion of his analysis: The ratio of masses of the two objects is equal to the ratio of differences between their initial and final velocities. Because velocities are visually specified, differences in velocities can be computed and their ratios taken. Thus, Runeson showed that the gap between visible properties of the colliding objects and the seemingly nonvisible property of their relative masses can be bridged, at least in theory. But is the visual system actually sensitive to this specific relation between mass and velocity so that the heavier object actually looks heavier?

This question has been studied by having subjects view collisions of various types and then make judgments of which object is heavier and (sometimes) how much heavier it is. Initial results were encouraging, showing that subjects were indeed correct in making judgments of relative mass from purely visual information (e.g., Kaiser & Proffitt, 1984, 1987; Todd & Warren, 1982).

However, investigation of a wider range of collision types revealed that subjects were actually not making full use of the mass ratio information specified in the equations that describe the physical interaction (Gilden & Proffitt, 1989). Rather, they appeared to make their judgments on the basis of two simpler heuristics:

1. **Ricochet heuristic.** When the incoming ball ricochets (moves backward) at a higher velocity than the forward motion of the initially stationary ball (Figure 10.4.4A), the stationary ball is heavier than the incoming one.

2. **Clobbering heuristic.** When the stationary ball moves off with high velocity ("gets clobbered") (Figure 10.4.4B), the incoming ball is heavier than the stationary one.

The informative data came from studying situations in which the two heuristics conflicted, that is, when the ricocheting ball moved more slowly than the ball it struck. Everyone thought that *one* ball was much heavier, but they didn't agree about which one. This is inconsistent with relative mass being correctly perceived. Therefore, people appear to be recovering information about mass from visual information, as Runeson (1977) proposed, but not with the quantitative precision and sophistication his analysis implied. Further studies have indicated that heuristics are involved in perception of most dynamical situations, not just colliding balls (Gilden, 1991; Pittenger, 1991).

10.4.3 Intuitive Physics

This early research by Michotte and Runeson on perception of collisions opened the general question of how people perceive the nature of simple physical events involving moving objects. In the 1980s, psychologist Michael McCloskey (1983) and his colleagues reported some surprising findings about what came to be called **intuitive physics** (or **naive physics**): the nature of people's untutored beliefs about seemingly simple physical events such as the trajectory of moving objects. They investigated college students' intuitions by asking them to predict the outcome of different physical situations from static pictures and accompanying verbal descriptions (e.g., McCloskey, Caramazza, & Green, 1980).

One classic problem is illustrated in Figure 10.4.5 It shows a ball rolling through a C-shaped tube lying flat on a tabletop. Subjects were asked to draw the trajectory the ball would follow after it exited the end of the tube. The correct answer is that it would move in a straight line, as indicated by the solid line, because once the ball leaves the tube, there is no force acting on it in the plane of the table. Surprisingly, about one-third of the college students they studied—including some who had taken

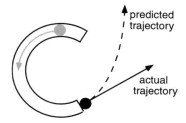

Figure 10.4.5 The C-tube problem. A ball rolling through a C-shaped tube will exit along a straight trajectory (solid line), but people often predict that its path will continue to curve (dashed line).

formal coursework in physics—indicated that the ball would continue to follow a curved trajectory, as indicated by the dashed line.

A similar result was obtained for the pendulum problem shown in Figure 10.4.6 (Caramazza, McCloskey, & Green, 1981). Subjects were asked to predict what would happen if the string of the pendulum were cut when the bob was exactly at its highest point (apex). The correct answer is that the bob would fall straight down. Because the bob is actually motionless at this point in its trajectory, there is no force acting on it except gravity once the string has been severed. Again, nearly one-third of college students indicated that the bob would continue to move laterally in some fashion as it fell, as illustrated by the dashed curve in Figure 10.4.6.

Recognizing versus Generating Answers. These results seem to indicate a rather surprising degree of ignorance of basic physical events. How are we to under-

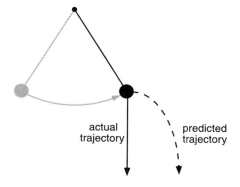

Figure 10.4.6 The pendulum problem. If the string of a pendulum is cut at its highest point, the weight will fall straight down (solid line), but people often predict that it will follow a curved path (dashed line).

stand this failing, especially in light of the visual system's demonstrated sensitivity to certain aspects of causality and dynamics in research on collisions? One possibility is that the high-level cognitive system that is responsible for generating solutions to statically stated problems simply does not have access to the perceptual system's expertise in these domains. If this were the case, people should be much more accurate at picking out the correct answer from among a set of dynamic simulations of the event than at imagining what would happen given just the static display.

Kaiser, Proffitt, and Anderson (1985) tested this hypothesis for the C-tube problem. They showed their subjects both a static version of the problem, consisting of several static drawings of possible paths for the ball, and a dynamic version, consisting of a series of computer-generated animations showing the same possible events unfolding in real time. They found that many of the same people who favored the curved trajectory when presented with the static version of the C-tube problem chose the correct, straight trajectory in the dynamic version. (Interestingly, men performed better than women on the static version of the problem, but there were no gender-related differences in the dynamic version.) Essentially the same results were found for the pendulum problem: Dynamic animation displays produced substantially better performance than static displays (Kaiser, Proffitt, Whelan, & Hecht, 1992). These findings support the view that the visual system is reasonably good at discriminating between physically natural and unnatural versions of dynamic events as they unfold over time but relatively poor at doing so when the problem is presented statically.

Similar experiments investigating other physical situations contradict this conclusion, however. In one study, for example, subjects saw computer animations of satellites rotating in space as they extended or contracted their solar panels, as illustrated in Figure 10.4.7 (Proffitt, Kaiser, & Whelan, 1990). A principle of physics known as *conservation of angular momentum* requires that as the panels are extended, the rate of rotation must decrease, and as they are contracted, the rate of rotation must increase. The same principle is at work when an ice skater spins, slowly with arms outstretched and rapidly with arms pulled in. Some of the animations showed the physically correct change in rotation rate, and others showed incorrect changes. In striking con-

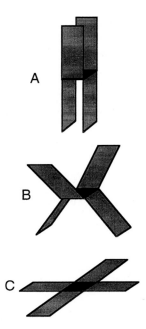

Figure 10.4.7 The satellite problem. A spinning satellite will spin fastest with its solar panels closed (A), slower with them partly open (B), and slowest with them fully open (C). Few human observers are sensitive to this fact, however.

trast to the results with the C-tube and pendulum problems, subjects showed almost no appreciation of which events were physically correct, even when viewing real-time animations. The only alternatives people clearly recognized as incorrect were animations in which extending or contracting the panels caused the satellites to stop spinning completely or to stop spinning and then start to spin in the opposite direction.

A similar failure to find benefits from viewing dynamic simulations was found for the effects of different distributions of mass as a wheel rolls down a ramp (Proffitt et al., 1990). Analogously to the case of a rotating satellite or ice skater, the more mass is concentrated toward the outside of the wheel, the more slowly the wheel will roll. However, college students showed virtually no evidence of sensitivity to this variable, even when shown animations of "races" between two different wheels (see Figure 10.4.8). In the one case in which their responses were significantly affected by mass distribution, they systematically favored the incorrect alternative. Even more striking is the fact that physics professors at the University of Virginia were not much better at this task than naive undergraduates, as long as they were

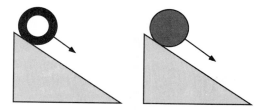

Figure 10.4.8 The wheel race problem. The wheel with its mass concentrated toward the outside rim (A) rolls more slowly than one with the same mass evenly distributed (B), but most people are insensitive to this fact. The two wheels are identical in both radius and total mass, the hollow wheel being made of denser material (e.g., aluminum) than the solid wheel (e.g., wood).

not allowed to solve the problems analytically. The perceptual intuitions tapped by viewing the simulations thus seem to be quite distinct from the high-level cognitive abilities shaped by formal training in physics.

Particle versus Extended Body Motion. It appears that the visual system has the ability to make discriminations about the naturalness of some kinds of dynamic events but not others. The obvious question, then, is what distinguishes the cases in which it succeeds from those in which it fails? Proffitt and Gilden (1989) have suggested that it arises from differences in the perception of two kinds of physical motions:

1. **Particle motion** is the change in position of an object that depends only on the location of its center of mass. The reason for calling it "particle motion" is not that the object in question has to be particlelike, but that it would behave in the same way if all its mass were concentrated (particlelike) at its center. No other variables are dynamically relevant to particle motion problems.

2. **Extended body motion** is the change in position of an object that depends on additional variables, such as its spatial distribution of mass, size, and orientation. These variables define an object as an extended body in space and are therefore incompatible with the object's behavior being the same as that of a particle. Examples include rolling wheels, the precession of tops and gyroscopes, the orientation of balances, liquid displacements, and object collisions.

Note that the same object can undergo either particle motion or extended body motion, depending on the physical situation in which it is considered. For example, consider a wheel in the two situations depicted in Figure

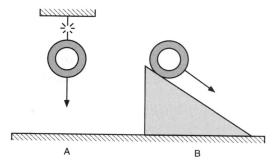

Figure 10.4.9 Particle motion versus extended body motion in different contexts. The same object undergoes particle motion in free fall (A) but extended body motion when it rolls down an inclined plane (B).

10.4.9. A wheel undergoing simple gravitational free fall (part A) is a case of particle motion because the only thing that matters is the position of its center of mass: It falls straight downward just like a particle of equivalent mass would. However, the same wheel rolling down an inclined plane (part B) is a case of extended body motion because the radial distribution of its mass influences how quickly it rolls, as noted above.

The C-tube and pendulum problems described previously are examples of particle motion. According to Proffitt and Gilden's hypothesis, that is why viewing simulations of them evokes more accurate judgments of naturalness. These problems are complicated, however, by the fact that just before the moment in question, they were undergoing extended body motion. That is, while the ball is rolling through the tube and while the pendulum bob is attached to the string, the forces that act on them via the tube and the string, respectively, give them dynamic qualities of extended body motion. But once the ball leaves the tube and once the pendulum string is cut, they behave just as particles having the same position, mass, and velocity would behave. Not so for the spinning satellites and rolling wheels, however, because the equations describing their rotational motions involve parameters concerning mass distribution. The problem is not that the visual system is insensitive to the spatial distribution of mass in these objects, for people can draw or recognize the shapes of the wheels and satellites quite accurately. Rather, the visual system apparently fails to appreciate the relevance of mass distribution for dynamic behavior in situations in which it actually does matter. Why this should be so is a fascinating, but as yet unanswered, question.

517

Perceiving Motion and Events

Suggestions for Further Reading

Anstis, S. (1986). Motion perception in the frontal plane: Sensory aspects. In K. R. Boff, L. Kaufman, & J. P. Thomas (Eds.), *Handbook of perception and human performance: Vol. 1: Sensory processes and perception*. New York: Wiley. This chapter provides an excellent review of image-based motion processing from a psychophysical perspective.

Cutting, J. E. (1986). *Perception with an eye for motion*. Cambridge, MA: MIT Press. Cutting presents and expands Gibson's ecological framework for perceiving motion in depth based on optic flow information in an engaging and well written monograph.

Mack, A. (1986). Perceptual aspects of motion in the frontal plane. In K. R. Boff, L. Kaufman, & J. P. Thomas (Eds.), *Handbook of perception and human performance: Vol. 1: Sensory processes and perception*. New York: Wiley. This chapter reviews higher-level aspects of motion processing from a perceptual perspective.

Proffitt, D. R., & Kaiser, M. K. (1995). Perceiving events. In W. Epstein & S. Rogers (Eds.), *Perception of space and motion*. New York: Academic Press, pp. 227–261. This chapter covers the literature on event perception in a comprehensive and insightful way.

Ullman, S. (1979). *The interpretation of visual motion*. Cambridge, MA: MIT Press. This ground-breaking book presents a computational approach to the correspondence problem of apparent motion and Ullman's important structure-from-motion theorem.

Warren, W. H. (1995). Self-motion: Visual perception and visual control. In W. Epstein & S. Rogers (Eds.), *Perception of space and motion*. New York: Academic Press, pp. 263–325. This chapter provides an up-to-date review of research on how people perceive their own motion through the environment from optic flow information.

Visual Selection: Eye Movements and Attention

Visual perception is inherently selective. When we look around our environment to understand where we are and what opportunities it affords us, we necessarily focus our visual resources more fully on some objects than on others. The result is that the visual system appears to get more or better information about the selected objects and perhaps more vivid visual experiences of them as well. Which objects we choose to focus on and the order in which we do so are determined largely by their relevance to the activities and task in which we are currently engaged. Even so, the choice of what to select next is usually made quite automatically at a nonconscious level. While driving your car toward an intersection, for example, you are more likely to focus on the stoplight at the corner than the mailbox just below it. This makes sense because stoplights are more important in driving toward intersections than are mailboxes. If you were walking around trying to mail a letter, however, the reverse would be true, and you would be correspondingly more likely to focus on the mailbox. You do not have to "tell yourself" to focus on the stoplight or the mailbox, you just do it. And you engage in such selective visual processes every waking moment of your life.

Acts of visual selection can be either *overt* (external and observable by others) or *covert* (internal and unobservable by others). Overtly, we move our eyes frequently—sometimes as often as several times per second—directing them back and forth over the visual world to pick up useful information about whatever parts of the environment are most relevant and/or interesting. Each fixation produces a different visual image on the retina and a different portion of it falls on the fovea. Although the world does not appear to jump about when we move our eyes, different aspects of the environment enter our awareness as we fixate on different objects. Covertly, we can also shift our attention from one object to another, more or less as we do with our eyes. But with attention, we can also select first one property of an attended object and then another, even when our eyes are quite still. In this chapter we will examine what is known about both overt and covert forms of visual selection and how they affect our perceptions.

11.1 Eye Movements

One of the most important facts about selection in vision is that we can see what is in front of us and not what is behind. (This is not true of hearing, for example, which is nearly omnidirectional.) The directionality of our visual sense is a form of selection because the human eye does not register all the information in the ambient optic array that is available at a given stationpoint. Rather, the visual field maps a large portion of the region in front of the observer, subtending approximately 130° vertically and 180° horizontally. Human perceivers therefore have control over what is selected visually by directing their eyes toward objects and situations of interest and relevance to them.

The major functions of eye movements are twofold:

1. *Fixation:* to position target objects of interest on the fovea where visual acuity is highest.

2. *Tracking:* to keep fixated objects on the fovea despite movements of the object or the observer's head.

Positioning an object on the fovea and keeping it there can also be accomplished by turning the body or the head. Moving the eyes within the head is more efficient, however, because it not only is faster and more precise, but also requires a great deal less muscular effort.

The mobility of the eye allows the visual system to explore the environment by selectively sampling information in different directions. This fact is important for a number of reasons, the foremost of which is that spatial acuity is highest in the central degree or two of the retina (the *fovea*) and then falls off rapidly toward the periphery. As we discussed in Chapter 1, the receptors in the fovea, consisting exclusively of color-sensitive cones, are much more densely packed than those in the periphery. As a result, spatial and chromatic resolution are much higher in the small central fovea than elsewhere. If detailed information is needed from many different areas of the visual environment, it can only be obtained by redirecting the eye so that the relevant objects fall sequentially on the fovea.

Until now we have implicitly been assuming that all the information we obtain from a given visual scene is processed simultaneously. This is obviously untrue. Even though a large amount of visual processing occurs in parallel over the expanse of the retinal image, normal visual perception of almost any object or scene is a temporally extended event, as our gaze shifts repeatedly from one object to another. After processing an object as a whole, we may then focus sequentially on various of its parts to examine them more closely. Because these eye movements and fixations take time and result in significantly different retinal images, the visual system must somehow integrate this spatio-temporal patchwork of partially overlapping images to construct a unified, coherent representation of the 3-D scene. In this section we will examine what is known about how this happens.

11.1.1 Types of Eye Movements

Physiological Nystagmus. The eyes can be moved because the back of them is approximately spherical and is situated in an approximately spherical socket. They can be rotated rapidly within the sockets by the action of six strong, precisely controlled *extraocular muscles*. Although you are not aware of it, your eyes are constantly making tiny involuntary movements, called **physiological nystagmus**, that are caused by tremors in these extraocular muscles. They cause the optical image to move slightly with respect to the retina all the time. You cannot detect this motion under normal conditions even if you try, but you can under special circumstances. For example, stare at the black dot in the middle of Figure 11.1.1 for about 30 s, and then fixate on the white dot. You will perceive a negative afterimage of the grid—caused by adaptation from the extended exposure—that will wander around slightly, no matter how hard you try to hold your eyes still. This motion is caused by eye tremor. You perceive movement because the grid's afterimage is precisely fixed in position on your retina, and the eye tremor therefore moves your retina relative to the fixated grid. This causes the afterimage of the grid to appear to move.[1]

Psychologists have developed techniques that eliminate these tiny eye movements to find out whether they play any important role in vision. The answer is both dramatic and surprising. If a patterned stimulus is presented to the eyes without any retinal motion whatsoever for more than a few seconds, the pattern completely disappears! Such retinally fixed stimuli are called **stabilized images**. They can be produced by either optical or electronic devices. The original method, developed by Pritchard (1961), involves having subjects wear an astonishing contact lens (see Figure 11.1.2). The lens is

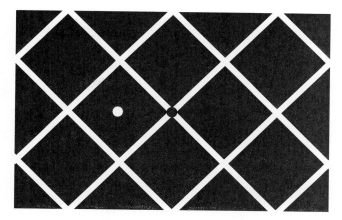

Figure 11.1.1 Demonstration of physiological nystagmus. Stare at the black dot for 30 seconds or more, then fixate the white dot. The movement you perceive in the position of your afterimage relative to the grid is due to tremor in the eye muscles.

molded to the eye so that it stays fixed in position, and attached to it is a tiny projector system that shines an image directly onto the retina. Because the projector is fixed in position relative to the lens and the lens is fixed relative to the eye, the image does not move on the retina, even when muscular tremor causes physiological nystagmus. Within a few seconds after the stimulus is turned on, the perception of the image mysteriously fades away.

The other technique for stabilizing images requires a fairly sophisticated computer graphics system and a device to sense the position of the eye. An image is presented to an observer on the computer's monitor while a complex eye tracking system simultaneously measures the observer's eye movements. As soon as the computer detects a change in eye position, it almost instantly compensates for the eye movement by shifting the image in the same direction and over the same distance. The image thus follows the eye so that it remains in the same retinal position at all times. Under these conditions, the perception of a stabilized image also fades away within a few seconds.

Research on stabilized images has led to a number of remarkable discoveries. One of the most fascinating is that the visual system appears to construct regions

---

[1] When you think about this phenomenon carefully, it seems puzzling that the afterimage should appear to move when it is actually stationary on the retina. Likewise, it is strange that the image of the grid appears to be stationary when eye tremor actually causes it to move on the retina. Clearly, the perception of motion is not determined purely by what is moving on the retina, as we discovered in Section 10.1.

Visual Selection: Eye Movements and Attention

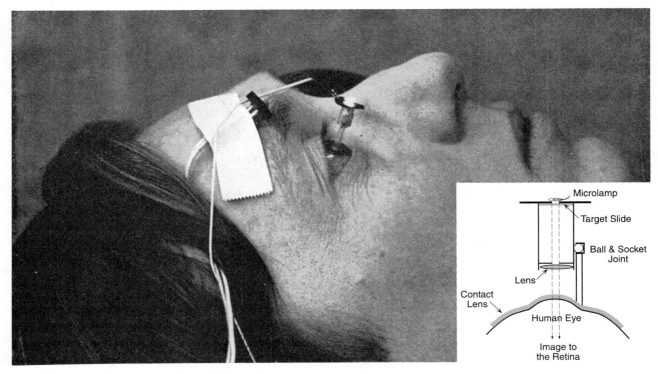

Figure 11.1.2 A device that produces a stabilized image on the retina. Because the contact lens is coupled to the eye, the tiny projector always projects the target image onto the same retinal location. After a few seconds of viewing, such stabilized images disappear. (Photo from Pritchard, 1961.)

within the visual field just from contour information, much as one might have predicted from our previous discussion of luminance edges in lightness constancy (e.g., Land & McCann, 1971). Krauskopf (1963) demonstrated this by presenting observers with a central red circle surrounded by a green disk. Under normal viewing conditions, this is just what it looked like. But Krauskopf then stabilized the inner contour between the red and green portions of the visual field without stabilizing the outer contour of the green disk. The astonishing result was that the inner red disk disappeared and was filled in by green to create the perception of a single large green disk!

The improbable conclusion from such experiments is that the visual system works largely by detecting moving edges and reconstructing the visual world from that information. This conception suggests a picture of the visual system that is very different from the usual idea that it is some sort of biological camera that faithfully records static images. To the extent that this is true at all, it is true only of the very earliest step of vision: the reg-

istration of light by photoreceptors. Almost immediately, adaptation and motion processing begin to take effect. The visual system seems to work by detecting spatial and temporal structure: finding moving contours and other spatio-temporal changes in the stimulation it receives. From this primitive information it apparently fills in and otherwise constructs the conscious visual experiences we have, as evidenced by Krauskopf's dramatic findings with the stabilized images of the red and green disks.

This view of vision is generally consistent with our current knowledge about early spatial and temporal processing of image-based information as it occurs in the retina and visual cortex, as we discovered in Chapter 4. Although some retinal ganglion cells (the P cells) appear most sensitive to static stimuli, other cells (the M cells) appear to be specialized for optimal processing of motion. By the time the information gets to visual cortex, very few cells produce sustained responses to unchanging stimulation. Thus, the temporal characteristics of cortical cells in area V1 appear to explain the disappearance of stabilized images. The physiological mechanisms that fill in sensory experience after adaptation to unmoving contours are not yet known, although cortical cells that respond appropriately to the filled-in sensory information in the blind spot have recently been discovered (Fiorani, Rosa, Gattass, & Rocha-Miranda, 1992).

Physiological nystagmus is an unusual kind of eye movement because it has no selective function. The other types of eye movements are all clearly selective in the sense that they control the object on which the eyes are fixated. As we will discover, each type has different characteristics and functions, as well as distinct neural mechanisms that control it.

Saccadic Movements. Saccades are very rapid, abrupt eye movements whose function is to bring new objects of interest to the fovea. They are the eye movements that normally occur most often when you look around a stationary environment. The movements your eyes are making while you read this sentence, for example, are saccades.

A saccade is essentially a **ballistic movement**: Once it has begun, its trajectory cannot be altered. If the eye misses its intended target object, another saccade can always be made to fixate it, but once a saccade is in progress, its destination appears to be fixed. Figure 11.1.3 shows graphs of two saccades to a target. No corrective saccade is required in the first case (Figure 11.1.3A), but an additional saccade is made in the second case to correct for the undershoot of the initial one (Figure 11.1.3B).

Saccades are a very rapid form of eye movement. A single saccade takes only about 150–200 ms to plan and execute. The ballistic movement of the eye itself is exceedingly fast, typically taking only about 30 ms and reaching speeds of up to 900° per second (Goldberg, Eggers, & Gouras, 1991). Between saccades, the eyes fixate the object of interest for a variable period of time, averaging about 300 ms per fixation, so that the visual system can process the optical information available in that location. Most of visual perception occurs during such sequences of fixations.

Although everyone knows that they move their eyes in looking around the environment, it is interesting that no one consciously perceives the image motion that results from saccadic eye movements. This is partly explained

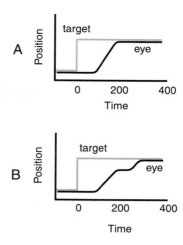

Figure 11.1.3 Saccadic eye movements. The position of the eye is plotted (black line) as it attempts to follow the position of the target (gray line). Trace A shows a successful saccade; trace B shows a case in which undershooting the target required a second, corrective saccade.

by perceptual constancy mechanisms: The displacement due to the eye movement is added to the displacement in the image to yield constancy of object position, as explained in Chapter 7. Even so, it is somewhat surprising that people do not perceive a moment of blurred vision while the eyes are actually moving, much as photographs are blurred if the camera moves while the shutter is open. Visual blurring is not perceived during saccades because perception appears to be attenuated during saccades. This phenomenon is called **saccadic suppression.**

Different explanations for saccadic suppression have been advanced. Perhaps the most obvious hypothesis is that the image motion resulting from saccades might be so fast that it cannot be perceived. However, experiments have shown that people readily perceive the motion of large, high-contrast objects moving at the same rate as images do during a saccade (Burr & Ross, 1982). Some other mechanism must therefore be responsible.

A more likely explanation of the lack of blurred vision during a saccade can be stated in terms of visual masking. Most generally, masking refers to the dominance of one kind of information over another (see Section 12.1.2). In the case of saccadic suppression, the masking hypothesis suggests that motion during saccades is not perceived because the sharp, clear images that arise from fixations immediately before and after the saccade

Visual Selection: Eye Movements and Attention

dominate the blurred images that arise during the saccade itself (Matin, 1974). Empirical support for this idea comes from experiments in which the stimulus conditions are arranged so that the visual field is completely dark just before and just after a saccade is executed, with a strobe light turned on only during the eye movement itself. Under these unusual conditions, observers do indeed perceive the retinal motion that occurs during the eye movement, thus supporting the theory that saccadic suppression is caused by the dominance of prior and subsequent fixations. The physiological mechanisms of this kind of masking are currently unknown, however.

Smooth Pursuit Movements. A third type of eye movement is used to track the position of a moving object to keep it in foveal vision once it is there. Such tracking movements are called **smooth pursuit eye movements**, and an example is shown in Figure 11.1.4. Because the image of a successfully tracked object is nearly stationary on the retina, pursuit movements enable the visual system to extract maximum spatial information from the image of the moving object itself. If it were not tracked, its retinal image would be smeared because of the object's motion and would spend most of its time in the periphery where acuity is poor. Pursuit movements thus serve an important evolutionary function of facilitating identification of moving objects. Both predator and prey need to be able to see what kinds of objects are moving about in their environment, a task that would be difficult without smooth pursuit eye movements.

Pursuit eye movements differ from saccades in several important respects:

1. *Smoothness.* Pursuit movements are typically smooth and continuous, rather than jerky and abrupt like saccades. Pursuit eye movements can be jerky to some degree, especially if the motion of the tracked object is jerky, but such motions are difficult to track.

2. *Feedback.* Pursuit movements are not ballistic like saccades but require constant correction based on visual feedback from the image. The signals sent from the brain to the eye muscles must be constantly updated with information from the image to keep the target object's image on the fovea. Smooth pursuit movements therefore cannot be made in the absence of a moving target to pursue.

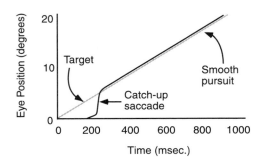

Figure 11.1.4 Pursuit eye movements. Eye position is plotted as a function of time (black line) as the eye attempts to track a moving target (gray line). After an initial saccade to intercept the target, the eye smoothly follows it.

3. *Speed.* Pursuit movements are slow in comparison with saccades. Saccades can reach speeds of 900° per second, whereas pursuit movements have a maximum velocity of about 100° per second.

4. *Acuity.* In pursuit movements, the image of the tracked object is clear, whereas images of untracked objects—including all stationary objects and those moving objects whose direction and speed differ from the target—are experienced as smeared and unclear because of their motion on the retina. (To experience this phenomenon for yourself, simply place your finger on this page and move it fairly quickly from one side to the other. As soon as you track your moving finger, the letters and words appear so blurred you are unable to read them, but your finger is clear. The words become sharp and clear again as soon as you stop moving your finger.) Blurring does not occur during saccades because of saccadic suppression.

Not surprisingly, the visual system's ability to track an object depends on its speed. If an object moves very slowly, the eye can follow its path almost exactly. The faster it goes, however, the more likely it is that the corrective feedback signals will not have time to be made with full accuracy. As a result, the image of the target is likely to deviate from the center of the fovea as tracking proceeds. This slippage accounts for the fact that visual acuity while tracking a moving display is usually worse than acuity for stationary displays. If tracking is essentially perfect, visual acuity does not suffer (Murphy, 1978).

Such findings imply that people who can execute more accurate pursuit eye movements should have better dynamic acuity and hence be able to see moving objects better. An interesting fact supporting this idea is that among a group of college students, members of the baseball team had considerably better dynamic visual acuity than the rest (Horner, 1982). This may be due to innate ability, practice, or both. Studies have shown that people can indeed improve their dynamic visual acuity with practice, but some improve more than others (Ludvigh & Miller, 1958).

Vergence Movements. Saccades and pursuit movements select primarily for the egocentric direction of the target object relative to the observer's head. The distance of the target from the observer is selected by **vergence eye movements**. As discussed in Chapter 5, when an observer fixates an object, the eyes are positioned so that the object falls on the center of each fovea. The eyes therefore converge to a degree that depends on how far away the object is, and this angle of convergence is a binocular source of information about the distance to the object: Near objects produce strong convergence and far objects produce little or no convergence, as illustrated in Figure 11.1.5. When an observer fixates an object that moves in depth, vergence eye movements are required to track it.

Vergence eye movements are slow, rarely exceeding 10° per second. They are initiated either by the presence of disparity in the target object (i.e., nonfoveal images of the target in one or both eyes) or by the presence of optical blur due to inaccurate accommodation (see Section 5.2.1). The primary difference between pursuit and vergence eye movements is that binocular pursuit movements are **conjugate** (in the same direction in both eyes), whereas vergence movements are **disconjugate** (in different directions). When an object approaches the observer's head, the angle of convergence increases as the two eyes move toward each other. When it recedes, the angle of convergence decreases as the eyes move away from each other. If the target's motion contains a directional component as well as one in depth, then conjugate and disconjugate components of pursuit movements must be made at the same time to track the object accurately.

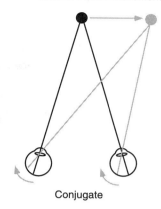

Smooth Pursuit Movement

Conjugate

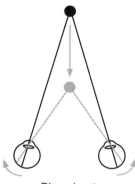

Vergence Movement

Disconjugate

Figure 11.1.5 Conjugate versus disconjugate eye movements. When tracking an object moving in the frontal plane, both eyes rotate in the same direction at the same rate (conjugate movements). When tracking an object moving in depth, the eyes rotate in opposite directions at the same time (disconjugate movements).

Vestibular Movements. The three types of selective eye movements we have considered thus far—saccadic, pursuit, and vergence movements—are used to put or keep the image of the target object on the fovea when the head is *still*. The last two types—vestibular and optokinetic movements—work together to keep the target image fixed on the fovea when the head *moves*.

Vestibular eye movements keep the eyes fixated on a particular environmental object when the head or body is being rotated. Although you are probably unaware of it, you make use of such eye movements all the time. To demonstrate them, simply move your head abruptly to the right and left while you are reading this

Visual Selection: Eye Movements and Attention

WORD. You somehow manage to keep fixating on the same word as your head rotates. When your head moved to the right, the image of the object remained stationary in central vision, so your eyes must have moved to the left just enough to compensate for the turning of your head. You can verify this by watching yourself in a mirror. Fixate on one of your eyes, and then rotate your head quickly. You will see that your eye rotates considerably in its socket to offset your head rotation.

Such eye movements are called "vestibular" because they are controlled via information coming from the vestibular system in the inner ear. As we explained in Section 7.3.1 while discussing orientation constancy, the vestibular system provides information about changes in the position and orientation of the head. Vestibular output is sent to the brain structures that control eye movements, and they, in turn, send compensatory signals to the eyes that keep them fixated on the target object.

Vestibular eye movements are extremely rapid and accurate, much more so than pursuit movements. You can demonstrate this fact by comparing the following two experiences. First, raise your index finger and fixate on it. Then start shaking your head side to side, slowly at first but speeding up over time. The image of your finger should stay in central vision and be clear and sharp for all but the very fastest head rotations you can make. Compare this experience with what happens when you keep your head still and move your finger back and forth while you try to track it with your eyes. Even at relatively modest speeds, the image of your finger becomes blurred because your eyes are unable to keep up with it. Shaking your head at the same speed, however, produces no blurring whatsoever.

You probably never thought about the fact that your eyes must move to fixate an object when you rotate your head, but it is true. You would discover it quickly enough if your vestibular system were damaged, because your vision would be seriously impaired. Overdoses of certain antibiotics can temporarily impair vestibular function, and when this happens, even small head movements disrupt the ability to fixate on stationary objects when the head is in motion. While you are walking, for example, the eye movement system cannot compensate for head movements, so images of objects in the environment jiggle and smear enough that you cannot do things that require high acuity, such as reading signs or recognizing faces of friends.

Optokinetic Movements. The final type of eye movement is an involuntary tracking movement that occurs when a large portion of the visual field moves uniformly across the retina. It normally occurs in conjunction with vestibular eye movements when the head rotates through large angles to keep a target object fixated. The primary difference between these two kinds of eye movements concerns the source of the information. Whereas vestibular movements are driven by kinesthetic signals from the inner ear, indicating that the head is moving, optokinetic movements are driven by optical translations of the whole visual field, which also arise when the head is moving. The purpose of the optokinetic response, like the vestibular response, is to track the fixated object in the visual field.

In a classic laboratory demonstration of optokinetic eye movements, a stationary observer is placed within a rotating striped cylinder. As the cylinder turns around the head, the stripes sweep past in the same way they would if the head were turning in the opposite direction. Even though the head is not actually rotating, the eyes track one of the stripes. If the full-field visual translation continues for more than a few seconds, the **optokinetic reflex** takes effect: After tracking a stripe through a large angle in the direction of the image motion, the eyes snap back in a rapid, saccadelike jump in the direction opposite to the image motion and then fixate and track another stripe. Figure 11.1.6 shows an example of this involuntary reflex at work.

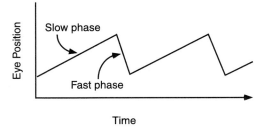

Figure 11.1.6 The optokinetic reflex. When the entire image translates across the visual field, the eye reflexively fixates an object and tracks it during the slow phase, then snaps back during the fast phase to fixate another object.

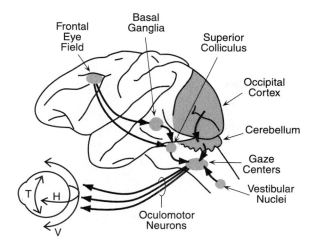

Figure 11.1.7 Brain areas involved with eye movements. Different types of eye movements are determined by activity in several different brain centers, all of which have a final common pathway in the brain stem gaze centers that control the eye muscles. (H = horizontal; V = vertical; T = torsional.)

11.1.2 The Physiology of the Oculomotor System

The different types of eye movements work together smoothly when the human visual system functions normally. One might therefore think that the neural centers that control them would constitute a neat package of nearby physiological structures. Somewhat surprisingly, this is untrue. The different kinds of eye movements have quite different neural mechanisms, which are scattered far and wide within the brain. We will now consider what is known about how eye movements are controlled by these disparate sites in the brain, although much remains to be discovered.

The eyes rotate in their sockets because of the action of the three pairs of extraocular muscles, which are among the fastest-acting in the body. They control eye rotations in three directions (see Figure 11.1.7): horizontal (left and right), vertical (up and down), and torsional (clockwise and counterclockwise in the plane of the cornea). Torsional rotations are relatively small compared with the other two. There are separate nuclei in the brain stem, often called the **gaze centers**, that control the extraocular muscles via the **oculomotor neurons**. These neurons constitute the final common pathway of the oculomotor system, originating in the gaze centers of the brain stem and projecting to the extraocular mus-

cles, as diagrammed schematically in Figure 11.1.7 for a monkey's brain. The superior colliculus of the midbrain is also involved in controlling eye movements, although its effects on the oculomotor neurons appear to be indirect.

Although a good deal is known about the neural circuits that control the different types of eye movements, the precise mechanisms for most of them are not yet known in detail. The best understood is the three-neuron reflex arc underlying the relatively simple vestibular-ocular reflex. The following provides a simplified description of the physiology underlying oculomotor control. (See Goldberg et al., 1991, for a more complete summary.)

• *Saccades.* Control of voluntary saccades can be traced to the **frontal eye fields** located in the frontal cortex (area 8). Its axons project both directly to the brain stem gaze centers and indirectly to them through the superior colliculus.

• *Smooth pursuit movements.* Because smooth pursuit movements require constant visual feedback, they are controlled by using information from the motion channels in visual cortex, including areas MT and MST (see Section 1.3.3). This input appears to project through the cerebellum and pons to the brain stem gaze centers, where a gaze velocity signal is generated to track the moving target.

• *Vergence movements.* Vergence movements also require visual feedback for control and also originate in occipital cortex, more specifically in the binocular disparity channels of area V2. They have their effect via neurons in the midbrain in the region of the oculomotor nucleus.

• *Vestibular movements.* The vestibular-ocular reflex is driven by a three-neuron reflex arc that begins with the output of hair cells in the vestibular system indicating disturbances in the fluid of the semicircular canals of the inner ear due to head rotations. This output goes to the vestibular nuclei, which then provide the oculomotor neurons with the correct eye velocity signal.

• *Optokinetic movements.* Optokinetic movements are generated partly in the cortical motion pathway (including areas MT and MST) and partly in a subcortical pathway (including a nucleus in the pretectum and the vestibular nucleus). Thus, both visual and vestibular inputs from head rotations converge on the vestibular nucleus, which then projects to the gaze centers.

It might seem surprising that these different types of eye movements are controlled by neural systems located in such diverse parts of the brain. Their main commonality is simply the fact that they all control the position of the eye. As we noted earlier, they have quite different purposes and make use of different kinds of information in determining direction of gaze. The distribution of control in different parts of the brain that specialize in the different kinds of information required therefore makes sense, as does the final common pathway in the oculomotor neurons.

11.1.3 Saccadic Exploration of the Visual Environment

Saccades are probably the most interesting type of eye movement because of their frequency and importance in understanding the dynamically selective nature of perceiving complex images. When you think about the limited nature of the visual information available from a single fixation, for example, it becomes obvious that perceiving realistic scenes requires a sequence of many different fixations, which must be integrated into a single unified perception. Foveal information is clear and fully chromatic, whereas peripheral information is blurry and color-weak to a degree that depends on distance from the fovea. To get high-resolution information about spatial and/or chromatic attributes, the visual scene must therefore be explored via eye movements that put different information in the fovea at different times.

Patterns of Fixations. The study of saccadic exploration of complex images was pioneered by the Russian psychologist Yarbus (1965). Using relatively crude equipment, he was able to record the fixations and saccades observers made while viewing natural objects and scenes. By superimposing the eye movements on the stimulus picture, he was able to determine which aspects of the image observers found most informative. For example, Figure 11.1.8 shows the record of fixations made by one observer to the face of a young girl over a 3-minute interval. As you can see, most fixations are allocated to inspecting the eyes, nose, mouth, and general outline of the face. Indeed, the pattern of fixations is so clear in this example that most people can guess what kind of object was being examined just by looking at the saccadic record.

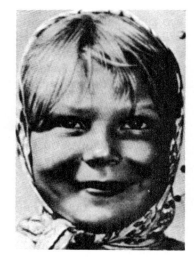

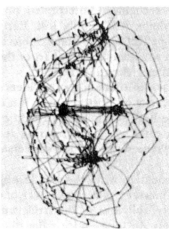

Figure 11.1.8 Saccadic exploration of a young girl's face. Free inspection of this picture shows a sequence of many fixations, the majority of which focus on the girl's facial features and the outline of her head. (From Yarbus, 1965.)

How the eyes explore a complex picture cannot be predicted simply from the structure of the stimulus itself, however. One also needs to know the observer's task. Figure 11.1.9A shows another picture studied by Yarbus (1967) together with the saccadic records produced when observers were given different questions to answer prior to viewing it. In one condition, the observer was allowed to examine the picture freely without any specific objective (part B). In other conditions, the observer was asked to estimate the material circumstances of the family (part C), to estimate the ages of the people (part D), to guess what the family had been doing before the

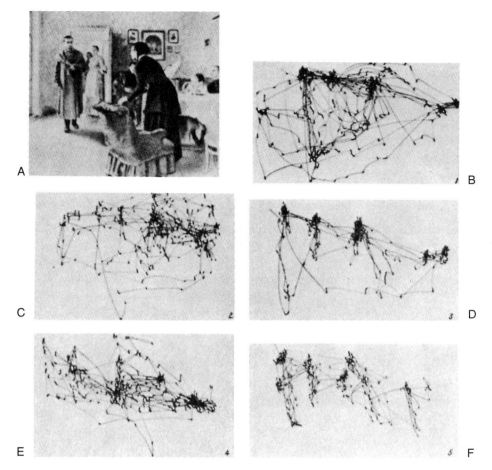

Figure 11.1.9 Effects of task on eye movements. The same picture (A) was examined by subjects with different instructions: free viewing (B), estimate the economic level of the people (C), judge their ages (D), guess what they had been doing before the visitor's arrival (E), and remember the clothes worn by the people (F). (From Yarbus, 1967.)

arrival of the "unexpected visitor" (part E), and to remember the clothes worn by the people (part F). The fact that the patterns of saccades vary considerably for different questions clearly demonstrates that the structure of the picture strongly interacts with the conscious perceptual goals of the observer in determining how it will be explored through saccadic eye movements.

More sophisticated eye-tracking equipment has allowed later investigators to determine the specific sequence of fixations that observers execute when exploring pictures. Noton and Stark (1971a, 1971b) analyzed the order of fixations as observers viewed simple line drawings such as the one shown in Figure 11.1.10. Although there was a great deal of variability, they were often able to identify recurring sequences of saccades for a given image which they called **scan paths**. In Figure 11.1.10, several individual fixation sequences from the same observer are shown in parts B–E, and Noton and Stark's idealized version of this scan path in part F. Scan paths are highly idiosyncratic. They differ markedly from one observer to the next and from one picture to the next. But when the same person viewed the same picture at a later time, highly similar sequences of fixations were observed with 65% of the pictures.

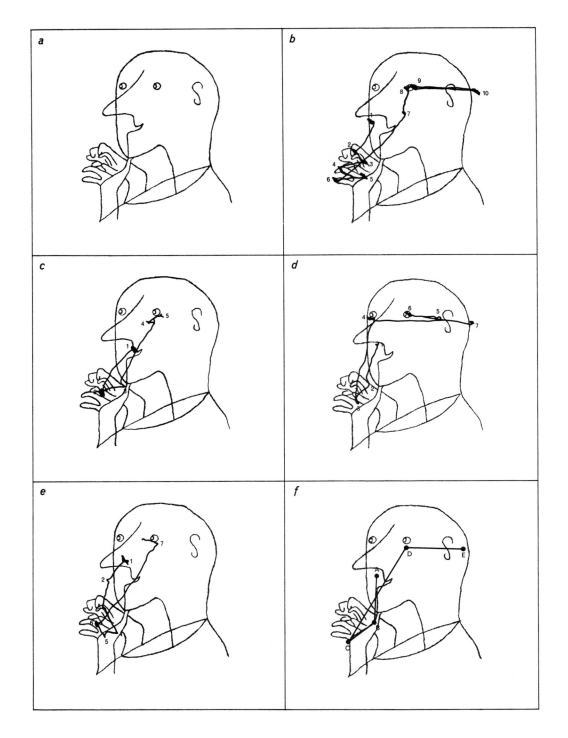

Figure 11.1.10 Scan paths. Several individual sequences of fixations (B–E) are shown for the same observer together with an idealized version of this scan path (F). Scan paths differ from one observer to another and from one picture to another. (From Noton & Stark, 1971a.)

Transsaccadic Integration. The fact that people explore a complex visual scene by making a sequence of many fixations on different informative parts amply demonstrates that normal perception is a dynamic, temporally extended process. But the perceptual result of this sequence of saccades does not resemble even remotely the piecemeal series of images it produces on the retina. Rather, the perception seems to be that of a single, unified scene. This perception must therefore be constructed by integrating the information extracted from the sequence of exploratory eye movements into some coherent internal representation of a single scene (Hochberg, 1970). Moreover, this perception must involve some brief form of memory to bridge the gap between fixations.

One possibility for integrating the contents of sequences of saccades is that they are mapped into a larger, spatially organized memory array according to their positions. The result would be an integrated, composite representation of the visual environment, each fixation being superimposed in its proper location of the array, as illustrated in Figure 11.1.11. As plausible as this **spatiotopic fusion hypothesis** might sound, experimental results show that the visual system does not make use of it (Irwin, 1992), as we will discuss in some detail in Section 12.1.3. Rather, the integration appears to be performed at the level of more abstract representations of objects within the scene.

In addressing this problem of saccadic integration, Hochberg (1970) postulated what he called a **schematic map**: a representation consisting of possible samplings of a spatially extended scene together with contingent expectancies of what will be seen as a result of those samplings. Hochberg never described the internal structure of his schematic maps in detail, but it seems quite likely that structural descriptions, as described in Chapters 8 and 9, would fit the requirements. They explicitly encode the spatial relations among the various parts of an object, effectively specifying the direction and distance at which various configurations of features would be found. In Palmer's face schema (Figure 8.2.16), for example, vectors specify the information required to get from one facial feature to another. This information could be used to support recognition via overt eye movements or covert shifts of visual attention to appropriate places in the image. This information is also encoded redundantly enough to support a variety

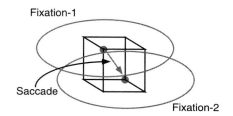

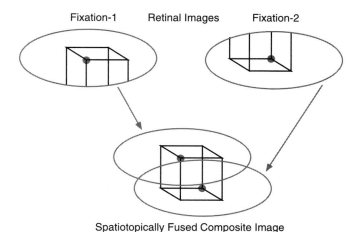

Figure 11.1.11 The spatiotopic fusion hypothesis. When the same scene is viewed by using more than one fixation, the retinal images from the multiple fixations might somehow be fused spatially into a single image in a visual memory.

of different scan paths. Thus, structural descriptions appear to be well suited to serve as the internal structure that accumulates information gathered from a number of different fixations and that integrates it into a coherent, unified whole. This description could then be used to recognize the same object or scene despite a different sequence of eye fixations, provided the proper components and spatial relationships were verified in the input.

11.2 Visual Attention

Even while our eyes are fixated on a particular location, it does not appear that the visual system passively processes all the information available within the image. Rather, we selectively attend to different aspects of it at different times. Sometimes we attend globally to the whole scene; at other times we attend to a selected object or set of objects; at still other times we attend locally to a specific object part. We may even concentrate on a particular property of a particular object, such as the color or texture of a shirt we are considering buying. Our ability to engage in these flexible strategies for processing different information within the visual field—generally referred to as *attention*—is therefore an important component of vision. Indeed, recent experiments suggest that attention may be required for us to consciously perceive anything at all (Mack & Rock, 1998).

Overt eye movements determine what optical information is available to the visual system; covert selective attention determines what subset of this information gets full processing. Attention is such a complex process (or set of processes) that it is difficult to define adequately. For the purposes of this book, however, we will consider **visual attention** to be those processes that enable an observer to recruit resources for processing selected aspects of the retinal image more fully than nonselected aspects.

Notice that this definition implies two different but related functions of attention: *recruiting* resources and *focusing* them on selected aspects of visual information. These correspond to two different properties of attention that theorists often distinguish:

1. *Capacity*. Capacity is the amount of perceptual resources that is available for a given task or process. Attentional capacity can vary with a number of factors, such as alertness, motivation, and time of day (Kahneman, 1973).

2. *Selectivity*. Even at a given moment, when the total capacity is fixed, the amount of attention paid to different subsets of visual information can be allocated flexibly to some degree. This ability allows attention to be selective in terms of what gets processed and what does not.

Of these two aspects, selectivity has been more intensively studied by vision scientists. In the remainder of this chapter, we will mainly be discussing selectivity, although capacity issues will sometimes arise as well.

Complex visual scenes like the ones that we normally look at contain a staggering amount of information, far more than we can be aware of at one time. As a result, we have to sample visual information over time in a series of distinct perceptual acts, each of which is inherently selective. As we discussed in the previous section of this chapter, voluntary eye movements are the first line of visual selection. But even when our eyes are

stationary and we are processing a single retinal image, we selectively sample the information it contains for further processing.

This second level of selectivity does not consist of overt, physical acts of orienting such as turning our heads or eyes toward objects of interest, but of covert, internal acts of orienting toward different information available within the retinal image. You can demonstrate the selective effect of attention without eye movements simply by focusing on some small object in your field of view and then attending to (or noticing) various nearby objects—without moving your eyes. This is not particularly easy because eye movements and shifts in attention are normally performed together, but they can be separated with effort. The fact that they can is evidence for the existence of selective attention in vision, independent of eye movements.

A more compelling and rigorous demonstration of our ability to attend to different things without fixating them can be achieved with the help of a camera flash. At night or in a windowless room, turn off the lights and adapt to the dark for a few minutes. Face the flash toward the room (away from yourself) and press the button. This brief burst of intense light will "paint" a single unmoving image of the environment on your retina. It cannot be selectively sampled by foveal fixations due to eye movements, because the afterimage necessarily moves with your eyes whenever you make an eye movement. Even so, you will be able to direct your attention to a number of different objects within the scene before it fades from view. This covert sampling is the work of **spatial selection**, the process of concentrating attentional resources on information from a restricted region of the visual field. At least to a first approximation, such attentional changes seem to be like movements of an internal eye—the so-called "mind's eye"—that can sample different locations within the stationary afterimage. Given the retinotopic organization of much of visual cortex (see Section 4.1.3), spatial selection can be thought of as internally sampling information from a restricted portion of a cortical map.

Spatial selection is only one aspect of visual attention, however. Attention is also at work when we selectively perceive different properties or features of the same object. Keeping a steady gaze on a complex object, for example, you can focus your attention sequentially on its color, its shape, its texture, its size, and so on. This demonstration illustrates **property selection**. It is at first difficult to understand property selection in terms of attention being an internal "mind's eye," for eyes have no physical structure that enables them to select among properties other than space. If different properties have spatially distinct representations within the brain, however, as suggested by the discovery of many different retinotopic maps in visual cortex to encode different visual properties (see Section 1.3.3), then property selection may also be understood in terms of covertly sampling information in different locations of these maps.

11.2.1 Early versus Late Selection

Why do we have the ability to selectively attend to different aspects of visual information? A plausible answer is that it protects the visual system from being overloaded by the massive amount of information available in the visual field. To be effective, however, attention must somehow manage to focus on the most important information given the organism's current goals, needs, and desires. Otherwise, selective sampling would be essentially random, and random selection is not very useful to an organism. Attention is therefore likely to have some means of selecting the most relevant information to process further so that only irrelevant information is rejected.

But how can the visual system choose the most important information without first processing all the information to determine what is most important? This is the *paradox of intelligent selection*. If attention operates very early in the visual system, before much processing has been done, it is unclear how the attentional system can determine what is important. If attention operates relatively late, after a good deal of processing has already been done, it is easy to determine what is important, but much of the advantage of selection would have been lost because most of the irrelevant information has already been processed to perform the selection.

Selective attention to important information is possible by using heuristics based on either innate principles or ones learned through individual experience. It is evolutionarily advantageous to attend to some kinds of information before others. Moving objects are generally important for survival, for example, especially objects that are coming toward you. It therefore makes sense for moving objects to attract your attention for further

analysis and for objects that are headed in your general direction to have priority. This attentional heuristic might even be hard-wired at birth through evolutionary processes of natural selection, and it seems plausible that it could be performed very early in visual processing.

In other cases, however, the importance of information is highly specific to an individual. Most people have had the experience of seeing their own name "pop out" of a page of text, for example, and grab their attention before any of the other words. This kind of selection clearly cannot be innate; it must be learned through experience by the individual. By the same token, it seems unlikely that it could be selected at a very early stage of processing, for it seems to presuppose the identification of the letters that make up the name. These theoretical considerations are suggestive, but whether (or how much) attentional selection takes place at early versus late stages of processing is an empirical question toward which many experiments have been directed.

Auditory Attention. The first research on whether attention operates early or late in human perception was conducted in the auditory domain. We will describe it briefly because many of the key questions and theoretical issues were originally explored there.

Auditory researchers began studying attention by asking subjects to perform a **shadowing task** in which they had to repeat aloud the message coming through either the left or right channel of a pair of headphones. The question of interest was what information subjects perceived about the other, unattended channel while performing this shadowing task. Initial results showed that they could perceive gross sensory features without attention, such as whether the unattended channel contained speech sounds or not and whether the voice was male or female. More specific features, such as what was being said or even whether the message was in English or French, were not perceived unless attention was diverted to the unattended channel (Cherry, 1953; Cherry and Taylor, 1954).

On the basis of such findings, British psychologist Donald Broadbent (1958) proposed that auditory attention operated early, analyzing the input to both ears only for gross sensory features and then selecting one ear for further processing of higher-level features to reach the level of meaning. This theory was called **filter theory** because it assumed that selection was due to an all-or-none blocking mechanism (or filter) that passed only the selected channel (see Figure 2.2.5).

Subsequent studies showed that auditory attention was not quite this complete or simple, however. Moray (1959) found that subjects were very likely to hear their own name if it was presented in the unattended channel. This phenomenon may be familiar to you from personal experience. If you are at a party talking with one person, for example, and someone nearby says your name, you are very likely to notice it and to shift your attention to find out why your name was mentioned. Note that this fact causes problems for an early selection theory of auditory attention because it suggests that recognition of your name occurs before selection, not after it, as Broadbent's filter theory would predict.

This difficulty was overcome by supposing that selection operates both early and late in auditory processing (see Figure 11.2.1). According to the most widely accepted theory, often called **attenuator theory** (Treisman, 1960), the initial phase of selection based on gross physical properties is only partial. That is, in contrast to Broadbent's filter theory, early selection merely attenuates (or reduces) the signals in the unattended channels rather than blocking them completely.[2] Attenuator theory can therefore be thought of as a "leaky" version of filter theory.

The second phase of attentional selection in attenuator theory operates during the process of identifying auditory events. Input information first activates **dictionary units**: internal representations of meaningful words and sounds that enable them to be identified. According to attenuator theory, words from both channels activate their corresponding dictionary units, but to different degrees. The units whose input comes from the attended channel are strongly activated, whereas those from the unattended channel are more weakly activated, owing to prior attenuation in the early selection phase. Many dictionary units can thus be active to different degrees at the same time.

The mechanism of late selection within attenuator theory is that dictionary units have dynamic thresholds that must be exceeded for conscious perception to oc-

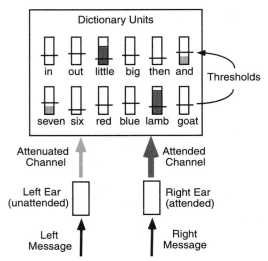

Figure 11.2.1 Treisman's attenuator theory of auditory attention. The message coming from the unattended left ear is attenuated, but both messages activate central dictionary units, only one of which typically exceeds threshold to become conscious. This theory contains mechanisms for both early and late selection.

cur. Highly salient items, such as one's own name, have dictionary units with permanently lowered thresholds. Even weak activation from the unattended channel will therefore be sufficient to exceed its threshold and attract attention. This enables attenuator theory to account for Moray's (1959) finding that subjects often hear their name when it occurs in the unattended channel. Less meaningful items will have higher thresholds, so they will tend to be perceived only if they arrive on the attended channel. Treisman also suggested that the thresholds of dictionary units could vary dynamically over time according to context. This would enable contextually expected words to be more easily identified than unexpected words, as reported in other auditory attention experiments (Gray & Wedderburn, 1960).

The Inattention Paradigm. Psychologists Arien Mack and Irvin Rock have recently begun investigating

---

[2] Equivalently, the information arriving from the attended channel might be amplified rather than those from the unattended channels being attenuated. It is also possible that both amplification of attended information and attenuation of unattended information might occur. The important

proposal is that some attentional mechanisms result in relatively more activation from the attended channel than from the unattended ones, regardless of how this effect is achieved.

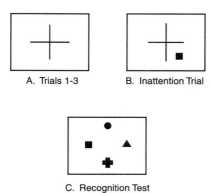

A. Trials 1-3   B. Inattention Trial

C. Recognition Test

Figure 11.2.2 The inattention paradigm. Subjects are instructed to determine whether the horizontal or the vertical line of a briefly presented cross is longer (A), but on the inattention trial, an extra unexpected element is presented (B). Subjects are asked whether they saw anything besides the cross and are then given a recognition test (C) to evaluate their perception of the extra element.

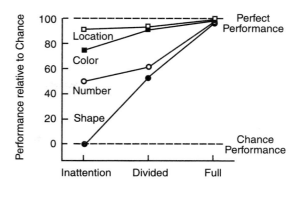

Attentional Condition

Figure 11.2.3 Results from the inattention paradigm. Subjects perform better than chance at recognizing location, color, and number of elements but not shape. (Data replotted from Rock et al., 1992, to equate chance levels.)

similar questions about early versus late selection in the visual domain (Mack & Rock, 1998). They began by asking what visual features could be perceived without attention. To find out, they had to develop a procedure—which they called the **inattention paradigm**—in which attention would not be focused on the object whose properties they wished to study, even though the object would be clearly visible within the visual field if it had been attended. The task they used was a relatively difficult discrimination in which subjects had to determine whether the vertical or horizontal line of a large cross was longer (see Figure 11.2.2A). The cross was presented briefly (200 ms) and followed by a mask. Several trials of this task were presented with nothing except the cross on the computer screen so that subjects would not expect anything else to be presented.

Then, on the third or fourth trial, the experimenters presented an *inattention trial* in which an additional object was displayed near the cross (Figure 11.2.2B). After the subject said which line of the cross was longer, the experimenter asked whether the subject had seen anything in addition to the cross. Perception of various properties of the unattended object was assessed in this inattention trial through a recognition test in which subjects were asked to pick out the alternative that corresponded to the extra object. An example is given in Figure 11.2.2C for an experiment studying shape perception under conditions of inattention.

After a few more trials of just presenting the cross task, subjects were again shown an extra object and again asked whether they had seen anything. This *divided attention trial* was included because subjects would have been alerted to the possibility of the extra object by the questioning that they received after the inattention trial shortly before. Subjects were given a final trial in which they were told to forget about the cross task entirely and to focus on perceiving anything else that might be present in the display. This *full attention trial* was designed to determine the perceptibility of the extra object under the same presentation conditions as the inattention and divided attention trials but without having to divide attention.

Initial results suggested that simple sensory properties were perceived without attention but that more complex ones were not. Specifically, the results indicated that color, position, and approximate number of objects could be perceived without attention but that shape could not (Rock, Linnett, Grant, & Mack, 1992). This conclusion was based on the fact that subjects performed no better than chance at picking out the correct shape alternative after the critical inattention trial but were almost perfect at doing so after the divided attention trial (see Figure 11.2.3). With properties such as color and position, however, subjects were nearly as good at choosing the correct alternative following the inattention trial as the divided attention trial. These results are reminiscent of early selection phenomena in auditory

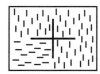

A. Trials 1-3   B. Inattention Trial

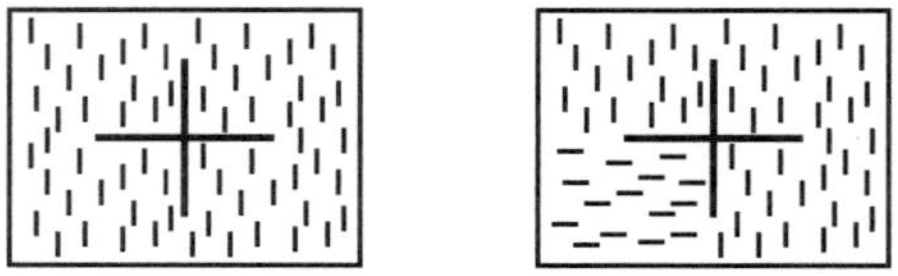

Figure 11.2.4 Texture segregation requires attention. When background texture elements unexpectedly differed in one quadrant on the inattention trial, subjects did no better than chance at reporting which quadrant was different. Conscious experience of grouping therefore appears to require attention.

attention, much like being able to tell whether the unattended voice was male or female without being able to understand what was being said (Cherry, 1953). Further experiments, to be described shortly, led Mack and Rock (1998) to believe that late selection was also occurring, however.

Other questions that have been examined to clarify the role of attention in perception were whether perceptual grouping or texture segregation occurs under conditions of inattention (Mack, Tang, Tuma, Kahn, & Rock, 1992). In the latter case, for example, the displays contained a texture of randomly placed vertical lines in the background of the cross for all of the initial trials (see Figure 11.2.4A). Then, on the crucial inattention trial, the orientation of all the lines in one quadrant was changed (Figure 11.2.4B), and subjects were asked whether they saw anything different. They did not. On the full attention trial, however, all subjects correctly reported the different quadrant. This indicates that the conscious perception of texture segregation requires attention, contrary to Julesz's (1984) claim that it is preattentive. Gestalt grouping by proximity and lightness were also found to be absent in the inattention trial but clearly present in the full attention trial.

One surprising result from the early studies with single objects was that about 25% of the subjects reported *not perceiving anything at all* on the inattention trial (Mack & Rock, 1998; Rock & Mack, 1994). Mack and Rock refer to this phenomenon as **inattentional blindness**. It cannot be attributed to sensory factors because virtually everyone reported seeing the target on the divided attention and full attention trials. These trials were optically identical to the unattended trial but differed in terms of the subject's expectation. On the inattention trial, they expected only the cross, but on the divided

and full attention trials, they were also monitoring for anything else that might be presented. The much higher incidence of missing the target on the inattention trials therefore strongly suggests that expectation is an important component of inattentional blindness.

Subsequent studies demonstrated a number of even more surprising effects concerning the degree of inattentional blindness. For instance, the amount of attentional blindness was actually greater (typically 50–75%) when the extra object was presented foveally at fixation than when it was presented about 2 degrees off center, as in the usual procedure. Most surprising of all, however, was the finding that the degree of attentional blindness depends greatly on the personal meaningfulness of the extra stimulus. As in the auditory domain, Mack and Rock found that only about 5% of subjects were blind to their own name when it was presented under conditions of inattention. Presenting someone else's name under the same conditions led to 35% inattentional blindness, and presenting letter strings with only one different letter—e.g., "Kon" instead of "Ken" or "Jeck" instead of "Jack"—led to about 60% inattentional blindness. Similar, but weaker effects of superior perception for meaningful visual stimuli under conditions of inattention were obtained for certain words (such as RAPE and STOP) and for a standard cartoon "happy face" (but not a sad, neutral, or scrambled face).

Clearly, these results from the inattention paradigm suggest that some form of late selection must be at work in visual as well as auditory attention. Unattended objects must be receiving fairly detailed visual processing for inattentional blindness to be so sensitive to the difference between one's own name and a slight modification of it. Notice that this conclusion actually seems to contradict the earlier empirical finding that shape information is not perceived without attention (Rock et al., 1992). It is not yet clear what the resolution of this conflict will be. Perhaps shape does get *processed* without attention but does not become *consciously perceived* unless attention is then drawn to the object because of its high salience, as would be the case with one's own name. Meaningless shapes would seldom attract attention and therefore fail to become conscious. If their activation dissipates over a matter of seconds, no trace would remain when subjects were asked to report whether they saw anything different. (We will consider some further evidence from the inattention paradigm supporting this view in Chapter 13 when we tackle the topic of visual awareness.) It is puzzling from this hypothesis that properties such as color and position of meaningless shapes are sometimes perceived even when subjects are not expecting them.

Although these and other results suggest that late selection is possible in vision, the early/late question may not have a single solution. Lavie (1995) has recently proposed that both early and late selection occur, but under different conditions. When the task places a high load on visual processing, she finds evidence that selection operates at an early stage of processing, effectively blocking out stimuli other than those within the current focus of attention. When perceptual load is low, however, selection appears to operate at a later stage, allowing the processing of stimuli outside the focus of attention. The task and stimulus conditions in the inattention paradigm are consistent with a low perceptual load, which may explain why Mack and Rock's results largely conform to the predictions of late selection.

Mack and Rock's hypothesis that people are literally blind to unattended visual information, even though such information may be processed extensively at a nonconscious level, is a radical one. Is there any other evidence that bears on it? One compelling source of evidence comes from patients with certain kinds of brain damage who appear not to consciously perceive some of the objects in their visual field because of an inability to attend to them. We will discuss these conditions, known as *unilateral neglect* and *Balint's syndrome*, a bit later in this chapter when we consider neurological mechanisms of attention. But there is also relevant evidence from other studies of normal perceivers who fail to see what would otherwise be clearly perceivable under conditions in which their attention has been captured by some other object or event. We will now examine two of these phenomena, known as the *attentional blink* and *change blindness*.

The Attentional Blink. The **attentional blink** refers to the fact that perception of a second target item is greatly reduced if it is presented within a half second of a first target item (Raymond, Shapiro, & Arnell, 1992; Shapiro, Raymond, & Arnell, 1994). It is typically studied in a **rapid serial visual presentation (RSVP)** search task, in which subjects are shown a very rapid sequence of visual stimuli, all at fixation where

acuity is greatest, and are asked to report targets of a specific type (Forster, 1970). For example, subjects might be shown a series of 15 alphanumeric characters at fixation in a period of only 1.5 s (100 ms per character), 13 of which were digits and 2 of which were letters. Their task would be to report the identity of any letters that they saw in the RSVP stream.

If the rate of presentation is no faster than about 11 items/s, the first target can almost always be correctly identified. If the second target is presented more than about 500 ms after the first target, it too is well perceived and reported. But if the second target is presented within about 200–500 ms of the onset of the first target, subjects are very likely to miss the second one completely. They appear simply not to see it.

This phenomenon has been dubbed the *attentional blink* because one interpretation is that after the first target captures the subject's attention, there is a period during which no attention is available for processing the incoming items that immediately follow it, much as blinking keeps visual information from being perceived while the eye is shut. If attention is indeed completely absorbed by processing the first target, then subjects' failure to identify or even detect a second target can be counted as further evidence for Mack and Rock's theoretical interpretation of inattentional blindness: People do not see the second target because it cannot be attended to at the same time the first target is being processed. Other interpretations are possible, however, including ones based on failure of memory rather than perception (e.g., Wolfe, 1999). We will discuss this proposal shortly.

Subsequent results indicate that during an attentional blink an unperceived target nevertheless receives nonconscious processing to the level of meaning. This fact has been demonstrated both behaviorally and electrophysiologically. Behaviorally, the target that appears during the blink has been shown to prime (facilitate) a semantically related third target item that occurs after the blink is over (Shapiro, Driver, Ward, & Sorenson, 1996). Electrophysiologically, the target during the blink has also been shown to influence a component in the evoked potential (called *N400*) that is known to be sensitive to semantic factors (see Shapiro & Luck, 1999). It therefore appears that the attentional blink, like inattentional blindness, operates at a fairly late stage of selection.

Change Blindness. Another phenomenon that may support Mack and Rock's hypothesis that lack of attention to an object causes failure to perceive it comes from a series of recent studies on what has come to be called **change blindness**. The basic finding is that people are surprisingly poor at detecting even gross changes in a visual stimulus if they occur in objects that are not the focus of attention (e.g., Rensink, O'Regan, & Clark, 1995a, 1995b).

A basic change blindness experiment goes like this. Subjects are alternately shown two complex scenes that are identical except for one object or feature that changes. If the two pictures are spatially aligned and presented right after one another with no black interval or distracting event, this task is extremely easy. Attention is immediately called to the stimulus change, which can then be accurately reported. But if a brief blank interval is inserted between the presentations, the task becomes extremely difficult. The same difference that was found effortlessly without a blank interval can now take 20 s or more of repeated alternations while the subject laboriously searches, object by object, for the change.

To experience a version of change blindness for yourself, look back and forth between Figures 11.2.5A and 11.2.5B until you notice the difference between them. If you are like most people, you will find this task surprisingly hard. Once you find the change, you will probably be amazed at how long it took you to spot such a big difference. In this case, there is no blank interval, but the eye movements you have to make between fixations on the target pictures appear to serve the same function and cause blindness to such changes (Blackmore, Brelstaff, Nelson, & Troscianko, 1995; Grimes, 1996). Other abrupt stimulus modifications, such as the sudden appearance of a distracting visual "mudsplash" will produce the same effect (Resnink, O'Regan, & Clark, 1997).

Further experiments show that this insensitivity to change over a short period of time is not a mere laboratory curiosity, but can occur even under normal perceptual conditions. In one study, a subject was approached by a stranger with a map who was asking directions to a location on campus (Simons & Levin, 1997). During their conversation, two workmen, carrying a door lengthwise, walked between the subject and person asking directions. In the few seconds during which the subject could not see the questioner, one of the workmen

A

B

Figure 11.2.5 Change blindness. There is a fairly obvious difference between these two pictures, but people have a hard time detecting it unless they attend directly to the relevant area. (Courtesy of Ron Rensink.)

carrying the door deftly switched places with the person so that after the door passed, the subject was talking to a different person wearing different clothes. Only about 50% of the subjects noticed that any change had occurred when they were asked about it moments later.

One interesting interpretation of this literature on the various conditions under which we fail to see things that are quite clearly visible—including inattentional blindness, attentional blinks, and change blindness of various sorts—is that our impression of normal conscious perceptions of our environment as being rich, complete, and detailed is just a grand illusion (O'Regan, 1992). In fact, it is claimed, we experience only the things to which we specifically attend for whatever purposes we currently have in mind, and the rest is simply not perceived because of the lack of focused attention. In this view, the unattended portion of the world *seems* to be there in our perceptions, at least under normal circumstances, because when we examine any given object to see whether it is fully represented in our perception, we necessarily attend to it. Once we have done so, the richly detailed information becomes part of our conscious perception, and seems as though it must have been there all along—even though it hasn't been. The piecemeal nature of our perceptions can therefore be revealed only under ecologically unusual circumstances when the target object changes quickly.

A different interpretation is possible, however, and in some ways preferable. Wolfe (1999) has argued that these phenomena are evidence of **inattentional amnesia** rather than inattentional blindness. He claims that all of these supposedly unseen objects and changes are actually experienced perceptually, albeit very briefly. But without the benefit of focussed attention, he suggests, there is absolutely no memory of them, even over very short time intervals. This account has the advantage of not having to explain away the fact we have conscious perceptual experiences everywhere in our visual field rather than just where we are attending: It is simply because we do have conscious perceptions of unattended objects. The problem comes in reporting these fleeting and fragile perceptions when any sort of memory is required. The unattended perceptions are simply gone by the time we can divert attention to them from either the cross-task in the inattention paradigm, the first target in the attentional blink paradigm, or the blank interval, mudsplash, or interrupting door in the change blindness experiments.

The proper interpretation of these intriguing and important findings is not yet clear. What is clear is that attention somehow plays a very important role in our conscious perception of visual events, by enabling nonconscious visual processing to reach consciousness and/or by creating durable representations in memory that can be used to report fleeting conscious perceptions that would otherwise disappear without a trace.

Intentionally Ignored Information. Thus far, we have concentrated on what happens to objects that are

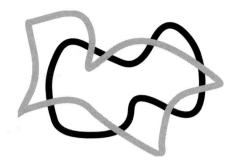

Figure 11.2.6 The overlapping figures experiment by Rock and Gutman (1981). Subjects attended to one of two overlapping novel figures and made a rating of its aesthetic appeal while they ignored the other. Subsequent memory tests revealed good memory for the attended figure but essentially no memory for the ignored one.

not attended because of lack of expectation (as in the inattention paradigm), lack of resources (as in the attentional blink) or some sort of distraction (as in change blindness). But what about objects that are *intentionally* ignored? What properties, if any, are perceived under these circumstances, and what is their fate?

The seminal experiment on this topic was performed by Rock and Gutman (1981). They constructed displays containing two novel outline figures that overlapped spatially, one red and the other green, as illustrated in Figure 11.2.6. Half of the subjects were told to attend just to the red figures and to rate them for aesthetic appeal; the other half were told to do the same for the green ones. After seeing a series of such displays, subjects were tested on their memory for the presented shapes using black versions of both sets of figures. Memory for the shape of the attended figures was quite good, but memory for the shape of unattended figures was essentially at chance. Rock and Gutman (1981) concluded that shape was not perceived unless a figure was attended.

There are alternative interpretations of this result, however. Perhaps shape was perceived perfectly well but forgotten so quickly that it was not recognized in the memory test. Or perhaps it was perceived initially but then was suppressed in order to process the attended figure. Although these hypotheses are more complex than assuming that shape was not perceived initially, both are consistent with Rock and Gutman's results.

Using sophisticated experimental procedures, Tipper and his associates have found evidence that the ignored

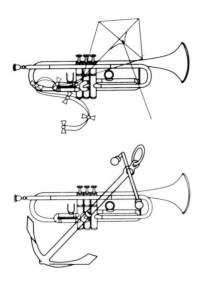

Figure 11.2.7 The negative priming effect. Subjects had to name one of two overlapping familiar figures. On trials in which the target figure was ignored on the previous trial, subjects took longer to name the target than they did when that figure was not present on the previous trial. (From Rock, 1995.)

shape is perceived at some level but not remembered because of active suppression (Allport, Tipper, & Chmiel, 1985; Tipper, 1985; Tipper & Cranston, 1985). The evidence supporting this interpretation is fascinating. Subjects were presented with two meaningful objects using Rock and Gutman's overlapping-contours method (see Figure 11.2.7 for examples in this task) and instructed to name just the ones in a given color (e.g., red), ignoring the other. On *repetition trials*, the target object on a given trial was preceded by a trial in which the same object was presented in the un-attended color (see Figure 11.2.7). On *unrelated trials*, the target object was preceded by a trial in which an unrelated object was presented in the unattended color. The surprising result was that naming the target object took significantly longer in the repetition trials (when the same object had been ignored on the immediately preceding trial) than on the unrelated trials (when it had not). This increase in response time has come to be known as the **negative priming effect** because the result is the opposite of what is usually found when a to-be-perceived object has been primed by prior exposure.

The existence of negative priming strongly suggests that subjects must have registered the shape of the un-attended object, but suppressed its perception in order

to correctly name the target object on that trial. The effect of this suppression is then measured on a repetition trial by slowing the process of naming the same object when it is presented in the attended color. Further experiments showed that the unattended figure appears to be processed at least to the level of meaning, because the slowing of responses also occurred for semantic associates of the suppressed object. For example, if a picture of a dog were presented in the unattended color on one trial, the time to name a cat figure presented in the attended color on the next trial would also be measurably slowed (Tipper & Driver, 1988).

These findings are theoretically interesting for at least two reasons. First, they indicate that intentionally ignored objects receive extensive perceptual processing, at least to the semantic level, because for them to slow responses to a related object on the next trial, they must have been identified on the previous trial. Second, they suggest that attention operates not only by *facilitating* processing of the attended object, but also by *inhibiting* processing of ignored objects. Although it has always been acknowledged that selection can occur either by facilitating the attended object or by inhibiting the un-attended ones, Tipper's results have provided strong evidence that both mechanisms are at work, at least in this situation.

What is responsible for the difference between the findings of Rock and Gutman versus Tipper and his associates? There are several possibilities:

1. *Long versus short retention interval.* Rock and Gutman typically assessed perceptual effects by measuring memory after a long delay, after several figures had been presented. Tipper's negative priming paradigm assessed them much more quickly, in the very next trial after only a few seconds had passed.

2. *Indirect versus direct measures.* Rock and Gutman asked their subjects to make direct assessments of perceptual memory, whereas Tipper assessed perceptual memory indirectly by measuring performance on a task in which the effects of a previously seen stimulus could be measured as an increase in response time. The latter may be a much more sensitive index of visual processing than simply asking what subjects remember.

3. *Novel versus familiar stimuli.* To study negative priming effects on naming latencies, Tipper used figures that could be named, and this required familiar, meaningful

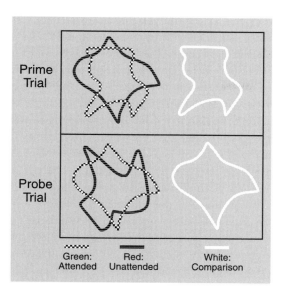

Green: Red: White:
Attended Unattended Comparison

Figure 11.2.8 Negative priming with novel figures. Subjects had to decide whether the green (checkered) and white figures on each trial had the same shape or not. On some sequences of trials, the previous prime trial required subjects to ignore the same figure that had to be attended in the present probe trial. (See text for details.) (After Treisman & DeSchepper, 1996.)

stimuli rather than the novel, meaningless ones that Rock and Gutman typically studied.

Surprising answers to these and other questions have come from a series of experiments by Treisman and DeSchepper (1996; DeSchepper & Treisman, 1996). To address the third possibility, they looked for negative priming effects using novel figures like Rock and Gutman's. They did so by changing the task from naming individual figures to deciding whether pairs of figures were the same or different. Each trial's display contained three figures: an attended figure in the target color (green in Figure 11.2.8) overlapping with an unattended figure in the unattended color (red in Figure 11.2.8), and a comparison figure (always white). Subjects had to indicate whether the green and white figures had the same shape or not, and reaction time was measured. The important question was whether the unattended red figure in the "prime" trial would affect performance on a later "probe" trial in which it reappeared as the attended (green) figure.

The critical experimental conditions were defined by the relation between the attended (green) figure on the probe trial and the unattended (red) figure on a previous

prime trial after some number of intervening trials. When they were on consecutive trials (lag = 1), a negative priming effect of 55 ms was obtained for trials in which the same shape was repeated (versus control trials in which a different shape preceded it). This result shows that the difference between Rock and Gutman's findings and Tipper's was not due to the novelty/familiarity of the stimulus materials because negative priming was obtained with novel meaningless figures very much like Rock and Gutman's.

Next, DeSchepper and Treisman investigated the effects of delay. Would the negative priming effect last for only a few trials, as Tipper (1985) had found with his familiar shapes, or would it last as long as the memory delays in Rock and Gutman's experiments? Being careful to show each critical figure in only two trials, they found the same amount of negative priming at lags of 1, 100, and 200 trials. Additional experiments showed that measurable effects of a previous exposure could be obtained up to one month later!

These results indicate that the processes underlying negative priming can be very long-lasting indeed if the figures in question are novel. Moreover, they demonstrate how sensitive indirect measures of memory can be. When explicit memory was tested at comparable delays of 72–104 trials using four-alternative forced-choice recognition procedures—that is, picking the one previously shown figure from among four alternatives—memory for unattended shapes was 26%, no higher than chance (25%). Even attended novel figures were recognized only a bit better than chance (34%) at these delays. The primary reason for the difference between the results of Rock and Gutman and those of Tipper and his associates therefore appears to be the use of direct versus indirect measures of visual memory.

11.2.2 Costs and Benefits of Attention

We now turn to the nature of spatial selection under conditions of explicit attention when the observer is expecting the possibility of some event that contains needed information. We have been presuming that if such an event occurs in a location that is attended, it is processed in ways that are somehow different from how it would be if it were not attended. But precisely what are the consequences of explicitly attending to one object or place rather than another?

Selective attention certainly sounds like a good thing if it enables an organism to focus the bulk of its visual processing capacity on objects, locations, and properties of interest. But this concentration of visual resources presumably comes at a price: Unattended objects and/or properties receive correspondingly *less* processing. This is the "double-edged sword" of selective attention: It may have significant costs as well as significant benefits. For it to be evolutionarily useful, the benefits should outweigh the costs.

The Attentional Cuing Paradigm. The question of how to measure the costs and benefits of selective attention has been studied most extensively by psychologist Michael Posner and his colleagues at the University of Oregon. Posner, Nissen, and Ogden (1978) developed an **attentional cuing paradigm** that has proven to be particularly well suited to examining costs and benefits. The task is simplicity itself: Subjects must press a button as soon as they detect a brief flash of light. The light is presented either to the left or to the right of a central fixation point, as shown in Figure 11.2.9.

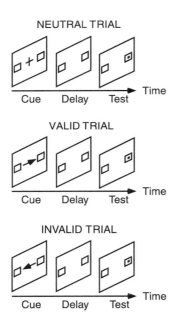

NEUTRAL TRIAL

Cue   Delay   Test   Time

VALID TRIAL

Cue   Delay   Test   Time

INVALID TRIAL

Cue   Delay   Test   Time

Figure 11.2.9 The attentional cuing paradigm. An arrow pointing toward the left or right box is used to cue subjects to attend there for a target stimulus. On valid trials, the target occurs in the cued location. On invalid trials, it occurs in the uncued location. On neutral trials, the cue is a plus sign.

The crucial manipulation that allowed the costs and benefits of selective attention to be studied was a cue presented in the center of the visual field before the test flash. This cue gave subjects information about where the test flash was likely to appear. A left-pointing arrow ($\leftarrow$) indicated that the flash would occur to the left of fixation on 80% of the left-arrow trials. A right-pointing arrow ($\rightarrow$) indicated that the flash would occur to the right of fixation on 80% of the right-arrow trials. A plus ($+$) indicated that the flash was equally likely to occur on either side of the fixation point. The cue was shown 1 second before the test flash appeared, and the subject's reaction time (RT) to respond to the flash was measured. Subjects were instructed to keep their eyes fixated on the center of the screen. To be sure that eye movements did not contaminate the results, however, all trials on which subjects moved their eyes were discarded.

The relation between the central cues ($\leftarrow$, $\rightarrow$, or $+$) and the position at which the test flash appeared (on the left or right side of the screen) defines three attentional conditions of interest:

1. *Neutral trials.* When the $+$ cue was presented, subjects got no prior information about the position of the test flash, so they presumably attended equally to both locations. RTs in this divided attention condition constitute a baseline against which RTs in the other two conditions can be compared to evaluate costs and benefits of focused attention.

2. *Valid trials.* On 80% of the arrow-cued trials, the flash appeared on the side to which the arrow pointed. On these "valid" trials, subjects are presumed to move their attention to the location cued by the arrow. If there are measurable benefits of selectively attending to the cued location, detection of the test flash should be faster on these valid trials than on the neutral trials.

3. *Invalid trials.* On 20% of the arrow-cued trials, the flash appeared on the side opposite the arrow, where subjects were *not* expecting it. If there are measurable costs of selectively attending to the cued location, detection of the test flash should be slower on these invalid trials than on both the neutral and the valid trials.

The results of this study are shown in Figure 11.2.10. Posner, Nissen, and Ogden (1978) found that RTs to the valid cues were about 30 ms faster than RTs to the neutral cues and that RTs to the invalid cues were about 30

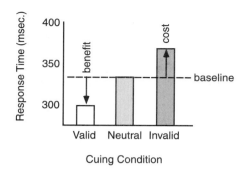

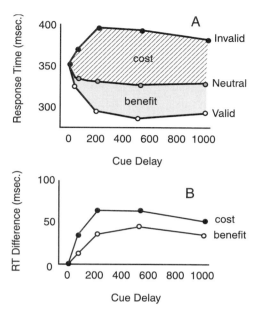

Figure 11.2.10 Costs and benefits of attention. The results in the cuing paradigm show that valid trials are faster than neutral trials (the benefit of correctly directing attention), whereas invalid trials are slower than neutral trials (the cost of misdirecting attention). (Data from Posner, Nissen, & Ogden, 1978.)

ms slower. This indicates that both costs and benefits are present in this particular task and that they are about equal. Given that the 30-ms benefit was obtained on 80% of the cued trials (the valid ones) and the 30-ms cost was obtained on only 20% (the invalid ones), the net benefits outweighed the net costs, at least in this objective sense.

Beyond measuring the basic costs and benefits due to attention, Posner and his associates also wanted to measure how long it takes subjects to shift attention to the cued location. They did this by performing a second experiment in which they varied the time interval between the presentation of the arrow cues and the test flashes (Posner, Nissen, & Ogden, 1978). The shortest interval was 50 ms, and the longest was 1000 ms. The experimenters reasoned that if the test flash were presented too soon after the cue, subjects would not have enough time to shift their attention to the cued location, and neither costs nor benefits would result. As the interval between cue and test increases, however, subjects would be increasingly likely to have completed the shift of attention by the time the test flash appeared. Thus, Posner and his colleagues predicted that both costs and benefits would increase as a function of the cue-to-test interval until some maximum level was reached, indicating the completion of the attentional shift.

The results of this experiment are shown in Figure 11.2.11A. Look first at the neutral trials in the middle. RTs to test flashes after the + cues were not much affected by the cue-test interval, presumably because they provided no information about the location of the test

Figure 11.2.11 Temporal development of costs and benefits. Graph A shows the response times for valid, invalid, and neutral conditions as a function of the delay between cue and test displays. Graph B plots the cost (invalid RT minus neutral RT) and benefit (neutral RT minus valid RT) of selective attention. (Part A after Posner, Nissen, & Ogden, 1978.)

flash. This is the baseline to which performance in the other two conditions should be compared. As in the first experiment, performance on valid trials was faster than that on neutral trials. The difference between these two curves therefore measures the benefit of selective attention (Figure 11.2.11B). Notice that the magnitude of this benefit increases steadily as the cue-to-test interval increases, reaching its highest level at about 400 ms. Performance on invalid trials is again slower than that on neutral trials. The difference between these two curves therefore measures the cost of selective attention (Figure 11.2.11B). Notice that the magnitude of this cost increases as the cue-to-test interval increases, reaching its highest level by 200 ms. Thus, we conclude that attentional shifts from one location to another accrue benefits to the attended location and costs to the unattended location. Moreover, we infer that it takes about 400 ms for people to complete such an attentional shift and that the costs seem to accrue slightly before the benefits.

Voluntary versus Involuntary Shifts of Attention. Attention researchers have extended this experi-

Visual Selection: Eye Movements and Attention

mental paradigm to study the effects of different kinds of attentional cues. You have probably noticed that when there is a sudden change in your field of view, such as the appearance of a new object, it seems to draw your attention automatically. This involuntary summoning of attention appears to be quite different from the voluntary, effortful process of directing attention according to the arrow cues in the experiments just described.

Jonides (1981) extended the cost/benefit paradigm to find out what kind of differences there might be between voluntary and involuntary shifts of attention. He examined voluntary shifts of attention using centrally presented symbolic cues such as the arrows at fixation as described above. These are sometimes called **push cues** because attention must be "pushed" from the symbolic cue to the cued location. He also examined involuntary shifts of attention by presenting peripheral arrows right next to the cued location. Because it was expected that these peripheral cues could effectively summon attention directly to that location, they are sometimes called **pull cues**. Valid and invalid trials for each cue type were constructed by presenting the target object in the cued location or some other location, respectively.

Several differences have been reported between voluntary and involuntary shifts of attention using push and pull cues:

1. *Pull cues produce benefits without costs.* Push cues produced both benefits and costs relative to the neutral condition. In contrast, pull cues produced benefits without corresponding costs.

2. *Pull cues work faster.* When the cue-to-test interval was varied, the results indicated that an equivalent shift of attention took only about 100 ms instead of 200–400 ms.

3. *Pull cues cannot be ignored.* When the validity of push cues was lowered to chance level (50%), subjects were able to ignore them. When the validity of pull cues was comparably reduced, they still produced significant benefits. Indeed, they did so even when subjects were instructed to actively ignore them.

Three Components of Shifting Attention. The results of these experiments on attentional cuing clearly demonstrate that attention has measurable effects on a task as simple as detecting the onset of a visual signal. They also show that it can be moved under either voluntary or involuntary control. Moving attention from one object to another seems intuitively simple enough, but how exactly does it happen?

Posner has suggested that a sequence of three component operations is required to shift attention from one object to another (e.g., Posner & Petersen, 1990; Posner, Walker, Friedrich, & Rafal, 1984):

1. *Disengagement.* Since attention is normally focused on some object, the first thing that must happen is to disengage it from that object.

2. *Movement.* Once it is disengaged, attention is free to move and must be directed toward the new object.

3. *Engagement.* After reaching the target, attention must be reengaged on the new object.

Moving attention from one object to another seems so simple that it is hard to believe that it is composed of these separate processes. However, evidence from neuropsychology suggests not only that they are distinct operations, but that they are controlled by three widely separated brain centers.

Patients with damage to parietal cortex (see Figure 11.2.12) show a pattern of costs and benefits on the cuing task, indicating that they have difficulty *disengaging* their attention from objects. Patients with damage to the superior colliculus in the midbrain show a different pattern of results, suggesting that they have difficulty *moving* their attention. (These patients are also severely impaired in making voluntary eye movements, a fact that suggests an important connection between attention and eye movements to which we will return at the end of this chapter.) Finally, patients with damage to certain centers in the thalamus, including the lateral pulvinar nucleus, appear to have difficulty *engaging* their attention on a new object. Thus, the seemingly simple and unitary operation of shifting attention from one object to another actually requires a coordinated effort among three widely separated regions of the brain. When neural functioning in these areas is impaired, attentional movements fail in predictable ways (see Posner & Raichle, 1994, for a review).

11.2.3 Theories of Spatial Attention

How can we understand visual attention theoretically? As is often the case in cognitive science, the first step in theorizing about a mental process is to find an appropri-

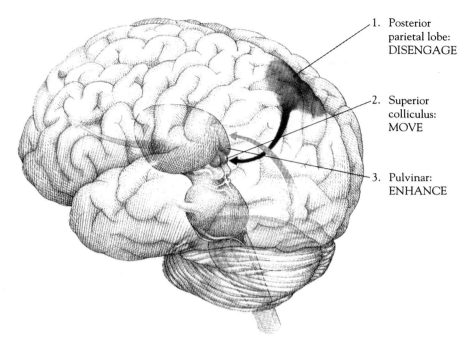

1. Posterior
   parietal lobe:
   DISENGAGE

2. Superior
   colliculus:
   MOVE

3. Pulvinar:
   ENHANCE

Figure 11.2.12 Three brain centers that are involved in orienting attention. Areas of parietal cortex control the disengagement of attention from objects; circuitry in the superior colliculus in the midbrain controls the movement of attention from one location to another; and certain centers in the thalamus, including the lateral pulvinar nucleus, control the engagement of attention on a new object. (From Posner & Raichle, 1994.)

ate metaphor. Because attention is a rather mysterious, unobservable entity, theorists have tried to understand it in terms of physical systems they can observe directly and therefore understand better. We have already encountered one such metaphor: Attention is like an internal eye. The internal eye metaphor captures some important facts about attention. Two of these facts are that it appears to move from object to object and that it has a fovealike center where processing is concentrated.

The internal eye metaphor is of limited theoretical utility, however, because there is a sense in which it is the operation of the eyes (i.e., vision) that we are trying to explain in the first place. The eye metaphor therefore has the potential problem of infinite regress: If attention is like an internal eye and if the real eye has an internal eye of attention, then does the internal attentional eye also have its own internal eye? And what about the internal eye of that internal eye? Even if the answers to these questions are negative—there may be just one internal eye of attention—many theorists find it preferable to liken attention to something simpler and better understood than an eye.

The Spotlight Metaphor. Among the most crucial aspects of the internal eye metaphor are the selection of one region on which to concentrate processing and the ability to move from one region to another over time. A simpler metaphor that captures both of these characteristics is that attention is like a spotlight (e.g., Posner, 1978). According to this **spotlight theory**, the object at the location where the spotlight of attention is focused is "illuminated" so that it stands out and can be processed more effectively than the less illuminated objects in other regions. Once that object has been processed, the attentional spotlight can be shifted to a different location by moving along a path from the present object to the next one, presumably through the disengage/move/ engage sequence of elementary attentional operations mentioned earlier.

The spotlight metaphor of attention has proved both popular and productive. Many experimental results can be understood in terms of it, and new experiments have been devised to test some of its predictions. Consider how Posner's cuing results might be explained, for example. On a cued trial, subjects use the cue to move the attentional spotlight from the central cue to the appropriate location. If the test flash occurs there (a valid trial), it is already in the spotlight of attention, so it can be processed quickly without requiring any subsequent attentional shift. However, if the test flash occurs on the unexpected side (an invalid trial), the spotlight is in the wrong location and must be moved to the correct one before the response can be made. If there is no directional cue (a neutral trial), the spotlight stays in the center and would be moved only half as far as it would on an invalid trial. The spotlight metaphor can thus account for the basic pattern of results shown in Figure 11.2.10. It can also account for the results obtained when the cue-to-test interval is varied, because it will take some amount of time for the attentional spotlight to reach the cued side from the center.

Further experiments have tested a number of predictions derived from the spotlight metaphor. Some have received strong support, but others are controversial. Among the most interesting predictions are the following:

1. *Rate of motion.* The amount of time it takes to shift attention to a target object should increase systematically with the distance over which it must be moved, as though a spotlight were scanning from one place to another. Tsal (1983) has obtained evidence supporting this prediction and has estimated the rate of motion experimentally at about 8 ms per degree of visual angle.

2. *Trajectory.* When a spotlight is moved from one object to another, it illuminates the objects along the path between them. Some evidence suggests that the same is true when attention is moved (e.g., Shulman, Remington, & McLean, 1979).

3. *Size.* Spotlights are generally fixed in size. Eriksen and Eriksen (1974) reported evidence suggesting that the attentional spotlight is about 1 degree of visual angle in size. (As we will see, however, there is also evidence that it can vary in size.)

4. *Unitariness.* A spotlight can be moved from place to place, but it cannot be divided into two or more separate regions. Eriksen and Yeh (1985) reported evidence

suggesting that the same is true of attention. (But again there is also evidence for the opposite conclusion.)

Despite its successes, there are a number of problems with the simple spotlight metaphor that have led theorists to consider alternatives. One difficulty is that, despite Eriksen and Eriksen's (1974) conclusion that attention covers only about 1 degree of visual angle in their particular experiment, it seems that under normal viewing conditions attention can cover a much wider area of the visual field, such as when you look globally at a large object or even a whole scene. It also seems that attention can be narrowed to a tiny region of the visual field, as when you scrutinize a small detail. These considerations have led to an alternative metaphor.

The Zoom Lens Metaphor. The **zoom lens theory** likens attention to the operation of a zoom lens on a camera that has variable spatial scope (Eriksen & St. James, 1986). The analogy is not exact, however, for the idea is that attention can cover a variable area of the visual field is usually coupled with the further assumption that varying the size of the attended region changes the amount of visual detail available within it. With a relatively wide attentional scope, only coarse spatial resolution is thought to be possible, whereas with relatively narrow scope, fine resolution is possible.

Shulman and Wilson (1987) tested this idea experimentally. They showed subjects large letters made up of small letters, like the stimuli Navon (1977) used to study global and local processing (see Section 7.6.3), as illustrated in Figure 7.6.9. On some trials, subjects had to identify the large letters, and on other trials the small ones. Shortly after each such trial, they had to respond to a sinusoidal grating that was either low in spatial frequency (wide fuzzy stripes) or high in spatial frequency (thin fuzzy stripes) (see Section 4.2.1). Shulman and Wilson found that responses to low-spatial-frequency gratings were enhanced after subjects had attended to the large global letter and that responses to high-spatial-frequency gratings were enhanced after subjects had attended to the small local letters. This is precisely what would be expected if attention worked like a zoom lens that took time to be adjusted to different sizes and spatial resolutions, large sizes being associated with coarse resolution (low spatial frequencies) and small sizes with fine resolution (high spatial frequencies). These findings are therefore widely cited as supporting the zoom lens metaphor.

Notice that the spotlight metaphor is actually compatible with the zoom lens metaphor in the sense that they can be usefully combined. One can easily conceive of a spotlight that is variable in size as well as position. If the total power of the spotlight is fixed, then a wide beam will illuminate a large region dimly, and a narrow beam will illuminate a small region intensely. This connection between beam width and brightness is not exactly the same as the presumed relation between attentional scope and resolution, but it provides a relatively simple metaphor for thinking about how attention might be distributed over space in a way that includes position, scope, and effectiveness.

Space-Based versus Object-Based Approaches.

The metaphors for attention that we have considered thus far—an internal eye, a spotlight, and a zoom lens—all have one important thing in common: They assume that attention selects a region of space. A spotlight, for example, illuminates whatever lies within its beam, whether it is an object, part of an object, parts of two or more nearby objects, or nothing at all. An important alternative to these **space-based theories** is the possibility that attention actually selects a perceptual object (or group of objects) rather than a region of space (e.g., Duncan, 1984). Notice that these **object-based theories** of attention allow a good deal of leeway in how attention might be deployed, because of differences in what constitutes a perceptual object. It could be directed at a single complete object, part of an object, or even an aggregation of objects, as discussed in Chapter 6 when we considered the hierarchical structure of perceptual organization.

Identifying perceptual objects as the domain of selective attention might make object-based accounts seem too ill-defined to be useful, but it does impose significant constraints on the distribution of attention. Unlike space-based theories, for example, object-based theories of attention cannot account for selection of arbitrary portions of two or more different objects, even if they are located within a spatially circumscribed region such as might be illuminated by a spotlight. Also unlike space-based theories, object-based theories can, under certain conditions, account for attentional selection of several discontinuous regions of space. These conditions require that the "object" of attention be a perceptual grouping of several objects whose members are typically defined by some common property (such as color or motion) with other objects interspersed between them. If attention can be allocated just to the set of objects within such a group, it need not occupy a connected region of space. The spotlight and zoom lens metaphors require that a unified region of space be selected.

Some of the strongest evidence for an object-based view of attention comes from a neurological condition known as Balint's syndrome, in which patients are unable to perceive more than one object at any time. We will discuss this syndrome later (in Section 11.2.7) when we consider the physiology of attention, but there is also good experimental evidence for object-based attention with normal perceivers. One of the most widely cited studies is an experiment by Duncan (1984). He reasoned that if attention is allocated to objects rather than to regions of space, it should be easier for subjects to detect two different properties of the same object than two properties of different objects that lie within the same region of space. He showed subjects displays like the one illustrated in Figure 11.2.13. Each stimulus consisted of two objects: a box with a gap in one side and a line running through the box. Each object had two relevant attributes. The box was either short or long and had the gap slightly to the left or right of center. The line was either dotted or dashed and tilted clockwise or counterclockwise from horizontal. After a brief presentation, subjects had to report either one or two attributes. When two attributes were tested, they could belong to the same object or different objects. Duncan found that if the two attributes belonged to different objects, subjects were worse at detecting the second property than

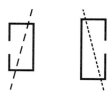

Figure 11.2.13 Stimuli for Duncan's experiment on object-based attention. Subjects had to report two features of a stimulus display that varied on four dimensions: line slant (left or right), line type (dashed or dotted), box length (long or short), and gap placement (left or right). Performance was better when the two features belonged to the same object than to different objects.

the first. But if they belonged to the same object, no such difference was obtained.

These results can easily be explained within an object-based view of attention. When the two properties come from the same object, no shift of attention is required because attention is defined by the single object. When they come from different objects, an attentional shift is required to detect the second property, taking additional time and therefore reducing accuracy. This pattern of results is more difficult to square with space-based theories, however, because the two objects occupy essentially the same region of space. A roughly circular spotlight that illuminates either the box or the line, for instance, will necessarily illuminate the other object. It is therefore not clear how such a difference in detecting properties would arise unless objects were somehow implicated in the allocation of attention. Notice that if a space-based theory allows the attentional spotlight to be shaped tightly around specific objects (e.g., LaBerge & Brown, 1989), they take on a significantly object-based flavor.

There is also recent evidence from a Posner-type cuing experiment suggesting that attention operates at an object-based level. Egly, Driver, and Rafal (1994) showed subjects displays containing two rectangles oriented either horizontally or vertically, as shown in Figure 11.2.14. After the initial presentation, the edges of one end of one rectangle brightened briefly, providing a pull cue to attend to that location. Subjects were then to make a response as quickly as possible when a dark square appeared anywhere in the display. When the cue was valid, the target square appeared briefly in the cued end of the cued object. There were two different types of invalid cues trials, however. In the *same object condition*, the target square appeared in the opposite end of the cued rectangle. In the *different object condition*, it appeared in the uncued object but at the same end as the cue.

As usual in the cuing paradigm, responses were faster when the target appeared at the cued location than when it appeared at either of the uncued locations. The results for the uncued locations showed object-based attentional effects, however, in that the same object condition was faster than the different object condition,

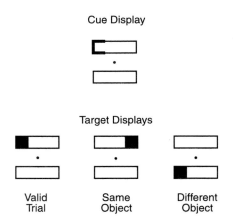

Figure 11.2.14 Stimuli for an experiment showing both space- and object-based attention. One end of two rectangular boxes was cued before presentation of the target in one of three locations. Same-object responses were faster than different-object responses, indicating an object-based attentional effect.

even though their distances from the cued location were equal. This finding suggests that switching from one object to another incurs an additional cost that cannot be attributed to distance.[3]

A third finding that lends credence to the object-based view concerns an observer's ability to keep track of several moving objects at once. Pylyshyn and Storm (1988) showed subjects a random array of static dots and designated several of them as target objects to be attended by flashing them on and off. All the dots then began to move in quasi-random (but continuous) trajectories, and subjects were instructed to try to keep track of the ones that were initially designated as targets. After several seconds of such motion, one of the elements flashed, and subjects were asked whether or not that particular dot was one of the initially designated targets. Pylyshyn and Storm found that subjects could track as many as five dots at once.

If one believes that this tracking task requires attention (and Pylyshyn and Storm do not), these results pose significant problems for space-based theories of attention. First, most space-based theories assume that the region to which attention can be allocated is a unitary,

---

[3] More recent experiments have shown that the "objects" in question are perceptually completed objects rather than retinally defined objects. Moore, Yantis, and Vaughan (1998) concluded this after finding results similar to those of Egly, Driver, and Rafal when the different ends of the same-object stimuli had been retinally separated by an occluding object. They also found this pattern of results when the two ends of the same object were defined only by illusory contours.

convex, connected area. However, the tracking task seems to require observers to attend to a number of disconnected spatial regions at the same time. Equally important, the trajectories of regions through space are defined only by virtue of the objects that traverse them. How else could attention be allocated to the proper regions of space at the proper times?

These results have another feature that is at least somewhat troubling from the object-based perspective, however: They seem to indicate that attention can be split among multiple objects. One could, of course, extend the object-based view specifically to allow for attention to be divided among some small number of objects. Indeed, this is how Pylyshyn and Storm (1988) interpreted their results. But there is another possibility that does not require giving up the unitary nature of attention. Perhaps observers keep track of the multiple dots by grouping them initially into a single superordinate object and attending to that group as a unitary entity. The designated dots could then be perceived, for example, as the corners of a virtual polygon whose shape changes over time as the dots move. Yantis (1992) has tested predictions from this hypothesis and found support for them in several experiments.

The current debate between object-based and space-based theories of attention often implies that they are mutually exclusive—that one or the other is correct but not both. This would presumably be the case if attention operates at just one level in the visual system. But what if attention operates at multiple levels? At an early image-processing level, such as Marr's primal sketch, a space-based definition of attention is the only thing that makes much sense, because in this low-level representation, coherent "perceptual objects" have not yet been designated. But at a higher level, after organizational processes have identified figures against grounds, objects could certainly be the basis for allocating attention. Both hypotheses may therefore be correct, just at different levels of the visual system.

11.2.4 Selective Attention to Properties

The theories of selective attention we have just discussed —including spotlights, zoom lenses, and even object-based theories—are designed to account for spatial selection. They cannot be the whole story of visual attention if its capabilities extend to selection of different properties, however. When you inspect a prospective purchase at a clothing store, for example, you seem to be able to focus selectively on its color, style (shape), texture, and size as you consider the garment. This ability appears to imply that attention must have important nonspatial components that select for other sorts of properties. Such evidence is anecdotal at best, however. Can people really attend to different properties of the same object independently or does attending to one necessarily result in perceiving them all? In this section we will consider experimental evidence that bears on this question.

The Stroop Effect. Early experiments seemed to indicate that if an object is attended, certain properties are processed automatically, even if the observer is trying to ignore them. This implies that selection by properties is either nonexistent or incomplete.

The best-known evidence for this conclusion comes from the **Stroop effect**, named for the psychologist, J. Ridley Stroop, who discovered it in 1935. The Stroop effect refers to the fact that when subjects are required to name the color of ink in which color words are printed, they show massive interference when the color word itself conflicts with the ink color to be named (Stroop, 1935). Examples of stimuli that produce this effect are shown in Color Plate 11.1.

You can demonstrate the Stroop effect for yourself by timing how long it takes you to name the ink colors in the column of X's on the left (the control condition) versus the conflicting color-word condition in the center versus the compatible color-word condition on the right. Even without timing yourself with a stopwatch, you will find it much more difficult to get through the middle column than the other two. This fact indicates that shape information is being processed automatically whenever the color of the word is attended and that the response to the identity of the word interferes with naming the ink color. This finding seems to imply that, unlike our intuitions based on everyday experience, selective attention to color, independent of shape, may not be possible after all.

One might wonder whether this interference is specific to color. Further research has shown that it is not. Stroop interference occurs, for instance, if the subject's task is to name an object that is drawn in outline around the name of a different object, as illustrated in Figure 11.2.15A. It also occurs when subjects have to name the

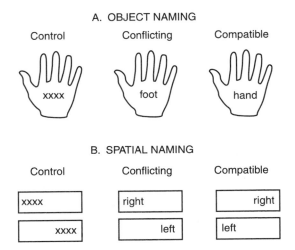

A. OBJECT NAMING

Control Conflicting Compatible

xxxx foot hand

B. SPATIAL NAMING

Control Conflicting Compatible

xxxx

xxxx

right

left

right

left

Figure 11.2.15 Additional Stroop effects. Stroop compatibility effects are also found in naming drawings of objects when object names are presented inside them (A) and in naming spatial locations when location names are the objects to be located (B).

location of letter strings (LEFT, RIGHT, or XXXX) when they are presented on either the left or right side of the display, as shown in Figure 11.2.15B (Clark & Brownell, 1975, 1976).

Interestingly, interference in the reverse direction does not occur in the standard Stroop task: Color words can be read just as quickly when they are printed in a conflicting color of ink as when they are printed in the compatible color. This shows that some selective attention to properties is indeed possible. It also suggests that there may be something special about reading printed words. One important consideration is that reading is a salient and highly practiced perceptual task. Educated people spend a significant portion of their waking hours reading printed words, and this degree of practice may result in highly automatic processing of letters and words. Another relevant factor is that there is a much more direct association between the printed color word and the sound of the color name (which is what the subject must produce) than there is between the color itself and the sound of the color name. That is, the letter-to-sound correspondences of English may provide more direct access to the name than the color does. The importance of this fact is supported by the finding that Stroop interference is reduced significantly when subjects must press different buttons to indicate ink color rather than when they must say color names. It

also explains why noncolor words that begin with the same letters as color words also produce Stroop interference, such as ROD instead of RED or BLOB instead to BLUE. (See MacLeod, 1991, for a review of Stroop effects.) These factors suggest that we should consider evidence from other kinds of tasks that do not depend so heavily on the special properties of reading printed words before we draw conclusions from what may be a very special case.

Integral versus Separable Dimensions. Psychologist Wendell Garner of Yale University has also attempted to answer questions about selective attention to different properties, including both discrete features and continuous dimensions. From an extensive series of experiments, he concluded that there is no single, simple answer. Different patterns of results arise, depending on the particular pair of dimensions being studied. His findings led him to distinguish between two different relations that can hold between pairs of properties or dimensions: *separability* and *integrality* (Garner, 1974).

1. *Separable dimensions.* Pairs of dimensions are **separable** if people can selectively attend to one or the other at will, without interference from the unattended property. The internal representations of separable dimensions therefore appear to be completely independent. Classic examples of separable dimensions are the color and shape of an object, both of which Garner found could be perceived selectively.

2. *Integral dimensions.* Pairs of dimensions are **integral** if people cannot selectively attend to one without also perceiving the other. Classic examples of integral dimensions are the saturation and lightness of a color. These two dimensions seem to be processed together whenever one attends to the color of an object.

The integral/separable dichotomy arose in a number of different experimental paradigms that Garner developed. The most powerful and widely studied method concerned a set of closely related tasks requiring speeded classification. Subjects were presented with various subsets of four stimuli defined by two different dimensions and were asked to classify them in different ways on different tasks. The speed of the perceptual discrimination was measured by reaction time. We will illustrate these conditions using the example of figures

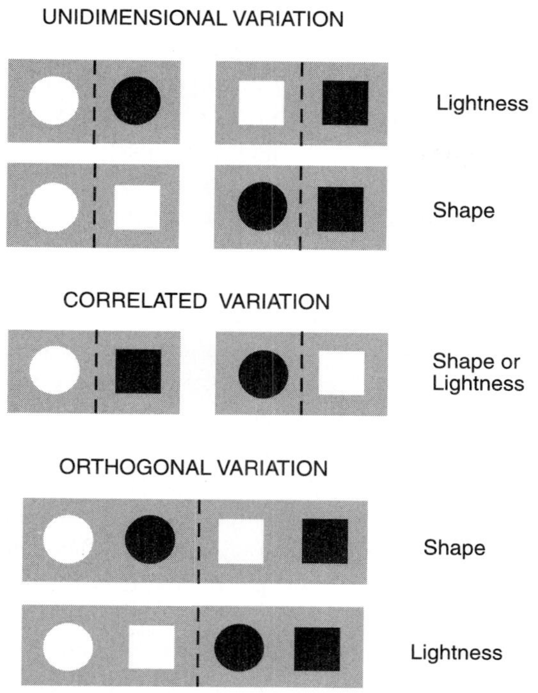

UNIDIMENSIONAL VARIATION

Lightness

Shape

CORRELATED VARIATION

Shape or Lightness

ORTHOGONAL VARIATION

Shape

Lightness

Figure 11.2.16 Three speeded classification tasks studied by Garner. Subjects were required to discriminate between two values of one dimension when the other dimension was held constant (unidimensional variation), when the other dimension covaried (correlated variation), or when the other dimension varied independently (orthogonal variation).

defined by their lightness and shape, as depicted in Figure 11.2.16. Each gray rectangle represents a block of many trials in which subjects had to classify the individual stimuli within it into two classes according to the rule implied by the dashed line. For example, in the first two blocks of trials the task might be to classify individual stimuli according to lightness alone, as indicated in the first row of stimuli in Figure 11.2.16. In this case, subjects would have to press one button for white figures and another for black figures. In later blocks of trials, the task would be to classify according to shape alone, as indicated in the second row of stimuli in Figure 11.2.16. In this case, they would have to press one button for squares and another for circles. Other blocks of trials would require the other discriminations indicated in the other rows of Figure 11.2.16.

There are three critical conditions for determining whether the two given dimensions are integral or separable. These conditions are defined in terms of how the unattended property varies with respect to the attended one within different blocks of trials, as illustrated in Figure 11.2.16.

1. **Unidimensional variation condition**. Subjects are told to classify the stimuli according to their value on one of the two dimensions while the other dimension is held constant.

On a unidimensional block of trials subjects would classify white squares and black squares according to lightness; on another block of trials they would classify white circles and black circles according to lightness. Thus, the shape of the figures is constant within each block of trials in which lightness is the dimension of classification. The same procedure would be followed for the other dimension on further blocks of trials—for example, white squares and white circles would be classified by shape in one block, and black squares and black circles by shape in another block. Note that in these unidimensional variation conditions, only two of the four stimuli are presented in any given block.

2. **Correlated variation condition**. Subjects again are told to classify the stimuli according to the value on just one dimension, but the other dimension varies in a correlated fashion.

For instance, white squares would be discriminated against black circles in one block of trials. In another block, black squares would be discriminated against white circles. In the correlated condition, therefore, subjects could use either of the two properties—or both simultaneously—to perform the classification task. If performance in these correlated conditions is faster than in either of the two unidimensional conditions, the difference in reaction time is called a **redundancy gain** because the two properties in the correlated condition are redundant with each other. As in the unidimensional case, only two of the four stimuli are presented in any one block.

3. **Orthogonal variation condition**. Subjects again have to classify according to a single specified dimension, but this time the other dimension varies independently (orthogonally) so that all four stimuli are presented within each block of trials.

On one block of trials subjects would have to classify all four stimuli according to shape alone (square versus

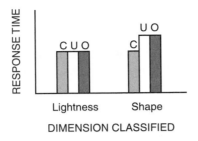

A. SEPARABLE DIMENSIONS

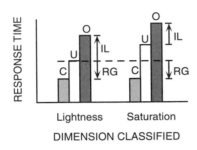

B. INTEGRAL DIMENSIONS

Figure 11.2.17 Characteristic patterns of results for separable versus integral dimensions. (C = correlated, U = unidimensional, O = orthogonal, IL = interference loss, RG = redundancy gain; see text for details.)

circle), and in another block according to lightness alone (black versus white). In these orthogonal conditions, subjects have to actively ignore the second dimension to perform accurately. It therefore might take additional time to effectively separate the relevant dimension from the irrelevant one. If performance in these orthogonal conditions is slower than for the corresponding unidimensional case, the difference in reaction time is called an **interference loss**.

Figure 11.2.17A shows idealized results that might be found for these three conditions. Reaction times in the unidimensional conditions (U) give the baseline data for each dimension and show that discriminating shape takes longer than discriminating lightness. Comparing these times to those of the correlated conditions (C) shows no significant differences from the faster unidimensional case (in this case, lightness), indicating that there is no redundancy gain when either or both properties could be used to make the discrimination. The results of the orthogonal condition also show no significant difference from the corresponding unidimensional case,

indicating no interference loss. This is the pattern of results expected for separable dimensions, assuming they can be selectively attended at will: neither redundancy gain nor interference loss. Such results therefore support the view that selective attention to properties is possible.

When the stimuli are single color chips that vary in saturation and lightness, however, the pattern of results changes dramatically to that characteristic of integral dimensions. As shown in Figure 11.2.17B, the correlated (C) condition produces a significant redundancy gain (RG) compared to the unidimensional (U) condition in both cases. The orthogonal (O) condition also produces a significant interference loss (IL) relative to the corresponding unidimensional (U) condition in both cases. It is as though subjects cannot pay attention to either one of the properties without automatically perceiving the other. If the two properties vary together, they help performance; if they vary independently, they hurt performance. Quite a different pattern of results emerges, however, if the same two dimensions of color are used in two spatially separated color chips. There is now no redundancy gain and no interference loss (that is, the same pattern as in Figure 11.2.17A). Thus, when lightness and saturation are spatially separated, they are attentionally separable. This fact reflects the efficiency of spatial selection.

Garner developed several other tasks using pairs of properties whose results he expected to support the distinction between separable and integral dimensions. One such task was to have subjects make a particular kind of similarity judgment. On each trial they were presented with three stimuli and asked to indicate which two seemed most similar. The three stimuli differed on two dimensions, as shown in Figure 11.2.18. The question was which pair subjects would see as most similar: Y and Z, which were closer together in the two-dimensional space of stimulus attributes but differed on both dimensions, or X and Y, which had exactly the same value on one dimension but were farther apart in the stimulus space. The results of many experiments showed that subjects tend to choose the "close" pair (Y and Z) as being most similar when the two dimensions were found to be integral in the speeded classification tasks described above. This situation is illustrated in Figure 11.2.18B by the dimensions of a rectangle's width and height. Most people see Y as being more similar to Z than to X in this example. In contrast, people tend to

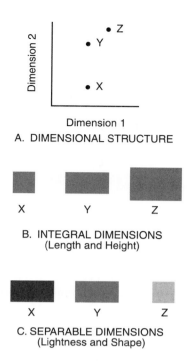

A. DIMENSIONAL STRUCTURE

B. INTEGRAL DIMENSIONS
(Length and Height)

C. SEPARABLE DIMENSIONS
(Lightness and Shape)

Figure 11.2.18 Garner's similarity classification task. Three two-featured stimuli are presented such that one pair (X and Y) share the same value on one dimension, whereas another pair (Y and Z) are closer together in the dimensional space. Integral dimensions tend to produce classification based on overall similarity (Y and Z are judged most similar), whereas separable dimensions produce classification based on identity on one dimension (X and Y are judged most similar).

choose the "same-value" pair as being most similar when the two dimensions were found to be separable in the speeded classification tasks. This situation is illustrated in Figure 11.2.18C by the dimensions of shape and lightness. Here, most people see Y as being more similar to X than to Z. The remaining pair (X and Z) is almost never chosen as being most similar in either case.

These results make sense in terms of Garner's attentional interpretation of integrality versus separability. If people cannot selectively attend to either dimension alone, as in the case of integral dimensions, then both dimensions should affect their perceptions of similarity. If it is easy to attend selectively to either dimension alone, however, it makes sense to select the pair that has exactly the same value on one dimension.

Developmental theorists have often suggested that perceptual processing in children develops from an early "holistic" mode to a later "analytic" one (e.g., Gibson,

1969). This idea has been tested most rigorously within Garner's framework of integral versus separable dimensions and has received considerable support. Children younger than about 6 years of age process almost all dimensions integrally, whereas older children process some integrally and others separably. The usual task for assessing this developmental trend is similarity judgment with triads of stimuli, as shown in Figure 11.2.18. The critical result is that for the same separable pair of dimensions, adults and older children choose the dimensionally identical pair (X and Y) as being more similar, whereas young children choose the closest pair (Y and Z) as being more similar (Shepp & Swartz, 1976; Smith & Kemler, 1977; Smith & Evans, 1989).

Garner's results from many experiments exploring the relations among different features and dimensions eventually led him to posit two other types of relations:

3. **Asymmetrically integral dimensions** are pairs of dimensions in which one property can be selectively attended to the exclusion of the other, but the reverse is not true. In other words, the first property is separable from the second, but the second is integral with the first. This pattern of results corresponds to the relation of color and word identity in the Stroop task: Color naming is strongly influenced by word identity, but word naming is not influenced by color identity.

4. **Configural dimensions** are pairs of properties—usually parts rather than features—that combine to produce a new, emergent property, such as symmetry or closure. A classic example is the combination of left- and right-facing parentheses, for which particular combinations produce vertically symmetrical configurations that are either closed "()" or open ")(" versus asymmetrical configurations that are left-facing "))" or right-facing "((" (Pomerantz & Garner, 1973). (We considered this kind of configural effect in Section 9.6.3 when we discussed the configural superiority effect.)

Garner's findings as well as Stroop interference effects show that selective attention to different properties is possible for some pairs of dimensions but not for others. They therefore indicate that metaphors based solely on the spatial distribution of attention are inadequate to account for selective phenomena of perception. A broader theoretical framework is needed to integrate spatial and property aspects of attention. Such an approach has been developed and tested by psychologist

Anne Treisman in her feature integration theory. To understand how she arrived at and tested this theory, we must first consider how visual processing might differ when attention is spatially distributed versus when it is focused.

11.2.5 Distributed versus Focused Attention

We claimed at the outset of this section that attention can function as a mechanism of perceptual selection. We reasoned that because there is far more information in a single visual scene than any observer can perceive at once, only a portion of it is selected for further processing to avoid sensory overload. This view of the function of attention implies that visual processing before attentional selection is somehow fundamentally different from the processing that occurs after it. This distinction is classically referred to as *preattentive* versus *attentive* (or sometimes *postattentive*) processing (e.g., Treisman, 1985). We will avoid this terminology because Mack and Rock (1998) have made a convincing case that all experimental tasks normally used to define so-called "preattentive" vision constitute conditions in which attention is explicitly deployed to perceive an expected target at an unknown location. Instead, we will call the mode of processing that occurs when subjects are prepared for the target to appear in any location **distributed attention** and we will call that which occurs when they have selected a single perceptual object **focused attention**. We thus take the view that both distributed attention and focused attention constitute examples of attentive processing, but ones that nevertheless differ in important respects.

The key difference between distributed attention and focused attention is **parallel processing** versus **serial processing**. The distributed processing that occurs before focused attention occurs in *parallel*, that is, simultaneously over the whole visual field. Processing that occurs after focused attention is *serial*, that is, a sequence of attentional fixations, each of which covers a limited region of space. Image-processing operations—such as finding edges and regions defined by luminance, color, texture, motion, and so forth—are generally thought to be performed automatically and in parallel. They would be sufficient to construct all the structures in Marr's (1982) primal sketch, for example. It is less clear whether information about surfaces in depth is also processed in

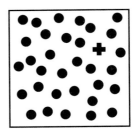

Figure 11.2.19 Pop-out in visual search. An element that differs from all others in a single feature pops out effortlessly from the display.

this way. But certainly by the time discrete perceptual objects have been created, attention can be selectively focused on one object (or a group of them) to the exclusion of other objects in the visual field. The closer scrutiny afforded by focused attention is thought to allow more detailed information about the chosen object to be processed.

Visual Pop-Out. A question of considerable theoretical interest is: What kinds of information can be processed in parallel without focused attention? In a series of influential papers, Treisman and her colleagues proposed that the phenomenon of **visual pop-out** indicates distributed attentional processing (e.g., Treisman, 1985; Treisman & Gelade, 1980; Treisman & Gormican, 1988). Pop-out occurs when an observer is looking at a field of similar objects, and one of them appears simply to "pop out" of the rest phenomenologically because it is very different from the others. In effect, the different item calls attention to itself, much as a moving object does in an otherwise stationary visual environment or a single red element does among a field of blue ones. Consider Figure 11.2.19, for example. All except one of the objects are circles, but the one cross effortlessly pops out from everything else. No laborious scrutiny of individual elements is required to detect its presence.

The phenomenon of visual pop-out for a given pair of mutually exclusive properties (such as a diagonal line within a field of many vertical lines or a red square in a field of many green squares) implies that the visual system can detect these properties in parallel over the whole visual field. If it did not, the different element would not pop out immediately but would require a sequential search through individual elements in the

A. PARALLEL SEARCH

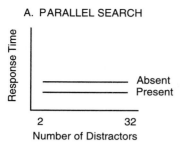

B. SERIAL SEARCH

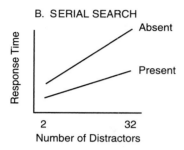

Figure 11.2.20 Patterns of response times for parallel and serial search. In parallel search, response times do not vary as the number of distractors increases. In serial search, response time increases linearly, the slope of the target-absent displays being twice that of target-present displays.

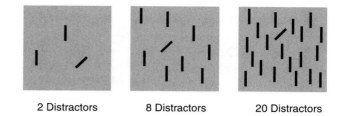

| 2 Distractors | 8 Distractors | 20 Distractors |

Figure 11.2.21 An example of parallel search. The tilted line segments can be detected as quickly among 20 distractors as among 2, indicating a parallel search process.

display. Effortful serial search is a process that is believed to characterize focused attentional processing.

This line of thinking led Treisman and Gelade (1980) to develop a specific experimental method for determining whether properties are processed serially or in parallel. Its logic is that if a property can be analyzed simultaneously over the whole visual field (that is, with distributed attention), a single target object with that property should be detected in the same amount of time, no matter how many other objects are in the display. However, if the display must be searched sequentially for a target object having that property (that is, with focused attention), the time required to find it should increase linearly with the number of items in the display.

These two patterns of predicted results are illustrated in Figure 11.2.20. Example stimuli for such a task are shown in Figure 11.2.21, in which line orientation is the relevant search dimension within displays containing 2, 8, and 20 distractor elements. Detecting the presence of the diagonal target line within these stimuli produces a flat response time function like that shown in Figure

11.2.20A. Such results indicate that the diagonal line can be detected among vertical lines simultaneously over all spatial locations. Making such a discrimination thus appears to be within the capabilities of distributed attentional vision. Similar results indicate that pop-out occurs when subjects search for targets that differ from distractors in color, shape, size, and a host of other simple visual properties.

Treisman and her colleagues interpret visual pop-out of a given feature as evidence that it is elementary in visual processing, that is, that it is one of the basic properties used by the visual system in constructing its initial representation of the image. They further argue that the findings from visual pop-out experiments are broadly consistent with what might be expected from the known physiology of the visual system. Explorations of visual cortex using single-cell recording and autoradiographic techniques (see Section 2.2.3) have identified many different regions that code distinct visual properties (Zeki, 1978). We have already discussed the fact that cells that are sensitive to different orientations and spatial frequencies are present in V1. Other cortical regions appear to code properties such as color, binocular disparity, and motion (see Section 4.4). One of the striking aspects of the architecture of these cortical regions is that their cells are arranged in clear *retinotopic maps*: sheets of cells whose spatial arrangement corresponds topographically to the 2-D positions of their receptive fields on the retina. Thus, the visual system appears to analyze the visual image into separate representations for different properties, each of which is organized by position. Activity within such maps could account for the spatially parallel detection of the odd element in a pop-out experiment if unique activity in a retinotopic map calls focused attention to that location.

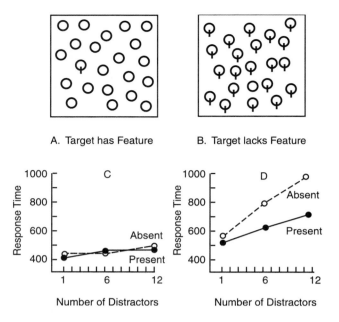

A. Target has Feature   B. Target lacks Feature

Figure 11.2.22 Search asymmetry. A circle with a line through it can be detected within a background of circles (A) much more quickly than a circle can be detected within a background of circles with lines through them (B). (Data from Treisman & Souther, 1985.)

Search Asymmetry. Treisman and Souther (1985) extended the investigation of visual pop-out by asking whether this phenomenon was symmetrical. For example, would a single circle with a line through its contour pop-out of a display containing a background of many circles without such lines (Figure 11.2.22A) as easily as a single circle does against a background of many circles with intersecting lines (Figure 11.2.22B)?

Treisman and Souther measured the time required to detect targets among distractors for several pairs of features, systematically varying which feature was the target and which was the distractor. In many cases, they found a marked asymmetry in the detection time. For example, when subjects had to detect a circle with a line through it against a background of simple circles, the target popped out, as evidenced by flat search functions (Figure 11.2.22C). When they had to detect a simple circle against a background of circles with lines through them, however, the search function increased steeply as a function of the number of distractors (Figure 11.2.22D), the pattern indicative of serial search. Similar asymmetries have been reported for other dimensions: A tilted line can be detected more quickly against

a background of vertical lines than the reverse; a circle with a gap in it can be detected more quickly against complete circles than the reverse; an ellipse can be detected more quickly against circles than the reverse; and a curved line can be detected more quickly against a background of straight lines than the reverse (Treisman & Gormican, 1988; Treisman & Souther, 1985).

Treisman has interpreted such results as indicating that a target defined by the presence of a feature can be detected against a background of distractors defined by its absence more quickly than the reverse. To understand why this might be true, consider the case of the circle with a line through it (Figure 11.2.22A). Here the discriminative feature is the straight line segment. When a circle-with-line is the target, the retinotopic map for straight vertical lines contains neural activity at only one location, regardless of the number of distractors. This activity calls focused attention to that location, and the target can thus be detected as quickly among many distractors as among few. But when a circle-without-line is the target (Figure 11.2.22B), the feature map for straight vertical lines contains activity at all locations in which a display element is present. The wide distribution of activity in this feature map cannot lead to visual pop-out of the location in which there is no such line, and indeed it does not.

One important implication of this account is that there is no feature map defined by the *absence* of a line. If there were, then no search asymmetry would be found; the circle-without-line would pop out due to unique activity at the target's location in the hypothetical no-straight-line map. Assuming that something like this explanation in terms of presence versus absence of features is correct, it can then be used to infer how elements are coded in terms of visual features.

11.2.6 Feature Integration Theory

Physiological evidence for the presence of retinotopic feature maps contains substantial support for the proposal that the visual system divides input information into many distinct subsystems that analyze different properties. But if this is true, how do all these properties get put back together into unified perceptual objects? This is a problem because we do not perceive unconnected attributes at different positions in the visual field (e.g., disconnected redness and verticalness); we perceive their conjunction in unified perceptual objects (a red horizontal line). The process of conjoining different properties into visual objects is called **binding**. Binding is an important theoretical problem because without some mechanism to bind properties into objects properly, an observer would not be able to tell the difference between a display containing a red circle and a blue triangle and a display containing a blue circle and a red triangle. Because people seldom bind features in the wrong way—at least under normal conditions—there must be some mechanism that does the job of producing conscious perceptions of unified objects.

Anne Treisman recognized the importance of the binding problem and proposed a theory of focused visual attention to solve it. The theory is called **feature integration theory** because it concerns how unitary perceptual objects are constructed by attentional acts that conjoin features into objects (Treisman, 1988, 1993; Treisman & Gelade, 1980; Treisman & Gormican, 1988). Consistent with the physiological evidence that different retinotopic maps code different visual properties, Treisman began with the assumption that before focused attention, the visual system contains separate representations of stimulus features such as redness, greenness, verticality, horizontality, and so on, as illustrated in Figure 11.2.23. Each of these **feature maps** is retinotopically organized according to locations in space and is constructed independently of all others. Thus, when there are red horizontal lines in the visual field, activity occurs at the appropriate corresponding locations in both the "red" feature map and the "horizontal" feature map. But simultaneous activity in both maps is not sufficient, according to feature integration theory, for an observer to perceive them as red horizontal lines. These two separate features must be conjoined by some additional process to bind them together.

Treisman theorized that feature binding is accomplished by selectively attending to specific locations in the visual field, as illustrated in Figure 11.2.23. This is done by focusing an attentional "spotlight" on a region of a master location map, which results in the conjunction of all features that are registered at the corresponding location in all the various feature maps. This conjunction then constitutes the unified perceptual object we consciously experience.

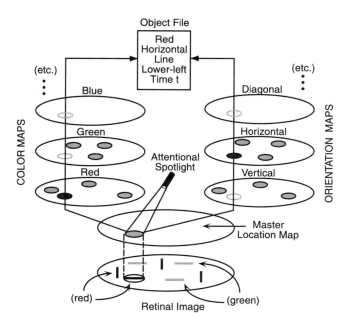

Figure 11.2.23 Feature integration theory. Treisman proposes that stimuli are analyzed into feature maps, which can then be accessed by a master map of locations. Focused attention selects a location in the master map and thus gains access to all the features that are present at that location. (After Treisman, 1988.)

To bind features correctly, the spotlight of attention must be narrowly focused on a limited region of the location map so that just the corresponding features are selected and bound together. Perceiving multiple objects in the field of view therefore requires that focused attention be moved sequentially from one location to another to construct the complex, multifeatured objects of conscious perceptual experience. This is the point at which visual processing changes from being parallel and nonselective (distributed attention) to being serial and selective (focused attention).

Feature integration theory has made a number of interesting experimental predictions that have been confirmed in extensive empirical testing. Here we list three of the most important findings: conjunction search, texture segregation, and illusory conjunctions.

Conjunction Search. The first prediction of feature integration theory is that pop-out should occur in visual search for target objects that can be discriminated from distractor objects by an elementary feature but not for objects that require conjunctions of features (Treisman & Gelade, 1980). For example, a black vertical line

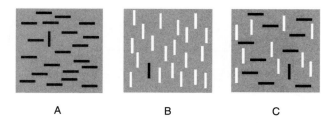

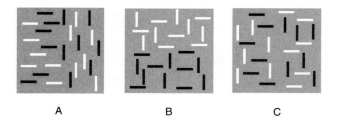

Figure 11.2.24 Examples of elementary and conjunction search displays. In part A, the target differs from the distractors only in orientation. In part B, it differs only in color. In part C, it differs by a conjunction of orientation and color: a black vertical target among white vertical and black horizontal distractors.

Figure 11.2.25 Texture segregation by elementary features versus feature conjunctions. In part A, the stimulus is easily segregated by orientation alone (vertical boundary). In part B, they are easily segregated by color alone (horizontal boundary). In part C, it is difficult to perceive whether the boundary between regions defined by conjunction of these features (white vertical and black horizontal versus white horizontal and black vertical) is vertical or horizontal.

should pop out against a set of distractors consisting of just black horizontal lines because of its orientation (see Figure 11.2.24A) or among just white vertical ones because of its color (see Figure 11.2.24B), but it should not pop out against distractors consisting of both black horizontal lines and white vertical ones (see Figure 11.2.24C).

Treisman and Gelade (1980) tested this prediction about conjunction search using the visual search paradigm described in the previous section. Targets defined by the conjunction of two features (e.g., black *and* vertical in Figure 11.2.24C) could be distinguished from the distractors (white vertical and black horizontal lines) only by attending to both features at the same time. These conjunction trials produced the increasing response time pattern predicted by serial search using focal attention (Figure 11.2.20B). Targets defined by the disjunction of the same two features (vertical *or* black in Figures 11.2.24A and 11.2.24B) could be distinguished from distractors by a single feature. These disjunction trials showed the flat response time function predicted by parallel search using diffuse attention (Figure 11.2.20A). This pattern of results is just what feature integration theory predicts.

Texture Segregation. Another prediction of feature integration theory is that although effortless texture segregation should be possible for displays in which simple features are sufficient for the discrimination, it should not be possible for displays in which feature conjunctions define the different textures. For example, it was already known that effortless feature discrimination is possible when a texture boundary is defined by horizontal versus vertical lines (regardless of color), as in Figure

11.2.25A, or by black versus white lines (regardless of line orientation), as in Figure 11.2.25B. But what happens when the boundary is defined by feature conjunctions, such as black vertical and white horizontal elements on one side and white vertical and black horizontal elements on the other? This type of conjunction display, shown in Figure 11.2.25C, does not support effortless texture segregation, a finding that is consistent with the prediction of feature integration theory (Treisman & Gelade, 1980).

Illusory Conjunctions. Perhaps the most startling prediction of feature integration theory is that if attention is spread over a region including several different objects, the features may not be correctly conjoined. As a result, these "free-floating" features can form **illusory conjunctions**: perceptions of objects in which features are bound into objects in the wrong way. Treisman and Schmidt (1982) first tested this prediction by flashing a 200-ms display containing a red X, a blue S, and a green T between two black digits, as shown in Figure 11.2.26. It was followed by a masking display of randomly arranged colored letter fragments to eliminate any afterimage of the test display. Subjects were told first to report the two digits (to spread attention over the portion of display including the colored letters) and then to report any of the colored letter targets that they could perceive. Illusory conjunctions—such as reporting a blue X or a red T—occurred on 39% of the trials, compared with only 15% of the trials on which subjects erroneously reported a color or letter that was not present

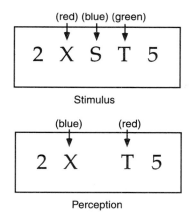

Figure 11.2.26 Illusory conjunctions. When subjects spread attention over the entire array to report the two numerals, they perceive incorrect pairings of letters and colors more often than is expected by chance guessing.

in the display at all. Illusory conjunctions thus appear to occur, as predicted by feature integration theory, under conditions in which short exposure and broad spatial focus prevent attention from being directed narrowly on the individual objects in a sequence of fixations.

The results from such experiments converge in supporting the hypotheses that there is an early parallel-processing stage at which primitive visual features are registered independently at different locations and that putting them together requires focusing attention sequentially on the locations of individual objects. Figure 11.2.23 shows the structure of feature integration theory that is able to account for many of these results. The incoming image is initially analyzed into many different retinotopically defined maps for different features, such as redness, greenness, verticality, horizontality, and so forth. Each of these maps can be monitored independently in the initial stage before attention is focused on individual objects. If the map required to discriminate the target from distractors contains activity at only one location, attention can be directed at the target very quickly, regardless of the number of distractors. This allows pop-out to occur, because a red horizontal line among a field of green horizontal lines will activate a single location in the red feature map.

Detecting a conjunction of two or more features (within appropriate distractors) is much more complicated in this processing architecture. No single location will pop out of any feature map because all relevant maps are activated by many objects. For example, a red horizontal line in a field of red vertical lines and green horizontal lines will activate many locations in the red, green, horizontal, and vertical maps. The red horizontal element can be detected only by the conjunction of both redness and horizontalness at the same location.

In feature integration theory, conjunctions are accomplished by moving the attentional spotlight to a specific location on the master attentional map. Once attention is focused on that location, all the features at corresponding locations in all the independent feature maps are properly bound into a coherent object. This object representation can then be checked for the presence of the target conjunction. If it is found, the search can be terminated. If it is not, attention must be moved to a different location to check for the presence of the target conjunction there. This process must be continued sequentially until either the target is found or all locations have been examined. Because conjunction targets require this serial search process, response time should increase approximately linearly with the number of distractors in the display, and numerous experimental results have shown that it does.

Problems with Feature Integration Theory. Feature integration theory has been tested many times in many ways by many investigators. For several years its predictions held up remarkably well, but systematic discrepancies eventually began to emerge. These problems have caused Treisman to make a number of modifications to her initial theory (Treisman, 1988, 1993).

One of the most important developments was the finding that conjunctions can sometimes be detected in parallel rather than requiring serial search. For example, Nakayama and Silverman (1986) reported that conjunctions of color and depth plane (e.g., a red target square in the near depth plane) produced strong pop-out against a background of distractors containing both features that were differently conjoined (e.g., green distractor squares in the near plane and red distractor squares in the far plane). In a similar experiment, they also found evidence of parallel search for conjunctions of color and direction of motion.

Such findings raise serious questions about Treisman's claim that attention is necessary to conjoin features. There are several ways in which such results could be obtained within the processing architecture defined by feature integration theory. Later experiments by Treisman (1988) and by Wolfe, Cave, and Franzel (1989) supported the hypothesis that highly distinctive features allow selective access to their intersection. They found that when the features within the same pair of dimensions were dramatically different, conjunctions could be searched in parallel, whereas when they were similar, conjunctions were searched serially. Consider conjunctions of color and line length, for example. When differences in color and line length are small (e.g., pink versus beige and 3 mm versus 4 mm in length), conjunctions require serial search. When they are large (e.g., red versus green and 2 mm versus 5 mm), conjunctions pop out in parallel search.

Such findings have caused Treisman (1988; Treisman & Sato, 1990) and others (e.g., Cave & Wolfe, 1990) to revise the search mechanism of the original feature integration theory. The main change is to assume that highly distinctive features allow nontarget features to be actively inhibited.[4] For example, if the target is a green vertical line, inhibiting all locations containing red elements and all locations containing horizontal elements will leave the target uninhibited, regardless of the number of distractor items. Thus, it will pop out, as evidenced by flat search time functions.

Other findings that require an important modification in feature integration theory concern the level of the visual system at which features are defined. In Treisman's early writings, feature maps were discussed as early image-based representations, much like the features of Marr's retinotopically organized primal sketch (see Section 4.3.1). But such representations are not consistent with some findings in the visual search paradigm for at least two reasons. One is that subjects move their eyes rapidly around the array during search, and this would cause the locations of the elements to shift every time subjects made an eye movement. Keeping track of which items had been examined in a serial search would be extremely difficult. It therefore seems likely that the master location map (at least) is coded in terms of perceived locations in the environment rather than retinal locations.

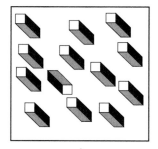

A

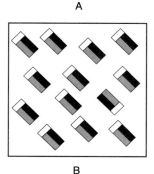

B

Figure 11.2.27 Pop-out of high-level features. The odd element pops out from distractors when they depict coherent 3-D objects that differ in spatial orientation (A) but not when they are similarly colored 2-D patterns (B). (After Enns & Rensink, 1990.)

Another problem is that recent research has shown that pop-out can occur for high-level, postconstancy properties. For example, Enns and Rensink (1990) found pop-out among objects that appear to be 3-D prisms with differently colored (or shaded) surfaces (Figure 11.2.27A) but serial search for 2-D patterns that are matched with the prisms in terms of complexity (Figure 11.2.27B). If the feature maps were based on image-level properties, the prisms would be processed in much the same way as the 2-D patterns. Other recent findings also show that pop-out occurs after stereoscopic depth perception and visual completion have been achieved (He & Nakayama, 1992). Therefore, we conclude that the features involved in visual search can come from relatively late perceptual representations.

The original story of visual search in feature integration theory has obviously been complicated by these new findings. Nevertheless, feature integration theory has

---

[4] The same effect can also be produced by facilitation of target features rather than inhibition of nontarget features. This is actually the mechanism suggested by Wolfe et al. (1989) and Cave and Wolfe (1990). Unfortunately, there is no easy way to distinguish between these two alternatives empirically.

provided the basic framework for understanding the integrative function of visual attention for many years and is still viable, albeit in a more complex form. Future research will undoubtedly require further modifications in its structure, but the insights it has provided have revolutionized the understanding of visual attention.

Object Files. Spatially focused attention appears to bind independently registered features into the representation of a unitary multifeatured object. In many experimental situations, this may be sufficient to characterize the brief perception of a stationary display. But in the real world, as well as in more complex experimental tasks, perception is dynamic and temporally extended.

As we discussed earlier in this chapter, eye movements are used to sample information in different locations via a sequence of fixations. An object whose gross features were perceived initially in the periphery may later be fixated, adding more detailed information about its specific shape, color, texture, and so on. Sometimes the new information that is perceived may substantially modify earlier information, although the perceiver almost always realizes that it is the same object. For example, I just saw a dark blob in my peripheral vision that I initially thought was my cat. But when I made a saccade to that object, it turned out to be a paper bag of roughly the same size and shape as a sitting cat. Such new information must be integrated with old to keep knowledge of the environment coherent and current.

Some objects in the environment change their visible properties over time. People, animals, and even inanimate objects move in a variety of complex ways, and such changes must be tracked by the visual system to maintain an accurate, up-to-date representation of the environment. If an object changes its location, for example, we see it not as a new object in its new location, but as the same one, even if some new features are visible after it has moved. How are we to understand the visual system's ability to cope with these dynamic changes in visual information?

Kahneman and Treisman (1984) have suggested that the results of perceptual analyses are integrated into temporary representations of objects and events called **object files**. They view object files as being analogous to the case files maintained in a police station to keep track of incidents currently being monitored. Initial in-

OBJECT FILE 421

LOCATION: on the mat
TIME: present
SIZE: 12" long x 8" wide x 6" high
COLOR: gray and black
TEXTURE: striped
SHAPE: oval
CATEGORY: cat
IDENTITY: Motor

Figure 11.2.28   An object file. Object files are memory representations of objects that are used to keep track of basic perceptual information—in this case, about a cat named "Motor." As this information changes, the object file is updated.

formation about a theft or shooting is used to open a new file. As further information and evidence become available, they are entered into the same file, updating its previous contents by either adding new information or modifying existing information.

An object file would likewise be opened for each new object that is perceived. It initially holds the conjunctions of features provided by focused attention to the object's location, more or less as hypothesized by Treisman's feature integration theory. At this point, the file might include information about the time, the object's location, its gross shape, and its approximate color (see Figure 11.2.28). As further information accumulates about it, as when it is fixated following a saccade, the newly visible features are integrated into the existing object file. At some point the object may be identified as an instance of a known category (e.g., a cat) or even a known exemplar (e.g., my cat Motor). If the object moves, its new location and direction of motion would be entered into its existing object file. The object file thus maintains the coherence of an object's representation over time, even though the contents of the file may change rather dramatically as a result of updating.

Although Kahneman and Treisman (1984) were not specific about precisely what kind of representations are contained within an object file, it is reasonable to think of them as dynamically changing structural descriptions of some sort, because they presumably support object categorization. Once the object has been identified, appropriate categorical information from memory can be added to the object file. Such information can provide expectations about what might occur in the future: what new parts might come into view as the viewpoint changes, what sort of motion it might exhibit, and so forth. Object files are thus a representational structure that can mediate between incoming low-level sensory information and internally generated high-level expectations. Once formed, object files may allow top-down unconscious monitoring of changes. That is, as long as the features of an object stay constant or change only in expected ways, the object file may be able to keep track of such changes without requiring the deployment of focused attention. If unexpected changes occur, however, attention may be directed to the object in question to update the new information.

What sort of evidence is there for the existence of object files and the role of attention in setting them up? One interesting experimental prediction is that once an object file has been established for an object, there will be some processing benefit from reperceiving it as having the *same* properties rather than new ones. Kahneman, Treisman, and Gibbs (1992) have examined this possibility using a priming technique called the **reviewing paradigm**. The structure of trials in the reviewing paradigm is illustrated in Figure 11.2.29 for an experiment involving motion. Subjects are initially presented with two simple geometrical objects in a static *preview display*. Letters are flashed briefly within these objects and then turned off. In the *linking display*, the two objects move continuously from their initial positions to their final positions in the *target display*. When the objects stop moving, a single letter is presented in one of the objects. The subjects' task is to name this target letter as quickly as possible, and response time is measured.

The crucial factor is the relationship between the target letter and the preview letters. On *same-object trials* the target letter is the one that was initially presented in the same object of the preview display. On *different-object tri-*

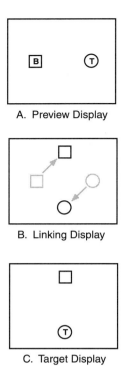

Figure 11.2.29 The reviewing paradigm. Subjects are initially shown simple objects with letters inside (A). The objects are then moved (B), after which subjects are tested for the identity of the letter in one of the objects (C). (After Kahneman, Treisman, & Gibbs, 1992.)

als the target is the letter that was initially presented in the other object. And on *no-match trials*, the target is a new letter, one that does not match either of the initially presented letters. Kahneman, Treisman, and Gibbs (1992) reasoned that if there were separate object files for each object that tracked them over time, subjects would be faster at naming the target in the same-object condition than in the different-object condition because the target letter would be contained in the object file for the same object. This prediction was confirmed for both slow- and fast-moving objects. Subjects were 23 ms faster at naming the target in the same-object condition than in the different-object condition when the objects moved quickly and 41 ms faster when they moved slowly.

Comparing performance on the different-object trials with that on the no-match trials provides a measure of how specific the letter priming effect is. If merely presenting the target letter in the initial preview display produced priming, subjects should be faster at naming the target in the different-object trials. In fact, however, performance was almost exactly the same on different-object and no-match trials. Consistent with the predictions based on object files, the facilitating effect of previewing the target letter in the initial display is quite specific to the object in which it was presented.

Kahneman, Treisman, and Gibbs (1992) reported the results of many experiments similar to this. In each case, they found significant object-specific facilitation in naming the target letter. It occurred both when the preview objects did not move and when they did, when they were seen in apparent motion and in continuous motion, and when as many as four (but not eight) objects were contained in the preview display. The object-specific reviewing effect is therefore robust experimental evidence for the existence of temporary object representations that track attended objects over time and space. This is precisely the rationale for postulating object files in the first place.

11.2.7 The Physiology of Attention

We have surveyed a sampling of what is known about human visual attention from behavioral methods. We now turn to what is known about the physiology of attention: How is visual attention accomplished by neural mechanisms in the brain?

Until recently, the only source of evidence about the physiology of attention came from studies of brain lesions due to strokes, tumors, gunshot wounds, and other neurological traumas. Patients with functional deficits of attention from such injuries are still the main source of information about the gross location of attentional mechanisms in the brain, but recent technological advances have brought other methods to bear, such as brain imaging and single-cell recording. Functional brain imaging techniques (including PET, and fMRI; see Section 2.2.3) not only have enriched the study of neurological patients, but also have brought physiological studies to the domain of normal perceivers. And although single-cell recording techniques have been available for many years, they have only recently been used to study awake, behaving animals. Almost all previous studies were performed on anaesthetized animals that were essentially comatose and therefore not attending at all.

Unilateral Neglect. The most common neurological condition in which attention is impaired is called **unilateral neglect** (or **hemineglect**).[5] Neglect is a name for a complex, clinically defined constellation of neurological symptoms. Whether it has a single underlying neurological cause is as yet unknown. However, the symptoms of neglect are commonly associated with brain injuries in certain locations, principally in the parietal lobe of the right hemisphere. It can also happen with parietal damage in the left hemisphere, although this condition is less severe and therefore less frequently reported. Acute neglect is often manifest only during the first few weeks following a stroke or other injury, when brain tissues swell in the vicinity of the damage. In the following weeks, it usually diminishes and may even disappear entirely as the swelling subsides. In some cases a permanent but less severe attentional disability remains, depending on the site and size of the irreversible portion of neurological damage.

The primary symptom of neglect is that patients systematically fail to notice objects on the side of the world opposite (contralateral) to their brain injury. For example, typical neglect patients with right parietal damage will orient toward the right side of the world by keeping their head turned noticeably to the right, fail to look at people on the left side of their hospital bed, and fail to eat food on the left side of their plate, even when they are hungry. A classical perceptual finding in patients with unilateral neglect is that when they are asked to draw a scene or copy a picture, they will draw only the right side of it or only the right sides of each object, as illustrated in Figure 11.2.30. This also happens when they draw something from memory, as exemplified by their drawings of a clock. A patient with right hemisphere damage either will draw only the right half of the clock or will try to squeeze all 12 numbers into the right side (see Figure 11.2.30). This clock-drawing task is a standard bedside diagnostic test for the presence of

---

[5] Unilateral neglect is sometimes called *inattention*, but we will reserve that term for the nonpathological conditions in which someone is not attending to or expecting a particular target object in the field of view, as studied by Mack and Rock (1998) and discussed in Section 11.2.1.

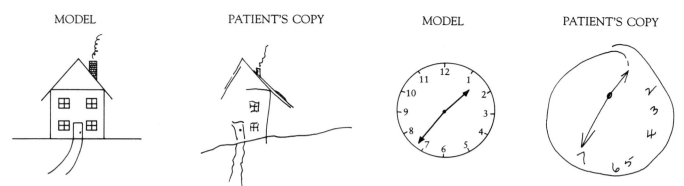

MODEL PATIENT'S COPY   MODEL PATIENT'S COPY

Figure 11.2.30 Drawings by patients with unilateral neglect. Neglect patients typically fail to reproduce the side of the model on the opposite side from their brain damage, which is usually in the right parietal lobe. Such failures also occur when neglect patients draw familiar objects from memory. (From Posner & Raichle, 1994.)

neglect. Another standard clinical test is to ask patients to cross out all the lines drawn on a page. They do fine with the lines on the same side of the page as their lesion (the **ipsilateral** lines) but fail to cross out the ones on the opposite side (the **contralateral** lines). Interestingly, if they are asked to *erase* all the lines, rather than cross them out, they will begin on the right but eventually erase them all.

Such findings indicate that neglect patients have severely impaired perception of objects or parts of objects on the side contralateral to their lesion, as though they were blind in that region of the visual field. However, more refined tests show that the problem is not sensory in nature. Rather, neglect patients appear not to be able to attend to objects on the contralateral side or appear to be able to do so only with great difficulty.

One intriguing piece of evidence that the problem in unilateral neglect is not sensory is that the same problems occur in visual imagery of scenes that were well known to the patients before their brain injury (Bisiach & Luzzati, 1978). When two neglect patients with right parietal damage were asked to imagine the buildings in the Piazza del Duomo in Milan from a vantage point on one side of the plaza, they systematically failed to report the ones that would have been on the left side of their image. When they were then asked to imagine the same scene from the opposite side of the plaza, they named the buildings they had failed to report previously (because these now fell in the intact right half of their image) and failed to report the buildings they had successfully reported previously (because these now fell in the neglected left half of their image). Therefore, ne-

glect appears to operate at a level high enough to affect imagery as well as perception and therefore cannot be solely a problem of low-level sensory input.

Further evidence of the nonsensory nature of neglect is that the neglected half can be defined relative to an object rather than to the field of view (Driver & Halligan, 1991). An object can be presented entirely within their "good" (ipsilateral) field, yet neglect patients do not perceive aspects of the object on the side of the object contralateral to their lesion. This finding is particularly interesting because it implicates object-based frames of reference in neglect. It appears that patients neglect not only the contralateral portion of the frame defined by the whole visual field, but also the contralateral portion of frames centered on individual objects. This is consistent with the so-called object-based theories of attention we discussed earlier in this chapter (see Section 11.2.3).

Posner and his colleagues have studied neglect patients using the attentional cuing paradigm (see Section 11.2.2) to find out how attention is impaired. Through careful analysis of the results from a series of experiments, they determined that neglect patients are able to move attention normally and engage attention to a new object but are impaired in disengaging attention from the currently attended object (Posner, Walker, Friedrich & Rafal, 1987). To explain the directionality of this syndrome, the disengage deficit must be specific to the direction of the required movement. That is, it must be difficult to disengage attention from objects on the unimpaired side to detect objects on the impaired side. This appears to be the case. It explains, among other things, why patients act as though they see only the lines on the good side of the page in the cross-out test yet appear to see all of them in the erasure test. The crossed-out lines are still present on the good side of the page, and so patients have great difficulty disengaging attention from them to cross out the lines on the bad side. But in the erasure test, the lines on the good side disappear from the page once they are erased. Eliminating them thus provides a kind of physical disengagement—since they are not there any more—allowing the patient eventually to see and erase all the lines on the page.

When acute neglect subsides, it sometimes leaves a permanent disability called **extinction**. In extinction, unlike full-blown neglect, a patient can see objects on either side of the visual field without difficulty. However, if patients are shown two objects at once, one on the good side and one on the bad side, they will report seeing only the one on the good side. This appears to be a less debilitating residue of neglect, but it can be explained by the same kind of disengagement problems.

Balint's Syndrome. An even more severe neurological condition related to attentional deficits is **Balint's syndrome** (Balint, 1909; Holmes & Horax, 1919; Rafal, in press). It results in what seems to be an almost complete inability to see anything except a single fixated visual object. Such patients take little interest in events occurring around them, staring instead at inconsequential objects for extended periods of time. The condition is often so debilitating that those who suffer from it are functionally blind. They must use conscious strategies such as closing their eyes to break fixation from one object so that they can look at another.

Patients with Balint's syndrome typically suffer from four main symptoms:

1. **Ocular apraxia**: the inability to change fixation from one object to another, as though the gaze were stuck on the currently fixated object. This renders impossible any visual task requiring more than one fixation. Because almost all real-world activities require multiple fixations, Balint's patients are severely impaired in everyday life.

2. **Simultagnosia**: the inability to perceive more than one object at a time during a single fixation. Even in a complex field of many objects, patients suffering from Balint's syndrome perceive only the object they are currently fixating. This is true even when two objects occupy the same location, as when a patient can see a person's face but cannot tell whether that person is wearing glasses.

3. *Spatial disorientation*: the inability to orient and localize objects correctly, including both their egocentric direction and their depth. This results in profound inaccuracy not only in perceiving the visible environment, but also in comprehending visual memories of places that were well known before the brain injury.

4. **Optic ataxia**: the inability to reach out and touch an object in space. This is perhaps not too surprising, given that patients are unable to localize objects correctly in space, but it is one of the most profoundly debilitating symptoms of the condition.

The first two symptoms may result from an underlying inability to disengage attention from the fixated object (Farah, 1990; Posner et al., 1987). If attentional shifts precede and direct eye movements, as some researchers believe (e.g., Rizzolatti, Riggio, Dascola, & Umilta, 1987), then a complete inability to disengage attention from its current object would produce ocular apraxia. And if attention is required for conscious perception of objects, as Mack and Rock (1998) suggest, restricting attention narrowly to the fixated object would also explain simultagnosia, the inability to perceive more than one object at once.

An alternative hypothesis to explain the nature of Balint's syndrome is that these problems can be understood as resulting from the loss of the master spatial map within Treisman's feature integration framework. If attention binds features into individuated object tokens by selecting locations in this map, and if Balint's patients cannot differentiate locations because there is no master map, it follows that they should form many illusory conjunctions in the one object that they do see. The Balint's syndrome patient whom Friedman-Hill, Robertson, and Treisman (1995) studied was found to do so quite noticeably.

Balint's syndrome is important from a theoretical standpoint because it provides powerful neurological evidence for the existence of an object-based attentional system. Its most significant perceptual symptom is that only one object is perceived at any time, even when two or more objects spatially overlap. For example, when

Balint's patients view a comb and a spoon in an overlapping cross configuration, they see only the comb or only the spoon, never both (Rafal, in press). This is hard to understand in terms of space-based theories based on metaphors of spotlights or zoom lenses but easy to understand in terms of object-based theories, for it is exactly what would be predicted. Another intriguing and relevant fact is that although one Balint's syndrome patient was completely unable to determine which of two separate lines was longer (because he could see only one of them at any one time), he could always report whether a rectangle was square or elongated (Holmes & Horax, 1919). That is, he had no trouble attending to the square holistically as a unitary figure even though it was composed of four line segments, but he was unable to attend to just two line segments when they were presented as separate objects.

Another finding that supports the object-based attention hypothesis concerns the performance of two Balint's syndrome patients on a task requiring them to determine whether a display contained circles of just one color (either all red or all green) or two colors (half red circles and half green circles). If the circles were separate and intermixed with randomly positioned, disconnected black lines, their performance was essentially at chance. However, if each line in the two-color display connected a red circle and a green circle, they performed much better. The connecting lines apparently unified the two circles into a single dumbbell-shaped object whose color could then be processed as a single object (Humphreys & Riddoch, 1992). This finding supports the powerful role of element connectedness in object formation (Palmer & Rock, 1994a), as discussed in Section 6.1.2.

Unlike unilateral neglect, Balint's syndrome typically involves bilateral lesions in the parietal and/or nearby occipital cortex. This fact suggests the possibility that Balint's syndrome may be the result of a bilateral deficit in disengaging attention (e.g., Farah, 1990). This idea fits with the hypothesis that unilateral neglect results from an inability to disengage attention from objects in the good side to objects in the bad side: If the brain damage were bilateral (as it is in Balint's syndrome), the patient would be unable to disengage attention to move to either side, thus freezing it on the currently attended object. Other indications suggest that Balint's syndrome

may be different from a bilateral version of neglect, however. The locations of the bilateral lesions that produce Balint's syndrome are slightly different from the unilateral lesions of neglect, being more likely to occur in the parieto-occipital junction than in the temporo-parietal junction, where neglect lesions are typically found (Rafal, 1996).

Brain Imaging Studies. The physiological basis of attention has also been studied in normal perceivers. Using sophisticated neuroimaging techniques, researchers have been able to determine which areas of the brain are active when people engage in activities involving attention. In general, they have corroborated conclusions previously drawn from studies of focal brain damage: The parietal lobe, particularly the right parietal lobe, is especially important in moving attention from one object to another.

One imaging study provides evidence of why damage to the right parietal lobe is so much more likely to produce unilateral neglect than damage to the left. PET images were used to examine what parts of the brain were active when normal subjects performed a continuous version of Posner's cuing task among several locations in the right or the left half of the visual field (Corbetta, Meizin, Dobmeyer, Shulman, & Petersen, 1991). As the subjects fixated their gaze overtly on a single box in the center of the display, they covertly attended to targets that were presented in a sequence of different boxes in the right visual field for one PET scan and in the left visual field for another. As Figure 11.2.31 shows, when attention was directed to the left visual field, the right parietal lobe showed greatly increased activity, as would be predicted from studies of neglect. When attention was directed to the right visual field, however, both the left and right parietal lobes were highly active. Thus, the right parietal lobe appears to be involved in attending to both halves of the visual field, whereas the left parietal lobe is involved only in attending to the right visual field. This helps to explain why the symptoms of neglect are so much more pronounced following damage to the right parietal lobe. Right parietal damage destroys the ability to attend to the left visual field but leaves the right visual field intact (owing to the unharmed left parietal lobe), whereas left parietal damage allows attention to both the right and left visual

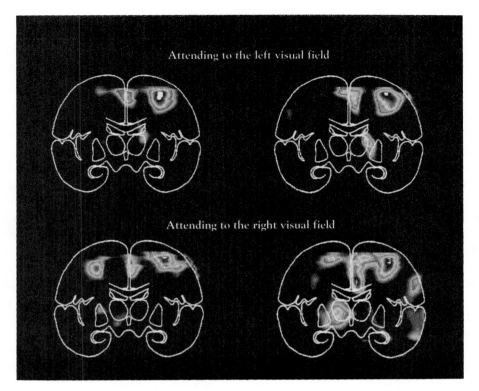

Attending to the left visual field

Attending to the right visual field

Figure 11.2.31 Brain activity while attending to the right versus left visual field. PET scans show activity in the right parietal lobe when subjects were attending to the left visual field but activity in both left and right parietal lobes when they were attending to the right visual field. (From Posner & Raichle, 1994.)

fields (owing to the unharmed right parietal lobe), as indicated in Figure 11.2.32.

Electrophysiological Studies. At a much smaller scale of analysis, single-cell physiologists have recently begun to study attentional effects by applying their techniques to awake behaving animals. The results have begun to provide a glimpse of the effects of attention on the responses of individual neurons. Only a little is known yet, but there are already clear indications that selective attention to a given spatial location or object can restrict the functional size of a cell's receptive field and increase its resolution for responding to specific features.

The reader may recall from Section 1.3.3 that the size of cells' receptive fields increases by a factor of 100 or more as one traces the flow of information from LGN to primary visual cortex (area V1) to inferotemporal cortex (area IT) where pattern recognition is thought to occur. A cell that is sensitive to a monkey's face in IT, for ex-

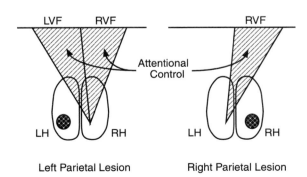

Left Parietal Lesion   Right Parietal Lesion

Figure 11.2.32 Attentional control with left versus right parietal damage. When the left parietal lobe is damaged, the right parietal lobe can still control attention on both sides of the visual field. When the right parietal lobe is damaged, the left parietal lobe can control attention only in the right visual field.

ample, may have a receptive field as large as 25°, firing rapidly when a monkey face appears anywhere within that area. But how is the monkey to know where this face is located? And how is it to be combined with other features that are coded by other cells in other visual areas? This is the binding problem of feature conjunction that we considered in Section 11.2.6. Moran and Desimone (1985) have reported physiological evidence that the response of an individual neuron is *gated* by the locus of the animal's attention—that is, that the cell's functional receptive field is restricted to the region to which the animal is attending.

Moran and Desimone found that the responses of cells in areas V4 and IT were strongly affected by the locus of the monkey's attention. The firing rate to the very same stimulus was only one-third as great when the monkeys did not attend to it as when they did. Because the sensory conditions in the experiment were carefully controlled to be identical in these two cases, the difference in the cell's response can be due only to the locus of the animal's attention. Therefore, cells in V4 and IT are strongly affected by attention, almost as though their effective receptive field were restricted to the attended location. This suggests a suppressive function of attention in which it blocks processing of non-attended information. Cells in areas V1 and V2 were not affected by attention, however. Such results suggest that V4 may be the first visual area in the occipito-temporal pathway where attention has this suppressive effect.

Later studies have shown that attention can also have an enhancing effect when the amount of attention is manipulated (Spitzer, Desimone, & Moran, 1988). The amount of attention that was paid to the stimuli was manipulated by having one block of trials require an "easy" discrimination between dissimilar stimuli (e.g., red versus aqua and orange versus blue) and another block require a "difficult" discrimination between similar stimuli (e.g., red versus orange and blue versus aqua). Recordings from V4 cells showed responses that were larger and more tightly tuned to the same stimulus in the difficult task than in the easy one. The same results were found for similar versus dissimilar orientations as for colors.

These two studies demonstrate some of the ways in which attention can influence the firing of individual cells in the visual system, but they do not identify the source of these effects. Presumably, there is an attentional subsystem somewhere in the brain that sends signals to these regions that modulate their responses depending on how attention is deployed, in both direction and amount. Where might this subsystem be located?

Desimone, Wessinger, Thomas, and Schneider (1990) reasoned that the lateral pulvinar nucleus (Figure 11.2.12) might be a good bet because it projects directly to visual cortex and because humans with lesions in this area have difficulty engaging attention (Rafal & Posner, 1987). They tested their conjecture by deactivating this region chemically in monkeys to see what effect it would have on selective attention. After injecting a drug (muscimol) into the lateral pulvinar that stopped all neural activity there, they found that the monkey was impaired in attending selectively to one stimulus in the presence of a distractor, but not to the same stimulus without a distractor. When the effects of the drug dissipated, the monkey was again able to selectively attend to the relevant stimulus in the presence of another. These results suggest that deactivating the lateral pulvinar nucleus eliminates the gating effect of attention that Moran and Desimone (1985) had found on the response of IT cells. This is just what they predicted would happen if this region were controlling selective attention to different regions of space. Similar results were found when portions of the superior colliculus were deactivated, suggesting that this region is also involved in controlling selective attention (Desimone et al., 1990).

11.2.8 Attention and Eye Movements

We began this chapter by considering the nature of overt selection through eye movements that change the optical content of the retinal image. We then discussed what is known about covert selection through attentional effects, including how it can be moved from one location to another within a single retinal image. We will now consider the relation between these two selective systems. It seems intuitively likely that they are linked, because attention is normally directed at whatever is fixated by the eyes. But what precisely is the relation? Does attention follow eye movements, do eye movements follow attention, or is there some more complex relation between them? And how are the physiological mechanisms of these two systems related? These are questions that we will address in the final section of this chapter.

The similarities between eye movements and attention are so compelling that we briefly considered the idea that attention is like an internal eye that can be moved around to sample the visual field much as the eye can be moved around to sample the visual world. Although this metaphor has limited utility for reasons we discussed, it underscores the intuitively close relation between the two. This relation is strengthened by the fact that shifts of attention normally occur more quickly than saccadic eye movements (Posner, 1980). Benefits of valid cues and costs of invalid ones in Posner's cuing paradigm begin to occur in less than 100 ms, long before a saccadic eye movement can be initiated. It also appears that the same kinds of stimulus conditions that lead to involuntary eye movements to an event also lead to involuntary capture of attention via so-called pull cues (Jonides, 1981).

Despite these connections, insight into the precise relation between attention and eye movements is a recent development. The dominant view, called the **premotor theory**, suggests that overt orienting through eye movements and covert orienting through attentional movements are controlled by closely related mechanisms and that eye movements normally *follow* attentional movements. This relation can be broken when you attend to something you are not looking at directly, but that is an unusual occurrence outside of attention experiments. Such covert orienting of just the attentional system would occur when the eye movement that normally would follow an attentional shift is inhibited, leaving only the attentional shift (Rizzolatti, Riggio, Dascola, & Umilta, 1987). According to this theory, attention normally drives the saccadic eye movement system, directing it to appropriate objects given the stimulus conditions and the task at hand. The hypothesis is that visual attention is first either summoned to a salient event (by the equivalent of a pull cue) or internally directed to an important location (by something akin to an internally generated push cue), and then the eyes follow attention.

This pre-motor theory of the relation between attention and eye movements makes several predictions. Behaviorally, it suggests that when an observer executes a saccade to a particular location, attention will enhance perception of events occurring there before the eye movement is actually executed. It also suggests that if an eye movement is made to a particular location, attention

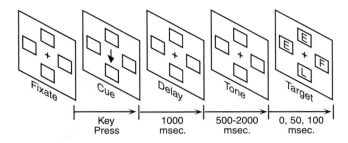

Figure 11.2.33 Enhanced visual discrimination before making a saccade. If subjects intend to make an eye movement to a given location as the result of a cue to move the eye, they are better at detecting target letters there than in other locations, long before the eye movement has begun.

will necessarily precede that eye movement and therefore cannot be sent in some other direction. Unequivocal support for such hypotheses proved difficult to find for many years (e.g., Klein & Pontefract, 1994), but recent studies have found good evidence for both of these predictions using a cuing paradigm similar to Posner's (see Section 11.2.2).

In one experiment, Hoffman and Subramaniam (1995) investigated whether preparing to make a saccade to a cued location facilitated perception in that location before the eye movement was actually executed. As shown in Figure 11.2.33, subjects were first shown a computer-generated display containing four empty rectangles. Immediately after they pressed a key, an arrow was presented that indicated to which box an eye movement was to be made. Then, after a randomly determined delay of 500–2000 ms, a brief tone signaled the subject to execute the cued saccade. After this cue, it took subjects at least 200 ms to actually begin the saccade. To test whether preparing for this eye movement enhanced perception in the cued location, letters were presented in the boxes at 0, 50, or 100 ms after the tone cue, well before any eye movement could be made. The subject's task was to discriminate which target letter had been presented (T or L) in one of the boxes when E's and F's were presented in the other boxes as distractors. The crucial question is whether subjects were better at discriminating which target was presented if it appeared in the box toward which the eye movement was programmed than if it appeared in the other boxes.

The results showed a substantial advantage for the location for which the eye movement was intended. Discrimination performance was about 90% correct when the target's location matched the intended saccade's location but about 70% in the other three locations. On control trials in which no arrow was presented and no saccade was made, performance was about 80% correct, intermediate between the two cuing conditions. Thus, Hoffman and Subramaniam's results indicate that both benefits and costs are associated with preparing for an eye movement, much like the benefits and costs associated with purely covert attentional shifts as measured by Posner's cuing paradigm. This finding thus supports the pre-motor theory.

In a second experiment, Hoffman and Subramaniam (1995) examined whether attention could be directed toward a location different from the one to which an eye movement was planned. Using the same series of displays and a slightly modified procedure, they decoupled eye movements from the expected target location. In this study, subjects always had to make a saccade to a given box throughout a block of trials, for example, to the box on the left. The arrow now provided information about the likely location of the target letter, as in Posner's original attentional cuing paradigm: On 75% of the trials it was valid, and on 25% of the trials it was invalid. On control trials, when no eye movement was required, normal costs and benefits of attentional cuing were found. When eye movements were required, however, performance was always better at the location toward which an eye movement was planned than at other locations and was unaffected by where attention should have been directed on the basis of the cue. This finding shows that attention is locked into the planning of saccades and cannot be redirected to a different location even if that is the optimal strategy. Similar conclusions hold for making slow pursuit eye movements (Kowler & Zingale, 1985).

In the physiological domain, the pre-motor theory predicts close correlations between the centers that control eye movements and those that control attention. Indeed, this is the case. The superior colliculus, for example, is known to be involved in controlling movements of both attention and the eye. Two other structures thought to play a major role in high-level motor control of the eye—the frontal eye fields in the frontal cortex and the posterior parietal cortex—also appear to be involved in controlling spatial attention (Desimone, Wessinger, Thomas, & Schneider, 1990). More specifically, the pre-motor theory predicts that damage to the brain centers involved in making eye movements should lead to corresponding deficits in shifting attention covertly. In support of this prediction, patients whose superior colliculus is damaged not only have been found to have difficulty making voluntary saccades, but are also impaired in covert attentional orienting as measured by Posner's cuing paradigm (Rafal, Posner, Friedman, Inhoff, & Bernstein, 1988). At a cellular level, evidence is also accumulating that the superior colliculus is involved in covert shifts of attention (Desimone, Wessinger, Thomas, & Schneider, 1990; Gattas & Desimone, 1992).

Although the subject is far from well understood, it is becoming increasingly clear that there is an intimate relationship between eye movements and attention as mechanisms of visual selection. Somewhat counterintuitively, the relation appears not to be that attention follows eye movements but that it precedes eye movements as an integral step in preparing to move the eyes. On reflection, this relation makes sense. One reason is that attentional shifts are purely neural operations and can therefore be executed more rapidly than ocularmotor responses that require actually rotating an eye in its socket. Another reason is that because attention is a central (rather than peripheral) process, it is better suited to controlling where the eye should be directed. Attention can therefore gain access to information about what locations contain important information and should thus be selected for higher resolution processing. Because attentional movements appear to drive eye movements rather than the other way around, attention may legitimately be viewed as the primary mechanism of visual selection, with eye movements playing an important but supporting role.

Suggestions for Further Reading

Eye Movements

Goldberg, M. E., Eggers, H. M., & Gouras, P. (1991). The ocularmotor system. In E. R. Kandel, J. H. Schwartz, & T. H. Jessel (Eds.), *Principles of neural science* (3rd ed., pp. 660–679). Norwalk, CT: Appleton & Lange. This chapter gives a good overview of the nature of eye movements and what is known about their physiological basis.

Kowler, E. (1995). Eye movements. In S. M. Kosslyn & D. N. Oshersohn (Eds.), *Visual cognition* (2nd ed., pp. 215–255). Cambridge, MA: MIT Press. This chapter provides a basic introduction to eye movements and their relation to attention.

Attention

Garner, W. R. (1974). *The processing of information and structure.* Hillsdale, NJ: Erlbaum. This research monograph presents Garner's original experiments on integral versus separable dimensions.

Mack, A., & Rock, I. (1998). *Inattentional blindness.* Cambridge, MA: MIT Press. This research monograph presents the important series of experiments by the authors on what is perceived under conditions of inattention.

Pashler, H. E. (1998). *The psychology of attention.* Cambridge, MA: MIT Press. Pashler's book is a very recent and up-to-date survey of attention from the perspective of a cognitive psychologist.

Posner, M. I. (1978). *Chronometric explorations of mind.* Hillsdale, NJ: Erlbaum. This book is a classic on the subject of visual attention, written by one of the most important researchers in the field.

Posner, M. I., & Raichle, M. E. (1994). *Images of mind.* New York: Scientific American Books. This volume is a lovely introduction to human cognitive neuroscience that focuses on visual attention, with major coverage of both behavioral and brain imaging studies.

Rafal, R., & Robertson, L. (1995). The neurology of visual attention. In M. S. Gazzaniga (Ed.), *The cognitive neurosciences* (pp. 625–648). Cambridge, MA: MIT Press. This chapter by two leading cognitive neuroscientists reviews the literature on attentional deficits in human patients with brain damage.

Visual Memory and Imagery

12.2.5 The Relation of Imagery to Perception
      Behavioral Evidence
      Neuropsychological Evidence
      Brain Imaging Studies

From the outset we have been considering visual perception as a temporally extended event: a process that unfolds over time as different stages of processing extract and represent new information. Thus far we have concentrated on the events that lead up to the creation of a given perception. But what happens after this perception has been achieved? Are the effects of a given perceptual experience over as soon as the visual environment changes or our attention turns elsewhere, as suggested by the old adage "Out of sight, out of mind," or do our perceptions have more lasting effects on our visual system? And if they do have more extended effects, what are they, and how long do they last?

Both everyday experience and careful experiments indicate that perceptions produce significant learning of and memory for visual information. The most salient of these visual memories can be very long-lasting indeed. You can probably remember what your childhood bedroom looked like, for example, and perhaps your third-grade teacher as well. You may even retain these visual memories for the rest of your life. But there are also many visual memories that have a much briefer duration yet are nevertheless important in governing your behavior in the short term. When you encounter a new acquaintance for the second time at a party, for example, you recognize the person and act accordingly. You don't reintroduce yourself as though you had never seen him or her before. This can only be because your brain has retained a memory of his or her appearance. It is unlikely, however, that this visual memory will last a lifetime—although it might. In the first half of this chapter we will examine the nature of visual memories, from ones that last from fractions of seconds to ones that last for decades.

In the second half we will consider the relation of visual memory to *visual imagery*: the quasi-visual experiences people have when they recall objects or events visually and when they engage in visual thinking. When you recall the appearance of your third-grade teacher or your childhood bedroom, for example, you typically experience visual images. Many people also use imagery

when they solve problems that have significant spatial and/or visual components, such as thinking about how to rearrange their living room furniture or how to avoid traffic problems in driving across town. The information on which such images are based must have been stored from prior perceptual experiences and somehow be recalled or reconstructed as needed at a later time.

12.1 Visual Memory

Perhaps the most obvious residual effects of previous visual experiences are specific visual memories. We know about such memories because at least some of them are relatively permanent, allowing us to "reexperience" visual information after days, weeks, months, years, or even decades. Consider the example of your childhood bedroom or your third-grade teacher. Your ability to call up such visual images of objects and events from many years ago is clear and compelling evidence of the existence of long-term visual memory. Somewhat surprisingly, however, there are other, more fleeting forms of visual memory as well, some lasting only fractions of a second. These are not obvious phenomenologically under normal conditions and have been identified only through the development of well-controlled experimental methods.

It might seem odd to call something that lasts less than a second a "memory," but that is just a matter of definition. For purposes of this book, **visual memory** can be defined as the preservation of visual information after the optical source of that information is no longer available to the visual system. The period of time over which this visual information is preserved is entirely unspecified, allowing for the possibility of memories lasting anywhere from a millisecond to an entire lifetime.

12.1.1 Three Memory Systems

Historically, the vast majority of memory research has been conducted with verbal materials. As a result, far more is known about how people remember letters, words, and sentences than about how they remember parts, objects, and scenes. The primary reasons for this imbalance are methodological: Words are easy to present to subjects in either visual or auditory form, easy to record when subjects recall them, and easy to score as correct or incorrect. This strong bias toward verbal materials in memory studies led to memory theories that were correspondingly biased toward verbal information. Still, many of the theoretical concepts that resulted from this work with letters and words have generalized successfully to memory for visual materials.

From the pioneering work of Hermann Ebbinghaus in 1885 until the 1960s, most verbal memory researchers believed that human memory performance was subserved by a single, undifferentiated memory system. According to this unitary memory view, information was "forgotten" when other, similar items interfered with retrieving it at some later time (e.g., Underwood & Postman, 1960). An important dissenting voice against this monolithic view of memory was that of the noted philosopher and psychologist William James. Mainly on phenomenological grounds, he argued for the existence of two kinds of memory: **primary memory**, which lasted only tens of seconds, and **secondary memory**, which could last for years (James, 1890/1950). Primary memory, for example, is the kind of memory one uses in remembering a telephone number long enough to dial it after looking it up in the phone book. The number can be maintained in primary memory almost indefinitely by rehearsing it (silently saying it over to oneself), but it is generally forgotten within a few seconds after rehearsal stops.

The controversy over whether memory was a single undifferentiated system or two (or more) different systems heated up in the 1960s (cf. Melton, 1963). Around this time, a number of new findings emerged that tended to support James's view that there was a distinct kind of memory that lasted for about 30 seconds or less (e.g., Peterson & Peterson, 1959; Waugh & Norman, 1965). This briefer memory is now standardly called **short-term memory (STM)**, but also has also been referred to as *immediate memory* as well as primary memory. Although STM can be distinguished from **long-term memory (LTM)** in many ways, the two systems work together so closely that their distinct contributions are not obvious without careful study.

As a result of literally thousands of experiments using dozens of procedures to tease apart the contributions of different memory systems, modern information processing theorists typically distinguish three components:

1. **Sensory information stores (SIS)** are very brief "buffer" memory stores for information in specific mo-

dalities, including visual information (*iconic memory* or *visual information store, VIS*) and auditory information (*echoic memory* or *auditory information store, AIS*).

2. Short-term memory (STM) is a limited-capacity memory store of longer duration (on the order of many seconds) for information that is currently being processed. Some theorists equate the contents of STM with consciousness. Others incorporate STM into a more comprehensive "executive system" (often called *working memory*) that oversees all active processing.

3. Long-term memory (LTM) is a large-capacity and temporally extended storage system for knowledge of general facts (*semantic memory*) and skills (*procedural memory*) as well as specific past experiences of one's personal history (*episodic memory*).

As we will see, the same distinctions seem to apply to visual memory as well, leading modern memory theorists to posit a three-layered system underlying visual memory: iconic memory (or visual information store, VIS), visual STM, and visual LTM.

Trying to decide how many memory systems there might be leads to the problem of defining a memory system. There is as yet no simple, agreed-upon answer, but one fruitful approach has been to define different memory systems by differences in their basic characteristics. Five of the most important are the following:

1. *Duration:* the length of time the memory lasts. This is the characteristic according to which human memory systems are most frequently named (e.g., "very short-term" versus "short-term" versus "long-term" memory).

2. *Content:* the kind of information that the memory contains, such as visual versus auditory versus semantic memory. In the case of visual memory systems, the information content is visual, although the specific type of visual information may differ in a variety of ways across different memory stores.

3. *Loss:* how the information is lost from memory, if indeed it is lost at all. The primary possibilities are autonomous decay over time versus interference due to other items in memory.

4. *Capacity:* how much information of a given type the memory can hold. Capacity may vary with duration, however, as when items decay over time or as the result of interference from other items in storage.

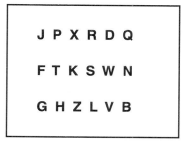

Figure 12.1.1 Stimulus for an experiment on iconic memory. In the whole report procedure, subjects are shown displays like this for 100 ms or less and asked to report as many letters as they can. In the partial report procedure, they are asked to report just the letters from a single cued row or an individual position.

5. *Maintenance:* how information can be refreshed, if at all, when it would otherwise be forgotten. Information in some memory systems cannot be voluntarily maintained, whereas that in others can be.

Armed with these five characteristics, we can evaluate the assertion that there are three visual memory systems rather than just one. In the pages that follow, we will examine how they are studied and differentiated.

12.1.2 Iconic Memory

One of the most striking early discoveries of the emerging information processing approach to psychology was of the existence of a very brief visual memory of high capacity known as **iconic memory**. In the late 1950s psychologist George Sperling, working at Bell Telephone Laboratories, became interested in studying the nature of brief visual memories. Previous research relevant to this topic had been performed to determine what was called the **span of apprehension**: the number of letters a person could perceive in a single, very brief visual presentation (e.g., Catell, 1881). Subjects were asked to report as many letters as they could from an array containing up to 20 letters that had been presented for less than 100 ms (see Figure 12.1.1). When the display contained only a few letters, subjects could report all of them, but when larger arrays were presented, subjects could typically identify only about four or five items correctly, as illustrated in Figure 12.1.2A.

When Sperling ran himself in this experiment, he found that he too could report only a few letters from such displays. But this result did not square with his vi-

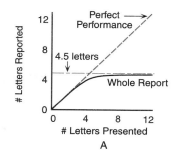

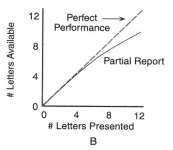

Figure 12.1.2 Typical results of experiments on iconic memory. Only four or five letters can be correctly reported when a whole report procedure is used (A), but many more letters appear to be available in iconic memory when a partial report procedure is used (B).

sual experience during the experiment of being able to see virtually all of the letters for a very short period of time before they "faded away." The problem, he reasoned, was not the capacity of this brief visual memory, but the **whole report procedure** used to study it. When subjects were asked to report every letter they could perceive in the display, the memory had faded to the point at which no more could be identified by the time a subject had reported about four letters. What was needed was a method of estimating the number of letters that were available in visual memory without requiring a lengthy reporting procedure.

The Partial Report Procedure. Sperling (1960) devised an ingenious method, known as the **partial report procedure**, to test his hypothesis. He showed subjects an array containing three rows of letters as before, but just when the display disappeared, a tone was presented indicating which row of letters to report: a high, medium, or low tone to cue report of the top, middle, or bottom row, respectively. Subjects could not use the cue to attend selectively to one row during

Visual Memory and Imagery

presentation because the tone occurred only after the array had disappeared. And because only one-third as many items needed to be reported, limitations related to the time required to report them should be considerably reduced. Indeed, if there were no more than four items per row, subjects should be able to report each row in its entirety.

To estimate the number of letters available in iconic memory using this partial report procedure, Sperling multiplied the number of items correctly reported in the target row by the number of rows. The logic of this calculation is that if all the letters in the one target row could be reported, and if the target row was cued only after the display itself was gone, then all the letters in the entire display must be potentially reportable from iconic memory. When the number of letters available in memory was plotted as a function of the number of items that were actually presented, a much larger estimate of the capacity of iconic memory was obtained, as shown in Figure 12.1.2B. By the time the arrays reached 12 items, there were four items in each row, thus approaching the same four-item limit observed in the whole report procedure.

More accurate estimates of the capacity of iconic memory were later made by using a visual bar marker just below a single letter (Averbach & Coriell, 1961). In this case there are no limitations on performance due to reporting multiple letters, and estimates of the number of letters available in iconic memory are correspondingly higher, reaching 16 of the 18 letters displayed under optimal conditions. If allowances are made for momentary lapses of attention and other processes that might reduce performance for reasons other than memory capacity, it appears that iconic memory can hold virtually complete visual information for a very short time.

Earlier we mentioned five important characteristics of a memory system: duration, information content, loss, capacity, and maintenance. We will now consider research that has attempted to measure these important characteristics of iconic memory.

Duration. To measure the duration of iconic memory precisely, Averbach and Sperling (1960) introduced a delay between the termination of the letter display and the onset of the tone cuing the target row. The rationale for this modification was that if the cue was delayed un-

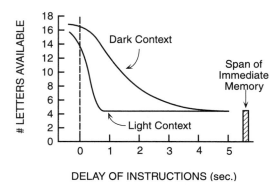

Figure 12.1.3 Effects of cuing delay and stimulus context on iconic memory. When the partial report cue is delayed from 0 to 5 s, the number of letters estimated to be available in iconic memory decreases at a rate that depends on whether the prestimulus and poststimulus fields are dark or light. Iconic memory lasts longer for dark than light conditions. (Redrawn from Averbach & Sperling, 1960.)

til after the information in iconic memory had decayed completely, then the estimate of the number of letters available from the partial report procedure would fall to the level measured by using the whole report procedure: about four letters. The effects of delaying the cue are shown in Figure 12.1.3 for two conditions that differ only in the brightness of the visual field presented before and after the letter display. The data effectively track the decay of information in iconic memory, showing that it lasts more than two seconds if the prestimulus and poststimulus fields are dark but only about half a second if they are light. Thus, the duration of iconic memory is on the order of a second, the exact time depending on the precise conditions. Typically, it is half a second or less, because preexposure and postexposure conditions are usually light rather than dark.

Content. The information content of iconic memory is surely visual in nature, but what kinds of visual information does it explicitly contain? One method of addressing this question is to study the effectiveness of different kinds of cues. The rationale is that a cue will be effective in increasing performance above the level of whole report only if that type of information is explicitly represented in iconic memory and can be used to selectively access the to-be-reported letters. The fact that spatial cues (e.g., tones cuing rows or bar markers cuing single letters) increase performance in partial report is evidence that spatial position is an important kind of information in iconic memory. The informational content of iconic memory can then be studied by finding out what other sorts of cuing properties lead to superiority of partial report over whole report.

Experiments by von Wright (1970, 1972) elegantly illustrate the differential effectiveness of different kinds of cues. Subjects were shown arrays of eight colored items in two rows of four. Four of the items were letters, and four were digits. Also, four of the items were red and four were black. The experimenter used one of two tones on each trial to cue the four items to be reported. In the spatial cue condition, one tone cued the subject to report the upper row, and the other tone cued the subject to report the lower row. In the color cue condition, one tone cued subjects to report the red items, and the other tone cued them to report the black items. In the category cue condition, one tone cued subjects to report the letters, and the other tone cued them to report the digits. Thus, the cuing conditions were formally the same except for the type of information to which they directed attention.

The results for these different cuing conditions were compared to the results of the whole report procedure to determine which ones were effective cues. Both the spatial and color cues significantly increased performance above the level of whole report, but the category cue did not. Other experiments have shown that both size (von Wright, 1968) and shape (Turvey & Kravetz, 1970) are also effective cues. From such results, we conclude that location, color, size, and shape are features that are represented in iconic memory and can be used to access it. Category information (e.g., letter versus digit or vowel versus consonant) either is not represented or cannot be used to access the memory. To determine the category of an item, subjects presumably have to attend serially to each and identify it through its spatial properties. It is worth noting, however, that categorical cuing effects have sometimes been observed in partial report experiments (Merikle, 1980). It is unclear how or why this happens if the content of iconic memory is actually precategorical.

Maintenance. Information in iconic memory appears to be lost via either decay or interference from subsequent items, as described in the next section, but there does not appear to be any way to voluntarily maintain information in iconic memory. It cannot be prolonged to avoid autonomous decay and cannot be reinstated once it has been interfered with by a subsequent display.

Loss. The fact that performance decreases gradually as the cue delay is extended (e.g., Averbach & Sperling, 1960) suggests that information is lost from iconic memory via autonomous decay. However, further experiments show that information in iconic memory can also be lost through interference due to subsequently presented visual items. This interference is called **masking**.

One of the most dramatic forms of masking was discovered unexpectedly when Averbach and Coriell (1961) were investigating different kinds of spatial cues for partial report of single letters. When they tried to cue a particular letter by surrounding it with a circle, they found that at certain delays, the circle effectively erased the letter inside it: Subjects reported seeing only an empty circle! This curious phenomenon is known as either **metacontrast masking** or **erasure**.

Careful experiments have shown that metacontrast masking is most effective when the circle is presented about 100 ms *after* the target display. Averbach and Coriell showed subjects two rows of letters and cued a single item by presenting a circle around it or a bar marker immediately above or below it. They varied the time between the onset of the array and the cue (circle or bar) from 100 ms before the target display to 500 ms after it. The results are graphed in Figure 12.1.4. When the circle was presented during the target display, subjects had no more trouble reporting the cued letter inside it than they did with a bar marker. But when presentation of the circle cue was delayed for 50 ms or more, subjects did much worse with the circle than with the bar. And at about 100 ms, they often saw nothing inside the circle. The presentation of the circle appears somehow to "erase" the letter inside it!

Even more surprising is the finding that if the masking circle is itself masked by presenting an even larger circle around it, the target letter is unmasked: The letter is perceived inside the larger circle alone and can be identified much more accurately than it is if the outer circle is not present (Dember & Purcell, 1967; Robinson, 1966). This remarkable result implies that the larger circle effectively erases the smaller one, thereby removing the perceptual object that caused the letter to

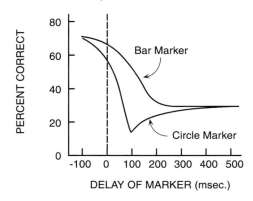

Figure 12.1.4 Metacontrast masking. After a given delay interval, single letters were cued with either a bar next to the letter or a circle around it. The results showed that both cues produce the usual decay, but circle markers produce additional masking that peaks at about a 100-ms delay. (Redrawn from Averbach & Coriell, 1961.)

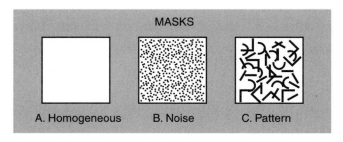

Figure 12.1.5 Types of masks. Stimulus displays can be followed by homogeneous light masks (A), randomly distributed noise masks (B), or pattern masks made from disconnected and randomly distributed pieces of more complex figures (C).

be masked in the first place. The larger circle does not erase the letter because it is too large and presented too long after the letter to have much effect on it.

How can a circle that is presented *after* a target letter obliterate the letter that preceded it? Theories of this phenomenon are complex, requiring a more extensive discussion of masking phenomena in general, the topic to which we now turn.

Masking. Some of the most striking and well-studied phenomena associated with iconic memory are masking effects: how various kinds of visual displays presented in close temporal contiguity to a target display degrade its perception. In its most general form, the fundamental question of masking is how two temporally contiguous displays interact with each other perceptually. The answer is extremely complex, depending on factors such as the spatial structure of the mask, its similarity to the target, the temporal delay between the target and the masker, the relative brightness of the target and the masker, and whether target and masker are presented to the same or different eyes. We will not attempt an exhaustive review of such masking effects, for that would require a good-sized book of it own (e.g., Breitmeyer, 1984). Rather, we will briefly discuss a few of the most important phenomena.

Before we begin, it will be useful to make some distinctions in terminology.

1. *Forward versus Backward Masking.* As the terms imply, **forward masking** obtains when a mask is presented before the target, and **backward masking** obtains when the mask is presented after the target. Both sorts of masking occur to degrees that depend on the specific type of mask.

2. *Homogeneous versus Noise versus Pattern Masks.* The spatial characteristics of the mask itself are critical. **Homogeneous masks** are spatially uniform flashes of light (see Figure 12.1.5A); **noise masks** are patterns of tiny, randomly distributed dots (Figure 12.1.5B); and **pattern masks** consist of many randomly distributed line segments or more complex configurations of several segments that are similar to the targets being masked (Figure 12.1.5C).

Turvey (1973) has argued that there are at least two different mechanisms that result in two different kinds of masking: integration masking and interruption masking. **Integration masking** is a process whereby the target and mask images are effectively added together to form a single composite image. Such addition occurs physically if the target and masker are optically superimposed by being presented at the same time. But integration may also occur in iconic memory if the masker is presented soon enough after the target is turned off or just before the target is turned on. In either case, the masker and target are added together in iconic memory rather than being physically added in a composite optical image. Integration effects therefore should be strongest when target and masker are presented close together in time and diminish as the delay between them increases.

This type of masking function is illustrated by the dashed curve in Figure 12.1.6 (Turvey, 1973). This

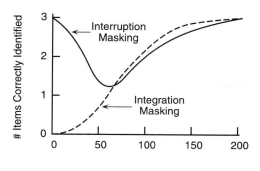

Figure 12.1.6 Integration versus interruption masking. The pattern of results expected from integration masking occurs when a bright pattern mask is presented at the specified delay (or SOA), as shown in the dashed curve. The pattern expected from interruption masking occurs when a dim pattern mask is presented at the same delays. (After Turvey, 1973.)

graph shows the results of an experiment in which subjects had to report as many letters as they could from a three-letter row in the presence of a pattern mask that was twice as bright as the target display. The target and masking displays were presented for just 10 ms each. The time between onset of the target and onset of the mask—the **stimulus onset asynchrony (SOA)**—was varied from 0 to 184 ms. When the SOA was 0 ms, there was true optical integration of target and mask, but when the SOA was longer than 10 ms, any masking effects could be occurring only in iconic memory. The results show that when the mask is optically integrated with the target at the 0 ms SOA, its effects are devastating: No letters can be identified. The same result is found, however, when the mask appears immediately after the target at an SOA of 16 ms. As the SOA increases further, the effect of the mask diminishes until about 200 ms, at which time report is essentially perfect.

The solid curve shows a masking function with a very different time course: no masking initially, followed by maximal masking at around 50 ms, and diminishing after that. These results were obtained when the same pattern mask was presented at the same SOAs as described above but at a lower brightness level than the target (at a target:mask ratio of 2:1). In this case, there is no masking initially, indicating that integration masking is minimal. But when the dimmer mask was presented about 50 ms after the target, it had its maximal masking effect. Such results suggest that at least two dif-

ferent mechanisms must underlie masking. The second type of masking is called **interruption masking** because it is thought to arise from the masking display interrupting the ongoing perceptual processing of the target display. Metacontrast masking appears to be of this type.

Integration masking is thought to be produced by fairly low-level sensory mechanisms, whereas interruption masking appears to occur more centrally. An important source of evidence in favor of this distinction comes from studies of interocular masking. Homogeneous masks typically do not degrade performance when presented to a different eye from the target, whereas they do when presented to the same eye (e.g., Turvey, 1973). This means that such effects probably occur prior to area V1 of visual cortex, because this is the first level at which information from the two eyes converges. Since homogeneous masks are generally thought to produce primarily integration masking, this result suggests that integration processes occur relatively early in visual processing.

The absence of interocular masking with homogeneous masks stands in contrast to the presence of interocular masking with pattern masks, which degrade performance even if they are presented to a different eye from the target. This means that pattern masking probably occurs more centrally than homogeneous masking, at or after the level of V1. Pattern masks may also have more peripheral effects, of course, but their primary action seems to be central.

Persistence versus Processing. Thus far, we have been assuming that the conscious persistence of a briefly flashed visual display—the "icon" itself—is responsible for a subject's ability to report letters after the display has been turned off. Given that there is phenomenological visual persistence, it is only natural to suppose that people can report cued items after the display is terminated because they can still see them. There is reason to doubt this conclusion, however. The evidence comes from differences in how cued memory performance and visual persistence are affected by variables such as stimulus duration and brightness (Coltheart, 1980, 1983).

Researchers have measured the visible persistence of the icon by having subjects adjust the timing of a brief

Visual Memory and Imagery

tone so that it coincides with the perceived onset or off-set of the displayed items. The difference between these two settings then corresponds to the apparent duration of the display. If the actual duration of the display is subtracted from this estimate, one obtains a measure of the visual persistence of the icon itself. Using this technique, Haber and Standing (1970) found that when the actual duration of the display was lengthened, the phenomenal duration of the icon *decreased*. Similarly, increasing the intensity of the display appeared to decrease visual persistence.

When the effects of these same two variables were assessed on memory performance by using partial report techniques, however, the results were quite different. Lengthening the display had no effect on partial report superiority (Di Lollo & Wilson, 1978; Sperling, 1960), and brightening it had either no effect (Eriksen & Rohrbaugh, 1970) or a positive effect (Adelson & Jonides, 1980). These differences between measurements of persistence and cued report therefore dictate caution in equating memory performance in partial report experiments with subjective persistence of the visual display.

Coltheart (1983) has argued that although the precategorical icon indeed underlies the phenomenon of visual persistence, the beneficial effects of cuing in partial report experiments probably occur at a higher level. In particular, he suggested that cuing effects may facilitate transfer from a postcategorical representation to a response buffer. His candidate for these postcategorical representations are the object files proposed by Kahneman and Treisman (1983) and discussed at the end of Chapter 11.

The existence of iconic memory is well documented, and many of its properties are well understood. Much less clear, however, is its functional role in ongoing visual processing: What is it for? One possibility is that iconic memory is used to process information during saccadic eye movements. As we mentioned in Section 11.1, visual input appears to be suppressed during saccades. Iconic memory might allow these gaps in input to be used for processing during the downtime between fixations. Although this sounds like a plausible hypothesis, research indicates that some perceptual encoding processes are actually inhibited during saccadic eye movements (e.g., Sanders & Houtmans, 1985). This does not mean that all perceptual processing ceases during saccades, because priming and word recognition processes appear

to continue while the eyes are in motion (Irwin, 1998; Irwin, Carlson-Radvansky, & Andrews, 1995), but it would be a stretch to claim that current evidence supports the hypothesis that iconic memory exists to facilitate processing during saccades.

Another possibility is that this brief form of visual memory may be related to the motion processing system. As we stated in Section 10.1.5, several computational theories of motion postulate a comparison between two spatially separate regions over a temporal delay. This temporal delay implies a brief visual memory for prior stimulation to which present stimulation can be compared for evidence of image motion. Perhaps iconic memory is this memory component of the motion perception system, which manifests itself under conditions of nonmotion as a brief but detailed memory of recent retinal stimulation.

Another possibility is that iconic memory is just a benign by-product of some other mechanism that does have functional significance. One such hypothesis is that iconic memory arises from residual retinal activity in the rods (Sakitt, 1976). The functional significance of rods is that they are much more sensitive to light than cones are and therefore can support vision under low levels of illumination. Because rods also have a much slower neural decay rate than cones, they will remain active for some time after the offset of a brief visual display. The rod-based theory of iconic memory, then, is that this form of memory arises from the continued firing of retinal rods after the cones have stopped firing. As simple and intriguing as this hypothesis may be, however, subsequent tests have shown that the partial report advantage attributed to iconic memory is evident under conditions in which retinal rods could not mediate it, although they may contribute to visible persistence under conditions of dark adaptation (Adelson, 1978, 1979). The functional role of iconic memory therefore remains an enigma after nearly 40 years of investigation.

12.1.3 Visual Short-Term Memory

Iconic memory is widely believed to be a very brief form of precategorical visual memory, generally lasting no more than a second or so. Is this extremely short, low-level form of visual memory sufficient to bridge the gap to long-term visual memory, or is there some intermediate form? Experimental evidence supports the existence of such an intermediate visual memory system. We will call it **visual short-term memory** (or *visual STM*) to emphasize its relation to the construct of STM in the classical memory literature as described in Section 12.1.1.

Visual STM versus Iconic Memory. Given that iconic memory is thought to be precategorical, there is a pretty obvious experiment that seems as though it would demonstrate the existence of visual STM. People would be shown meaningful displays, consisting of letters, words, or pictures of known objects, and their memory would be tested after retention intervals greater than the 1-s duration of iconic memory. Unfortunately, when subjects in a memory task are presented with such meaningful visual materials, they usually categorize and name them. If the first item were a picture of a dog, for example, it would quickly be categorized as a dog, and this would, in turn, provide access to its name and to semantic information (e.g., what nonvisual properties the object has, what it is used for, what other objects it tends to be found with, and so on). Naming provides access to the sequence of phonemes that make up the names and therefore an alternative coding in terms of acoustical structure. Both of these consequences of categorization thus add new kinds of information that are not strictly visual, and these other forms of information could also be used to span the temporal interval between visual presentation and memory test. Because findings based on memory for meaningful, nameable items may be contaminated by these other forms of information, they cannot be taken as pure measures of visual memory.

One solution to this problem is to use meaningless visual materials: items that cannot be categorized or named in the first place. This was the approach taken by British psychologist William Phillips in his pioneering studies of visual STM. He constructed meaningless patterns of black and white squares in matrices that varied in complexity from 4×4 to 8×8 (Phillips, 1974). Figure 12.1.7 shows some examples. He then showed subjects a series of trials in which one such matrix was followed by a second matrix after a specified retention interval ranging from 0 to 9 s. The two matrices were either identical or differed by just one square. Subjects were required to make same/different judgments of the second (test) pattern with respect to the first

4 x 4 Grid

Figure 12.1.7 Stimuli for a visual short-term memory experiment. Random patterns of varying complexity were presented and later tested for recognition memory using the identical pattern or one differing by only one square, as illustrated in the right column.

(study) pattern, and their accuracy in doing so was measured.

The results are plotted in Figure 12.1.8. At very short retention intervals of less than 0.5 s, memory was essentially perfect for all matrix sizes. This level of memory performance was presumably mediated by iconic memory, since the stimulus parameters are within the bounds that define this form of memory. At longer retention intervals, however, memory declined substantially and depended strongly on the complexity of the matrices. The 8×8 matrices dropped to near-chance levels (50% correct) by a 3-s retention interval, but the 6×6 and 4×4 matrices both provided clear evidence of above-chance performance to at least 9 s, far beyond the temporal limits of iconic memory. Phillips suggested that this performance was mediated by a different form of memory: visual STM.

In other experiments Phillips (1974) investigated additional properties of visual STM. For example, he studied the nature of the spatial coordinates in iconic

Visual Memory and Imagery

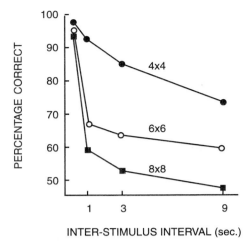

Figure 12.1.8 Recognition memory for random patterns as a function of retention interval and complexity. Memory decreases over a 9-s interval, with greater forgetting of the more complex patterns. (From Phillips, 1974.)

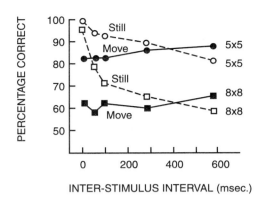

Figure 12.1.9 Recognition memory for random patterns as a function of retention interval and displacement. When matrices of two levels of complexity were tested in the same position ("still" condition), memory decreased as the retention interval increased, but when they were displaced one square to the right ("move" condition), the retention interval did not affect memory performance. (From Phillips, 1974.)

memory and visual STM by looking at what happened when the position of the pattern changed between the study and test presentations. Iconic memory is generally thought to be specified in terms of absolute retinal coordinates, so changing the position of the pattern between study and test should greatly disrupt performance based on iconic memory. Spatial information in visual STM, on the other hand, might be coded in object-based reference frames and so might be relatively immune to changes in position.

This is indeed what Phillips found, as illustrated in Figure 12.1.9. When the positions of the matrices were not changed (as was the case in the initial experiment described above), retention decreased as a function of time. Performance at less than 0.5 s was again excellent, as expected from iconic memory, and then declined to lower levels as the retention interval increased. When the positions were changed, however, the retention curves were essentially flat. This suggests that performance in this condition was mediated completely by visual STM with no contribution from iconic memory, as would be expected under the hypothesis just described. Therefore, we conclude that visual STM represents spatial information in terms of relative positions, whereas iconic memory does so in terms of absolute retinal positions.

Visual STM versus Visual LTM. The distinction between visual STM and visual LTM was justified largely by analogy to corresponding differences that had been found in verbal memory. To understand the relation, we will digress briefly to illustrate how verbal memory researchers teased apart these different memory systems using a memory paradigm known as **free recall.**

In a verbal free recall experiment, subjects are presented with a list of words, typically 10–30 of them, and are then asked to recall as many words as possible in any order they wish. The results of such an experiment can be summarized in the **serial position curve**: a plot of the probability of correctly recalling an item as a function of its serial position in the list. Typical serial position curves are illustrated by the solid curves in Figure 12.1.10 for lists containing 10 or 20 words (Postman & Phillips, 1965). They begin at an elevated level, decline to a relatively constant middle region, and then rise steeply at the end. Why does this graph of free recall performance have this particular shape?

Memory theorists currently believe that different portions of the serial position curve reflect retrieval from STM and LTM. The elevated recall level for the last four to five words of the list, called the **recency effect**, is widely believed to reflect mainly retrieval from STM. Recall of earlier items is attributed to retrieval from LTM, including both the elevated **primacy effect** at

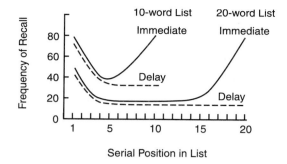

Figure 12.1.10 Typical effects of delay on the serial position curve for recall of verbal materials. When lists of 10 or 20 words were tested immediately, recall of the last five or six items is elevated in a classic recency effect. When rehearsal is prevented during a 30-s delay prior to recall, the recency effect disappears for both list lengths. (Redrawn from data of Postman & Phillips, 1965.)

the beginning of the list and the lower portion in the middle. The reason these parts of the serial position curve are thought to arise from different memory systems is that they respond quite differently to specific changes in the free recall procedure.

Normally, subjects are instructed to begin recalling as soon as the last word of the list has been presented. This procedure results in a strong recency effect because subjects almost always recall the last few items in the list immediately. This fact is attributed to subjects retrieving as many items as possible from STM before they start searching LTM. If they are prevented from doing so by having to perform some other cognitively demanding task during a 20- to 30-s delay—such as counting backward by threes from a given three-digit number—the recency portion of the curve disappears entirely, as indicated by the dashed curves in Figure 12.1.10 (Postman & Phillips, 1965). Counting backward has much less of an effect on the level of recall in the primacy or middle portions of the serial position curve, however, a result suggesting that it is selectively affecting the contribution of STM.

Other manipulations in the free recall paradigm change the primacy and middle portions of the serial position curve without much affecting the recency portion. One such factor is the presentation rate. When the word list is presented at a slower rate, recall in the early part of the list is higher, but the recency effect is unchanged (Murdock, 1962). This presumably reflects bet-

ter storage of semantic information in LTM when there is more time to encode it but no corresponding effect on storage in verbal STM, which is typically thought to represent the sounds of the words. Other variables, such as the relatedness of the words, have similar effects, increasing the level of recall in the beginning and middle of the list without much affecting that at the end.

Many related differences of this kind eventually convinced memory researchers in the 1960s that there are two types of memory underlying our ability to remember verbal information over normal time spans from several seconds to several years. The question to which we now turn is whether a similar distinction between visual STM and visual LTM is also required to account for visual memory results.

Phillips and Christie (1977) investigated the relation of visual STM to visual LTM using matrices of black and white squares similar to those employed in earlier studies of visual STM. They reasoned that if there were a visual STM analogous to standard verbal STM, then similar operations might be used to distinguish it from visual LTM. They therefore studied the serial position curve, but using a visual recognition memory task like the one Phillips (1974) had used before rather than a recall task. After the list of matrices had been presented, they tested recognition for matrices that either were identical to ones they had seen before or differed by only one square.

Their results showed that there was a recency effect, as in verbal memory, but just for the very last item, as illustrated in the solid curve in Figure 12.1.11. This suggests that visual STM has a capacity of only one visual display and that each time a new display is presented, it overwrites the previous one. When subjects were required to perform a mental arithmetic task after the end of the list and before the recognition test (dashed curve in Figure 12.1.11), the single-item recency effect was entirely eliminated, whereas the earlier items were unaffected. Analogous to the corresponding results with verbal materials, this finding suggests that the recency effect is due to visual STM, whereas memory for earlier items is due to visual LTM. It also seems to indicate that visual STM can be actively rehearsed by visualization, but not if attention is diverted to some other distracting task. Phillips and Christie (1977) also examined the effect of changing the rate at which the matrices were presented. Faster rates reduced recognition performance

Visual Memory and Imagery

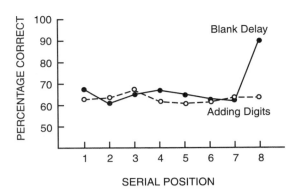

Figure 12.1.11 Effects of mental arithmetic on the serial position curve for recognition of visual materials. When visual recognition memory is tested after a blank delay interval, a recency effect of one item is present. When subjects had to add digits during the delay interval, the recency effect disappeared. (From Phillips & Christie, 1977.)

for the earlier items but did not affect the level of the recency effect, much as has been found in similar experiments on verbal memory.

The findings on visual STM can be summarized in terms of our five characteristics of memory systems as follows:

1. *Duration*. Information in visual STM appears to last at least 10 s, probably longer if no additional visual input replaces it. Its duration is surely much longer than the half-second or so of iconic memory. This inference is based on the fact that the curves in Figure 12.1.8 for the simpler items are clearly above chance at the 9-s retention interval and show only modest decreases with time. The limiting duration of visual STM depends on maintenance activities, as is evidenced by the loss of information when rehearsal was blocked by a concurrent mental arithmetic problem.

2. *Content*. The information in visual STM is clearly spatial and appears to be represented in an abstract, object-based coordinate system, as suggested above. Because the meaning of visually presented information is available in less than 1 s, the content of visual STM is almost certainly postcategorical if the to-be-remembered materials are meaningful, although this related semantic information is presumably contained in other memory systems.

3. *Capacity*. The capacity of visual STM is limited to the most recent display. There appear to be capacity limi-

tations within this single display, however, as evidenced by the large differences in level of memory for different-sized matrices (see Figure 12.1.8). The precise nature of these limitations is not yet clear.

4. *Loss*. Information in visual STM appears to be lost mainly through replacement, as evidenced by the single-item recency effect described above. It may also be lost through decay if the most recent item is not rehearsed, however, as is suggested by the slow decrease in accuracy with increasing retention intervals.

5. *Maintenance*. Unlike iconic memory, information in visual STM appears to be rehearsable. The evidence is the disappearance of the one-item recency effect when subjects are required to perform a difficult mental arithmetic task. Information in visual STM therefore appears to be actively visualized in a way that requires processing resources.

The Visuo-Spatial Scratch Pad. There is another theoretical construct in the memory literature that may refer to the same underlying system as visual STM. It is the visuo-spatial scratch pad (or sketchpad) proposed by Baddeley and Hitch (1974) as one component of their concept of working memory.

Working memory is a theoretical construct that is closely related to classical STM. Indeed, working memory is sometimes used simply as an alternative name for STM, but the two underlying conceptions differ importantly in emphasis. The standard view of STM is as a unitary memory storage system whose primary purpose is to bridge the gap between very short-term SIS and the more permanent LTM. Working memory is a broader construct that emphasizes the role of STM structures in executive control of processing in virtually all cognitive tasks (Baddeley, 1986).

Consistent with this broader and more complex view, working memory is conceived as having important internal structure. Specifically, it is proposed to contain a **central executive** that controls the processing of information in all kinds of cognitive tasks—including comprehension and problem solving as well as memory tasks—plus a number of **"slave" memories**: subservient memory systems that code recently accessed information in a specific sensory modality. These slave memories function much like cache memories in modern digital computers in the sense that they are much

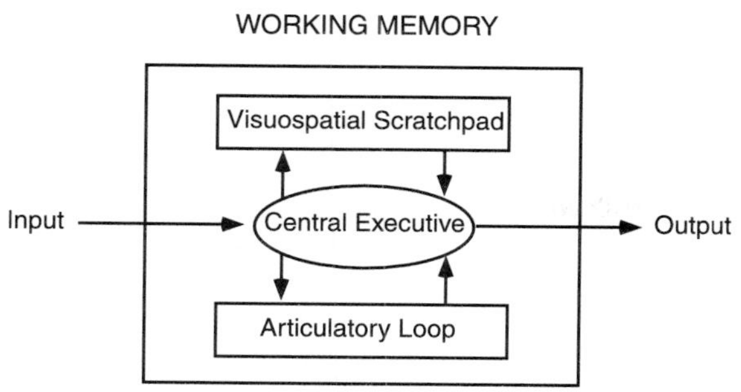

WORKING MEMORY

Input → Central Executive → Output

Visuospatial Scratchpad

Articulatory Loop

Figure 12.1.12 A flow diagram of working memory. Working memory is an elaboration of STM in which there is a central executive function plus separate memory stores for visual/spatial and auditory/articulatory information.

faster and easier to access than LTM. Within working memory, verbal information in phonemic form is stored in the **articulatory loop**, and visual and/or spatial information is stored in the **visuo-spatial scratch pad (VSSP)**. There may be other storage systems for information in other modalities as well, but these two are the most important and intensively studied. Figure 12.1.12 shows a flow diagram of working memory as conceived by Baddeley and Hitch (1974).

The rationale for postulating a multistore system within working memory can be illustrated by experiments investigating modality-specific interference effects in a variety of tasks. In one such experiment, Logie (1986) instructed some subjects in a memory task to use an imagery strategy of forming visual images of the objects named by the words and told other subjects to use a rote rehearsal strategy of repeating the words silently to themselves. He then measured the effect of different kinds of distractor stimuli—either irrelevant visual patterns or irrelevant words—while subjects were trying to memorize the list. He found that the visual patterns decreased memory for subjects engaged in imagery processing but not for those engaged in rote rehearsal. Irrelevant words, on the other hand, disrupted recall for subjects engaged in rote rehearsal but not for those engaged in imagery processing. These findings indicate selective interference within memory modalities, as would be expected if there were modality-specific stores within working memory. Given the role of the visual sketchpad in working memory, it is natural to equate it with visual STM.

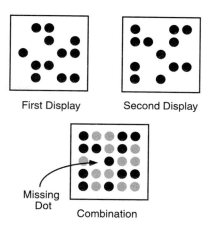

First Display   Second Display

Missing Dot   Combination

Figure 12.1.13 Stimuli for an experiment on transsaccadic memory. Subjects are presented with two displays separated by a delay. Each display consists of 12 dots from a 5×5 matrix such that, when they are combined, only one dot is missing. When no eye movement is required, subjects are excellent at this task, but when an eye movement is made between the two presentations, performance is poor.

Transsaccadic Memory. Another kind of visual memory that may be closely related to visual STM is that which mediates the integration of information across saccades, sometimes called **transsaccadic memory**. In Section 11.1.3 we noted that creating a coherent perception of a unified scene from multiple fixations requires some form of memory. Rayner, McConkie, and Erlich (1978) hypothesized that there might be an integrative visual buffer that effectively superimposes the contents of successive fixations, as illustrated in Figure 11.1.11. This would require a large-scale spatiotopically organized memory, much like an enlarged, longer-lasting version of iconic memory, plus procedures to place the contents of the fixations appropriately within it. As plausible as this spatiotopic fusion hypothesis seems, however, its predictions have generally failed to be confirmed in experiments that were designed to test them.

Irwin, Yantis, and Jonides (1983) reasoned that if an integrative visual buffer exists in which the contents of multiple fixations can be superimposed, subjects should be able to perceive the composite of two different stimuli presented in the same environmental location but in different fixations. As illustrated in Figure 12.1.13, they presented subjects with 12 dots from a 5×5 array in the first display and 12 others in the second display. The task was to report the location of the "missing dot" that was not present in either display. When the two displays are presented to a stationary eye, so that their locations are retinally superimposed, subjects do very well on this task (Di Lollo, 1980). Performance begins to deteriorate when the time between the two displays approaches the limits of iconic memory, but this is consistent with the hypothesis that fusion can occur in iconic memory as long as no eye movement takes place.

In the transsaccadic condition, however, subjects had to make an eye movement to a target cross after the first display and before the second so that the two parts were no longer retinally aligned, even though they were still environmentally aligned. Under these conditions, subjects reported no experience of visual integration into a single array, and accuracy was very low. The results thus contradict the predictions of spatiotopic fusion in an integrative visual buffer.

Further experiments by Irwin and his colleagues examined the characteristics of transsaccadic memory using a partial report procedure with a bar marker as described in Section 12.1.2. The experimental events are diagrammed in Figure 12.1.14 (Irwin, 1992). The main differences from previous experiments on iconic memory were that eye fixations were measured and that

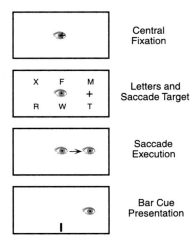

Figure 12.1.14 Procedure for an experiment on transsaccadic partial report. After fixating a central point for 1.5 s, a 2 × 3 array of letters is presented until the subject makes a saccade to a target (+), usually within about 250 ms. After a 40- to 750-ms delay, a bar marker is presented under one of the originally presented letters, and subjects are required to name the cued letter and report its position ("W-5" in the case depicted).

after the initial presentation of the letter array, subjects had to make a saccade to a target cross before the bar cue was presented. The eye movement caused the position of the bar not to be *retinally* aligned with the to-be-reported letter, even though it was *environmentally* aligned with it. The results showed that report of the correct letter in this task was substantially worse than when no saccade was made. Further results using this procedure indicate that transsaccadic memory is limited to about four items in a single display, decays little in nearly a full second, and is better for identity than location information (Irwin & Gordon, 1998). Note that these properties correspond far more closely to those of visual STM than to those of iconic memory. This fact suggests that visual STM may be the memory system that supports integration of visual information across fixations.

If memory for objects across saccadic eye movements is so poor, why then do we have such a strong impression that we perceive a single, stable, spatially integrated environment over many fixations? Experimental results undercut the possibility that it is because the visual system creates a single, stable, spatially integrated representation from many fixations, so the most plausible alternative is that it is because the environment itself is unitary, stable, integrated, and coherent. That is, the stability and unity may come largely from the nature of the world rather than from the nature of our visual representation of it (O'Regan, 1992).

Recent evidence for this hypothesis comes from experiments in which subjects have to make a saccade from an initial fixation point to a designated object in a picture and the stimulus is changed during the saccade (Currie, McConkie, Carlson-Radvansky, & Irwin, 1995). The location of either the entire picture, just the target object, or just the background behind the object was shifted while the eye was in motion. Subjects usually detected the shift if the target object was moved. If the target object was stationary, however, subjects usually perceived stability, even if everything else in the picture shifted. Therefore, perceived stability across fixations seems to depend mainly on processes involving the perceived location of the target object stored in visual STM. Much of the rest of the stability in our perceptions depends on the stability of what we are looking at.

Conceptual Short-Term Memory. To firmly establish the existence of visual STM independent of confounding memories for any information of a nonvisual sort, experimenters took great pains to use meaningless visual materials such as the black-and-white grid matrices devised by Phillips (1974) and the paired missing-dot matrices employed by Irwin et al. (1983). Such materials are well suited to their intended purpose but highly unrepresentative of the kind of visual material we experience and remember in our daily lives. Almost all the visual objects we perceive as we locomote through the environment, play sports, read books, watch TV, eat meals, and so forth are *meaningful* in the sense of having semantic or conceptual content over and above strictly visual features. Indeed, we argued in Chapter 1 that extracting this conceptual information from optical structure is a primary function of vision.

None of the visual memory experiments we have described thus far address questions about the time course of extracting and remembering this conceptual information. When does it become available? How long does it last? Under what conditions is it forgotten? Only recently have such issues begun to be studied, primarily by using an experimental paradigm known as **rapid serial visual presentation (RSVP)**. RSVP requires presenting a series of many visual displays, usually centered at fixation, at rates of many displays over a few seconds (Forster, 1970). This technique has been employed by Potter, Intraub, and their associates to investigate the activation, structuring, and retention of conceptual representations based on visual input in both pictorial and linguistic forms.

In an RSVP experiment, subjects might be shown a series of, say, 16 color photographs of a wide variety of scenes at a presentation rate selected from the range between 1 picture every 2 seconds (2000 ms per picture) to 10 pictures per second (100 ms per picture). Before seeing a stream of pictures, they would be asked either to try to detect the presence of any picture fitting a fairly abstract conceptual description (e.g., "a picnic scene" or "two people drinking") or to try to remember them for a later old/new recognition memory task. At slow presentation rates (1 or 2 seconds each), people are easily able to detect and recognize a conceptually described picture. At fast presentation rates (100 ms each), they can still detect conceptually described pictures reasonably well, but cannot recognize them at better than chance levels (Potter & Levy, 1969; Potter, 1976). People thus appear to be able to compehend such meaningful pictures within 100–200 ms, but not to be able to form stable memory traces for them during this time span.

Is this because such short durations are simply not long enough to support memory performance, or is there something about seeing several pictures in rapid succession that blocks the formation of memories? Further experiments showed that memory for pictures presented singly at durations of only 100 ms is quite good, even when the pictures are followed by a visual noise mask (Potter, 1976). The problem in remembering a picture in an RSVP stream is therefore not caused either by the short duration of the picture itself or by purely the visual masking that arises from the immediately following picture (Intraub, 1980, 1984; Loftus & Ginn, 1984; Potter, 1976). Rather, it appears to be caused by **conceptual masking**: the reduction in memory performance for a meaningful picture that is produced by the subsequent presentation of another novel, meaningful picture. Conceptual masking occurs when subsequent pictures are presented within about 500 ms of the previous picture's onset.

To account for such findings, Potter and her associates have proposed a brief memory system for conceptual information that they call **conceptual short-term memory (CSTM)**. CSTM is claimed to be different from classical STM and the various forms of purely visuo-spatial memory we have just considered. It contains semantic representations of recognized objects in meaningful contexts that are structured by rapid processes requiring no more than 100–200 ms. To turn these transitory representations into durable memories that will last for periods within the range of classical STM requires some additional encoding or consolidation process that takes at least another 400 ms and may require focusing attention on the item. If attention is somehow diverted from the current conceptual representation or if another conceptual representation is constructed of the next picture before this 400 ms is up, conceptual masking takes place, and the subject will not be able to remember having seen the picture at all.

These two phases of CSTM—an initial encoding phase of about 100 ms and a second consolidation phase of about 400 ms—may also be able to account for other phenomena, such as inattentional blindness, the attentional blink, and change blindness. In each case, a clearly visible stimulus is not reported as having been seen under conditions in which attention is absorbed by

Visual Memory and Imagery

another task or shifted to another stimulus event. In such cases, the account in terms of CSTM is that the initial event was indeed perceived during the first 100 ms or so, but was not remembered because the consolidation phase did not have the time and resources it needed to occur. Only fractions of a second after having seen and comprehended an object or event, the observer claims not to have seen it because this fleeting and fragile representation vanished as quickly as it was constructed.

It is not yet clear exactly how CSTM might relate to and be integrated with other information-processing constructs such as attention, object files, iconic memory, visual STM, the visuo-spatial scratchpad, transsaccadic memory, and classical STM. Nor is it clear whether or in what sense the representations in CSTM are conscious. What is clear is that conceptual understanding of coherent pictures and sentences takes place very quickly but appears to leave no memory trace unless some form of further attentive processing is performed. Once attention is turned to these conceptual representations, they can be transformed into some more durable form that may last anywhere from seconds to decades.

We see that visual STM appears to be heavily involved in the important function of integrating visual information across saccades and other brief interruptions of visual information. In the final section of this chapter, we will consider the possibility that visual STM is also involved in the creation and manipulation of visual images. Some models of imagery postulate a visual buffer within which images are constructed and processed (e.g., Kosslyn, 1980). Such an imagery buffer has properties that are similar to those we have just described for visual STM, leading to the conjecture that visual STM, the visuospatial scratch pad, transsaccadic memory, and the imagery buffer may all be minor variants of a single underlying visual memory system. Before we turn to visual imagery, however, we must first consider how visual information might be stored in a more permanent form than we have yet discussed.

12.1.4 Visual Long-Term Memory

Clearly, we are able to remember visual information for more than the tens of seconds it is thought to reside in visual STM. We will follow general memory theorists in calling this more permanent storage system long-term memory (LTM) and its visual components **visual LTM**.

Consistent with our treatment of visual memory thus far, we will frame our discussion of visual LTM as though it simply concerned visual aspects of a much more comprehensive memory system that contains information from other sensory modalities (auditory, olfactory, kinesthetic, etc.) as well as more abstract conceptual information.

Three Types of LTM. For a variety of reasons, modern memory theorists distinguish between several different kinds of LTM, usually called semantic, episodic, and procedural memory. Because we will follow this framework in our discussion, it will be useful to review these general concepts before narrowing our focus to visual LTM.

1. **Semantic memory** includes information in LTM that concerns general knowledge of generic concepts. A good analogy for semantic memory is the kind of information that one typically finds in a dictionary or encyclopedia. In the case of the concept "hammer," for example, semantic memory would contain the information that hammers are tools, that they are used for driving nails into objects, that they always have a handle and a head and sometimes claws opposite the head, and that if they have claws, they can also be used to remove nails from objects.

2. **Procedural memory** includes information in LTM concerning general knowledge about generic skills—that is, knowing how to use something rather than knowing what it is. It contains the kind of information one typically finds in a user's manual. In the case of hammers, procedural memory would contain information about how to hold a hammer by the handle with your hand, how to swing it backward and forward with your arm to bring the head into contact with a nail, and how to grip a partly hammered nail by its head using the claw and then rock the hammer back against the head to remove nails.

3. **Episodic memory** includes information in LTM about specific objects and events that one has experienced as part of one's personal life history. A good analogy for episodic memory is the kind of information one would find in a diary. In the case of hammer-related knowledge, it might contain information about the time your dad gave you a plastic hammer for your sixth

birthday, the time you smashed your thumb with a hammer when you were putting up the fence in your back yard, and so forth.

There are visual analogs to all three kinds of LTM. The kind of visual LTM that is analogous to semantic memory concerns the visual appearance of generic object types. It is the vast storehouse of visual representations that we use to categorize perceived objects, as discussed at length in Chapter 9. It is also presumed to be the source of visual information about the appearance of objects that we use in producing spatial patterns, such as drawing or imaging well-known types of objects. Consistent with our discussion in Chapters 8 and 9, we will assume that this form of visual LTM consists of a complex, interconnected network of structural descriptions that can be accessed either by incoming visual input (for categorizing objects) or by internal search (for imagining objects). We will return to this form of visual LTM at the end of this chapter when we discuss imagery in detail.

Visual Routines. Part of the storehouse of procedural memory in vision is the set of processes that people have for extracting useful information from optical information. Ullman (1984) has distinguished between those early visual processes that are performed in parallel, bottom-up, and without focused attention versus those later processes that operate only with the benefit of focused attention to a single object or group. He calls the latter processes **visual routines**. Although Ullman's discussion of visual routines focused on the processes that might be used in analyzing complex properties of incoming visual information, the concept can be extended to include the processes that operate on visual images retrieved from memory, such as generating and transforming images for a variety of tasks. The latter operations are most closely related to the study of visual imagery, and so we will defer their discussion until later.

Ullman (1984) suggests that the perception of shape and spatial relations among various parts is supported by sophisticated visual routines that are constructed from a set of primitive routines or elemental operations. These primitives, as well as useful sequences of them that are programmed into more complex routines, are stored in procedural visual memory and used in identifying objects and performing many other specific visual

tasks. Ullman suggested five plausible elemental operations and gave a computational analysis of how they might be carried out:

1. *Shifting the focus of processing.* This operation allows all visual routines to be applied to any location in the visual field simply by shifting the center of processing. It corresponds to changing the position of focal attention as discussed in Section 11.2.

2. *Indexing.* Indexing involves selection of a location where something is "different," as in visual pop-out (Section 11.2.5) and various pull cues that summon attention (Section 11.2.2).

3. *Bounded activation (or "coloring").* Coloring is used to find the interior of a region by spreading activation within its boundaries.

4. *Boundary tracing.* This operation is used to determine whether two locations are on the boundary of the same object.

5. *Marking.* Marking a location is an operation that designates it as one to be remembered so that it can be accessed quickly at a later time.

Obviously, there must be many more elemental operations and a huge number of complex visual routines based on them. Ullman has called attention to the general problem of what they might be and how they might be carried out, but very little other work has been done on procedural aspects of visual LTM.

The analog to visual episodic memory is what we normally think about as being long-term visual memory: information about the appearance of objects and events from specific prior experiences in one's life. This will be the topic of discussion for the remainder of this section.

Recall versus Recognition. Everyday experience suggests that LTM for visual information is very good. We have all had the experience of recognizing a person as someone we know without being able to recall the person's name or even how we know him or her. Similarly, many people say, "I may forget a name, but I never forget a face," indicating more confidence in their visual than their verbal memory. But is this faith really justified?

The answer turns out to depend on a number of factors, including how memory is tested. In verbal memory experiments, the generally favored method of assessing memory is a **recall memory task**: the reproduction of the to-be-remembered words by writing or speaking. This works well for verbal materials because everyone is quite adept at producing spoken and written words, and two words are easy to score categorically as being the same or different. Neither holds true for recall of visual material, however. Few people draw well enough to be sure that discrepancies between the figure they saw and the figure they reproduce from memory are due to limitations of the memory rather than the act of reproducing it. One method for overcoming this problem is to have subjects copy the to-be-remembered figure while it is perceptually present and then to compare the reproduction from memory with the copied version (Hanawalt, 1937). The degree to which the recalled version is less similar to the original figure than is the copied version can be taken as a measure of how poor the visual memory is.

Although this comparison procedure provides a good control for drawing limitations, there is another problem with recall procedures for visual figures that is not so easily overcome. Once the experimenter has the perceptual copy and memory reproduction in hand, he or she must make some assessment of how similar they are to the original figure. This is difficult because there are always perceptible differences to some degree. If there were a well-defined and well-accepted theory of visual similarity, it could be used to score the degree of difference. Unfortunately, there is no such theory, as we discovered in Chapter 8.

For these reasons, there have been few definitive studies of visual memory using recall procedures. What few have been done are difficult to interpret. Researchers on visual memory have therefore turned to a different method for testing memory that overcomes most of these problems.

In a visual **recognition memory task**, subjects are shown an initial set of visual items and are later tested by being shown another set of items, some of which they have seen before and others of which they have not. There are two major variants of this procedure. In a **yes-no** (or **old-new**) **recognition test**, subjects are shown test items individually and asked to say for each one whether it is one they have seen before ("old") or not ("new"). Subjects are often asked to rate their confidence in each response once they have made it. In a **forced-choice recognition test**, subjects are shown two or more alternative items and asked to indicate which they think they saw before. Confidence ratings can also be made following each choice.

Recognition overcomes both problems with trying to measure recall of visual material. First, subjects do not have to draw anything, so drawing ability is irrelevant. Second, coding correct versus incorrect responses is easy because there is an unambiguous classification of each test item as having been presented in the initial learning phase or not. This is not to say that recognition memory tests are without problems; they are just different problems. The most difficult is the nature of the **distractors** (sometimes called **foils**): the test items that were not previously presented, for which the correct response is "new." Whether a subject will make an error on, say, a two-alternative forced-choice test is very highly dependent on the nature of the distractors.

Consider a picture of a beach scene shown during the initial presentation phase. In the testing phase, the distractor for this picture could be a close-up of a tulip, a picture of people at poolside, a picture of a different beach scene, or a picture of the same beach scene taken a few moments later when some of the people had moved or some new object had appeared in the scene. Clearly, the likelihood of someone mistaking the tulip for the beach scene is lowest and that of mistaking the same beach scene a few moments later for the original is highest, with the others in between. But the problem goes deeper than just overall similarity. Certain aspects of the initial beach scene were presumably encoded and present in memory at testing, whereas others were not. Suppose the subject remembered that the beach umbrella was red but not that the dog was a poodle. He or she would then not make an error when the distractor was an otherwise identical beach scene with a green umbrella but might make an error when it was an otherwise identical beach scene with a cocker spaniel. Such problems are inherent in recognition memory tests. Even so, recognition tests are generally considered sufficiently superior to recall tests that recognition procedures are used almost exclusively in modern studies of visual memory.

How Good Is Episodic Visual LTM? One of the earliest demonstrations that visual recognition memory is excellent, even when recall is poor, came from an experiment by Rock and Engelstein (1959). They showed subjects a single meaningless shape and tested memory for it up to a month later. By that time, almost no subjects could reproduce the shape from memory, yet almost all were able to recognize it from a set of similarly meaningless distractors.

Subsequent studies pushed the limits of visual recognition memory a great deal further. For example, Shepard (1967) had subjects look through 600 vacation pictures at their own rate. Using a testing procedure in which subjects were required to decide which of two pictures they had seen before, he found that people were 98% correct immediately after seeing the original slides. Under comparable conditions, subjects shown 600 words were only 90% correct, and those shown 600 sentences only 88% correct. Even more impressive results were reported in a study using 2,560 slides shown for 10 seconds each. After several days, recognition memory was still above 90% (Standing, Conezio, & Haber, 1970).

It is difficult to know exactly what to make of such results, however, because recognition memory depends on so many different factors. One is the similarity of the to-be-remembered items to each other. The more dissimilar they are, the better memory performance will be. Another crucial variable, already mentioned, is the similarity of the distractors in the recognition test. Again, the more dissimilar they are, the better memory performance will be, since any difference between them could be sufficient to discriminate the one seen before from the new one. Therefore, on both counts, one would expect recognition memory for pictures in the just-cited studies to be excellent, given that the slides they used as targets and distractors were about as dissimilar as pictures can be. It is not even certain that recognition memory in these cases was necessarily based on visual rather than verbal information, for subjects could have named scenes or objects and discriminated between the two tested alternatives on that basis.

A more stringent test of visual LTM was conducted by Goldstein and Chance (1971) using highly similar, difficult-to-name objects such as snowflakes, inkblots, and women's faces. They showed their subjects just 14 stimuli for only 2–3 seconds each and then tested recognition memory either immediately or 48 hours later. When the 14 old items were embedded in 70 new distractors, subjects were correct on 33% of the snowflakes, 46% of the inkblots, and 71% of the faces, with almost no forgetting during the two-day retention period.

Superficially, these results appear to contradict those of earlier studies, for the levels of accuracy are not nearly as impressive. A more careful look, however, suggests that they are not so contradictory, because visual memory is clearly better than chance and is surely much superior to what could possibly have been achieved by using purely verbal encodings of the complex and highly similar patterns under comparable presentation and testing conditions.

Given that visual memory for these briefly presented objects is as good as it is, one might think visual recognition memory for common objects that are seen every day would be essentially perfect. This is not necessarily the case, however, as demonstrated in a study of memory for the appearance of an American penny (Nickerson & Adams, 1979). Without cheating by looking at one, try to pick the correct penny from among the highly similar distractors shown in Figure 12.1.15. If you are like the subjects in this experiment, you will find it difficult; only 42% chose the correct one. Although this is more than the 7% expected by chance, it is a far cry from 100%.

How can this finding be squared with the otherwise superior memory for visual information? Perhaps the most important factor is that most of our daily encounters with pennies involve only the most cursory perception of their features. With the exception of coin collectors and makers, people generally determine that a given coin is a penny simply by perceiving its size and color, only occasionally even noticing the central picture on its side. The arrangement of the fine spatial details that are manipulated in the distractors appears not to be very well encoded in memory. This is an interesting fact because it suggests that registration of visual information in memory is not completely automatic. Rather, it appears to depend heavily on which features of an object one attends to when perceiving it.

Visual Imagery as a Mnemonic Device. Another indication that visual memory is indeed excellent comes from the effectiveness of **mnemonic devices** (memory strategies) based on visual imagery. One of the best ways to improve memory performance for verbal information is by engaging in visualization. This technique, which is described in virtually every self-help book on memory, is far from a modern discovery. It was well known to ancient Greek and Roman orators, who made frequent use

Visual Memory and Imagery

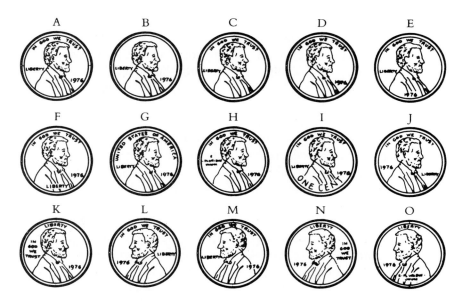

Figure 12.1.15 Fifteen test stimuli in an experiment on visual recognition memory for a penny. Subjects were asked to choose the drawing that most closely conformed to their visual memory of a penny. Despite the high level of visual experience with pennies, only 42% chose the correct alternative. (From Nickerson & Adams, 1979.)

of the **method of loci** to remember the sequence of topics in their speeches.

The method of loci works well for remembering any ordered list of items, such as your plan for doing your activities for the day. Suppose, for example, that you decide to go first to the post office to buy stamps, then to the library to work on your term paper, then to the gym, then to chemistry class, and so on. To apply the method of loci, you first identify a well-known route in your environment, say, the walk from your apartment to the university. Then you imagine an object that is associated with each activity at salient locations along the route in the order you want to recall them. On the door of your apartment building, you might imagine a huge stamp being pasted. At the entrance to the laundromat down the street, you might imagine a pile of library books. At the next corner, you might imagine a pair of giant sneakers hanging from the traffic light, and so on. Then, during the day, when you want to recall what to do next, you take a mental walk along this route, remembering the sequence of images that you constructed earlier and decoding them to recover the intended activity.

A related mnemonic device that relies heavily on visual imagery is the use of peg words. One first learns a simple rhyme: "One is a bun, two is a shoe, three is a tree, four is a door, five is a hive," and so on, each number being associated with a common object whose name rhymes with the number. Then, to remember an ordered list of items, each item is imagined paired with the corresponding object named by the peg word in the prescribed order. To use our previous example, a stamp might be imagined pasted to the top of a hamburger bun, a book stuffed into a very large shoe, a pair of sneakers hanging from the branch of a tree, and so forth. Then, when you wish to recall the list, the rhyme is used to generate the peg word images—first a bun, then a shoe, then a tree, and so on—with the other images (ideally) being retrieved at the same time. Then all that remains is remembering or reconstructing what activities the objects signify.

Dual Coding Theory. Modern psychological studies of visual imagery began with experiments that were designed to investigate their effects on memory. Some of the earliest findings concerned the memorability of different kinds of words in verbal learning tasks. It had long been known that the frequency with which a given word is used in the language is an important factor in how well it will be remembered. However, Canadian psychologist Alan Paivio found that an even more potent variable was the concreteness versus abstractness of words. He had subjects rate the probability that a given word would evoke a visual image and then showed that concrete, imageable words (e.g., book, hammer, telephone, elephant) were remembered much better than abstract, nonimageable words (e.g., truth, life, freedom, intelligence) in large part because the visual appearance of concrete words can easily be imagined during learning (Paivio, 1969). The interesting theoretical question was why using visual imagery might improve memory.

Paivio (1969) proposed the **dual coding theory** of memory to explain his results. His basic claim was simply that there are two separate storage systems in LTM: one for verbal/linguistic information and another for visual/imagistic information. Highly concrete, imageable words were hypothesized to be encoded in both the verbal and visual memory stores, whereas abstract, nonimageable words were hypothesized to be encoded in just the verbal memory store. Words that have been imaged during the learning phase are better remembered in the testing phase because they can be retrieved from either the visual store, the verbal store, or both, whereas words that have not been imaged at encoding are available only in the verbal store.

This theory implies that using both verbal and visual encoding strategies will always lead to better memory than either one alone, but more recent research has shown this prediction to be incorrect. Schooler and his colleagues (Dodson, Johnson, & Schooler, 1997; Schooler & Engstler-Schooler, 1990) investigated the effects of verbal description on memory for faces and found that it degrades rather than improves subsequent recognition performance. In a typical experiment all subjects are initially shown a visual display containing faces. Half the subjects are then asked to verbally describe the face in detail, and the other half are asked to perform a control task, such as naming states, for an equal period of time. In the later recognition memory task, subjects had to choose the previously seen face from among several other similar faces. The surprising result is that the subjects who verbally described the face selected the correct face much *less* frequently than the control subjects did. This so-called **verbal overshadowing effect** is obtained not just with faces, but also with other visual materials, such as colors, for which visual information appears to be much finer grained than verbal descriptions.

Such findings suggest that dual coding of information is not always better. When the to-be-remembered information is visual and requires fine perceptual discriminations, verbal descriptions can actually be harmful to later recognition accuracy. This implies, for example, that an eyewitness is likely to be less accurate in picking the correct suspect from a police line-up if the eyewitness is required to give a detailed verbal description of the criminal's face beforehand. Exactly why this verbal overshadowing effect occurs is not yet clear. It may well result from lower-resolution verbal information competing with the higher-resolution perceptual information, although other interpretations are possible (Dodson et al., 1997). In any event, it certainly implies that visual recognition memory for certain kinds of information is much more effective than even extended verbal descriptions of the same stimulus.

Photographic Memory. Another source of evidence for the potency of visual memory is the existence of people who have extremely vivid and detailed visual memories, popularly known as **photographic memory** and technically known as **eidetic imagery**. One of the most fascinating facts about eidetic images is that the people who have them typically experience them as "outside the head" and therefore as phenomenologically different from normal memory images. Consistent with this claim, they can usually be scanned by eye movements, as though the object or scene were actually being viewed. Very few people actually possess this incredibly vivid and accurate form of visual memory, but it has nevertheless been subjected to scientific study. It appears to be more frequent in children than adults, for example, but even so, only 7% of children were classified as eidetic imagers in a large-scale study of 500 children (Leask, Haber, & Haber, 1969).

By far the most dramatic demonstration of eidetic imagery was reported by Stromeyer and Psotka (1970). A young woman with striking eidetic abilities was presented with one image of a random dot stereogram (see Figure 5.3.8) to just one eye. On the next day, she was shown the other image of the stereo pair and was able to fuse it with the eidetic image of the first random dot pattern so that the correct figure stood out in depth as it would have had both images been viewed simultaneously under appropriate conditions! This is a truly amazing feat of purely visual memory, for no verbal description could possibly have mediated her ability to see the figure in depth. Unfortunately, this subject has not been studied subsequently by others, and no comparable feats of eidetic imagery have been reported.

Mnemonists. Other individuals with remarkable memory abilities—called **mnemonists**—also show a strong visual component. Perhaps the best-known example is S, a mnemonist who was studied by the great Russian neuropsychologist A. R. Luria (1968). S was able to learn a matrix of 50 digits perfectly in just 3 minutes of study. Once they were learned, he could recall the digits in any specified order, as though he was reading them from a page. Moreover, he could retain such seemingly meaningless information for years.

S's mental functioning has many unusual aspects that appear to be closely related to his remarkable memory. One is his extraordinary degree of **synesthesia**, the tendency for sensory experiences in one modality to evoke correlated experiences in other modalities. For example, when S heard a pure tone of 2000 Hz, he reported the following synesthetic experiences: "It looks something like fireworks tinged with a pink-red hue. The strip of color feels rough and unpleasant and it has an ugly taste—rather like that of a briny pickle ... you could hurt your hand on this" (Luria, 1968, p. 23). Perhaps his synesthesia helped S to remember things, in part, because they were encoded into memory in several sensory modalities rather than just one, as is normally the case.

S typically reported using vivid and sometimes bizarre visual images in remembering even meaningless material. For example, in memorizing a complex mathematical formula that began $(\mathcal{N} \cdot \sqrt{d^2})$, he described the following imagery:

Neiman (N) came out and jabbed at the ground with his cane (·). He looked up at a tall tree which resembled the square-root sign ($\sqrt{\ }$), and thought to himself: "No wonder the tree has withered and begun to expose its roots. After all, it was here when I built these two houses (d^2)." (Luria, 1968, p. 49)

(The Russian word for house begins with "d.") This unusual sequence of images enabled S not only to remember the equation at the time he learned it, but to recall it 15 years later!

It is worth noting that S's remarkable powers of memory were not entirely a blessing. His vivid visual imagery, for example, caused him to have unusual difficulty in understanding simple prose passages. In his own words, S complained, "Each word calls up images; they collide with one another, and the result is chaos" (Luria, 1968, p. 65). In trying to comprehend the simple phrase, "the work got underway normally," S reported the following imagery:

As for "work," I see that work is going on ... there's a factory ... but there's that word "normally." What I see is a big, ruddy-cheeked woman—a "normal" woman ... then that expression "get underway." Who? What is all this? You have industry ... that is a factory, and this normal woman—but how does all this fit together? How much I have to get rid of to get the simple idea of the thing! (Luria, 1968, p. 128)

Neuropsychology of Visual Memory. In contrast to such individuals with extraordinarily good memory are those with extraordinarily bad memory, usually as the result of brain damage. There is now a large literature documenting that lesions in certain areas of cortex characteristically cause **amnesia**: a profound reduction in the ability to remember due to organic brain damage. When the problem is remembering old information that was known before the brain was damaged, it is called **retrograde amnesia**. This is the sort of amnesia that is widely portrayed in books and movies when someone receives a blow to the head and forgets who he or she is and what he or she has done. There is another form of amnesia, called **anterograde amnesia**, that is theoretically just as interesting. It occurs when the patient has difficulty remembering new information that occurred after the brain was damaged.

Anterograde amnesia is one of the classic phenomena cited to support the distinction between STM and LTM. It typically follows from severe bilateral damage to the temporal lobes. A patient known as H.M., for example, had portions of both temporal lobes surgically removed to relieve severe epilepsy (Milner, 1966). The operation succeeded in reducing his epilepsy but left H.M. completely unable to form new long-term memories. He could remember his personal experiences quite normally up to a time very near the operation but was profoundly incapable of forming any new memories after that, either visual or verbal. If you spoke with H.M. and were forced to leave the room for more than a minute, when you returned, he would have totally forgotten both the conversation and you.

Later studies by Milner (1968) and Ross (1980, 1982) showed that damage to the two temporal lobes was functionally asymmetrical. Lesions in left temporal cortex selectively impaired verbal memory, whereas those in right temporal cortex selectively impaired visual memory. Visual memory deficits in the right temporal lobe were studied carefully by Hanley, Pearson, and Young (1990), who compared the visual and verbal memory performance of a 55-year-old patient with age- and sex-matched controls. The patient, known as E.L.D., suffered a stroke in 1985 when she was 49 years old that damaged her right frontotemporal region. After the stroke, she complained of memory problems, particularly of difficulty in remembering new faces and learning new routes. She had difficulty following television programs because she could not remember the faces of the different characters, for example, and had trouble finding her way home.

Preliminary behavioral tests showed that she had no visual agnosia (inability to categorize objects visually; see Section 9.2.5) unilateral neglect (inability to attend to half the visual field; see Section 11.2.7), or loss of basic visual functions. To assess her visual memory before versus after her stroke, she was shown 26 faces of people who became famous before 1985 and 26 others who became famous after 1985. E.L.D. was no different from control subjects in remembering the names and occupations associated with pre-1985 faces, but she was much worse for post-1985 faces. When she was presented with the names, however, her ability to recall occupations was as good as that of controls for both pre-1985 and post-1985 celebrities. Further tests indicated that her impairment was not limited to faces, but affected her memory for unfamiliar objects as well. Therefore, she appears to be a pure case of anterograde visual amnesia. The most likely explanation of this condition is that the brain structures responsible for transferring information from visual STM to visual LTM were severely damaged by the stroke.

E.L.D.'s spatial memory was also severely impaired. Although she could find her way to and get around in her parents' and sister's houses, which she knew before 1985, she had great trouble remembering how to get to her own post-1985 home and could not remember her

way around new houses that she visited. If she had to leave the room at her day-center, she would often return to the wrong seat, much to her friends' amusement.

The fact that both visual and spatial memory are impaired in E.L.D. suggest that her problem might lie in damage to the visuo-spatial sketchpad of working memory as postulated by Baddeley and Hitch (1974) (see Section 12.1.3). To explore this possibility, Hanley, Young, and Pearson (1991) tested her memory for spatial sequences using a board on which nine randomly positioned wooden blocks were glued. The experimenter tapped some number of blocks in a specified sequence, which she was then asked to reproduce. She did well when the to-be-remembered series was three blocks or fewer, but her performance fell to zero for sequences of five blocks or more. In contrast, normal control subjects were correct on more than 80% of the five-block sequences and more than 60% of the six-block sequences. In a task requiring memory for sequences of four unfamiliar faces, E.L.D.'s performance was also systematically worse than controls, particularly for the last face, which is the one most recently held in visual STM. This result is in striking contrast to her sequential memory for letters, which was systematically better than that of controls. The overall pattern of findings are thus consistent with the hypothesis that E.L.D.'s visuo-spatial sketchpad in working memory is impaired, whereas her articulatory loop is intact.

Hanley, Young, and Pearson (1991) also examined the possibility that E.L.D.'s visual imagery might suffer as a result of her visual memory deficit. They found that her memory for word lists was not improved by imagery instructions, as it typically is in normal subjects (Paivio, 1970), and that she was very poor at performing mental rotations of 3-D block configurations (see Section 12.2.2). These results thus support the possibility mentioned earlier that the visual buffer of Kosslyn's (1980) imagery theory (see Section 12.2.4) is the same as Phillips's visual STM and Baddeley and Hitch's visuo-spatial sketchpad.

Interestingly, E.L.D.'s problems with imagery do not appear to stem from difficulty in retrieving information from visual LTM. Further tests showed that she was able to perform normally on questions that required reporting the characteristic color of named objects (e.g., a golf ball), deciding which of two named objects is bigger (e.g., a toothbrush or a banana), and which of a pair of faces is most like a target (e.g., whether Winston Churchill or Adolph Hitler looks more like Charlie Chaplin). This result is in contrast to another patient, L.H., who could perform normally on imagery tasks such as mental rotation but could not answer questions like these that required retrieval of information from visual LTM (Farah, Hammond, Levine, & Calvanio, 1988).

These findings support the hypothesis that the right temporal lobe of the brain contains the neural substrate of short-term memory for visual and spatial information and their transfer or consolidation into long-term memories. Damage to this structure can profoundly impair memory for unfamiliar visuo-spatial information as well as visual imagery abilities but does not affect short-term verbal memories, previously learned long-term visual memories, or the ability to retrieve previously learned information from visual LTM. Thus, visual STM appears to be distinct from visual LTM and from verbal STM, at least by neuropsychological criteria.

12.1.5 Memory Dynamics

Research has established that visual memory is very good and that it can last a long time. Even so, memories change with the passage of time. That they become "weaker" in some sense seems undeniable, whether this weakening is due to autonomous decay with time or interference from other information. Regardless of the mechanism, the dominant view has always been that this weakening is essentially neutral and undirected.

There have been several dissenting views in the literature, however, suggesting that visual memory may not simply become weaker over time, but undergo systematic changes or distortions. The general idea that memories may change systematically in time is called **memory dynamics**. The notion that memory is dynamic in this way has always been regarded with suspicion by mainstream memory theorists. Perhaps for this reason, empirical claims of dynamic effects in memory have usually been subjected to severe methodological scrutiny. In many cases, this scrutiny has turned out to be justified, resulting in the reversal of opinion about whether or not memories actually change systematically over time. In this section we examine a number of different claims for memory dynamics that have appeared in the literature quite independently over the years.

Tendencies toward Goodness. Gestalt psychologists were among the first to suggest that visual memories might undergo systematic distortions over time. They theorized that visual information in memory would gradually become "better" in the Gestalt sense (i.e., simpler, more symmetric, and more regular, as described in Section 8.3 on figural goodness). Their belief in the Law of Prägnanz—that perception will be as "good" as the prevailing conditions allow—was the basis of this prediction, because Gestaltists believed that a pervasive "force toward goodness" operated in memory as well as in perception. In perception, this force is counterbalanced by the constraints of the visual stimulus on the retina (called "the prevailing conditions"). But once information is in memory, such stimulus constraints were thought to be less effective, thus providing an opportunity for systematic distortions to occur toward better, more regular, more symmetrical figures.

The pioneering experiments on this topic were performed by the Gestalt psychologist Wulf (1922). He showed subjects 20 figures and later asked them to reproduce the figures from memory after retention intervals of 30 seconds, 1 day, and 1 week. He analyzed their reproductions and claimed substantial support for the hypothesis of systematic, progressive change in the direction of regularity and symmetry. However, his experiment had several major methodological flaws that clouded its interpretation (Riley, 1962).

One problem was using reproduction to test visual memory. As mentioned above, it seems entirely possible that subjects' drawing abilities might limit their ability to express the degree of irregularity and asymmetry in their memories of the figures. Subsequent studies therefore used recognition memory procedures, although this method introduces other problems. Another difficulty with Wulf's study was the repeated testing of the same subject at different retention intervals. On the second memory test, for example, were subjects remembering the original stimulus, their attempted reproduction on the first memory test, or some combination of the two? Yet another problem was determining which changes Gestalt theory actually predicted, for there was no well-defined theory of figural goodness that could be used to unequivocally determine which changes were in the direction of greater goodness and which were not.

Many experiments were performed to test the Gestalt hypothesis that figures in memory autonomously become "better" over time. To illustrate the lengths to which researchers have gone to eliminate methodological problems, we will consider an experiment by Hanawalt (1952). Subjects were shown a single figure in which there was just one salient dimension along which the figure could become either "better" or "worse": a circle with a 5° gap in it. The presumption was that since a complete circle is a very "good" figure, dynamic forces toward goodness in memory should cause the gap to close over time. Visual memory was then tested by using a particularly clever recognition procedure. Subjects were shown a comparison figure that was actually identical to the initial figure (i.e., one having a 5° gap) and were then asked to say whether the gap in this test figure was bigger or smaller than the one they had seen before. The Gestalt hypothesis predicts that, if the initial gap had gotten smaller over time in memory, subjects should say that the gap in the test stimulus was bigger. The results of this carefully controlled study failed to find the predicted effect.

Further studies by the Gestalt psychologist Erich Goldmeier (1982) garnered additional support for the Gestalt hypothesis of greater figural goodness, but only under restricted conditions. Goldmeier's results are somewhat difficult to interpret, however, because his predictions are based on an intuitive rather than a formal theory of goodness. Moreover, the effects he did find were small. The bottom line appears to be that such effects, if they exist at all, are relatively minor and rare. The tendency for figures in LTM to become better over time therefore does not appear to be a major force in visual memory.

Effects of Verbal Labels. Another suggestion of systematic distortions in visual memory concerns the effects of verbal labels. The hypothesis underlying this line of research is that verbal labels interact with visual information in memory in such a way that the visual information becomes more consistent with the verbal label with the passage of time.

The hypothesis that such effects might occur was supported in a classic study by Carmichael, Hogen, and Walter (1932). They presented subjects with 12 ambiguous figures, such as the ones shown in the central column of Figure 12.1.16, together with a label that corresponded to one of the figure's two most obvious possible interpretations. For example, the rectangle with four

interior lines in Figure 12.1.16 was presented with the label "curtains in a window" to one group of subjects and "diamond in a rectangle" to another. Later reproductions of these forms from memory showed systematic distortions toward the presented label, a result that seems to support the hypothesis that memory is dynamic under these circumstances.

As in the case of Wulf's study of goodness dynamics, however, this experiment has significant methodological flaws. One problem is whether the effect is due to actual distortions in visual memory or to some aspect of the process of recall and reproduction. Prentice (1954) therefore repeated the experiment using recognition memory instead of recall—that is, asking subjects to choose which of several pictures had actually been presented—and found no distortions due to labels. This result suggests that the label affected neither the initial storage of visual information nor its nature during retention but retrieval processes during recall. Other evidence supporting this possibility comes from a study in which labels were not presented initially with the visual figure but were introduced only at testing (e.g., "Draw the figure that looked like eyeglasses"). Under these conditions, distortions similar to those reported by Carmichael et al. (1932) were obtained. Since the labels were presented *only* at recall, they cannot have affected either initial encoding or the stored information during retention. It appears, then, that although verbal information can affect visual memory performance in a recall paradigm, it does so at the retrieval stage and therefore is not consistent with the existence of dynamic effects in memory per se.

The Misinformation Effect. A related case for which it has been suggested that visual information in LTM is systematically distorted by verbal information comes from studies of what has come to be called the **misinformation effect**. These experiments were conducted to investigate biases that might be introduced by leading questions such as attorneys often use in interrogating eyewitnesses. Such questions typically presuppose some piece of potentially inaccurate information that may then distort the original unbiased memory. For example, in a trial of an alleged shooting incident, a witness who heard a loud noise might be asked, "At what time did you hear the gunshot?" when it had not yet been established that the loud noise was, in fact, a

Visual Memory and Imagery

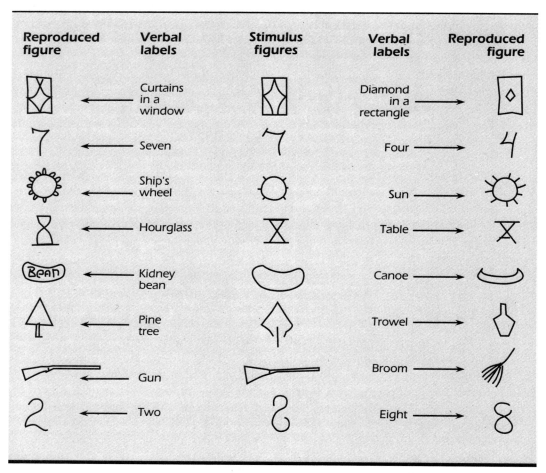

Figure 12.1.16 Examples of stimuli and reconstructions in an experiment on verbal labeling of visual information. Subjects were initially shown the stimulus figures in the central column to- gether with one of two verbal labels shown next to them. Representative distortions are shown for each case. (From Sternberg, 1996.)

gunshot. Is it possible that the witness's memory for the event will subsequently distort in the direction of the re- membered noise sounding more like a gunshot than it actually did?

This type of memory scenario has been investigated extensively by psychologist Elizabeth Loftus and her colleagues at the University of Washington. In one of the earliest studies, all subjects were shown the same videotape of an automotive collision (Loftus & Palmer, 1974). Half the subjects were then asked to estimate the speed of the cars "when they smashed into each other"; the other half were asked to estimate the speed "when they hit each other." Consistent with the fact that the term "smashed" clearly presupposes that the cars were going faster than the more neutral term "hit," subjects in the "smashed" condition gave higher estimates of the speed (10.5 miles per hour) than those in the "hit" con- dition (8.0 miles per hour). Moreover, subjects in the "smashed" condition were more likely to (inaccurately) report the presence of broken glass when tested a week later.

The classic misinformation study has the following basic design, diagrammed in Figure 12.1.17. All subjects are shown an initial event, usually an accident of some sort, in a videotape or sequence of slides. This event contains some information that will later be tested, such as whether the traffic sign at the scene of the accident was a stop sign or a yield sign. Let us suppose that it was

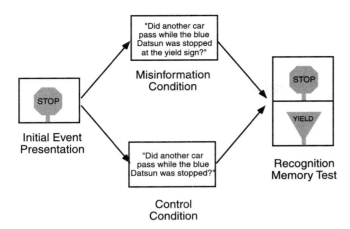

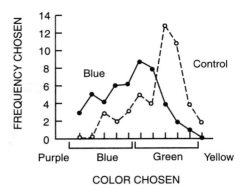

Figure 12.1.18 A blending effect on color memory due to misinformation. Subjects were initially shown a visual scene containing a green car. After exposure to misleading verbal information presupposing that the car was blue, more subjects chose bluer color chips as matching the car than did control subjects who did not receive such misinformation. (From Loftus, 1977.)

Figure 12.1.17 The misinformation paradigm in visual memory. Subjects see a videotape containing visual information (e.g., the stop sign on the left) followed by either misleading verbal information (top quotation) or neutral verbal information (bottom quotation). Their memory for the original object is later tested by using forced-choice recognition procedures. Subjects in the misinformation condition are more likely to misrecognize the yield sign than controls.

actually a stop sign. Half of the subjects are then assigned to the "misinformation condition" in which they are exposed to a verbal presupposition that it was a yield sign, such as, "Did another car pass the blue Datsun while it was stopped at the yield sign?" The other half of the subjects are assigned to the control condition, in which they are given the same question but without any reference to a traffic sign. After some period of time has passed, memory for the sign is tested in both groups, typically by a forced-choice visual recognition test between a stop sign and a yield sign.

The misinformation effect in this case would be that the misinformed subjects are more likely to choose the yield sign than the control subjects, and this is indeed the case (Loftus, Miller, & Burns, 1978). In the actual experiment this entire design was also repeated with a yield sign being presented in the initial visual event and a stop sign being suggested verbally in the misinformation condition. Again, the verbal suggestion increased the number of false recognitions of the corresponding object.

Further experiments have shown interesting "blending effects" on visual information due to postevent verbal descriptions. In one such experiment, Loftus (1977) showed subjects a series of slides of an accident in which

a green car drove past the scene of the mishap. Half the subjects later answered the question, "Did the blue car that drove past the accident have a ski rack on the roof?" The control subjects answered the same question without the word "blue" in it. Loftus found that subjects exposed to the "blue" description picked bluer color chips from among a set of 30 alternatives than did control subjects, as shown in Figure 12.1.18. This result is consistent with the possibility that the misinformation actually distorts the original memory in the direction of becoming bluer, but it is not conclusive in this regard. The problem is that memories for the target event and the postevent description might be stored quite separately and accurately, yet still produce a blending effect at testing.

Numerous experiments using the misinformation paradigm have firmly established that such memory effects exist and can lead eyewitnesses to alter their reports of what they remember. This fact has clear and important implications for the nature of eyewitness testimony and the conditions under which it is elicited during interrogations both inside and outside of the courtroom. But the issue that will concern us here is the theoretical question of whether the postevent misinformation actually causes changes in the initial visual memory by overwriting or distorting it or whether it simply produces a distinct memory for the misleading postevent information that influences later recall of the incident, much as the verbal labeling effect apparently does.

Loftus and her colleagues favor the **distortion hypothesis**, which states that postevent misinformation becomes inextricably integrated into the original memory, irreversibly distorting it (e.g., Loftus, Schooler, & Wagenaar, 1985). Other researchers oppose the distortion hypothesis. Some favor the idea that separate memory representations exist for the original perceptual event and the later verbal misinformation but that the misinformation somehow reduces the accessibility of the original memory (e.g., Bekerian & Bowers, 1983). Others dispute the claim that postevent misinformation has any effect whatsoever on the original memory (McCloskey & Zaragoza, 1985).

As in the case of verbal labeling, the critical issues concern methodology. The most radical challenge is McCloskey and Zaragoza's (1985) contention that Loftus's results contain no evidence that any change has taken place in memory at all. The logic of their argument is that all of the misinformation effect can be attributed to biasing the performance of subjects who had no initial memory of the crucial fact at all. To see how this can happen, let us suppose that 40% of the subjects encode and retain the information that the traffic sign in the initial event was a stop sign and 60% do not. Let us further suppose that all of those who truly remember the stop sign choose it in the recognition test, regardless of whether they are in the misinformed or control group. The control subjects who do not remember the stop sign will, of course, be forced to guess randomly because they have no source of other information. Random guessing between the two alternatives will produce responding at about 50% correct. This will result in a total of 70% correct in the control condition: the 40% who actually remember it plus the half of the 60% who don't (that is, 30% who correctly guess it by chance).

But what about the 60% of the misinformed subjects who have no memory of the traffic sign from the original event? They have subsequently heard a verbal description involving a yield sign, a description that they have no particular reason to doubt, given their lack of visual memory for the stop sign. For the sake of argument, let us suppose that half of these subjects remember the verbal description and use it in responding to the memory test. None of these subjects will be correct. The other half (or 30% of the total), who do not remember the verbal description of the yield sign, will be forced to guess randomly at a rate of 50% correct. The mis-

informed group will therefore be correct in the memory test only 55% of the time (the 40% of the subjects who actually remember the sign plus only 15% from the subjects who do not). This total is substantially less than the 70% correct for the control group, a difference that is consistent with the misinformation effect. McCloskey and Zaragoza (1985) therefore argued that a sizable difference in memory performance can be predicted without assuming that the postevent misinformation has affected the original memory of any subjects at all. Rather, it may have its effect simply by influencing the response of subjects who either did not encode or later forgot the crucial feature of the original event.

McCloskey and Zaragoza (1985) went on to propose a slightly modified recognition procedure that they argued would be a more accurate test of whether the original visual memory was changed by the postevent misinformation. The modification was simply to use a third object type as the distractor in the recognition memory test. In the example described above, for example, the recognition test would be between the originally presented stop sign and, say, a no-parking sign (or some other familiar traffic sign) so that misinformed subjects who had no memory of the original stop sign would not be biased to choose the incorrect alternative based on their memory of the verbally described yield sign. If the misinformation had actually changed the original memory of the stop sign into a yield sign, subjects should still be less likely to choose the stop sign. In a series of six experiments, they replicated the classic misinformation effect using the standard recognition test (72% correct in the control condition versus 37% correct in the misled condition) and failed to replicate it using their own procedure (75% correct in the control condition versus 72% correct in the misled condition). They argued, therefore, that the misinformation effect is not evidence of distorting the original memory at all, but rather a complex biasing effect due to a distinct memory for the postevent misinformation that occurs in the absence of memory for the original event.

Despite the compelling nature of McCloskey and Zaragoza's argument and their experimental demonstration, the question of whether memory distortions are caused by subsequent misleading information is not completely settled. Loftus, Schooler, and Wagenaar (1985) countered that McCloskey and Zaragoza's all-or-none kind of analysis was inappropriate and could not deal with the memory blending effects for color information reported by Loftus (1977). Moreover, they claimed that more sensitive methods for testing memory using McCloskey and Zaragoza's modified recognition procedure showed a significant misinformation effect. Nevertheless, there is now substantial doubt about the validity of the original claim that misleading postevent information can cause permanent and irreversible changes in the original memory. As in the case of the goodness effect and the verbal labeling effect, better methods suggest that such changes either do not occur or, if they do, are much less robust than was initially claimed.

Representational Momentum. Yet another claim for dynamic distortions in visual memory arose from Freyd and Finke's (1984) discovery of **representational momentum**. This phenomenon is rather different from those we have just discussed in that it is intrinsically tied to the dynamics of objects perceived or inferred to be moving. Simply stated, representational momentum is a memory distortion akin to physical momentum in moving objects: The final position of an abruptly halted object is misremembered as being farther along its path of motion than it actually was.

Figure 12.1.19A shows a sequence of stimuli that illustrate the basic phenomenon. Subjects are first shown the sequence of three static pictures, each for 250 ms with a 100- to 900-ms interval between presentations. Each picture depicts a rectangle in a different orientation, as though it were undergoing a rotation. Subjects were told to remember the third (target) picture on each trial and then to decide whether a fourth (test) figure was identical to the target or not. The test figures were rectangles in orientations similar to that of the last presented figure. Freyd and Finke discovered that subjects were much more likely to say that the test figure matched the target if the test figure was a bit farther along the implied path of motion than the target had been. Figure 12.1.20 shows the choice percentages for each tested orientation in the solid curve. Notice that the responses are not symmetrical and are biased toward orientations in the direction of continued motion, as if the object's (implied) momentum carried over into its memory representation. This is the signature of representational momentum.

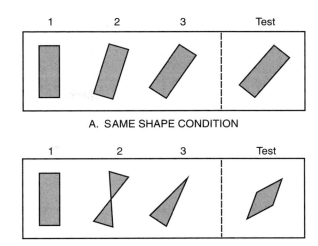

A. SAME SHAPE CONDITION

B. DIFFERENT SHAPE CONDITION

Figure 12.1.19 Stimuli for two experiments on representational momentum. Subjects are shown a series of three visual displays in which an object's orientation changes systematically. After a variable delay, subjects are shown a test stimulus and asked whether it was identical to the final display of the series. Part A depicts an experiment in which all three figures are identical in shape. Part B depicts an analogous experiment in which they differ dramatically. (After Kelly & Freyd, 1987.)

This representational momentum effect does not require that the object be actually perceived in (apparent) motion, but it does require the sequence of pictures to be consistent with a coherent motion trajectory for a single object. If the order of the initial two pictures is reversed, for example, no momentum effect is obtained (Freyd & Finke, 1984). The momentum effect also disappears if the three pictures are of different shapes rather than the same one, even when the orientations of those objects correspond exactly to conditions that produce the momentum effect, as illustrated in Figure 12.1.19B (Kelly & Freyd, 1987). The results from this different-shapes condition are graphed in the dashed curve of Figure 12.1.20. Notice that it is quite symmetrical, with no hint of the momentum effect.

Further experiments have examined the time course of the momentum effect. It occurs for very brief intervals between target and test, on the order of 10–100 ms. Within this range, the amount of displacement increases linearly with the retention interval. Another important finding is that the momentum effect appears to be impervious to feedback about the correct answer and to

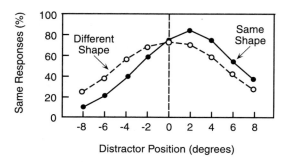

Figure 12.1.20 The representational momentum effect. The percentage of subjects who judged the test figure (see Figure 12.1.19) to have the same orientation as the final (third) figure is plotted as a function of the orientation of the test figure relative to the correct orientation. When the figures are identical in shape (solid curve), subjects tend to choose test figures whose orientation is beyond that of the last shown object. When the figures differ in shape, no such tendency is found (dashed curve). (Data from Kelly & Freyd, 1987.)

extended practice. Both of these results suggest that it is automatic and unavoidable.

Therefore, it appears that representational momentum is a true dynamic effect. It occurs during the first hundred or so milliseconds after the target picture is turned off, as though prior displacements of the same object carry over into the memory representation. Perhaps the most serious theoretical issue is whether it is appropriate to think of it as a memory effect at all. Rather, it is possible to think of it as a perceptual extension of the stimulus event that has continued beyond the actual end of sensory stimulation. Once the perception has ended, the final perceived location of the object is stored in a more durable memory. If the effect occurs in the first 100 ms, it surely is a change not in the visual LTM representation, but in some earlier memory system, possibly even iconic memory.

Although somewhat far afield, representational momentum can be conceived as a dynamic analog to the occlusion illusion in size perception. As illustrated in Figure 7.1.15, when the visual system interprets one object as being occluded by another, the visible portion of the occluded object is extrapolated slightly into its unseen portion behind the occluder so that it appears larger than it actually is. Similarly, representational momentum can be viewed as the temporal extrapolation of an unfinished event into its unseen completion so that it appears to have gone farther than it actually did.

We have now considered four different examples in which claims have been made that visual memory is dynamic in the sense of changing systematically over time: toward "better" structure, toward consistency with a verbal label, toward consistency with an indirect verbal presupposition, and toward completion of a motion event. There is little firm evidence that visual memories change in systematic ways once they are encoded, either by themselves or because of later related events. Performance on visual memory tasks can certainly be influenced by subsequent events, but careful studies indicate that these effects appear to occur primarily at testing rather than by changing the visual memory itself. The possible exception to this generalization, representational momentum, occurs during a very brief period of time, a finding that rules out the possibility that it is caused by dynamic properties of visual LTM.

12.2 Visual Imagery

When we recall visual information stored in LTM, we often have vision-related experiences that are typically called **visual images**. The processes that are involved in generating, examining, and manipulating these images are usually referred to as **visual imagery**. To demonstrate some important features of visual imagery, imagine the shape of the Taj Mahal. Almost everybody knows what it looks like to some degree and reports some attendant visual experience of its general shape in response to this instruction. But the experience of imagining the Taj Mahal is not the same as actually perceiving it either. The perception is much richer and more detailed than the image, for example, and has solid, palpable, and external qualities that the image lacks. The image, in contrast, is vague, ill-defined, and internal. You can count the spires when you perceive the Taj Mahal, for example, whereas your image may contain only the vague sense that it has "several" or "many" of them. The study of visual imagery attempts to understand the nature and use of such visual images.

Visual imagery has played an interesting and important role in the history of psychology. In the early part of this century, it was central to the downfall of introspection as the dominant method of the field and to the rise of behaviorism. Then in the 1960s, it somewhat paradoxically was also instrumental in bringing about the demise of behaviorism and the emergence of cognitivism as the guiding theoretical approach for much of psychology.

At the end of the nineteenth century, much of psychology was grounded only in introspective analyses of experience. The role of sensory images in mental life was then a hotly debated issue that proved to be the downfall of introspection. Some psychologists (e.g., Wundt) maintained that all of human thought processes consisted of nothing but a succession of sensory images—visual, auditory, tactile, and so on—whereas others (e.g., Külpe) claimed that thought was essentially "imageless." It would seem that such a simple and basic dispute should be easy to settle, but it turned out to be impossible. The problem was that introspective methods contained no mechanism to settle such disputes scientifically. Because images are internal experiences with no direct, outward manifestation, they are available only to one's self. (We will have much more to say about the private nature of conscious experience in Chapter 13.) Because images are private, they are not directly accessible to scientific study and therefore cannot be used to resolve such controversies.

Behaviorists objected strenuously to introspection as a method for the scientific study of psychology for precisely this reason. They insisted on tying all psychological concepts to directly observable behavior. This made imagery a difficult topic to study, and during the reign of behaviorism in the 1920s to 1950s, imagery was virtually outlawed as too "mentalistic." Research on visual imagery reemerged only during the "cognitive revolution" of the 1960s, which made the study of internal, mentalistic entities scientifically respectable again. Indeed, imagery research played an important role in establishing the advantages of the cognitive approach over the behavioristic one.

The first experiments to reintroduce imagery as an acceptable topic of study were described earlier in this chapter when we discussed the effects of imagery on memory. It was found, for example, that people remembered word lists better if they consisted of nouns naming concrete objects that could easily be imagined and/or if subjects were given instructions to construct visual images of the objects named (e.g., Paivio & Yuille, 1967; Yuille & Paivio, 1968). Such experiments had a substantial impact because they were scientifically respectable owing to their objective measurements of

memory performance. They became the wedge that ultimately opened up a whole new field of imagery research by showing that these unobservable mentalistic images were clearly important in understanding human memory. The 1970s unleashed a flood of further studies about the role of imagery in other cognitive processes and eventually about the nature of imagery processes themselves. In fact, the reintroduction of visual imagery into psychology was an important factor that led to the overthrow of theoretical behaviorism as the dominant approach in human experimental psychology.

12.2.1 The Analog/Propositional Debate

Once the study of imagery was legitimized by experiments on its role in human memory, the questions that cognitive psychologists began asking concerned the nature of visual images themselves rather than their role as an aid to memory or problem solving or some other cognitive process. By far the most important theme in this line of research was the so-called **analog/propositional debate**. The fundamental issue in this controversy was whether images were picturelike (analog) representations or languagelike (propositional) representations. Although this seemed a fairly easy distinction to draw initially, it turned out to be surprisingly difficult to pin down both theoretically and experimentally.

The Analog Position. The analog position is grounded in the idea that visual images are essentially "pictures in the head." It is therefore also called the **picture metaphor theory** of imagery. It fits with most people's naive introspections about their imagery experiences because images have distinctly visual and spatial qualities that are most easily described as being picturelike. But the idea that images are like pictures in the head raises the tricky question of who or what might be "viewing" these mental pictures. The standard answer is that they are examined by "the mind's eye," some internal processing system, such as visual attention, that presumably also "views" incoming sensory information during perception.

This position was largely implicit in the early literature on imagery, although its assumptions underlay much of the research about imagery effects on memory. It was brought to the fore in an important article by cognitive scientist Zenon Pylyshyn (1973) titled "What

Visual Memory and Imagery

the Mind's Eye Tells the Mind's Brain: A Critique of Mental Imagery."[1] This paper launched the analog/propositional debate by making the picture metaphor explicit and criticizing it on a number of grounds. Pylyshyn's arguments against the picture metaphor included several serious objections:

1. *Image retrieval.* Pylyshyn took issue with the prevailing view in the memory literature—based on Paivio's dual coding theory (see Section 12.1.4)—that images are stored as uninterpreted pictures in the head. The problem is that if this were true, we couldn't possibly retrieve the right image without "looking through" them sequentially with our mind's eye. This would be a staggeringly difficult and time-consuming task. Rather, it seems that images must be interpreted so that they can be accessed by some kind of symbolic description.

2. *Interpretation of images.* Pictures are simply objects containing optical information that must be interpreted by a perceiver. If images are like pictures, then they also must be uninterpreted and rely on some perceiver (the mind's eye) to interpret them. But images, Pylyshyn claims, are intrinsically interpreted. Your image of the Taj Mahal, for example, represented the Taj Mahal from its inception; it did not require an interpretative act to be seen as the Taj Mahal.

3. *Indeterminate information.* As we noted in the Taj Mahal example, images appear to contain less information than a normal picture. But the way in which it is incomplete is unlike ways in which a normal picture can be informationally incomplete. The image of the Taj Mahal has spires but not a determinate number of spires. Normal pictures can be incomplete—for example, if a corner is torn off or part of it has faded—but cannot be indeterminate in this way.

The Propositional Position. Because of these problems with the analog view of images, Pylyshyn (1973) suggested that images were better considered as descriptions constructed of abstract propositions. Propositional representations (e.g., the structural descriptions we considered in Chapters 8 and 9) were becoming increasingly

Figure 12.2.1 The duck/rabbit ambiguous figure. Analog theorists claimed that a mental image of such a figure can be ambiguous in the same way that pictures can be ambiguous. Propositional theorists claimed that mental images were inherently interpreted and therefore unambiguous, being either clearly a duck or clearly a rabbit, and not subject to reinterpretation.

popular in theories of perception in the 1970s, and it made sense to suppose that the kinds of representations that underlay visual perception would also underlie visual imagery. Propositional representations were also consistent with the hypothesis that all of cognition was subserved by a single internal symbolic form of languagelike representation (Fodor, 1979). Rather than images being stored as pictures, Pylyshyn suggested that they were stored as propositional descriptions and then reconstructed in more detail at retrieval.

Because they are symbolic, propositional representations necessarily have the property of being interpreted and unambiguous. That is, propositions are thought to express meaning in a way that is not subject to different interpretations. A picture such as the ambiguous duck-rabbit (see Figure 12.2.1) can be interpreted either as a duck or as a rabbit, but a proposition, such as that expressed by the sentence "This object is a duck," cannot be reinterpreted as meaning that this object is a rabbit. Pylyshyn argued that this was a desirable property for the representations of images to have because, he claimed, it was also a property of images. As we will see shortly, there has been some debate about this claim in the subsequent experimental literature.

Because propositions are abstract descriptions rather than concrete spatial objects, they also have the desirable property of being able to represent incomplete information in an appropriately indeterminate way. It is possible for a propositional description of the Taj Mahal to express that it has "many spires," for example, without being committed to a specific number. Pylyshyn

---

[1] This title was a spoof of a famous article on visual processing in the frog's retina, entitled "What the Frog's Eye Tells the Frog's Brain" by Lettvin, Maturana, McCullough, and Pitts (1959).

Table 12.2.1

Analog Theories	Propositional Theories
Picturelike	Languagelike
Uninterpreted	Interpreted
Determinate	Indeterminate
Spatial format	Spatial Content
Continuous	Discrete

argued that this was another distinct advantage for propositional representations of images.

But what of the overriding subjective impression that images are like pictures rather than like sentences? Pylyshyn argued that this meant only that the representations that underlay images were very much like the representations that underlay perception, and the latter, he asserted, are more likely to be propositional than picturelike. Because they are propositions about visual and spatial structure, it is not surprising that they have the feature of being experienced as visual and spatial. That is, their subjective nature is explained by their information *content* rather than by their representational *format*.

There was a heated exchange in the imagery literature during the 1970s and 1980s debating the advantages and disadvantages of analog and propositional representations of images. This debate had the desirable result of clarifying some of the theoretical issues behind the controversy. The key stands taken by each position are summarized in Table 12.2.1. Still, answers to such questions are seldom to be found solely in theoretical arguments; they are settled by experimental evidence. Let us now take a look at what properties of imagery have been studied and how cognitive scientists have managed to discover the properties of these private cognitive events.

12.2.2 Mental Transformations

One potential source of information about whether images are analog or propositional comes from how they are transformed. Analog theorists claimed that if images were picturelike, then they should be transformed continuously, as objects in pictures might be rotated, enlarged, moved, and so forth. They also claimed that the same kinds of transformations on propositional representations should be executed in a single discrete step simply by changing a parameter. The earliest experi-

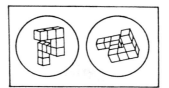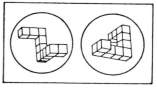

A. Picture Plane Rotations   B. Depth Rotations

Figure 12.2.2 Stimuli for an experiment on mental rotation. Subjects were shown pairs of 3-D figures that were related by picture-plane rotations (A) or rotations in depth (B). They were required to discriminate pairs that were identical (related by pure rotations as in parts A and B) from pairs that were left-right isomers (related by rotations plus reflections). (From Shepard & Metzler, 1971.)

ments aimed at determining whether images were analog or propositional examined the nature of such transformations using new and ingenious methods that yielded some of the most elegant results in cognitive psychology.

Mental Rotation. The first finding to be widely cited as supporting the analog position was **mental rotation**: people's ability to imagine objects changing their orientation continuously in 3-D space. Shepard and Metzler (1971) showed their subjects pairs of 3-D objects made out of cubes, as illustrated in Figure 12.2.2. The two objects presented on a trial were either identical objects or mirror images (left-right isomers), and the subjects' task was to determine which kind they were as quickly as they could. The amount of time subjects took to perform this task was measured.

The key to understanding the mental rotation paradigm and its results is that if two objects are identical, like two left hands, they can be rotated into complete correspondence. If they are left-right isomers, like a left hand and a right hand, there is no rotation that will bring them into complete correspondence. The identical pairs of objects differed systematically from trial to trial in terms of the smallest angle though which they could be rotated to achieve complete correspondence. The main question was how subjects' reaction times would vary as a function of this angle. Would larger rotations take longer, as the analog position implied, or would all transformations take the same amount of time, as the propositional position implied? A secondary question under investigation was whether the results would differ

Visual Memory and Imagery

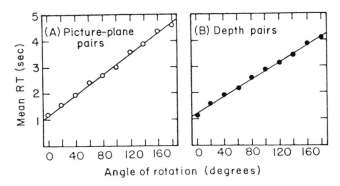

Figure 12.2.3 Results of an experiment on mental rotation. Mean response times for identical pairs of 3-D figure increased linearly as a function of the angle of rotation between them for both picture-plane rotations (A) and depth rotations (B). (From Shepard & Metzler, 1971.)

when the shortest rotation path was within the picture plane, as in Figure 12.2.2A, or required a rotation in depth through three-dimensional space, as in Figure 12.2.2B.

Shepard and Metzler's (1971) results, graphed in Figure 12.2.3, were strikingly clear. Reaction time increased linearly with increasing angles of rotation up to a maximum of 180°, just as one would expect if subjects were rotating one object into correspondence with the other through the shortest rotational path. Moreover, it didn't matter whether the rotation was in the picture plane or in depth; both conditions resulted in linear functions with almost exactly the same slope. This pattern of results is consistent with what subjects reported introspectively, as the reader can verify in trying to perform the task. What is so remarkable about the results is that the data conform precisely to the predictions of an analog theory of imagery. If images of these objects exist in an intrinsically continuous representation of 3-D space and are transformed continuously within this representation of space, then one would expect the time to complete such imagined rotations to have exactly this form.

Many subsequent experiments were performed to test various aspects of this explanation (see Shepard and Cooper, 1982, for a collection of these studies). They generally confirmed the essential predictions of the analog theory, including the following:

1. Mental rotation results occur with a wide variety of different visual stimuli, including letters and 2-D random polygons as well as 3-D cube-based objects (Cooper, 1975; Cooper & Shepard, 1973).

2. People rotate images of specific concrete objects, not abstract frames of reference (Cooper & Shepard, 1973).

3. Mental rotation consists of a continuous path of internal representations at different orientations, not just one orientation at the beginning and a different one at the end (Cooper, 1976).

4. Subjects continue to use mental rotation to perform the mirror-reversal task even after thousands of trials with the same stimuli; they do not seem to be able to learn the orientation-invariant features that can be used to perform the task (Cooper & Shepard, 1973).

These and other experiments have provided overwhelming evidence that images are transformed continuously through intermediate orientations during mental rotation tasks. It is less clear, however, that the representations being transformed in this fashion are picturelike rather than propositional. A structural description that contains quantitative parameters specifying the positions and orientations of various parts could certainly undergo changes in these parameters that would effectively simulate rotation of the object. Although such a propositional account is consistent with the obtained results, it is less satisfying than analog accounts because it doesn't explain why the parameters change continuously rather than in a single discrete jump. Analog theories explain this as an inherent property of the imagistic representations arising from the medium in which visual imagery takes place.

Other Transformations. Other investigators have extended the work on mental rotation to other image transformations. For example, Bundesen and Larsen (1975) had subjects make decisions about whether pairs of figures that differed in size were otherwise identical or mirror-image reflections. The central question was analogous to that in mental rotation experiments: Would more time be required to compensate for larger differences in size? The results showed that reaction times increased approximately linearly with the difference in size between the two figures. These results suggest that subjects are imagining one figure becoming smaller (or larger) so that the two are the same size when such comparisons are made. This result is easily explained by an analog theory of imagery, although it is also compatible with propositional accounts that include quantitative parameters for size-related information. Again, however, the analog explanation is more satisfying because it actually predicts this result rather than merely being consistent with it.

12.2.3 Image Inspection

Psychologist Stephen Kosslyn conducted another line of experiments that produced many results confirming predictions that were derived explicitly from the picture metaphor. The guiding idea behind this research was that if images are mental pictures that are viewed by the mind's eye, then the amount of time the mind's eye takes to inspect the image will vary systematically with analog properties of the image being inspected. This general idea was developed in several different lines of research, the most important of which investigated the effects of image scanning and image size.

Image Scanning. Kosslyn (1973) first tested the prediction that if the mind's eye inspects images as a real eye does pictures, then the time required to get from one part of the image to another should increase systematically with distance. In a later, more elegant experiment of this type, Kosslyn, Ball, and Reiser (1978) taught subjects a map of a fictitious island called Bora-Bora. As indicated in Figure 12.2.4, the map showed several objects whose locations were chosen so that pairs of objects gave a wide variety of different distances. In the first phase of the experiment, subjects had to learn the positions of the different objects until they could reproduce them all with a high degree of accuracy. In the second phase of the experiment, subjects were shown the names of pairs of objects on the island (e.g., ROCK and BEACH). They had to scan their image by imagining a spot moving from the first object to the second one and press a button when the spot arrived. The results of this **image-scanning task** are shown in Figure 12.2.5. They reveal a highly linear relation between response times and the distance between the pair of objects. Such results from image-scanning experiments support the predictions of the picture metaphor for processes involved in image inspection.

Image Size Effects. Kosslyn also reasoned that extracting information from an image might be influenced

Figure 12.2.4 Stimulus for an experiment on image scanning. Subjects were required to learn this map of a fictional island ("Bora-Bora") and then to use it in subsequent trials in which they had to scan their mental image from one object to another. (From Kosslyn et al., 1978.)

by other analog properties of images, such as their size. Just as it is difficult to perceive parts of an object if its retinal size is small, so too it might be difficult to discern information in a visual image if its size is small. To induce subjects to create large or small images of a specified object, he had them imagine a pair of objects in their natural relative sizes. For example, a medium-sized animal, such as a goose, would be relatively small when imagined next to an elephant but relatively large when imagined next to a fly. Once the subjects had imagined the two objects, they were asked to inspect their image to verify the presence of a specific part of one of the two objects, such as the goose's beak. On half the trials, one of the objects contained the target part; on the other half, neither did. Consistent with his prediction based on the picture metaphor, Kosslyn (1975) found that it took subjects significantly longer to verify the presence of the same part when it was imagined next to a much larger object than when it was imagined next to a much smaller object.

Visual Memory and Imagery

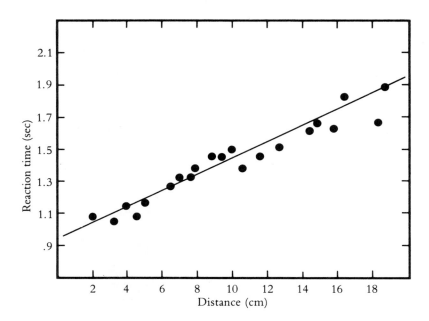

Figure 12.2.5 Results of an experiment on image scanning. Mean reaction time to scan from one object to another is plotted as a function of the distance between them on the map (Figure 12.2.4). The relationship is strongly linear, consistent with predictions based on the analog view of imagery. (From Kosslyn, Ball, & Reiser, 1978.)

Mental Psychophysics. Kosslyn embarked on a third line of research based on the picture metaphor in which he measured the properties of visual images using the kind of procedures that have been used in visual psychophysics. For example, he measured the "visual angle" of the mind's eye by having subjects imagine a given type of animal (e.g., a horse) against a blank background and then imagine moving closer to it until the horse "overflowed" the image, that is, until the entire horse could no longer be "seen" in the image. At that point, Kosslyn had subjects estimate how far away they were from the horse. Since the approximate size of horses is known in advance and the distance to the horse at the point of overflow was given by the subject, the angle subtended by the horse's image can be calculated. When subjects used a strict criterion for overflow, this angle averaged about 20°. Larger estimates of 40–60° were obtained by using a laxer criterion for overflow.

Several aspects of this result are interesting. One is that subjects apparently found it a meaningful task and gave consistent data on the size of their visual image despite differences in the initial sizes of animals. It is not obvious that this task would make sense to subjects if their images were propositional. Another is that the measured size of the visual image is considerably smaller than the field of normal vision, which typically subtends nearly 120° vertically and 180° horizontally. A third aspect is that different criteria give different estimates because the boundaries of the image field appear to be fuzzy, more like the visual field than like a picture that ends abruptly. It is unclear how a propositional theory could account for such findings.

Reinterpreting Images. Thus far, it appears that the analog theory of image representation very much dominates experimental results. Is there any evidence supporting a propositional account? One of the main claims of the propositional view is that images, unlike pictures, are intrinsically interpreted: They do not require subsequent interpretation by a perceptionlike process (Pylyshyn, 1973). Propositional theories therefore predict that images cannot be ambiguous, whereas pictures can be.

This hypothesis was tested by Chambers and Reisberg (1985). First, they had subjects learn an ambiguous figure given just one description. For example, they would show all subjects the drawing in Figure 12.2.6A and tell half that it was a duck and the other half that it

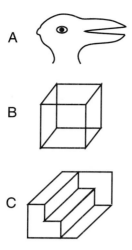

Figure 12.2.6 Stimuli for an experiment on ambiguity in visual imagery. Subjects learned to reproduce the ambiguous drawing in part A accurately after being told that it was either a duck or a rabbit. They were later unable to reinterpret it from inspecting their visual image of it but were able to do so from inspecting their own drawing of it. Similar results were obtained with the Necker cube (B) and the Shroder staircase (C).

was a rabbit. They had subjects draw the figure until they could reproduce it accurately. Then they took away the drawing and had subjects imagine the drawing and asked them whether they could see it as anything else. Almost nobody could do so. They then asked subjects to draw the figure from memory and again asked whether they could see it as anything else. Almost everybody could now do so. The results were similar using the ambiguous Necker cube and Shroder staircase (see Figures 12.2.6B and 12.2.6C). From these striking results, they concluded that the image was fundamentally an interpreted representation that was incapable of reinterpretation, as claimed by propositional theorists.

Further research has limited the generality of this conclusion, however. Finke, Pinker, and Farah (1989) challenged it on the grounds that the figures that Chambers and Reisberg used were too complex. They thought that images could indeed be reinterpreted, provided that they were simple enough. You can try some of their tasks yourself. First, imagine the letter N. Rotate it 90° clockwise. What does it look like now? Or imagine the letter D, rotate it 90° counterclockwise, and place the letter J directly underneath. What object does it look like? (The answers are: a Z and an umbrella.) Virtually all subjects could reinterpret simple images that were

constructed or transformed in this way. Such results appear to show that simple, geometrical images can be reinterpreted as if they were pictures being inspected by the mind's eye. Exactly why simple and complex figures should differ in this way is not clear, but the findings of Finke et al. (1989) indicate that images can, in principle, be reinterpreted, contrary to the predictions of propositional theories.

12.2.4 Kosslyn's Model of Imagery

The analog/propositional debate was one of the most hotly contested topics in cognitive psychology during the 1970s and early 1980s. Although it has never been fully resolved, in the sense that one view has been shown to be completely true and the other completely false, it was largely diffused by movement of both camps. Pylyshyn and the propositionalists scored points mainly on logical grounds. It was clear that completely uninterpreted images could not be stored in memory without some way to access them by their content or they could never be retrieved. And regardless of whether or not images can be reinterpreted, they surely are interpreted when they are generated. Shepard, Kosslyn, and the analog theorists scored points for a wide variety of experimental results that conformed to their predictions. There does seem to be some intrinsic representation of spatial structure in imagery that is difficult, if not impossible, to capture by purely propositional data structures.

Many of the findings on mental imagery can be accounted for within a computational theory of imagery proposed by Kosslyn (1980, 1981; Kosslyn & Schwartz, 1977). Although Kosslyn is one of the central figures in the analog camp of imagery theorists, his theory is most accurately viewed as a hybrid with both analog and propositional aspects, as we shall see. It consists of the three basic components illustrated in Figure 12.2.7:

1. *Visual buffer.* The **visual buffer** is a spatially organized array within the visual system that constitutes the medium or format for visual images. It corresponds to what Kosslyn had previously called "the CRT screen in the head." Visual images are short-term, analog representations that are constructed, inspected, and transformed within this buffer.

2. *Long-term stored representations.* The LTM data structures that Kosslyn proposed contain both propositional and analog components. The propositional components

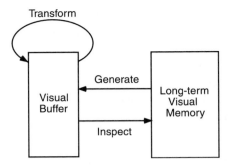

Figure 12.2.7 Kosslyn's model of imagery. Visual images are generated by retrieving information from long-term visual memory and constructing it in a spatial format in the visual buffer. Images in the buffer can be transformed (e.g., by rotation or scanning) and then be inspected for new information.

are very much like the hierarchical structural descriptions we discussed in Chapter 9 as representations for object categories. They specify parts of a given size at a particular location and orientation. The analog components are stored representations of primitive picturelike entities that constitute the parts of propositionally encoded object descriptions. The result is a structural description that is very similar to those described by Palmer (1975a), such as the face schema shown in Figure 8.2.16.

3. *Image-processing operations.* Active processes are required to initiate imagery when appropriate to the task, to generate images in the visual buffer from the stored descriptions, to inspect images for the presence of specific information, and to transform images within the visual buffer for different tasks. These operations are stored as visual routines in procedural LTM and are used whenever they are required for an imagery task.

To understand how the theory works, we will run through a few examples. Consider first Shepard and Metzler's (1971) mental rotation task. The images of the two objects are initially registered in the visual buffer, and inspection processes determine the correspondence of some salient part or parts. The difference in orientation between these parts suggests that a rotation of one of the images in the buffer in a particular direction will bring them into alignment. This rotation process is initiated and continued in an incremental fashion until the corresponding parts have the same orientation. Further inspection processes are then called upon to compare

the rest of the two images for complete identity. A positive response is executed if they are the same, and a negative response is executed if they are different. In this task, no retrieval of visual information in LTM was necessary because both objects were presented optically in the task.

Now consider Kosslyn, Ball, and Reiser's (1978) image-scanning task. We will assume that the subject has already learned the map of Bora Bora and has stored its representation propositionally in visual LTM. When the subject is given the name of the first object, he or she retrieves the visual information about the island from LTM, constructs an image of it in the visual buffer, and focuses attention on the named object. When the name of the second object is given, its location is accessed, and the subject uses a scanning operation to move from the first object to the second, simultaneously imagining a spot flying along the scanned path. When inspection processes indicate that the spot has reached the second object, the subject responds.

These examples give some idea of how this theory works in accounting for imagery phenomena. The contents of the visual buffer give it the "picture-in-the-head" quality of imagery, the inspection and transformation routines give it the "mind's eye" quality of introspective experiences, and the stored propositional descriptions provide the interpretive framework for images from stored spatial knowledge.

Notice that most of what is needed to construct this theory exists in the visual memory components we discussed earlier in this book. The visual buffer that holds the current image sounds very much like visual STM and the visuo-spatial sketchpad, the stored descriptions are very much like the hierarchical structural descriptions of visual LTM, and the inspection, transformation, and identification routines are very much like the ones required for object classification (see Section 9.3) and the visual routines described earlier in the present chapter. The only further requirements are image-generation routines used to construct images in visual STM from the structural descriptions in visual LTM and some image-manipulation routines to carry out the necessary image transformations such as rotation and scanning. Thus, Kosslyn's theory fits nicely within the general framework for visual memory that we have been discussing to account for other findings.

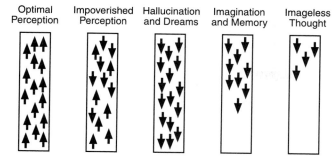

Figure 12.2.8 A schematic depiction of relations among several forms of visual activity. Five examples of visual processes are compared in terms of their bottom-up (upward arrows) and top-down components (downward arrows). (From Shepard, 1984.)

12.2.5 The Relation of Imagery to Perception

Kosslyn's model, like many other theories of visual imagery, assumes quite explicitly that imagery shares important representations and processes with normal visual perception (e.g., Finke, 1980, 1985; Shepard, 1984). The general hypothesis underlying such theories is that imagery and perception are similar except for the source of the information and the direction of processing. This view is somewhat impressionistically illustrated in a diagram by Shepard (1984), shown in Figure 12.2.8. It indicates that images are the result of top-down retrieval of internal visual information from LTM without supporting low-level sensory stimulation, whereas normal perception (under ideal conditions) results from the bottom-up processing of external visual information. Note that perception under impoverished conditions is depicted as a combination of bottom-up and top-down processing but includes the low-level sensory information lacking in imagery. A good example of how processing structures might be shared by both perception and imagery is the hypothesis that Kosslyn's image buffer may be the same processing structure as visual STM. This all makes intuitive sense, but is there any empirical evidence that visual imagery shares processing mechanisms with visual perception?

Behavioral Evidence. Perhaps the most direct behavioral evidence for a close relation between perception and imagery comes from experiments in which interactions have been found between these two types of processing. One line of evidence comes from studies in which the modality of an imagery task (e.g., visual versus auditory) produces differential effects on some perceptual task that is either visual or auditory in nature.

Among the first modern studies to document such effects were those by Segal and associates. They examined the effect of imagery tasks on people's performance on sensory detection tasks. For example, subjects were asked to construct either a visual or an auditory image at the same time as they tried to detect a faintly presented visual or auditory stimulus in a perceptual task. The results show that visual imagery reduced performance on the visual detection task more than it did the auditory detection task and that auditory imagery had the opposite effect (Segal & Fusella, 1969). Thus, imagery interacts with perception in the sense that it interferes with perception in the same modality more than it does with perception in a different modality.

Perhaps the most elegant and convincing behavioral evidence of interactions between perceptual and imaginal mechanisms comes from a recent study of the effects of adaptation on imagining visual motion (Gilden, Blake, & Hurst, 1995). The experimenters reasoned that if perception and imagery share the same mechanisms, adapting subjects to real motion in one direction would slow down subsequently imagined motion in that direction and speed it up in the opposite direction. Testing this simple hypothesis required a fairly complex experiment, however.

First, subjects were adapted for a few minutes to motion in a specific direction by having them stare at a fixation cross in the middle of a field of dots moving at a constant rate within a square region of a computer display. They then saw a series of trials in which the following events occurred (see Figure 12.2.9): They readapted to the same motion for 10 s and then were shown a single dot in real motion approaching the square region where the adapting field of moving dots had been. This single dot disappeared when it reached the nearest border of the adapted region. Subjects were instructed to imagine it continuing to move at the same rate and in the same direction through the square region and to press a button when the dot reached the other side.

If adaptation to perceived motion affects imagined motion, then the dot should take longer to go through the square when subjects adapted to motion in the same direction than when they adapted to motion in the opposite direction. This prediction is based on the hypothesis that adaptation fatigues neurons that are sensitive to

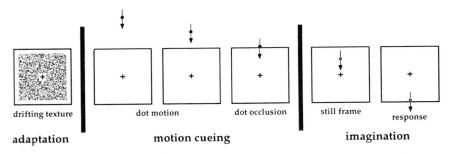

drifting texture   dot motion   dot occlusion   still frame   response

adaptation   **motion cueing**   **imagination**

Figure 12.2.9 Procedure for an experiment on the relation between visual aftereffects and imagery. Subjects are first adapted to a moving texture. While they are experiencing motion aftereffects, they are shown a dot moving toward and behind an oc- cluder and asked to imagine it continuing at the same speed be- hind the occluder. They are told to respond as soon as it would reappear from behind the occluder. (From Gilden, Blake, & Hurst, 1995.)

the adapted direction of motion. This would make the system generally less sensitive to motion in that direction and more sensitive to motion in the opposite direction. This is a well-documented phenomenon in visual per- ception (e.g., Thompson, 1981), but it is not clear that it would affect imagined motion in the same way. If imag- ery and perception share motion-processing operations, it is reasonable to predict that it would.

Gilden et al. (1995) found the pattern of results they predicted. The speed of imagined motion was slower when it was in the same direction as the prior adapted motion, it was faster when it was in the direction oppo- site to the adapted motion, and it was unaffected when it was perpendicular to the adapted motion. The detailed pattern of results further suggested that although real and imagined motion engage some common neural mechanisms, they are not functionally equivalent.

Neuropsychological Evidence. If imagery and per- ception share common neural mechanisms, one would expect neurological damage that impairs perception to impair imagery as well. Indeed, this appears to be the case. Farah (1988) examined a number of cases in which there were related deficits in visual perception and im- agery. Agnosic patients, for example, who are unable to recognize certain classes of objects often (but not always) report difficulty in generating images of those same ob- jects. Similarly, patients with deficits in color perception often also have difficulty with color imagery tasks, such as reporting the color of common objects from memory (DeRenzi & Spinnler, 1967). Yet another example is that patients with unilateral neglect due to damage in

their right parietal lobe (see Section 11.2.7) who report seeing objects only on the right side also report objects only from the right side when describing visual images of scenes they knew before the onset of their neurologi- cal problem (Bisiach & Luzzatti, 1978).

Additional connections can be made between Kos- slyn's imagery model and the specific deficits found in neuropsychological patients. For instance, some patients can both describe and recognize visually presented ob- jects but cannot describe the visual appearance of ob- jects from memory. Farah (1984) argues that this implies a selective impairment in image-generation processes. Figure 12.2.10 shows how she arrives at this conclusion. According to Kosslyn's theory, the ability to describe a percept implies that both the inspection processes that encode input from the retina and the visual buffer are intact. The ability to recognize objects further implies that visual knowledge in LTM and the inspection proc- esses that access this information are also intact. The in- ability to describe visual appearances from memory

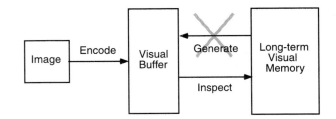

Figure 12.2.10 Analyzing visual deficits in imagery within Kosslyn's model of visual imagery (see Figure 12.2.7). Farah (1984) argues that patients who can describe and recognize ob- jects presented visually but cannot describe their appearance from memory have a selective deficit in the image-generation process.

therefore implies that the image-generation process is selectively impaired in these patients. Using similar logic, Farah was able to identify other patients who had intact generation processes but impaired image inspection processes. The consistency of these cases supports not only the existence of a close connection between perception and imagery, but also the plausibility of Kosslyn's model.

Another finding that links deficits of imagery with known neural mechanisms of normal perception comes from a study that dissociates the "what" and "where" systems in imagery. The reader will recall that in Chapter 1 we reviewed evidence that there are two distinct visual pathways in the brain. The ventral path, leading from the occipital cortex to the temporal cortex, is involved in identifying objects (*what* they are), and the dorsal path, leading from occipital to parietal cortex, is concerned with processing the location of objects (*where* they are).

Levine, Warach, and Farah (1985) described two patients who had quite different deficits of visual imagery as a result of damage to the dorsal and ventral pathways. The patient whose lesion was ventral (in the junction between the occipital and temporal lobes) was unable to imagine the appearance of objects from memory but could imagine going from one place to another well enough to give detailed directions. The one whose lesion was dorsal (in the junction between the occipital and parietal lobes) was able to correctly describe the details of objects from memory but could not describe even the simple route from his home to the corner grocery store. Significantly, both patients had perceptual difficulties of the corresponding sort. The patient with temporal involvement had great difficulty in identifying people he knew unless they wore some kind of distinctive clothing, and the patient with parietal involvement had great difficulty in getting around in the world. Thus, the what and where pathways of visual perception also appear to be involved in comparable functions in visual imagery.

Brain Imaging Studies. One problem with studies of neurological patients is that their brains are, by definition, abnormal. This can make it difficult to generalize conclusions based on their behavior to normal people. Fortunately, the development of functional neuro-imaging techniques (PET and fMRI, as described in Section 2.2.3) has allowed researchers to examine normal processing in the brains of normal people while they carry out well-defined tasks.

Some of the earliest studies to examine the regions of the brain involved in visual imagery were conducted by the Scandinavian neurologist Per Roland, who helped to pioneer cognitive studies of blood flow via PET images. Roland and Friberg (1985) asked subjects to imagine walking along a well-known route and to "observe" landmarks along the way. They were also asked to imagine stopping at every second street corner and then turning to the right and the left. The PET scans that were obtained while they engaged in this imagery task caused high amounts of activation in both the temporal and parietal lobes, which is just what one would expect if this task engaged both the "what" and the "where" pathways of the visual system, as indeed it should. Interestingly, this task failed to generate significant activation in early visual areas of the occipital lobe (Roland, Eriksson, Stone-Elander, & Widen, 1987).

Better-controlled studies of visual imagery using PET, fMRI, and ERP techniques have since been carried out by a number of researchers (e.g., Farah, Peronnet, Gonon, & Giard, 1988; Goldenberg, Steiner, Podreka, & Deecke, 1992; Kosslyn et al., 1993; Le Bihan et al., 1993). In virtually every case, they have found that imagery tasks produce activation in visual regions of the brain, often including occipital cortex itself. Moreover, perceptual tasks with related material generally produce increased blood flow and electrical activity in essentially the same regions of the brain as the imagery tasks.

Neuroimaging studies are beginning to provide converging evidence that visual perception and imagery are very closely related processes, as many cognitive theorists proposed well before such techniques were available. No single technology yet provides sufficient detail in either the spatial or temporal domain to allow fine-grained tests of specific imagery models such as Kosslyn's, but newer techniques may eventually allow researchers to do so. At this point, it is clear that there are close connections, both physiologically and functionally, between visual perception and visual imagery. Just how much overlap there is and what specific mechanisms are shared are exciting topics for future research.

Suggestions for Further Reading

Visual Memory

Baddeley, A. D. (1998). *Human memory: Theory and practice.* Boston: Allyn & Bacon. This book, written by one of the world's leading experts, gives an up-to-date survey of the field of human memory in general.

Loftus, E. F. (1979). *Eyewitness testimony.* Cambridge, MA: Harvard University Press. Loftus's book describes her experiments on how performance on visual memory tasks can be influenced by misleading questions and presuppositions.

Coltheart, V. (Ed.). (1999). *Fleeting memories: Cognition of brief visual stimuli.* Cambridge, MA: MIT Press. The chapters in this edited volume review some of the most recent evidence about what can be detected and remembered from briefly presented visual images.

Visual Imagery

Finke, R. (1989). *Principles of mental imagery.* Cambridge, MA: MIT Press. This book gives a succinct presentation of many of the basic phenomena of visual imagery and their theoretical interpretations.

Kosslyn, S. M. (1980). *Image and mind.* Cambridge, MA: Harvard University Press. This is Kosslyn's classic statement of his theory of visual imagery and its relation to important imagery phenomena.

Kosslyn, S. M. (1994). *Image and brain: The resolution of the imagery debate.* Cambridge, MA: MIT Press. This book purports to resolve the propositional/analog debate of visual imagery by appealing to recent findings from brain imaging studies.

Shepard, R. N., & Cooper, L. A. (1982). *Mental images and their transformations.* Cambridge, MA: MIT Press. This volume reprints the well-known and influential series experiments by Shepard, Cooper, and their associates on mental rotation and its implications for visual imagery.

Visual Awareness

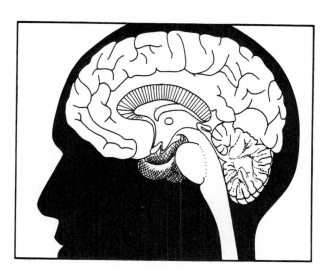

The previous 12 chapters contain an enormous amount of information about visual perception, attention, and memory. Oddly, though, none of it directly addresses what is perhaps the single most fascinating aspect of vision: the conscious, phenomenological component that we will call *visual awareness* or *visual experience* or *visual consciousness*, all of which we will take to mean essentially the same thing. At this point, a definition of visual awareness should follow, but such a definition turns out to be almost impossible to formulate for reasons that we will consider shortly. The best we can do right now is to say that visual awareness is what it "feels like" for a sighted organism to see. This is woefully inadequate as a definition because we cannot state what "feels like" means at all, and we have presupposed knowing what vision is by referring to a "sighted organism" and "seeing." Still, this definition seems to make intuitive sense to people who can see, so it will have to do for now.

We have talked all around the topic of visual experience, appealing at every turn to the reader's intuitions about his or her own conscious visual experiences. But as far as the precise nature of these experiences, how they arise, and why they are important, we have said almost nothing. The situation was aptly described by Nobel laureate Francis Crick, who observed,

There are two rather surprising aspects of our present knowledge of the visual system. The first is how much we already know—by any standards the amount is enormous. . . . The other surprising thing is that, in spite of all this work, we really have no clear idea how we see anything. (Crick, 1994, pp. 23–24)

Although Crick's assessment is accurate, it does not mean that the foregoing 12 chapters all have been for naught. In fact, many of the processes involved in vision—perhaps even most of them—are quite unconscious. If they were not, ancient philosophers would presumably have solved all the problems of visual perception, attention, and memory long ago simply by introspecting about their own conscious experiences. But most of what goes on during visual perception appears to be quite inaccessible to consciousness. This explains why most people are so surprised to discover the enormous complexity of vision: They are totally unaware of most of the processes that underlie it. All the unconscious visual processes can be treated simply as garden-variety neural information processing and are none the worse for it.

It is startling just how much of visual processing is unconscious. Consider, for example, the activity of retinal receptors, which most people assume is conscious. In fact, it appears not to be. Our visual experiences are *derived* from receptor activity, but this activity itself does not appear to be conscious. Awareness appears to arise somewhere farther along a complex chain of neural information processing, rather than in the receptors themselves.

We have already discussed several facts that support this conclusion. Some of the most compelling evidence concerns the ability of higher visual processes to fill in visual experiences in ways that are different from the pattern of firing on the retina. One phenomenon we have already mentioned is the fact that we do not experience a hole in our vision at the blind spot. As we discussed in Chapter 1, there is an absence of visual information in that region because there are no receptors where the axons of ganglion cells leave the retina. We fail to experience any sensory gap at the blind spot, however, because higher-level processes fill it in appropriately. We know that it is filled in because of demonstrations like the lower one shown in Figure 1.3.14. The line on the retina actually has a gap in it at the blind spot, but we experience it as complete and uninterrupted when the gap falls within the blind spot. The important point is that what we experience visually conforms not to the firing of retinal receptors, but to some higher level of neural activity. Similarly, we do not experience the shadows due to blood vessels on our retinas because some higher-level process fills in these regions as well.

More dramatic evidence of a similar sort comes from filling-in processes in patients who have **scotomas**: limited regions of blindness due to damage to part of the retina or visual cortex. Vision scientist V. S. Ram-

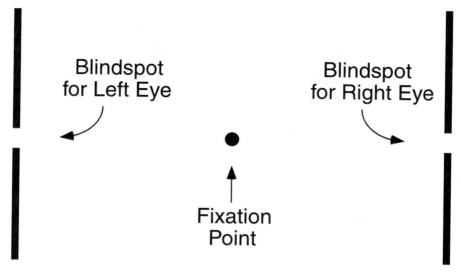

Figure 13.0.1 Filling in the blind spot. Close your right eye and fixate the central point while holding this figure about 4 inches from your face. When the gap falls on the blind spot of your left eye, the left line will fill in and appear solid. Doing the same with your left eye closed will cause the right line to fill in and appear solid.

achandran (1993) has studied patients with cortical scotomas and found remarkable filling in of perceptual qualities that are not retinally present. Figure 13.0.2 shows some examples that are essentially extensions of the blind spot demonstration in Figure 13.0.1. Patients with scotomas also experience the gap in an interrupted straight line as being filled in appropriately. More strikingly, they report that two misaligned lines fill in so that the resulting percept is of a single straight line through the scotoma, as indicated in Figure 13.0.2A. Even more surprising is the fact that these patients report filling in textured patterns such as the double column of X's shown in Figure 13.0.2B. This does not happen immediately; but within a few seconds after being shown the interrupted pattern, they begin to see X's in their scotoma, none of which are present in the retinal image. There are limits to this filling-in process, however. If the column consists of just a single line of large X's (see Figure 13.0.2C), the single large X that should appear in the scotoma is not filled in perceptually. Exactly why this should be true is not yet known. The important point is that these filling-in phenomena provide convincing evidence that what people experience visually is not the pattern of receptor firings in the retina, but activity at some higher level in the brain.

If some visual processes are conscious and others are not, what determines which ones are? At what level do these visual experiences arise? And how do they arise? Surely consciousness is related to which neurons are firing in the brain and/or how they are firing. But what exactly is the relation?

In truth, vision scientists do not yet know. We do not even know whether the explanation is to be found in facts about how information is being processed at the algorithmic level or about underlying neurophysiological

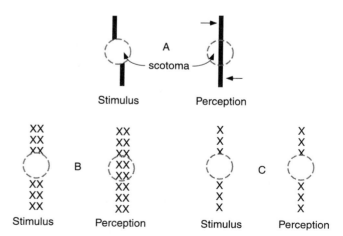

Figure 13.0.2 Filling in scotomas. Patients with restricted damage in the retina or cortex experience more dramatic filling-in phenomena. Misaligned segments are perceived as continuous and straight (A), configural lines of many texture elements also fill in (B), but lines of fewer elements do not (C).

events at the implementation level. Many theorists believe that it must be the physiological events in the brain (e.g., Crick, 1994; Searle, 1993). But suppose one could make an artificial brain out of millions of microprocessors, each of which simulated the input/output behavior of a neuron in every respect. Suppose further that one could then connect them together in exactly the same way as the neurons are connected in a real brain. Would the artificial brain so constructed have visual experiences? This is an important question, but one to which we do not yet have a good answer.

To be brutally honest, scientists do not yet have even the remotest idea of how visual experiences—or indeed any other kinds of experiences—arise from physical events in the brain. How is it that even a very complex and extensive network of neurons that is undergoing the purely physical events involved in propagating electrochemical activity among neurons could possibly give rise to a phenomenon that has the properties of conscious experience? We will use the term **explanatory gap** to refer to this major theoretical impasse (Levine, 1983). The problem is not that scientists cannot figure out which gap-filling theory is correct; it is that there are not yet any serious contenders.

This level of ignorance is admittedly a bit surprising, especially given all the physiological studies that have been performed to examine the neural activity of living animals. Do they tell us nothing at all about visual consciousness? Unfortunately, the answer is that they probably don't. Hubel and Wiesel's ground-breaking experiments, in which they recorded the activity of single neurons in visual cortex of cats and monkeys, told us volumes about how these animals' nervous systems respond to retinal stimulation in terms of visual information processing. But they did not necessarily tell us anything about visual experience because the animals were deeply anesthetized and quite unconscious during the experiments. They were effectively asleep and therefore (presumably) experienced nothing at all when the bars and edges caused their cortical neurons to fire. The same is true of most physiological experiments that were carried out before the 1990s. More recently, experimenters have begun to explore physiological responses in awake, behaving animals (see Maunsell & Newsome, 1987). Unfortunately, these experiments have not yet yielded very much information about the neural correlates of visual consciousness and none at all about the ultimate causes of consciousness.

In the present chapter we will discuss the scientific understanding of visual awareness. First, we will summarize the philosophical literature about the relation between mind and brain. Then we will describe several conditions that produce dissociations between unconscious processing and conscious experience, first in neurological patients and then in normal observers. Finally, we will consider several representative theories that have been proposed to explain consciousness.

13.1 Philosophical Foundations

The first work on virtually all scientific problems was done by philosophers, and the nature of human consciousness is no exception. The issues they raised have framed the discussion for modern theories of awareness. Philosophical treatments of consciousness have primarily concerned two issues that we will discuss before considering empirical facts and theoretical proposals: The *mind-body problem* concerns the relation between mental events and physical events in the brain, and the *problem of other minds* concerns how people come to believe that other people (or animals) are also conscious.

13.1.1 The Mind-Body Problem

Although there is a long history to how philosophers have viewed the nature of the mind (sometimes equated with the soul), the single most important issue concerns what has come to be called the **mind-body problem**: What is the relation between mental events (e.g., perceptions, pains, hopes, desires, beliefs) and physical events (e.g., brain activity)? The idea that there is a mind-body problem to begin with presupposes one of the most important philosophical positions about the nature of mind. It is known as **dualism** because it proposes that mind and body are two different kinds of entities. After all, if there were no fundamental differences between mental and physical events, there would be no problem in saying how they relate to each other.

Dualism. The historical roots of dualism are closely associated with the writings of the great French philosopher, mathematician, and scientist René Descartes. Indeed, the classical version of dualism, **substance**

dualism, in which mind and body are conceived as two different substances, is often called **Cartesian dualism**. Because most philosophers find the notion of physical substances unproblematic, the central issue in philosophical debates over substance dualism is whether mental substances exist and, if so, what their nature might be. Vivid sensory experiences, such as the appearance of redness or the feeling of pain, are among the clearest examples, but substance dualists also include more abstract mental states and events such as hopes, desires, and beliefs.

The hypothesized mental substances are proposed to differ from physical ones in their fundamental properties. For example, all ordinary physical matter has a well-defined position, occupies a particular volume, has a definite shape, and has a specific mass. Conscious experiences, such as perceptions, remembrances, beliefs, hopes, and desires, do not appear to have readily identifiable positions, volumes, shapes, and masses. In the case of vision, however, one might object that visual experiences *do* have physical locations and extensions. There is an important sense in which my perception of a red ball on the table is located on the table where the ball is and is extended over the spherical volume occupied by the ball. What could be more obvious? But a substance dualist would counter that these are properties of the physical object that I perceive rather than properties of my perceptual experience itself. The experience is in my mind rather than out there in the physical environment, and the location, extension, and mass of these mental entities are difficult to define—unless one makes the problematic move of simply identifying them with the location, extension, and mass of my brain. Substance dualists reject this possibility, believing instead that mental states, such as perceptions, beliefs, and desires, are simply undefined with respect to position, extension, and mass. In this case, it makes sense to distinguish mental substances from physical ones on the grounds that they have fundamentally different properties.

We can also look at the issue of fundamental properties the other way around: Do experiences have any properties that ordinary physical matter does not? Two possibilities merit consideration. One is that experiences are **subjective phenomena** in the sense that they cannot be observed by anyone but the person having them. Ordinary matter and events, in contrast, are **objective phenomena** because they can be observed by anyone, at least in principle. The other is that experiences have what philosophers call **intentionality**: They inherently refer to things other than themselves.[1] Your experience of a book in front of you right now is about the book in the external world even though it arises from activity in your brain. This *directedness* of visual experiences is the source of the confusion we mentioned in the previous paragraph about whether your perceptions have location, extension, and so forth. The physical objects to which such perceptual experiences refer have these physical properties, but the experiences themselves do not. Intentionality does not seem to be a property that is shared by ordinary matter, and if this is true, it provides further evidence that conscious experience is fundamentally different.

It is possible to maintain a dualistic position and yet deny the existence of any separate mental substances, however. One can instead postulate that the brain has certain unique properties that constitute its mental phenomena. These properties are just the sorts of experiences we have as we go about our everyday lives, including perceptions, pains, desires, and thoughts. This philosophical position on the mind-body problems is called **property dualism**. It is a form of dualism because these properties are taken to be nonphysical in the sense of not being reducible to any standard physical properties. It is as though the physical brain contains some strange nonphysical features or dimensions that are qualitatively distinct from all physical features or dimensions.

These mental features or dimensions are usually claimed to be **emergent properties**: attributes that simply do not arise in ordinary matter unless it reaches a certain level or type of complexity. This complexity is certainly achieved in the human brain and may also be achieved in the brains of certain other animals. The situation is perhaps best understood by analogy to the

---

[1] The reader is warned not to confuse intentionality with the concept of "intention" in ordinary language. Your intentions have intentionality in the sense that they may refer to things other than themselves—for example, your intention to feed your cat refers to your cat, its food, and your-self—but no more so than other mental states you might have, such as beliefs, desires, perceptions, and pains. The philosophical literature on the nature of intentionality is complex and extensive. The interested reader is referred to Bechtel (1988) for an overview of this topic.

Visual Awareness

emergent property of being alive. Ordinary matter manifests this property only when it is organized in such a way that it is able to replicate itself and carry on the required biological processes. The difference, of course, is that being alive is a property that we can now explain in terms of purely physical processes. Property dualists believe that this will never be the case for mental properties.

Even if one accepts a dualistic position that the mental and physical are somehow qualitatively distinct, there are several different relations they might have to one another. These differences form the basis for several varieties of dualism. One critical issue is the direction of causation: Does it run from mind to brain, from brain to mind, or both? Descartes's position was that both sorts of causation are in effect: events in the brain can affect mental events, and mental events can also affect events in the brain. This position is often called **interactionism** because it claims that the mental and physical worlds can interact causally with each other in both directions. It seems sensible enough at an intuitive level. No self-respecting dualist doubts the overwhelming evidence that physical events in the brain cause the mental events of conscious experience. The pain that you feel in your toe, for example, is actually caused by the firing of neurons in your brain. Convincing evidence of this is provided by so-called **phantom limb pain**, in which amputees feel pain—sometimes excruciating pain—in their missing limbs (Chronholm, 1951; Ramachandran, 1996).

In the other direction, the evidence that mental events can cause physical ones is decidedly more impressionistic but intuitively satisfying to most interactionists. They point to the fact that certain mental events, such as my having the intention of raising my arm, appear to cause corresponding physical events, such as the raising of my arm—provided I am not paralyzed and my arm is not restrained in any way. The nature of this causation is scientifically problematic, however, because all currently known forms of causation concern physical events causing other physical events. Even so, other forms of causation that have not yet been identified may nevertheless exist.

Not all dualists are interactionists, however. An important alternative version of dualism, called **epiphenomenalism**, recognizes mental entities as being different in kind from physical ones yet denies that mental states play any causal role in the unfolding of physical events. An epiphenomenalist would argue that mental states, such as perceptions, intentions, beliefs, hopes, and desires, are merely ineffectual side effects of the underlying causal neural events that take place in our brains. To get a clearer idea of what this might mean, consider the following analogy: Imagine that neurons glow slightly as they fire in a brain and that this glowing is somehow akin to conscious experiences. The pattern of glowing in and around the brain (i.e., the conscious experience) is clearly caused by the firing of neurons in the brain. Nobody would question that. But the neural glow would be causally ineffectual in the sense that it would not cause neurons to fire any differently than they would if they did not glow. Therefore, causation runs in only one direction, from physical to mental, in an epiphenomenalist account of the mind-body problem. Although this position denies any causal efficacy to mental events, it is still a form of dualism because it accepts the existence of the "glow" of consciousness and maintains that it is qualitatively distinct from the neural firings themselves.

Idealism. Not all philosophical positions on the mind-body problem are dualistic. The opposing view is **monism**: the idea that there is really just one sort of stuff after all. Not surprisingly, there are two sorts of monist positions—**idealism** and **materialism**—one for each kind of stuff there might be. A monist who believes there to be no physical world, but only mental events, is called an idealist (from the "ideas" that populate the mental world). This has not been a very popular position in the history of philosophy, having been championed mainly by the British philosopher Bishop Berkeley.

The most significant problem for idealism is how to explain the commonality of different people's perceptions of the same physical events. If a fire engine races down the street with siren blaring and red lights flashing, everyone looks toward it, and they all see and hear pretty much the same physical events, albeit from different vantage points. How is this possible if there is no physical world that is responsible for their simultaneous perceptions of the sound and sight of the fire engine? One would have to propose some way in which the minds of the various witnesses happen to be hallucinating exactly corresponding events at exactly corresponding times. Berkeley's answer was that God was responsible for this grand coordination, but such claims have held little sway in modern scientific circles. Without a cogent scientific explanation of the commonality of shared experiences of the physical world, idealism has largely become an historical curiosity with no significant modern following.

Materialism. The vast majority of monists believe that only physical entities exist. They are called materialists. In contrast to idealism, materialism is a very common view among modern philosophers and scientists. There are actually two distinct forms of materialism, which depend on what their adherents believe the ultimate status of mental entities will be once their true physical nature is discovered. One form, called **reductive materialism**, posits that mental events will ultimately be reduced to material events in much the same way that other successful reductions have occurred in science (e.g., Armstrong, 1968). This view is also called **mind-brain identity theory** because it assumes that mental events are actually equivalent to brain events and can be talked about more or less interchangeably, albeit with different levels of precision.

A good scientific example of what reductive materialists believe will occur when the mental is reduced to the physical is the reduction in physics of thermodynamic concepts concerning heat to statistical mechanics. The temperature of a gas in classical thermodynamics has been shown to be equivalent to the average kinetic energy of its molecules in statistical mechanics, thus replacing the qualitatively distinct thermodynamic concept of heat with the more general and basic concept of molecular motion. The concept of heat did not then disappear from scientific vocabulary; it remains a valid concept within many contexts. Rather, it was merely given a more accurate definition in terms of molecular motion at a more microscopic level of analysis. According to reductive materialists, then, mental concepts will ultimately be redefined in terms of brain states and events, but their equivalence will allow mental concepts to remain valid and scientifically useful even after their brain correlates are discovered. For example, it will still be valid to say, "John is hungry," rather than, "Such-and-such pattern of neural firing is occurring in John's lateral hypothalamus."

The other materialist position, called **eliminative materialism**, posits that at least some of our current concepts concerning mental states and events will eventually be eliminated from scientific vocabulary because they will be found to be simply invalid (e.g., Churchland, 1990). The scenario eliminative materialists envision is thus more radical than the simple translation scheme we just described for reductive materialism. Eliminative materialists believe that some of our present concepts about mental entities (perhaps including perceptual experiences as well as beliefs, hopes, desires, and so forth) are so fundamentally flawed that they will someday be entirely replaced by a scientifically accurate account that is expressed in terms of the underlying neural events. An appropriate analogy here would be the elimination of the now-discredited ideas of "vitalism" in biology: the view that what distinguishes living from nonliving things is the presence of a mysterious and qualitatively distinct force or substance that is present in living objects and absent in nonliving ones. The discovery of the biochemical reactions that cause the replication of DNA by completely normal physical means ultimately undercut any need for such mystical concepts, and so they were banished from scientific discussion, never to be seen again.

In the same spirit, eliminative materialists believe that some mental concepts, such as perceiving, thinking, desiring, and believing, will eventually be supplanted by discussion of the precise neurological events that underlie them. Scientists would then speak exclusively of the characteristic pattern of neural firings in the appropriate nuclei of the lateral hypothalamus and leave all talk about "being hungry" or "the desire to eat" to historians of science who study archaic and discredited curiosities of yesteryear. Even the general public would eventually come to think and talk in terms of these neuroscientific explanations for experiences, much as modern popular culture has begun to assimilate certain notions about DNA replication, gene splicing, cloning, and related concepts into movies, advertising, and language.

Behaviorism. Another position on the mind-body problem is **philosophical behaviorism**: the view that the proper way to talk about mental events is in terms of the overt, observable movements (behaviors) in which an organism engages. Because objective behaviors are measurable, quantifiable aspects of the physical world, behaviorism is, strictly speaking, a kind of materialism.

It provides such a different perspective, however, that it is best thought of as a distinct view. Behaviorists differ markedly from standard materialists in that they seek to reduce mental events to behavioral events or dispositions rather than to neurophysiological events. They shun neural explanations not because they disbelieve in the causal efficacy of neural events, but because they believe that behavior offers a higher and more appropriate level of analysis. The radical behaviorist movement pressed for nothing less than redefining the scientific study of mind as the scientific study of behavior. And for many years, they succeeded in changing the agenda of psychology.

The behaviorist movement began with the writings of psychologist John Watson (1913), who advocated a thoroughgoing purge of everything mental from psychology. He reasoned that what made intellectual inquiries scientific rather than humanistic or literary was that the empirical data and theoretical constructs on which they rest are objective. In the case of empirical observations, objectivity means that, given a description of what was done in a particular experiment, any scientist could repeat it and obtain essentially the same results, at least within the limits of measurement error. By this criterion, introspective studies of the qualities of perceptual experience (see Chapter 2) were unscientific because they were not objective. Two different people could perform the same experiment (using themselves as subjects, of course) and report different experiences. When this happened—and it did—there was no way to resolve disputes about who was right. Both could defend their own positions simply by appealing to their private and privileged knowledge of their own inner states. This move protected their claims but blocked meaningful scientific debate.

According to behaviorists, scientists should study the behavior of organisms in a well-defined task situation. For example, rather than introspect about the nature of the perception of length, behaviorists would perform an experiment. Observers could be asked to discriminate which of two lines was longer, and their performance could be measured in terms of percentages of correct and incorrect responses for each pair of lines (see Appendix A). Such an objective, behaviorally defined experiment could easily be repeated in any laboratory with different subjects to verify the accuracy and generality of its results. Watson's promotion of objective, behavior-

ally defined experimental methods—called **methodological behaviorism**—was a great success and strongly shaped the future of psychological research.

Of more relevance to the philosophical issue of the relation between mind and body, however, were the implications of the behaviorist push for objectivity in theoretical constructs concerning the mind. It effectively ruled out references to mental states and processes, replacing them with statements about an organism's propensity to engage in certain behaviors under certain conditions. This position is often called theoretical behaviorism or philosophical behaviorism. Instead of saying, "John is hungry," for example, which openly refers to a conscious mental experience (hunger) with which everyone is presumably familiar, a theoretical behaviorist would say something like "John has a propensity to engage in eating behavior in the presence of food." This propensity can be measured in a variety of objective ways—such as the amount of a certain food eaten when it was available after a certain number of hours since the last previous meal—precisely because it is about observable behavior.

But the behaviorist attempt to avoid talking about conscious experience runs into trouble when one considers all the conditions in which John might fail to engage in eating behavior even though he was hungry and food was readily available. Perhaps he could not see the food, for example, or maybe he was fasting. He might even have believed that the food was poisoned. It might seem that such conditions could be blocked simply by inserting appropriate provisions into the behavioral statement, such as "John had a propensity to engage in eating behavior in the presence of food, provided he perceived it, was not fasting, and did not believe it was poisoned." This move ultimately fails, however, for at least two reasons:

1. *Inability to enumerate all conditionals.* Once one begins to think of conditions that would have to be added to statements about behavioral dispositions, it quickly becomes apparent that there are indefinitely many. Perhaps John fails to eat because his hands are temporarily paralyzed, because he has been influenced by a hypnotic suggestion, or whatever. This problem undercuts the claim that behavioral analyses of mental states are elegant and insightful, suggesting instead that they are fatally flawed or at least on the wrong track.

2. *Inability to eliminate mental entities.* The other problem is that the conditionals that must be enumerated frequently make reference to just the sorts of mental events that are supposed to be avoided. For example, whether John *sees* the food or not, whether he *intends* to fast, and what he *believes* about its being poisoned are all mentalistic concepts that have now been introduced into the supposedly behavioral definition. The amended version is therefore unacceptable to a strict theoretical behaviorist.

For such reasons, theoretical behaviorism ultimately failed. The problem, in a nutshell, was that behaviorists mistook the **epistemic status** of mental states (how we come to know about mental states in other people) for the **ontological status** of mental states (what their inherent nature is) (Searle, 1992). That is, we surely come to know about other people's mental states through their behavior, but this does not mean that the nature of these mental states is inherently behavioral.

Functionalism. Functionalism was a movement in the philosophy of mind that began in the 1960s in close association with the earliest stirrings of cognitive science (e.g., Putnam, 1960). Its main idea is that a given mental state can be defined in terms of the causal relations that exist among that mental state, environmental conditions (inputs), organismic behaviors (outputs), and other mental states. Note that this is very much like behaviorism, but with the important addition of allowing other mental states into the picture. This addition enables a functionalist definition of hunger, for example, to refer to a variety of other mental states, such as perceptions, intentions, and beliefs, as suggested above. Functionalists are not trying to explain away mental phenomena as actually being propensities to behave in certain ways, as behaviorists did. Rather, they are trying to define mental states in terms of their relations to other mental states as well as to input stimuli and output behaviors. The picture that emerges is very much like the information processing analyses in which we have been engaged throughout this book. This is not surprising because functionalism is the philosophical foundation of modern computational theories of mind.

Functionalists aspired to more than just the overthrow of theoretical behaviorism, however. They also attempted to block reductive materialism by suggesting new criticisms of mind-brain identity theory. The basis of this criticism lies in the notion of **multiple realizability**: the fact that many different physical devices can serve the same function, provided they causally connect inputs and outputs in the same way via internal states (Putnam, 1967). As we saw in Chapter 3, for example, there are many different ways of building a thermostat. They all have the same function—to control the temperature in the thermostat's environment—but they realize it through very different physical implementations.

Multiple realizability poses the following challenge to identity theory. Suppose there were creatures from some other galaxy whose biology was based on silicon molecules rather than on carbon molecules, as ours is. Let us also suppose that they were alive (even though the basis of their life was not DNA, but some functionally similar self-replicating molecule) and that they even look like people. And suppose further not only that their brains were constructed of elements that are functionally similar to neurons, but also that these elements were interconnected in just the way that neurons in our brains are. Indeed, their brains would be functionally isomorphic to ours, even though they were made of physically different stuff.

Functionalists then claim that these alien creatures would have the same mental states as we do—that is, the same perceptions, pains, desires, beliefs, and so on that populate our own conscious mental lives—provided that their internal states were analogously related to each other, to the external world, and to their behavior. This same approach can be generalized to argue for the possibility that computers and robots of the appropriate sort would also be conscious. Suppose, for example, that each neuron in a brain was replaced with a microcomputer chip that exactly simulated its firing patterns in response to all the neuron chips that provide its input. The computer that was thus constructed would fulfill the functionalist requirements for having the same mental states as the person whose brain was "electronically cloned." You should decide for yourself whether you believe that such a computer would actually have mental states or would merely act as though it had mental states. Once you have done so, try to figure out what criteria you used to decide. (For two contradictory philosophical views of this thought experiment, the reader is referred to Dennett (1991) and Searle (1993).)

Multiple realizability is closely related to the differences between the algorithmic and implementation levels that we discussed in Chapter 2. The algorithmic level corresponds roughly to the functional description of the organism in terms of the relations among its internal states, its input information, and its output behavior. The implementation level corresponds to its actual physical construction. The functionalist notion of multiple realizability thus implies that there could be many different kinds of creatures that would have the same mental states as people do, at least defined in this way. If true, this would undercut identity theory, since mental events could not then be simply equated with particular neurological events; they would have to be equated with some more general class of physical events that would include, among others, silicon-based aliens and electronic brains.

The argument from multiple realizability is crucial to the functionalist theory of mind. Before we get carried away with the implications of multiple realizability, though, we must ask ourselves whether it is true or even remotely likely to be true. There is not much point in basing our understanding of consciousness on a functionalist foundation unless that foundation is well grounded. Is it? More important, how would we know if it were? We will address this topic shortly when we consider the problem of other minds.

Supervenience. There is certainly some logical relation between brain activity and mental states such as consciousness, but precisely what it is has obviously been difficult to determine. Philosophers of mind have spent hundreds of years trying to figure out what it is and have spilled oceans of ink attacking and defending different positions. Recently, however, philosopher Jaegwon Kim (1978, 1993) has formulated a position with which most philosophers of mind have been able to agree. This relation, called **supervenience**, is that any difference in conscious events requires some corresponding difference in underlying neural activity. In other words, mental events supervene on neural events because no two possible situations can be identical with respect to their neural properties while differing in their mental properties. It is a surprisingly weak relation, but it is better than nothing.

Supervenience does not imply that all differences in underlying neural activity result in differences in consciousness. Many neural events are entirely outside awareness, including those that control basic bodily functions such as maintaining gravitational balance and regulating heartbeat. But supervenience claims that no changes in consciousness can take place without some change in neural activity. The real trick, of course, is saying precisely what kinds of changes in neural events produce what kinds of changes in awareness. We will return to this crucial problem at the end of the chapter.

13.1.2 The Problem of Other Minds

The functionalist arguments about multiple realizability are merely thought experiments because neither aliens nor electronic brains are currently at hand. Even so, the question of whether or not someone or something is conscious is central to the enterprise of cognitive science because the validity of such arguments rests on the answer. Formulating adequate criteria for consciousness is one of the thorniest problems in all of science. How could one possibly decide?

Asking how to discriminate conscious from nonconscious beings brings us face to face with another classic topic in the philosophy of mind: the **problem of other minds**. The issue at stake is how I know whether another creature (or machine) has conscious experiences. Notice that I did not say "how *we* know whether another creature has conscious experiences," because, strictly speaking, I do not know whether *you* do or not. This is because one of the most peculiar and unique features of my consciousness is its internal, private nature: Only I have direct access to my conscious experiences, and I have direct access only to my own. As a result, my beliefs that other people also have conscious experiences—and your belief that I do—appear to be inferences. Similarly, I may believe that dogs and cats, or even frogs and worms, are conscious. But in every case, the epistemological basis of my belief about the consciousness of other creatures is fundamentally different from knowledge of my own consciousness: I have direct access to my own experience and nobody else's.

Criteria for Consciousness. If our beliefs that other people—and perhaps many animals as well—have experiences like ours are inferences, on what might such inferences be based? There seem to be at least two criteria.

1. *Behavioral similarity.* Other people act in ways that are roughly similar to my own actions when I am having conscious experiences.

When I experience pain on stubbing my toe, for example, I may wince, say "Ouch!," and hold my toe while hopping on my other foot. When other people do similar things under similar circumstances, I presume they are experiencing a feeling closely akin to my own pain. Dogs also behave in seemingly analogous ways in what appear to be analogous situations in which they might experience pain, and so I also attribute this mental state of being in pain to them. The case is less compelling for creatures like frogs and worms because their behavior is less obviously analogous to our own, but many people firmly believe that their behavior indicates that they also have conscious experiences such as pain.

2. *Physical similarity.* Other people—and, to a lesser degree, various other species of animals—are similar to me in their basic biological and physical structure.

Although no two people are exactly the same, humans are generally quite similar to each other in terms of their essential biological constituents. We are all made of the same kind of flesh, blood, bone, and so forth, and we have roughly the same kinds of sensory organs. Many other animals also appear to be made of similar stuff, although they are morphologically different to varying degrees. Such similarities and differences may enter into our judgments of the likelihood that other creatures also have conscious experiences.

Neither condition alone is sufficient for a convincing belief in the reality of mental states in another creature. Behavioral similarity alone is insufficient because of the logical possibility of **automatons**: robots that are able to simulate every aspect of human behavior but have no experiences whatsoever. We may think that such a machine acts as if it had conscious experiences, but it could conceivably do so without actually having them. (Some theorists reject this possibility, however [e.g., Dennett, 1991].) Physical similarity alone is insufficient because we do not believe that even another living person is having conscious experiences when they are comatose or in a dreamless sleep. Only the two together are convincing. Even when both are present to a high degree, I still have no guarantee that such an inference is warranted. I only know that I myself have conscious experiences.

But what then is the status of the functionalist argument that an alien creature based on silicon rather than carbon molecules would have mental states like ours? This thought experiment is perhaps more convincing than the electronic-brained automaton because we have presumed that the alien is at least alive, albeit using some other physical mechanism to achieve this state of being. But logically, it would surely be unprovable that such silicon people would have mental states like ours, even if they acted very much the same and appeared very similar to people. In fact, the argument for functionalism from multiple realizability is no stronger than our intuitions that such creatures would be conscious. The strength of such intuitions can (and does) vary widely from one person to another.

The Inverted Spectrum Argument. We have gotten rather far afield from visual perception in all this talk of robots, aliens, dogs, and worms having pains, but the same kinds of issues arise for perception. One of the classic arguments related to the problem of other minds—called the **inverted spectrum argument**—concerns the perceptual experience of color (Locke, 1690/1987). It goes like this: Suppose you grant that I have visual awareness in some form that includes differentiated experiences in response to different physical spectra of light (i.e., differentiated color perceptions). How can we know whether my color experiences are the same as yours?

The inverted spectrum argument refers to the possibility that my color experiences are exactly like your own, except for being spectrally inverted. In its literal form, the inversion refers to reversing the mapping between color experiences and the physical spectrum of wavelengths of light, as though the rainbow had simply been reversed, red for violet (and vice versa) with everything in between being reversed in like manner. The claim of the inverted spectrum argument is that no one would ever be able to tell that you and I have different color experiences.

This particular form of color transformation would not actually work as intended because of the shape of the color solid (Palmer, in press). As you may recall from Chapter 3, the color solid is asymmetrical in that the most saturated blues and violets are darker than the most saturated reds and greens, which, in turn, are darker than the most saturated yellows and oranges (see

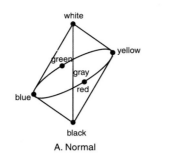

A. Normal

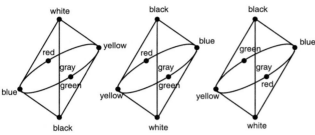

B. R/G Reversed   C. Complementary   D. B/Y & Bl/Wh Reversed

Figure 13.1.1 Sophisticated versions of the inverted spectrum argument. Transformations of the normal color solid (A) that would not be detectable by behavioral methods include (B) red-green reversal, which reflects each color about the blue-yellow-black-white plane; (C) the complementary transformation, which reflects each color through the central point; and (D) blue-yellow and black-white reversal, which is the combination of both the two other transformations (B and C). (After Palmer, in press.)

Figure 13.1.1A). The problem this causes for the literal inverted spectrum argument is that if my hues were simply reversed, your experience of yellow would be the same as my experience of blue-green, and so you would judge yellow to be darker than blue-green, whereas I would do the reverse. This difference would allow the spectral inversion of my color experiences (relative to yours) to be detected.

This problem may be overcome by using more sophisticated versions of the same color transformation argument (Palmer, in press). The most plausible is red-green reversal, in which my color space is the same as yours except for reflection about the blue-yellow plane, thus reversing reds and greens (see Figure 13.1.1B). It

does not suffer from problems concerning the differential lightness of blues and yellows because my blues correspond to your blues and my yellows to your yellows. Our particular shades of blues and yellows would be different—my greenish yellows and greenish blues would correspond to your reddish yellows (oranges) and reddish blues (purples), respectively, and vice versa—but gross differences in lightness would not be a problem.

There are other candidates for behaviorally undetectable color transformations as well (see Figures 13.1.1C and 13.1.1D). The crucial idea in all these versions of the inverted spectrum argument is that if the color solid were symmetric with respect to some transformation—and this is at least roughly true for the three cases illustrated in Figures 13.1.1B–13.1.1D—there would be no way to tell the difference between my color experiences and yours simply from our behavior. In each case, I would name colors in just the same way as you would, because these names are only *mediated* by our own private experiences of color. It is the sameness of the physical spectra that ultimately causes them to be named consistently across people, not the sameness of the private experiences. I would also describe relations between colors in the same way as you would: that focal blue is darker than focal yellow, that lime green is yellower than emerald green, and so forth. In fact, if I were in a psychological experiment in which my task was to rate pairs of color for similarity or dissimilarity, I would make the same ratings you would. I would even pick out the same unique hues as you would—the "pure" shades of red, green, blue, and yellow—even though my internal experiences of them would be different from yours. It would be extremely difficult, if not impossible, to tell from my behavior with respect to color that I experience it differently than you do.[2]

I suggested that red-green reversal is the most plausible form of color transformation because a good biological argument can be made that there should be some very small number of seemingly normal trichromats who should be red-green reversed. The argument for such **pseudo-normal color perception** goes as follows (Nida-Rümelin, 1996). As we discussed in Section 3.2.3,

---

[2] One might think that if white and black were reversed, certain reflexive behaviors to light would somehow betray the difference. This is not necessarily the case, however. Whereas you would squint your eyes when you experienced intense brightness in response to bright sunlight, I would also squint my eyes in response to large amounts of sunlight. The only difference is that my experience of brightness under these conditions would be the same as your experience of darkness. It sounds strange, but I believe it would all work out properly.

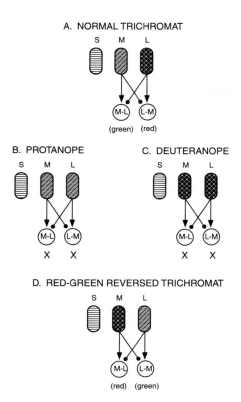

A. NORMAL TRICHROMAT

S   M   L

(M-L) (L-M)
(green) (red)

B. PROTANOPE

S   M   L

(M-L) (L-M)
X   X

C. DEUTERANOPE

S   M   L

(M-L) (L-M)
X   X

D. RED-GREEN REVERSED TRICHROMAT

S   M   L

(M-L) (L-M)
(red) (green)

Figure 13.1.2 A biological basis for red-green-reversed tri-chromats. Normal trichromats have three different pigments in the retinal cones (A), whereas red-green color blind individuals have the same pigment in their L and M cones (B and C). People with the genes for both forms of red-green color blindness, however, would be red-green-reversed trichromats (D).

normal trichromats have three different pigments in their three cone types (Figure 13.1.2A). Some people are red-green color blind because they have a gene that causes their long-wavelength (L) cones to have the same pigment as their medium-wavelength (M) cones (Figure 13.1.2B). Other people have a different form of red-green color blindness because they have a different gene that causes their M cones to have the same pigment as their L cones (Figure 13.1.2C). In both cases, people with these genetic defects lose the ability to experience both red and green because the visual system codes both colors by taking the difference between the outputs of

these two cone types (see Figure 3.2.15). But suppose that someone had the genes for *both* of these forms of red-green color blindness. Their L cones would have the M pigment, and their M cones would have the L pigment (Figure 13.1.2D). Such doubly colorblind individuals would therefore not be red-green color blind at all, but red-green-reversed trichromats.[3] Statistically, they should be very rare (about 14 per 10,000 males), but they should exist. If they do, they are living proof that this color transformation is either undetectable or very difficult to detect by purely behavioral means, because nobody has ever detected one!

These color transformation arguments are telling criticisms against the completeness of any definition of conscious experience based purely on behavior. Their force lies in the fact that there could be identical behavior in response to identical environmental stimulation without there being corresponding identical experiences underlying them, even if we grant that the other person has experiences to begin with. We will come back to this problem at the end of the chapter to examine certain of its implications about possible limits on scientific theories of consciousness.

Phenomenological Criteria. Let us return to the issue of criteria for consciousness: How are we to tell whether a given creature is conscious or not? Clearly, phenomenological experience is key. In fact, it is the defining characteristic, the necessary and sufficient condition, for attributing consciousness to something. I know that I am conscious precisely because I have such experiences. This is often called **first-person knowledge** or **subjective knowledge** because it is available only to the self (i.e., the first-person or subject). In his classic essay "What Is It Like to Be a Bat?" philosopher Thomas Nagel (1974) identifies the phenomenological position with what it is like to *be* some person, creature, or machine in a given situation. In the case of color perception, for example, it is what it is like for you to experience a particular shade of redness or pale blueness or whatever. This much seems perfectly clear. But if it is so

---

[3] One could object that the only thing that differentiates M and L cones is the pigment that they contain, so people with both forms of red-green color blindness would actually be normal trichromats rather than red-green-reversed ones. There are two other ways in which M and L cones might be differentiated, however. First, if the connections of M and L

cones to other cells of the visual system are not completely symmetrical, they can be differentiated by these connections independently of their pigments. Second, they may be differentiable by their relation to the genetic codes that produced them.

Visual Awareness

clear, then why not simply define consciousness with respect to such phenomenological criteria?

As we said before, the difficulty is that first-person knowledge is available only to the self. This raises a problem for scientific explanations of consciousness because the scientific method requires its facts to be objective in the sense of being available to any scientist who undertakes the same experiment. In all matters except consciousness, this appears to work very well. But consciousness has the extremely peculiar and elusive property of being directly accessible only to the self, thus blocking the usual methods of scientific observation. Rather than observing consciousness itself in others, the scientist is forced to observe the correlates of consciousness, the "shadows of consciousness," as it were. Two sorts of shadows are possible to study: behavior and physiology. Neither is consciousness itself, but both are (or seem likely to be) closely related.

Behavioral Criteria. The most obvious way to get an objective, scientific handle on consciousness is to study behavior, as dictated by methodological behaviorism. Behavior is clearly objective and observable in the third-person sense. But how is it related to consciousness? The link is the assumption that if someone or something behaves enough like I do, it must be conscious like I am. After all, I believe I behave in the ways I do because of my own conscious experiences, and so (presumably) do others. I wince when I am in pain, eat when I am hungry, and duck when I perceive a baseball hurtling toward my head. If I were comatose, I would not behave in any of these ways, even in the same physical situations.

Behavioral criteria for consciousness are closely associated with what is called **Turing's test**. This test was initially proposed by the brilliant mathematician Alan Turing (1950), inventor of the digital computer, to solve the problem of how to determine whether a computing machine could be called "intelligent." Wishing to avoid purely philosophical debates, Turing imagined an objective behavioral procedure for deciding the issue by setting up an *imitation game*. A person is seated at a computer terminal that allows her to communicate either with a real person or with a computer that has been programmed to behave intelligently (i.e., like a person). This interrogator's job is to decide whether she is communicating with a person or the computer. The termi-

nal is used simply to keep the interrogator from using physical appearance as a factor in the decision, since appearance presumably does not have any logical bearing on intelligence.

The interrogator is allowed to ask anything she wants. For example, she could ask the subject to play a game of chess, engage in a conversation on current events, or describe its favorite TV show. Nothing is out of bounds. She could even ask whether the subject is intelligent. A person would presumably reply affirmatively, but then so would a properly programmed computer. If the interrogator could not tell the difference between interacting with real people and with the computer, Turing asserted that the computer should be judged "intelligent." It would then be said to have "passed Turing's test."

Note that Turing's test is a strictly behavioral test because the interrogator has no information about the physical attributes of the subject, but only about its behavior. In the original version, this behavior is strictly verbal, but there is no reason in principle why it needs to be restricted in this way. The interrogator could ask the subject to draw pictures or even to carry out tasks in the real world, provided the visual feedback the interrogator received did not provide information about the physical appearance of the subject.

The same imitation game can be used for deciding about the appropriateness of any other cognitive description, including whether the subject is "conscious." Again, simply asking the subject whether it is conscious will not discriminate between the machine and a person because the machine can easily be programmed to answer that question in the affirmative. Similarly, appropriate responses to questions asking it to describe the nature of its visual experiences or pain experiences could certainly be programmed. But even if they could, would that necessarily mean that the computer would *be* conscious or only that it would *act as if it were* conscious?

If one grants that physical appearance should be irrelevant to whether something is conscious or not, Turing's test seems to be a fair and objective procedure. But it also seems that there is a fact at issue here rather than just an opinion—namely, whether the target object is actually *conscious* or merely simulating consciousness—and Turing's test should stand or fall on whether it gives the correct answer. The problem is that it is not clear that it will. As critics readily point out, it cannot distinguish between a conscious entity and one that only acts as if it were conscious—an automaton or a zombie. To assert that Turing's test actually gives the correct answer to the factual question of consciousness, one must assume that it is impossible for something to act as if it is conscious without actually being so. This is a highly questionable assumption, although some have defended it (e.g., Dennett, 1991). If it is untrue, then passing Turing's test is not a sufficient condition for consciousness, because automatons can pass it without being conscious.

Turing's test also runs into trouble as a necessary condition for consciousness. The relevant question here is whether something can be conscious and still fail Turing's test. Although this might initially seem unlikely, consider a person who has an unusual medical condition that disables the use of all the muscles required for overt behavior yet keeps all other bodily functions intact, including all brain functions. This person would be unable to behave in any way yet would still be fully conscious when awake. Turing's test thus runs afoul as a criterion for consciousness because behavior's link to consciousness can be broken under unlikely but easily imaginable circumstances.

We appear to be on the horns of a dilemma with respect to the criteria for consciousness. Phenomenological criteria are valid by definition but do not appear to be scientific by the usual yardsticks. Behavioral criteria are scientific by definition but are not necessarily valid. The fact that scientists prefer to rely on respectable but possibly invalid behavioral methods brings to mind the streetlight parable: A woman comes upon a man searching for something under a streetlight at night. The man explains that he has lost his keys, and they both search diligently for some time. The woman finally asks the man where he thinks he lost them, to which he replies, "Down the street in the middle of the block." When she then asks why he is looking here at the corner, he replies, "Because this is where the light is." The problem is that consciousness does not seem to be where behavioral science can shed much light on it.

Physiological Criteria. Modern science has another card to play, however, and that is the biological substrate of consciousness. Even if behavioral methods cannot penetrate the subjectivity barrier of consciousness, perhaps physiological methods can. In truth, few impor-

tant facts are yet known about the biological substrates of consciousness. There are not even very many hypotheses, although several speculations have recently been proposed (e.g., Baars, 1988; Crick, 1994; Crick & Koch, 1990, 1995, 1998; Edelman, 1989). Even so, it is possible to speculate about the promise such an enterprise might hold as a way of defining and theorizing about consciousness. It is important to remember that in doing so, we are whistling in the dark, however.

Let us suppose, just for the sake of argument, that neuroscientists discover some crucial feature of the neural activity that underlies consciousness. Perhaps all neural activity that gives rise to consciousness occurs in some particular layer of cerebral cortex, or in neural circuits that are mediated by some particular neurotransmitter, or in neurons that fire at a temporal spiking frequency of about 40 times per second. If something like one of these assertions were true— and, remember, we are just making up stories here—could we then define consciousness objectively in terms of that form of neural activity? If we could, would this definition then replace the subjective definition in terms of experience? And would such a biological definition then constitute a theory of consciousness?

The first important observation about such an enterprise is that biology cannot really give us an objective definition of consciousness independent of its subjective definition. The reason is that we need the subjective definition to determine what physiological events correspond to consciousness in the first place. Suppose we knew all of the relevant biological events that occur in human brains. We still could not provide a biological account of consciousness because we would have no way to tell which brain events were conscious and which ones were not. Without that crucial information, a biological definition of consciousness simply could not get off the ground. To determine the biological correlates of consciousness, one must be able to designate the events to which they are being correlated (i.e., conscious ones), and this requires a subjective definition.

For this reason, any biological definition of consciousness would always be derived from the subjective definition. To see this in a slightly different way, consider what would constitute evidence that a given biological definition was incorrect. If brain activity of type C were thought to define consciousness, it could be rejected for either of two reasons: if type C brain activity were found to result in nonconscious processing of some sort or if consciousness were found to occur in the absence of type C brain activity. The crucial observation for present purposes is that neither of these possibilities could be evaluated without an independent subjective definition of consciousness.

Correlational versus Causal Theories. In considering the status of physiological statements about consciousness, it is important to distinguish two different sorts, which we will call *correlational* and *causal*. Correlational statements concern what type of physiological activity takes place when conscious experiences are occurring that fail to take place when they are not. Our hypothetical examples in terms of a specific cortical location, a particular neurotransmitter, or a particular rate of firing are good examples. The common feature of these hypotheses is that they are merely correlational: They only claim that the designated feature of brain activity is associated with consciousness; they don't explain why that association exists. In other words, they provide no causal analysis of how this particular kind of brain activity produces consciousness. For this reason they fail to fill the explanatory gap that we mentioned earlier. Correlational analyses merely designate a subset of neural activity in the brain according to some particular property with which consciousness is thought to be associated. No explanation is given for this association; it simply is the sort of activity that accompanies consciousness.

At this point we should contrast such correlational analyses with a good example of a causal one: an analysis that provides a scientifically plausible explanation of how a particular form of brain activity actually causes conscious experience. Unfortunately, no examples of such a theory are available. In fact, to this writer's knowledge, nobody has ever suggested a theory that the scientific community regards as giving even a remotely plausible causal account of how consciousness arises or why it has the particular qualities it does. This does not mean that such a theory is impossible in principle, but only that no serious candidate has been generated in the past several thousand years.

A related distinction between correlational and causal biological definitions of consciousness is that they would differ in generalizability. Correlational analyses would very likely be specific to the type of biological system

within which they had been discovered. In the best-case scenario, a good correlational definition of human consciousness might generalize to chimpanzees, possibly even to dogs or rats, but probably not to frogs or snails because their brains are simply too different. If a correlational analysis showed that activity mediated by a particular neurotransmitter was the seat of human consciousness, for example, would that necessarily mean that creatures without that neurotransmitter were nonconscious? Or might some other evolutionarily related neural transmitter serve the same function in brains lacking that one? Even more drastically, what about extraterrestrial beings whose whole physical make-up might be radically different from our own? In such cases, a correlational analysis is almost bound to break down.

An adequate causal theory of consciousness might have a fighting chance, however, because the structure of the theory itself could provide the lines along which generalization would flow. Consider the analogy to a causal theory of life based on the structure of DNA. The analysis of how the double helical structure of DNA allows it to reproduce itself in an entirely mechanistic way suggests that biologists could determine whether alien beings were alive in the same sense as living organisms on earth by considering the nature of their molecular basis and its functional ability to replicate itself and to support the organism's lifelike functions. An alien object containing the very same set of four component bases as DNA (adenine, guanine, thymine, and cytosine) in some very different global structure that did not allow self-replication would not be judged to be alive by such biological criteria, yet another object containing very different components in some analogous arrangement that allowed for self-replication might be. Needless to say, such an analysis is a long way off in the case of consciousness.

13.2 Neuropsychology of Visual Awareness

Now that we have set the philosophical stage for discussing visual awareness, let us consider some facts about it. To begin, we will reconsider our initial definition of vision from Chapter 1: the process of acquiring knowledge about environmental objects and events by extracting information from the light they emit or reflect. One interesting feature of this definition is that it does not contain any reference to visual awareness or experience. This might seem like an oversight, but it was not. Conscious visual experience was left out because it is logically possible for vision to occur in the absence of awareness. Many aspects of vision do occur in the absence of awareness, as when an object coming toward us automatically draws our attention. A nonconscious analysis of its motion must have been carried out to cause the shift in attention, and this is surely an important visual ability. Is it possible that a full perceptual analysis can occur without visual awareness? This question is important not only for the issue of whether a machine (e.g., a computer or a robot) can perceive without awareness, but also for the issue of whether people can. There are several neurological conditions in which dissociations between visual abilities and visual awareness actually occur in humans, and these provide important clues about the basis of visual awareness.

13.2.1 Split-Brain Patients

In the nineteenth century, the pioneering psychophysicist Gustav Fechner (1860/1996) speculated on purely anatomical grounds that a brain structure called the **corpus callosum**—a large tract of fibers connecting the two cerebral hemispheres (see Figure 13.2.1)—was necessary for the "unity of consciousness." If this were true, he reasoned, cutting the corpus callosum might allow two different consciousnesses to develop. Fortunately, experiments of this nature cannot be carried out purely to satisfy Fechner's (or our) curiosity. But they can if they provide medical treatment in which there is reason to believe the patient will benefit substantially.

In the 1940s the first surgeries to sever the corpus callosum were performed to relieve or reduce epileptic seizures. Major seizures usually begin in one hemisphere and then spread to the corresponding location in the other hemisphere through the corpus callosum, gaining in intensity as the two foci of the seizure reinforce one another. Neurosurgeons reasoned that cutting the corpus callosum could drastically reduce the frequency and severity of seizures, and in many individuals, this was true. But what happened to the patient's consciousness? Did it split in two, as Fechner suggested?

Informal questioning of these **split-brain patients** after surgery revealed that severing the corpus callosum had surprisingly little effect on consciousness—so little,

in fact, that the famous biological psychologist Karl Lashley joked that perhaps the function of the corpus callosum was simply to hold the two hemispheres together! However, more careful testing under the scrutiny of neuropsychologists Roger Sperry (1961), Michael Gazzaniga (1970), and their colleagues began to uncover a fascinating story of the different perceptual, cognitive, and linguistic functions housed in the left and right hemispheres. Here is an example of the kind of experiment conducted to shed light on the nature of conscious visual perception in the left and right hemispheres (see Springer & Deutsch, 1981).

A split-brain patient, N.G., was presented with a fixation point in the middle of a screen. Once she fixated it, a picture of a cup was briefly flashed to the right of the dot. She was asked what she saw, and she replied, "A cup." On the next trial, a spoon was flashed to the left of the dot. Again she was asked what she saw, but this time she replied, "Nothing." She was then asked to reach under the screen with her left hand and pick out the object that had just been shown in her left visual field but without being able to see the objects. She reached under and felt each object, finally holding up the spoon. When she was asked what she was holding, she replied, "A pencil."

Why did patient N.G. behave in this way in these perceptual tests? How could she have picked the correct object with her left hand when she consciously perceived nothing and did not know what her left hand had chosen? To understand, we first need to review the way in which optical information is projected from the environment to the retinas and how the resulting neural information gets from the retinas to visual cortex. As shown in Figure 13.2.2, the left visual field (LVF) projects exclusively to the right visual cortex, and the right visual field (RVF) projects exclusively to the left visual cortex. The only exception is a narrow strip down the middle of the visual field, just 1° wide, that projects to both sides of the brain, presumably to "stitch together" the two separate cortical representations.

The net result of these crossed pathways is that the cup in the RVF is processed in the left hemisphere (LH) and the spoon in the LVF is processed in the right hemisphere (RH). N.G. appeared to consciously perceive the cup but not the spoon. Does this mean that only the LH is conscious? Possibly, but not necessarily. Other studies have shown that in most people, the speech centers of

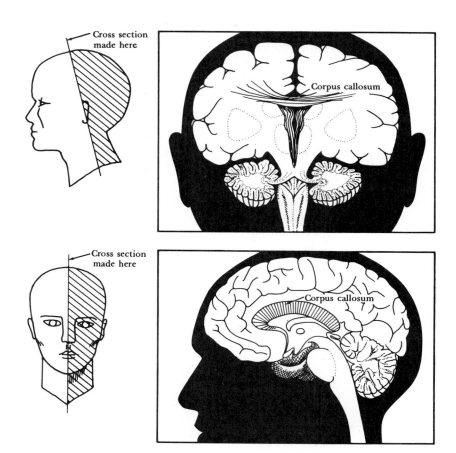

Figure 13.2.1 Two views of the corpus callosum. The corpus callosum is a large tract of fibers that connects the left and right cerebral hemispheres. When the corpus callosum has been severed, so-called split-brain patients reveal evidence of different functions in the two hemispheres. (From Lindsay & Norman, 1972.)

the brain are located in the LH. This means that N.G. could report the conscious experience of the cup verbally because it projected to the LH, which contains the major linguistic areas. The spoon was not named because it projected to the RH, which has much more limited linguistic capabilities. Normal subjects can name objects that are presented in the LVF because, after initially projecting to the RH, information crosses via the corpus callosum to the LH, where it can be named. In N.G., however, this could not occur because the corpus callosum had been severed.

The difficult question is whether N.G.'s inability to name the spoon—or indeed, to say that she saw anything at all in the LVF—means that the RH is not conscious or that it has its own form of consciousness without expressive linguistic capabilities. The most likely explanation of N.G.'s behavior is that each hemisphere

was aware of the object projected to it, but only the LH could talk about it. This brings us face to face with the previously discussed problem of criteria for consciousness: What are we willing to count as evidence that someone or something is conscious? In this case, the "something" is the RH of a person whose LH we are willing to grant consciousness because it is able to talk about its experiences. Should we deny that the RH has visual experiences simply because it is not able to talk about them?

Unfortunately there is no easy answer. We cannot ask the "person" because in the case of split-brain patients, we have an interesting situation in which the problem of other minds exists within a single person. The linguistic LH that can answer our question about RH consciousness appears not to know what, if anything, the RH experiences. The fact that the RH was able to pick out the

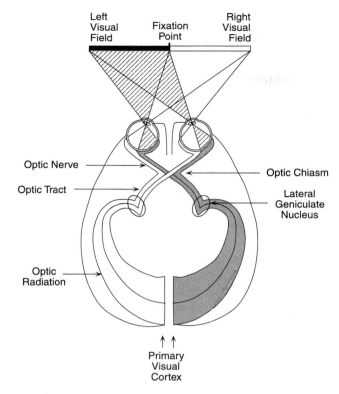

Figure 13.2.2 Projections of the left and right visual fields to the left and right hemispheres. Axons from retinal ganglion cells on the nasal side project to the opposite side of the brain, so the left visual field projects entirely to the right hemisphere and the right visual field projects entirely to the left hemisphere.

correct object by touch certainly suggests that it may have been visually aware of the spoon. But how do we know that this behavior was accompanied by consciousness? Certainly the critical issue in this case is behavioral similarity of the LH and RH, because physically speaking, the RH is almost identical to the LH, at least in gross morphology. If nothing else, this example points out the critical importance of linguistic report in deciding issues of consciousness. We are particularly apt to believe that someone or something is conscious if we ask it to report its experiences and it says what we would say under comparable circumstances. This is an exceedingly chauvinistic attitude but one that fits with the general notion that "similarity to me" is the ultimate dimension on which people decide their beliefs about consciousness in others.

13.2.2 Blindsight

One of the most unusual and fascinating neurological phenomena ever reported is **blindsight**: the ability of certain patients with damage to primary visual cortex to respond with greater than chance accuracy on visual tasks at the same time as they report having no visual experience whatever. The first documented case of blindsight was described by neuropsychologist Lawrence Weiskrantz (1980; Weiskrantz, Sanders, & Marshall, 1974), although several other cases have since been reported.

The discovery of blindsight resulted from attempts to reconcile discrepancies between the effects of lesions in striate cortex in monkeys and humans. When striate cortex is removed in monkeys, they are still able to make a number of visual discriminations (Humphrey, 1974). When similar operations are performed in humans (for purely medical reasons), they report complete absence of visual experiences in the corresponding area of the visual field. Suspecting that at least part of the reason for the difference might lie in the testing, Weiskrantz et al. (1974) first examined a human patient using the same kinds of procedures they had devised for monkeys. What they found was quite remarkable.

The Case History of D.B. The patient in whom blindsight was first fully documented, known as D.B., suffered from severe and persistent migraine headaches from the age of 14. They were always preceded by a visual disturbance in which a flashing light appeared in his lower-left visual field. After about 15 minutes, the flashing stopped, and the region became a white, opaque oval that was blind to stimulation, with a colored fringe around the lower and outer edges. A severe headache ensued on the right side of his head, followed by vomiting about 15 minutes later. The headaches persisted up to 48 hours, although D.B. usually slept through much of the attack and awakened to find his headache gone and his vision restored. By the time D.B. was in his twenties, the frequency of the headaches had increased to one every three weeks, on average. By that age, he also reported a persisting scotoma (blind area) in his left visual field, considerably smaller than the blind region that preceded the headaches but constantly present. As you might imagine, these headaches and visual prob-

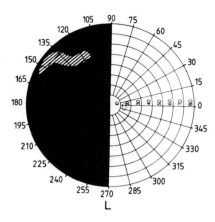
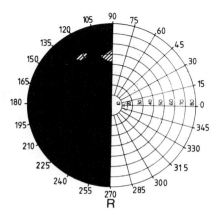

Figure 13.2.3 Visual field maps for the left (L) and right (R) eyes of a patient with blindsight. Patient D.B. could see almost nothing in his left visual field (black region) because his right occipital cortex was removed. The only exception was in a small region in the upper left quadrant (shaded region) where he had unclear visual experiences. (From Weiskrantz et al., 1974.)

lems were severely debilitating to both his work and his personal life.

Neurologists determined that the cause of D.B.'s headaches was a torturous mass of enlarged blood vessels in the right visual cortex. Several different forms of treatment were attempted, but none gave him relief. Finally, at age 33, the part of his brain containing the malformed blood vessels was surgically removed, including much of the striate cortex in his RH. The medical result was decidedly positive: D.B.'s symptoms were relieved, and the quality of his life improved markedly. As expected from the large amount of primary visual cortex removed, however, the operation left him phenomenologically blind over most of his LVF. Figure 13.2.3 shows that he reported seeing nothing at all in his LVF except for a crescent of hazy vision in the upper left quadrant. This result was obtained by presenting small lights at different locations and asking D.B. to say simply whether he saw them or not. By such standard measures, D.B. was almost completely blind in his LVF. (Note that this half-field blindness is not the same as being blind in just one eye. It would be like being blind in just the right half of both retinas. In fact, both of D.B.'s eyes were quite normal.)

Accurate Guessing without Visual Experience. By running D.B. on nonstandard tests—much like the tests given to cortically lesioned monkeys—Weiskrantz et al. (1974) discovered that he had considerable visual abilities despite his professed lack of visual experience. They gave D.B. well-defined tasks and asked him to guess where something was presented or what was presented on every trial, even though he reported seeing absolutely nothing. In one experiment, they presented a small light at various positions along the horizontal midline of his blind left field or his sighted right field for 3 s and then asked him to point to its location. Figure 13.2.4 shows the remarkable results: D.B. was very nearly as accurate in his blind field as in his sighted field. There were small systematic errors and slightly larger variability in the blind field, but nothing like what would be expected if D.B. had no visual information from his consciously blind region.

Subsequent experiments showed that he could also make a surprising number of visual discriminations for stimuli presented to his blind field by "guessing." For example, he could accurately distinguish between horizontal versus vertical lines, diagonal versus vertical lines, and X's versus O's without consciously seeing them. In each case, his performance improved as a function of the size and duration of the stimuli: Larger lines and letters resulted in better performance, as did longer stimulus durations (up to about 250 ms).

During all of these experimental sessions, D.B. was conscientious about reporting visual experiences that arose when any portion of the stimulus figure intruded into his small area of preserved vision in the upper left quadrant. The rest of the time, he maintained that he

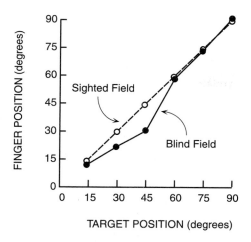

Figure 13.2.4 Accurate finger-pointing performance. D.B.'s ability to point to lights in his blind field (by guessing) was almost as good as that in his sighted field (by conscious seeing).

saw nothing at all. When pressed, he sometimes said that he had a feeling of "smoothness" versus "jaggedness" in discriminating the O's and X's, but he denied that these feelings were based on visual experience. When he was informed of his high level of accuracy, he was openly astonished and reiterated that all his responses had been mere guesses. The data show that they were extremely accurate guesses, however, demonstrating the dissociation between visual experience and visual performance that is the hallmark of blindsight. How is this possible? How could D.B. "see" nothing yet perform as though he did?

The Two Visual Systems Hypothesis. One intriguing possibility that Weiskrantz and others have suggested is that although the primary pathway to visual cortex was largely destroyed by the surgery, a secondary visual pathway to the superior colliculus in the thalamus was still very much intact. If the cortical system were somehow responsible for visual awareness and the collicular system performed significant nonconscious visual functions, the main features of blindsight could be explained. D.B. would lack visual experience in the LVF because primary visual cortex in his RH had been surgically removed. He would retain the ability to make visual discriminations in the LVF, however, because the visual pathway through the superior colliculus was still able to process enough relevant visual information. The

fact that the pathway through the superior colliculus is much smaller than the cortical system could also explain why stimuli had to be larger and presented for a longer time: The collicular system presumably has much lower spatial resolution than visual cortex. Therefore, a number of important facts are neatly explained by the hypothesis that blindsight results from activity in the collicular system.

Because physiological experiments cannot ethically be performed on people, it is of some importance for future research on this subject whether monkeys who have residual visual abilities after removal of striate cortex also have blindsight. The question is tricky, of course, because monkeys cannot talk to us about their visual experiences—or lack of them. However, Cowey and Stoerig (1995) recently reported an interesting result suggesting that monkeys also have blindsight. First, they removed area V1 of one cerebral hemisphere from three monkeys and verified that they had residual visual abilities in the opposite visual half-field. Next, they trained the monkeys to discriminate between real visual events and blank (no-stimulus) events in their intact visual hemifield. Finally, they tested whether the monkeys would respond to a real stimulus event in their impaired hemifield as a blank. They did, a result suggesting that despite their residual visual ability in that hemifield, they do not have visual experiences there.

Methodological Challenges. As usually happens with claims of visual ability without visual awareness, blindsight has been subjected to intense methodological scrutiny. Many of the experiments with D.B. were indeed less than perfectly executed, often having been carried out in the rooms and corridors of hospitals with makeshift apparatus. Because D.B.'s eye movements were not monitored during the experiments, for example, one cannot rule out the possibility that on some trials, he might have moved his eyes so that the stimulus that the experimenters thought was presented entirely to his blind LVF actually fell partly on his intact RVF or on the island of unclear vision in his upper LVF. This account of blindsight seems unlikely, however, especially in light of D.B.'s seemingly scrupulous reports of any trials in which he had visual experiences. More sophisticated objections have also been raised, such as the possibility that D.B.'s performance could have been based on light from the target stimulus in the blind LVF scattering within the eye itself into his sighted RVF (Campion, Latto, & Smith, 1983). Subsequent experiments have shown this explanation to be false for at least some aspects of blindsighted performance (Zihl & Werth, 1984).

Improved methods for studying eye movements in a blindsight patient have recently called into question the two visual systems hypothesis (Fendrich, Wessinger, & Gazzaniga, 1992). The patient (C.L.T.) had suffered a stroke in his right occipital region six years before the study and was phenomenologically blind in his LVF. Magnetic resonance imaging (see Section 2.2.3) showed widespread damage to visual cortex, but with some islands of intact tissue. The superior colliculus, being a subcortical structure with a different blood supply, was entirely unaffected by the stroke. Using sophisticated equipment for measuring eye position and presenting stimuli to precise locations, the experimenters tested for residual visual function throughout the retina and found it to be present only within certain specific regions. That is, performance was at chance in many regions of the LVF but substantially and systematically above chance in others. Because C.L.T. reported no visual sensations in these islands of spared visual function, they are legitimate instances of blindsight.

The interesting fact about this preserved visual function is that it was spotty but consistently localized. Because the superior colliculus was fully intact, the authors argued that it was unlikely that the spotty residual functioning they measured was due to collicular processing. Rather, it seems more plausible that it was caused by the islands of spared tissue in visual cortex (see also Campion et al., 1983). The results of this study therefore do not seriously question the existence of blindsight as a phenomenon, since C.L.T. reported no visual experience in the locations where his performance was consistently above chance. However, they do challenge the interpretation that blindsight is mediated by a separate, nonconscious visual system involving the superior colliculus.

Does this finding rule out the subcortical explanation of blindsight? The answer is far from clear. If monkeys without area V1 have true blindsight, as Cowey and Stoerig's (1995) previously described findings suggest, it cannot be mediated by intact striate cortex, because this tissue was surgically removed in its entirety. But that was in monkeys, not in humans, and the mechanisms might conceivably be different for these two species. In humans, there is further evidence that the collicular pathway is involved in blindsight, at least in the case of eye movements. Careful studies have shown that eye movements of blindsight patients can be influenced by stimulation in the blind field and that these effects are mediated by the subcortical collicular pathway (Rafal, Smith, Krantz, Cohen, & Brennan, 1990). Another possibility is that some aspects of blindsight may arise within the geniculo-striate system but from a pathway that bypasses primary visual cortex. Cowey and Stoerig (1989) have argued that blindsight may be mediated by a population of cells in the LGN that project directly to extrastriate cortical areas, such as V4 and MT. Although such connections have been shown to exist anatomically, their function is still uncertain.

Whatever the neurological substrates of blindsight turn out to be—and there may be more than one—certain aspects of its nature suggest possible functions for visual awareness because the "residual" visual abilities present in blindsight are limited in interesting ways. Although it is true that the quality of visual performance in the blind field is usually worse than that in the sighted field, it can be at least as good. For example, whereas form discrimination is better in the sighted field, stimulus detection is sometimes actually better in the blind field (Weiskrantz, 1986). The most striking fact about blindsight is that the patient can achieve better than chance performance only if he or she is given a specific discrimination task among a small number of concrete alternatives and is forced to guess. What is oddly missing is the open-ended capability of seeing what is in the blind field based on bottom-up processing of sensory information. The residual visual function in blindsight appears to require top-down testing of a specific hypothesis, one that is provided by the experimenters rather than the patient's own visual system. Blindsight is therefore not very useful to the patient, as it does not seem able to support spontaneous intentional actions (Marcel, 1983b).

13.2.3 Unconscious Processing in Neglect and Balint's Syndrome

In Chapter 11 we discussed the phenomenon of unilateral neglect, a neurological syndrome that is usually caused by brain damage to the posterior part of the right hemisphere (RH) but without damage to primary visual cortex. In its classical form, neglect patients appear to be unaware of objects presented in their LVF, although there is also more recent evidence for neglect of just the left side of objects presented in their RVF (e.g., Driver & Halligan, 1991). Neglect is generally thought to be a deficit of attention in which objects or parts of objects fail to be perceived because patients cannot shift attention to them. Whatever the cause, neglected objects or parts of objects are not consciously perceived. The existence of blindsight following occipital damage suggests the possibility that neglected objects might also be processed unconsciously following parietal damage. Is there any evidence that this might be so?

Several recent studies have reported effects that are compatible with this hypothesis. Marshall and Halligan (1988) presented a patient simultaneously with drawings of two houses, vertically aligned in the center of vision. The houses were identical except that red flames emanated from the left side of one of them. Because of the patient's neglect, she reported that the two houses looked identical. When she was asked which house she would prefer to live in, however, she repeatedly chose the house without the flames. The obvious interpretation of this result is that although the patient did not perceive the flames consciously, she unconsciously recognized them—and the danger they implied—and therefore chose the other house. Although this finding has proven somewhat controversial (e.g., Bisiach & Rusconi, 1990), other experiments point to the same conclusion.

Cohen, Ivry, Rafal, and Kohn (1995) recently reported a particularly convincing experiment. They used a modified version of the Stroop task that was discussed in Section 11.2.4. The patient was required to name the color of a red or green O presented centrally at fixation. Just to the left or right of this target was a distractor element: another O whose color was either congruent with that of the target (e.g., a second red O if the target was red) or incongruent with it (e.g., a green O to one side or the other of the central red O). The distractor could be presented either in the intact field to the right of the target or in the neglected field to the left of it. The experimenters found that patients showed faster color responses to the target with congruent distractors and slower responses with incongruent distractors when they were presented in either the neglected or the intact field.

This could happen only if the patients registered the color of the distractor in the neglected field as well as the intact one. The methodology of this study is particularly clean and rules out virtually all alternative interpretations. The conclusion is that the objects that neglect patients deny perceiving consciously are nevertheless processed unconsciously to relatively high levels in the visual system, at least to the point of identification.

Patients with the debilitating condition known as Balint's syndrome also show evidence of nonconscious processing of unattended objects. As we discussed in Section 11.2.7, patients with Balint's syndrome appear to be able to perceive only one object at a time and to have a greatly impaired ability to disengage attention from that object to fixate another. Even so, evidence from a color-naming task shows that unseen objects in the visual field affect their performance (Rafal & Robertson, 1995). One such patient was presented with a central square whose color he was to name as quickly as possible. On every trial, another colored square was flashed for 16 ms near the central square. Although the patient could not tell whether anything other than the central square was presented, his response times were longer when the color of the second square was inconsistent with the central one than when it was the same. This shows that even patients with Balint's syndrome, who are phenomenologically blind to everything but the one object they are fixating, are nonconsciously processing other objects in their visual field. That this processing is carried to a semantic level is suggested by the fact that such patients are more likely to be able to name both of two simultaneously presented objects if they are semantically related than if they are not (Coslett & Saffran, 1991).

13.2.4 Unconscious Face Recognition in Prosopagnosia

Another fascinating neurological syndrome that shows evidence of dissociation between visual performance and visual awareness is prosopagnosia. As described in Section 9.2.5, prosopagnosia is a form of visual agnosia in which patients can see quite well and identify many objects but cannot recognize faces, even those of their spouses and immediate family members. Nevertheless, there is mounting evidence that, despite their inability to consciously identify faces or even to experience them as familiar, these patients are unconsciously able to discriminate known from unknown faces and even to identify ones they know.

One line of evidence for unconscious perception of facial familiarity comes from experiments in which subjects must decide, as quickly as possible, whether two faces are the same or different. Prosopagnosic patients are measurably faster at deciding that two familiar faces are the same than that two unfamiliar faces are (de Haan, Young, & Newcombe, 1987). This result shows some residue of facial familiarity in the patient's visual system despite his or her inability to name any of the (previously) familiar faces in an identification test.

Another result indicating residual effects of facial familiarity in prosopagnosic patients arises when they are required to categorize names (not faces) as belonging to famous versus nonfamous people. Normals are faster at performing this task when they are shown the face of a related person just before the target name. For instance, subjects would be faster at indicating that "Diana Spencer" was a famous name when it was preceded by a picture of Prince Charles than when it was not. The startling result with a prosopagnosic patient was that not only were responses speeded by such face primes, but the size of the effect was the same as that for normals (Young, Hellawell, & de Haan, 1988). Explicit testing showed that the patient could name just two of the twenty faces used as primes. The face primes thus appear to be identified at a nonconscious level, and this information appears to access associations to memory representations of related people.

New findings of strange dissociations between visual ability and visual consciousness in neuropsychological patients are being reported at an ever increasing rate. Given the number of unexpected effects discovered in the past decade, one suspects that vision scientists have barely begun to scratch the surface of this fascinating topic.

13.3 Visual Awareness in Normal Observers

Fortunately, insights into the nature of visual awareness are not limited to results with patients who have brain damage. Normal people also show interesting evidence of some forms of dissociation between visual processing and visual awareness, although the conditions under which these effects can be observed are more restrictive and difficult to achieve than those in studies of neuropsychological patients. Partly for this reason, studies claiming to show evidence of perception without awareness in normals have been subjected to even more intense methodological scrutiny than studies of patient populations.

13.3.1 Perceptual Defense

The first phenomenon related to visual awareness that raised the hackles of methodologists was **perceptual defense**. The claim was that the visual system could resist unwanted, anxiety-producing stimuli by reducing its sensitivity to their conscious perception (e.g., Bruner & Postman, 1947), much as Sigmund Freud (1915) claimed that the ego could dynamically repress disturbing thoughts and desires that arose internally. In support of perceptual defense, experimenters found that subjects required longer exposures to identify "disturbing" words (e.g., Kotex, penis, raped, whore) than to identify "normal" control words (e.g., apple, glass, broom) (e.g., McGinnies, 1949). This phenomenon unleashed a firestorm of controversy, in large part because it seemed to imply a level of nonconscious perception prior to conscious perception. The problem is that for the visual system to defend against disturbing words, it seemed that it would first have to identify them.

The experiments were attacked on numerous methodological grounds, most of which turned out to be valid. For example, critics showed that the disturbing words were less frequent in printed English text than the control words and that word frequency was a potent factor in word perception (Howes & Solomon, 1950). Other critics argued that subjects might actually perceive the disturbing words at the same exposure level as the control words but simply be embarrassed to say them aloud to the experimenter. This form of response bias is a serious problem (see Appendix A), and so subsequent experiments tried to control for its effects. They often showed reliable defense effects but of much smaller magnitude (e.g., Bootzin & Natsoulas, 1965). The initial backlash of criticism gave perceptual defense a bad name from which it never fully recovered, and the empirical question of whether it exists has never been satisfactorily settled (Erdelyi, 1974). Rather, the debate simply ran out of steam as researchers moved on to study other phenomena.

Interestingly, the scientific community's willingness to accept nonconscious perception in normals appears to have increased greatly following the discovery of blindsight. The reason appears to be that most scientists are far more willing to believe a person's verbal report that he or she has no visual experience from a given optical event if there is incontrovertible evidence of neurological damage to visual areas of the brain than if the visual system is entirely intact. This bias is understandable for at least two reasons. First, the nature of the brain damage in cases like D.B.'s is such that one would predict severe deficits in visual experience before the patient's report of it. D.B. was surely warned by his neurosurgeon that the operation would cause substantial blindness in his LVF. Second, the blindsight patient has a persistent symptom of never having any visual experience in a specific region of the visual field. Normal people, in contrast, have visual experiences in all parts of the visual field under normal conditions. When a visual stimulus is presented under conditions that result in the subject reporting no visual experience of it—for example, flashing it very briefly and masking it immediately with another stimulus—the subject still has visual experiences. The crucial question is whether anything in those experiences corresponded to the briefly flashed target stimulus. The conclusion that there was not is therefore a much more subtle and debatable proposition than that D.B. has no visual experience in response to a stimulus in his blind field.

13.3.2 Subliminal Perception

By far the most dramatic and important claim about unconscious perception in normal observers is for the existence of **subliminal perception**: the ability to register and process information that has been presented under conditions in which it is below the threshold of awareness. (The term "subliminal" is derived from the prefix *sub*, meaning "below," and the root *limen*, meaning "threshold.") Blindsight is a clear case of subliminal perception but with neurological patients rather than normal perceivers. Many readers will be familiar with the idea of subliminal perception in the guise of **subliminal advertising**: the attempt to influence people's consumer decisions by very rapid or subtle presentation of information below the threshold of awareness. Although we will not tackle the issue of subliminal advertising directly, we will consider the closely related issue of the scientific status of subliminal perception under conditions similar to some used in subliminal advertising.

The basic paradigm for investigating the existence of subliminal perception requires subjects to engage in two different tasks in two different phases of the experiment using the same stimulus materials. The *direct task* is designed to assess the subject's conscious awareness of a visual presentation. It often involves a simple detection task in which subjects are asked to indicate on every trial whether they saw something or nothing. When performance in the direct task is just at the level of chance—for example, 50% correct in a two-alternative forced-choice detection—it is usually assumed that the subject has no visual awareness of the stimulus presented. The *indirect task* is designed to tap some process that can be influenced by registered information about the stimulus even when there is no visual awareness of it. Many different indirect tasks have been used in studies of visual subliminal perception, only a few of which will be discussed here.

Marcel's Experiments. British psychologist Anthony Marcel (1983a) performed a series of well-known and influential experiments in which he claimed to have demonstrated subliminal perception in normal observers. Although he reported a number of studies, we will consider only one. Marcel used yes/no detection performance as the direct measure of conscious experience and performance on a Stroop color-naming task (see Section 11.2.4) as the indirect measure of unconscious processing.

The experiment consisted of two phases. In the first (direct task) phase Marcel attempted to find each subject's individual threshold for consciously detecting the presence (versus absence) of briefly flashed words. On each trial he presented either a color name (RED, BLUE, GREEN, or YELLOW) or a blank slide for a variable period of time, immediately followed by a pattern mask. Marcel adjusted the duration of the word or blank field until the subject was just slightly above chance at detecting the difference, around 60% or less. (He erred on the side of being above chance, reasoning that if performance were actually at chance, the

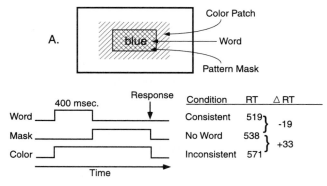

A.

Color Patch
Word
Pattern Mask

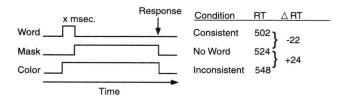

Condition	RT	△RT
Consistent	519	-19
No Word	538	
Inconsistent	571	+33

B. SUPRATHRESHOLD CONDITION (CONSCIOUS)

Condition	RT	△RT
Consistent	502	-22
No Word	524	
Inconsistent	548	+24

C. SUBTHRESHOLD CONDITION (UNCONSCIOUS)

Figure 13.3.1 Subliminal perception in Marcel's modified Stroop experiment. A color word that is presented before a color patch facilitates or interferes with response time (*RT*) to name the patch when the word is presented consciously, as indicated by *RT* changes (Δ*RT*) relative to the no-word condition. Suprisingly, the same effects are present when subjects are not conscious of seeing the prior color word because of the rapid presentation of a pattern mask.

stimulus might be substantially below threshold.) The presentation durations that elicited this level of performance varied from 30 to 80 ms, depending on the subject.

The second (indirect task) phase of the experiment examined Stroop effects: the influence of irrelevant color words on the speed with which patches of color can be named. There were two different types of trials, which Marcel called *suprathreshold* and *subthreshold*. On the suprathreshold trials, he showed subjects one of four color words (or no word at all) on a background of a larger rectangular patch of color, as illustrated in Figure 13.3.1A. After 400 ms, a pattern mask was presented over the color word, but the initial display was long enough for subjects to see the color word clearly and consciously. The task was to name the color patch, regardless of the color word that was presented with it,

and to do so as quickly and accurately as possible. On some trials, the color word was consistent with the color patch (e.g., a red patch on which the word RED appeared); on other trials, the word was inconsistent with the color (e.g., a red patch on which the word BLUE appeared). As Figure 13.3.1B shows, subjects in this task were 33 ms slower in naming the color patch when the color word was inconsistent than when there was no word at all. When the color word was consistent, they were 19 ms faster than when there was no word at all. Therefore, both interference and facilitation are present in this modified version of the Stroop task when subjects consciously perceive the color word.

The results in this suprathreshold condition of the Stroop task were contrasted with other trials in the same experiment in which subjects saw exactly the same thing, except that the color word was followed by the pattern mask at the time interval Marcel had determined to be the threshold for detecting the presence of the word. Notice that in this condition, the subjects presumably saw nothing but the pattern mask and the color patch. If such were the case, there should be no difference between the consistent, inconsistent, and neutral conditions. However, what Marcel actually found was that subjects showed significant interference and facilitation effects in these conditions, as indicated in Figure 13.3.1C. Even more surprising, the size of the effect was not reliably smaller than in the suprathreshold condition: 24 ms of interference with inconsistent color words and 22 ms of facilitation with consistent color words. Therefore, Marcel concluded that the color words had been registered and processed to the level of identification in the subthreshold condition, even though detection measures indicated that subjects were not aware of them.

Marcel's (1983a) claim to have demonstrated subliminal perception unleashed a flood of controversy and stimulated a great deal of further research into the existence and nature of this phenomenon. Despite his seemingly careful methods of measuring the threshold of awareness and subsequent replications of his main results by other researchers (e.g., Fowler, Wolford, Slade, & Tassinary, 1981), Marcel's studies were heavily criticized for a variety of reasons (e.g., Cheesman & Merikle, 1984; Holender, 1986). As usual, much of the controversy surrounded methodology, particularly the question of whether the subjects actually had no visual experience of the color words or were merely reticent to say that they had. This is an extremely thorny issue. It concerns nothing less than how one defines an adequate experimental procedure to measure the threshold of visual awareness. Given the apparently ironclad subjective nature of consciousness, it is perhaps not surprising that trying to define it objectively through behavioral measures gives rise to vexingly difficult problems. To see just how intractable the issues are, we will now consider an experiment that Cheesman and Merikle (1984) performed in an attempt to improve on Marcel's methods.

Objective versus Subjective Thresholds of Awareness. Cheesman and Merikle (1984) argued that Marcel's direct measure of conscious perception was inadequate because subjects may simply have been too conservative in reporting that they saw a word rather than a blank. They reasoned that the best way to find the actual threshold of conscious perception would be to have subjects make a forced-choice discrimination among the four color words (ORANGE, BLUE, GREEN, and YELLOW), guessing if they were unsure. On each trial of the first phase of their experiment, they showed subjects one of the four color words, followed by a pattern mask, and had them guess which it was. They adjusted the delay between the word and the mask until subjects were at chance (25%). Then they measured performance on the Stroop test, as Marcel had done, and found no Stroop effects at all (i.e., no difference between the consistent and inconsistent conditions). Therefore, they concluded that subliminal perception does not really exist.

Cheesman and Merikle (1984) called their forced-choice discrimination measure—"which of these four words did you see"—the **objective threshold of awareness**. Following Eriksen (1960), they believed that consciousness should be defined relative to an objective measure showing that the subject has *no* visual information from the stimulus in a direct perceptual task. They contrasted their approach with Marcel's yes/no detection measure—"Did you see anything or not?"—which they called the **subjective threshold of awareness**. They argued that this method allowed subjects to get some visual information from the stimulus at the measured threshold because they were too conservative in saying that they saw something rather than

nothing. Which threshold is the right one for assessing the presence of visual experience?

Cheesman and Merikle (1984) argued that the objective threshold is the correct one, but the issue is far from clear. For example, it might be that subjects in the discrimination task were responding on the basis of nonconscious visual information when the words were presented at the so-called objective threshold of awareness. In fact, subjects in experiments like these invariably report that near the objective threshold, they believe that they are guessing randomly on every trial, even when their actual performance is substantially better than chance. This means that their guessing behavior based on nonconscious visual processing is included in Cheesman and Merikle's definition of the objective threshold of awareness. But should it be?

Many researchers would argue that it should not. When D.B. claimed that he was guessing randomly about stimuli presented in his blind field and yet was actually performing almost perfectly, most people believe that he saw nothing. By Cheesman and Merikle's objective threshold criterion, however, D.B.'s accurate guesses should be taken as evidence that he was consciously perceiving things. If we believe D.B.'s claim that he was guessing even though his performance was above chance, why should we not also believe normal subjects when they say that they are guessing and yet are performing above chance? If we do believe them and decide that accurate guessing does not constitute evidence of conscious perception, then Cheesman and Merikle's objective threshold method is inappropriate for defining visual awareness, and Marcel's subjective threshold method is far better.

Ideally, a direct measure of conscious perception should satisfy two criteria (Merikle & Reingold, 1992):

1. *Exhaustiveness.* The measure should exhaust the contents of consciousness. That is, it should wring out every last bit of information the observer has in his or her conscious experience of the stimulus event. Anything less opens the door to the objection that performance in the indirect task may reflect conscious information that has escaped measurement by the direct task. These are the grounds on which Marcel's (1983a) original detection measure of the so-called subjective threshold of awareness can be criticized.

2. *Exclusiveness.* The measure should reflect exclusively

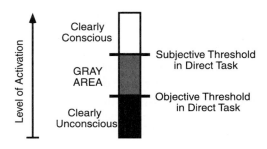

Figure 13.3.2 The gray zone between conscious perception and lack of visual information. There is a region of visual phenomena below the subjective threshold of awareness and above the objective threshold that some claim is subliminal and others claim is supraliminal.

the contents of consciousness. That is, it should measure only aspects of conscious experience. It is not appropriate if it also taps nonconscious processes that underlie true guessing behavior. These are the grounds on which Cheesman and Merikle's (1984) discrimination measure of the so-called objective threshold of awareness can be criticized.

A scientist who is trying to define consciousness experimentally is thus on the horns of this dilemma. Both criteria are important, yet they seem nearly impossible to satisfy simultaneously.

We are left with a gray zone lying between two different thresholds, as depicted in Figure 13.3.2. The lower bound is Cheesman and Merikle's objective threshold of awareness. Surely, no one is aware of anything below this level, for it is defined as the point at which visual input has no measurable effect on behavior in direct perceptual tasks. The upper bound is Marcel's subjective threshold of awareness, the point at which people are willing to assert that they have had a visual experience. We will presume that every sighted person is aware of visual input above this level and will report it as conscious—unless they are intentionally lying. The gray area in between is bona fide subliminal perception to those who advocate identifying consciousness with subjective thresholds but bogus subliminal perception to those who advocate objective thresholds. It appears that an impasse has been reached. Is there any way around it?

Functional Correlates of Consciousness. Even though experts disagree about which definition is most appropriate for the threshold of visual awareness, it should be possible for them to agree on the functional properties of "gray zone" perception, regardless of whether it is called "subliminal" or not. The key question is whether there is anything that people cannot do with visual information in this gray zone that they can do once it crosses the subjective (upper) threshold into clearly conscious perception?

In a series of later experiments, Cheesman and Merikle (1986) took this approach. They reasoned that subjects would not be able to engage in intentional cognitive strategies unless they were aware of what they had seen. They investigated this possibility in a Stroop experiment in which they varied the probability of congruent trials (e.g., RED on red) and incongruent trials (e.g., RED on blue). In some blocks, 75% of the trials had congruent words and colors; in other blocks, only 25% of the trials did. Previous experiments had shown that when there is a high proportion of congruent trials, subjects tend to engage in a strategy whereby they rely on the word more heavily than they do when there is a low proportion of congruent trials. The typical result is a dramatic increase in the amount of both facilitation on congruent trials and interference on incongruent ones. But this change in performance would seem to require conscious knowledge of the relative frequency of consistent and inconsistent trials. Would this kind of manipulation have similar effects when the word was presented in the gray area between the objective and subjective thresholds?

Cheesman and Merikle (1986) measured response times to name the color patch on which the color words were presented under two masking conditions. In the *suprathreshold condition*, the mask was presented 300 ms after the color word, a delay at which all subjects clearly and consciously perceived the word. In the *subjective threshold condition*, the mask was presented at a delay that had previously been measured for each subject to be in the gray zone, just below the subjective threshold of awareness. The results of this experiment are shown in Figure 13.3.3. First, notice that even in the subjective threshold (gray zone) conditions, there is a clear Stroop effect: Naming latencies are faster in congruent trials than in incongruent trials. Next, notice that in these gray zone conditions, it did not matter much whether the probability of congruent trials was 25% or 75%. Stroop effects were also evident in the suprathreshold conditions, but

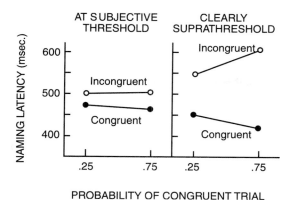

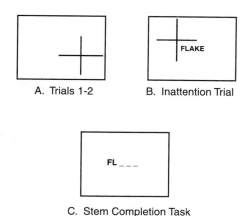

A. Trials 1-2   B. Inattention Trial

C. Stem Completion Task

Figure 13.3.3 Differences in strategic effects in a Stroop task due to awareness. When color words are presented below the subjective threshold, probability of a congruent trial does not affect naming latencies. Above the subjective threshold, they do. (Data from Cheesman & Merikle, 1986.)

Figure 13.3.4 Subliminal effects in the inattention paradigm. Many subjects report no awareness of a word presented briefly under conditions of inattention (see Section 11.2.1). When tested on a stem completion task, however, they are much more likely to respond with the word that they did not consciously experience than are control subjects who were not shown the word on the inattention trial.

here the size of the Stroop effect increases dramatically with increasing probability of congruent trials. Thus, the results support the hypothesis that conscious perception of the words causes the subject to employ strategic differences that are not invoked when the same words are presented in the gray zone of visual perception.

There are presumably many more such differences between conscious and unconscious visual processing that have yet to be discovered. Cheesman and Merikle's (1986) experiments are just an example of the first such difference to be discovered and how one could go about finding others. It is interesting to speculate about what might be common to these functional properties that exist only above the subjective threshold of awareness, because it may provide clues to the functional significance of consciousness itself: what it is *for*. One interesting possibility is that visual awareness is required for stimulus-driven generation of perceptual hypotheses (Marcel, 1983b). D.B., for example, could not initiate intentional actions based on his blindsight unless the experimenter framed a specific set of hypotheses for him. He could not tell what, if anything, was presented in his blind field unless he was forced to guess between a small number of choices: X versus O, horizontal versus vertical lines, and so on. This conjecture is just one possibility among a large number of alternatives, however, and there are scarcely enough data to constrain them meaningfully as yet.

13.3.3 Inattentional Blindsight

Another dissociation between visual awareness and visual processing in normal subjects appears to occur in the phenomenon of inattentional blindness described in Section 11.2.1. Mack and Rock (1998) have repeatedly found that when subjects are performing the reasonably difficult perceptual task of deciding which line of a nonfoveally presented cross is longer (see Figure 13.3.4A) and have been led not to expect any additional stimulus in the display by being given several trials in which nothing but the cross appears, as many as 90% of subjects are blind to the suprathreshold presentation of an additional stimulus such as a geometrical figure or even a meaningful word (Figure 13.3.4B). As surprising as this phenomenon is, it is eclipsed by the finding that indirect tasks provide evidence that these unseen objects appear to be processed at least to the level of identification, a phenomenon we will call **inattentional blindsight**.

Support for this claim comes from results using an indirect **stem completion task** that was administered after subjects showed inattentional blindness to a presented word. Subjects were presented with a five-letter word (e.g., FLAKE) at fixation as an unexpected additional stimulus on the third trial of the cross task (Figure 13.3.4B). Asking subjects whether they had seen anything except the cross and explicit forced-choice recognition tests that were given right after subjects responded to the cross showed that most of them were inattentionally blind to its presence in that they gave no indication of having perceived the word. Indirect tests using a stem completion task, however, provided evidence that many of these inattentionally blind subjects identified the target word subliminally.

In the stem completion task (Figure 13.3.4C), subjects were shown part of a word with blanks substituted for some of the letters (e.g., FL_ _ _) and were asked to complete it with the first two words that came to mind. When these stems were given to control subjects who had not taken part in the inattention task, they were completed as FLAKE only about 4% of the time. When the experimental subjects who had shown inattentional blindness with explicit recognition tests were given the same task, however, they completed the same stem 40% of the time. This tenfold increase can be attributed only to subjects having unconsciously perceived (or registered) the word that they professed not to have consciously seen.

This result is clearly related to classical subliminal perception but is different in crucial ways. Most important, it occurs under stimulus conditions that are fully adequate for conscious perception when subjects are not performing the cross task, as Mack and Rock (1998) have shown in a wide variety of studies. Under conditions of inattention, subjects appear not to be aware that a word was presented—or anything at all, for that matter—yet still show indirect effects on unrelated tasks. Therefore, some form of dissociation between visual processing and visual awareness appears to be operating in normal perceivers in this situation as well as in classical subliminal perception.

13.4 Theories of Consciousness

We now come to the really hard question: How can the phenomena of consciousness we have just reviewed be explained theoretically? This is a very tall order, one that is unlikely to be achieved even in the next several decades. Still, it is a problem to which theorists have begun to turn their attention, and the suggestions that they have made are worthy of serious consideration. Even if all of these suggestions are wrong—and they almost certainly are—we can learn something by considering their strengths and weaknesses.

At the heart of virtually all theories of consciousness is the **activation assumption** that awareness is associated with the behavior of neurons or neuronlike entities. This is not too surprising, given the seemingly incontrovertible evidence that consciousness is somehow caused by physiological events in the brain. The firing of neurons is by far the most plausible candidate. Neural firing alone is insufficient to explain consciousness, however, because all neural information processing involves the firing of neurons, whereas only a relatively small subset of this processing appears to be conscious. We argued at the beginning of this chapter, for example, that the firing of retinal receptors is not conscious. It is also true that highly practiced tasks that were initially performed consciously can ultimately become unconscious. When you first learned to drive a car, for instance, every movement you made was under active conscious control. After several years of practice, however, most low-level driving skills are executed quite unconsciously and more effectively than when they were performed consciously. Surely there is neural activity going on in both cases. What is it that leads some neural events to give rise to clear conscious experiences, whereas others do not?

Some further constraints are obviously required to identify what types of neural activity give rise to consciousness and what types do not. Two main approaches have been advocated:

1. The **functional approach to consciousness** assumes that the additional constraints concern the computational structure of the mind. In this view, it is the functional role of certain types of activation that determines what is conscious and what is not. In this view, the explanation of consciousness lies at what Marr (1982) called the algorithmic level rather than the implementation level.

2. The **physiological approach to consciousness** assumes that the additional constraints concern particular biological properties of the neurons or neural circuits or neural activity in the brain that underlie consciousness. In this view, certain brain locations or types of neural firing lead to consciousness, whereas others do not, placing explanations of consciousness squarely at the implementation level.

It is worth mentioning that these two possibilities are not mutually exclusive. Functional explanations generally have identifiable physiological correlates, and physiological explanations generally have functional correlates as well. A causal theory of consciousness may therefore be likely to have both functional and physiological components.

There is a third kind of theory, based on a purely **physical approach to consciousness**, that is worth considering briefly. The basic idea is that consciousness arises from some unusual property of matter in general rather than neurons in particular. In its most extreme form, called **panpsychism**, such theories posit that all matter has some very small or weak form of consciousness and that experiences arise in people's brains because lots of matter gets hooked up in just the right way. Exactly what it is about matter that gives rise to consciousness or what constitutes the "right way" to hook it up is, of course, unknown. It is perhaps not surprising that physical approaches to consciousness generally appeal to bizarre properties of matter that either have not yet been discovered or are not yet well understood.

One physical theory within which speculations about consciousness tend to arise is quantum mechanics, the highly successful but intuitively opaque formal theory that currently dominates particle physics. One example of this type of approach to consciousness is due to mathematician and cosmologist Roger Penrose, who suggests that the secret of consciousness will be found in a theory of quantum gravity (Penrose, 1989). The rationale for proposing such a theory is well beyond the scope of this book, requiring an understanding of complex and sophisticated physical constructs such as Heisenberg's uncertainty principle and the role of the "observer" in determining the outcome of subatomic physical experiments. The reader is referred to Penrose's (1989) book and related writings (e.g., Lockwood, 1989) for further information.

In the next two sections, we will consider a sampling of functional and biological theories of consciousness. This survey makes no pretense of being exhaustive. The goal is simply to illustrate the variety of different approaches that have been suggested and see how they fare in accounting for the facts about conscious and unconscious perception we have considered in this book, especially those described in this final chapter.

13.4.1 Functional Architecture Theories

The first class of theories that we will consider are based on functional analyses of consciousness in terms of what sort of information processing subsystems might be identified with it. Typically, they posit abstract computational structures and/or processes as the determinants of consciousness rather than the neural mechanisms that implement them.

The STM Hypothesis. When cognitive psychologists first began to consider the relation between their information processing theories of mind and the nature of consciousness, they discussed how consciousness related to the various types of memory stores they proposed. In this context, consciousness seems to be most naturally identified with short-term memory (STM) because the most recent item in STM is almost invariably the one most centrally represented in a person's current experience. In the case of visual STM, only the most recent item is thought to be present in the store, and so the contents of visual STM seem quite appropriately identified with the contents of visual awareness. The sequence of items in all STM systems would then be equated with the "stream of consciousness" about which William James (1890/1950) wrote so eloquently.

The contents of long-term memory, in contrast, are not generally conscious. Although much of the information LTM contains can be brought to consciousness by appropriate retrieval operations, that information is not present in consciousness until some process accesses or activates it. Note that this process of retrieving information from LTM is generally modeled as transferring it to STM, so this operation also fits the identification of STM with consciousness. In the case of visual awareness, we have suggested that retrieving visual memories from visual LTM results in the creation of visual images in visual STM. Visual images are certainly one kind of visual awareness, even though they lack the richness and vivid detail of perceiving the external world through optical stimulation.

But what about very brief sensory memories, such as iconic and echoic memory? They too seem to have a reasonable claim on being part of awareness, since sensory information is clearly an important aspect of consciousness. One potential problem with equating sensory memories with consciousness is that we are seldom aware of all the information available in them. As we argued at length in Section 12.1.2, iconic memory contains virtually an unlimited amount of visual information, albeit for a short period of time. Equating the contents of sensory memories with awareness is problematic because doing so appears to greatly overestimate what is actually conscious. On the other hand, one might only claim that certain uninterpreted sensory features of this information are conscious. This hypothesis is consistent with the fact that after a brief exposure, visual information is phenomenologically present until it fades away within fractions of a second.

A more serious problem with identifying iconic memory as the functional correlate of visual awareness is that it is reasonably easy to ignore incoming sensory information either by focusing on another modality or by focusing on internally generated information. Everybody has had the experience of concentrating so intently on inner thoughts and plans that we later realize that we were quite unconscious of visual information that was present throughout. Since this information is presumably registered in iconic memory, it would also have to be conscious, according to the iconic memory hypothesis, but it is not. Yet another problem is that the information in sensory memories is generally thought to be precategorical—and thus nonsemantic—so their contents are perhaps less appropriate for consciousness than that of STM, which is usually thought to include meaning. Still, there is something to be said for including brief sensory memories in the contents of awareness, albeit for a very short period of time, simply because sensory information itself is such a vivid aspect of consciousness.

Regardless of what particular memory might be identified with consciousness, information processing theories of consciousness usually boil down to assuming the existence of a "consciousness box" (or "C-box") in an information processing diagram (see Figure 13.4.1). In this conception, information is shuffled around from box to box according to the arrows between boxes, being transformed in various ways as it goes. Whatever information happens to be in the C-box (say, STM) at any particular time is taken to be conscious, and everything else is not. With sufficient elaboration of what information would be in the C-box for a particular task, this hypothesis might eventually provide a good description of

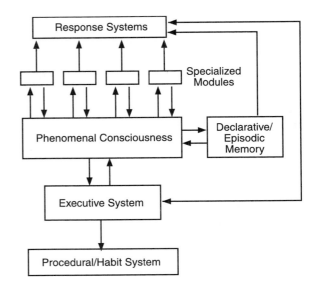

Figure 13.4.1 A C-box theory of consciousness. An information processing theory in which consciousness is identified with a processing stage labeled "Phenomenal Consciousness" (the C-box) whose contents are proposed to be conscious. (After Schacter, McAndrews, & Moscovitch, 1988.)

the contents of consciousness at any given moment. A full-blown computer simulation of the underlying processes would therefore constitute a model of consciousness within this framework. But would this be an adequate explanation of consciousness? What is it about the C-box that makes its contents conscious, for example? The central aspect of consciousness—namely, phenomenal awareness—appears to be pure unadulterated magic in the C-box conception. This approach to consciousness thus fails to fill the explanatory gap in any coherent way.

An Activation-Based Conception of STM. There is another conception of STM that is a bit more satisfying as an approach to consciousness, however. It also makes a close connection between the STM hypothesis and the activation assumption. In this view, sometimes called the **display-board model**, information in STM is conceived not as a separate processing structure (or box), but as a state of activation (e.g., Norman, 1968; Reddy & Newell, 1974). The idea is that information in LTM becomes activated when it is accessed either externally or internally through spreading activation within neural networks. If that activation exceeds a certain threshold, the information is, by definition, in STM.

Because the current item is the most recently activated, it has the greatest activation. Previous items have correspondingly less activation as they decay over time. This decay accounts for the decrease in accessibility for successively older items in the stream of consciousness.

Given this continuum of levels of activation, however, some further assumption is required to specify what is conscious and what is not, for recent items that are still in the 7 ± 2 capacity of STM are surely not present in consciousness in the same way as is the current item. One possible further assumption is that only the single most active item is conscious. Another is that only items above some high threshold of activation, either absolute or relative, achieve conscious status. Whatever the mechanism, the current item in STM is presumed to achieve this criterial level of activation. This view suggests that there are three qualitatively different states for information:

1. *Conscious*: items in STM that are the most highly activated ones at a given moment, probably limited to the single most active item. Its high level of activation is due to its being the most recently accessed item, but its activity decays as other items become activated subsequently.

2. *Inactive*: items in LTM that have not been accessed recently and therefore are essentially unactivated.

3. *Activated*: items in LTM that have been recently accessed and are therefore activated to some degree. Two different histories can be associated with this activated, but nonconscious state:

3a. *Previously conscious*: items that were recently conscious but have decayed to a level insufficient for current focal awareness.

3b. *Primed*: items that have been recently activated but not sufficiently to have reached awareness.

The primed case (3b) is required to account for unconscious priming effects due to items that have not been consciously perceived, as in Marcel's (1983a) subliminal perception experiment or Mack and Rock's (1998) finding of inattentional blindsight. Measurable effects of these items on the indirect task are due to the fact that they have been activated to some intermediate level (in what we have called the gray zone) that is sufficient to influence ongoing processing of other information without ever having reached a high enough level

of activation to achieve consciousness on their own. Thus, even though Marcel's masked color words were never consciously perceived by subjects, they may have been activated sufficiently to speed the naming of congruent color patches and slow that of incongruent ones.

The activation-based version of the STM hypothesis has somewhat better potential as an explanation of consciousness than the C-box version does, mainly because it is grounded explicitly in the concept of activation. Its answer to why not all neural activity gives rise to consciousness is simply that only activation above some high threshold produces conscious experience.

The Attention Hypothesis. A somewhat different functional view of consciousness specifically in perceptual domains associates awareness with the operation of attention. The simplest version of the hypothesis is that the currently attended "object" defines the contents of visual consciousness. The word "object" is in quotation marks because a perceptual object can be just part of an object, a group of several objects, or even a whole scene, as discussed in Section 6.1. But visual experience is not this simple. When we attend specifically to one object in a visual scene, for example, its visual properties and structure are clearly and forcefully represented in consciousness, but it is not as though it were the only object of which we have any visual awareness. The surrounding objects and background also register to some degree in our awareness, at least in the sense that our perceptual experience would be noticeably different if the scene consisted only of the attended object.

The spotlight metaphor of attention (see Section 11.2.3) is perhaps particularly appropriate for capturing this aspect of visual awareness. Just as spotlights have a central region in which their light is most intense and a surrounding region in which the intensity of their light diminishes to darkness, so too does visual consciousness appear to have a central focus of clear consciousness surrounded by a *fringe* of more vaguely experienced visual information. This fleeting, elusive fringe of consciousness was discussed by the great philosopher/psychologist William James, who claimed,

Every definite image in the mind is steeped and dyed in the free water that flows around it. With it goes its sense of relations, near and remote, the dying echo of whence it came to us, the drawing sense of whither it is to lead. The significance, the value of the

image is all in this halo or penumbra that surrounds and escorts it. (James, 1890/1950, p. 246)

The fringe of consciousness has recently been the subject of renewed interest in cognitive science (e.g., Mangan, 1993), although it remains a particularly elusive concept.

One difficulty with simple spotlight theories of attention is that they have difficulty in coping with the selective awareness of subsets of objects that all lie within a spatially contiguous region. In Figure 13.4.2, for example, one can attend to the upward-pointing triangle and experience its shape, to the downward-pointing triangle and experience its shape, or to both at once and experience the six-pointed star figure. All three figures encompass essentially the same area and therefore would presumably be associated with the same spotlight of attention. Some more complex notion of attention is therefore required to account for this kind of experience, one that includes selectivity by objects or features other than gross spatial location.

This problem can perhaps be solved by appealing to the separate retinotopic maps of properties such as orientation, color, and motion. But if the various features of objects are represented separately in different feature maps in the brain (see Section 1.3.3), how does our conscious perception achieve the unity it so obviously has on most occasions? This is called the *binding problem* because it concerns how different features get "bound" into coherent objects. Without proper binding, for example, it would be impossible to distinguish between one display consisting of a red square and a blue circle and another one containing a blue square and a red circle. As discussed in Section 11.2.6, psychologist Anne Treisman theorized that focal attention is necessary to integrate (or "bind") the various features of an object so that a single unified entity is perceived. Her experiments have succeeded in making a convincing case that this is true. Because objects in visual awareness are unified, it is reasonable to suppose that the sort of attention that solves the binding problem is closely related to consciousness.

There are also links between the attention hypothesis and the STM hypothesis. Primary among these is the fact that attending focally to any given object usually causes it to be registered in STM. Therefore, the most recent item in STM is almost invariably the most recently attended item. Because of this close connection, it is inappropriate to think of these two hypotheses as independent conceptions of consciousness. Rather, they are like different sides of the same coin.

Working Memory Theories. In the past decade or so, cognitive theorists have begun to develop more comprehensive theories of consciousness than the sort of general hypotheses that associate it with STM or attention. A number of these theories appear to converge on a similar conception of the functional nature of consciousness that are elaborations and extensions of the crude STM/attention hypothesis we have just considered. These include Bernard Baars's (1988) *global workspace theory,* Philip Johnson-Laird's (1983, 1988) *mental operating system theory,* and Daniel Dennett's (1991) *multiple drafts theory.* Although there are significant differences in content and emphasis among them, they share a family resemblance that makes it useful to consider them together. We will refer to them collectively as *working memory theories of consciousness* because this name is neutral with respect to particular versions and because it is descriptive of them as elaborations of the simpler STM and attention hypotheses.

The general idea behind working memory theories is that consciousness arises from interactions among many simultaneously active specialist processes that communicate through a working memory—which is also called a global workspace (Baars, 1988) and a mental blackboard (Reddy & Newell, 1974) as well as STM—whose contents can be broadcast to the system as a whole. Taking off from Minsky's (1980) analogy that the mind is like a complex society, Baars (1988) likens the operation of the cognitive system to a human community equipped with a television station. Most routine interactions within the

Figure 13.4.2 A problem for a spotlight theory of attention and awareness. If observers are aware of whatever lies within a spotlight of attention, it is unclear how they can selectively experience the six-pointed star versus the upward-pointing triangle versus the downward-pointing triangle in this figure.

community can occur simply by people talking to relevant other people. This is especially true when the tasks being carried out are routine in the sense of being well practiced with appropriate lines of communication having already been established. But when something novel happens and many people must be mobilized to cooperate together who have not previously done so, it is enormously helpful for the television station to broadcast the information to the community at large. Conscious experience is like the broadcasting of information by the television station; it enables the information to be shared by many different processors at widely disparate locations.

In some working memory theories of consciousness, there is no single, unified stream of consciousness that is played out in some central unitary location (e.g., Dennett's multiple drafts theory). Rather, consciousness is the result of temporary coalitions among specialist processes working in widely distributed locations in the brain that cause a series of different contents to dominate at different times and for different purposes. The stream of consciousness is just the result of the activity of all these spatially distributed processors. Most of the time there is a coherent, consistent content to the activity, but sometimes there is not.

The 2.5-D Sketch Theory of Consciousness. A different approach to visual awareness is taken by linguist Ray Jackendoff (1987), who associates it with an intermediate level of representation. Roughly speaking, he identifies visual awareness with Marr's 2.5-D sketch, which, the reader will recall from Sections 2.4.3 and 5.1.2, is a viewer-centered representation of the visible surfaces of objects arrayed in depth—or "surface slant-at-a-distance," as Gibson (1950) called it. It is not that Jackendoff believes that people are unaware of higher-level representations, such as object-based or category-based ones, but that these are not, strictly speaking, perceptual. After all, if one takes care in specifying exactly what one can actually see in viewing a complex scene from a particular perspective, it is just the visible surfaces of objects. The unseen surfaces must be inferred, to be sure, but even when they are, the form of experience they produce is qualitatively different from that of visible surfaces. Jackendoff calls these higher levels of visual processing "visual understanding."

To clarify this distinction, consider your visual experience when you are looking at the back of a woman's head. You experience her hair visually in Jackendoff's view, and although you naturally infer that she has a face, you do not experience it directly. Moreover, unless you recognize her from the back as someone you know, the particular face you expect her to have is largely indeterminate. When she turns around so that you can actually see her face, your visual experience is qualitatively different from what it was when her back was toward you. For reasons like this, Jackendoff associates consciousness with intermediate levels of visual representation.

The line Jackendoff draws between visual experience and visual understanding is clear enough. It is essentially the distinction between the part of visual experience that has direct sensory support and the part that does not. What is less clear is whether visual awareness should be restricted to mental content that has direct sensory support. By this criterion, much of the information we normally take to be visually conscious would not be, including the 3-D shape of objects as well as their categorical identity.

Several implications of this intermediate-level view are worth pointing out. One is that a basketball should not produce the visual experience of being a spherical object, but as being half-spherical, the back half being inferred and therefore nonconscious. Another is that the visual experience of a prosopagnosic does not change as a result of his or her disability, for such patients often appear to have intact visual abilities in all matters other than identifying faces. One can argue about whether such differences are "visual consciousness" or "visual understanding," but it seems unequivocal that it is a difference in experience based on visual information. Therefore, it seems that high-level visual information is strongly implicated in consciousness, although one may still wish to keep different aspects of it separate, as Jackendoff does.

13.4.2 Biological Theories

Theories of consciousness based on functional analyses are, by definition, independent of the specific neural hardware on which they might be implemented. Such theories are therefore compatible with multiple realizability as proposed by functionalists: Computers, robots, or other information processing devices with the appropriate architecture and algorithms might have the same kind of conscious states and processes as people do. But consciousness may not reside at this abstract computational level at all. If it is possible for any truly non-conscious organism or machine to pass Turing's test legitimately, then the ultimate explanation of consciousness must lie elsewhere. The rationale is that successfully simulating consciousness (without producing it) would provide an existence proof that something more than the correct algorithm and architecture are required. (How we could *know* that the organism or machine in question actually lacked consciousness is a serious matter, of course, as the problem of other minds indicates, but we are taking a god's-eye view of the situation right now and assuming we somehow know what is truly conscious and what is not.)

If the functional architecture of the perceptual system is not sufficient to account for visual awareness, the obvious place to look for such an explanation is at the implementation level of biological mechanisms. After all, people are biological creatures who have reached their present level of cognitive functioning through evolution, and it is at least plausible to suppose that consciousness may be inextricably bound up in the biological processes that occur in our nervous systems. As we said earlier, there are two sorts of biological theories: correlational and causal. Since there are as yet no serious candidates for causal theories, we will describe some attempts to capture consciousness in terms of its biological correlates.

Activation Thresholds. Perhaps the most prevalent assumption in biological theories of consciousness is that any neural activity that is "something enough"— for example, strong enough, lasts long enough, or whatever—will produce consciousness. This threshold approach to modeling consciousness has the nontrivial advantage of simplicity: Consciousness is just a matter of having enough of the crucial property, and any neural activity that meets this criterion will be conscious. At least implicitly, this suggests that all neural activity may be slightly conscious, with clear and coherent states of consciousness arising only when enough of that kind of activity is present for a long enough period of time. As the foregoing statement implies, there are at least two different kinds of activation thresholds that can be dis-

cerned: one concerning its *amount* and the other concerning its *duration*.

The most intuitively obvious version of threshold activation theories is that the firing rate must be above some minimum level. The threshold could be absolute, such as some number of spikes per second that must be exceeded for the information that it carries to become conscious, or it could be relative. An absolute threshold seems rather unlikely, because many neurons have about the same maximal rate of firing, which is determined by the biochemical properties of the neurons, and many neurons can be firing at their maximal rate. It seems more likely that a conscious threshold for neural activity would be defined relative to the background level of firing by other neurons. One kind of formulation of a relative threshold rule is in terms of the *signal-to-noise ratio*, expressing the ratio between the conscious activity (the "signal") and all the other nonconscious neural firing that competes with it (the "noise"). There might even be a continuum of degrees of consciousness above this threshold, with higher signal-to-noise ratios indicating clearer, more vivid consciousness. Notice that this general approach is closely related to the activation-based conception of STM we described earlier.

The most obvious strengths of this notion of consciousness are its simplicity and its straightforward correspondence with behavioral analyses of subliminal perception. We spoke earlier of the idea that there might be a threshold for consciousness that was significantly higher than that required for indirect perceptual effects, leading to the gray zone of subliminal effects. A threshold activation theory can assume that the lower bound of the gray area is simply the level at which the signal-to-noise ratio for the target stimulus exceeds unity—that is, that its activation level is slightly greater than competing alternatives. This level of activation would be insufficient for consciousness, however, which has a higher threshold. Similar analyses might also apply to other phenomena described in the previous section of this chapter, such as blindsight and perceptual defense. Important details remain to be worked out, however, not the least of which is why removing a large section of visual cortex in blindsight patients would have the effect of reducing the level of activation to the gray zone rather than obliterating it altogether.

Thus far, we have been speaking as though the unit over which activation is integrated to determine the total amount of activity were individual neurons, but this may not be the case. It seems fairly implausible that one neuron, no matter how rapidly it was firing, would be sufficient to give rise to a clear, coherent, conscious experience. It seems more likely that consciousness would require high levels of activity in many different neurons, all of which are mutually consistent with one another. This might correspond to the sum of the activity within a more complex neural network or even across several such networks. This raises the problem of how the brain binds different neural events together into a coherent unity, an issue about which we are almost totally ignorant at this time. Recently, some suggestions have been made that different neurons coding the same visual object may fire synchronously (von der Malsburg, 1981). If so, the amount of activation may be integrated over neurons firing in the same temporal pattern. We will return to this possibility shortly.

Duration Thresholds. Activation threshold theories can be augmented by adding the temporal dimension. Perhaps for a given pattern of neural activity to become conscious, it must dominate activation for some critical period of time. This idea arose explicitly from work with connectionist models that used distributed representations—that is, networks in which the most important characteristic of activity is not the activity level in any particular unit, but the overall pattern of activity across many units (Rumelhart & McClelland, 1986). In studying the dynamic properties of such distributed networks with feedback loops, it was found that when they are stimulated by input activation, they tend to undergo a dynamic process of settling into an optimal pattern of activation. This pattern depends on both the input activation and the connections in the network, and settling into it takes time (see Section 6.5 and Appendix B). A new or changing input can therefore disrupt the pattern of activity before it has had time to settle into the optimal state for long enough to become conscious.

It is not difficult to imagine that such mechanisms could operate in subliminal perception experiments in which a masker is introduced after a brief presentation of the target stimulus. The target would initiate activity in the critical network, beginning the process of dynamic settling that would normally end in the stable pattern of activity corresponding to conscious perception of the target. When this process is only partly completed, how-

ever, the presentation of the masker blocks the full emergence of this activity pattern. Even so, activation initiated by the target will have strongly influenced the network's state before the onset of the masker. This information has therefore "entered the system" and certainly could propagate to other networks with sufficient strength to produce priming or other indirect effects on subsequent processing. How theories of stable activation might account for blindsight is more difficult to envision, but it may have a different underlying cause in any case.

One suggested feature of consciousness that theories based on stable states of activation are particularly adept at capturing is the fact that consciousness generally reflects the *results* of processing rather than the processes themselves (Shallice, 1972). Evidence for this assertion in visual perception abounds. One example is the fact that we are conscious of the depth and slant of surfaces in the environment but not of the complex processes that lead us to this representation, such as stereopsis and shape-from-shading (see Chapter 5). Another is that we are conscious of the category to which perceived objects belong but are quite unaware of the process of classification that gives rise to this representation (see Chapter 9). The fact that we are conscious of results rather than processes follows directly within stable state theories because the surface manifestation of the "process" is the dynamic flux of activation that leads to the stable state, and the "result" is the stable state itself. Since the stable state is, by definition, conscious in such theories and the flux leading to it is nonconscious, it follows that results will be conscious and processes will not be.

The Cortical Hypothesis. Another fairly simple and obvious biological hypothesis about the neural basis of consciousness is that it arises from activity in the cortex. Although this proposal is enormously diffuse, given the size and complexity of human cortex, it is at least a start, rather like the hypothesis that the mechanism of heredity lay in the cell nucleus.

The cortical hypothesis makes biological sense for a number of reasons. One is that the single most distinctive feature of the human brain, relative to those of other animals, is the enormous development of cortex. The lower portions of the human brain are not too different from those of many mammals, but cortical differences are vast. If one takes the chauvinistic stance that

Visual Awareness

consciousness is most highly developed in humans, it is a reasonable bet that cortical activity is heavily involved in consciousness. Moreover, the other animals that seem to behave in ways most suggestive of consciousness, including chimps, apes, and monkeys, also have well-developed cortices.

More specific evidence for the cortical hypothesis comes from the neuropsychological findings we discussed earlier in this book. Virtually all the cases in which visual experience appears to be impaired are caused by damage to areas of the cortex involved in vision. Damage to primary visual cortex results in phenomenal blindness; diffuse damage to right posterior parietal region of cortex produces neglect of the left side of space and objects; and damage to infero-temporal cortex leads to various forms of agnosia in which people fail to recognize faces or other classes of objects. Moreover, as we discussed in Section 13.2, each of these syndromes shows some evidence of residual visual ability in the phenomenally absent function. This residual function suggests that other areas of the brain may be mediating related visual abilities but without conscious access to the results. All of these phenomena point to the cortex as the seat of consciousness.

A few words about the logic of lesions and consciousness are in order at this point. It is tempting to conclude that if absence of a given brain structure, S, eliminates awareness of some particular feature, F, then S is the locus of awareness of F. At first blush, for example, it seems sensible to conclude that blindsight constitutes evidence that area V1 is the seat of visual awareness. But this conclusion would be a grave mistake. Damage to receptors also causes lack of visual awareness, but we have argued that retinal firing is not sufficient for visual awareness. Blindsight provides clear evidence of this fact, for retinal receptors appear to work perfectly well in blindsight patients, who are, nevertheless, phenomenologically blind. Indeed, the fact that blindsight patients can guess accurately in the absence of visual experience is evidence that their receptors must be working; otherwise, they could not possibly perform better than chance.

The logic of the relation between brain lesions and their function is thus a bit more complex. The correct inference is that if damage to brain structure S destroys awareness of visual feature F, awareness of F must take place in or after S in the flow of neural processing. The reason is that lesioning S will disrupt neural processing not only in S, but also in any brain structure that receives input from S. Thus, blindsight does not eliminate the possibility that visual awareness arises in extrastriate occipital cortex, in the visual portions of the temporal or parietal lobes, or even in the frontal lobes, because all of them receive input directly or indirectly from V1. Although this eliminates only the few brain structures below V1 from consideration, it does imply that visual awareness is a cortical phenomenon. We just do not know which part of cortex is responsible.

The cortical hypothesis is too vague a constraint on consciousness to be very useful by itself. One of the biggest problems is that most of the visual processes to which we have no conscious access—for example, stereopsis, shape-from-shading, edge interpretation, and the various constancies—also take place in cortex. If cortex is indeed the seat of consciousness, then some further biological constraints are required to narrow the field in some appropriate way. Activation and duration thresholds are one kind of additional constraint, but others are possible as well. We will now consider some recent suggestions.

The Crick/Koch Conjectures. Biologists Francis Crick and Christoff Koch (1990, 1992, 1995, 1998) have recently put forward a series of conjectures about the **neural correlate of consciousness** (or **NCC**, as they have come to call it). In the course of their speculations, they have suggested three quite different hypotheses about the NCC for vision. One is based on the layer of cortex in which they believe the cells that are implicated in consciousness might reside, the second on the type of neural activity those cells produce, and the third on the gross location of those cells in the brain.

1. *The lower layers conjecture.* The cells Crick and Koch suggest as most plausibly giving rise to visual awareness are those in the lower layers of visual cortex, particularly layers 5 and 6.

2. *The 40 Hertz conjecture.* Within the lower cortical layers, Crick and Koch suggest that the signature of consciousness is neural firing at about 40 Hz (cycles per second), or within a range of about 35–75 Hz.

3. *The frontal lobes conjecture.* Crick and Koch argue that the most likely brain area in which the neural correlates of consciousness might reside is in the frontal lobes.

Why did they choose these specific hypotheses? Interestingly, it was because of a particular fit between certain computational functions that Crick and Koch deemed necessary for consciousness and corresponding biological structures that might support them. The functional requirements were a temporal memory, a solution to the binding problem, and global mediation between perception and action. Note that these requirements are closely related to the STM and attentional hypotheses discussed earlier.

Crick and Koch speculated that visual awareness requires at least a brief memory component, arguing that neural activity in visual cortex would not become conscious unless it persisted for some minimum period of time, as discussed above. Crick and Koch speculate that such a memory is likely to arise in a **reverberatory circuit**: a closed loop of neurons that fire each other sequentially so that the firing "reverberates" (echoes around and around) through the neural loop. Minimally, this can be accomplished by a pair of neurons that activate each other: A causes B to fire, and B causes A to fire. Crick and Koch focus on layers 5 and 6 of visual cortex because these layers in V1 have reciprocal connections to and from the LGN of the thalamus that suggest a reverberatory circuit capable of supporting a brief visual memory.

Their 40 Hertz conjecture was motivated by a possible solution to the binding problem mentioned previously: How do the different features of different objects get properly combined or bound together? We considered this problem in Section 11.2.6 when we discussed Treisman's feature integration theory of attention, but we did not consider the biological mechanisms through which it might be accomplished. Following an earlier proposal by neural network theorist Christoph von der Malsburg (1981), Crick and Koch speculated that binding may be accomplished by synchronizing the firing of all neurons responding to the same object. Observations of neural oscillations in the 35 to 75-Hz range in the visual cortex of cats (Gray & Singer, 1989) suggest this as a plausible neural implementation of the synchronized firing scheme, and Crick and Koch incorporated it into their theory.

The frontal lobe conjecture arose in large part from their speculation that the function of visual awareness is to make the best interpretation of the visual scene directly available to the parts of the brain that plan voluntary motor output. Frontal cortex receives input from many visual areas of the brain, including both the ventral ("what") and dorsal ("where" or "how") pathways, and it sends much of its output to the motor areas of cortex. These connections make it a prime candidate for the locus of the NCC from Crick and Koch's point of view, and there is at least some suggestive evidence supporting it (Nakamura & Mishkin, 1980, 1986). Crick and Koch explicitly reject the possibility that cells in area V1 produce visual awareness, despite the phenomenon of blindsight described earlier, arguing that although they may well be *necessary* for consciousness, they are not *sufficient* for it.

Although Crick and Koch promote their theoretical ideas as centrally biological, they are actually an interesting hybrid of computational and biological hypotheses. Indeed, the computational/functional analysis is primary in the sense that it provides the main motivation for their biological speculations. Since there is as yet no direct biological evidence linking any of their conjectures to visual awareness, the plausibility of their hypotheses arises mainly from the fit between their computational/functional arguments and their physiological speculations. It is the synergy between these two levels of analysis that is attractive, but other as-yet-untold stories may be equally, or even more, plausible.

As an example of a promising approach to identifying the NCC for vision, Crick and Koch (1998) point to the fascinating research of Logothetis and his colleagues in studying the neural basis of binocular rivalry (Leopold & Logothetis, 1996; Logothetis & Schall, 1989; Sheinberg & Logothetis, 1997). As we noted in Section 5.3.2, when grossly different images are presented to the left and right eye, such as the horizontal and vertical gratings in Figure 5.3.15, conscious perception is bistable. The observer typically reports seeing only one pattern at a time and alternates between the two possibilities. Logothetis trained monkeys to report what they saw by making different motor responses for the two perceptions and then recorded from individual cells in different areas of visual cortex while they did so. Responses in relatively few cells in early visual cortex (e.g., V1, V2, V4, and MT) are tightly coupled with the monkey's reported perceptions. But about 90% of the cells in the superior temporal sulcus (STS) and inferotemporal cortex (IT) reliably predicted its perceptual state.

Figure 13.4.3 shows a compelling example of such a cell (Sheinberg & Logothetis, 1997). This cell fires

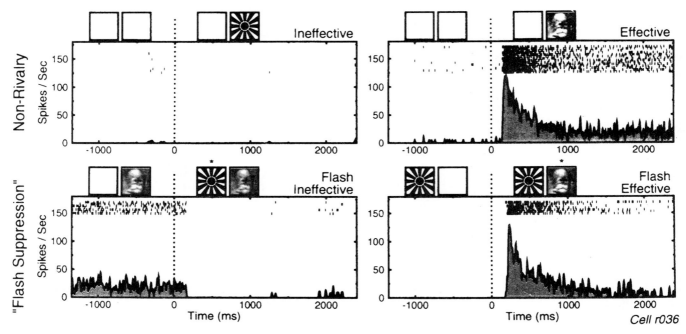

Figure 13.4.3 Activity of a face-sensitive neuron in the superior temporal sulcus (STS) of macaque monkey to binocular rivalry. This cells does not fire to a sunburst pattern alone (upper left) but does fire to a monkey face alone (upper right). When the face stimulus competes with the onset of the sunburst stimulus, the latter supresses the cell's response (lower left), but when the sunburst competes with the onset of the face, the cell fires to the face (lower right). In all cases, the cell's response correlates with the animal's motor responses, indicating its visual perceptions. (From Sheinberg & Logothetis, 1997.)

rapidly to a monkey face (upper right) but not to a sunburst pattern (upper left) when each is shown alone, without a competing rivalrous pattern. When the monkey face is shown first alone and then in rivalry with a sunburst pattern (lower left), the cell fires to the monkey face initially, but it stops firing when the sunburst appears, precisely following the monkey's on-line motor report of what it is perceiving. If the sunburst pattern is shown first and then in rivalry with the monkey face, the cell begins firing just when the monkey face appears, again mirroring the animal's motor reports of what it sees. Although this does not prove that these cells are the NCC for these perceptions, their behavior is strikingly close to what the monkey appears to perceive, certainly much closer than that of cells earlier in the flow of visual processing.

ERTAS: The Extended Reticular-Thalamic Activating System. Baars (1988) has conjectured that his global workspace theory might be implemented in the brain by certain types of relations among neural struc-

ture in the **extended reticular-thalamic activating system (ERTAS)**. Briefly, he suggests that the parallel, distributed specialist processors of his theory reside in cortex, that the limited resources of the global workspace may be identified with a midbrain structure called the reticular activating system, and that the broadcasting of workspace information occurs through the diffuse projections of the thalamus. The locations of these brain structures are shown schematically in Figure 13.4.4.

Despite the dominance of the cortical hypothesis in theories of consciousness, the reticular formation has long been thought to be somehow involved, because it appears to play an important role in wakefulness, alertness, orienting, and attention (Magoun, 1962). All of these mental functions appear to be related to consciousness, although in a nonspecific way. They may be produced by the reticular formation amplifying a subset of cortical activity. It is well situated to perform such functions, receiving input from all sensory and motor systems and projecting back to the cortex through the thalamus, which sits just below the cortex and projects diffusely to it, as indicated in Figure 13.4.4. Therefore, it

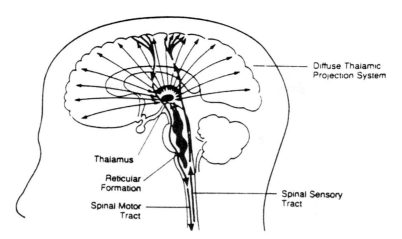

Diffuse Thalamic
Projection System

Thalamus

Reticular
Formation

Spinal Motor
Tract

Spinal Sensory
Tract

Figure 13.4.4 The extended reticular-thalamic activating system (ERTAS). ERTAS has a gross anatomical structure that suggests a possible implementation of Baars's (1988) global workspace theory. The reticular formation in the midbrain provides the limited resources of consciousness, and the thalamus broadcasts information globally to the cortex. (From Baars, 1988.)

seems a plausible candidate for the function of the limited capacity workspace in Baars's theory.

One can easily see some global correspondence between the gross structure of this (greatly oversimplified) diagram of the ERTAS and the functional architecture Baars describes in his theory. Still, the involvement of these particular structures in the physiological basis of consciousness is currently an unsubstantiated speculation. The enormous body of painstaking work that would be required to test it has not even begun to be carried out. And even if it were true, it does not provide a causal theory of consciousness. It merely claims to designate the neural correlates of consciousness in terms of gross interactions among vast subsystems of the brain. Why neural activity in these particular regions of this particular type might give rise to experience remains a mystery.

Causal Theories of Consciousness: An Analogy.
There are many more speculations about the neural substrate of consciousness that we do not have space to discuss here. None of them fills the explanatory gap, however. Crick and Koch, for example, have no explanation of how activity in layers 5 and 6 (as opposed to that in layers 3 and 4) gives rise to experience or of how activity around 40 Hz (as opposed to that around 20 Hz or 80 Hz) does either. Whether they are true or not, they are good examples of correlational theories, since they

identify structures or features of brain activity that might be intimately involved with consciousness yet fail to provide a causal explanation. This does not mean that correlational hypotheses are worthless in the quest for causal ones, however. Quite the contrary, they are probably necessary milestones along the path to a causal theory, for before detailed biological mechanisms can be worked out, one must know where to look for them. Correlational theories suggest places to look.

To see more clearly the relation between the phenomena to be explained and different kinds of theorizing about consciousness, it is instructive to consider once again an analogy to the search for a scientific understanding of the basis of life (e.g., Dennett, 1996; Palmer, in press; Searle, 1984). The facts about life to be explained concern certain differences in macroscopic properties of living organisms versus nonliving objects, particularly their abilities to grow, sustain their internal functions, and reproduce. The basic mechanisms available for a truly causal theory to explain such life functions are all the physical interactions of which ordinary matter is capable. Before Crick and Watson's discovery of the structure of DNA, however, there was a huge explanatory gap between the known physical laws and these molar properties of living organisms. The gap was large enough that, as noted earlier, some theorists claimed that there must be a special "vital force" that pervades living tissue and magically endows it with the required properties. Other theorists rejected this view,

Visual Awareness

insisting on a mechanistic theory devoid of mysterious, nonphysical forces.

The fact about living organisms that turned out to be most important for understanding the basis of life is their ability to reproduce. One of the most important features of reproduction is inheritance: the fact that properties of offspring bear lawful statistical relations to those of their parents. The general shape of these regularities was worked out by the brilliant Austrian monk Gregor Mendel in his painstaking experiments breeding different varieties of garden peas and other plants. His results enabled him to propose, test, and refine a theory of inheritance based on hypothetical physical entities, now called genes, that are combined in reproduction and expressed in offspring according to lawful principles. He worked out this genetic theory without ever directly observing the physical basis of these genes. Mendel's work is a beautiful example of how a molar analysis of experimental outcomes can provide brilliant insights into underlying mechanisms without direct observation of those mechanisms.

Mendel's genetic theory did not fill the explanatory gap, however, for it did not specify the physical basis of life. Once sufficiently powerful microscopes enabled biologists to observe the internal machinery of cells directly, correlational hypotheses correctly suggested that the nucleus of cells was crucial in their self-replicating abilities. More refined correlational conjectures focused on the strands of chromosomes within the nucleus as the crucial structures involved in cell reproduction. Even so, the explanatory gap remained, since there were no good theories about how the reproductive properties of living cells might arise from chromosomes.

The gap-filling discovery was made by Crick and Watson when they determined the double helical structure of DNA. It revealed how this complex molecule, which was made of more basic building blocks, could unravel and replicate itself in a purely mechanical way. As the further implications of its structure were worked out, it became increasingly clear how purely physical processes could form the basis of genetics as well as the other unique and previously inexplicable properties of living tissue. The current biological theory of life is thus a good example of how a truly causal theory can fill an explanatory gap in science. It did not appear magically but was historically preceded by molar analyses of or-

ganismic phenomena and by correlational observations of the underlying biological structures. If Crick and Watson had discovered the structure of DNA before these other findings, its importance would very likely have gone completely unnoticed. All levels of theorizing were important in the historical development of a scientific theory of life.

In this analogy, our present knowledge of consciousness is best thought of as being pre-Mendelian. After decades of actively ignoring the problem of consciousness, scientists of many persuasions are finally beginning to work on it. Behavioral scientists are looking for functional correlates of consciousness in the hope of discerning regularities that would form the basis of algorithmic-level theories of consciousness. These theories can be thought of as being akin to Mendelian genetics: hypotheses about the nature of consciousness at an abstract information processing level distinct from the actual physical mechanisms that produce it.

Biologists are also beginning to look for biological correlates of consciousness in the hope of narrowing the problem to some relevant subset of the brain where conscious experiences arise. This work can be likened to microscopic studies that identified the special importance of the nucleus, particularly of the chromosomes in cellular division and reproduction. This biological analysis of the neural correlates of consciousness is barely in its infancy, and much work will be required before we even begin to know where to look for the relevant mechanisms. Needless to say, we are still very much in the pre-DNA phase of our quest to provide a causal explanation of conscious experience. Nobody yet has a clue about what such a theory might look like. When and if it is discovered, it will be a scientific breakthrough of staggering importance and implications, for it will unlock one of the deepest scientific problems of all time: the secret of how conscious experience arises from purely physical events.

13.4.3 Consciousness and the Limits of Science

The goal of this book has been to explain the nature of visual perception within the general framework of modern vision science. We have learned a great deal about the kind of optical information on which perception is based and about how this information is processed by the visual system, in terms of both abstract algorithms and concrete neural mechanisms. The final question to which we now turn is how this sort of scientific analysis is related to visual awareness and whether it is likely to succeed in explaining that awareness.

Relational Structure. To understand the relation between visual information processing and visual awareness, it will be useful to divide mental events into two conceptually distinct aspects (Palmer, in press). Both are present in visual experience and are normally so completely intertwined that it may seem artificial to separate them.

1. *Individual experiences.* One aspect of visual awareness is the nature of experiences themselves. Philosophers often call such experiences **qualia** or **raw feels** in attempting to convey what it "feels like" to experience different sensory qualities, such as redness and circularity, to pick just two relevant examples. Experiences have the drawback of being very difficult (perhaps even impossible) to define objectively, given that nobody has access to anyone's except his or her own.

2. *Relational structure.* The other aspect of visual awareness is the relations among these experiences: how two or more experiences are structured with respect to each other. Regardless of what the experience of red itself is like, everyone with normal color vision would agree that red is more like orange than like green. And everyone with normal spatial vision would agree that a circle is more like a regular octagon than like an equilateral triangle.

Sensory experiences are the raw stuff of visual awareness and are generally the focus of discussions of consciousness. Indeed, it is tempting to think that this is all there is to know about visual experience. But the relations among such experiences are just as important— probably even more so—because they determine the structure of experience. If experiences had no relational structure, they would simply be a collection of completely different and totally unrelatable mental states, like the "blooming buzzing confusion" of which William James (1890/1950) spoke in describing his conception of the sensory experience of infants.

Without relational structure we would not experience different colors as being more closely related to each other than they are to shapes: Redness would be as much like circularity as it is like greenness. Nor would we experience gray as being intermediate between white and black; we would experience them only as different. Because of relations among experiences, however, we are aware of colors as a class of experiences and the ordering of colors in terms of a whole continuum of lightness levels, stretching from black to white. Indeed, the entire structure of color space is determined by relations among colors. Relations among individual experiences thus provide the rich, complex, and interwoven dimensional superstructure of experience. It is quite literally unimaginable what visual experience would be like without this superstructure.

To illustrate the distinction, we will once again consider the case of color experiences. We have argued that it may be impossible to be sure that my experience of red is the same as your experience of red, for it might conceivably be the same as your experience of green. This is the revised version of the inverted spectrum argument we discussed in Section 13.1.2. More radically, though, my experience of red could be totally different from any experience you have ever had or are capable of having. The same argument applies to all other color experiences as well. As long as we are dealing with individual color qualia, there is not much more we can say about their experiential qualities. We can (and do) agree on basic color terms that refer to them— roses are "red," violets are "blue," and so forth—so that we can communicate effectively about them. This is an objective fact about individual color experiences, but it is the weakest kind of structure in that it does not constrain the nature of either your or my experiences in any useful way. We just learn to attach the same names to our corresponding internal experiences that arise from viewing the same environmental objects, regardless of what those particular internal experiences might be like.

Further constraints *are* introduced once we begin to consider relations among experiences. Both you and I can make judgments about the relative similarity of pairs or triples of colors, for example. These judgments are inherently relational, and the relations on which they are based determine the superstructure of color experience. We both agree, for example, that red is more like orange than like yellow and more like purple than like blue. Indeed, all normal trichromats agree on such statements. We can therefore infer that there is an objective aspect to such relational aspects of experience as well, because it clearly can be verified across individuals. This is not to say that my relational experiences are objectively the same as yours, for my experience of color similarity relations might be as wildly different from yours as my individual color experiences are from yours. Rather, all we can claim is that the abstract *structure* of our color experiences is the same. This abstract structure is what is captured so well by the three-dimensional color space within which all color experiences can be related.

The same color solid models color experience for all normal trichromats for exactly this reason: It captures the relational structure among color experiences. Indeed, this is what allows the color solid, which is a purely geometrical object, to function as a model of color experiences in the first place. It works because spatial relations among the points in the space have the same structure as corresponding relations among color experiences. This is not to say that my experience of white is "above" my experience of black, even though the point representing white in the color solid is above the one representing black in the conventional color solid. But my experience of white is lighter than that of black, and the spatial relation *above* in canonical color space corresponds to the experiential relation *lighter-than* in visual awareness.

The Isomorphism Constraint. At this point the reader may begin to feel some vague sense of familiarity with this line of argument, for we covered much of the same ground in Section 2.3.4 when we discussed representations in terms of homomorphisms. To reiterate, we said that one set of objects could represent (or model) another set of objects if there is a mapping of objects in one world to those of the other such that corresponding relations are preserved (Palmer, 1978; Tarski, 1954). This situation is diagrammed in Figure 13.4.5. In the present case, the geometrical color solid can serve as a representation (or model) of color experiences because color experiences can be mapped onto points in color

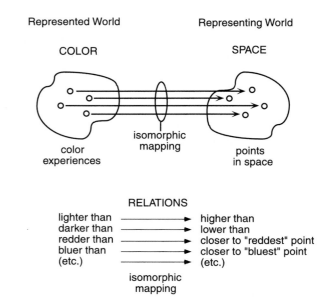

Figure 13.4.5 The color solid isomorphism. Color experiences are mapped to points in a three-dimensional space such that color relations among experiences are preserved by spatial relations among points.

space such that relations among color experiences are preserved by spatial relations among points in the color solid. *Lighter-than* corresponds to *higher-than*; *more-saturated-than* corresponds to *farther-from-the-central-axis-than*; *more-similar-to* corresponds to *closer-to*; and so forth.

The situation is much the same when we consider the relation between my color experiences and yours. Your color experiences might actually be the same as mine, but then again, they might not. If they are different, however, they must have the same relational structure as mine in exactly the sense that the color solid has the same relational structure as both of our sets of color experiences. This sameness of structure is called **isomorphism** (from *iso*, meaning "same," and *morphism*, meaning "form" or "structure").[4]

The picture that emerges from our extended discussion of this example is that even if the nature of individual color experiences cannot be fixed by objective behavioral means, their structural relations can be. This means that any set of underlying experiences will do for

[4] Shepard and Chipman (1970) called this relation "second-order isomorphism" to emphasize that the first-order properties of representations do not have to be identical. The representation of a green object thus does not have to be itself green; but whatever it is, it must be more like the rep-

resentation of something that is turquoise than like that of something that is red. Strictly speaking, the "second-order" qualifier is unnecessary because isomorphisms are, by definition, abstracted from the "first-order" properties of individual objects (see Palmer, 1978).

color, provided they relate to each other in the required way. The same argument can be extended quite generally into other perceptual and conceptual domains, although the underlying experiential components will necessarily be different and the relational structure will be much more complex. We can summarize the argument thus far in terms of what Palmer (in press) calls the **isomorphism constraint**: Objective behavioral methods can determine the contents of awareness up to, but not beyond, the criterion of isomorphism.

There is an interesting analogy between this analysis of color experience and axiomatic formulations in mathematics. In classical mathematics, a given domain is formalized by specifying a set of primitive elements (e.g., points, lines, and planes in Euclidean geometry) and a set of axioms that specify the relations among them (e.g., two points uniquely determine a line, and three noncolinear points uniquely determine a plane). Given a set of primitives elements, a set of axioms, and the rules of mathematical inference, mathematicians can prove theorems that specify many further relations among mathematical objects in the domain. These theorems are guaranteed to be true if the axioms are true. But the primitive elements to which all the axioms and theorems refer cannot be fixed in any way except the nature of the relations among them; they refer equally to any entities that satisfy the set of axioms. That is why mathematicians sometimes discover that there is an alternative interpretation of the primitive elements, called a *dual system*, that also works. An axiomatic mathematical system can therefore be conceived as a complex superstructure of mathematical relations on an underlying, but otherwise undefined, set of primitives. Any primitives can be substituted, as long as they have the proper relational structure. The brilliant French mathematician Poincaré (1952) put it very clearly: "Mathematicians do not study objects," he said, "but the relations between objects. To them it is a matter of indifference if these objects are replaced by others, provided that the relations do not change" (p. 20).

We have just argued that the same situation applies to color experiences. There is an objective relational superstructure that holds among individual experiences for every person with normal trichromatic vision. These relations constrain the experiences in important ways, but they do not fix the experiences uniquely. This is why red-green inversion of color experiences would be diffi-cult or impossible to detect. Any primitive experiences for color will do, as long as they have the proper relational superstructure. Poincaré's statement can therefore be modified to apply to consciousness: Behavioral scientists do not study experiences, but the relations among experiences.

Relation to Functionalism. The analysis that we have just given is largely consistent with the tenets of functionalism. We said that what matters in functionalist accounts is the relations among mental states and their connections to the external world. Two cognitive systems that have the same relations among all their mental states and the same relations to the external world (on both the input and the output ends) are thus functionally equivalent. But the bottom line of the previous discussion about color experiences and the isomorphism constraint is that functional equivalence does not necessarily imply phenomenological equivalence. In other words, there can be many other cognitive systems with the same relational structure as my own cognitive system that would not necessarily have the same conscious states I have.

There are at least two ways in which this can fail to be true. One we have just discussed: the possibility that the individual conscious states may be quite different, as exemplified in the inverted spectrum argument. The other is that some cognitive system might have the same relational structure on its representational states yet have no conscious experiences whatsoever. Let us now consider this latter case.

We have just argued that the color solid represents color experience because it has the same relational structure. Does this mean that functionalism must claim that the points in the color solid *are* color experiences rather than merely representing them? No, because although the color solid has the proper relations among its "internal states," it does not have the proper causal relations to the external world. Indeed, a physical model of the color solid would have *no* causal relations to the external world. To provide this link, one would have to create a working "color machine" that actually processes information in light and responds as people typically do.

Figure 13.4.6 illustrates one way to construct such a machine, or at least its front end. It analyzes incoming light using prisms, masks, photometers, electronic add-

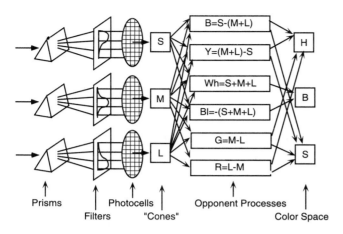

Figure 13.4.6 A color machine. A simple optico-electrical device that produces an output that is isomorphic with experiences of hue, saturation, and brightness of color samples. The prisms break the light into spectral components; the filter masks mimic the absorption spectra of S, M, and L cones; the photocells convert the signal to electrical form to mimic the output of these cone types; the opponent processors integrate cone responses as indicated; and the color space processors further combine opponent responses. The output thus mimics the hue, saturation, and brightness experiences of human color perception under reduction conditions.

ing and subtracting circuits, and so forth to process color information according to the principles described in Chapter 3. To enable it to respond, one could extend it to produce basic color terms for the colors it is shown so that it would name them in the same way as normal trichromats do. Supposing such a causal color machine were constructed—and it would not be hard to do—it seems almost bizarre to argue that the fact that it derived the three values corresponding to, say, focal red and named it as "red" necessarily implies that it has a corresponding experience of intense redness (Palmer, in press). This is at least one way in which a functionalist account can hold without warranting the further inference that the system that has the appropriate relational structure actually *has* mental states rather than merely simulating them.

It would seem that one cannot *prove* that this machine fails to have color experiences because of the problem of other minds. We cannot get access to the inner experiences of a machine—supposing that it has them to begin with—any more than we can get access to those of another person. But a clever argument by philosopher John Searle (1980) purports to show that appropriate experiences cannot arise from the purely syntactic calculations carried out by such a machine, even if they are the same calculations carried out by the brain. His original argument, called the "Chinese room argument," involves the process of understanding natural languages, which is a topic rather far afield from that of this book. But a simpler version that makes the same point has recently been described by Palmer (in press) in the domain of color perception. This "color room argument" is based on a thought experiment concerning whether doing the computations that the visual system does in arriving at color perceptions is sufficient to give rise to conscious experiences of colors. It goes like this.

Imagine yourself inside a room. Through a door on one side, you receive an ordered set of three numbers. You then consult a rule book that tells you how to perform various numerical calculations necessary to arrive at three other numbers. The book further tells you how to use these three values to select one of a particular set of letter strings to hand out a second door on the other side of the room. If the language of color naming is German, and if you do not know German, these would be meaningless strings of letters to you: "schwartz," "weiss," "rot," "grün," "blau," etc. You sit in the color room, carrying out your computations flawlessly, but totally mechanically, as nothing you are doing has any meaning—other than the fact that you are performing various arithmetical operations and following certain logical rules that govern which letter strings you pass out the second door.

Unbeknownst to you, however, people outside the room interpret the three numbers you receive through the first ("input") door to be the quantum catches of the three types of wavelength-sensitive receptors in the retina in response to a colored light. They also interpret the letter strings you send out the second ("output") as basic color terms in German. Thanks to the formulas and rules in the book, the letter strings you send out in response to the three input numbers turn out to be the appropriate basic color terms in German for the color patch that produced the three input numbers. The set of three numbers you computed from the three input values actually correspond to the perceived hue, saturation, and brightness values of the colored light that produced the quantum catches. This "color room" therefore appears to be perceiving colors and naming them by their basic color terms.

Let us further suppose that you become so well practiced at this task that your performance is indistinguishable from that of native German speakers with normal color vision. Let us also suppose, for the sake of argument, that the rules you are following in the book conform precisely to the established operations that the visual nervous system uses to arrive at internal representations of colors and their color names. These two facts mean that you have satisfied the standard functionalist criteria for claiming that you have mental states associated with color perception and naming: You have the same input-output function as a real perceiver, and you arrive at this output by carrying out the same computations that a real perceiver's visual system does. The key question is whether carrying out these computations would necessarily cause you to have the color experiences you normally would have when viewing the colored light that produced the three input numbers.

Most people's intuitions on this question are perfectly clear. Performing these computations, no matter how closely they might correspond to visual information processing in response to patches of color, would not give rise to anything like the experiences of color that would spontaneously arise if you were actually looking at the patch of light.

Like Searle's Chinese room argument, the power of this scenario is that it avoids the problem of other minds in deciding whether the color room has color experiences by inserting *you* into the color room system of rules and computations. You therefore know that there is a conscious agent within the room who could have color experiences, if that were indeed a necessary consequence of doing the right computations. If you think you would not have appropriate chromatic experiences as a consequence of doing these calculations, then it is reasonable to suppose that the machine does not either.[5]

Biology to the Rescue? What then of visual experience? Is it simply beyond the reach of science? The preceding argument suggests that the nature of experience itself may be beyond the reach of *behavioral* science, even though its relational superstructure clearly is not. At this juncture we should consider the possibility that biological science might succeed where behavioral science fails.

It is surely conceivable that we will someday attain a full enough understanding of the brain that the biological mechanisms underlying conscious experience will be discovered and understood to some significant extent. We currently have no clue as to what this explanation might be like. The best we can do right now is to appeal to the previously mentioned analogy with the understanding of life that was gained by the discovery of the molecular structure of DNA. Perhaps some as-yet-unknown structures and processes will be discovered in the biochemical events that take place within neurons that can explain how experiences arise from certain forms of neural activity. Most vision scientists believe this to be possible, at least in principle (e.g., Crick, 1994).

But there are also serious "in principle" problems that are likely to arise in trying to execute the biological program required to pin down the nature of qualia (Palmer, in press). If all our brains were identical, it would be easy to argue, on the basis of Kim's (1978, 1993) principle of supervenience, discussed at the end of Section 13.1.1, that our subjective experiences must therefore also be identical. But the fact of the matter is that individual brains differ from one another in a multitude of ways, and small physiological differences might conceivably cause important differences in experience. Even this would not prove fatal if there were some way of studying the correlations of biological differences between people's brains with experiential differences between their qualia. But here we run into serious problems.

There is surely no "in principle" problem in specifying the biological differences between two brains. That is just a matter of inventing and then applying appropriate state-of-the-art neurobiological techniques. But if two people have different brains, as surely they must, how are we to discover the corresponding differences in their subjective experiences? That would require some direct comparisons of, say, my experience and yours under identical stimulus conditions. As we have seen, this goal is blocked by the subjectivity barrier. If there

---

[5] Many have attempted to rebut Searle's Chinese room argument. The reader is referred to the numerous commentaries following his original article and his replies to them for a more thorough discussion of this topic than can be provided in this book (Searle, 1980).

are objective differences in relational structure, such as occur in the various forms of color blindness, they can clearly be detected behaviorally. But if two people's relational structures are identical, then their qualia are free to vary up to the constraint of isomorphism without being detected behaviorally, even in principle. One way science could deal with this situation would be to invoke Ockham's razor and simply state that if no objectively detectable differences in relational structure exist, scientists should assume their experiences to be identical. Unfortunately, assuming something does not make it so.

One avenue that seems open to scientific study in this otherwise bleak scenario is to avoid the subjectivity barrier at least partially by using within-subject experimental designs (Palmer, in press). The basic idea is simple. Use a biological intervention—such as a drug, surgery, or genetic manipulation—on individual subjects and ask each for reports about any changes in color experience from before to after the intervention. Suppose, for instance, that there were a drug called invertacillin that exchanged the light-sensitive pigments in M and L cones, as suggested earlier for pseudo-normal color vision. If the drug acted reasonably quickly and it didn't also mysteriously alter people's long-term memories for object colors or the associations between internal experiences and color names, subjects would indeed notice, and could reliably report, changes in their color experiences due to taking the drug. They would presumably report that blood now looks green and grass now looks red. These are extreme examples, of course, and it is hoped that subtler changes in experience would also be detectable. But the crucial point is that the same sub-isomorphic color transformations that are impossible to detect between individuals should be, at least in principle, easy to detect within individuals. Notice that we have not penetrated the individual's subjectivity barrier, for we don't actually know how blood or grass or anything else appeared to the subject either before or after the change. We know only that it changed by reversing the red-green dimension of color experience, whatever that dimension might be like for that observer.

To see how far this approach might take us, let us suppose that we know what the biological effects of the drug are and that it affects all trichromats' color experiences in the same way: by reversing the red-green dimension of their internal color space. We can then divide the set of behaviorally defined trichromats into two biological classes: "invertomats" who normally have the biological structure associated with the result of the invertacillin intervention (i.e., reversed M and L cones) and "normals" who do not (i.e., normal M and L cones).

Notice that this biologically defined class does not imply equivalent color experiences for individuals within it. We know that people in different classes have different color experiences, but we do not know whether people in the same class have the same color experiences or not, for there might be other biological factors that also matter. To infer that two people have the same color experiences, we would have to exhaust the set of all the relevant biological factors—and all their possible interactions. This is a very large set. But in principle, if two people were the same in all relevant biological respects, we could reasonably infer that they actually have the same color experiences. And if all the relevant factors and their effects were known, people in different equivalence classes could even be inferred to have color experiences that differ in specific ways. If I am a red-green invertomat, for example, and you are a normal trichromat, and if the corresponding physiological difference were the only one in our chromatic neurobiology, then our experiences could be inferred to differ specifically by the red-green inversion reported by subjects who took invertacillin.

I keep saying that we could "infer" that two people have the same color experiences or that they differ in some specific way because such claims could not be tested directly. The subjectivity barrier would still be very much in place, even if we were able to carry out this incredibly difficult research program. They would be inferences we have discussed because you cannot *have* my experiences in any direct fashion, nor can I *have* yours. The inferences are based on at least two important assumptions. One is that any difference in experience must necessarily rest on some biological difference; the other is that all relevant biological variables have been identified. If either is false, then the conclusion that you would know what my color experiences are like by taking invertacillin is also false. Given the dubious nature of such assumptions—especially the second—the chances of being able to bring this project off in reality are vanishingly small, even in the long run.

Such practical considerations cast doubt on the possibility of sciences ever being able to give a complete and testable explanation of all aspects of consciousness. Perhaps the nature of an individual's experience will turn out to be the ultimate mystery, the one that will never yield its deepest secrets to the seemingly inevitable advance of science. But then again, maybe it will.

Suggestions for Further Reading

Philosophical Approaches

Chalmers, D. J. (1996). *The conscious mind*. New York: Oxford University Press. This book provides an informed, up-to-date view of the cognitive science of consciousness from a philosophical perspective.

Churchland, P. M. (1988). *Matter and consciousness*. Cambridge, MA: MIT Press. Churchland's engagingly written text surveys the philosophical literature from a modern perspective.

Block, N., Flanagan, O., & Güzeldere, G. (Eds.). (1997). *The nature of consciousness: Philosophical debates*. Cambridge, MA: MIT Press. This edited volume reprints an excellent selection of classic papers about consciousness written by many outstanding philosophers and philosophically oriented cognitive scientists from other fields.

Cognitive and Neuroscientific Approaches

Baars, B. (1988). *A cognitive theory of consciousness*. Cambridge, England: Cambridge University Press. This book presents Baars's global workspace theory of consciousness.

Crick, F. H. C. (1994). *The astonishing hypothesis: The scientific search for the soul*. New York: Scribner. The man who co-discovered the structure of DNA writes about the prospects of understanding the problem of visual awareness from a biological perspective.

Springer, S. P., & Deutsch, G. (1981). *Left brain, right brain*. San Francisco: Freeman. This engaging book surveys the differences between the function of the left and right hemispheres.

Weiskrantz, L. (1986). *Blindsight*. Oxford, England: Oxford University Press. This research monograph is Weiskrantz's classic presentation of the phenomenon of blindsight in patient D.B. and his original ideas about the brain mechanisms that support it.

Psychophysical Methods

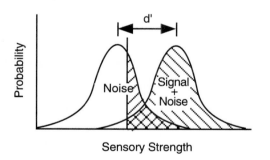

In Chapter 4 we mentioned a highly sophisticated and quantitative branch of perceptual psychology known as *psychophysics*: the behavioral study of quantitative relations between people's perceptual experiences and corresponding physical properties. In this appendix we will describe a few of the experimental methods on which psychophysics is based. We will also describe an important theory, called signal detection theory (or SDT), that is closely related to certain of these methods.

A.1 Measuring Thresholds

Psychophysical methods were originally developed to find the **threshold** for perceiving a stimulus: the weakest stimulus that could just barely be perceived. There are number of ways to measure such a threshold in classical psychophysics. Gustav Fechner, the father of this field, described three of them in 1860: the method of adjustment, the method of limits, and the method of constant stimuli.

A.1.1 Method of Adjustment

The quickest and easiest way to find a threshold is the **method of adjustment**. The subject is given a dial or some other mechanism that controls the magnitude or intensity of the stimulus along some dimension of interest. For example, suppose one is interested in measuring the threshold for seeing a very dim spot of light. On *ascending trials*, the stimulus is initially set substantially below threshold (e.g., completely off), and the subject slowly increases the spot's intensity until it is just barely visible. On *descending trials*, the stimulus is initially set substantially above threshold, and the subject slowly decreases its intensity until it is no longer visible. Each type of measurement is usually taken several times, and the values are averaged to obtain more stable estimates of the subject's true threshold.

Threshold values for ascending adjustments tend to be systematically higher than those for descending adjustments. In general, there seems to be a tendency for something already perceived to continue to be perceived and for something not yet perceived to remain unperceived. This tendency toward perceptual inertia is called **hysteresis**. If a single estimate of the threshold is needed from the method of adjustment, it is usually taken as the average of the ascending and descending thresholds.

The method of adjustment is a convenient way to measure thresholds because it can be done very quickly and easily. This is sometimes important, especially in studying a time-varying phenomenon such as adaptation. For example, in tracing the course of dark adaptation (see Figure 1.3.12), the absolute threshold must be found for seeing a dim spot at many different points in time. Other methods would take too long, so adjustment is the method of choice.

A.1.2 Method of Limits

The **method of limits** is essentially a discrete-trial version of the method of adjustment. On each trial, the experimenter presents a stimulus at a particular intensity level, and the subject indicates whether he or she detects it or not. The trials are arranged in sequences in which the stimulus intensity is either ascending or descending. In an ascending sequence, the initial trial uses a stimulus that is substantially below threshold. On each subsequent trial, the intensity is increased until the subject

responds that he or she saw the stimulus. In descending sequences, the initial trial uses a stimulus that is substantially above threshold. On each subsequent trial, the intensity is decreased until the subject responds that he or she did not see the stimulus.

Hysteresis effects are also present in the method of limits: The threshold for ascending sequences tends to be systematically higher than that for descending sequences. As in the method of adjustment, the value of the threshold is taken as the average value for the thresholds of all ascending and descending sequences.

A.1.3 Method of Constant Stimuli

The **method of constant stimuli** is a modification of the method of limits in which the order of the trials is randomized rather than fixed in ascending or descending sequences. It uses a series of discrete trials in which the subject's task on each trial is to indicate whether or not he or she detects the presence of a stimulus. Since this method is the point of departure for later psychophysical methods, we will describe it in somewhat greater detail.

A classical experiment to find the absolute threshold for seeing a given-sized spot of light using the method of constant stimuli goes like this: The stimulus is a very dim spot of light that is presented briefly under conditions of complete darkness so that the subject is maximally sensitive to light. One spot is presented to the subject on each trial, randomly selected from a range of stimulus values that are expected to bracket the threshold (i.e., from clearly below the threshold to clearly above the threshold). At the end of the experiment, the percentage of detection responses ("Yes, I saw the spot" or an equivalent button press) is computed for each stimulus intensity value.

The results can be summarized in a **psychometric function**: a graph that plots the percentage of detection responses on the y axis as a function of stimulus intensity on the x axis. A typical psychometric function is shown in Figure A.1.1. Notice that for very dim lights (clearly below threshold), detection is at 0%. For very bright lights (clearly above threshold), detection is at 100%. If there were a single, unvarying absolute threshold, the transition from 0% to 100% detections would be very sharp, occurring right at the threshold intensity. Psychometric functions are invariably smooth S-shaped curves, however, in which there is no single threshold

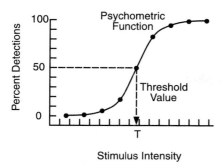

Figure A.1.1 A psychometric function and the threshold of detection. The psychometric function plots percentage of detections as a function of stimulus intensity and almost always produces an S-shaped curve. The threshold for the studied dimension is the intensity value (T) at which the observer detects the stimulus 50% of the time (dashed line and arrow).

value, but merely a region of gradual transition from absence to presence of visual experience. The standard practice is to define the absolute threshold as the intensity value at which the psychometric function crosses the 50% detection level, as indicated in Figure A.1.1.

A.1.4 The Theoretical Status of Thresholds

In the absolute threshold experiment we described above, the term "threshold" was defined methodologically in terms of a measurement of the minimal stimulus intensity that can be seen according to a certain procedure. But **threshold** is also a theoretical construct, one that indicates the particular stimulus value at which the internal response goes from absence to presence of visual experience, as illustrated in Figure A.1.2. The

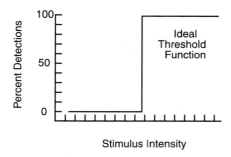

Figure A.1.2 An ideal threshold function. If there were a discrete and perfect sensory threshold, there would be a change from no sensory experience to clear sensory experience at a particular value, at which point the threshold function would jump discretely from 0 to 100% detections. Such functions are never actually found, however.

theoretical status of a visual threshold is controversial, however. Technically, it implies that a specific amount of stimulus energy is required to produce a visual experience such that below that amount, experience is absent and above it, experience is present. Many vision scientists doubt the reality of such thresholds because of one or more of the following potential problems.

1. *Smooth transitions.* As just mentioned, psychometric functions do not show sharp changes from absence to presence of experience; they show smooth transitions. Superficially, at least, this appears to be incompatible with the assumption of a discrete threshold value.

2. *Subliminal perception.* People sometimes behave as though they have seen something even when detection is at or below the supposed sensory threshold (see Section 13.3.2). If there were a single sensory threshold, this would not be true.

3. *Response bias.* Performance in detection tasks can be affected systematically by strategic factors such as payoffs and motivation. These biases can systematically change the measured threshold in experiments like the one described above.

Of these three problems, response bias is perhaps the least obvious but the most important theoretically. The smooth transitions in psychometric functions can be explained within classical threshold theory by assuming that the psychometric function necessarily represents an average over many trials in which the threshold is variable. If the precise value of a discrete threshold varies randomly from trial to trial according to a normal (bell-shaped) distribution, for example, the average performance over many trials would show exactly the kind of smooth S-shaped transition that is normally found in psychometric functions. Subliminal perception can be explained by the existence of two different thresholds: a higher one for producing visual awareness and a lower one for affecting behavior (see Section 13.3.2). But the presence of response biases in detection tasks and their effects on measured thresholds have had a profound influence on both theories and methods in psychophysics. Indeed, they have led to a very different conception of how detection responses are made, one in which there is no discrete sensory threshold at all. We now will consider this alternative view in some detail, for it provides the basis for the modern information processing view of sensory detection performance.

Psychophysical Methods

A.2 Signal Detection Theory

Signal detection theory (SDT) replaces the single concept of a discrete sensory threshold with two separate concepts: an immutable **sensory process** that cannot be influenced by strategic factors and a later **decision process** that can be (Green & Swets, 1966). We will consider these constructs in detail shortly. But SDT is more than just a theory of how detection responses are made; it also prescribes a different experimental method for studying detection performance, one that is closely tied to its theoretical assumptions. This method has become the modern standard for studying a wide variety of perceptual and memory phenomena. To understand SDT and its associated methodology, we must first understand how response bias effects occur and why they affect threshold measures obtained by using the methods described above.

A.2.1 Response Bias

Suppose the dim spots you were trying to detect in the threshold experiment described above were blips on a sonar screen that indicated the presence of a submarine nearby. Suppose further that you were trying to detect these blips on a battleship in the midst of a raging sea battle. Because of the high probability of encountering an enemy submarine in such a situation and the dire consequences of failing to detect one, you would say "Yes, I saw a blip" whenever you had the faintest possible experience of the blip being present. This **liberal response strategy** would lead you to a strong bias toward saying "yes," and your threshold would be measured as lower (i.e., more sensitive) than it would if you were equally likely to say "yes" and "no."

Now suppose you were trying to detect the same sonar blips on a freighter in Lake Michigan during peacetime. The probability of there being a submarine in the area would be exceedingly low, and even if there were one, the consequences of failing to detect it would be slight. In this situation, chances are good that you would say "No, I didn't see a blip" unless you had a very strong experience of the spot being present, because if you were wrong, you would risk being laughed off the ship. This **conservative response strategy** would lead to a strong response bias toward saying "no," and

your threshold would be measured as higher (i.e., less sensitive) than it would be on a battleship in wartime.

The crucial question is whether your visual experiences actually changed as a result of the different probabilities of a submarine being present and your different levels of motivation to detect the faint blips on the screen. Classical threshold theory would have to claim that your sensory threshold for the minimum visual experience was indeed lower on the wartime battleship than on the peacetime freighter. It is possible that the retinal receptors or subsequent sensory processes actually change as a function of knowledge and motivation, but SDT provides a more plausible alternative explanation. It suggests that the sensory response was actually the same in both cases but that your internal **criterion** for saying "Yes, I saw a blip" was simply lower on the battleship than on the freighter.

A.2.2 The Signal Detection Paradigm

The problem of response bias had been recognized long before SDT was formulated. Classical methods for finding thresholds included ways to identify such response biases in a detection task by including a few **catch trials** in which no stimulus is presented at all. The percentage of "yes" responses on these catch trials can then be used to estimate the influence of response biases. SDT extends the idea of catch trials to become an integral and indispensable part of any detection experiment. In a typical SDT experiment, a weak stimulus is presented on half the trials (called **signal trials**), and no stimulus is presented on the other half (called **noise trials**, which are the same as catch trials). The subject's task is to discriminate between signal trials and noise trials by responding "yes" (a signal was presented) or "no" (it was not) on each trial.

The basic experimental design advocated by SDT methodology is given in Figure A.2.1. On each trial a signal is either present or absent, and the subject responds by saying either "yes" or "no." All trials can thus be classified as falling into one of the four cells shown in Figure A.2.1 **hits**, **misses**, **false alarms**, or **correct rejections**, depending on both the stimulus condition and the subject's response.

Notice what happens in this design if the subject has a bias to say "yes," as when detecting submarines in the midst of a naval battle. As indicated in Figure A.2.2A,

RESPONSE

	"Yes"	"No"
STIMULUS		
Signal + Noise	HIT	MISS
Noise only	FALSE ALARM	CORRECT REJECTION

Figure A.2.1 The design of signal detection experiments. On every trial, either a signal is presented (signal + noise) or it is not (noise only). Subjects must respond that a signal was present ("Yes") or that it was not ("No"). The resulting 2 × 2 matrix defines the set of possible outcomes: hits, misses, false alarms, and correct rejections.

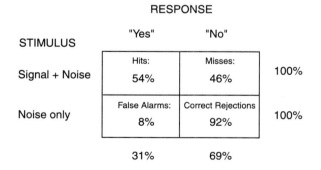

RESPONSE

	"Yes"	"No"	
STIMULUS			
Signal + Noise	Hits: 92%	Misses: 8%	100%
Noise only	False Alarms: 46%	Correct Rejections 54%	100%
	69%	31%	

A. RESPONSE BIAS TOWARD "YES"

RESPONSE

	"Yes"	"No"	
STIMULUS			
Signal + Noise	Hits: 54%	Misses: 46%	100%
Noise only	False Alarms: 8%	Correct Rejections 92%	100%
	31%	69%	

B. RESPONSE BIAS TOWARD "NO"

Figure A.2.2 Results of a signal detection experiment in which the same subject's bias changes from saying "Yes" to saying "No." Part A shows that using a liberal (or lax) criterion produces many hits but also many false alarms. Part B shows that using a conservative (or strict) criterion produces fewer hits but also fewer false alarms.

the percentage of hits will be high (92%), but so will the percentage of false alarms (46%). The high rate of false alarms arises because the sonar operator is taking even the slightest possibility of a signal as indicating the presence of a submarine. In this case, the bias toward detecting signals is very strong; the subject has given more than twice as many "yes" responses (69%) as "no" responses (31%).

If the subject has a bias toward saying "no," as when detecting enemy submarines in Lake Michigan during peacetime, the percentage of hits will be low (54%), but so will the percentage of false alarms (8%) (see Figure A.2.2B). Here the subject requires a great deal of sensory evidence before he or she will say that a signal was present. Note that under these conditions, the subject has given more than twice as many "no" responses as "yes" responses.

SDT provides an analysis of such data that combines the percentages of hits and false alarms to extract separate estimates of two underlying factors. There is one parameter for **discriminability**, called d' (pronounced "d-prime"), and another for **response bias**, called ß (pronounced "beta"). In the present example, d' is the same for both data sets, indicating equal sensory responses to the optical signals reaching the eye. However, β is different, because of the very different tendencies to respond yes versus no in the two situations.

A.2.3 The Theory of Signal Detectability

Theoretically, SDT proposes that detection decisions are based on an initial sensory process followed by a decision process that operates on the output of the sensory process, as indicated in Figure A.2.3. In the sensory stage, the stimulus event (signal trial or noise trial) produces an internal response within the subject, the strength of which reflects only sensory information. In particular, the strength of the sensory response depends only on the intensity of the stimulus (e.g., brighter spots of light will result in higher values of d' in a threshold detection task) and the state of the sensory system (e.g., longer periods of dark adaptation lead to higher values of d' in an absolute threshold detection task). The output of this sensory system does not depend on strategies, motivational factors, the probability of a signal, or any other factors that might affect response bias. You can think of the output of the sensory system as reflecting the strength of an early neural response to the stimulus

Psychophysical Methods

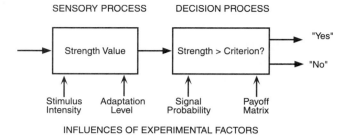

SENSORY PROCESS   DECISION PROCESS

Strength Value → Strength > Criterion? → "Yes" / "No"

Stimulus Intensity   Adaptation Level   Signal Probability   Payoff Matrix

INFLUENCES OF EXPERIMENTAL FACTORS

Figure A.2.3 The theory of signal detectability. Stimulus events are detected by a two-stage process. The sensory process produces a strength value that depends on factors such as the intensity of the stimulus and the adaptational state of the sensory system. The decision process compares the strength of the sensory response to an internally set criterion and responds "Yes" if it is above the criterion and "No" otherwise. The decision process can be influenced by knowledge of the probability of signal events and payoff factors.

event. (Strictly speaking, SDT does not propose specific neural mechanisms but specifies abstract information processing operations that might be carried out neurally in many different ways.) This strength value is the output of the initial sensory process and provides the only stimulus information that the subject has for deciding whether or not a signal was presented on that particular trial.

SDT assumes that the sensory system is "noisy," meaning that it is subject to random fluctuations that are unrelated to the stimulus event. The sensory response will therefore not be the same on every signal trial (or on every noise trial) even if the physical stimulus events are identical. Rather, SDT assumes that the sensory response will vary randomly over trials around an average value, producing an aggregate distribution of strength values over many trials, such as the normal (bell-shaped) curve labeled "noise alone distribution" shown in Figure A.2.4. Because the signal adds to the strength of the noisy sensory process, the signal + noise distribution has greater strength than the noise-alone distribution but about the same amount of variability. If the signal is weak—as it usually is in detection experiments—the distributions of strength values for these two sensory events will overlap to some degree (see Figure A.2.4), so the upper end of the noise-alone distribution has greater sensory strength than the lower end of the signal+noise distribution. This overlap is the source of errors in detection tasks.

The decision process must try to determine whether the strength value it receives from the sensory process on

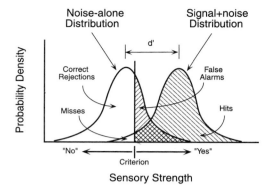

Figure A.2.4 Deriving responses from signal + noise and noise-only distributions. Signal trials produce sensory strength values from the signal + noise distribution; nonsignal trials produce strength values from the noise-only distribution. If the sensory strength value is above the criterion, the decision process detects a signal ("Yes"); otherwise it does not ("No"). This leads to hits, false alarms, misses, and correct rejections proportional to the areas indicated by different shadings.

a given trial resulted from a trial on which the signal was present or absent. SDT assumes that the decision stage accomplishes this by setting a criterion somewhere along the continuum of sensory strength (the vertical line in Figure A.2.4): a strength value above which the subject will respond "yes" and otherwise will respond "no." Much of the time, this decision rule will lead to correct "yes" responses (hits) resulting from signal+noise values above the criterion and correct "no" responses (correct rejections) resulting from noise-alone values below the criterion. Notice that if the distributions overlap, however, there are bound to be errors. Sometimes, the sensory value on signal trials will fall below the criterion, resulting in incorrect "no" responses (misses); other times, the sensory value on noise trials will fall above the criterion, resulting in incorrect "yes" responses (false alarms).

Given the same two distributions of sensory values, the numbers of hits, misses, false alarms, and correct rejections will depend on precisely where the criterion is placed, and it is the placement of this criterion that reflects the subject's strategy. Using a low (liberal or lax) criterion results in many "yes" responses and a high hit rate but also a high false-alarm rate, as depicted in Figure A.2.4. Using a high (conservative or strict) criterion results in few "yes" responses and a low hit rate but also a low false-alarm rate. Many factors can influence the setting of this criterion in the decision process. Some of the most potent are informing the subject of the probabilities of signal versus noise trials, paying the subject differently for hits versus correct rejections (or fining the subject differently for misses versus false alarms), and simply instructing the subject to use a lax versus a strict criterion for saying "yes."

SDT provides a mathematical description of how these sensory and decision factors jointly determine the percentages of hits, misses, false alarms, and correct rejections. The mathematical details of the theory are more technical than need concern us here (see Green & Swets, 1966, for the classic presentation), but the conceptual basis is rather simple. As we said before, SDT identifies two variables in a detection task: d', which is a measure of discriminability, and β, which is a measure of response bias. In terms of the overlapping distributions of sensory strength shown in Figure A.2.4, d' is a numerical estimate of the distance between the signal and noise distributions calculated in units of the standard deviation (width) of the noise distribution. β is a numerical estimate of the position of the decision criterion along the continuum of sensory strength. (By convention, threshold is defined as the stimulus intensity at which $d' = 1$, so that the signal + noise distribution is one standard deviation above the noise-alone distribution, regardless of the value of β.)

Notice that d' and β are independent: Either can be changed without affecting the other. Of particular interest is the fact that when the decision criterion is varied without changing the distance between the signal and noise distributions, detection performance can vary greatly in terms of the percentages of hits and false alarms (e.g., as illustrated in Figures A.2.2A and A.2.2B), yet d' will remain constant. This finding has been consistently obtained with human observers in detection experiments when the stimuli and subjects are kept constant while response bias is changed in a variety of different ways (see Green & Swets, 1966). SDT is generally agreed to be a very good theory of human detection performance.

A.3 Difference Thresholds

The experiment we described initially was designed to determine an absolute threshold in which the subject is trying to discriminate the difference between the presence and absence of visual experience. But **difference thresholds** can also be measured by asking subjects to discriminate the difference between two stimuli rather than the difference between one stimulus and nothing. The experimental situation is generally similar to that for measuring an absolute threshold except that each trial consists of a *pair* of stimuli and subjects are asked to detect the presence of a *difference* between them.

A.3.1 Just Noticeable Differences

For example, suppose you wanted to measure the difference threshold between a line of a given length and one slightly longer. On each trial, the subject would see two lines: one of some standard length (I) and one just a bit longer ($I + \Delta I$), where ΔI indicates the small increment in length and is read "delta-I." For each pair, the subject would say whether the two lines looked the same or different in length. After many such trials, a psychometric function can be plotted by graphing the proportion of "different" responses on the y axis as a function of the difference in length (ΔI) on the x axis. The difference threshold is taken as the length difference (value of ΔI) at which this function crosses 50%. This measurement is also known as the **just noticeable difference** (**jnd**) because it represents the smallest difference that can be detected.

A.3.2 Weber's Law

Suppose you have determined that the jnd for a standard line of 10 mm is 1 mm. If you repeated the experiment with a standard line of 20 mm, would the size of the jnd be the same? In fact, it would be about 2 mm. Figure A.3.1 shows some examples of jnds at several line lengths. Notice that although the size of the jnd increases steadily with the length of the standard line, the ratio of the size of the jnd (ΔI) to the length of the standard line (I) remains constant. If we plot the relation between the size of the jnd (ΔI) and the magnitude of the standard line (I), as shown in Figure A.3.2, we obtain a straight line whose slope is the constant ratio of ΔI to I.

Ernst Weber discovered this lawful relation in 1846 and found that it held for a wide variety of stimulus dimensions. The only difference between dimensions was the particular value of this constant ratio. Fechner

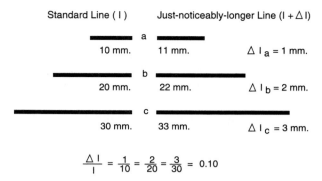

Standard Line (I) Just-noticeably-longer Line (I + ΔI)

a
10 mm.   11 mm.   ΔI$_a$ = 1 mm.

b
20 mm.   22 mm.   ΔI$_b$ = 2 mm.

c
30 mm.   33 mm.   ΔI$_c$ = 3 mm.

$$\frac{\Delta I}{I} = \frac{1}{10} = \frac{2}{20} = \frac{3}{30} = 0.10$$

Figure A.3.1 Just noticeable differences (jnds) at different stimulus magnitudes for line length. At 10 mm, an additional 1 mm of length is needed to detect a difference; at 20 mm, an additional 2 mm; and at 30 mm an additional 3 mm. Thus, the ratio of additional length required (ΔI) to the stimulus magnitude (I) is constant at a value of 0.1.

summarized all Weber's findings in a single equation, which he called **Weber's law**:

$$\Delta I / I = k, \tag{A.1}$$

where I is the intensity of the standard stimulus, ΔI is the size of the jnd (and value of the difference threshold) for the given value of I, and k is the value of the constant ratio for the particular dimension being studied. In words, Weber's law means, roughly, that the bigger or more intense the stimulus is, the bigger or more intense the increment must be to be detected. More precisely, the relation between these two quantities is linear, as Figure A.3.2 illustrates.

The procedure just described for finding a difference threshold is also subject to response bias effects, however, and better methods for measuring it have been

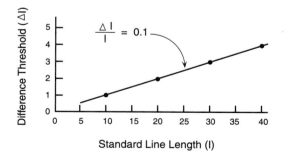

Figure A.3.2 A graph of difference thresholds exhibiting Weber's law. The additional line length (ΔI) required for detecting a difference in line length between two lines increases linearly as a function of stimulus intensity (I) with a slope of 0.10.

devised. Rather than simply having subjects say whether they detect a difference or not on each trial, they can be asked to indicate which line is longer. In this case, there is a correct answer on each trial, and a psychometric function can be plotted in terms of the percentage of correct responses as a function of the size of the difference (ΔI). Values of ΔI at which the subject is correct only 50% of the time must be at or below threshold because he or she cannot discriminate which is longer any better than chance (as though guessing). Values of ΔI at which the subject is correct 100% of the time must be above threshold. By convention, the threshold in a difference threshold experiment with two alternatives is normally taken as the value of ΔI at which this psychometric function crosses 75% correct. (Note that this is different from the 50% definition of threshold when the y axis represents percentage of detection responses rather than percentage of *correct* responses.)

A.4 Psychophysical Scaling

One of the important goals of psychophysics is to specify the quantitative relation between physical and psychological dimensions. The principal way of representing physical dimensions is in terms of measurement scales, such as the metric scales for length (expressed in meters) and weight (expressed in grams), to mention just two. Are these scales also appropriate for measuring psychological experiences or are new and different **psychophysical scales** required?

A.4.1 Fechner's Law

When you think about it, Weber's law suggests that standard physical scales are not appropriate for reflecting psychological experiences. Physically, for instance, the difference between 1 and 2 mm is the same as the difference between 101 and 102 mm—1 mm in each case. But Weber's law tells us that the first difference would be easy to detect perceptually, whereas the second would be almost impossible. Therefore, the perceptual difference between 101 and 102 mm is very much smaller than the perceptual difference between 1 and 2 mm. Is there any way to construct a psychologically meaningful scale that would accurately reflect such differences?

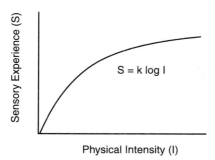

Figure A.4.1 Fechner's law of psychophysical scaling. If one assumes that all jnds are psychologically equal, the relation between physical dimensions and sensory experience can be described by a logarithmic function of the general form given. Such equations produce a negatively accelerated curve like the one shown.

Weber's law suggests that a perceptually meaningful scale might be derived directly from jnds. The key assumption is that all jnds are psychologically equal. Using our line-length example, the 1-mm jnd for a 10-mm line is assumed to be perceptually equal to the 2-mm jnd for a 20-mm line and the 4-mm jnd for a 40-mm line. If this is so, one can construct an equal interval perceptual scale by laying out jnds end to end, as it were. As the perceptual scale of line length increases by single (and presumably equal) jnds, the physical stimulus increases by larger and larger amounts, as shown in Figure A.4.1.

This relation between psychological and physical scales was proposed by Gustav Fechner in 1860. It can be expressed mathematically as an equation known as **Fechner's law**:

$$S = k \log(I), \tag{A.2}$$

where S is the magnitude of the sensory experience, I is the physical magnitude or intensity, and k is a constant specific to the given dimension. This relation between psychological and physical scale values is graphed in Figure A.4.1.

A.4.2 Stevens's Law

Fechner's method of constructing perceptual scales is indirect in the sense that subjects are never asked to indicate the magnitudes of their perceptual experiences directly. Rather, the scale is inferred indirectly from discrimination responses. A more direct approach to psychophysical scaling, called **magnitude estimation**, was developed by S. S. Stevens (1956), who asked sub-

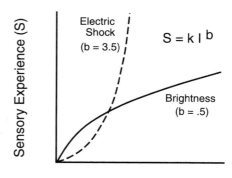

Figure A.4.2 Stevens's law of psychophysical scaling. Magnitude estimation procedures produce results that conform to the power law shown. Such equations produce either negatively accelerated functions (e.g., for brightness) when the exponent is less than unity or positively accelerated functions (e.g., for electric shock) when the exponent is greater than unity.

jects to assign numbers to their experiences of stimuli. For example, subjects would be presented with an initial stimulus (say, a light of some intensity) and were told to assign it some value (say, 10). Then they would be presented with another light of a different physical magnitude and would be told that if it were twice as bright, they should call it 20; if it were half as bright, they should call it 5; and so on.

There was no guarantee that subjects would be able to do this at all or, if they did, that different subjects would agree with each other. But, in fact, people can perform this task with great consistency. Further, Stevens found that the ratings from magnitude estimation tasks could be summarized by a single equation:

$$S = kI^b, \tag{A.3}$$

where S is again the magnitude of the sensory experience, I is the physical intensity of the stimulus, k is a constant (different from Fechner's constant), and b is an exponent that is characteristic of the given sensory dimension. Figure A.4.2 shows two examples of psychophysical scales with very different exponents. Notice that doubling the physical intensity of a light less than doubles the experience of brightness. This result is at least qualitatively consistent with Fechner's law. Other dimensions produce much different patterns of ratings, however. Electric shock is a classic case in which doubling the physical intensity of the shock more than doubles the experience of discomfort. Fechner's law cannot predict such results.

Of all these psychophysical methods, the most useful and important in studying vision are the ones for determining thresholds, either absolute or differential. They underlie many of the results we discussed throughout this book. In several chapters, for example, we discussed experiments in which the effects of adaptation were studied. The way in which adaptation was assessed was to measure the observer's threshold once before adaptation and then again after adaptation. The elevation in threshold is then taken as a measure of the amount of adaptation. This general technique is so frequently used in psychophysical studies of vision that it is sometimes referred to as the "psychophysicist's electrode."

Suggestions for Futher Reading

Fechner, G. (1860/1966). *Elements of psychophysics* (H. E. Adler, Trans.). New York: Holt, Rinehart & Winston. This is the classic reference work on psychophysical methods. It also introduces both Weber's Law and Fechner's Law.

Green, D. M., and Swets, J. (1966). *Signal detection theory and psychophysics*. New York: Wiley. This is the classic book on signal detection theory written by two of the psychophysicists who developed it.

Connectionist Modeling

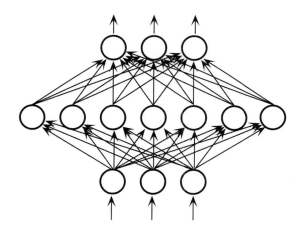

In Chapter 2 we noted that classical information processing models of visual perception are quite purposely abstracted from any reference to brain events. This approach to visual theory is sanctioned by the computer metaphor (mind:brain::program:computer; see Section 2.3.1) and the functionalist doctrine of multiple realizability (the same mental processes can be implemented equally well in many different kinds of hardware; see Section 13.1.1). The usual inference from these assumptions is that the hardware of the mind doesn't matter because the same mental events could occur in many different physical devices, of which brains are but one.

In stark contrast with this abstract, symbolic approach to computational theory is an explicitly brain-oriented approach based on **connectionist** or **neural networks**. (We will use the term "connectionist" to describe these computational models, reserving "neural networks" to refer to models of actual neuronal interactions.) Connectionist models are based on the assumption that human cognition, including vision, depends heavily on the massively parallel structure of neural circuits in the brain. If so, accurate models of human capabilities will require brainlike computational architectures, a feature that is central to connectionist models.

A connectionist model consists of a network of interconnected units that spread activation to each other via their connections. Such models have four key parallels with brain structure.

1. *Units* ⟷ *neurons*. The basic building blocks of connectionist networks are densely interconnected computing elements (usually called **units**), each of which works much like a simplified neuron.

2. *Activation* ⟷ *firing rate*. Each unit's current state is characterized by its **activation level**, which corresponds roughly to a neuron's firing rate.

3. *Connections* ⟷ *synapses*. Activation is spread throughout the network by **connections** between units, much like the synapses through which neurons communicate (see Figure 2.2.4).

4. *Connection weights* ⟷ *synaptic strength*. Each connection is characterized by a **connection weight** that can be positive (excitatory) or negative (inhibitory) to different degrees, much as the strength of synapses can vary in neural circuitry.

The correspondence between connectionist models and neural structures and events is far from complete, however. For example, most connectionist models fail to represent different neural transmitters, the fine structure of temporal spiking events, spatial interactions due to distances between synapses on dendritic trees, and a host of other potentially important phenomena in the behavior of real neurons. Such factors could be incorporated into connectionist models, however, if they were found to be crucial in understanding the computational properties of neural events.

The behavior of connectionist models is determined by the weights of the connections between units in a network. Indeed, the same set of units can perform very different computations if the connection weights are different. It is often not easy to determine exactly how such a network will behave without running a computer simulation. The basic principles that underlie the behavior of individual units are simple enough to understand, but their interactions can be exceedingly complex, sometimes leading to quite unexpected and counterintuitive results. In the first half of this appendix, we will describe the basic principles that determine the behavior of individual units and simple networks that are composed of such units.

One of the reasons connectionist models have become so popular in the past decade is that they can be programmed to learn to perform nontrivial computations automatically. This is accomplished by defining rules that specify how to adjust the connection weights to increase the accuracy of the network in performing the desired task. The second half of this appendix will describe one of the most popular schemes for learning by automatic adjustment of weights, called *back propagation*. There are many other algorithms for adjusting weights that depend on the details of different mathematical rules, but many bear a strong family resemblance to back propagation. Others, such as unsupervised learning algorithms, are quite different and will not be described here (see Bishop, 1995, for a description).

The reader is forewarned that this appendix is not intended to be a comprehensive treatment or even a general primer on the rapidly expanding field of connectionist modeling. Rather, it is designed to provide useful background material to help readers understand in more detail the connectionist models described elsewhere in this book. For a more complete exposition of connectionist networks, the reader is referred to Anderson (1995) or Caudhill (1992).

B.1 Network Behavior

It is easy to understand the behavior of individual units in a connectionist network. Although we will minimize the presentation of specific equations in favor of a more general conceptual understanding, even the mathematics are fairly simple at this level. This might seem surprising because, as we have seen in the various cases considered in this book, connectionist models are capable of exhibiting quite complex behaviors. In fact, this complexity arises from the interactions between units, depending on the pattern of connection between units and the weights of those connections. In an effort to understand how these behaviors arise, we will first consider basic principles governing the behavior of an individual unit and then discuss further principles that underlie the interactive behavior of multiunit networks.

B.1.1 Unit Behavior

The current state of any arbitrarily chosen unit in a connectionist network (call it "unit j") can be represented by a number that represents its *activation level*, or simply its *activation*, denoted a_j. This number typically takes values from a bounded interval, such as 0 to 1. It is interpreted as corresponding to the firing rate (number of spikes per second) of a neuron, where an activation of 1 is arbitrarily taken to represent the maximum firing rate, whatever that might be.[1]

Connection weights can be positive, zero, or negative. Connections with negative weights represent inhibitory synapses between neurons, and those with positive weights represent excitatory synapses. A weight of zero can denote either no connection at all or a neutral connection that is neither excitatory nor inhibitory. In this section, we will see how these simple numerical representations for unit activations and connection weights can be combined to achieve interesting computational capabilities.

Figure B.1.1 shows the basic structure of a unit (j) in the context of other units in a network. It receives input either from other units in the network (as shown) or directly from environmental stimulation. It modifies its activation state according to this input and sends its output activation to other units. In understanding the activation behavior of such a unit, it will be helpful to distinguish two aspects of its functioning: combining input activation and determining output activation.

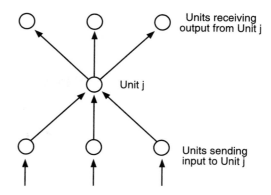

Figure B.1.1 The computational environment for an arbitrarily selected unit (unit j) in a simple feedforward connectionist network. Unit j receives input from a subset of the units in the network and provides output to another subset. (These two subsets are illustrated as nonoverlapping for clarity, but they need not be.)

Combining Input Activation. The inputs of all units connected to unit j must be combined by some rule, usually addition. Before the activations (a_i) from each of its input units are added together, each is multiplied by the connection weight between it and unit j, denoted w_{ji}. The combined input to unit j, c_j, can then be specified as the following weighted sum:

$$c_j = \sum_{i=1}^{n} w_{ji} a_i$$

$$= w_{j1} a_1 + w_{j2} a_2 + w_{j3} a_3 + \cdots + w_{jn} a_n.$$

(B.1)

This equation can be interpreted as specifying that some proportion (depending on the value of w_{ji}) of the activation coming from each input to unit j gets passed to it, either adding it (for positive connection weights) or subtracting it (for negative weights) from the combined input.[2]

---

[1] Some connectionist models use discrete activation levels, such as 0 versus 1, which indicate that the unit is either inactive (0) or active (1). We will not consider such discrete models in this appendix, however, and will take the continuous interval from 0 to 1 as the default range of activation values.

[2] In some cases, more complex combination rules are required to specify conjunctions of two (or more) inputs (e.g., in the Marr-Hildreth theory of edge detection; see Figure 4.3.9 and Section 4.3.2). If one input is used to "gate" another, so that both units need to be active before any input goes to the receiving unit, an obvious way of combining them is by multiplication (i.e., $a_x a_y$) before weighting them and adding their weighted product to the combined input. In the most general case, any number of input

units can be conjoined in this way, not just pairs. Such multiplicatively conjoined units are sometimes called *sigma-pi units* because the formula for their combined input includes the uppercase Greek letters sigma and pi:

$$c_j = \sum_{i=1}^{n} w_{ji} \prod_{k=1}^{m} a_{ki},$$

where k indexes the number of input units whose activations are to be conjoined. The rationale for multiplication is that if any of the conjoined units is inactive (has zero activation), the product will be zero activation, so no input will come from the conjoined ensemble. When all the conjoined units are maximally active, however, they will provide maximum output.

Connectionist Modeling

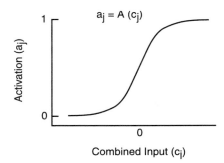

Figure B.1.2 An S-shaped activation function. The activation function for a network specifies the transformation from the combined input, which can range from large negative to large positive values, to the unit's activation, which is restricted in range. This activation function squashes the input at very high and very low values to produce values between 0 and 1.

Determining Output Activation. Because the combined input, representing the total current influences on unit j from external sources,[3] can be much greater or much less than the range of activations available to unit j, one must also specify an activation function (A) that maps the combined input to the output activation level, a_j:

$$a_j = A(c_j). \qquad (B.2)$$

This mapping is typically nonlinear, having a form like that illustrated in Figure B.1.2. Such activation functions typically squash extreme values of the combined input toward a maximum (1) and minimum (0) bound, resulting in a smooth, S-shaped function. Notice that this kind of activation function is a smooth approximation to a threshold function such that low combined input values have almost no effect on a unit's output, medium values have a gradually increasing effect, and high values have almost equal effects.

These two aspects of the function of individual units are sufficient to specify how any given unit will behave, assuming that all of its input activations and weights are known. How the network as a whole behaves is a very different matter, however, one that depends on all the interactions that take place among all the units in the network over an extended period of time.

B.1.2 System Architecture

To construct a connectionist network, one must define its **architecture**: the number of units and the pattern of connections among them. There is an infinite number of different possible architectures, but some factors have particularly important implications for the kinds of behavior a given network exhibits. Here we list just a few types of network architectures that are important in understanding the models described in this book.

Feedforward Networks. One of the most crucial factors is whether the network contains any feedback loops: paths of connections in which one unit, either directly or indirectly, affects itself. If such connections exist, the unit is ultimately influenced by its own previous behavior, thus forming a functional loop. Networks that do not contain such loops are called **feedforward networks**. Feedforward networks are dynamically simple because activation propagates through the network along unidirectional chains of connections, starting at the input units and proceeding, connection by connection, to the output units. In this case, the activation of a unit changes only once, going from its initial to its final state after its inputs change. Feedforward networks are often used in connectionist research, such as Lehky and Sejnowski's (1988) study of computing surface curvature from shading information (see Section 4.3.3).

Feedback Networks. Feedback (or **recurrent**) **networks** are sets of units in which there are loops. Recurrent networks exhibit more complex temporal behavior than feedforward networks do because activation passes cyclically through the loop rather than stopping at the end of the forward chain of connections. Recurrent networks therefore tend to have interesting dynamic properties, such as settling into minimum energy states or oscillating among two or more different states. We will say more about such dynamic properties shortly. McClelland and Rumelhart's (1981) interactive activation model of letter and word recognition (see Section 9.4.3) and Marr and Poggio's (1977) first stereo algorithm (see Section 5.3.3) are good examples of re-

---

[3] The activation of a given unit can also be influenced by its own prior activation. Adaptation effects can be modeled, for example, by subtracting some proportion of a unit's prior activation from its current activation.

Such influences are usually modeled with a self-loop: a connection from the unit to itself so that the unit's prior activation becomes one of its own inputs.

current networks that reach their solutions by settling into a stable activation state over time.

Symmetric Networks. The connections within recurrent networks can be either symmetrical or asymmetrical. In a **symmetric network**, the weights between two units in the two opposite directions are the same ($w_{ji} = w_{ij}$); in asymmetric networks, they are not. Symmetry turns out to be important in determining whether activation in a recurrent network will converge to a single stable state or not. Activation in symmetric recurrent networks necessarily converges to a single stable state, whereas that in asymmetric networks may or may not converge (Hopfield, 1982). Symmetric recurrent networks are sometimes called **Hopfield nets**.

Winner-Take-All Networks. One particular form of symmetric recurrent network (or subnetwork within a large network) is worth special mention. It consists of a set of units in which all units mutually inhibit each other with the same negative weight. This symmetrical mutual inhibition causes a particular behavior in which the single unit with the highest activation eventually comes to dominate that of all the other units, whose activations drop to a minimum level. Such sets of units are called **winner-take-all (WTA) networks** because their dynamic behavior is that the most active unit (the "winner") eventually has all the activation ("takes all").

To see why this happens, consider just two units that inhibit each other. For simplicity, we will assume that both units receive constant input from other units while they interact. Whichever unit has more initial activation necessarily inhibits the other more than it is inhibited by the other. This leads to its having a greater advantage in activation after the initial cycle of inhibition. This advantage again leads to its inhibiting the other unit more than it is inhibited, further increasing its prior advantage. And so it goes until a stable state is reached in which the initially more active unit reaches a relative maximum in activation and the initially less active one reaches a relative minimum in activation. McClelland and Rumelhart's (1981) interactive activation model employs WTA networks at both the letter and the word levels (see Section 9.4.3), Marr and Poggio's (1977) first stereo algorithm uses them to implement the opacity constraint (see Section 5.3.3), and Rumelhart, Smolensky, McClelland, and Hinton's (1986) Necker cube

model uses them to implement mutually exclusive interpretations of sensory input (see Section 6.5.1).

B.1.3 Systemic Behavior

Properly configured neural networks are capable of solving many interesting computational tasks. Among the examples that are discussed in this book are connectionist models of stereoscopic correspondence (Marr & Poggio, 1977), texture discrimination (Malik & Perona, 1990), surface curvature from shading (Lehky & Sejnowski, 1988), and letter recognition (McClelland & Rumelhart, 1981; Rumelhart & McClelland, 1982). Such networks exhibit a variety of important emergent properties that cannot be understood in terms of the behavior of individual units but clearly emerge from the behavior of the network as a whole. Several of these properties make them particularly attractive as models of visual phenomena. Interestingly, none of these features are directly built into the networks. They arise serendipitously from the ways in which the units interact as activation spreads throughout the network. In the following subsections, we discuss a few of the most important of these properties.

Graceful Degradation. When individual connections or even whole units are randomly destroyed within a densely connected network, its ability to perform its task does not immediately plummet to zero but degrades gracefully. As more connections or units are eliminated, performance decreases, but not catastrophically. This fact is consistent with current knowledge of brain function. Neurons in our brains die all the time, yet people do not suffer any noticeable loss of function unless a major trauma, such as a stroke, gunshot wound, tumor, or surgery, causes the death of large numbers of neurons in a localized region. In symbolic computational theories, however, the deletion of a single rule often has catastrophic effects on performance. It either produces bizarre errors of the sort that people seldom, if ever, make or brings the entire process to a sudden halt. This is one reason connectionist models appear preferable to symbolic ones as theories of human cognitive capabilities.

Connectionist models also tend to exhibit **graceful degradation** in the presence of random variability (noise) in their input data. If small random deviations are added to the correct input values, the resulting output is usually quite close to the correct values. Large deviations produce worse performance but in a graded manner that is qualitatively consistent with human performance under noisy stimulus conditions. Rule-based systems, in contrast, tend to break down dramatically when noise above a certain level is introduced.

Settling into a Stable State. As mentioned above, recurrent networks have interesting dynamic properties. Unlike feedforward networks, they change over time because of internal feedback loops. In theory, activation in such networks might never stop changing, continually transforming in unpredictable ways. In fact, however, many networks have a very strong tendency to settle into a single stable state (called an **attractor**) and stay there until different input values initiate further interactions. The behavior of winner-take-all networks is an example of such settling: The initial pattern of activation changes in predictable ways until the initially most active unit has the lion's share of activation and the rest have little or none. Once it is in this state, it stays there until new conditions change its inputs. It has been shown that when the connections in a recurrent network are symmetric (see above), as they are in WTA networks, activation will settle into a pattern that corresponds to a local minimum in a well-defined "energy" function (Hopfield, 1982). This energy function is a mathematically defined quantity that represents a kind of metaphorical energy rather than real physical energy.[4] Even so, the close relation between Hopfield's formulation and Gestalt ideas about the brain being a physical system that settles into minimum energy states (Wertheimer, 1924/1950) is quite remarkable (see Palmer, 1995).

Soft Constraint Satisfaction. A number of interesting problems in vision can be cast as requiring the simultaneous satisfaction of many **soft constraints**.

Soft constraints are conditions that are desirable to meet in a computational solution rather than ones that absolutely *must* be met. Depth perception in the face of multiple possibly conflicting cues is one good example. Recurrent networks have proven to be extremely useful for finding solutions to such problems. Soft constraints can be encoded in the connections between units, and the input data are represented in the inputs to the units. Activation then spreads through the recurrent network, and the connections allow the system to settle (or "relax") into the solution most compatible with the set of constraints. The connectionist model of multi-stability in the perception of a Necker cube (Rumelhart, Smolensky, McClelland, & Hinton, 1986) is a good example in this book (see Section 6.5.1). The connections between units are either mutually excitatory (when they are constrained to be part of the same coherent interpretation) or mutually inhibitory (when they are constrained to be alternative interpretations of the same sensory input). Marr and Poggio's (1977) first stereo algorithm is another example in which soft constraints are encoded in connection weights. Surface opacity constraints are encoded in the mutually inhibitory connections among units on the same line of sight, and surface continuity constraints are encoded in the mutually facilitory connections between units in the same depth plane (see Section 5.3.3). In each case, the settling of a recurrent network into a stable state finds a best-fit solution to the simultaneous soft constraints encoded in its connection weights.

Pattern Completion. Objects are often represented in connectionist models by patterns of activation over a set of several units. Typically, each unit represents a feature of some sort, so a pattern of activation represents the degree to which a given object has each of the features. Once the interdependencies of these features within known objects becomes encoded in the con-

---

[4] Hopfield (1982) defined the global energy at a given moment for a symmetric network consisting of units whose discrete activation levels are -1 and $+1$ as

$$E = -\sum_{i<j} w_{ji} s_i s_j + \sum_i \Theta_i s_i,$$

where w_{ji} is the strength of the connection between units i and j, s_i is the state of the ith unit, and Θ_i is a threshold for unit i. Hopfield's model was derived from physical systems called "spin glasses" in which spins are

either "up" or "down." They begin in random spins but settle into stable states as they "cool down." Energy is at a minimum in spin glasses when all of them are the same, either up or down. In spin glasses, the energy function that is minimized corresponds to real physical energy. In Hopfield nets, the energy function (defined here) corresponds to something like the degree to which the activations of pairs of units match the weights of the connections between them. That is, energy will be low when the sign of the weight (+ or −) between two units is the same as the sign of the product of their activations (+ or −).

nections among the units, recurrent networks can often complete known patterns on the basis of partial information. If several units from a particular well-known pattern are activated but a few are not, the activation reverberates through the network, causing the missing information to be completed in the manner most consistent with the stimulus information given. This is another example of soft constraint satisfaction operating within recurrent networks by settling into minimum energy configurations of activation.

Connectionist networks have many further properties, but these four are among the most important for models of visual processing. A crucial further feature is their ability to learn, the topic to which we now turn.

B.2 Connectionist Learning Algorithms

What enables a given connectionist network to accomplish a given computational task are the particular connections and weights that exist between units. Together, they determine the patterns of activation that arise from input information and how this activation changes over time. Given this basic fact of systemic behavior, it appears possible that a network could learn to perform a task by modifying the weights and/or connections between units. The trick—and it is by no means easy—is to devise a rule that specifies how to adjust the weights as a function of past performance so that improvement (learning) takes place. This endeavor has opened up a whole new field of modeling activities in which teachable connectionist networks have been used to generate possible theories about how the brain might accomplish difficult computational tasks. Lehky and Sejnowski's (1988) analysis of surface curvature from shading information (Section 4.3.3) is one interesting example, even though the learning rule they used is not a biologically plausible one.

B.2.1 Back Propagation

Most connectionist learning algorithms assume that the network's architecture (i.e., the connections among its units) is fixed and that learning occurs by adjusting the weights of existing connections. The increments or decrements that are made to the weights are typically small, resulting in relatively slow learning over many presentations. The primary question is how each particular

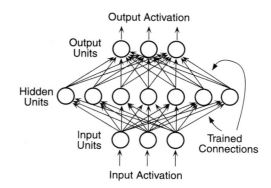

Figure B.2.1 A three-layer feedforward network. Activation flows "upward" through this network from input units to hidden units to output units. Each layer is connected to the next layer and to no other layers. The connections to and from the hidden middle layer are trained during back propagation learning by adjusting the weights of the connections to minimize error.

weight should be adjusted: up or down, and by how much? There are many different learning schemes, of which we will consider only one: **back propagation** (**BP**) (Rumelhart, Hinton, & Williams, 1986). We focus on BP not because it is biologically plausible (it is not), but because of its historical importance. The development of BP was a watershed event for connectionist learning algorithms, one that marked the beginning of the modern explosion of research into network learning. Another reason to focus of BP is that many other learning schemes bear a strong family resemblance to it.

BP learning typically operates on a simple three-layer feedforward network such as the one shown in Figure B.2.1. The input units receive activation from "outside" the network. The connection strengths from these input units then determine the pattern of activation that arises in the "hidden units" in the middle layer. This activation then spreads to the output units via the connection strengths to the output units, producing the final pattern of activation for the network as a whole. Because there are no feedback loops, the activation behavior of such networks has no interesting dynamic properties. The learning behavior of such networks is an entirely different matter, however.

One can think of such networks as transforming one representation (the pattern of activation in the input units) to another representation (the pattern of activation in the output units) via the connections to and from the hidden units. The classic task for BP learning is

Connectionist Modeling

pattern classification. In this case, the activation of input units is viewed as a representation of some predesignated set of features or dimensions for which each object has some defined set of values. For example, if the stimuli were uppercase letters, the input units might represent features such as the segments of which they are composed, as in the interactive activation model of letter recognition (see Section 9.4.3). The output units are viewed as representing the set of categories into which the input patterns are to be classified, typically (but not always) one unit for each category. In the case of uppercase letters, there would thus be 26 output units. The job of BP learning is to adjust the weights to and from the hidden middle layer in a three-layer feedforward network so that the input representation activates the output unit that corresponds to the proper category. This is by no means the only task for which BP has been used, but it is perhaps the most common.

The Delta Rule. To make the network learn to perform a classification, BP requires feedback from the correct output.[5] This is represented in an additional set of units, called **teacher units**, that stand in one-to-one correspondence with the output units. The pattern of activation in the output units is compared to the correct pattern of activation in the teacher units to derive an **error signal** (e_j) for each output unit, defined as the difference between the teacher output activation (t_j) and the actual output activation (a_j),

$$e_j = t_j - a_j. \tag{B.3}$$

This error signal for unit j is then used to determine how the weights on the connections leading to that unit should be adjusted for the current stimulus input. For a two-layer feedforward network, one method for adjusting the weight on the connection from input unit i to output unit j is the classic **delta rule** (Widrow & Hoff, 1960):

$$\Delta w_{ji} = r e_j a_i = r(t_j - a_j)a_i, \tag{B.4}$$

where Δw_{ji} is the change in the weight from input unit i to output unit j, r is a (positive) constant that reflects the rate at which learning will occur, e_j is the error signal for output unit j, and a_i is the activation value of input unit i. This is called the delta rule because the Greek letter delta (Δ) is often used in mathematics to represent a difference or change in a quantity, such as the change in weight this equation specifies.

Let us take a moment to understand why the delta rule has the desired effect. It says that if the output is too low (i.e., if the teacher unit, t_j, is more active than the corresponding output unit, a_j), so the error signal (e_j) is positive, then the change in weight from unit i to unit j (Δw_{ji}) will be positive. This makes sense because under these circumstances, the output activation needs to be increased to bring it closer to the desired value. If the output of unit j is too high (i.e., if the teacher unit, t_j, is less active than the corresponding output unit, a_j), so the error signal (e_j) is negative, then the change in weight from unit i to unit j (Δw_{ji}) will be negative. This also makes sense because decreasing the weight will decrease the activation of the output unit, thereby bringing it closer to the desired value. If there is no error for the current input pattern ($e_j = 0$), then the weights are not changed at all because there is no need to change them.

The product of the error signal (e_j) and the rate parameter (r) is multiplied by the activation of input unit i (a_i) for the current pattern to scale the weight change in proportion to unit i's contribution to the activation of output unit j. For example, if the activation of input i was zero, it could not affect the activation of j at all, and so the weight from it to unit j does not change. If the activation of unit i was high, then it could contribute a lot and therefore its weight to unit j changes proportionally to the amount of error. In effect, multiplying the error signal by the input activation is a way of differentially assigning "blame" for the error to the units that were most responsible.

This simple rule thus specifies how to change the weight between each input/output pair of units in such

---

[5] The requirement of feedback means that BP (and similar learning schemes) can model learning that takes place when the correct answer is somehow provided. It might be a parent or teacher explicitly providing the correct answer (e.g., "This is a dog"), or it might be some further environmental stimulus that allows the child to figure out the correct answer (e.g., when an animal that the child thought was a cat begins to bark).

Learning in the absence of feedback about which particular pattern of output activations is correct cannot be modeled by BP or other learning algorithms that depend on knowing the correct answer. Other types of connectionist learning schemes have been developed for such "unsupervised" learning, but they are beyond the scope of this presentation.

a way as to reduce the error signal the next time this particular stimulus is given to the system. When this rule is followed for many presentations of a given set of stimuli, the overall effect is that the network learns to perform the transformation from input representation to output representation more accurately with each additional presentation. The size of each weight adjustment depends on the value of the rate constant, r, which scales the product of the error signal and the input value to produce larger or smaller weight changes, depending on the value of r. We have presented the learning rate, r, as a simple constant, but in some learning algorithms, its value changes over time during learning. Learning can often be made more efficient by starting with a large value of r and decreasing it as learning progresses. This has the effect of making large adjustments initially and small ones later.

The Generalized Delta Rule. The delta rule was designed for two-layer feedforward networks and cannot be directly applied to networks with three or more layers. It can be used to adjust the weights from the hidden middle layer units to the output units but not to adjust those from the input units to the hidden units. The problem is that there is no rule for deriving an error signal for the hidden units akin to the error signal for the output units. Rumelhart, Hinton, and Williams (1986) derived the **generalized delta rule** that underlies BP by proposing a procedure to do just this.[6] It works, in effect, by propagating the error signal at the output units backward through the network very much as the input signal is propagated forward, but in reverse. The error at each output unit is, in effect, divided up among the hidden units in the middle layer according to a scheme for apportioning "blame." This attributed error signal at each hidden unit can then be used to adjust the weights from input units to hidden units. Because the mathematical details of the generalized delta rule are more complex than the simple delta rule, we will not describe them here. The interested reader should consult the original description by Rumelhart, Hinton, and Williams (1986).

B.2.2 Gradient Descent

The delta rule works by a method of reducing errors called gradient descent. To understand what this means and how it works, we will have to go back and explain how classifier networks accomplish their task in somewhat more detail. Rather than presenting the principles through complex equations, however, we will aim for a more intuitive understanding that can be achieved through figures and graphs. To do so, however, we must consider a much simpler network than the one in Figure B.2.1.

The network that we will examine is the two-level, three-unit feedforward network shown in Figure B.2.2A. We will interpret it as a pattern classifier network that will learn to distinguish between triangles and other simple geometric figures. The two input units represent two crucial features that bear on such a classification: Unit 1 represents whether the figure is closed (high activation) or not (low activation), and unit 2 represents whether it contains three straight lines (high activation) or not (low activation). Triangles have both features, so the output unit (3) should be highly active when both input features are activated and not otherwise, as is indicated in Figure B.2.2B. In other words, the output unit should learn to compute something akin to the logical AND of the two inputs, responding only if both are "on."

Input Vector Space. The input state of the network at any moment in time can be represented as a vector consisting of an ordered set of input values, one for each input unit of the network. In the present case, there are only two inputs, so the input vector is just an ordered pair of activation values (a_1, a_2). This input vector can be understood as the coordinates of a point in a multidimensional space—the **input vector space**—in which each dimension corresponds to the activation of a particular input unit. In the current example, the input vector space is only two-dimensional because there are only two input units. Figure B.2.3 shows the input vector space for the triangle network and indicates the locations of several different stimuli within it. Because a

---

[6] Although Rumelhart, Hinton, and Williams (1986) popularized the BP learning algorithm, formally equivalent rules were derived earlier by Werbos (1974), Parker (1985), and LeCun (1986).

Connectionist Modeling

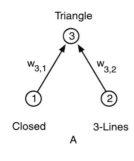

Triangle

Closed   3-Lines

A

Activation of Unit

1 (Closed)	2 (3-Lines)	3 (Triangle)
low	low	low
low	high	low
high	low	low
high	high	high

B

Figure B.2.2 A network for recognizing triangles. Part A shows a simple three-unit, two-layer feedforward network that can be used to distinguish triangles from other simple geometric figures on the basis of the features of closedness and containing three straight lines. Part B shows the desired behavior of the network, where the output unit (3) is highly active only when both input units (1 and 2) are highly active—that is, when the figure both is closed and contains three straight lines.

triangle has both features, it corresponds to a point in the upper right corner of the space. A circle lies in the lower right corner because it is closed but does not contain three straight lines. An arrow lies in the upper left corner because it contains three straight lines but is not closed, and a plus sign lies in the lower left corner because it has neither feature. In theory, any simple geometric figure maps to a point somewhere within this 2-D space, usually near one of the four corners, with all the triangles being located near the top right corner.

Partitioning the Input Vector Space. Pattern classification corresponds to partitioning (or dividing) the input vector space into a set of nonoverlapping regions, each of which corresponds to a category. Because there is a single output unit with a linear input function in the present case, the classification it can achieve is limited to dividing the input vector space into two regions along a straight-line boundary. Because the output unit should

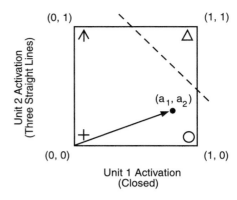

Figure B.2.3 Input vector space. Each input to a network can be defined by the ordered set (or vector) of activation values that it produces in the input units. These values define a dimensional space in which the activation of each input unit is represented by its own dimension. The input vector space shown here corresponds to the three-unit triangle network of Figure B.2.2. Each possible input is represented by a point (a_1, a_2) defined by the activation that it produces in the two input units. The locations of four stimuli (triangle, circle, arrow, and plus) within this space are illustrated. The dashed line indicates a possible partition into triangles versus nontriangles.

be "on" when both input units are highly active, the partition should occur along the dashed line running diagonally across the input vector space. Any patterns that fall in the upper right region are classified as triangles, and any patterns that fall into the rest of the space are classified as nontriangles. This partition will be accomplished by establishing a threshold for the activation of the output (triangle-detecting) unit. Values above the threshold will represent the presence of a triangle, and values below it will represent a nontriangle.

State Space. The state of the entire network can be captured by a single point in a **state space** in which there is a dimension for the activation level of every unit in the network. (The input vector space is a subspace of the state space because it represents only activation of the input units.) Figure B.2.4 shows the 3-D state space for the current three-unit network. Any given network with a particular set of connection weights can occupy only a subset of the positions in this space, however, because for each point in the input vector space (see Figure B.2.3), there is just one activation level in the output unit. Which activation the output unit will have for each input vector depends on the specific weights from input units to the output unit. If we fix the weights

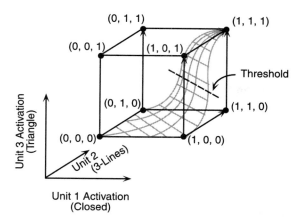

Figure B.2.4 State space. The state of an entire network can be represented by a space in which the activation of each unit is represented by a corresponding dimension. This illustration shows the 3-D state space for the three-unit triangle network of Figure B.2.2, defined by the activations of units 1, 2, and 3. When the connection weights have fixed values, this network can occupy only positions on a single surface within this space. The surface shown here corresponds to the states of the network when the two connections both have weights of +1.

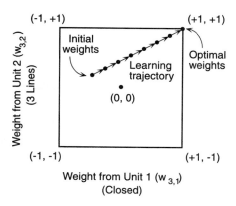

Figure B.2.5 Weight space. The set of possible weights in a network can be represented by a dimensional space in which each weight corresponds to a single dimension. Each point in weight space thus represents a particular setting of all the weights. The 2-D space illustrated shows the weight space for the three-unit (two-connection) triangle network shown in Figure B.2.2. Learning by incremental weight adjustment then corresponds to a trajectory of points in weight space leading from the point corresponding to the initial weight settings to the point corresponding to the final (and, it is hoped, optimal) weight settings.

at some particular values and plot the output level for each possible input vector, the result will be a surface within the state space. These are the only positions of the state space a given network can occupy with its particular set of weights. Figure B.2.4 shows the surface that would result from weights of +1 on both connections by the grid of gray lines. The S-shaped curvature of this surface results from the S-shaped activation function shown in Figure B.1.2.

Notice that this particular surface achieves the desired relation between inputs and output: Output activation is high only when both input units have high activation. Notice also that if we define a threshold on the activation of the output unit, as indicated by the dashed black line along the surface, that threshold can be used to partition the input space as required. Figure B.2.3 is just the projection of Figure B.2.4 onto the 2-D input vector space, as though you were looking down on Figure B.2.4 from directly above. Thus, if the weights on the two connections are both +1, yielding a surface in state space like that depicted in Figure B.2.4, and if a threshold is defined on the activation of the output unit corresponding to the dashed line in Figure B.2.4, the desired classification into triangles versus nontriangles can be achieved.

Weight Space. We have now specified the *goal* of learning within this network—namely, to arrive at a state space like the one shown in Figure B.2.4—but we have not yet begun to say how this might be *achieved*. The problem of learning within such networks is really just the question of how to adjust the weights to reach optimal performance. To understand how this might happen in the present triangle example, it will be useful to consider an entirely different graph of the network, called its **weight space**.

Thus far, the graphs we have used to represent the network have represented only one particular setting of the weights. We now want to construct a graph that will represent all possible settings of the weights. We therefore define weight space as a multidimensional space in which each dimension represents the weight on a particular connection. Because weights will vary over the range from −1 to +1, Figure B.2.5 shows the 2-D weight space for our simple two-weight network. Each possible setting of the two weights thus corresponds to a single point in this weight space. For instance, the optimal configuration of weights (+1 on both connections) is the point at the upper right corner of this weight space.

If each possible setting of weights corresponds to a single point in weight space, and if learning takes place

Connectionist Modeling

by a series of small changes in weights, then learning corresponds to a sequence of points that follows a path within weight space, as indicated in Figure B.2.5. The question of how to learn by weight adjustment can now be reformulated in terms of devising a rule that will adjust the weights to follow a path from the initial point in weight space, whatever that might be, to the optimal point for the task, which in this case is at the upper right corner of weight space. How might this be accomplished?

Weight-Error Space. The key to the answer lies in realizing that the goal of learning by weight adjustment is to reduce the system's *error* on the given task with each change in the weights. This can be conceptualized in an augmented version of weight space, called **weight-error space**, in which there is one extra dimension that represents the amount of error the system will produce for each possible setting of the weights.

Recall that error is just the difference between the correct (teacher) output values and the actual output values, as defined in Equation B.3 for a single output unit on a single input pattern. The total error for all stimuli can be computed by adding the squared errors generated by all the output units over all input patterns. If these total errors are plotted for each point in weight space, one obtains a surface in weight-error space, as depicted in Figure B.2.6. Lower points on this surface correspond to better solutions, and higher points correspond to worse solutions. The lowest point, called the **global minimum**, thus represents the best possible solution within the given network architecture. In the present example, this global minimum is located at $(+1, +1, 0)$ in the lower right corner.

Gradient Descent. The error surface provides a way to ensure that performance on the set of training examples improves with each weight adjustment: Simply adjust the weights so that the system moves as far downward on the error surface as possible. One way to accomplish this is to examine the effect of small adjustments in each direction for each weight and use the particular combination of weight changes that leads to the greatest reduction in error, as indicated by the sequence of black dots in Figure B.2.6. In terms of weight-error space, this means that from the present position along the error surface, the algorithm will change the weights

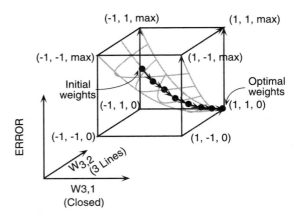

Figure B.2.6 Weight-error space. The accuracy of different possible settings of a network's weights can be represented in an augmented version of weight space in which the error of the system at each possible weight setting (from the restricted range of -1 to $+1$) forms an additional dimension. The error values define an error surface that has a global minimum at the lowest error value. The space illustrated is for the triangle network of Figure B.2.2, which has its lowest error (i.e., best performance) when both weights are set at $+1$.

to produce the steepest descent along the error surface. This method is called **gradient descent**. The delta rule (Equation B.4) and the generalized delta rule are both gradient descent methods. They are guaranteed to follow a path down the error surface until any further weight adjustment produces an increase in error rather than a decrease, at which point they stop. Notice that Figure B.2.5 is just the projection of Figure B.2.6 onto the two dimensions of weight space, as though one were viewing Figure B.2.6 from directly above.

Local versus Global Minima. The particular set of final weights achieved by gradient descent may indeed be the desired global minimum, but it might only be a **local minimum**: the lowest point in the immediate vicinity but at a higher error level than the global minimum for the entire error surface (much like a valley high in the mountains). Figure B.2.7 shows a one-dimensional weight-error space in which learning from an initial state at point A leads to a local minimum at point B. Note that if the initial state had been at point C, gradient descent would have reached the global minimum at point D. Finding the global minimum rather than some merely local minimum is a significant theoretical problem for gradient descent methods, such as

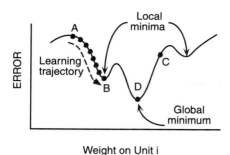

Figure B.2.7 Local versus global minima. Back propagation is guaranteed to find a local minimum on the error surface but not necessarily the global minimum. This graph shows an error surface with two local minima as well as a global minimum.

the delta rule and the generalized delta rule. They are guaranteed to find a local minimum, but the global minimum may well elude them (unless there are no local minima in the error surface, as is the case in Figure B.2.6). This is generally viewed as a weakness of gradient descent learning rules, but only as optimal models of learning. Indeed, if people get stuck in the same sorts of local minima as the learning rule does, then it can be considered a strength of the rule as a model of human learning because it accurately reflects human performance.

Learning by back propagation in connectionist networks is by no means limited either to simple feed-forward networks or to pattern classification tasks. We have used this example because it is simple enough to understand and because it is a representative task. In principle, any network with any architecture can learn to improve its performance at a given task by back propagation, as long as the network gets accurate error signals from the teacher units. The problem of local minima means that it might not achieve the best possible performance within its given architecture, but it is guaranteed to improve its performance unless it happens to start at a local or global minimum. A variety of different learning schemes have been developed to help solve the problem of local minima, but these are beyond the scope of this presentation. Interested readers should consult Haykin (1994) for an up-to-date discussion of connectionist learning algorithms.

We have seen that connectionist networks have many intriguing properties as models of human perception and cognition. Several of the models described in this book are specified in an explicitly connectionist framework, and many of the others could be. Perhaps because of their brainlike structure, they lend themselves well to capturing the kind of approximate yet powerful computational abilities that the visual system needs to deal with the underconstrained problem of interpreting visual input and the heuristics needed to do so. Future research will no doubt reveal more about the capabilities and limitations of such models in achieving the astounding levels of performance of which the human visual system is capable.

Connectionist Modeling

Suggestions for Further Reading

General Texts

Anderson, J. (1995). *An introduction to neural networks*. Cambridge, MA: MIT Press. This volume is a basic textbook at an introductory level.

Bishop, C. (1995). *Neural networks for pattern recognition*. Oxford, England: Clarendon Press. This book is a more advanced treatment of connectionist networks with an emphasis on solving pattern recognition problems.

Caudhill, M. (1992). *Understanding neural networks: Computer explorations*. Cambridge, MA: MIT Press. This work, comprising a textbook and workbook, includes neural net software for both PCs and Macintosh computers.

Psychological Applications

Hummel, J. E., & Biederman, I. (1992). Dynamic binding in a neural network for shape recognition. *Psychological Review, 99,* 480–517. This paper describes a connectionist model of Biederman's recognition by components theory of visual classification into entry-level categories and includes a detailed proposal about how temporal synchrony of neural firing could solve the binding problem.

McClelland, J. L., Rumelhart, D. E., & the PDP Research Group (1986). *Parallel distributed processing: Explorations in the microstructure of cognition. Vol. 2: Psychological and biological models.* Cambridge, MA: MIT Press.

Rumelhart, D. E., McClelland, J. L., & the PDP Research Group (1986). *Parallel distributed processing: Explorations in the microstructure of cognition. Vol. 1: Foundations.* Cambridge MA: MIT Press. The publication of these two volumes launched the great resurgence of interest in connectionist models of cognitive phenomena. Volume 1 covers a broad range of basic issues. Volume 2 describes applications in many diverse fields.

APPENDIX

Color Technology

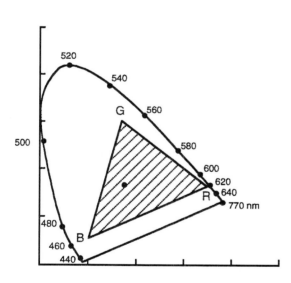

Nature exhibits an enormous variety of colors, from the azure blue of a clear sky to the deep red of a rose petal. Modern technology provides nearly as extensive a palette for human artifacts. Just think for a moment of the wide range of man-made colors that we encounter every day in our clothing, interior decor, books, magazines, paintings, photographs, movies, television, computer displays, and so forth. Although we seldom consider how such colors are produced, sophisticated chromatic engineering techniques are usually at work behind the scenes. In this appendix we will consider some basic facts about color technologies and find out how they relate to human color perception as described in Chapter 3.

The dawn of color technology occurred before recorded history when primitive people used simple dyes and paints to draw pictures of important objects and events on cave walls. Indeed, paints and dyes formed the basis of color technology for most of human existence. It was only very recently, on a global time scale, that radically different techniques—such as color printing, photography, and television—have become available. These technologies have dramatically increased our ability to create (and recreate) colored objects and images.

Much of color technology is directed at accurately reproducing the colors of existing objects. The goal is to create something that people perceive as having the same color as the object depicted—that is, to create a **metamer** of the object's natural color (see Section 3.2.1), or at least a reasonable approximation of it. Happily, one does not need to reproduce the exact spectrum of light reflected from the target object to create the perception of its color in human observers. The reason is that people have (at most) three kinds of color-sensitive receptors, and as discussed in Section 3.2.1, any colored light can be matched with some mixture of three appropriately chosen lights. This is true in a formal rather than a practical sense, however, because highly saturated colors can be matched only by using the "negative colors" trick (see Section 3.2.1). This trick cannot be played in the technology of color reproduction because the color of the target object is fixed and unchangeable. But supposing that one can get away without having to reproduce all of the most saturated colors, human trichromacy implies that acceptable color reproduction can be achieved with just three appropriately chosen primary colors. What these primaries are and how they can be combined to form different colors depends critically on whether the color mixture process is *additive* or *subtractive*.

C.1 Additive versus Subtractive Color Mixture

All forms of color technology are based on the ability to create a multitude of different colors by combining a reasonably small set of basic colors. How these colors combine, however, depends on the physics of the situation. The two basic forms of color mixture are called "additive" and "subtractive" because the main difference lies in whether mixing a second color causes wavelengths of light to be added to or subtracted from those of the first color. The results can be dramatically different, as we shall see.

Perhaps the easiest way to demonstrate the difference between additive and subtractive color mixture is to consider the two situations depicted in Color Plate C.1. In part A, two identical spotlights are directed at a screen so that their beams overlap. (We will assume for simplicity that both spotlights produce light containing the same number of photons at all visible wavelengths.) Before hitting the screen, one beam goes through a blue

gel (or filter) that mainly passes light in the short- and medium-wavelength regions, absorbing light mainly in the long-wavelength end of the spectrum. The other beam goes through a yellow gel that mainly passes light in the medium- and long-wavelength regions, absorbing light mainly in the short-wavelength end of the spectrum. If only beam A is on, the spot on the screen looks blue; if only beam B is on, it looks yellow. The question is: What happens in the region of overlap where both lights are present? In this situation, the photons coming through the blue filter are added to the photons coming through the yellow filter, so their combination contains nearly equal amounts of light at all wavelengths. As a result, the overlapping region on the screen looks essentially white, as illustrated on the left side of Color Plate C.1A. This "blue + yellow = white" phenomenon is an example of additive color mixture.

Now suppose that we change the situation by combining the gels in what seems like only a slightly different way. Instead of superimposing the *light* after it has passed through the colored gels, as in Color Plate C.1A, we can superimpose the *gels* in the paths of the beams of light, as in part B. We know that the blue gel passes mainly light in the short and medium wavelengths. Of this reduced spectrum, the yellow gel absorbs most of the short-wavelength light, thus passing primarily light in the medium wavelengths, the long-wavelength light having already been removed by the blue gel. Thus, the light transmitted through both filters lies mainly in the medium wavelength region and therefore looks green. This "blue + yellow = green" phenomenon is an example of subtractive color mixture. Comparing the two beams in Color Plate C.1B shows that the result of superimposing gels does not depend on their order. Placing the blue gel before the yellow one (beam C) produces results identical to those of placing the yellow gel before the blue one (beam D).

Notice that the same apparatus (two lights and two kinds of filters) were used to produce both the additive combination of a white spot and the subtractive combination of a green spot. The critical issue is therefore not the apparatus, but whether what is being "mixed" or "combined" is the *light* (i.e., the photons at different wavelengths), as in the additive situation of Part A, or the *filters* (i.e., the pigments), as in the subtractive situation of Part B. This basic distinction holds for all forms of color technology, although the details differ from case

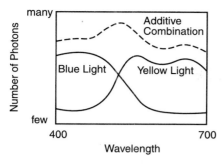

A. ADDITIVE COLOR MIXTURE

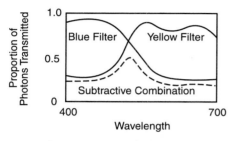

B. SUBTRACTIVE COLOR MIXTURE

Figure C.1.1 Combining physical spectra in additive versus subtractive color mixture. Additive mixture of lights (A) produces a combined spectrum that is the *sum* of the component light spectra. Subtractive mixture of pigments (B) produces a combined spectrum that is the *product* of the component transmission spectra.

to case and are seldom as pure and simple as in this example.

C.1.1 Adding versus Multiplying Spectra

To understand what is happening in additive versus subtractive color mixture more precisely, let us consider this example in terms of the relevant physical spectra. The solid curves in Figure C.1.1A show the spectra for the light coming through the blue gel alone and that coming through the yellow gel alone. When these lights are combined by superimposing them on the screen, their combination is literally additive: It is the simple sum of the photons from both beams. Notice that the additive combination (the dashed curve) is brighter than either component alone and that its spectral shape is such that the sum is nearly uniform across wavelengths. The highest value in the middle wavelengths is less than 20% higher than the lowest value. This is why the additive mixture of this particular blue and yellow appears essentially white (i.e., neutral in hue).

The solid curves in Figure C.1.1B show the **transmission spectra** of the blue and yellow gels alone. Transmission spectra are graphs of the proportion of photons that pass through an optical filter for each wavelength of light. (These spectra have the same shape as the light spectra in Figure C.1.1A because we assumed that the light from the spotlights was perfectly uniform across wavelengths.) When the gels are combined by superimposing them, light must get through both filters, so there will be less of it than came through either filter alone. The mathematical rule for determining the combination of two color filters, when expressed as fractions or probabilities, is simple multiplication. To understand why, consider what happens if half the photons at some wavelength get through the blue gel and half of the remaining photons at that wavelength get through the yellow gel. When the two gels are superimposed, only one quarter of the initial number of photons will pass through both filters (i.e., $0.5 \times 0.5 = 0.25$). Notice that, in contrast to the additive combination of lights, when the blue and yellow filters are superimposed, the transmission spectrum of the combined filter passes twice as many photons in the middle wavelengths as in the high or low wavelengths. White light passing through both filters therefore appears green.

C.1.2 Maxwell's Color Triangle

The basic facts about additive mixture of lights were known by the mid-1800s from Maxwell's (1855) systematic experiments. He was able to match an enormous number of colors by mixing just three "primary" lights: orangish red (at 700 nm, the upper end of the spectrum), bluish violet (at 436 nm, the lower end of the spectrum), and an intermediate green (at 546 nm). He was able to summarize the results of these experiments within a color mixture space known as **Maxwell's triangle**. As Figure C.1.2 shows, the vertices of Maxwell's triangle represent the three primary colors that he used, and each point within the triangle represents a color that he could match by some mixture of these three primaries. Colors are then represented in terms of their triangular coordinates with respect to the vertices: The proportion of light of each primary in its mixture corresponds to the proximity of its point relative to each vertex of the triangle. White lies at the center, for example, because it contains equal amounts of the orange-red, green, and blue-violet primaries. The complements

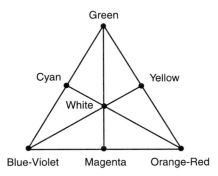

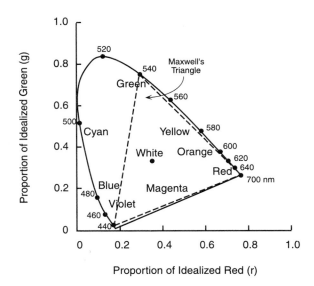

Figure C.1.2 Maxwell's triangle. Maxwell's results about light mixture can be predicted from this diagram. The vertices of the equilateral triangle are the three primaries, their complements are located on the opposite side, and their various mixtures lie along straight lines between them. All colors within the triangle can therefore be created by mixtures of the three primaries.

Figure C.1.3 The C.I.E. chromaticity diagram. Colored lights are represented by two coordinates that specify the proportion of an idealized red and the proportion of an idealized green in a given light. Pure (monochromatic) spectral colors from the rainbow lie along the outer contour where wavelengths from 440 to 700 nm are shown as points. The approximate locations of color experiences are indicated by English color names. All experiences of color lie within the solid curve. The dashed figure shows Maxwell's triangle embedded in the C.I.E. diagram.

of the primaries—cyan (bluish green), magenta (purplish red), and yellow—lie opposite them along the straight line passing through white and the corresponding primary. As we will see, both the three primaries at the vertices and their complements on the opposite side figure prominently in color technologies.

The most important fact about Maxwell's triangle as a representation of color is that the mixture of any two lights on or within its perimeter lies along the straight line connecting the corresponding pair of points. This property is not actually true in other color spaces, as we pretended it was in Section 3.2.1, but it is true in Maxwellian color space and its close relative, C.I.E. color space.

C.1.3 C.I.E. Color Space

Maxwell's triangle provides an elegant representation of how lights combine additively, but it has certain practical limitations, especially as an easily usable standard for color mixture. First, it cannot represent all colors that people can experience because many highly saturated colors lie outside the triangle (see Section 3.2.1). Most monochromatic lights (e.g., in a rainbow) cannot be formed by mixing Maxwell's primaries, except by using the negative colors trick described in Section 3.2.1. Second, triangular coordinates are much harder to use than standard Cartesian (x, y) coordinates.

In an attempt to solve these and other problems, the International Commission on Illumination (Commission

Internationale de l'Eclairage, or C.I.E.) defined a standardized system for representing the color and mixture of lights that is widely used in color research and technology. Figure C.1.3 shows the **C.I.E. chromaticity diagram** defined according to these standards. It solves the first problem with Maxwell's triangle by using idealized primaries that lie outside actual color experience. This allows all actually experienced colors to be represented as a mixture of positive amounts of these imaginary primary lights, which we will call idealized red (R_i), idealized green (G_i), and idealized blue (B_i). It solves the second problem by representing colored lights as the proportions of these idealized primaries relative to the total amount of light. By convention, the x axis represents the proportion of idealized red (i.e., $r = R_i/(R_i + G_i + B_i)$), and the y axis represents the proportion of idealized green (i.e., $g = G_i/(R_i + G_i + B_i)$). Because the C.I.E. coordinates are proportions of the primaries and because all lights in this system are composed of just these three primaries, the three proportions must sum to 1. This means that if one knows the proportion of idealized red (r) and the proportion of idealized green (g), the proportion of idealized blue (b) is simply $1 - (r + g)$. White light, for example, has C.I.E. coordinates (0.33, 0.33) because it is an equal mixture of the three idealized primaries. All real colors lie within the boundary of the solid curve shown in Figure C.1.3. Beyond it lie "imaginary" colors, including the idealized primaries.

Notice that the C.I.E. chromaticity diagram is only two-dimensional. This is convenient for representing chromaticity diagrams on a flat page, but it obviously fails to represent some aspects of human color experience. As the reader may have already realized, C.I.E. space captures the dimensions of hue and saturation but not overall brightness. This is because C.I.E. coordinates are defined as proportions of light rather than absolute amounts. As a result, white and all shades of gray map onto the same neutral point in the C.I.E. diagram: (0.33, 0.33). Many browns will also map to the same points as yellows and oranges, because browns are just dark versions of yellows and oranges. If brightness were added to the C.I.E. diagram, it would come out of the plane of the page. The C.I.E. color space is therefore akin to a flattened version of the color space that we discussed in Section 3.1.2, in which the brightness dimension has been collapsed by projecting all colors onto the color circle.

It is instructive to ask why the C.I.E. chromaticity curve is not circular, like the color circle in Color Plate 3.3. Its particular shape arises because of the constraint that all mixtures of any pair of lights must lie along the straight line between them. It has one flat side because the most saturated purples can be created only by mixing the shortest (violet) and longest (orange-red) wavelengths visible to the eye, and all mixtures of any two lights are constrained to lie along the straight line connecting them. These nonspectral purples therefore define the straight boundary of the C.I.E. curve.

C.1.4 Subtractive Color Mixture Space?

Given that additive color mixture can be specified within simple, elegant models of color experience like Maxwell's triangle and C.I.E. color space, is there any corresponding system for specifying subtractive color mixture? Unfortunately, the answer is "no" for reasons that can be demonstrated by a simple experiment.

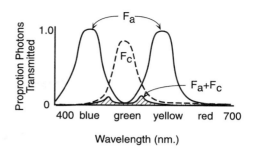

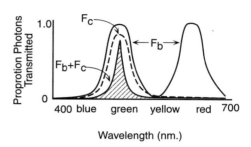

Figure C.1.4 Subtractive mixture of "metameric" filters. When full-spectrum white light is passed through two filters, F_a and F_b, they produce the same color experience of white light. When a third filter, F_c, is superimposed on each of the other two, the combinations are quite different. This demonstrates why subtractive color mixture cannot be predicted within psychological color spaces.

One of the key facts that makes it possible to formulate laws of additive light mixture in terms of a psychological color space is that we do not have to worry about physical differences between metamers. If two lights, L_a and L_b, have different physical spectra but look identical to us, then adding a third light, L_c, to either of them will always produce the same color experience. That is, if $C(L_a) = C(L_b)$, then $C(L_a + L_c) = C(L_b + L_c)$, where $C(L)$ denotes the color of light L and = denotes perceptual equivalence. This property of metameric invariance means that the effects of adding two lights can be predicted entirely within psychological color space without any reference to their physical spectra.

The same is not true of subtractive color mixture, however. Suppose we take three filters and perform the same kind of "metameric" experiment by superimposing them in the same beam of light. Figure C.1.4 shows the transmission spectra of the filters we will use. Filters F_a and F_b are "metameric matches" in the sense that full-spectrum white light looks identical after it has passed through each alone, even though the luminance spectra of these lights are different because the transmission spectra of the filters are different. As Figure C.1.4 shows, filter F_a passes light about equally in two wavelength regions of the spectrum: blue and yellow. The light coming through this filter will appear white (uncolored) because blue and yellow are complementary colors, and equal amounts of light of complementary colors add to make white light. Filter F_b passes light about equally in the red and green wavelength regions. This light will also appear white because red and green are complementary colors too. Therefore, even though F_a and F_b have quite different physical effects on white light passing through them, they produce the same visible result.

Notice that the perceptual equivalence of these two filters will not hold for all illuminating lights, because the light that passes through the filter depends on an interaction between the wavelengths present in the illuminating light and those passed by the filter. For instance, a light whose spectrum is strongly peaked in the middle (green) or long (red) wavelengths will not pass through F_a, which filters out energy in these regions of the spectrum, but it will pass through F_b, which transmits them. This is why two filters cannot be called "metameric" except with respect to specified illumination conditions.

Now let's perform the crucial experiment to determine whether superimposing filters depends on their physical spectra or only on their perceptual results after transmitting an illuminating light. We superimpose on each of these two filters a third filter, F_c, that passes light only in the green region of the spectrum and see what happens. Figure C.1.4 illustrates the result in the shaded spectra. When F_a and F_c are superimposed, virtually *no* light gets through the pair because F_a has already removed all the light in the green region where F_c transmits light. (Remember that when we superimpose filters, we must multiply corresponding values of their transmission spectra to find the spectrum of the result.) When F_b and F_c are superimposed, however, light in the green region passes through both largely intact, so we see their mixture as moderately bright and green. Therefore, these two "metameric" filters in this particular light have very different effects when added to the same third filter. This means that in predicting the subtractive mixture of filters (or dyes, paints, inks, or any subtractive medium), the precise spectral characteristics of the com-

ponents can matter a great deal, and the effect of the combination cannot be predicted solely within any psychological color space.

Now that we understand at least some of the differences between additive and subtractive color mixture, we can consider several different forms of color technology. Some (such as color television) are fundamentally additive, others (such as color photography) are fundamentally subtractive, and still others (such as color printing and painting) can be used to take advantage of either form of color mixture (or both), depending on how they are carried out.

C.2 Color Television

All televisions produce their picture by scanning an electron beam across the face of the screen. The beam's position is controlled by magnetic fields that bend the trajectories of the negatively charged particles in the beam as they pass through it. By rapidly changing the strength of the field in just the right ways, the beam scans across the entire screen 30 times per second. It starts at the top left, scans rightward across a row, and then moves down and left to the next row while the beam is off (Figure C.2.1). After it reaches the bottom right corner, it returns to the top left position and begins again. The beam moves in this zigzag pattern so rapidly that we perceive the image it creates as being presented instantaneously and continuously (see Section 10.1.3).

The beam actually produces the image on the screen by colliding with **phosphors**, substances that emit elec-

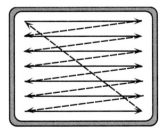

Figure C.2.1 The scan path for TV and video displays. An electron bean scans rightward across the screen (solid lines), changing intensity as it moves. At the end of each row, it is turned off (dashed lines) and repositioned at the left end of the next row. When it reaches the lower right corner, it is turned off and repositioned at the left end of the top row.

tromagnetic energy in the visible spectrum when excited by absorbing an electron from the beam. The amount of light the phosphors emit depends on the intensity of the beam; the greater the number of electrons per second, the brighter the light emitted by the phosphor. The color of the light the phosphors emit depends on their physical nature.

To produce a black-and-white image using this technology, the intensity of a single electron beam is modulated (i.e., increased and decreased) very rapidly to create different levels of gray at each pixel, at the same time as the strength of the magnetic field is modulated to change the beam's position on the screen from one pixel to the next. If these two events are properly coordinated, the result is a coherent picture on the screen composed of about 480 horizontal lines whose brightness varies across the screen in roughly the same way as the scene it depicts.

When electrons strike the screen of a black-and-white TV, photons are emitted by a mixture of two different phosphors: a blue one and a yellow one. There is only one electron gun, however, whose beam strikes both phosphors equally. The result is the additive combination of the two lights, which is a slightly bluish white. (See Color Plate C.2 for a simulation of this effect.) Darker shades of gray and black are produced by decreasing the intensity of the beam, and lighter shades of gray and white are produced by increasing the intensity of the beam.

Color TVs produce chromatic light by using three guns whose electron beams strike three different phosphors with different intensities. The phosphors emit light that we see as particular shades of orange-red, green, and blue-violet. Their various additive combinations cover the interior of the triangle defined by these primaries in C.I.E. color space, as illustrated in Figure C.2.2. (These primaries are actually quite similar to those in Maxwell's triangle, as can be seen by comparing Figure C.2.2 with Figure C.1.3.) The electron guns are often called "red," "green," and "blue" (or simply "R," "G," and "B"), but the beams that they emit are not actually colored at all. They produce different colors only by virtue of the kind of phosphor they strike on the screen. This means that to accomplish their desired effect, the "red" gun must strike only red phosphors, the "green" gun only green phosphors, and the "blue" gun

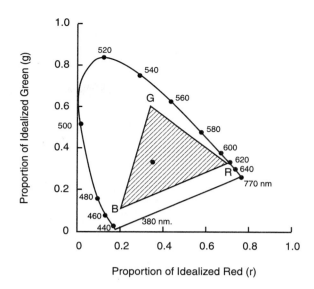

Figure C.2.2 The approximate location of color television phosphors in C.I.E. color space. Lights emitted by three common phosphors in color TVs (europium yttrium vanadate (R), zinc cadmium sulphide (G), and zinc sulphide (B)) are shown in the C.I.E. chromaticity diagram. Their various additive mixtures fill the triangle they define.

only blue phosphors. This is accomplished by a mask or grill that aligns the beams precisely with the regions of the screen that contain the appropriate phosphors. One such arrangement is shown in Figure C.2.3A. Many newer TVs use thin vertical stripes of phosphors, as illustrated in Figure C.2.3B. Proper alignment must be maintained among the position of the three guns, the holes in the mask, and the mosaic of phosphors on the screen to ensure that each gun strikes only the appropriate region of the screen.

This description of the physical situation does not square very well with our perceptions of TV pictures, however, in that we do not perceive a mosaic of little patches of red, green, and blue when we look at a color TV screen under normal viewing conditions. The reason, as we mentioned in Section 3.2.1, is that the dots are too small and too close together for the human visual system to resolve at normal viewing distances. If you get close enough to a stable TV picture or use a magnifying glass, you will actually be able to see the tiny colored dots or stripes. When the visual system cannot resolve the dots of light, they have much the same effect as a physically superimposed mixture of the three corre-

Color Technology

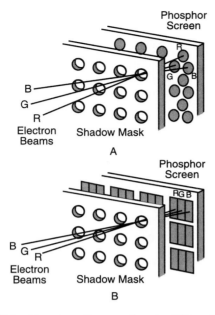

Figure C.2.3 Phosphor alignment in color TV and video displays. The three electron guns (R, G, and B) produce electron beams that excite corresponding red, green, and blue phosphors on the screen. A shadow mask is used to ensure that the guns strike only the proper phosphors. Parts A and B show different spatial arrangements of phosphors and guns.

sponding lights. The seemingly endless variety of colors that you perceive in TV images therefore results from the laws of additive color mixture that were discussed in Section 3.2.1.

C.3 Paints and Dyes

Paints reflect and absorb different amounts of light at different wavelengths because of the presence of millions of tiny colored particles, called pigments, that are suspended in their liquid medium. A variety of different liquids can be used (water, oil, latex, etc.), and the pigments come from a wide variety of sources. The earliest pigments were prepared by grinding colored minerals and other natural substances into a fine powder and mixing them in a liquid medium—for example, chalk for white, charcoal for black, iron oxide for red, and copper carbonate for green. Modern pigments are largely synthetic and come in a much wider range of colors.

Regardless of the specific nature of either the pigments or the medium, the process of painting is basically the same. A surface is covered with a thin layer of the pigmented liquid, which then hardens into an opaque "skin" as it dries. The pigments in this skin then determine which wavelengths of light are reflected and absorbed, since they cover the surface below it. Dyes work in much the same way except that the pigments they contain are much smaller, usually molecules that are fully dissolved in the liquid. Dyes color materials by staining, just as cranberry juice or red wine stains most fabrics on contact. Because dyes are absorbed into the material itself and are only partly opaque, the natural color and texture of the object show through much more than they would if the object were painted.

C.3.1 Subtractive Combination of Paints

The usual method of combining paints is by physically mixing them into a uniform liquid. This is fundamentally a subtractive mixture process because it combines pigments rather than lights. When two paints are mixed together, both pigments absorb light, much as when colored gels are superimposed (see Color Plate C.1B). There are two important differences, however. One is that opaque paints reflect the unabsorbed photons instead of transmitting them as translucent gels do. The other is that when gels are superimposed, the total amount of light coming through two filters is always less than either one alone, whereas when paints are mixed, the amount of light reflected by the combination is intermediate between the components. Mixing black and white paints, for example, results in an intermediate shade of gray, rather than an even darker black.

This process can be understood in terms of the physical mixture of pigment particles suspended in liquid, as illustrated in Figure C.3.1. What determines the reflectance of paint is primarily the density of pigment particles in a given volume. Imagine mixing idealized white and black paints, each of which contains just one kind of pigment. Suppose the white paint contains 100 white pigment particles per unit of volume (call it a "microdrop") that reflect all wavelengths of light completely, and the black paint contains 100 black pigment particles per microdrop that reflect no light at all. (Such "perfect" pigments do not exist, of course, but these are only hypothetical paints.) If we mix these two paints equally, two microdrops will contain 100 white particles and 100 black particles, or 50 particles of each per

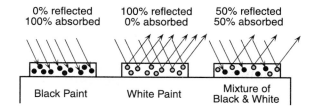

Figure C.3.1 Mixing paints is an averaging process. If idealized black paint is mixed with idealized white paint, their mixture is the average of the particle densities of the components.

microdrop. The resulting pigment densities are therefore just the arithmetic average of the component densities—that is, $(100 + 0)/2 = 50$—and they will reflect an intermediate amount of light.

Paints, dyes, and inks act as filters in the sense that they selectively reflect or transmit light at different wavelengths, removing the wavelengths that are absorbed. As mentioned above, physically different filters—and therefore physically different paints, dyes, and inks—can be considered "metameric" only with respect to certain specific lighting conditions. Pragmatically, this means that two paints, dyes, or inks that look the same in one light may look different in another light. For example, two articles of clothing that appear to be perfectly matched under the fluorescent lights of a store may look noticeably different in daylight or incandescent light. *Caveat emptor*: "Let the buyer beware!"

Another consequence of the fact that paints act as filters on light is that paints that look the same under some lighting conditions but have different reflection spectra may actually combine differently with a third paint. The situation is analogous to that for translucent gels as illustrated in Figure C.1.4. If the two paints actually contain the same pigment, they will necessarily have the same physical spectrum and will therefore mix in the same way with any other paint. But if they have different pigments, they can combine differently with other paints even if they look identical under some specific lighting condition.

C.3.2 Additive Combination of Paints

Somewhat surprisingly, there are ways of using two paints together that produce additive rather than subtractive color mixture. Instead of being mixed as liquids before they are applied to a surface, the paints must be applied separately in small regions at adjacent but non-overlapping positions. An example of this is shown in Color Plate C.2, where several areas filled with blue and yellow squares of different sizes are displayed side by side. When viewed from far enough away that the distinct regions of blue and yellow cannot be resolved by the visual system, the squares fuse perceptually, more or less as the individual blue and yellow dots in a black-and-white TV set do. The perceived color of the fusion is the one that is predicted by additive mixture (gray) instead of subtractive mixture (green). Notice that as you move farther away, the regions with larger squares begin to lose their checkerboard appearance and fuse into neutral gray. In the artistic domain, this technique of producing additive color mixture by applying distinct dots of color is known as **pointillism** (pronounced "*pwan*-til-ism"). It was made famous in large part by the French impressionists, such as Paul Signac, whose painting, *The Dining Room* is shown in Color Plate C.3.

C.4 Color Photography

Color photography of all sorts is a subtractive color technology. In color slides, movies, and prints, the color is produced by passing white light through a series of layers of partially transparent gelatine, each of which contains pigments of a particular color, before it strikes a white surface. The layers of gelatine act as filters, removing light selectively at different wavelengths so that initially white light ends up colored. In color movies or slides, the colored gelatine filters are placed close to the white light source (the projector bulb) and far from the white surface (the screen), as illustrated in Figure C.4.1A. This is exactly analogous to superimposing colored gels on spotlights, as described above and illustrated in Color Plate C.1. In color prints, however, the colored gelatine filters are located far from the light source (the sun or artificial lighting) and adjacent to the white surface (the paper on which it is printed), as illustrated in Figure C.4.1B. This situation is similar, except that the light now passes through each translucent layer twice rather than once.

Color prints are made in a complex two-stage process that will be easier to understand if we first describe the corresponding process in black-and-white photography. The first step in making a black-and-white print consists

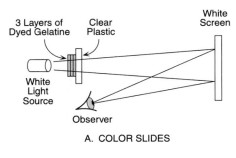

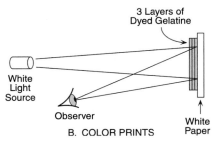

Figure C.4.1 Viewing color slides versus color prints. In color slides (A), the three layers of dyed gelatine are close to the light source and far from the white screen. In color prints (B), the three layers of dyed gelatine are attached to the white backing paper and are far from the light source.

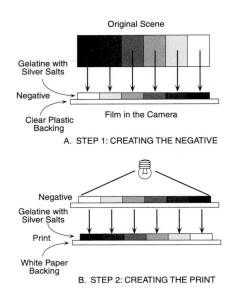

Figure C.4.2 The two-step process of making a black-and-white photographic print. After the scene is photographed, the exposed film is processed to create a negative image of the scene. This negative is then turned into a positive image by producing the negative of the negative. (See text for details.)

of making a **photographic negative**. Light from the scene enters the camera and is focused on the flat surface of the film, where it exposes a thin layer of gelatine on the surface of the film. The gelatine contains silver salts that are sensitive to light. When these salts are exposed to light in the camera and are later treated with a chemical developer, they turn black. The unexposed silver salts in regions where little or no light exposed the film are washed away by a chemical fixer. The net result of exposing, developing, and fixing the film is that the exposed areas of the film are dark to varying degrees and the unexposed areas are clear to varying degrees, as illustrated in Figure C.4.2A. Film that is processed in this way is called a *negative* because the degree of transparency of regions of the developed film is the "negative" of the luminance of the corresponding regions of the scene: White regions are black (fully opaque) on the negative, black regions are clear, and gray regions are translucent to intermediate degrees.

In the second stage of making a black-and-white print, an enlarger is used to create a positive print from the negative film. As illustrated in Figure C.4.2B, light shines through the negative onto a sheet of white paper

that is covered by another layer of gelatine containing light-sensitive silver salts. Exposure to this light, followed by chemical processing similar to that for negatives, produces dark silver grains in the gelatine layer of the print paper. Because the light was passed through the negative image of the scene, however, this process now produces the negative of the negative image, which is the positive image of the initial scene. Black regions in the negative (corresponding to white regions in the scene) produce clear regions in the gelatine, which therefore allow white light to be reflected from the paper into the observer's eye. Clear regions in the negative (corresponding to black regions in the scene) produce black regions in the gelatine layer, which do not allow white light to be reflected into the eye.

Color prints are produced by a similar two-stage process, except that there are now *three* layers of gelatine, each of which is sensitive to different wavelengths of light. In the early days of color photography and in some current professional applications, the three layers are actually three separate pieces of film. Advances in the technology of color photography allow all three layers to be present on a single piece of film, called an **integral tripack**. How such film produces a color print of a pattern consisting of black, white, red, green, blue, and yellow stripes is illustrated in Color Plate C.4. Each of the three layers of light-sensitive gelatine in the tripack works like its black-and-white counterpart, except that instead of being sensitive to all wavelengths of light, one layer is selectively sensitive to short wavelengths (blue), another to medium wavelengths (green), and the third to long wavelengths (red). Making the positive print still requires the intermediate stage of producing the negative film, but in this case the color of the negative is the complement of the positive: Blue sky is yellow on the negative, green grass is magenta (purplish red), and a red apple is cyan (bluish green). The "primitive" colors of subtractive technology are cyan, magenta, and yellow because these are the result of removing the additive primitives of red, green, and blue from white light, that is, white − red = cyan, white − green = magenta, and white − blue = yellow, as illustrated in Color Plate C.4A.

The positive print is then made by passing full-spectrum white light through this negative film onto the printing paper, which is also covered with three layers of gelatine containing substances that are sensitive to the same three bands of wavelength: short (blue), medium (green), and long (red), as illustrated in Color Plate C.4B. After exposure and chemical processing, particles of yellow, magenta, and cyan appear in the corresponding layers of gelatine. Thus, each layer on the white paper creates the negative version of its corresponding layer in the color negative. Then, when white light from the printing paper is transmitted through this second set of pigmented layers, it creates the negative of the negative image—that is, the positive image—thus converting the sky back to blue, the grass to green, and the apple to red. The details of this conversion are not intuitively obvious, but the important thing is that it works!

Although standard color prints require a negative image to be produced in an initial stage, the same is not true of color slides, color movies, and "instant" prints. They are still based on subtractive color mixture and still require three layers of gelatine sensitive to different wavelengths of light, but the dyes in the layers are different, and result in positive images after a single stage of photographic processing. There are various methods for accomplishing this, and they differ for different forms of one-stage color photography.

C.5 Color Printing

Printing color reproductions using various colored inks on paper is a complex process that can include both additive and subtractive color mixture. The printing process involves the application of pigmented translucent inks in thin layers, usually on white paper. The transparency of the inks means that when the print is viewed in white light, the light that enters your eye actually passes through the layers of ink to the paper and is reflected back through the inks again on their way to your eye, just as in color prints (see Figure C.4.1B and Color Plate C.4B). The inks thus filter the light, differentially absorbing various wavelengths as light passes through them. This means that when two colors of ink are printed on top of each other, they combine subtractively, since both inks remove some of the light. The usual primitives for color printing are therefore cyan, magenta, and yellow, although different inks can be used if only a restricted number or range of colors is required. When two inks are printed in small dots that do not overlap, however, they combine additively, just as the colored dots on your color TV screen do.

Because the layers of ink are of uniform thickness and have uniform densities of pigment, the amount of each color is varied by applying it in a pattern of tiny dots. The intensity of the given color is then determined by the density of these ink dots. In high-quality color reproductions, the dots are far too small to be seen when viewed normally with the unaided eye but are clearly visible with a good magnifying glass. In crude color printing, such as comic strips in the Sunday paper, you can see the dots with the naked eye if you just look closely.

Color prints are sometimes made with black ink in addition to three colored ones. With cyan, magenta, and yellow inks, black is made by overlaying all three. This works, but it is expensive and produces blacks that are seldom as dark as can be achieved by using black ink. Printing black separately with a single black ink thus produces "better" blacks and more detailed shadows as well as economizing on the more expensive colored inks. Very high-quality color reproductions, such as those found in expensive art and photography books, often use even more than four inks to increase the range of highly saturated colors that can be recreated.

You can now appreciate how fundamentally all forms of color technology depend on the basic physiological and psychological mechanisms of color vision. The ubiquity of highly saturated hues of red, green, and blue as the primitives for additive color technology is determined by the absorption spectra of the long-, medium-, and short-wavelength receptors in the human eye. The use of cyan, magenta, and yellow for subtractive color technology is determined by their complementary relation to red, green, and blue. The way in which red, green, and blue are combined to create a broad spectrum of colors within the psychological color space depends on the laws of color mixture, which are based on the existence of metamers. Thus, color technology is finely tuned to match the physiological mechanisms of human color vision.

Suggestions for Further Reading

Kaiser, P. K., & Boynton, R. M. (1996). *Human color vision*. Washington, DC: Optical Society of America. This is the classic reference to human color vision, including detailed references to various color spaces.

Rossotti, H. (1983). *Colour: Why the world isn't grey*. Princeton, NJ: Princeton University Press. This book is a general presentation of the physics of light and the perception of color intended for a nontechnical audience.

Glossary

Note: All words in italics are defined elsewhere in this glossary.

Absolute depth information is *information* about the distance to objects in which the source determines the actual distance from the observer to the object rather than just its distance relative to other objects.

Absolute threshold is a measurement of the least intense stimulus an observer can reliably detect under a given set of conditions.

Absorption spectrum of a substance is the percentage of *light* that it absorbs for each wavelength within the *visible spectrum* (see Figure 3.2.13).

Accommodation is the process by which the optical properties of the *lens* of an eye can be altered by temporarily changing its shape using the *ciliary muscles*.

Accretion/deletion of texture is a source of *depth information* provided by a textured surface moving behind another surface. The appearing/disappearing texture belongs to the farther surface, and the occluding *edge* belongs to the closer surface.

Achromatic colors are *colors* of zero *saturation* that lie along the central axis of *color space*: white, black, and all intermediate grays.

Achromatopsia, is a neurological syndrome in which patients report not being able to see *colors*, as though they were looking at the world on a black-and-white TV, or that *colors* have lost their vividness.

Action potentials (or **nerve impulses** or **spikes**) are all-or-none differences in electrical potential that are propagated along the *axon* of a *neuron*.

Activation (see *activation level*).

Activation assumption is the hypothesis that *consciousness* is associated with the firing of *neurons* or neuronlike entities.

Activation level is the parameter in a *connectionist network* that characterizes the state of a single *neuron*-like *unit*, corresponding to the *firing rate* of a *neuron*.

Adaptation is the process of becoming less sensitive to a given type of stimulation because of prolonged exposure to that stimulation.

Aerial (or **atmospheric**) **perspective** is a systematic decrease in the contrast and increase in short-wavelength light (bluish color) that occurs when objects are viewed from greater distances, as when looking at mountains from afar (see Color Plate 5.1).

Afferent theory (or **input theory** or **feedback theory**) of *position constancy* proposes that after the brain signals the eye to move to a particular position, sensors in the eye muscles register *information* about muscular tension, which is then sent to the brain to provide feedback about the actual position of the eye (see Figure 7.4.4).

Affordances are functions of an object that an observer can perceive directly from its visible structure (e.g., whether it affords grasping by the observer's hand or sitting-upon by the observer's body) rather than indirectly by categorizing it.

Aftereffect is the visual result of any stimulus presentation once that stimulus has been removed, including *adaptation* and *afterimages*.

Afterimage is the visual persistence of a retinal *image* after the stimulus is gone because of either intense or prolonged stimulation with constant eye *fixation* (see Color Plate 2.1).

AI (see *artificial intelligence*).

Alberti's window is an artistic device for recreating a realistic depiction of depth in a drawing of a scene by viewing it through a pane of glass with one eye at a fixed position and then tracing all the contours directly onto the glass (see Figure 5.5.2).

Algorithm is a well-defined procedure for performing a computation: a program.

Algorithmic level of an *information processing* system specifies how a computation is accomplished in terms of *representations* and *processes*, independent of their physical embodiment.

Alignment with 2-D views is a theoretical approach to object *identification* in which an incoming *image* is matched to internally stored 2-D views by aligning it with a combination of those views.

Alignment with 3-D models is a theoretical approach to object *identification* in which an incoming *image* is matched to internal 3-D models by finding the optimal alignment that brings the *image* into correspondence with a *perspective projection* of the model.

Alternation rate of *apparent motion* is the speed at which a pair of static *images* are interchanged.

Amacrine cells are *neurons* in the *retina* that indirectly connect *bipolar cells* to *ganglion cells*.

Ambient optic array (**AOA**) is the convergence of *light* on a single *viewpoint* from all directions. It contains all the optical *information* available about the environment at that position.

Ambiguous figures are single *images* that can give rise to two or more distinct perceptual interpretations (see Figure 1.1.5).

Ames room is a greatly distorted room that produces the illusion of a normal, rectangular room from just one particular *viewpoint* (see Figure 5.5.32).

Amnesia is a profound reduction in a person's ability to remember because of organic brain damage.

Amodal completion (see *visual completion*).

Amplitude (or **contrast**) of a *sinusoidal grating* is the difference in *luminance* between its lightest and darkest regions, specified as a percentage of the maximum possible difference (see Figure 4.2.1).

Amplitude spectrum (see *power spectrum*).

Analog/propositional debate is a controversy about whether *visual images* are picturelike (analog) representations or languagelike (propositional) representations of visual *information*.

Anatomy is the biological study of the physical structure of organisms.

Anchor points are a small set of salient positions on an object (such as points of *maximum concavity*) that are used to bring it into alignment with an internal *representation* by a spatial *transformation* (such as *translation*, *rotation*, and *dilation*).

Anchoring heuristic of *lightness* perception assumes that the region of highest *luminance* is white and that all other regions are scaled relative to it.

Anomalous trichromacy (see *color weakness*).

Anorthoscopic perception is a phenomenon of spatio-temporal integration in which an object seen passing behind a thin slit is perceived as an integral whole, even though it is never registered on the retina at one time (see Figure 10.2.21).

Anterograde amnesia is a form of *amnesia* in which the patient has difficulty remembering new *information* that occurred after the brain damage.

AOA (see *ambient optic array*).

Aperture color (or **film color**) is the filmy quality of *color experiences* when lights or surfaces are viewed through a *reduction tube*.

Aperture problem is the difficulty posed by local ambiguity in the direction and speed of *motion* whenever the stimulus that is visible within a restricted region (the aperture) lacks *unique points* whose correspondences can be unambiguously determined.

Apparent distance theory of the *moon illusion* is that the horizon moon looks larger than the zenith moon because observers perceive the horizon moon to be farther away (see Figure 7.1.8).

Apparent motion (or **stroboscopic motion**) is the *illusion* of *motion* that results from rapid presentation of purely static *images* that show the same perceived object in different positions.

Apparent rotation is a form of *apparent motion* in which the observer sees a continuous change in *orientation* in a rapidly presented series of purely static *images* in which the same perceived object is shown discretely at different *orientations*.

Apperceptive agnosia is a neurological condition in which there appears to be damage to the later stages of sensory processing, such that patients are unable to recognize objects because they do not see them normally.

Aqueous humor is the clear liquid in the cavity behind the *cornea*.

Architecture of a neural or *connectionist network* is the pattern of *connections* among *units* within the *network*.

Arcs (see *connections*).

Articulatory loop is the *slave memory* system for verbal *information* in phonemic form within Baddeley and Hitch's theory of *working memory*.

Artificial intelligence (**AI**) is the branch of computer science that is concerned with how computers can be programmed to simulate intelligent behavior. *Computer vision* is a subbranch of AI.

Aspect graphs are *representations* of objects containing all topologically distinct 2-D views (or aspects) of the same object in a single *network*, where each aspect is represented by a graph of the set of *edges* and *vertices* in the projected *image* (see Figure 9.3.9).

Aspect ratio is the ratio of width to length of shapes, such that shapes that are about equal in length and width have an aspect ratio near 1.0; long, thin shapes have aspect ratios greater than 1.0; and short, fat shapes have an aspect ratio less than 1.0.

Associative agnosia is a neurological condition in which the patient sees normally, but the perceptions are stripped of their meaning because of the patient's inability to categorize them correctly.

Asymmetrically integral dimensions are pairs of *dimensions* in which one property can be given *selective attention* to the exclusion of the other, but the reverse is not possible.

Atomism is the theoretical view that complex perceptions are built up from elementary sensations, such as the *experience* of tiny points of *color* at particular retinal locations.

Atmospheric perspective (see *aerial perspective*).

Attention is the act of allocating mental resources selectively to some subset of *processes*, the result of which is relative facilitation of the selected *process* in speed and/or accuracy.

Attentional blink is the phenomenon in which subjects fail to report seeing a second target in a *rapid serial visual presentation* search task if it is presented within 500 ms of the onset of the first target in the same *RSVP* stream.

Attentional cuing paradigm is an experimental procedure devised by Posner for studying the costs and benefits of *selective attention*. Subjects are able to detect a stimulus more quickly when it occurs in a precued location than when it does not (see Figure 11.2.9).

Attenuator theory is a theory of auditory *attention* proposed by Treisman in which an initial phase of partial selection is based on gross physical properties and a later phase of selection is based on salience and expectancy.

Attractor is a stable state in the dynamic behavior of a *connectionist network* toward which nearby unstable states tend to gravitate.

Attribute (see *feature*).

Autokinetic effect is the perception of a stationary spot of light as moving when it is viewed for an extended period of time in total darkness.

Automatons are robots that are able to simulate some aspects of human behavior but have no *experiences* whatsoever.

Autoradiography is a technique for studying simultaneous activity in large areas of brain tissue by first injecting an animal with radioactive sugar (e.g., 2-deoxyglucose) that accumulates within active *neurons* and then making a photographic *image* of the pattern of radioactivity (see Figure 2.2.10).

Autostereograms (or **magic-eye stereograms**) are computer-generated *images* that produce compelling *illusions* of stereoscopic depth when viewed with the appropriate misconvergence of the eyes (see Figure 5.3.12).

Awareness is the *experience* of one's own mental states and *processes*: what it feels like to be you.

Axis of a coordinate system is a line that defines a reference *orientation*.

Axon is a long, thin projection of a *neuron* along which *action potentials* are propagated to other *neurons*, often over a considerable distance.

Back propagation (**BP**) is a learning *algorithm* for *connectionist networks* that enables them to program themselves to perform well-defined tasks by automatic adjustment of *connection weights*.

Backward masking is interference in perceiving a target object because of the subsequent presentation of a different stimulus (the mask) that reduces performance in seeing the target.

Balint's syndrome is a neurological condition in which the patient is unable to see anything except a single, fixated visual object.

Ballistic movement is a movement that cannot be altered once it has been initiated, such as a *saccade*.

Bar detectors (see *line detectors*).

Barberpole illusion is the *illusion* that the stripes on a rotating barberpole are moving vertically up the pole rather than rotating laterally around it (see Figure 10.1.14A).

Basic color terms are linguistic descriptors of *color* in a given language that are single lexical items, have primary color reference, are not object-specific, and are frequently used. (In English they are red, green, blue, yellow, black, white, gray, orange, purple, brown, and pink.)

Basic level categories are *categories* at a privileged intermediate level in the *categorical hierarchy* (below *superordinate categories* and above *subordinate categories*) as defined by Rosch's criteria.

Basis functions are sets of orthogonal *vectors* in a *dimensional* space that fully span the space.

Behaviorism (see *methodological behaviorism* and/or *philosophical behaviorism*).

Best-fit decision rule (see *maximum decision rule*).

Beta (β) is a parameter in *signal detection theory* that reflects the observer's *criterion* for making a "yes" decision.

Beta motion is a form of *apparent motion* in which the alternation between two lights is experienced as a single light moving continuously back and forth from one position to the other (Figure 10.1.6C).

Binding is a *process* by which different *features* detected by the visual system are associated together in the perception of a single, unified object.

Binocular cells are *neurons* in the visual system that receive input from both eyes.

Binocular depth information is *depth information* that requires both eyes.

Binocular disparity is the relative lateral displacement of the *images* of the same environmental object in the left and right eyes (see Figure 5.3.1).

Binocular rivalry (or **binocular suppression**) is a *process* by which grossly mismatched *images* in the two eyes result in the observer experiencing only one of them at a time.

Binocular suppression (see *binocular rivalry*).

Bipolar cells are *neurons* in the retina that form the second major layer between the *receptors* and *ganglion cells*.

Blind spot (or **optic disk**) is the region of the *retina* in which there are no *receptors* because the *axons* of the *ganglion cells* exit the eye into the *optic nerve*.

Blindsight is the name given to residual visual capability in people who have no visual *experiences* because of damage to *primary visual cortex* resulting from disease, surgery, or stroke.

Blob regions are subregions within layers 2 and 3 in each *hypercolumn* of *V1*, defined anatomically by the fact that they are rich in the enzyme *cytochrome oxidase* (see Figure 4.4.2, in which the dark spots are the blobs).

Blocks world is a greatly restricted visual environment for which early computer vision programs were written, consisting of simple, uniformly colored geometrical solids on a flat tabletop, like a child's set of blocks.

Bottom-up processing (or **data-driven processing**) is the direction of *processes* that take a "lower-level" (more peripheral or sensory) *representation* as *input information* and create or modify a "higher-level" (more central or cognitive) *representation* as *output information*.

Boundary rule is a procedure used in *parsing* objects into *parts* by applying a set of criteria that specify where boundaries between *parts* are located, such as at *deep concavities*.

Boundary tracing is a primitive of Ullman's *visual routines* that is used to determine whether two locations are on the boundary of the same object.

Bounded activation (or **"coloring"**) is a primitive of Ullman's *visual routines* used to find the interior of a region by spreading activation within the boundaries of a *topographic representation* of the *image*.

BP (see *back propagation*).

Brightness is the vertical dimension of *color space* for *lights* (as opposed to surfaces).

British Empiricism was an influential school of philosophy—whose members included Locke, Berkeley, and Hume—noted for promoting the *empiricist* view that perceptions are determined by learning through interaction with the world.

Canonical perspective is the "best," most easily identified view of an object (see Figures 9.2.4 and 9.2.5).

Capacity is the amount of perceptual resources that is available for a given task or *process*. Capacity can vary with factors such as alertness, motivation, and time of day.

Cartesian dualism (see *substance dualism*).

Cast shadow is a darker region on the surface of a given object that is caused by another object blocking *light* that would otherwise fall on the given object (see Figure 5.5.30).

Cataract is a medical condition in which the *lens* of an eye becomes cloudy or opaque, leading to partial or complete blindness.

Catch trials are test intervals in a perceptual experiment on which no stimulus is presented to assess the strength of a response bias toward saying "yes."

Categorization (or **classification**) is the *process* of interpreting objects as being members of known types to allow observers to respond to them in appropriate ways via *informa-*

tion stored in memory from previous experiences with similar objects.

Categorical hierarchy is the nested structure of embedded inclusion relations among *categories* viewed as sets of objects (e.g., collies are dogs and dogs are animals).

Category is a collection of objects that are alike in some important way.

Category-based stage is the set of *representations* and *processes* involved in inferring the functional properties of objects from their intrinsic physical properties via *categorization*.

Cell body is the part of a cell that contains the nucleus and cellular machinery. In *neurons*, the membrane around the cell body integrates the electrical signals arriving from all the *dendrites*.

Center/surround organization of a cell in the visual system is a rotationally symmetric *receptive field* in which the central region and outer annulus are antagonistic in whether they respond to light by *excitation* or *inhibition* (see Figure 4.1.2).

Central executive is a complex *process* that controls cognitive strategies and the order of nonautomatic *information processing* in all kinds of cognitive and perceptual tasks.

Cerebral hemispheres are the two approximately symmetrical halves of the *cortex* of the brain.

Ceteris paribus rules are systematic principles that can predict the outcome of some *process* (such as *perceptual grouping* or *figure/ground organization*) with certainty only when everything else is equal; that is, when there is no other factor influencing the outcome.

Change blindness is a phenomenon in which observers fail to perceive quite obvious changes from one presentation to the next if they are separated by a transient event, such as a blank interval, an eye movement, or a mudsplash (see Figure 11.2.5).

Chroma (see *saturation*).

Chromatic adaptation is a temporary reduction in the visual system's sensitivity to perceiving a particular *color* immediately following prolonged exposure to *light* perceived as that *color* (see Color Plate 3.8).

Chromatic color constancy is the ability of an observer to perceive the invariant properties of a surface's *reflectance spectrum* despite changes in *illumination* and viewing conditions.

C.I.E. chromaticity diagram is a *color space* in which *colors* are defined by the amounts of three idealized primary lights—idealized red, blue, and green—that are needed to produce them (see Figure C.1.3).

Ciliary muscles are the muscles that control the shape of the *lens* by exerting force via attachment to its edge.

Classification (see *categorization*).

Clobbering heuristic is the tendency of an observer to perceive an incoming object as heavier than a stationary one in a collision event when the stationary one moves off with high velocity ("gets clobbered").

Closure is a principle of *perceptual grouping* that states that, all else being equal, elements that form a closed region are more likely to be grouped together (see Figure 6.1.2J).

Codes are internal *representations* in *structural information theory* that describe how to generate the figures they represent.

Coding theory (see *structural information theory*).

Cognitive constraints are influences on perception that are caused by high-level goals, plans, and expectations of the perceiving organism.

Cognitive reference points are salient standards around which concepts are organized and encoded in memory, such as *focal colors* in color *categories*.

Cognitive science is the scientific study of knowledge (including perception, attention, memory, language, decision, reasoning, and thought) using interdisciplinary techniques from biology, psychology, computer science, linguistics, cognitive anthropology, philosophy, and related fields.

Color is the visual experience arising from the distribution of *light* intensity across the *visible spectrum* of *electromagnetic energy*.

Color afterimage is an *aftereffect* of viewing highly *saturated colors* for a prolonged period of time. Each *color* produces its *complementary color* in the *afterimage* (see Color Plate 2.1).

Color anomia is a neurological syndrome in which patients are unable to produce appropriate linguistic labels for *colors*.

Color blindness is a dysfunction of *color* vision in which *color space* contains fewer than three dimensions.

Color circle is a two-dimensional slice through *color space* that includes the *colors* of maximum *saturation* around the edge (see Color Plate 3.3).

Color constancy is the ability to perceive the *reflectance spectrum* of surfaces despite changes in *illumination* and other viewing conditions.

Color opponent cells are *neurons* that are *excited* and *inhibited* by opposed pairs of primaries: red versus green and blue versus yellow (see Figure 3.2.14).

Color scission (or **color splitting**) is a phenomenon in which *image colors* in the region of translucent surfaces are perceived as the combination of two other colors, one belonging to the farther opaque surface and the other to the nearer translucent surface (see Figure 6.4.14).

Color solid (or **color spindle**) is a geometrical model of the complete set of *colors* that people with normal color vision can experience within *color space*. It looks rather like a lopsided child's top (see Color Plate 3.2).

Color space is a spatial model or *representation* of color *experiences* in which the dimensions are *hue*, *saturation*, and *lightness* (or *brightness*) (see Color Plate 3.2).

Color spindle (see *color solid*).

Color splitting (see *color scission*).

Color triangles are two-dimensional slices through *color space* that contain all colors of the same *hue*, regardless of *saturation* or *lightness* (see Color Plate 3.4).

Color weakness (or **anomalous trichromacy**) is a visual condition in which an observer is less sensitive to certain chromatic differences because of pigments in the *cones* that are slightly different from those of normal *trichromats*.

"Coloring" (see *bounded activation*).

Combinatorial explosion is the enormous increase in the number of alternatives that occurs when one considers all the possible combinations of multiple independent factors.

Combinatorial structure is the set of alternatives that are derived by orthogonally combining all possible values of each factor with all possible values of every other factor.

Command theory of position constancy (see *efferent copy theory*).

Common fate is a principle of *perceptual grouping* that states that, all else being equal, elements that move together are more likely to be grouped together (see Figure 6.1.2F).

Common motion component of *configural motion* is a *vector* component that is shared by the *motion* of all objects in a perceived group.

Common region is a principle of *perceptual grouping* that states that, all else being equal, elements that are located within the same bounded region are more likely to be grouped together (see Figure 6.1.6).

Compact coding is a scheme for recoding the output of the *receptor* array so that the number of units needed to represent the *image* is minimized (see Figure 4.3.23A).

Competition in *connectionist networks* arises when two *units* are connected by mutually inhibitory *connections* such that increased *activation* in one tends to decrease *activation* in the other, and vice versa.

Complementary colors are *colors* located on opposite sides of the *color circle*.

Complex cells are the most common type of *neuron* in *striate cortex*. They have elongated *receptive fields* that are nonlinear, sensitive to *motion*, and less sensitive to position than *simple cells*.

Component cells are cells in visual *cortex* that respond to the *motion* of component *sinusoidal gratings* in a moving plaid stimulus rather than to the *motion* of the whole pattern.

Composite color categories are categories defined from two adjacent *primary color categories* by the *fuzzy union* (the OR operation of *fuzzy logic*) (see Figure 3.4.4).

Computational level of an *information processing* system specifies the informational constraints that map *input information* to *output information*, thus defining the computation and its informational basis without specifying how it is accomplished.

Computer graphics is the branch of computer science that investigates how to render *images* on a computer display screen to depict scenes of objects, usually by modeling the optical process of *image* formation.

Computer metaphor is an analogy in which the brain is likened to a computer and the mind to a program that runs on the brain. It is often expressed as the analogy "mind:brain::program:computer."

Computer tomography (**CT**) is a brain imaging technique in which X-rays that are directed through the brain and measured on the other side are used to reconstruct the 3-D structure of the brain with the aid of powerful computer *algorithms*.

Computer vision is the branch of computer science that investigates how computers can be programmed to interpret optical *images* to extract *information* about the environmental objects and events that produced to them.

Concave discontinuities are places where a surface, edge, or line is not smooth but angles sharply inward toward the interior of the object (see Figure 6.2.6).

Concave discontinuity rule is a procedure for *parsing* objects into *parts* at abrupt changes in surface orientation toward the interior of the object (i.e., *concave discontinuities*).

Concave orientation edges are *edges* of an object where its surfaces meet at an interior angle greater than 180°.

Conceptual short-term memory (**CSTM**) is the brief retention of meaningful information extracted from a visual scene that can be disrupted by *conceptual masking* if another scene is presented within about 500 msec.

Conceptual masking is the reduction in memory performance for a meaningful picture that is produced by the subsequent presentation of another meaningful picture within about 500 ms of the onset of the previous picture, usually using the *rapid serial visual presentation* (*RSVP*) method.

Conclusions are logically certain statements derived by rules of *deductive inference* from *premises*.

Cones are three types of short, thick, cone-shaped *photoreceptors* that are responsible for the perception of *color*. They are heavily concentrated in the center of the *retina* (the *fovea*), but some are found throughout the periphery (see Figures 1.3.8 and 1.3.9).

Configural dimensions are pairs of properties—usually parts rather than features—that combine to produce a new, *emergent property*, such as symmetry or closure.

Configural motion is the *perceptual organization* of two or more moving objects into a group with a *common motion component* of the whole group and *relative motion components* of the individual objects with respect to the group.

Configural orientation effects are certain types of contextual influences demonstrating that perception of local spatial *orientation* is influenced by more global orientational structure.

Configuration is a perceived entity that contains several elements whose spatial relations to each other are perceived as structured and systematic, often giving rise to *emergent properties*.

Configural superiority effect is a phenomenon in which subjects are better able to perceive single elements when they are presented as part of *configurations* that produce *emergent properties* than when they are presented alone.

Conjugate eye movements are movements in which both eyes travel in the same direction, as in saccades and pursuit eye movements in the frontal plane.

Connection weights are the strengths of *links* between *units* in a *connectionist network* that can be positive (*excitatory*) or negative (*inhibitory*) to different degrees, much as the strength of *synapses* can vary in neural circuitry.

Connectionist networks (or **neural networks**) are massively parallel models consisting of many densely interconnected computing *units* (or *elements*), each of which works like a simplified *neuron* whose state is characterized by an *activation level* (like the firing rate of a *neuron*) that is spread throughout the network by *connections* that are either *excitatory* or *inhibitory* (like the *synapses* between *neurons*) (see Figure 2.2.4).

Connections (or **links** or **arcs**) are the linkages between *units* in a *connectionist network* that allow *activation* to be passed from one *unit* to another.

Consciousness is the *experience* of one's own mental states and *processes*: what it feels like to be you.

Conservative response strategy in *signal detection theory* corresponds to setting a high *criterion* for saying "yes," leading the observer to a *response bias* toward saying "no."

Constructivism is a theory of perception based on Helmholtz's idea that the visual system performs a kind of *unconscious inference*, using the retinal *image* plus a set of *heuristic assumptions* to reach *conclusions* about the most likely state of affairs in the world.

Contextual effects are changes in performance of a task due to the (logically irrelevant) spatial structure surrounding the target object.

Continuity (see *good continuation*).

Contour is a boundary of a region. Normally it is an *edge* that is assigned to the region on one side or the other, depending on factors influencing *figure/ground organization*.

Contour cells are *neurons* in area *V2* of visual *cortex* that respond to both *luminance edges* and *illusory contours* (see Figures 6.4.12 and 6.4.13).

Contralateral is a description of the relative location of two referenced objects or events that are on opposite sides of the brain's plane of symmetry (e.g., the left visual field is contralateral to the right hemisphere).

Contrast between two adjacent regions is their relative *luminance* levels.

Contrast sensitivity function (**CSF**) is the standard measurement of how sensitive observers are to *sinusoidal gratings* at different *spatial frequencies* (see Figure 4.2.5B).

Convergence is the angle through which the two eyes are turned inward (toward each other) to fixate an object (see Figure 5.2.2).

Convergence of parallels (see *linear perspective*).

Convex orientation edges are *edges* of an object whose surfaces meet at an interior angle less than 180°.

Convolution is a mathematical *transformation* in which a *filter* (or *operator*) is combined with an *image* by a sequence of multiplications and summations (see Figure 4.3.2).

Cooperation in a *connectionist network* arises when two units are connected by mutually *excitatory* links such that increased *activation* in one *unit* tends to increase *activation* in the other, and vice versa.

Coordinate system is a formal structure that allows each point in an *n*-dimensional space to be represented as an ordered set of *n* numbers, called its *coordinates* (see Figure 8.1.5).

Coordinates of a point in an *n*-dimensional space are an ordered set of *n* numbers, each of which represents its position along one spatial dimension.

Cornea is a transparent bulge on the front of the eye that bends *light* inward to help focus it in a clear *image* on the *retina*.

Corollary discharge is the hypothetical copy of a brain command to move the eyes. It is believed to be sent to brain centers that compensate for eye movements, according to the *efferent copy theory* of *position constancy*.

Corpus callosum is a large tract of axons connecting the two *cerebral hemispheres* (see Figure 13.2.1).

Correct rejections are negative ("no") responses on *noise trials* in a *signal detection* experiment.

Correlated variation condition in a Garnerian *classification* task requires subjects to classify the stimuli according to the value on just one dimension, while the other dimension varies in a correlated fashion (see Figure 11.2.18).

Correspondence problem (of stereopsis) is the task of determining which *features* in the left retinal *image* arise from the same environmental location as which *features* in the right retinal *image*.

Correspondence problem (of apparent motion) is the task of determining which objects in one frame of *apparent motion* should be mapped to which objects in the next frame.

Corresponding positions on the two *retinae* are positions that would coincide if the two *foveae* were superimposed by simple lateral displacement.

Cortical magnification factor is the proportional enlargement of the central area of vision (around the *fovea*) in the *topographic map* of *striate cortex* (see Figure 1.3.15).

Cortex is the evolutionarily most recent part of the brain. In humans, it is the largest brain structure, consisting of the highly convoluted layers of cells that surrounds the top and sides of the rest of the brain.

Criterion for a *decision* is the value of a variable at or above which one alternative is selected and below which the other alternative is selected.

Critical period is a developmental interval during which an organism undergoes rapid development when exposed to the right sort of environmental stimulation.

Crossed disparity is the outward direction of *binocular disparity* that occurs when a given object is closer than the fixated object (see Figure 5.3.2).

CSF (see *contrast sensitivity function*).

CT scan (see *computer tomography*).

Cultural relativism (or the **Sapir-Whorf hypothesis**) is the hypothesis that each culture (and language) imposes its own idiosyncratic structure on an individual's perceptual *experiences*.

Cyclopian eye is a metaphorical, phenomenological eye midway between an observer's two physical eyes from which a unitary view of the world is available after *stereopsis*.

Cytochrome oxidase is an enzyme concentrated in some cortical *neurons* that enables anatomical differentiation of regions. In *V1*, differences in its levels defines the *blob regions* versus interblob regions.

d′ (pronounced **"d-prime"**) is the parameter in *signal detection theory* that reflects the sensitivity of the sensory system to the studied stimulus dimension.

Da Vinci stereopsis is a source of *binocular depth information* arising from the *viewing geometry* adjacent to an occluding depth edge. The portion of the surface that appears in only one *image* is always farther than the surface that appears in both eyes (see Figure 5.3.23).

Dark adaptation is the *process* of becoming less sensitive to the dark (that is, more sensitive to *light*) because of a prolonged period of being in the dark.

Data-driven processing (see *bottom-up processing*).

Decision process is an *operation* that attempts to select the "best" among two or more alternatives according to a set of well-defined criteria.

Decomposable system (or **modular system**) is a system in which the interactions between components are negligible in comparison to those within components, enabling the components to function largely as independent subsystems.

Deductive inference is a form of *logical inference* in which conclusions are certain as long as its *premises* are true.

Deep concavity is a point at which a contour undergoes a sharp bend toward the interior of the region.

Deep concavity rule specifies a procedure for *parsing* objects that divides a surface where its surface is maximally curved inward (concave), even if these curves are smooth and continuous (see Figure 7.6.8A).

Default value is the particular value of a *feature* that is assumed to be true in the absence of information.

Delay-and-compare theories of *motion* detection compare what happens in one region of the *retina* with what happened shortly before in a nearby area, using some form of time delay mechanism to perform the comparison (see Figure 10.1.18).

Deletion of texture (see *accretion/deletion of texture*).

Delta rule is a learning rule for two-layer *feedforward networks* that specifies how to adjust the *connection weights* between input and output *units* to improve performance on a given task.

Dendrites are thin protrusions from the *cell body* of a *neuron* that collect chemical signals from other *neurons* at *synapses* and convert them into electrical activity along the thin membrane that encloses the cell.

Depth is the radial distance from an observer to a surface of an object in the 3-D environment.

Depth edges are changes in *luminance* between two regions of an *image* that result from a spatial discontinuity between the corresponding two environmental surfaces (see Figure 5.5.16).

Derived color categories are *categories* formed from *primary color categories* by the operation of *fuzzy intersection* (see Figure 3.4.3).

Deuteranopia is a form of red-green *color blindness* that is caused by the absence of the medium-wavelength *cone* pigment.

Dichromats are partially *color blind* people who can match any color with some mixture of just two (rather than three) others. They fail to experience differences either between red and green or between blue and yellow (see Color Plate 3.6).

Dictionary units are internal *representations* of meaningful words and sounds in Treisman's *attenuator theory* of auditory *attention* that are activated by sensory *information* during the *process* of *identification*.

Difference threshold (or **just noticeable difference** or **jnd**) is the measure of the smallest difference along some dimension that an observer can detect between two stimuli.

Diffuse illumination is a lighting condition in which *light* radiates from a spatially extended region of space, such as the *light* of the sun filtered through the clouds on an overcast day (see Figure 1.2.1B).

Dilation is a geometrical *transformation* of size scaling (expansion or contraction) in which every point of an *image* is mapped to one whose new coordinates relative to the center of expansion are multiplied by a constant (the scaling factor).

Dimension is a *feature* or *attribute* of an object that can take on a continuous range of values, such as length, *lightness*, or *orientation*.

Diplopia is the experience of seeing double *images* because of unresolved *binocular disparity*.

Dipole statistics of a binary *image* are the probabilities that for a randomly chosen pair of points, both are black, both white, or one is black and one white for each possible distance between and orientation of the two points.

Direct perception is Gibson's claim that visual perception of the environment is fully specified by the *optical information* that is available at the *retina* of a moving, actively exploring organism without mediating inferential *processes* or internal *representations*.

Disconjugate eye movements are movements in which the two eyes travel in different directions, toward each other or away from each other, as in *vergence eye movements*.

Discriminability is a measure of the ease with which observers can tell the difference between two or more stimuli, often measured by d'.

Discrimination task is an experimental procedure in which subjects are shown two stimuli and required to indicate whether they are the same or different.

Dishabituation is a phenomenon in which an organism whose response to a given stimulus has previously been *habituated* produces an increased response to a different stimulus.

Display-board model is a conception of *short-term memory* as an activated state of *information* in *long-term memory* rather than as a separate box in a flow diagram.

Distal mode is a strategy for perceiving in which the properties of the environmental object, or *distal stimulus*, dominate those of the *image*, or *proximal stimulus*.

Distal stimulus is the scene in the external world that emits or reflects *light*, thus beginning the causal chain of events that results in vision.

Distortion hypothesis is the claim, due to Loftus, that postevent misinformation becomes inextricably integrated into the original memory for the event, irreversibly altering it.

Distractors (or **foils**) are test items in a *recognition memory task* that were not initially presented.

Distributed attention is a mode or strategy of visual *processing* without *spatial selection* that occurs when subjects are prepared for targets anywhere in the visual field.

Dorsal is the cranial direction toward the top of the head.

Double opponent cells are cells in visual *cortex* that have a spatially opponent *center/surround organization* as well as a chromatically opponent structure (see Figure 3.2.24).

Dual coding is Paivio's theory of memory that assumes the existence of two separate storage systems in *long-term memory*: one for verbal/linguistic *information* and the other for visual/imagistic *information*.

Dual process theory is Hurvich and Jameson's two-stage theory of *color* perception that there is an initial *trichromatic* stage whose outputs are recombined into a second *opponent process* stage (see Figure 3.2.12).

Dualism is a philosophical position on the *mind-body problem* that is based on the idea that mind and body are two completely different kinds of entities.

Dynamic binding (see *binding*).

Dynamic depth information is *information* about the distance to an object that depends on changes over time as the observer and/or the objects move relative to each other.

Ecological optics is Gibson's theory that the *informational* basis of *visual perception* is the dynamic structure of ambient *light* that is *reflected* into the eye from surfaces as an active organism explores its environment.

Ecological validity is the degree to which the conditions of perceptual observation conform to the natural environment of an organism, particularly to the conditions in which its species evolved.

Ecology is the relationship between an organism and its natural environment.

Edge is a local spatial gradient in a sensory continuum, usually used as a shorthand for *luminance edge* (local changes in luminance) but also used to refer to changes in *color*, *texture*, *motion*, *binocular disparity*, etc.

Edge detectors are hypothetical neural elements that respond to the presence of a *luminance edge* in the proper *orientation*, retinal position, and polarity (light to dark or dark to light).

Edge discontinuity is an abrupt change in the direction of a contour, formally defined as a discontinuity in the first derivative of the mathematical function that describes the *edge* over space.

Edge operator is a computational scheme for integrating *luminance* values over a local region of an *image* to arrive at a single number representing the likelihood that there is a *luminance edge* at that location (see Figure 4.3.1)—that is, a computational version of an *edge detector*.

Efferent copy theory (or **output theory** or **command theory**) of *position constancy* is the proposal that whenever the brain sends an outgoing (efferent) command to move the eyes, it also sends a copy of that command to the brain centers that compute the *egocentric positions* of environmental objects (see Figure 7.4.4).

Egocentric position of an object is its location relative to the observer in terms of radial direction and distance.

Egocentric position constancy (see *position constancy*).

Eidetic imagery (or **photographic memory**) is the ability to form extremely vivid and detailed visual *experiences* from *visual long-term memory*.

Electrical brain stimulation is a technique for studying localization of function in the brain by delivering a mild electrical current via an electrode to determine what behavior or reportable *experience* it causes.

Electromagnetic energy is the form of physical energy that includes *light*. It can be characterized by the number of *photons* at each *wavelength*.

Electromagnetic spectrum is the full range of *wavelengths* of *electromagnetic energy* from extremely short (10^{-14} m) to extremely long (thousands of km).

Element aggregations are loose confederations of perceptual objects that result from *perceptual grouping* operations.

Element connectedness is a principle of *perceptual grouping* that states that, all else being equal, elements that share a common border (i.e., are connected) are more likely to be grouped together (see Figure 6.1.7).

Eliminative materialism is a form of *materialism* in which it is claimed that current folk concepts about mental states and events will eventually be dropped from scientific vocabulary as fundamentally flawed and be replaced by statements about underlying brain events.

Emergent properties are aspects of an entity that arise only at the level of some larger *configuration*, such as the *orientation* of a line composed of points, each of which has no orientation, and the conscious properties of brain states that are not present in the physical events that underlie them.

Emmert's law is a rule that states that the perceived size of a retinal *image* of constant size is proportional to its perceived distance: The farther away it appears to be, the bigger it appears to be.

Empiricism is the theoretical view that perceptions are determined by learning that accumulates knowledge through personal interactions with the world.

End-stopped cells (see *hypercomplex cells*).

Entraining effect is a form of perceived causation in which the first object in a collision does not stop moving upon contact with the second object but continues to move along with the second object (see Figure 10.4.3C).

Entry-level categories are the *categories* into which objects are initially classified.

Entry-level units are the first regions designated as *figures* (against a *ground*), which then provide the initial entry into the *part/whole hierarchy* (see Figure 6.2.7) according to Palmer and Rock's theory.

Epiphenomenalism is a kind of *dualism* that recognizes mental entities as being different in kind from physical ones yet denies that mental states play any causal role in the unfolding of physical events.

Episodic memory is a form of *long-term memory* that encodes specific knowledge about specific objects and events in a person's life history; the kind of *information* that one would find in a person's diary.

Epistemic status of something refers to how people come to know about it, rather than what it is. For example, the epistemic status of mental states in others refers to the *problem of other minds*.

Erasure (see *metacontrast masking*).

Error signal is the difference in activation between each output *unit* of a *connectionist network* and the corresponding *teacher unit* when the network is learning through *back propagation*.

ERTAS (see *extended reticular activating system*).

Excitation is an increase in the *firing rate* of *neurons* in the brain or in the *activation* of units in a *connectionist network*.

Expectation-driven processing (see *top-down processing*).

Experience is the *awareness* of one's own mental states and *processes*; what it feels like to be you.

Experience error is the false (and usually implicit) belief that the structure of perceptual *experience* is somehow directly given in the array of *light* that falls on the *retina*.

Explanatory gap refers to the lack of any adequate hypotheses about how the complex physical events involved in producing electrochemical neural activity could possibly give rise to *conscious experience*.

Extended body motion refers to any physical *motion* of an object that depends on variables other than its mass and center of gravity, such as its spatial distribution of mass, size, and *orientation* (see Figure 10.4.9).

Extended reticular-thalamic activating system (ERTAS) is a set of brain structures that Baars has suggested to be the neural substrate of his global workspace theory of *consciousness*, including the reticular activating system, the diffuse projections of the thalamus, and the *cortex* to which they project (see Figure 13.4.4).

Extinction is a neurological condition in which a patient can see single objects on either side of the visual field but will report seeing only the object on the "good side" (*ipsilateral* to the brain *lesion*) if two objects are shown simultaneously.

Extracellular recordings are single-cell recordings made from outside a *neuron* but near enough to pick up its *action potentials*.

Extraocular muscles are six small, strong muscles that control the position and movement of the eye.

Extraretinal theory of perceived heading assumes that *information* about *eye movements* is taken into account in computing heading by effectively subtracting its contribution from the *optic flow* field.

Extremal edge (or **limb**) is a kind of *depth edge* that results when a surface curves smoothly around to partly *occlude* itself (see Figure 5.5.22).

Eye fixation is either (1) the *process* of directing the eyes at a particular target object so that its *image* falls on both *foveae*, or (2) the period of time during which the eyes are immobile following the process of fixation.

Eye movement is the process of changing the direction of the eyes by rotating them in the *eye sockets*.

Eye sockets are the two nearly hemispherical holes in the skull that hold the eyes securely in position, yet allow them to be rotated via the *extraocular muscles*.

False alarms are positive ("yes") responses on *noise trials* in a *signal detection* experiment.

Familiar size is a source of *absolute depth information* arising from prior knowledge of the absolute size of an object, which allows its distance from the observer to be determined from its retinal size.

Farsightedness (see *hyperopia*).

Feature is a characteristic or property of an object or event.

Feature integration theory is a theory of *visual attention* due to Treisman that is based on the hypothesis that unitary perceptual objects are constructed by attentional acts that conjoin (or *bind*) *features* into objects (see Figure 11.2.23).

Feature lists are symbolic *representations* of objects in terms of a simple set of attributes.

Feature maps are *representations* that pair *features* with their *retinotopic* positions in the *image* (see Figures 8.2.14 and 11.2.23).

Fechner's law is the psychophysical relation between sensory experience and physical magnitude, $S = k \log(I)$, where S is the magnitude of the sensory experience, I is the physical magnitude or intensity, and k is a constant specific to the given dimension (see Figure A.4.1).

Feedback networks (or **recurrent networks**) are sets of interconnected *units* in which there are closed loops of *connections* that cause complex temporal behavior as *activation* passes cyclically through the loops.

Feedback theory of position constancy (see *afferent theory*).

Feedforward networks are sets of interconnected *units* in which *activation* propagates through the network along unidirectional chains of *connections*, starting at the input units and proceeding, *connection* by *connection*, to the output units with no feedback.

Figural goodness is an aspect of perceptual *experience* emphasized by Gestalt theorists that is best described as a composite of (at least) simplicity, order, and regularity (see Figures 8.3.1 and 8.3.2).

Figural scission is a phenomenon in which a single homogeneous region is split perceptually into two figures of the same *color* with one in front of and occluding the other along an *illusory contour* (see Figure 6.4.16).

Figure refers to an *image* region to which its contours have been assigned, producing the perception of being a "thing-like" perceptual element whose *shape* is defined by the contour (see Figure 6.3.1).

Figure/ground organization is either (1) the *process* by which contours are assigned to regions, thereby distinguishing between *figure* and *ground* or (2) the result of that *process*.

Film color (see *aperture color*).

Filters are a set of general purpose analyzers that decompose an *image* into a useful set of primitives that can be used to represent any possible *image*.

Filter theory is Broadbent's theory of auditory *attention* that proposes that selection operates early, first analyzing input to both ears for gross sensory features and then selecting one ear for further *processing* (see Figure 2.2.5).

Firing rate is the number of electrical impulses a *neuron* generates in a given amount of time (e.g., *spikes* per second), which corresponds to the strength of the integrated signal it transmits to other *neurons*.

First derivative of a *luminance function* is the change in light intensity as a function of spatial position (see Figure 4.3.4C).

First-order differential operators are *edge operators* that compute the signed difference between adjacent *pixels*, thereby computing the slope of the *luminance function* along a particular direction (see Figures 4.3.1A and 4.3.1B).

First-person knowledge (see *subjective knowledge*).

Fixation (see *eye fixation*).

Flicker fusion is the minimum rate at which a light can be flickered (turned rapidly on and off) so that it appears to be on continuously.

FLMP (see *fuzzy logical model of perception*).

Focal color is the best example (or *prototype*) of a given color *category*.

Focal point of a *lens* is the point behind the *lens* through which all *light* rays pass, forming a virtual pinhole.

Focus of optical expansion is the stationary point at the center of a pattern of enlarging *optic flow* that indicates the observer's heading, provided that the observer is also *fixating* on this point.

Focused attention is a mode of perception that occurs after *spatial selection*, once the observer has selected a single perceptual object or group for more intensive *processing*.

Foils (see *distractors*).

Forced-choice recognition is a *recognition memory task* in which subjects are presented with two or more alternative items and asked to indicate which they believe they saw before.

Form (see *shape*).

Forward masking refers to interference in perceiving a target object due to the prior presentation of a masking stimulus.

Fourier analysis is a *transformation* that maps any two-dimensional *luminance image* into the sum of a set of *sinusoidal gratings* that differ in *spatial frequency*, *orientation*, *amplitude*, and *phase* (see Figures 4.2.1 and 4.2.2).

Fourier spectrum is the *transformation* of an *image* into a numerical structure consisting of a *power spectrum* and a *phase spectrum*.

Fourier synthesis is the inverse *transformation* of *Fourier analysis*, such that an *image* can be reconstructed from the complete set of *sinusoidal gratings* into which it was analyzed (i.e., its *power spectrum* and *phase spectrum*).

Fovea is a small region in the center of the retina, about 2° of visual angle in diameter, that contains exclusively *cones* and is responsible for highest spatial acuity.

Frame of reference in visual perception is a set of standards with respect to which the properties of visual objects can be described. Its effects are particularly salient in *orientation* and *shape* perception.

Free recall is an experimental procedure in which subjects are presented with a list of items and are then asked to reproduce as many items as possible in any order they wish.

Frequency hypothesis of perspective effects in object *categorization* is the assumption that response speed is a function of the number of times the object has been seen from the particular viewpoint in which it is presented.

Frontal eye fields are regions in the frontal *cortex* (area 8) that control saccadic eye movements via *axons* projecting to the brain stem *gaze centers* both directly and indirectly through the *superior colliculus*.

Frontal plane is the plane perpendicular to the line of sight on which the eyes are *fixated*.

Full primal sketch is Marr's second *image-based representation* that includes global *perceptual grouping* and *organization* among the local *image features* present in the *raw primal sketch*.

Functional approach to consciousness (see *functionalism*).

Functionalism is an approach to the *mind-body problem* based on the idea that a given mental state can be defined in terms of the causal relations that exist among that mental state, environmental conditions (inputs), organismic behaviors (outputs), and other mental states.

Fuzzy intersection is an operation of *fuzzy set theory* corresponding to the *fuzzy logical* AND operation. The membership function of the result is the minimum of the membership functions of the two initial fuzzy sets.

Fuzzy logic is an alternative to standard logic in which propositions can have different degrees of truth rather than being simply true or false.

Fuzzy logical model of perception (**FLMP**) is an approach to perception that is based on *fuzzy set theory* and *fuzzy logic*. It assumes a continuous range of possible values for features which are then integrated mathematically during the *process* of *identification* (see Figure 9.4.3).

Fuzzy set theory is a modification and extension of classical set theory in which membership of elements in a set is continuously graded (degrees of membership) rather than binary (member or nonmember).

Fuzzy union is an operation of *fuzzy set theory* corresponding to the *fuzzy logical* OR operation. The membership function of the result is the maximum of the membership functions of the two component fuzzy sets.

Gabor function (or **wavelet**) is a local patch of a *sinusoidal grating* whose *contrast* (*amplitude*) decreases with distance from the center (see Figure 4.2.12). It is constructed by multiplying a global *sinusoidal grating* by a bell-shaped Gaussian weighting function.

Ganglion cells are the last layer of *neurons* in the *retina*, whose *axons* exit the eye as the *optic nerve*.

Ganzfeld is a visual environment in which equal amounts of *light* from all directions arrive at a *viewpoint*, producing the perception of an all-encompassing gray fog.

Gaze centers are nuclei in the brain stem that control the six *extraocular muscles* via the *oculomotor neurons* (see Figure 11.1.7).

General viewpoint refers to viewing conditions in which the *stationpoint* is representative in the sense that small changes in its location will not cause qualitative differences in image structure, such as introducing hidden surfaces or edge discontinuities.

Generalized cylinders are a generalization of standard geometric cylinders in which the base (cross section), the *axis*, and the sweeping rule are variable rather than fixed (see Figure 8.2.17).

Generalized delta rule is a learning rule for *connectionist networks* that underlies *back propagation*. It works by propagating the *error signal* at the output *units* backward through the network.

Genericity (see *nonaccidentalness*).

Geon theory (see *recognition by components theory*).

Geons are *generalized cylinders* whose inherently continuous parameters have been divided into discrete categories that are easy to distinguish by *nonaccidential features* from *general viewpoints* (see Figure 9.3.1).

Gestaltism is a school of perceptual theory that arose as a reaction against *structuralism*, proposing that perception is organized, *holistic*, and innate. Its principle advocates were Max Wertheimer, Wolfgang Köhler, and Kurt Koffka.

Global minimum is the point in *weight-error space* with the lowest error, thus representing the best possible solution within a given network *architecture*.

Global precedence is either (1) the theoretical claim that large-scale spatial structure (global information) is perceived before small-scale structure (local information), or (2) the empirical finding that *global properties* are perceived more rapidly than local properties.

Global properties are attributes of whole *figures* or *configurations*, such as symmetry, closedness, connectedness, and overall *shape*.

Good continuation (or **continuity**) is a principle of *perceptual grouping* that states that, all else being equal, elements that are aligned in *orientation* and position are more likely to be grouped together (see Figure 6.1.2I).

Goodness-of-example ratings (see *typicality ratings*).

Graceful degradation is a property of the brain and *connectionist networks* in which computational power is lost slowly in the face of added noise or random deletions of components rather than abruptly and catastrophically as many symbolic programs do.

Graded potential is continuously variable electrical activity in *neurons* that transmits signals from the *dendrites* to the *cell body*. In early retinal neurons without *myelin sheaths* it is also used to transmit signals along the *axon*.

Gradient descent is an *algorithm* for connectionist learning by making small adjustments in each *connection weight* to produce the steepest decrease in error along the surface of *weight-error space*.

Ground refers to regions to which *contours* have not been assigned, producing the perception of being in the background and extending behind the *figure* (see Figure 6.3.1).

Grouping (see *perceptual grouping*).

Habituation is a phenomenon in which an organism's natural response to a stimulus decreases over time with continued presentation.

Habituation paradigm is an experimental procedure for studying perceptual development in which babies are exposed to an initially novel stimulus, *habituate* to it, and then are tested with other stimuli to determine how much they *dishabituate*.

Hardware primitives are a set of physiologically plausible components (e.g., *neurons*) into which a complex *process* can be *recursively decomposed*.

Hemineglect (see *unilateral neglect*).

Heuristic assumptions are propositions that are taken to be true in *probabilistic inference* to reach *conclusions* that are valid only if the heuristic assumptions are actually true.

Heuristic processes are *probabilistic inferences* that make use of "rules of thumb," usually based on additional *hidden assumptions* that are usually, but not always, valid.

Hidden assumptions are statements that, if assumed to be true, can convert *inductive inferences* to *deductive inferences*.

Hierarchical clustering programs are computer *algorithms* that convert a *proximity matrix* into the best-fitting *hierarchical tree* structure.

Hierarchical templates are complex *templates* that are constructed by concatenating *standard templates* into a *hierarchical tree* structure.

Hierarchical tree is a *network* in which the *terminal nodes* correspond to individual *objects* or *parts*, nonterminal nodes to sets of objects or parts, and *links* to set inclusion relations among the sets represented by *nodes* (see Figures 8.2.12 and 9.2.1 for categorical structure and Figure 6.2.7 for part/whole structure).

Hits are positive ("yes") responses on *signal trials* of a *signal detection* experiment.

Holism is the theoretical view that a complex perception is fundamentally different from, and cannot be reduced to, the simple concatenation of its parts.

Homogeneous masks are spatially uniform flashes of *light* presented just before, during, or after the target stimulus (see Figure 12.1.5A).

Homomorphism is a mapping from objects in a source domain to objects in a target domain such that relations among objects in the source domain are mirrored by corresponding relations among corresponding objects in the target domain (see Figure 2.3.7).

Homunculus is a fictitious "man-in-the-head" who examines the output of some low-level *process* and then engages in some higher-level *process* through mysterious and unspecified mechanisms.

Hopfield nets are symmetric *recurrent networks*.

Horizon ratio is a mathematical relation between the height of an object, the distance of the *viewpoint* from a ground plane, and the visual angles from the horizon line to the top and bottom of the object (see Figure 7.1.7).

Horizontal cells are *neurons* in the *retina* that connect *receptors* to *bipolar cells*.

Horopter is the set of environmental points that stimulate corresponding points on the two *retinae* (see Figures 5.3.3 and 5.3.4).

Hue is the directional dimension of *color space* that corresponds to the basic *color* of a *light* or surface (see Color Plates 3.2 and 3.3).

Hypercolumns are long, thin columns of tissue in area *V1*, about 1 mm × 1 mm on the surface of the *cortex*, that run perpendicularly through all six cortical layers and whose cells have *receptive fields* that are tuned to the same retinal location (see Figure 4.1.15).

Hypercomplex cells (or **end-stopped cells**) are *neurons* in area *V1* that reduce their firing to *lines* or *edges* that extend beyond a certain optimal length (see Figure 4.1.11).

Hyperopia (or **far-sightedness**) is a condition in which people can see well far away but cannot focus properly on nearby objects because their *lens* is too thin relative to the depth of their eye (see Figure 1.3.5D).

Hyperspace is a dimensional space of more than three spatial dimensions.

Hypersphere is surface in *hyperspace* analogous to a sphere in 3-D space.

Hypotheses are theoretical statements, assumptions, or conjectures that characterize the object of scientific study. They may be either true or false.

Hypothesis driven processing (see *top-down processing*).

Hysteresis is a kind of "perceptual inertia" in threshold experiments, producing the tendency for something that is already perceived to continue to be perceived as intensity is reduced and for something that has not yet been perceived to remain unperceived as intensity is increased.

Iconic memory is a very brief form of *visual memory* in which a great deal of uninterpreted visual *information* from the most recent *image* is stored for periods up to about 1 second.

Idealism is a *monist* approach to the *mind-body problem* in which only mental phenomena are believed to exist.

Identification is the *process* of perceptually recognizing that a given target object is a particular known object. It is also often used as a synonym for *classification* and *categorization*.

Illumination refers to the lighting conditions in the environment: how objects are struck by *photons* either directly from light sources or indirectly from reflections by other objects.

Illumination edges are changes in *image luminance* that are caused by different amounts of *light* falling on a surface of homogeneous *reflectance*, such as those caused by *cast shadows*, reflected highlights, or changes in *surface orientation* (see Figure 5.5.16).

Illumination map is a hypothesized *representation* of *image* regions according to how much *light* is falling on them.

Illumination spectrum is the number of *photons* at each visible *wavelength* falling on a given region of a surface per unit of time from a light source.

Illusions are systematically *nonveridical perceptions* of environmental objects and events (see Figure 1.1.4).

Illusory conjunctions are perceptions of objects in which *features* are bound into objects in the wrong way, resulting in false perceptions. They usually arise when *attention* is spread over two or more nearby objects.

Illusory contours (or **subjective contours**) are visual experiences of *edges* where no corresponding physical *luminance edges* are present in the *image* (see Figures 4.3.15 and 6.4.6).

Image is either (1) a 2-D optical projection of an environmental scene, or (2) an actively generated internal *representation* of environmental objects and events that has been generated by accessing *visual long-term memory*.

Image-based stage is a set of *representations* and *processes* that extract features of 2-D image structure, such as detecting *edges* and *lines*, matching corresponding parts of the left and right *images*, partitioning *images* into two-dimensional regions, and detecting other 2-D features, such as line terminations.

Image-scanning task is an experimental paradigm for studying *visual imagery* in which subjects are asked to change the focus of their *attention* from one object to another in a *visual image* and to press a button when they arrive at the target object.

Implementational level of an *information processing* system specifies how an *algorithm* is actually embodied in physical processes within a physical system.

Impossible objects are two-dimensional line drawings that initially give the perception of coherent three-dimensional objects that are physically impossible (see Figure 1.1.8).

Inattention paradigm is an experimental method for studying perception without *attention*. Subjects have to perform a relatively difficult discrimination task for several trials before an unexpected extra stimulus is presented and then tested immediately afterward (see Figure 11.2.2).

Inattentional amnesia is a theoretical interpretation of phenomena such as *inattentional blindness*, the *attentional blink*, and *change blindness* as resulting from the failure to construct a durable, reportable memory *representation* of a target object or event because of a lack of *attention* (rather than the failure to consciously perceive it because of inattention).

Inattentional blindness is either (1) the phenomenon that many subjects fail to report having seen the extra stimulus in the critical trial of the *inattention paradigm* or (2) the theoretical interpretation that such failures result from the absence of conscious perception because of a lack of *attention* (rather than inadequate memory).

Inattentional blindsight is the phenomenon that subjects who are *inattentionally* blind to a presented stimulus nevertheless appear to *process* it to the level of *identification*, as indicated by performance on an indirect task such as *stem completion*.

Indexing is a *visual routine* that selects of a location where something is "different," as exemplified in *visual pop-out* and various *pull cues* that summon *attention*.

Induced color (see *simultaneous color contrast*).

Induced motion is an *illusion* in which a small stationary object surrounded by a larger moving frame produces the perception of a small moving object within a large stationary frame (see Figure 10.2.17).

Induced self-motion is an observer's *experience* of himself or herself as moving through the environment because of the pattern of *optic flow* on the *retina*.

Inductive inference is probabilistic reasoning in which likely *conclusions* are based on an accumulation of many similar occurrences (e.g., that the sun always rises because it always has in the past).

Inference is a *process* whereby two or more pieces of *information* are combined by some set of well-defined rules (e.g., mathematical proof, propositional logic, or statistical calculation), to reach a *conclusion* that follows from them. (See also *deductive inference*, *inductive inference*, *logical inference*, and *probabilistic inference*.)

Information is the structure of an object, scene, or event relative to the set of possible alternatives.

Information flow diagram is a schematic picture in which informational events are depicted as boxes and the transfer of *information* is depicted as directed arrows between corresponding boxes.

Information load in *structural information theory* is a measure of the symbolic complexity of a code and is used to determine the "best" possible code, roughly as advocated in the *Gestalt principle of Prägnanz*.

Information pickup is Gibson's theory about how an actively exploring organism can perceive the environment unambiguously by a *process* metaphorically akin to mechanical resonance.

Information processing is a *metatheoretical* approach to understanding vision (and other forms of cognition) in terms of a complex set of *computational processes* that operate on *representations* of visual structure.

Information theory is a mathematical theory of communication that measures a commodity (in "bits") that depends on the degree of uncertainty associated with a given possible signal among a set of alternatives in a particular communication context.

Informational equivalence is a relation that can hold between two internal *representations* if they reflect the same facts about the structure of the external world and therefore carry identical *information* about it.

Informational event is a description of a physical event in terms of an *operation* that transforms *input information* to *output information*.

Inhibition refers to decreases in the *firing rate* of *neurons* in the brain or in the *activation* of *units* in a *connectionist network*.

Inner segment is the portion of a *photoreceptor* that contains the nucleus and other cellular machinery (see Figure 1.3.10).

Input information is the initial data structure that is transformed by an *information processing operation* into *output information*.

Input theory of position constancy (see *afferent theory*).

Input vector space is a geometric representation of the set of all possible inputs to a *connectionist network* in which each input *unit's activation* corresponds to a dimension of the space.

Instantiation is the *process* whereby a token is created to represent an instance of a type, as when a particular *edge* is encoded at a particular location, *orientation*, and polarity.

Integral dimensions are pairs of properties with respect to which people cannot *selectively attend* one without also perceiving the other.

Integral tripack is a type of photographic color film in which the required three layers of gelatine are all attached to a single piece of film (see Color Plate C.4).

Integration masking refers to a hypothesized *process* whereby the target and mask *images* are effectively added together to form a single composite *image*.

Intentionality is the property of conscious states by which they inherently refer to or are directed toward things other than themselves: namely, objects and events in the external world.

Interactionism is a form of *dualism* in which it is claimed that the mental and physical worlds can interact causally with each other in both directions: Physical events cause mental events, and mental events also cause physical events.

Interactive activation (IA) model is a theory of letter and word perception based on a multilayer *connectionist network* consisting of *units* representing *features*, letters, and words, with feedback between the letter and word levels to model context effects in letter perception (see Figure 9.4.6).

Interblob regions are subregions within layers 2 and 3 in each *hypercolumn* of *V1* that are defined anatomically by the fact that they are relatively poor in the enzyme *cytochrome oxidase* (see Figure 4.4.2).

Interference loss is an increase in classification time for *orthogonal variation conditions* relative to that in the corresponding *unidimensional variation conditions* in a Garnerian *classification* task (see Figure 11.2.17).

Interocular transfer effects are phenomena in which *adaptation* in one eye causes *aftereffects* in the other.

Interposition (see *occlusion*).

Interpretive process is an *inference* that some state of affairs exists in the environment based on *probabilistic* sensory *information* (e.g., that two otherwise similar *images* of different sizes are actually projections of two identical objects at different distances).

Interruption masking is a type of *masking* that is thought to arise from the masking display interrupting the ongoing perceptual *processing* of the target display.

Intracellular recordings are *single-cell recordings* made from inside a *neuron*, where *graded potentials* can be measured.

Intrinsic images refer to Barrow and Tennenbaum's *surface-based representations*, named to emphasize the fact that they represent intrinsic properties of surfaces in the external world rather than properties of the input *image*.

Introspection is a method that is used to study conscious perception (and other cognitive *processes*) by systematic self-examination of internal *experiences* under controlled conditions.

Intuitive physics refers to people's untutored beliefs about everyday physical events such as the trajectories of moving objects under various conditions.

Invariant feature is a property of an object that does not change as a result of applying a specified *transformation*.

Invariant features hypothesis of *shape equivalence* is the claim that two objects are perceived to have the same shape if and only if they have the same set of "shape features."

Inverse problem refers to the difficulty in reversing a well-defined functional mapping when the solution is underconstrained and therefore not unique. In vision, it usually refers to the problem of getting from realistic 2-D *images* of scenes to knowledge of the 3-D array of objects that gave rise to them.

Inverse projection is the extrapolation of optical rays from a retinal *image* "backward" into environmental space to solve the correspondence problem of stereoscopic *depth* perception (see Figure 5.3.17).

Inverted spectrum argument is a philosophical claim that one can never know whether one's own *experiences* of *color* are the same as someone else's or whether they are systematically transformed.

Ipsilateral is the property of two specified objects or events being located on the same side of the brain's plane of symmetry (e.g., the left visual field is ipsilateral to the left hemisphere).

Iris is the opaque structure behind the *cornea* that keeps *light* from entering the eye and that gives the eye its external color (see Figure 1.3.4).

Isomorphism is a mapping from objects in a source domain to objects in a target domain such that their relational structure is the same (see Figure 13.4.5).

Isomorphism constraint is the hypothesis that objective behavioral methods can determine the contents of awareness up to, but not beyond, the criterion of *isomorphism*.

IT is an acronym for *InferoTemporal* cortex, an area that is part of the *ventral "what" system* (see Figure 1.3.19).

jnd (see *just noticeable difference*).

Junctions (see *vertices*).

Just noticeable difference (**jnd**) is the size of the smallest difference that an observer can detect in some stimulus dimension.

Kanizsa triangle is a well-known *image* that produces strong perception of *illusory contours* along the sides of a white triangle on a white background (see Figure 6.4.6).

KDE (see *kinetic depth effect*).

Kinesthetic feedback refers to incoming signals from joints that specify the relative spatial positions and orientations of limbs.

Kinetic completion is a phenomenon that is analogous to standard visual completion, except that the *information* about *occlusion* is dynamic rather than static (see Figure 10.2.20).

Kinetic depth effect (**KDE**) is the perception of a rigidly rotating 3-D object in depth from viewing its 2-D back-projected shadow (see Figure 5.4.3).

Korte's laws are empirical generalizations about the pairwise relations among separation, intensity, and *alternation rate* in the perception of two-point *apparent motion*.

Kurtosis is a measure of the peakedness of a probability distribution. High kurtosis is characteristic of *sparse distributed coding* schemes for *neural networks*.

Lambertian surface is a surface of a homogeneous *matte* material that reflects *light* uniformly in all directions (see Figure 5.5.25).

Laminar structure is the organization of certain brain regions into anatomically defined layers (e.g., area *V1* has six major layers).

Lateral geniculate nucleus (LGN) is the visual center in the thalamus that receives the majority of axons from retinal *ganglion cells* and that projects its axons to area *V1* (see Figure 1.3.1).

Lateral inhibition refers to an *architecture* for *neural networks* in which *neurons* inhibit spatially neighboring *neurons* (see Figure 3.2.17).

Launching effect is a form of perceived causality in which one object strikes another and is perceived to cause the subsequent *motion* of the second object (see Figure 10.4.3A).

Laws of grouping are *ceteris paribus rules* that specify certain principles (or factors) that govern *perceptual grouping* (see Figures 6.1.2, 6.1.5, 6.1.6, and 6.1.7).

Lens is an optically transparent object that focuses *light* in a coherent *image* on a surface at the appropriate distance.

Lesion is a wound or injury that causes tissue damage.

Lesion experiments are studies in which areas of animals' brains are surgically removed or otherwise destroyed to determine what function they perform.

LGN (see *lateral geniculate nucleus*).

Liberal response strategy in *signal detection theory* corresponds to setting a low *criterion* for saying "yes," leading the observer to a *response bias* toward saying "yes."

Light is physical energy in a restricted range of the *electromagnetic spectrum* with wavelengths between 400 and 700 nm (see Color Plate 3.1).

Light adaptation refers to the visual system's temporary loss of sensitivity to *light* following prolonged exposure to it.

Light mixture is the process of physically superimposing beams of colored *light* to produce different colors via additive color mixture.

Lightness (or **value**) is the vertical dimension of *color space* for surface reflection, corresponding to the overall perception of reflectance from white to black (see Color Plate 3.2).

Lightness constancy is the ability to perceive the constant achromatic reflectance properties of surfaces despite changing conditions of *illumination* and *viewing geometry* (see Figure 3.3.1).

Likelihood principle is Helmholtz's proposal that the visual systems arrives at the most likely state or event in the external world that could have caused the retinal *image* or event.

Limb (see *extremal edge*).

Line detectors (or **bar detectors**) are hypothetical *neurons* that respond to the presence of bars or lines at the proper *orientation*, retinal position, and polarity (light-dark-light or dark-light-dark) (see Figure 4.1.6).

Linear perspective (or **convergence of parallels**) is a fact of projective geometry that parallel lines in depth converge toward a *vanishing point* on the horizon in the *image* plane (see Figure 5.5.4).

Linguistic universality is the idea that language is determined either by invariant physical characteristics in the structure of the stimulus, invariant biological features in the structure of the organism, or both.

Links (see *connections*).

Local minimum in *weight-error space* is the lowest point in the immediate vicinity of the error surface but one that is at a higher level than the global minimum for the entire error surface (see Figure B.2.7).

Local parts are features specifying spatially restricted subsets of objects, such as containing a straight line, a curved line, or an acute angle.

Local spatial frequency theory is a variation of *spatial frequency theory* in which each small region of an *image* is hypothesized to be analyzed into a set of localized sinusoidal components (that is, *Gabor functions*).

Logical inference is a process by which *conclusions* are derived from *premises* by applying rules of deduction.

Long-range motion system is a visual *process* that is hypothesized to be responsible for classical phenomena of *apparent motion* with large-scale, individual figures and to be capable of detecting *motion* with relatively large displacements and slow alternation rates.

Long-term memory (**LTM**, also called **secondary memory**) is a very large-capacity and temporally extended storage system for knowledge of general facts (*semantic memory*) and skills (*procedural memory*) as well as specific past experiences of one's personal history (*episodic memory*).

Looming (see *optic expansion*).

LTM (see *long-term memory*).

Luminance is a measure of the amount or intensity of visible *light* energy emitted or reflected from a given source or surface.

Luminance edges are abrupt changes in the amount of *light* that falls on two adjacent regions of an *image*.

Luminance function is a graph of the intensity of *light* plotted as a function of spatial position (see Figure 4.3.4B).

Luminance spectrum is the amount of *light* that is reflected into the eye in a given region, determined jointly by the *reflectance spectrum* of the surface viewed and the *illumination spectrum* of *light* incident on it (see Figure 3.3.2).

M ganglion cells are *neurons* in the *retina* whose *axons* project to the *magnocellular layer* of the *lateral geniculate nucleus*.

Mach bands are illusory variations in perceived *lightness* (or *brightness*) that occur at *edges* between two regions of highly different *lightness* (or *brightness*) levels (see Figure 3.2.6).

Magic-eye stereograms (see *autostereograms*).

Magnetic resonance imagery (**MRI**) is a brain imaging technique in which the brain is placed in a strong magnetic field and pulsed with radio waves so that its molecules emit radio energy that can be detected and used to reconstruct the 3-D structure of the brain (see Figure 2.2.11).

Magnitude estimation is Stevens's method of constructing *psychophysical scales*, in which observers are asked to assign numbers to their *experiences* of stimuli to reflect the ratios of the magnitudes of their *experiences* (e.g., if light A is twice as bright as light B, A should be assigned a number twice as large as the number assigned to B).

Magnocellular layers of the *lateral geniculate nucleus* are the lower two layers that contain large cell bodies (see Figures 4.1.4 and 4.1.5).

Marking a location is one of Ullman's primitive *visual routines* that designates a particular location as one to be remembered so that it can be accessed quickly at a later time.

Masking refers to the dominance or interference of one visual event (presenting the mask) on measuring another event (detecting a target), typically when the interfering event comes just before or after the target event.

Materialism is a form of *monism* in which only physical phenomena are believed to exist.

Matte surfaces are dull surfaces that reflect incident *light* diffusely in many directions, such as a typical piece of typing or construction paper (see Figure 1.2.4A).

Maturation is the theoretical view that perception is genetically determined from birth but unfolds in part during development in a preprogrammed sequence.

Maximal concavities are local negative minima of curvature.

Maximal information hypothesis of perspective effects in object *categorization* is that such effects are caused by differences in the amount of *information* different views contain about the *shape* and function of the object.

Maximum (best-fit) decision rule is a *categorization* procedure whereby the alternative that has the highest value (best fit) on the outcome of some evaluation *process* is chosen over all other alternatives.

Maximum-over-threshold decision rule is a *categorization* procedure that sets a *criterion* (the *threshold*) below which an object is assigned to no existing category and above which it is assigned to the category with the highest value (best fit).

Maxwell's triangle is a color space that summarizes the results of additive color mixture experiments using three primary colors (the vertices). Each point within the triangle represents a color that can be matched by additive color mixture as specified by its triangular coordinates (see Figure C.1.2).

MDS (see *multidimensional scaling*).

Memory dynamics is a *process* by which memories are hypothesized to change systematically over time.

Mental rotation is a *process* by which people are able to imagine an object changing its *orientation* continuously in 3-D space to perform certain kinds of visual tasks, such as deciding whether two figures are identical to or mirror images of each other.

Metacontrast masking (or **erasure**) is a form of *backward masking* that occurs when the target stimulus is replaced by a surrounding stimulus about 50–100 ms after the target is removed.

Metamers are pairs of *lights* or surfaces that look the same but have physically different *illumination spectra* or different *reflectance spectra*, respectively.

Metatheory is an abstract characterization of the concepts and assumptions that underlie a coherent set of possible theories, such as *information processing* theories.

Method of adjustment is a *psychophysical* procedure for finding the *threshold* for some stimulus dimension in which the subject adjusts the level to the lowest level that he or she can detect in both ascending and descending sequences.

Method of constant stimuli is a modification of the *method of limits* in which the order of the trials is randomized rather than fixed in ascending and descending sequences.

Method of limits is a discrete-trial version of the *method of adjustment*. On each trial, a stimulus at a particular intensity level is presented, and the subject indicates whether or not he or she detects it.

Method of loci is a *mnemonic device* for remembering sequences of several items using *visual imagery* techniques.

Methodological behaviorism is a scientific method of studying mental events in which objective, observable behaviors (rather than *experiences* based on *introspection*) are taken as the phenomena to be explained.

Microelectrode is an extremely thin glass or metal shaft with a tip diameter of about 0.001 cm that is used to make *extracellular recordings* from single *neurons*.

Mind-body problem is the philosophical issue of how to explain the relation between mental events (e.g., perceptions, pains, hopes, desires, and beliefs) and physical events (e.g., brain activity).

Mind-brain identity theory (see *reductive materialism*).

Minimum code is the simplest code for a given figure in *structural information theory* as measured by its having the lowest *information load*.

Minimum principle (see *principle of Prägnanz*).

Misinformation effect is the finding that *recall* and *recognition* of visual *information* in *long-term memory* can be systematically distorted by subsequently presenting misleading verbal information.

Misses are negative ("no") responses on *signal trials* in a *signal detection* experiment.

Mnemonic devices are strategies that are used to improve memory performance.

Mnemonists are individuals with remarkably superior memory abilities.

Modified weak fusion is a theoretical position on integration of *depth information* that allows for certain limited kinds of interactions among *depth* sources.

Modular system (see *decomposable system*).

Modularity hypothesis is Fodor's claim that the mind is a strongly *decomposable system*, consisting of separate modules for different sensory modalities and various higher-level components.

MOMS filters (see *multiorientation, multiscale filters*).

Mondrians are complex two-dimensional displays of overlapping rectangles of different *colors* or *lightnesses* that are used to study *color constancy* (see Figure 3.3.7A). They are named after artist Piet Mondrian, whose abstract paintings they resemble.

Monism is a philosophical position on the *mind-body problem* based on the idea that mind and body are essentially the same kind of thing.

Monochromat is a completely *color blind* individual who can match any *color* with some intensity of a single *light* of another *wavelength*.

Monochromatic light is *electromagnetic energy* in which all the *photons* have the same *wavelength*, such as the *light* emitted by lasers (see Figure 3.1.2A).

Monocular depth information is *information* about *depth* that is available from optical structure in the *image* of a single eye.

Moon illusion is the inaccurate perception that the moon is larger when it is near the horizon than it is when it is high in the night sky (see Figure 7.1.8).

Motion is a property of an object in which all or part of it changes in position over time.

Motion aftereffects are phenomena caused by prolonged viewing of consistent *motion*, after which subsequent *motion* perception is significantly altered (e.g., the *waterfall illusion*).

Motion constancy is the ability to perceive the *veridical* movement of physical objects in the environment despite variations in *image motion* due to viewing factors such as movements of the eyes, head, and body.

Motion gradients are systematic differences in *image motion* that occur over extended regions of the *ambient optic array* because of relative movement of the observer with respect to its environment (see Figure 5.4.2).

Motion parallax is differential *image motion* of pairs of points due to their different *depths* relative to the *fixation point* when viewed by a moving observer.

MRI scan (see *magnetic resonance imagery*).

MST is an acronym for *Medial Superior Temporal cortex*, which is a major center for processing *information* about *motion* (see Figure 1.3.19).

MT is an acronym for *Medial Temporal cortex* (also called *V5*), which is part of the *ventral "what" system* for object recognition (see Figure 1.3.19).

Multidimensional representations are encodings of objects consisting of several continuous *features* (i.e., *dimensions*) such that each object corresponds to a point in a multidimensional space whose coordinates reflect its value on those features (see Figure 8.2.8).

Multidimensional scaling (MDS) program is a computer *algorithm* that constructs *representations* of objects within a *multidimensional space* automatically from similarity (or dissimilarity) measures of pairs of objects (see Figure 8.2.8).

Multidimensional space is a way of representing objects that can be described along a common set of continuous parameters. Each object corresponds to a point in such a space, and its position is determined by the coordinates corresponding to its parameter values.

Multifeatural representation of an object is typically conceived as a set (unordered list) of discrete *features* that characterize the object.

Multiorientation, multiscale (MOMS) filters are a set of computational *units* that are selectively tuned to *luminance* energy at different *orientations* and sizes for each retinal location (e.g., *Gabor function filters*).

Multiple realizability is the *functionalist* doctrine that many different physical devices can serve the same function, provided that they causally connect inputs and outputs in the same way via corresponding internal states.

Multiple scales of resolution refer to different descriptions of the same object from local (small) to global (large) spatial perspectives.

Multistable perception is perception in which two (or more) interpretations of the same *ambiguous image* alternate while an observer looks at them. It is thought to arise from competition between two (or more) models (see Figure 1.1.5).

Myelin sheath is a fatty covering over the *axons* of most *neurons* that speeds the conduction of *action potentials* as they travel toward the *synapse*.

Myopia (or **nearsightedness**) is a condition in which people can see well over short distances but cannot focus properly on distant objects because their *lens* is too thick relative to the depth of their eye (see Figure 1.3.5C).

Nativism is the theoretical view that perception is determined through innate mechanisms that have evolved through natural selection.

Naive physics (see *intuitive physics*).

Naive realism is the philosophical belief that the external world has the same objective structure and properties that are evident in our normal, everyday perception of it.

Nearly decomposable system is an *information processing* device in which the interactions among components are weak but not negligible.

Nearsightedness (see *myopia*).

Necessary and sufficient conditions for *category* membership are a set of *features*, all of which an object must have to be counted as a member of that *category*.

Negative priming effect is a phenomenon in which intentionally ignoring a stimulus on one trial interferes with its conscious perception on subsequent trials (see Figure 11.2.7).

Nerve impulses (see *action potentials*).

Network is a data structure consisting of a set of *nodes* (or *units*) connected by *links* (or *arcs*).

Neural correlate of consciousness is the physiological mechanism that produces *awareness*.

Neural fatigue hypothesis is the proposal that perception of *ambiguous figures* alternates among different interpretations because different sets of *neurons* get "tired" after firing for a long time.

Neural networks are assemblies of *neurons* that are heavily interconnected; sometimes used as a synonym for *connectionist networks*.

Neuron is the main cellular component of the nervous system, a specialized type of cell that integrates electrochemical activity of the other neurons that are connected to it and that propagates that integrated activity to other neurons.

Neurotransmitter is a chemical substance that is released into the *synapse* between two *neurons* that enables the first *neuron* to affect the activity of the second *neuron* by stimulating its *dendrites*.

Neutral point of *color blind* individuals is the *wavelength* of *monochromatic light* that is perceived as uncolored (gray).

Node is a *unit* in a *network* or graph structure that is connected to other nodes by *connections* (or *links* or *arcs*).

Noise masks are patterns of tiny, randomly distributed dots that are used to interfere with the perception of an immediately preceding or succeeding stimulus (see Figure 12.1.5B).

Noise trials are experimentally defined intervals during which no stimulus is presented (rather than a weak stimulus, as on *signal trials*).

Nonaccidental features are aspects of an object's *image* structure that are robust over *viewpoints* in the sense that they do not depend on rare "accidents" of perspective.

Nonaccidentalness (or **genericity** or **rejection-of-coincidence** principle) is the hypothesis that the visual system avoids interpreting structural regularities as arising from unlikely accidents of *viewing geometry* that violate the assumption of *general viewpoint*.

Nonspectral hues are the *hues* not found in *monochromatic light*, including purples, magentas, and deep, pure reds (see Color Plate 3.3). These hues can be created only by combining two or more *wavelengths* of light.

Nonterminal nodes are *nodes* in a *hierarchical tree* between the *root node* and the *terminal nodes* that represent different levels of subsets of objects.

Nonveridical perception is perception that is inconsistent with the actual state of affairs in the environment (i.e., an *illusion*).

Normalization is the *process* of transforming incoming *images* into "standard form," such as requiring a standard position, size, and orientation, prior to further processing by *template* matching, *alignment with 2-D views*, or *alignment with 3-D models*.

Object-based stage is the set of *representations* and *processes* that construct a visual *representation* of fully three-dimensional *information*, including unseen surfaces and volumetric *shape*.

Object-based theories of visual *attention* propose that *attention* selects a perceptual object (rather than a region of space) on which additional processing resources are then focused.

Object-centered reference frames are analogous to geometric *coordinate systems* within which the locations of *features* and *parts* are believed to be represented relative to aspects of the intrinsic structure of the object itself.

Object-centered reference frames hypothesis is the claim that *shape* equivalence is assessed by comparing objects within *reference frames* defined by the intrinsic properties of the objects.

Object files are temporary, integrated representations of the cumulative results of perceptual analyses of an object or event that are used to keep track of it over time (see Figure 11.2.8).

Object recognition (**object identification**, **object categorization**, or **object classification**) is the *process* of perceptual *classification* into *entry-level categories*.

Object-relative power spectrum is a *power spectrum* that encodes the *amplitudes*, *spatial frequencies*, *phases*, and *orientations* of *sinusoidal gratings* relative to some object-defined standard component, such as the fundamental frequency of the pattern.

Object superiority effect is the phenomenon in which subjects are better able to perceive individual lines when they are presented as part of 3-D objects than when they are presented alone or in meaningless 2-D *configurations*.

Objective knowledge is knowledge of public events that can be observed by anyone, at least in principle.

Objective shape is the spatial structure of an object that does not change when it is subjected to *transformations* of the *similarity group*: *translations, rotations, dilations, reflections*, and their combinations (see Figure 8.1.1).

Objective threshold of awareness refers to a measure of awareness based on the stimulus level at which the subject's performance falls to chance in the most sensitive possible discrimination task.

Occipital cortex (or **primary visual cortex** or **occipital lobe**) is the most posterior cortical lobe of the brain (see Figure 1.3.2). It receives visual input from the *lateral geniculate nucleus* of the thalamus and contains six major, anatomically distinct layers and numerous functionally distinct *retinotopic maps* of visual information (see Figure 1.3.19).

Occipital lobe (see *occipital cortex*).

Occlusion (or **interposition**) is the condition in which *light* reflected from a farther object is blocked from reaching the viewer's eye by an opaque object between the viewer and the occluded object.

Ockham's razor is the assumption that the best explanation of a set of facts is the one with the fewest assumptions (that is, the one with greatest *parsimony*).

OCR (see *optical character recognition*).

Ocular apraxia is a symptom of *Balint's syndrome* in which the patient cannot change *fixation* from one object to another, as though the gaze were stuck on the currently fixated object.

Ocular depth information is *information* about *depth* arising from the state of the eyes themselves (rather than from the optical *information* they register; see *optical depth information*).

Ocular dominance slabs are columns of binocular cells in *striate cortex* that are perpendicular to the cortical surface within which the same eye is dominant (see Figure 4.1.14).

Oculomotor neurons are the final common pathway of the eye movement system, originating in the *gaze centers* of the brain stem and projecting to the *extraocular muscles* (see Figure 11.1.7).

Off-center cells are *neurons* that are excited when the light at the center of the *receptive field* is turned off (Figure 4.1.2B). They have a *center/surround organization* that is *inhibitory* in the center and *excitatory* in the surround.

Old-new recognition (see *yes-no recognition*).

On-center cells are *neurons* that are excited when the *light* at the center of the *receptive field* is turned on (Figure 4.1.2A).

They have a *center/surround organization* that is *excitatory* in the center and *inhibitory* in the surround.

Ontological status refers to the inherent nature of the object of study (as opposed to its *epistemic status* which pertains to how one comes to know about it).

Operation is the active component in an informational event that transforms *input information* into *output information*.

Opponent process theory of color perception, due to Hering, states that there are six psychologically primary *colors* structured into three pairs of opposites: red versus green, blue versus yellow, and black versus white.

Opposite slope sign condition is evidence that an *edge* is due to differences in *reflectance* (rather than *illumination*). It holds when the graph of the changes in intensity at two *wavelengths* for the two regions go in the opposite directions (see Figures 3.3.11A and 3.3.11B).

Optic ataxia is a symptom of *Balint's syndrome* in which the patient cannot reach out and touch an object in space.

Optic chiasm is an anatomical X-shaped structure where the *axons* of the *optic nerve* from the inner (nasal) side of each *retina* cross to the opposite side of the brain.

Optic disk (see *blind spot*).

Optic expansion (or **looming**) occurs when an observer moves directly toward a surface in the frontal plane, *fixating* on the point toward which he or she is heading (see Figure 5.4.2B).

Optic flow is the dynamic pattern of *information* available in the *ambient optic array* along a moving trajectory of *viewpoints*.

Optic nerve is the bundle of *axons* of *ganglion cells* that leaves the back of the eye and carries visual *information* to visual centers in the brain.

Optic radiations are the *axons* through which visual *information* is projected from the *lateral geniculate nucleus* to the visual *cortex*.

Optical character recognition (**OCR**) is a branch of computer science whose goal is to program computers to be able to read text from optical *images*.

Optical depth information is *depth information* arising from the structure of the *light* entering the eyes (rather than from the state of the eyes themselves; see *ocular depth information*).

Optics is the branch of physics concerned with the behavior of *light*.

Optokinetic reflex is an automatic response to maintain *fixation* during full field *image translations*. After the eyes have tracked an object through a large angle in the direction of *image motion*, they snap back in a rapid, *saccade*-like jump in the opposite direction and then *fixate* and track another object (see Figure 11.1.6).

Orientation is a property of objects concerning their alignment with respect to some reference line, such as gravity or the medial axis of the head.

Orientation aftereffect is the result of prolonged exposure to viewing retinally tilted lines, which causes distortions in the perceived orientation of subsequently viewed lines (see Figure 1.1.3).

Orientation at a distance is the perception of optical invariants that define *surface layout* within the 3-D environment according to Gibson's theory of *ecological optics.*

Orientation constancy is the ability to perceive the gravitational *orientation* of objects *veridically* despite changes in head orientation.

Orientation edges are changes in *luminance* in an *image* due to discontinuities in surface *orientation* in environmental surfaces (see Figure 5.5.16).

Origin of a *coordinate system* is a point that defines the reference (zero) position in all dimensions.

Orthogonal variation condition in a Garnerian *classification* task requires that subjects classify according to a single specified dimension while the other dimension varies independently (orthogonally) (see Figure 11.2.17).

Orthographic projection (or **parallel projection**) is a method of *image* formation in which the *light* rays striking the image plane travel parallel to each other and perpendicular to the image plane.

Outer segment of *photoreceptors* is the portion that contains billions of light-sensitive pigment molecules embedded in the membranes of hundreds of disks stacked perpendicular to its long axis (see Figure 1.3.10).

Output information is the structure that results from *input information* being acted upon by an *information processing operation.*

Output theory of *position constancy* (see *efferent copy theory*).

Overconstancy is the tendency to overcompensate for viewing factors in constancy judgments.

P ganglion cells are *neurons* in the *retina* whose *axons* project to the *parvocellular layer* of the *lateral geniculate nucleus.*

Panpsychism is a physical approach to *consciousness* positing that all matter has some very small or weak form of *consciousness* and that *experiences* arise in people's brains because lots of matter gets hooked up in just the right way.

Panum's fusional area is the region around the *horopter* within which disparate binocular *images* are perceptually fused into single *stereoscopic images* (see Figure 5.3.5).

Paradoxical motion is an odd experience in *motion aftereffects*, which produce a clear perception of *motion* without any global change in the perceived position of the objects that seem to be moving.

Parallel distributed processing (PDP) models are a kind of *connectionist network* model in which *information* is represented by the simultaneous activation of many interconnected *units.*

Parallel processing refers to *operations* that occur simultaneously rather than sequentially (see *serial processing*).

Parallel projection (see *orthographic projection*).

Parietal lobe is the lobe of *cortex* just above and in front of *occipital (primary visual) cortex* (see Figure 1.3.2) and is part of the *dorsal "where" system.*

Parsimony is a criterion for evaluating scientific theories in terms of simplicity: The theory that accounts for the same empirical facts with the fewest assumptions is best (see *Ockham's razor*).

Parsing is the *process* of dividing a single unit of *perceptual organization* into two or more parts.

Partial report procedure is an experimental task devised by Sperling to study brief *visual memory*. At or shortly after the termination of a briefly presented multielement array, subjects are cued to report only a small subset of the elements.

Particle motion is any *motion* of an object that depends only on its mass and the position of its center of mass (see Figure 10.4.9).

Partition is the division of an *image* into a set of mutually exclusive regions, rather like a stained-glass window.

Part refers to a restricted portion of an object that has semiautonomous, objectlike status in visual perception.

Part/whole hierarchy is a structure of nested inclusion relations that hold between different levels of perceptual objects and parts as represented in a *hierarchical tree* with the smallest units at the bottom and the largest at the top.

Parvocellular layers of the *lateral geniculate nucleus* are the upper four layers that contain small *cell bodies* (see Figures 4.1.4 and 4.1.5).

Past experience is a principle of *perceptual grouping* in which elements that have been previously associated in prior viewings tend to be seen as grouped in the present situation (see Figure 6.1.15).

Path-guided apparent motion is a phenomenon in which a gray path is briefly flashed between two alternated objects, resulting in *apparent motion* that follows the path induced by the gray region (see Figure 10.2.12A).

Path impletion is the *process* of traversing a continuous series of points between two given points in a dimensional space.

Pathways are large-scale neural structures for processing *information* about different visual properties, such as *color, shape, depth,* and *motion.*

Pattern cells are cortical *neurons* that respond to the *motion* of a whole plaid grating rather than that of the individual component gratings.

Pattern masks are *images* consisting of many randomly distributed line segments or meaningless pieces of figures that interfere with perception of a previous or subsequent target *image* (see Figure 12.1.5C).

PCA (see *principle components analysis*).

PDP models (see *parallel distributed processing models*).

PET scan (see *positron emission tomography*).

Perceived translucency (see *perceived transparency*).

Perceived transparency (or **perceived translucency**) is the perception of some portion of the visual field as being viewed through a closer object that transmits some portion of the *light* striking it (see Figure 6.4.14).

Perceptrons are a particular class of *neural network* models studied intensively in the 1960s that were able to learn how to identify examples of *categories* by adjusting the *weights* on their *connections* according to explicit rules, such as the *delta rule*.

Perceptual adaptation is a process that induces semi-permanent changes in perception or perceptual-motor coordination to reduce discrepancies between or within sensory modalities that have been caused by global optical *transformations* such as *image* inversion or displacement.

Perceptual constancy is the ability to perceive the properties of environmental objects, which are largely invariant over different viewing conditions, rather than the properties of their projected retinal *images*, which vary greatly with viewing conditions.

Perceptual defense is the hypothesis that the visual system can resist unwanted, anxiety-producing stimuli by reducing its sensitivity to their conscious perception, much as Freud claimed that the ego could dynamically repress disturbing thoughts and desires.

Perceptual grouping refers to the *processes* by which the various elements in an *image* are perceived as "going together" in the same perceptual unit of experience (see Figure 6.1.2).

Perceptual organization refers to *processes* by which the bits and pieces of visual *information* that are available in the retinal *image* are structured into the larger *units* of perceived objects and their interrelations.

Perspective projection (or **polar projection**) is a method of *image* formation in which *light* from the environment converges toward a single focal point (or pole) before striking the *image* plane.

Phantom limb pain is a phenomenon in which some people who have had an appendage amputated feel pain—sometimes excruciating pain—in the limb that is missing.

Phase of a *sinusoidal grating* is a measure of the position of the sinusoid relative to a reference point, as specified in degrees from the reference point to the positive-going inflection point of the grating: $0°$ = sine phase, $90°$ = cosine phase, $180°$ = anti-sine phase, and $270°$ = anti-cosine phase.

Phase spectrum of *Fourier analysis* for an *image* specifies the *phase* of each constituent *sinusoidal grating* at each particular *spatial frequency* and *orientation*.

Phenomenology is either (1) the *experience* of one's own mental states and *processes*, or (2) the systematic study of *consciousness* through *introspection*.

Phi motion (or **phi phenomenon**) is a form of *apparent motion* in which *motion* is perceived between two lights without the perception of its traveling through intermediate positions (Figure 10.1.6B).

Philosophical behaviorism is a position on the *mind-body problem* that claims that statements about mental events can be reduced to statements about the environmental conditions under which an organism behaves in certain ways or exhibits the disposition to behave in those ways.

Phosphors in a television screen are substances that emit *electromagnetic energy* in the *visible spectrum* when excited by absorbing an electron.

Photographic memory (see *eidetic imagery*).

Photographic negative is a piece of film that has been exposed to light, developed, and fixed such that regions on the film are complementary in color to the corresponding regions in the *image* (see Figure C.4.2A).

Photons are the discrete, indivisible packets of *electromagnetic energy* of which *light* is composed. Photons behave like waves in some respects and like particles in others.

Photopic conditions are viewing conditions under high levels of *illumination* (e.g., normal daylight or adequate artificial room lighting) when the *cones* are active and *color* is perceived.

Photoreceptors (or **receptors**) are the tiny nerve cells that densely cover the back of the eye (*retina*) and that convert *light* energy into *graded potentials*.

Phrenology is the study of the shape of people's skulls in the belief that the size of the lumps, bumps, and bulges of the head indicated the size and development of the brain structures underneath (see Figure 1.3.16).

Physical affordances are directly perceivable, observer-relative properties of objects in which function follows form.

Physical approach to consciousness is that awareness arises from some unusual property of matter in general rather than of *neurons* in particular (see *panpsychism*).

Physical Gestalt is a dynamic physical system that converges toward a stable state of minimum energy, such as a soap bubble becoming perfectly spherical over time.

Physiognomic character is the perception of functional properties of objects from their visible characteristics without first categorizing them, as suggested by *Gestalt* theorists.

Physiological approach to consciousness assumes that *awareness* is determined by particular biological properties of the *neurons* or neural activity that underlie *consciousness*, such that its explanation lies at the *implementational level*.

Physiological nystagmus refers to tiny involuntary eye movements that are caused by tremors in the *extraocular muscles*.

Physiology is the biological study of life processes and functions.

Pictorial depth information is a collection of many sources of *depth information* available in static, monocularly viewed *images*.

Picture metaphor theory of *visual imagery* is the idea that *visual images* are "pictures in the head" that are *experienced* when they are viewed by "the mind's eye."

Pigment bleaching is the process that occurs when molecules of *rhodopsin* absorb *photons* of *light*, causing it to turn from deep purple to almost transparent.

Pigment epithelium is the layer of tissue in the eye just behind the *retina*, whose main function is to restore bleached pigment molecules to their unbleached state by the action of enzymes.

Pinhole camera is an optical device for creating a focused, upside-down, and backward *image* of a 3-D scene on a 2-D plane by placing a pinhole in an otherwise light-tight box (see Figure 1.2.7).

Pixel (a shortened form of "picture element") is the most primitive, indivisible, explicitly represented visual unit of *information* in computer *images*, corresponding to an individual *receptor* in retinal *images*.

Point-source illumination is an idealized situation in which all the *light* illuminating a scene comes from a single, point-sized source of *light* at a specific location (see Figure 1.2.1A).

Pointillism is an artistic technique for producing additive color mixture by applying many small, adjacent, but spatially distinct dots of color (see Color Plate C.3)

Polar coordinates are an ordered set of numbers that specify the location of a point in terms of its radial direction and distance from a reference point.

Polar projection (see *perspective projection*).

Polychromatic light is *electromagnetic energy* whose *photons* are a mixture of two or more *wavelengths* (see Figures 3.1.2B and 3.1.2C).

Ponzo illusion is a famous illusion of size in which converging lines induce distortions of equally long lines between them (see Figure 7.1.10).

Pop-out (see *visual pop-out*).

Position constancy is the ability to perceive the correct egocentric direction to an object *veridically* despite rotations of the head and eye.

Positive direction along an *axis* of a *coordinate system* is the direction along that *axis* that is taken as the positive reference standard.

Positron emission tomography (**PET**) is a brain imaging technique in which a radioactive substance is injected into the blood so that blood flow to active brain regions can be detected and used to reconstruct a 3-D map of brain activity (see Figure 2.2.11D).

Power spectrum of *Fourier analysis* for an *image* specifies the *amplitude* of each *sinusoidal grating* at each particular *spatial frequency* and *orientation*.

Preferential looking paradigm is a method of studying visual *discriminability* in infants by measuring how long they look at two different visual displays. If they look longer at one than at the other, they can tell the difference between them.

Premises are the given *information* for *processes* of *logical inference* from which *conclusions* are drawn.

Pre-motor theory of *attention* claims that *eye movements* and *attentional* movements are controlled by closely related mechanisms and that *eye movements* normally follow *attentional* movements (rather than vice versa).

Presbyopia is a visual condition in which the *lens* gradually loses its elasticity as a person ages normally, so it cannot become thick enough for close vision.

Primacy effect is the elevated portion of the serial position curve in verbal memory experiments at the beginning of the list (see Figure 12.1.10).

Primal sketches are Marr's *image-based representations* in his theory of vision, consisting of the *raw primal sketch* (which includes detected *edges*, bars, blobs, and line terminations) and the *full primal sketch* (which adds global grouping and organization among the local *image features*).

Primary color categories are the result of classifying *colors* into the six biological primitives of the visual system: black, white, red, green, blue, and yellow.

Primary memory (see *short-term memory*).

Primary visual cortex (see *occipital cortex*).

Priming effects are experimental phenomena in which a previously performed perceptual task speeds a later task with related stimuli in a *priming paradigm*.

Priming paradigm is an experimental procedure in which processing a particular *image* of an object is faster and more accurate if the same *image* (or one very much like it) is presented a second time, because the *processes* that accomplish its perception are in a state of heightened readiness.

Primitive code is the initial *representation* of a figure in *structural information theory*. It is generated by tracing the *contour* of the figure and describing it symbolically as a sequence of line segment lengths and the angles between them (see Figure 8.3.5).

Principle components analysis (**PCA**) is a method for achieving compact coding of *images*. It identifies a reduced set of orthogonal *vectors* (also called *basis functions*) that capture the maximum variance of the subset of points corresponding to the set of natural *images* within the *state space*.

Principle of Prägnanz (or **minimum principle**) is the *Gestalt* proposal that the basis for selecting among possible perceptual interpretations of a given retinal *image* is the "goodness" or "simplicity" of the alternatives: the percept will be as "good" as the prevailing conditions allow.

Probabilistic inference (or **statistical inference**) is a form of statistical reasoning based on the rules of probability and Bayes' theorem.

Problem of other minds is the philosophical issue of how you know whether another person, creature, or machine has *conscious experiences* or not.

Procedural memory is the retention of *information* in *long-term memory* concerning general knowledge about how to use something (e.g., the kind of *information* that one typically finds in a user's manual).

Processes are the active components in an *information processing* system that *transform* (or perform *operations*) on *information* by changing one *representation* into another.

Projective field of a *neuron* in the visual system is the set of higher-level cells to which it projects (see Figure 3.2.18A).

Projective geometry is the mathematical study of how a higher-dimensional space is mapped onto lower-dimensional ones.

Property dualism is a philosophical position on the *mind-body problem* based on the idea that physical and mental events differ in their *features* or characteristics, even though they do not constitute different substances (as claimed in *substance dualism*).

Property selection is the *process* of concentrating *attention* on specific visual *dimensions* or *features* or objects, such as their *color*, *shape*, or *orientation*.

Proportionality hypothesis is the proposal that *size constancy* can be accounted for by the *invariant feature* of relative size of adjacent objects independent of their distance from the observer (see Figure 7.1.5).

Proprioceptive system is the set of biological structures that are responsible for (among other things) the sense of upright and balance within the gravitational field of the earth.

Prosopagnosia is a specific form of *visual agnosia* in which the patient is unable to recognize individual faces, even if they were very familiar before the brain was damaged.

Protanopia is one of two conditions of red-green *color blindness*. It is caused by the lack of the long-*wavelength* pigment in *cones* of the *retina*.

Prototype is the "best" or "most representative" example of a given *category*. It plays a special role in structuring color and other natural categories in Rosch's theory of categorization.

Proximal mode is a strategy for perceiving in which the properties of the retinal *image*, or *proximal stimulus*, dominate those of the environmental object, or *distal stimulus*.

Proximal stimulus is the immediate physical cause of perception: the projected optical *image* that falls on the *retina*.

Proximity is a principle of *perceptual grouping* that states that, all else being equal, closer elements are more likely to be grouped together (see Figure 6.1.2B).

Proximity matrix is a square table consisting of n rows and n columns in which each entry is a number that represents the similarity (or dissimilarity) of the item in that row to the item in that column (see Figure 8.2.9).

Pseudo-normal color perception is a hypothetical condition of the visual system in which the pigments in the long-*wavelength* (**L**) and medium-*wavelength* (**M**) *cones* are exchanged because of two simultaneous genetic abnormalities (see Figure 13.1.2). It has been claimed that such observers would have red-green reversed color *experiences* relative to standard normal *trichromats*.

Pseudoscope is an optical device that reverses *binocular disparity* by reversing the *images* that are projected to the left and right eyes (see Figure 5.5.33).

Psychometric function is a graph that plots the percentage of detection responses on the y axis as a function of stimulus intensity on the x axis (see Figure A.1.1).

Psychophysical channel is a hypothetical neural mechanism that is selectively tuned to a limited range of values within some continuum, such as *spatial frequencies* or *orientations* of *sinusoidal gratings*.

Psychophysical correspondence is a mapping that specifies how physical measurements map onto psychological measurements of corresponding *experiences*.

Psychophysical scales are quantitative relations between experiential magnitude and physical magnitude, such as *Fechner's law*.

Psychophysics is the behavioral study of quantitative relations between people's conscious *experiences* and corresponding properties of the physical world.

Psychophysiological isomorphism is the *Gestalt hypothesis* that one's psychological *experiences* have the same abstract structure as the physiological mechanisms that cause those *experiences*.

Pull cues are peripherally presented changes in stimulus *images* that draw *attention* to the location at which they appear, thereby producing involuntary shifts of *attention*.

Pupil is the variably sized opening in the opaque *iris* of the eye.

Push cues are centrally presented symbols (such as an arrow at fixation) that direct a subject's *attention* to a different location, thereby producing voluntary shifts of *attention*.

Qualia (or **raw feels**) refer to the qualities of *conscious experience*: what it "feels like" to experience different sensory qualities, such as redness versus circularity.

Qualitative depth information is *information* that specifies just the ordinal *depth* relations (closer/farther) between objects.

Quantitative depth information is *information* that specifies the numerical distance relations between objects (e.g., ratios of distances or absolute distances).

Random dot kinematograms are experimental stimuli in which many randomly positioned elements change position rapidly and are perceived to be in *motion* (see Figure 10.1.12).

Random dot stereogram is a pair of *images* consisting of thousands of randomly placed dots whose lateral displacements produce a convincing illusion of *depth* when viewed stereoscopically so that one *image* stimulates the left eye and the other *image* stimulates the right eye (see Figures 5.3.8 and 5.3.9).

Rapid serial visual presentation (**RSVP**) is an experimental procedure in which a sequence of many visual stimuli is presented at *fixation* for brief exposure durations, typically at rates of 3 to 10 items per second.

Raw feel (see *qualia*).

Raw primal sketch is Marr's initial *representation* in the *image-based stage* which includes symbolic encoding of *luminance edges*, bars, blobs, and terminators as the primitive elements (see Figure 4.3.14).

RBC theory (see *recognition by components theory*).

Recall memory task is an experimental paradigm in which subjects' memories are assessed by requiring them to reproduce the to-be-remembered items.

Recency effect is the elevation in performance on a *recall memory task* for the last few items of the list, widely believed to reflect mainly retrieval from *short-term memory* (see Figure 12.1.10).

Receptive field of a *neuron* in the visual system is the region of the *retina* that influences the *firing rate* of the target *neuron* by increasing it (*excitation*) or decreasing it (*inhibition*).

Receptors (see *photoreceptors*).

Recognition by components (**RBC**) **theory** (or **geon theory**) is a *structural description* theory of *object classification* into *entry-level categories* based on a discrete set of *shape primitives* derived from *nonaccidental properties* of *generalized cylinders*.

Recognition memory task is an experimental paradigm in which subjects' memories are assessed by showing them an initial set of items and later testing them by showing another set of items, for each of which they must decide whether or not it was presented previously.

Recurrent networks (see *feedback networks*).

Recursive decomposition is the description of a complex (nonprimitive) *informational event* at one level as consisting of two or more component *informational events* and the temporal ordering relations among them at a lower level (see Figure 2.3.6).

Recursive operations are *operations* that refer to themselves in their own definitions or are able to take their own output as input.

Reduced codes are simplified representations in *structural information theory* that result from applying *semantic operators* to *primitive codes* or other reduced codes (see Figure 8.3.5).

Reduction tube (or **reduction screen**) is a device for eliminating contextual factors in visual perception. It consists of a neutral gray aperture that blocks out everything in the visual field except a specified target region.

Reduction screen (see *reduction tube*).

Reductive materialism (or **mind-brain identity theory**) is a version of *materialism* in which mental events are believed to be ultimately reducible to material events in much the same way that other successful reductions have occurred in science.

Redundancy gain is facilitation in a Garnerian *classification* task in a *correlated variation condition* relative to the faster of the two corresponding *unidimensional variation conditions* (see Figure 11.2.17).

Reflectance (see *reflectance spectrum*).

Reflectance edges are changes in *image luminance* caused by changes in the *reflectance* of two retinally adjacent surfaces, such as occur when surfaces are made of different materials or are painted different *colors* (see Figure 5.5.16).

Reflectance map is a hypothesized *representation* of *image* regions that correspond to surfaces that differ in the percentage of *light* they reflect.

Reflectance spectrum of a surface is the percentage of incident *photons* at each *wavelength* reflected by the surface.

Reflection about a given *axis* is a geometrical *transformation* of handedness (or "sense") in which every point of an *image* is mapped to one that is the same in perpendicular distance from the axis of reflection but opposite in direction.

Refraction of *light* is the bending of the trajectory of *photons* as they travel from one medium to another (see Figure 1.2.3).

Region segmentation is the *process* of dividing an *image* into mutually exclusive areas based on uniformity of *image-based properties*, such as *luminance, color, texture, motion,* or *binocular disparity*.

Regions of an *image* are bounded, 2-D areas that constitute spatial subsets of the *image*.

Rejection-of-coincidence principle (see *nonaccidentalness*).

Relatability theory is Kellman and Shipley's theory of *visual completion* based mainly on the *perceptual grouping* principle of *good continuation* (see Figure 6.4.5).

Relational determination is the principle that perception is dominated by configural relations among properties and parts rather than by absolute properties.

Relative depth information refers to *information* that specifies how far objects are relative to each other.

Relative motion component of *configural motion* refers to the *vectors* that specify how each object is moving relative to the group as a whole (i.e., relative to its *common motion component*).

Relative size is a source of *relative depth information* arising from the fact that the closer of two identical objects will project a larger *image* than the farther object (see Figure 5.5.8).

Reparameterization is the *process* of changing the variables that directly control a system's behavior from one *representation* to another.

Replication of *templates* refers to constructing a different *template* for each shape in every possible position, *orientation*, size, and *reflection*.

Representation refers to a state of the visual system that stands for an environmental object or event by virtue of having the same relational structure with respect to other objects or events.

Representational momentum is a memory distortion in which the final position of an abruptly halted object is misremembered as being farther along its path of *motion* than it actually was.

Representational system is a relation of *homomorphism* that holds between two related but distinct worlds: the represented world (or source domain) and the representing world (or target domain).

Represented world is the set of objects and events outside an *information processing* system (usually called the "external world" or "environment") that is modeled by an internal representation.

Representing world is the set of objects and events within the *information processing* system (usually called "the internal *representation*" or simply "the *representation*") that models the external world.

Resonance metaphor is Gibson's analogy that an organism picks up *information* about the environment much as a tuning fork vibrates in the presence of acoustical energy at or near its resonant frequency.

Response bias (β) refers to the tendency of observers to raise or lower their internal criterion for detecting a signal due to strategic *information* about the probability of a signal, the costs of *misses* versus *false alarms*, and so on.

Retina is the curved surface at the back of the eye that is densely covered with over 100 million light-sensitive *photoreceptors* plus *amacrine, bipolar, ganglion,* and *horizontal cells* that *process* the *output* of the *receptors*.

Retinal densitometry is a technique for measuring *pigment bleaching* in the eyes of living humans by determining how much *light* is absorbed by the *receptors*.

Retinal image theory of perceived heading claims that the visual system is able to factor out the *translational* component produced by the *eye movements* from purely *image*-based *information*.

Retinex theory is a theory of *color constancy* and *lightness constancy* developed by Land and McCann in which *luminance* ratios are taken at *edges* and integrated across the visual field (see Figure 3.3.7B).

Retinoscope is a device that allows the examiner to determine how well the eye focuses *light*.

Retinotopic mapping (or **topographic mapping**) is a spatial correspondence between the *retina* and various sheets of *neurons* in the visual system (e.g., *LGN* or *V1*) such that nearby regions on the *retina* project to nearby regions of the sheet, thus preserving qualitative (but not quantitative) spatial relations in the map.

Retrograde amnesia is a form of *amnesia* in which the patient has difficulty remembering old *information* that was known before the brain was damaged.

Reverberatory circuit is a closed loop of *neurons* that fire each other sequentially so that the firing "reverberates" (echoes around and around) through the neural loop.

Reviewing paradigm is an experimental method for studying temporal integration in object perception. Subjects are presented with two or more static objects with letters inside them, and the objects begin to move. When they stop, a target letter is presented in one, and subjects must name this target letter as quickly as possible (see Figure 11.2.29).

Rewrite rules (see *semantic operators*).

Rhodopsin is the photosensitive pigment in *rods*.

Ricochet heuristic is the tendency for observers to see the initially stationary ball in a collision event as being heavier than the incoming one if the incoming ball ricochets (moves backward) at a higher velocity than the resulting forward *motion* of the initially stationary ball (see Figure 10.4.4A).

Rigidity heuristic is a bias toward perceiving rigid *motions* in 3-D space rather than plastic deformations, provided that the sensory stimulation is consistent with such an interpretation.

Rod-and-frame effect is an *illusion* in which the gravitational *orientation* of a luminous rod within a large, tilted, luminous rectangle is misperceived toward the direction of the rectangle's *orientation* (see Figure 7.3.4).

Rods are long, rod-shaped *photoreceptors* in the *retina* (see Figure 1.3.8) that are extremely sensitive to *light* and are located everywhere in the retina except at its very center (*fovea*). They are used exclusively for vision at low levels of *illumination*.

Roelofs' effect is an *illusion* in which the *egocentric position* of an object within a rectangle is displaced in the direction of the rectangle's center (see Figure 7.4.7).

Root node is the *node* at the top of a *hierarchical tree*. It represents the set of all objects at the *terminal nodes*.

Rotation about a point is a geometrical *transformation* of *orientation* in which every point of an *image* is mapped to one that is the same distance from the center of rotation but whose direction from it differs by the angle of rotation.

Rotation and reflection (R & R) subsets is a theory of *figural goodness* in which *shapes* are predicted to be "good" to a degree that depends on the number of different versions generated by central *rotations* and central *reflections* (see Figure 8.3.4).

RSVP (see *rapid serial visual presentation*).

Saccades are very rapid, abrupt, ballistic *eye movements* whose function is to bring new objects of interest to the *fovea* (see Figure 11.1.3).

Saccadic suppression is the phenomenon that the visual system is less sensitive to stimulation during a *saccade*, including the visual blurring produced by the *eye movement* itself.

Saccule is a fluid-filled sac in the inner ear which, along with the *utricle*, signals the orientation of the head (see Figure 7.3.2A).

Sapir-Whorf hypothesis (see *cultural relativism*).

Saturation (or **chroma**) is the radial dimension of *color space* (that is, the distance from the central *axis*) corresponding to the vividness of *color* in a *light* or surface (see Color Plate 3.2).

Scale integration is the *process* by which the visual system determines how *edges* at different scales of resolution match up to determine which ones correspond to the same environmental *edge* and which ones do not (see Figure 4.3.12).

Scale space is a continuous representation of *edge* scales (sizes) hypothesized by Witkin to facilitate solving the problem of *scale integration* by following *edges* throughout this dimension (see Figure 4.3.13).

Scaling problem of *lightness* perception is to determine how *luminance* ratios should be mapped onto the white-to-black scale of achromatic *lightnesses*.

Scan paths are stereotyped sequences of *saccades* that are used to explore a given *image* (see Figure 11.1.10).

Schematic map is Hochberg's conception of a *representation* consisting of possible samplings of a spatially extended scene together with contingent expectancies of what will be seen as a result of those samplings.

Scientific paradigm is a set of working assumptions that a community of scientists share (often implicitly) in conducting research, usually involving pretheoretical or *metatheoretical* ways of conceptualizing the major issues and standard ways of approaching them.

Scotomas are limited regions of blindness due to damage to part of the *retina* or visual *cortex*.

Scotopic conditions refer to vision under low levels of illumination when *rod* activity dominates vision, particularly at night.

Second derivative of a *luminance* function is the slope of the first derivative of the *luminance* function (see Figure 4.3.4E).

Second-order differential operators are *edge operators* that take the difference between the differences of neighboring *pixels* (see Figures 4.3.1C, 4.3.1D, and 4.3.1E).

Secondary light sources are surfaces that reflect *light* onto other surfaces, thereby illuminating them indirectly.

Secondary memory (see *long-term memory*).

Selectivity refers to the flexible allocation of *attentional* resources (*capacity*) to different subsets of visual information, including filtering by location and other properties.

Self-occluded surfaces are the surfaces of an object that are hidden from view by its visible surfaces, such as the back sides of a cube (see Figure 1.1.7).

Semantic memory is *information* in *long-term memory* that concerns general knowledge of generic concepts and *categories*, the kind of *information* that one typically finds in a dictionary or encyclopedia.

Semantic operators (or **rewrite rules**) are *operations* in *structural information theory* to simplify *primitive codes* by removing structural redundancies (see Figure 8.3.5).

Semicircular canals are three fluid-filled tubes in the inner ear that signal changes in the orientation of the head (see Figure 7.3.2A).

Sensory atoms are the primitive, indivisible elements of *experience* in a given sense modality that were postulated by *structuralist* theorists to be the basis of all perception.

Sensory information stores (SIS) are very brief "buffer" memory stores for *information* in specific modalities, including visual *information* (see *iconic memory*).

Sensory processes are the responses of low-level mechanisms within a given modality (such as vision or audition) that depend on the magnitude of the stimulus, the adaptation state of the system, and internal noise.

Separable dimensions are pairs of continuous properties for which people can selectively *attend* to one or the other at will, without interference from the unattended property.

Serial position curve is a graph of the probability of correctly recalling an item as a function of its serial position in the originally presented list of items (see Figure 12.1.10).

Serial processing refers to two or more *operations* that occur sequentially, one following another.

Shadowing task is an experimental method for studying auditory *attention* in which subjects have to repeat aloud the message coming through either the left or right channel of a pair of headphones.

Shape (or **form**) is a complex *feature* of objects that refers to its relative distribution in space.

Shape constancy is the ability to perceive the same object as having the same *shape* when observed from different viewpoints, even though its retinal *shape* changes (see Figure 7.2.1).

Shape equivalence is the perception of two different objects as having the same *shape* despite other differences between them, such as their positions, orientations, and sizes.

Shape primitives are a set of simple, indivisible shapes (e.g., *generalized cylinders*) that constitute the complete set of the most basic parts into which more complex objects can then be analyzed.

Short-range motion system is Braddick's proposed subsystem of the *motion* perception system that is assumed to be sensitive to relatively short displacements and rapid alternation rates, such as occur in *random dot kinematograms*.

Short-term memory (**STM**, also called **primary memory**) is a limited-*capacity* memory store of longer duration than *sensory information stores* (on the order of many seconds) for *information* in the image that is currently being *processed*.

Signal detection theory (**SDT**) is a *psychophysical* theory that replaces the concept of a discrete sensory *threshold* with two separate concepts: an immutable *sensory process* that cannot be influenced by strategic factors and a later *decision process* that can be.

Signal-to-noise ratio is a relative measure of detectability expressed by dividing the level of the designated source (the signal) by the level of irrelevant background variation (the noise). Highly detectable signals have high signal-to-noise ratios.

Signal trial is an experimentally defined interval in which a weak stimulus (the signal) is presented either alone or embedded in noise.

Similarity is either (1) a relation of the relative degree of sameness between two perceptual objects or (2) a principle of *perceptual grouping* that states that, all else being equal, more

similar elements (in size, *shape, color, orientation*, etc.) are more likely to be grouped together (see Figures 6.1.2C, 6.1.2D, and 6.1.2E).

Similarity group is a mathematically defined set of geometrical *transformations* consisting of *translations, rotations, dilations, reflections*, and their various combinations (see Figure 8.1.1).

Simple cells are *neurons* in area *V1* whose responses to complex stimuli can be predicted from their responses to individual spots of *light*. They fire primarily to stationary *edges* or bars of *light* at a particular *orientation* and retinal position (see Figure 4.1.6).

Simultagnosia is the inability to perceive more than one object at a time during a single *fixation*.

Simultaneous color contrast (or **induced color**) is a spatial context effect in which a vivid *color* in one region influences its neighboring regions toward the *complementary hue* (see Color Plate 3.7).

Simultaneous lightness contrast is a spatial context effect in which a very light *color* in one region influences its neighboring regions toward a darker *color* (see Figure 3.2.5).

Simultaneous motion contrast is a spatial context effect on *motion* perception in which a field of dots moving steadily in one direction causes an adjacent region of stationary dots to appear to drift in the opposite direction (see Figure 10.1.5).

Single-cell recording is a technique that is used to explore *neuron*-level *information processing* by positioning an extremely thin *microelectrode* close to a *neuron's axon* to register its *spiking* behavior in response to specific stimulus conditions (see Figure 2.2.6).

Sinusoidal gratings are two-dimensional patterns whose *luminance* varies according to a sine wave over one spatial dimension and is constant over the perpendicular dimension. Each grating is characterized by four parameters: *spatial frequency, orientation, phase*, and *amplitude* (or *contrast*) (see Figure 4.2.1).

SIS (see *sensory information stores*).

Size constancy is the ability to perceive the true environmental size of objects despite changes in the size of their *images* on the *retina* because of differences in viewing distance.

Size-distance paradox refers to the conflict between the *apparent distance theory* of the *moon illusion* and the fact that people report that the horizon moon seems closer (rather than farther) than the zenith moon.

Size-distance relation is the mathematical relation among the environmental size of an object, the optical size of its *image*, and the distance between the object and its *image* (see Figure 5.5.9).

Sketchpad (see *visuo-spatial scratchpad*).

Slant refers to the size of the angle between the observer's line of sight and the surface normal (the line perpendicular to the surface at that point): The larger is the angle, the greater is the surface slant (see Figure 5.0.1).

"Slave" memories are subservient buffer memory systems in *working memory* that code recently accessed *information* in a specific sensory modality, such as the *visuo-spatial scratchpad* and the *articulatory loop*.

Smooth pursuit eye movements are *eye movements* that track the position of a moving object to keep it in *foveal* vision once it is there (see Figure 11.1.4).

SOA (see *stimulus onset asynchrony*).

Soft constraints are informational restrictions, varying from weak to strong, that should be taken into account in making an inference but may be overridden by other considerations.

Software primitives are a set of computationally plausible operations into which a complex *process* can be decomposed.

Space-based theories of *visual attention* assume that *attention* selects a region of space (rather than a perceptual object) on which resources are focused.

Space-time diagrams are multidimensional spatial *representations* of dynamic *image* structure that include temporal *information* in an extra spatial dimension (see Figure 10.1.1).

Span of apprehension is the number of letters that a person can perceive in a single, very brief visual presentation.

Sparse distributed coding is a scheme for recoding the output of *receptors* so that the number of active *units* is minimized (see Figure 4.3.23B).

Spatial frequency of a *sinusoidal grating* refers to the width of its fuzzy light and dark stripes: Low-frequency gratings have thick bars, and high-frequency gratings have thin ones. It is specified in terms of the number of light/dark cycles per degree of visual angle (see Figure 4.2.1).

Spatial frequency theory is a *psychophysical* theory of spatial vision in which it is claimed that complex *images* are analyzed into *sinusoidal gratings* at different *spatial frequencies*, *orientations*, *phases*, and *amplitudes*.

Spatial selection is the *process* of concentrating *attentional* resources on *information* from a restricted region of the visual field.

Spatiotopic fusion hypothesis is the conjecture that retinal *images* from different *saccades* are mapped into a larger, spatially organized *transsaccadic memory* array according to their positions to produce an integrated, composite representation of the visual environment (Figure 11.1.11).

Spectral crosspoint condition is evidence that a chromatic *edge* is due to differences in *reflectance* rather than *illumination*. It holds when the graphs of the changes in intensity at two *wavelengths* for two adjacent regions cross each other (see Figures 3.3.11A and 3.3.11C).

Spectral diagram of a *light* is a graph of the number of *photons* at each *wavelength* in the range from 400 to 700 nm (see Figure 3.1.2).

Specular surfaces are shiny, polished surfaces, such as mirrors, that reflect incident *light* in the single direction symmetric to that from which it came: The angle of incidence is equal to the angle of reflection (see Figure 1.2.4B).

Spikes (see *action potentials*).

Spiral aftereffect is a *motion aftereffect* in which sustained perception of a spiral rotating outward (or inward) produces the opposite *motion* in a stationary field.

Split-brain patients are people whose *corpus callosum* has been partially or completely severed, thus disconnecting large portions of their two *cerebral hemispheres*.

Spotlight theory of spatial *attention* is the proposal that *attention* is like a spotlight, so the object at the location where *attention* is focused can be processed more effectively than objects in other regions.

Stabilized images are *images* that are presented so that they are completely stationary with respect to the *retina* (see Figure 11.1.2).

Stages are discrete sets of closely related *information processing* events that work as a unit in the sense of being highly interdependent among themselves but largely independent of those in other stages.

Standard template (see *template*).

State space is a multidimensional *representation* of the set of possible states of a computational system, within which the state of each *unit* corresponds to a different dimension and the current state of the whole system corresponds to a single point whose coordinates represent the current states of all the *units*.

Static depth information is *information* about the distances to objects that is available in a motionless *image*.

Stationpoint (see *viewpoint*).

Statistical inference (see *probabilistic inference*).

Stem completion task is an indirect method for assessing memory for presented material. Subjects are shown part of a word with blanks substituted for some of the letters (e.g., FLA __) and are asked to complete it with letters from the first few words that come to mind.

Stereoacuity threshold is the smallest *binocular disparity* that an organism is able to detect.

Stereoblindness is the inability to perceive *depth information* from *binocular disparity*.

Stereogram is a pair of slightly different *images* that produce compelling *illusions* of *depth* when viewed so that one *image* projects to the left eye and the other to the right eye (see Figure 5.3.6).

Stereo-kinetic effect is a phenomenon in which observers perceive *motion* of a 3-D cone (or tunnel) in *depth* even though the actual display is a set of nested circles rigidly *rotating* in the *frontal plane*.

Stereopsis is the *process* of perceiving the relative distance to objects based on their relative lateral displacement (*binocular disparity*) in the two retinal *images*.

Stereoscopic vision is the perception of a layout of surfaces in 3-D that is based on interpreting the relative *binocular disparity* of corresponding image features in two laterally displaced retinal images as relative depth.

Stimulus-driven processes (see *bottom-up processes*).

Stimulus onset asynchrony (**SOA**) is the time delay between the onset of a target stimulus and the onset of another stimulus, often a *mask*.

STM (see *short-term memory*).

Strabismus is the misalignment of the two eyes so that they do not *fixate* on the same object.

Stress is a measure of how badly the distances between pairs of points in a *multidimensional scaling* solution fit the measured similarities (or dissimilarities) of corresponding pairs of objects in the *proximity matrix*.

Striate cortex (or area **V1**) is the first cortical visual area of the brain. It receives input directly from the *lateral geniculate nucleus* and sends its *output* to a large number of different visual areas (see Figure 1.3.19).

Stroboscopic motion (see *apparent motion*).

"Strong AI" is the so-called "strong" view of *artificial intelligence* that assumes that a properly programmed machine actually has mental *processes*, including *conscious experiences*.

Stroop effect is the phenomenon that occurs when subjects are required to name the *color* of ink in which color words are printed: They show massive interference when the color word conflicts with the ink *color* to be named.

Structural descriptions are *representations* of *parts* and relations between *parts*, usually as *networks* in which *nodes* represent the whole object and its various *parts* and labeled *links* (or *arcs*) between *nodes* represent the relations between *parts* (see Figure 8.2.15).

Structural information theory (or **coding theory**) is a *structural description* theory of *shape representation* that determines *perceptual organization* in a context-sensitive way by finding the "best," most economical symbolic description. It is based on the *Gestalt principle of Prägnanz*.

Structuralism is the earliest psychological theory of perception, developed largely from the views of the *British Empiricists* and based on principles of *empiricism*, *atomism*, and *introspection*.

Structure-from-motion theorem is a mathematical relation that if one knows the correspondence of points from each view to the next and if one assumes that the object is rigid, it is possible to recover both the 3-D location and the *motion* of the object from four non-coplanar points in three distinct *orthographic projections*.

Structure from shading (also called **shape from shading**) is the *process* by which *information* about the curvature of surfaces can be extracted from changes in *luminance* in the *image* that result from differences in surface *depth* and *illumination* (see Figure 4.3.17).

Subjective contours (see *illusory contour*).

Subjective knowledge is knowledge of private events that cannot be observed by anyone except the person who is having them.

Subjective threshold of awareness is a measure based on the subject's introspective report of the presence or absence of *conscious* states of perception to a question, such as, "Did you see anything or not?"

Subliminal advertising is the attempt to influence people's consumer decisions by very rapid or subtle presentation of *information* below the *threshold* of *awareness*.

Subliminal perception is the ability to register and *process* *information* that has been presented under conditions in which it is below the *threshold* of *awareness*.

Subordinate categories are *categories* below the basic level in Rosch's theory of *category* structure.

Substance dualism (or **Cartesian dualism**) is a form of *dualism* that is based on the idea that mind and body are two completely different kinds of things.

Superior colliculus is the nucleus in the brain stem to which the smaller bundle of *axons* of retinal *ganglion cells* project. It *processes information* about location and *eye movements* (see Figure 11.1.7).

Supervenience is a relation between mind and body due to Kim that states that any difference in conscious events requires some corresponding difference in underlying neural activity (whereas there can be many differences in neural activity that produce no differences in conscious events).

Superordinate categories are *categories* above the *basic level* in Rosch's theory of category structure.

Surface-based stage is a set of *representations* and *processes* that are concerned with recovering the intrinsic properties of visible surfaces in the environment that might have produced the features discovered in the *image-based stage*.

Surface layout is the name Gibson used to refer to the spatial distribution of visible surfaces within the three-dimensional environment.

Surface normal at a point on an object's surface is the direction perpendicular to the local surface region around that point and pointing away from the object's interior.

Surface orientation is the *slant* and *tilt* of a surface with respect to the viewer's line of sight.

Swinging room is an experimental device that is used to study visual effects on balance and posture. It consists of a large, movable, bottomless box suspended from the ceiling of a larger room. The floor of the larger room is thus stationary, but the walls and ceiling of the box can be swung forward and backward or side to side (see Figure 10.3.3).

Symmetric networks are *connectionist networks* in which the *connection weights* between each pair of *units* is the same in both directions.

Symmetry is a global property of a figure with respect to a given *transformation* (e.g., *reflection* or *rotation*) if applying that transformation leaves the figure unchanged.

Symmetry subgroup of a given figure is the subset of spatial *transformations* that leave it unchanged (see Figure 8.3.4).

Synapse is a small gap that exists between the *terminals* of one *neuron* and the *dendrites* of another, into which *neurotransmitters* are released (see Figure 1.3.6).

Synchrony is a principle of *perceptual grouping* that states that, all else being equal, elements that change at the same time are more likely be grouped together (see Figure 6.1.5).

Synesthesia is the tendency for sensory experiences in one modality to evoke correlated experiences in other modalities.

Taking account of distance is an indirect theory of *size constancy* in which prior perception of the distance to an object is used to calculate its environmental size from the *size-distance relation*.

Tau function is the ratio of any spatial variable (e.g., the position of a point relative to the *focus of optical expansion*) divided by its temporal derivative (e.g., the point's *velocity* relative to the *focus of expansion*).

Teacher units are an additional set of *units* in a *connectionist network* that stand in one-to-one correspondence with the *output units* and encode the correct output.

Templates are *representations* in which *shape* is specified by the concatenation of *receptor cells* on which the *image* of an object with that particular shape would fall (see Figure 8.2.1).

Temporal lobe is the lobe of the brain that extends downward and forward from *occipital (primary visual) cortex* (see Figure 1.3.2). It is part of the *ventral "what" system* of visual processing and appears to be concerned primarily with object *categorization* and *identification*.

Terminal nodes are the *nodes* at the bottom of a *hierarchical tree* that represent individual objects or parts.

Terminals are the branching ends of the *axon* of a *neuron* at which the electrical activity of the *axon* is converted into a chemical signal, via *neurotransmitters*, by which it can stimulate another *neuron*.

Terminator boundaries are divisions between illuminated and shadowed regions of an *image* where the *surface normal* is known to be perpendicular to the direction of incident *light* (see Figure 5.5.29).

Textons are the elemental local *features* of *texture* proposed by Julesz.

Texture is a statistical property of the local spatial structure of *image* regions and/or surfaces to which the visual system is sensitive.

Texture analysis is the *process* by which the visual system defines *image* regions that differ in the statistical properties of local spatial structure (see Figure 4.3.16).

Texture gradient is a gradual change in the size, density, and/or 2-D shape of projected environmental elements as the surface of which they are part recedes in the distance (see Figures 2.1.9, 5.5.11, and 5.5.12).

Texture segregation is the *process* by which an *image* is *partitioned* into a set of *regions* solely on the basis of *texture information* (see Figure 6.2.8).

Theory is an integrated set of statements (called *hypotheses*) about underlying mechanisms or principles that not only organizes and explains known phenomena, but also makes predictions about new ones.

Threshold (empirical) for perceiving a given stimulus dimension is the weakest stimulus that can just barely be detected according to some specified *psychophysical* method.

Threshold (theoretical) is the particular stimulus value at which the internal response is hypothesized to change from the absence of any visual *experience* to the presence of some visual *experience* (see Figure A.1.2).

Threshold rule is a procedure for making a *decision* by setting a *criterion* on the outcome of some *process* and assigning the target object or event to whatever alternative outcome, if any, has a value equal to or exceeding the *criterion*.

Tilt refers to the direction of a *depth* gradient relative to the *frontal plane* (see Figure 5.0.1).

Time to contact is the length of time it will take the observer to reach the surface toward which he or she is heading under present movement conditions.

Tokens in a symbolic *representation* are individual instances of a symbolic *type*, such as the particular *edges* that are encoded in Marr's *raw primal sketch* as instances of the general type known as *edges*.

Top-down processing (or **hypothesis-driven** or **expectation-driven processing**) refers to *processes* that operate by taking as *input* a "higher-level" (more central or cognitive) *representation* and producing or modifying a "lower-level" (more peripheral or sensory) *representation* as *output*.

Topographic mapping (see *retinotopic mapping*).

Trained introspection is the method of studying perception by turning one's mind inward (*introspecting*) and carefully observing one's own *experiences* after studying with a qualified expert.

Transformation is a systematic change in structure according to some well-defined function.

Transformational alignment hypothesis is the proposal that *shape equivalence* is analyzed by determining whether two objects can be brought into exact correspondence by one of an allowable set of *transformations* such as those of the *similarity group*.

Transformational invariance is a *feature* of an object when applying a particular *transformation* to the object leaves it unchanged.

Translation is a geometrical *transformation* in which every point of an *image* is mapped to one that differs by the same direction and distance.

Transmission spectra are graphs of the proportion of *photons* that pass through an optical filter for each *wavelength* of *light*.

Transparency or **translucency** (see *perceived transparency*).

Transsaccadic memory is a memory structure that mediates the integration of *information* across *saccades* into a unified perception of the visual world.

Transversality regularity refers to the fact that when one object penetrates another, they tend to meet in *concave discontinuities* where their composite surface is not smooth but angles sharply inward toward the interior of the composite object (see Figure 7.6.7).

Trichromatic theory is a theory of *color* vision due to Young and Helmholtz stating that all color experiences can be explained by the pattern of response in three types of color *receptors* with overlapping spectral sensitivities that peak at *wavelengths* in the red, green, and blue regions of the *electromagnetic spectrum* (see Figures 3.2.7 and 3.2.8).

Trichromats are people with "normal" *color* vision who can match any *light* with some mixture of three appropriately chosen others.

Triggering effect is a form of perceived causation that occurs when the speed of the second object in a collision exceeds that of the first object, as though some additional force acted on the second object to make it move so quickly (see Figure 10.4.3B).

Tritanopia is the condition of blue-yellow *color blindness* that is caused by the lack of the short-*wavelength cone* pigment.

Turing machine is a finite state device, such as a modern digital computer, that can be programmed to *process information* automatically in a theoretically infinite variety of ways.

Turing's test is a behavioral test due to Turing that attempts to solve the problem of how to determine whether a computing machine could be called "intelligent" by determining whether a person can tell the difference, just from behavior, between a real person and a computer that has been programmed to behave intelligently.

2.5-D sketch is the name of the *surface-based* representations in Marr's theory of vision (see Figure 2.4.5).

Type in a symbolic *representation* is the *category* of an *image feature* or element (as opposed to an individual *token* of those types), such as *edges*, bars, blobs, and terminations in Marr's *raw primal sketch*.

Typicality (or **goodness-of-example**) **ratings** are judgments of how representative (or "good") a given example is as a member of a specific category.

Unconscious inference is Helmholtz's proposal that vision bridges the logical gap between optical *information* and perceptual knowledge using hidden *heuristic assumptions* in conjunction with the retinal *image* to reach perceptual *conclusions* about the environment.

Uncrossed disparity is the nasal (inward) direction of *binocular disparity* that occurs when the target object is farther than the *fixated* object (see Figure 5.3.2).

Undecomposable system is an *information processing* device in which the interactions between components are as strong as those within components.

Underconstancy is incomplete *perceptual constancy* in which the perception is a compromise between *proximal* and *distal* matches.

Unidimensional variation condition in a Garnerian *classification* task requires subjects to classify the stimuli according to their value on one of two dimensions while the second dimension is held constant (see Figure 11.2.17).

Uniform connectedness is the principle by which connected regions of uniform *image* properties—for example, *luminance, color, texture, motion,* and *binocular disparity*—become the initial units of perceptual organization, according to Palmer and Rock.

Unilateral neglect is a complex pattern of symptoms that includes the inability to *attend* to objects in the half of the visual field opposite to their brain damage.

Unique-point heuristic is a procedure in which the unambiguous *motion* of unique points in some parts of an object's image are extrapolated to other parts of the same object whose image *motion* is ambiguous.

Unit is the basic building block of *connectionist networks*, each of which works much like a simplified *neuron*.

Unit formation is the *process* of fusing a number of underlying elements into a single coherent object.

Unit size of a *coordinate system* is a distance taken as the reference standard.

Utricle is a fluid-filled sac in the inner ear which, along with the *saccule*, signals the orientation of the head (see Figure 7.3.2A).

V1 is another name for *striate cortex*, the first visual area in cortex (see Figure 1.3.19).

V2 is another name for the second visual area, adjacent to area *V1* (see Figure 1.3.19).

V4 is another name for the fourth visual area, which appears to *process information* about *color* and *shape* (see Figure 1.3.19).

V5 is another name for the fifth visual area, also called area *MT* (see Figure 1.3.19).

Value in color space (see *lightness*).

Vanishing point is the point at which a set of parallel lines on the same plane converge in depth on the horizon of that plane.

Variant features are properties of an object that change as a result of applying a specified *transformation*.

Vector is a mathematical quantity completely specified by a magnitude and a direction, typically symbolized by an arrow.

Velocity is a quantity that indicates both the speed and direction of *motion*, conveniently represented as a mathematical *vector* (see Figure 10.1.3).

Velocity constancy is the ability to perceive the environmental speed of moving objects rather than their speed in the retinal *image*.

Venn diagrams are *representations* of set relations that are often used to depict *category* structure, representing *categories* as bounded areas within which all members of that *category* fall (see Figure 9.2.18).

Ventral is the cranial direction toward the bottom of the head.

Verbal overshadowing effect is the finding that subjects who verbally describe a face while studying it in a memory task select the correct face less frequently than do subjects who studied it silently.

Vergence eye movements are *eye movements* that control eye *convergence*, which selects for the distance of the target from the observer.

Veridical perception is perception that is consistent with the actual state of affairs in the environment.

Vertices (or **junctions**) are intersections that are formed by the *convergence* of line segments at a point.

Vestibular eye movements are *eye movements* controlled by feedback from the *vestibular system* to keep the eyes fixated on a particular environmental object when the head or body is being rotated.

Vestibular system is the principle organ of balance, located in the middle ear. It contains three interconnected fluid-filled tubes, called the *semicircular canals*, and two fluid-filled sacs, called the *utricle* and the *saccule* (see Figure 7.3.2A).

Vieth-Müller circle is the theoretical *horopter* in the horizontal plane of the eyes, consisting of the set of all corresponding points in that plane. This set forms a circle that passes through the *fixation* point and the nodal points of both eyes (see Figure 5.3.3).

Viewer-centered reference frame is a *coordinate system* within which the 3-D layout of surfaces is specified relative to the direction and distance from the observer's *stationpoint* to the surface.

Viewing geometry is the mathematical analysis of the spatial structure of the observer's *stationpoint* relative to surfaces in the environment.

Viewpoint (or **stationpoint**) is the point from which an environmental scene is observed.

Viewpoint-specific theories of *object identification* are theories based on different *representations* for the same object as seen from different perspectives.

Virtual reality (VR) displays are computer-generated visual displays that change in appropriate ways when the observer changes his or her viewpoint, producing compelling *illusions* of objects existing in a 3-D environment that does not physically exist.

Visible spectrum is the portion of the *electromagnetic spectrum* in which *light* affects the behavior of *receptors* in the retina, roughly between *wavelengths* between 400 and 700 nm (see Color Plate 3.1).

Vision science is the interdisciplinary scientific study of how organisms know about their environment by processing *information* from emitted or reflected *light*. The disciplines include biology, psychology, computer science, cognitive anthropology, philosophy, and other related fields.

Visual agnosia is a deficit in identifying certain kinds of objects by sight because of damage in parts of the *temporal cortex*.

Visual angle is a measure of *image* size on the *retina*, corresponding to the number of degrees the *image* subtends from its extremes to the *focal point* of the eye.

Visual attention is a *process* that enables an observer to recruit greater resources for processing selected aspects of the retinal *image* more fully than unselected aspects.

Visual buffer is a spatially organized array proposed by Kosslyn to constitute the "medium" or "format" for *visual images*, much like a "CRT screen in the head."

Visual capture is a phenomenon in which vision dominates other sensory modalities when they are in conflict about the properties of objects.

Visual cliff is an apparatus that is used to study *depth* perception in infants. It consists of a glass-topped table with a central board separating a shallow side and a deep side (see Figure 5.6.1).

Visual completion (or **amodal completion**) is the *process* of perceptually filling in parts of objects that are hidden from view (see Figures 1.1.6 and 6.4.1).

Visual imagery refers to the *processes* involved in generating, examining, and manipulating *visual images*.

Visual images are quasi-visual experiences people have when they recall objects or events from *visual memory* and when they engage in visual thinking.

Visual information store (VIS) (see *iconic memory*).

Visual interpolation is the *process* by which the visual system infers the nature of hidden parts of environmental surfaces and objects from visible ones.

Visual kinematics are the laws of *motion* that are derived from purely visual constraints on possible solutions to *apparent motion transformations*.

Visual long-term memory (visual LTM) is the visual component of *long-term memory*.

Visual memory is the preservation of visual *information* over periods of time lasting from fractions of seconds to decades after the optical source of the *information* is no longer available.

Visual perception is the *process* of acquiring knowledge about environmental objects and events by extracting *information* from their emitted or reflected *light*.

Visual pop-out is a phenomenon that occurs when an observer looks at a field of many objects and the one that is different from the rest automatically draws *attention* to itself (see Figure 11.2.19).

Visual routines are general-purpose *processes* in *visual perception* and *imagery* proposed by Ullman that operate only with the benefit of focussed *attention* to a single object or group.

Visual short-term memory (visual STM) is an intermediate *visual memory* system akin to standard *short-term memory* but restricted to visual *information* from the most recently presented *image*.

Visuo-spatial scratch pad (or **sketchpad**) is a visual buffer store proposed by Baddeley to be a component of *working memory*.

Vitreous humor is the clear liquid that fills the central chamber of the eye (see Figure 1.3.4).

Volumetric primitives are sets of basic 3-D volumes (e.g., *geons* or *generalized cylinders*) that can be used to represent the *shape* of complex objects.

VR (see *virtual reality displays*).

Wagon wheel illusion is the experience of seeing a wheel turning backward in a movie or TV program when the real wheel is actually turning forward (see Figures 10.1.8 and 10.1.9).

Waterfall illusion is a *motion aftereffect* that occurs after watching a field in uniform *motion* for several minutes (e.g., a waterfall), following which a stationary field appears to move in the opposite direction.

Wavelength is a variable that distinguishes different *photons* from each other in terms of the frequency of their electromagnetic vibration (see Color Plate 3.1).

Wavelet (see *Gabor function*).

"Weak AI" is the "weak" claim for *artificial intelligence (AI)* that a properly programmed machine would only simulate mental events, conscious or otherwise, not duplicate them.

Weak fusion is the theoretical position that different estimates of the distance to an object can be integrated without considering interactions between different *information* sources.

Weber's law is the *psychophysical* relation between stimulus intensity (I) and the *difference threshold* (ΔI), $\Delta I / I = k$, where and k is the value of the constant ratio for the particular dimension that is being studied (see Figure A.3.2).

Weight-error space is an augmentation of *weight space* in which the extra dimension represents the amount of error the system will produce for each possible setting of the weights (see Figure B.2.6).

Weight space is a multidimensional space for representing the current set of *connection weights* by using a different dimension for the weight on each connection (see Figure B.2.5).

Weights (see *connection weights*).

"What" system is the popular name for the *ventral* pathway of the visual system extending from area *V1* to the *temporal lobe* that is believed to support the *categorization* and *identification* of objects (see Figure 1.3.17).

"Where" system is the popular name for the *dorsal* pathway of the visual system extending from area *V1* to the *parietal lobe* that is believed to support the perception of spatial location (see Figure 1.3.17).

Whole report procedure is an experimental method that is used to study *visual memory* by showing subjects an array of many items and asking them to report as many items as possible.

Whorfian hypothesis (see *cultural relativism*).

Winner-take-all network (**WTA network**) is a *network* of *units* all of which mutually *inhibit* each other with the same negative *connection weight*. Such a network causes the single *unit* with the highest *activation* eventually to dominate all the other *units*, whose *activations* drop to a minimum level.

Word-letter effect is the experimental phenomenon that subjects perceive an individual target letter less accurately than the same letter within a meaningful word.

Word-nonword effect is the experimental phenomenon that subjects perceive individual letters more accurately when they are presented as part of meaningful words than when they are presented in meaningless strings.

Word superiority effect is the fact that subjects perceive individual letters more accurately when they are presented as part of meaningful words than when they are presented either alone (the *word-letter effect*) or in meaningless strings (the *word-nonword effect*).

Working memory is a theoretical concept that is closely related to classical *short-term memory*. It consists of a *central executive* that controls the *processing* of *information* in all kinds of cognitive tasks plus a number of *slave memories* that code recently accessed *information* in a specific sensory modalities (see Figure 12.1.12).

Yes-no (or **old-new**) **recognition** is a *recognition memory task* in which subjects are shown test items individually and asked to say whether each is one that they have seen before ("old") or not ("new").

Zero-crossing detectors are the mechanism that Marr and Hildreth proposed to detect *luminance edges* in *images*.

Zero-crossings of the second derivative of the *luminance function* are the points at which *luminance edges* are located. Marr and Hildreth exploited this fact in their *edge detection algorithm*.

Zoom lens theory of spatial attention likens *attention* to a camera's zoom lens, which is able to cover either a large region with coarse resolution or a small region with high resolution.

References

Adams, H. F. (1912). Autokinetic sensations. *Psychological Monographs, 14*, 1–45.

Adelson, E. H. (1978). Iconic storage: The role of rods. *Science, 201*(4355), 544–546.

Adelson, E. H. (1979). Visual persistence without the rods. *Perception & Psychophysics, 26*(3), 245–246.

Adelson, E. H., & Bergen, J. K. (1985). Spatio-temporal energy models for the perception of motion. *Journal of the Optical Society of America, 2*, 284–299.

Adelson, E. H., & Jonides, J. (1980). The psychophysics of iconic storage. *Journal of Experimental Psychology: Human Perception & Performance, 6*(3), 486–493.

Adelson, E. H., & Movshon, J. A. (1982). Phenomenal coherence of moving visual patterns. *Nature, 300*(5892), 523–525.

Agin, G. J., & Binford, T. O. (1976). Computer description of curved objects. *IEEE Transactions on Computers, C-25*, 439–449.

Agostini, T., & Proffitt, D. R. (1993). Perceptual organization evokes simultaneous lightness contrast. *Perception, 22*(3), 263–272.

Albert, M. K. (1993). Parallelism and the perception of illusory countours. *Perception, 22*(5), 589–596.

Albert, M. K., & Hoffman, D. D. (1995). Genericity in spatial vision. In R. D. Luce, M. D'Zmura, D. D. Hoffman, G. J. Iverson, & A. K. Romney (Eds.), *Geometric representations of perceptual phenomena: Papers in honor of Tarow Indow on his 70th birthday* (pp. 95–112). Mahwah, NJ: Erlbaum.

Allen, J. M. (1967). *Molecular organization and biological function.* New York: Harper & Row.

Allport, D. A., Tipper, S. P., & Chmiel, N. R. (1985). Perceptual integration and post-categorical filtering. In M. I. Posner & O. S. M. Marin (Eds.), *Attention and performance* (Vol. 11). Hillsdale, NJ: Erlbaum.

Ames, A. (1951). Visual perception and the rotating trapezoidal window. *Psychological Monographs, 65*(7 [Whole No. 324]).

Anderson, J. A. (1995). *An introduction to neural networks.* Cambridge, MA: MIT Press.

Anstis, S. M. (1980). The perception of apparent movement. *Philosophical Transactions of the Royal Society, London, B, 290,* 153–168.

Anstis, S. M. (1986). Motion perception in the frontal plane: Sensory aspects. In K. R. Boff, L. Kaufman, & J. P. Thomas (Eds.), *Handbook of perception and human performance: Vol. 1. Sensory processes and perception* (pp. 16-1–16-27). New York: Wiley.

Anstis, S. M., & Duncan, K. (1983). Separate motion aftereffects from each eye and from both eyes. *Vision Research, 23*(2), 161–169.

Armstrong, D. M. (1968). *A materialist theory of the mind.* London: Routledge & Kegan Paul.

Asch, S. E., & Witkin, H. A. (1948a). Studies in space orientation: I. Perception of the upright with displaced visual fields. *Journal of Experimental Psychology, 38,* 325–337.

Asch, S. E., & Witkin, H. A. (1948b). Studies in space orientation: II. Perception of the upright with displaced visual fields and with body tilted. *Journal of Experimental Psychology, 38,* 455–477.

Aslin, R. N. (1977). Development of binocular fixation in human infants. *Journal of Experimental Child Psychology, 23*(1), 133–150.

Atkinson, J., Braddick, O., & Moar, K. (1977). Development of contrast sensitivity over the first 3 months of life in the human infant. *Vision Research, 17*(9), 1037–1044.

Attneave, F. (1954). Some informational aspects of visual perception. *Psychological Review, 61,* 183–193.

Attneave, F. (1968). Triangles as ambiguous figures. *American Journal of Psychology, 81,* 447–453.

Aubert, H. (1861). Eine scheinbare bedeutende Drehung von Objekten bei Neigung des Kopfes nach rechts oder links. *Virchows Archives, 20,* 381–393.

Aubert, H. (1886). Die Bewegungsempfindung. *Archiv für die Gesamte Physiologie, 39,* 347–370.

Averbach, E., & Coriell, A. S. (1961). Short-term memory in vision. *Bell System Technical Journal, 40,* 309–328.

Averbach, E., & Sperling, G. (1960). Short-term storage of information in vision. In C. Cherry (Ed.), *Information theory.* London: Butterworth.

Baars, B. (1988). *A cognitive theory of consciousness.* Cambridge, England: Cambridge University Press.

Baddeley, A. (1986). *Working memory.* Oxford, England: Clarendon Press/Oxford University Press.

Baddeley, A. (1998). *Human memory: Theory and practice.* Boston: Allyn & Bacon.

Baddeley, A. D., & Hitch, G. (1974). Working memory. In G. Bower (Ed.), *The psychology of learning and motivation* (Vol. 8). New York: Academic Press.

Balint, R. (1909). Die Seelenlahmung des Schauens, optische Ataxie, räumliche Störung der Aufmerksamkeit. *Monatsschrift für Psychiatrie und Neurologie, 25,* 51–81.

Banks, M. S. (1980). The development of visual accommodation during early infancy. *Child Development, 51*(3), 646–666.

Banks, M. S., Aslin, R. N., & Letson, R. D. (1975). Sensitive period for the development of human binocular vision. *Science, 190*(4215), 675–677.

Barlow, H. B. (1953). Summation and inhibition in the frog's retina. *Journal of Physiology, 119,* 69–88.

Barlow, H. B. (1961). The coding of sensory messages. In W. H. Thorpe & O. L. Zangwill (Eds.), *Current problems in animal behavior.* Cambridge, England: Cambridge University Press.

Barlow, H. B. (1972). Single units and sensation: A neuron doctrine for perceptual psychology? *Perception, 1,* 371–394.

Barlow, H. B. (1983). Understanding natural vision. In O. J. Braddick & A. C. Sleigh (Eds.), *Physical and biological processing of images* (Vol. 11, pp. 2–14). Berlin: Springer-Verlag.

Barlow, H. B. (1995). The neuron doctrine in perception. In M. S. Gazzaniga (Ed.), *The cognitive neurosciences* (pp. 415–435). Cambridge, MA: MIT Press.

Barlow, H. B., Blakemore, C., & Pettigrew, J. D. (1967). The neural mechanisms of binocular depth discrimination. *Journal of Physiology (London), 193,* 327–342.

Barlow, H. B., & Levick, W. R. (1965). The mechanism of directionally selective units in rabbit's retina. *Journal of Physiology, 178,* 477–504.

Baron, J., & Thurston, I. (1973). An analysis of the word-superiority effect. *Cognitive Psychology, 4*(2), 207–228.

Barrow, H. G., & Tenenbaum, J. M. (1981). Interpreting line drawings as three dimensional surfaces. *Artificial Intelligence, 17,* 75–116.

Barrow, H. G., & Tenenbaum, J. M. (1986). Computational Approaches to Vision. In L. Kaufman, K. R. Boff, & J. P. Thomas (Eds.), *Handbook of perception and human performance: Vol. 2. Cognitive processes and performance* (pp. 38-1–38-70). New York: John Wiley & Sons.

Barrow, H. G., & Tenenbaum, J. M. (1978). Recovering intrinsic scene characterists from images. In A. Hanson & E. Riseman (Eds.), *Computer vision systems.* New York: Academic Press.

Bartram, D. J. (1974). The role of visual and semantic codes in object naming. *Cognitive Psychology, 6*(3), 325–356.

Beardsworth, T., & Buckner, T. (1981). The ability to recognize oneself from a video recording of one's movements without seeing one's body. *Bulletin of the Psychonomic Society, 18*(1), 19–22.

Bechtel, W. (1988). *Philosophy of mind: An overview for cognitive science.* Hillsdale, NJ: Erlbaum.

Beck, J. (1966). Effects of orientation and shape similarity on perceptual grouping. *Perception & Psychophysics, 1,* 300–302.

Beck, J. (1972). Similarity grouping and peripheral discriminability under uncertainty. *American Journal of Psychology, 85*(1), 1–19.

Beck, J. (1975). The relation between similarity grouping and perceptual constancy. *American Journal of Psychology, 88*(3), 397–409.

Beck, J. (1982). Textural segmentation. In J. Beck (Ed.), *Organization and representation in perception* (pp. 285–318). Hillsdale, NJ: Erlbaum.

Bekerian, D. A., & Bowers, J. M. (1983). Eyewitness testimony: Were we misled? *Journal of Experimental Psychology: Learning, Memory, & Cognition, 9*(1), 139–145.

Bekesey, G. von. (1967). *Sensory inhibition.* Princeton, NJ: Princeton University Press.

Benary, W. (1924). Beobachtungen zu einen Experiment über Helligkeitskontrast. *Psychologishe Forschung, 5,* 131–142.

Berlin, B., & Kay, P. (1969). *Basic color terms: Their universality and evolution.* Berkeley: University of California Press.

Biederman, I. (1972). Perceiving real-world scenes. *Science, 177*(4043), 77–80.

Biederman, I. (1981). On the semantics of a glance at a scene. In M. Kubovy & J. R. Pomerantz (Eds.), *Perceptual organization* (pp. 213–224). Hillsdale, NJ: Erlbaum.

Biederman, I. (1985). Human image understanding: Recent research and a theory. *Computer Vision, Graphics, and Image Understanding, 32,* 29–73.

Biederman, I. (1987). Recognition-by-components: A theory of human image understanding. *Psychological Review, 94*(2), 115–117.

Biederman, I., & Cooper, E. E. (1991a). Evidence for complete translational and reflectional invariance in visual object priming. *Perception, 20*(5), 585–593.

Biederman, I., & Cooper, E. E. (1991b). Priming contour-deleted images: Evidence for intermediate representations in visual object recognition. *Cognitive Psychology, 23*(3), 393–419.

Biederman, I., & Cooper, E. E. (1992). Size invariance in visual object priming. *Journal of Experimental Psychology: Human Perception & Performance, 18*(1), 121–133.

Biederman, I., & Gerhardstein, P. C. (1993). Recognizing depth-rotated objects: Evidence and conditions for three-dimensional viewpoint invariance. *Journal of Experimental Psychology: Human Perception & Performance, 19*(6), 1162–1182.

Biederman, I., & Gerhardstein, P. C. (1995). Viewpoint dependent mechanisms in visual object recognition: Reply to Tarr and Bulthoff (1995). *Journal of Experimental Psychology: Human Perception & Performance, 21*(6), 1506–1514.

Biederman, I., Glass, A. L., & Stacy, E. W. (1973). Searching for objects in real-world scenes. *Journal of Experimental Psychology, 97*(1), 22–27.

Biederman, I., & Ju, G. (1988). Surface versus edge-based determinants of visual recognition. *Cognitive Psychology, 20*(1), 38–64.

Binford, T. O. (1971). *Visual perception by computer.* Paper presented at the IEEE Conference on Systems and Control, Miami, FL.

Bishop, C. (1995). *Neural networks for pattern recognition.* Oxford, England: Clarendon Press.

Bisiach, E., & Luzzatti, C. (1978). Unilateral neglect of representational space. *Cortex, 14*(1), 129–133.

Bisiach, E., & Rusconi, M. L. (1990). Breakdown of perceptual awareness in unilateral neglect. *Cortex, 26,* 643–649.

Blackmore, S. J., Brelstaff, G., Nelson, K., & Troscianko, T. (1995). Is the richness of our visual world an illusion? Transsaccadic memory for complex scenes. *Perception, 24*(9), 1075–1081.

Blakemore, C., & Campbell, F. W. (1969). On the existence of neurons in the human visual system selectively responsive to the orientation and size of retinal images. *Journal of Physiology, 203,* 237–260.

Blakemore, C., Carpenter, R. H. S., & Georgeson, M. A. (1970). Lateral inhibition between orientation detectors in the human visual system. *Nature, 228,* 37–39.

Blakemore, C., & Nachmias, J. (1971). The orientation specificity of two visual aftereffects. *Journal of Physiology (London), 213,* 157–174.

Blakemore, C., & Van Sluyters, R. C. (1975). Innate and environmental factors in the development of the kitten's visual cortex. *Journal of Physiology, 248*(3), 663–716.

Block, N. (1995). On a confusion about a function of consciousness. *Behavioral & Brain Sciences, 18*(2), 227–287.

Block, N., Flanagan, O., & Güzeldere, G. (Eds.) (1997). *The nature of consciousness: Philosophical debates.* Cambrige, MA: MIT Press.

Bootzin, R. R., & Natsoulas, T. (1965). Evidence for perceptual defense uncontaminated by response bias. *Journal of Personality & Social Psychology, 1*(5), 461–468.

Boring, E. G. (1953). A history of introspectionism. *Psychological Bulletin, 50,* 169–189.

Bornstein, M. H., Ferdinandsen, K., & Gross, C. G. (1981). Perception of symmetry in infancy. *Developmental Psychology, 17*(1), 82–86.

Bower, T. G. (1974). *Development in infancy*. San Francisco: W. H. Freeman.

Bower, T. G., Broughton, J. M., & Moore, M. K. (1970). The coordination of visual and tactual input in infants. *Perception & Psychophysics, 8*(1), 51–53.

Bower, T. G., Broughton, J. M., & Moore, M. K. (1971). Infant responses to approaching objects: An indicator of response to distal variables. *Perception & Psychophysics, 9*(2), 193–196.

Bozzi, P. (1975). Osservazione su alcuni casi di trasparenza fenomica realizzabili con figure a tratto. In G. d'Arcais (Ed.), *Studies in perception: Festschrift for Fabio Metelli* (pp. 88–110). Milan/Florence: Martelli-Giunti.

Braddick, O. (1974). A short-range process in apparent motion. *Vision Research, 14*, 519–528.

Bradley, A., Switkes, E., & De Valois, K. K. (1988). Orientation and spatial frequency selectivity of adaptation to color and luminance gratings. *Vision Research, 28*, 841–856.

Brainard, D. H., & Wandell, B. A. (1991). A bilinear model of the illuminant's effect on color appearance. In M. S. Landy & J. A. Movshon (Eds.), *Computational models of visual processing* (pp. 171–186). Cambridge, MA: MIT Press.

Brainard, D. H., & Wandell, B. A. (1992). Asymmetric color matching: How color appearance depends on the illuminant. *Journal of the Optical Society of America A, 9*(9), 1433–1448.

Braunstein, M. L. (1976). *Depth perception through motion*. New York: Academic Press.

Bregman, A. S. (1978). The formation of auditory streams. In J. Requin (Ed.), *Attention and performance* (Vol. 7). Hillsdale, NJ: Erlbaum.

Breitmeyer, B. G. (1984). *Visual masking: An integrative approach*. New York: Oxford University Press.

Brindley, G. S., & Merton, P. A. (1960). The absence of position sense in the human eye. *Journal of Physiology, 153*, 127–130.

Broadbent, D. E. (1958). *Perception and communication*. New York: Pergamon Press.

Brown, J. F. (1931). The visual perception of velocity. *Psychologishe Forschung, 14*, 199–232.

Brown, P. K., & Wald, G. (1964). Visual pigments in single rods and cones of human retina. *Science, 144*, 45–52.

Bruner, J. S. (1973). *Beyond the information given: Studies in the psychology of knowing* (1st ed.). New York: Norton.

Bruner, J. S., & Postman, L. (1947). Emotional selectivity in perception and reaction. *Journal of Personality, 16*, 69–77.

Bruner, J. S., & Postman, L. (1949). Perception, cognition, and behavior. *Journal of Personality, 18*, 14–31.

Bruno, N., & Cutting, J. E. (1988). Minimodularity and the perception of layout. *Journal of Experimental Psychology: General, 117*(2), 161–170.

Brunswik, E. (1956). *Perception and the representative design of psychological experiments* (2nd ed., rev. and enl. ed.). Berkeley: University of California Press.

Bucher, N. M., & Palmer, S. E. (1985). Effects of motion on perceived pointing of ambiguous triangles. *Perception & Psychophysics, 38*(3), 227–236.

Buffart, H., Leeuwenberg, E., & Restle, F. (1981). Coding theory of visual pattern completion. *Journal of Experimental Psychology: Human Perception & Performance, 7*(2), 241–274.

Buffart, H., & Leeuwenberg, E. L. J. (1981). Structural information theory. In H. G. Geissler, E. L. J. Leeuwenberg, S. Link, & V. Sarris (Eds.), *Modern issues in perception*. Berlin, Germany: Erlbaum.

Bülthoff, H. H., & Edelman, S. (1992). Psychophysical support for a two-dimensional interpolation theory of object recognition. *Proceedings of the National Academy of Science, USA, 89*, 60–64.

Bundesen, C., & Larsen, A. (1975). Visual transformation of size. *Journal of Experimental Psychology: Human Perception & Performance, 104*(1), 214–220.

Bundesen, C., Larsen, A., & Farrell, J. E. (1983). Visual apparent movement: Transformations of size and orientation. *Perception, 12*(5), 549–558.

Burr, D. C., & Ross, J. (1982). Contrast sensitivity at high velocities. *Vision Research, 22*(4), 479–484.

Burt, P., & Sperling, G. (1981). Time, distance, and feature trade-offs in visual apparent motion. *Psychological Review, 88*(2), 171–195.

Byrne, A., & Hilbert, D. R. (Eds.) (1997). *Readings on color: Vol. 2. The science of color*. Cambrige, MA: MIT Press.

Campbell, F. W., & Robson, J. G. (1968). Application of Fourier analysis to the visibility of gratings. *Journal of Physiology, 197*, 551–566.

Campion, J., Latto, R., & Smith, Y. M. (1983). Is blindsight an effect of scattered light, spared cortex, and near-threshold vision? *Behavioral & Brain Sciences, 6*(3), 423–486.

Campos, J. J., Langer, A., & Krowitz, A. (1970). Cardiac responses on the visual cliff in prelocomotor human infants. *Science, 170*(3954), 196–197.

Canny, J. F. (1986). A computational approach to edge detection. *IEEE Transactions on Pattern Analysis and Machine Intelligence, 8*, 769–798.

Caramazza, A., McCloskey, M., & Green, B. (1981). Naive beliefs in "sophisticated" subjects: Misconceptions about trajectories of objects. *Cognition, 9*(2), 117–123.

Carlson, V. R. (1953). Satiation in a reversible perspective figure. *Journal of Experimental Psychology, 45*, 442–448.

Carlson, V. R. (1960). Overestimation in size constancy judgements. *American Journal of Psychology, 73*, 199–213.

Carlson, V. R. (1977). Instructions and perceptual constancy judgements. In W. Epstein (Ed.), *Stability and constancy in visual perception* (pp. 217–254). New York: Wiley.

Carlton, E. H., & Shepard, R. N. (1990a). Psychologically simple motions as geodesic paths: I. Asymmetric objects. *Journal of Mathematical Psychology, 34*(2), 127–188.

Carlton, E. H., & Shepard, R. N. (1990b). Psychologically simple motions as geodesic paths: II. Symmetric objects. *Journal of Mathematical Psychology, 34*(2), 189–228.

Carmichael, L., Hogen, H. P., & Walter, A. A. (1932). An experimental study of the effect of language on the reproduction of visually perceived form. *Journal of Experimental Psychology, 15*, 73–86.

Carroll, J. D., & Chang, J. J. (1970). Analysis of individual differences in multidimensional scaling via an N-way generalization of "Eckart-Young" decomposition. *Psychometrica, 35*, 283–319.

Casati, R., & Varzi, A. C. (1994). *Holes and other superficialities.* Cambridge, MA: MIT Press.

Cataliotti, J., & Gilchrist, A. (1995). Local and global processes in surface lightness perception. *Perception & Psychophysics, 57*(2), 125–135.

Cattell, J. M. (1886). The time taken up by cerebral operations. *Mind, 11*, 220–242; 377–392; 524–538.

Caudhill, M. (1992). *Understanding neural networks: Computer explorations: A workbook in two volumes with software for the Macintosh and PC.* Cambridge, MA: MIT Press.

Cavanagh, P. (1991). Short-range vs long-range motion: Not a valid distinction. *Spatial Vision, 5*(4), 303–309.

Cavanagh, P., & Anstis, S. (1991). The contribution of color to motion in normal and color blind observers. *Vision Research, 31*(12), 2109–2148.

Cavanagh, P., & Mather, G. (1989). Motion: The long and short of it. *Spatial Vision, 4*(2–3), 103–129.

Cavanagh, P., Tyler, C. W., & Favreau, O. E. (1984). Perceived velocity of moving chromatic gratings. *Journal of the Optical Society of America A, 1*(8), 893–899.

Cave, K. R., & Wolfe, J. M. (1990). Modeling the role of parallel processing in visual search. *Cognitive Psychology, 22*(2), 225–271.

Chalmers, D. J. (1996). *The Conscious Mind.* New York: Oxford University Press.

Chambers, D., & Reisberg, D. (1985). Can mental images be ambiguous? *Journal of Experimental Psychology: Human Perception & Performance, 11*(3), 317–328.

Cheesman, J., & Merikle, P. M. (1984). Priming with and without awareness. *Perception & Psychophysics, 36*(4), 387–395.

Cheesman, J., & Merikle, P. M. (1986). Distinguishing conscious from unconscious perceptual processes. *Canadian Journal of Psychology, 40*(4), 343–367.

Cherry, E. C. (1953). Some experiments on the recognition of speech with one and two ears. *Journal of the Acoustical Society of America, 25*, 975–979.

Cherry, E. C., & Taylor, W. K. (1954). Some further experiments upon the recognition of speech with one or two ears. *Journal of the Acoustical Society of America, 26*, 554–555.

Chipman, S. F. (1977). Complexity and structure in visual patterns. *Journal of Experimental Psychology: General, 106*(3), 269–301.

Chubb, C., & Sperling, G. (1988). Drift-balanced random stimuli: A general basis for studying non-Fourier motion perception. *Journal of the Optical Society of America A, 5*(11), 1986–2007.

Churchland, P. M. (1990). Current eliminativism. In W. G. Lycan (Ed.), *Mind and cognition: A reader* (pp. 206–223). Oxford, England: Basil Blackwell.

Cicerone, C. M., & Nerger, J. L. (1989). The density of cones in the fovea centralis of the human dichromat. *Vision Research, 29*(11), 1587–1595.

Clark, H. H., & Brownell, H. H. (1975). Judging up and down. *Journal of Experimental Psychology: Human Perception & Performance, 104*(1), 339–352.

Clark, H. H., & Brownell, H. H. (1976). Position, direction, and their perceptual integrality. *Perception & Psychophysics, 19*(4), 328–334.

Clark, J. J., & Yuille, A. L. (1990). *Data fusion for sensory information processing systems.* Boston, MA: Kluwer.

Clowes, M. B. (1971). On seeing things. *Artificial Intelligence, 2*, 79–116.

Cohen, A., Ivry, R. B., Rafal, R. D., & Kohn, C. (1995). Activating response codes by stimuli in the neglected visual field. *Neuropsychology, 9*(2), 165–173.

Cohen, J. (1964). Dependency of the spectral reflectance curves of the Munsell color chips. *Psychonomic Science, 1*, 369–370.

Coltheart, M. (1980). The persistence of vision. *Philosophical Transactions of the Royal Society of London, B, 290*, 57–69.

Coltheart, M. (1983). Iconic memory. *Philosophical Transactions of the Royal Society, London, B, 302*, 283–294.

Coltheart, V. (Ed.) (1999). *Fleeting memories: Cognition of brief visual stimuli.* Cambridge, MA: MIT Press.

Cooper, L. A. (1975). Mental rotation of random two-dimensional shapes. *Cognitive Psychology, 7*(1), 20–43.

Cooper, L. A. (1976). Demonstration of a mental analog of an external rotation. *Perception & Psychophysics, 19*(4), 296–302.

Cooper, L. A., & Shepard, R. N. (1973). Chronometric studies of the rotation of mental images. In W. G. Chase (Ed.), *Visual information processing* (pp. 75–166). New York: Academic Press.

Corballis, M. C. (1988). Recognition of disoriented shapes. *Psychological Review, 95*(1), 115–123.

Corbetta, M., Meizin, F. M., Dobmeyer, S., Shulman, G. L., & Peterson, S. E. (1991). Selective and divided attention during visual discrimination of shape, color, and speed: Functional anatomy by positron emision tomography. *Journal of Neuroscience, 11*, 2383–2402.

Coren, S., & Girgus, J. S. (1978). *Seeing is decieving: The psychology of visual illusions.* Hillsdale, NJ: Erlbaum.

Coslett, H. B., & Saffran, E. (1991). Simultagnosia: To see but not two see. *Brain, 113*, 1523–1545.

Cowey, A., & Stoerig, P. (1989). Projection patterns of surviving neurons in the dorsal lateral geniculate nucleus following discrete lesions of striate cortex: Implications for residual vision. *Experimental Brain Research, 75*, 631–638.

Cowey, A., & Stoerig, P. (1995). Blindsight in monkeys. *Nature, 373*(6511), 247–249.

Craik, K. J. W. (1943). *The nature of explanation.* Cambridge, England: Cambridge University Press.

Crick, F. H. C. (1994). *The astonishing hypothesis: The scientific search for the soul.* New York: Scribner.

Crick, F. H. C., & Koch, C. (1990). Toward a neurobiological theory of consciousness. *Seminars in the Neurosciences, 2*, 263–275.

Crick, F. H. C., & Koch, C. (1992). The problem of consciousness. *Scientific American, 267*, 152–159.

Crick, F. H. C., & Koch, C. (1995). Are we aware of neural activity in primary visual cortex? *Nature, 375*, 121–123.

Crick, F. H. C., & Koch, C. (1998). Consciousness and neuroscience. *Cerebral Cortex, 8*, 97–107.

Cronholm, B. (1951). Phantom limbs in amputees. *Acta Psychiatrica Scandinavica, 72*(Suppl.).

Currie, C., McConkie, G. W., Carlson-Radvansky, L. A., & Irwin, D. E. (in preparation). Maintaining visual stability accross saccades: Role of the saccade object. *Perception & Psychophysics.*

Cutting, J. E. (1978). Generation of synthetic male and female walkers through manipulation of a biomechanical invariant. *Perception, 7*(4), 393–405.

Cutting, J. E. (1982). Blowing in the wind: Percieving structure in trees and bushes. *Cognition, 12*, 25–44.

Cutting, J. E. (1991). Why our stimuli look as they do. In G. R. Lockhead & J. R. Pomerantz (Eds.), *The perception of structure* (pp. 41–52). Washington, DC: American Psychological Association.

Cutting, J. E., & Proffitt, D. R. (1982). The minimum principle and the perception of absolute, common, and relative motions. *Cognitive Psychology, 14*(2), 211–246.

Cutting, J. E., Proffitt, D. R., & Kozlowski, L. T. (1978). A biomechanical invariant for gait perception. *Journal of Experimental Psychology: Human Perception & Performance, 4*(3), 357–372.

Cutting, J. E., Vishton, P., Flückiger, M., Baumberger, B., & Gerndt, J. D. (1997). Heading and path information from retinal flow in naturalistic environments. *Perception & Psychophysics, 59*(3), 426–441.

Dacey, D. M. (1996). Circuitry for color coding in the primate retina. *Proceedings of the National Academy of Science, USA, 93*, 582–588.

Damasio, A. (1985). Disorders of complex visual processing: Agnosias, achromatopsia, Balint's syndrome, and related difficulties of orientation and construction. In M. Mesulam (Ed.), *Principles of Behavioral Neurology* (pp. 259–288). Philadelphia, PA: F. A. Davis.

Dannemiller, J. L. (1989). A test of color constancy in 9- and 20-week-old human infants following simulated illuminant changes. *Developmental Psychology, 25*(2), 171–184.

Daugman, J. G. (1980). Two-dimensional spectral analysis of cortical receptive field profiles. *Vision Research, 20*(10), 847–856.

Davidoff, J. B., & Østergaard, A. L. (1984). Color anomia resulting from weakened short-term color memory. *Brain, 107*, 415–431.

Daw, N. W., & Wyatt, H. J. (1976). Kittens reared in a unidirectional environment: Evidence for a critical period. *Journal of Physiology, 257*(1), 155–170.

de Angelis, G. C., Ohzawa, I., & Freeman, R. D. (1995). Receptive-field dynamics in the central visual pathways. *Trends in Neurosciences, 18*(10), 451–458.

de Haan, E. H. F., Young, A. W., & Newcombe, F. (1987). Face recognition without awareness. *Cognitive Neuropsychology, 4*, 385–415.

De Valois, R. L. (1965). Analysis and coding of color in the primate visual system. *Cold Spring Harbor Symposium on Quantitative Biology, 30,* 567–579.

De Valois, R. L., Abramov, I., & Jacobs, G. H. (1966). Analysis of response patterns in LGN cells. *Journal of the Optical Society of America, 56,* 966–977.

De Valois, R. L., Albrecht, D. G., & Thorell, L. G. (1982). Spatial frequency selectivity of cells in macaque visual cortex. *Vision Research, 22*(5), 545–559.

De Valois, R. L., & De Valois, K. K. (1980). Spatial vision. *Annual Review of Psychology, 31,* 309–341.

De Valois, R. L., & De Valois, K. K. (1988). *Spatial vision.* New York: Oxford University Press.

De Valois, R. L., & De Valois, K. K. (1993). A multi-stage color model. *Vision Research, 33*(8), 1053–1065.

De Valois, R. L., & Jacobs, G. H. (1968). Primate color vision. *Science, 162*(3853), 533–540.

de Weert, C. M. M., & Sadza, K. J. (1983). New data concerning the contribution of colour differences to stereopsis. In J. D. Mollon & L. T. Sharpe (Eds.), *Colour Vision* (pp. 553–562). New York: Academic Press.

Delis, D. C., Robertson, L. C., & Efron, R. (1986). Hemispheric specialization of memory for visual hierarchical stimuli. *Neuropsychologia, 24*(2), 205–214.

DeLucia, P. R., & Hochberg, J. (1991). Geometrical illusions in solid objects under ordinary viewing conditions. *Perception & Psychophysics, 50,* 547–554.

Dember, W. N., & Purcell, D. G. (1967). Recovery of masked visual targets by inhibition of the masking stimulus. *Science, 157,* 135–136.

Dennett, D. (1991). *Consciousness explained.* Boston: Little, Brown.

Dennett, D. (1996). *Kinds of minds: Toward an understanding of consciousness.* New York: Basic Books.

DeRenzi, E., & Spinnler, H. (1967). Impaired performance on color tasks in patients with hemispheric lesions. *Cortex, 3,* 194–217.

Deriche, R. (1987). Using Canny's criteria to derive an optimum edge detector recursively implemented. *International Journal of Computer Vision, 2,* 167–187.

DeSchepper, B., & Treisman, A. (1996). Visual memory for novel shapes: Implicit coding without attention. *Journal of Experimental Psychology: Learning, Memory, & Cognition, 22*(1), 27–47.

Desimone, R., Albright, T. D., Gross, C. G., & Bruce, C. (1984). Stimulus-selective properties of inferior temporal neurons in the macaque. *Journal of Neuroscience, 4*(8), 2051–2062.

Desimone, R., Moran, J., & Spitzer, H. (1988). Neural mechanisms of attention in extrastriate cortex of monkeys. In M. Arbib & S. Amari (Eds.), *Dynamic interactions in neural networks: Models and data* (pp. 169–182). New York: Springer-Verlag.

Desimone, R., & Schein, S. J. (1987). Visual properties of neurons in area V4 of the macaque: Sensitivity to stimulus form. *Journal of Neurophysiology, 57*(3), 835–868.

Desimone, R., Wessinger, M., Thomas, L., & Schneider, W. (1990). Attentional control of visual perception: Cortical and subcortical mechanisms. *Cold Spring Harbor Symposium on Quantitative Biology, 55,* 963–971.

DeYoe, E. A., & Van Essen, D. C. (1988). Concurrent processing streams in monkey visual cortex. *Trends in Neurosciences, 11*(5), 219–226.

Di Lollo, V. (1980). Temporal integration in visual memory. *Journal of Experimental Psychology: General, 109,* 75–97.

Di Lollo, V., & Wilson, A. E. (1978). Iconic persistence and perceptual moment as determinants of temporal integration in vision. *Vision Research, 18*(12), 1607–1610.

DiLorenzo, J. R., & Rock, I. (1982). The rod-and-frame effect as a function of the righting of the frame. *Journal of Experimental Psychology: Human Perception & Performance, 8*(4), 536–546.

Dodson, C. S., Johnson, M. K., & Schooler, J. W. (1997). The verbal overshadowing effect: Why descriptions impair face recognition. *Memory & Cognition, 25*(2), 129–139.

Dosher, B. A., Sperling, G., & Wurst, S. A. (1986). Tradeoffs between stereopsis and proximity luminance covariance as determinants of percieved 3D structure. *Vision Research, 26*(6), 973–990.

Driver, J., & Halligan, P. W. (1991). Can visual neglect operate in object-centered co-ordinates? An affirmative single-case study. *Cognitive Neuropsychology, 8*(6), 475–496.

Duda, R., & Hart, P. (1973). *Pattern classification and scene analysis.* New York: Wiley.

Duncan, J. (1984). Selective attention and the organization of visual information. *Journal of Experimental Psychology: General, 113*(4), 501–517.

Duncker, K. (1929/1937). Induced motion. In W. D. Ellis (Ed.), *A sourcebook of Gestalt psychology* (pp. 161–172). London: Routledge & Kegan Paul.

Ebbinghaus, H. (1885). *On memory* (H. Ruger & C. Bussineus, Trans.). Leipzig: Duncker & Humblot.

Ebenholtz, S. M. (1977). Determinants of the rod-and-frame effect: The role of retinal size. *Perception & Psychophysics, 22*(6), 531–538.

Edelman, G. M. (1987). *Neural Darwinism: The theory of neuronal group selection.* New York: Basic Books.

Edelman, G. M. (1989). *The remembered present: A biological theory of consciousness.* New York: Basic Books.

Edelman, S., & Bülthoff, H. H. (1992). Orientation dependence in the recognition of familiar and novel views of three-dimensional objects. *Vision Research, 32*(12), 2385–2400.

Egly, R., Driver, J., & Rafal, R. D. (1994). Shifting visual attention between objects and locations: Evidence from normal and parietal lesion subjects. *Journal of Experimental Psychology: General, 123*(2), 161–177.

Ellis, A. W., & Young, A. W. (1988). *Human cognitive neuropsychology.* Hillsdale, NJ: Erlbaum.

Enns, J. T., & Rensink, R. A. (1990). Sensitivity to three-dimensional orientation in visual search. *Psychological Science, 1*(5), 323–326.

Enterprises, N. E. Thing (1993). *Magic eye: A new way of looking at the world.* Kansas City: Andrews and McMeel.

Epstein, W. (1965). The known-size apparent-distance hypothesis. *American Journal of Psychology, 74,* 333–346.

Epstein, W. (1973). The process of "taking into account" in visual perception. *Perception, 2,* 267–285.

Epstein, W., & Broota, K. D. (1986). Automatic and attentional components in perception of size-at-a-distance. *Perception & Psychophysics, 40,* 256–262.

Epstein, W., & Lovitts, B. E. (1985). Automatic and attentional components in perception of shape-at-a-slant. *Journal of Experimental Psychology: Human Perception & Performance, 11,* 355–366.

Epstein, W., Park, J., & Casey, A. (1961). The current status of the size-distance hypothesis. *Psychological Bulletin, 58,* 491–514.

Erdelyi, M. H. (1974). A new look at the new look: Perceptual defense and vigilance. *Psychological Review, 81*(1), 1–25.

Eriksen, B. A., & Eriksen, C. W. (1974). Effects of noise letters upon the identification of a target letter in a nonsearch task. *Perception & Psychophysics, 16*(1), 143–149.

Eriksen, C. W. (1960). Discrimination and learning without awareness: A methodological survey and evaluation. *Psychological Review, 67,* 279–300.

Eriksen, C. W., & Rohrbaugh, J. W. (1970). Some factors determining efficiency of selective attention. *American Journal of Psychology, 83*(3), 330–342.

Eriksen, C. W., & St. James, J. D. (1986). Visual attention within and around the field of focal attention: A zoom lens model. *Perception & Psychophysics, 40*(4), 225–240.

Eriksen, C. W., & Yeh, Y. Y. (1985). Allocation of attention in the visual field. *Journal of Experimental Psychology: Human Perception & Performance, 11*(5), 583–597.

Exner, S. (1888). Uber optische bewegungsemfindungen. *Biologische Cantralblatt, 8,* 437–448.

Fantz, R. L. (1958). Pattern vision in young infants. *Psychological Record, 8,* 43–47.

Fantz, R. L. (1961). A method for studying depth perception in infants under six months of age. *Psychological Records, 11,* 27–32.

Fantz, R. L. (1965). Visual perception from birth as shown by pattern selectivity. *Annals of the New York Academy of Sciences, 118,* 793–814.

Fantz, R. L., Fagan, J. F., & Miranda, S. B. (1975). Early visual selectivity. In L. B. Cohen & P. Salapatek (Eds.), *Infant perception: From sensation to cognition* (Vol. 1, pp. 249–346). New York: Academic Press.

Fantz, R. L., & Nevis, S. (1967). Pattern preferences and perceptual-cognitive development in early infancy. *Merrill-Palmer Quarterly, 13*(1), 77–108.

Farah, M. J. (1984). The neurological basis of mental imagery: A compential analysis. *Cognition, 18*(1–3), 245–272.

Farah, M. J. (1988). Is visual imagery really visual? Overlooked evidence from neuropsychology. *Psychological Review, 95,* 307–317.

Farah, M. J. (1990). *Visual agnosia: Disorders of object recognition and what they tell us about normal vision.* Cambridge, MA: MIT Press.

Farah, M. J. (1992). Is an object and object an object? Cognitive and neuropsychological investigations of domain specificity in visual object recognition. *Current Directions in Psychological Science, 1,* 164–169.

Farah, M. J., Hammond, K. L., Levine, D. N., & Calvanio, R. (1988a). Visual and spatial mental imagery: Dissociable systems of representation. *Cognitive Psychology, 20,* 439–462.

Farah, M. J., Peronnet, F., Gonon, M. A., & Giard, M. H. (1988b). Electrophysiological evidence for a shared representational medium for visual images and percepts. *Journal of Experimental Psychology: General, 117*(3), 248–257.

Farah, M. J., Rochlin, R., & Klein, K. L. (1994). Orientation invariance and geometric primitives in shape recognition. *Cognitive Science, 18*(2), 325–344.

Faugeras, O., & Maybank, S. J. (1990). Motion from point matches: Multiplicity of solutions. *International Journal of Computer Vision, 4*(3), 225–246.

Fechner, G. (1860/1966). *Elements of psychophysics* (H. E. Adler, Trans.) (Vol. 1). New York: Holt, Rinehart & Winston.

Feldman, J. A. (1981). A connectionist model of visual memory. In G. E. Hinton & J. A. Anderson (Eds.), *Parallel models of associative memory* (pp. 49–81). Hillsdale, NJ: Erlbaum.

Feldman, J. A., & Ballard, D. H. (1982). Connectionist models and their properties. *Cognitive Science, 6,* 205–254.

Fendrich, R., & Mack, A. (1980). Anorthoscopic perception occurs with a retinally stabilized image. *Supplement in Investigative Ophthalmology and Vision Science, 19*, 166.

Fendrich, R., Wessinger, C. M., & Gazzaniga, M. S. (1992). Residual vision in a scotoma: Implications for blindsight. *Science, 258*, 1489–1491.

Ferrier, D. (1878). *The localisation of cerebral disease.* London, England: Smith, Elder.

Field, D. J. (1993). Scale-invariance and self-similar "wavelet" transforms: An analysis of natural scene and mammalian visual systems. In M. Farge, J. Hunt, & J. C. Vassilicos (Eds.), *Wavelets, fractals, and Fourier transforms* (pp. 151–193). Oxford, England: Oxford University Press.

Field, D. J. (1994). What is the goal of sensory coding? *Neural Computation, 6*, 559–601.

Finke, R. A. (1980). Levels of equivalence in imagery and perception. *Psychological Review, 87*(2), 113–132.

Finke, R. A. (1985). Theories relating mental imagery to perception. *Psychological Bulletin, 98*, 236–259.

Finke, R. A. (1989). *Principles of mental imagery.* Cambridge, MA: MIT Press.

Finke, R. A., Pinker, S., & Farah, M. J. (1989). Reinterpreting visual patterns in mental imagery. *Cognitive Science, 13*(1), 51–78.

Fiorani, M., Rosa, M. G. P., Gattass, R., & Rocha-Miranda, C. E. (1992). Dynamic surrounds of receptive fields in primate striate cortex: A physiological basis for perceptual completion. *Proceedings of the National Academy of Science USA, 89*, 8547–8551.

Fodor, J. A. (1979). *The language of thought.* Cambridge, MA: Harvard University Press.

Fodor, J. A. (1983). *The modularity of mind: An essay on faculty psychology.* Cambridge, MA: MIT Press.

Forster, K. I. (1970). Visual perception of rapidly presented word sequences of varying complexity. *Perception & Psychophysics, 8*, 215–221.

Foster, D. H. (1975). Visual apparent motion and some preferred paths in the rotation group SO(3). *Biological Cybernetics, 18*, 81–89.

Fowler, C. A., Wolford, G., Slade, R., & Tassinary, L. (1981). Lexical access with and without awareness. *Journal of Experimental Psychology: General, 110*(3), 341–362.

Fox, R., Aslin, R. N., Shea, S. L., & Dumais, S. T. (1980). Stereopsis in human infants. *Science, 207*(4428), 323–324.

Freud, S. (1915). Repression. In J. Stachey (Ed.), *The standard edition of the complete psychological works of Sigmund Freud* (Vol. 14). London: Hogarth Press.

Freyd, J. J., & Finke, R. A. (1984). Representational momentum. *Journal of Experimental Psychology: Learning, Memory, & Cognition, 10*(1), 126–132.

Friedman-Hill, S. R., Robertson, L. C., & Treisman, A. (1995). Parietal contributions to visual feature binding: Evidence from a patient with bilateral lesions. *Science, 269*(5225), 853–855.

Frisby, J. P. (1979). *Seeing: Illusion, brain and mind.* Oxford, England: Oxford University Press.

Gallant, J. L., Braun, J., & Van Essen, D. C. (1993). Selectivity for polar, hyperbolic, and Cartesian gratings in macaque visual cortex. *Science, 259*, 100–103.

Gardner, H. (1985). *The mind's new science: A history of the cognitive revolution.* New York: Basic Books.

Garner, W. R. (1974). *The processing of information and structure.* Hillsdale, NJ: Erlbaum.

Garner, W. R., & Clement, D. E. (1963). Goodness of pattern and pattern uncertainty. *Journal of Verbal Learning & Verbal Behavior, 2*(5–6), 446–452.

Gattas, R., & Desimone, R. (1992). Stimulation of the superior colliculus (SC) shifts the focus of attention in the macaque. *Society for Neuroscience Abstracts, 18*, 703.

Gazzaniga, M. S. (1970). *The bisected brain.* New York: Appleton-Century-Crofts.

Geisler, W. S., & Super, B. J. (in press). *Psychological Review.*

Geldard, F. A. (1972). *The Human Senses* (2nd ed.). New York: Wiley.

Geman, S., & Geman, D. (1984). Stochastic relaxation, Gibbs distributions, and the Bayesian restoration of images. *IEEE Transactions of Pattern Analysis and Machine Intelligence, 6*(6), 721–741.

Gerbino, W. (1994). Achromatic transparency. In A. L. Gilchrist (Ed.), *Lightness, brightness, and transparency* (pp. 215–255). Hillsdale, NJ: Erlbaum.

Geschwind, N., & Fusillo, M. (1966). Color naming deficits in association with alexia. *Archives of Neurology, 15*, 137–146.

Gibson, E. J. (1969). *Principles of perceptual learning and development.* New York: Appleton-Century-Crofts.

Gibson, E. J., & Walk, R. D. (1960). The "visual cliff." *Scientific American, 202*(4), 64–71.

Gibson, J. J. (1950). *The perception of the visual world.* Boston: Houghton Mifflin.

Gibson, J. J. (1966). *The senses considered as perceptual systems.* Boston: Houghton Mifflin.

Gibson, J. J. (1979). *The ecological approach to visual perception.* Boston: Houghton Mifflin.

Gibson, J. J., Kaplan, G. A., Reynolds, H. N., & Wheeler, K. (1969). The change from visible to invisible: A study of optical transition. *Perception & Psychophysics, 5,* 113–116.

Gilchrist, A. L. (1988). Lightness contrast and failures of constancy: A common explanation. *Perception & Psychophysics, 43*(5), 415–424.

Gilden, D. L. (1991). On the origins of dynamical awareness. *Psychological Review, 98*(4), 554–568.

Gilden, D. L., Blake, R., & Hurst, G. (1995). Neural adaptation of imaginary visual motion. *Cognitive Psychology, 28*(1), 1–16.

Gilden, D. L., & Proffitt, D. R. (1989). Understanding collision dynamics. *Journal of Experimental Psychology: Human Perception & Performance, 15*(2), 372–383.

Gilinsky, A. (1955). The effect of attitude on the perception of size. *American Journal of Psychology, 68,* 173–192.

Gillam, B. (1973). The nature of size scaling in the Ponzo and related illusions. *Perception & Psychophysics, 14,* 353–357.

Gillam, B. (1981). False perspectives. *Perception, 10*(3), 313–318.

Ginsburg, A. P. (1971). *Psychological correlates of a model of the human visual system.* Paper presented at the IEEE Transactions on Aerospace and Electronic Systems, New York.

Ginsburg, A. P. (1986). Spatial filtering and visual form perception. In K. R. Boff, L. Kaufman, & J. P. Thomas (Eds.), *Handbook of perception and human performance: Vol. 2. Cognitive processes and performance* (pp. 1–41). New York: Wiley.

Girgus, J. J., Rock, I., & Egatz, R. (1977). The effect of knowledge of reversibility on the reversibility of ambiguous figures. *Perception & Psychophysics, 22*(6), 550–556.

Gleason, H. A. (1961). *An introduction to descriptive linguistics.* New York: Holt, Rinehart & Winston.

Gleitman, H. (1981). *Psychology.* New York: Norton.

Glickstein, M. (1988). The discovery of the visual cortex. *Scientific American, 259*(3), 118–127.

Gogel, W. C. (1965). The equidistance tendency and its consequences. *Psychological Bulletin, 64,* 195–221.

Gogel, W. C. (1978). The adjacency principle in visual perception. *Scientific American, 238*(5), 126–139.

Goldberg, M. E., Eggers, H. M., & Gouras, P. (1991). Ch 43. The Ocular Motor System. In E. R. Kandel, J. H. Schwartz, & T. H. Jessell (Eds.), *Principles of neural science* (3rd ed., pp. 660–679). Norwalk, CT: Appleton & Lange.

Goldenberg, G., Steiner, M., Podreka, I., & Deeke, L. (1992). Regional blood flow patterns related to verification of high-imagery sentences. *Neuropsychologia, 30,* 581–586.

Goldiamond, I. (1958). Indicators of perception: I. Subliminal perception, subception, unconscious perception: An analysis in terms of psychophysical indicator methodology. *Psychological Bulletin, 55,* 373–411.

Goldmeier, E. (1936/1972). Similarity in visually perceived forms. *Psychological Issues, 8*(1), 1–135.

Goldmeier, E. (1982). *The memory trace: Its formation and its fate.* Hillsdale, NJ: Erlbaum.

Goldstein, A. G. (1957). Judgments of visual velocity as a function of length of observation time. *Journal of Experimental Psychology, 54,* 457–461.

Goldstein, A. G., & Chance, J. E. (1971). Visual recognition memory for complex configurations. *Perception & Psychophysics, 9*(2), 237–241.

Goldstein, E. B. (1989). *Sensation and perception.* New York: Wiley.

Goodale, M. A. (1995). The cortical organization of visual perception and visuomotor control. In S. M. Kosslyn & D. N. Osherson (Eds.), *Visual cognition* (pp. 167–214). Cambridge, MA: MIT Press.

Gottschaldt, K. (1929). Uber den Einfluss der Erfahrung auf die Wahrnemung von Figuren, II. *Psychologische Forschung, 12,* 1–87.

Graham, N., & Nachmias, J. (1971). Detection of grating patterns containing two spatial frequencies: A comparison of single-channel and multiple-channel models. *Vision Research, 11,* 251–259.

Granrud, C. E. (1987). Size constancy in newborn human infants. *Investigative Ophthalmology and Visual Science, 28*(Suppl.), 5.

Granrud, C. E., & Yonas, A. (1984). Infants' perception of pictorially specified interposition. *Journal of Experimental Child Psychology, 37*(3), 500–511.

Gray, C. M., & Singer, W. (1989). Stimulus-specific neuronal oscillations in orientation columns of cat visual cortex. *Proceedings of the National Academy of Sciences, USA, 86,* 1698–1702.

Gray, J. A., & Wedderburn, A. A. I. (1960). Grouping strategies with simultaneous stimuli. *Quarterly Journal of Experimental Psychology, 12,* 180–184.

Green, D. M., & Swets, J. (1966). *Signal detection theory and psychophysics.* New York: Wiley.

Gregory, R. L. (1966). *Eye and brain: The psychology of seeing.* New York: McGraw-Hill.

Gregory, R. L. (1970). *The intelligent eye.* New York: McGraw-Hill.

Gregory, R. L. (1972). Cognitive contours. *Nature, 238,* 51–52.

Grimes, J. (1996). On the failure to detect changes in scenes across saccades. In K. Akins (Ed.), *Perception* (pp. 89–110). New York: Oxford University Press.

Grimson, W. E. L., & Lozano-Perez, T. (1987). Localizing overlapping parts by searching the interpretation tree. *IEEE Transactions on Pattern Analysis and Machine Intelligence, 9*(4), 469–482.

Gross, C. G., Rocha-Miranda, C. E., & Bender, D. B. (1972). Visual properties of neurons in inferotemporal cortex of the macaque. *Journal of Neurophysiology, 35*(1), 96–111.

Grossberg, S. (1982). *Studies of mind and brain: Neural principles of learning, perception, development, cognition, and motor control.* Hingham, MA: D. Reidel.

Grossberg, S., & Mingolla, E. (1985). Neural dynamics of form perception: Boundary completion, illusory figures, and neon color spreading. *Psychological Review, 92*(2), 173–211.

Gruber, H. E. (1954). The relation of perceived size to perceived distance. *American Journal of Psychology, 67*, 411–426.

Guilford, J. P., & Dallenbach, K. M. (1928). A study of the auto-kinetic sensation. *American Journal of Psychology, 40*, 83–91.

Guzman, A. (1968). *Computer recognition of three-dimensional objects in a visual scene.* Unpublished doctoral dissertation, Massachusetts Institute of Technology, Cambridge, MA.

Guzman, A. (1969). Decomposition of a visual scene into three-dimensional bodies. In A. Griselli (Ed.), *Automatic interpretation and classification of images* (pp. 243–276). New York: Academic Press.

Haber, R. N., & Standing, L. G. (1970). Direct estimates of the apparent duration of a flash. *Canadian Journal of Psychology, 24*(4), 216–229.

Hamilton, C. R. (1964). Intermanual transfer of adaptation to prisms. *American Journal of Psychology, 77*(3), 457–462.

Hanawalt, N. G. (1937). Memory trace for figures in recall and recognition. *Archives of Psychology (Columbia University)* (216), 89.

Hanawalt, N. G. (1952). The method of comparison applied to the problem of memory change. *Journal of Experimental Psychology, 43*, 37–42.

Hanley, J. R., Pearson, N. A., & Young, A. W. (1990). Impaired memory for new visual forms. *Brain, 113*, 1131–1148.

Hanley, J. R., Young, A. W., & Pearson, N. A. (1991). Impairment of the visuo-spatial sketch pad. *Quarterly Journal of Experimental Psychology, 43A*, 101–125.

Harkness, L. (1977). Chameleons use accomodation cues to judge distance. *Nature, 267*, 346–349.

Harmon, L. D., & Julesz, B. (1973). Masking in visual recognition: Effects of two-dimensional filtered noise. *Science, 180*(4091), 1194–1196.

Harris, C. S. (1965). Perceptual adaptation to inverted, reversed, and displaced vision. *Psychological Review, 72*(6), 419–444.

Haykin, S. (1994). *Neural networks: A comprehensive foundation.* New York: Macmillan.

He, Z. J., & Nakayama, K. (1992). Surfaces versus features in visual search. *Nature, 359*(6392), 231–233.

Hebb, D. O. (1964). *Organization of behavior.* New York: Wiley.

Heeger, D. J. (1988). Optical flow using spatio-temporal filters. *International Journal of Computer Science, 1*(4), 279–302.

Heider, E. R. (1972). Universals in color naming and memory. *Journal of Experimental Psychology, 93*(1), 10–20.

Held, R. (1965). Plasticity in sensory-motor systems. *Scientific American, 213*(5), 84–94.

Held, R., Birch, E. E., & Gwiazda, J. (1980). Stereoacuity in human infants. *Proceedings of the National Academy of Sciences, USA, 77*, 5572–5574.

Held, R., & Freedman, S. J. (1963). Plasticity in human sensorimotor control. *Science, 142* (Whole No. 3591), 455–462.

Helmholtz, H. von (1867/1925). *Treatise on physiological optics* (from 3rd German edition, Trans.) (3rd ed., Vol. III). New York: Dover Publications.

Hering, E. (1878/1964). *Outlines of a theory of the light sense* (L. M. Hurvich & D. J. Jameson, Trans.). Cambridge, MA: Harvard University Press.

Hershenson, M. (1989). *The moon illusion.* Hillsdale, NJ: Erlbaum.

Hess, E. H., & Polt, J. M. (1960). Pupil size as related to interest value of visual stimuli. *Science, 132*, 349–350.

Hess, E. H., & Polt, J. M. (1964). Pupil size in relation to mental activity during simple problem-solving. *Science* (3611), 1190–1192.

Hill, A. L. (1972). Direction constancy. *Perception & Psychophysics, 11*, 175–178.

Hinton, G. E. (1979). Some demonstrations of the effects of structural descriptions in mental imagery. *Cognitive Science, 3*, 231–250.

Hinton, G. E. (1981). *A parallel computation that assigns canonical object-based frames of reference.* Paper presented at the Proceedings of the International Joint Conference on Artificial Intelligence, Vancouver, Canada.

Hinton, G. E., & Anderson, J. A. (1981). *Parallel models of associative memory.* Hillsdale, NJ: Erlbaum.

Hochberg, J. (1950). Figure-ground reversal as a function of visual satiation. *Journal of Experimental Psychology, 40,* 682–686.

Hochberg, J. (1964). *Perception.* Englewood Cliffs, NJ: Prentice-Hall.

Hochberg, J. (1968). In the mind's eye. In R. N. Haber (Ed.), *Contemporary theory and research in visual perception* (pp. 309–331). New York: Holt, Rinehart & Winston.

Hochberg, J. (1970). Attention, organization and consciousness. In D. L. Mostofsky (Ed.), *Attention: Contemporary theory and analysis.* New York: Appleton-Century-Crofts.

Hochberg, J. (1971). Perception: Space and movement. In J. W. Kling & L. A. Riggs (Eds.), *Experimental psychology* (pp. 475–550). New York: Holt, Rinehart & Winston.

Hochberg, J., & McAlister, E. (1953). A quantitative approach to figural "goodness." *Journal of Experimental Psychology, 46,* 361–364.

Hoffman, D. D., & Richards, W. A. (1984). Parts of recognition. Special Issue: Visual cognition. *Cognition, 18*(1–3), 65–96.

Hoffman, J. E., & Subramaniam, B. (1995). The role of visual attention in saccadic eye movements. *Perception & Psychophysics, 57*(6), 787–795.

Hofsten, C. von. (1976). The role of convergence in visual space perception. *Vision Research, 16*(2), 193–198.

Hofsten, C. von. (1977). Binocular convergence as a determinant of reaching behavior in infancy. *Perception, 6*(2), 139–144.

Holender, D. (1986). Semantic activation without conscious identification in dichotic listening, parafoveal vision, and visual masking: A survey and appraisal. *Behavioral & Brain Sciences, 9*(1), 1–66.

Holmes, G., & Horrax, G. (1919). Disturbances of spatial orientation and visual attention with loss of stereoscopic vision. *Archives of Neurology and Psychiatry, 1,* 385–407.

Holway, A. H., & Boring, E. G. (1941). Determinants of apparent visual size with distance variant. *American Journal of Psychology, 54,* 21–37.

Hopfield, J. J. (1982). Neural networks and physical systems with emergent collective computational abilities. *Proceedings of the National Academy of Sciences, USA, 79*(8), 2554–2558.

Horn, B. K. P. (1971). *The Binford-Horn linefinder* (MIT–AI Memo 285). Cambridge, MA: MIT.

Horn, B. K. P. (1974). Determining lightness from an image. *Computer Graphics and Image Processing, 3*(1), 277–299.

Horn, B. K. P. (1975). Obtaining shape from shading information. In P. H. Winston (Ed.), *The psychology of computer vision* (pp. 115–156). New York: McGraw-Hill.

Horn, B. K. P. (1977). Understanding image intensities. *Artificial Intelligence, 8,* 201–231.

Horner, D. G. (1982). Can vision predict baseball players' hitting ability? *American Journal of Optometry and Physiological Optics, 59,* 69P.

Howes, D. H., & Solomon, R. L. (1950). A note on McGinnies' "Emotionality and perceptual defense." *Psychological Review, 57,* 229–234.

Hubel, D. H. (1995). *Eye, brain, and vision.* New York: Scientific American Library/Scientific American Books.

Hubel, D. H., & Wiesel, T. N. (1959). Receptive fields of single neurons in the cat's striate cortex. *Journal of Physiology (London), 148,* 574–591.

Hubel, D. H., & Wiesel, T. N. (1962). Receptive fields, binocular interaction, and functional architecture of the cat's visual cortex. *Journal of Physiology (London), 160,* 106–154.

Hubel, D. H., & Wiesel, T. N. (1963). Receptive fields of cells in striate cortex of very young, visually inexperienced kittens. *Journal of Neurophysiology, 26*(6), 994–1002.

Hubel, D. H., & Wiesel, T. N. (1968). Receptive fields and functional architecture of monkey striate cortex. *Journal of Physiology, 195,* 215–243.

Hubel, D. H., & Wiesel, T. N. (1970). Stereoscopic vision in macaque monkey. Cells sensitive to binocular depth in area 18 of the macaque monkey cortex. *Nature, 225*(227), 41–42.

Hubel, D. H., & Wiesel, T. N. (1977). Functional architecture of macaque visual cortex. *Proceedings of the Royal Society of London, B, 198,* 1–59.

Hubel, D. H., Wiesel, T. N., & Stryker, M. P. (1977). Orientation columns in macaque monkey visual cortex demonstrated by the 2-deoxyglucose autoradiographic technique. *Nature, 269*(5626), 328–330.

Huffman, D. A. (1971). Impossible objects as nonsense sentences. In M. Meltzer & D. Michie (Eds.), *Machine intelligence* (Vol. 6). Edinburgh, Scotland: Edinburgh University Press.

Hume, D. (1777/1966). *An Enquiry concerning human understanding.* La Salle, IL: Open Court.

Hummel, J. E. (in press). Where view-based theories break down: The role of structure in shape and object recognition. In E. Dietrich & A. Markman (Eds.), *Cognitive dynamics: Conceptual change in humans and machines.* Cambridge, MA: MIT Press.

Hummel, J. E., & Biederman, I. (1992). Dynamic binding in a neural network for shape recognition. *Psychological Review, 99*(3), 480–517.

Hummel, J. E., & Stankiewicz, B. J. (1996). Categorical relations in shape perception. *Spatial Vision, 10*(3), 201–236.

Hummel, J. E., & Stankiewicz, B. J. (1998). Two roles of attention in shape perception: A structural description model of visual scrutiny. *Visual Cognition, 5*(1–2), 49–79.

Humphrey, N. K. (1974). Vision in a monkey without striate cortex: A case study. *Perception, 3*(3), 241–255.

Humphreys, G. W., & Riddoch, J. (1992). Interactions between object and space systems revealed through neuropsychology. In D. E. Meyer & S. Kornblum (Eds.), *Attention and Performance* (pp. 143–162). Cambridge, MA: MIT Press.

Humphreys, G. W., & Riddoch, M. J. (1984). Routes to object constancy: Implications from neurological impairments of object constancy. *Quarterly Journal of Experimental Psychology: Human Experimental Psychology, 36*(3), 385–415.

Humphreys, G. W., & Riddoch, M. J. (1985). Author's corrections to "Routes to object constancy." *Quarterly Journal of Experimental Psychology: Human Experimental Psychology, 37A*, 493–495.

Hurvich, L. M. (1981). *Color vision.* Sunderland, MA: Sinauer Associates.

Hurvich, L. M., & Jameson, D. (1957). An opponent process theory of color vision. *Psychological Review, 64*, 384–404.

Huttenlocher, D. P., & Ullman, S. (1987). *Object recognition using alignment* (MIT–AI Memo 937). Cambridge, MA: MIT.

Intraub, H. (1980). Presentation rate and the representation of briefly glimpsed pictures in memory. *Journal of Experimental Psychology: Human Learning & Memory, 6*, 1–12.

Intraub, H. (1984). Conceptual masking: The effects of subsequent visual events on memory for pictures. *Journal of Experimental Psychology: Learning, Memory, & Cognition, 10*, 115–125.

Irwin, D. E. (1992). Memory for position and identity across eye movements. *Journal of Experimental Psychology: Learning, Memory, & Cognition, 18*(2), 307–317.

Irwin, D. E. (1998). Lexical processing during saccadic eye movements. *Cognitve Psychology, 36*(1), 1–27.

Irwin, D. E., Carlson-Radavanski, L. A., & Andrews, R. V. (1995). Information processing during saccadic eye movements. *Acta Psychologica, 90*, 261–273.

Irwin, D. E., & Gordon, R. D. (1998). Eye movements, attention and trans-saccdic memory. *Visual Cognition, 5*(1–2), 127–155.

Irwin, D. E., Yantis, S., & Jonides, J. (1983). Evidence against visual integration across saccadic eye movements. *Perception & Psychophysics, 34*(1), 49–57.

Ittelson, W. H. (1951). Size as a cue to distance. *American Journal of Psychology, 64*, 54–67.

Jackendoff, R. (1987). *Consciousness and the computational mind.* Cambridge, MA: MIT Press.

James, W. (1890/1950). *Principles of psychology.* New York: Holt.

Janez, L. (1983). Stimulus control of the visual reference frame: Quantitative theory. *Informes de Psicologia, 2*, 133–147.

Johansson, G. (1950). *Configuration in event perception.* Uppsala, Sweden: Almqvist & Wiksell.

Johansson, G. (1973). Visual perception of biological motion and a model for its analysis. *Perception & Psychophysics, 14*, 210–211.

Johansson, G. (1975). Visual motion perception. *Scientific American, 232*(6), 76–88.

Johnson, S. P., & Aslin, R. N. (1995). Perception of object unity in 2 month old infants. *Developmental Psychology, 31*, 739–745.

Johnson-Laird, P. N. (1983). A computational analysis of consciousness. *Cognition and Brain Theory, 6*, 499–508.

Johnson-Laird, P. N. (1988). A computational analysis of consciousness. In A. J. Marcel & E. Bisiach (Eds.), *Consciousness in contemporary science* (pp. 357–368). Oxford, England: Clarendon Press/Oxford University Press.

Jolicoeur, P. (1985). The time to name disoriented natural objects. *Memory & Cognition, 13*(4), 289–303.

Jolicoeur, P., Gluck, M. A., & Kosslyn, S. M. (1984). Pictures and names: Making the connection. *Cognitive Psychology, 16*(2), 243–275.

Jones, D. G., & Malik, J. (1992). Computational framework for determining stereo correspondence from a set of linear spatial filters. *Image Vision Computation, 10*, 699–708.

Jonides, J. (1981). Voluntary versus automatic control over the mind's eye. In J. Long & A. D. Baddeley (Eds.), *Attention and Performance* (Vol. 9). Hillsdale, NJ: Erlbaum.

Judd, D. B., McAdam, D. L., & Wyszecki, G. (1964). Spectral distribution of typical daylight as a function of correlated color temperature. *Journal of the Optical Society of America, 23*, 1031–1040.

Julesz, B. (1971). *Foundations of cyclopean perception.* Chicago: University of Chicago Press.

Julesz, B. (1975). Experiments in the visual perception of texture. *Scientific American, 232*, 34–43.

Julesz, B. (1981). Textons, the elements of texture perception, and their interactions. *Nature, 290*(5802), 91–97.

Julesz, B. (1984). A brief outline of the texton theory of human vision. *Trends in Neurosciences, 7*(2), 41–45.

Kabrisky, M. (1966). *A proposed model for visual information processing in the human brain.* Urbana, IL: University of Illinois Press.

Kahneman, D. (1973). *Attention and effort.* Englewood Cliffs, NJ: Prentice-Hall.

Kahneman, D., & Beatty, J. (1967). Pupillary responses in a pitch discrimination task. *Perception & Psychophysics, 2*, 101–105.

Kahneman, D., & Treisman, A. (1984). Changing views of attention and automaticity. In R. Parasuraman & D. R. Davies (Eds.), *Varieties of attention* (pp. 29–62). New York: Academic Press.

Kahneman, D., Treisman, A., & Gibbs, B. J. (1992). The reviewing of object files: Object-specific integration of information. *Cognitive Psychology, 24*(2), 175–219.

Kaiser, M. K., & Phatak, A. V. (1993). "Things that go bump in the light: On the optical specification of contact severity": Correction. *Journal of Experimental Psychology: Human Perception & Performance, 19*(4), 743.

Kaiser, M. K., & Proffitt, D. R. (1984). The development of sensitivity to causally relevant dynamic information. *Child Development, 55*(4), 1614–1624.

Kaiser, M. K., & Proffitt, D. R. (1987). Observers' sensitivity to dynamic anomalies in collisions. *Perception & Psychophysics, 42*(3), 275–280.

Kaiser, M. K., Proffitt, D. R., & Anderson, K. (1985). Judgments of natural and anomalous trajectories in the presence and absence of motion. *Journal of Experimental Psychology: Learning, Memory, & Cognition, 11*(1–4), 795–803.

Kaiser, M. K., Proffitt, D. R., Whelan, S. M., & Hecht, H. (1992). Influence of animation on dynamical judgments. *Journal of Experimental Psychology: Human Perception & Performance, 18*(3), 669–689.

Kaiser, P. K., & Boynton, R. M. (1996). *Human color vision.* Washington, DC: Optical Society of America.

Kanizsa, G. (1955). Margini quasi-percettivi in campi con stimolazione omogenea. *Rivista di Psicologia, 49,* 7–30.

Kanizsa, G. (1974). Contours without gradients or cognitive contours. *Italian Journal of Psychology, 1,* 93–112.

Kanizsa, G. (1979). *Organization in vision: Essays on Gestalt perception.* New York: Praeger.

Kanizsa, G., & Gerbino, W. (1976). Convexity and symmetry in figure-ground organization. In M. Henle (Ed.), *Vision and artifact.* New York: Springer.

Kant, E. (1781/1929). *Critique of pure reason* (N. Kemp-Smith, Trans.). London: Macmillan.

Kaufman, L., & Rock, I. (1962). The moon illusion: I. *Science, 136,* 953–961.

Kay, P., & McDaniel, C. K. (1978). The linguisitc significance of the meanings of basic color terms. *Language, 54,* 610–646.

Kellman, P. J. (1984). Perception of three-dimensional form by human infants. *Perception & Psychophysics, 36*(4), 353–358.

Kellman, P. J. (1995). Ontogenesis of space and motion perception. In W. Epstein & S. J. Rogers (Eds.), *Perception of space and motion. Handbook of perception and cognition* (2nd ed., pp. 327–364). San Diego, CA: Academic Press.

Kellman, P. J. (1996). The origins of object perception. In R. Gelman & T. K.-F. Au (Eds.), *Perceptual and cognitive development. Handbook of perception and cognition* (2nd ed., pp. 3–48). San Diego, CA: Academic Press.

Kellman, P. J., & Cohen, M. H. (1984). Kinetic subjective contours. *Perception & Psychophysics, 35*(3), 237–244.

Kellman, P. J., Gleitman, H., & Spelke, E. S. (1987). Object and observer motion in the perception of objects by infants. Special Issue: The ontogenesis of perception. *Journal of Experimental Psychology: Human Perception & Performance, 13*(4), 586–593.

Kellman, P. J., & Loukides, M. G. (1987). An object perception approach to static and kinetic subjective contours. In S. Petry & G. E. Meyer (Eds.), *The perception of illusory contours* (pp. 151–164). New York: Springer-Verlag.

Kellman, P. J., & Shipley, T. F. (1991). A theory of visual interpolation in object perception. *Cognitive Psychology, 23*(2), 141–221.

Kellman, P. J., & Spelke, E. S. (1983). Perception of partly occluded objects in infancy. *Cognitive Psychology, 15*(4), 483–524.

Kelly, M. H., & Freyd, J. J. (1987). Explorations of representational momentum. *Cognitive Psychology, 19*(3), 369–401.

Kender, J. R. (1979). *Shape from texture: A computational paradigm.* Paper presented at the Proceedings of the DARPA Image Understanding Workshop.

Kennedy, J. M. (1988). Line endings and subjective contours. *Spatial Vision, 3*(3), 151–158.

Kersten, D., Knill, D. C., Mamassian, P., & Bulthoff, I. (1996). Illusory motion from shadows. *Nature, 379*(6560), 31.

Kienker, P. K., Sejnowski, T. J., Hinton, G. E., & Schumacher, L. E. (1986). Separating figure from ground with a parallel network. *Perception, 15*(2), 197–216.

Kim, J. (1978). Supervenience and nomological incommensurables. *American Philosophical Quarterly, 15,* 149–156.

Kim, J. (1993). *Supervenience and mind.* Cambridge, England: Cambridge University Press.

Kinchla, R. A., & Wolfe, J. M. (1979). The order of visual processing: "Top-down," "bottom-up," or "middle-out." *Perception & Psychophysics, 25*(3), 225–231.

King, M., Meyer, G. E., Tangney, J., & Biederman, I. (1976). Shape constancy and a perceptual bias towards symmetry. *Perception & Psychophysics, 19*(2), 129–136.

Kinsbourne, M., & Warrington, E. K. (1964). Observations on color agnosia. *Journal of Neurology, Neurosurgery, and Psychiatry, 27,* 296–299.

Klein, R. M., & Pontefract, A. (1994). Does oculomotor readiness mediate cognitive control of visual attention?

Revisited. In C. Umilta & M. Moscovitch (Eds.), *Attention and performance 15: Conscious and nonconscious information processing* (pp. 333–350). Cambridge, MA: MIT Press.

Kleiner, K. A., & Banks, M. S. (1987). Stimulus energy does not account for 2-month-olds' face preferences. Special Issue: The ontogenesis of perception. *Journal of Experimental Psychology: Human Perception & Performance, 13*(4), 594–600.

Koenderink, J. J., Kappers, A. M. L., Pollick, F. E., & Kawato, M. (1997). Correspondence in pictoral space. *Perception & Psychophysics, 59*(6), 813–827.

Koenderink, J. J., & van Doorn, A. J. (1976a). Geometry of binocular vision and a model for stereopsis. *Biological Cybernetics, 21*(1), 29–35.

Koenderink, J. J., & van Doorn, A. J. (1976b). Local structure of movement parallax of the plane. *Journal of the Optical Society of America, 66*(7), 717–723.

Koenderink, J. J., & van Doorn, A. J. (1979). The internal representation of solid shape with respect to vision. *Biological Cybernetics, 32*, 211–216.

Koenderink, J. J., van Doorn, A. J., & Kappers, A. M. L. (1992). Surface perception in pictures. *Perception & Psychophysics, 52*(5), 487–496.

Koenderink, J. J., van Doorn, A. J., & Kappers, A. M. L. (1996). Pictorial surface attitude and local depth comparisons. *Perception & Psychophysics, 58*(2), 163–173.

Koffka, K. (1935). *Principles of Gestalt psychology*. New York: Harcourt, Brace.

Kohler, I. (1962). Experiments with goggles. *Scientific American, 206*(5), 62–86.

Köhler, W. (1920/1950). Physical Gestalten. In W. D. Ellis (Ed.), *A sourcebook of Gestalt psychology* (pp. 17–54). New York: The Humanities Press.

Köhler, W. (1940). *Dynamics in psychology*. New York: Liveright.

Köhler, W. (1947a). *Gestalt psychology: An introduction to new concepts in modern psychology*. New York: Liveright.

Köhler, W. (1947b). Sensory organization. In W. Kohler (Ed.), *Gestalt psychology*. New York: Liveright.

Kolb, B., & Whishaw, I. Q. (1996). *Fundamentals of human neuropsychology*. New York: Freeman.

Kolers, P. A. (1972). *Aspects of motion perception*. London: Pergamon Press.

Kolers, P. A., & Pomerantz, J. R. (1971). Figural change in apparent motion. *Journal of Experimental Psychology, 87*, 99–108.

Kopferman, H. (1930). Psychologishe Untersuchungen uber die Wirkung Zwei-dimensionaler korperlicher Gebilde. *Psychologische Forschung, 13*, 293–364.

Korte, A. (1915). Kinematoskopische Untersuchungen. *Zeitschrift fur Psychologie, 72*, 193–206.

Kosslyn, S. M. (1973). Scanning visual images: Some structural implications. *Perception & Psychophysics, 14*(1), 90–94.

Kosslyn, S. M. (1975). Information representation in visual images. *Cognitive Psychology, 7*(3), 341–370.

Kosslyn, S. M. (1980). *Image and mind*. Cambridge, MA: Harvard University Press.

Kosslyn, S. M. (1981). The medium and the message in mental imagery: A theory. *Psychological Review, 88*(1), 46–66.

Kosslyn, S. M. (1994). *Image and brain: The resolution of the imagery debate*. Cambridge, MA: MIT Press.

Kosslyn, S. M., Alpert, N. M., Thompson, W. L., Maljkovic, V., & others. (1993). Visual mental imagery activates topographically organized visual cortex: PET investigations. *Journal of Cognitive Neuroscience, 5*(3), 263–287.

Kosslyn, S. M., Ball, T. M., & Reiser, B. J. (1978). Visual images preserve metric spatial information: Evidence from studies of image scanning. *Journal of Experimental Psychology: Human Perception & Performance, 4*(1), 47–60.

Kosslyn, S. M., & Schwartz, S. P. (1977). A simulation of visual imagery. *Cognitive Science, 1*(3), 265–295.

Kowler, E. (1995). Eye movements. In S. M. Kosslyn & D. N. Osherson (Eds.), *Visual cognition* (pp. 215–255) Cambridge, MA: MIT Press.

Kowler, E., & Zingale, C. (1985). Smooth eye movements as indicators of selective attention. In M. I. Posner & O. S. M. Marin (Eds.), *Attention and performance: Vol. 11. Mechanisms of attention* (pp. 285–300). Hillsdale, NJ: Erlbaum.

Krauskopf, J. (1963). Effect of retinal image stabilization on the appearance of heterochromatic targets. *Journal of the Optical Society of America, 53*, 741–744.

Kröse, B. J. (1986). *A Description of Visual Structure*. Unpublished Ph.D. dissertation, Delft University of Technology, Delft, Netherlands.

Kröse, B. J. (1987). Local structure analyzers as determinants of preattentive pattern discrimination. *Biological Cybernetics, 55*(5), 289–298.

Krumhansl, C. (1978). Concerning the application of geometric models to similarity data: The interrelationship between similarity and spatial density. *Psychological Review, 85*, 445–463.

Kruskal, J. B. (1964). Multidimensional scaling by optimizing goodness of fit to a nonmetric hypothesis. *Psychometrika, 29*, 1–27.

Kubovy, M., & Holcombe, A. O. (1998). On the lawfulness of grouping by proximity. *Cognitive Psychology, 35*(1), 71–98.

Kubovy, M., & Wagemans, J. (1995). Grouping by proximity and multistability in dot lattices: A quantitative Gestalt theory. *Psychological Science, 6*(4), 225–234.

Kuffler, S. W. (1953). Discharge patterns and functional organization of mammalian retina. *Journal of Neurophysiology, 16*, 37–68.

Kuffler, S. W., & Nicholls, J. G. (1976). *From neuron to brain: A cellular approach to the function of the nervous system.* Sunderland, MA: Sinauer Associates.

Kuhn, T. S. (1962). *The structure of scientific revolutions.* Chicago: University of Chicago Press.

LaBerge, D., & Brown, V. (1989). Theory of attentional operations in shape identification. *Psychological Review, 96*(1), 101–124.

Lachman, R., Lachman, J. L., & Butterfield, E. (1979). *Cognitive psychology and information processing: An introduction.* Hillsdale, NJ: Erlbaum.

Lamb, M. R., Robertson, L. C., & Knight, R. T. (1989). Attention and interference in the processing of global and local information: Effects of unilateral temporal-parietal junction lesions. *Neuropsychologia, 27*(4), 471–483.

Land, E. H., & McCann, J. J. (1971). Lightness and retinex theory. *American Journal of Optical Society of America, 61*, 1–11.

Landy, M. S., Maloney, L. T., Johnston, E. B., & Young, M. (1995). Measurement and modeling of depth cue combination: In defense of weak fusion. *Vision Research, 35*(3), 389–412.

Lappin, J. S., & Preble, L. D. (1975). A demonstration of shape constancy. *Perception & Psychophysics, 17*(5), 439–444.

Lashley, K. S. (1929). *Brain mechanisms of intelligence.* Chicago: Chicago University Press.

Lashley, K. S. (1931). Mass action in cerebral function. *Science, 73*, 245–254.

Lashley, K. S. (1950). In search of the engram. *Symposium of the Society for Experimental Biology, 4*, 454–482.

Lashley, K. S., Chow, K. L., & Semmes, J. (1951). An examination of the electrical field theory of cerebral integration. *Psychological Review, 58*, 123–136.

Lavie, N. (1995). Perceptual load as a necessary condition for selective attention. *Journal of Experimental Psychology: Human Perception & Performance, 21*(3), 451–468.

Le Bihan, D., Turner, R., Zeffiro, T. A., Cuenod, C. A., Jezzard, P., & Bonnerot, V. (1993). Activation of human primary visual cortex during visual recall: A magnetic resonance imaging study. *Proceedings of the National Academy of Sciences, USA, 90*(24), 11802–11805.

Leask, J., Haber, R. N., & Haber, R. B. (1969). Eidetic imagery in children: II. Longitudinal and experimental results. *Psychonomic Monograph Supplements, 3*(3), 25–48.

LeCun, Y. (1985). Une procedure d'apprentisage pour reseau a seuil assymetrique. *Cognitiva, 85*, 599–604.

Lee, D. N. (1976). A theory of visual control of braking based on information about time-to-collision. *Perception, 5*(4), 437–459.

Lee, D. N. (1980). Visuo-motor coordination in space-time. In G. E. Stelmach & J. Requin (Eds.), *Tutorials in motor behavior* (pp. 281–295). Amsterdam: North Holland.

Lee, D. N., & Aronson, E. (1974). Visual proprioceptive control of standing in human infants. *Perception & Psychophysics, 15*(3), 529–532.

Lee, D. N., & Lishman, J. R. (1975). Visual and proprioceptive control of stance. *Journal of Human Movement Studies, 1*, 87–95.

Lee, D. N., & Young, D. S. (1985). Visual timing of interceptive action. In D. Ingle, M. Jeannerod, & D. N. Lee (Eds.), *Brain mechanisms and spatial vision* (pp. 1–30). Dordrecht, Netherlands: Martinus Nijhoff.

Leeuwenberg, E. L. J. (1971). A perceptual coding language for visual and auditory patterns. *American Journal of Psychology, 84*(3), 307–349.

Leeuwenberg, E. L. J. (1978). Quantification of certain visual pattern properties: Salience, transparency and similarity. In E. L. J. Leeuwenberg & H. F. J. M. Buffart (Eds.), *Formal theories of visual perception.* New York: Wiley.

Lehky, S. R., & Sejnowski, T. J. (1988). Network model of shape-from-shading: Neural function arises from both receptive and projective fields. *Nature, 333*(6172), 452–454.

Lehky, S. R., & Sejnowski, T. J. (1990). Neural network model of visual cortex for determining surface curvature from images of shaded surfaces. *Proceedings of the Royal Society, London, B, 240*, 251–278.

Lehky, S. R., & Sejnowski, T. J. (1992). Network model of shape-from-shading: Neural function arises from both receptive and projective fields. In S. M. Kosslyn & R. A. Andersen (Eds.), *Frontiers in cognitive neuroscience* (pp. 187–189). Cambridge, MA: MIT Press.

Leibowitz, H. (1955). Effect of reference lines on the discrimination of movement. *Journal of the Optical Society of America, 45*, 829–830.

Leopold, D. A., & Logothetis, N. K. (1996). Activity changes in early visual cortex reflect monkey's percepts during binocular rivalry. *Nature, 379*, 549–553.

Lettvin, J. Y., Maturana, H. R., McCullough, W. S., & Pitts, W. H. (1959). What the frog's eye tells the frog's brain. *Proceedings of the Institute of Radio Engineers, 47*, 1940–1951.

Leung, T., & Malik, J. (1998). *Contour continuity in region based image segmentation.* Paper presented at the Proceedings of the 5th European Conference on Computer Vision, Freiburg, Germany.

LeVay, S., Hubel, D. H., & Wiesel, T. N. (1975). The pattern of ocular dominance columns in macaque visual cortex revealed by a reduced silver stain. *Journal of Comparative Neurology, 159*, 559–575.

Levelt, W. J. M. (1968). *On binocular rivalry.* The Hague: Mouton.

Levine, D. N., Warach, J., & Farah, M. J. (1985). Two visual systems in mental imagery: Dissociations of "what" and "where" in imagery disorders due to bilateral posterior cerebral lesions. *Neurology, 35*, 1010–1018.

Levine, J. (1983). Materialism and qualia: The explanatory gap. *Pacific Philosophical Quarterly, 64*, 354–361.

Lewis, D. (1966). An argument for the identity theory. *Journal of Philosophy, 50*, 249–258.

Lewis, E. R., Zeevi, Y. Y., & Werblin, F. S. (1969). Scanning electron microscopy of vertibrate visual receptors. *Brain Research, 15*, 559–562.

Li, X., & Gilchrist, A. (in press). Relative area and relative luminance combine to anchor surface lightness values. *Perception & Psychophysics.*

Lindsay, P. H., & Norman, D. A. (1977). *Human information processing.* New York: Academic Press.

Linsker, R. (1988). Self-organization in a perceptual network. *Computer, 21*(3), 105–117.

Lissauer, H. (1890/1988). A case of visual agnosia with a contribution to theory. *Cognitive Neuropsychology, 5*(2), 157–192.

Livingstone, M. S., & Hubel, D. H. (1984). Specificity of intrinsic connections in primate primary visual cortex. *Journal of Neuroscience, 4*(11), 2830–2835.

Livingstone, M. S., & Hubel, D. H. (1987). Psychophysical evidence for separate channels for the perception of form, color, movement, and depth. *Journal of Neuroscience, 7*(11), 3416–3468.

Livingstone, M. S., & Hubel, D. (1988). Segregation of form, color, movement, and depth: Anatomy, physiology, and perception. *Science, 240*(4853), 740–749.

Locke, J. (1690/1987). *An essay concerning human understanding.* Oxford, England: Clarendon Press.

Lockwood, M. (1989). *Mind, brain, and the quantum: The compound 'I.'* Oxford, England: Basil Blackwell.

Loftus, E. F. (1977). Shifting human color memory. *Memory & Cognition, 5*(6), 696–699.

Loftus, E. F. (1979). *Eyewitness testimony.* Cambridge, MA: Harvard University Press.

Loftus, E. F., Miller, D. G., & Burns, H. J. (1978). Semantic integration of verbal information into a visual memory. *Journal of Experimental Psychology: Human Learning & Memory, 4*(1), 19–31.

Loftus, E. F., & Palmer, J. C. (1974). Reconstruction of automobile destruction: An example of the interaction between language and memory. *Journal of Verbal Learning & Verbal Behavior, 13*(5), 585–589.

Loftus, E. F., Schooler, J. W., & Wagenaar, W. A. (1985). The fate of memory: Comment on McCloskey and Zaragoza. *Journal of Experimental Psychology: General, 114*(3), 375–380.

Loftus, G. R., & Ginn, M. (1984). Perceptual and conceptual masking of pictures. *Journal of Experimental Psychology: Learning, Memory & Cognition, 10*, 435–441.

Logie, R. H. (1986). Visuo-spatial processing in working memory. *Quarterly Journal of Experimental Psychology: Human Experimental Psychology, 38*(2), 229–247.

Logothetis, N., & Schall, J. (1989). Neuronal correlates of subjective visual perception. *Science, 245*, 761–763.

Longuet-Higgins, H. C., & Prazdny, K. F. (1980). The interpretation of a moving retinal image. *Proceedings of the Royal Society, London, B, 208*, 385–397.

Loomis, J. M., & Nakayama, K. (1973). A velocity analogue of brightness contrast. *Perception, 2*(4), 425–428.

Lowe, D. G. (1985). *Perceptual organization and visual recognition.* Boston, MA: Kluwer Academic Publishers.

Lowe, D. G. (1987). The viewpoint consistency constraint. *International Journal of Computer Vision, 1*, 57–72.

Lu, C., & Fender, D. H. (1972). The interaction of color and luminance in stereoscopic vision. *Investigative Ophthalmology, 11*(6), 482–490.

Lu, Z.-L., & Sperling, G. (1995). The functional architecture of human visual motion perception. *Vision Research, 35*(19), 2697–2722.

Luck, S. J., Vogel, E. K., & Shapiro, K. L. (1996). Word meanings can be accessed but not reported during the attentional blink. *Nature, 383*, 616–618.

Ludvigh, E., & Miller, J. W. (1958). Study of visual acuity during the ocular pursuit of moving test objects: I. Introduction. *Journal of the Optical Society of America, 48*, 799–802.

Luria, A. R. (1968). *The mind of a mnemonist: A little book about a vast memory.* New York: Basic Books.

Mace, W. M. (1977). James J. Gibson's strategy for perceiving: Ask not what's inside your head, but what your head's inside of. In R. Shaw & J. Bransford (Eds.), *Perceiving, acting, and knowing* (pp. 43–66). Hillsdale, NJ: Erlbaum.

Mach, E. (1865/1965). Uber die Wirkung der raumlichen Vertheilung des Lichterizes auf die Netzhaut, I. In F. Ratliff (Ed.), *Mach bands: Quantitative studies on neural networks in the retina.* San Francisco: Holden-Day.

Mach, E. (1914/1959). *The analysis of sensations*. Chicago: Open Court.

Mack, A. (1978). Three modes of visual perception. In M. H. Pick (Ed.), *Modes of percieving and information processing* (pp. 171–186). Hillsdale, NJ: Erlbaum.

Mack, A., Hill, J., & Kahn, S. (1989). Motion aftereffects and retinal motion. *Perception, 18*(5), 649–655.

Mack, A., & Rock, I. (1998). *Inattentional blindness*. Cambridge, MA: MIT Press.

Mack, A., Tang, B., Tuma, R., Kahn, S., & Rock, I. (1992). Perceptual organization and attention. *Cognitive Psychology, 24*(4), 475–501.

MacLeod, C. M. (1991). Half a century of research on the Stroop effect: An integrative review. *Psychological Bulletin, 109*(2), 163–203.

MacLeod, D. I. A., & Lennie, P. (1976). Red-green blindness confined to one eye. *Vision Research, 16*, 691–712.

Magoun, H. W. (1962). *The waking brain* (2nd ed.). Springfield, IL: Charles C. Thomas.

Malik, J. (1987). Interpreting line drawings of curved objects. *International Journal of Computer Vision, 1*(1), 73–103.

Malik, J., & Perona, P. (1990). Preattentive texture discrimination with early vision mechanisms. *Journal of the Optical Society of America A, 7*(5), 923–932.

Malik, J., & Rosenholtz, R. (1994). *A computational model for shape from texture*. Paper presented at the Higher-order processing in the visual system. Ciba Foundation symposium, 184, Chichester, England.

Maloney, L. T., & Wandell, B. A. (1986). Color constancy: A method for recovering surface spectral reflectance. *Journal of the Optical Society of America A, 3*(1), 29–33.

Mangan, B. (1993). Taking phenomenology seriously: The "fringe" and its implications for cognitive research. *Consciousness and Cognition, 2*, 89–108.

Marcel, A. J. (1983a). Conscious and unconscious perceptions: An approach to the relations between phenomenal experience and perceptual processes. *Cognitive Psychology, 15*, 238–300.

Marcel, A. J. (1983b). Conscious and unconscious perceptions: Experiments on visual masking and word recognition. *Cognitive Psychology, 15*, 197–237.

Marks, W. B., Dobelle, W. H., & MacNichol, M. F. J. (1964). Visual pigments of single primate cones. *Science, 143*, 1181–1183.

Marr, D. (1978). Representing visual information. In A. Hanson & E. M. Riseman (Eds.), *Computer vision systems*. New York: Academic Press.

Marr, D. (1982). *Vision: A computational investigation into the human representation and processing of visual information*. San Francisco: W. H. Freeman.

Marr, D., & Hildreth, E. C. (1980). Theory of edge detection. *Proceedings of the Royal Society of London, B, 207*, 187–217.

Marr, D., & Nishihara, H. K. (1978). Representation and recognition of the spatial organization of three-dimensional shapes. *Proceedings of the Royal Society of London, 200*, 269–294.

Marr, D., & Poggio, T. (1977). Cooperative computation of stereo disparity. *Science, 194*, 283–287.

Marr, D., & Poggio, T. (1979). A computational theory of human stereo vision. *Proceedings of the Royal Society of London, B, 204*, 301–328.

Marr, D., & Ullman, S. (1981). Directional selectivity and its use in early processing. *Proceedings of the Royal Society of London, B, 211*, 151–180.

Marshall, J. C., & Halligan, P. W. (1988). Blindsight and insight in visuo-spatial neglect. *Nature, 336*(6201), 766–767.

Massaro, D. W. (1973). The perception of rotated shapes: A process analysis of shape constancy. *Perception & Psychophysics, 13*(3), 413–422.

Massaro, D. W. (1987). *Speech perception by ear and eye: A paradigm for psychological inquiry*. Hillsdale, NJ: Erlbaum.

Massaro, D. W. (1988). Ambiguity in perception and experimentation. *Journal of Experimental Psychology: General, 117*(4), 417–421.

Massaro, D. W. (1989). Testing between the TRACE model and the fuzzy logical model of speech perception. *Cognitive Psychology, 21*(3), 398–421.

Massaro, D. W., & Friedman, D. (1990). Models of integration given multiple sources of information. *Psychological Review, 97*, 225–252.

Massaro, D. W., & Hary, J. M. (1986). Addressing issues in letter recognition. *Psychological Research, 48*(3), 123–132.

Matin, E. (1974). Saccadic suppression: A review and an analysis. *Psychological Bulletin, 81*(12), 899–917.

Matin, L., & MacKinnon, G. E. (1964). Autokinetic movement: Selective manipulation of directional components by image stabilization. *Science, 143*(3602), 147–148.

Maunsell, J., & Felleman, D. (1987). Visual processing in monkey extrastriate cortex. *Annual Review of Neuroscience, 10*, 363–401.

Maxwell, J. C. (1855). Experiments on colour, as perceived by the eye, with remarks on colour-blindness. *Transactions of the Royal Society, Edinborough, 21*, 275–298.

McClelland, J. L. (1976). Preliminary letter identification in the perception of words and nonwords. *Journal of Experimental Psychology: Human Perception & Performance, 2*(1), 80–91.

McClelland, J. L. (1991). Stochastic interactive processes and the effect of context on perception. *Cognitive Psychology, 23*(1), 1–44.

McClelland, J. L., & Johnston, J. C. (1977). The role of familiar units in perception of words and nonwords. *Perception & Psychophysics, 22*, 249–261.

McClelland, J. L., & Miller, J. (1979). Structural factors in figure perception. *Perception & Psychophysics, 26*(3), 221–229.

McClelland, J. L., & Rumelhart, D. E. (1981). An interactive activation model of context effects in letter perception: I. An account of basic findings. *Psychological Review, 88*(5), 375–407.

McClelland, J. L., Rumelhart, D. E., & the PDP Research Group (Eds.) (1986). *Parallel distributed processing: Explorations in the microstructure of cognition: Vol. 2. Psychological and biological models.* Cambridge, MA: MIT Press.

McClelland, J. L., & Rumelhart, D. E. (1988). *Explorations in parallel distributed processing: A handbook of models, programs, and exercises.* Cambridge, MA: MIT Press.

McCloskey, M. (1983). Intuitive physics. *Scientific American, 248*(4), 122–130.

McCloskey, M., Caramazza, A., & Green, B. (1980). Curvilinear motion in the absence of external forces: Naive beliefs about the motion of objects. *Science, 210*(4474), 1139–1141.

McCloskey, M., & Zaragoza, M. (1985). Misleading postevent information and memory for events: Arguments and evidence against memory impairment hypotheses. *Journal of Experimental Psychology: General, 114*(1), 1–16.

McGinnies, E. (1949). Emotionality and perceptual defense. *Psychological Review, 56*, 244–251.

Meadows, J. C. (1974). Disturbed perception of colors associated with localized cerebral lesions. *Brain, 97*, 615–632.

Melton, A. W. (1963). Implications of short term memory for a general theory of memory. *Journal of Verbal Learning & Verbal Behavior, 2*, 1–21.

Merikle, P. M. (1980). Selection from visual persistence by perceptual groups and category membership. *Journal of Experimental Psychology: General, 109*(3), 279–295.

Merikle, P. M., & Reingold, E. M. (1992). Measuring unconscious perceptual processes. In R. F. Bornstein & T. S. Pittman (Eds.), *Perception without awareness: Cognitive, clinical, and social perspectives* (pp. 55–80). New York: Guilford Press.

Mervis, C. B., Catlin, J., & Rosch, E. (1975). Development of the structure of color categories. *Developmental Psychology, 11*(1), 54–60.

Mervis, C. B., & Rosch, E. (1981). Categorization of natural objects. *Annual Review of Psychology, 32*, 89–115.

Metelli, F. (1974). The perception of transparency. *Scientific American, 230*(4), 90–98.

Metzger, F. (1953). *Gesetze des Sehens.* Frankfurt-am-Main: Waldemar Kramer.

Michael, C. R. (1978). Color vision mechanisms in monkey striate cortex: Dual-opponent cells with concentric receptive fields. *Journal of Neurophysiology, 41*, 572–588.

Michotte, A. (1946/1963). *The perception of causality* (T. R. Miles and E. Miles, Trans.). London: Methuen.

Miller, J. (1981). Global precedence in attention and decision. *Journal of Experimental Psychology: Human Perception & Performance, 7*(6), 1161–1174.

Milner, A. D., & Goodale, M. A. (1995). *The visual brain in action.* Oxford: Oxford University Press.

Milner, B. (1966). Amnesia following operation on the temporal lobes. In C. W. M. Whitty & O. L. Zangwill (Eds.), *Amnesia.* London: Butterworths.

Milner, B. (1968). Visual recognition and recall after right temporal-lobe excision in man. *Neuropsychologia, 6*, 191–209.

Milner, P. M. (1974). A model for visual shape recognition. *Psychological Review, 81*, 521–535.

Minsky, M. (1975). A framework for representing knowledge. In P. H. Winston (Ed.), *The psychology of computer vision.* New York: McGraw-Hill.

Minsky, M. (1980). *The society of mind.* New York: Simon & Schuster.

Minsky, M., & Papert, S. (1969). *Perceptrons: An introduction to computational geometry.* Cambridge, MA: MIT Press.

Mishkin, M., Ungerleider, L., & Macko, K. (1983). Object vision and spatial vision: Two central pathways. *Trends in Neuroscience, 6*, 414–417.

Mollon, J. D., Newcombe, F., Polden, P. G., & Ratcliff, G. (1980). On the presence of three cone mechanisms in a case of total achomatopsia. In G. Verriest (Ed.), *Color vision deficiencies.* Bristol: Hilger.

Mollon, J. D., & Polden, P. G. (1979). Post-receptoral adaptation. *Vision Research, 19*, 35–40.

Moore, C. M., Yantis, S., & Vaughn, B. (1998). Object-based visual selection: Evidence from perceptual completion. *Psychological Science, 9*(2), 104–110.

Moran, J., & Desimone, R. (1985). Selective attention gates visual processing in the extrastriate cortex. *Science, 229*(4715), 782–784.

Moray, N. (1959). Attention in dichotic listening: Affective cues and the influence of instructions. *Quarterly Journal of Experimental Psychology, 11*, 56–60.

Morgan, M. J., Findlay, J. M., & Watt, R. J. (1982). Aperture viewing: A review and a synthesis. *Quarterly Journal of*

Experimental Psychology: Human Experimental Psychology, 34(2), 211–233.

Movshon, J. A., Adelson, E. H., Gizzi, M. S., & Newsome, W. T. (1985). The analysis of moving visual patterns. In C. Chagas, R. Gattass, & C. Gross (Eds.), *Pattern recognition mechanisms* (pp. 117–151). New York: Springer-Verlag.

Müller, G. E. (1896). Zur Psychophysik der Gesichtsempfindungen [Concerning the psychophysics of visual sensations]. *Zeitschrift für Psychologie, 10*, 1–82.

Munsell, A. H. (1905). *A color notation*. Boston: G. H. Ellis.

Murdock, B. J. (1962). The serial position curve in free recall. *Journal of Experimental Psychology, 64*, 482–488.

Murphy, B. J. (1978). Pattern thresholds for moving and stationary gratings during smooth eye movement. *Vision Research, 18*, 521–530.

Musatti, C. I. (1924). Sui fenomeni stereocinetici. *Archivo Italiano Psicologia, 3*, 105–120.

Musatti, C. I. (1975). Stereokinetic phenomena and their interpretation. In G. B. Flores d'Arcais (Ed.), *Studies in perception: Festschrift for Fabio Metelli* (pp. 166–189). Milan: Martello-Giunti.

Nagel, T. (1974). What is it like to be a bat? *The Philosophical Review, 83*, 435–450.

Nakamura, R. K., & Mishkin, M. (1980). Blindness in monkeys following lesions in nonvisual cortex. *Brain Research, 188*, 572–577.

Nakamura, R. K., & Mishkin, M. (1986). Chronic blindness following lesions of nonvisual cortex in the monkey. *Experimental Brain Research, 62*, 173–184.

Nakayama, K. (1977). *Geometrical and physiological aspects of depth perception*. Paper presented at the 3-D image processing, Proceedings of the Society of Photo-optical Instrumentation Engineers.

Nakayama, K., He, Z. J., & Shimojo, S. (1995). Visual surface representation: A critical link between lower-level and higher-level vision. In S. M. Kosslyn & D. N. Osherson (Eds.), *Visual cognition: An invitation to cognitive science* (2nd ed., Vol. 2, pp. 1–70). Cambridge, MA: MIT Press.

Nakayama, K., & Shimojo, S. (1990). DaVinci stereopsis: Depth and subjective contours from unpaired monocular points. *Vision Research, 30*, 1811–1825.

Nakayama, K., & Silverman, G. H. (1986). Serial and parallel processing of visual feature conjunctions. *Nature, 320*, 264–265.

Nalwa, V. S. (1993). *A guided tour of computer vision*. Reading, MA: Addison-Wesley.

Nathans, J. (1987). Molecular biology of visual pigments. *Annual Review of Neuroscience, 10*, 163–194.

Nathans, J. (1989). The genes for color vision. *Scientific American, 260*(2), 42–49.

Navon, D. (1976). Irrelevance of figural identity for resolving ambiguities in apparent motion. *Journal of Experimental Psychology: Human Perception & Performance, 2*, 130–138.

Navon, D. (1977). Forest before trees: The precedence of global features in visual perception. *Cognitive Psychology, 9*(3), 353–383.

Neisser, U. (1967). *Cognitive psychology*. Englewood Cliffs, NJ: Prentice-Hall.

Neisser, U. (1989). *Direct perception and recognition as distinct perceptual systems*. Paper presented at the Annual Meeting of the Cognitive Science Society, Ann Arbor, MI.

Neitz, J., Neitz, M., & Jacobs, G. H. (1993). More than three different cone pigments among people with normal color vision. *Vision Research, 33*(1), 117–122.

Neuhaus, W. (1930). Experimentelle Untersuchung der Scheinbewegung [Experimental investigation of apparent movement]. *Archiv für die Gesamte Psychologie, 75*, 315–458.

Newell, A. (1973). You can't play 20 questions with nature and win. In W. G. Chase (Ed.), *Visual information processing* (pp. 283–310): New York, NY: Academic.

Newell, A., Shaw, J. C., & Simon, H. A. (1958). Elements of a theory of human problem solving. *Psychological Review, 65*, 151–166.

Newell, A., & Simon, H. A. (1963). GPS, a program that simulates human thought. In E. A. Feigenbaum & J. Feldman (Eds.), *Computers and thought*. New York: McGraw-Hill.

Newell, A., & Simon, H. A. (1972). *Human problem solving*. Englewood Cliffs, NJ: Prentice-Hall.

Nickerson, R. S., & Adams, M. J. (1979). Long-term memory for a common object. *Cognitive Psychology, 11*(3), 287–307.

Nida-Rümelin, M. (1996). Pseudonormal vision: An actual case of qualia inversion? *Philosophical Studies, 82*, 145–157.

Norman, D. A. (1968). Toward a theory of memory and attention. *Psychological Review, 75*(6), 522–536.

Nothdurft, H.-C. (1992). Feature analysis and the role of similarity in preattentive vision. *Perception & Psychophysics, 52*(4), 355–375.

Noton, D., & Stark, L. (1971a). Eye movements and visual perception. *Scientific American, 224*(6), 34–43.

Noton, D., & Stark, L. (1971b). Scanpaths in eye movements during pattern perception. *Science, 171*(3968), 308–311.

Nowlan, S. J., & Sejnowski, T. J. (1995). A selection model for motion processing in area MT of primates. *Journal of Neuroscience, 15*(2), 1195–1214.

O'Regan, J. K. (1992). Solving the "real" mysteries of visual perception: The world as an outside memory. Special Issue:

Object perception and scene analysis. *Canadian Journal of Psychology, 46*(3), 461–488.

Ober-Thompkins, B. A. (1982). *The effects of typicality on picture perception and memory.* Unpublished Ph.D. Dissertation, University of California, Berkeley, CA.

Oden, G. C., & Massaro, D. W. (1978). Integration of featural information in speech perception. *Psychological Review, 85*(3), 172–191.

Ogle, K. N. (1950). *Binocular vision.* Philadelphia: Saunders.

Olshausen, B. A., & Field, D. J. (1996). Emergence of simple-cell receptive field properties by learning a sparse coade for natural images. *Nature, 381,* 607–609.

Olson, R. K., & Attneave, F. (1970). What variables produce similarity grouping? *American Journal of Psychology, 83*(1), 1–21.

Paivio, A. (1969). Mental imagery in associative learning and memory. *Psychological Review, 76*(3), 241–263.

Paivio, A., & Yuille, J. C. (1967). Mediation instructions and word attributes in paired-associate learning. *Psychonomic Science, 8*(2), 65–66.

Pallis, C. A. (1955). Impaired identification of faces and places with agnosia for colours: Report of a case due to cerebral embolism. *Journal of Neurology, Neurosurgery & Psychiatry, 18,* 218–224.

Palm, G. (1980). On associative memory. *Biological Cybernetics, 36,* 19–31.

Palmer, G. (1777). *Theory of light.* London: Leacroft.

Palmer, S. E. (1975a). The effects of contextual scenes on the identification of objects. *Memory & Cognition, 3*(5), 519–526.

Palmer, S. E. (1975b). Visual perception and world knowledge: Notes on a model of sensory-cognitive interaction. In D. A. Norman & D. E. Rumelhart (Eds.), *Explorations in cognition* (pp. 279–307). San Francisco: W. H. Freeman.

Palmer, S. E. (1977). Hierarchical structure in perceptual representation. *Cognitive Psychology, 9*(4), 441–474.

Palmer, S. E. (1978). Fundamental aspects of cognitive representation. In E. Rosch & B. Lloyd (Eds.), *Cognition and categorization* (pp. 261–304). Hillsdale, NJ: Erlbaum.

Palmer, S. E. (1980). What makes triangles point: Local and global effects in configurations of ambiguous triangles. *Cognitive Psychology, 12*(3), 285–305.

Palmer, S. E. (1983). The psychology of perceptual organization: A transformational approach. In J. Beck, B. Hope, & A. Baddeley (Eds.), *Human and machine vision* (pp. 269–339). New York: Academic Press.

Palmer, S. E. (1985). The role of symmetry in shape perception. Special Issue: Seeing and knowing. *Acta Psychologica, 59*(1), 67–90.

Palmer, S. E. (1989). Reference frames in the perception of shape and orientation. In B. E. Shepp & S. Ballesteros (Eds.), *Object perception: Structure and process* (pp. 121–163). Hillsdale, NJ: Erlbaum.

Palmer, S. E. (1991). Goodness, Gestalt, groups, and Garner: Local symmetry subgroups as a theory of figural goodness. In G. R. Lockhead & J. R. Pomerantz (Eds.), *The perception of structure: Essays in honor of Wendell R. Garner* (pp. 23–39). Washington, DC: American Psychological Association.

Palmer, S. E. (1992). Common region: A new principle of perceptual grouping. *Cognitive Psychology, 24*(3), 436–447.

Palmer, S. E. (1995). Gestalt psychology redux. In P. Baumgartner & S. Payr (Eds.), *Speaking minds: Conversations with twenty eminent cognitive scientists* (pp. 156–176). Princeton, NJ: Princeton University Press.

Palmer, S. E. (in press). Color, consciousness, and the isomorphism constraint. *Behavioral & Brain Sciences.*

Palmer, S. E., & Beck, D. (in preparation). The repetition detection task: A quantitative method for studying grouping.

Palmer, S. E., & Bucher, N. M. (1981). Configural effects in perceived pointing of ambiguous triangles. *Journal of Experimental Psychology: Human Perception & Performance, 7*(1), 88–114.

Palmer, S. E., & Bucher, N. M. (1982). Textural effects in perceived pointing of ambiguous triangles. *Journal of Experimental Psychology: Human Perception & Performance, 8*(5), 693–708.

Palmer, S. E., & Hemenway, K. (1978). Orientation and symmetry: Effects of multiple, rotational, and near symmetries. *Journal of Experimental Psychology: Human Perception & Performance, 4*(4), 691–702.

Palmer, S. E., & Kimchi, R. (1986). The information processing approach to cognition. In T. J. Knapp & L. C. Robertson (Eds.), *Approaches to cognition: Contrasts and controversies.* Hillsdale, NJ: Erlbaum.

Palmer, S. E., & Levitin, D. (in preparation). Synchrony: A new principle of perceptual organization.

Palmer, S. E., Neff, J., & Beck, D. (1996). Late influences on perceptual grouping: Amodal completion. *Psychonomic Bulletin & Review, 3*(1), 75–80.

Palmer, S. E., & Rock, I. (1994a). On the nature and order of organizational processing: A reply to Peterson. *Psychonomic Bulletin & Review, 1,* 515–519.

Palmer, S. E., & Rock, I. (1994b). Rethinking perceptual organization: The role of uniform connectedness. *Psychonomic Bulletin & Review, 1*(1), 29–55.

Palmer, S. E., Rosch, E., & Chase, P. (1981). Cannonical perspective and the perception of objects. In J. Long & A. Baddeley (Eds.), *Attention and Performance* (Vol. 9) (pp. 135–151). Hillsdale, NJ: Erlbaum.

Palmer, S. E., Simone, E., & Kube, P. (1988). Reference frame effects on shape perception in two versus three dimensions. *Perception, 17*(2), 147–163.

Pantle, A. J., & Picciano, L. (1976). A multi-stable movement display: Evidence for two separate motion systems in humans. *Science, 193*, 500–502.

Parker, D. B. (1985). *Learning-logic: Casting the cortex of the human brain in silicon* (Technical Report TR-47). Cambridge, MA: Center for Computational Research in Economics and Management Science, MIT.

Parks, T. E. (1965). Post-retinal visual storage. *American Journal of Psychology, 78*, 145–147.

Pashler, H. E. (1998). *The psychology of attention.* Cambridge, MA: MIT Press.

Penrose, L. S., & Penrose, R. (1958). Impossible objects: A special type of visual illusion. *British Journal of Psychology, 49*, 31–33.

Penrose, R. (1989). *The emperor's new mind.* Oxford, England: Oxford University Press.

Pentland, A. (1986). Perceptual organization and the representation of natural form. *Artificial Intelligence, 28*, 293–331.

Pentland, A. (1989). Shape information from shading: A theory about human perception. *Spatial Vision, 4*(2–3), 165–182.

Peterhans, E., & von der Heydt, R. (1989). Mechanisms of contour perception in monkey visual cortex. II. Contours bridging gaps. *Journal of Neuroscience, 9*(5), 1749–1763.

Peterhans, E., & von der Heydt, R. (1991). Subjective contours: Bridging the gap between psychophysics and physiology. *Trends in Neurosciences, 14*(3), 112–119.

Petersik, J. T. (1991). Comments on Cavanagh and Mather (1989): Coming up short (and long). *Spatial Vision, 5*(4), 291–301.

Peterson, L. R., & Peterson, M. J. (1959). Short-term retention of individual verbal items. *Journal of Experimental Psychology, 58*, 193–198.

Peterson, M. A. (1994). The proper treatment of uniform connectedness. *Psychological Bulletin & Review, 1*, 509–514.

Peterson, M. A., & Gibson, B. S. (1991). The initial identification of figure-ground relationships: Contributions from shape recognition processes. *Bulletin of the Psychonomic Society, 29*(3), 199–202.

Peterson, M. A., & Gibson, B. S. (1993). Shape recognition inputs to figure-ground organization in three-dimensional grounds. *Cognitive Psychology, 25*(3), 383–429.

Peterson, M. A., Harvey, E. M., & Weidenbacher, H. J. (1991). Shape recognition contributions to figure-ground

reversal: Which route counts? *Journal of Experimental Psychology: Human Perception & Performance, 17*(4), 1075–1089.

Peterson, M. A., & Hochberg, J. (1983). Opposed-set measurement procedure: A quantitative analysis of the role of local cues and intention in form perception. *Journal of Experimental Psychology: Human Perception & Performance, 9*(2), 183–193.

Phillips, W. A. (1974). On the distinction between sensory storage and short-term visual memory. *Perception & Psychophysics, 16*(2), 283–290.

Phillips, W. A., & Christie, D. F. (1977). Components of visual memory. *Quarterly Journal of Experimental Psychology, 29*(1), 117–133.

Pierce, C. S., & Jastrow, J. (1884). On small differences in sensation. *Memoirs of the National Academy of Science, 3*, 75–83.

Pinker, S. (Ed.) (1985). *Visual cognition.* Cambridge, MA: MIT Press.

Piotrowski, L. N., & Campbell, F. W. (1982). A demonstration of the visual importance and flexibility of spatial-frequency amplitude and phase. *Perception, 11*(3), 337–346.

Pirenne, M. H. (1970). *Optics, painting & photography.* London: Cambridge University Press.

Pittenger, J. B. (1991). Cognitive physics and event perception: Two approaches to the assessment of people's knowledge of physics. In R. R. Hoffman & D. S. Palermo (Eds.), *Cognition and the symbolic processes: Applied and ecological perspectives* (pp. 233–254). Hillsdale, NJ: Erlbaum.

Pitts, W., & McCullough, W. S. (1947). How we know universals: The perception of auditory and visual forms. *Bulletin of Mathematical Biophysics, 9*, 127–147.

Poggio, G. F., & Fischer, B. (1977). Binocular interaction and depth sensitivity in striate and prestriate cortex of behaving rhesus monkey. *Journal of Neurophysiology, 40*(6), 1392–1405.

Poggio, T., & Edelman, S. (1990). A neural network that learns to recognize three-dimensional objects. *Nature, 343*, 263–266.

Poincaré, H. (1952). *Science and hypothesis.* New York: Dover.

Pomerantz, J. R., & Garner, W. R. (1973). The role of configuration and target discriminability in a visual search task. *Memory & Cognition, 1*(1), 64–68.

Pomerantz, J. R., & Kubovy, M. (1986). Theoretical approaches to perceptual organization: Simplicity and likelihood principles. In K. R. Boff, L. Kaufman, & J. P. Thomas (Eds.), *Handbook of perception and human performance: Vol. 2. Cognitive processes and performance* (pp. 1–46). New York: Wiley.

Pomerantz, J. R., Sager, L. C., & Stoever, R. J. (1977). Perception of wholes and of their component parts: Some configural superiority effects. *Journal of Experimental Psychology: Human Perception & Performance, 3*(3), 422–435.

Posner, M. I. (1978). *Chronometric explorations of mind.* Hillsdale, NJ: Erlbaum.

Posner, M. I. (1980). Orienting of attention. *Quarterly Journal of Experimental Psychology, 32*(1), 3–25.

Posner, M. I., Nissen, M. J., & Ogden, W. C. (1978). Attended and unattended processing modes: The role of set for spatial locations. In H. L. Pick & B. J. Saltzman (Eds.), *Modes of perceiving and processing information* (pp. 137–158). Hillsdale, NJ: Erlbaum.

Posner, M. I., & Petersen, S. E. (1990). The attention system of the human brain. *Annual Review of Neuroscience, 13*, 25–42.

Posner, M. I., & Rafal, R. D. (1987). Cognitive theories of attention and the rehabilitation of attentional deficits. In M. J. Meier, A. L. Benton, & L. Diller (Eds.), *Neuropsychological rehabilitation* (pp. 182–201). New York: Guilford Press.

Posner, M. I., & Raichle, M. E. (1994). *Images of mind.* New York: Scientific American Books.

Posner, M. I., Walker, J. A., Friedrich, F. A., & Rafal, R. D. (1984). Effects of parietal injury on covert orienting of attention. *Journal of Neuroscience, 4*(7), 1863–1874.

Posner, M. I., Walker, J. A., Friedrich, F. A., & Rafal, R. D. (1987). How do the parietal lobes direct covert attention? *Neuropsychologia, 25*(1), 135–145.

Postman, L., & Phillips, L. W. (1965). Short-term temporal changes in free recall. *Quarterly Journal of Experimental Psychology, 17*(2), 132–138.

Potter, M. C. (1976). Short-term conceptual memory for pictures. *Journal of Experimental Psychology: Human Learning & Memory, 2*, 509–522.

Potter, M. C., & Levy, E. I. (1969). Recognition memory for a rapid sequence of pictures. *Journal of Experimental Psychology, 81*, 10–15.

Prazdny, K. (1980). Egomotion and relative depth from optical flow. *Biological Cybernetics, 36*, 87–102.

Prazdny, K. (1982). *Computing motions of planar surfaces from spatiotemporal changes in image brightness.* Paper presented at the Proceedings for the IEEE Conference on Pattern Recognition and Image Processing, New York.

Prazdny, K. (1984). *A (computational) study of stereo disparity detection* (FLAIR Technical Report 34). Palo Alto, CA: Fairchild Laboratory for Artificial Intelligence Research.

Prentice, W. C. H. (1954). Visual recognition of verbally labeled figures. *American Journal of Psychology, 67*, 315–320.

Prinzmetal, W., & Silvers, B. (1994). The word without the tachistoscope. *Perception & Psychophysics, 55*, 296–312.

Pritchard, R. M. (1958). Visual illusions viewed as stabilized retinal images. *Quarterly Journal of Experimental Psychology, 10*, 77–81.

Pritchard, R. M. (1961). Stabilized images on the retina. *Scientific American, 204*(6), 72–78.

Proffitt, D. R., & Gilden, D. L. (1989). Understanding natural dynamics. *Journal of Experimental Psychology: Human Perception & Performance, 15*(2), 384–393.

Proffitt, D. R., & Kaiser, M. K. (1995). Perceiving events. In W. Epstein & S. J. Rogers (Eds.), *Perception of space and motion. Handbook of perception and cognition* (2nd ed., pp. 227–261). San Diego, CA: Academic Press.

Proffitt, D. R., Kaiser, M. K., & Whelan, S. M. (1990). Understanding wheel dynamics. *Cognitive Psychology, 22*(3), 342–373.

Proffitt, D. R., Rock, I., Hecht, H., & Schubert, J. (1992). Stereokinetic effect and its relation to the kinetic depth effect. *Journal of Experimental Psychology: Human Perception & Performance, 18*(1), 3–21.

Putnam, H. (1960). Minds and machines. In S. Hook (Ed.), *Dimensions of mind.* New York: Collier Books.

Putnam, H. (1967). Psychological predicates. In W. Capitan & D. Merrill (Eds.), *Art, mind, and religion* (pp. 35–48). Pittsburgh: University of Pittsburgh Press.

Pylyshyn, Z. W. (1973). What the mind's eye tells the mind's brain: A critique of mental imagery. *Psychological Bulletin, 80*(1), 1–24.

Pylyshyn, Z. W. (1984). *Computation and Cognition.* Cambridge, MA: MIT Press.

Pylyshyn, Z. W., & Storm, R. W. (1988). Tracking multiple independent targets: Evidence for a parallel tracking mechanism. *Spatial Vision, 3*(3), 179–197.

Rafal, R. (1996). Balint's syndrome. In T. E. Feinberg & M. J. Farah (Eds.), *Behavioral Neurology and Neuropsychology* (pp. 337–356). New York: McGraw-Hill.

Rafal, R., & Posner, M. I. (1987). Defects in human visual spatial attention following thalamic lesions. *Proceedings of the National Academy of Sciences, USA, 84*, 7349–7353.

Rafal, R., Posner, M. I., Friedman, J. H., Inhoff, A. W., & Bernstein, E. (1988). Orienting of visual attention in progressive supranuclear palsy. *Brain, 111*, 267–280.

Rafal, R., & Robertson, L. (1995). The neurology of visual attention. In M. S. Gazzaniga (Ed.), *The cognitive neurosciences* (pp. 625–648). Cambridge, MA: MIT Press.

Rafal, R., Smith, J., Krantz, J., Cohen, A., & Brennan, C. (1990). Extrageniculate vision in hemianopic humans: Saccade inhibition by signals in the blind field. *Science, 250*, 118–121.

Ramachandran, V. S. (1993). Filling in gaps in perception: II. Scotomas and phantom limbs. *Current Directions in Psychological Science, 2*(2), 56–65.

Ramachandran, V. S., & Gregory, R. L. (1978). Does colour provide an input to human motion perception? *Nature, 275,* 55–56.

Ramachandran, V. S., Levi, L., Stone, L., Rogers-Ramachandran, D., McKinney, R., Stalcup, M., Arcilla, G., Zweifler, R., Schatz, A., & Flippin, A. (1996). Illusions of body image: What they reveal about human nature. In R. R. Llinas & P. S. Churchland (Eds.), *The mind-brain continuum: Sensory processes* (pp. 29–60). Cambridge, MA: MIT Press.

Ramachandran, V. S., Rao, V. M., & Vidyasagar, T. R. (1973). Apparent movement with subjective contours. *Vision Research, 13*(7), 1399–1401.

Ratliff, F. (Ed.) (1965). *Mach bands: Quantitative studies on neural networks in the retina.* San Francisco: Holden-Day.

Raymond, J. E., Shapiro, K. L., & Arnell, K. M. (1992). Temporary suppression of visual processing in an RSVP task: An attentional blink? *Journal of Experimental Psychology: Human Perception & Performance, 18*(3), 849–860.

Rayner, K., McConkie, G., & Erlich, S. (1978). Eye movements and integrating information across fixations. *Journal of Experimental Psychology: Human Perception & Performance, 4*(4), 529–544.

Reddy, R., & Newell, A. (1974). Knowledge and its representation in a speech understanding system. In L. W. Gregg (Ed.), *Knowledge and cognition.* Potomac, MD: Erlbaum.

Reed, S. K., & Johnsen, J. A. (1975). Detection of parts in patterns and images. *Memory & Cognition, 3*(5), 569–575.

Regan, D. M., & Beverly, K. I. (1982). How do we avoid confounding the direction we are looking with the direction we are moving? *Science, 215,* 194–196.

Reichard, W. (1957). Autokorrelationsauswertung als funktionsprinzip des zentralnervensystems. *Zeitschrift Naturforschung, 12b,* 447–457.

Reichard, W. (1961). Autocorrelation: A principle for the evaluation of sensory information by the central nervous system. In W. A. Rosenblith (Ed.), *Sensory communication.* New York: Wiley.

Reicher, G. M. (1969). Perceptual recognition as a function of meaningfulness of stimulus material. *Journal of Experimental Psychology, 81*(2), 275–280.

Rensink, R. A., & Enns, J. T. (1995). Preemption effects in visual search: Evidence for low-level grouping. *Psychological Review, 102*(1), 101–130.

Rensink, R. A., O'Reagan, J. K., & Clark, J. J. (1995a). Image flicker is as good as sacades in making large scene changes invisible. *Pereption, 24*(Suppl.), 26–27.

Rensink, R. A., O'Regan, J. K., & Clark, J. J. (1995b). Visual perception of scene changes disrupted by global transients. *Nature* (manuscript).

Rensink, R. A., O'Reagan, J. K., & Clark, J. J. (1997). To see or not to see: The need for attention to perceive changes in scenes. *Psychological Science, 8*(5), 368–373.

Restak, R. M. (1984). *The brain.* New York: Bantam Books.

Richards, W. (1970). Stereopsis and stereoblindness. *Experimental Brain Research, 10*(4), 380–388.

Riley, D. A. (1962). Memory for form. In L. Postman (Ed.), *Psychology in the making.* New York: Knopf.

Rizzolatti, G., Riggio, L., Dascola, I., & Umilta, C. (1987). Reorienting attention across the horizontal and vertical meridians: Evidence in favor of a premotor theory of attention. Special Issue: Selective visual attention. *Neuropsychologia, 25*(1), 31–40.

Ro, T., & Rafal, R. D. (1996). Perception of geometric illusions in hemispatial neglect. *Neuropsychologia, 34,* 973–978.

Roberts, L. G. (1965). Machine perception of three-dimensional solids. In J. T. Tippett, D. A. Berkowitz, L. C. Clapp et al. (Eds.), *Optical and electro-optical information processing.* Cambridge, MA: MIT Press.

Robertson, L. C., & Lamb, M. R. (1991). Neuropsychological contributions to theories of part/whole organization. *Cognitive Psychology, 23*(2), 299–330.

Robertson, L. C., Lamb, M. R., & Knight, R. T. (1988). Effects of lesions of the temporal-parietal junction on perceptual and attentional processing in humans. *Journal of Neuroscience, 8,* 3757–3769.

Robins, C., & Shepard, R. N. (1977). Spatio-temporal probing of apparent rotational movement. *Perception & Psychophysics, 22*(1), 12–18.

Robinson, D. N. (1966). Disinhibition of visually masked stimuli. *Science, 154,* 157–158.

Rock, I. (1966). *The nature of perceptual adaptation.* New York: Basic Books.

Rock, I. (1968). The basis of position-constancy during passive movement. *American Journal of Psychology, 81*(2), 262–265.

Rock, I. (1973). *Orientation and form.* New York: Academic Press.

Rock, I. (1975). *An introduction to perception.* New York: Macmillan.

Rock, I. (1983). *The logic of perception.* Cambridge, MA: MIT Press.

Rock, I. (1984). *Perception.* New York: Scientific American Library.

Rock, I. (1990). The frame of reference. In I. Rock (Ed.), *The legacy of Solomon Asch: Essays in cognition and social psychology* (pp. 243–268). Hillsdale, NJ: Erlbaum.

Rock, I. (1995). *Perception* (2nd ed.). New York: Scientific American Library.

Rock, I. (Ed.) (1997). *Indirect perception.* Cambridge, MA: MIT Press.

Rock, I., & Brosgole, L. (1964). Grouping based on phenomenal proximity. *Journal of Experimental Psychology, 67,* 531–538.

Rock, I., & DiVita, J. (1987). A case of viewer-centered object perception. *Cognitive Psychology, 19*(2), 280–293.

Rock, I., DiVita, J., & Barbeito, R. (1981). The effect on form perception of change of orientation in the third dimension. *Journal of Experimental Psychology: Human Perception & Performance, 7*(4), 719–732.

Rock, I., & Ebenholtz, S. (1959). The relational determination of perceived size. *Psychological Review, 66,* 387–401.

Rock, I., & Ebenholtz, S. (1962). Stroboscopic movement based on change of phenomenal rather than retinal location. *American Journal of Psychology, 75,* 193–207.

Rock, I., & Englestein, P. (1959). A study of memory for visual form. *American Journal of Psychology, 72,* 221–229.

Rock, I., Gopnik, A., & Hall, S. (1994). Do young children reverse ambiguous figures? *Perception, 23*(6), 635–644.

Rock, I., & Gutman, D. (1981). The effect of inattention on form perception. *Journal of Experimental Psychology: Human Perception & Performance, 7*(2), 275–285.

Rock, I., Hill, A. L., & Fineman, M. (1968). Speed constancy as a function of size constancy. *Perception & Psychophysics, 4*(1), 37–40.

Rock, I., & Kaufman, L. (1962). The moon illusion: II. *Science, 136,* 1023–1031.

Rock, I., Linnett, C. M., Grant, P., & Mack, A. (1992). Perception without attention: Results of a new method. *Cognitive Psychology, 24*(4), 502–534.

Rock, I., & Mack, A. (1994). Attention and perceptual organization. In B. Soledad (Ed.), *Cognitive approaches to human perception.* (pp. 23–41). Hillsdale, NJ: Erlbaum.

Rock, I., & Mitchener, K. (1992). Further evidence of failure of reversal of ambiguous figures by uninformed subjects. *Perception, 21*(1), 39–45.

Rock, I., Nijhawan, R., Palmer, S., & Tudor, L. (1992). Grouping based on phenomenal similarity of achromatic color. *Perception, 21*(6), 779–789.

Rock, I., Palmer, S. E., & Hume, Q. (in preparation).

Roelofs, C. O. (1935). Die optische Lokalisation. [Visual localization.] *Archiv für Augenheilkunde, 109,* 395–415.

Rogers, B., & Graham, M. (1979). Motion parallax as an independent cue for depth perception. *Perception, 8*(2), 125–134.

Roland, P. E., Eriksson, L., Stone-Elander, A., & Widen, L. (1987). Does mental activity change the oxidative metabolism of the brain? *Journal of Neuroscience, 7,* 2373–2389.

Roland, P. E., & Friberg, L. (1985). Localization of cortical areas activated by thinking. *Journal of Neurophysiology, 53,* 1219–1243.

Rosch, E. (1973a). Natural categories. *Cognitive Psychology, 4*(3), 328–350.

Rosch, E. (1973b). On the internal structure of perceptual and semantic categories. In T. E. Moore (Ed.), *Cognitive development and the acquisition of language.* New York: Academic Press.

Rosch, E. (1975a). Cognitive reference points. *Cognitive Psychology, 7*(4), 532–547.

Rosch, E. (1975b). Cognitive representations of semantic categories. *Journal of Experimental Psychology: General, 104*(3), 192–233.

Rosch, E., & Mervis, C. B. (1975). Family resemblances: Studies in the internal structure of categories. *Cognitive Psychology, 7*(4), 573–605.

Rosch, E., Mervis, C. B., Gray, W. D., Johnson, D. M., & Boyes-Braem, P. (1976). Basic objects in natural categories. *Cognitive Psychology, 8*(3), 382–439.

Rosenblatt, F. (1962). *Principles of neurodynamics: Perceptrons and the theory of brain mechanisms.* Washington, DC: Spartan Books.

Rosenfeld, A., Thurston, M., & Lee, Y.-H. (1972). Edge and curve detection: Further experiments. *Proceedings of IEEE Transactions on Computers, 21,* 677–715.

Ross, E. D. (1980). Sensory-specific and fractional disorders of recent memory in man: Isolated loss of recent visual memory. *Archives of Neurology, 37,* 193–200.

Ross, E. D. (1982). Disorders of recent memory in humans. *Trends in Neurosciences, 5,* 170–173.

Rossotti, H. (1983). *Colour: Why the world isn't grey.* Princeton, NJ: Princeton University Press.

Royden, C. S., Banks, M. S., & Crowell, J. A. (1992). The perception of heading during eye movements. *Nature, 360*(6404), 583–585.

Royer, F. L. (1981). Detection of symmetry. *Journal of Experimental Psychology: Human Perception & Performance, 7*(6), 1186–1210.

Rubens, A. B., & Benson, D. F. (1971). Associative visual agnosia. *Archives of Neurology, 24,* 305–316.

Rubin, E. (1921). *Visuell Wahrgenommene Figuren.* Kobenhaven: Glydenalske boghandel.

Rubin, J. M., & Richards, W. A. (1982). Color vision and image intensities: When are changes material? *Biological Cybernetics, 45,* 215–226.

Rubin, J. M., & Richards, W. A. (1989). Color vision: Representing material categories. In W. A. Richards (Ed.), *Natural computation* (pp. 194–213). Cambridge, MA: MIT Press.

Rumelhart, D. E., Hinton, G. E., & Williams, R. J. (1986). Learning internal representations by error propagation. In D. E. Rumelhart, J. L. McClelland, & the PDP Research Group (Eds.), *Parallel distribution processing: Explorations in the microstructure of cognition: Vol. 1. Foundations* (pp. 318–362). Cambridge, MA: MIT Press.

Rumelhart, D. E., & McClelland, J. L. (1982). An interactive activation model of context effects in letter perception: II. The contextual enhancement effect and some tests and extensions of the model. *Psychological Review, 89*(1), 60–94.

Rumelhart, D. E., McClelland, J. L., & the PDP Research Group (Eds.) (1986). *Parallel distributed processing: Explorations in the microstructure of cognition: Vol. 1. Foundations.* Cambridge, MA: MIT Press.

Rumelhart, D. E., Smolensky, P., McClelland, J. L., & Hinton, G. E. (1986). Schemata and sequential thought processes in PDP models. In J. L. McClelland, D. E. Rumelhart, & PDP Research Group (Eds.), *Parallel distributed processing: Explorations in the microstructure of cognition: Vol. 2. Psychological and biological models* (pp. 7–57). Cambridge, MA: MIT Press.

Runeson, S. (1977). On visual perception of dynamic events. *Acta Universitatis Upsaliensis: Studia Psychologia Upsaliensis (Series 9).*

Rushton, W. A. H., & Campbell, F. W. (1954). Measurement of rhodopsin in the living human eye. *Nature, London, 174,* 1096–1097.

Sacks, O. W. (1985). *The man who mistook his wife for a hat and other clinical tales.* New York: Summit Books.

Sakitt, B. (1976). Iconic memory. *Psychological Review, 83*(4), 257–276.

Sanders, A. F., & Houtmans, M. J. M. (1985). There is no central stimulus encoding during saccadic eye shofts: A case against general parallel processing notions. *Acta psychologica, 60,* 323–338.

Sanger, T. D. (1989). An optimality principle for unsupervised learning. In D. Touretzky (Ed.), *Advances in Neural Information Processing Systems* (Vol. 1, pp. 11–19). San Mateo, CA: Morgan-Kaufmann.

Schacter, D. L., McAndrews, M. P., & Moscovitch, M. (1988). Access to consciousness: Dissociations between implicit and explicit knowledge in neuropsychological syndromes. In L. Weiskrantz (Ed.), *Thought without language.* Oxford, England: Oxford University Press.

Schiller, P. H., & Lee, K. (1991). The role of the primate extrastriate area V4 in vision. *Science, 251*(4998), 1251–1253.

Schnapf, J. L., Kraft, T. W., & Baylor, D. A. (1987). Spectral sensitivity of human cone photoreceptors. *Nature, 325*(6103), 439–441.

Schooler, J. W., & Engstler-Schooler, T. Y. (1990). Verbal overshadowing of visual memories: Some things are better left unsaid. *Cognitive Psychology, 22*(1), 36–71.

Schubert, J., & Gilchrist, A. L. (1992). Relative luminance is not derived from absolute luminance. *Investigative Ophthalmology and Visual Science, 33*(4), 1258.

Schumann, F. (1904). Beitrage zur Analyse der Gesichtswahrnehmungen. *Zeitschrift für Psychologie, 36,* 161–185.

Searle, J. R. (1980). Minds, brains, and programs. *Behavioral & Brain Sciences, 3*(3), 417–457.

Searle, J. R. (1984). *Minds, brains, and science.* Cambridge, MA: Harvard University Press.

Searle, J. R. (1992). *The rediscovery of mind.* Cambridge, MA: MIT Press.

Searle, J. R. (1993). The problem of consciousness. *Consciousness & Cognition: An International Journal, 2*(4), 310–319.

Sedgwick, H. A. (1986). Space perception. In K. R. Boff, L. Kaufman, & J. P. Thomas (Eds.), *Handbook of perception and human performance: Vol. 1. Sensory processes* (pp. 23.21–23.44). New York: Wiley.

Segal, S. J., & Fusella, V. (1969). Effects of imagery on signal-to-noise ratio with varying signal conditions. *British Journal of Psychology, 60,* 459–464.

Sejnowski, T. J., & Nowlan, S. J. (1995). A model of visual motion processing in area MT of primates. In M. S. Gazzaniga (Ed.), *The cognitive neurosciences* (pp. 437–449). Cambridge, MA: MIT Press.

Sekuler, A., & Blake. (1985). *Perception*: Alfred A. Knopf.

Sekuler, A. B., & Palmer, S. E. (1992). Perception of partly occluded objects: A microgenetic analysis. *Journal of Experimental Psychology: General, 121*(1), 95–111.

Selfridge, O. G. (1957). Pattern recognition and learning. In C. Cherry (Ed.), *Information theory* (pp. 345–353). New York: Academic Press.

Selfridge, O. G., & Neisser, U. (1960). Pattern recognition by machine. *Scientific American, 203*(2), 60–68.

Sergent, J. (1982). The cerebral balance of power: Confrontation or cooperation. *Journal of Experimental Psychology: Human Perception & Performance, 8,* 253–272.

Shallice, T. (1972). Dual functions of consciousness. *Psychological Review, 79,* 383–393.

Shannon, C. E. (1948). A mathematical theory of communication. *Bell System Technical Journal, 27,* 279–423; 623–656.

Shannon, C. E., & Weaver, W. (1949). *The mathematical theory of communication*. Urbana: University of Illinois Press.

Shapiro, K. L., Driver, J., Ward, R., & Sorensen, R. E. (1996). Priming from the attentional blink: A failure to extract visual tokens but not visual types. *Psychological Science, 8*(2), 95–100.

Shapiro, K. L., & Luck, S. J. (1999). The attentional blink: A front-end mechanism for fleeting memories. In V. Coltheart (Ed.) *Fleeting memories: Cognition of brief visual stimuli*. Cambridge, MA: MIT Press.

Shapiro, K. L., Raymond, J. E., & Arnell, K. M. (1994). Attention to visual pattern information produces the attentional blink in RSVP. *Journal of Experimental Psychology: Human Perception & Performance, 20*(2), 357–371.

Shapley, R. (1995). Parallel neural pathways and visual function. In M. S. Gazzaniga (Ed.), *The cognitive neurosciences* (pp. 315–324). Cambridge, MA: MIT Press.

Shapley, R., & Perry, V. H. (1986). Cat and monkey retinal ganglion cells and their visual functional roles. Special Issue: Information processing in the retina. *Trends in Neurosciences, 9*(5), 229–235.

Shatz, C. J., & Stryker, M. P. (1978). Ocular dominance in layer IV of the cat's visual cortex and the effects of monocular deprivation. *Journal of Physiology, 281*, 267–283.

Sheinberg, D. L., & Logothetis, N. K. (1997). The role of temporal cortical areas in perceptual organization. *Proceedings of the National Academy of Sciences, USA, 94*, 3408–3413.

Shepard, R. N. (1962a). The analysis of proximities: Multidimensional scaling with an unknown distance function: Part I. *Psychometrika, 27*, 125–140.

Shepard, R. N. (1962b). The analysis of proximities: Multidimensional scaling with an unknown distance function: Part II. *Psychometrika, 27*(3), 219–246.

Shepard, R. N. (1967). Recognition memory of words, sentences, and pictures. *Journal of Verbal Learning & Memory, 6*(156–163).

Shepard, R. N. (1981). Psychophysical complementarity. In M. Kubovy & J. R. Pomerantz (Eds.), *Perceptual organization* (pp. 279–342). Hillsdale, NJ: Erlbaum.

Shepard, R. N. (1984). Ecological constraints on internal representation: Resonant kinematics of perceiving, imagining, thinking and dreaming. *Psychological Review, 91*(4), 441–447.

Shepard, R. N. (1992). The perceptual organization of colors: An adaptation to regularities of the terrestrial world? In J. H. Barkow, L. Cosmides, & J. Tooby (Eds.), *The adapted mind: Evolutionary psychology and the generation of culture* (pp. 495–532). New York: Oxford University Press.

Shepard, R. N., & Chipman, S. (1970). Second-order isomorphism of internal representations: Shapes of states. *Cognitive Psychology, 1*, 1–17.

Shepard, R. N., & Cooper, L. A. (1982). *Mental images and their transformations*. Cambridge, MA: MIT Press.

Shepard, R. N., & Judd, S. A. (1976). Perceptual illusion of rotation of three-dimensional objects. *Science, 191*, 952–954.

Shepard, R. N., Kilpatric, D. W., & Cunningham, J. P. (1975). The internal representation of numbers. *Cognitive Psychology, 7*(1), 82–138.

Shepard, R. N., & Metzler, J. (1971). Mental rotation of three dimensional objects. *Science, 171*, 701–703.

Shepard, R. N., & Zare, S. L. (1983). Path-guided apparent motion. *Science, 220*(4597), 632–634.

Shepp, B. E., & Swartz, K. B. (1976). Selective attention and the processing of integral and nonintegral dimensions: A developmental study. *Journal of Experimental Child Psychology, 22*(1), 73–85.

Shi, J., & Malik, J. (1997). *Normalized cuts and image segmentation*. Paper presented at the Proceedings of the IEEE Conference on Computation: Vision and Pattern Recognition, San Juan, Puerto Rico: IEEE.

Shimaya, A. (1997). Perception of complex line drawings. *Journal of Experimental Psychology: Human Perception & Performance, 23*(1), 25–50.

Shulman, G. L., Remington, R. W., & McLean, J. P. (1979). Moving attention through visual space. *Journal of Experimental Psychology: Human Perception & Performance, 5*(3), 522–526.

Shulman, G. L., & Wilson, J. (1987). Spatial frequency and selective attention to spatial location. *Perception, 16*(1), 103–111.

Sigman, E., & Rock, I. (1974). Stroboscopic movement based on perceptual intelligence. *Perception, 3*(1), 9–28.

Simon, H. A. (1969). *The sciences of the artificial*. Cambridge, MA: MIT Press.

Simons, D. J., & Levin, D. T. (1997). Failure to detect changes to attended objects. *Investigative Ophthalmology and Visual Science, 38*(4), S707.

Singh, M., Seyranian, G., & Hoffman, D. (in press). Parsing visual shapes: The short-cut rule. *Perception & Psychophysics*.

Slater, A., Johnson, S. P., Brown, E., & Badenoch, M. (1996). Newborn infants' perception of partly occluded objects. *Infant Behavior and Development, 19*, 145–148.

Slater, A., Mattock, A., & Brown, E. (1990). Size constancy at birth: Newborn infants' responses to retinal and real size. *Journal of Experimental Child Psychology, 49*, 314–322.

Slater, A., & Morison, V. (1985). Shape constancy and slant perception at birth. *Perception, 12*, 707–718.

Sloan, L. L., & Wollach, L. (1948). A case of unilateral deuteranopia. *Journal of the Optical Society of America, 38*, 501–509.

Smith, L. B., & Evans, P. (1989). Similarity, identity, and dimensions: Perceptual classification in children and adults. In B. E. Shepp & S. Ballesteros (Eds.), *Object perception: Structure and process* (pp. 325–356). Hillsdale, NJ: Erlbaum.

Smith, L. B., & Kemler, D. G. (1977). Developmental trends in free classification: Evidence for a new conceptualization of perceptual development. *Journal of Experimental Child Psychology, 24*(2), 279–298.

Smolensky, P. (1988). On the proper treatment of connectionism. *Behavioral & Brain Sciences, 11*(1), 1–74.

Spacek, L. A. (1985). *The detection of contours and their visual motion.* Unpublished Ph.D., University of Essex at Colchester, Colchester, England.

Spelke, E. S. (1990). Principles of object perception. *Cognitive Science, 14*(1), 29–56.

Sperling, G. (1960). The information available in brief visual presentations. *Psychological Monographs, 74*(11) [whole No. 498]), 29.

Sperry, R., & Miner, N. (1955). Pattern recognition following insertion of mica plates into the visual cortex. *Comparative and Physiological Psychology, 48*, 463–469.

Sperry, R. W. (1961). Cerebral organization and behavior. *Science, 133*, 1749–1757.

Spitzer, H., Desimone, R., & Moran, J. (1988). Increased attention enhances both behavioral and neuronal performance. *Science, 240*(4850), 338–340.

Springer, S. P., & Deutsch, G. (1981). *Left brain, right brain.* San Francisco: W. H. Freeman.

Standing, L., Conezio, J., & Haber, R. N. (1970). Perception and memory for pictures: Single trial learning of 2560 visual stimuli. *Psychonomic Science, 19*, 169–179.

Stankiewicz, B. J., Hummel, J. E., & Cooper, E. E. (1998). The role of attention in priming for left-right reflections of object images: Evidence for a dual representation of object shape. *Journal of Experimental Psychology: Human Perception & Performance, 24*(3), 732–744.

Sternberg, R. J. (1996). *Cognitive Psychology.* Fort Worth, TX: Harcourt Brace.

Sternberg, S. (1966). High-speed scanning in human memory. *Science, 153*, 652–654.

Sternberg, S. (1969). The discovery of processing stages: Extension of Donders' method. In W. G. Koster (Ed.), *Attention and Performance* (Vol. 2). Amsterdam: North Holland.

Stevens, J. K., Emerson, R. C., Gerstein, G. L., Kallos, T., Neufeld, G. R., Nichols, C. W., & Rosenquist, A. C. (1976). Paralysis of the awake human: Visual perceptions. *Vision Research, 16*(1), 93–98.

Stevens, K. A. (1979). *Surface perception from local analysis of texture and contour.* Unpublished Ph.D. Dissertation, MIT, Cambridge, MA.

Stevens, S. S. (1956). The direct estimation of sensory magnitudes: Loudness. *American Journal of Psychology, 69*, 1–25.

Stratton, G. M. (1896). Some preliminary experiments on vision without inversion of the retinal image. *Psychology Review, 3*, 611–617.

Stromeyer, C. F., & Psotka, J. (1970). The detailed texture of eidetic images. *Nature, 225*, 346–349.

Stroop, J. R. (1935). Studies of interference in serial verbal reactions. *Journal of Experimental Psychology, 18*, 643–662.

Tanaka, J. W., & Farah, M. J. (1993). Parts and wholes in face recognition. *Quarterly Journal of Experimental Psychology: Human Experimental Psychology, 164A*, 225–245.

Tanaka, J. W., & Taylor, M. (1991). Object categories and expertise: Is the basic level in the eye of the beholder? *Cognitive Psychology, 23*(3), 457–482.

Tarr, M. J., & Bülthoff, H. H. (1995). Is human object recognition better described by geon structural descriptions or by multiple views? Comment on Biederman and Gerhardstein (1993). *Journal of Experimental Psychology: Human Perception & Performance, 21*(6), 1494–1505.

Tarr, M. J., & Pinker, S. (1989). Mental rotation and orientation-dependence in shape recognition. *Cognitive Psychology, 21*(2), 233–282.

Tarr, M. J., & Pinker, S. (1990). When does human object recognition use a viewer-centered reference frame? *Psychological Science, 1*(4), 253–256.

Tarr, M. J., & Pinker, S. (1991). Orientation-dependent mechanisms in shape recognition: Further issues. *Psychological Science, 2*(3), 207–209.

Tarski, A. (1954). Contributions to the theory of models: I and II. *Indigationes Mathematicae, 16*, 572–588.

Teller, D. Y., Peeples, D. R., & Sekel, M. (1978). Discrimination of chromatic from white light by two-month-old human infants. *Vision Research, 18*(1), 41–48.

Ternus, J. (1926/1955). The problem of phenomenal identity. In W. D. Ellis (Ed.), *A sourcebook of Gestalt psychology* (pp. 149–160). London: Routledge & Kegan Paul.

Teuber, H. L. (1968). Alteration of perception and memory in man. In L. Weiskrantz (Ed.), *Analysis of Behavioral Change.* New York: Harper and Row.

Thompson, I. D., Kossut, M., & Blakemore, C. (1983). Development of orientation columns in cat striate cortex revealed by 2-deoxyglucose autoradiography. *Nature, 301*(5902), 712–715.

Thompson, P. (1981). Velocity aftereffects: The effects of adaptation to moving stimuli on the perception of subsequently seen moving stimuli. *Vision Research, 21*, 337–345.

Thouless, R. H. (1931). Phenomenal regression to the real object. I. *British Journal of Psychology, 21*, 339–359.

Tipper, S. P. (1985). The negative priming effect: Inhibitory priming by ignored objects. *Quarterly Journal of Experimental Psychology: Human Experimental Psychology, 37*(4), 571–590.

Tipper, S. P., & Cranston, M. (1985). Selective attention and priming: Inhibitory and facilitatory effects of ignored primes. *Quarterly Journal of Experimental Psychology: Human Experimental Psychology, 37*(4), 591–611.

Tipper, S. P., & Driver, J. (1988). Negative priming between pictures and words in a selective attention task: Evidence for semantic processing of ignored stimuli. *Memory & Cognition, 16*(1), 64–70.

Todd, J. T. (1995). The visual perception of three-dimensional structure from motion. In W. Epstein & S. Rogers (Eds.), *Perception of space and motion: Handbook of perception and cognition* (2nd ed., pp. 201–226). San Diego: Academic Press.

Todd, J. T., Koenderink, J. J., van Doorn, A. J., & Kappers, A. M. L. (1996). Effects of changing viewing conditions on the perceived structure of smoothly curved surfaces. *Journal of Experimental Psychology: Human Perception & Performance, 22*(3), 695–706.

Todd, J. T., & Warren, W. H. (1982). Visual perception of relative mass in dynamic events. *Perception, 11*(3), 325–335.

Todorovic, D. (1997). Lightness and junctions. *Perception, 26*(4), 379–394.

Tootell, R. B. H., Silverman, M. S., Switkes, E., & De Valois, R. L. (1982). Deoxyglucose analysis of retinotopic organization in primate striate cortex. *Science, 218*(4575), 902–904.

Tootell, R. B. H., Silverman, M. S., De Valois, R. L., & Jacobs, G. H. (1983). Functional organization of the second visual area in primates. *Science, 220*, 737–739.

Toyoda, J., Nosaki, H., & Tomita, T. (1969). Light-induced resistance changes in single photoreceptors of *Necturus* and *Gekko*. *Vision Research, 9*(4), 453–463.

Treisman, A. (1960). Contextual cues in selective listening. *Quarterly Journal of Experimental Psychology, 12*, 242–248.

Treisman, A. (1969). Strategies and models of selective attention. *Psychological Review, 76*, 282–299.

Treisman, A. (1985). Preattentive processing in vision. *Computer Vision, Graphics, and Image Processing, 31*, 156–177.

Treisman, A. (1988). Features and objects: The Fourteenth Bartlett Memorial Lecture. *Quarterly Journal of Experimental Psychology: Human Experimental Psychology, 40*(2), 201–237.

Treisman, A. (1993). The perception of features and objects. In A. D. Baddeley & L. Wieskrantz (Eds.), *Attention: Selection, awareness, and control: A tribute to Donald Broadbent* (pp. 5–35). Oxford, England: Clarendon Press/Oxford University Press.

Treisman, A., & DeSchepper, B. (1996). Object tokens, attention, and visual memory. In T. Inui & J. L. McClelland (Eds.), *Attention and performance: Vol. 16. Information integration in perception and communication* (pp. 15–46). Cambridge, MA: MIT Press.

Treisman, A., & Gelade, G. (1980). A feature-integration theory of attention. *Cognitive Psychology, 12*(1), 97–136.

Treisman, A., & Gormican, S. (1988). Feature analysis in early vision: Evidence from search asymmetries. *Psychological Review, 95*(1), 15–48.

Treisman, A., & Sato, S. (1990). Conjunction search revisited. *Journal of Experimental Psychology: Human Perception & Performance, 16*(3), 459–478.

Treisman, A., & Schmidt, H. (1982). Illusory conjunctions in the perception of objects. *Cognitive Psychology, 14*(1), 107–141.

Treisman, A., & Souther, J. (1985). Search asymmetry: A diagnostic for preattentive processing of separable features. *Journal of Experimental Psychology: General, 114*(3), 285–310.

Tresilian, J. R. (1991). Empirical and theoretical issues in the perception of time to contact. *Journal of Experimental Psychology: Human Perception & Performance, 17*(3), 865–876.

Tsal, Y. (1983). Movement of attention across the visual field. *Journal of Experimental Psychology: Human Perception & Performance, 9*(4), 523–530.

Turing, A. M. (1937). On computable numbers with an application to the Entscheidungsproblem. *Proceedings of the London Mathematical Society, 42*, 230–265.

Turing, A. M. (1950). Computing machinery and intelligence. *Mind, 59*(236), 433–460.

Turing, S. (1959). *Alan M. Turing*. Cambridge, England: W. Heffer.

Turvey, M. T. (1973). On peripheral and central processes in vision. *Psychological Review, 80*, 1–52.

Turvey, M. T., & Kravetz, S. (1970). Retrieval from iconic memory with shape as the selection criterion. *Perception & Psychophysics, 8*(3), 171–172.

Tversky, A. (1977). Features of similarity. *Psychological Review, 84*(4), 327–352.

Tversky, A., & Gati, I. (1982). Similarity, separability, and the triangle inequality. *Psychological Review, 89*(2), 123–154.

Tyler, C. W., & Chang, J.-J. (1977). Visual echoes: The perception of repetition in quasi-random patterns. *Vision Research, 17*(1), 109–116.

Tyler, C. W., & Clarke, M. B. (1990). *The autostereogram.* Paper presented at the The International Society for Optical Engineering, Santa Clara, CA.

Tyler, C. W., & Nakayama, K. (1984). Size interactions in the perception of orientation. In L. Spillman & B. R. Wooten (Eds.), *Sensory experience, adaptation, and perception* (pp. 529–546). Hillsdale, NJ: Erlbaum.

Ullman, S. (1979). *The interpretation of visual motion.* Cambridge, MA: MIT Press.

Ullman, S. (1980). Against direct perception. *Behavioral & Brain Science, 3,* 373–415.

Ullman, S. (1984). Visual routines. Special Issue: Visual cognition. *Cognition, 18*(1–3), 97–159.

Ullman, S. (1989). Aligning pictorial descriptions: An approach to object recognition. *Cognition, 32,* 193–254.

Ullman, S. (1996). *High level vision.* Cambridge, MA: MIT Press.

Ullman, S., & Basri, R. (1991). Recognition by linear combinations of models. *IEEE Transactions on Pattern Analysis and Machine Intelligence, 13*(10), 992–1006.

Underwood, B. J., & Postman, L. (1960). Extraexperimental sources of interference in forgetting. *Psychological Review, 67,* 73–95.

Ungerleider, L. G., & Mishkin, M. (1982). Two cortical visual systems. In D. G. Ingle, M. A. Goodale, & R. J. Q. Mansfield (Eds.), *Analysis of visual behavior* (pp. 549–586). Cambridge, MA: MIT Press.

Vaina, L. (Ed.) (1991). *From the retina to the neocortex: Selected papers of David Marr.* Boston: Birkhauser.

Van der Helm, P. A., & Leeuwenberg, E. L. (1991). Accessibility: A criterion for regularity and hierarchy in visual pattern codes. *Journal of Mathematical Psychology, 35*(2), 151–213.

Van Essen, D. C., Anderson, C. H., & Felleman, D. J. (1992). Information processing in the primate visual system: An integrated systems perspective. *Science, 255*(5043), 419–423.

Van Essen, D. C., & DeYoe, E. A. (1995). Concurrent processing in the primate visual cortex. In M. S. Gazzaniga (Ed.), *The cognitive neurosciences* (pp. 383–400). Cambridge, MA: MIT Press.

Van Essen, D. C., Felleman, D. J., DeYoe, E. A., Olavarria, J., & Knierim, J. J. (1990). Modular and hierarchical organization of extrastriate visual cortex in the macaque monkey. *Cold Spring Harbor Symposium on Quantitative Biology, 55,* 679–696.

Van Essen, D. C., & Maunsell, J. H. (1983). Hierarchical organization and functional streams in the visual cortex. *Trends in Neuroscience, 6*(9), 370–375.

Van Giffen, K., & Haith, M. M. (1984). Infant visual response to Gestalt geometric forms. *Infant Behavior & Development, 7*(3), 335–346.

Van Santen, J. P., & Sperling, G. (1984). Temporal covariance model of human motion perception. *Journal of the Optical Society of America A, 1*(5), 451–473.

Vecera, S. P., & O'Reilly, R. C. (1998). Figure-ground organization and object recognition processes. *Journal of Experimental Psychology: Human Perception & Performance, 24*(2), 441–462.

Vetter, T., Poggio, T., & Bülthoff, H. H. (1994). The importance of symmetry and virtual views in three-dimensional object recognition. *Current Biology, 4,* 18–23.

von der Heydt, R., & Peterhans, E. (1989a). Mechanisms of contour perception in monkey visual cortex. I. Lines of pattern discontinuity. *Journal of Neuroscience, 9*(5), 1731–1748.

von der Heydtr, R., & Peterhans, E. (1989b). Cortical contour mechanisms and geometrical illusions. In D. M. Lam & C. D. Gilbert (Eds.), *Neural mechanisms of visual perceptions* (pp. 157–170). The Woodlands, TX: Portfolio Publishing.

von der Heydt, R., Peterhans, E., & Baumgartner, G. (1984). Illusory contours and cortical neuron responses. *Science, 224*(4654), 1260–1262.

von der Malsburg, C. (1981). *The correlation theory of brain function* (Internal Rep. No. 81-2). Gottingen, Germany: Max Plank Institute for Biophysical Chemistry, Department of Neurobiology.

von der Malsburg, C. (1987). Synaptic plasticity as a basis of brain organization. In J. P. Changeaux & M. Konishi (Eds.), *The neural and molecular bases of learning* (pp. 411–432). New York: Wiley.

von Holst, E. (1954). Relations between the central nervous system and the peripheral organs. *British Journal of Animal Behaviour, 2,* 89–94.

von Kries, J. (1905). Die Gesichtsempfindungen. In W. Nagel (Ed.), *Handbuch der Physiologie der Menschen* (pp. 109–282). Brunswick: Vieweg.

von Neumann, J. (1951). The general and logical theory of automata. In L. A. Jeffress (Ed.), *Cerebral mechanisms in behavior: The Hixon Symposium.* New York: Wiley.

von Senden, M. (1960). *Space and sight: The perception of space and shape in the congenitally blind before and after operations* (P. Heath, Trans.). London: Methuen.

von Wright, J. M. (1968). Selection in visual immediate memory. *Quarterly Journal of Experimental Psychology, 20*(1), 62–68.

von Wright, J. M. (1970). On selection in visual immediate memory. *Acta Psychologica, 33,* 280–292.

von Wright, J. M. (1972). On the problem of selection in iconic memory. *Scandinavian Journal of Psychology, 13*(3), 159–171.

Wallace, M. A., & Farah, M. J. (1992). Savings in relearning face-name associations as evidence for "covert recognition" in prosopagnosia. *Journal of Cognitive Neuroscience, 4*(2), 150–154.

Wallach, H. (1935). Uber visuell Wahrgenommene Bewegungrichtung. *Psychologishe Forschung, 20,* 325–380.

Wallach, H. (1939). On the constancy of speed. *Psychological Review, 46,* 541–552.

Wallach, H. (1948). Brightness constancy and the nature of achromatic colors. *Journal of Experimental Psychology, 38,* 310–324.

Wallach, H. (1959). The perception of motion. *Scientific American, 201,* 56–60.

Wallach, H., & Floor, L. (1971). The use of size matching to demonstrate the effectiveness of accomodation and convergence as cues for distance. *Perception & Psychophysics, 10,* 423–428.

Wallach, H., & O'Connell, D. N. (1953). The kinetic depth effect. *Journal of Experimental Psychology, 45,* 205–217.

Wallach, H., Weisz, A., & Adams, P. A. (1956). Circles and derived figures in rotation. *American Journal of Psychology, 69,* 48–59.

Waltz, A. L. (1972). *Generating semantic descriptions from drawings of scenes with shadows* (AI-TR-271). Cambridge, MA: MIT Press.

Waltz, D. (1975). Understanding line drawings of scenes with shadows. In P. H. Winston (Ed.), *The psychology of computer vision* (pp. 19–92). New York: McGraw-Hill.

Wann, J. P. (1996). Anticipating arrival: Is the tau margin a specious theory? *Journal of Experimental Psychology: Human Perception & Performance, 22*(4), 1031–1048.

Warren, W. H. (1995). Self motion: Visual perception and visual control. In W. Epstein & S. Rogers (Eds.) *Perception of space and motion* (pp. 263–325). New York: Academic Press.

Warren, W. H., & Hannon, D. J. (1988). Direction of self-motion is perceived from optical flow. *Nature, 336*(6195), 162–163.

Warrington, E. K., & Shallice, T. (1984). Category specific semantic impairments. *Brain, 107,* 829–854.

Warrington, E. K., & Taylor, A. M. (1973). The contribution of the right parietal lobe to object recognition. *Cortex, 9*(2), 152–164.

Warrington, E. K., & Taylor, A. M. (1978). Two categorical stages of object recognition. *Perception, 7*(6), 695–705.

Watson, A. B., & Ahumada, A. J. (1985). Model of human visual-motion sensing. *Journal of the Optical Society of America, 2*(2), 322–341.

Watson, J. B. (1913). Psychology as the behaviourist views it. *Psychological Review, 20*(2), 158–177.

Waugh, N. C., & Norman, D. A. (1965). Primary memory. *Psychological Review, 72*(2), 89–104.

Weber, E. H. (1846). Der Tastsinn und das Gemeinfühl [The sense of touch and general sensation]. In R. Wagner (Ed.), *Handwörterbuch der Physiologie* (Vol. 3, pp. 481–588). Braunshweig: Vieweg.

Weber, J., & Malik, J. (1992). *Robust computation of optical flow in a multi-scale differential framework* (92/709). Berkeley, CA: Computer Science Division (EECS), University of California, Berkeley.

Weber, J., & Malik, J. (1995). Robust computation of optical flow in a multi-scale differential framework. *International Journal Of Computer Vision, 14*(1), 67–81.

Weiskrantz, L. (1980). Varieties of residual experience. *Quarterly Journal of Experimental Psychology, 32,* 365–386.

Weiskrantz, L. (1986). *Blindsight: A case study and implications.* Oxford, England: Oxford University Press.

Weiskrantz, L., Sanders, M. D., & Marshall, J. (1974). Visual capacity in the hemianopic field following a restricted cortical ablation. *Brain, 97,* 709–728.

Weisstein, N., & Harris, C. S. (1974). Visual detection of line segments: An object-superiority effect. *Science, 186*(4165), 752–755.

Welch, R. B. (1978). *Perceptual modification: Adapting to altered sensory environments.* New York: Academic Press.

Welch, R. B. (1986). Adaptation of space perception. In K. R. Boff, L. Kaufman, & J. P. Thomas (Eds.), *Handbook of Perception and Human Performance* (Vol. 1, pp. 24.21–24.45). New York: Wiley.

Wenderoth, P. M. (1974). The distinction between the rod-and-frame illusion and the rod-and-frame test. *Perception, 3*(2), 205–212.

Werblin, F. S., & Dowling, J. E. (1969). Organization of the retina in the mudpuppy, *Necturus maculosus*: II Intracellular recording. *Journal of Neurophysiology, 32,* 339–355.

Werbos, P. J. (1974). *Beyond Regression: New tools for prediction and analysis in the behavioral sciences.* Unpublished Ph.D. Dissertation, Harvard, Cambridge, MA.

Wertheimer, M. (1912). Über das Sehen von Scheinbewegunen und Scheinkorporen. *Zeitschrift fur Psychologie, 61,* 463–485.

Wertheimer, M. (1923/1950). Untersuchungen zur Lehre von der Gestalt. *Psychologishe Forschung, 4,* 301–350.

Wertheimer, M. (1924/1950). Gestalt theory. In W. D. Ellis (Ed.), *A sourcebook of Gestalt psychology* (pp. 1–11). New York: The Humanities Press.

Weyl, H. (1952). *Symmetry*. Princeton: Princeton University Press.

Wheeler, D. D. (1970). Processes in word recognition. *Cognitive Psychology, 1*, 59–85.

White, M. (1979). A new effect of pattern on perceived lightness. *Perception, 8*(4), 413–416.

Widrow, G., & Hoff, M. E. (1960). *Adaptive switching circuits*. Paper presented at the Institute of Radio Engineers, Western Electronic Show and Convention, Convention Record Part 4.

Wiesel, T. N., & Hubel, D. H. (1963). Single-cell responses in striate cortex of kittens deprived of vision in one eye. *Journal of Neurophysiology, 26*(6), 1002–1017.

Winston, P. H. (1975). Learning structural descriptions from examples. In P. H. Winston (Ed.), *The psychology of computer vision*. New York: McGraw-Hill.

Wiser, M. (1981). *The role of intrinsic axes in shape recognition*. Paper presented at the Third Annual Conference of the Cognitive Science Society, Berkeley, CA.

Wish, M., Deutsch, M., & Biener, L. (1970). Differences in conceptual structures of nations: An exploratory study. *Journal of Personality & Social Psychology, 16*(3), 361–373.

Witkin, A. P. (1981). Recovering surface shape and orientation from texture. *Artificial Intelligence, 17*, 17–45.

Witkin, A. P. (1983). Scale-space filtering. *Proceedings of the Eighth International Joint Conference on Artificial Intelligence, 2*, 1019–1022.

Wittgenstein, L. (1953). *Philosophical investigations*. London: Macmillan.

Wohlgemuth, A. (1911). On the aftereffect of seen movement. *British Journal of Psychology Monographs, (Supplement No. 1)*.

Wolfe, J. M. (1999). Inattentional amnesia. In V. Coltheart (Ed.), *Fleeting memories: Cognition of brief visual stimuli*. Cambridge, MA: MIT Press.

Wolfe, J. M., Cave, K. R., & Franzel, S. L. (1989). Guided search: An alternative to the feature integration model for visual search. *Journal of Experimental Psychology: Human Perception & Performance, 15*(3), 419–433.

Woodworth, R. S. (1938). *Experimental psychology*. New York: Holt.

Wulf, F. (1922). Uber die Veranderung von Vorstellungen. *Psychologie Forschung, 1*, 333–373.

Yakimovsky, Y. Y. (1976). Boundary and object detection in real world images. *Journal of the Association for Computing Machinery, 23*, 599–618.

Yantis, S. (1992). Multielement visual tracking: Attention and perceptual organization. *Cognitive Psychology, 24*(3), 295–340.

Yarbus, A. L. (1965). *Role of eye movements in the visual process*: Moscow, USSR: Nauka, 1965.

Yarbus, A. L. (1967). *Eye movements and vision* (L. A. Riggs, Trans.). New York: Plenum Press.

Yonas, A. (1981). Infants' response to optical information for collision. In R. N. Aslin, J. Alberts, & M. Petersen (Eds.), *Development of Perception: Psychobiological perspectives: The visual system* (Vol. 2, pp. 313–334). New York: Academic Press.

Yonas, A., Arterberry, M., & Granrud, C. (1987). Space Perception in Infancy. *Annals of Child Development, 4*, 1–34.

Yonas, A., Bechtold, A. G., Frankel, D., Gordon, F. R., McRoberts, G., Norcia, A., & Sternfels, S. (1977). Development of sensitivity to information for impending collision. *Perception & Psychophysics, 21*(2), 97–104.

Young, A. W., Hellawell, D., & de Haan, E. H. (1988). Cross-domain semantic priming in normal subjects and a prosopagnosic patient. *Quarterly Journal of Experimental Psychology: Human Experimental Psychology, 40*(3), 561–580.

Young, T. (1802). *On the theory of light and colors*. London: The Society.

Yuille, J. C., & Bülthoff, H. H. (1995). A Bayesian framework for the integration of visual modules. In T. Inui & J. L. McClelland (Eds.), *Attention and Performance: Vol. 16. Information integration in perception and communication* (pp. 49–70). Cambridge, MA: MIT Press.

Yuille, J. C., & Paivio, A. (1968). Imagery and verbal mediation instructions in paired-associate learning. *Journal of Experimental Psychology, 78*(1), 436–441.

Zadeh, L. A. (1965). Fuzzy sets. *Information and Control, 8*, 338–353.

Zadeh, L. A. (1976). A fuzzy-algorithmic approach to the definition of complex or imprecise concepts. *International Journal of Man-Machine Studies, 8*(3), 249–291.

Zeki, S. M. (1974). Functional organization of a visual area in the posterior bank of the superior temporal sulcus of the rhesus monkey. *Journal of Physiology, 236*, 549–573.

Zeki, S. M. (1978). Functional specialisation in the visual cortex of the rhesus monkey. *Nature, 274*(5670), 423–428.

Zeki, S. M. (1980). The representation of colours in the cerebral cortex. *Nature, 284*(5755), 412–418.

Zeki, S. M. (1983). Colour coding in the cerebral cortex: The reaction of cells in monkey visual cortex to wavelengths and colours. *Neuroscience, 9*(4), 741–765.

Zeki, S. M. (1993). *A vision of the brain*. Oxford: Blackwell.

Zihl, J., Von Cramon, D., & Mai, N. (1983). Selective disturbance of movement vision after bilateral brain damage. *Brain, 106*, 313–340.

Zihl, J., & Werth, R. (1984). Contributions to the study of blindsight I: Can stray light account for saccadic localization in patients with postgeniculate field defects? *Neuropsychologia, 22*(1), 1–11.

Zollner, F. (1860). Uber eine neue Art von Pseudoskopie und ihre Beziehung zu den von Plateau und Oppel beschreibenen Bewegungsphaenomenon. *Poggendorf's Annalen der Physik und Chemie, 110*, 500–525.

Zollner, F. (1862). Uber eine neue Art anorthoskopischer Zerrbilder. *Poggendorf's Annalen der Physik und Chemie, 117*, 477–484.

Name Index

Judd, D. B., 134, 493–495
Julesz, B., 177, 212–213, 276–277, 536

Kabrisky, M., 383
Kahn, S., 476, 536
Kahneman, D., 27, 532, 561–563, 580
Kaiser, M. K., 514–515
Kanizsa, G., 282–283, 292–293, 326
Kant, E., 514
Kaplan, G. A., 229
Kappers, A. M., 61, 185, 243–244
Kaufman, L., 8, 322–324
Kawato, M., 185
Kay, P., 83, 137–142, 418
Kellman, P. J., 252, 290–291, 293–294, 299, 306–309, 502
Kelly, M. H., 601–602
Kemler, D. G., 553
Kender, J. R., 235–236
Kennedy, J. M., 293
Kersten, D., 246
Kienker, P. K., 283
Kilpatric, D. W., 389
Kim, J., 624, 661
Kimchi, R., 70, 73–77, 112
Kin, H., 687
Kinchla, R. A., 356
King, M., 329
Kinsbourne, M., 121
Klein, K. L., 330, 569
Klein, R. M., 569
Kleiner, K. A., 385
Knight, R. T., 356–357
Knill, D. C., 246
Koch, C., 629, 652–656
Koenderink, J. J., 61, 185, 243–245, 434, 444, 446
Koffka, K., 47, 50, 91–92, 268n.1, 410
Kohler, I., 346
Köhler, W., 52–53, 59, 220, 256, 301, 303
Kohn, C., 637
Kolers, P. A., 475, 496
Kopferman, H., 375–376
Korte, A., 472
Kosslyn, S. M., 419–420, 588, 595, 607–613
Kossut, M., 157
Kowler, E., 570
Kozlowski, L. T., 512
Kraft, T. W., 112
Krantz, J., 636
Krauskopf, J., 273, 522
Kravetz, S., 577
Kröse, B. J., 279
Krowitz, A., 250
Krumhansl, C., 390
Kruskal, J. B., 389
Kube, P., 376
Kubovy, M., 57, 258, 261–262
Kuffler, S., 65, 147, 151, 154
Kuhn, T. S., 70
Külpe, 603

LaBerge, D., 548
Lachman, J. L., 70
Lachman, R., 70
Lamb, M. R., 356–357
Land, E. H., 128–132, 522
Landy, M. S., 248–249
Langer, A., 250
Lappin, J. S., 329
Larsen, A., 495, 606
Lashley, K. S., 37, 53, 631
Latto, R., 636
Lavie, N., 537
Leask, J., 593
Le Bihan, D., 613
LeCun, Y., 683n.6
Lee, D. N., 506, 509–510
Lee, K., 197
Lee, Y.-H., 179
Leeuwenberg, E. L. J., 398, 402, 405–406
Lehky, S. R., 116, 184–187, 678–679, 681
Leibowitz, H., 470
Lennie, P., 105
Leopold, D. A., 653
Letson, R. D., 209
Lettvin, J. Y., 604
Leung, T., 271–272
LeVay, S., 155–156
Levelt, W. J. M., 216
Levick, W. R., 484–485
Levin, D. T., 538
Levine, D. N., 596, 613, 618
Levitin, D., 259
Levy, E. I., 587
Lewis, D., 623
Li, X., 130
Lindsay, P. H., 632
Linnett, C. M., 535
Linsker, R., 190
Lishman, J. R., 506
Lissauer, H., 431
Livingstone, M. S., 43, 146, 149, 193–195, 197, 482
Locke, J., 625
Lockwood, M., 645
Loftus, E., 598–601
Loftus, G. R., 587
Logie, R. H., 585
Logothetis, N., 653–654
Longuet-Higgens, H. C., 227, 342, 508
Loomis, J. M., 471
Loukides, M. G., 293, 502
Lovitts, B. E., 312
Lowe, D. G., 299, 381, 393, 436, 444, 448–452
Lozano-Perez, T., 397
Lu, C., 197, 479
Lu, Z.-L., 477
Luck, S. J., 537
Ludvigh, E., 525
Luria, A. R., 594
Luzzati, C., 564, 612

Mace, W. M., 53
Mach, E., 52, 106, 341, 366, 368–369, 371–373, 375–376
Mack, A., 313n.1, 476, 504, 532, 534–537, 554, 563n.5, 565, 643–644, 647
MacKinnon, G. E., 471
MacLeod, C. M., 550
MacLeod, D. I. A., 105
MacNichol, M. F. J., 112
Magoun, H. W., 654
Mai, N., 196, 483
Malik, J., 171, 184, 186–187, 221–223, 225, 236–238, 241, 271–272, 278–280, 679
Maloney, L. T., 134, 248–249
Mamassian, P., 246
Mangan, B., 648
Marcel, A. J., 255, 361, 636, 639–643, 647
Marks, W. B., 112
Marr, D., 10, 61, 71–72, 74, 76, 88–89, 91–92, 96, 112, 146, 169, 171–172, 175–183, 186–187, 202–203, 217–221, 270, 277, 351–352, 369, 375, 382, 396, 433, 443–444, 485, 554, 644, 649, 678–680
Marshall, J. C., 633, 637
Massaro, D. W., 83, 248, 329, 387, 454, 457, 460
Mather, G., 477–478
Matin, L., 471, 524
Mattock, A., 251, 321
Maturana, H. R., 604
Maunsell, J. H., 193, 618
Maxwell, J. C., 102, 108, 691
Maybank, S. J., 490
McAdam, D. L., 134
McAlister, E., 289, 399, 405
McAndrews, M. P., 646
McCann, J., 128–132, 522
McClelland, J. L., 62, 301, 360, 454, 457–460, 678–680
McCloskey, M., 511, 515, 600–601
McConkie, G., 585–586
McCullough, W. S., 366, 604
McDaniel, C., 83, 140–142
McGinnies, E., 638
McLean, J. P., 546
Meadows, J. C., 121
Meizin, F. M., 566
Melton, A. W., 574
Mendel, G., 656
Merikle, P. M., 577, 640–643
Merton, P. A., 341
Mervis, C. B., 140, 417–419
Metelli, F., 297–298
Metzger, F., 282
Metzler, J., 605–606, 610
Meyer, G. E., 329
Michael, C. R., 120
Michotte, A., 511, 513–515
Miller, D. G., 599
Miller, J., 356, 360
Miller, J. W., 525
Milner, A. D., 412
Milner, B., 39, 412, 595
Milner, P. M., 438

Miner, N., 53
Mingolla, E., 296
Minsky, M., 62, 442, 648
Miranda, S. B., 308
Mishkin, M., 38–39, 193, 412, 653
Mitchener, K., 304–305
Moar, K., 165
Mollon, J. D., 119, 121
Moore, C. M., 548n.3
Moore, M. K., 252
Moran, J., 42, 567–568
Moray, N., 534
Morgan, M. J., 504
Morison, V., 251, 331
Moscovitch, M., 646
Movshon, J. A., 481–483, 486–487
Müller, G. E., 52, 110
Munsell, A. H., 98
Murdock, B. J., 583
Murphy, B. J., 525
Musatti, C. I., 491–492

Nachmias, J., 166–168, 383
Nagel, T., 627
Nakamura, R. K., 653
Nakayama, K., 208, 224, 338, 471, 559–560
Nathans, J., 121
Natsoulas, T., 638
Navon, D., 355–356, 475–476, 546
Neff, J., 265
Neisser, U., 64, 366, 411–412
Neitz, J., 133
Neitz, M., 133
Nelson, K., 538
Nerger, J. L., 113
Neuhaus, W., 478
Newcombe, F., 121, 638
Newell, A., 60, 76, 646, 648
Newsome, W. T., 482, 618
Newton, I., 96–97
Nicholls, J. G., 154
Nickerson, R. S., 591–592
Nida-Rümeln, M., 626
Nijhawan, R., 264–265
Nishihara, H. K., 89, 91, 369, 375, 433, 444
Nissen, M. J., 542–543
Norman, D. A., 574, 632, 646
Nosaki, H., 34
Nothdurft, H.-C., 280
Noton, D., 304, 529–530
Nowlan, S. J., 483

Ober-Thompkins, B. A., 418
O'Connell, D. N., 228, 489
Oden, G. C., 387, 454
Ogden, W. C., 542–543
Ogle, K. N., 208
Ohzawa, I., 154
Olshausen, B. A., 188, 192–193
Olson, R. K., 266

Sacks, O. W., 433
Sadza, K. J., 197
Saffran, E., 637
Sakitt, B., 580
Sanders, A. F., 580
Sanders, M. D., 633
Sanger, T. D., 190
Sapir, E., 137
Sato, S., 560
Schachter, D. L., 646
Schein, S. J., 197
Schiller, P. H., 197
Schmidt, H., 558
Schnapf, J. L., 112
Schneider, W., 568, 570
Schooler, J. W., 593, 600
Schrödinger, 110
Schubert, J., 127, 492
Schumacher, L. E., 283
Schumann, F., 292
Schwartz, S. P., 609
Searle, J. R., 71, 618, 623, 655, 660–661
Sedgwick, H. A., 232, 321
Segal, S. J., 611
Sejnowski, T. J., 116, 184–187, 283, 483, 678–679, 681
Sekel, M., 122
Sekuler, A. B., 292
Selfridge, O. G., 366
Semmes, J., 53
Sergent, J., 357
Seyranian, G., 354
Shallice, T., 432, 651
Shannon, C. E., 399
Shapiro, K. L., 537–538
Shapley, R., 149
Shatz, C. J., 158
Shaw, J. C., 60
Shcall, J., 653
Shea, S. L., 251
Sheinberg, D. L., 653–654
Shepard, R. N., 134, 332, 388–389, 493–497, 591, 605–606, 609–611, 658n.4
Shepp, B. E., 553
Shi, J., 271–272
Shimojo, S., 224
Shipley, T. F., 290–291, 293–294, 299, 502
Shulman, G. L., 546, 566
Sigman, E., 497–498
Silverman, M. S., 155–156, 559
Silvers, B., 458
Simon, H. A., 60, 75–76
Simone, E., 376
Simons, D. J., 538
Singale, C., 570
Singer, W., 653
Singh, M., 354
Slade, R., 640
Slater, A., 251, 309, 321, 331
Sloan, L. L., 105
Smith, J., 636
Smith, L. B., 553

Smith, Y. M., 636
Smolensky, P., 62, 301, 651, 679–680
Solomon, R. L., 638
Sorenson, R. E., 538
Souther, J., 556
Spacek, L. A., 175, 180
Spelke, E., 306–309
Sperling, G., 63–64, 248, 477–479, 484–486, 575–577, 580
Sperry, R., 53, 631
Spinnler, H., 612
Spitzer, H., 42, 568
Springer, S. P., 631
St. James, J. D., 546
Stacy, E. W., 430
Standing, L. G., 580, 591
Stankiewicz, B. J., 425, 440, 444, 452
Stark, L., 304, 529–530
Steiner, M., 613
Sternberg, R. J., 68
Sternberg, S., 63
Stevens, J. K., 341
Stevens, K. A., 234
Stevens, S. S., 673–674
Stoerig, P., 635–636
Stone-Elander, A., 613
Storm, R. W., 548–549
Stratton, G. M., 345–346
Stromeyer, C. F., 593
Stroop, J. R., 549–550, 642–643
Stryker, M. P., 67, 158
Subramaniam, B., 569–570
Swartz, K. B., 553
Swets, J., 668, 671
Switkes, E., 155–156, 166

Tanaka, J. W., 420, 444
Tang, B., 536
Tangney, J., 329
Tarr, M. J., 425–426, 441, 444–445, 452
Tarski, A., 77, 658
Tassinary, L., 640
Taylor, A. M., 432, 436
Taylor, M., 420
Taylor, W. K., 533
Teller, D. Y., 122
Tennenbaum, J. M., 89, 241–243
Ternus, J., 476
Teuber, H. L., 431
Thomas, L., 568, 570
Thompson, I. D., 157, 612
Thompson, P., 612
Thorell, L. G., 169
Thouless, R. H., 329
Thurston, M., 179
Tipper, S. P., 539–541
Todd, J. T., 490, 514
Todorovic, D., 118
Tomita, T., 34
Tootell, R. B. H., 155–156, 194–195
Toyoda, J., 34
Treisman, A., 196, 393, 534, 541, 554–563, 565, 580, 648, 653

Subject Index

Bar detectors, in striate cortex, image-based spatial processing in, 151–153
Barrier-induced curved apparent motion, perception of, 495–496
Basic color terms, category-based color processing and, 138
Basic-level categories
   properties of, 418–419
   region segmentation and, 275
Basis functions, natural image structure and, 190–192
Bayes theorem
   hidden assumptions and, 83
   likelihood principle and, 57n.4
Behavioral criteria, for visual awareness, 628–629
Behavioral similarity, as consciousness criteria, 624–625
Behaviorism. *See also* Methodological behaviorism; Theoretical behaviorism
   classical vision theory and, 48
   information processing psychology and, 63–64
   mind-body problem and, 621–623
   visual imagery and perception and, 611–612
Beta motion, apparent motion alternation rate and, 472
Binary membership, categorical hierarchies and, 417–418
Binding. *See also* Feature integration theory
   in feature integration theory, 557
   problem, attention hypothesis of consciousness and, 647–648
Binocular cells
   depth perception mechanisms and, 222–224
   image-based spatial processing in, 148–150
Binocular convergence, development of, 250–251
Binocular depth information. *See also* Binocular disparity; Stereopsis
   convergence as, 205–206
   in depth perception, 203–204
Binocular disparity. *See also* Stereopsis
   corresponding retinal positions and, 207–208
   crossed vs. uncrossed disparity, 207–208
   depth perception and, 206–211
   horopter and, 208–210
   motion parallax and, 225–226
   pseudoscope and, 248
   stereograms and, 210–211
   vertical disparity, 224
   visual pathways physiology and, 197
Binocular pathway, visual pathways physiology and, 195
Binocular rivalry, correspondence problem and, 216
Binocular suppression, 216
Binocular vision, eye anatomy and, 26–27
Biological consciousness theory
   activation thresholds and, 650–651
   causal theories and, 655–656
   cortical hypothesis and, 651–652
   Crick/Koch conjectures and, 652–654
   duration thresholds and, 651
   extended reticular-thalamic activating system (ERTAS) and, 654–655
   principles of, 649–656, 661–663
Biological image processing, of spatial information, 146–147
Biological information processing
   autoradiography and, 66
   brain imaging techniques for, 66–70
   classical vision theory and, 64–70

historical background of, 64
   single-cell recording and, 64–66
Biological motion, perception of, 511–513
Bipolar cells
   image-based spatial processing in, 148–149
   in retinal neurons, 29–30
Bit, defined, 399n.4
Black box diagrams
   information descriptions and, 75
   recursive decomposition assumptions and, 74–76
Blindness, eye-brain interaction and, 24–25
Blindsight
   challenges to research on, 635–636
   eye-brain interaction and, 25
   guessing without visual experience, accuracy of, 634–635
   inattentional blindsight, 643–644
   two visual systems hypothesis of, 635
   unconscious processing in neglect and Balint's syndrome patients, 636–637
   visual awareness and, 633–636
Blind spot
   retinal design and, 33–34
   visual awareness and, 617
Blob region, in hypercolumn architecture, visual pathways physiology and, 194–196
Blocks world environment
   computer vision systems and, 60–61
   edge interpretation and, 237, 239–241
Blue/yellow balance, chromatic color constancy and, 134
Bottom-up processing
   blindsight research and, 636
   information processing theory and, 84–85
Boundary-based region segmentation, perceptual organization and, 270–271
Boundary colors method, color categories and, 139
Boundary rule
   continuous motion analysis and, 469–471
   part segmentation and, 351, 353–354
Boundary tracing, long-term memory (LTM) and, 589
Bounded activation, long-term memory (LTM) and, 589
Brain
   attention physiology and, 563–568
   biological information processing and, 64
   consciousness theory and research on, 661–663
   cortical mechanisms of color processing and, 120–121
   electrical fields in, Gestalt theory on, 53
   eye function and, 24–25
   oculomotor system and, 526–527
   perceptual organization theory and brain damage, 255
   retinal design and, 34–35
Brain imaging techniques
   attention physiology and, 566–567
   biological information processing theory and, 67–70
   blindsight research and, 636
   motion perception neuropsychology and, 484
   neuropsychology of visual imagery and, 613
   visual pathways hypothesis and, 43
Brightness
   defined, 99n.1
   vs. lightness, in color perception, 99
British empiricism, structuralism and, 49

Conclusions, implicit information as, 80
Conditionals, elimination of, behaviorist theory and, 622–623
Cones. *See also* Photo receptors
  anatomy of, 32
  inner and outer segment of, 31
  regeneration of, 32–33
  as retinal photoreceptors, 29, 31
  three-cone color processing system, 112–113
Configural dimensions, selective attention theory and, 553–554
Configural motion, components of, 499–501
Configural orientation effects, global-local perception and, 357–359
Configural superiority effect, global-local perception and, 360–361
Conjugate eye movements, characteristics of, 525
Conjunction search, feature integration theory, 557–558
Connectedness, parts perception and, 351n.4
Connectionist networks. *See also* Neural networks
  back propagation and, 681–682
  behavior of, 676–681
  computational analysis of image structure and, 171–172
  computer vision systems and, 62
  delta rule and, 682–683
  generalized delta rule and, 683
  gradient descent and, 683–687
  input vector space of, 683–684
  learning algorithms and, 681–687
  local vs. global minima of, 686–687
  models of, 675–676
  multistability and, 301–302
  recursive decomposition theory and, 76
  state space of, 684–685
  system architecture of, 678–679
  systemic behavior of, 679–681
  unit behavior of, 677–678
  weight-error space of, 686
  weight space of, 685–686
Connection weight, in connectionist networks, 676–677
Consciousness
  activation-based STM and, 646–647
  activation thresholds and, 650–651
  attention hypothesis of, 647–648
  behaviorism and, 63
  biological theories of, 649–656, 661–663
  causal theories of, 655–656
  C-box theory of, 646
  correlational vs. causal theories of, 630
  cortical hypothesis of, 651–652
  Crick/Koch conjectures about, 652–654
  criteria for, 624–625
  duration thresholds and, 651
  extended reticular-thalamic activating system (ERTAS) and, 654–655
  functional approach to, 644
  functional architecture theories of, 645–649
  functional correlates of, 642–643
  functionalism and, 659–661
  global vs. local perceptual processing and, 354–355
  isomorphism constraint and, 658–659
  limits of science and, 656–663
  physical approach to, 645
  physiological approach to, 644
  physiological criteria for, 629–630

  relational structure and, 657–658
  short-term memory hypothesis of, 645–647
  theories of, 644–663
  Turing's test for, 629
  2.5D sketch theory of, 649
  visual awareness and, 616
  visual perception and, 13–15
  working memory theories of, 648–649
Conservation of angular momentum, intuitive physics and, 516–517
Conservative response strategy, in signal detection theory (SDT), 668
Consistent conditions, of configural orientation effects, 358
Consistent configurations, global precedence and, 355
Constancy, definition of, 312
Constant stimuli method, of threshold measurement, 666
Constant velocity, image motion analysis of, 467–468
Constraint lines, local image motion analysis and, 486–487
Constructivism, principles of, 55–59
Content
  of iconic memory, 576–577
  short-term vs. long-term memory and, 584
  of visual memory, 574
Contextual effects
  in object categorization, 428–431
  in recognition by components theory, 442–443
Contextual orientation, heuristics in reference frame selection and, 375–376
Continuity constraint
  multiorientation, multiscale (MOMS) filters, 221–222
  part perception and, 351n.4
Continuous motion, image motion analysis and, 469–471
Contour cells, illusory contour physiology and, 295–297
Contralateral neglect, attention physiology and, 564
Contrast
  figure/ground organization and, 282
  lightness constancy and, 127–128
  lightness vs. brightness, in color perception and, 99, 116–118
  square wave vs. sine waves, grating thresholds and, 167–168
Contrast sensitivity function (CSF)
  channel physiology and, 169–171
  development of spatial frequency channels and, 168–169
  selective channel adaptation and, 165–166
  spatial frequency channels and, 163–169
Convergence of eyes
  crossed and uncrossed convergence methods of stereoscopic fusion, 210–211
  depth perception and, 205–206
  development of, 250–251
Convergence of parallels, 231
  hidden assumptions and, 81–84
  part perception and, 350–351
Convexity, figure/ground organization and, 282–283
Convex orientation edges, classification of, 238
Convolution, edge operators and, 173–175
Cooperation, multistability, connectionist network model and, 302
Coordinate systems, object-centered reference frame hypothesis and, 369–370
Cornea, anatomy of, 27
Corollary discharge, efferent copy theory and, 340–341
Corpus callosum
  anatomy and physiology of, 37–38
  visual awareness in split-brain patients and, 631–633

Developmental processes
   color constancy development, 136–137
   depth perception and, 249–253
   habituation paradigm and, 306
   image-based color processing and, 121–122
   perceptual grouping and, 306–309
   perceptual organization and, 305–309
   preferential looking paradigm and, 122, 168–169
   receptive field development, image-based spatial processing and, 157–158
   shape constancy and, 331–332
   size constancy and, 321–322
   spatial frequency channels and, 168–169
Diagnostic information, canonical perspective and, 421–424
Dichromats
   color blindness and, 104
   cone deficits with, 113n.8
Dictionary units, in auditory attention theory, 534
Difference threshold
   just noticeable differences and, 671
   principles of, 671–672
   Weber's law and, 671–672
Different-exemplar priming, part structure, categorization and, 427–428
Differential geometry, computer vision systems and, 61–62
Diffuse illumination, defined, 16
Dilations
   apparent rotation and, 495
   objective shape definition and, 364
   similarity transformation group and, 364–365
Diplopia, binocular disparity and, 210
Dipole statistics, texture segregation and, 277
Direction
   launching effect and, 513
   perception of, 338–339
   self-motion and perception of, 506–509
Directional selectivity, in cortical motion analysis, 482–483
Direct perception
   affordances and, 409–411
   ecological optic theory and, 54–55
   self-motion perception and, 510–511
Direct task, subliminal perception and, 639
Disconfirmed expectations, predictive modeling and, 12–13
Disconjugate eye movements, characteristics of, 525
Discriminability, in signal detection theory (SDT), 668
Disengagement
   attention shifts and, 544
   unilateral neglect and, 564–565
Dishabituation phenomenon, perceptual organization development and, 306
Display-board model, short-term memory (STM) processing and, 646–647
Distal mode of perception, defined, 313–314
Distal stimulus
   ecological optic analysis of, 53–54
   optical images and, 20
   properties of, 312–313
Distance perception. See also Depth perception
   egocentric position and, 338
   size-distance relation and, 317–318
   size illusions and, 323

Distortion hypothesis, of misinformation effect, 600–601
Distractors, long-term memory (LTM) and, 590
Distributed attention, vs. focused attention, 554–556
Distribution operator, redundancy removal and, 404
Divided attention trial, inattention paradigm and, 535–536
Dominance, depth perception and, 247–248
Dorsal action-based system, physical affordances theory and, 412–413
Dot lattices, perceptual grouping measurement and, 261–262
Double opponent cells, color processing physiology and, 119–120
Double vision. See Diplopia
Dual coding theory, long-term memory and, 592–593
Dualism concept, mind-body problem and, 618–619
Dual process theory
   possible neural circuits of, 114–115
   principles of, 110–112
Duration
   of iconic memory, 576
   of short-term vs. long-term memory, 584
   of visual memory, 574
Duration threshold, biological consciousness theory and, 651
Dyes. See Paints and dyes
Dynamic binding, object categorization by recognition by components theory, 438–440
Dynamic occlusion, long-range apparent motion and, 497–498
Dynamic perceptual organization
   anorthoscopic perception, 502–504
   configural motion, 499–501
   depth perception and, 203–204, 225–229
   development of depth perception and, 252
   induced motion, 501–502
   kinetic completion and illusory figures, 502
   Marr-Poggio algorithm and, 220
   movement grouping, 498–499
   object motion analysis and, 498–504
Dynamic vision theory, projective geometry in, 20–21

Ebbinghaus illusion, 326–327
Ecological constraint theories, visual completion and, 290–292
Ecological optics
   computational approaches to, 61–62
   constructivism and, 56
   information processing theory and, 71
   principles of, 53–55
   recursive decomposition theory and, 76
   self-motion perception and, 510–511
Ecological perception, self-motion perception and, 510–511
Ecological validity
   classical vision theory and, 53
   figure/ground organization and, 283–284
   vs. hidden assumptions, 83–84
Edge-based models
   depth perception and, 220–221
   image motion analysis and, 485
   Marr-Poggio algorithm and, 220–221
Edge detection
   boundary-based region segmentation and, 270–271
   computational analysis of image structure and, 172–183
   convolution of edge operators and, 173–175
   correspondence problem, random dot stereograms and, 212–214

Gradient descent
  connectionist networks and, 683–687
  input vector space and, 683–684
  local vs. global minima and, 686–687
  natural image structure, learning algorithms and, 190n.3
  state space and, 684–685
  weight-error space and, 686
  weight space and, 685–686
Graph theory, regional analysis and, 271–273
Grating stimuli, spatial frequency aftereffects and, 167–168
Gravitational orientation, heuristics in reference frame selection and, 375
Gray-scale images
  in computer vision systems, 60
  retinal image stage of visual perception and, 86–87
  structural information theory and, 405–406
  template-based shape representation and, 377–378
  zero-crossing algorithms and, 176–177
Gray zone perception
  activation thresholds, biological consciousness theory and, 650–651
  subliminal visual awareness and, 642–643
Ground continuity, hole perception and, 287
Guessing, role in visual awareness, 634–635

Habituation paradigm, perceptual organization development and, 306
Hallway illusion, size constancy and, 315–317
Hardware primitives, recursive decomposition theory and, 76
Harmonic motion, image motion analysis and, 468
Head orientation, orientation constancy and, 333–336
Hemineglect. *See* Unilateral neglect
Helmholtz, Hermann von
  constructivism and, 55
  trichromatic theory of color processing and, 107
  unconscious inference and, 56
Hering, Ewald
  lightness constancy and, 126–127, 132–133
  opponent process theory of, 109–111
Hermann grid illusion, lateral inhibition and, 117–118
Heuristic processes
  clobbering heuristic, 515
  constructivist theory and, 57–58
  depth perception and, 202
  failures in shape equivalence and, 371
  illumination vs. reflectance edges and, 132–133
  information processing theory and, 83–84
  inverse projection and, 23–24
  objected-centered reference frame hypothesis and, 374–377
  orientation illusions and, 336–338
  relative size and, 233–234
  ricochet heuristic, 515
  rigidity heuristic, 228–229
  surface orientation from shading and, 244
  texture gradients and, 234–236
  unique-point heuristic in apparent motion, 480–481
Hidden assumptions
  vs. ecological validity, 83–84
  information processing theory and, 81–84
Hierarchical clustering programs, multifeatural representations and, 391–394

Hierarchical templates
  shape representation and, 381–382
  structural descriptions and, 394–395
Hierarchical tree, multifeatural representations and, 390
High-dimensional solutions, in multidimensional scaling (MDS) programs, 389–390
High frequency color terms, defined, 138
Holes, figure/ground organization and, 285–287
Holism
  classical vision theory and, 47
  configural motion and, 500
  Gestaltism and, 50–52
Homogeneous masks, iconic memory and, 578
Homomorphic mapping, in representation systems, 77–79
Homunculus process, categorization theory of functional perception, 415
Hopfield nets, connectionist architecture and, 679
Horizon, position relative to, 231–232
Horizon ratio, size constancy and, 321
Horizontal cells, in retinal neurons, 29–30
Horizontal edge operators, convolution of, 174–175
Horn's computational analysis, of shading information, 245
Horopter, binocular disparity and, 208–210
Hue
  color space and, 98
  complementary hues, 106
  dual process theory and cancellation experiments on, 110–112
  mean spectral wavelength and, 100
Huffman-Clowes physical constraints analysis, edge interpretation and, 241–243
Human eye
  anatomy of, 25–26
  brain and, 25–26
  cross sectional drawing of, 27
  physiological optics of, 26–28
Human visual system, components of, 24–25
Hybrid images, Fourier analysis of shape representation and, 385–386
Hypercolumns
  multiorientation, multiscale (MOMS) filters and, 221–222
  spatial frequency channel physiology and, 171
  striate architecture and, 156–157
  visual pathways hypothesis, image structure and, 194–196
Hypercomplex cells, in striate cortex, image-based spatial processing theory and, 153–154
Hyperopia, lens focusing abilities and, 28
Hypersphere/hyperspace, apparent rotation and, 494
Hypotheses, in vision theory, 46
Hypothesis-driven processing. *See* Top-down processing
Hysteresis, in threshold measurement, 666

Iconic memory
  content of, 576–577
  defined, 575
  duration of, 576
  functional architecture of consciousness and, 646
  information processing psychology and, 64
  loss of, 577–578
  maintenance of, 577
  masking of, 578–579
  partial report procedure and, 575–576
  persistence vs. processing, 579–580
  vs. short-term memory (STM), 581–582

Idealism, mind-body problem and, 620
Identity priming, part structure, categorization theory and, 427
Illumination
  chromatic color constancy in, 133–134
  defined, 15–16
  diffuse illumination, 16
  point-source illumination, 15–16
Illumination edges
  classification of, 238
  vs. reflectance edges, 130–136
Illumination map, lightness constancy and, 132
Illusions. *See also* Orientation illusions; Shape illusions; Size illusions; Position illusions
  characteristics of, 312–313
  visual perception and, 7–10
Illusory conjunctions, feature integration theory, 558–559
Illusory contours
  dynamic perceptual organization and, 502
  figural scission and, 298–299
  raw primal sketch and, 182
  visual interpolation through, 292–296
Image-based color processing
  chromatic adaptation and, 107
  color afterimages and, 105–106
  color blindness and, 104–105
  color vision theories of, 107–112
  developmental characteristics of, 121–122
  light mixture and, 101–104
  physiological mechanisms of, 112–121
  simultaneous color contrast and, 106–107
Image-based representation
  characteristics of, 87–88
  color processing and, 101–122
  image-based primitives, 88
  spatial processing and, 146–197
Image-based spatial processing
  computational analysis of, 171–193
  physiological mechanisms of, 146–158
  psychophysical channels and, 158–171
  research background of, 146
  theoretical synthesis of, 186–192
  visual pathways and, 194–197
Image blur, accommodation and depth perception and, 205
Image formation
  of optical images, 20
  optical information and, 19–24
  projective geometry and, 20–21
  prospective and orthographic projection and, 21–22
Image inspection, visual memory and, 607–609
Image interpretation, analog position on visual imagery and, 604
Image motion
  adaptation to and aftereffects of, 470
  aperture problem and, 479–481
  apparent motion, 471–481
  autokinetic effect and, 471
  computational problem of, 466–469
  computational theories of, 484–487
  continuous motion, 469–471
  correspondence problem and, 474–477
  delay-and-compare networks and, 484–485
  edge-based models of, 485

flicker fusion and, 473–474
  local motion integration and, 486–487
  physiological mechanisms of, 481–484
  simultaneous motion contrast and, 470–471
  spatial-frequency-based models of, 485–486
Image partitioning
  regional analysis and, 271–273
  uniform connectedness and, 269
Image processing operations, Kosslyn's imagery model, 610–611
Image reinterpretation, visual memory and, 608–609
Image retrieval, analog position on visual imagery, 604
Image scanning task, visual imagery and, 607
Image size effects, visual imagery and, 607–608
Imitation games, Turing's test and, 628–629
Implementational level of information processing, 73
Implicit information, vs. explicit information, 80
Impossible objects
  edge interpretation and, 240–241
  environmental modeling and, 11–12
Inactive items, activation-based short-term memory (STM) processing and, 647
Inattention. *See* Unilateral neglect
Inattentional amnesia, visual attention theory and, 539
Inattentional blindness, visual attention theory and, 536–537
Inattentional blindsight, defined, 643
Inattention paradigm
  visual attention and, 534–537
  visual awareness and, 643–644
Inconsistent conditions, configural orientation effects and, 358
Inconsistent configurations, global precedence and, 355
Indeterminate information, analog position on visual imagery, 604
Indexing, long-term memory (LTM) and, 589
Indirect perception, perceptual constancy and, 312–313
Indirect task, subliminal perception and, 639
Individual experience, consciousness theories and, 657
Induced color. *See* Simultaneous color contrast
Induced motion
  dynamic perceptual organization and, 501–502
  self-motion as, 504–506
Inductive inference, information processing and, 81
Infant development. *See* Developmental processes
Inference, processing as, 80–81
Infero temporal (IT) cortex, visual pathways hypothesis and, 43
Informational basis of perception, ecological optics and, 53
Informational description, assumptions based on, 73–74
Informational equivalence, in representation systems, 79
Informational events
  assumptions based on, 73–74
  in representation systems, 79
Information flow diagrams
  informational descriptions and, 75
  recursive decomposition assumptions and, 75–76
Information load, figural goodness and, 402, 404–405
Information pickup
  computer metaphor of information processing and, 71
  ecological optic theory and, 54
Information processing
  algorithmic level of, 72–73
  biological processing, 64–70
  computational level of, 72
  computer metaphor for, 71

computer vision and, 59–63
depth perception and integration of, 247–249
heuristics and, 83
hidden assumptions and, 81–83
hidden assumptions vs. ecological validity and, 83–84
historical background of, 59–70
implementational level of, 73
implicit vs. explicit information and, 80
inference as process in, 80–81
informational description assumption and, 73–74
motion perception and, 511–517
paradigm of, 70–71
physical embodiment in, 76
psychology of, 63–64
recursive decomposition and, 74–76
representational system and, 77–79
theoretical principles of, 70–85
top-down vs. bottom-up processes in, 84–85
visual perception and, 6
Information sources, of depth perception, 203–204
Information theory, figural goodness and, 399–400
Inheritance, biological consciousness theory and, 656
Input activation, of connectionist networks, 677–678
Input information
    information descriptions and, 74–75
    template-based shape representation and, 378–379
Input theory of position constancy. *See* Afferent theory
Input vector space, of connectionist network gradient descent, 683–684
Instance-based representation, categorical hierarchies and, 418
Instantiated tokens, edge detection and, 182
Instructions, role of, in multistability, 304–305
Interference loss, selective attention theory and, 552
Integral dimensions
    asymmetrically integral dimensions, 553
    selective attention and, 550–554
Integral tripack film, color photography technology, 698–699
Integration masking, of iconic memory, 578–579
Intentionality, philosophical problem of, 619
Intentionally ignored information, visual attention theory, 539–541
Interactionism, mind-body problem and, 620
Interaction mechanisms, depth perception information and, 249
Interactive activation (IA) model
    limits of, 460–461
    word/letter perception and, 458–461
Interblob region, in hypercolumn architecture, visual pathways physiology and, 194–196
Interocular transfer effects, continuous image motion analysis and, 470
Interposition, edge interpretation and, 236
Interpretive process, visual illusion and, 9
Interruption masking, iconic memory and, 579
Intracellular recording techniques, for image-based spatial processing in bipolar cells, 148
Intrinsic biases, shape equivalence and, 371
Intrinsic images, surface-based stage of visual perception and, 89
Introspection, classical vision theory and, 48
Intuitive physics, motion perception and, 515–517
Invalid trials, in attentional cuing paradigm, 542
Invariant features hypothesis, of shape equivalence, 365–367

Inverse problem
    optical information and, 23–24
    perceived transparency and, 297–298
    surface-based color processing and, 125
Inverse projection, Marr-Poggio algorithm, 217–220
Inverted spectrum argument, visual awareness and, 625–627
Ipsilateral neglect, attention physiology and, 564
Iris, anatomy of, 27
Isomorphism constraint, consciousness theory and, 658–659
Isotropy, texture gradients and, 235–236
Iteration operator, redundancy removal and, 403–404

JIM neural network model, connectionist implementation of recognition by components theory, 438–440
Julesz, Bela, 276–277
Just noticeable differences, difference thresholds and, 671

Kanizsa triangle, illusory contours and, 292–294
Kepler, Johannes, on the human eye, 24
Kinesthetic feedback, orientation constancy and, 335–336
Kinetic completion effect, dynamic perceptual organization and, 502
Kinetic depth effect (KDE)
    correspondence problem and rigidity heuristic and, 490–491
    object motion and, 228, 489–490
Knowledge acquisition, visual perception and, 5
Korte's laws
    of apparent motion, 473
    apparent rotation and, 494–495
Kosslyn's model of visual imagery, 609–611
Kuhnian paradigm, information processing as, 70
Kurtosis, natural image structure and, 191–192

Lambertian surface
    Horn's computational analysis of, 245
    shading information from, 242–244
Laminar structure, visual cortex anatomy and physiology and, 42
Landmark discrimination, visual cortex physiology and, 39
Lateral geniculate nucleus (LGN)
    anatomy of, 35–36
    color opponent cells and, 113–114
    image-based spatial processing in, 148–150
    image motion analysis and, 481–482
    laminar structure and, 42
    neural implementation of edge operators in, 179–180
    primary visual cortex and, 40
    striate cortex physiology and, 37
    structure from shading and, 184–185
    visual pathways physiology and, 194–196
Lateral inhibition
    color processing physiology and, 115–116
    image-based spatial processing in ganglion cells and, 147–148
Launching effect, causality and motion perception and, 511–512
Law of mass action, localization of function and, 37
Learning algorithms
    in connectionist networks, 681–683
    natural image structure and, 190
Left visual field (LVF)
    in blindsight patient, 635–636
    in split-brain patients, 631–633
    in unilateral neglect, 563–565

image-based stage of visual perception and, 88
lightness constancy and, 128–130
local spatial frequency filters and, 187–188
Marr-Hildreth zero-crossing algorithm and, 175–179
natural image structure and, 188–193
neural implementation and, 179–180
Luminance gratings, contrast sensitivity function and, 164
Luminance information
apparent motion research and, 479
perceptual grouping and, 264–266
uniform connectedness and, 268–269
Luminance ratios
illumination vs. reflectance edges, 132–133
lightness constancy and, 127–130
Luminance spectrum
properties of, 15
spatial frequency channel physiology and, 164, 169
surface-based color processing and, 123–125
visual pathways physiology and, 197

Mach bands
image-based spatial processing in ganglion cells and, 147–148
lateral inhibition mechanism in color processing and, 116
simultaneous contrast and, 106–107
Magic Eye: A New Way of Looking at the World, 215–216
Magic-eye stereograms, depth perception and, 215–216
Magnetic resonance imagery (MRI). *See also* Functional magnetic
resonance imagery (fMRI)
biological information processing and, 68–70
Magnocellular layers in LGN, image-based spatial processing in,
149–150
Magno system, image motion analysis and, 481–482
Maintenance
of iconic memory, 577
short-term vs. long-term memory and, 584
of visual memory, 575
Malik-Perona algorithm
of texture analysis, 184
of texture segregation, 277–280
Mammalian vision systems, single-cell recording experiments with,
65
Marcel's experiments on subliminal perception, 639–641
Marking, long-term memory (LTM) and, 589
Marr-Hildreth zero-crossing algorithm
boundary-based region segmentation and, 270–271
connectionist networks and, 677n.2
edge detection by, 175–179
image motion analysis and, 485
neural implementation of, 179–180
raw primal sketches and, 180–182
viewpoint-specific categorization theories and, 448
Marr-Poggio algorithms
correspondence problem and, 217–220
edge-based techniques, 220–221
point-based techniques, 217–220
Masking, in iconic memory, 577–579
Mass relations, event perception and, 514–515
Materialism, mind-body problem and, 620–621
Matte surfaces, light interaction with, 17
Maturation, empiricism vs. nativism and, 47
Maximal concavities, role in boundary rule, 354

Maximal information hypothesis, of canonical perspective, 421–424
Maximum (best fit) rules, in categorization theory of functional
perception, 415
Maximum-over-threshold rule, in categorization theory of functional
perception, 415
Maximum speed parameters, apparent rotation and, 494–495
Maxwell's color triangle, properties of, 691–692
Meaningfulness, figure/ground organization and, 284–285
Mean wavelength, hue correspondence with, 100
Measuring thresholds, 665–667
adjustment method of, 665–666
constant stimuli method of, 666–667
limits method of, 666
Mechanistic basis of perception, ecological optics and, 53
Medial superior temporal (MST) cortex, visual pathways hypothesis
and, 43
Medial temporal (MT) cortex, visual pathways hypothesis and, 43,
194–196
Mediated perception of function, affordances and, 409–410
Memory dynamics
defined, 596
misinformation effect and, 597–601
representational momentum and, 601–602
tendencies toward goodness and, 596–597
verbal labeling and, 597
Mendel, Gregor, 46, 656
Mental entities, elimination of, behaviorist theory and, 622–623
Mental operating system theory, working memory theories of
consciousness and, 648–649
Mental psychophysics, visual memory and, 608
Mental rotation, visual imagery and, 605–606
Mental transformations, visual imagery and, 605–607
Metacontrast masking, in iconic memory, 577–578
Metamers
color technology based on, 690
light mixtures and, 102–103
Metatheory, information processing levels and, 71–72
Method of loci, as mnemonic device, 592
Methodological behaviorism, 622
constructivism and, 56
Mexican hat receptive fields
image-based spatial processing in ganglion cells, 147–148
neural implementation of edge operators and, 185
receptive field structure of, 176–177
structure from shading and, 185
M ganglion cells, image-based spatial processing in, 149–150
Middle-out processing, global precedence and, 356
Mind-body problem, of consciousness, 618–624
Mind-brain identity theory, consciousness and, 621
Minimum coding principles, in figural goodness and structural
information theory, 402–403
Minimum principle. *See also* Prägnanz principle
figural simplicity theory and, 289–290
vs. likelihood principle, 57
Mirror-image environment, Marr-Poggio algorithm and, 217–220
Misinformation effect
distortion hypothesis of, 600–601
memory dynamics and, 597–601
Mnemonic devices
synesthesia and, 594
visual imagery as, 591–592

Modularity hypothesis, information processing theory and, 76
Modular systems, information processing in, 75–76
Mondrians
    chromatic color constancy in, 133–134
    retinex theory and, 128–129
    scaling problem and, 130
Monism, mind-body problem and, 620
Monkey cortex, visual pathways hypothesis and, 42–43
Monochromatic light
    color perception theory and, 97
    variance in wavelength and, 100
Monochromats
    color blindness and, 104
    trichromatic theory and, 108
Monocular information, depth perception and, 203–204
Monolexemic color terms, defined, 138
Moon illusion
    Emmert's law and, 323
    size constancy and, 322
    visual perception and, 7–10
Motion constancy, object motion analysis and, 487
Motion detectors, long-range apparent motion and, 497–498
Motion gradients
    development of, 252
    optic flow and depth perception and, 226–228
Motion hyperspace, apparent rotation and, 494
Motion parallax, depth perception and, 225–226
Motion pathway, visual pathways physiology and, 195
Motion perception. *See also* Apparent motion; Image motion; Object motion; etc.
    apparent motion, 471–481
    biological motion, 511–513
    causation and, 513–515
    color vision and, 197
    computational analysis of, 466–469, 484–487
    continuous motion, 469–471
    depth and, 488–493
    dynamic perceptual organization and, 498–504
    heuristics in reference frame selection and, 376
    iconic memory and, 580
    image motion, 466–487
    information processing and, 511–517
    intuitive physics and, 515–517
    long-range apparent motion, 493–498
    object motion, 487–504
    physiological mechanisms of, 481–484
    self-motion and optic flow, 504–511
    transformational alignment theory and, 367–368
Motion picture technology, apparent motion research and, 473–474
Motion sensitivity
    computational theory of image motion, 484–486
    in striate cortex complex cells, image-based spatial processing in, 153
Movement, attention shifts and, 544
Multidimensional representations of shape, 387
Multidimensional scaling (MDS) programs
    letter identification and, 454–455
    shape representation and, 387–390
Multidimensional space, shape representation and, 387
Multifeatural representations of shape, 390–394

Multiorientation, multiscale (MOMS) filters
    depth perception and, 221–222
    texture perception and, 277–280
Multiple drafts theory, working memory theories of consciousness and, 648–649
Multiple perspectives
    shape constancy and, 330–331
    viewpoint-specific categorization theories and, 444–445
Multiple realizability, visual awareness and, 623–624
Multiple scales
    edge-based algorithms and, 220
    shape primitives and, 352–353
Multiple sensory channels, template theories and, 379
Multiple spatial frequency channels hypothesis, 165–166
Multistability
    in connectionist network behavior, 680
    connectionist network models of, 301–302
    eye fixations and, 304
    figural scission and, 299
    instructions and, 304–305
    neural fatigue and, 302–304
    perceptual organization and, 300–305
Multistable perceptions, ambiguous figures and, 10
Munsell Book of Color, 98
Munsell color chips, category-based color processing and, 139
Mutual excitation, neural fatigue hypothesis and, 303
Mutual exclusion process, ambiguous figures and, 9–10
Mutual inhibition, neural fatigue hypothesis and, 303
Myelin sheath, around neurons, 29
Myopia, lens focusing abilities and, 28

Naive physics. *See* Intuitive physics
Nativism
    in classical vision theory, 47
    constructivism and, 56
Natural image structure, image-based spatial processing and, 188–192
Nearly decomposable systems, information processing in, 76
Necessary and sufficient conditions principle, categorical hierarchies and, 417–418
Necker cube
    connectionist network behavior and, 680
    eye fixations and, 304
    multistability, connectionist network model of, 301–302
    neural fatigue hypothesis and, 303–304
Negative aftereffect, perceptual adaptation and, 344–345
Negative priming effect, intentionally ignored information and, 540–541
Nerve impulses, in retinal neurons, 29
Neural correlate of consciousness (NCC), biological consciousness theory and, 652–656
Neural fatigue hypothesis, multistability and, 301–304
Neural networks. *See also* Connectionist networks
    connectionism and, 62
    edge operator convolution and, 174–175
    illusory contour physiology and, 296n.8, 297
    lateral inhibition mechanism in color processing and, 115–116
    Marr-Hildreth zero-crossing algorithm and, 179–180
    Marr-Poggio algorithm and, 218–220
    motion detection and, 484–487
    multistability and, 301–302
    natural image structure, learning algorithms and, 190

neural correlate of consciousness (NCC) and, 652–656
recognition by components theory and, 438–440
structure from shading and, 184–185
Neural pathways
anatomy of, 35–36
recursive decomposition theory and, 76
Neurons
oculomotor system physiology, 527
retinal neurons, 28–29
structure of, 29
Neurotransmitters, in retinal neurons, 29
Neutral points, color blindness and, 104
Neutral trials
attentional cuing paradigm, 542
quantitative perceptual grouping measurement, 262–263
Noise trials, in signal detection theory (SDT), 668
No-match trials, feature integration theory, 562–563
Nonaccidentalness
figure/ground organization and, 284
hole identification and, 287
recognition by components (RBC) theory and, 435–436
visual completion and, 299–300
Non-Cartesian gratings, visual pathways physiology and, 196
Nonhuman eye, anatomy of, 26
Nonlinearity, in striate cortex complex cells, image-based spatial
processing in, 153
Nonreflected light, surface interactions of, 16
Nonrigid motion, perception of, 492–493
Nonspatial transformations, objective shape definition, 364n.1
Nonspectral hues, in color circle, 98
Normalization strategy, for template-based shape representation,
380–381
Novel objects
categorization theory of functional perception and, 414
intentionally ignored information and, 540–541
viewpoint-specific categorization theories and, 451–452
Numerical arrays, retinal image stage of visual perception and, 86–87

Object-based attention theory
Balint's syndrome and, 565–566
vs. space-based theories, 547–549
Object-based representation, as a stage of visual perception, 90–92
Object categorization
canonical perspective and, 421–424
categorical hierarchies and, 420
contextual effects in, 428–431
empirical phenomena, accounting for, 440–444
orientation effects in, 426–427
part structure and, 427–428
priming effects in, 424–426
recognition by components (RBC) theory of, 434–440
theories of, 433–453
viewpoint-specific theories of, 444–453
visual agnosia and, 431–433
Object-centered reference frame hypothesis
geometric coordinate systems and, 369–370
heuristics processes and, 374–377
object-based representation and, 91
orientation and shape in, 373–374
perceptual reference frames, 370–371
shape equivalence and, 365, 368–377

shape equivalence failures and, 371–373
visual agnosia and object categorization and, 433
Object classification. *See* Object categorization
Object discrimination, visual cortex physiology and, 38–39
Object files
feature integration theory and, 561–563
iconic memory and, 580
reviewing paradigm and, 562–563
Object identification
categorical hierarchies and, 420
visual cortex physiology and anatomy and, 38–39
visual perception and, 6
Objective phenomena, visual awareness and, 619
Objective shape, definition of, 364–367
Objective threshold of awareness, subliminal perception and, 641
Object location, visual cortex physiology and anatomy and, 38–39
Object motion
depth perception and, 488–493
dynamic perceptual organization and, 498–504
kinetic depth effect (KDE) and, 489–490
nonrigid motion perception, 492–493
rigidity heuristic and correspondence problem of, 490–491
rigid motion in depth, 489
stereo-kinetic effect and, 491–492
velocity perception and, 487–488
Object recognition. *See also* Object categorization
categorical hierarchies and, 420
perceptual grouping and, 266
Object-relative power spectrum, Fourier analysis of shape
representation and, 383–384
Object representation, categorization theory and, 413
Object schemas, in recognition by components theory, 442–443
Object superiority effect, global-local perception and, 359–360
Observer relativity, affordances theory and, 411
Occipital cortex
anatomy of, 35–36
physiology of, 37–38
Occluded images
development of depth perception and, 252
edge interpretation and, 236
size illusion and, 326–327
structural information theory and, 405–407
visual completion and, 10–11, 288–292
Ockham's razor, scientific theory and, 47
Ocular apraxia, Balint's syndrome and, 565
Ocular dominance columns, 155n.1
Ocular dominance slabs, striate architecture and, 155–156
Ocular information for depth perception
accommodation, 203–205
convergence, 205–206
depth perception based on, 203–206
development of depth perception and, 250–251
Oculomotor system, physiology of, 527–528
Off-center ganglion cells, image-based spatial processing in, 147–
148
On-center ganglion cells, image-based spatial processing in, 147–
148
One-dimensional edges
boundary-based region segmentation and, 270–271
region analysis and, 267–268
Ontological status, visual awareness and, 623

Protanopia
  characteristics of, 104
  cone deficits with, 113
  trichromatic theory and, 108
Prototype structure, categorical hierarchies and, 417–418
Prototypical colors, category-based color processing and, 139–140
Proximal mode of perception, defined, 313–314
Proximal stimulus
  ecological optic analysis of, 53–54
  optical images and, 20
  properties of, 312–313
Proximity
  part perception and, 351n.4
  perceptual grouping and, 257–258, 264
Proximity matrix, multidimensional scaling (MDS) programs and, 388–390
Pseudo-normal color perception, visual awareness and, 626–627
Pseudoscope, depth perception and, 248
Psychological perception theories, 47–59
  color perception and, 97–99
  constructivism, 55–59
  defined, 46–47
  ecological optics, 53–55
  Gestaltism, 50–53
  information processing psychology and, 63–64
  motion perception neuropsychology and, 483–484
  part perception and, 350–351
  psychophysical correspondence and, 99–101
  structuralism, 48–50
Psychometric function, threshold measurement and, 666–667
Psychophysical channels
  image-based spatial processing and, 158–171
  local spatial frequency filters and, 186–187
  selective channel adaptation and, 165–166
  spatial frequency channels, 162–171
  visual imagery and mental psychophysics and, 608
Psychophysical scaling
  Fechner's law, 672–673
  principles of, 672–674
  Steven's law, 673–674
Psychophysiological isomorphism, Gestaltism and, 51–53
Pull cues, attention shifts and, 544
Pupil, anatomy of, 27
Push cues, attention shifts and, 544

Qualia, consciousness theories and, 657
Qualitative information, for depth perception, 203–204
Quantitative information
  for depth perception, 203–204
  in perceptual grouping measurement, 261–263
Quantum mechanics
  consciousness and, 645
  Newtonian paradigm and, 70

Radial direction, egocentric position and, 338
Random dot kinematograms, apparent motion research and, 477–478
Random dot stereograms, correspondence problem and, 212–214
Rapid serial visual presentation (RSVP)
  attentional blink and, 537
  conceptual short-term memory (CSTM) and, 587–588

Rate of motion, spotlight attention theory and, 545
Rate vs. intensity, in apparent motion, 473
"Raw feel," consciousness and, 657
Raw primal sketch. *See also* Full primal sketch; Primal sketches
  computational analysis of image structure and, 172
  edge detection and, 180–183
  image-based stage of visual perception and, 88
  local spatial frequency filters and, 187
  part segmentation and, 351–352
Ray-tracing algorithm, "inverse" problem of vision and, 23
Real images, in computer vision systems, 60
Reality, visual perception and, 7–10
Recall memory task, long-term memory (LTM) and, 589–590
Recency effect, short-term vs. long-term memory and, 582–584
Receptive fields
  development of, image-based spatial processing and, 157–158
  in ganglion cells, image-based spatial processing in, 147–148
  lateral inhibition mechanism in color processing and, 116
  local spatial frequency filters and, 186–187
  neural implement of edge operators and, 179–180
  principle components analysis (PCA) and, 190–193
  in striate cortex, image-based spatial processing in, 151–153
  structure from shading and, 185
Recognition by components (RBC) theory
  geons and, 434–437
  neural network implementation of, 438–440
  nonaccidental features and, 435–436
  object categorization and, 434–440
  stages of object categorization and, 437–438
  weaknesses of, 443–444
Recognition memory task, long-term memory (LTM) and, 589–591
Recursive decomposition
  color perception models and, 95–96
  dual process color theory and, 112
  information processing theory and, 74–77
Red/green balance, chromatic color constancy and, 134
Reduction screen, image-based color processing and, 101
Reduction tube, image-based color processing and, 101
Reductive materialism, mind-body problem and, 621
Redundancies, removal of, structural information theory and, 403–404
Redundancy gain, correlated variation condition, 551
Reference frames. *See also* Frames of reference
  failure of shape equivalence and, 372–373
  image-based representation and, 88
  object-based representation and, 91
  structural descriptions and, 395–396
  surface-based representation and, 89–90
Reflectance edges
  classification of, 238
  illumination edges vs., 130–136
Reflectance mapping, lightness constancy and, 132
Reflectance spectrum
  chromatic color constancy and, 134
  surface-based color processing and, 123
Reflected light, surface interactions of, 16–18
Reflectional symmetry
  axes, heuristics in reference frame selection and, 375–377
  geon theory and, 434–435
Reflections, objective shape definition and, 364
Refraction, of transmitted light, 16–17

Signal detection theory (SDT) (cont.)
  response bias in, 668
  signal detection paradigm and, 668–669
Signal-to-noise ratio
  activation thresholds, biological consciousness theory and, 650–651
  natural image structure, sparse codings and, 192
Signal trials, in signal detection theory (SDT), 668
Similarity classification task, selective attention theory and, 551–553
Similarity group, objective shape definition and, 364–365
Similarity
  categorical hierarchies and, 419
  multidimensional scaling (MDS) programs and, 390
  perceptual grouping and, 258–259
  shape representation theories and, 377
  template-based shape representation and, 380–381
  texture segregation algorithms and, 280
  uniform connectedness and, 268–269
Simple cells
  spatial frequency channel physiology and, 171
  in striate cortex, image-based spatial processing in, 151–153
Simplicity theory, visual completion and, 289–290
Simultagnosia, Balint's syndrome and, 565
Simultaneous color contrast, 106–107
Simultaneous flickering, apparent motion and, 472
Simultaneous lightness contrast, 106–107
Simultaneous motion contrast, continuous motion analysis and, 470–471
Simultaneous orientation contrast, orientation perception and, 337–338
Sine waves
  harmonic motion and, 468
  sinusoidal gratings, spatial frequency theory and, 160
  vs. square waves, grating thresholds and, 167–168
Single-cell recording
  biological information processing and, 64–65
  motion perception physiology and, 483–484
  in retinal cells, 147–149
  in striate cortex, 151–153
Single-pass operations, edge-based algorithms and, 220–221
Sinusoidal gratings
  contrast sensitivity function (CSF) and, 164–166
  Fourier analysis and, 160–162
  image-based spatial processing and, 159–160
  selective channel adaptation and, 165–166
  sine wave vs. square wave thresholds and, 167–168
  spatial frequency aftereffects of, 166–167
  spatial frequency theory and, 159–160
Size
  apparent motion and correspondence problem, 476–477
  familiar size in depth perception, 234
  figure/ground organization and, 282
  perceptual constancy and, 314–321
  relative size in depth perception, 232–234
  spotlight, in attention theory, 545
  variation in, geon theory and, 434–435
Size constancy
  approximations to, 317
  demonstrations of, 315–317
  departures from, 317
  development of, 321–322
  distance and, 317–318

horizon ratio and, 321
  properties of, 315–322
  relative size and, 319–321
  size-distance relation and, 315
  texture occlusion and, 318–319
Size-distance paradox, size illusions and, 323
Size-distance relation
  relative size and, 233–234
  size constancy and, 315–317
Size illusions
  apparent distance theory, 322–323
  Emmert's law and, 323
  moon illusion, 322–323
  occlusion illusions, 326
  Ponzo illusion, 324–325
  properties of, 322–327
  relative size illusions, 325–326
  size-distance paradox and, 323–324
Slant, defined, 200
"Slave" memories, visuo-spatial scratch pad and, 584–585
Smoothness assumption edge interpretation and, 243
Smooth pursuit eye movements
  characteristics of, 524–525
  oculomotor system physiology of, 527
Smooth transitions, in threshold experiments, 667
Soft constraints
  connectionist network behavior and, 680
  hidden assumptions as, 83
Software primitives, recursive decomposition and, 76
Space-based attention theory vs. object-based theories, 547–549
Space-time diagrams, image motion analysis and, 467–468
Span of apprehension, iconic memory and, 575
Sparse distributed coding, natural image structure and, 189–192
Spatial attention theories
  feature integration theory, 556–563
  object files theory, 561–563
  research issues in, 544–549
  space-based vs. object-based approaches, 547–549
  spotlight metaphor, 544–545
  zoom lens metaphor, 546–547
Spatial dimensions
  depth perception and, 200–201
  optical images and, 20
Spatial disorientation, Balint's syndrome and, 565
Spatial extension, in striate cortex complex cells, 153
Spatial frequency theory
  aftereffects and, 166–167
  channel physiology and, 169–171
  channels in, 162–163
  contrast sensitivity functions (CSF) and, 163–164
  development of channels and, 168–169
  Fourier analysis and, 160–162
  image motion models based on, 485–486
  local spatial frequency analysis and, 169
  psychophysics of image-based spatial processing and, 159–168
  selective channel adaptation and, 165–166
  sine wave vs. square wave grating thresholds and, 167–168
  visual pathways physiology and, 197
Spatial processing. *See also* Image-based spatial processing
  image-based spatial processing, 171–193
  primary visual cortex and, 40

Surface orientation
  depth perception and, 200
  shading information from, 243–245
  slant vs. tilt, 200
  texture gradients and, 234–236
Surface primitives, surface-based representation and, 89
Surface recovery, depth processing and, 202–203
Surroundedness
  figure/ground organization and, 282
  hole perception and, 286–287
  induced motion and, 501–502
Swinging room experiment, induced self-motion and, 506
Symmetric networks, connectionist architecture, 679
Symmetry
  figural goodness and subgroups, 401–402
  figure/ground organization and, 282
  geon theory and, 434
  redundancy removal of, 403–404
Synapse, in retinal neurons, 29
Synchrony, perceptual grouping and, 259–260
Synesthesia, mnemonists with, 594
Systemic behavior, in connectionist networks, 679–681

Tau function, speed of self-motion and, 509–510
Teacher units, connectionist network learning algorithms and, 682
Template representation
  hierarchical templates, 381–382
  in letter identification, 453–455
  normalization and, 380–381
  part structure and, 381–382
  replication strategy and, 380
  shape representation theory and, 377–383
  standard templates, 377–378
  strengths of, 378–379
  three-dimensionality and, 382–383
  viewpoint-specific categorization theories, aspect graphs of, 447
  weaknesses of, 379–380
Temporal cortex, anatomy and physiology of, 38–39
Terminals, in retinal neuron axons, 29
Termination boundaries, shading information and, 245–246
Ternus display, apparent motion and correspondence problem, 476–477
Tetrahedron
  aspect graphs of, 446–447
  edge interpretation of, 240–241
Textons, defined, 277
Textural orientation, heuristics in reference frame selection and, 375
Texture analysis
  apparent motion research and, 479
  image-based spatial processing and, 184
Texture gradients
  depth perception and, 234–236
  ecological optic analysis of, 53–54
  relative size and, 233–234
Texture occlusion, size constancy and, 318–319
Texture segregation
  feature integration theory and, 558
  inattention paradigm and, 536
  Malik/Perona theory of, 277–280
  region analysis and, 275–280
Theoretical horopter, 208

Theory, defined, 46
Thermostat as an information processing device
  algorithmic levels of, 71–73
  homomorphism in, 78
Three-dimensional environment. *See also* Two-dimensional environment
  computer vision systems and, 61–62
  constancy and illusion in, 312–313
  constructivism and, 57
  depth perception and, 200–202
  ecological optics theory and, 55
  ecological validity vs. hidden assumptions in, 84n.6
  Fourier analysis of shape representation and, 384–385
  heuristics in reference frame selection and, 375n.2
  image motion analysis and, 466–469
  impossible objects and perceptual errors, 12
  inverse projection and, 23–24
  kinetic depth effect (KDE) and, 489–490
  multifeatural representations and, 391–394
  object-based representation in, 90–91
  objective shape definition in, 364–365
  optical image formation in, 20
  perceptual grouping and, 264–266
  perspective projection in, 230–231
  predictive models and, 12–13
  projective geometry in, 20–21
  shape constancy, perspective changes in, 327–331
  shape perception and, 363
  stereo-kinetic effect and, 491–492
  structural information theory and, 406
  template-based shape representation and, 382–383
  transformational alignment theory and, 368
  viewpoint-specific categorization theories and, 444–453
Three-dimensional geometry
  object-based representation and, 91
  surface-based representation and, 89
Threshold rule, categorization theory of functional perception, 415
Thresholds
  adjustment measurement methods for, 665–666
  constant stimuli measurement method for, 666–667
  defined, 665
  limits measurement method for, 666
  measurement of, 665–667
  square wave vs. sine waves, grating thresholds, 167–168
  theoretical status of, 667
Tilt
  aftereffects, spatial frequency aftereffects, 167
  defined, 200
Tilted room illusion, orientation perception, 336–338
Time to contact parameter, speed of self-motion and, 509–510
Timing conditions, launching effect and, 513
Tokens of images, edge detection and, 182
Top-down processing
  blindsight research and, 636
  information processing theory and, 84–85
Topographic mapping
  image-based spatial processing and, 149–150
  occipital cortex physiology and, 37–38
Tracking, eye movements and, 520
Trained introspection, structuralist theory and, 50
Trajectory, spotlight attention theory and, 545

Transformational alignment hypothesis
   vs. object-centered reference frame hypothesis, 377
   shape equivalence and, 365, 367–368
Transformational invariance, figural goodness and symmetry
      subgroups, 401–402
Translations, objective shape definition and, 364
Transmission spectra, 691
Transmitted light, surface interactions and, 16
Transsaccadic integration, eye movements and, 531
Transsaccadic memory, visual short-term memory as, 585–586
Transversality regularity, boundary rules and, 353–354
Treatise on Physiological Optics, 56
Trichromatic theory
   dual process theory and, 111–112
   opponent process theory and, 109–110
   principles of, 107–108
Trichromats
   anomalous trichromats, 105–106
   color blindness and, 104
   cone systems in, 112–113
   visual awareness and, 626–627
Triggering effect, causality perception, 512
Trigonometric equations
   binocular convergence and depth perception, 205–206
   relative size and, 233–234
Trihedral angles, vertex classification of, 239–240
Tritanopia
   characteristics of, 105
   cone deficits in, 113
   trichromatic theory and, 108
Turing machines
   development of, 59–60
   recursive decomposition theory and, 76
Turing's test
   behavioral criteria using, 628–629
   biological consciousness theory and, 650
Two-dimensional environment. *See also* Three-dimensional
      environment
   computer vision systems and, 61–62
   constructivism and, 57
   depth effects in motion analysis and, 488–489
   depth perception and, 200–201
   ecological optic theory and, 55
   ecological validity vs. hidden assumptions in, 84n.6
   figure/ground organization and, 284
   heuristics in reference frame selection and, 375n.2
   image motion analysis and, 466–469
   inverse projection and, 23–24
   letter and word identification and, 453
   multifeatural representations and, 391–394
   perceptual grouping and, 264–266
   perspective projection in, 230–231
   projective geometry in, 20–21
   region analysis and, 267–268
   shape constancy, perspective changes in, 328–329
   stereo-kinetic effect in, 491–492
   structural information theory and, 406
   transformational alignment theory and, 367–368
   uniform connectedness and, 269
   viewpoint-specific categorization theories and, 444–453

Two-dimensional geometry, of image-based stage, 88
Two-dimensional light patterns, visual perception and, 4
2.5-D sketch
   consciousness theory based on, 649
   depth perception and, 202–203
   Marr-Poggio algorithm and, 217n.3
   shape perception and, 363
   surface-based stage of visual perception and, 89, 201
Two visual systems hypothesis
   blindsight research and, 635
   physical affordances theory and, 412
Types, vs. tokens in edge detection, 182
Typicality effects
   categorical hierarchies and, 418
   recognition by components theory and, 440

Uncertainty, inductive inferences and, 81
Unconscious depth, Ponzo illusion and, 324–325
Unconscious inference
   constructivism and, 56–59
   lightness constancy and, 126–128
   relative size and, 233–234
   size constancy and, 317–319
Unconscious visual processing
   blindsight and, 634–636
   face recognition in prosopagnosia and, 637–638
   inattentional blindsight and, 643–644
   self-motion perception and, 510–511
   subliminal perception and, 639–643
   visual awareness and, 616, 636–638
Uncrossed convergence method, stereograms and, 210–211
Uncrossed disparity, corresponding retinal positions and, 208
Undecomposable systems, information processing in, 76
Underconstancy, defined, 314
Underdetermination, figural scission and, 298–299
Underspecification, inverse projection and, 23
Unidimensional variation condition, selective attention theory and,
      551
Uniform connectedness
   parsing and, 274
   region analysis and, 268–269
   texture segregation and, 275–280
Unilateral neglect
   attention physiology and, 563–565
   neuropsychology of visual imagery and, 612–613
   unconscious visual awareness and, 636–637
   visual cortex physiology and anatomy and, 39
Uniqueness problem, of categorization, 414–415
Unique-point heuristics
   apparent motion research and, 480–481
   correspondence problem and, 490–491
   nonrigid motion perception and, 492–493
Unitariness, of attentional spotlight, 545
Unit formation principles, perceptual grouping and, 261
Units, in connectionist networks, 676–678
Unsupervised learning algorithms
   in connectionist networks, 682n.5
   natural image structure and, 190n.3, 191–193
Upside-down phenomenon, perceptual adaptation and, 345–346
Utricle (vestibular system), orientation constancy and, 334–336

Waterfall illusion, motion aftereffects and, 470
Wavelength-sensitive receptors
    color perception theory and, 96–97
    trichromatic theory and, 108
Wavelet functions
    Fourier analysis of shape representation and, 384
    spatial frequency channel physiology and, 169–171
"Weak" AI (artificial intelligence) theory, 71
Weak fusion
    depth perception information and, 248–249
    modified weak fusion, 249
Weber's Law
    difference thresholds and, 671–672
    psychophysical scaling and, 672
Weight-error space, connectionist learning, 686
Weight space, connectionist learning, 685–686
Wertheimer, Max, 50, 52, 256–261, 263, 266–267, 400, 472–473,
    680
"What" system
    physical affordances theory and, 412
    visual cortex physiology and anatomy and, 38–39
Wheel race problem, intuitive physics and motion perception, 516–
    517
"Where" system
    physical affordances theory and, 412
    visual cortex physiology and anatomy and, 38–39
Whole report procedure, iconic memory and, 575
Winner-take-all (WTA) networks
    behavior of, 680
    connectionist network architecture and, 679
    Marr-Poggio algorithm and, 218–220
Witkin's scale space algorithm, edge detection and, 180–182
Word identification
    categorization theory and, 456–458
    interactive activation (IA) model of, 459–460
Word-letter effect, categorization and, 457–458
Word-letter perception, interactive activation model of, 458–461
Word-nonword effect, categorization and, 457–458
Word superiority effect
    global-local perception and, 359
    word/letter identification and, 456–457
Word-to-letter feedback, interactive activation (IA) model of, 460
Working memory
    consciousness theory and, 648–649
    visuo-spatial scratch pad model, 584–585

Yes-no (old-new) recognition test, long-term memory (LTM) and, 590
Young-Helmholtz trichromatic theory. *See* Trichromatic theory

Zero-crossings, of luminance edges
    boundary-based region segmentation and, 270–271
    Marr-Hildreth algorithm and, 175–179
    neural implementation of, 179–180
Zöllner illusion, orientation perception and, 337–338
Zoom lens metaphor, spatial attention theory and, 545–546

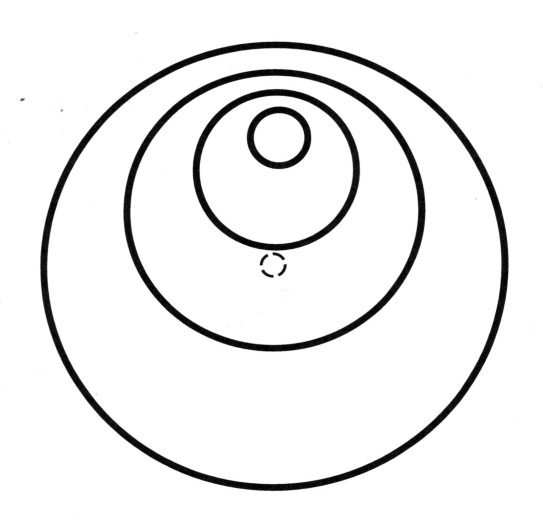